AF708957

The Marketplace of Ideas: Twenty Years of *Cardozo Arts & Entertainment Law Journal*

The Marketplace of Ideas: Twenty Years of *Cardozo Arts & Entertainment Law Journal*

Edited by
Peter K. Yu

Benjamin N. Cardozo School of Law
Yeshiva University

Kluwer Law International
The Hague/London/New York

Published by
Kluwer Law International
233 Spring Street, 7th Floor
New York, NY 10013 USA
sales@kli.wkap.nl
http://www.kluwerlaw.nl

Sold and Distributed in North, Central, and South America by:
Kluwer Law International
101 Philip Drive
Norwell, MA 02061 USA

Sold and Distributed in all other countries by:
Kluwer Law International
Distribution Center, P.O. Box 322,
3300 AH Dordrecht, The Netherlands

Library of Congress Cataloging-in-Publication Data

The marketplace of ideas: twenty years of Cardozo arts & entertainment law journal / edited by Peter K. Yu.
p. cm.
Includes bibliographical references and index.
ISBN 9041188819 (acid-free paper)
1. Law and art—United States. 2. Performing arts—Law and legislation—United States. 3. Mass media—Law and legislation—United States. I. Yu, Peter K.

KF4288.A75 M37 2002
344.73'097—dc21

2002024137

Printed on acid-free paper
Cover design by Lai Yu Fung

ISBN 9041188819
2002 Kluwer Law International

Kluwer Law International Incorporates the imprint of Martinus Nijhoff Publishers

This publication is protected by international copyright law.
All rights reserved. No part of this publication may be reproduced, stored in a retrieval system, or transmitted in any form or by any means, electronic, mechanical, photocopying, recording, or otherwise, without the prior permission of the publisher.

TABLE OF CONTENTS

THE WHITE HOUSE

WASHINGTON

May 10, 1982

I was delighted to learn that the Benjamin N. Cardozo School of Law of Yeshiva University has established the Cardozo Arts & Entertainment Law Journal.

Benjamin Cardozo exemplified the highest traditions of legal scholarship throughout his distinguished career, culminating with his service on the New York Court of Appeals and the United States Supreme Court. In carrying forward those traditions, the faculty and students of the School of Law named for Justice Cardozo honor his life and memory.

I know that the Journal will display the same devotion to excellence to which Justice Cardozo was, and Yeshiva University remains, committed. As you know, I have a special interest in the arts and entertainment, and you have my congratulations and best wishes as you launch a publishing venture that will contribute to learning and scholarship in this field.

Sincerely,

Ronald Reagan

PREFACE

Scholars and jurists have repeatedly emphasized how an "uninhibited, robust, and wide-open" marketplace of ideas can promote social progress by facilitating open discussion and free exchange of ideas. In the same tradition of this metaphorical "marketplace," the *Cardozo Arts & Entertainment Law Journal* has provided, in the past twenty years, a forum for jurists, scholars, practicing attorneys, policymakers, and members of the intellectual property and communications industries to debate, discuss, and disseminate ideas in the fields of art, media and intellectual property law.

The origin of the *Journal* can be traced back to the early 1980s, when a group of visionary students founded the first student-edited entertainment law journal in the United States. Published in spring 1982, the inaugural issue contained an article by Frederick F. Greenman, Jr. and Alvin Deutsch that was entitled *The Copyright Royalty Tribunal and the Statutory Mechanical Royalty: History and Prospect*. The issue also included student works on direct broadcast satellites, artists' resale royalties, and the right of first refusal. Preceding these writings was the *Journal*'s Statement of Purpose, which is reprinted in full below:

> During the past several decades the importance of the arts in American life has increased dramatically. Technological achievements have expanded communication capabilities and have created new legal relationships and issues. Many of the traditional legal concepts associated with arts and entertainment are being reexamined by legislators and courts. Few law school journals specialized in the areas of entertainment and the arts and the Benjamin N. Cardozo School of Law seeks to fill this void.
>
> The *Cardozo Arts & Entertainment Law Journal* will be a lively, issue-oriented forum for the exploration of current problems in the growing field of arts and entertainment law. Legal scholars, jurists, practicing attorneys and students will provide original articles on the full range of legal issues affecting the arts and the entertainment industry, both in this country and abroad.

Over the course of the years, the *Journal* has grown to be one of the most widely-subscribed journals in the field and has published articles, essays, notes, comments, and book reviews on a large variety of issues, including art, entertainment, intellectual property, sports, First Amendment, communications, and cyberspace law. Featuring distinguished members of the academia, the legal community, and the intellectual property and communications industries, writings in the *Journal* have been cited by the United States Supreme Court, the United States Courts of Appeals, jurists, scholars, attorneys, students, and the mass media.

Every year, the *Journal* sponsors a distinguished lecture on a cutting-edge issue in the field of intellectual property and entertainment law. Shortly after the *Journal* was created, Cardozo established the Herman Finkelstein Lecture to honor the former general counsel of the American Society of Composers, Authors, and Publishers (ASCAP) and director of the Nathan Burkan Memorial Competition. Lecturers included the late Professor Ralph Brown of Yale Law School, the late Simon Rifkind of Paul, Weiss, Rifkind, Wharton & Garrison, and Ralph Oman, the former Register of Copyrights of the United States.

A decade later, Cardozo established the Annual Tenzer Distinguished Lecture in Intellectual Property Law in memory of the late Herbert Tenzer, one of Cardozo's founders and benefactors. Since its inception, the Tenzer Lecture has become a premier event for which jurists, scholars, practitioners, alumni, and students gather. Past speakers include Under Secretary of Commerce Q. Todd Dickinson; Assistant Secretary of Commerce Bruce Lehman; Judges Jon Newman and Pierre Leval of the United States Court of Appeals for the Second Circuit; Dean Brian Fitzgerald of the Faculty of Law and Justice of Southern Cross University, New South Wales, Australia; Professor Jane Ginsburg of Columbia Law School; Professor J. Thomas McCarthy, author of *McCarthy on Trademarks and Unfair Competition*; and William Patry, former counsel to the Subcommittee on Intellectual Property and Judicial Administration, Committee on the Judiciary, U.S. House of Representatives.

In addition, the *Journal* sponsors and publishes a large variety of symposia. Topics covered include artists' rights, the Berne Convention, regulation of cable television, the construction of authorship, the jurisprudence of ratings for television and motion pictures, Russian media law and policy, European responses to media ownership and pluralism, the right of publicity, early publication of patent applications, Internet domain names, the extension of copyright term, and government funding of the arts. Most recently, the *Journal* sponsored two highly-acclaimed and well-attended symposia: "Report from the Front Lines of the Art and Cultural Property Wars" and "Copyright Law as Communications Policy: Convergence of Paradigms and Cultures."

This year marks the twentieth anniversary of the *Cardozo Arts & Entertainment Law Journal.* To celebrate this milestone, the present volume brings together some of the most widely-cited articles published in the *Journal* in the past twenty years and the numerous distinguished lectures sponsored by the Law School. These articles and lectures not only demonstrate the breadth and depth of contemporary scholarship on intellectual property, art, and media law, but also reflect the various issues that dominated the scholarly debate in the past twenty years. In sum, the *Journal* is as much about the marketplace of ideas as it is the marketplace itself.

Many of the writings collected in this volume were written before the Information Age. Yet, as Professor Marci Hamilton pointed out in her introduction, these writings are highly relevant to our current debate on the protection and regulation of expressions. Reproduced as they originally appeared in the *Journal*, these articles and lectures enable us "to understand and to succeed in the Information Era."

Last but not the least, I would like to express my profound gratitude to Deans Paul Verkuil and Stewart Sterk and Professor Marci Hamilton for their enthusiastic support of this project. I also would like to thank Matthew Bower, Kevin Fritz, and Peter Wilner for providing excellent editorial and administrative assistance. In addition, I would like to thank the authors included in this volume for granting permission to reprint their articles and the past and present members of the *Cardozo Arts & Entertainment Law Journal* for their superb editing and devoted efforts. This volume is dedicated to all those who founded the *Journal*, who helped the *Journal* grow and flourish, and who continue to promote the full and free discussion in this "marketplace of ideas."

Peter K. Yu

INTRODUCTION

THE DISTANT DRUMBEAT: WHY THE LAW STILL MATTERS IN THE INFORMATION ERA

MARCI A. HAMILTON*

Utopias tempt devotion to simple formulae, and there was a time when the Information Era appeared to introduce a utopia. It was supposed to offer freedom to all. Instead of simplicity, however, we have landed in the midst of a pitched political, legal, and ideological struggle that arises out of the technological changes of this era.

The truth is that simple formulae work no better now than they ever did, and they should not displace our nuanced legal regime despite novel technology. A matrix of legal principles—many of which are explored in this collection—that ensure accountability of government, the rule of law, and liberty are as important now as they were a decade or even two centuries ago. However technologically advanced they are, the Internet and the technology that travels across it remain tools that are humanly manipulable for good or bad.

The fundamental principle underlying the Constitution—that all those holding power may abuse it—remains invulnerable to disproof. As we have learned, governments intent on censorship will suppress information traveling via the Internet as readily as that traveling via the post, and individuals are more than capable of turning the Web to their own, sometimes criminal, ends. The honeymoon of the Information Era is over, and humans—not technology or code—remain the factor determining good or bad results. While the technology is new, human nature remains disarmingly complex and the law a necessary antecedent to society.

The Information Era, then, does not guarantee democracy. Nor does the technology inevitably let the people rule. Rather they will rule, or will only be ruled by those they choose as in the United States, only if law and public policy conform the uses of the new technologies to those ends. Democracy on or through the Internet is no inevitability, but rather must be affirmatively chosen if it is

Copyright © 2001 Marci A. Hamilton

* Paul R. Verkuil Chair in Public Law & Director, Intellectual Property Law Program, Benjamin N. Cardozo School of Law, Yeshiva University.

going to be realized. Thus, even this wondrous collection of new technology cannot relieve us of the heavy burden of choosing how we will be governed.

The Information Era was officially initiated when Stewart Brand of the Electronic Frontier Foundation declared that "[i]nformation wants to be free."[1] This mesmerizing, utopian call has had a powerful impact, leading otherwise law-abiding citizens to declare that copyright law—the hackers' most hated legal regime—was dead, that national boundaries are ephemeral, and that privacy was impossible. They have treated the collection of new technologies we have dubbed an "era" as the path to democracy, the path to free creative products, and the path to radical egalitarianism.

The hackers who initiated the Information Era have touted an anti-government, anti-law, and anti-big business mentality that challenges the fundamentals of the modern legal, creative culture. The fertile ground of their radical posture has generated arguments against any regulation of the Web (even including child pornography regulations), arguments against sales taxes on the Web as though sales that happen to occur via the Web are categorically different from other types of sales, and, most vociferously of all, arguments that copyright laws are simply obsolete. While challenges to existing powers can be constructive, if successful, such challenges could lead to less liberty.

In fact, the logical structure of the hackers' utopia is socialist, despite its adolescent foot-stomping about government regulation. The futuristic quality of the Information Era with its new technologies, its new businesses, and its new jobs has led most of us to treat it as an utterly new phenomenon, but this era is actually part and parcel of some of the most important ideological battles being waged around the world, in particular the intertwined battles between socialism and capitalism, and between extremism and the rule of law.

It should come as no surprise that dominant political, intellectual constructs have been translated into the hackers' philosophy, for ideas and philosophies are not the products of immaculate conception, but rather reconfiguration of the available intellectual materials. When the Berlin Wall fell, the people of East Germany were demanding not only an escape from the political structure of communism, but, even more vehemently, an open door to the

---

1 Stewart Brand, *Finding a Balance in the Slippery Economics of an Information Age: Depending on Your Perspective, Data's Free—Or Priceless*, L.A. TIMES, Nov. 8, 1987, at C3.

world's fabulous marketplace of goods. American television, especially shows like *Dallas*, had whetted appetites for luxury items and a luxurious life clearly unattainable under the existing regime. The crystalline promises of a better life under communism, with shared resources and centralized planning, were shattered by the demand for products. The same was true for countries like Hungary. Indeed, one of the most difficult challenges the new democracies faced was the disappointment of their people that fighting off communism did not result automatically in increased consumer goods.

The other serious hurdle posed to each emerging democracy is the identical problem facing the Information Era: the institution of the rule of law. The American Bar Association's Central and Eastern European Law Initiative (CEELI), led by Justice Sandra Day O'Connor, has dedicated its mission to assist the Eastern European countries to institute the rule of law. Russia, China, and South American and African countries labor under the same requirement that they construct a path to the rule of law, which yields just and predictable application of the laws to all.

The deep irony is that, as the Internet has shrunk the world, making it more feasible for political reform and the principle of the rule of law to spread, some of its founders have constructed a vision of a lawless world, controlled by code, not law. Their vision is a world in which code rules, as Professor Lawrence Lessig has argued, but it rules in the absence of human capacity to choose the good over the bad. For them, engineering dictates results, rather than moral or policy choices. Not only is this "new world" lawless, it is a world where products valued and owned by others are free and where everyone is permitted, in fact encouraged, to take from an unlimited commons. The borderless world has deconstructed the ownership fences around each intellectual product to open them to all. There is no meaningful theoretical distinction between this vision of the relationship between the people and the market and communism.

Like communism, the hackers' utopia is fatally flawed, because it is built on the empirically disproved proposition that such a commons will be replenished as it is siphoned off. In the absence of a reward for contributions to the commons, the commons is inevitably depleted. In contrast, the capitalist structure at the heart of the American copyright system creates the potential for reward for creative products delivered to the people. The dynamic relationship between reward and the author of an existing work, which results in incentives to further creation, has engendered a marketplace that is regularly restocked with new, original works. In contrast, when the online supermarket is plundered under the hackers' world view, there is no reason for any creative person to release her works into the commons out of any motivation other than ideological devotion to the commons. The sad fate of the citizens of the former communist countries, especially East Germany and Russia, proves that such ideological devotion will not engender a thriving marketplace of consumer goods or even ideas, but rather a citizenry dependent on a structure centrally controlled and necessary to deliver even the minimum necessities. Lack of reward for individual effort—the insight at the heart of capitalism—generates dependence.

The hackers, of course, began as the central controllers in the Information Era. Like the communist leaders, they are not elected, but self-appointed, and, like the communist leaders, they lead with an ideology that does not mandate accountability to the common good.

That communist ideology is fundamentally opposed to copyright law is seen most vividly in China, where piracy has been rampant. Because of the resistance in communist dogma to private property barriers, especially those surrounding intellectual products, the Chinese are having to do contortions to become part of the world's expanding global market, a market they deeply desire. Having literally begged to be part of the World Trade Organization ("WTO"), and then included because of its huge market potential, China is now at a crossroads. To satisfy the demands of the Western countries that led the way for their WTO membership, China must institute a rule of law. At the same time, its leaders are not willing to release the centralized control of the communist party that impedes the development of the rule of law.

Like the stories of the fall of communism around the world, the emerging story of the Information Era is a story about power. In the early days of the Internet, when the control of the system lay in their hands, the hackers' vision was the only vision, and the supposed freedom of information transmogrified into a freedom of the people. The Internet became the typical utopian promise: cost-free, freedom-enhancing, and a solution for the downtrodden. But, of course, hackers promoted this vision of freedom in the context of their own de facto control of the Internet. While believing in their ideal, borderless world, they had no need to face the necessity of boundaries, legal or otherwise, because no one was challenging their hegemony in their self-created world. Like all utopias, this was a utopia with an underbelly.

For the last twenty years, technological change has been rapid and its potential shocking to pre-existing legal and economic structures, leaving the hackers' mantra significant time to grow roots into the Internet culture, where it continues to bloom today. The creators of freenet.com, for example, continue to treat their software product as a free product. They believe it should not be subject to copyright law, which ironically means that they cannot make money on it (despite its clear market value). Instead, they support themselves by selling freenet T-shirts, a socialist approach to family support if there ever was one.

Not all hackers have taken the freenet route, of course. The free-information concept extended cover for those early participants who seamlessly turned from thinking of their creations as engineers of freedom to engines of profit. While the world was marveling at these new technological miracles, Bill Gates was building an empire that would challenge the power of presidents and foreign governments, simultaneously attempting to corner the Internet market and lobbying worldwide to extend the scope and content of his legal rights in information. And he was not the only one.

The hackers' philosophy led to a Wild West stage in the Information Era during which hackers, e-businesses, and consumers boldly violated copyright, trademark, and even national security laws. E-commerce businesses constructed their business plans on the assumption that information is free. The hackers declared that no law could stop them while those, like Gates, who took early advantage of this new market, assumed that the pre-existing power structures and laws simply did not apply to them. Microsoft's culture was nearly as anti-law as the hackers' world, with few lawyers and even less deference to lawyer-like concerns, including antitrust compliance policies.

Like the gunslingers of the Wild West, though, hackers, Microsoft, e-business, and consumers are finding that the law can catch up to them. As a result of this potent challenge to the status quo, this is a time in which everyone is looking for solid ground for analysis. For example, Professor Lawrence Lessig sought footing in the way that computer code is constructed on the Global Information Infrastructure[2] while Professor Jeffrey Rosen focused on privacy.[3] These are just two of the many arenas that are necessary to

---

[2] LAWRENCE LESSIG, CODE AND OTHER LAWS OF CYBERSPACE (1999).

[3] JEFFREY ROSEN, THE UNWANTED GAZE: THE DESTRUCTION OF PRIVACY IN AMERICA (2000).

understand where the Information Era has taken us and where we are or ought to be headed.

A reexamination of information principles is absolutely necessary today, because every judicial or policy decision implicating information needs to be legally contextualized. The moral, political, and policy questions regarding how to or whether to regulate new technology need to be made with full awareness of the backdrop of this amalgam of legal principles. Although this new era would seem to indicate otherwise, we have had a species of information jurisprudence for over 200 years. Absence of this rich context in the debate over information can short-circuit public and scholarly discussion and hinder the development of constructive information policies.

While it may come as a surprise, this futuristic era desperately needs the context provided by the Framers of the U.S. Constitution. Their wisdom provides solid ground for the legal treatment of issues in the Information Era. The Framers built the Constitution, and therefore the U.S. polity, on the cornerstone that every entity holding power will be tempted to abuse it, that humans are capable of good, but inclined to abuse power. The same focus on the exercise of power and its relation to the public good retains force. When read against the Framers' understanding of the polity they were building, this era is a revolution in technology, but not a revolution in human nature or legal and constitutional principles.

The Framers constructed the most successful constitutional experiment in history by starting at their enduring insight that any person or any institution that holds power will be sorely tempted to abuse that power. The temptation of power was the background assumption of the Constitutional Convention. Framer James Madison remarked that "[t]he truth was that all men having power ought to be distrusted to a certain degree"[4] and that the ends of the Constitution "were first to protect the people against their rulers."[5] This sentiment was frequently invoked with George Mason stating that "those who have power in their hands . . . will always [not give it up] when they can rather increase it,"[6] and Elbridge Gerry declaring that any who "acquire power [will] abuse it."[7] Gouverneur Morris summed up the perspective of the Framers neatly when he referred to humans' "love of power . . . [and]

---

[4] JAMES MADISON, NOTES OF DEBATES IN THE FEDERAL CONVENTION OF 1787, at 272 (Adrienne Koch ed., Ohio Univ. Press 1966).

[5] *Id.* at 193.

[6] *Id.* at 266.

[7] *Id.* at 288.

oppression."[8]

The distrust of those in power was a theme of *The Federalist Papers* as well. Alexander Hamilton wrote in *The Federalist No. 6* that "momentary passions, and immediate interests, have a more active and imperious control over human conduct"[9] while James Madison concluded in *The Federalist No. 51* that "[i]f angels were to govern men, neither external nor internal controls on government would be necessary."[10]

The Framers had good reason to trust no entity holding power. Their generation had witnessed cardinal abuses of power by the Church in England, the guild monopolies in England, by Parliament, by King George III, by the state legislatures during the Articles of Confederation, and, immediately before the Convention, by the people. And for most, the Reformation and the Inquisition were fresh historical antecedents proving that even the Church was capable of falling by the wayside. Their utopian expectations, including faith in organized religion and faith in direct democracy, were dashed in a remarkably short period of time, leaving the fledgling states reeling and the Framers in a desperate position: either construct a form of government that can meet all of the abuses they knew so well or fail, with the union of the states disintegrating into a collection of principalities and the promise of international trade and military self-defense an impossible dream.

It would be an overstatement, however, to say that the Framers held out no hope of human achievement in the public good. Their belief was twofold: expect tyranny, but hope for the good in each man to prevail over his baser instincts. In the footsteps of the great Reformation systematic theologian, John Calvin, the Framers believed that the governmental structure could deter the temptation to abuse and turn individuals' sights on a higher good. In this way, they combined a sage distrust of human motives with a hope in properly crafted structures. Thus, the system was built on this paradox of distrust and hope.

Distrust and hope drove the Framers to divide power, to disperse power, and to set power structures against each other for the purpose of checking abuses of power. The President, the Congress, and the Judiciary received distinct powers. The states reserved power distinct from the new federal government. Church and State were to be divided. The people were to have the power

---

[8] *Id.* at 323.

[9] THE FEDERALIST No. 6, at 56 (Alexander Hamilton) (Clinton Rossiter ed., 1961).

[10] THE FEDERALIST No. 51, *supra* note 10, at 322 (James Madison).

to vote and the power to communicate with their rulers, but no power directly to rule. Business monopolies also were hated, explicitly in the Copyright and Patent Clause of Article I of the Constitution, which limits property rights in innovative inventions and writings to "Authors" alone and thereby cuts out the industry, guilds, and the government from initial control over these valuable works.

When the Framers' belief in the temptation to abuse power fades into the background, the empty promises of utopian visions can gain a toehold and, inevitably, disappoint. The blinding excitement of the new technologies temporarily eclipsed the Framers' comparatively mundane insights. Yet, technological tools, which are no more than other tools despite their novelty, need not and should not control how we construct the world we want.

The need to check illegal and immoral behavior simply has not been diminished. The Internet may have sped up our communication and increased our dissemination potential, but it has made no inroads into human nature. For that reason, the Framers' vision, which is premised on distrust of and hope for human endeavors and which is embedded in the Constitution, continues to have direct relevance.

In spectacular fashion, the pre-existing legal regime has collided with the hackers' mantra in three arenas: (1) music copying, (2) copying of DVD versions of motion pictures, and (3) disputes over the balance of power in the marketplace of Internet control technologies.

The War in the Courtroom Between the Hackers and the Law

New technologies of reproduction and distribution over the Internet have made it possible to disseminate copyright-protected works en masse at lightning speed. Firmly situated in the hackers' utopian mindset, early and successful e-businesses built their business plans on the assumption that the deployment of this fabulous technology need not take into account the copyright interests of the content being copied and distributed. Because the technology has made it possible to copy and distribute content with ease and with close-to-perfect quality, the two most popular copyrighted works to copy to date are sound recordings and motion pictures. As these are the two most powerful copyright industries in the world, the clash between free use of music and movies on the Internet with the legal owners of the content being copied was destined for a legal showdown.

While newspapers have been able to establish websites with some success, the longer written works like novels and nonfiction books have lagged in Web copying potential because hard copy continues to be preferable to reading lengthy works on-screen or even having to download and print such works. Even among my most tech-savvy colleagues, snail mail has continued to be the favored mode of exchanging scholarly drafts in most instances.

Whether the focus is print or sound recordings or motion pictures, however, the same issue is posed by the clash of the hackers' mantra with the pre-existing legal regime. Copyright law, which is an enumerated power of Congress under Article I of the Constitution, vests power over written works in "Authors" and no others. The scheme instituted by the Constitution has been a fabulously successful, capitalist regime in which authors are given the power to commodify their intellectual products, i.e., to build fences around their creative property, and therefore to be capable of being compensated by a market. Their compensation is not the entitlement of socialist systems, however, but rather is keyed directly to the market. If the marketplace demands the product, the author may profit. If not, the author learns a lesson. What he does with that lesson is completely up to him. In this way, the American system has made it unnecessary for the government to engage in patronage to foster creative activity and, through the First Amendment, has built in a bias against government funding of the arts and a bias in favor of private, creative entrepreneurship.

The market *rewards* original expression, a regime that replaces the enervating concept of the need for government to create incentives for artists to create as though artists find their Muse in the same way that Pavlov's dogs responded to stimulus. As a result, authors and artists in the United States are freer than they are anywhere else in the world. They have more potential to earn wealth, and the market is richer in products, both pop and high art. The key to the United States' successful copyright industry is the Framers' decision in the Copyright Clause of Article I of the Constitution to decentralize control over creative works by vesting power over such works in "Authors." Fully aware that other choices (e.g., publishers or the government) were available, the Framers placed control in the least centralized hands possible as they directed income streams to the creative source of the product.

The hackers, however, would turn this system on its head, by arguing that the authors and artists may not control copying, use, or distribution of their works. Even worse, they may not profit from the same and would divest individuals of such control. The authors' only means of eliciting profit from their creative contributions to society is through enforcement of copyright, so the hackers have not only instituted a utopian vision that is anti-government, anti-law, and anti-big business, but also anti-author. This is a turn that, if left unchecked by the reimposition of the copyright law in the Information Era, will generate one of two results: a socialist system in which artists will have to beg the government for support or a creative drought as talented authors and artists turn to other careers to support their families and needs.

Naspter / MP3. The clashes between the music industry and the hackers have been explicitly understood as a battle between the hacker ethos and entrenched copyright principles. When digital compression technology, which allows audio recordings to be stored digitally using far less memory than otherwise, found MP3, a popular, standardized, and high-quality compressed file format, it became possible to upload and download high-quality audio files on the Internet faster and easier than ever before. To say that, however, was not to say that it was fast and easy. The process of finding a server that stored a certain MP3 file a user wanted to download was often very time-consuming and frustrating. Napster aimed to resolve this problem with software that would provide its users with an unprecedented ability to locate specific audio files on the Internet. Users log onto the Napster system and can immediately and easily share files with any other user who is logged onto the system. While Napster attempts to improve the quality of its service and increase its user base (which increases the quantity of files available for download on the service since individuals are sharing files with each other), it remains a free service. Eventually, however, its plan is to become a revenue-generating endeavor, with potential future sources of revenue, including targeted email, advertising, commissions from links to commercial websites, and the direct marketing of CDs, Napster products, and equipment for creating MP3 files and storing them on CDs. Napster built a business plan on becoming *the* distributor of music over the Internet, a sharing of copyright-protected works that then permitted college students (and others) around the country to download CD-quality sound, to copy it, and to distribute it.

The MP3.com site worked differently. Instead of providing a service allowing individuals to freely share their audio files, the MP3.com site's purpose was to allow the owners of music to digitally access the music they owned from anywhere in the world. It required users to prove that they already owned a hard CD copy of a song or album by either purchasing it from one of its cooperating online retailers or by using the site's "Beam-it Service" which required the user to insert her hard copy of the CD into her computer's CD-ROM drive, where the site could scan it. Once the user proved that she owned the song or album in CD form, the site provided that individual with the file in digital form, which could be easily accessed, via the Internet, from anywhere. In order to provide this service to its users, the site purchased CD copies of tens of thousands of CDs that it copied onto its computer servers without authorization. MP3 argued, however, that it was not displacing a market in music, but rather making already-owned music capable of Internet accessibility—that it merely provided functional equivalent storing its users' CDs. Similar to Napster, MP3.com does not currently charge its subscribers any fee for use of the service, but seeks to create a sufficient clientele to draw advertisers and eventually become profitable.

Reimerdes. The motion picture industry invested heavily in technology research to create the means of sending motion pictures over the Web, an effort that resulted in the DVD technology. To prevent the unauthorized copying of motion pictures on DVD, the motion picture companies utilized an encryption-based technology, CSS, which allows users only to play back movies on licensed players. In order to circumvent this technological limitation on the copying of movies, a group of well-known computer hackers developed a software utility, DeCSS, which enabled users to decrypt the CSS protection system. DeCSS was then widely and freely disseminated over the Internet, allowing anyone to view DVDs on unlicensed players or make digital copies of them with very minimal quality loss.

The court in *Universal City Studios v. Reimerdes*[11] understood that it was being asked to choose between the hackers' utopia and the copyright law, noting:

> Plaintiffs have invested huge sums over the years in producing motion pictures in reliance upon a legal framework that, through the law of copyright, has ensured that they will have the exclusive right to copy and distribute those motion pictures for economic gain. They contend that the advent of new technology should not alter this long established structure.
>
> Defendants, on the other hand, are adherents of a movement that believes that information should be available without

[11] Universal City Studios, Inc. v. Reimerdes, 111 F. Supp. 2d 294 (S.D.N.Y. 2000).

> charge to anyone clever enough to break into the computer systems or data storage media in which it is located. Less radically, they have raised a legitimate concern about the possible impact on traditional fair use of access control measures in the digital era.[12]

The court had no problem, however, in deciding that the hackers lost this time. First, it concluded that, although tensions could arise between access-control measures and fair use, Congress properly resolved those tensions when it passed the Digital Millennium Copyright Act, and that there was really no serious contention that the hackers' dissemination of DeCSS did not violate the Act. The court also easily disposed of defendant's First Amendment claims. While computer code is in part expressive, the court argued, it also can cause computers to perform in ways that would create serious harm to society. Thus, society must be able to regulate the use and dissemination of code in appropriate circumstances such as these, where the government is protecting "copyrighted works stored on digital media from the vastly expanded risk of privacy in this electronic age."[13] In a testimony to the reach of the hackers' world view in the Information Era, however, the court was careful to preserve the hackers' arguments for other factual scenarios, noting that under a different set of facts some of the hackers' claims would be "[p]otentially more troublesome"[14] and that "[g]iven the *peculiar* characteristics of computer programs for circumventing encryption and other access control measures, the DMCA *as applied to posting and linking here* does not contravene the First Amendment."[15]

Microsoft. Unlike the copyright disputes in the music and motion picture cases, Microsoft found not just its actions with copyrighted products, computer programs, under attack by the Department of Justice, but rather its entire approach to the law, and specifically antitrust law. This case is a battle between a corporation with elements of the hacker philosophy and the rule of law. It is also the clearest reaffirmation in the Information Era of the Framers' belief that power is dangerous and that concentrated power is the shortest route to tyranny.

While the first two types of conflict involve copying generated by new technologies, this last example of the confrontation of law and the Information Era involves power, pure and simple. Bill

---

12 *Id.* at 346.
13 *Id.* at 330.
14 *Id.* at 325.
15 *Id.* at 346 (emphasis added).

Gates built an Information Era empire, the basis of which was that technology mattered, not law. He transported the hackers' anti-government mantra into a Fortune 500 company, a move that would explain his apparently genuine, if tragic, surprise when he was treated by the Antitrust Enforcement Division of the Department of Justice as a Fortune 500 company capable of abusing its power in the marketplace. If John Heileman's reports are correct, Microsoft not only did not have a well-developed legal culture for many years, but it was in fact the hackers' antinomian shell. Technology was its business, period. Indeed, there seems to have been a fear that if the company took its eyes off the technology to comply with the status quo law, it would lose competitive advantage.

Yet, Microsoft grew in size and political influence to a stage where Bill Gates declared that he was more powerful than the President of the United States, when Microsoft became a worldwide lobbyist to expand its information empire and when it could muscle its competition into tying agreements no other company in this fast-moving era could compel. This is the single, best testimony of the enduring relevance of the Framers' understandings. Microsoft, as it developed, heedless of the law, was destined to fall in the American scheme not only because it violated antitrust doctrine, though that of course is relevant, but also because it violated the fundamental principle at the base of the Constitution: all monopolies of power must be divided, dispersed, and then deterred. This is an instinctual, rational fear on the part of the American polity, and it is no less justified in the Information Era than it was at the Framing or during the Civil War or during the 1960s. The fact that Bill Gates was surprised that he could not wield Microsoft's market power with abandon, even in the Information Era, is proof that the hackers' utopian mantra has made it more necessary than usual to invoke the Framers' insights on power.

Here is where the philosophy of the hackers met hard reality. If there was to be no law in the Information Era that could stop the technology creators, and if those same technology creators could amass as much as power as they could grab, then the market ceased to determine whether a contributor to the storehouse of creative products was successful, and raw power would determine the same. Thus, there would be large hackers and small hackers, and the large had carte blanche to silence or stop the production of the small. From a system operating on merit determined by market demand, the American technological industries evolved into a regime in which creativity was not rewarded, but squelched. This is extremist capitalism, a business world in which Thomas Hobbes is the patron philosopher and the people do not receive the rich marketplace of products on which they can place bids that determine true market valuation. Capitalism is driven not by market demand, but rather by power to squelch. What is missing is the necessary principle that even business can abuse its power and that the American polity cannot tolerate such abuses.

There are two ways out of this conundrum. Either let Microsoft retain its power as government attempts to spur other creative juices through government grants, i.e., the socialist path, or penalize Microsoft and forbid it from exercising its power in ways that are contrary to a free market. The latter is the only choice consistent with the roots of the successful American market in creative products.

The relevance of the Framers' simple insight is truly remarkable. It is also consistent with sophisticated, contemporary economic analysis. Robert Bork, whom one might have expected to have supported a free market, as in a let-the-powerful-control-the-market approach to Microsoft, sided with the government. He and many other economists described Microsoft as a "predator" in the market. While it was perfectly acceptable for Microsoft to be large and to be successful, it was not permissible for it to wield its monopoly power through exclusionary contracts to exclude any meaningful competition from the market, thereby keeping competitive, and potentially better, products from consumers.

Bork cited truly damning evidence of Microsoft executives in internal memoranda saying "that it will be very hard to increase browser market share on the merits of Internet Explorer alone." By tying the browser to the operating program, Microsoft was able to leverage Internet Explorer into its monopoly position already established by the dominance of its operating program. Netscape was the victim, as were the programs, like Java, that would have made possible an endrun around Microsoft's hegemony.

Microsoft's business plan was not driven by a plan to engage in superior marketing or superior product introduction, but rather by the sheer exercise of monopoly power. It was not the technological product that was driving market results, but rather Microsoft muscle. Thus, Microsoft was guilty of abusing its power, which it was irresistibly tempted to abuse because of its monopoly position.

Many defended Microsoft in the early stages of the antitrust lawsuit, before the economists weighed in, saying that Microsoft was a hero for introducing the marvels of the Information Era to so many. The technology's potential blinded those early defenders to the reality that, behind the technology, Microsoft was really no different from any other schoolyard bully or unchecked monarch. Regardless of the magnificence of the product, and there are those who argue that Microsoft's products are in fact the mediocre of Silicon Valley's offerings, the focus must be swung from technology to people to avoid tyranny.

Bare technology and its marvels too long solely shaped how we understand the Internet, the new technologies, and all of their potential. We are being introduced to these novelties through the hackers' lens. And we are disabled in our ability to fully test their hypotheses, because the next wave of technology is just now emerging, and that wave is going to change the borderless quality of the Internet and profoundly shake the ground underneath their claims about pure democracy, free information, and freedom from the law.

Technology Today vs. Technology Tomorrow

The current war between the hackers' mantra and the rule of law has occurred against a backdrop of this era's development in technology. Conclusions are being reached based on an incomplete universe of technological possibilities. For example, the borderless world advocated by the hackers is only borderless until the technologies that introduce fences, walls, and locked gates are widely deployed, an era not far in the future, if the market is not squelched by the government's overzealous willingness to protect existing technology. The sound recordings carried by Napster are only capable of free, endless copying and distribution because those files did not have embedded codes that would prevent, or record, such copying. The future tools of distribution on the Internet will prevent the massive, global copying in this intermediate stage of the Information Era, and instead will introduce an era troubling in its own right, in which the owner of a creative work can prevent all free uses, including fair use, browsing, or personal use. Once again, the rule of law will be necessary, but this time to free information locked up, rather than to ensure authors' remuneration.

The key issue of concern in the next stage of the Information Era will be whether the tools of information disclosure and secrecy are available to the people, or only to the government or big business. It is not in the interest of our now oligopolistic publishers to share information-control technologies with authors or the people, because they could then be cut out of the process (though their power to brand and promote works still will carry value). The federal government has stepped forward for those with encrypted information by making de-encryption devices illegal in the Digital Millennium Copyright Act. The result of this action is to stunt technological development in information-hiding or information-sharing technologies. In a world in which publishers and authors can exert perfect control over their works through digitized information-feedback that tells them precisely what the user is doing with the work and charges the user accordingly, the millions of marginal, fair, and necessary uses made of creative works every day will decline. The only weapon against such technology will be other technology that makes private browsing or fair use feasible, as it prohibits massive redistribution and piracy. The people will need to have access to such technologies to be able to withstand the tyranny of government and big business, but there will be no market in such if the government continues to outlaw such tools. Like the Second Amendment, which was intended to arm the people against government tyranny, a right to information tools, grounded in the First Amendment, can protect the people from the tyrannical exercise of power over information.

The Information Era should not drown out the distant drumbeat of the pre-existing legal regime. Until human nature changes, a complex structure of information/privacy jurisprudence will be needed to deter tyranny and maximize liberty. The existing legal landmarks should continue to be the need for information about government, the necessity of a public storehouse of information, and the need for a measure of personal privacy, all three principles to be mutually considered in the judicial and legislative policy discussions implicating information. The legal challenge in this era is not so much the construction of a new world as it is how to sustain time-tested and cherished *legal* principles.

The hackers are simply wrong. Information is not inherently free, Web access does not guarantee either freedom or democracy, and the Internet does not necessarily level the playing field. To the contrary, the hackers, including those transformed into the big business magnates the hackers profess to hate, like Bill Gates, have used new technology and the Internet as a base of control, not liberty for all. Behind the curtain of their utopian vision, they have lobbied the European Union and the United States to expand their power and have been successful in ways the people have yet to comprehend. The existing two centuries of information law in the United States needs to be demythologized and the legal moves of the hackers analyzed to reach a clearer understanding.

Information "wants" nothing. Like technology, it is nothing

more than a tool that can be used by humans for good and for evil. The hackers' utopia is a seductive but dangerous dream. The daily battle for liberty from tyrants continues, and the legal tools of the past should be ready to hand, even if they are in need of fine-tuning.

Hence, I highly recommend the following thoughtful, challenging, and invaluable intellectual property works written for the *Cardozo Arts and Entertainment Law Journal* before and during the tornado of technological change. The *Journal* and its editors deserve high praise for the sizable contribution they have made to our ability to understand and to succeed in the Information Era.

THE WIDENING GYRE: ARE DERIVATIVE WORKS GETTING OUT OF HAND?

RALPH S. BROWN*

Turning and turning in the widening gyre
The falcon cannot hear the falconer;
Things fall apart; the center cannot hold
Mere anarchy is loosed upon the world. . . .[1]

I. INTRODUCTION

The passage I have just read came to mind when I was obliged to provide a label for something that was not yet written. It was of course utterly presumptuous for me to take my title from one of the noblest poems of this century, William Butler Yeats' *The Second Coming*. I had an uneasy feeling from recent cases and commentaries that a certain escape from control marked the sphere of copyright. Yet if the falcon, flying high and wide, could not hear the falconer, it was not because our chief falconer, Herman Finkelstein, was any less clear in voice or acute in discernment than when he first took to this field more than half a century ago. While his primary attention has always been devoted to his clients—grateful clients, I trust—namely the thousands of composers, authors and publishers who make up ASCAP, he has ardently concerned himself with the welfare of all creative people, and with the body of law surrounding copyright that is intended to create and protect their rights.

Among his contributions to the enrichment of copyright law none has been more fruitful than the essay competition that honors the memory of Herman's mentor Nathan Burkan. Generously fertilized by ASCAP, the green shoots of young scholars have produced a rich foliage of writing that has no parallel that I can think of, in the 30 volumes of the Burkan national prize papers, and the numberless law review contributions bearing the Burkan imprimatur.

As you will hear, on reflection I do not think that mere anarchy has been loosed upon the copyright world. But I am somewhat troubled, because of the following developments that I perceive in some of the cases and some of the commentators:

---

* Simeon Baldwin Professor of Law, Emeritus, Yale Law School; B.A., 1935, LL.B., 1939, Yale University. This lecture is printed essentially as it was delivered on October 19, 1983, when the Benjamin N. Cardozo School of Law honored Herman Finkelstein, Director, Nathan Burkan Memorial Competition; retired General Counsel, American Society of Composers, Authors and Publishers.

[1] W. B. YEATS, *The Second Coming*, in COLLECTED POEMS 184 (1956).

First, the exclusive right of a copyright owner "to prepare derivative works based upon the copyrighted work"[2] is an expansive one, because of the definition of derivative work in section 101.[3]

> A "derivative work" is a work based upon one or more preexisting works, such as a translation, musical arrangement, dramatization, fictionalization, motion picture version, sound recording, art reproduction, abridgement, condensation, or any other form in which a work may be recast, transformed, or adapted. A work consisting of editorial revisions, annotations, elaborations, or other modifications which, as a whole, represent an original work of authorship, is a "derivative work."[4]

It is not only expansive, it is still expanding. We have come a long way from 1853, when, in the absence of an express statutory right, Justice Grier could tell Harriet Beecher Stowe that a German translation did not infringe her most famous work, *Uncle Tom's Cabin.*[5] Most of the rights now protected seem to most of us, I'm sure, to reflect little more than simple justice. But the nineteenth century judges who were uneasy about enlarging copyright saw a difference that still has force. Copyright is not patent. The scuttling crabwise movement of copyright into any and all other media and forms sometimes looks as though copyright is outdoing patent law when it protects "equivalents".[6] Such enlargements engender the same fears as far more timid steps did in our forbears. I do not need to belabor the reasons why a patent should cast a wider net of protection than a copyright. It is hard (and expensive) to get. It requires an inventive step that is far more difficult than the simple copyright test of originality, that you did it yourself. Its duration is only 17 years, compared to our approximately 75.[7] And so on.

Second, maybe we are calling on copyright to do the work of unfair competition, and of design patents. When you have a produc-

---

[2] 17 U.S.C. § 106(2) (1982).

[3] *Id.* § 101 (1982).

[4] *Id.*

[5] Stowe v. Thomas, 23 F. Cas. 201 (C.C.E.D. Pa. 1853) (No. 13,514). For further discussion on the history before and after 1853, consult the first of Professor-Justice Kaplan's delicious lectures in AN UNHURRIED VIEW OF COPYRIGHT (1967).

[6] *See* Graver Tank & Mfg. Co. v. Linde Air Prods. Co., 339 U.S. 605 (1950). A broad range for "equivalents" is reserved for "pioneer" patents. *See* 4 D. CHISUM, PATENTS §§ 18.02[2], 18.04 (1983).

[7] *See* Graham v. John Deere Co. of Kansas City, 383 U.S. 1 (1966); Alfred Bell & Co. v. Catalda Fine Arts, 191 F.2d 99 (2d Cir. 1951).

tion of great popularity with enormous potential for exploitation of all its derivative bits and pieces—the T-shirt market, the cocktail coaster market, etc.,—appropriate protection in those markets should perhaps come from other quarters. Paul Goldstein has pointed this out,[8] but you will see that I do not always follow him down certain garden paths.

Third, and related to the second concern, derivative works are edging into what I think should be the forbidden area of useful articles. Paul Goldstein does not mind this either;[9] I do.

Fourth, the new copyright in a derivative work may be misused to block access to a public domain original. This despite the fact that section 103 of the new law could hardly be more emphatic in stating that the derivative right "does not imply any exclusive right in the preexisting material."[10]

Fifth, there is a bold attempt to claim that some derivative works, notably movies, have a life of their own that overrides claims of an underlying work in copyright. Then these derivate works can doubtless spawn their own derivatives, *ad infinitum*. This is a process I shall address.

Sixth and finally, I am troubled because there are too many reported cases. Not only is it hard to keep up with them—that's a personal disability—rather, it seems to me that the sheer numbers may signify undue pressures and strains. This is a shaky conjecture, I know. Let me dubiously objectify it with some numbers.

This chart[11] shows, in the black columns, all the cases in United States Code Annotated, from 1847 to 1960, under section 7 of the old law. The white columns show, for five-year periods, the number of cases, derived from Lexis, that use the phrase "derivative works" in conjunction with "copyright". The first one was in 1965. The white and black column, 1960-75, is a composite of USCA and Lexis. The last column still has more than a year to go. The two measures, USCA and Lexis, are of course not the same, but they are indicative.

---

[8] Goldstein, *Derivative Rights and Derivative Works in Copyright*, 30 J. COPYRIGHT SOC'Y 209, 224 (1983).

[9] *Id.* at 227–32.

[10] 17 U.S.C. § 103 (1982). Certain cases and practices in the field of musical arrangements typify this concern. *See* B. KAPLAN & R. BROWN, CASES ON COPYRIGHT 224–56 (1978) (access to public domain folk music).

[11] *See infra* app. Table I. These numbers are not adjusted to reflect an increase in population, in litigation generally, or in copyright litigation in particular. They are, therefore, only illustrative of a crude trend.

After all this portentous introduction, do not be alarmed. I shall, if fact, address only two lines of recent cases. In the second part, those that deal with claims of rights *in* derivative works, stemming from *G. Ricordi & Co. v. Paramount Pictures, Inc.*.[12] In the first part, three cases: *L. Batlin & Son, Inc. v. Snyder,*[13] *Durham Industries, Inc. v. Tomy Corp.*[14] and *Gracen v. Bradford Exchange,*[15] which attempt to define or redefine what it takes to legitimate a derivative copyright.

II. Obtaining a Derivative Copyright

L. Batlin & Son v. Snyder is the most important of this trilogy, I think, because it was decided by the Second Circuit, *en banc*, to be sure with a substantial dissent.[16] In a dispute between two vendors of plastic mechanical banks copied from the familiar public domain figure of Uncle Sam, the court found no "substantial variation" between the public domain figure and the version which Batlin had copied. Judge Oakes' opinion, while reciting the usual platitudes about how modest the copyright requirement of "originality" is, actually raises that requirement a notch or two.

Durham Industries, Inc. v. Tomy Corp. is also about tawdry toys (though I realize they are important to those who make a living from them). Both vendors in *Durham* were Disney licensees, so that we do not have the public domain background of the Uncle Sam case. Judge Meskill, who wrote for the dissenters in the Uncle Sam case,[17] writes for the court in the Disney case. He holds part of his dissenting ground by maintaining that the Tomy figures have no originality and are, therefore, not copyrightable. The significant element, to me, is a passage where he points out the impediments created when one licensee harasses another.[18] Durham, like Batlin, was impelled to bring a declaratory judgment action to subdue its pugnacious competitor. If Durham had not succeeded, derivative replicas of the familiar Disney figures (in this case windup toys) would, in order to avoid infringement charges, have to deviate from the originals, and would thus be unsaleable! "Thus it is clear," Judge Meskill concluded, "that the originality requirement imposed by the Constitution and the Copy-

---

[12] 189 F.2d 469 (2d Cir. 1951).

[13] 536 F.2d 486 (2d Cir. 1976).

[14] 630 F.2d 905 (2d Cir. 1980).

[15] 698 F.2d 300 (7th Cir. 1983).

[16] *Batlin*, 536 F.2d at 492.

[17] *Id.*

[18] *Durham*, 630 F.2d at 910–11.

right Act has particular significance in the case of derivative works based on copyrighted preexisting works."[19]

The redoubtable Judge Posner, in *Gracen v. Bradford Exchange*,[20] picked up the ball and ran with it. But it is just possible that he ran in the wrong direction. The case was given summary judgment in the district court,[21] with the familiar result that one has some unsatisfied curiosity about the facts, which in any case are off-beat. Let me recall them to you. Miss Gracen's employer, Bradford, licensed by MGM to produce "collectors' plates" with scenes from The Wizard of Oz, ran a contest for the best painting of Judy Garland as Dorothy. Miss Gracen, an amateur artist, won. A falling-out about contract terms arose and Bradford hired another one of the contestants who worked from Miss Gracen's painting. Miss Gracen sued for copyright infringement and oddly joined MGM as a defendant. This led to a nasty shock, because the trial court held that Miss Gracen had no authority to make or exhibit her painting, and awarded damages against her on a counterclaim. There are musty agency problems here of apparent authority, but they are not for us. The main point is that the Seventh Circuit, via Judge Posner, concluded that even if Miss Gracen was authorized to make the painting, she was not entitled to a copyright. "[E]specially as applied to derivative works," he said, "the concept of originality in copyright law has as one would expect a legal rather than aesthetic function—to prevent overlapping claims."[22] It must, he continued, "assure a sufficiently gross difference between the underlying and the derivative work to avoid entangling subsequent artists depicting the underlying work in copyright problems."[23]

The court found no such difference in this case. Three exhibits in the case, two of them publicity shots of Judy Garland (Miss Gracen did not work from a single source), the other her realization, vividly illustrate that the court meant the difference to be quite considerable.[24]

The announced goal here, which is to let other artists represent the original work without getting entangled, sounds commendable; and I for one was initially pleased with the decision. But after I submitted it to a higher court, as an examination question, I was

---

[19] *Id.* at 911.

[20] 698 F.2d 300 (7th Cir. 1983).

[21] *Gracen*, 698 F.2d at 302.

[22] *Id.* at 304.

[23] *Id.* at 305.

[24] One of the MGM photographs and the Gracen painting are illustrated in the case. *Id.* at 306–07.

shaken to find that an overwhelming majority of my students rejected the Posner position. They said it went beyond the precedents, and the statute; that it put too much power in the judges. As one student expressed it, "[I]n the name of artistic freedom, Judge Posner is clearly erecting a barrier to artistic freedom"—that is, by denying the benefits of copyright to people who think they have created something.

If I am persuaded that Judge Posner went too far,—and I am—why do I commend *Batlin* and *Durham*, the Uncle Sam and Mickey Mouse cases? I do because they bear down—a little—on claims of copyright in mass-produced essentially mechanical variations in objects that stand on the fringe of copyright anyway. Miss Gracen may not have been a gifted painter, but she was a flesh-and-blood person who made a portrait. Although intended for use on multi-copy plates, it never got there. In another direction, how do we distinguish between Batlin-like objects and the mezzotints that were the subject of our lodestar case on questions of originality, Judge Frank's magisterial 1951 opinion in *Alfred Bell & Co. v. Catalda Fine Arts*?[25] We note that there, putting aside some overblown dicta,[26] what the decision actually rewarded was "a tedious process requiring skill and patience."[27] Similarly, we can recognize the admitted talents of the copyist who produced a faithful replica of Rodin's *Hand of God*.[28]

Now these distinctions do involve line-drawing; but it is not line-drawing that says this is art and this is not art. We can be faithful to Justice Holmes in *Bleistein v. Donaldson Lithographing Co.*,[29] and recognize copyright in circus advertisements. But when we are dealing with the creation of rights in avowedly derivative works, it is proper to require a certain distance—a "substantial variation" as the *Batlin* court put it[30]—between the derived work and its antecedent. This is especially so when the derived work approaches the status of a useful article.

---

[25] 191 F.2d 99 (2d Cir.1951). The plaintiff made and copyrighted mezzotint reproductions of old master paintings. Defendants photographed the mezzotints and copied them lithographically. The Court of Appeals held that it was sufficient that the mezzotints " 'originated' with those who make them." *Id.* at 104.

[26] *E.g.*, "A copyist's bad eyesight or defective musculature, or a shock caused by a clap of thunder, may yield sufficiently distinguishable variations. Having hit upon such a variation unintentionally, the 'author' may adopt it as his and copyright it." *Id.* at 105 (footnotes omitted).

[27] Alfred Bell & Co. v. Catalda Fine Arts, Inc., 74 F. Supp. 973, 975 (S.D.N.Y. 1947), *modified*, 191 F.2d 99 (2d Cir. 1951). *Accord* Kuddle Toy, Inc. v. Pussycat-Toy Co., 183 U.S.P.Q. (BNA) 642, 658 (E.D.N.Y. 1974).

[28] *See* Alva Studios, Inc. v. Winninger, 177 F. Supp. 265 (S.D.N.Y. 1959) (copyright valid).

[29] 188 U.S. 239 (1903).

[30] *Batlin*, 536 F.2d at 490.

Useful articles are not copyrightable, with respect to their useful attributes,[31] Uncle Sam banks and windup Mickey Mice are essentially toys; and it has been held that toys are not useful objects,[32] a conclusion that I find difficult to understand; they are useful as toys. We got into this quicksand in the aftermath of *Mazer v. Stein*[33] while wandering from Balinese maidens to chimpanzees to model airplanes which were all called "works of art." There anarchy *was* loosed upon the world.[34]

Let me clarify my complaint by going back to the statute. We know that it recognizes derivative works as copyright subject-matter in section 103.[35] Section 106,[36] without any later limitations, creates the exclusive right "to prepare derivative works"—a curious verb, prepare, with a cryptic legislative history;[37] and we have already noted that the definition of derivative works is expansive.

I would argue, that when derivative works take any of the forms specified in section 102[38]—literary, dramatic, musical, and so on, they should not be permitted to escape the limits on those forms. I think this is especially so when derivative works approach "pictorial, graphic, or sculptural works." The statute then takes great pains to keep copyright away from useful articles. It does so in the definition of "pictorial, graphic, and sculptural" works. There, we are told that

---

[31] *See infra* text accompanying note 39.

[32] Gay Toys, Inc. v. Buddy L Corp., 703 F.2d 970 (6th Cir. 1983) (model airplane).

[33] 347 U.S. 201 (1954).

[34] *See* Note, *Copyright Protection for Mass-Produced, Commercial Products: A Review of the Developments Following Mazer v. Stein*, 38 U. CHI. L. REV. 807 (1971). I must concede that a classification of toys as useful objects becomes blurred as one moves from mechanical models to dolls and stuffed animals, which after all, are a form of sculpture. Can one distinguish between "played with" and "looked at"? Not at all clearly. Still, that is the kind of problem that the copyright statute has to wrestle with in section 113 and in the definition of "pictorial, graphic, and sculptural works" in section 101, in the absence of a separate design protection statute. *Compare* Denicola, *Applied Art and Industrial Design: A Suggested Approach to Copyright in Useful Articles*, 67 MINN. L. REV. 707 (1983) *with* Reichman, *Design Protection after the Copyright Act of 1976: A Comparative View of the Emerging Interim Models*, 31 J. COPYRIGHT SOC'Y 267 (1984).

[35] 17 U.S.C. § 103 (1982).

[36] *Id.* § 106 (1982).

[37] HOUSE COMM. ON THE JUDICIARY, 89TH CONG., 1ST SESS., THE SUPPLEMENTARY REPORT OF THE REGISTER OF COPYRIGHTS, COPYRIGHT LAW REVISION, pt. 6, at 17 (Comm. Print 1965), *reprinted in* 4 OMNIBUS COPYRIGHT REVISION LEGISLATIVE HISTORY 351 (1976), declares that this language makes the preparation of a derivative work an infringement even if it is not fixed—as distinct from the protection in section 106(1) of copies and reproductions, which do have to be fixed. This interpretation further appears in the authoritative House Report, H.R. REP. No. 94-1476, 94th Cong., 2d Sess. 62, *reprinted in* 1976 U.S. CODE CONG. & AD. NEWS 5659, 5675–76. It would be surprising if it had any practical application.

[38] 17 U.S.C. § 102 (1982).

copyright is not available for the "mechanical or utilitarian aspects" of applied art.[39] The policy is so strong that protected elements of design have to be separable from utilitarian aspects—you must be able, as it were, to peel them off.[40] This leads to the reproach that the law is not neutral as to aesthetics—it is positively anti-aesthetic in its unwillingness, for example, to recognize the inseparability of form from function in much of modern design. This is a reproach that must be endured.[41]

I can not go further into the bramble bush of design and useful articles. Professor Goldstein, if I read him correctly, would let derivative works go where they will, in the interest of stimulating investment.[42] If a drawing of a dress is copyrightable, then why not the dress?

Why not? Because of the statute, and because, even on Goldstein's economic grounds, there is no reason to think that we need more investment in the apparel industries. Matthew Nimetz demonstrated this in a Burkan paper 16 years ago.[43]

I do agree with Goldstein that we are creating a likelihood of confusion by invoking copyrights where we should use trademarks, especially in the merchandising of derivative works.[44] An egregious example of a trademark case gone wrong comes to hand in a Texas case concerning *E.T.*[45] The defendant, who blithely testified that he never applies for licenses because they cost too much, manufactured

---

[39] *Id.* § 101 (1982).

[40] *See* Esquire, Inc. v. Ringer, 591 F.2d 796 (D.C. Cir. 1978), *cert. denied*, 440 U.S. 908, *reh'g denied*, 441 U.S. 917 (1979). *Cf.* Kieselstein-Cord v. Accessories By Pearl, Inc., 632 F.2d 989 (2d Cir. 1980).

[41] *See* Kieselstein-Cord v. Accessories By Pearl, Inc., 632 F.2d at 994 (Weinstein, J., dissenting).

[42] Goldstein, *supra* note 8, at 230.

[43] Nimetz, *Design Protection*, 15 Copyright L. Sym. (ASCAP) 79 (1976). Professor Goldstein, in correspondence, says that I have misread him:

> All that I tried to suggest in my analysis of *Jack Adelman* [Jack Adelman, Inc. v. Sonner's & Gordon, Inc., 21 U.S.P.Q. (BNA) 218 (S.D.N.Y. 1934)] was that I would let derivative works go where the logic and the design of the Act would take them, entirely apart from the very difficult question of investment effects. I really have a hard time determining whether we need more or less investment in the apparel industries and would prefer to treat the issue from a viewpoint of economic indifference—allowing the general logic of the Act to control until someone can rigorously demonstrate that we have too much or too little investment in this form of subject matter.

Letter from Paul Goldstein to Ralph S. Brown (Dec. 5, 1983).

[44] Goldstein, *supra* note 8, at 227.

[45] Universal City Studios, Inc. v. Kamar Indus., Inc., 217 U.S.P.Q. (BNA) 1162 (S.D. Tex. 1982).

mugs that said "I love E.T.," and "E.T. phone home." We have a set of memorandum findings of fact and law that should never have seen print, because it is too clear that they meticulously parrot every theory the plaintiff's lawyers could think of—statutory trademark, common-law trademark, Lanham Act section 43(a), misappropriation, and copyright. Yes, copyright. That is absurd. Now I must allow that if the mug-maker had embossed his product with the lightning-bug lineaments of E.T., that could infringe a copyright. But do the initials "E.T." copy the character E.T.? The court so held.[46] As for the captions, there is no occasion at all to recognize copyright in phrases and slogans, especially when, standing alone, they are commonplace. For that matter, "phone home" is a basic idea of *E.T.*, is it not?

That invocation, perhaps over-simplified, of the fundamental divide between unprotectable idea and protectable expression, leads me to the last of the comments I want to make on this half of our subject. Some kinds of derivative works that claim copyright stem-from a work of exposition—how to do it. Expository expressions are certainly protected, but the plan or system that they are trying to express is not. One example is the limited protection given to legal forms. The classic example is the mysterious bookkeeping system in *Baker v. Selden*,[47] which Goldstein suggests should be "viewed as a threshold decision on derivative rights."[48] That vigorous Supreme Court decision of 1879, though outmoded in some of its examples, drew a firm line between exposition and substance that survives despite upstart attacks by some academics. I merely want to point out, smugly, that it is now embedded in the statute, right up front in section 102(b):

> In no case does copyright protection for an original work of authorship extend to any idea, procedure, process, system, method of operation, concept, principle, or discovery, regardless of the form in which it is described, explained, illustrated, or embodied in such work.[49]

Could a statement be more emphatic? Can there be any doubt that it extends to every kind of work? Yet it seems to be suffering from benign neglect. Even if, as the influential House Committee Report states, it neither "enlarges or contracts the scope of copyright protection under

---

[46] *Id.* at 1166.
[47] 101 U.S. 99 (1879).
[48] Goldstein, *supra* note 8, at 230.
[49] 17 U.S.C. § 102(b) (1982).

the present law,"[50] *Baker v. Selden* was and is very much the foundation of that law.

To sum up thus far: The proliferation of derivative works is not ground for dismay; their variety and profitability indeed enhance the attractions of authorship.

But, first, it is reasonable for courts faced with squabbles between competitors in crowded markets, to set perceptible thresholds of originality for derivative products that are mass-produced and mass-merchandised, especially when the base work is in the public domain, or is a well-known work that is widely licensed. That threshold can take account of the skill and effort reflected in the derivative work. "Trivial variations" should not impede the competitive production of other variations.

Second, derivative works cannot escape certain basic boundaries of copyright, especially one that seeks "to draw as clear a line as possible between copyrightable works of applied art and uncopyrighted works of industrial design."[51] In addition, they must respect still another boundary that leaves ideas, systems, methods of operation, and so on in the public domain, unless they qualify for patent protection.

Third, copyright should not be distorted to protect interests in names, symbols, undeveloped characters and other popular magnets that can seek protection by way of well-established headings of unfair competition, chiefly trademark and misrepresentation.

III. Rights in Derivative Works

We now turn to the rights of makers of derivative works, and of the public. Movie-makers provide most of the problems, because they seem to have been extraordinarily careless about renewing their copyrights, if we can so infer from a run of cases in the last few years.[52] (I ask, parenthetically, what is there about the industry that permits such indifference? Is it a fixation on the next blockbuster, a contempt for its past? I wish somebody could explain this.) When the makers have failed to renew and have accordingly lost copyright, and when

---

[50] H.R. Rep. No. 94-1476, 94th Cong., 2d Sess. 57, *reprinted in* 1976 U.S. Code Cong. & Ad. News 5659, 5670–71.

[51] *Id.* at 55.

[52] *See, e.g.*, Rohauer v. Killiam Shows, Inc., 551 F.2d 484 (2d Cir.), *cert. denied*, 431 U.S. 949 (1977); Russell v. Price, 612 F.2d 1123 (9th Cir. 1979), *cert. denied*, 446 U.S. 952 (1980); Classic Film Museum, Inc. v. Warner Bros., Inc., 597 F.2d 13 (1st Cir. 1979).

the films have turned out to have continuing artistic or commercial vitality, an urgent problem has surfaced: What if the film was derived from an underlying literary or dramatic work in which copyright still subsists? On the one hand, if the copyright in the film was not renewed, or if its total term has expired,[53] the work should be in the public domain. The public's privilege to exhibit and to see it should be asserted. On the other hand, the owner of the underlying work has rights too. Does not the making of new prints, and any public performance of the film, reproduce or perform the underlying work?

This issue has been generalized, and elevated to a high level of controversy. In this corner, the defender of the primacy of the underlying work, and accordingly of the subordination of the derivative work. Let us hear it for Professor Nimmer and his trusty seconds![54] In that corner, the contenders for old movie fans everywhere, who see new property rights in derivative works. Whom shall we designate as *the* challenger? I would choose Professor Jaszi,[55] who also has able seconds such as Professors Ellingson and Nevins.[56] But I will not bewilder you with the blow-by-blow confusion as the contestants belabor each other. I will, lifting Judge Woolsey's phrase in the Letty Lynton case, take a "more Olympian viewpoint",[57] and just as the

---

[53] Works published before January 1, 1978, have a first term of 28 years, renewable for 28 years under the old law, 17 U.S.C. § 24 (Supp. 1964), *amended by* 17 U.S.C. §§ 302–305(1982), but the renewal term is extended to 47 years under the 1976 Act section 304, thus providing a total term of 75 years. Seventy-five years is also the duration of a work made for hire, under section 302(c), a category into which all corporately produced movies would fall. But if the underlying work has a natural author, its copyright duration will be the life of the author plus 50 years. 17 U.S.C. § 302(a). So, if the author survives for more than 25 years after the derivative work is made, copyright in the underlying work will still subsist when the derivative work's expires.

Example: an author born in 1965 publishes a novel in 1990. A movie based on the novel appears in 1995. The copyright in the movie will expire in 2070. But if the author dies in 2050 (aged 85), the copyright in the novel will last till 2100.

So the problems created under the old law, by failure to renew a derivative work, can still arise; one should live so long.

[54] 1 M. Nimmer, Nimmer on Copyright § 3.07 (1983); Stoll, *Derivative Copyright and the 1909 Act—New Clarity or Confusion?* 44 Brooklyn L. Rev. 905 (1978); Comment, *Derivative Copyright Proprietor May Continue to Exhibit Derivative Work Notwithstanding Termination of License to Use Underlying Copyrighted Work Employed by the Derivative Work—Rohauer v. Killiam Shows, Inc.*, 11 Suffolk U. L. Rev. 1374 (1977).

[55] *See* Jaszi, *When Works Collide: Derivative Motion Pictures, Underlying Rights and the Public Interest*, 28 UCLA L. Rev. 715 (1981).

[56] *See* Ellingson, *The Copyright Exception for Derivative Works and the Scope of Utilization*, 56 Ind. L.J. 1 (1980); Nevins, *The Doctrine of Copyright Ambush: Limitations on the Free Use of Public Domain Derivative Works*, 25 St. Louis U.L.J. 58 (1981).

[57] Sheldon v. Metro-Goldwyn Pictures Corp., 7 F. Supp. 837, 842 (S.D.N.Y. 1934), *rev'd*, 81 F.2d 49 (2d Cir.), *cert. denied*, 298 U.S.669 (1936).

Olympian gods intervened in duels upon the dusty plains of Troy, so will I try to determine several outcomes; never mind that I am in real life a mere mortal.

Let us first give some attention to the cases. The starting-point is *Ricordi & Co. v. Paramount Pictures, Inc.*,[58] the *Madam Butterfly* case, decided in 1951 by an exceptionally strong bench—Judges Learned Hand, Swan, and Frank. I know that the new property people reach back to *Edmonds v. Stern*,[59] of 1918. But I do not find there all that they do;[60] and in any event I do not give much weight even to the Second Circuit's decisions in the decade following the 1909 statute. With all respect, they were floundering in the heavy wake of a new statute, just as courts and commentators may be doing now.

Ricordi was a casebook classic. John Luther Long, a Philadelphia lawyer and a part-time writer, published a story in 1897.[61] The flamboyant David Belasco made a one-act play of it in 1900. These are both forgotten. Puccini and his lyricists, with licenses from Long and Belasco, gave us the immortal *Madame Butterfly* in 1904. The play did not claim statutory copyright until 1917; it was not renewed, and, therefore, it lost copyright in 1945. Copyright in the story, however, was renewed—Long, let us not forget, *was* a Philadelphia lawyer—and accordingly still subsisted at the time of the litigation.

Paramount had been diligent in acquiring movie rights from both Long and Belasco. Indeed, in one of his often intriguing 351 footnotes, Professor Jaszi tells us that Paramount did make a movie of *Madame Butterfly* in 1915, starring Mary Pickford![62] Would not that be fun to see?

Ricordi, Puccini's publisher, launched this action to establish *its* movie rights. It learned what it should have expected: that, though it had a copyright in what Puccini had added to the story, notably the glorious music, it had no movie rights in the underlying story. Paramount and Ricordi both learned that whatever Belasco had added was in the public domain. So there was a standoff, not an unusual one: Paramount could make a movie, but not with Puccini's music, while Ricordi could not make a movie with Long's story imbedded in it.

What we all learned were two important things. First, that "[a] copyright renewal creates a new estate . . . clear of all rights, interests or licenses granted under the original copyright."[63] Even if Ri-

---

58 189 F.2d 469 (2d Cir. 1951).

59 248 F. 897 (2d Cir. 1918).

60 *See* Jaszi, *supra* note 55, at 760, 797.

61 *See* M. Carner, Puccini: A Critical Biography 120 (1959).

62 Jaszi, *supra* note 55, at 797 n. 291.

63 *Ricordi*, 189 F.2d at 471.

cordi had acquired movie rights in Long's first term, it did not get them after he renewed. The separate integrity of the second term, under the 1909 law, has always seemed to be dictated by the statute itself, and in any event to have been affirmed by the Supreme Court, albeit by a shaky 5-4 decision, in the *Moonlight and Roses* case of 1960.[64] Indeed, Long might have demanded a new license for the opera when he renewed in 1925. If he had died before then, whoever had the renewal right could have said, "New license, or no opera." (As we will see, Judge Friendly mussed up the clarity of this insight in the *Son of the Sheik* case.)[65]

We now learn the second lesson of *Ricordi*. Prodded by Paramount for clarification, the court agreed that it should not have said that after Belasco's copyright in his play was not renewed "the play was in the public demesne." Rather, it amended the opinion to read that when the copyright expired, "the *copyrightable new matter in the play* was property in the public demesne . . ."[66] Surely Long's underlying story did not lose its copyright when Belasco's play did. As a general proposition, this is unexceptionable. But it has led to much puzzlement.

The case that first tested the implications of *Ricordi*'s second lesson was *Grove Press Inc. v. Greenleaf Publishing Co.*,[67] a district court opinion which has had remarkable influence. An authorized English translation of Genet's *A Thief's Journal* did not attain United States copyright because of a supposed failure to comply with the *ad interim* provisions of our law for imported books in English, pending compliance with our regressive manufacturing clause.[68] This is not an appealing way for a work to enter the public domain; but there it was. When Grove published a revised translation, Greenleaf attempted to compete with the public domain version. Judge Bartels held that this was an infringing copy of the French original. He said that although the first translation "like any other derivative work . . . is separate and apart from the underlying work . . . a dedication to the public of the derivative work did not, without more, emancipate the pattern of the underlying work from its copyright."[69]

---

[64] Miller Music Corp. v. Charles N. Daniel's, Inc., 362 U.S. 373 (1960).

[65] *See infra* text accompanying notes 85–90.

[66] *See* Nevins, *supra* note 56, at 66 (emphasis supplied).

[67] 247 F. Supp. 518 (E.D.N.Y. 1965).

[68] 17 U.S.C. § 16 (Supp. 1964), *repealed by* Copyright Revision Act of 1974, Pub. L. No. 94-553, 90 Stat. 2541.

[69] *Grove Press*, 247 F. Supp. at 525. This case, incidentally, is the second reported case to use the familiar phrase "derivative work." It follows six months after the first one, Nom Music, Inc. v. Kaslin, 343 F.2d 198, 200 (2d Cir. 1965).

It is clear from other passages in the opinion that Judge Bartels thought he had to face the question whether the unprotected publication of the translation in this country "destroyed the author's copyright protection in his literary composition."[70] For example, he read *Ricordi* as raising the same question, "the differentiation between dedicating the underlying work and the derivative work to the public."[71] There was nothing in that opinion about dedicating the underlying work to the public. The question was just what Belasco's failure to renew left open to the parties. It is worth emphasizing that these parties were not interested at all in printing or producing Belasco's play; they both wanted exclusive rights to make a motion picture.

Judge Bartels correctly quoted Nimmer's first edition, then fresh off the press, which stated, "[I]t would seem that any *authorized* publication of a derivative work must necessarily also constitute a publication of the basic work upon which it is based."[72] But it should have been clear, from the stated facts in the *Thief's Journal* case, that Genet's publisher had not authorized any publication of the first translation in the United States, and, assuredly, not the defendant's publication.

I do not want to quibble about the nuances of a district court opinion, even an influential one, but mischief has followed it. While Nimmer's text still contains the quoted statement about the effect of an authorized publication, the heading of that section now reads: "The General Rule: Publication of a Derivative Work Constitutes Publication of the Basic Work."[73] However, I assert that there is no such general rule; and I can think of no reason why courts would not be alert to protect the underlying work from loss of its copyright, when by the act of another or by operation of law a derivative work came into the public domain.

Any fear that free use of the public domain derivative work would divest copyright in an underlying work should be allayed. When the movie cases came along, notably *Russell v. Price*,[74] the *Pygmalion* case, the Ninth Circuit did not raise that bugaboo. There, copyright in the 1938 film, starring Wendy Hiller and Leslie Howard, had not been renewed. But, you can be sure, George Bernard Shaw had renewed his copyright in the play—it doesn't expire until 1988—[75]

---

[70] *Grove Press*, 247 F. Supp. at 524.

[71] *Id.* at 526.

[72] *Id.* at 525 (emphasis added).

[73] 1 M. NIMMER, *supra* note 54, § 4.12[A], at 4-57.

[74] 612 F.2d 1123 (9th Cir. 1979), *cert. denied*, 446 U.S. 952 (1980).

and his successors sued a would-be distributor. The court held flatly that "established doctrine prevents unauthorized copying or other infringing use of the underlying work or any part of that work contained in the derivative product so long as the underlying work itself remains copyrighted."[76] The court did not explicitly address the claims of the public domain, perhaps because the defendant vainly argued for a new property right in the derivative work.

The Second Circuit expressly agreed with the *Pygmalion* case in *Filmvideo Releasing Corp. v. Hastings*,[77] better known as the *Hopalong Cassidy* litigation. There, copyright had not been renewed on no fewer than 23 westerns; and they had ostensibly come into the public domain.[78] As the court viewed defendant's claims, defendant "contended . . . that it was entitled to make free and untrammeled use of the movie prints in all media."[79] (It is clear that the television late-night market was really in mind.) If that was the defendant's contention, then the court was only slightly exaggerating when it said that:

> The principal question on this appeal is whether a licensed, derivative, copyrighted work and the underlying copyrighted matter which it incorporates both fall into the public domain where the underlying copyright has been renewed but the derivative copyright has not. We agree with the Ninth Circuit, *Russell v. Price*, that the answer is "No".[80]

However, that was not the way *Russell v. Price*, the *Pygmalion* court put the question, and the *Hopalong Cassidy* court did not, I think, advance the analysis by observing that the proprietor of a derivative copyright "cannot release that which he does not own into the public domain."[81] Here we are, plagued again with the false notion that if the derivative work becomes available to the public, the underlying work must be pushed into the public domain. I would urge that in all these cases—Belasco's *Butterfly*, Genet's *Thief's Journal*, *Pygmalion*, and *Hopalong Cassidy*—the precise derivative work that is in the public domain can be copied and exhibited. But that does not diminish, let along divest, any other rights of the author or owner of

---

[75] Jaszi, *supra* note 55, at 769 n. 158.

[76] *Russell*, 612 F.2d at 1128.

[77] 668 F.2d 91 (2d Cir. 1981).

[78] This case was confused by serious issues about whether all the films really were copies of Clarence Milford's cowboy novels. *See* Nevins, *supra* note 56, at 83.

[79] *Filmvideo*, 668 F.2d at 92.

[80] *Id.*

[81] *Id.* at 93.

the underlying work. No one may, without license, make another derivative work. I would further protect the underlying work by limiting the public domain uses to those the derivative grantee had. Thus, in *Hopalong Cassidy*, where the novelist had reserved television rights, I would say that the non-renewal did not open up television rights to the public. To the extent that the underlying author is still injured, she should sue the original movie-maker for breach of an implied covenant to keep the derivative work in copyright.[82]

This limited opening, I suggest, should resolve the seeming paradox that a work that has come into the public domain can still not be in the public domain. One could, however, live with paradoxes. What is more persuasive, it seems to me, are the arguments of Jaszi and Nevins that old films, not in copyright, should be available for critical and entertainment uses without having to negotiate with the owner of an underlying work—but not because of some "new property" theory as they propose.[83] Rather, I would insist that there is *no* property in these public domain works, because that is what it means to be in the public domain. Nonetheless, the property in the underlying works should be respected in that the holders of copyright in the underlying works should control, among other rights, the preparation of any other derivative works.

The policy arguments in favor of access to derivative works that are no longer in copyright are especially appealing on behalf of movies, because film-makers often transform and transcend the underlying work. However, the recognition of public domain status should not depend on the medium, nor on the extent of the transformation since that would entangle courts with qualitative judgments.

Can this position be reconciled with the cases discussed? Not entirely. One could say of the *Thief's Journal* case that a translation, unlike a film version, so parallels the original, that the original is so completely embedded in it, as to leave nothing for the public domain. But that is to belittle the art of translation.[84] Furthermore, one could diminish the *Hopalong Cassidy* precedent by arguing that the court properly kept the defendant from what it wanted in that case—

---

[82] This remedy is also proposed by Jaszi, *supra* note 55, at 811. A farsighted draftsman would include an express covenant binding the movie-maker to renew, which could be backed up by a power of attorney authorizing the licensor to do so.

[83] *See* Jaszi, *supra* note 55; Nevins, *supra* note 56. Professor Ellingson also espouses the "new property" right. Ellingson, *supra* note 56. Professor Nevins and I came to very similar conclusions about what can be done with derivative works. Nevins, *supra* note 56, at 79–80.

[84] *But cf.* Nevins, *supra* note 56, at 80, arguing for continuing control over translations and thus reconciling the outcome in *Grove Press* with his (and my) positions.

television rights that the derivative licensee never had. The privilege of exhibiting the old movies (which is all that should be allowed) was not really at issue.

However, *Russell v. Price*, the *Pygmalion* case, still stands squarely in the way. It blocks exhibition of what should be a public domain film. All one can say is that the defendant there (and likewise in the *Hopalong Cassidy* case) misdirected the court's attention and caused the court to place misguided reliance on a faulty foundation, *Rohauer v. Killiam Shows, Inc.*[85] In this 1977 case, the author of a novel on which a Rudolph Valentino film, *The Son of the Sheik*, was based, had promised to assign the renewal term to the film-maker; but the author died before renewal time. Her only child renewed and, as one would have thought was her clear right under the old statute,[86] assigned movie and television rights in the novel to another. In the meantime, the film-maker renewed its copyright. There was no public domain issue in the case—it was a quarrel about who had the renewal rights. In a stunning display of his powers, Judge Friendly in writing for the court stood *Madame Butterfly* on her head, threw dust in everyone's eyes, and held that the film-maker's assignee was entitled to the renewal right. The outcome is perhaps defensible in that it anticipated the similar arrangement that was about to come into existence in the new Act. That compromised cousin of renewal rights, the right to terminate a grant, includes a massive exception in favor of the continued exploitation of a derivative work.[87] One could say that the Second Circuit, as it had done before,[88] was only trying to correct an anomaly that legislation also was about to correct.

But the analytic road it took in *Rohauer* seemed to offer aid and comfort to the proponents of a new property in derivative works; they rode down it to their doom in the public domain cases. The *Pygmalion* court, easily distinguishing *Rohauer*, said that it "express[ed] no opinion about the merits" of that case.[89] In *Hopalong Cassidy*, another panel of the Second Circuit in a kindly way referred to the "aberration" in *Rohauer* as "a minor one."[90]

---

[85] 551 F.2d 484 (2d Cir.), *cert. denied*, 431 U.S. 949 (1977).

[86] *See supra* text accompanying notes 58–65.

[87] 17 U.S.C. §§ 203(b)(1), 304 (1982). *See* 2 M. Nimmer, *supra* note 54, § 9.07, at 9–88; Ellingson, *supra* note 56.

[88] *See, e.g.*, Goodis v. United Artists Television, Inc., 425 F.2d 397 (2d Cir. 1970) (notice in name of magazine publisher protects contributors, anticipating § 403(a)).

[89] *Russell*, 612 F.2d at 1126 n.10.

[90] *Filmvideo*, 668 F.2d at 93.

The commentators have been less kind.[91] Even Professor Jaszi, who appeared for the winner in *Rohauer*, which Judge Friendly said was "well briefed and argued"[92]—praise from Sir Henry is praise indeed!—concedes that there are "major objections"[93] to the opinion. I will not add to the bloodletting.

Nor need I say much about one other recent case that winds through this sequence, *Classic Film Museum, Inc. v. Warner Bros.*,[94] where the First Circuit in 1979 affirmed Judge Gignoux's "learned and succinct opinion" below.[95] Warner, having let the copyright on the 1937 production of *A Star is Born* lapse, now tried to assert its supposed common-law copyright in its script in order to prevent defendant from showing the film. Judge Gignoux said that the film was "dedicated in its entirety to the public use."[96] To hold otherwise, he said, "would frustrate the whole concept of limited monopoly in copyright law."[97] *A Star is Born* is as right as *Son of a Sheik* is wrong.

We have no way of knowing how many other public domain films may be blocked by persisting copyrights in underlying works. Eventually their copyrights too will expire. Looking ahead, the 1976 exemption that will permit the continued exploitation of a derivative work despite the exercise of grant termination ought to suffice to keep derivative works available. On grounds of incompetence, I will spare you any discussion of the angularities of grant termination.

Note that it is almost taken for granted that owners of the derivative and the underlying rights will not make deals at renewal time, if a deal is necessary, or that the Shaw estate will not offer a license at a price that will make it worth some entrepreneur's while to peddle *Pygmalion*. Deadlock is the feared outcome, and long deadlocks.

A contrary expectation, namely that rational parties will not stay deadlocked, is reflected in a line of cases that have dealt with the rights of existing licensees when new uses emerged that would diminish the old ones. The first of these, *Harper Bros. v. Klaw*,[98] in 1916, death with the effect on the exclusive licensee of dramatic rights to *Ben Hur* when a movie-maker came on the scene. Judge Hough's

---

[91] *See, e.g.*, 1 M. NIMMER, *supra* note 54, § 3.07A; Mimms, *Reversion and Derivative Works Under the Copyright Acts of 1909 and 1976*, 25 N.Y.L. SCH. L. REV. 595 (1980).

[92] *Rohauer*, 551 F.2d at 485.

[93] Jaszi, *supra* note 55, at 777.

[94] 597 F.2d 13, 15 (1st Cir. 1979).

[95] Classic Film Museum, Inc. v. Warner Bros., 453 F. Supp. 852 (D. Me. 1978).

[96] *Id.* at 856.

[97] *Id.*

[98] 232 F. 609 (S.D.N.Y. 1916); *See* B. KAPLAN & R. BROWN, *supra* note 10, at 369–86.

solution was to invoke an implied covenant not to undercut the dramatic license. The publisher of the novel could not grant movie rights without the play producer's consent, and the play producer could not expand his license and make a movie. Somehow, the world still turned. But courts and commentators are often remote from the world. Possibly the avarice of authors does prevent us from seeing old movies.

There is another reason why the author of an underlying novel may want to get hold of the movie at renewal time. Maybe she hated it. Professor Nevins tells us that Clarence Mulford would complain bitterly of the ways he thought Hollywood was distorting his creation, *Hopalong Cassidy*. But all he got in reply was soothing words, and a box of cigars.[99] There are authors more famous than he who after one bitter experience turned their backs on Hollywood; Willa Cather, for one; J.D. Salinger, for another.[100] Let's face it, many movies are terrible.

Such authors, through their copyrights, are able to invoke the moral rights that the law otherwise grants so imperfectly. The author's interest in the integrity of his work, even if it is often dissolved by dollars, stands as an obstacle to other people's notions of how to exploit it. It also, we should note, gums up unvarnished economic analysis of copyright interests. Can economics measure something that, to the author, is priceless?

I have taken a pretty stern line about the extent of rights in derivative works, vis-à-vis the owner of the renewed term in the underlying work. I think *Rohauer* was an aberration, and not a minor one. Cranky as the old law was in its disposition of renewal rights, its outcomes had become fairly settled, and should be respected. If the new statute had swept away the whole jerry-built structure and had transmuted all existing terms to the new span of duration, I for one would have applauded. But it did not; and it seems over-activist for judges to try to convert old grants into the shape they would have *if* they had arisen under the new law.

"Stern" also describes my attitude toward the new property thesis. New property in what the derivative author has added, certainly; but not enough new property to create a forced license to copy the underlying work. Proponents of the moviemakers seize upon Justice Kaplan's observation that:

---

[99] *See* Nevins, *supra* note 56, at 68.

[100] Fosburgh, *Why More Top Novelists Don't Go Hollywood*, N.Y. Times, Nov. 21, 1976, § 2 (Arts and Leisure), at 1, col. 1.

> It is surely wrong to assume that what Hollywood is content to call a dramatization or screen treatment of a novel or play would necessarily be an infringing copy if not licensed.[101]

Some treatments would not infringe. Sometimes, as we know, the film-maker is really buying only the title and its pulling-power; what initially followed the title may be not at all the stuff of dream merchants. In other cases the law will, I think, apply to derivative works, as to any others, Learned Hand's hard-boiled precept that if "substantial parts were lifted[,] no plagiarist can excuse the wrong by showing how much of his work he did not pirate."[102]

IV. Remedies

Still, I have concessions to offer. As the last part of this essay, I would like to make a few observations about adjusting remedies with respect to derivative works. Procedure, substance, remedies—why do our eyes glaze over when remedies are mentioned? Perhaps because they come at the end—of a trial, of a text, of a lecture. Yet considerable subtlety of outcomes can be achieved by flexibility of remedies, especially by tempering injunctions to the perceived equities of a situation. When you have flatout reproduction of a work, even in another medium, an injunction should follow as a matter of course. When ambiguities arise, not so fast.

Here I am in such extensive agreement with Professor Goldstein that I will do little more than paraphrase his suggestions.[103] First, injunctions, especially preliminary injunctions, should not be awarded so routinely. Now and then a district judge in this circuit will withhold a preliminary injunction, only to have the court of appeals give short shrift to the trial court's supposed discretion[104]—a discretion confirmed by section 502 of the new statute. As Alan Latman neatly summed up the situation:

> In copyright cases, such relief is often close to automatic; in patent cases, it is close to impossible; in trademarks, and unfair competition, it depends.[105]

---

[101] B. Kaplan, An Unhurried View of Copyright 56 (1967).

[102] Sheldon v. Metro Goldwyn Pictures Corp., 81 F.2d 49, 56 (2d Cir.), *cert. denied*, 298 U.S. 669 (1936).

[103] Goldstein, *supra* note 8, at 236–39. Similar proposals are found in B. Kaplan, *supra* note 101, at 70–73.

[104] *See, e.g.*, Concord Fabrics, Inc. v. Marcus Bros. Textile Corp., 296 F. Supp. 736 (S.D.N.Y.) (preliminary injunction denied), *rev'd per curiam*, 409 F.2d 1315 (2d Cir. 1969).

[105] Latman, *Preliminary Injunctions in Patent, Trademark and Copyright Cases*, 60 Trade-Mark Rep. 506 (1970).

I have never understood why this is so; but it is not too late to mend.

When the infringed work is only a part of a larger work, as would usually be true of a movie, the court should limit any award of profits to the portion that the plaintiff contributed. This is settled law. May it not then also consider whether a permanent injunction against further copying is appropriate? Even if an injunction is viewed as a matter almost of right, surely we have learned a lot in the civil rights decades about how injunctions can be shaped to fit the case.

One approach was heralded by Professor Calabresi and Mr. Melamed in their pioneering article, *One View of the Cathedral*,[106] and boldly applied in the Arizona nuisance case of *Spur v. Webb.*[107] There, the developer who had built up to defendant's smelly cattle-feeding lot was awarded an injunction; but he had to pay the lot operator's moving costs. Such an approach would give the injunction to the infringed author but require him to compensate the loser for her losses that were independent of the infringement. That would really create pressure to avoid deadlock and come to terms, would it not?

What about my incorruptible author who wants nothing to do with a derivative medium and whose rights have been invaded? Must such a plaintiff be required by an equity court to submit to an involuntary license? Surely not; but it would, I submit, be reasonable to require the author to satisfy the judge that she is indeed clinging to principles, not to the other party's checkbook.

The mere mention of involuntary licenses—and that is the outcome, even if the plaintiff gets carefully allocated damages, a conditional injunction, and nothing more—may cause many a heart in this room to skip a beat. I do not want to bring on any chest pains, and I quickly concede that the issue is not a laughing matter. I have read with care Register Ladd's eloquent lecture of last April.[108] But, as Professor Goldstein points out, we are not talking about statutory licenses that lie crudely on whole industries or segments of them.[109] Ours is a utopian prescription that we share for individual cases where there are equities on both sides.

What Paul Goldstein and I do not share is his confidence in the flexibility of state unfair competition law to take care of odd cases that

---

[106] Calabresi & Melamed, *Property Rules, Liability Rules, and Inalienability: One View of the Cathedral*, 85 HARV. L. REV. 1089, 1105–24 (1972).

[107] Spur Indus. Inc. v. Del E. Webb Dev. Co., 108 Ariz. 178, 494 P.2d 700 (1972).

[108] Ladd, *The Harm of the Concept of Harm in Copyright*, 30 J. COPYRIGHT SOC'Y 421 (1983).

[109] Goldstein, *supra* note 8, at 238 n. 94.

stretch copyright out of recognition.[110] My lack of confidence stems from the tendency of state law to take under its wing plaintiffs who want relief not just from unfair competition, but simply from competition.[111] The drafters of the 1976 copyright law tried to check these end-runs with a powerfully preemptive section 301. This is not the time to inquire how section 301 was weakened, and what its future is.[112]

But one is not encouraged when one notes the persistent sapping, especially by New York courts, of the foundations of preemption. Consider a recent appellate division decision upholding state court jurisdiction.[113] Plaintiff charged defendant, a competitor in licensing transparencies of art masterworks, with "misappropriating" some of its slides, with a view to selling reproduction rights. Sounds like a copyright claim, does it not? However, the court, dividing 3 to 2, said that "obtaining a copy for the purpose of copying is not necessarily copyright violation,"[114] so that this claim was not preempted. This is cause for sorrow, because the presiding justice who wrote for the majority surely yields to no one, in any court, in his grasp of copyright law.

A very able federal judge in this District writes as follows, in private correspondence (I have permission to quote him, with appropriate deletions.):

> One aspect of the subject that I think needs more stress is that Congress has permitted the states to legislate in ways that greatly extend protection. Ironically, the state statutes involved end up being construed primarily by federal courts, by way of pendent jurisdiction. While I strongly felt no protection should be afforded the [widgets] discussed in the enclosed opinion, for example, I felt compelled to give protection under state law. I have reached similar conclusions in other cases.[115]

It may be that federal judges can be more faithful to their convictions by a more vigorous application of preemptive doctrines, but that, as I said, is another subject.

---

110 *Id.* at 222–24.

111 *See* Brown, *Product Simulation: A Right or a Wrong?*, 64 COLUM. L. REV. 1216 (1964).

112 *See* Brown, *Unification: A Cheerful Requiem for Common Law Copyright*, 24 UCLA L. REV. 1070, 1089–1106 (1977).

113 Editorial Photocolor Archives, Inc. v. Granger Collection, 94 A.D. 2d 347, 464 N.Y.S. 2d 506 (1st Dept. 1983).

114 *Id.* at 350, 464 N.Y.S. 2d at 508.

115 Letter from federal district court judge to Ralph S. Brown. *Cf.* Bi-Rite Enters., Inc. v. Button Master, 555 F. Supp. 1188, 1196 (S.D.N.Y. 1983) (court denied relief on Lanham Act claims, but recognized state law publicity right).

I have strayed from derivative works to vent long-standing spleens. To return just for a moment to the theme of flexibility within the copyright system, I must say something about fair use. Where would we be without it? Consider this heavily derivative lecture. Fair use is my shield. To change the metaphor, it is a marvelous safety-valve to relieve the pressures of literal insistence on rights.

As you know, four "factors" are to be considered, according to the statute: the purpose of the use, the nature of the work, the substantiality of the taking, and—now I quote—"the effect of the use upon the potential market for or value of the copyrighted work."[116]

There is a movement afoot, it seems to me, to single out and exalt the fourth factor—the effect upon *potential* markets and values.[117] For many derivative works, potential markets are as unlimited as hucksters' imaginations. But it is not a seller's desire to monopolize markets that creates values. It is the law's readiness to exclude others that is decisive, and that readiness calls for a sensitive awareness of the scope of incentives that copyright is intended to evoke.

A recent student note in the *Harvard Law Review* makes the impertinent assertion that "copyright law can now be viewed as simply an anti-misappropriation scheme that protects the fruits of intellectual labor."[118]

No such thing. Let me cite an authority that arguably outweighs the *Harvard Law Review*, namely the Supreme Court of the United States.

> Creative work is to be encouraged and rewarded, but private motivation must ultimately serve the cause of promoting broad public availability of literature, music, and the other arts. The immediate effect of our copyright law is to secure a fair return for an author's creative labor. But the ultimate aim is, by this incentive, to stimulate artistic creativity for the general public good.[119]

---

[116] 17 U.S.C. § 107(4) (1982).

[117] These issues are ably examined in Gordon, *Fair Use as Market Failure: A Structural and Economic Analysis of the Betamax Case and its Predecessors*, 82 Colum. L. Rev. 1600 (1982). The Betamax case, at last decided, Sony Corp. of Am. v. Universal City Studios, Inc., 52 U.S.L.W. 4090 (U.S. Jan. 17, 1984), gives primacy to the nature of the use, whether commercial or non-commercial. It gives little guidance concerning derivative uses, which are usually commercial.

[118] Note, *Copyright Protection of Computer Program Object Code*, 96 Harv. L. Rev. 1723, 1741 (1983).

[119] This passage, which has many counterparts, is from Twentieth Century Music Corp. v. Aiken, 422 U.S. 151, 156 (1975).

On this elevated note, we may conclude. Copyright does serve the public interest. But it is a fragile thing. Technology has vastly extended its reach beyond the maps, charts, and books that were the sole subject-matter of our first statute of 1790. Technology can also destroy copyright because of the ease of evasion by cunning predators.

Yeats went on, in his *Second Coming*, to decry a time when

> The best lack all conviction, while the worst
> Are full of passionate intensity.[120]

Fortunately for copyright, the best, exemplified by people like Herman Finkelstein, do have convictions, and act on them. As for the worst, I leave them to your judgments; and I thank you for your attention.

---

[120] W. B. YEATS, *supra* note 1.

TABLE 1

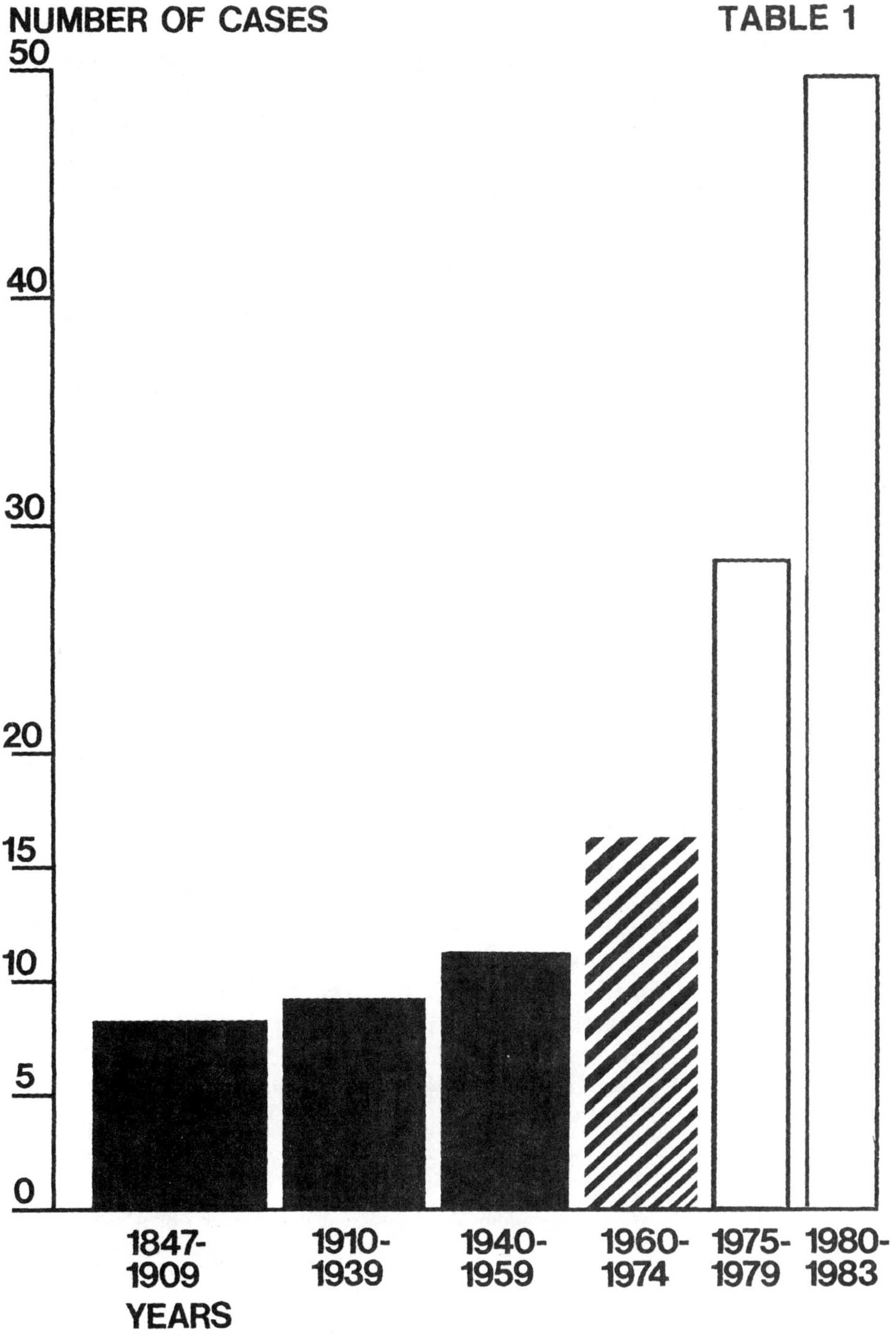
NUMBER OF CASES
50
40
30
20
15
10
5
0
1847-1909
1910-1939
1940-1959
1960-1974
1975-1979
1980-1983
YEARS

THE COMPULSORY LICENSE REDUX: WILL IT SURVIVE IN A CHANGING MARKETPLACE?

RALPH OMAN*

I. INTRODUCTION

Long ago, the Copyright Act could comfortably fit in one's pocket without disturbing one's profile.[1] This Act contained only one explicit limitation on a copyright owner's otherwise exclusive power to negotiate (or to decline) a license for all uses of a copyrighted work. The "mechanical compulsory license"[2] provided the owner of a copyright in a musical work who had authorized the creation and publication, of what the current law calls phonorecords, a right to statutorily determined compensation if others made different recordings of his music. As most copyright practitioners know, Congress enacted this restriction on authors' rights out of fear that the few existing manufacturers would monopolize the market for "mechanical rights" if it were left unregulated.[3]

This compulsory license and those that followed owed their creation to the *combination* of a desire to capture royalties from new technological uses of copyrighted works, and a fear that a purely private market for those uses would result in one or more aspects of a monopolized market. These aspects are artificially high prices, restricted output, or reduced public access to works of authorship. As technology has ratcheted forward, we have periodically discovered new ways in which to use copyrighted works, and, almost always, we have commercially exploited them. That exploitation has virtually always preceded a modification of the copyright law making clear that copyright would govern the

---

* Register of Copyrights and Associate Librarian of Congress for Copyright Services; B.A., 1962, Hamilton College; J.D., 1973, Georgetown University.

This Article is printed essentially as it was delivered at the Herman Finkelstein Lecture, Benjamin N. Cardozo School of Law, March 20, 1986. This Lecture honors the retired General Counsel of the American Society of Composers, Authors and Publishers, and Director, Nathan Burkan Memorial Competition.

In preparing this Article, the author received valuable assistance from Christopher A. Meyer, a Senior Attorney and Policy Planning Advisor in the Copyright Office.

[1] The Copyright Act of 1909, as revised through 1973, was 25 pages long. Ch. 320, 35 Stat. 1075 (1909) (repealed and superseded by the Copyright Act of 1976, 17 U.S.C. §§ 101-810 (1982, Supp. I 1983, & Supp. II 1984)). Copyright Office Circular 91. The 1976 Act is 68 pages long and gets longer with each amendment. U.S. Gov't Printing Office Doc. No. 0-39-006.

[2] 17 U.S.C. § 1(e) (1974) (superseded by 17 U.S.C. § 106 (1982)).

[3] *See* H.R. REP. No. 83, 90th Cong., 1st Sess., 66-67 (1967).

new use.[4]

If one examines the history of United States copyright law in this century, it becomes clear that however long it takes Congress to provide some measure of copyright relief for a new technological use,[5] that relief will likely appear in the form of a limited right to remuneration rather than a "classical" grant of complete copyright rights. Why this has happened, whether it shall remain so, and whether we should always complain about it, are subjects that others have addressed at greater lengths than I have. What I propose to examine is *how* the current law's licenses have functioned. This is more a sociological than a legal exposition. Today's question is not "should we have compulsory licenses at all?" or "could Congress draft these licenses more artfully?" but, much more simply, "how goes it?" After looking at our experiences with compulsory licensing, I will briefly discuss how Congress may solve tomorrow's problems.

II. BACKGROUND

Before turning to the first question, I will review the creation of the current law. I will not embark on a detailed review of the legislative history of the 1976 Act. Instead, I will just recall how the struggle which preoccupied many of us for years appeared to this congressional staffer who got in on the tail end. Commentators have often recounted that a variety of technology-related issues prevented Congress from quickly completing the process of modernizing the copyright law soon after publication of the Copyright Office's initial report recommending its possible revision.[6] The Office prepared that report[7] in 1961, fifteen years before the Congress enacted the current law. As time passed,

---

4 For example, motion pictures were invented in the 19th century but were not included in the copyright law until the 1912 revisions of the 1909 Act. 17 U.S.C. § 5(l)-(m) (1974) (subsequent history omitted). Sound recordings were commercially viable long before their inclusion in the law in 1971. 17 U.S.C. § 5(n) (1974) (subsequent history omitted).

5 It bears noting that it took 67 years in the case of jukeboxes and 10 years in that of cable television. 17 U.S.C. § 1(e) (1974) (subsequent history omitted) (jukebox performances exempted outright). Since 1978, 17 U.S.C. § 116 has provided a basis for compensation for such performances under a compulsory license. *Cf.* Teleprompter Corp. v. CBS, Inc., 415 U.S. 394 (1974); Fortnightly Corp. v. United Artists Television, Inc., 392 U.S. 390 (1968). Cable retransmissions were held exempt from copyright liability until 1978, when 17 U.S.C. § 111 provided the cable compulsory license.

6 H.R. REP. No. 1476, 94th Cong., 2d Sess. 359 (1976); 122 CONG. RECORD 31,984 (1976) (remarks of Rep. Railsback); *see* National Cable Television Ass'n v. CRT, 689 F.2d 1077 (D.C. Cir. 1982); *see, e.g.*, Greene, *The Cable Television Provisions of the Revised Copyright Act*, 27 CATH. U.L. REV. 263, 279 (1978).

7 REPORT OF THE REGISTER OF COPYRIGHTS ON THE GENERAL REVISION OF THE U.S. COPYRIGHT LAW, 87th Cong., 1st Sess. (1961).

new technologies created new controversies, so that arguments about library photocopying,[8] cable television,[9] and computer uses[10] crowded the dockets. While the issues and the protagonists changed, the arguments had a strong family resemblance; a use of a copyrighted work to which the 1909 statute did not apply became a matter of commercial success, then of great dispute, and often of extended litigation.

To most Members of Congress, compromise solutions are almost always the most attractive. Thus, when copyright owners tried to reverse Congress' decades-old decision exempting jukeboxes from copyright liability, and to reverse legislatively the Supreme Court's more recent decisions that cable television systems were not publicly performing the works that they rebroadcast, the compulsory license mechanism, having "solved" the mechanical-monopoly problem, provided an obvious model for this latter-day compromise. Copyright owners believed with justification that a right to remuneration was a small fraction of a loaf as compared with a right to control all uses of their works. From the congressional perspective this was a practicable compromise. After all, Congress itself initially had determined that jukebox performances were exempt, and the Supreme Court simultaneously had held likewise for cable performances and had called on Congress to clarify the law.[11] Few Members of Congress felt that clarification necessarily meant full copyright liability, particularly where, as in the cable and jukebox industries, literally millions of transactions a year were to be brought within the ambit of copyright for the first time.

The idea that some restraints on the market for copyrighted works are appropriate is as old as statutory copyright itself. The first copyright law, the Statute of Anne,[12] contained a provision that if the Archbishop of Canterbury, the Lord Bishop of London, or certain other officials found a book's price "High and Unreasonable," they then had the power and authority to limit the price to one which, to them, seemed "Just and Reason-

---

8 Williams and Wilkins Co. v. United States, 487 F.2d 1345 (Ct. Cl. 1973), *aff'd by an equally divided court*, 420 U.S. 376 (1975).

9 *See, e.g.*, Fortnightly Corp. v. United Artists Television, Inc., 392 U.S. 390 (1968).

10 Questions concerning computer storage of "traditional" works, copyright for computer software, and works created with the assistance of a computer were assigned to the National Commission on New Technological Uses of Copyrighted Works by Pub. L. 93-573 (1974). Its recommendations were largely followed and are substantially contained in 17 U.S.C. § 117.

11 *See, e.g.*, Fortnightly Corp. v. United Artists Television, Inc., 392 U.S. 390 (1968).

12 Statute of Anne, 8 Anne ch. 19 (1710) (subsequent history omitted). *reprinted in* A. Latman, R. Gorman, & J. Ginsburg, Copyright for the Eighties 2 (1985).

able."[13] Recent debates about the ratemaking policies of the Copyright Royalty Tribunal (CRT) can trace their lineage back to eighteenth century England.

If one leaps from the Statute of Anne to the current law's four compulsory licenses,[14] one learns four slightly different lessons, a number of which are intimately related to the history of the CRT. The unexpected thread common to most is the extent to which the parties involved have negotiated solutions that modify or partially supplant the provisions of the compulsory licenses.

III. The Compulsory Licenses

A. *The Mechanical License*

The oldest example of a compulsory license is the mechanical license,[15] a lineal descendant of a compromise forged in 1909 between those who opposed any recognition of mechanical reproduction rights and those who favored full liability. Today the market for mechanical rights is one in which most transactions are, in a limited manner, consensual rather than regulated. Most of the contracts for the manufacture of phonograph records and tapes are made on terms set by the copyright owners in conjunction with record producers.[16] Given the regulated price for which a license may be had without negotiation, it is hardly surprising that the price terms of the negotiated licenses are always below the rates specified in 1978 by the statute, and now by the CRT.

The world in which prices could only be negotiated under a regulatory ceiling has recently become less harsh for copyright owners than it was from 1909 to 1978, when the rate stayed frozen at two cents per record.[17] Under the current law, we have made some progress on that front. The rate became two and three-fourths cents per record or one-half cent per minute, whichever was higher, in 1978.[18] The present rate is five cents per record or just under one cent per minute, whichever is

[13] 8 Anne ch. 19.

[14] 17 U.S.C. § 111 (cable license secondary transmissions); *id.* § 115 (mechanical license for phonorecords); *id.* § 116 (jukebox license); *id.* § 118 (public broadcasting license).

[15] *Id.* § 115.

[16] S. Shemel & M. Krasilovsky, This Business of Music 147 (5th ed. 1977).

[17] 17 U.S.C. § 1(e) (1974) (superseded by 17 U.S.C. § 106 (1982)) (rate as it had been adopted in 1909).

[18] 17 U.S.C. § 115.

higher.[19] While there is still a "cap," it does increase, and thus offers fairer compensation, albeit not full rights, to composers and music publishers.

As the Copyright Office neither collects the royalties paid under this license, nor, except in rare circumstances, receives notice when the license is invoked,[20] we have no concrete evidence of the number of purely compulsory transactions as opposed to partly consensual ones. However, it seems likely that most transactions are based on agreements arrived at after non-price negotiations.

B. *The Jukebox License*

The 1976 Act gave us a more modern compromise between the advocates of no liability and those of full liability with respect to jukebox licenses.[21] For a flat fee, initially set out in the law[22] and thereafter adjusted by the CRT,[23] a jukebox operator is granted a license to publicly perform the musical compositions on its records. However, since copyright liability of *any* type was a new wrinkle for the jukebox industry, compliance has long been a primary concern with the operation of this license and remains a substantial problem to this day, particularly for the performing rights societies.

Surprisingly, in a society where we have a governmental or private statistic for almost everything, jukebox numbers, and their growth or diminution, are immune from exact quantification. Over time, there has been literally no agreement between jukebox operators and the representatives of the composers whose works are performed for the music-hungry public. During the early debate, prior to revision of the copyright law in 1976, the jukebox operators accepted the estimate that placed the number of boxes in use in this country at 500,000.[24] Later, as the likelihood of liability for jukebox performances loomed larger and larger, they revised that estimate downward to 250,000. Current industry estimates apparently range from 144,000-

---

19 37 C.F.R. § 307.3(c) (1985).

20 17 U.S.C. § 115(b)(1).

21 *Id.* § 116.

22 *Id.* § 116(b)(1)(a).

23 *Id.* § 801(b)(1).

24 *See Hearings before the Subcommittee on Patents, Trademarks, and Copyrights of the Committee on the Judiciary United States Senate*, 90th Cong., 1st Sess. 259 (1967), *reprinted in* 9 G. GROSSMAN, OMNIBUS COPYRIGHT REVISION LEGISLATIVE HISTORY 259 (1976) (statement of Nicholas Allen, Counsel to the Music Operators of America).

250,000.[25] Whatever are the correct numbers, the Copyright Office records reflect a steady decline in jukebox registrations since 1978.[26] In recounting this history, I do not want to be unfair to the operators. They point out that the social habits of the country are changing, with more people staying home and spending less time feeding quarters into machines in the local gin mills. Moreover, with the increased rates, they have retired some marginally profitable boxes.

In 1978, the operators registered almost 140,000 boxes for an eight dollar fee for each one, generating a pot of roughly $1.1 million.[27] Through 1981, while the statutory fee of eight dollars was in force, there was a slight but consistent downward trend in the number of certificates issued annually, but the annual revenues, when rounded off, remained at $1.1 million.[28] When the fee was raised to twenty-five dollars in 1982, the number of registered jukeboxes declined more sharply than ever before. During the two years in which that fee was in effect, certificates declined by 15.7%.[29] In 1983, the year with the fewest registrations up to that time, due to the increase in the fee, the revenue was $2.8 million. Since the fee became fifty dollars in 1984, registrations have continued to decline, however, revenues substantially increased. In 1985, although only 97,000 jukeboxes were registered, the operators deposited $4.8 million with the Copyright Office.[30] This is more than four times the 1978 revenue, despite

[25] Letter from Corinne Jones Gorzo, Senior Licensing Specialist, United States Copyright Office to Elana L. Gershen, Editor-in-Chief, *Cardozo Arts & Ent. L.J.* (Apr. 3, 1986):

JUKEBOXES CERTIFICATES ISSUED AS OF FEBRUARY 21, 1986

	FULL YEAR	HALF YEAR	TOTAL	ADDITIONAL NOTES
1978	139,569	3,827	143,396	4,287 operators
1979	135,763	2,395	138,158	3,959 operators
1980	135,046	2,121	137,167	4,058 operators
1981	133,702	1,637	135,339	3,922 operators
1982	125,218	1,182	126,400	4,007 operators
1983	112,700	1,641	114,341	4,068 operators
1984	102,468	1,845	104,313	4,317 operators
1985	97,424	1,942	99,366	4,164 operators
1986	24,124	0	24,124	1,056 operators

[26] *Id.*

[27] *Id.*

[28] *Id.*

[29] *Id.*

[30] *Id.*

the fact that the number of licensed machines had declined by thirty percent.

While we have no clear data indicating the *extent* of operator noncompliance, the fact that some jukeboxes are unlicensed is clear to anyone who occasionally inspects a jukebox looking for the signature of the Register of Copyrights. (I wonder what my law school professors would have thought had they known that one day I would hold a position in which the broadest public dissemination of my name would be via tiny certificates intended for display in dimly lit corners of bars and diners throughout the land).

More scientifically, data from state and local governments reflect a higher number of jukeboxes than the number of certificates issued by the Copyright Office.

With the leadership and strong encouragement of Representative Robert Kastenmeier of Wisconsin, the problem of unlicensed machines has been dealt with in part by negotiations between the performing rights societies and the jukebox operator trade association. At present, the timely registration of a jukebox entitles its operator to a ten dollar rebate from the performing rights societies. Since the previous fee increases have all led to a reduction in registrations, it is plausible that the rebate method should do for the American Society of Composers, Authors and Publishers (ASCAP), Broadcast Music, Inc. (BMI), and SESAC what it does for your friendly neighborhood car dealer. Whatever will happen, a pool of approximately five million dollars a year has been created now. Under the 1909 Copyright Act, there was nothing. While it is probably impossible to estimate what the pool would look like if there were full copyright liability for jukebox performances, it is clear that this compulsory license, notwithstanding all the arguments about the numbers of jukeboxes and fair prices, has served to provide a small but real contribution to the annual income of composers, lyricists, and music publishers.

C. *The Cable License*

The compulsory license for certain rebroadcasts by cable television systems provides a pie about twenty times larger than does the jukebox license. It comes as no great surprise, then, to see that this cable license[31] has been the subject of legislative initiatives, commercial debates, and protracted litigation to a

---

31 17 U.S.C. § 111.

greater extent than the jukebox license. In addition, the number of claimants who seek and receive their share of this pie is also substantially larger. In examining the history of copyright in the United States over the last twenty years, one might reasonably conclude that the largest *economic* shift in copyright policy occurred when Congress created this license.

To be sure, the 1976 Act arguably makes more fundamental *legal* changes in copyright policy: a unified federal system,[32] a display right,[33] a reduction in the importance of the copyright notice,[34] and a tortuous transition from a renewal-based duration scheme to the international norm of the life of the author plus fifty years.[35] But now that the passions of the revision wars have largely cooled, it safely can be said that it is hard to identify large sums of money either created anew or distributed differently because of the death of state common law copyright or a change in the rules for calculating when a copyright expires.

It is not hard to identify new sums with respect to the cable license. In 1984, $86.9 million was received by the Copyright Office. An additional $7.3 million was added, which reflected interest and appreciation in the value of the treasury instruments in which the funds were invested.[36] For 1985, incomplete returns show $98.7 million in receipts as of January 31, 1986.[37] As Everett Dirksen once said, "100 million here, 100 million there; sooner or later you're talking about real money." The substantial stakes can be attested to by examining the appellate litigation concerning cable ratemaking and distribution in which the CRT has been a party.[38]

Whenever the CRT has adjusted the rates, there has been litigation. Although the 1976 Act provides claimants with antitrust immunity as an incentive to work together to allocate shares among themselves and to present a plan to the CRT, every distribution has been the subject of a controversy involving the CRT and has gone to a court of appeals before final distribution could occur.[39] In these cases, television and radio broadcasters, together with a variety of copyright owners, have clamored for the

---

32 *Id.* § 301.
33 *Id.* § 106(5).
34 *Id.* §§ 405-406.
35 *Id.* §§ 302-304.
36 C. Gorzo, *supra* note 25.
37 *Id.*
38 *See, e.g.*, National Cable Television Ass'n v. CRT, 724 F.2d 176 (D.C. Cir. 1983); National Cable Television Ass'n v. CRT, 689 F.2d 1077 (D.C. Cir. 1982).
39 *See, e.g.*, National Ass'n of Broadcasters v. CRT, 772 F.2d 922 (D.C. Cir. 1985) (subsequent history omitted).

recognition of their right to some compensation. If that claim was recognized, they then have clamored for a share of the pie larger than that decreed by the CRT.

For all the trouble that the CRT's practices and records have given the Court of Appeals for the District of Columbia Circuit, virtually all of the CRT's cable-related actions have been upheld, albeit somewhat grudgingly. The list of issues the court has had to deal with is instructive. These cases reflect, among other things, the creativity of the copyright and communications bars when $100 million is at issue. Without attempting to review every issue from every case, I would like to highlight a few of those issues which the CRT and the courts have considered. It is fair to say that hardly any of these were anticipated by Congress when it enacted the cable license.

One of the most long-standing and unsuccessful arguments made by the television broadcasters alleges that an individual station's broadcast day is itself somehow a copyrighted compilation of copyrighted programs. They argue that a separate copyright exists in the order in which various shows are presented. The court described the broadcast day argument as "quantitatively de minimis" in 1982[40] and twice rejected the notion that compensation was required.[41]

Commercial radio broadcasters suffered a similar result with respect to their claim that something other than the copyrighted music which they broadcast—and for which the performing rights societies receive royalties—was worthy of compensation.[42] One of the devotional television broadcasters argued, without success, that its share of the cable royalties was too small due to the CRT's "unconstitutional hostility toward broadcasting carried on as part of [our] Christian ministry."[43]

If one moves off the well-trodden path connecting the CRT and the Court of Appeals for the District of Columbia Circuit, other arguments concerning cable and copyright have been the subject of major battles. While I cannot speak for the whole 94th Congress, I am confident that neither Senator Scott nor Senator Mathias suspected that questions about the satellite delivery of baseball game broadcasts,[44] the "customizing" of a broadcast

---

40 National Ass'n of Broadcasters v. CRT, 675 F.2d 367, 379 (D.C. Cir. 1982).

41 *Id.*; National Ass'n of Broadcasters v. CRT, 772 F.2d 922.

42 National Ass'n of Broadcasters v. CRT, 675 F.2d at 379-80.

43 National Ass'n of Broadcasters v. CRT, 772 F.2d at 939.

44 Eastern Microwave, Inc. v. Doubleday Sports, Inc., 691 F.2d 125 (2d Cir.), *cert. denied*, 459 U.S. 1226 (1982).

signal for national distribution,[45] and the "stripping" and replacement of an invisible portion of a television signal by a satellite service[46] would concern both bench and bar to the extent that they have. Is it pure coincidence that these cases each involve one of the three "superstations" which have become staples of cable programming?

Finally, the question whether the definition of a "local service area" in the 1976 Act[47] included the then-unknown phenomenon of the low power broadcaster was hardly foreseeable. However, it is important to note that all of these controversies are rooted in the language of the copyright law which created the cable compulsory license.

In selecting the compulsory license compromise, Congress shaped the present market in ways that no one could have predicted in 1976. The advent of the superstation and the ratemaking practices of the CRT have directly affected the mix and quantity of distant signals available on cable systems. The idea that there would be near-universal interest in watching an out-of-town local station several thousand miles from its source might have seemed preposterous in 1976. Similarly, the notion that 3.75% of a cable system's gross receipts should be paid for retransmitting an additional distant station seemed ludicrous.

The effect of imposing such a rate has been twofold. First, it makes it prohibitively expensive for a cable system to import additional distant signals, because operators cannot pass along increased expenses to their customers if license fees increase every time revenues do. Second, this rate has made the creative accounting mechanism known as "tiering" even more attractive. By tiering, a cable system will offer a loss leader package of programs for a very low fee—that tier, of course, containing all distant signals for which the compulsory license fees must be paid—in the belief that 3.75% of a lesser amount of money is better. While the present rate was adopted on the theory that it reflected the free market price for distant signal equivalents,[48] it is nearly impossible to determine that price for any service if prices in its market are now strongly regulated. It is, however, a safe bet that a free market price would be expressed in dollars per subscriber rather than as a percentage off the top. In fact, if I can trust the

---

45 Hubbard Broadcasting, Inc. v. Southern Satellite Sys., 777 F.2d 393 (8th Cir. 1985).

46 WGN v. United Video, Inc., 693 F.2d 622 (7th Cir. 1982).

47 17 U.S.C. § 111(f).

48 47 Fed. Reg. 52,159 (1982).

Washington rumor mill, this turns out to be the direction in which parties are tending to supplant, at least, the ratemaking functions of the CRT in their negotiations. If this comes to pass, then the cable license, which has been the source of tremendous controversy since its inception, will become, along with the mechanical and jukebox licenses, a statutory starting point for negotiations among the industries rather than a tariff demanding blind obedience.

D. *The Public Broadcasting License*

The final compulsory license in the current law concerns certain public broadcasting activities.[49] At first blush, it appears to be unlike the other "new" compulsory licenses. It is not immediately clear that it was enacted contemporaneously with the granting of new rights, but to a large degree it was. To be sure, the tradeoff between the creation of cable and jukebox rights, and their limitation via a compulsory license, is more obvious. But when Congress amended the law to provide a right of public display[50] and to remove the "for-profit" condition from the right of public performance,[51] public broadcasters felt threatened with dramatic and potentially expensive changes. The license, therefore, is a limited response to some of those changes.

It explicitly differs from the other licenses by stating Congress' desire that the parties make their own arrangements, by providing that voluntary license agreements supersede any CRT determinations,[52] and by granting copyright owners and public broadcasters antitrust exemptions so that they may negotiate collectively.[53] Thus, such negotiations and agreements have been the order of the day since 1978. Although the first round of negotiations took an immense amount of effort by both sides, from the government's perspective the benefits appear to have been worth it.

The Code of Federal Regulations contains an exhaustive schedule of rates with respect to the performance and display of various works by the Public Broadcasting System and local public radio and television broadcasters.[54] Yet, the overwhelming majority of copyright clearances for all types of public broadcasting

49 17 U.S.C. § 118.
50 *Id.* § 106(5).
51 *Id.* § 106(4); *cf.* 17 U.S.C. § 1(c), (e) (1974) (subsequent history omitted).
52 17 U.S.C. § 118(b)(2).
53 *Id.* § 118(b).
54 *See* 37 C.F.R. § 304 (1985).

entities are accomplished by what the copyright law describes as "[l]icensed agreements voluntarily negotiated."[55]

IV. The Future of Compulsory Licenses

In the long run, there is no telling how these four licenses will fare. It is clear that in each instance, private arrangements can supplement or supersede the government's determinations. Large segments of the cable market, for example, are unaffected by the compulsory license. On an eighty-channel system it is not uncommon to find several local signals for which no copyright permission or payment is required, two or three distant signals imported and paid for via the license, with the balance of the programming consisting of cable-originated services for which private contracts are a necessity. Most public broadcasting transactions are paid for at rates to which the parties acquiesce, and the jukebox rebate system is in place, at least for the moment. Thus one sees the general preference of both copyright owners and their customers for making their own arrangements. This is clear even with the availability of a license which requires no communication between licensee and licensor.

Does this mean that these compulsory licenses have outlived their usefulness and that they will wither away? Will no others come to occupy a place in our copyright future? I know that that would be a popular message in some quarters, but it is not mine today. In large measure, the harsh reality of the existing compulsory licenses has motivated the negotiations that have occurred. To abolish compulsory licenses would dramatically alter the relationships between the parties and the circumstances under which the current system functions. Furthermore, Congress has not put the dramatic alteration of the copyright system high on its agenda. Members of Congress have introduced bills to abolish the CRT[56] and substantially curtail the cable license,[57] but none of these bills seems close to enactment.[58]

My task in this Article has been to report where we are and

---

[55] 17 U.S.C. § 118(a)(2).

[56] H.R. 2752, 99th Cong., 1st Sess. (1985). Congress would transfer CRT's functions to the Copyright Office. H.R. 2784, 99th Cong., 1st Sess. (1985) would create a copyright royalty court to replace the CRT.

[57] H.R. 3339, 99th Cong., 1st Sess. (1985) would retain the cable license only for small systems while letting market forces determine the price for retransmission by large systems.

[58] On the "high-tech" front, the 98th Congress legislated a "pseudo-compulsory" license by according some retroactive protection to semi-conductor chips. 17 U.S.C. § 913(d).

to peer tentatively into the unknown. While the "ghost of copyright future" casts no shadow and speaks with less clarity than Congress, we can examine the shards in the dustbin of Capitol Hill.

I suspect we all remember the cartoons that filled the editorial pages after the Ninth Circuit's opinion in the *Betamax*[59] case; they portrayed copyright police forcibly removing a videocassette recorder (VCR) from Blackacre. Those cartoons were premature and slightly ridiculous. Premature, because the Supreme Court decreed the home-taping at issue non-infringing; and ridiculous, because Congress (not to mention the courts) would never have dreamed of permitting such intrusions into the sanctity of our homes.

Congressional response to the copyright issue is worth mentioning here. A number of bills were introduced during the pendency of the *Betamax* litigation and more have followed.[60] All would have made clear, as a matter of statutory law, the non-infringing nature of home taping. Some bills would have compensated copyright owners by providing a compulsory license with respect to equipment and recording media,[61] but no one gave any serious consideration to forbidding the importation, sale, or use of VCR's. Similar bills concerning compulsory licenses for audio-recording have also been introduced.[62]

As the United States considers whether to adhere to the Berne Convention,[63] it is worth noting that of our four current licenses, only the jukebox license looms as a serious impediment to our adherence to that strong pro-author treaty. Mechanical compulsory licenses are specifically authorized and are widely used among Berne member states.[64] The cable and public broadcasting licenses appear compatible under the rubric of "equitable remuneration for broadcasts and rebroadcasts."[65] In fact, some Berne members provide no compensation whatsoever for cable

---

59 Sony Corp. of America v. Universal City Studios, Inc., 464 U.S. 417 (1984).

60 *See, e.g.*, H.R. 4783, 97th Cong., 1st Sess. (1981); S.1758, 97th Cong., 1st Sess. (1981).

61 S.31, 98th Cong., 1st Sess. (1983); H.R. 1030, 98th Cong., 1st Sess. (1983).

62 S.1739, 99th Cong., 1st Sess. (1985); H.R. 2911, 99th Cong., 1st Sess. (1985).

63 *See* Duboff, Winter, Flacks & Keplinger, *Out of UNESCO and into Berne: Has United States Participation in the Berne Convention for International Copyright Protection Become Essential?*, 4 CARDOZO ARTS & ENT. L.J. 203 (1985).

64 Article 13(1), Berne Convention for the Protection of Literary and Artistic Works (Paris 1971), *reprinted in* 4 M. NIMMER, NIMMER ON COPYRIGHT, app. 27-5 to -6 (1985).

65 *Id.* at art. 11*bis*(2).

retransmissions.[66] Aside from the jukebox license, it appears that the licenses we have are not only the product of hard-fought domestic battles, but are also well within international standards.

None of this is to say that compulsory licenses are a panacea. If one were to set out today to design a copyright system *de novo*, one might be able to strike a balance between the rights of creators and the needs of users[67] without constraining markets for uses of copyrighted works. We do not have, and probably never will have, the luxury our founding fathers had back in 1790—starting from scratch. Instead, we find ourselves enmeshed in the present system, with an awkward mixture of pure copyright, random limitations such as fair use, and compulsory licensing.

Copyright progress in the recent past has been substantial; cable and jukebox performances are now part of the warp and woof of copyright life, generating more than $100 million annually for copyright owners. The search for relief on the home taping front continues. More likely than not, it will be governed by a compulsory license. As long as technology develops in ways that provide individuals with the capacity to do what publishers or recording studios used to do, then the right to remuneration is probably the maximum attainable goal. It may not have the appeal of a full-fledged exclusive right, however it is, I suspect, more attractive than no right at all.

V. Conclusion

The title of this Article asked whether compulsory licensing will survive in a changing market. Like a law professor, I have provided the question but not the answer. In thinking about that answer, it is important to remember that the licenses we now have, and those that are being proposed, are themselves the products of changed markets. If compulsory licensing disappears, it will do so because mechanisms will develop that make full liability transaction costs low enough to meet the demands of the user community. If the licenses survive, they will do so because the majority of those who rely on them view them, not as the best of all possible solutions, but as the least drastic alternative in a world where pure choices between clear options can rarely be made.

---

66 Canada, for example, is now considering whether to compensate copyright owners for broadcast retransmissions.

67 17 U.S.C. § 108(i).

THE IMPACT OF BERNE ON UNITED STATES COPYRIGHT LAW*

DAVID NIMMER**

I. INTRODUCTION

Nineteen eighty-eight was a milestone year for intellectual property legislation.[1] Congress enacted ten bills last year falling within the general subject matter of copyrights, patents, and trademarks. Five of these new laws exert an integral impact on United States copyright protection.[2] I will focus on the most important piece of new legislation—the Berne Convention Implementation Act of 1988 ("BCIA").[3]

The BCIA, as its name denotes, is an act whose purpose is to implement the Berne Convention for the Protection of Literary and Artistic Works, initially adopted in Berne, Switzerland, on September 9, 1886.[4] The Berne Convention is the world's oldest

---

* Copyright © 1989 by David Nimmer. The author delivered this speech at an international copyright symposium held at Cardozo School of Law on March 16, 1989, under the auspices of the Melville B. Nimmer Memorial Fund.

** A.B., 1977, Stanford University; J.D., 1980, Yale University. Current author of NIMMER ON COPYRIGHT, Mr. Nimmer is Of Counsel to Irell & Manella, Los Angeles, California.

1 1988 was significant for the United States with regard to international copyright relations in other ways as well. The United States formally suggested that the General Agreement on Tariffs and Trade ("GATT") be supplemented to include an intellectual property code. *See* General Agreement on Tariffs and Trade, Oct. 30, 1947, 61 Stat. A3, T.I.A.S. No. 1700, 55 U.N.T.S. 187 (entered into force Jan. 1, 1948). Also, the United States pursued and quietly resolved a trade complaint filed against South Korea by the Motion Picture Export Association of America. Sobel, *U.S. Enters New Era in International Copyright Relations*, 10 ENT. L. REP. 3 (Nov. 1988).

2 Berne Convention Implementation Act of 1988, Pub. L. No. 100-568, 102 Stat. 2853 (1988) (codified at 17 U.S.C. §§ 101, 104, 116, 301, 401-02, 404-08, 801 (1988)); Satellite Retransmission Act of 1988, Pub. L. No. 100-667, 102 Stat. 3949 (1988) (codified as amended at 17 U.S.C. § 119 (1988)); the Record Rental Amendment of 1988, Pub. L. No. 100-617, 102 Stat. 3194 (1988) (amending 17 U.S.C. § 109 (1988)); the National Film Preservation Act of 1988, Pub. L. No. 100-446, 102 Stat. 1782 (1988) (codified at 2 U.S.C. § 178 (1988)); and the Intellectual Property Bankruptcy Protection Act, Pub. L. No. 100-506, 102 Stat. 2538 (1988) (codified at 11 U.S.C. § 101 (1988)).

3 Berne Convention Implementation Act of 1988, Pub. L. No. 100-568, 102 Stat. 2853 (1988). The BCIA contains 13 sections, most of which amend United States copyright law. *See* Symposium Appendix at 73.

4 Since 1886, the Berne Convention has been revised approximately at 20-year intervals. *See* Jaszi, *A Garland of Reflections on Three International Copyright Topics*, 8 CARDOZO ARTS & ENT. L.J. 49, 52 n.11 (1989) [hereinafter Jaszi]. The current text is adopted at Berne Convention For the Protection of Literary and Artistic Works, Sept. 9, 1886, *revised* Paris, July 24, 1971, 25 U.S.T. 1341, T.I.A.S. No. 7868, 828 U.N.T.S. 221. The text is reproduced in 4 M. NIMMER & D. NIMMER, NIMMER ON COPYRIGHT Appendix 27 (1989) [hereinafter NIMMER ON COPYRIGHT]. The preceding text of the Berne Conven-

and most comprehensive copyright treaty.[5] Among the seventy-seven members of the Berne Union are virtually all of the principal nations of the world, with the notable exceptions of the Soviet Union and the People's Republic of China.[6] It has taken the United States a full century[7] to bring our laws into compliance with Berne.[8] The BCIA finally completes that process, started[9] by the Copyright Act of 1976.[10] As of the effective date of the BCIA, March 1, 1989, the United States has taken its place in the international copyright community as a full-fledged member of the Berne Union.

The underlying philosophy of the BCIA, which Congress has repeatedly emphasized, is minimalism.[11] This minimalist philosophy dictates that to the extent that United States copyright law was clearly incompatible with the strictures of the Berne Convention, Congress amended that portion of United States law, but only to the minimum extent required to bring it into conformity with Berne.[12] By way of illustration, if ten experts and industry representatives testified before Congress, seven stating that United States law needed to be changed and three opining that United States law was adequate, then Congress, in accordance with its minimalist approach, left the law unaltered.[13] Congress

---

tion, the Brussels Act of June 26, 1948, is reproduced in 4 NIMMER ON COPYRIGHT Appendix 26.

[5] *See generally* RICKETSON, THE BERNE CONVENTION FOR THE PROTECTION OF LITERARY AND ARTISTIC WORKS: 1886-1986 (1987).

[6] The Soviet Union belongs to the other great multilateral copyright treaty, the Universal Copyright Convention ("UCC"), Sept. 6, 1952, 6 U.S.T. 2731, T.I.A.S. No. 3324, 735 U.N.T.S. 368, *revised* July 24, 1971, Paris Text, 25 U.S.T. 1341, T.I.A.S. No. 7868. China, by contrast, belongs to no international copyright organization and has yet to enact a comprehensive copyright statute. *See* Simone, *Copyright in the People's Republic of China: A Foreigner's Guide*, 7 CARDOZO ARTS & ENT. L.J. 1 (1988).

[7] Actually, the United States and Japan both participated as observers at the initial 1886 conference in Berne. The United States delegate indicated rather obliquely that American participation in Berne might be forthcoming: "The position and attitude of the United States is one of expectancy and reserve." *See* Ricketson, *The Birth of the Berne Union*, 11 COLUM.-VLA J. L. & ARTS 9, 29-30 (1986).

[8] In a little-known historical sidelight, the United States Senate actually ratified the Berne Convention on April 19, 1935. 79 CONG. REC. 6032 (1935). On April 22, 1935, however, Congress withdrew ratification after recognizing the significant modification United States copyright law would need to undergo in order to conform to Berne. 79 CONG. REC. 6099 (1935). *See* Sandison, *The Berne Convention and the Universal Copyright Convention: The American Experience*, 11 COLUM.-VLA J. L. & ARTS 89, 103 (1986).

[9] *See generally* Nimmer, *Implications of the Prospective Revisions of the Berne Convention and the United States Copyright Law*, 19 STAN. L. REV. 499 (1967).

[10] *See, e.g.*, 2 NIMMER ON COPYRIGHT, *supra* note 4, at § 9.01[A][2].

[11] *See* H.R. Rep. No. 100-609, 100th Cong., 2d Sess. 20 (1988) [hereinafter H. R. Rep. No. 100-609].

[12] *Id.*

[13] For instance, a group of interested representatives from both industry and government comprised the Ad Hoc Working Group on United States Adherence to the Berne Convention. *See id.* at 7. *See also Final Report of Ad Hoc Working Group on U.S. Adherence to*

acted only if all ten agreed that there was a clear inconsistency.[14] Even then, Congress acted only to the minimum extent required to bring the United States into compliance with Berne Convention requirements by eliminating overt impediments to Berne adherence.[15]

Given that the Senate has now ratified the Berne Convention and Congress, as a whole, has signaled its approval by amending United States copyright law to conform to the Berne Convention, the minimalist approach is disappointing. Assuming accession to the Berne Convention to be a positive development for our country, one would have imagined that after a century of effort, Berne proponents could secure greater changes to United States copyright law than the tepid provisions contained in the BCIA.[16] As an example, consider the juke box compulsory license,[17] about which widespread recognition of its incompatibility with the Berne Convention existed.[18] Congress acted in the BCIA by adding a very lengthy provision to the Copyright Act,[19] but upon careful examination, it is apparent that this lengthy provision will virtually maintain the *status quo ante*.[20] In essence, Congress has added some legislative twists and turns to the juke box provision which are designed to forestall almost any practical application.[21]

The irony here is that a primary motivation of the United States in joining the Berne Convention was to make an international statement about our moral posture in adhering to the world's foremost multilateral copyright treaty.[22] Given that desire, it is not only unfortunate, but self-defeating, for our govern-

---

the Berne Convention, 10 COLUM.-VLA J.L. & ARTS 513 (1986) [hereinafter *Final Report of Ad Hoc Working Group*]. The Ad Hoc Working Group rendered the opinion that the cable compulsory license of 17 U.S.C. § 111(c) (1988) is Berne-compatible. *See Final Report of Ad Hoc Working Group* at 519. The BCIA leaves the cable compulsory license wholly unaffected.

14 The requirement of a notice for copyright subsistence is a primary example of a feature of United States law which, by consensus of congressional witnesses, is incompatible with the Berne Convention. *See infra* Part II(A).

15 Congress kept the notice formality largely intact, rather than merely eliminating copyright notices altogether. *See infra* notes 29-45 and accompanying text.

16 As noted by the House subcommittee, "[i]deal solutions to issues take much congressional time, require careful examination of often conflicting interest, and generally lead to the legislative processing of a bill designed to solve a carefully defined question. That methodology is *not* used for the [Berne Convention Implementation] Act." H.R. Rep. No. 100-609, *supra* note 11, at 20 (emphasis added).

17 17 U.S.C. § 116 (1988).

18 H.R. Rep. No. 100-609, *supra* note 11, at 47.

19 *See* 17 U.S.C. § 116A (1988).

20 *See* 2 NIMMER ON COPYRIGHT, *supra* note 4, at § 8.17[A].

21 *See also* 1 NIMMER ON COPYRIGHT, *supra* note 4, § 2.08[D][2][a] n.163.4 (minimal adjustment of United States copyright law to Berne Convention requirement regarding architectural works).

22 *See generally* Jaszi, *supra* note 4.

ment to implement Berne only through the most stingy means available.

II. Bread and Butter Issues: Provisions of the BCIA Concerning Copyright Formalities

Representative Robert Kastenmeier, the chief congressional architect of the BCIA, stated that "the central feature of Berne is its prohibition of formalities."[23] Although the thrust of the Berne Convention is unquestionably anti-formal, Representative Kastenmeier's characterization is nonetheless a bit too broad. The Berne Convention does not prohibit formalities. While allowing formalities to exist *per se*, Berne forbids only those formalities that stand as a condition to the exercise and enjoyment of a copyright.[24]

For example, in the United States, those who register their works prior to infringement may, following a favorable judgment, obtain attorneys' fees and statutory damages.[25] Those two *remedies*—attorneys' fees and statutory damages—hinge on the *formality* of registration, which is perfectly compatible with the Berne Convention because they do not interfere with the exercise and enjoyment of a copyright. In other words, it does not contravene the Berne Convention to make *remedies* dependent upon formalities.[26] Alternatively, however, to make "the exercise or the enjoyment of a copyright" dependent upon a formality would be incompatible with the Berne Convention.[27] The primary example of hinging copyright *subsistence* on a formality is copyright notice, which has been a feature of every United States

---

23 134 Cong. Rec. H3082 (daily ed. May 10, 1988).

24 The Berne Convention states that "the enjoyment and the exercise of [copyright] shall not be subject to any formality" in "countries of the Union other than the country of origin. . . . " Berne Convention For the Protection of Literary and Artistic Works, Sept. 9, 1886, *revised* Paris, July 24, 1971, art. 5(1)-(2), 25 U.S.T. 1341, T.I.A.S. No. 7868, 828 U.N.T.S. 221.

25 17 U.S.C. § 412 (1988).

26 Indeed, capitalizing on this feature, the BCIA doubled all statutory damages, meaning that, concurrent with Berne adherence, the formality of registration actually assumed heightened significance. *See* 3 Nimmer on Copyright, *supra* note 4, at § 14.04[B][1][b].

27 The Berne Convention provides:

> The enjoyment and the exercise of these rights shall not be subject to any formality; such enjoyment and such exercise shall be independent of the existence of protection in the country of origin of the work. Consequently, apart from the provisions of this Convention, the extent of protection, as well as the means of redress afforded to the author to protect his rights, shall be governed exclusively by the laws of the country where protection is claimed.

Berne Convention For the Protection of Literary and Artistic Works, Sept. 9, 1886, *revised* Paris, July 24, 1971, art. 5(2), 25 U.S.T. 1341, T.I.A.S. No. 7868, 828 U.N.T.S. 221.

copyright act since the original Copyright Act of 1791.[28]

A. *Copyright Notice*

Because of a near unanimity that our notice strictures violate Berne standards, the United States has finally abandoned its two century-old copyright notice requirement. Works first published two weeks ago, or today, or at any point in the future, need not bear any copyright notice to satisfy United States domestic law[29] or to receive protection under the Berne convention.[30] Nonetheless, affixing a copyright notice remains not only a good idea,[31] but a necessity for a copyright owner who wishes to command protection throughout the nations of the other major treaty, the Universal Copyright Convention ("UCC").[32] In addition to the above reasons, I would recommend continuing to affix a copyright notice because those who use copyright notices may preclude a defense of innocent infringement in mitigation of statutory or actual damages.[33] Conversely, those who do not use a copyright notice today may not invoke that remedy.[34]

Given that the nations of the Berne Union have eschewed any type of copyright notice for decades and that the United States now accedes to Berne membership, logic would indicate that our laws should now be in harmony with those of the rest of the world. Unfortunately, experience proves the opposite. In implementing the Berne Convention, Congress has left an extraordinarily complex system of formalities extant during this

---

28 Act of May 31, 1790, ch. 15, 1 Stat. 124 (1790). *See* 2 NIMMER ON COPYRIGHT, *supra* note 4, at § 7.01 n.1.

29 17 U.S.C. § 401 (1988).

30 Berne Convention For the Protection of Literary and Artistic Works, Sept. 9, 1886, *revised* July 24, 1971, art. 2(2), 25 U.S.T. 1341, T.I.A.S. No. 7868, 828 U.N.T.S. 221.

31 Even during the Berne era, copyright notice remains "in all probability, the cheapest deterrent to infringement which a copyright holder may take." H.R. Rep. No. 100-609, *supra* note 11, at 27.

32 *See* Universal Copyright Convention, Sept. 6, 1952, 6 U.S.T. 2731, T.I.A.S. No. 3324, 735 U.N.T.S. 368, *revised* July 24, 1971, Paris Text, art. III, para. 1, 25 U.S.T. 1341, T.I.A.S. No. 7868. Nations that are party to the UCC but not the Berne Convention may, like the United States prior to March 1, 1989, require a valid UCC copyright notice in order to excuse compliance with other copyright formalities.

33 17 U.S.C. §§ 401(d), 402(d) (1988).

34 17 U.S.C. § 401(d) (1988) provides:

> If a notice of copyright in the form and position specified by this section appears on the published copy or copies to which a defendant in a copyright infringement suit had access, then no weight shall be given to such a defendant's interposition of a defense based on innocent infringement in mitigation of actual or statutory damages, except as provided in the last sentence of section 504(c)(2).

Id.

supposedly anti-formal Berne era. Congress did not sweep aside all of the jurisprudence of copyright notice. Instead, it reenacted the existing sections of the Copyright Act with respect to formerly published works and added a new level of analysis with respect to post-March 1, 1989 publications.

As an example, suppose that after today's lecture, a member of the audience walks down Fifth Avenue to a book shop and purchases a cassette book-on-tape, which bears the following notice: "Copyright XYZ Publisher." Because that notice includes no date, which is required by United States notice provisions,[35] that defective notice is tantamount to publishing the work without a copyright notice.[36] However, given that the customer purchased the item today, March 16, 1989, the absence of the copyright notice is largely insignificant—under the Copyright Act of 1976 as amended by the BCIA, notice is strictly voluntary. Therefore, a conclusion about the copyright status of the work cannot be drawn.

Suppose further research reveals that the subject book-on-tape has never been registered with the United States Copyright Office and that it was first published in 1980 with the same notice specified above. Since the law in 1980 required defective notices to be cured by registration within five years, it would appear that this work is now in the United States public domain because it was not registered by 1985.[37] Thus, one may go to the United States Copyright Office, commission a search, determine that the work has not been registered, and thereupon conclude that it is not protected by copyright today.[38]

---

35 17 U.S.C. § 401(b) (1988) provides:

> If a notice appears on the copies, it shall consist of the following three elements:
>
> (1) the symbol ©, or the word "Copyright", or the abbreviation "Copr."; and
>
> (2) the year of first publication of the work;
>
> . . . .
>
> (3) the name of the owner of copyright in the work, or an abbreviation by which the name can be recognized, or a generally known alternative designation of the owner.

Id.

36 *See* E. Mishan & Sons, Inc. v. Marycana, Inc., 662 F. Supp. 1339, 1344 (S.D.N.Y. 1987).

37 Section 405 of The Copyright Act of 1976, 17 U.S.C. § 405 (1976) [hereinafter 1976 Act] states that "[t]he omission of the copyright notice . . . does not invalidate the copyright in a work" if "the registration for the work has been made before or is made within five years after the publication without notice . . . ." *Id.*

38 *Id.* at § 401(a)(2). *See* Lifshitz v. Walter Drake & Sons, Inc., 806 F.2d 1426 (9th Cir. 1986); Donald Frederick Evans and Assoc. v. Continental Homes, Inc., 785 F.2d 897 (11th Cir. 1986); M. Kramer Mfg. Co. v. Andrews, 783 F.2d 421 (4th Cir. 1986); Disenos Artisticos E Industriales, S.A. v. Work, 676 F. Supp. 1254 (E.D.N.Y. 1987).

But now, suppose that even more research reveals that the subject book-on-tape was first published in 1970. Under this scenario an entirely different set of rules applies, because the Copyright Act of 1909 governed at that time.[39] Section 19 of the 1909 Act required a copyright notice to consist of the word "copyright" and the proprietor's name.[40] No date was required except for certain categories of work, such as printed, literary, musical or dramatic works.[41] Because our cassette tape does not fit within any of the excepted categories, no date was required in the copyright notice for this work. Consequently, when this work was first issued in 1970, it did bear a proper copyright notice. But what about its further publication in 1980? When the work was reissued with an undated copyright notice in 1980, the 1976 Act, which required dates in the copyright notices for this category of works, as for all works, governed. Consequently, it would seem that the 1980 publication doomed the work absent curing registration. Nonetheless, the 1976 Act contains a saving provision, which states that any work republished with a copyright notice that was valid under the 1909 Act may still bear that same copyright notice, notwithstanding that such a notice is insufficient to meet the guidelines of the 1976 Act.[42] Accordingly, the work, when first published in 1970, had valid notice. When it was republished in 1980 without changing its notice, that notice was still effective, and hence, the work remains protected today even if never the subject of a copyright registration.

The foregoing illustrates the complexities of United States copyright law, despite the "abolition" of the copyright notice requirement. Three levels of analysis govern the placement and effect of copyright notice. First, the BCIA does not require copyright notice for works first published after March 1, 1989.[43] Second, Congress left the notice provisions intact "[w]ith respect to copies and phonorecords publicly distributed by authority of the copyright owner before the effective date" of the BCIA.[44] Third, the 1976 Act preserved the 1909 Act's notice provisions.[45] Therefore, as in the foregoing example, one must refer to the

---

39 The Copyright Act of 1909, ch. 320, 35 Stat. 1075-88 (1909) (revised at 17 U.S.C. § 1 (1976)).

40 17 U.S.C. § 18 (1909).

41 *Id.*

42 17 U.S.C., Trans. Supp. Prov., § 108 (1976). *See* 2 NIMMER ON COPYRIGHT, *supra* note 4, at § 7.04.

43 *See supra* note 26.

44 17 U.S.C. §§ 404(b), 405(a)-(b), 406(a)-(c) (1989).

45 *See supra* note 42.

1909 Act and the original 1976 Act, as well as the BCIA, when determining in 1990 whether, for example, a work first published in 1969 and republished in 1983 remains protected by United States copyright. So much for the elimination of the notice formality.

B. *Registration*

Registration is another formality which underwent change when the United States joined the Berne Convention.[46] To place the Berne Convention's registration requirements in perspective, one must first understand the operation within the American framework of two doctrines of international copyright law which Berne brings to the fore: *national treatment* and *minimum standards*.

The requirement of *national treatment* is based on the principle that each given country ought not disadvantage foreigners.[47] Under the Berne Convention, those copyright privileges that a country affords its own citizens must equally extend to Convention claimants seeking copyright protection within that country.[48] For example, if an American can obtain statutory damages in the United States merely by virtue of registering her song with the Copyright Office, then a Brazilian and an Italian must also be allowed to obtain statutory damages in the United States after having registered their songs with the United States Copyright Office.

In the United States, national treatment has never been an issue. Once a foreigner's works qualified for protection, such works have historically been afforded every right pertaining to American-authored works. Thus, returning to the foregoing example, Brazilians and Italians have been accorded statutory damages for decades on precisely the same terms and conditions as Americans.[49]

The Berne Convention also sets forth certain *minimum re-*

---

46 Berne Convention Implementation Act of 1988, § 9, Pub. L. No. 100-568, 102 Stat. 2853 (1988) (amending 17 U.S.C. §§ 408 & 411 (1988)).

47 *See* Sobel, *The Framework of International Copyright*, 8 CARDOZO ARTS & ENT. L.J. 1, 7 (1989).

48 Art. 5(1) of the Berne Convention provides:

> Authors shall enjoy, in respect of works for which they are protected under this Convention, *in countries of the Union other than the country of origin*, the rights which their respective laws do now or may hereafter grant to their nationals, as well as the rights specially granted by this Convention.

Berne Convention For the Protection of Literary and Artistic Works, Sept. 9, 1886, *revised* Paris, July 24, 1971, art. 5(1), 25 U.S.T. 1341, T.I.A.S. No. 7868, 828 U.N.T.S. 221 (emphasis added).

49 *See* 17 U.S.C. § 504(c) (1988).

quirements that each adhering state must accord. For example, the United States Congress has created the right to have infringing goods impounded and destroyed.[50] This right is protected under the Berne Convention,[51] and any abrogation of it by the United States Congress would run afoul of its Berne Convention obligations. However, Congress is not barred from changing its copyright law to eliminate rights not set forth and established under Berne.[52]

A word of caution is in order here. The minimum standard requirement only applies to Berne Convention claimants; it does not reach a country's internal laws as applied to its own citizens.[53] Accordingly, a country could eliminate a Berne Convention protection affecting its own citizens by revising its domestic copyright law. Congress, for instance, could eliminate the minimum standard of impoundment vis-a-vis only American claimants. Such a course would not violate the Berne Convention because litigants entering United States courts as Berne Convention claimants would still be able to invoke the minimum standard of impoundment. In effect, United States courts would grant Berne Convention claimants rights superior to American claimants, who would only receive national treatment.

With that background in mind, we can appreciate the changes that Congress wrought in United States registration provisions. Congress eliminated the requirement of registration solely for Berne Convention claimants, leaving United States citizens obligated to register their works as a jurisdictional prerequisite before filing suit.[54] This curious situation arose because the House bill that led to the BCIA left registration unaffected.[55] All claimants coming into United States district court, whether American or foreign, under that bill would have continued to be

---

50 One can go to court in this country and, after securing judgment in favor of plaintiff in a copyright infringement suit, have the court order the infringing goods impounded and destroyed. 17 U.S.C. § 503(b) (1988).

51 Berne Convention For the Protection of Literary and Artistic Works, Sept. 6, 1886, *revised* Paris, July 24, 1971, art. 16, 25 U.S.T. 1341, T.I.A.S. No. 7868, 828 U.N.T.S. 221.

52 *Id.* at Art. 5(1).

53 The Berne Convention applies to those authors cited in articles 3 and 4 of the Convention.

54 "[R]egistration is not a condition of copyright protection." Berne Convention Implementation Act of 1988, § 9(a)(1), Pub. L. No. 100-568, 102 Stat. 2853 (1988) (codified at 17 U.S.C. § 408(a) (1989)). This adds an exception to § 411(a) "for actions for infringement of copyright in Berne Convention works whose country of origin is not the United States." *Id.* at § 9(b)(1)(B) (codified at 17 U.S.C. § 411(a) (1989)). *See* 2 NIMMER ON COPYRIGHT, *supra* note 4, at § 7.16[B][1][b].

55 *See* H. R. Rep. 100-609, *supra* note 11, at 41 n.93.

under the jurisdictional prerequisite of tendering the registration certificate for the work on which the suit was based. By contrast, the Senate bill, viewing the registration prerequisite as a barred formality under Berne, completely eliminated the statutory provision[56] requiring registration.[57] To resolve the tension between the House and the Senate bills, Congress compromised by invoking the doctrine of minimum standards, outlined above, and providing that American claimants who come to court to sue for violations of their copyrights must, as they always had to, produce a registration certificate bearing the seal of the United States Copyright Office.[58] However, plaintiffs who come into United States courts as Berne Convention claimants are excused from the jurisdictional requirement of offering a registration certificate. In that way, no one from another Berne nation can claim that the United States has breached its treaty obligations by imposing a prohibited formality on Berne Convention claimants.

Once again, an irony must be noted. In addition to the reasons noted above, registration has other significant consequences. Only those who register their works are entitled to statutory damages,[59] attorneys' fees within the discretion of the court,[60] and a *prima facie* presumption of copyright validity.[61] Therefore, to avail herself of these additional privileges, which go beyond Berne minima, a foreigner must register her copyright. This seeming leniency for Berne Convention claimants ought actually be viewed as a hidden trap that only a foolish foreign copyright owner would invoke. For instance, if a Belgian author wishes to sue for violation of his copyright in United States court, he must hire an American lawyer, pay approximately $120.00 as a filing fee to a United States district court, and complete all the other procedural and logistical requirements for filing suit. However, based on the BCIA, this author could say, "I want to save myself from spending $10 and from filling out a registration form. Therefore, I am going to take advantage of this loophole, even though it is going to cost me recovery of statutory damages, attorneys' fees, and the *prima facie* presumption of va-

---

56 17 U.S.C. § 411(a) (1976).

57 Section 7(c)(1) of S1301 provided that "[r]egistration is not a prerequisite to the institution of a civil action for infringement of copyright." S. Rep. 352, 100th Cong., 2d Sess., *reprinted in* 1988 U.S. CODE CONG. & ADMIN. NEWS 3706, 3710, 3735.

58 The Berne Convention allows members to apply their domestic copyright laws to their citizens. *See supra* note 47 and accompanying text.

59 17 U.S.C. § 412(2) (1988).

60 *Id.*

61 *Id.* at § 410(c) (1988).

lidity." It is difficult to foresee that this new provision will be commonly invoked. Accordingly, the change is more illusory than real.

C. *Recordation*

Another aspect of the United States copyright law that the BCIA has changed is the law governing the recordation of transfers. Moreover, unlike the registration change discussed above, this change will be more real than illusory.

In addition to registering copyright for a work, the 1976 Act provided that a transferee from the author had to file a recordation of transfer with the United States Copyright Office.[62] Such recordation, like a registration, served as a jurisdictional prerequisite to filing suit. The BCIA has now abolished that jurisdictional requirement. Moreover, this change applies to Berne Convention and American claimants alike.[63]

III. Ethereal and Constitutional Issues

A. *Public Domain Recapture*

Article 18 of the Berne Convention provides that upon accession to the treaty, an adhering state must accord protection to works that are still protected in their countries of origin.[64] This rule differs dramatically from the standard applicable under the UCC.[65] Thus, last year's Berne ratification posed a dilemma for the United States that we did not face upon joining the UCC in 1955. More specifically, the United States has never recognized copyright protection for Egyptian-authored works published in Egypt in 1970, for example. Yet those works are probably protected in Egypt today. The question therefore arises: Upon joining the Berne Union, of which Egypt is also a member, must the United States recapture the copyright of such Egyptian works out of the public domain?

Regardless of the answer to that question as a matter of in-

---

62 *See* 17 U.S.C. § 205(d) (1987).

63 Berne Convention Implementation Act of 1988, § 109(a), Pub. L. No. 100-568, 102 Stat. 2853 (1988) (amending 17 U.S.C. § 501(b) (1989)).

64 Article 18(1) provides: "This Convention shall apply to all works which, at the moment of its coming into force, have not yet fallen into the public domain in the country of origin . . . . " Berne Convention For the Protection of Literary and Artistic Works, Sept. 9, 1886, *revised* Paris, July 24, 1971, art. 18(1), 25 U.S.T. 1341, T.I.A.S. No. 7868, 828 U.N.T.S. 221.

65 Universal Copyright Convention, Sept. 6, 1952, 6 U.S.T. 2731, T.I.A.S. No. 3324, 735 U.N.T.S. 368, *revised* July 24, 1971, Paris Text, art. II, 25 U.S.T. 1341, T.I.A.S. No. 7868.

ternational treaty law, Congress has provided the answer as a matter of internal legislation. The BCIA provides that works in the United States public domain remain in the public domain.[66] As a practical matter,[67] therefore, the Egyptian works under consideration will not benefit from United States accession to the Berne Convention.[68]

B. *Moral Rights*

Almost a third of the new law's thirteen sections are designed, in whole or in part, to forestall any claim that the Berne Convention is self-executing under United States law.[69] In addition, this issue played a key role in the bill's deliberation in both houses.[70] The issue of self-execution merited such close attention not because of its intrinsic jurisprudential significance, but rather because of its intimate relationship to the controversial issue of moral rights. To appreciate the significance of this issue, Article 6*bis* of the Berne Convention must first be understood:

> Independently of the author's economic rights, and even after the transfer of the said rights, the author shall have the right to claim authorship of the work and to object to any distortion, mutilation or other modification of, or other derogatory action in relation to, the said work, which would be prejudicial to his honor or reputation.[71]

Many advanced nations, such as France and Japan, for example, incorporate Article 6*bis* of the Berne Convention into their domestic

---

66 Section 12 of the BCIA explicitly states that it "does not provide copyright protection for any work that is in the public domain in the United States." Berne Convention Implementation Act of 1988, § 12, Pub. L. No. 100-568, 102 Stat. 2853 (1988). Taken literally and minimally, this provision merely expresses the truism that works in the public domain are *ipso facto* not protected by copyright. Its intent, nonetheless, is clearly not merely to legislate a tautology, but to avoid according retroactive protection by virtue of Berne adherence. S. Rep. No. 100-352, 100th Cong., 2d Sess. 48 (1988) [hereinafter S. Rep. 100-352]; H.R. Rep. No. 100-609, *supra* note 11, at 51-52.

67 Even as a treaty matter, there appears to be some justification for the United States' position. Some long-standing Berne members, evidently also do not recapture public domain works.

68 The contrary conclusion could arise if the United States courts applied the Berne Convention as governing law, rather than the BCIA. This issue raises the question of treaty self-execution. *See infra* notes 82-106 and accompanying text.

69 *See* Berne Convention Implementation Act, §§ 2-3, 4(a)(3), 6, Pub. L. No. 100-568, 102 Stat. 2853 (1988).

70 *See* H.R. Rep. No. 100-609, *supra* note 11, at 28-38; 134 Cong. Rec. S14553 (daily ed. Oct. 5, 1988) (statement of Senator DeConcini).

71 Berne Convention For the Protection of Literary and Artistic Works, Sept. 9, 1886, *revised* Paris, July 24, 1971, art. 6*bis*(1), 25 U.S.T. 1341, T.I.A.S. No. 7868, 828 U.N.T.S. 221.

copyright laws, either *in haec verba* or in substance. In the United States, by contrast, moral rights are in their infancy.[72] The issue therefore arose as to whether the United States would adopt the moral rights envisioned by Article 6*bis* in the course of joining the Berne Convention.

Before discussing Congress' resolution of this issue, I will elaborate on the foregoing moral minima of the Berne Convention. Berne contains two moral rights, *attribution* (paternity) and *integrity*. The *attribution* right is a right to claim credit, such that each time an artistic work is utilized the author's name must be listed. The right arises in all sorts of contexts. For instance, when a song is broadcast over the air on a radio station, the attribution right, if applied literally, would require that the singer's name be credited on the air. If applied even more broadly, it would mean that the instrumentalist's name, back-up vocalists' names, and the sound engineer's name must all be stated on the air. Consider an actual case, filed in Brazil, in which a Brazilian newspaper published a photograph of Joseph Mengele. The photograph had been taken from a British documentary, which had obtained the photograph from a Czech film crew, which, in turn, had received the photograph from an unknown provenance. Ponder the complexities of attribution under that scenario![73]

The *integrity* right is a right to prevent distortion or mutilation of an artistic work itself. In another actual case from foreign jurisprudence, the son of the producer of an Italian movie sued RAI, the Italian television network, for breach of the subject film's integrity right. RAI had put the film on television and interrupted the continuity of the film with commercials. The filmmaker's son claimed the showing of commercials constituted unconscionable mutilation of his father's work and thus should be barred as a violation of the integrity right.[74]

---

[72] *See* 2 NIMMER ON COPYRIGHT, *supra* note 4, at § 8.21 (cited in H.R. Rep. No. 100-609, *supra* note 11, at 33 n.63). The Ad Hoc Working Group concluded that United States law is in compliance with the Berne Convention's moral rights requirements, citing at length from Professor Nimmer's report prepared for the predecessor organization to the World Intellectual Property Organization ("WIPO"). *See Final Report of Ad Hoc Working Group, supra* note 13, at 548-57 (citing Nimmer, *Implications of the Prospective Revisions of the Berne Convention and the United States Copyright Law*, 19 STAN. L. REV. 499 (1967)). The House Report draws the same conclusion. H. R. Rep. No. 100-609, *supra* note 11, at 34 & n.67.

[73] "[T]he recognition of the right to claim authorship in each such potential 'author' would require an index of unmanageable size." *Hearing on S. 1301 and S. 1971 Before the Subcomm. on Patents, Copyrights and Trademarks of the Senate Judiciary Comm.*, 100th Cong., 2d Sess. 398 (1988) (statement of David Ladd on behalf of The Coalition to Preserve the American Copyright Tradition).

[74] "Preparation of works for commercial television necessarily entails cutting for in-

A useful contrast in understanding the integrity right stems from juxtaposing treatment of the same case in this country and in a jurisdiction with a highly developed *droit moral*, i.e. France. Dmitri Shostakovich, the celebrated Soviet composer, instituted suit in New York state court in 1941,[75] well before the U.S.S.R. first undertook international copyright relations in 1973.[76] Shostakovich acknowledged that he lacked copyright protection in the United States.[77] He nonetheless claimed that the defendant's exhibition of an anti-Soviet film entitled *The Iron Curtain* violated his moral rights by synchronizing his music in a manner offensive to his sensibilities.[78] The New York court rejected Shostakovich's contention that use of his music in an offensive context contravened his rights.[79] Nonetheless, the almost identical case was brought in France, which ruled *au contraire*.[80]

During the Congressional debate over the Berne bill, an avalanche of opposition to moral rights was registered, including by some of the bill's most vociferous advocates.[81] If the bill had any hope of passage, the task was presented of fashioning a method for the United States to join the Berne Union without incorporating its moral rights provisions into the fabric of American law. The law as passed purports to satisfy that goal.

C. *Self-Execution*

Against the background of the foregoing "parade of horribles," one can understand Congress' fear that moral rights, as contained in the Berne Convention, could be argued to have been imported into United States law by virtue of Berne adher-

---

sertion of commercials, time limitations or indecency concerns. The [filmmaker's son is delaying] presentation by objecting to such cut or the inclusion of commercials." *Id.* at 399.

75 Shostakovich v. Twentieth Century Fox Film Corp., 80 N.Y.S.2d 575 (Sup. Ct. 1948), *aff'd*, 87 N.Y.S.2d 430 (1st Dep't 1949).

76 *See* 4 NIMMER ON COPYRIGHT, *supra* note 4, at Appendix 21.

77 *Id.* at 577.

78 The film depicted KGB infiltration of Canada. *Id.* at 576. The composers were given credit lines and their works were "reproduced . . . for a total of approximately 45 minutes. The entire running time of the film [was] 87 minutes." *Id.* Additionally, one of the plaintiff's names was shown when a character in the movie "plac[ed] a recording of th[e] particular plaintiff's music on a phonograph." *Id.* at 577.

79 *Id.*

80 Societe Le Chant du Monde v. Societé Fox Europe et Societé Fox Americaine Twentieth Century, Cour d'appel, Paris, Jan. 13, 1973 (discussed in Strauss, *The Moral Right of the Author*, 4 AM. J. COMP. L. 506, 534-35 n.56 (1955)).

81 Representatives of the magazine publishing industry opposed the Berne bill precisely out of a fear that it would lead to increasing recognition of moral rights in this country. S. Rep. 100-352, *supra* note 66, at 6. Representatives of the Writers' and Directors' Guilds of America supported the bill, but also believed that it had to be supplemented by additional legislation protecting moral rights to satisfy their concerns. *Id.*

ence. Congress stated its position on this subject without ambiguity:

> The provisions of the Berne Convention, the adherence of the United States thereto, and satisfaction of United States obligations thereunder, do not expand or reduce any right of an author of a work, whether claimed under Federal, State, or the common law — (1) to claim authorship of the work; or (2) to object to any distortion, mutilation, or other modification of, or other derogatory action in relation to, the work, that would prejudice the author's honor or reputation.[82]

The unambiguous intent of Congress is that no litigant can come into a United States court and prevail on an argument that the Berne Convention is self-executing. The President of the United States and members of the Executive branch have gone on record with essentially the same declaration.[83]

The question remains how courts will construe United States ratification of the Berne Convention with regard to whether, in fact, the treaty is self-executing. On the one hand, moral right opponents need go no further than to cite the fact that the legislative and executive branches have stated that moral rights are not self-executing in the United States. But on the other hand, Article 6, clause 2 of the United States Constitution states that "[t]his Constitution, and the Laws of the United States which shall be made in Pursuance thereof; *and all Treaties made*, or which shall be made, *under the Authority of the United States*, shall be the supreme Law of the Land. . . . "[84]

A recent case involving the sculpture "Tilted Arc" is helpful in resolving the dilemma.[85] This work by sculptor Richard Serra was placed on display some blocks from here in Federal Plaza in lower Manhattan. After determining that the sculpture's location was inappropriate, the General Services Administration, which owned the sculpture, decided to move it. Serra attempted to invoke a moral right to have the sculpture remain where it was designed to be displayed.[86] He lost his case last year, based on constitutional

---

[82] Berne Convention Implementation Act, § 3(b), Pub. L. No. 100-568, 102 Stat. 2853 (1988). *See also id.* at § 2 (Berne Convention is "not self-executing under the Constitution and laws of the United States").

[83] *Hearings on H.R. 1623 before Subcomm. on Courts, Civil Liberties, and the Administration of Justice of the Comm. on the Judiciary*, 100th Cong., 2d Sess. 1229 (1986) (letter from Ronald Reagan to Senate dated June 18, 1986). *See also* House Joint Explanatory Statement on House-Senate Compromise Incorporated In Senate Amendment to H.R. 4262, 134 Cong. Rec. H10095 (daily ed. Oct. 12, 1988).

[84] U.S. Const. art. VI, cl. 2 (emphasis added).

[85] Serra v. United States General Serv. Admin., 847 F.2d 1045 (2d Cir. 1988).

[86] *Id.* at 1048.

grounds.[87] But as of March 1, 1989, the United States entered a new era, raising the possibility that Serra could go back to court. In response to a claim of *res judicata*, Serra could argue that his prior case was decided on the basis of ancient law, i.e. the copyright statute applicable in 1988, and that he would be entitled to justice based on current law, i.e. the BCIA.

Before addressing the merits of this hypothetical, I will examine an analogous case from France, where moral rights are taken quite seriously. In this case, Renault contracted with a sculptor to construct a statue for the road leading up to the Renault corporate headquarters.[88] The contract contained a liquidated damages clause, providing that if Renault did not perform completely, it would pay the sculptor x francs. Renault began to construct the statue, but in the middle of the project decided to stop. One could have merely looked to the contract to pay the liquidated damages. Instead, the French courts held that having undertaken construction of the statue, Renault was obligated to finish the statue and the statue would remain for an indefinite period in the location for which it was designed.[89]

Thus, I will assume for the sake of discussion that the issue is live. A Berne Convention view of moral rights, assuming it to be congruent with the French approach,[90] would mean that Serra should prevail. By contrast, a reaffirmation of pre-Berne United States law would mean that Serra would continue to be without a remedy. Thus, depending on whether or not the Berne Convention is viewed as self-executing, different results could emerge.

The jurisprudence in this country on treaty self-execution is complex. One can go back as far as 1833 to find a United States Supreme Court opinion stating that the Florida Cession treaty is self-executing and creating a private cause of action based on the treaty.[91] By the same token, the Ninth Circuit in 1974 recognized a private cause of action under a treaty with respect to Former Japa-

---

[87] *Id.* at 1048-52.

[88] Dubuffet v. Regie Renault, Trib. Gr. Inst. Paris, Mar. 23, 1977, July 1977 RIDA 191, *aff'd*, Paris, June 2, 1978, 1979 D. Jur. 14, *rev'd*, Civ. 1re, Jan. 8, 1980, 1980 D. Jur. 89, *on remand*, Versailles, July 8, 1981, Oct. 1981 RIDA 201, 1982 D.I.R. 45, *aff'd*, Civ. 1re, Mar. 16, 1983, July 1983 RIDA 80, 1983 D.I.R. 432.

[89] Francon & Ginsberg, *Authors' Rights in France: The Moral Right of the Creator of a Commissioned Work to Compel the Commissioning Party to Complete the Work*, 9 COLUM. J.L. & ARTS 381 (1985).

[90] The assumption does not necessarily pertain. France implements moral rights to a much greater extent than the minimum standards of the Berne Convention. *See* Plaisant, *France*, M. NIMMER & P. GELLER, INTERNATIONAL COPYRIGHT LAW AND PRACTICE § 7 (1989) [hereinafter INTERNATIONAL COPYRIGHT LAW]. The issue is simplified here for the sake of clarifying the issues.

[91] United States v. Percheman, 32 U.S. (7 Pet.) 51 (1833) (Marshall, Ch. J.).

nese Mandated Islands.[92]

One can also find authority to the contrary. In 1979, the Third Circuit decided that the 1883 Paris Convention for Intellectual Property was not self-executing.[93] The Berne Convention is in some respects similar to, but in others dissimilar to, the Paris Convention.[94] Without exhaustive analysis on the subject at this juncture, suffice it to say that it is unclear whether Mr. Serra's interests should be vindicated.

However, a vital difference exists between United States ratification of the Berne Convention, on the one hand, and our ratification of the Florida Cession treaty and the treaty with respect to Former Japanese Mandated Islands, on the other. The Senate ratified the latter two without any statement by Congress that such treaties are not self-executing. By contrast, as already noted, Congress implemented the Berne Convention with an explicit declaration that the treaty is not self-executing.[95] What role does this difference play? There is no authority on how to construe such a legislative determination. In fact, Congress has made a determination of non-self-execution in only one other instance in the United States Code: implementation of the Convention on Psychotropic Substances.[96] Given that that treaty has never been ruled self-executing or non-self-executing, a judge would have to forge new law in order to upset the explicit Congressional declaration and the explicit Presidential declaration that the Berne Convention is not to be deemed self-executing.

But assuming that the foregoing objections are brushed away by a court eager to rule in Serra's favor and that the Berne Convention as a whole is deemed self-executing within United States law, the more limited question remains as to whether Article 6*bis* of the Berne Convention is self-executing. The answer to this limited

---

92 People of Saipan v. Dep't of Interior, 502 F.2d 90, 97 (9th Cir. 1974), *cert. denied*, 420 U.S. 1003 (1975).

93 Mannington Mills, Inc. v. Congoleum Corp., 595 F.2d 1287, 1299 (3d Cir. 1979) ("Both [Article 17 of the Paris Convention, 13 U.S.T. 1, 41, T.I.A.S. No. 4931 and Article IX of the Pan-American Convention, Aug. 20, 1910, 38 Stat. 1811, 1815] are at odds with a contention that they are self-executing").

94 *Final Report of Ad Hoc Working Group, supra* note 15, at 600-01.

95 *See* Berne Convention Implementation Act of 1988, §§ 2 & 3(a), Pub. L. No. 100-568, 102 Stat. 2853 (1988) (codified at 17 U.S.C. § 101 (1988)). The legislative history also indicated Congress' intention that the treaty not be self-executing in nature. The Senate committee included declarations of this intent "to make it absolutely clear to courts that any claim that Berne is self-executing be rejected." S. Rep. No. 100-352, 100th Cong., 2d Sess. 38, *reprinted in* 1988 U.S. CODE CONG. & ADMIN. NEWS 3735. The Senate Report also explains that although the question of whether a treaty is self-executing is one for the United States courts to decide, the courts should look to these declarations of legislative intent for guidance. *Id.*

96 Pub. L. No. 95-633, 92 Stat. 3768 (codified at 21 U.S.C. § 801(a) (1988)).

question appears to be negative, meaning that Serra's hypothetical initial victory would be Pyrrhic. Article 6*bis* of the Berne Convention itself provides that "[t]he means of redress for safeguarding the rights granted by this Article shall be governed by the legislation of the country where protection is claimed."[97] Thus, even if the Berne Convention as a whole is construed to be self-executing, Article 6*bis* intrinsically is not self-executing. Finally, even if all these problems were avoided, the fact remains that Berne Convention minimum standards, as already noted, apply only to Convention claimants. In other words, if he is an American, Serra cannot claim protection under the Berne Convention within the United States.

Thus, our lengthy speculation about Serra's renewal of his case shows that the BCIA is extremely unlikely, in the short run, to vindicate moral rights. Nonetheless, in the long term, although we have seen that moral rights have not been *ipso facto* legislated, they are arguably becoming implemented within United States law. This has been seen not only in the Kennedy Bill,[98] but in other laws as well. For example, the National Film Integrity Act of 1988[99] was enacted into law at around the same time as the BCIA. Its preamble includes a declaration by Congress of the cultural importance of motion pictures to the United States. Such recognition falls under the broad rubric of protecting the integrity right, even though the teeth in this new law are undeniably blunt. A few days after the BCIA was enacted, a New York court upheld a moral right in a book, despite the terms of the book contract.[100] Moral rights have arisen at the state level and are included by statute in the laws of six states.[101]

Bearing in mind the perils of prediction, the experience of the United Kingdom offers a worthwhile benchmark. Although that country joined the Berne Convention at its inception in 1887, moral rights were not then part of the fabric of British law. Even as recently as 1952, a special committee advising Parliament emphasized the foreignness of the idea of moral protection.[102] A generation

---

97 Berne Convention For the Protection of Literary and Artistic Works, Sept. 9, 1886, *revised* Paris, July 24, 1971, art. 6*bis*(3), 25 U.S.T. 1341, T.I.A.S. No. 7868, 828 U.N.T.S. 221.

98 Visual Artists Rights Act of 1987, S. 1619, 100th Cong., 1st Sess., 133 CONG. REC. 11502 (daily ed. Aug. 6, 1987).

99 2 U.S.C. § 178 (1988).

100 Soc'y of Survivors of the Riga Ghetto, Inc. v. Huttenbach, 141 Misc. 2d 921, 535 N.Y.S.2d 670 (Sup. Ct. 1988). The court held that, although the publisher was the copyright owner, it did not have the right to drastically alter or revise the manuscript and publish it with the author's name. Additionally, the court did not prevent the plaintiff from seeking to enforce his contractual and common-law rights. *Id.* at 674.

101 *See* 2 NIMMER ON COPYRIGHT, *supra* note 4, at § 8.21[G][2]-[7].

102 Cornish, *United Kingdom*, INTERNATIONAL COPYRIGHT LAW, *supra* note 90, at § 7[1].

later, however, the Copyright, Designs and Patent Act of 1988[103] contains strong moral rights provisions.[104] With the increased tempo of internationalization, the recognition of moral rights within American law may occur much sooner than a generation hence. Moreover, the very "culture" of the Berne Union[105] to which the United States now adheres may also affect the American way of copyright protection, including judicial decisions regarding moral rights.[106]

IV. Conclusion

As stated at the outset, 1988 was a banner year for American copyright protection. We have now seen that a number of changes of a formal nature have entered our law as of March 1, 1989. In addition, a number of areas of a more theoretical or constitutional nature have also been implicated. As to those ethereal matters, by and large, no overt change was abruptly instituted upon United States accession to the Berne Convention. However, in the months and years ahead, I believe that we will see an evolution of United States copyright law directly affected by our adherence to the Berne Convention. I hope that my reflections today have offered a framework for viewing that evolution in context.

---

[103] S.I. 1988, No. 48, *reprinted in* 11 Halsbury's Statutes 5 (Current Statutes Service 1988). Coincidentally, this British act received the royal assent on November 15, 1988, only two weeks after the President signed the BCIA into law in the United States.

[104] Chapter 4 of the 1988 United Kingdom law is entirely devoted to moral rights. It includes the attribution right to be identified as the author and not to be falsely attributed with authorship, and the integrity right to object to derogatory treatment of a work, as well as provisions concerning divulgence, duration, and waiver. Copyright, Designs, and Patent Act of 1988, ch. 4.

[105] One of the primary accomplishments of the Berne Convention in 1886, which persists until this day, was the formation of all the constituent states into the Berne Union, an undertaking as political as it was legal. H.R. Rep. No. 100-609, *supra* note 11, at 12. This political unit is constituted at the very outset of the Convention. *See* Berne Convention For the Protection of Literary and Artistic Works, Sept. 9, 1886, *revised* Paris, July 24, 1971, art. 1, 25 U.S.T. 1341, T.I.A.S. No. 7868, 828 U.N.T.S. 221.

[106] *See generally* Jaszi, *supra* note 4. *Cf.* Geller, *International Copyright: An Introduction*, International Copyright Law, *supra* note 90, at § 3[4] n.334 (possibility of "porous" seepage of treaty principles into United States law).

TELEPHONE COMPANIES HAVE FIRST AMENDMENT RIGHTS TOO: THE CONSTITUTIONAL CASE FOR ENTRY INTO CABLE*

LAURENCE H. WINER**

I. INTRODUCTION

It has become a cliche to speak of this as the "Information Age," but a cliche that nonetheless is accurate.[1] The impact of virtually instantaneous, largely uncensored global communication cannot be doubted by anyone watching the historic transformation of the political world as one revolution leads to the next. Another revolution, that of astounding advances in computer science and technology, promises equally profound effects on human society.[2] Combining communications and computer technologies has limitless potential. We may be on the threshold of a futuristic "super-pipe" link among homes, businesses and other institutions through which will flow, in all directions, an integrated panorama of voice, data, print, video, and computing services.[3]

One normally would expect the United States telephone industry, which always has been at the forefront of telecommunications science, to have a major role in developing and providing such services. Currently, however, there is at least one significant, artificial barrier to telephone companies' full participation. Through somewhat different but overlapping restrictions, the various telephone companies ("telcos") are effectively excluded from the cable television industry. Without the lucrative opportunity of being cable operators, the telcos may not have sufficient incentive to help develop the technological infrastructure neces-

---

* Copyright © 1990 by Laurence H. Winer.

** Professor, Arizona State University College of Law. B.A., 1967; M.A., 1970; Ph.D, 1973, Boston University; J.D., 1977, Yale University.

[1] *See* Golshani & Regulinski, *Prologue* to ON THE SYNERGISM OF COMPUTERS AND COMMUNICATION (Communications of the ACM, Jan. 1990) (describing the current era as "set off by processes involved in the acquisition, storage, retrieval, transmission, reception, and security of information"). *See generally* Wright, *On the Road to the Global Village*, SCIENTIFIC AMERICAN, Mar. 1990, at 83 [hereinafter Wright].

[2] *See generally* Peled, *The Next Computer Revolution*, SCIENTIFIC AMERICAN, Oct. 1987, at 57 (introduction to symposium issue on the next phase of computer science and technology).

[3] *See infra* notes 248-53 and accompanying text (discussing information age technologies).

sary for true information age services. Their participation may be crucial.

The argument against participation proceeds from the apprehension that local telephone companies that enjoy regulated monopoly status in their common carrier functions will use this market power in anticompetitive ways, through cross-subsidization or discriminatory practices, to unfairly compete against cable companies. Indeed, the ban originated as a way of promoting the development of an independent cable industry free from the threat of being swallowed by the all-powerful telephone companies. Similarly, the telcos' presumed power as cable operators may dominate or even drown out other voices in the electronic video marketplace. Further, allowing the telcos to participate only in the transmission aspects of cable but not the content related activities may be sufficient for development of advanced technology.

These arguments, however, seem not only wrong but backwards. Cable today is hardly the poor orphan it once was perceived as. Cable arguably has developed into a powerful, unregulated monopoly that could use the market discipline of competition from telcos rather than re-regulation by Congress. Artificially excluding cable's major, natural competitors then makes no sense. Moreover, telco entry into the cable industry may greatly enrich, rather than restrict, the diversity of the "marketplace of ideas," particularly if it leads to vastly expanded capacity with new products and services. This would serve an important public interest while also respecting the telcos' rights and interests.

While this Article generally favors the latter approach, its real thrust is elsewhere. We need to place the debate over telco entry into cable in the proper context, that of the first amendment. The telephone companies are willing speakers, with no mass media position, wishing to enter an important electronic mass media market. They have a first amendment right to do so that cannot be curtailed in the absence of a demonstrated and compelling need effectuated only by narrowly tailored means. Government denial of that right is a prior restraint of the most repressive kind that cannot be justified by speculative fear of untoward results. Such entry, of course, may be subject to regulations, such as those proposed by the Federal Communications Commission ("FCC" or "the Commission") that do not infringe first amendment freedoms and are designed to monitor and control anti-competitive activities.

This Article addresses what in some respects is the most disappointing aspect of the debate, the relegation of constitutional principles to secondary or tertiary status. It may seem strange to stress the first amendment rights of the "big, bad telephone companies," especially since freedom of expression is too often associated only with that of individuals or the established media. But the first amendment fundamentally concerns our common interest in assuring freedom of expression to all, not just officially preferred, speakers. Thus, the challenge is to begin from the premise that telephone companies have a right to develop, own, and operate cable systems. Government should allow their participation in the media without infringing their first amendment freedoms or stifling technological progress, while taking appropriate steps to avoid possible excesses.

Part II of this Article surveys the FCC rules, statutory provisions, and court decrees that constitute the ban on telephone companies entering the cable business and the justifications offered for it. Part II also discusses the current regulatory climate. Part III begins the constitutional analysis by demonstrating that the telcos' first amendment rights are not qualified by their corporate nature, their common carrier status, or other existing media cross-ownership restrictions. Part IV first considers the proper relationship between antitrust and first amendment principles and then establishes that the ban should be treated as a prior restraint. As such it cannot be justified by hypothetical fears about anti-competitive behavior or dislocation of the marketplace of ideas. Finally, Part V considers briefly the possible technological benefits from telco entry into cable which may be jeopardized by continuation of the ban.

II. Current Restrictions

To understand the constitutional infirmities of a ban on telephone companies entering a mass media market such as cable television, one first must consider the various restrictions currently in force, their genesis, and the justifications generally offered for them. There are three somewhat overlapping sets of prohibitions: FCC rules, codifications in the Cable Communications Policy Act of 1984,[4] and provisions of the *Modified Final Judgment* ("MFJ") as interpreted and applied by Judge Greene.

---

[4] Cable Communications Policy Act of 1984, Pub. L. No. 98-549, 98 Stat. 2779 (codified at 47 U.S.C. §§ 521-559 (Supp. V 1987)).

A. *FCC Rules*

The Commission's telephone company — cable television cross-ownership restrictions[5] date back to 1970.[6] At that time, the cable industry was a mere shadow of its present stature. Indeed, it was then still referred to as "Community Antenna Television" ("CATV"), reflecting its primary function of receiving broadcast signals and redistributing them to subscribers by coaxial cables in areas that otherwise were inaccessible or had only poor reception.[7]

The Commission feared that telephone company control of telephone poles and conduit space, needed to accommodate coaxial cables, could be used to favor cable companies owned by or affiliated with the phone companies to the competitive disadvantage of independent cable operators.[8] This could lead to a "concentration of control of broadband cable facilities and . . . thwart the introduction of new and different services."[9] This concern

---

5 The current FCC rules appear at 47 C.F.R. §§ 63.54-63.58 (1989).

6 *See* Applications of Telephone Common Carriers for Section 214 Certificates for Channel Facilities Furnished to Affiliated Community Antenna Television Systems, Final Report and Order, 21 F.C.C.2d 307, *modified*, 22 F.C.C.2d 746 (1970), *aff'd sub. nom.* General Tel. Co. of S.W. v. United States, 449 F.2d 846 (5th Cir. 1971).

7 *See General Tel. Co. of S.W.*, 449 F.2d at 850-51. At the time of the Commission's fundamental cable rulemaking in 1972, Cable Television Report and Order, 36 F.C.C.2d 143, *reconsid.*, 36 F.C.C.2d 326 (1972), *aff'd sub. nom.* ACLU v. FCC, 523 F.2d 1344 (9th Cir. 1975), there were only 2,841 local cable systems serving about six million subscribers and penetrating only 9.5% of all television households. J. GOODALE, ALL ABOUT CABLE § 1.14 (rev. ed. 1988). Cable did not begin developing into the sort of mass media we know today until Home Box Office pioneered satellite distribution of its programming in 1976. C. FERRIS, F. LLOYD & T. CASEY, CABLE TELEVISION LAW ¶ 5.05[7] (1989) [hereinafter CABLE TELEVISION LAW]. For a description of the dramatic growth in the cable industry, see Nat'l Telecommunications and Information Admin., United States Dep't of Commerce, Video Program Distribution and Cable Television: Current Policy Issues and Recommendations, NTIA Report 88-233, at 8-17 (June 1988) [hereinafter NTIA Report]. *See also infra* notes 209-13, 223-24 and accompanying text.

8 *See* Northwestern Indiana Tel. Co. v. FCC, 872 F.2d 465, 469 n.2 (D.C. Cir. 1989) ("[t]he need to eliminate favored treatment of telephone company affiliates is, of course, the cross-ownership rules' *raison d'etre*."), *cert. denied*, 110 S. Ct. 757 (1990).

9 Telephone Company — Cable Television Cross-Ownership Rules, Notice of Inquiry, 2 F.C.C. Rcd. 5092, 5092, ¶ 3 (1987). *See* Telephone Company — Cable Television Cross-Ownership Rules, Further Notice of Inquiry and Notice of Proposed Rulemaking, 3 F.C.C. Rcd. 5849 (1988). Such anticipated services included "the distribution of data, information storage and retrieval, and visual, facsimile and telemetry transmission of all kinds." *Final Report and Order*, 21 F.C.C.2d at 324-25, ¶ 47. By and large such services on cable systems have not materialized despite the Commission's rules. *Telco Notice of Inquiry*, 2 F.C.C. Rcd. at 5097 n.33; *Telco Further Notice of Inquiry*, 3 F.C.C. Rcd. at 5857, ¶ 35.

Indeed, the FCC's concern was something of a *non sequitur*. It never really explained how telephone entry into cable, even at a commanding market level, would inhibit the development of broadband technology and services that independent cable companies alone otherwise might produce. *See Final Report and Order*, 21 F.C.C.2d., at 324-25. One could argue contrarily that a telephone company with substantial market power, and advanced research and development capabilities, would seek to extend its monopoly profits into any related product markets it could develop. Nonetheless, an avowed pur-

about monopolization resulted in the Commission's basic prohibition on any telephone common carrier, subject to the 1934 Communications Act,[10] providing video programming to the viewing public in its telephone service area either directly or through an "affiliate."[11] If such a carrier wishes to construct and maintain, as a common carrier, distribution facilities for lease to a cable system in its service area, *i.e.* provide "channel service"[12] it must obtain "Section 214 authorization"[13] and show that the

---

pose of the cross-ownership ban was to "preserve an environment for the development of new and different broadband services . . . ." *Telco Notice of Inquiry*, 2 F.C.C. Rcd. at 5093, ¶ 12. The Commission is now reexamining this issue. *Id.* at 5095, ¶ 23, 5097 n.33; *Telco Further Notice of Inquiry*, 3 F.C.C. Rcd. at 5857.

[10] 47 U.S.C. §§ 201-220 (1934). Such common carriers include the long-distance, interexchange carriers such as AT&T and its reinvigorated competitors like MCI and US Sprint; the seven Regional Holding Companies, comprised of the twenty-two Bell Operating Companies ("BOCs") spun off from AT&T in the 1984 divestiture pursuant to the 1982 Modified Final Judgment, *infra* note 64; and the 1500 or so independent, local exchange telephone companies. *See Telco Notice of Inquiry*, 2 F.C.C. Rcd. at 5096 n.26. The telephone service areas of these entities, and therefore the extent of the prohibition, vary.

Most long distance interexchange carriers such as AT&T no longer control access to local distribution facilities—poles and conduit space—that was considered essential for cable service. There is, therefore, an argument that the term "telephone service area" (*see* 47 C.F.R. § 63.54 (1989); Cable Act § 613(b), 47 U.S.C. § 533(b) (Supp. V 1987)) should be taken to mean "local exchange service area," with the effect of exempting the interexchange carriers from the rules and the statute. *See Telco Further Notice of Inquiry*, 3 F.C.C. Rcd. at 5862-63, ¶ 70. *See also infra* note 69.

[11] 47 C.F.R. § 63.54. Recently the Commission seems to be narrowing somewhat the previously broad scope it gave to the term "affiliate." *See* Century Fed., Inc. v. FCC, 846 F.2d 1479, 1481-82 (D.C. Cir. 1988) (FCC enlarging exception to its affiliation rule); Northwestern Indiana Tel. Co. v. FCC, 824 F.2d 1205, 1209-10 (D.C. Cir. 1987), *following remand*, 872 F.2d 465, 468 (D.C. Cir. 1989) (discussing FCC's indicia of affiliation), *cert. denied*, 110 S. Ct. 757 (1990).

[12] *See Telco Notice of Inquiry*, 2 F.C.C. Rcd. at 5097 n.35; *Telco Further Notice of Inquiry*, 3 F.C.C. Rcd. at 5870 n.2. Under the Cable Act, the lessee may need a cable franchise to be able to provide "cable service." *See* Cable Act §§ 602 (4)-(6), 621(b), 47 U.S.C. §§ 522(4)-(6), 541(b); H.R. REP. No. 934, 98th Cong., 2d Sess. 57, *reprinted in* 1984 U.S. CODE CONG. & ADMIN. NEWS 4655, 4694 [hereinafter H.R. REP. No. 934]. *See generally* NTIA Report, *supra* note 7, at 40-43.

On the other hand, a customer of tariffed video transmission services provided by a common carrier, much like a user of a "PEG" (public, educational, or governmental) channel under Section 531 of the Cable Act, or a user of a commercial leased access channel under Section 532, might not own, control or manage a cable system "facility" and therefore might not need a franchise as a "cable operator." *See Telco Notice of Further Inquiry*, 3 F.C.C. Rcd. at 5863. At the same time, a carrier when providing channel service also may not need a cable franchise as it has no role in producing, selecting, or marketing programming, nor any relationship with subscribers, and thus may not be providing cable service. *Id.*

[13] Section 214 requires such a carrier to obtain a certificate from the FCC. 47 U.S.C. § 214 (1982). *See* General Tel. Co. of California, 13 F.C.C.2d 488 (1968), *aff'd*, General Tel. Co. of California v. FCC, 413 F.2d 390 (D.C. Cir.), *cert. denied*, 396 U.S. 888 (1969) (upholding Commission's jurisdiction to regulate channel service). Section 214 authorization is the vehicle through which the FCC enforces its cross-ownership rules. *See* NTIA Report, *supra* note 7, at 45.

Outside a carrier's telephone service area the Commission has granted blanket Section 214 authority for channel service. Blanket Section 214 Authorization for Provision by a Telephone Carrier of Lines for its Cable Television and other Non — Common

cable operator is unrelated and unaffiliated.[14] Focusing on the potential for anticompetitive effect, the rules also allow for waivers in communities where independent cable service otherwise "demonstrably could not exist" or upon "other showing of good cause" if the public interest would be served.[15] Furthermore, there is a general exemption for rural areas,[16] now without regard for whether alternative, independent cable service would be available in such areas.[17]

In 1987, however, the Commission determined that recent changes in the telecommunications industry and the tremendous development of cable television warrant reexamination of these cross-ownership rules.[18] For example, in originally formulating its rules the Commission did take notice of the general competitive relationship between cable and the telephone industry. This included the possibility of a telephone company cross-subsidizing its cable operations from its telephone revenues and the potential adverse social and economic effects of concentration of control over cable by the already powerful telephone companies.[19] But the Commission focused on the particular problem of access to poles and conduit space.[20]

Then, in 1978, the Pole Attachments Act gave the FCC the right to assure that the rates, terms, and conditions for pole at-

---

Carrier Services Outside its Telephone Service Area, Report and Order, FCC 84-28, 49 Fed. Reg. 21333 (1984). *See Telco Further Notice of Inquiry*, 3 F.C.C. Rcd. at 5870 n.2.

14 47 C.F.R. §§ 63.54-.55 (1989). Few such arrangements seem to have been made. *See* D. BRENNER, M. PRICE & M. MEYERSON, CABLE TELEVISION AND OTHER NONBROADCAST VIDEO § 11.03[4][a], at 11-24 to 11-28 (1989) [hereinafter BRENNER, PRICE & MEYERSON].

As of mid-1988, Centel, the nation's twelfth largest local telephone company, was the largest telephone company providing cable service *outside* its service area. It owned and operated cable systems in seven states serving 521,000 subscribers, placing it among the top 25 cable operators. NTIA Report, *supra* note 7, at 44 n.127, 58-59.

15 47 C.F.R. § 63.56. In a recent controversial proceeding, based on its assessment of the public interest benefits the FCC granted a conditional, good-cause waiver to General Telephone Company of California to construct and maintain broadband, coaxial and fiber optic cable facilities in Cerritos, California. General Tel. Co. of California, 4 F.C.C. Rcd. 5693 (1989), *appeal docketed sub nom.*, National Cable Television Ass'n v. FCC, No. 89-1517 (D.C. Cir. Aug. 2, 1989).

16 47 C.F.R. § 63.58.

17 *See Telco Notice of Inquiry*, 2 F.C.C. Rcd. at 5096 n.12; *Telco Further Notice of Inquiry*, 3 F.C.C. Rcd. at 5850-51.

18 *Telco Notice of Inquiry*, 2 F.C.C. Rcd. at 5093, ¶ 8.

19 Applications of Telephone Common Carriers for Section 214 Certificates for Channel Facilities Furnished to Affiliated Community Antenna Television Systems, Final Report and Order, 21 F.C.C.2d 307, 308, 323-24 (1970).

20 *Id.* at 323-27. *See Telco Notice of Inquiry*, 2 F.C.C. Rcd. at 5094, ¶ 13 (potential for cross-subsidization was a "serious concern" but not an "explicit rationale" for adopting the 1970 cross-ownership rules); *Telco Further Notice of Inquiry*, 3 F.C.C. Rcd. at 5849, ¶ 3.

tachments are "just and reasonable."[21] This Act does not guarantee access, which remains a matter of contract negotiation between the cable operator and the utility owning the poles or conduits.[22] Nonetheless, the Commission does have some authority to mandate access in specific cases of denial or termination.[23] So while the Commission is not persuaded that all concerns over access to poles and conduits have been eliminated,[24] the ability of cable to wire over eighty percent of the nation's residences is a good indication that the purpose of the Pole Attachments Act is being achieved.[25]

Other issues remain concerning the relationship between telephone companies and the cable industry, including the possibility of telco cross-subsidization. A 1981 FCC staff report considered possible efficiencies from telco entry into cable and the development of new technologies and services, but concluded that necessary safeguards did not then exist to allow elimination of the cross-ownership ban.[26] In launching its current inquiry after further evolutions in the industries, the Commission describes the "central issue" as "whether it is still necessary or desirable to restrict entry of telephone companies in order to preserve an environment that encourages competitive provision of cable facilities and services."[27]

In June 1988, the Commerce Department's National Telecommunications and Information Administration (NTIA) released a report on Video Program Distribution and Cable Television.[28] A key recommendation was to allow local telephone companies greater freedom in providing non-discrimina-

---

21 Pub. L. No. 97-130, 95 Stat. 1687 (codified at 47 U.S.C. § 224 (1982 & Supp. V 1987)).

22 Indeed, in sustaining the Pole Attachments Act against a constitutional challenge as an uncompensated taking of property, the Supreme Court relied on the absence of compulsory access in the Act stating, "The language of the Act provides no explicit authority to the FCC to require pole access for cable operators, and the legislative history strongly suggests that Congress intended no such authorization." FCC v. Florida Power Corp., 480 U.S. 245, 251 n.6 (1987) (citations to legislative history omitted).

23 *See Telco Further Notice of Inquiry*, 3 F.C.C. Rcd. at 5871 n.16.

24 *Id.* at 5871 n.17.

25 *See* National Cable Television Ass'n, Inc. v. FCC, 747 F.2d 1503, 1505, 1506 & n.1 (D.C. Cir. 1984). In upholding the FCC's rural exemption, the court noted that the opportunities for phone companies to use control over pole attachments to extract a monopolist's premium from providers of cable services have diminished with passage of the Pole Attachments Act. *Id. See Telco Notice of Inquiry*, 2 F.C.C. Rcd. at 5093-94, ¶ 13 (discussing ameliorating effect of the Pole Attachments Act).

26 FCC Policy on Cable Ownership, A Staff Report, released Nov. 1981, FCC Office of Plans and Policy, *described in Telco Further Notice of Inquiry*, 3 F.C.C. Rcd. at 5850, ¶ 6.

27 *Telco Notice of Inquiry*, 2 F.C.C. Rcd. at 5093, ¶ 10; *Telco Further Notice of Inquiry*, 3 F.C.C. Rcd. at 5851, ¶ 10.

28 NTIA Report, *supra* note 7.

tory, video common carriage — a "video dial tone" — within their service areas.[29] While the NTIA was clearly in favor of continuing to prohibit the phone companies from providing video programming directly to local subscribers,[30] the users of the recommended video transport services no longer would have to be franchised cable operators. They also could be more closely affiliated with the telephone companies in that the latter could provide ancillary services such as billing, order taking, service maintenance and the like.[31] Not too surprisingly, development of widely available video dial tone service was generally supported in a more sweeping NTIA study released later in 1988.[32]

The Commission now has gone even further in tentatively concluding that the public interest would be best served by greater telco participation in the provision of cable television service, because this would foster increased competition in the cable industry.[33] The Commission thus seems ready to recommend removal of the cross-ownership ban subject to appropriate safeguards against anticompetitive cross-subsidies.[34] This would go beyond the "video dial tone" proposal in allowing telephone companies to directly market video programming to subscribers.[35] However, the video dial tone does not address the telephone companies' first amendment concerns discussed below. Moreover, the Commission believes that full entry is necessary to give the telcos sufficient financial incentives to develop and offer video and other services and achieve efficiencies of operation.[36]

Similarly, the Commission has proposed specifying particu-

---

29 *Id.* at 32-60.

30 *Id.* at 36.

31 *Id.* at 35-36, 39-43.

32 Nat'l Telecommunications and Information Administration, United States Dept. of Commerce, NTIA TELECOM 2000, at 150, 161-62 (Oct. 1988).

33 *Telco Further Notice of Inquiry*, 3 F.C.C. Rcd. at 5849.

34 *Id.* at 5860. Alfred C. Sikes became Chairman of the FCC after the Telco Further Notice of Inquiry was released. Mr. Sikes had been Assistant Secretary of Commerce for Communications and Information and as such supervised NTIA's narrower recommendation in terms of video dial tone service. His current position is not clear. *See Sikes Focuses a Critical Gaze on Cable's Franchise Foundations*, CABLEVISION, Dec. 4, 1989, at 48, 55; *The "Irreversible Momentum" of Al Sikes*, BROADCASTING, Oct. 9, 1989, at 35, 36-37. *See infra* notes 226-31 and accompanying text (further discussing proposed safeguards).

35 In this capacity the telephone company presumably would be subject to the same franchising requirements of any other cable operator. *See Telco Further Notice of Inquiry*, 3 F.C.C. Rcd. at 5863. *Cf. supra* note 12.

Commissioner Dennis filed a separate statement expressing her preference on the present record for the NTIA "video dial-tone" approach rather than the open entry favored by the majority. Separate Statement of Commissioner Patricia Diaz Dennis, 4 F.C.C. Rcd. 2400, 2401 (1989).

36 *Telco Further Notice of Inquiry*, 3 F.C.C. Rcd. at 5857 n.23. *But cf.*, NTIA Report, *supra* note 7, at 39. *See infra* note 261 and accompanying text.

lar standards under which it will grant "good cause" waivers, making such waivers more accessible. Thus, the Commission tentatively "concluded that construction and operation of technologically advanced, integrated broadband networks by carriers for the purpose of providing video programming and other services will constitute good cause for waiver."[37] The Commission reached this conclusion despite both the legislative history of the 1984 Cable Act codifying the cross-ownership rules, which indicates the Commission's waiver authority should be narrowly construed,[38] and the general requirement for a "hard look" at waiver requests.[39] Finally, and toward much the same end, the Commission plans to modify its broad definition of affiliation to focus on ownership or control as the prohibited relationships between a carrier and a cable system, even though the Commission earlier had determined that nothing in the 1984 Cable Act or its legislative history suggests Congress thought any such change necessary then.[40] The effect will be to ameliorate the previous stringent application of the cross-ownership rules.[41]

B. *The 1984 Cable Act*

The FCC is constrained in eliminating the cross-ownership ban by the codification of its rules in the 1984 Cable Act. This has several practical ramifications for the effort to allow telephone entry into cable.

The Cable Act[42] was the FCC's first explicit statutory grant

---

[37] *Telco Further Notice of Inquiry*, 3 F.C.C. Rcd. at 5849 ¶ 1, 5861 ¶ 60. *See infra* notes 250-59 and accompanying text (describing integrated broadband networks). Such an approach was anticipated in Revision of the Processing Policies for Waivers of the Telephone Company — Cable Television Cross-Ownership Rules, 69 F.C.C.2d 1097, 1110 (1978). In addition to such integrated systems capable of providing cable television service and traditional common carrier services, the Commission will consider other waiver proposals for technologically advanced communications services. *Telco Further Notice of Inquiry*, 3 F.C.C. Rcd. at 5873 n.48.

The Commission's proposal to generally remove the ban, however, is not contingent upon the construction of any particular technologically advanced facilities. *Id.* at 5858.

[38] *See Telco Further Notice of Inquiry*, 3 F.C.C. Rcd. at 5850, 5861 (citing 130 Cong. Rec. H10,444 (daily ed. Oct. 1, 1984)).

[39] *See id.* at 5861 (citing WAIT Radio v. FCC, 418 F.2d 1153 (D.C. Cir. 1969)).

[40] *Id.* at 5865-66. *See* Amendment of Parts 1, 63 and 76 of the Commission's Rules to Implement the Provisions of the Cable Communications Policy Act of 1984, 58 Rad. Reg. 2d (P&F) 1, 16-17 (1985).

[41] The current federal regulations prohibit *any* financial, business or other relationship between telephone and cable companies beyond the basic carrier-user relationship. 47 C.F.R. § 63.54 n.1. Such relationship contemplates a general offer to provide substantially the same services to all similarly situated entities or individuals on a non-discriminatory basis. *See Telco Further Notice of Inquiry*, 3 F.C.C. Rcd. at 5865, 5874 n.64.

[42] Cable Act §§ 601-39, 47 U.S.C. §§ 521-59 (Supp. V 1987).

of authority over cable.[43] In this context Congress essentially codified[44] the FCC's telephone — cable cross-ownership rules, relying on the Commission's findings to support them without independent analysis.[45] This may make it easier for Congress simply to defer to a new recommendation from the FCC. Moreover, with respect to policy and constitutional analysis the rules and the statute can be treated alike.

As a practical and legal matter, therefore, the FCC cannot act unilaterally to eliminate the statutory ban but can only make such a recommendation to Congress. This has two consequences. First Congress must be persuaded to act, and this may be a propitious time. Congress is considering re-regulation of the cable industry[46] in the context of a widespread perception that the cable industry has become too powerful, monopolistic, and vertically integrated, with adverse competitive effects and excessive rates for consumers.[47] One important aspect of new legislation addressing these issues may be the creation of more diversity and competition in the cable industry by letting telephone companies enter.[48]

---

43 Prior to the Cable Act, the FCC could regulate cable only on the theory and to the extent such regulation was "reasonably ancillary" to its effective regulation of broadcasting. United States v. Southwestern Cable Co., 392 U.S. 157, 178 (1968). This approach had clear limits. *See* United States v. Midwest Video Corp., 406 U.S. 649, 676 (1972) (Burger, C.J. concurring in result) (FCC's local origination cable rule "strains the outer limits" of its jurisdiction over cable); FCC v. Midwest Video Corp., 440 U.S. 689 (1979) (mandatory access and minimum channel capacity requirements for cable systems exceed FCC's statutory authority).

44 Cable Act § 613(b), 47 U.S.C. § 533(b) (Supp. V 1987).

45 *See* Telephone Company — Cable Television Cross-Ownership Rules, Notice of Inquiry, 2 F.C.C. Rcd. 5092, 5092-93 (1987); H. R. REP. No. 934, *supra* note 12 at 4693-94 (indicating congressional intent to codify FCC rules). Congress, however, did wish to provide an unqualified rural exemption, *id.*, and the Commission complied. *See Telco Further Notice of Inquiry*, 3 F.C.C. Rcd. at 5851.

46 The Cable Act itself requires the FCC to report to Congress by October 30, 1990, on rate regulation of cable services and the effect of competition in the marketplace. Cable Act § 613(h), 47 U.S.C. § 543(h) (Supp. V 1987). The FCC has launched a broad notice of inquiry on the status of cable television that it hopes to complete early in the summer of 1990. Competition, Rate Deregulation and the Commission's Policy Relating to the Provision of Cable Television Service, Notice of Inquiry, 5 F.C.C. Rcd. 362 (1989). *See FCC to Review State of Cable TV*, BROADCASTING, Dec. 18, 1989, at 81.

47 *See generally Competition, Rate Deregulation*, 5 F.C.C. Rcd. at 362-63; *Cable TV: The New Big Kid Confronts Re-Regulation*, 49 CONG. Q. 3361, 3361 (1989) [hereinafter *Cable TV: The New Big Kid*]. For a study of recent basic cable rate increases, see NTIA Report, *supra* note 7, at App. A; *General Accounting Office, Telecommunications: National Survey of Cable Television Rates and Services, Report to the Chairman, Subcomm. on Telecommunications and Finance, House Comm. on Energy and Commerce*, (GAO/RCED-89-193) (Aug. 3, 1989) [hereinafter *GAO Survey*]. The Commission has initiated a separate proposed rulemaking on basic cable rates. Reexamination of the Effective Competition Standard for the Regulation of Cable Television Basic Service Rates, Notice of Proposed Rulemaking, 5 F.C.C. Rcd. 259 (1990).

48 *See Competition, Rate Deregulation*, 5 F.C.C. Rcd. at 365-67. *See, e.g.*, S.1068, 101st Cong., 1st Sess. § 4 (1989) and H.R. 2437, 101st Cong., 1st Sess. § 4 (1989). (These

The necessity for congressional action also means that much of the friction in recent years between Congress and the Commission may be avoided with smoother and more definite results. As just one example of this recently difficult relationship, consider the uncertain status of the fairness doctrine over the past several years. In its 1985 Fairness Doctrine Report, the FCC finally recognized the probable constitutional infirmity of the doctrine.[49] It refrained from eliminating the doctrine, however, out of concern that it might have been codified by a 1959 amendment to the Communications Act.[50] A panel of the Court of Appeals for the District of Columbia Circuit then announced that the doctrine was only an "administrative construction, not a binding statutory directive."[51] Another panel of the same court told the Commission that, in the face of a constitutional challenge in a specific fairness doctrine enforcement proceeding, it was obliged to resolve the status of the doctrine despite intense political pressure from Congress.[52] That pressure included a statutory directive that the Commission "consider alternative means of administering and enforcing the Fairness Doctrine" and report to Congress, presumably *before* altering the doctrine.[53]

Following this mandate the FCC proceeded with a notice of inquiry and report,[54] but *simultaneously* with release of its report the Commission eliminated the doctrine in a pending enforcement proceeding.[55] Both this result and the manner in which it

---

companion measures would partially reregulate cable but allow telcos to offer cable services).

49 1985 Fairness Doctrine Report, 102 F.C.C.2d 143, 148-57 (1985), *petition for review dismissed as to constitutional challenge but not otherwise,* Radio-Television News Directors Ass'n v. FCC, 809 F.2d 860 (D.C. Cir.) (per curiam), *vacated,* 831 F.2d 1148 (D.C. Cir. 1987). The two-pronged obligation of the Commission's fairness doctrine required broadcast licensees to provide coverage of important and controversial issues of local community interest and to provide a reasonable opportunity for the presentation of contrasting viewpoints on such issues. *1985 Fairness Doctrine Report,* 102 F.C.C.2d at 146.

50 *1985 Fairness Doctrine Report,* 102 F.C.C.2d at 227-46.

51 Telecommunications Research and Action Center v. FCC, 801 F.2d 501, 517, *reh'g en banc denied,* 806 F.2d 1115 (D.C. Cir. 1986), *cert. denied,* 107 S. Ct. 3196 (1987).

52 Meredith Corp. v. FCC, 809 F.2d 863, 872-74 (D.C. Cir. 1987).

53 Making Continuing Appropriations for Fiscal Year 1987, Pub. L. No. 99-500, 132 CONG. REC. H10,619 (daily ed. Oct. 15, 1986). *See Meredith Corp.,* 809 F.2d at 873 n.11 (citing H.R. REP. No. 1005, 99th Cong., 2d Sess. (1986), *reprinted in* 132 CONG. REC. H10,720 (daily ed. Oct. 15, 1986)).

54 Inquiry into Section 73.1910 of the Commission's Rules and Regulations Concerning Alternatives to the General Fairness Doctrine of Broadcast Licensees, Notice of Inquiry, 2 F.C.C. Rcd. 1532 (1987); Report of the Commission, 2 F.C.C. Rcd. 5272 (1987), *reconsid. denied,* 3 F.C.C. Rcd. 2050 (1988).

55 Syracuse Peace Council v. Television Station WTVH, 2 F.C.C. Rcd. 5043, 5057 (1987), *reconsid. denied,* 3 F.C.C. Rcd. 2035 (1988) ("fairness doctrine, on its face, violated the first amendment and contravened the public interest"), *aff'd,* Syracuse Peace Council v. FCC, 867 F.2d 654 (D.C. Cir. 1989), *cert. denied,* 110 S. Ct. 717 (1990).

was achieved greatly angered many in Congress.[56] The reaction has included repeated and ongoing attempts to write the doctrine into law,[57] one of which would have succeeded but for a presidential veto.[58] Such contretemps between Congress and the Commission sours their relationship and affects and distracts from other issues as well.[59]

The message here is clear. Whatever inconvenience results from the uncertain status of the fairness doctrine pales in comparison to what would occur if there were a similar dispute between the FCC and Congress over telephone entry into cable. The present paralysis would continue, as no one would undertake substantial investment to enter an industry where the right to remain was at all questionable. Cooperation, not acrimony, between Congress and the Commission is essential and far wiser politically.

Nonetheless, the Commission may be positioning itself to partially supplant continued congressional inaction. By proposing to grant certain waivers more liberally and adopting a more flexible notion of affiliation, despite some contra-indications from Congress,[60] the Commission may be perceived as again trying to usurp congressional prerogative.[61] Much, of course,

---

56 *See Official Reaction to Fairness Doctrine Repeal: The Good, the Bad and the Ugly*, BROADCASTING, Aug. 10, 1987, at 59; *A Question of Priorities*, BROADCASTING, Aug. 10, 1987, at 28. The fairness doctrine is intimately related to 47 U.S.C. § 315 (1982), the provision mandating equal broadcast opportunities for political candidates. *See* Winer, *The Signal Cable Sends — Part I: Why Can't Cable Be More Like Broadcasting?*, 46 MD. L. REV. 212, 268-76 (1987) [hereinafter Winer, *The Signal Cable Sends*]. This may partly explain the particular affinity for the fairness doctrine many in Congress exhibit.

57 *See Fairness Excised As Congress Exits*, BROADCASTING, Nov. 27, 1989, at 40.

58 Veto of the Fairness in Broadcasting Act of 1987, 23 WEEKLY COMP. PRES. DOC. 715 (June 19, 1987). President Reagan characterized the doctrine as unconstitutional content-based regulation. *Id.* President Bush may take a similar approach. *See Bush Seen As Sending Signal On Fairness Doctrine*, BROADCASTING, Apr. 17, 1989, at 31.

59 *See, e.g.*, *Fairness Doctrine Law Still "Quid" To Broadcasters' "Pro Quo"*, BROADCASTING, May 8, 1989, at 36. For descriptions of other similar incidents between Congress and the FCC, see Emrod, *The First Amendment Invalidity Of FCC Ownership Regulations*, 38 CATH. U.L. REV. 401, 425-27 (1989) (Congressional disfavor of FCC's attempt to change the multiple ownership rules) [hereinafter Emrod]; Winter Park Communications, Inc. v. FCC, 873 F.2d 347, 350-51 (D.C. Cir. 1989) (congressional action to forestall possible Commission changes in comparative preferences based on gender and race), *cert. granted sub nom.* Metro Broadcasting, Inc. v. FCC, 110 S. Ct. 715 (1990); and Shurberg Broadcasting of Hartford, Inc. v. FCC, 876 F.2d 902, 925 n.39 (D.C. Cir. 1989) (Silberman, J.) (same; Congress obliged FCC to disregard court order), *cert. granted sub nom.* Ltd. Astroline Communications Co. Ltd. Partnership v. Shurberg Broadcasting of Hartford, Inc., 110 S. Ct. 715 (1990).

60 *See supra* notes 37-41 and accompanying text. This is not to say that the FCC's interpretation of Congress' current positions on these issues may not be both supportable and correct.

61 Such a charge is being made in the appeal of the Cerritos waiver granted to GTE. General Tel. Co. of California, 4 F.C.C. Rcd. 5693 (1989), *appeal docketed sub nom.*, National Cable Television Ass'n v. FCC, No. 89-1517 (D.C. Cir. Aug. 2, 1989). *See NCTA*

would depend upon how the FCC actually implements its proposed changes.[62] The far better approach, however, would be for Congress and the Commission to agree upon an end to the cross-ownership ban and allow open entry with appropriate safeguards. This is the value of reliance upon the constitutional arguments to be developed, since they apply equally to Congress and the FCC (and to judicial supervision of the *Modified Final Judgment* discussed below) and depend less on variable policy evaluations.

C. *The Modified Final Judgment*

Even if Congress and the Commission agree on eliminating or substantially relaxing the telco-cable cross-ownership ban, one must still contend with Judge Greene.[63] The *Modified Final Judgment* ("MFJ"),[64] which divested AT&T of what now are called the Bell Operating Companies ("BOCs"), imposed various lines of business restrictions. In particular, AT&T was excluded from "electronic publishing" over its own transmission facilities for seven years,[65] and the BOCs generally were restricted through-

---

Says FCC Overstepped Bounds in Cerritos Case, BROADCASTING, Jan. 22, 1990, at 60; *supra* note 15.

62 The Commission, for example, might conclude that the statutory ban does not apply to interexchange carriers or that waivers often should be available to such carriers. *See* Telephone Company — Cable Television Cross-Ownership Rules, Further Notice of Inquiry and Notice of Proposed Rulemaking, 3 F.C.C. Rcd. 5849, 5862-63 (1988).

63 Congress may essentially overrule Judge Greene through legislation. The antitrust consent decree process is a creature of statute, Antitrust Procedures and Penalties Act, 15 U.S.C. § 16(b)-(h) (Supp. V. 1987) (also known as the Tunney Act), and there is little doubt Congress has the power to intervene. *See* United States v. AT&T, 552 F. Supp. 131, 149 n.76 (D.D.C. 1982), *aff'd sub nom.* Maryland v. United States, 460 U.S. 1001 (1983). Indeed, Congress might even remove continued supervision of the BOCs from the district court and place it where many believe it belongs, namely, with the FCC, the agency that presumably has the expertise and resources to manage the telephone industry. *See, e.g.*, H.R. 2140, 101st Cong., 1st Sess. (1989) ("Consumer Telecommunications Services Act of 1989"). Judge Greene, however, has some doubts about the Commission's commitment and ability here. *See infra* notes 228-29 and accompanying text. *Cf.* Maryland v. United States, 460 U.S. 1001, 1005 (1983) (Rehnquist, J., Burger, C.J., and White, J., dissenting) (question of whether an antitrust consent decree is in the public interest, assigned to district courts by statute, "is a classic example of a question committed to the Executive"). This broader controversy, however, is beyond the scope of this Article.

64 United States v. AT&T, 552 F. Supp. 131 (D.D.C. 1982), *aff'd sub nom.* Maryland v. United States, 460 U.S. 1001 (1983).

65 The MFJ defines "electronic publishing" as the "provision of any information which AT&T or its affiliates has, or has caused to be, originated, authored, compiled, collected, or edited, or in which it has a direct or indirect financial or proprietary interest, and which is disseminated to an unaffiliated person through some electronic means." *AT&T*, 552 F. Supp. at 231. *See id.* at 180-85; United States v. Western Elec. Co., 714 F. Supp. 1, 12 n.39, *amendment and clarification denied*, 1988-1 Trade Cas. (CCH) ¶ 68,094 (D.D.C. 1988).

The MFJ defines "information" as "knowledge or intelligence represented by any

out the country from providing "information services."[66] This was based on fear that the BOCs, through their continued control over the local network, could discriminate against competitors by providing their own services more favorable access to the network. Also, they might shift costs and use revenues from their local exchange monopoly to cross-subsidize their other services at anti-competitive prices.[67] There has been no specific judicial or regulatory ruling whether these decree prohibitions include cable television.[68] The language of Judge Greene's opinion, however, strongly suggests that cable is included.[69]

---

form of writing, signs, signals, pictures, sounds, or other symbols." *AT&T*, 552 F. Supp. at 229. This prohibition now has been lifted. United States v. Western Elec., 1989-2 Trade Cas. (CCH) ¶ 68,673 (D.D.C. 1989).

66 The MFJ defines "information service" as the

> offering of a capability for generating, acquiring, storing, transforming, processing, retrieving, utilizing, or making available information which may be conveyed via telecommunications, except that such service does not include any use of any such capability for the management, control, or operation of a telecommunications system or the management of a telecommunications service.

AT&T, 552 F. Supp. at 229. These sometimes are referred to as "enhanced services." *Id.* at 178 n. 198. *See id.* at 189-90.

The MFJ defines "telecommunications" as

> the transmission, between or among points specified by the user, of information of the user's choosing, without change in the form or content of the information as sent and received, by means of electromagnetic transmission medium, including all instrumentalities, facilities, apparatus, and services (including the collection, storage, forwarding, switching and delivery of such information) essential to such transmission.

Id. at 229.

67 *AT&T*, 552 F. Supp. at 189. *See* United States v. Western Elec. Co., 673 F. Supp. 525, 563-67 (D.D.C. 1987). In subsequently denying requests for waivers from the restrictions, the court described several forms of harmful cross-subsidization. United States v. Western Elec., 1989-1 Trade Cas. (CCH) ¶ 68,619, at 61,269 (D.D.C. 1989).

68 NTIA Report, *supra* note 7, at 49; Telephone Company — Cable Television Cross-Ownership Rules, Further Notice of Inquiry and Notice of Proposed Rulemaking, 3 F.C.C. Rcd. 5849, 5873 n.51. One BOC, Pacific Telesis, however, has requested waivers of the MFJ restrictions to enable it to buy controlling interests in Chicago cable systems. Request of Pacific Telesis Group, United States v. Western Elec. Co., Civ. No. 82-1092 (HHG) (D.D.C. Dec. 19, 1989). *See Pac Tel Asks Waivers To Buy Chicago Cable Systems*, 7 CABLE T.V. & NEW MEDIA 3 (Jan. 1990).

69 Judge Greene referred to "information services" as an "umbrella description of a variety of services including electronic publishing and other enhanced uses of telecommunications." *AT&T*, 552 F. Supp. at 189. He expressly incorporated his earlier discussion of "electronic publishing," *id.* at 189 n.237, which rather clearly includes cable. *Id.* at 180-81.

On the other hand, AT&T disavowed any intention of competing with newspapers, broadcasting, or traditional cable television. *Id.* at 185 n.221. Instead, AT&T agreed to the future restrictions on the BOCs as part of the overall settlement. *Id.* at 186 nn.227, 220-22. Moreover, Judge Greene's rationale for prohibiting the BOCs from providing information services is based on their control over the local telephone networks. *Id.* at 189-90. It may be possible to argue, therefore, that the unqualified language of the decree prohibition was not meant to constrain BOC activity outside their local service areas. *But see* United States v. Western Elec. Co., 1989-1 Trade Cas. (CCH) ¶ 68,619 at 61,266, 61,270-72 (waivers of line of business restrictions denied because BOC bottleneck monopolies and their ability to cross-subsidize would permit them to engage in

Upon the first triennial review of the MFJ,[70] the court found the information services restrictions more problematic.[71] Judge Greene struck a distinction between control over the content of information and the means for its transmission. Again, this was based on the perceived temptation for a company that both generates and transmits information, especially time-sensitive material, to discriminate against competitors that rely on it for the transmission function.[72] As generation or control of information involves the exercise of editorial discretion, however, such activity is at the core of first amendment freedoms. Nonetheless, the court maintained the information services prohibition as far as the generation or manipulation of information content is concerned, while allowing the BOCs to construct and operate a sophisticated network infrastructure for the transmission of information services where others generate and control the content.[73] Operating a cable system in the usual sense of programming channels still seems forbidden.[74]

Thus, Judge Greene's continued supervision of the BOCs under the MFJ will keep the largest and quite likely the most important, effective and innovative potential competitors out of the cable industry.[75] The telcos probably are best situated to play the leading role in development of a fiber-optic, integrated broadband communications network and the new technologies and services associated with it.[76] They also have the capital and

---

anticompetitive activities even with respect to out-of-region information services activities); United States v. Western Elec., 627 F. Supp. 1090, 1110 (D.D.C. 1986) (rejecting argument that BOCs are free to provide voice storage and retrieval services outside their own regions).

70 *See AT&T*, 552 F. Supp. at 195 (Department of Justice will report to court every three years on the continued need for the decree's restrictions).

71 United States v. Western Elec. Co., 673 F. Supp. 525, 563 (D.D.C. 1987).

72 *Id.* at 595, 603.

73 *Id.* at 603. The court cited videotex (interactive data services), such as provided on the French Teletel system, as a model for the sort of transmission services it had in mind. *See* United States v. Western Elec. Co., 714 F. Supp. 1 (D.D.C.), *amendment and clarification denied*, 1988-1 Trade Cas. (CCH) ¶ 68,094 (D.D.C. 1988).

74 *See Western Elec.*, 714 F. Supp. at 11-22 (Judge Greene's description of what BOCs may do by way of information "gateway" services under his more liberal approach).

75 The BOCs comprise about two-thirds of the domestic telecommunications industry and serve approximately 77% of United States local exchange customers. P. HUBER, THE GEODESIC NETWORK: 1987 REPORT ON COMPETITION IN THE TELEPHONE INDUSTRY 1.34 (Report prepared for first triennial review of the MFJ) [hereinafter HUBER]. *See Western Elec.*, 673 F. Supp. at 528 n.1, 537 n.44). *See also* Pepper, *Through the Looking Glass: Integrated Broadband Networks, Regulatory Policies, and Institutional Change, Office of Plans and Policies*, FCC, Nov. 1988, at 26-27 [hereinafter Pepper]. The preclusive effect of the MFJ, coupled with the FCC rules and the Cable Act provision, therefore amounts to virtually a total ban on telephone companies providing cable service domestically.

76 Even Judge Greene recognizes the importance of BOCs' participation, at least on the transmission side, for the development of a vigorous, nationwide market in informa-

technical experience and expertise to compete competently with powerful, entrenched cable systems.[77] As with continued enforcement of the FCC rules and the statutory prohibition, the main basis for this Draconian exclusionary approach is the speculative fear of anticompetitive activities in that industry[78] and the concern for diversity in the media marketplace discussed below. While there are a number of issues peculiar to continuing judicial review of the MFJ,[79] the constitutional issues which Part III addresses are common to all three sources of restrictions and compel rectifying congressional action.

III. Constitutional Issues

The most disappointing aspect of the debate over telco entry into cable is the paucity of weight given to first amendment principles and analysis. If any other non-media entity wished to enter the field and thereby serve its own interests as well as those of potential subscribers, an overwhelming first amendment presumption would support its right to do so. With the telephone companies, however, constitutional principles are relegated to a subsidiary role. Why should this be so? As this Section shows, nothing in the corporate nature of the telcos, nor their general status as common carriers, nor other existing media cross-owner-

---

tion services. *Western Elec. Co.*, 714 F. Supp. at 6. But he claims they are "not needed" on the information side. *Id.* at 3 n.4. *See infra* notes 243-59 and accompanying text (discussing the technology and services).

77 The BOCs each rank in the top 20 American corporations in terms of assets and in the Fortune 50 in terms of sales. *Western Elec. Co.*, 714 F. Supp. at 4 n.9. *See* United States v. AT&T, 552 F. Supp. 131, 187 n.230 (D.D.C. 1982) *aff'd sub. nom.* Maryland v. United States, 460 U.S. 1001 (1983); *infra* note 265 (referencing BOCs' foreign cable experience).

78 Because the mere possession of monopoly power in one market is not a sufficient antitrust justification to restrict competition generally, Judge Greene explicitly based his restrictions upon "the *assumption* that the Operating Companies, were they allowed to enter the forbidden markets, would use their monopoly power in an anticompetitive manner." *AT&T*, 552 F. Supp. at 187 (emphasis added).

79 One key issue is the appropriate standard for lifting the restrictions, whether it is to be a liberal public interest test for modifying an antitrust consent decree or the specific, stricter language of Section VIII(C) of the MFJ. Section VIII(C) requires a petitioning BOC to make a showing that "there is no substantial possibility that it could use its monopoly power to impede competition in the market it seeks to enter." *Western Elec. Co.*, 673 F. Supp. at 532. A related issue is the extent to which the BOCs, or more accurately AT&T on behalf of the BOCs, waived their first amendment or other rights.

The Court of Appeals now has ruled that the public interest standard should be applied to the BOCs unopposed motion to lift entirely the information services restriction and therefore remanded this matter to Judge Greene without addressing any first amendment issues. United States v. Western Elec. Co., 900 F.2d 283 (D.C. Cir. Apr. 3, 1990). The "public interest" standard, however, at least under the Communications Act, "necessarily invites reference to First Amendment principles." FCC v. National Citizens Committee for Broadcasting, 436 U.S. 775, 795 (1978), *quoting* Columbia Broadcasting System, Inc. v. Democratic National Committee, 412 U.S. 94, 122 (1973).

ship restrictions qualifies their first amendment rights. Moreover, the following Section establishes that the same is true of applicable antitrust principles. Thus, rather than viewed as a mere incidental restriction on speech, as the FCC maintains, the ban on telco entry should be recognized for what it clearly is — a prior restraint, the most onerous and least supportable abridgment of first amendment freedoms. Particularly in light of the substantial benefits telco entry into cable promises,[80] the heavy burden of justifying continuation of the ban cannot be met. Congress therefore should act to remove the exclusionary provisions.

A. *Corporate Speech*

At least since *First National Bank of Boston v. Bellotti*,[81] the Supreme Court's leading case on the free speech rights of corporations, it is difficult to claim that the mere corporate status of a willing speaker denies it the protection of the first amendment. In *Bellotti*, the Massachusetts legislature wished to enact a graduated individual income tax, but was stymied in several electoral attempts to approve the necessary constitutional amendment. To stifle opposition, the legislature passed a criminal statute prohibiting any contributions or expenditures by banks and business corporations to influence the vote on referendum issues, other than one "materially affecting" the corporation. The legislature tied the knot by simultaneously decreeing that no individual income tax issue materially affects corporations.[82]

Upon a constitutional challenge, the Supreme Court re-

---

80 *See infra* notes 243-59 and accompanying text.

81 435 U.S. 765, *reh'g denied*, 438 U.S. 907 (1978).

82 Even in dissenting, Justice Rehnquist acknowledged that the Massachusetts legislature blatantly tried to "muzzle" corporate speech on core political issues to achieve its tax objective. *Id.* at 826 n.6 (Rehnquist, J., dissenting). The Massachusetts statute provided in relevant part:

> No corporation carrying on the business of a bank, trust, surety, indemnity, safe deposit, insurance, railroad, street railway, telegraph, telephone, gas, electric light, heat, power, canal, aqueduct, or water company . . . shall directly or indirectly give, pay, expend or contribute, or promise to give, pay, expend or contribute any money or other valuable thing for the purpose of aiding, promoting or preventing the nomination or election of any person to public office, or aiding, promoting or antagonizing the interests of any political party, or influencing or affecting the vote on any question submitted to the voters other than one materially affecting any of the property, business or assets of the corporation. . . .

MASS. GEN. LAWS ANN. ch. 55, st. 8 (West Supp. 1977).

The Massachusetts statute further provided:

> No question submitted to the voters solely concerning the taxation of the income, property or transactions of individuals shall be deemed materially to affect the property, business or assets of the corporation.

MASS. GEN. LAWS ANN. ch. 55, st. 8 (West Supp. 1977).

jected the Massachusetts Supreme Court's approach of asking generally whether and to what extent corporations enjoy first amendment rights. Rather, the Supreme Court found the speech in question clearly entitled to protection and asked whether the corporate identity of the speaker somehow deprived it of that protection. The Court could find no basis for such a denigration of the liberty interest in free speech protected, for both media and non-media entities,[83] against state abridgment by the due process clause.[84] The Court therefore applied the "exacting scrutiny" demanded by the first amendment to see if Massachusetts could demonstrate the sort of compelling interest, achieved only by narrowly drawn means, necessary to justify its legislation.[85] Most pertinent for present purposes, the Court rejected the asserted justification that, absent the legislation, corporate participation would exert an undue influence on the outcome of referenda, thereby diminishing the active role of the individual citizen in the electoral process and destroying confidence in the democratic process and the integrity of government.[86]

The Court has reinforced its support for corporate free speech, even for privately owned but government regulated monopolies. It would not allow, for example, the Public Service Commission of New York to prohibit Consolidated Edison Company from including inserts in its monthly electric bills discussing

---

83 The Court declined to distinguish media and non-media corporate entities for purposes of its decision. "[T]he press does not have a monopoly on either the First Amendment or the ability to enlighten." *Bellotti*, 435 U.S. at 782. Chief Justice Burger wrote separately to emphasize the difficulty of such a distinction. *Id.* at 795. This separate opinion was likely in reaction to a well-known speech by Justice Stewart, who developed the thesis that the press clause gives special status and privileges to the institutional press. Stewart, *Or of the Press*, 26 HASTINGS L.J. 631 (1975).

A majority of the Court continues to reject any such distinction. *See* Dunn & Bradstreet, Inc. v. Greenmoss Builders, Inc., 472 U.S. 749, 759 (1985); *id.* at 765 (White, J., concurring in judgment); *id.* at 774-96 (Brennan, Marshall, Blackmun, Stevens, JJ., dissenting). *But see* infra note 97.

84 The inherent worth of the speech in terms of its capacity for informing the public does not depend upon the identity of its source. . . . In the realm of protected speech, the legislature is constitutionally disqualified from dictating the subjects about which persons may speak and the speakers who may address a public issue.

Bellotti, 435 U.S. at 777, 784-85.

85 *Id.* at 786.

86 *Id.* at 789-92. *See infra* notes 232-41 and accompanying text (further discussing the diversity issue). The Court also rejected the argument that the legislation was needed to protect corporate shareholders' interests. *Bellotti*, 435 U.S. at 792-95. *But see infra* note 101.

For a criticism of *Bellotti's* alleged abstract and formalistic approach to corporate free speech, see Schneider, *Free Speech and Corporate Freedom: A Comment on First National Bank of Boston v. Bellotti*, 59 S. CAL. L. REV. 1227 (1986) [hereinafter Schneider].

controversial issues of public importance.[87] Indeed, the Court has found that first amendment protection for such entities extends even to their purely commercial speech in the form of promotional advertising.[88]

First amendment protection must extend, therefore, to telephone companies as cable system operators. As with broadcasting, cable activities "plainly implicate First Amendment interests" through original programming and the exercise of editorial discretion.[89] In fact, much of what cable operators presently do fits the Court's previous definition of core editorial activity, namely "selection and choice of material."[90]

As cablecasters, telcos should be entitled to such constitutional protection not only because they would be affording the public "access to discussion, debate, and the dissemination of information and ideas,"[91] but also because of the telcos' own interests in self-expression.[92] The Court has recognized that *both*

---

87 Consolidated Edison Co. of New York, Inc. v. Public Serv. Comm'n of New York, 447 U.S. 530, 534 n.1 (1980) ("Nor does Consolidated Edison's status as a privately owned but government regulated monopoly preclude its assertion of First Amendment rights.").

88 Central Hudson Gas & Elec. Corp. v. Public Serv. Comm'n of New York, 447 U.S. 557 (1980).

89 Los Angeles v. Preferred Communications, Inc., 476 U.S. 488, 495 (1986). Since it was reviewing the dismissal of a complaint, the Court appropriately refrained from a detailed analysis of the precise first amendment standard to apply to cable. In ruling on motions for summary judgment the district court subsequently found that "[t]he programming of a cable television network, like the publishing of a newspaper, involves editorial discretion." Preferred Communications, Inc. v. Los Angeles, No. CV 83-5846 (CBM), slip op. at 18 (C.D. Cal. Jan 5. 1990) *See* FCC v. Midwest Video Corp., 440 U.S. 689, 707 (1979) ("Cable operators now share with broadcasters a significant amount of editorial discretion."); Quincy Cable TV, Inc. v. FCC, 768 F.2d 1434, 1452 (D.C. Cir. 1985) (describing cable operators' dramatically expanded editorial role), *cert. denied*, 476 U.S. 1169 (1986); Tele-Communications of Key West Inc. v. United States, 757 F.2d 1330, 1336-37 (D.C. Cir. 1985) ("Whether or not [cable] produces any original programming of its own, its activities of transmitting and packaging programming mandate that it receive First Amendment protection.").

90 "For better or worse, editing is what editors are for; and editing is selection and choice of material." CBS, Inc. v. Democratic Nat'l Comm., 412 U.S. 94, 124 (1973). Requirements that cable operators produce local origination programming further emphasize their editorial function. *See* Chicago Cable Communications v. Chicago Cable Comm'n, 879 F.2d 1540 (7th Cir. 1989) (such requirements do not violate the first amendment), *cert. denied*, 110 S. Ct. 839 (1990). Moreover, cable operators' vertical integration into programming has expanded programming availability for the viewing public and is yet another aspect of their first amendment activity. *See* Klein, *The Competitive Consequences of Vertical Integration in the Cable Industry*, at 4 (June 1989) (unpublished manuscript).

91 First Nat'l Bank of Boston v. Bellotti, 435 U.S. 765, 783, *reh'g denied*, 438 U.S. 907 (1978).

92 *See id.* at 777 n.12 ("The individual's interest in self-expression is a concern of the First Amendment separate from the concern for open and informed discussion, although the two often converge."). *See also* Consolidated Edison Co. of New York, Inc. v. Public Serv. Comm'n of New York, 447 U.S. 530, 534 n.2 ("Freedom of speech also protects the individual's interest in self-expression.").

considerations apply to the first amendment rights of corporations and that by protecting corporate self-expression — specifically, the "wish to enter the marketplace of ideas" — the public's interest in receiving information is also protected.[93]

For at least a plurality of the Court, a corporation has autonomy interests analogous to those of natural persons, which are an important part of the rationale for first amendment freedoms. This was a major reason why, in *Pacific Gas & Electric Co. v. Public Utilities Commission of California*,[94] the Court held that a privately owned, regulated utility could not be forced to include in its billing envelopes speech of a third party with which it disagreed. At least for the plurality such forced association with objectionable ideas violates the first amendment because it offends the underlying autonomy interest — the interest in affirmative self-expression and the "concomitant freedom *not* to speak publicly, one which serves the same ultimate end as freedom of speech in its affirmative aspect."[95] Thus, "[f]or corporations as for individuals, the choice to speak includes within it the choice of what not to say."[96]

Recognition of this full scope of first amendment interests of corporations is only natural. Otherwise how could we distinguish, as we surely would want, the expansive first amendment freedoms of media entities, most of which operate in the corpo-

---

93 Pacific Gas & Elec. Co. v. Public Utils. Comm'n of California, 475 U.S. 1, 8 (1986). *See* Virginia State Bd. of Pharmacy v. Virginia Citizens Consumer Council, Inc., 425 U.S. 748 (1976). In holding that corporate commercial speech is entitled to first amendment protection, the Court stated, "[W]here a speaker exists, . . . the protection afforded is to the communication, to its source and to its recipients both. This is clear from the decided cases." *Id.* at 756.

94 475 U.S. 1, *reh'g denied*, 475 U.S. 1133 (1986).

95 *Pacific Gas*, 475 U.S. at 11 (quoting Harper & Row Publishers, Inc. v. Nation Enter., 471 U.S. 524, 559 (1985)) (emphasis in original). Telephone companies in particular have been exercising just this sort of discretion in terminating certain "dial-a-porn" services with which they do not wish to be associated. Their autonomy interests in doing so, even with respect to telephone service, have been upheld so long as their action is not coerced or significantly encouraged by the state. Carlin Communications, Inc. v. Mountain States Tel. & Tel. Co., 827 F.2d 1291 (9th Cir. 1987) *cert. denied*, 485 U.S. 1029 (1988); Carlin Communication, Inc. v. Southern Bell Tel. & Tel. Co., 802 F.2d 1352 (11th Cir. 1986); United States v. Western Elec. Co., 1989-2 Trade Cas. (CCH) ¶ 68,710 (D.D.C. 1989) (court approved restrictions on billing and collection services). But state action here restricting access to non-obscene material might be unconstitutional censorship. Sable Comm'n of California, Inc. v. FCC, 109 S. Ct. 2829 (1989).

96 *Pacific Gas*, 475 U.S. at 16. *See* Miami Herald Publishing Co. v. Tornillo, 418 U.S. 241 (1974) (right of reply statute applied to a newspaper violates the first amendment). Dissenting in *Pacific Gas*, Justice Rehnquist described the plurality's "fundamental flaw" as extending to business corporations "negative" free speech rights which in his view depend on individual freedom of conscience. *Pacific Gas*, 475 U.S. at 32-33 (Rehnquist, J., dissenting). *See also* PruneYard Shopping Center v. Robins, 447 U.S. 74 (1980). The *PruneYard* case was distinguished in *Pacific Gas*, 475 U.S. at 12.

rate form.[97] Moreover, if membership corporations such as the ACLU or the NAACP actively enjoy such rights, either collectively or as representatives of their members,[98] why should the standard corporate form make any difference?[99] A corporation, after all, is constituted by a group of individuals with presumably some common interests and purposes. Today many expect corporations to reflect and support shareholders' views on a broad range of social, political, environmental and economic interests, which often are quite removed from the narrower business purposes of the firm.[100] The corporate structure should not defeat a first amendment autonomy interest collectively exercised by the corporation, particularly given free shareholder entry into and exit from the organization.[101]

This is not to say that corporations necessarily enjoy all constitutional rights coextensively with natural persons. As the *Bellotti* Court explains, certain "purely personal" guarantees, such as the fifth amendment privilege against compulsory self-incrimination, may be unavailable to corporations for reasons relevant to the particular constitutional provision.[102] But both the autonomy interest in self expression and the social utility of broad

97 The potential difficulty is well illustrated by the fact that in *Pacific Gas* the utility distributed its own newsletter in its billing envelopes, which occasioned the third party request for access to the envelopes. The plurality found this newsletter "[i]n appearance no different from a small newspaper," and therefore invoked *Miami Herald*, 418 U.S. at 241, as controlling precedent. *Pacific Gas*, 475 U.S. at 8-18. *See supra* note 83 and accompanying text. *But see* Austin v. Michigan Chamber of Commerce, 110 S. Ct. 1391, 1401-02 (1990) (under equal protection analysis, Court sanctions an exemption for media corporations in a state act limiting some corporate political expenditures); *Cf. id.* at 1414-15 (Scalia, J., dissenting).

98 *See, e.g.*, NAACP v. Button, 371 U.S. 415, 428 (1963) (NAACP can assert first amendment rights on its own behalf as well as for its members); ACLU v. FCC, 823 F.2d 1554 (D.C. Cir. 1987), *cert. denied*, 485 U.S. 959 (1988) (ACLU as lead petitioner for review of FCC's original orders implementing the Cable Act).

99 *But see Austin*, 110 S. Ct. at 1398-1400, in which the Court attempts to distinguish, at least in the context of corporate political expenditures, *some* nonprofit ideological corporations from ordinary business corporations. *Cf. id.* at 1419 (Kennedy, J., dissenting).

100 *Compare* C. STONE, WHERE THE LAW ENDS (1975) *with* Engel, *An Approach to Corporate Social Responsibility*, 32 STAN. L. REV. 1 (1979).

101 *But see Austin*, 110 S. Ct. at 1399 (discussing the economic disincentive in disassociating with a corporation). *Cf. id.* at 1411-12 (Scalia, J., dissenting). For a contrary argument in favor of substantially lessened free speech rights for traditional corporations, see Schneider, *supra* note 86, at 1252-61. *See* First Nat'l Bank of Boston v. Bellotti, 435 U.S. 765, 804-05 (1978) (White, Brennan, Marshall, JJ., dissenting).

102 *Belloti*, 435 U.S. at 778 n.14. There may also be some circumstances that justify different application of the first amendment to individuals and corporations. *Id.* at 777-78 n.13. For example, although reaffirming *Bellotti's* corporate free speech principle, the Court recently upheld a state campaign finance statute that prohibits corporations from using their general treasury funds, as opposed to special segregated funds, for independent expenditures supporting or opposing candidates in elections for state office. *Austin*, 110 S. Ct. at 1396. Corporate participation in partisan candidate elections is an area that the *Bellotti* opinion itself distinguished. *Bellotti*, 435 U.S. at 788 n.26.

communication and dissemination of information and ideas underlying the first amendment support constitutional protection for the telephone companies' desire to enter the cable industry. As Chief Justice Burger stated, "the First Amendment does not 'belong' to any definable category of persons or entities: It belongs to all who exercise its freedoms."[103]

B. *Common Carrier Status*

Telephone companies are not only regulated utilities, often with a monopoly position, but common carriers subject to extensive regulation under Title II of the Communications Act.[104] This, however, should not affect their ability to enter the cable industry, their status as cable operators, or their first amendment rights as such.

Cable television systems are not common carriers. Prior to the 1984 Cable Act the Supreme Court ruled that the FCC could not regulate cable systems as common carriers.[105] Congress reinforced this position in the Cable Act which unambiguously states that cable systems are not subject to common carrier or utility regulation by virtue of providing cable service.[106] Removal of the ban on telcos as cable operators, therefore, would allow such an entity to be a common carrier with respect to other telecommunications services it provides, while also providing cable service as to which it would not be treated as a common carrier.

Such a dual function is just what the legislative history of the Cable Act contemplates. Congress intended the Act's definition of "cable services"[107] to delineate between those services provided by a cable system that are exempt from common carrier regulation and all other communications services that could be provided by that system, with the inference that the latter might

---

103 *Belloti*, 435 U.S. at 802 (Burger, C.J., concurring).

104 47 U.S.C. §§ 151-609 (1982 & Supp. V 1987). The Communications Act's circular definition of a "common carrier," 47 U.S.C. § 153(h), has been given meaning by courts and the FCC. *See* FCC v. Midwest Video Corp., 440 U.S. 689, 701 (1979) (discussing the meaning of common carrier service in the communications context). *See generally* CABLE TELEVISION LAW, *supra* note 7, at ¶ 6.03.

105 *Midwest Video*, 440 U.S. 689, 708-09 (1979); United States v. Southwestern Cable, 392 U.S. 157, 169 n.29 (1968).

106 Cable Act § 621(c), 47 U.S.C. § 541(c) (Supp. V 1987). There is some confusion, however, as to the circumstances in which the Cable Act's definition of a cable system includes the facilities of a common carrier. *Id.* at § 602(6), 47 U.S.C. § 522(6). *See* BRENNER, PRICE & MEYERSON, *supra* note 14, at ¶ 11.03[3].

107 Cable Act § 602(5), 47 U.S.C. § 522(5). The term includes both "video programming," *id.* at § 602(16), 47 U.S.C. § 522(16), and "other programming service," *id.* at § 602(11), 47 U.S.C. § 522(11).

be subject to common carrier regulation.[108] Indeed, the legislative committee described some of these "other" communications services that might "compete with services provided by telephone companies."[109] Since such services can be provided by a cable system, but are not considered "cable services," the Act does not affect existing regulatory authority over them.[110] Thus it is clear that, under the Cable Act, cable operators can "provide any mixture of cable and non-cable service they chose [sic]."[111]

This is quite consistent with earlier understandings. The Supreme Court, for example, in its pre-Act ruling that the FCC cannot impose common carrier regulation on a cable system, noted that such a system can operate as a common carrier with respect only to another portion of its service.[112] Other courts have made a similar observation about telephone companies.[113] The term "common carrier," therefore, is better used to describe an activity as to which a particular entity is a common carrier rather than to describe the entity itself.[114]

In their capacity as cable operators, telephone companies should be entitled to the same first amendment rights as any other cablecasters. Nothing in their additional status as common carriers, with respect to other services and activities, detracts from such entitlement.[115] The Supreme Court has implicitly acknowledged this in its recent "dial-a-porn" decision.[116]

In operating a "976" or "Scoopline" dial-a-message network, a telephone company leases such a line to a business subscriber which then offers to the public, for a specified price per

---

108 H.R. Rep. No. 934, *supra* note 12, at 4678.

109 *Id.* at 4678-81. One example is voice communication between subscribers. A cable service, by contrast, must make its information available to all subscribers generally and may not include subscriber-specific information. *Id.*

110 *Id.* at 4678. In its Computer II Inquiry, the FCC decided not to impose Title II common carrier regulation on certain enhanced services, combining data processing and communications services, although it retained ancillary jurisdiction over them. Second Computer Inquiry, 77 F.C.C.2d 384, *reconsid.*, 84 F.C.C.2d 50 (1980), *further reconsid.*, 88 F.C.C.2d 512 (1981), *aff'd sub nom.* Computer and Communications Indus. Ass'n v. FCC, 693 F.2d 198 (D.C. Cir. 1982), *cert. denied*, 461 U.S. 938 (1983).

111 H.R. Rep. No. 934, *supra* note 12, at 4681. "The term 'cable system' is not limited to a facility that provides only cable service which includes video programming. Quite the contrary, many cable systems provide a wide variety of cable services and other communications services as well." *Id.*

112 FCC v. Midwest Video Corp., 440 U.S. 689, 701 n.9 (1979).

113 Carlin Communications, Inc. v. Mountain States Tel. & Tel. Co., 827 F.2d 1291, 1293 n.2 (9th Cir. 1987), *cert. denied*, 485 U.S. 1029 (1988).

114 *Computer and Communications Indus.*, 693 F.2d at 209 n.59.

115 *Cf.* United States v. Western Elec. Co, 673 F. Supp. 525, 586 n.273 (D.D.C. 1987) (treating the BOCs as common carriers with respect to information services and therefore "differently for First Amendment purposes than traditional news media"), *remanded*, 900 F.2d 283 (D.C. Cir. 1990).

116 Sable Communications of California v. FCC, 109 S. Ct. 2829 (1989).

call, various kinds of information services such as sports updates, weather reports or, more controversially, sexually explicit "adult" messages known as "dial-a-porn." In simultaneously connecting thousands of paying callers to a single recorded message, this service resembles cablecasting.[117] Whatever notion Congress might have had that a telephone company's common carrier status would allow greater regulation of this service was dashed by the Court's unanimous opinion that legislation banning indecent interstate commercial telephone messages violates the first amendment.[118]

Thus cable operators, including telephone companies, may act as hybrids with different regulatory schemes applicable to different activities.[119] As such, difficult first amendment issues will arise. Among the more significant of these is the question of access to the system.[120] It is probably a mistake to try and resolve these first amendment issues prior to substantial telephone entry. Such entry may affect, for example, the need for mandatory access as well as the capacity for and feasibility of providing it.[121] So, while telco entry may aid the resolution of some difficult issues, the constitutional considerations should not depend on the identity or other similar status of the operators.

---

[117] *See Carlin*, 827 F.2d at 1294. The court loosely spoke of broadcasting without considering the closer analogy to a subscriber cable system. *Cf. Sable*, 109 S. Ct. at 2837.

[118] *Sable*, 109 S. Ct. at 2837. A majority, however, upheld the prohibition of obscene telephone messages.

[119] *See* Brenner, *Cable Television and the Freedom of Expression*, DUKE L.J. 329, 331 (1988) ("The key to cable's first amendment regime lies in distinguishing, as reasonably as possible, among the expressive and nonexpressive activities of operators.").

[120] Section 531 of the Cable Act allows franchisors to require that cable operators make available channels for public, educational, or governmental use ("PEG" channels). Cable Act § 611, 47 U.S.C. § 531 (Supp. V 1987). Section 532 requires a cable operator to designate specified channel capacity for leased commercial use. *Id.* at § 612, 47 U.S.C. § 532. Both of these prohibit an operator's editorial control over the access channels.

The constitutionality of these provisions remains an open question. In holding that FCC cable access rules imposed prior to the Cable Act exceeded the Commission's statutory authority, the Supreme Court noted that the rules "significantly compromise" cable operators' editorial discretion and raise first amendment problems that are "not frivolous." FCC v. Midwest Video Corp., 440 U.S. 689, 707 n.17, 709 n.19 (1979). While the Eighth Circuit had held the rules unconstitutional, Midwest Video Corp. v. FCC, 571 F.2d 1025 (8th Cir. 1978), the Supreme Court suggested "less intrusive" access provisions might survive. *Midwest Video*, 440 U.S. at 705 n.14. *See* Century Fed., Inc. v. Palo Alto, 710 F. Supp. 1552, 1554-55 (N.D. Cal. 1987), *appeal dismissed*, 484 U.S. 1053 (1988) (mandatory access channels provision unconstitutional). *Accord* Group W Cable, Inc. v. Santa Cruz, 669 F. Supp. 954, 968-69 (N.D. Cal. 1987); Preferred Communications v. City of Los Angeles, CV 83-5846 (CBM) (C.D. Cal. Jan. 5, 1990). *Contra* Erie Telecommunications, Inc. v. Erie, 659 F. Supp. 580, 598-601 (W.D. Pa. 1987), *aff'd on other grounds*, 853 F.2d 1084 (3d Cir. 1988).

[121] *See infra* notes 243-59 and accompanying text (describing possible new technologies).

C. *Other Media Cross-Ownership Provisions*

There are numerous FCC "structural" rules that limit or preclude multiple or cross ownership interests among various mass media.[122] Many depend on the perceived scarcity of the broadcast spectrum, which is irrelevant to cable and telcos. This dependency, and dramatic changes in the video marketplace, also are rendering such rules increasingly outdated and suspect on constitutional and other grounds.[123] None is so drastic as to totally ban entry into a mass media market by a non-participant in any such market. These other structural rules, therefore, lend no support to a continued telco/cable cross-ownership ban.[124]

The idea of the FCC enforcing structural regulation of the media industry dates back at least to the chain broadcasting[125] regulations upheld in *National Broadcasting Co. v. United States*.[126] In substance, this was an antitrust case in which the Commission mandated certain business relationships between broadcast licensees and the networks to limit network dominance over the local affiliated stations. The narrow question presented by the case was simply whether specific statutory authority over chain broadcasting[127] encompassed the business regulations at issue. Writing for a bare majority of the Court, however, Justice Frankfurter laid the scarcity predicate for comprehensive broadcast regulation pursuant to the public interest. Moreover, in a single paragraph discussing the first amendment implications of such regulation, Justice Frankfurter inverted the proper relationship between Congressional power and the Constitution by suggesting that FCC action does not violate the first amendment if it is valid under the public interest standard of the Communications Act.[128]

This precedent[129] puts into perspective the other structural

---

122 For an extensive description of these rules, see generally Emrod, *supra* note 59, at 401-69.

123 *See id.*

124 *Cf.* United States v. American Tel. & Tel., 552 F. Supp. 131, 183-85 (D.D.C. 1982) (citing other cross-ownership provisions to support the public interest determination made).

125 "Chain broadcasting," the "simultaneous broadcasting of an identical program by two or more connected stations," 47 U.S.C. § 153(p) (1982), meant simply the network system of program distribution. *See* 47 C.F.R. § 73.658 (1989).

126 319 U.S. 190 (1943). *See* Winer, *The Signal Cable Sends*, *supra* note 56, at 220-27 (discussing NBC v. United States, 319 U.S. 190 (1943)).

127 47 U.S.C. § 303(i) (1982).

128 *NBC*, 319 U.S. at 227. One noted commentator responded, "The passage catches a great judge at an unimpressive moment." Kalven, *Broadcasting, Public Policy and the First Amendment*, 10 J. L. & ECON. 15, 43 (1967).

129 In United States v. Storer Broadcasting, 351 U.S. 192 (1956), the Court further

regulations most pertinent to a consideration of the telco/cable ban, namely the broadcast/cable and the newspaper/broadcast cross-ownership restrictions. As to the former, beginning in 1970 the FCC prohibited common ownership or control between a cable system and a local broadcast television station where their service areas sufficiently overlap.[130] At the same time the FCC prohibited the national broadcast networks from an ownership interest in any cable system, wherever located.[131] These regulations were in furtherance of the "Commission's policy favoring diversity of control over local mass communications media."[132] More recently, the Commission has described the goals on which it based its rules as "increasing competition in the economic and ideological marketplaces."[133]

The owner of a television station challenged the rules in *Marsh Media, Ltd. v. FCC*.[134] The court first determined that these rules, like those on newspaper/broadcasting cross-ownership, are an exercise of the Commission's authority over broadcast licensees.[135] It then ruled that Marsh Media's first amendment challenge was foreclosed by the Supreme Court's decision in *FCC v. National Citizens Committee for Broadcasting*[136] upholding the newspaper/broadcasting rules.

The Commission, however, is reviewing its position. The 1988 NTIA Report notes dramatic changes in today's video marketplace, such as a "clear trend towards greater competition in the local [video] distribution market"[137] and the emergence of

---

supported the Commission's ability to issue business regulations (multiple ownership rules) dealing with "concentration of control."

130 Second Report and Order in Docket No. 18397, 23 F.C.C.2d 816 (1970), *reconsid. denied in part*, 39 F.C.C.2d 377 (1973). This was codified in the Cable Act, at section 613(a), 47 U.S.C. § 533(a) (Supp. V 1987), which also gives the FCC the authority to make other cable ownership rules governing persons who own or control other co-located media of mass communications. *Id.* at § 613(c), 47 U.S.C. § 533(c). A number of broadcast entities now own cable systems outside their service systems. *See* NTIA Report, *supra* note 7, at 61.

131 *Second Report and Order*, 23 F.C.C.2d at 819. The FCC later made minor modifications as to a divestiture requirement. Second Report and Order in Docket No. 20423, 55 F.C.C.2d 540 (1975), *reconsid. denied*, 58 F.C.C.2d 596 (1976). The current version of the rules is at 47 C.F.R. § 76.501 (1989). The Cable Act did not codify the network provision. For an example of a waiver of the network rule based on changes in the cable industry, see In re CBS, Inc., 87 F.C.C.2d 587 (1981). The next year CBS sold its cable interests.

132 *Second Report and Order*, 23 F.C.C.2d at 820.

133 Third Report and Order in Docket No. 20423 (Postponement of Divestiture Requirement), 56 Rad. Reg. (P&F) 2d 87 (1984).

134 798 F.2d 772, *reh'g en banc denied*, 802 F.2d 455 (5th Cir. 1986), *cert. denied*, 479 U.S. 1085 (1987).

135 *Marsh Media*, 798 F.2d at 775.

136 436 U.S. 775 (1978).

137 NTIA Report, *supra* note 7, at 69.

cable as an important source of programming.[138] Because of such developments, "the bases for the network/cable cross-ownership rules cannot withstand empirical or theoretical analyses."[139] The NTIA therefore recommended FCC repeal of this rule.[140] It also urged amendment of the Cable Act to allow permanent waivers for local broadcast stations to own co-located cable systems on a showing that there will be no lessening of economic competition and diversity in that market.[141] Based on this and previous studies, the FCC has issued a Further Notice of Proposed Rulemaking on repeal of the network rule.[142]

Since the court in *Marsh Media* simply deferred to the Supreme Court's constitutional opinion in *National Citizens*, the first amendment analysis in *National Citizens* is relevant to both media cross-ownership rules under discussion. The newspaper/broadcasting ban at issue in *National Citizens* prospectively prohibited co-located daily newspaper/broadcast combinations. Also, absent waiver, it required divestiture over five years of such combinations in "egregious cases . . . [of] effective monopoly in the marketplace of ideas as well as economically."[143] In addition to favoring economic competition, this policy was based on the diversity principle — that is, the perceived negative "impact on the dissemination of ideas in a democratic society . . . [from] a lack of diversity of viewpoints and programming" feared to result from a "combination of media holdings held by a single entity."[144]

---

138 *Id.* at 72.

139 *Id.*

140 In doing so, the NTIA noted that allowing telephone companies greater flexibility in providing transport facilities for video programming, which it also was recommending, further supported elimination of the rule. *Id.* at 73 n.247.

141 *Id.* at 74-76.

142 3 F.C.C. Rcd. 5283 (1988).

143 Second Report and Order in Docket No. 18110, 50 F.C.C.2d 1046, 1080-81, *modified*, 53 F.C.C.2d 589 (1975). The rule is currently codified at 47 C.F.R. § 73.3555(c) (1989).

144 *Second Report and Order*, 50 F.C.C.2d at 1059, 1074. *See* FCC v. National Citizens Comm. for Broadcasting, 436 U.S. 775, 780 (1978). The potential for government abuse of the diversity principle is well illustrated by the recent attack Senator Kennedy orchestrated against publisher Rupert Murdoch. In the early morning hours as Congress was about to adjourn, the Senator attached an unnoticed and undiscussed rider to a catchall appropriations bill that prevented the FCC from extending any waiver of the newspaper/television cross-ownership ban. This was aimed squarely at Murdoch, the only person affected by it, and would have required him to sell either the newspaper or the television station he owned in both Boston and New York City. Senator Kennedy reportedly was motivated, at least in part, by criticism of him in Murdoch's Boston paper. *See Kennedy And Paper Battle In Boston*, N.Y. Times, Jan. 7, 1988, at A16, col. 4; *Congress Faces New Battle Over Media Ownership*, N.Y. Times, Jan. 11, 1988, at A13, col. 1. *See also* News America Publishing, Inc. v. FCC, 844 F.2d 800, 802, 806-10 (D.C. Cir. 1988). The court found that the bill violated the first and fifth amendments. Murdoch, however, subsequently sold his New York newspaper and his Boston television station. *See*

The Supreme Court upheld the Commission's rulemaking relying squarely on FCC authority to regulate *broadcasting* in the public interest since the Commission has no authority over newspapers. Such regulation, in turn, was justified despite a first amendment challenge because of the physical scarcity of the broadcast spectrum. Indeed, the Court cited its leading broadcasting cases establishing scarcity as the predicate for regulation that otherwise would violate the first amendment.[145] Such scarcity, however, is irrelevant to both the telephone and cable industries.[146] Even current cable systems have great multi-channel capacity.[147] Moreover, the hallmark of telco entry into cable and the development of a high-technology, fiber optic network is the potential for virtually unlimited capacity for the transmission of information, quite likely surpassing the needs of available programming.[148]

More fundamentally, the scarcity rationale itself is rapidly losing whatever legitimacy it once may have had. In *FCC v. League of Women Voters*,[149] the Court for the first time invalidated on constitutional grounds a statutory restriction on broadcasters' freedom of expression. In so doing, the Court once again referred to scarcity as the "fundamental distinguishing characteristic" of broadcasting,[150] but applied a standard of review of upholding only those restrictions that are "narrowly tailored to further a substantial governmental interest."[151] Although the Court disavowed a new approach, this is a stricter level of scrutiny than it has applied in the past.[152] Moreover, the Court noted

---

Murdoch to Sell TV Station to Owners of Boston Celtics, N.Y. Times, Sept. 22, 1989, at D15, col. 3.

145 *National Citizens*, 436 U.S. at 794-800 (citing Red Lion Broadcasting Co. v. FCC, 395 U.S. 367, 388 (1969) (there is no "unabridgeable First Amendment right to broadcast comparable to the right of every individual to speak, write, or publish"); and CBS, Inc. v. Democratic Nat'l Comm., 412 U.S. 94, 101 (1973) ("broadcast media pose unique and special problems not present in the traditional free speech case").

146 Quincy Cable TV, Inc. v. FCC, 768 F.2d 1434, 1449 (D.C. Cir. 1985), *cert. denied*, 476 U.S. 1169 (1986) ("[T]he 'scarcity rationale' has no place in evaluating government regulation of cable television."). *Accord* Century Communications Corp. v. FCC, 835 F.2d 292, 295 (D.C. Cir. 1987), *cert. denied*, 486 U.S. 1032 (1988).

147 86.8% of cable subscribers are served by systems with capacity exceeding 30 channels. Competition, Rate Dergulation and the Commission's Policy Relating to the Provision of Cable Television Service, Notice of Inquiry, 5 F.C.C. Rcd. 362, 363 (1989).

148 *See infra* notes 243-59 and accompanying text.

149 468 U.S. 364 (1984) (prohibition on editorializing by noncommercial educational broadcasters who accept funds from the Corporation for Public Broadcasting is unconstitutional).

150 *Id.* at 377.

151 *Id.* at 380. The Court did comment that ensuring adequate and balanced coverage of public issues is such an interest. *Id.*

152 *See* News America Publishing, Inc. v. FCC, 844 F.2d 800, 812, 814 (D.C. Cir. 1988).

the increasing criticism of scarcity as the prevailing rationale for broadcast regulation and suggested that it might reconsider its entire approach upon an appropriate signal from Congress or the FCC that technological developments in the electronic media warrant it.[153]

The Commission sent just such a signal the next year in its 1985 fairness doctrine Report.[154] There it documented the tremendous growth and development of both radio and broadcast television, as well as dramatic technological developments leading to a rich variety of alternatives in the electronic mass media, especially cable. The Commission therefore concluded that the fairness doctrine contravenes the public interest and is questionable as a matter of constitutional law, thereby undercutting the factual basis and rationale developed in *Red Lion* which the Court has relied on since.

Lower federal courts already have gotten the message. One panel of the Court of Appeals for the District of Columbia Circuit recently noted that a universal economic fact such as scarcity cannot be used to justify regulation in one media but not another. Rather, scarcity as an analytic tool is a "distinction without a difference . . . [that] inevitably leads to strained reasoning and artificial results."[155] Concurring in an even more recent opinion, another member of this Court acknowledged that "spectrum scarcity, without more, does not necessarily justify regulatory schemes which intrude into First Amendment territory."[156] Rather, in evaluating restrictions that tread on the editorial discretion of broadcasters, courts must carefully scrutinize application of the regulatory standard to the interests assertedly advanced.

One commentator, not addressing the telco ban, asserts that the "Commission has not written one word concerning the constitutional validity of its structural regulations," and questions how it could avoid applying its recent emphasis on first amendment concerns in other areas to a re-examination of the cross-ownership rules.[157] With regard to the telco/cable ban the point

---

[153] *League of Women Voters*, 468 U.S. at 376 n.11.

[154] 1985 Fairness Doctrine Report, 102 F.C.C.2d 143 (1985).

[155] Telecommunications Research and Action Center v. FCC, 801 F.2d 501, 508, *reh'g en banc denied*, 806 F.2d 1115 (D.C. Cir. 1986), *cert. denied*, 482 U.S. 919 (1987) (review of FCC's decision not to apply three forms of political broadcast regulation to teletext). Judge Bork wrote the opinion joined by Judge, now Justice, Scalia.

[156] Syracuse Peace Council v. FCC, 867 F.2d 654, 683 (D.C. Cir. 1989) (Starr, J., concurring), *cert. denied*, 110 S. Ct. 717 (1990).

[157] Emrod, *supra* note 59, at 431.

is even stronger. The scarcity predicate for regulation is irrelevant and dying out in legitimacy. But even on the Commission's own terms of ownership preference for new and different speakers, the telcos should be favored. The other ownership restrictions limit the share of some mass media market owned or controlled by a single entity *already* participating in the mass media. None of them goes so far as to entirely exclude from the media market an entity, such as a telephone company, that has essentially no mass media position. Such a drastic denial of first amendment rights is counter to the FCC's own diversity goals. Invoking other cross-ownership restrictions in support of the telco/cable ban is, therefore, not only wrong and outmoded, it is contradictory.

IV. Antitrust, Prior Restraint, and the First Amendment

Thus, the argument comes down to whether concern for competition, both in the economic marketplace and in the marketplace of ideas, is sufficient to justify a virtually complete ban on telco entry into cable. This depends upon the appropriate relationship between antitrust enforcement and first amendment considerations and, more importantly, upon a proper appreciation of the first amendment status and consequences of the ban as a prior restraint.

A. *Antitrust*

Antitrust, tax, and other economic regulations apply to media entities. The first amendment does not shield them from such generally applicable regulations, at least so long as there is no significant impact on the editorial process.[158] Differential treatment, however, that burdens certain elements of the media without particularized justification raises the specter of suppression of expression and is "presumptively unconstitutional."[159]

[158] *See* Minneapolis Star Tribune Co. v. Minnesota Comm'r of Revenue, 460 U.S. 575, 581 (1983) (examples of permissible regulation; but Court rules newspaper tax at issue is unconstitutional); Home Placement Serv., Inc. v. Providence Journal Co., 682 F.2d 274 (1st Cir. 1982), *cert. denied*, 460 U.S. 1028 (1983) (newspaper free to make decisions on accepting advertising based on legitimate editorial or business reasons, but not for anticompetitive reasons); Newspaper Guild v. NLRB, 636 F.2d 550, 558 (D.C. Cir. 1980) (otherwise valid laws may become invalid in application where they constitute interference by government with "matters lying at the heart of a newspaper's independence"). *Cf.* Pittsburgh Press Co. v. Pittsburgh Comm'n on Human Relations, 413 U.S. 376 (1973) (newspaper's editorial discretion to carry help-wanted advertisements in sex-designated columns may be restricted with respect to such commercial speech that aids illegal employment discrimination).

[159] *Minneapolis Star*, 460 U.S. at 585.

The Court recently found, for example, that selective taxation of the press designed to encourage "fledgling publishers" and "foster communication" violates the first amendment.[160]

The seminal case on the relationship between antitrust and the first amendment, and the one relied on by Judge Greene,[161] is *Associated Press v. United States*.[162] The facts of that case, however, demonstrate how misplaced and ironic such reliance is. The Associated Press was a non-profit membership organization for the gathering and dissemination of news to its member newspapers. Its by-laws allowed existing members to effectively restrict new membership by competitors who therefore were precluded from access to important, though not the only, sources of news — the association itself as well as each of the individual members. The by-laws were found to constitute a restraint of trade seriously limiting the opportunity for new entry by competing newspapers in cities already served by an existing member.[163] The Court therefore required the Associated Press to offer membership on a basis that did not discriminate against competitors.

In other words, the Court removed privately imposed restraints on entry into the print media. It *opened up* the market to greater competition from all sources, even in face of the argument that doing so would cause Associated Press to grow so large as to "become the only news service, and get a monopoly by driving out all the others."[164] The Court thus rejected precisely the speculative fear that is used to ban telco entry, and specifically avoided any restraint on the member newspapers' ability to publish as they pleased.[165] It is in this context that the Court's well-known endorsement of first amendment principles must be read:

> That Amendment rests on the assumption that the widest possible dissemination of information from diverse and antagonistic sources is essential to the welfare of the public, that a free press is a condition of a free society. Surely a command that the government itself shall not impede the free flow of ideas does not afford non-governmental combinations a ref-

---

160 Arkansas Writers' Project, Inc. v. Ragland, 481 U.S. 221, 222 (1987).

161 *See* United States v. American Tel. & Tel., 552 F.2d 131, 183-84 (D.C. Cir. 1982) *aff'd*, 460 U.S. 1001 (1983); United States v. Westinghouse Elec., 673 F. Supp. 525, 585-86 (D.D.C. 1987).

162 326 U.S. 1 (1945).

163 *Id.* at 12-13.

164 United States v. Associated Press, 52 F. Supp. 362, 374 (S.D.N.Y. 1943) (Hand, J.). Judge Learned Hand perceived no harm from this "exceedingly remote" possibility of a monopoly open to all. *Id.*

165 *Associated Press*, 326 U.S. at 20 n.18.

uge if they impose restraints upon that constitutionally guaranteed freedom. Freedom to publish means freedom for all and not for some. Freedom to publish is guaranteed by the Constitution, but freedom to combine to keep others from publishing is not.[166]

To be sure, should the telcos enter the cable industry and engage in monopolistic or other anti-competitive practices, the teaching of *Associated Press* is that the full range of the antitrust laws is available to rectify the problem.[167] The nature and scope of particular remedies, however, should be sensitive to first amendment concerns.[168] But the case cannot be read for the proposition that,

---

166 *Id.* at 20. Indeed, in Miami Herald Publishing Co. v. Tornillo, 418 U.S. 241, 252 (1974), the Supreme Court rejected reliance on this very language to support an argument for increased diversity and competition in the economic media marketplace and the marketplace of ideas, the same argument behind the telco ban.

167 *See, e.g.*, Lorrain Journal Co. v. United States, 342 U.S. 143 (1951) (injunction approved against newspaper attempting to maintain its local monopoly on mass dissemination on all news and advertising by forcing its advertisers to boycott a competing radio station); Citizen Publishing Co. v. United States, 394 U.S. 131 (1969) (joint operating agreement between two newspapers, that had the purpose and effect of monopolizing local newspaper business, required modification). The FCC has specific authority to further antitrust policies. 47 U.S.C. § 314 (1988). *See* FCC v. National Citizens Comm. for Broadcasting, 436 U.S. 775, 795-96 (1978).

168 It is well established that antitrust and similar economic regulation must take into account first amendment concerns. *See Lorrain Journal*, 342 U.S. at 156 ("[w]hile the decree should anticipate probabilities of the future, it is equally important that it do [sic] not impose unnecessary restrictions"); *Citizen Publishing*, 394 U.S. at 139 ("[n]either news gathering nor news dissemination is being regulated by the present decree"); United States v. National Soc'y of Professional Engineers, 555 F.2d 978, 984 (D.C. Cir. 1977) (antitrust decree requiring professional society to state affirmatively that it does not consider competitive bidding unethical violates the first amendment), *aff'd*, 435 U.S. 679, 686 n.8, 697-98 (1978) (noting, however, that the first amendment does not prevent antitrust remedies). *See also* Passaic Daily News v. NLRB, 736 F.2d 1543 (D.C. Cir. 1984) (while a newspaper is accountable for unfair labor practices against its editorial employees, Associated Press v. NLRB, 301 U.S. 103 (1937), it cannot be required to publish such an employee's material); Standard Oil Co. of California v. FTC, 577 F.2d 653, 662 (9th Cir. 1978) ("first amendment considerations dictate that the Commission exercise restraint in formulating remedial orders which may amount to a prior restraint on protected commercial speech"); Beneficial Corp. v. FTC, 542 F.2d 611, 620 (3d Cir. 1976), *cert. denied*, 430 U.S. 983 (1977) (government "must start from the premise that any prior restraint is suspect, and that a remedy, even for deceptive advertising, can go no further than is necessary").

The Court's recent opinion in FTC v. Superior Court Trial Lawyers Ass'n, 110 S. Ct. 768 (1990), is not to the contrary, particularly as applied to the telco/cable ban. In that case the Court of Appeals ruled that the FTC had to apply the antitrust laws "with a special solicitude for . . . First Amendment rights." *Superior Court Trial Lawyers Ass'n*, 856 F.2d 226, 233 (D.C. Cir. 1988). The scope of regulation could be no "greater than is essential to further the state's interest in maintaining competition." *Id.* at 248. The government had to "prove rather than presume" a "significant threat to competition." *Id.* at 250, 253. The Supreme Court reversed because it found the antitrust *per se* rule against the sort of boycott and horizontal price fixing arrangement at issue, even though it may have entailed a component of political expression, was justified by a "long-standing judgment that the prohibited practices by their nature have 'a substantial potential for impact on competition.'" 110 S. Ct. at 780 (quoting Jefferson Parish Hosp. District No. 2 v. Hyde, 466 U.S. 2, 16 (1984)). With a government imposed, absolute ban on

especially absent any significant, demonstrated violations, the government is free *ab initio* to ban all entry. Quite the contrary, the telcos, like any other willing speaker, are among the "diverse and antagonistic sources" enjoying first amendment rights. The government has no prerogative to selectively "impede the free flow" of their ideas. Rather, the "[f]reedom to publish . . . for all" must include the telephone companies.

B. *Prior Restraint*

This conclusion is all the more compelling when we consider the nature of the telco/cable ban. The FCC naturally wishes to emphasize the ordinary, regulatory nature of the ban designed to meet important goals of economic competition and diversity in the marketplace of ideas, with only an "incidental" effect on freedom of expression. Despite this attempt to invoke a particularly accommodating, but inapposite, trend in the Court's recent first amendment jurisprudence, the ban amounts to the worst kind of prior restraint — the most onerous and least supportable form of governmental regulation. If put to its proof, as the government should be, it is hard to imagine justification for the ban.

The concept of prior restraint is not well defined in first amendment jurisprudence. It has been invoked in a variety of arguably dissimilar situations to occasion the highest level of judicial scrutiny, with the almost immediate result of invalidating whatever restriction on free expression has been so characterized.[169] One indeed might argue that the doctrine of prior restraint has become simply an expression of fundamental policies in favor of expanding first amendment freedoms.[170] The linguistic characterization of the ban on telco entry into cable as a prior

---

telco entry which substantially restricts competition, the presumption is reversed. As the Court noted, the Sherman Act reflects a legislative judgment in favor of competition, including the "free opportunity to select among alternative offers." *Superior Court Trial Lawyers Ass'n*, 110 S. Ct. at 775 (quoting *National Soc'y of Professional Engineers*, 435 U.S. at 695). Rather than being "categorically prohibit[ed]," competition from telco entry is presumptively favored, and any restrictions imposed should require at least the scrutiny of the lower court's approach. *Id.* at 779.

169 *See* Jeffries, *Rethinking Prior Restraint*, 92 YALE L.J. 409, 419 (1983) (both judicial and academic commentators reinforce "the impression of elasticity and incoherence in the term 'prior restraint' ") [hereinafter Jeffries]; Scordato, *Distinction Without a Difference: A Reappraisal of the Doctrine of Prior Restraint*, 68 N.C.L. REV. 1, 2 (1989) (asserting the Supreme Court has "affixed the prior restraint label to an exceptionally diverse group of laws, regulations, and government actions").

170 *See* Jeffries, *supra* note 169, at 419-20. The Supreme Court, however, clearly continues to believe there is an identifiable concept meriting special treatment. *See, e.g.*, Minneapolis Star Tribune Co. v. Minnesota Comm'r of Revenue, 460 U.S. 575, 583-84 n.6 (1983) ("Prior restraints, for instance, clearly strike to the core of the Framers' concerns, leading this Court to treat them as particularly suspect.").

restraint on the telephone companies' freedom of expression need not trouble us, however. On any measure the presumptive unconstitutionality of the ban is apparent.

The ban is aimed directly at a categorically defined class of speakers and prohibits any and all use of a major electronic medium of mass communications of expanding reach and importance. An entity with no mass media presence is prohibited from what is likely its most natural and accessible *entre* into that general market. The simple identity of the willing speaker precludes it from clearly protected, basic, first amendment activity. While the ban apparently is not viewpoint specific, it can hardly be considered content-neutral,[171] thereby allowing greater room for regulation. For it would be perverse to consider a *total* ban on cablespeech by telcos content-neutral, and therefore less infringing, because it was not *more limited* to specific categories of expression.[172] Rather, absolute prohibitions on speech are presumptively unconstitutional.[173] Moreover, an articulated goal of the ban in terms of fostering diversity in the marketplace of ideas reveals the fundamental content-based nature of the regulation.[174]

Consequently, the ban on telco entry deserves to be treated

---

171 The Supreme Court's latest statement on content-neutrality in the first amendment context seems to conflate the notions of viewpoint discrimination and content-neutrality. Ward v. Rock Against Racism, 109 S. Ct. 2746, 2754 (1989). Taking the government's purpose as the controlling consideration, the Court states that incidental regulation of expressive activity is content-neutral so long as it is "*justified* without reference to the content of the regulated speech." *Id.* (citing Community for Creative Non-Violence, 468 U.S. 289, 293 (1989); Heffner Int'l Soc'y v. Krishna Consciousness, Inc., 452 U.S. 640, 648 (1981) (quoting Virginia Pharmacy Bd. v. Virginia Citizens Consumer Council, Inc., 425 U.S. 748, 711 (1976))) (emphasis in original). This background paragraph of the Court's opinion, citing numerous precedents, apparently was not meant to alter traditional analysis. At any rate, as discussed in the text, the telco ban is partly justified by reference to content and cannot be considered as having only an incidental effect on first amendment rights.

172 "The First Amendment's hostility to content-based regulation extends not only to restrictions on particular viewpoints, but also to prohibition of public discussion of an entire topic." Consolidated Edison Co. of New York, Inc. v. Public Serv. Comm'n of New York, 447 U.S. 530, 537 (1980). *A fortiori*, to be at all meaningful it must extend to prohibition of all public communication on any topic. *See also* Arkansas Writers' Project, Inc. v. Ragland, 107 S. Ct. 1722, 1728 (1987).

173 *See* Airport Comm'rs of Los Angeles v. Jews for Jesus, Inc., 107 S. Ct. 2568, 2572 (1987) (no conceivable governmental interest could justify prohibition on all first amendment activities at airport regardless of its status as a public or nonpublic forum).

174 Pacific Gas & Elec. Co. v. Public Util. Comm'n of California, 475 U.S. 1, 12-13 (1986) (access to utility's billing envelopes designed to "offer the public a greater variety of views" is not content neutral). *But cf.* United Video Inc. v. FCC, 890 F.2d 1173, 1189 n.13 (D.C. Cir. 1989) (FCC's syndicated exclusivity rules are justified by their encouragement of production of diverse programming and therefore are content-neutral). The lower court somehow viewed this as a justification "without reference to the content of the regulated speech." *Id.*

as a prior restraint. Indeed, it is the worst kind of prior restraint; it is far closer to a permit or licensing scheme that works a total exclusion than to the prototypical prior restraint in the form of an injunction that has more limited effect. As such, it suffers from many of the vices associated with the broad power to censor by administrative fiat.[175] The ban, therefore, must bear a "heavy presumption against its constitutional validity,"[176] and the government must meet the "heavy burden of showing justification for the imposition of such a restraint."[177]

To avoid this burden which it cannot meet, the FCC, in its brief discussion of constitutional issues raised by the ban, portrays it as content-neutral regulation affecting speech only incidentally.[178] As such, the Commission asserts that its rules can be sustained as narrowly tailored (no greater than essential) to achieve a substantial government interest under the *O'Brien* standard.[179] This is plausible as the Court has been eviscerating the protection it is willing to afford even political expression from regulation that it deems has only an "incidental" burden on speech.[180]

This approach is very similar to the FCC's unsuccessful attempt to sustain its cable "must-carry" regulations by invoking a lessened standard of review. The original must-carry regulations were held to violate the first amendment even under *O'Brien's* in-

---

175 *See* Jeffries, *supra* note 169, at 421-34. The overlapping administrative, statutory, and judicial components of the ban make it somewhat complicated to fit nicely into Jeffries' discussion of different types of prior restraints. Administrative discretion, for example, which Jeffries identifies as an especially troublesome factor, is present in the FCC's waiver policy. *Id.* at 423. *See* City of Lakewood v. Plain Dealer Publishing Co., 486 U.S. 750, 757 (1988) (licensing statute entailing governmental discretion may constitute prior restraint and result in censorship). Judge Greene's repeated judicial review, on the other hand, even though on a very broad level of regulation, may possess some ameliorating characteristics. *See* Jeffries, *supra* note 169, at 426-34. As described in the text, however, the problems with the ban are manifest.

176 New York Times Co. v. United States, 403 U.S. 713, 714 (1971) (per curiam) (quoting Bantam Books, Inc. v. Sullivan, 372 U.S. 58, 70 (1963)).

177 *Id.* (quoting Organization for a Better Austin v. Keefe, 402 U.S. 415, 419 (1971)). *See also* Nebraska Press Ass'n v. Stuart, 427 U.S. 539, 556-62 (1975).

178 Telephone Company — Cable Television Cross-Ownership Rules, Further Notice of Inquiry and Notice of Proposed Rulemaking, 3 F.C.C. Rcd. 5849, 5864 (1988).

179 United States v. O'Brien, 391 U.S. 367, 377 (1968). While Judge Greene never discussed the appropriate standard for evaluating the constitutionality of the telco ban, those opposing telco entry on appeal argued the *O'Brien* standard.

180 *See* United States v. Albertini, 472 U.S. 675, 689 (1985) (a neutral, incidental burden on speech need only promote a "substantial government interest that would be achieved less effectively absent the regulation"). *See also* Board of Trustees of the State University of New York v. Fox, 109 S. Ct. 3028, 3033-34 (1989) (rejecting, in the commercial speech context, a "least restrictive means" test for narrow-tailoring and suggesting the same applies to political expressive conduct). *Accord* Ward v. Rock Against Racism, 109 S. Ct. 2746, 2757-58 (1989).

terest-balancing formulation.[181] At the same time, the Court expressed its "serious doubts" about applying such an unexacting standard to these infringements on cable operators' editorial discretion.[182] In reformulating its rules[183], the Commission tried to rely on the Supreme Court's intervening decision in *City of Renton v. Playtime Theatres, Inc.*,[184] an adult theatre zoning case. In *Renton*, the Court maintained that the time, place and manner zoning ordinance at issue was content-neutral because it was not aimed at the content of the adult films but at the "secondary effects" adult theaters have on the surrounding community.[185] It therefore was "*justified* without reference to the content of the regulated speech."[186]

Renton is dangerous first amendment precedent. Just as it is becoming all too easy to describe clear content-based regulation as only incidentally burdening expression, so too does Justice Rehnquist's opinion for the Court in *Renton* demonstrate how easy it is to contrive secondary effects to justify suppression of free speech plainly directed at its content.[187] A majority of the Court may be retreating slightly in acknowledging that the impact of speech on its audience—the concern of the diversity principle supporting the telco ban—cannot be a mere "secondary effect" subject to *Renton* analysis.[188] At any rate, the fate of the FCC's prior attempts to rely on *O'Brien* and *Renton* should control here as well.

The must-carry rules invalidated in *Quincy* interfered with a cable operator's editorial discretion on only a portion of his available channels. The cable operator was entirely free to program as it wished on the rest of the channels. The court realized that, as with the telco ban, the goal of the rules could be framed in content-neutral terms of preserving competition and fostering

---

181 *See generally* Quincy Cable TV, Inc. v. FCC, 768 F.2d 1434, 1452 (D.C. Cir. 1985), *cert. denied*, 476 U.S. 1169 (1986).

182 *Id.* at 1448.

183 Amendment of Part 76 of the Commission's Rules Concerning Carriage of Television Broadcast Signals by Cable Television Systems, 1 F.C.C. Rcd. 864, 893-94 (1986), *reconsid. denied*, 2 F.C.C. Rcd. 3593, 3602-03 (1987), *rev'd*, Century Communications Corp. v. FCC, 835 F.2d 292 (D.C. Cir. 1987), *cert. denied*, 108 S. Ct 2014 (1988).

184 475 U.S. 41 (1986).

185 *Id.* at 47.

186 *Id.* at 48 (quoting Virginia Bd. of Pharmacy v. Virginia Citizens Consumer Council, Inc., 425 U.S. 748, 771 (1976) (emphasis in original)).

187 *See Renton*, 475 U.S. at 55-63 (Brennan, Marshall, JJ., dissenting); Boos v. Barry, 108 S. Ct. 1157, 1171-73 (1988) (Brennan, Marshall, JJ., concurring) (further describing the dangers and difficulties posed by the *Renton* analysis).

188 *Boos*, 108 S. Ct. at 1163. *But see* Ward v. Rock Against Racism, 109 S. Ct. 2746, 2754 (1989); *id.* at 2761 n.1 (Marshall, Brennan, Stevens, JJ., dissenting).

diversity in the electronic video marketplace.[189] Nonetheless, the rules were a "far cry" from a merely incidental burden on speech.[190] Although viewpoint neutral, they were "explicitly designed to 'favor[] certain classes of speakers over others.' "[191] Therefore, they "profoundly affect values that lie near the heart of the First Amendment."[192] If pressed, it is hard to see how the court in *Quincy* could have avoided treating the must-carry rules as a direct burden on the first amendment rights of cable operators subject to exacting scrutiny. Indeed, the Commission had no more success in invoking *Renton* to buttress its incidental/secondary effects argument in support of far less onerous modified rules.[193]

The telco ban does not just infringe editorial discretion it precludes any opportunity for its exercise by a telephone company. The ban keeps *all* potential cable channels from the telcos and reserves them for others. It "favors" certain classes of speakers in a particularly Draconian way by wholly eliminating another class. As a direct ban it is certainly a direct burden, and the question is whether the government can possibly justify such a prior restraint.

C. *The First Amendment*

One may assume, at least in the abstract, that the asserted goals of preserving economic competition in the electronic video marketplace and competition in this marketplace of ideas are substantial, even compelling, governmental interests.[194] Even so, and simply put, speculative fears about untoward consequences in these regards from telco entry into cable cannot begin to justify the total ban.

On one level, if neither plausible fear at the highest rank of

---

189 Quincy Cable TV, Inc. v. FCC, 768 F.2d 1434, 1451 (D.C. Cir. 1985), *cert. denied*, 476 U.S. 1169 (1980).

190 *Id.*

191 *Id.* (quoting HBO, Inc. v. FCC, 567 F.2d 9, 48 (D.C. Cir.), *cert. denied*, 434 U.S. 829 (1977)) (FCC's pay cable rules invalidated).

192 *Quincy TV*, 768 F.2d at 1453.

193 *See generally* Century Communications Corp. v. FCC, 835 F.2d 292 (D.C. Cir. 1987), *cert. denied*, 486 U.S. 1032 (1988). Once again, the court found the rules did not satisfy even the less-demanding *O'Brien* test and therefore did not have to decide whether to apply a stricter standard. *Id.* at 298.

194 *See* FCC v. League of Women Voters of California, 468 U.S. 364, 377-80 (1984). *But see* Shurberg Broadcasting v. FCC, 876 F.2d 902, 919-23, 923 n.33, 926 (D.C. Cir. 1989) (Silberman, J.), *cert. granted sub nom.* Astroline Communications Co. Ltd. Partnership v. Shurberg Broadcasting of Hartford, Inc., 110 S. Ct. 715 (1990) ("It is doubtful that the FCC has a compelling interest in fostering programming diversity."). *Cf. id.* at 930 n.11 (MacKinnon, J., dissenting).

government of a grave threat to national security during a time of war,[195] nor realistic concerns about preserving the fundamental constitutional right to a fair trial in a capital case,[196] justify a prior restraint on the media, the far more speculative and far less momentous interests asserted here cannot possibly justify the even broader prior restraint on the telephone companies. One need not go to such lofty heights, however. On their own terms the government's economic and diversity concerns are wholly inadequate to overcome the heavy presumption against "one of the most extraordinary remedies known to our jurisprudence."[197]

In upholding the FCC's limited divestiture requirement of co-located newspaper-broadcast combinations in *National Citizens*, the Supreme Court allowed the Commission to rely on factual economic determinations of a "judgmental or predictive nature" in circumstances where "complete factual support . . . is not possible or required."[198] In *Bellotti*, the Court indicated that an empirically-supported argument that a particular faction "threatened *imminently*" to overwhelmingly dominate the marketplace of ideas, "thereby denigrating rather than serving First Amendment interests," would at least merit the Court's consideration.[199] Neither of these approaches, however, supports the broad prior restraint on the telephone companies.

As a preliminary matter, even if the FCC and, by extension Congress, in reliance upon the Commission, were to maintain the need for continuing the ban, that cannot determine the first amendment issue. As the Court frequently states, "[d]eference to a legislative finding cannot limit judicial inquiry when First Amendment rights are at stake."[200] This principle has particular

195 *See generally* New York Times Co. v. United States, 403 U.S. 713, 717 (1971) (The Pentagon Papers Case). The standard from this case for sustaining a prior restraint usually is taken from Justice Stewart's opinion: the government must show that lack of prior restraint "surely will result in direct, immediate, and irreparable damage to our Nation or its people." *Id.* at 730 (Stewart, White, JJ., concurring). *See also id.* at 726-27 (Brennan, J., concurring).

196 *See generally* Nebraska Press Ass'n v. Stuart, 427 U.S. 539, 569-70 (1976).

197 *Id.* at 562.

198 FCC v. National Citizens Comm. for Broadcasting, 436 U.S. 775, 813-14 (1978). *See id.* at 796-97 (diversity and its effects are elusive concepts, not easily defined or measured; in these circumstances the Commission is entitled to rely on its judgment).

199 First Nat'l Bank of Boston v. Bellotti, 435 U.S. 765, 789 (1978) (emphasis added). *See also* Central Hudson Gas & Elec. Corp. v. Public Serv. Comm'n of New York, 447 U.S. 557, 577 (1980) (Blackmun, J., concurring) (absent an emergency that justifies repression, the remedy for alleged distortion in the marketplace of ideas is "more speech, not enforced silence").

200 Sable Communications of California v. FCC, 109 S. Ct. 2829, 2838 (1989) (quoting Landmark Communications, Inc. v. Virginia, 435 U.S. 829, 843 (1978)). *See also* Los Angeles v. Preferred Communications, Inc., 476 U.S. 488, 496 (1986); Century Communications Corp. v. FCC, 835 F.2d 292, 299 (D.C. Cir. 1987), *cert. denied*, 486 U.S. 1032

force when the asserted "finding" is in fact merely a presumption.

1. Economic Concerns

Concerns that telephone companies in the cable business will engage in cross-subsidization, unfair competition, or other monopolizing activities are not wholly ephemeral.[201] The telcos well may have both the ability and temptation to do so.[202] The point, rather, is that such *a priori* speculative fears cannot sustain a broad prior restraint.[203] Such fears do not simply constitute a well-accepted economic theory that may be relied upon in a specific instance without empirical support.[204] Instead they represent a conclusion about what necessarily will happen in a dynamic economic market, despite forewarning and available alternative means well short of prior restraint to prevent their occurrence or remedy excesses that do occur.

The appropriate approach again is typified by the must-carry cases. Although the court in *Quincy* was reviewing regulation that infringed the editorial discretion of cable operators far less than the telco ban, and it ultimately applied the less demanding *O'Brien* standard, it nonetheless distinguished the *National Citizens* approach.[205] Deference to the Commission's "concededly un-

---

(1988) ("[T]he substantial deference due in the administrative context has little relevance when first amendment freedoms are even incidentally at stake."); News America Publishing, Inc. v. FCC, 844 F.2d 800, 805 (D.C. Cir. 1988) ("even in broadcast regulation the First and Fifth Amendments demand" close fit between a law and its asserted legitimate purposes).

201 *But see* HUBER, *supra* note 75, at § 6.35 (indicating that the lack of overlap involved in many activities of running a local telephone exchange and a cable service presents little opportunity for cross-subsidization).

202 *See, e.g.*, *Wrong Numbers: Nynex Overcharged Phone Units For Years, An FCC Audit Finds*, Wall St. J., Jan. 9, 1990, at 1, col. 6 (findings of cost and revenue shifting by a BOC) [hereinafter *Wrong Numbers*]; In re New York Telephone Co., 67 Rad. Reg. (P & F) 588 (1990) (apparent violations of affiliate transaction rules and policies).

203 If one were to argue that "any given issue of Hustler [Magazine] may be found legally obscene" and that, therefore, the Magazine generally should be subject to sanction or prior restraint, *see* Herceg v. Hustler Magazine, Inc., 814 F.2d 1017, 1029 (5th Cir. 1987) (Jones, J., concurring in part and dissenting in part), *cert. denied*, 485 U.S. 959 (1988), loud first amendment alarms surely would sound. The telcos are entitled to at least as much first amendment solicitude as Larry Flint. *See* Austin v. Michigan Chamber of Commerce, 110 S. Ct. 1391, 1413-14 (1990) (Scalia, J., dissenting) (describing the long and powerful tradition that "the mere potential for harm does not justify a restriction upon speech").

204 *See* United Video Inc. v. FCC, 890 F.2d 1173, 1180 (D.C. Cir. 1989) (Commission's conclusion sufficiently in accord with accepted economic theory that it can stand without empirical support).

205 Quincy Cable TV, Inc. v. FCC, 768 F.2d 1434, 1458 (D.C. Cir. 1985), *cert. denied*, 476 U.S. 1169 (1986). The court found the FCC capable of the "most sophisticated analysis" of the effects of cable on conventional broadcasting. *See also* News America

supported determinations [was] plainly inappropriate."[206] Where first amendment rights are at stake "the Commission must do more than ask us to defer to its 'more or less intuitive model' and 'collective instinct.' "[207] In short, "speculative fears alone have never been held sufficient to justify trenching on first amendment liberties."[208]

Moreover, the empirical basis for the speculative fears is questionable. The cable industry has grown dramatically in recent years. Its audience and revenues have exploded,[209] and sales of cable systems command increasingly high prices.[210] Many consider the cable industry already too concentrated,[211] vertically integrated[212] and powerful. For example, multiple system owners ("MSOs") control over fifty percent of subscribers with the top ten controlling about 47% and the top four about 28%.[213] Currently, the Commission is undertaking major studies of the industry[214] in the wake of growing congressional sentiment for re-regulation.[215]

However, the best way to discipline the industry is through

Publishing, Inc. v. FCC, 844 F.2d 800, 811-12 (D.C. Cir. 1988) (rejecting FCC's broad reading of *National Citizens*).

206 *Quincy*, 768 F.2d at 1457.

207 *Id.* at 1458. Even in the criminal context, "cases firmly hold that mere probable cause to believe a legal violation has transpired is not adequate" to restrain expression. Fort Wayne Books, Inc. v. Indiana, 109 S. Ct. 916, 929 (1989).

208 Century Communications Corp. v. FCC, 835 F.2d 292, 300 (D.C. Cir. 1987), *cert. denied*, 486 U.S. 1032 (1988). *See also* Consolidated Edison Co. of New York, Inc. v. Public Serv. Comm'n of New York, 447 U.S. 529, 543 (1980) ("Mere speculation of harm [from cross-subsidization] does not constitute a compelling state interest"); Central Hudson Gas & Elec. Corp. v. Public Serv. Comm'n of New York, 447 U.S. 557, 569 (1980) ("conditional and remote eventualities simply cannot justify silencing appellant's promotional advertising").

209 *See* United Video Inc. v. FCC, 890 F.2d 1173, 1181 (D.C. Cir. 1989); Competition, Rate Deregulation and the Commission's Policy Relating to the Provision of Cable Television Service, Notice of Inquiry, 5 F.C.C. Rcd. 362, 362-63 (1989).

210 *See* Fabrikant, *For Cable Systems The Takeover Frenzy Cools*, N.Y. Times, Jan. 22, 1990, at C6, col. 3.

211 *See* NTIA Report, *supra* note 7, at 77-88 and Attachment 2 (concentration charts of top ten and top four MSOs for 1983-87); *Competition, Rate Deregulation*, 5 F.C.C. Rcd. at 362-63, 370-73.

212 NTIA Report, *supra* note 7, at 89-107; *Competition, Rate Deregulation*, 5 F.C.C. Rcd. at 373-74.

213 *See Cable TV: The New Big Kid*, *supra* note 47, at 3364; *Top 100 MSO's*, CABLEVISION, Jan. 29, 1990, at 80. Taking into account cross-ownership interests among MSOs these concentration figures can appear considerably higher. *See Competition, Rate Deregulation*, 5 F.C.C. Rcd. at 378 n. 68.

214 *See generally Competition, Rate Deregulation*, 5 F.C.C. Rcd. 362; Reexamination of the Effective Competition Standard for the Regulation of Cable Television Basic Service Rates, Notice of Proposed Rulemaking, 5 F.C.C. Rcd. 259 (1990).

215 *See, e.g.*, S.1880, 101st Cong., 1st Sess. (1989); H.R.3826, 101st Cong., 1st Sess. (1990). These companion measures would impose significant restrictions on cable operators.

increased competition.[216] To exclude the single best source of such competition, and in particular the two thirds of the domestic telecommunications industry represented by the BOCs,[217] is senseless and counterproductive. Indeed, the argument that we have to exclude these potential competitors to preserve competition in the industry is all too reminiscent of the logic regarding the Vietnamese village that had to be destroyed in order to save it.

It is axiomatic that the goal of antitrust policy is to protect competition, not competitors.[218] The best result from telco entry would be the creation of direct competition between systems serving the same customers and providing some roughly fungible services. This would create real choice and perhaps some diversity for consumers.[219] Cable, however, may be a local natural monopoly because economic factors in the industry may dictate that the long-range competitive market equilibrium would result in a single firm serving a given geographic area.[220] Even if so, and even if fears of telephone companies replacing cable operators through anticompetitive practices materialize, at worst one natural monopolist will replace another. While some cable operators might suffer, it is not clear the public would. Under this pessimistic scenario, however, maintaining the ban on telco entry not only does violence to the first amendment, it also forecloses potential competitive pressure to produce periodically, through market forces and not governmental edict, the "best" cable monopolist.[221]

The FCC now believes both that the cable industry is suffi-

---

216 *Competition, Rate Deregulation*, 5 F.C.C. Rcd. at 363 ("[I]n the long term, competitive market forces [as opposed to direct regulatory intervention] will best promote the interests of viewers or consumers.").

217 HUBER, *supra* note 75, at 1.34. Another study suggests the BOCs serve approximately 77% of United States local exchange customers. *See* Pepper, *supra* note 75, at 26-27.

218 *See, e.g.*, Cargill, Inc. v. Monfort of Colorado, Inc., 479 U.S. 104, 110 (1986).

219 *See* Hazlett, *Cable vs. Telcos: Technology Shaping Emerging Policy Options*, 7 CABLE T.V. AND NEW MEDIA 1 (May 1989).

> The real opportunity from a public policy perspective is to juxtapose two telecommunications giants in earnest rivalry in local markets. . . . [T]echnological evolution means that the separation of video service providers and common carrier voice or data transmission suppliers will become increasingly archaic. As in other areas of communications, convergence of distribution modes forces a reassessment of the separation of distribution functions.

Id. See also Pepper, *supra* note 75, at 78-79; *Reexamination of the Effective Competition Rulemaking*, 5 F.C.C. Rcd. at 267 n. 30.

220 *See* Winer, *The Signal Cable Sends*, *supra* note 56, at 245-52 (discussing this problematic issue).

221 *See id.* at 249-50.

ciently strong and mature to compete competently with the telephone companies and that it has available adequate, nonstructural accounting and related safeguards to monitor and detect improper anticompetitive behavior by the telcos.[222] It is hard to quarrel with this conclusion. Cable is now available to almost 82% (73.9 million) of the nation's television households with over 56% (50.8 million) actually subscribing.[223] In terms of revenues, profitability, ratings, market share, access to programming, and investor interest, cable has come of age.[224] The initial construction phase of cable is virtually complete leaving telephone companies the alternative of acquiring existing systems or overbuilding to compete. As the Commission concludes, "with respect to most of the country, there is no risk of telephone company preemption of broadband services."[225]

The situation may be less conclusive with respect to safeguards for preventing anticompetitive activity. The Commission apparently believes that provision of cable service by telephone companies would be sufficiently similar to their provision of other services that it can devise and apply adequate, nonstructural accounting and other safeguards analogous to those developed to protect against anticompetitive conduct by carriers in other areas.[226] Implementing such safeguards would not appear to raise any significant first amendment concerns, so long as they do not infringe upon editorial discretion.[227]

---

222 Telephone Company — Cable Television Cross-Ownership Rules, Further Notice of Inquiry and Notice of Proposed Rulemaking, 3 F.C.C. Rcd. 5849, 5853, 5858-60.

223 *By The Numbers*, BROADCASTING, Dec. 18, 1989, at 14.

224 *See generally Cable TV: The New Big Kid, supra* note 47, at 3361-66; *Competition, Rule Deregulation*, 5 F.C.C. Rcd. at 362.

225 *Telco Further Notice of Inquiry*, 3 F.C.C. Rcd. at 5853. *See also* NTIA Report, *supra* note 7, at 34 (concerns that telephone companies would displace the cable industry "overlook the strengths of the cable industry"). The BOCs, however, still dwarf the cable operators. The largest MSO had 1987 revenue of $1.71 billion compared with sixth-ranked Pacific Telesis' $9.13 billion. Amparano, *Phone Firms Battle Cable-TV Operators Over Providing Fiber-Optic Home Links*, Wall St. J., Sept. 9, 1988, at 23, col. 3.

226 *Telco Further Notice of Inquiry*, 3 F.C.C. Rcd. at 5858-60. These might include requiring the offering of unbundled basic services, explicit cost allocation standards, and the common carrier offering of underlying transmission capacity to others on the same terms and conditions the carrier takes such capacity for its own cable service. *See* Southwestern Bell Corp. v. FCC, 896 F.2d 1378 (D.C. Cir. 1990) (upholding FCC rules governing transfer of assets between a regulated telco and its nonregulated affiliates).

227 Ironically, the debate over regulation of cable seems driven, at least in part, by such lofty concerns as the siphoning of sports programming onto "pay" television, as if viewers have an inherent, fundamental right to "free" access to such programming. *See* Carnevale, *Congress Seeks To Rein In Cable TV*, Wall St. J., Dec. 11, 1989, at B1, col. 4; *Joe Sixpack: This One's For You*, CONG. Q., Dec. 9, 1989, at 3362 ("Congress knows no fury, it seems, like that of a frustrated sports fan"). Accounting safeguards are one thing, but government attempts to determine what is shown on television, on what channels, under what conditions, and when offend the first amendment and are inappropriate.

Judge Greene has been rather skeptical of the FCC's previous oversight abilities.[228] But specifically with regard to telco entry into cable, the FCC and others presumably are well aware of the possible problems and know what to look for in monitoring the industry.[229] Moreover, the Commission no longer is dealing with one enormous and monolithic telephone company. Instead there are many substantial, independent companies, prominently including the increasingly diversified BOCs all of whom may become horizontal competitors with each other as well as with the existing MSOs and independent cable operators.[230] In the past cable operators have not been hesitant to assert themselves against anticompetitive activities,[231] and there is no reason to believe the expanded and even more competitive industry will be any less vigilant in policing itself this way. If necessary, the Commission should apply increased regulatory resources before extinguishing the telephone companies' freedom of expression. Furthermore, deference to the FCC's expertise here is appropriate as it operates in favor of first amendment rights.

2. Diversity Considerations

Finally, appeal to an amorphous diversity principle in support of prior restraint is wholly inappropriate. First, it is as equally backwards as the economic argument. Allowing telco entry may well stimulate greater development of broadband facilities and networks making available more, new and better programs and services.[232] In particular, these might include the

---

228 United States v. Western Electric Co., 673 F. Supp. 525, 567-74 (D.D.C. 1987). *See Wrong Numbers*, *supra* note 202 (FCC has fewer than 20 auditors to police a $150 billion industry and could conduct a full audit of each major phone company only once every 16 years). The fact that the FCC has just fined Nynex $1.4 million and ordered it to disgorge $35 million in inflated profits earned through cost-shifting demonstrates both that problems exist and the FCC's ability to detect and remedy them. *See* In re New York Tel. Co., 67 Rad. Reg. (P & F) 558 (1990). *See also* Sims, *U.S. Accuses 2 Nynex Companies Of Overcharging And Fines Them*, N.Y. Times, Feb. 9, 1990, at 1, col. 1; *FCC: Nynex Telcos Overpaid $118.5 Million To Unregulated Subsidiary*, FCC Week, Feb. 12, 1990, at 1, 2 (FCC Chairman quoted as saying that Commission's action demonstrates "safeguards actually exist, and that they are being efficiently administered and vigorously enforced.").

229 *See* United States v. Western Electric Co., 714 F. Supp. 1, 17-18, *amendment and clarification denied*, 1988-1 Trade Cas. (CCH) ¶ 68,094 (D.D.C. 1988).

230 *See* United States v. American Tel. & Tel., 552 F. Supp. at 187 (distinguishing the BOCs from the former, monolithic Bell system). *See also* Lopez & Carnevale, *Phone Firms Are Becoming Poles Apart: Bells, In Varying Degrees, Diverge and Diversify*, Wall St. J., Feb. 9, 1990, at B5, col. 1.

231 *See, e.g.*, Central Telecommunications, Inc. v. TCI Cablevision, Inc., 800 F.2d 711 (8th Cir. 1986), *cert. denied*, 480 U.S. 910 (1987) (affirmance of multi-million dollar antitrust judgment for cable operator against a competitor).

232 A stated purpose of the Cable Act is the provision of "the widest possible diversity of information sources and services to the public." Cable Act § 601(4), 47 U.S.C.

considerable benefit of substantially increased opportunities for access to the medium in far less constitutionally troublesome ways. The Commission now seems persuaded of this basic view.[233]

More fundamentally, the diversity concept necessarily implies an inherently vague and subjective social-political-economic scale on which to measure programming and related services. Social scientists might think they can do this,[234] but the first amendment demands more precision.[235] Simple market fragmentation does not yield program diversity;[236] there is no necessary relationship between the two, as a comparison of the three major broadcast networks readily demonstrates. Moreover, as just discussed, the economics of the cable industry may well mean that telco entry will not much affect, one way or the other, the degree of market fragmentation. At most, the identity of some players may change.

A cable operator who "narrowcasts" a range of cable chan-

---

§ 521(4) (Supp. V 1987). The telcos certainly would qualify in terms of sources and services.

233 Telephone Company — Cable Television Cross-Ownership Rules, Further Notice of Inquiry and Notice of Proposed Rulemaking, 3 F.C.C. Rcd. 5849, 5857 (1988). Again, there seems little potential for a more restrictive industry even if telcos do displace present cable operators.

234 As an example of what passes for research in this general area, consider Lowry & Towles, *Prime Time TV Portrayals of Sex, Contraception and Venereal Diseases*, 66 JOURNALISM Q. 347 (Summer 1989). The authors' basic coding categories for selected prime time network programming included "erotic touching" ("heavy" kissing was counted but not a casual "peck" type of kiss, unless the context was ambiguous and the kiss lasted three seconds or longer), *id.* at 349, and "heterosexual intercourse" subdivided into verbal (*e.g.* spoken references to "an affair"), implied, or physically depicted. *Id.* In another category, "physical suggestiveness," three women in bikinis walking together directly in front of the camera counted as one instance, but three different camera shots of one woman in a bikini counted as three instances! *Id.* at 350. The authors performed modest statistical compilations of the data collected — that is, the number of "codable behaviors" observed in each category — and purported to draw conclusions such as: "[N]etwork TV presentation of sexual behaviors is more a disinformation campaign than a realistic source of information." *Id.* at 352. One must hope the first amendment would save us from any attempt to regulate based on such stuff.

235 *See, e.g.*, Winter Park Communications, Inc. v. FCC, 873 F.2d 347, 358-59 (D.C. Cir. 1989) (Williams, J., dissenting) (criticizing study purporting to show link between minority broadcast ownership and diverse programming for failing to define " 'minority-targeted programming' " and suggesting the inevitable collapse of any such evidence), *cert. granted sub nom.* Metro Broadcasting, Inc. v. FCC, 110 S. Ct. 715 (1990).

236 Even when particularized to the area of gender- and race-based preferences in awarding broadcast licenses, there is great controversy as to whether minority ownership leads to minority programming. *See, e.g.*, Shurberg Broadcasting of Hartford, Inc. v. FCC, 876 F.2d 902, 921-22 (D.C. Cir. 1989) (Silberman, J.) (calling this a "questionable premise" based on racial or ethnic stereotypes), *cert. granted sub nom.* Astroline Communications Co. Ltd. Partnership v. Shurberg Broadcasting of Hartford, Inc., 110 S. Ct. 715 (1990). *Cf. id.* at 932 (opinion of MacKinnon, J.) (citing legislative findings); *id.* at 944-48 (Wald, C.J., dissenting). *See also* Winter Park Communications, Inc. v. FCC, 873 F.2d 347 (D.C. Cir. 1989), *cert granted sub nom.* Metro Broadcasting, Inc. v. FCC, 110 S. Ct. 715 (1990).

nels, just like a broadcaster who programs a single channel, has to attract a sufficient audience (subscribers) to be profitable. The broadcaster with a single channel by and large does this with bland, average, lowest-common-denominator programming. For the cable operator the task is more complicated since it must determine the right mix of programming and prices to offer in various options. Still, consumer demand will produce substantial similarity among the services offered regardless of who the cable operator is.[237] As with any medium of information and entertainment there is room for diversity but, mainly, only at the margins. It is hard to imagine a coherent, let alone conclusive, argument that telco entry into cable will so distort the industry as to produce a uniformly deleterious marginal effect, or even that such a hypothetical effect would be of any consequence.

At any rate, the first amendment clearly precludes any governmental attempt to engineer the mass media for such content-based diversity. As the Court repeatedly stresses in a variety of contexts, "the concept that the government may restrict the speech of some elements of our society in order to enhance the relative voice of others is wholly foreign to the First Amendment."[238] Even more certainly, such distinctions cannot be made based on the identity of the speaker or the interests the speaker might represent.[239]

Ultimately one's view of the appropriateness of government "tinkering" with the mass media marketplace, as in the telco ban, depends on a reading of the first amendment as a prohibition on such government involvement, "Congress shall make no law," or on a belief that the amendment creates an affirmative power or obligation for the government to structure such markets to achieve perceived underlying goals.[240] First amendment free-

---

[237] *See Shurberg Broadcasting*, 876 F.2d at 923 (Silberman, J.) ("[I]t is not at all apparent why a station owner, be she minority or nonminority, would make programming decisions according to her personal tastes rather than in response to the demands of the marketplace.").

[238] Buckley v. Valeo, 424 U.S. 1, 48-49 (1976). *See* First Nat'l Bank of Boston v. Bellotti, 435 U.S. 765, 790-91 (1978); Pacific Gas & Elec. Co. v. Public Util. Comm'n of California, 475 U.S. 1, 14 (1986).

[239] *Bellotti*, 435 U.S. at 784; *Pacific Gas*, 475 U.S. at 15.

[240] *See* CBS, Inc. v. Democratic Nat'l Comm., 412 U.S. 94, 145 (Stewart, J., concurring) in which Justice Stewart warned of the "dangers that beset us when we lose sight of the First Amendment itself, and march forth in blind pursuit of its 'values.' " Even if one adopts the latter point of view, one also would have to believe the government can outperform the market in this regard, a dubious proposition at best. *See* Austin v. Michigan Chamber of Commerce, 110 S. Ct. 1391, 1415-16 (1990) (Scalia, J., dissenting) (discussing the appropriate first amendment roles of government and private institutions in managing the arena of public debate).

doms do create dangers including, perhaps, influence by certain interests over particular media. By and large, however, they are dangers contemplated by the framers of the first amendment and left to the people to resolve without the heavy hand of government intervention, an even greater danger.[241]

V. Technological Benefits From Telco Entry

The first amendment arguments for telephone companies' right to enter the cable market stand alone. They do not depend on an affirmative demonstration of the public benefits to be gained. Such benefits, however, already inhere in the actual or potential competition the telcos will represent, as well as the opportunities for greater diversity in the marketplace of ideas they may provide. It is also useful to consider briefly the technological developments telco entry may stimulate, resulting in new and better products and services.

The FCC has a statutory mandate to promote technological developments in the communications field.[242] And even Judge Greene emphatically acknowledged both the tremendous benefits from broad development of information services[243] and the practical necessity of BOC participation in creating the transmission infrastructure for such services.[244] The Judge focused on what he termed the "videotex industry," referring to a wide variety of easy-to-use interactive data services that he described in

---

241 *See Bellotti*, 435 U.S. at 791-92; Virginia State Bd. of Pharmacy v. Virginia Citizens Consumer Council, Inc., 425 U.S. 748, 770 (1976). *See also supra* note 144. Consider the difficulty the media in England is having with a supposedly conservative government in the absence of a first amendment. *See, e.g.*, Atlas, *Thatcher Puts A Lid On: Censorship In Britain*, N.Y. Times, Mar. 5, 1989, (Magazine) at 36.

242 *See* 47 U.S.C. § 218 (1982) (FCC should act so that "the benefits of new inventions and developments may be made available to the people of the United States."); 47 U.S.C. § 303(g) (1982) (FCC should "generally encourage the larger and more effective use of radio in the public interest.").

243 United States v. Western Elec. Co., 714 F. Supp. 1, *amendment and clarification denied*, 1988-1 Trade Cas. (CCH) ¶ 68,094 (D.D.C. 1988). Judge Greene wrote that

> If consumer-oriented videotex services were made available on a large scale, the economic and social welfare of the American people could be substantially advanced. It is difficult to overestimate the significance of this potential. Information services . . . can come in an amazing scope and variety. If developed to their full potential, these services could in some ways revolutionize American intellectual, social, cultural, and economic life.

Western Elec., 714 F. Supp. at 5-6 (footnote omitted).

244 *Id.* at 6. Judge Greene, however, felt that BOC participation in the provision of information content was unnecessary and would pose the danger of anticompetitive activity. *Id.* at 5-6; United States v. Western Elec. Co., 673 F. Supp. 525, 595 (D.D.C. 1987). For Judge Greene, such an infrastructure consists "primarily of various low-level gateway functions that do not involve control of or interaction with information content." *Id.* at 592. *See* United States v. Western Elec. Co., 714 F. Supp. 1, 11-17, *amendment and clarification denied*, 1988-1 Trade Cas. (CCH) ¶ 68,094 (D.D.C. 1988).

some detail.[245] Indeed, although noting that several efforts to provide videotex services in this country have failed,[246] the Judge looked to Teletel, the French videotex system, as one possible model for a "coherent information services network," but one that soon may be eclipsed.[247]

In fact, the brave, new, inevitable information world may well surpass whatever we dream of today. The marriage of computing capability and electronic communications holds limitless potential.[248] The head of MIT's Media Lab, for example, predicts that in twenty years the average television set will have the computing power of today's Cray supercomputer.[249]

The key, most likely, is the development of a fiber-optic system whose greatly expanded capacity and increased speed[250] will allow for broadband, integrated services digital networks ("B-ISDN"), for both business and residential use. This "envisions a universal and ubiquitous system designed to provide efficient broadband interconnection for all possible communication services," in particular integrating voice, data and video on a single system.[251] So far ISDN has been rather limited, encompassing only narrowband activities;[252] but telephone companies are ex-

---

245 *Western Elec.*, 714 F. Supp. at 5-7. Quoting the HUBER REPORT, Judge Greene explained that "videotex arranges information in a text or graphic format on a video display with user input through a keyboard." *Id.* at 5 n.12. This is distinguished from "audiotex" which "allows consumer access to information through a regular telephone line and the use of a touchtone keypad." *Id.* at 13 n.44. The court, however, did not distinguish between the two in allowing BOC involvement in the transmission of information services. *Id.* at 13.

246 *Western Elec.*, 673 F. Supp. 525, 587 (D.D.C. 1987). The telcos have not yet had much chance to develop it.

247 *Western Elec.*, 714 F. Supp. at 7-8; *id.*, 673 F. Supp. at 588-89. *See generally* Wright, *supra* note 1, at 83-94.

248 *See generally* S. BRAND, THE MEDIA LAB: INVENTING THE FUTURE AT MIT (1987) [hereinafter BRAND]; Baer, *New Communications Technologies and Services*, in 2 NEW DIRECTORS IN TELECOMMUNICATIONS POLICY 139 (P. Newberg ed. 1989) [hereinafter Baer].

249 BRAND, *supra* note 248, at 77-78 ("It will not be receiving pictures. It will be receiving data, and *it* makes the pictures").

250 *See* Pepper, *supra* note 75, at 6.

251 U.S. Congress, Office of Technology Assessment, *Critical Connections: Communication for the Future*, OTA-CIT-407 (U.S. Gov't Printing Office, Jan. 1990) at 50 [hereinafter *Critical Connections*]. Digitalization is "the process of transforming 'analog' messages (a spoken word, a picture, a letter) into signals made up of discrete pulses that can be transmitted, processed and stored electronically." *Id.* at 49. Not only is transmitting in digital form far more efficient and accurate, but in such form "audio, video, and textual messages can be combined and recombined, allowing information to be integrated in a way that previously was impossible." *Id.* at 49-50. This can lead to tremendous multimedia applications in videotex and elsewhere. *Id.* at 52-53. *See also* Frenkel, *HDTV and the Computer Industry*, 32 COMMUNICATIONS OF THE ACM, 1301, 1307-08 (1989) (describing the virtues of digital television) [hereinafter Frenkel].

252 The upper limit for standard copper cable ISDN lines is to provide two 64,000 bit-per-second voice channels and one 16,000 bit-per-second data channel. Digital transmission of regular television, however, requires 45 million bits-per-second (HDTV

pected to be in the forefront of developing this technology.[253]

We should allow market forces to promote development of such networks to their maximum extent. Even so, legitimate questions arise relevant to telco entry into the cable market.[254] For example, unlike business and other large users, it is not clear what residential services besides entertainment video will require broadband capacity.[255] Such capacity may be linked to advanced television technologies such as high definition television (HDTV), representing "the convergence of the television, computer, and telephone industries."[256] As one visionary describes a digital, interactive[257] world: "your workstation will probably become a large screen on a wall that is your port into information space, whether from telecomputing if you stay at home and work, or whether for entertainment."[258] The GTE experiment in Cerritos may provide useful information on what is currently possible and feasible, from both a technological and economic perspective, with certain integrated, broadband functions including video-on-demand.[259]

---

needs 150 Mbps). Fiber optic cable may be capable of carrying a trillion bits of information per second. Wright, *supra* note 1, at 91-93. By contrast, humans "are analog beasts . . . our brains can absorb only 50 bits per second." *Id.* at 93 (quoting AT&T vice president of customer relations).

253 *Critical Connections*, *supra* note 251, at 51. *See, e.g.*, Dawson, *With Sonet, Telcos Move Much Closer to Achieving BISDN and Video Dial Tone*, CABLEVISION, Nov. 20, 1989, at 38. Baer, *supra* note 248, at 141 ("Switched broadband ISDN services to business and homes remain a telephone company vision for the late 1990s or beyond.").

254 *See* Pepper, *supra* note 75, at 38. The cost-effectiveness of bringing fiber optics to the home also is a major uncertainty. *Id.* at 6-11.

255 *Id.* at 13-14. Broadband networks for large users will be necessary for "high speed data, video conferencing, high speed document transfer, and new applications using computer aided design and manufacturing, artificial intelligence, and graphic imaging." *Id.* at 14 n.20.

256 Frenkel, *supra* note 251, at 1303. Development of HDTV may have a significant impact on the United States semiconductor industry. *Id.* at 1304-05. More generally, a digital fiber optic infrastructure could "combine technologies in which the United States still has the leading edge . . . [and be] a longer term solution to retaining technological leadership." *Id.* at 1309. *See also U.S. Counts On Computer Edge in the Race For Advanced TV*, N.Y. Times, Nov. 28, 1989, at B5, col. 6 [hereinafter *U.S. Counts*].

257 The network probably will be a switched one and allow asymmetric two-way transmission. Pepper, *supra* note 75, at 5.

258 Frenkel, *supra* note 251, at 1308; *U.S. Counts*, *supra* note 256, at B8 ("Smart TV's . . . could automatically scan the digital airwaves for shows of interest, recording them when certain key words were present"). *See also* Riley and Berns, *Legal Issues, Judicial Limitations In Regard To "Switchable Video,"* N.Y.L.J., Nov. 3, 1989, at 5, col. 1.

> A switchable fiber system would be capable of carrying more than entertainment. The same line could simultaneously carry multiple picturephone conversations, numerical data for banking and energy management, and instantaneous FAX signals. The morning newspaper could be FAXed in less than a second, and shopping at home from an interactive video catalogue could become a reality.

Id.

259 General Tel. Co. of California, 4 F.C.C. Rcd. 5693, 5699-5700 (1989), *appeal dock-*

Continuation of the telco ban on entry into the cable market thus could have the serious detrimental effect of inhibiting, if not precluding, development of the residential network with all its attendant benefits. On the other hand, perhaps telco entry is not really necessary to spur cable industry development of its own fiber-optic network at a reasonable pace. The cable industry has its own incentives for near-term exploitation of fiber-optics.[260] Some also might question whether the telcos have to provide video programming in order for them to develop switched, fiber broadband networks.[261] Uncertainties abound, which is only to be expected since "we are not good at forecasting the demand for new telecommunications services."[262] We can expect, however, that "[f]uture services requiring large bandwidths and very high transmission rates are likely to develop as advanced information services employing expert systems and artificial intelligence develop."[263]

The point, therefore, is that the telcos have made their own determinations and most are anxious to expand into cable.[264] Some already are gaining cable experience in foreign markets.[265] They have the right to enter and such entry may very well make tremendous contributions to our telecommunications and infor-

---

eted sub nom. National Cable Television Ass'n v. FCC, No. 89-1517 (D.C. Cir. Aug. 2, 1989). GTE proposes to offer "near" video-on-demand on its coaxial cable, enabling customers to choose a program at intervals of 15-30 minutes using up to 30 channels. "Pure" video-on-demand service, using the full bandwidth of an optical fiber facility, can offer point-to-point distribution and telemetric control of programming to particular customers, a far greater service capacity. *Id.* *See GTE Test Offers View Of Video Future*, Wall St. J., Dec. 29, 1988, at B1, col. 3; *GTE Details Fiber Plans For Cerritos*, BROADCASTING, June 27, 1988, at 66.

260 *See Cable Sees A Shortcut The Telcos Can't Follow*, CABLEVISION, Aug. 15, 1988, at 39. *See also* Dawson, *Clearing The Fog Around Fiber*, CABLEVISION, Feb. 29, 1988, at 14, 16.

> [M]uch time will elapse before telcos are ready for video in the framework of their ISDN approach, and, in the meantime, the cable industry will be exploring the technological options fully in the context of perceivable and exploitable market demand for new services and in light of direct advantages in signal quality, operations savings and other factors that flow from use of fiber.

Id.

261 *See* Pepper, *supra* note 75, at 18-20, 72-73. In an analogous circumstance, however, the 1970 Sloan Commission on Cable concluded that a common carrier system would not provide sufficient economic incentive for the cable industry's development. *See* I. POOL, TECHNOLOGIES OF FREEDOM 169 (1983).

262 Elton, *Integrated Broadband Networks: Balancing The Risks*, 7 CABLE T.V. & NEW MEDIA 1 (Oct. 1989).

263 Pepper, *supra* note 75, at 14. The author goes on to note that "[a]s with many new technological advances, broadband networks will lead to applications and services unknown before increased speed and capacity make those new services possible." *Id.* at 15.

264 *See* Amparano, *Phone Firms Battle Cable-TV Operators Over Providing Fiber-Optic Home Links*, Wall St. J., Sept. 9, 1988, at 23, col. 3.

265 *See* Sim, *The Baby Bells Scramble For Europe*, N.Y. Times, Dec. 10, 1989, § 3, at 1, col. 3; *US West And International Cable*, BROADCASTING, Aug. 14, 1989, at 66.

mation industries. The artificial, regulatory barriers to entry should be removed.

VI. Conclusion

In the debate over telco entry into cable we should put the first amendment back where it belongs — into the position of primary importance. It is both necessary and appropriate that we begin from the premise that telephone companies enjoy the same first amendment right to develop, own and operate cable systems as any other individual or entity. Nothing resulting from their corporate nature, common carrier status, other existing media cross-ownership restrictions, or applicable antitrust principles affects this conclusion. To the contrary, the ban operates as a prior restraint on speech. A heavy presumption therefore favors its elimination and mandates allowing entry.

Moreover, this constitutional mandate accords with the substantial benefits likely from telco entry. The telephone companies will provide much needed economic competition to the cable industry. This is far preferable, from both a marketplace and constitutional perspective, than re-regulation by Congress,[266] particularly since the FCC believes it can monitor and control anticompetitive excesses by the telcos. Moreover, we can expect telco entry to stimulate rather than restrict diversity in the marketplace of ideas, whatever that rather ambiguous concept may mean. This is especially likely if telco entry furthers the developing links between communications and computer technologies leading to greatly expanded capacity and a wealth of new products and services.

One cannot be certain that the FCC's safeguards and regula-

---

266 There is considerable irony in the cable industry's shortsighted opposition to telco entry. *See, e.g.*, *The Evolution Of Cable's Anti-Telco Strategy*, Broadcasting, Mar. 6, 1989, at 30. For some time, cable companies properly have been asserting their own entitlement to full first amendment status. *See, e.g.*, Chicago Cable Communication v. Chicago Cable Comm'n, 879 F.2d 1540 (7th Cir. 1989), *cert. denied*, 110 S. Ct. 839 (1990) (constitutional challenge to requirements for local origination programming); Pacific West Cable Co. v. Sacramento, 672 F. Supp. 1322 (E.D. Cal. 1987) (city's single franchising policy violates first amendment); *supra* note 120. They should realize that in opposing first amendment rights of the telcos to enter cable they are acting analogously to broadcasters' efforts in the must-carry dispute to deny cable operators first amendment freedom. *See* Quincy Cable TV, Inc. v. FCC, 768 F.2d 1434, 1452 (D.C. Cir. 1985), *cert. denied*, 476 U.S. 1169 (1986); Century Communications Corp. v. FCC, 835 F.2d 292, 295 (D.C. Cir. 1987), *cert denied*, 108 S. Ct. 2014 (1988). Simultaneously the cable industry, by trying to exclude market competition, is reinforcing the need for its re-regulation by Congress, thereby undoing its hard-won freedom. One day, perhaps, *all* the electronic media will realize their symbiotic relationship with one another and that the only way for any of them to achieve true first amendment parity with the print media is for each to support full first amendment rights for all others. *See generally* Winer, *The Signal Cable Sends*, *supra* note 56.

tory approach will be adequate to curb the telcos' anticompetitive tendencies. Nor can one predict the benefits that actually will accrue from telco entry. But such risk and uncertainty are inherent in first amendment freedoms. Equally inherent in the first amendment is the principle that needs repeated emphasis: government must restrain itself from the constant temptation to engineer the "best" media marketplace. That is why the appropriate premise is so important here — namely, that telephone companies have first amendment rights too.

AN ANTITRUST PARADOX FOR THE 1990s: REVISITING THE ROLE OF THE FIRST AMENDMENT IN CABLE TELEVISION*

GLENN B. MANISHIN**

I. INTRODUCTION

More than a decade ago, then-professor Robert Bork authored the influential book *The Antitrust Paradox*,[1] arguing that courts had interpreted and applied the antitrust laws in ways which conflicted with economic efficiency. Bork's conservative precepts set the tone for antitrust doctrine throughout the 1980's, and may change forever the role of antitrust in the United States system of business regulation. Yet, while American media corporations have benefited greatly from the dominance of Bork's "Chicago School" of antitrust law,[2] they have now created a new, and quite different, sort of antitrust paradox. Applying the first amendment as a shield against governmental regulation, as well as a sword to attack restrictions on their right to enter new markets, cable television and telephone companies have been using the free speech principles of the Constitution to do the work the antitrust laws did in pre-Bork times.

The "antitrust paradox" of the 1990s is that these first amendment arguments—which lie at the heart of a growing public debate about the appropriate communications market structure for the next several decades—are really antitrust issues masquerading in constitutional clothes. What both the cable television and local telephone industries seek to achieve is not the advancement of any marketplace of ideas, but rather the constitutional elimination of restraints on their commercial activities in the video distribution market. Instead of basing regulatory and legislative decisions on the competitive and public policy issues presented by their proposals—for instance, whether cable televi-

* Copyright © 1990 by Glenn B. Manishin.

** Partner, Blumenfeld & Cohen, Washington, D.C.; B.A., 1977, Brandeis University; J.D., 1981, Columbia Law School. Mr. Manishin specializes in telecommunications and antitrust. He served with the Justice Department's Antitrust Division, 1982 through 1985, where he was the principal author of the Department's proposals for implementing the Cable Communications Policy Act of 1984. This Article is adapted from Mr. Manishin's presentation at a March 1990 Cardozo School of Law Symposium, "Cable Television: The Race to Reregulate."

1 R. BORK, THE ANTITRUST PARADOX (1978).

2 *See* Gerhart, *The Supreme Court and Antitrust Analysis: The (Near) Triumph of the Chicago School*, 1982 SUP. CT. REV. 319 (1983); Posner, *The Chicago School of Antitrust Analysis*, 127 U. PA. L. REV. 925 (1979).

sion systems should be limited in the prices they can charge consumers, or whether local telephone companies should be able to impose on ratepayers the costs of constructing cable television facilities—each of these industries asserts that the first amendment overrides proposed statutory restraints on the scope or conduct of their businesses.

The sophisticated and subtle constitutional constructs assembled in support of these efforts filled much of a recent Symposium issue of the *Cardozo Arts & Entertainment Law Journal*, where the constitutional case was framed by both cable and telephone company interests.[3] Scrutinizing the logic of these quasi-constitutional arguments, however, suggests that the first amendment, as reframed by these adversarial industries, is being misapplied. The real issues facing the courts and Congress are not who can "speak," but rather the competitive structure of the cable television market: the number of systems and programmers from which consumers can choose, the degree to which available alternatives in the market can achieve the most efficient and lowest-cost service possible, and the need for governmental regulation to prevent and redress the acquisition and use of monopoly power.

These are archetypal antitrust issues, qualitatively different from (although analogous to) the "diversity" considerations underlying first amendment precedent.[4] That the Supreme Court has properly ruled that regulators may not prohibit bill inserts[5] or promotional advertising by electric utilities,[6] however, says nothing about whether cable systems should be subject to rate regulation or, more precisely, whether the Constitution dictates the choice between competition and regulation. In making this leap, the logic used by first amendment advocates breaks down,

---

[3] *See* Robinowitz, *Cable Television: Proposals for Reregulation and the First Amendment*, 8 CARDOZO ARTS & ENT. L.J. 309 (1990) [hereinafter Robinowitz]; Winer, *Telephone Companies Have First Amendment Rights Too: The Constitutional Case for Entry into Cable*, 8 CARDOZO ARTS & ENT. L.J. 257 (1990) [hereinafter Winer].

[4] *See* Metro Broadcasting, Inc. v. FCC, 110 S. Ct. 2997 (1990); Shurberg Broadcasting, Inc. v. FCC, 876 F.2d 902 (D.C. Cir. 1989); *see also Federal Communications Commission: Cable Television Policies, Recommendations, and Initiatives Before the Subcomm. on Communications of the Senate Comm. on Commerce, Science, and Transportation* 1-2 (Nov. 17, 1989) (statement of Alfred C. Sikes, Chairman, Federal Communications Commission) ("For more than half a century, American mass media policies have been soundly grounded on competitive principles—and a belief that those actions which foster effective economic rivalry also yield a critical added dividend: namely, diversity in what Mr. Justice Holmes 70 years ago described as the 'free trade in ideas.' ") (footnote omitted).

[5] Consolidated Edison Co. v. Public Serv. Comm'n, 447 U.S. 530 (1980). *See* Winer, *supra* note 3, at 274-75.

[6] Central Hudson Gas & Elec. Corp. v. Public Serv. Comm'n, 447 U.S. 557 (1980). *See* Winer, *supra* note 3, at 274-75.

at least in part—as this Article suggests—because there is no real first amendment question in the first instance.

II. Shelf Space or Soap Boxes?

Throughout the first nine months of 1990, there raged in the halls of Congress a fierce debate in which both sides ritualistically wrapped their claims in the hallowed mantle of the first amendment. Cable television companies, flush with recent victories in the courts affirming constitutional protection against municipal franchise requirements,[7] threatened to undermine fast-moving efforts to regulate cable pricing by tying up proposed legislation in the knot of constitutional litigation.[8] Telephone companies, having just recently lost a thirty-year long battle in the antitrust courts to maintain the old Bell System monopoly,[9] are increasingly shrill about their purported first amendment right to enter unregulated (and highly profitable) communications markets. Ironically, but perhaps not unexpectedly, both advocates denigrate the competitive status—and first amendment basis—of the other's industry.[10]

Telephone companies ("telcos") and cable companies also contend that each alone can bring modern communications technologies (in this instance, fiber optic cable) to the curbs and homes of American consumers.[11] This intensely acrimonious debate illustrates the tenuous link between today's technologies for delivering communications and the legal status of those technol-

---

[7] *See, e.g.*, Pacific W. Cable Co. v. City of Sacramento, 798 F.2d 353 (9th Cir. 1986); Tele-Communications of Key West, Inc. v. United States, 757 F.2d 1330 (D.C. Cir. 1985); Group W. Cable, Inc. v. City of Santa Cruz, 669 F. Supp. 954 (N.D. Cal. 1987); Century Fed., Inc. v. City of Palo Alto, 579 F. Supp. 1553 (N.D. Cal. 1984), *later proceeding*, 648 F. Supp. 1465 (N.D. Cal. 1986), *appeal dismissed*, 484 U.S. 1053 (1988); Carlson v. Village of Union City, 601 F. Supp. 801 (W.D. Mich. 1985).

[8] *See* Kaplan, *Time Warner's Dynamic Duo: Bork and Tribe Tapped to Fight Cable Regulation*, Legal Times, May 7, 1990, at 2, col. 4 (" 'If legislation gets enacted and it's just horrendous, we would be ready to challenge it, perhaps on the First Amendment grounds.' ") (quoting Michael Hammer, Director of Communications Policy in Time Warner's Washington office); *House Approves Reins on Cable TV*, Chicago Tribune, Sept. 11, 1990, § 1, at 3, col. 4 (Office of Management and Budget would recommend a veto of cable reregulation legislation on first amendment grounds).

[9] *See* United States v. AT&T, 552 F. Supp. 131 (D.D.C. 1982), *aff'd mem. sub nom.* Maryland v. United States, 460 U.S. 1001 (1983).

[10] *See* Aversa, *Groups Debate Video Role in Growing Broadband Net*, Multichannel News, Apr. 16, 1990, at 9, col. 1.

[11] *See, e.g.*, Chiddix, *Don't Let Overreaction Slow Tech Advances*, Multichannel News, Apr. 16, 1990, at 51, col. 2 ("It is clear the cable industry will bring the benefits of fiber to the American public long before the telcos—MUCH LONGER."); Rep. R. Boucher, Cable Competition vs. Cable Regulation: White Paper on Telecommunications Policy 1 (1990) ("[T]elephone company entry into the market for cable services presents the best opportunity for such competition and is a positive step towards improving our telecommunications infrastructure.").

ogies. As America moves steadily into the technologically uncharted terrain of the so-called "Information Age,"[12] our notions of the proper relationship between the law and the commercial providers of the nation's information infrastructure become increasingly cloudy. Newspapers, magazines, movie studios, television networks, cable systems, and telephone companies, among others, all contribute to the wealth of information available to citizens. Yet the owners of these media vary in many ways, from the means of delivering communications, to the availability of governmental licenses for use of the airwaves and the streets, to their ability to control or exclude competition in the marketplace. While these differences should be central to the discussion of whether the first amendment undermines regulatory constraints on communications firms in these markets, they have not been, and the policy debate has suffered accordingly.

Cable television's vision of the first amendment posits that local cable system operators are the 20th Century equivalent of the pamphleteers and newspapers of the 18th and 19th Centuries. Thus, cable systems have convinced a number of federal courts that they are engaged in constitutionally protected "editorial" functions, precluding franchise limitations on which (and how many) cable firms can compete in a given market.[13] The problem is that to reach this conclusion, one must not only disregard the roots of the first amendment in the television industry, but also apply classical antitrust concepts to resolve purported freedom of speech issues.

Regulation of the broadcast television market, including the recently repealed "fairness doctrine" for broadcast television stations,[14] has long been premised on the notion of physical scarcity. Under this "scarcity" rationale, restrictions on the communications activities of licensees—from the license requirement itself to limits on station ownership to restrictions on network programming production—are justified by the need to preserve diversity in expression for all listeners in light of the limited resource of the electromagnetic spectrum in which over-

---

12 *See* United States v. Western Elec. Co., 673 F. Supp. 525, 590 (D.D.C. 1987), *aff'd in part, rev'd in part*, 900 F.2d 283 (D.C. Cir. 1990).

13 *See supra* note 7.

14 Syracuse Peace Council v. Television Station WTVH, 2 F.C.C. Rcd. 5043 (1987), *reconsideration denied*, 3 F.C.C. Rcd. 2035 (1988), *aff'd*, 867 F.2d 654 (D.C. Cir. 1989), *cert. denied*, 110 S. Ct. 717 (1990). *See also* Meredith Corp. v. FCC, 809 F.2d 863 (D.C. Cir. 1987), *cert. denied*, 110 S. Ct. 717 (1990); Telecommunications Research & Action Center v. FCC, 801 F.2d 501 (D.C. Cir. 1986), *cert. denied*, 482 U.S. 919 (1987).

the-air communications are broadcast.[15] In the cases raising first amendment questions in regulation of cable television systems, however, this concept of physical scarcity has been subtly transformed into one of "economic scarcity."[16] Instead of using limited airwave space as the justification for regulation, municipal franchisors have used the monopoly status of most cable systems as the basis for restricting market entry. The theory is that given the extraordinary costs of wiring communities with coaxial cable, local cable markets are "natural monopolies" in which competition is not sustainable, so municipal regulation of the cable provider is a constitutionally permissible substitute for market competition.[17]

With this twist, the first amendment debate becomes driven not by considerations of communications diversity and expressive freedom, the traditional values protected by the constitutional guarantees of speech and press freedom, but rather by paradigmatic (indeed, Borkean) antitrust concerns such as market structure, economics, and monopoly power. While the first amendment has often been defended with the "marketplace of ideas" metaphor,[18] the actual marketplace operations of first amendment speakers—in areas including corporate acquisitions and mergers, product distribution, and anticompetitive or exclusionary practices—have always been addressed under the antitrust laws.[19] The new learning pressed by the cable industry in its first amendment cases, namely that the Constitution prohibits franchise regulation limiting competitive entry in cable markets, thus appears fundamentally more akin to the Sherman Antitrust

---

[15] Red Lion Broadcasting Co. v. FCC, 395 U.S. 367 (1969). *See also* FCC v. League of Women Voters, 468 U.S. 364, 376-77 (1984).

[16] Preferred Communications, Inc. v. City of Los Angeles, 754 F.2d 1396 (9th Cir. 1985), *aff'd*, 476 U.S. 488 (1986).

[17] *See, e.g.*, Central Telecommunications, Inc. v. TCI Cablevision, Inc., 800 F.2d 711 (8th Cir. 1986), *cert. denied*, 480 U.S. 910 (1987); Community Communications Co. v. City of Boulder, 660 F.2d 1370 (10th Cir. 1981), *cert. dismissed*, 456 U.S. 1001 (1982).

[18] *E.g.*, Anderson v. Celebrezze, 460 U.S. 780, 794 (1983); Abrams v. United States, 250 U.S. 616, 630 (1919) (Holmes, J., dissenting).

[19] *See* Associated Press Co. v. United States, 326 U.S. 1 (1945) (antitrust laws applied to require newspaper wire service to disseminate stories to competitors of members); National Broadcasting Co. v. United States, 319 U.S. 190 (1943) (limitations imposed by the FCC on activities and stations' ownership of broadcast television networks permissible); United Video, Inc. v. FCC, 890 F.2d 1173 (D.C. Cir. 1989) (affirming "syndicated exclusivity" rules which would enable broadcast stations with exclusive rights to a syndicated program to forbid any cable television station from importing that program into the local broadcast area from a distant station); United States v. Columbia Pictures Indus., Inc., 507 F. Supp. 412 (S.D.N.Y. 1980) (movie studio joint venture into pay cable television market designed to be prime time showcase for exhibition of feature films prohibited by antitrust laws).

Act's prohibition of "monopolization"[20] and the Clayton Act's safeguard against mergers which "may substantially lessen competition"[21] than the artistic and political communications interests James Madison had in mind in 1798.[22]

In many ways, cable systems simply are not engaged in activities of significant first amendment value. Unlike cable *programmers* (Turner Broadcasting, Home Box Office, Music Television, etc.), cable *systems* by and large produce little or no programming and perform little or no expression of their own. Rather, cable systems serve as the television supermarkets of the 1990s, making "shelf space" decisions for communications developed, produced and marketed by others. Today's cable systems act more like grocers than speakers. In small systems (twelve to thirty-six channels), the system operator must allocate his channels among the programming services available, while in large systems (as many as 112 or 128 channels) the operator scrambles to find product to fill his shelves, frequently settling for filler material such as multiple channels of teletext services and community bulletin boards.

The "shelf space" activities of cable systems are hardly different from the decisions of local grocers as to which soup cans to stock in their stores, and at the same time are markedly different from the editorializing and reporting functions of newspapers and magazines and the entertainment-production functions of movie studios, television networks, and even television stations.[23] The transmission of cable programming over local cable

---

20 Section 2 of the Sherman Act makes it unlawful to monopolize, attempt to monopolize or conspire to monopolize any market. 15 U.S.C. § 2 (1988).

21 Section 7 of the Clayton Act makes unlawful mergers and acquisitions the effect of which may be to substantially lessen competition or tend to create a monopoly in any market. 15 U.S.C. § 12 (1988).

22 Since cable systems also require easements and other uses of the public streets, municipal police power supports at least some limitations on entry and market conduct notwithstanding any first amendment protection cable systems may enjoy. *See* Gannett Satellite Information Network v. Metropolitan Transp. Auth., 745 F.2d 767 (2d Cir. 1984) (upholding licensing fee imposed on newspaper racks in public train stations on the ground that the fees were content-neutral); Erie Telecommunications, Inc. v. City of Erie, 659 F. Supp. 580 (W.D. Pa. 1987), *aff'd on narrower grounds*, 853 F.2d 1084 (3rd Cir. 1988) (cable systems may constitutionally be assessed franchise fee for commercial use of public rights of way). The suggestion that rate regulation of monopoly cable systems would contravene the first amendment is accordingly specious. *See* Robinowitz, *supra* note 3, at 317-24. Ironically, proponents of this view must rely on the antitrust issue of natural monopoly in arguing that the governmental interest supporting price restrictions is constitutionally insufficient. *Id.* at 321-23.

23 Both Robinowitz and Winer rely on a series of lower federal court decisions which suggest that the channel carriage decisions of cable system operators are a constitutionally cognizable exercise of "editorial discretion." Winer, *supra* note 3, at 275; Robinowitz, *supra* note 3, at 313-14. Most of the cases have arisen in situations where the first amendment is being used to eliminate barriers to video competition by invalidating mu-

distribution facilities is not really an editorial or communications content activity, but a commercial one. At the very least, it is far removed from the core political, social and artistic values protected by the first amendment. That the "cans" stocked by cable systems contain communications—and sometimes even ideas—makes little difference, since the regulations challenged on first amendment grounds involve content-neutral economic regulation, such as pricing and distribution practices, and generally do not mandate or preclude any specific types of programming carriage.[24] Even where regulations mandate certain types of programming, as in the "must carry" requirements[25] that cable systems include local broadcast stations in channel line-up, the first amendment is not (or should not be) a barrier to governmental action designed to protect the communication rights of *listeners* and the ability of *others* to speak.[26] Indeed, as it becomes increasingly clear that cable systems exercise "bottleneck" or "gateway" power[27] over which television services will be delivered to local consumers, asserting that the first amendment encompasses an "editorial" right to withhold some of those services

---

nicipal franchising restrictions against cable entry. *See supra* notes 14-17 and accompanying text. By stretching the concept of "editorializing" to extend the first amendment into these competitive issues, courts trivialize the constitutional status of the first amendment "speaker." Indeed, as Robinowitz concedes, the courts did not extend first amendment protections to cable systems where they simply retransmitted broadcast television stations, although the cable operators did (and still do) "select" which stations to carry on their systems. Robinowitz, *supra* note 3, at 313. Under this approach, however, first amendment protection turns on *where the video programming comes from*, a matter that is plainly not of constitutional relevance.

24 Incidental regulation of expressive activity is considered content-neutral where it is "*justified* without reference to the content of the regulated speech." Ward v. Rock Against Racism, 109 S. Ct. 2746, 2754 (1989) (quoting Clark v. Community for Creative Non-Violence, 468 U.S. 288, 293 (1984)) (emphasis in original). Thus, for instance, arguments that regulation of cable system pricing would violate the first amendment are specious, because they are wholly unrelated to the content of the asserted first amendment conduct. *See* Robinowitz, *supra* note 3, at 319-20. In response to arguments that cable regulation would "discriminate" in favor of competing technologies, *id.*, one need only observe that rate regulation of cable systems has been justified on the ground that cable systems hold monopoly power because these purported "competitors" do not provide effective competition to cable systems.

25 Quincy Cable TV, Inc. v. FCC, 768 F.2d 1434 (D.C. Cir. 1985), *cert. denied*, 476 U.S. 1169 (1986); Century Communications Corp. v. FCC, 835 F.2d 292 (D.C. Cir. 1987), *cert. denied*, 486 U.S. 1032 (1988).

26 "[T]here is no 'unabridgeable First Amendment right to broadcast comparable to the right of every individual to speak, write, or publish.' " FCC v. National Citizens Comm. for Broadcasting, 436 U.S. 775, 799 (1978) (quoting Red Lion Broadcasting Co. v. FCC, 395 U.S. 367, 388 (1969)). Thus, to the extent that regulation of cable systems prevents the abuse of cable market power and the monopolization of the marketplace of ideas, denying listeners their right to the speech of others, first amendment and antitrust values parallel each other. Red Lion Broadcasting Co. v. FCC, 395 U.S. 367, 390 (1969).

27 Complaint at 16, Viacom International v. Time Inc., No. 89 Civ. 3139 (S.D.N.Y. filed May 9, 1989).

from consumers loses much of its policy legitimacy.[28]

III. Natural Monopoly and the Marketplace of Ideas

That the cable television first amendment debate is really an antitrust controversy becomes clear when one examines the key question in first amendment challenges to local franchise regulation of cable systems—whether or not the market is a "natural monopoly."[29] The answer to this question depends on the definition and underlying economics of the market, issues that antitrust enforcers and antitrust courts regularly grapple with in monopolization and merger cases.[30] Furthermore, the natural monopoly issues really comprise two questions: Is the market a natural monopoly, and who decides whether it is? The latter question is by far more important in the context of the first amendment debate.

Under the antitrust laws, there is no "natural monopoly" defense to an antitrust violation, and local governments have no license to create monopolies by regulatory fiat.[31] The antitrust laws require that the marketplace itself determine if a market is a natural monopoly; if the market cannot support more than one firm, then only one firm will survive the disciplining process of competition.[32] The cable industry's use of the first amendment to restrict municipalities from limiting entry by means of the franchising process thus implements antitrust values, not free speech interests. These first amendment cases, where the courts

---

[28] New York Citizens Comm. on Cable TV v. Manhattan Cable TV, Inc., 651 F. Supp. 802, 817 (S.D.N.Y. 1986).

[29] As FCC Chairman Alfred Sikes recently explained:

> Competition in the cable or multichannel video marketplace is controversial. Many say it is not possible to have competition because this is a natural monopoly business. . . .
>
> . . . .
>
> The end result of this "natural monopoly" attitude and obstructionist actions has been that many despair of ever seeing competition develop and consequently choose government regulations.

Statement of FCC Chairman Alfred C. Sikes on the Commission's Cable Television Report 1-2 (July 26, 1990). For a somewhat different perspective, see Kinsley, *Remote Control*, New Republic, Apr. 23, 1990, at 4 ("Whether cable needs to be a monopoly or always will be are open questions. Whether it's a monopoly now is indisputable (though the cable lobby preposterously disputes it).").

[30] *E.g.*, Central Telecommunications, Inc. v. TCI Cablevision, Inc., 800 F.2d 711 (8th Cir. 1986), *cert. denied*, 480 U.S. 910 (1987).

[31] *See* Town of Hallie v. City of Eau Claire, 471 U.S. 34 (1985); Community Communications Co. v. City of Boulder, 455 U.S. 40 (1982); *see also* Video Int'l Prod., Inc. v. Warner-Amex Cable Communications, 858 F.2d 1075 (5th Cir. 1988), *cert. denied*, 109 S. Ct. 1955 (1989).

[32] Omega Satellite Prods. Co. v. City of Indianapolis, 694 F.2d 119, 127 (7th Cir. 1982) ("[T]he antitrust laws protect competition not only in, but for, the market—that is, competition to be the firm to enjoy a natural monopoly . . . .").

discussed natural monopoly *only* in the constitutional context, are better considered antitrust cases.[33]

This paradox is not the only one presented by the cable industry in the 1990s. A second paradox is that federal policy toward the question of cable system competition is flawed because it is at war with itself over the question of natural monopoly.[34] Traditionally, the *quid pro quo* for natural monopoly is regulation, and that for competition is antitrust.[35] Where a market is a natural monopoly, *e.g.*, gas and electric distribution, local telephones, etc., regulation seeks to replicate the results of a competitive market. On the other hand, competitive markets are left unregulated, but are protected from becoming monopolies by the antitrust laws.

In cable television, federal policy has brought us the worst of both worlds. In 1985, the Justice Department decided it would not apply the antitrust laws to cable system mergers and acquisitions, on the ground that most cable markets are natural monopolies.[36] That same year, the Federal Communications Commission deregulated most cable systems, on the weak reed that there is "effective competition" for cable systems where viewers have three broadcast television stations from which to choose.[37] This policy conundrum means that cable television is treated as a natural monopoly for antitrust purposes—exempt from the antitrust laws—but as a competitive market for regulatory purposes—exempt from regulation. Instead of either regulation or antitrust, local cable systems are unregulated monopolies, facing neither competition nor regulation.[38]

---

[33] *See supra* notes 7, 16.

[34] *See* Manishin, *Antitrust and Regulation in Cable Television: Federal Policy at War with Itself*, 6 CARDOZO ARTS & ENT. L.J. 75 (1987).

[35] *See, e.g.*, Notice of Inquiry, In re Competition, Rate Deregulation and the Commission's Policies Relating to the Provision of Cable Television Service, 5 F.C.C. Rcd. 362, 369-70 (1989).

[36] The Justice Department, upon terminating a well-publicized investigation into a substantial cable system merger, announced that in light of cable television's "natural monopoly characteristics," it would defer to the decisions of municipal franchising authorities in lieu of applying the Clayton Antitrust Act. *See* 2 C. FERRIS, F. LLOYD & T. CASEY, CABLE TELEVISION LAW, ¶ 24.06[4] (1990) (discussing Justice Department Press Release, Apr. 2, 1985).

[37] Amendment of Parts 1, 63 and 76 of the Commission's Rules to Implement the Cable Communications Policy Act of 1984, 50 Fed. Reg. 18,637 (1985), *reconsidered*, 104 F.C.C.2d 386 (1986), *aff'd in part, rev'd in part sub nom.* ACLU v. FCC, 823 F.2d 1554 (D.C. Cir. 1987), *reconsideration pending*, 5 F.C.C. Rcd. 362 (1989).

[38] Another Symposium author argues that cable television systems are not unregulated monopolies because market definition analysis under the Justice Department's Merger Guidelines "shows conclusively cable's inability to exercise market power." Lloyd, *The FCC's Cable Inquiry: An Opportunity to Reaffirm the Cable Act*, 8 CARDOZO ARTS & ENT. L.J. 337, 347 (1990). Contrary to Lloyd's view that "[c]able is just one provider of

Worse still, the current regulatory climate allows municipalities to decide whether the market is a "natural" monopoly by determining how many, and which, cable systems will serve a market.[39] Not only does this lead to graft and related abuses of the political process, but it also prevents the attainment of any "regulatory dividend." While the 1984 Cable Act[40] and the 1985 Justice Department policy[41] allow a city to sanction a cable monopoly, the FCC's deregulation policy precludes cities from acting as surrogate consumers, namely, using the franchising process to achieve price and service concessions for the benefit of cable subscribers. Judges (and "Chicago School" adherents) Richard Posner and Frank Easterbrook have argued that cable systems should not be treated as public utilities on the ground that the ability of cities to drive a "hard bargain" in the franchising process makes regulation superfluous.[42] Nearly by definition, this defense of unregulated local cable monopolies collapses when, as in the current climate, those municipal bargains are by and large legally unenforceable.[43] This, among other things, is one reason why the second session of the 101st Congress was the scene of considerable rhetoric and legislative rumblings about "reregulation" of the cable industry.

IV. MA BELL "SPEAKS UP"

The final paradox in the confluence of antitrust and first amendment considerations in communications is that the cable industry's efforts to use the first amendment as a shield against governmental regulation have been turned against it by the telcos, which contend that the first amendment makes cross-ownership prohibitions on telephone company entry into the cable

---

entertainment and information services in a robust market," *id.*, the Justice Department recently reaffirmed that "neither conventional television broadcasting nor any of the alternative technologies presently available are close enough substitutes for basic and pay cable television services to prevent the providers of such cable services from exercising some degree of market power." Reply Comments of the United States Dep't of Justice, In re Competition, Rate Deregulation and the Commission's Policies Relating to the Provision of Cable Television Service, MM Docket No. 89-600, at 2 (filed Apr. 2, 1990).

39 *See* 47 U.S.C. § 541 (Supp. V 1987) (a franchising authority may award "1 or more franchises within its jurisdiction").

40 Cable Communications Policy Act of 1984, Pub. L. No. 98-549, 98 Stat. 2779 (codified at 47 U.S.C. §§ 521-559 (Supp. V 1987)).

41 For a discussion of the Justice Department policy, see *supra* note 36.

42 Easterbrook, *Antitrust and the Economics of Federalism*, 26 J.L. & ECON. 23, 32 (1983); Posner, *Natural Monopoly and its Regulation*, 21 STAN. L. REV. 548, 562 (1969).

43 *See* Tribune-United Cable v. Montgomery County, 784 F.2d 1227 (4th Cir. 1986) (upholding cable system's right to unilateral modification of franchise agreements under 1984 Cable Act).

market unconstitutional.[44] As a constitutional matter, the telcos insist (borrowing the cable industry's first amendment refrain) that because cable systems are "speakers," restrictions on their ability to enter the market are invalid.

The telco/cable issue illustrates the extraordinary implications of misapplying first amendment doctrine to market structure issues better suited to antitrust resolution. The telephone company position is essentially that the Constitution permits anyone to enter the cable market, and that since telcos are no different from anyone else, they too have a right to enter and "speak" cable. If the first proposition were correct, of course, there could be no franchise requirement for cable service, no restrictions on entry into the market or prices, and no Cable Act governing regulation of cable systems. More importantly, though, the antitrust history of the telephone industry demonstrates that the telco/cable ban protects competitive interests.[45] From an antitrust perspective, telcos are quite different from other potential cable "speakers."

The real issue in this aspect of the first amendment debate is whether a telephone company enjoys a first amendment right to act as *both* a local telephone monopoly and a cable operator.[46] Telephone companies enjoy a host of government-conferred advantages, including statutory protection of their franchise monopolies, guaranteed financial success and above-market rates-of-return, and access to competitively essential rights-of-way. The *quid pro quo* for these governmental privileges is that telcos are constrained from abusing the competitive advantages they are conferred.[47] Since the history of the telephone industry is

---

44 The 1984 Cable Act and FCC regulations both bar local telephone companies from providing cable television services within their service areas. 47 U.S.C. § 533(b) (Supp. V 1987); 47 C.F.R. § 63.54 (1989). In addition, the United States v. AT&T consent decree bars the Bell Operating Companies from providing "information services," which encompass cable television services, even beyond their service areas. *See* Winer, *supra* note 3, at 269-70.

45 *See, e.g.*, *'Baby Bell' Regulators Struggle for Power*, CONG. Q., Aug. 26, 1989, at 2210-11.

46 Plainly, nothing precludes a telco from relinquishing its local monopoly position in telephone service and, on that basis, qualifying to operate a cable television system under the current cross-ownership structure. Thus, the issue is not whether the Constitution grants a right to "cablespeech," but rather whether it requires government to permit a firm to engage in both the telephone and cable businesses in a single franchised location.

47 *See* § 214 Certificates, 21 F.C.C.2d 307 (1970), *aff'd sub nom.* General Tel. Co. v. United States, 449 F.2d 846 (5th Cir. 1971) (discussing competitive rationales underlying cable/telco cross-ownership rules). Professor Winer suggests that telcos' common carrier status and these government-conferred advantages should not be a factor in the constitutional analysis. Winer, *supra* note 3, at 279. However, as the Supreme Court has recognized, common carriers are different from other first amendment actors: "Unlike

one of continued frustration in regulatory and judicial efforts to control abuse of the telephone companies' local monopoly power,[48] the telco/cable prohibition makes sense as both an antitrust remedy and as a matter of competition policy.[49] So far, the telcos' efforts to use the first amendment to escape the strictures of the *United States v. AT&T* consent decree (which also prohibits telco cable service)[50] have accordingly been rebuffed by the courts.[51]

In this light, the underlying question in the telco/cable dispute is whether *competitive policy* warrants permitting telephone companies to provide cable service. Cable systems, seeking to protect themselves from telco competition, emphasize the antitrust risks attendant to telco entry into competitive markets.[52] Telcos, seeing rising populist fervor against abuses by unregulated cable monopolies as a wedge for advancing their own interests, contend that they are best-suited to bring effective competition to cable systems by combining telephone and cable service in an integrated, 21st Century fiber optic network into the home.[53]

---

common carriers, broadcasters are 'entitled under the First Amendment to exercise "the widest journalistic freedom consistent with their [sic] public [duties]." ' "). FCC v. League of Women Voters, 468 U.S. 364, 378 (1984) (quoting Columbia Broadcasting Sys. v. FCC, 453 U.S. 367, 395 (1981) (quoting Columbia Broadcasting Sys. v. Democratic Nat'l Comm., 412 U.S. 94, 110 (1973))).

48 *See, e.g.*, United States v. Western Elec. Co., 673 F. Supp. 525, 568-69, 571-76 (D.D.C. 1987) (FCC accounting and cost regulations are not a "substantial improvement" over procedures previously found inadequate to deter anticompetitive abuses), *rev'd in part on other grounds*, 900 F.2d 283 (D.C. Cir. 1990).

49 Thus, even if cable system operation raises first amendment values, a telco/cable cross-ownership ban would still pass constitutional muster. It is well-established that an antitrust remedy "may impinge upon [first amendment] rights that would otherwise be constitutionally protected." National Soc'y of Professional Eng'rs v. United States, 435 U.S. 679, 697-98 (1978).

50 For a discussion of the consent decree, see *supra* note 44.

51 United States v. Western Elec. Co., 900 F.2d 283 (D.C. Cir. 1990) (vacating in part decision upholding antitrust decree restrictions against the regional Bell companies' entry into "information services" without addressing or reaching first amendment arguments).

52 For instance, according to the National Cable Television Association, removal of the cross-ownership prohibition "would result in anticompetitive conduct that would adversely affect and radically transform television and the video marketplace." Comments of The National Cable Television Ass'n, In re Telephone Company-Cable Television Cross-Ownership Rules, §§ 63.54-.58, CC Docket No. 87-266, at 7 (filed Dec. 16, 1988).

53 *See* Comments of Pacific Bell and Nevada Bell, In re Telephone Company Cable Television Cross-Ownership Rules, §§ 63.54-.58, CC Docket No. 87-266, at 7 (filed Nov. 2, 1987); *see also* Aversa, *Telcos Call Senate Draft Too Restrictive*, Multichannel News, Apr. 9, 1990, at 40, col. 1. Since telephone companies are not prohibited from constructing these "high tech" fiber optic systems and leasing capacity on them to unaffiliated television programmers (including competitors of incumbent cable system monopolies), 47 C.F.R. § 63.57 (1985), it appears that their desire to enter the cable television service

Once again, these are antitrust and market structure issues, not first amendment questions.[54] Indeed, from a first amendment perspective, the governmental interest in preserving competitive markets would appear to be just the sort of "compelling" or "important" state interest necessary to support narrow, content-neutral restrictions on expression like the telco/cable cross-ownership restriction.[55] Moreover, the ban itself does not prohibit telcos from speaking (they can still engage in commercial speech, own newspapers, publish yellow pages, etc.), but only from a particular manner of purported speech, a characteristic sort of permissible "time, place and manner" restriction.[56] By silencing the telephone companies from speaking, we protect the ability of other competitors to do so.

The irony of this issue is illustrative. Telephone companies desire to lift the telco/cable ban not to provide more competition to cable systems, but instead to replace the existing cable monopolies with their own. Exchanging one monopolist for another has no effect on either the "marketplace for ideas" or the marketplace for cable television services.[57] Just as franchise and rate regulation of cable systems is largely content-neutral, so too is the impact of the telco/cable restriction constitutionally neutral. Both should be addressed not as first amendment matters, but as antitrust and competitive policy issues. Until this "antitrust paradox" is resolved, one can expect little more than continued *ad hoc* muddling as courts, legislatures, and observers struggle to fit the cable and telephone industries into the cubbyhole of the first amendment.

---

business must be based on some other, unstated strategic objective. *See* TV Signal of Aberdeen v. AT&T, 617 F.2d 1302 (8th Cir. 1980).

54 *See* FCC v. National Citizens Comm. for Broadcasting, 436 U.S. 775 (1978) (affirming constitutionality of newspaper/broadcast cross-ownership restriction).

55 The exacting scrutiny required by the "compelling state interest" standard, which applies when laws bar speech based on its effects or involve government in the choice of permissible communications content, may not be appropriate for cross-ownership restrictions, which lack the traditionally suspect characteristics of official control and discrimination. *See* Boos v. Barry, 108 S. Ct. 1157, 1164 (1988).

56 *See* Renton v. Playtime Theatres, Inc., 475 U.S. 41, 47 (1986) (time, place and manner restrictions are not subject to strict scrutiny and are sustainable if they are content-neutral, "designed to serve a substantial governmental interest, and do not unreasonably limit alternative avenues of communication"); Clark v. Community for Creative Non-Violence, 468 U.S. 288, 293 (1984).

57 As the National Telecommunications & Information Administration emphasized in proposing that telcos be authorized to provide "video dial tone" on a common carrier basis, "If telephone involvement would simply lead to replacement of one [cable] distributor with another, we would not consider the public to be greatly benefited." National Telecommunications and Information Admin., United States Dep't of Commerce, Video Program Distribution and Cable Television: Current Policy Issues and Recommendations, NTIA Report 88-233, at 32 (June 1988).

V. Conclusion

While there may be room for first amendment principles at the margin of the debate, regulation of cable television services and the cable/telco cross-ownership restrictions present market structure and competitive issues better suited to resolution under the antitrust laws. By injecting constitutional doctrine into this well-funded battle between two major industries, we devalue the protections accorded expressive conduct and divert attention from the more difficult—and in the long-term more important—question of competition in the delivery of video programming. Although no one could seriously argue that the Constitution permits government to dictate which television programming consumers can buy and view, that surely does not mean government cannot regulate this industry, even if first amendment actors are involved, if it is necessary to produce a competitive marketplace or arrest monopoly abuse that diminishes viewers' access to diverse and low-cost television. Whether the victors in this regulatory process are the cable systems or the telcos, however, is a matter of constitutional indifference. Paradoxically, courts, legislatures, and commentators keep looking for the answer in the first amendment.

CONTRADICTION AND CONTEXT IN AMERICAN COPYRIGHT LAW*

KEITH AOKI**

I. INTRODUCTION

We live in a profoundly designed world. In the late twentieth century, industrial design is so pervasive that it has become, in a certain sense, invisible. There are virtually no environments in which we work or relax where the effects of industrial design are not felt. Yet, the question of extending protection to works of industrial art has been a persistent conundrum in intellectual property law, particularly in the area of copyright.

This Article identifies distinctions[1] used in copyright law that purport to be useful in resolving cases, but which, in fact, have resulted in confusing, inconsistent, and erratic decisions.[2] Faced

---

* R. VENTURI, COMPLEXITY AND CONTRADICTION IN ARCHITECTURE 16 (1966):

> Everywhere . . . complexity and contradiction have been acknowledged, from Gödel's proof of ultimate inconsistency in mathematics to T.S. Eliot's analysis of difficult poetry and Joseph Albers' definition of the paradoxical quality of painting
>
> . . . .
>
> I am for richness of meaning rather than clarity of meaning; for the implicit function as well as the explicit function. I prefer 'both-and' to 'either-or,' black and white, and sometimes gray, to black or white.

** Associate, Hale and Dorr, Boston, Mass.; B.F.A., 1978, Wayne State University; M.A., 1986, Hunter College; J.D., 1990, Harvard Law School, *cum laude*. I wish to thank William W. Fisher III and Duncan Kennedy without whose insight, advice, and good humor this paper could not have been undertaken and completed. Mistakes are all my own.

1 For example, art/industry, or art/utility, which have evolved into applied art/industrial design. Note also that "applied art" is not defined by any copyright legislation, even though it is expressly mentioned among works which are protected.

Professor Reichman suggests that works of applied art are " 'intellectual works . . . [that] differ from graphic and plastic works in that they are no longer completely gratuitous, as solely the expression of the artist's message; they also have a utilitarian aspect.' " Reichman, *Design Protection in Domestic and Foreign Copyright Law: From the Berne Revision of 1948 to the Copyright Act of 1976*, 1983 DUKE L.J. 1143, 1146 n.7 (1983) [hereinafter Reichman I]. Another commentator suggests that "a clear definition of such works is not possible." S. LADAS, PATENTS, TRADEMARKS, AND RELATED RIGHTS: NATIONAL AND INTERNATIONAL PROTECTION 833 (1975) [hereinafter LADAS].

Professor Reichman believes that the term "industrial design" as used in commentary and cases is less satisfactory than the term "designs of useful articles" or "ornamental designs of useful articles." Reichman I, *supra*, at 1174 n.153. *See Design Protection Hearings* 1960: *Hearings on S.2075 and S.2852 Before the Senate Subcomm. on Patents, Trademarks, and Copyrights of the Senate Comm. on the Judiciary*, 86th Cong., 2d Sess. 56 (1960) (statement of Arthur Fisher, Register of Copyrights) [hereinafter *Design Protection Hearings*].

2 We often conceal from ourselves the fact that we "maintain, side by side as it were, beliefs which are inherently incompatible. . . . We seem to keep these antagonistic be-

with these contradictions, the courts, on the alleged mandate of Congress, have unsuccessfully sought to suppress the internal instability of their varying positions through the use of the doctrine of "conceptual separability."[3] In this twilight zone between applied art and industrial design, one can glimpse the acute tensions that pervade legal controversy.[4] Courts deciding cases in the area of industrial design routinely invoke Justice Holmes' famous 1903 admonition that strict "value neutrality" in terms of aesthetic judgments is the rule.[5] Yet, these same courts just as routinely find ways to rhetorically wriggle around Holmes' constraints, invoking standards of "value-neutrality" and "non-discrimination," while essentially ignoring them.[6] This privileging of one term in a set of contradictory arguments is used to justify frequent and confusing departures from the "neutral" norm as exceptional cases. Furthermore, out of these "privileged" norms, such as value-neutrality and non-discrimination, one can excavate not-so-latent elements of an individualist, rights-based, libertarian regime very much at odds with the trend toward increasing disintegration of the idea of "absolute property."[7] This contradiction is particularly ironic in light of the simultaneous intangibility of intellectual property rights and the enormous economic interests at stake in this area of art, commerce, and law. Joseph Story wrote that copyright law approaches "what may be called the metaphysics of the law, where the distinctions are, or at least may be, very subtile [sic] and refined, and, sometimes, almost evanescent."[8] There is no area of copyright where this is

---

liefs apart by putting them in 'logic-tight compartments.' " J. FRANK, LAW AND THE MODERN MIND 30 (1949).

[3] Professor Neil Boorstyn, in reference to *Brandir International*, *infra* note 255, says that " 'Conceptual separability' is alive and well, according to the majority, but diminished to the vanishing point, according to the dissent. We believe that while the concept may be alive, it is far from well." N. BOORSTYN, COPYRIGHT LAW § 2:10, at 36 (Supp. 1989) [hereinafter COPYRIGHT LAW].

[4] For example, the conflict between bright-line mechanical rules and situation sensitive *ad hoc* standards, or the traditional liberal idea that values and desires are subjective, while facts and reason are objective and therefore privileged in legal discourse. *See infra* note 346 and accompanying text. *See generally* Kennedy, *Form and Substance in Private Law Adjudication*, 89 HARV. L. REV. 1685, 1710-11 (1976).

[5] Bleistein v. Donaldson Lithographing Co., 188 U.S. 239, 251 (1903). *See infra* note 12 and accompanying text.

[6] For a discussion of these cases, see *infra* notes 49-64, 127-44, 185-220 and accompanying text.

[7] *See* Singer, *The Legal Rights Debate in Analytical Jurisprudence From Bentham to Hohfeld*, 1982 WIS. L. REV. 975; Gordon, *An Inquiry into the Merits of Copyright: The Challenges of Consistency, Consent, and Encouragement Theory*, 41 STAN. L. REV. 1343 (1989); Van de Velde, *The New Property of the Nineteenth Century: The Development of the Modern Concept of Property*, 29 BUFFALO L REV. 325 (1980).

[8] Folsom v. Marsh, 9 F. Cas. 342, 344 (C.C. Mass. 1841) (No. 4901).

more true than the area of conceptual separability.

This Article first describes the increasing incoherence in the industrial art cases.[9] Second, it examines the legislative history of the 1976 Copyright Revision Act[10] ("1976 Act") involving applied art and industrial design, with the purpose of casting doubt on the myth of "legislative intent," which has been used as a rationalization or command to the courts and the Copyright Office. Third, this Article examines the relationship between legal history and the history of industrial design, constructing an alternative explanation of why the split between applied art and industrial design occurred. Finally, this Article reviews and critiques the feasibility of using arguments from history to illuminate this deeply unsettled area of law.

II. Contradiction in the Cases, the Copyright Office, and Congress

A. *From* Bleistein *to the 1976 Copyright Act*

1. *Bleistein v. Donaldson Lithographing Co.*

Crucial to any discussion of the legal distinction between applied art and industrial design is the 1903 case, *Bleistein v. Donaldson Lithographing Co.*,[11] which involved the copyrightability of chromolithographs used as circus advertisements. Writing for the majority, Justice Holmes proclaimed:

9 Currently, there are at least three approaches in different circuits, each purporting to apply a correct interpretation of conceptual separability. One approach, supported by the Second Circuit, would allow partial cumulation. *See* Durham Indus. v. Tomy Corp., 630 F.2d 905 (2d Cir. 1980); Kieselstein-Cord v. Accessories by Pearl, 632 F.2d 989 (2d Cir. 1980); L. Batlin & Son, Inc. v. Snyder, 436 F.2d 486 (2d Cir. 1976). Noncumulation is supported by the D.C. and Eleventh Circuits. *See* Norris Indus. v. ITT, 696 F.2d 918 (11th Cir. 1983); Esquire, Inc. v. Ringer, 591 F.2d 796 (D.C. Cir. 1978). The Ninth Ciruit excludes nontraditional utilitarian designs, but expands federal unfair competition law. *See* Fabrica, Inc. v. El Dorado Co., 697 F.2d 890 (9th Cir. 1983).

Professor Reichman provides some useful definitions: "*Cumulation* means that concurrent protection is available for ornamental designs of useful articles in copyright and special design law." Copyright protection is *always* available. *Sui generis* law "augment[s] manufacturers' rights[] without forfeiting protection . . . of artistic property [rights]. This approach is followed in France and Belgium.

"Noncumulation" systems provide "virtually no possibility of concurrent protection for ornamental designs" of useful articles. "[S]hort-term [design] protection . . . [is] the only safe route regardless of the degree of artistic content." Italy follows this modified patent law paradigm.

"Partial cumulation" systems occasionally provide copyright protection for works "manifesting exceptional creativity." The aesthetic judgment necessary to determine exceptional creativity is an exception to the general rule of non-discrimination. Note also that "[a]s a rule, however, systems that allow partial cumulation attempt to relegate most industrial art to special design laws." *See* Reichman I, *supra* note 1, at 1168-69 (citations omitted).

10 17 U.S.C. §§ 101-810 (1988).

11 188 U.S. 239 (1903).

> It would be a dangerous undertaking for persons trained only to the law to constitute themselves final judges of the worth of pictorial illustrations, outside of the narrowest and most obvious limits. At the one extreme some works of genius would be sure to miss appreciation. Their very novelty would make them repulsive until the public had learned the new language in which their author spoke. It may be more than doubted, for instance, whether the etchings of Goya or the paintings of Manet would have been sure of protection when seen for the first time. At the other end, copyright would be denied to pictures which appealed to a public less educated than the judge. Yet if they command the interest of any public, they have a commercial value—it would be bold to say that they have not an aesthetic and educational value—and the taste of any public is not to be treated with contempt. . . . That these pictures had their worth and their success is sufficiently shown by the desire to reproduce them without regard to the plaintiffs' rights.[12]

Bleistein anticipated by six years the liberalized thrust of the Copyright Act of 1909 ("1909 Act").[13] The *Bleistein* court responded to the perceived narrowness of the statutory definition in force since 1870,[14] limiting copyright protection to "works connected with the fine arts."[15] From this decision, a nascent contradiction emerged. Holmes disclaimed the distinction between good and bad art, but set up an opposition between " 'illustrations or works connected with the fine arts' "[16] (including advertising posters), and " 'prints or labels designed to be used for any other articles of manufacture.' "[17] Holmes stated that "works are not the less connected with the fine arts because their pictorial quality attracts the crowd and therefore gives them a real use—if use means to increase trade and to help to make money."[18] Holmes' dicta indicates that "pictorial quality," which has the function of attracting consumers, could receive copyright protection under the Act of 1874 as it

---

[12] *Id.* at 251-52.

[13] Copyright Act of 1909, ch. 320, § 5(g), 35 Stat. 1076, 1076-77 (formerly codified at 17 U.S.C. §§ 1-216) [hereinafter 1909 Act]. Arguably, section 5(g) expanded protection to three-dimensional models. *See Hearings on S.6330 and H.R.19,583 Before the Comms. on Patents*, 59th Cong., 1st Sess. 11 (1906) (H. Putnam, the Librarian of Congress testified during the 1909 hearings that by eliminating the "fine arts" classification, the scope of copyright was being expanded.), *reprinted in* 4 LEGISLATIVE HISTORY OF THE 1909 COPYRIGHT ACT 11 (E. Bylawski & A. Goldman eds. 1976).

[14] Copyright Act of 1870, ch. 230, 16 Stat. 198.

[15] *Bleistein*, 188 U.S. at 251.

[16] *Id.* at 250 (quoting Copyright Act of 1874, ch. 301, 18 Stat. 78, 79).

[17] *Id.* at 251.

[18] *Id.*

was interpreted in 1903. Holmes emphasized that because of this principle of aesthetic non-discrimination, the threshold of originality needed to be low.

> The Constitution does not limit the useful to that which satisfies immediate bodily needs. . . . Personality always contains something unique. It expresses its singularity even in handwriting, and a very modest grade of art has in it something irreducible, which is one man's alone. That something he may copyright unless there is a restriction in the words of the act.[19]

Thus, aesthetic non-discrimination combined with a low threshold of originality meant a potentially expanded field of copyrightable material.

Justice Harlan's dissent argued that the chromolithographs' useful function of attracting an audience, which Holmes claimed was the basis for copyright protection, was precisely the reason why the advertisements should be denied protection. To Justice Harlan,

> [i]f a mere label simply designating or describing an article to which it is attached, and which has no value separated from the article, does not come within the constitutional clause upon the subject of copyright, it must follow that a pictorial illustration designed and useful only as an advertisement, and having no intrinsic value other than its function as an advertisement, must be equally without the obvious meaning of the Constitution.[20]

In *Bleistein*, key elements of the current argument over conceptual separability emerged. Since *Bleistein*, sharply divided courts have repeatedly mouthed variations of Justices Holmes' and Harlan's arguments.[21]

2. The 1909 Copyright Act

The 1909 Act was more liberal than its predecessor.[22] It classified "designs and models" as "works of art," thus granting copyright protection under section 5(g), and eliminating the 1870 exclusionary provision limiting protection to "works of fine art."[23] The 1909 Act allowed the Copyright Office to establish "rules and regulations for the registration of claims to copy-

---

19 *Id.* at 249-50 (citation omitted).

20 *Id.* at 252 (Harlan, J., dissenting).

21 *See* section II of this Article.

22 Copyright Act of 1870, *supra* note 14.

23 *Id.*

right,"[24] beginning a power struggle between the courts and the Copyright Office. From 1909 through 1949, the Copyright Office used its power to grant or withhold copyright protection in order to maintain a clear distinction between copyright law and design patent law,[25] which had stricter eligibility requirements, including "novelty" and "non-obviousness."[26] The Copyright Office sought to prevent manufacturers from skirting the stricter design patent requirements by satisfying the low creativity and originality thresholds of copyright protection.[27] During this period, the Copyright Office virtually always denied copyright protection for any three-dimensional object that "would fall within the category of multiple commercial production of works of the applied arts."[28]

In 1949, the Copyright Office changed its definition of "work of art" to include "works of artistic craftsmanship, insofar as their form but not their mechanical or utilitarian aspects are concerned, such as artistic jewelry, enamels, glassware, and tapestries, as well as works belonging to the fine arts."[29] This change marked the beginning of the Copyright Office's move towards the expansive Holmesian non-discrimination position of copyright protection developed in *Bleistein* for "less-than-artistic but more-than-utilitarian" mass-produced three-dimensional artifacts.

---

24 1909 Act, *supra* note 13, at 1085 § 53.

25 *See* Graham v. John Deere, 383 U.S. 1 (1966); *see also* Copyright Office, Rules and Regulations for the Registration of Claims to Copyright, Bull. No. 15, at 8 (1910), *reprinted in* Mazer v. Stein, 347 U.S. 201, 212 n.23 (1954) (" '*Works of art.*—This term includes all works belonging fairly to the so-called fine arts. (Paintings, drawings, and sculpture.) 'Productions of the industrial arts utilitarian in purpose and character are not subject to copyright registration, even if artistically made or ornamented.' ").

26 For a discussion of the novelty and non-obviousness requirements of patent law, see *John Deere*, 383 U.S. 1 (1965); *see infra* note 93; *see also infra* notes 145-82 and accompanying text.

27 Design Patent Law, Act of Aug. 29, 1842, ch. 263, 5 Stat. 544 (codified at 35 U.S.C. §§ 171-173 (1988)); *see also* Alfred Bell & Co. v. Catalda Fine Arts, Inc., 191 F.2d 99 (2d Cir. 1951) (originality required in order to receive protection). *But cf.* L. Batlin & Son, Inc. v. Snyder, 436 F.2d 486 (2d Cir. 1976); Bailie v. Fisher, 258 F.2d 425, 426 (D.C. Cir. 1958) (creativity required for work to receive protection).

28 Derenberg, *Copyright No-Man's Land: Fringe Rights in Literary and Artistic Property*, in 1953 COPYRIGHT PROBLEMS ANALYZED 215, 227 (1953).

29 37 C.F.R. § 202.10(a) (1959) (amended June 18, 1959) (repealed Jan. 1 1978, 43 Fed. Reg 6 (1978)). Professor Reichman plausibly contends that this was the result of pressure from the members of the Berne Union, of which the United States was not a member, when they met in 1948 in Brussels. At the 1948 Berne Union, advocates of protection for works of some applied and industrial art triumphed, forcing non-member countries like the United States "to review their positions in order to maintain the minimum degree of reciprocity that comity and the exigencies of international trade made advisable." Reichman I, *supra* note 1, at 1149.

3. *Mazer v. Stein*

The Copyright Office's shift toward protecting designs incorporated into useful objects was bolstered by *Mazer v. Stein.*[30] At issue in *Mazer* were copies of a lamp base made in the stylized shape of a Balinese dancer. The statuette of the dancer had previously been registered with the Copyright Office as a "work of art" under the expanded 1949 Copyright Office regulation.[31] The putative infringers contended that copyright protection was not appropriate for the unlimited industrial reproduction of an admittedly protected individual article.[32] These alleged infringers also claimed that there should be a mutually exclusive and strict division between design patent and copyright protection.[33] Justice Reed responded for the majority:

> We . . . hold that the patentability of the statuettes, fitted as lamps or unfitted, does not bar copyright as works of art. Neither the Copyright Statute nor any other says that because a thing is patentable it may not be copyrighted. . . .
>
> . . . [C]opyright protects originality rather than novelty or invention—conferring only 'the sole right of multiplying copies.' . . . The dichotomy of protection for the aesthetic is not beauty and utility but art for the copyright and the invention of original and ornamental design for design patents. We find nothing in the copyright statute to support the argument that the intended use or use in industry of an article eligible for copyright bars or invalidates its registration.[34]

The *Mazer* case was fecund with alternative interpretations and ambiguous implications. On one level it purported to extend *Bleistein*'s non-discrimination principle,[35] thus admitting that an object's aesthetic value is virtually irrelevant for copyright purposes. This extension signaled the Court's desire to avoid subjective evaluations. On another level, the *Mazer* court said that the commercial,

---

30 347 U.S. 201 (1954).

31 *Id.* at 202-03. The statuettes "were submitted . . . to the Copyright Office for registration as 'works of art' or reproductions thereof under § 5(g) or § 5(h) of the copyright law, and certificates of registration issued." *Id.* (citation omitted). *See* 17 U.S.C. § 5(g), (h) (Supp. V 1952) (section 5 has been incorporated into 17 U.S.C. § 102).

32 *Mazer*, 347 U.S. at 205.

33 *Id.* at 216.

34 *Id.* at 217-18 (citations omitted).

35 *Id.* at 214.

> Individual perception of the beautiful is too varied a power to permit a narrow or rigid concept of art. . . . [The articles] must be original, that is, the author's tangible expression of his ideas. . . . Such expression, whether meticulously delineating the model or mental image or conveying the meaning by modernistic form or color, is copyrightable.

Id. (citations omitted)

mass-produced nature of an object is irrelevant to the issue of its copyrightability and that the "intended use or use in industry of an article eligible for copyright" did not preclude an object's copyright registration.[36] Additionally, *Mazer* presented three possible interpretations of the development of industrial design protection. First, it could be read to suggest broad copyright protection to industrial art.[37] Second, *Mazer* could be interpreted to permit narrow access to copyright and to provide alternative protection for non-copyrightable designs under state unfair competition laws.[38] Third, it could be construed to permit narrow access to copyright while encouraging the protection of the majority of non-copyrightable designs under a new *sui generis* design law.[39]

Both *Bleistein* and *Mazer* redefined the issues with which the Court has grappled. In *Bleistein*, Holmes emphasized that the granting of copyright protection should not turn on whether the object is good or bad art, but whether the object is associated with fine art (even if it is functional), or is a manufactured item. In *Mazer*, Justice Reed stressed that "[t]he dichotomy of protection for the aesthetic is not beauty and utility but art for the copyright and the invention of original and ornamental design for design patents."[40] This fuzzy split widened in later cases[41] into a conceptual chasm resulting from the ambiguity of the definitions the Court employed. Indeed, this Article argues that while both Reed and Holmes were using words like "art" and "manufacturing," they were speaking in different historical contexts and intended different meanings. During the fifty-year period between *Bleistein* and *Mazer*, the meanings of the words changed as the world was transformed by the World Wars, the De-

---

36 *Id.* at 218.

37 *See* 1 M. NIMMER, NIMMER ON COPYRIGHT § 2.08[B], at 2-88, 2-96.3 (1989) [hereinafter NIMMER ON COPYRIGHT]; *Mazer*, 347 U.S. at 214.

38 Although this would have been foreclosed by the subsequent 1964 *Sears-Compco* cases. Sears, Roebuck & Co. v. Stiffel Co., 376 U.S. 225 (1964); Compco Corp. v. Day-Brite Lighting, Inc., 376 U.S. 234 (1964). *But see* Goldstein v. California, 412 U.S. 546 (1973) (states can prevent duplication of performances on phonograph records); Truck Equip. Serv. Co. v. Freuhauf Corp., 536 F.2d 1210, 1214 (8th Cir. 1976); *see also* Tomlin v. Walt Disney Prods., 18 Cal. App. 3d 226, 96 Cal. Rptr. 118 (1971) (titles); Sinatra v. Goodyear Tire & Rubber Co., 435 F.2d 711 (9th Cir. 1970) (vocalist's style); Columbia Broadcasting Sys. v. DeCosta, 377 F.2d 315 (1st Cir. 1967). *See* Note, *The Problem of Functional Features: Trade Dress Infringement Under Section 43(a) of the Lanham Act*, 82 COLUM. L. REV. 77 (1982).

39 "Under the 'copyright approach,' the basic criterion for [industrial design] protection should be originality in the sense of independent creation. . . . originality, meaning independent creation, is the basic criterion for protection. Under the 'patent approach' to design protection, standards of objective novelty must be satisfied." *See* Reichman I, *supra* note 1, at 1172 n.147 (citation omitted).

40 *Mazer*, 347 U.S. at 218.

41 See *infra* notes 183-220 and accompanying text.

pression, and revolutions in science, technology, and intellectual thought.

4. *Vacheron*, *Bailie* and Art in the "Ordinary and Historical Conception"

Initially, the courts gave *Mazer* a fairly broad reading. For example, in 1955, a court held that while a piece of costume jewelry was "a commonplace fashion accessory," and "not an expression of 'pure' or 'fine' art,"[42] it nonetheless could be copyrighted as long as the author had created an original, tangible expression of an idea, rather than a "merely pleasing form dictated solely by functional considerations."[43]

Expansive application of *Bleistein* and *Mazer* moved copyright law toward a broad "unity of art" theory.[44] In 1953, while *Mazer* was working its way up to the Supreme Court, experts began drafting a design protection bill for the United States, which the Copyright Register endorsed and supported.[45] Against the background of a possible American *sui generis* design protection law, the Copyright Office began advocating a non-cumulation model,[46] in which industrial designs would seek protection under a *sui generis* design law and not in copyright.[47]

The first post-*Mazer* Copyright Office regulation in 1956 cautioned courts that

> [w]hen the shape of an article is dictated by, or is necessarily responsive to, the requirements of its utilitarian function, its

---

42 Trifari, Krussman & Fischel v. Charel Co., 134 F. Supp. 551, 553 (S.D.N.Y. 1955). *See, e.g.*, Rushton v. Vitale, 218 F.2d 434, 436 (2d Cir. 1955) (chimpanzee doll modeled after a television chimp was held to be copyrightable).

43 *Id.*

44 In France, a cumulationist model exists in which designers and manufacturers can cumulate both the advantages of *sui generis* design legislation and copyright protection. Protection is extended to all industrial art. *See* Reichman I, *supra* note 1, at 1153-58.

45 *Id.* at 1176.

46 For a definition of non-cumulation, see *supra* note 9.

47 The 1956 regulation's "clearly a work of art in itself" language seemed to say that differences in the degree of qualitative creativity/aesthetic value could be critical factors in copyrightability. This idea seems to have been resurrected, to some degree, in the guise of "conceptual separability" under the 1976 Act. Professor Reichman contends that between 1955 and 1976, the Copyright Office may also have had "an administrative preference for a regime of partial cumulation." *See* Reichman I, *supra* note 1, at 1179.

Problems with a total cumulation regime include: overprotection because of the long duration of copyright protection; difficulties applying moral rights (or moral rights-like) reasoning to industrial designs; complication of the status of designs by employees and works made for hire; and the severity of copyright remedies. In general, the doctrine of total cumulation had the potential to deform and undermine copyright law, bringing it more in line with industrial property law. If copyright law becomes more like industrial property law, a conflict between the limited copyright monopoly and policies against restraints on competition in industrial property law will arise.

> shape, though unique and attractive, cannot qualify it as a work of art. If the sole intrinsic function of an article is its utility, the fact that it is unique and attractively shaped will not qualify it as a work of art. However, where the object is clearly a work of art in itself, the fact [that] it is also a useful article will not preclude its registration.[48]

In seeking to lay the foundation for a non-cumulation regime, the Copyright Office wanted to narrow *Mazer*'s holding without explicitly overriding it. In *Vacheron & Constantin-Le Coultre Watches, Inc. v. Benrus Watch Co.*,[49] for example, the District Court for the Southern District of New York responded to the new Copyright Office regulation, which mandated that the "work of art" be given a "colloquial rather than a philosophical significance."[50] The *Vacheron* court upheld the denial of copyright registration to a modernistic watch face, with the numerals represented by jewels and sticks.[51] The court speculated that while the watch face was not copyrightable, design patent protection might be available because the designer's rearrangement of stock elements had the "necessary beauty and originality born of the inventive faculty."[52]

On appeal, as was typical of the cases in which a Copyright Office regulation had to be threaded through the apparatus of the 1909 Copyright Act, the Second Circuit was split. Judge Hand, writing for the majority, evaded the question of the Copyright Office's legislative authority to make aesthetic evaluations of articles seeking registration. "It is true that 'works of art' is a loose phrase whose perimeter is hard to define" but the "decision here did not demand the exercise of a discretion that was conclusive with the Register."[53] In his dissent, Chief Judge Clark denied the Copyright Office's discretionary authority in registering articles, and was disturbed by the mounting inconsistencies in this area.[54]

In *Bailie v. Fisher*,[55] the District of Columbia Circuit approved the Register's movement to raise the copyright threshold. *Bailie* ad-

---

48 21 Fed. Reg. 6024 § 202.10(c) (1956), *repealed by* 37 C.F.R. 966 (1978).

49 155 F. Supp. 932 (S.D.N.Y. 1957), *modified on other grounds*, 260 F.2d 637 (2d Cir. 1958).

50 *Vacheron*, 155 F. Supp. at 934.

51 *Id.* at 933. "In place of numerals there are jeweled 'sticks' of equal length and width except the stick of the six o'clock position which is shortened to permit the introduction of the name 'Le Coultre (c̄).' " *Id.*

52 *Id.* at 935. While the Second Circuit affirmed the denial of copyright, a dissenting judge argued that the "highly ornamented watches" were copyrightable under *Mazer*. *Vacheron*, 260 F.2d at 643 (Clark, C.J., dissenting).

53 *Vacheron*, 260 F.2d at 640.

54 *Id.* at 644 (denying copyright to highly designed and aesthetic watch face, but granting copyright to costume jewelry is inconsistent).

55 258 F.2d 425, 426 (D.C. Cir. 1958).

dressed the scope of discretion the Copyright Office could exercise under the 1909 Act, implementing and legitimizing its discretionary judgments at the threshold of registration. The court upheld the Register's denial of copyright to a "cardboard star with a circular center bearing the photograph of an entertainer."[56] The court noted that " '[a] thing is a work of art . . . if it appears to be within the historical and ordinary conception of the term art,' " and that a "cardboard star which stands because of folded flaps does not fall within that conception."[57] Taken to its limit, this "historical conception" of art rationale could have undermined earlier decisions by holding items such as dolls and costume jewelry copyrightable.[58]

By 1958, two distinct positions had emerged. According to *Mazer*, a minimum quantum of originality or creativity was sufficient to obtain copyright protection.[59] By contrast, the Copyright Office adopted the position that if an item did not fall into the category of "the historical and ordinary conception of the term art" it was not copyrightable.[60] Part of the difficulty was caused by the contradictory nature of the Copyright Office's 1956 regulation,[61] which was too narrow and vague. For instance, in the phrase "the sole intrinsic function of an article is its utility,"[62] the Register seemed to be characterizing objects as utilitarian, yet allowing some non-utilitarian functions to be copyrightable. This test for copyright protection, that the object be "clearly a work of art in itself,"[63] was

---

56 *Id.* at 426.

57 *Id.* (citing Rosenthal v. Stein, 205 F.2d 633, 635 (9th Cir. 1953), one of the earlier lamp cases from the Ninth Circuit).

58 *See* Rushton v. Vitale, 218 F.2d 434 (2d Cir. 1955).

59 For a discussion of *Mazer*, see *supra* notes 30-39 and accompanying text; *see also* Alfred Bell & Co. v. Catalda Fine Arts, Inc., 191 F.2d 99 (2d Cir. 1951).

60 *See supra* notes 56-58 and accompanying text.

61 *See supra* note 47 and accompanying text; Reichman I, *supra* note 1, at 1177-79.

62 *Id.* at 1177 (quoting § 202.10(c) of 21 Fed. Reg. 6024 (1956)).

63 *Id.* For the views of the apologetic Consensus and Process Theorists, see H. HART & A. SACKS, THE LEGAL PROCESS: BASIC PROBLEMS IN THE MAKING AND APPLICATION OF LAW (1958) (This was a seminal "legal process" casebook which envisioned policy decisions as made by legislators with the law seen as only a "neutral procedural instrument," implementing policy decisions based on consensus.) [hereinafter BASIC PROBLEMS IN THE MAKING AND APPLICATION OF LAW]; Wechsler, *Toward Neutral Principles of Constitutional Law*, 73 HARV. L. REV. 1 (1959). The Consensus and Process Theorists provided a backdrop for the prevailing deference to "art in the ordinary and historical sense." These theorists endowed social custom with undue normativity and sought to draw a defensible line between applied art and industrial design. This trend continued in the 1970s and 1980s decisions which simultaneously deferred to the consumer market as a means of avoiding subjective preferences (this deference becomes meaningless because the consumer market is nothing but an aggregate of individual barely articulated subjective value preferences) and deference to institutional expertise (allowing experts to determine what is and what is not design). However, in Brandir Int'l v. Cascade Pacific Lumber Co., 834 F.2d 1142 (2d Cir. 1987), the court retreated into legalism to defend its judgment against modernist experts in order to prevent the disintegration of conceptual

subjective, giving credence to considerations of aesthetic merit which *Bleistein* proscribed.[64]

5. The Emergence of the Aesthetic Separability Test

By 1958, there seemed to be recognition that *Vacheron* and *Bailie* had reached the limits of the aesthetic merit test. To go any further risked blatant contradiction with *Bleistein* and the gutting of *Mazer*. While plans for the new *sui generis* design law were proceeding in Congress,[65] the Copyright Office abandoned the "clearly a work of art in itself" criterion, but avoided instituting a new scheme that completely overlapped with copyright law.

To mediate these conflicting positions, the Copyright Office amended its 1956 regulation.[66] In an effort to implement the *Mazer* decision, the Office deleted the "clearly a work of art in itself" language and substituted an aesthetic "separability" test in its regulation 202.10(c):

> If the *sole intrinsic function* of an article is its utility, the fact that the article is unique and attractively shaped will not qualify it as a work of art. However, if the shape of a utilitarian article incorporates features, such as artistic sculpture, carving, or pictorial representation, which can be *identified separately* and are capable of *existing independently* as a work of art, such features will be eligible for registration.[67]

Professor Reichman has suggested that the Copyright Office surreptitiously packed an American analogue of the Italian *scindibile*

---

separability. The decisions of the 1950s also deferred to expertise. *See Design Protection Hearings*, *supra* note 1.

64 *See supra* notes 11-21 and accompanying text.

65 The 1959 proposed design law would have excluded standard, commonplace, staple designs and would have implemented an administrative screening procedure, similar to trademark opposition procedure. The appearance, and not the utility of the article would have been the touchstone of protection. Designs dictated solely by function would be excluded. Protectable designs would receive five years of protection and registration would be required within six months from the time the design was made known. The line of demarcation between soft design protection (5 years), hard patent protection (14 years), and soft copyright protection (56 years) would have been "usefulness." This would have meant a strict quarantine of industrial design. This policy of drawing a strict line between copyright and design would have involved a rigorous exclusion of commercially exploited designs of useful articles. *See* Reichman I, *supra* note 1, at 1190-1191; *see also Design Protection Hearings*, *supra* note 1, at 57 (statement and testimony of Arthur Fisher, Register of Copyright) ("[T]he stretching of the copyright law to cover ornamental designs of useful articles is rapidly developing an attitude of vested interest in long-term rights of an undesirable nature in a diversity of articles and industries.").

66 37 C.F.R. § 202.10(c) (1959) (amended June 18, 1959) (repealed Jan. 1, 1978).

67 *Id.* (emphasis added). *See also* NIMMER ON COPYRIGHT, *supra* note 37, at 2-89 ("[The 1959 Regulation] offered no ready answer to the line drawing problem inherent in delineating the extent of copyright protection available for works of applied art.").

into a regime of total non-cumulation.[68] This *scindibile*, or separability, had different premises than the broad "unity of art" thesis which posited that industrial art *is art* and should be allowed copyright protection, as suggested by *Mazer*.[69] The first premise of separability is that industrial designs are inextricably bound up with industrial products and ought to be protected by industrial property law containing a design protection component.[70] Given a separability regime, the questions become: a) what elements of shape, design, and color that "embellish" an industrial product are "works of art applied" to a product and, therefore, copyrightable?; and b) which elements are inseparable from the product and subject to industrial property law? Professor Reichman suggested, in accordance with Italian separability theory, that an element is separable when "a work . . . contains its own message and conserves its artistic value independently of the material support in which it is embodied."[71]

If physical separability is the basic paradigm, then carvings on doors, caryatids supporting arches, and designs woven into carpet could be regarded as separable from their material support.[72] Conceptual separability, however, is more problematic because of its increasingly abstract and ethereal nature.[73] Conceptual separability requires only the mere possibility of conceiving of a work independently of the object in which it is embodied in an abstract or ideal sense. The objective of conceptual separability is to exclude functional shapes without ornamentation from copyright protection, while protecting figurative and superfluously ornamental objects. These distinctions are ephemeral, however, inviting arbitrary adjudication under the guise of a supposedly objective analysis based on a categorical scheme. Moreover, conceptual separability presupposes that the concepts of "art" and "industry" are stable qualities inherent in the objects themselves, and not arbitrary and contingent

---

68 *See* Reichman I, *supra* note 1, at 1183-84.

69 *See supra* notes 30-39 and accompanying text.

70 Conflicts arise because of the dual markets involved; "favoring the protection of the design of a useful article *qua* artistic work may thus interfere with policies favoring free competition in the 'material supports' in which . . . artistic work has been embodied." Applied art is capable of competing in both the artistic work market and the general products market: "[N]o facile invocation of general principles of copyright law will make this two-market conundrum disappear." Reichman I, *supra* note 1, at 1197. It is not "unreasonable to limit . . . the applicability of artistic copyrights to useful articles, when useful articles" are protected by a design law. However, protection would be in acute tension with the generally "stringent preconditions to restraints on free competition." *Id.*

71 *Id.* at 1183.

72 *Id.* at 1184-85.

73 Note the dissent's discussion in Brandir Int'l v. Cascade Pacific Lumber Co., 834 F.2d 1142 (2d Cir. 1987). See *infra* notes 282-83 and accompanying text for a catalog of at least six different versions of conceptual separability.

cultural constructs whose meanings shift significantly over time. Being conducive to such a high level of generality, the concept is indeterminate.[74] For example, separability "theory excludes virtually all three-dimensional designs, because only the design that has been added to the object without losing its autonomous character is ever copyrightable."[75] Conversely, most two-dimensional designs incorporated into manufactured objects " 'can rarely be considered part of the useful article' "integral.[76]

The underlying inadequacy of the Copyright Office's regulation 202.10(c) and its ambiguous separability test was described by former Register of Copyrights, Barbara Ringer:

> The borderline between copyrightable and uncopyrightable designs is extremely difficult to draw, although the Copyright Office Regulations, as recently amended . . . make the . . . attempt
>
> . . . .
>
> . . . Most important is the fact that at its present state of development the copyright law protects only those designs which can be separately identified as 'works of art,' and excludes many aesthetically superior designs of useful articles. This distinction seems difficult to justify on the grounds of logic or policy.[77]

Other critics, such as supporters of the 1959 O'Mahoney-Wiley-Hart Bill,[78] thought copyright protection for industrial design would be "too broad and vague," and that common law unfair competition protection could be dangerous because of the potential perpetuity of the protection.[79] Some experts thought that the line between industrial design and applied art should be based on the "usefulness"

---

[74] When confronting this indeterminacy, the Holmes aesthetic non-discrimination principle begins to sound attractive, even if ultimately illusory. The non-discrimination principle, however, removes precisely the tools needed in order to begin to make an intelligent analysis of values and then compels decisions that necessarily implicate values.

[75] Reichman I, *supra* note 1, at 1186. *See also* Esquire, Inc. v. Ringer, 591 F.2d 796 (D.C. Cir. 1978); Carol Barnhart v. Economy Cover Corp., 773 F.2d 411 (2d Cir. 1985); Norris Indus. v. ITT, 696 F.2d 918 (11th Cir. 1983). *But cf.* Kieselstein-Cord v. Accessories by Pearl, Inc., 632 F.2d 989 (2d Cir. 1980).

[76] Reichman I, *supra* note 1, at 1186.

[77] Ringer, *The Case for Design Protection and the O'Mahoney Bill*, 7 BULL. COPYRIGHT SOC'Y 25, 29-30 (1959)[hereinafter *Design Protection and the O'Mahoney Bill*].

[78] S.2075 (O'Mahoney-Wiley-Hart Bill), 86th Cong., 1st Sess. (1959), *refining* H.R.8873 (Willis Bill), 85th Cong., 1st Sess. § 1(b)(1), (2) (1957) [hereinafter S.2075]. *See also* Latman, *A Proposal for Effective Design Legislation: S.2075 Examined*, 6 BULL. COPYRIGHT SOC'Y 279, 280 (1959) ("[T]here no longer would remain the impossible task of determining what is a 'work of art.' Substituted is the inquiry as to utility which, while by no means a simple one, seems more appropriate and workable.").

[79] *Design Protection and the O'Mahoney Bill*, *supra* note 77, at 30.

of the article in which the design was embodied.[80] The proposed definition of a "useful article" was "an article normally having an intrinsic function other than merely to portray its own appearance or to convey information."[81] Under this definition, however, works of fine art were not "useful articles" "because their normal and intrinsic function is to portray their own appearance."[82]

Some opponents of the 1959 bill, claiming it was regressive, filed a complaint against the Justice Department alleging unnecessary restraint of trade.[83] Other interest groups feared that the bill would "maim" copyright law by terminating protection of subsequent works to which the originally protectable work had been applied.[84]

In 1960, Copyright Register Fisher warned presciently:

> If nothing is done, the problem will increase in complexity and without the protective features that have been carefully worked out . . . . And I believe that [this] is not only the experience here in the United States but in the world at large. . . . [T]he matter has become so urgent that we should deal with it

---

80 *See* S.2075, *supra* note 78.

81 *Id.* §§ 1(b)(2), 32. *But see* 17 U.S.C. § 101 (1988) (final definition of "useful article").

82 Bogsch, *Towards a More Effective Protection of Designs in the United States of America*, 1959 INDUS. PROP. Q. 3, 7 (1959). Professor Reichman states that the "useful article" line was drawn because " 'the impact of long term statutory protection upon the consuming public and the national economy is much greater in the field of useful commodities than . . . in the area of fine arts' " and also that " 'articles . . . bought for use have much greater economic significance than those . . . bought solely for display.' " Reichman I, *supra* note 1, at 1198-99 (citing Note, *Present Design Protection in the United States*, 5 BULL. COPYRIGHT SOC'Y 139-40 (1958)). Because designs and models are reproduced in series, commercial exploitation is largely determined by factors governing the market segment in which the useful object is to be sold rather than by economic factors operating on the market for works of art. *See id.*

83 Opposition to the 1959 design bill emanated from

> confirmed and irresponsible design pirates[;] . . . large firms whose business is not traditionally related to design or who apparently prefer to . . . 'shop' the creations of their smaller and often more original competitors, trusting to their greater selling power, size, and trade names, etc., to protect their interests; and . . . a few concerns who would like . . . to have their cake and eat it, that is, to have the benefit of a new sui generis design law where appropriate but at the same time to retain the unrestricted long term of the present copyright law.

Design Protection Hearings, *supra* note 1, at 58 (testimony of Arthur Fisher, Register of Copyrights). *See id.* at 19 (letter from Lawrence E. Walsh, Deputy Attorney General); *id.* at 85-88 (address by Harry R. Mayers, General Counsel to General Electric Co.). The garment industry was excluded from the scope of the proposed design bill. This exclusion was considered vital to the design bill's support. REGISTER OF COPYRIGHTS, 1961 REGISTER'S REPORT ON THE GENERAL REVISION OF THE U.S. COPYRIGHT LAW 13, *reprinted in* COPYRIGHT LAW REVISION pt.1, at 13, 87th Cong., 1st Sess. (Comm. Print 1961) (printed for the use of the House Comm. on the Judiciary).

84 For example, a copyrighted cartoon character subsequently embodied in a T-shirt could cease to be protected as embodied in other T-shirts as soon as the shorter term of design protection lapsed. *See* Reichman I, *supra* note 1, at 1196.

> promptly before we find vested interests in different industries, as we have found in other situations, and where it will be much more difficult in a few years to deal with the matter effectively.[85]

6. Legislative Procrastination, Compromise, and Confusion in the Courts

The Copyright Office, from 1954 to 1969, attempted to "limit the access of industrial art to copyright protection [under the 1909 Act,] while pressing Congress for a prompt enactment of a *sui generis* design law."[86] Then, from 1969 to 1976, the Copyright Office tried to limit the damage it perceived the courts had caused to the various obstacles the Copyright Office had erected to inhibit industrial design from being granted copyrights.[87] Despite the Office's pressure, Congress scuttled the design protection component from the 1976 Copyright Revision Act.[88]

During the 1960s and 1970s, copyright law was subject to increasing pressure to provide some type of interim protection for industrial design. This pressure arose partially from the reaction to the *Sears-Compco* cases,[89] which foreclosed state unfair

---

85 *Design Protection Hearings*, *supra* note 1, at 66 (testimony of Arthur Fisher, Register of Copyrights).

86 *See* Reichman I, *supra* note 1, at 1173.

87 *See generally id.* (discussing the tension between the Copyright Office, which attempted to set a threshhold for copyrightability of useful articles, and the courts, which, during this period, would punch holes in those threshholds by allowing copyrights in more and more articles).

88 Legislative foot-dragging from the mid-1950s to the mid-1970s occurred against a shift in background theories of legislative and administrative legitimacy from the consensus theory to interest group pluralist bargaining theory. *See* Stewart, *The Reformation of American Administrative Law*, 88 HARV. L. REV. 1667 (1975); Sunstein, *Interpreting Statutes in the Regulatory State*, 103 HARV. L. REV. 407 (1989); Easterbrook, *The Supreme Court, 1983 Term—Forward: The Court and the Economic System*, 98 HARV. L. REV. 4, 15 (1984).

89 Sears, Roebuck & Co. v. Stiffel Co., 376 U.S. 225, 231 (1964); Compco Corp. v. Day-Brite Lighting, Inc., 376 U.S. 234, 238 (1964). These cases truncated a growing common law trend towards extending misappropriation theory to protect industrial design. The *Sears-Compco* cases preempted state misappropriation actions for unpatentable designs of useful articles. *See also* Bonito Boats, Inc. v. Thunder Craft Boats, Inc., 489 U.S. 141, 165 (1989) (Florida anti-direct molding statute proscribing the copying of an unpatented item in general circulation preempted by federal patent laws which held the design to be unpatentable.).

> Congress has considered extending various forms of limited protection to industrial design either through the copyright laws or by relaxing the restrictions on the availability of design patents . . . Congress explicitly refused to take this step in the copyright laws . . . and despite sustained criticism . . . it has declined to alter the patent protections presently available for industrial design.

Id. at 986 (citations omitted). Justice O'Connor stressed that "the federal patent laws do create a federal right to copy and use" what is unpatentable).

competition law as an avenue for protecting designs. Another source of pressure stemmed from the courts' reaffirmation of a high threshold of non-obviousness in order to receive design patent protection.[90]

The Copyright Office found itself confronted with a dilemma. If it continued to staunchly resist granting copyright protection for articles of industrial design, it risked provoking a backlash from the courts. It was feared that the courts might grant broad protection to marginal items,[91] stemming from their belief that the Copyright Office's restrictive regulations violated *Bleistein.*[92] On the other hand, if the Copyright Office relaxed its tough line, there would be a proliferation of new vested interests with long-term copyright protection at odds with the anticipated short-term design protection in the pending congressional bills.[93]

During this period, the tension between the covert qualitative test in the Copyright Office's "sole intrinsic function" regulation and judicial allegiance to ideals of non-discrimination and advocacy of a minimal standard of originality produced a slew of copyrights for toys, dolls, jewelry, and other marginal items.[94]

---

90 The non-obviousness requirement was codified in 1952 at 35 U.S.C. § 103. *See* Graham v. John Deere, 383 U.S. 1, 14-17 (1966). Courts interpreting the non-obviousness requirement have applied it to industrial design in a strict fashion. *See, e.g.*, G.B. Lewis Co. v. Gould Prods., 436 F.2d 1176, 1178 (2d Cir. 1971); Rains v. Niaqua, Inc., 406 F.2d 275, 279 n.7 (2d Cir.), *cert. denied*, 395 U.S. 909 (1969).

91 *See infra* text accompanying note 94.

92 *See supra* notes 11-21 and accompanying text.

93 *See* Esquire, Inc. v. Ringer, 591 F.2d 796, 800 n.12 (D.C. Cir. 1978). "Since 1914, approximately seventy design protection bills have been introduced in Congress, none of which has been enacted into law." Each year that Congress failed to enact a design protection bill, the problem intensified, resulting in the heightening of four choices: copyright overprotection, overprotection under § 43(a) of the Lanham Act granting potential perpetuity, underprotection under design patent law because of its high standard of non-obviousness, and non-protection. These four alternatives could be viewed as parts of a vicious cycle: foot-dragging by Congress put pressure on the Copyright Office and the courts to lower the copyright threshold, which created vested interests in parties who now lobby Congress to continue dragging its feet, so that the vested interests are not divested. This intensifies pressures on the Copyright Office and the courts to step up their efforts. On the other hand, if the Copyright Office and the courts chose to maintain a higher copyrightability threshold, pressure would then be placed on federal unfair competition law to protect industrial design. This could create opposition because of its anti-competitive effects, leading to further lobbying for a design protection bill, which would be opposed by those with vested interests who had already obtained Lanham Act protection, leading to further congressional foot-dragging.

94 *See, e.g.*, Rushton v. Vitale, 218 F.2d 434, 434 (2d Cir. 1955) (doll in shape of television chimp copyrightable); Hassenfield Bros. v. Mego Corp., 150 U.S.P.Q. (BNA) 786, 788-89 (S.D.N.Y. 1966) (GI Joe dolls copyrightable); Remco Indus. v. Goldberger Doll Mfg. Co., 141 U.S.P.Q. (BNA) 898, 899 (E.D.N.Y. 1964) (Beatle dolls copyrightable); Royalty Designs, Inc. v. Thrifticheck Serv. Corp., 204 F. Supp. 702, 704 (S.D.N.Y. 1962) (plastic banks in shape of dogs copyrightable); Blazon, Inc. v. Deluxe Game Corp., 268 F. Supp. 416, 421 (S.D.N.Y. 1965) (hobby horse model copyrightable); Dan Kasoff,

These cases did not explicitly deal with separability and utilitarian function because the nature of the articles allowed the courts to avoid confronting the problem of copyright in modernist, functionalist, industrial design, but laid the doctrinal foundation for future inconsistencies to emerge. This growing number of items that the courts found to be copyrightable before *Mazer*[95] were examples of the vested interests the Copyright Office sought to limit. These cases involving copyrighted marginal items also served to weaken the Copyright Office's sole intrinsic function criterion.[96] Following the 1961-1964 Congressional compromises regarding the pending design bill,[97] the Copyright Office was foreclosed from ejecting the increasingly anomalous and growing body of already copyrighted objects from the proposed bill.[98] These inconsistencies both marred the Copyright Office's interim regulations and put cracks in the proposed noncumulation scheme.[99]

Three significant cases during this period foreshadowed later developments. *Prestige Floral, S.A. v. California Artificial Flower Co.*[100] held that a likeness of a natural flower could be copyrighted. The court determined that to be copyrightable, a "work of art" must be " 'a product of original creative authorship.' "[101]

Inc. v. Novelty Jewelry Co., 309 F.2d 745, 746 (2d Cir. 1962) (design of "garish trinket" copyrightable); Dan Kasoff, Inc. v. Gresco Jewelry Co., 204 F. Supp. 694, 695 (S.D.N.Y. 1962) (ornamental jewelry box copyrightable). *But see* L. Batlin & Son, Inc. v. Snyder, 536 F.2d 486, 492 (2d Cir. 1976) (Uncle Sam bank based on public domain image not copyrightable because it lacked substantial originality).

95 *See supra* notes 30-39 and accompanying text.

96 *See supra* note 47 and accompanying text.

97 HOUSE COMM. ON THE JUDICIARY, 89TH CONG., 1ST SESS., COPYRIGHT LAW REVISION PART 6: 1965 REVISION BILL 81 (Comm. Print 1965) ("The present situation is chaotic, and it is becoming worse all the time."). *See also Copyright Law Revision: Hearings on H.R.4347; H.R.5680; H.R.6831; H.R.6835 Before Subcomm. No. 3 of the House Comm. on the Judiciary*, 89th Cong., 1st Sess. 65-66 (1975) (testimony of A. Kaminstein, Register of Copyrights).

98 This was part of the "anti-maim" compromise which used the idea of separability to insure copyright holders such as Disney Studios, that they would not lose their copyright in their cartoon characters merely by printing them on a T-Shirt. *See* Waldheim, *Don't Maim Our Copyrights*, 7 BULL. COPYRIGHT SOC'Y 160, 161 (1960) ("Perhaps the drafters of [the design protection bill] inserted these provisions because it is difficult to define an exact dividing line between useful articles which embody works of art and those which embody merely design. So the proponents of the bill resolved the difficulty by erasing the line and by assuming that art ceases to be art when it becomes part of a useful article."); Waldheim, *The "Anti-Maim" Rule—New Design Bill Shares Majority View Among Nations*, 8 BULL. COPYRIGHT SOC'Y 359 (1961) (contending that the proposed design protection bill "maimed" copyright by terminating protection of later works to which an originally copyrighted work had been applied).

99 *See supra* notes 44-54.

100 201 F. Supp. 287, 291 (S.D.N.Y. 1962).

101 *Id.* at 289 (quoting HOUSE COMM. ON THE JUDICIARY, 87TH CONG., 1ST SESS., COPYRIGHT LAW REVISION 9 (Comm. Print 1961)).

According to the court, the "series of determinations" which were made by the artificial flower's designer reflected the requisite originality and the substantial degree of skill and independent judgment which copyright requires.[102] In *Doran v. Sunset House Distribution Corp.*,[103] the court held that a life-size, inflatable stand-up plastic Santa Claus was copyrightable. The court determined that the copier's use of the original assembly sheet with the original's logo infringed the original design's copyright. In *Ted Arnold Ltd. v. Silvercraft Co.*,[104] the court upheld the copyright in a pencil sharpener housed inside a replica of an antique telephone. The *Ted Arnold* court put forward a doctrine which attempted to rationalize separability on the grounds of consumer preference: "[W]e would not agree with defendant that its 'sole intrinsic function . . . is its utility.' Customers are paying fifteen dollars for it, not because it sharpens pencils uncommonly well, but because it is also a decorative conversation piece."[105] By trying to adhere to the *Bleistein* non-discrimination principle, the courts either had to continue lowering the thresholds of minimal creativity and originality, or engage in increasingly abstract and manipulable tests to invalidate copyright in useful objects.[106]

At the same time, the courts were growing increasingly confused over the issue of "trivial variations," resulting in part from problems arising in *Doran*.[107] Inevitably, the parsing of increas-

---

102 *Id.* at 291 (citation omitted). *But cf.* Gardenia Flowers, Inc. v. Joseph Markovits, 280 F. Supp. 771, 781-82 (S.D.N.Y. 1968) (commonplace, traditional arrangements of artificial flowers used in corsages did not embody sufficient creativity to constitute copyrightable works of art).

103 197 F. Supp. 940, 944 (S.D. Cal. 1961).

104 259 F. Supp. 733 (S.D.N.Y. 1966).

105 *Id.* at 736 (citation omitted).

106 Among other examples of specious tests was the practice of counting dissimilarities to find that insufficient substantial similarity had been shown to prove infringement. *See, e.g.*, Ideal Toy Corp. v Fab-Lu-Ltd., 360 F.2d 1021, 1022-23 (2d Cir. 1966). Other attempts to delimit the expansive scope of *Mazer* and *Bleistein* included ham-handed uses of the idea/expression dichotomy. *See, e.g.*, Uneeda Doll Co. v. P & M Doll Co., 241 F. Supp. 675, 677 (S.D.N.Y. 1965), *aff'd*, 353 F.2d 788 (2d Cir. 1965) (idea/expression dichotomy used to limit copyright of a doll on a pole in a display box). In the Second Circuit, Judge Clark, distressed over the pervasive indeterminacy in this area, urged that an "overall impression" test should be adopted. *See* Ideal Toy Corp. v. Sayco Doll Corp., 302 F.2d 623, 627 (2d Cir. 1963) (Clark, C.J., dissenting) ("[R]eproduction should be apparent on inspection and not be based upon a counting of similarities which do not constitute or leave a total impression of copying."). Ironically, though typical of these types of tests, the overall impression test produced results as arbitrary as the test it sought to replace. *See* Roth Greeting Cards v. United Card Co., 429 F.2d 1106, 1110 (9th Cir. 1970); Concord Fabrics, Inc. v. Marcus Bros. Textiles, 409 F.2d 1315, 1316 (2d Cir. 1969); Peter Pan Fabrics, Inc. v. Dan River Mills, Inc., 295 F. Supp. 1366, 1368-69 (S.D.N.Y. 1969).

107 Doran v. Sunset House Distrib. Corp., 197 F. Supp. 940 (S.D. Cal. 1961). *See also* Remco Indus. v. Goldberg Doll Mfg. Co., 141 U.S.P.Q. (BNA) 898, 899 (E.D.N.Y. 1964)

ingly fine variations between an original and a putatively infringing copy collided with industrial design practices during this period. Generally, design develops through small variations on existing style and market trends.[108] In terms of industrial design, this meant that during this period courts conflated a modicum of protectable originality and creativity into a protectable idea, thereby over-protecting extremely marginal articles.[109] By protecting small variations in designs falling into recognized traditional categories, such as toys, dolls, fabrics, and two-dimensional designs,[110] the courts ignored the possibility that the overall shape of a functional article might be eligible for copyright protection, thereby avoiding the problem of copyright for industrial design.

In granting registration to items such as rectangular architectural fixtures, geometric flower pots, and castings of fixtures,[111] the Copyright Office seemed to have begun extending the idea of physical separability to encompass conceptual separability. It explicitly did this in 1975.[112] The courts, however, seemed perplexed as to what basis the Copyright Office had used in allowing certain objects to be registered for copyright. As a result, by the mid-1970s, the distinction between art and utility had become an incoherent spectrum along which administrators and courts adopted contradictory, inconsistent and irreconcilable positions.[113]

(Beatle dolls); Hassenfield Bros. v. Mego Corp., 150 U.S.P.Q. (BNA) 786, 786-88 (S.D.N.Y. 1966) (GI Joe dolls).

108 This tendency towards incremental variation is a combination of both internal and external constraints, such as success in a particular submarket due to taste, fancy and other mixed motives, or the limited range of variations due to consumer tradition, custom or so-called functional considerations.

109 *See* Bleistein v. Donaldson Lithographing Co., 188 U.S. 239, 251 (1903). The tendency to protect the margins of copyright, in the name of protecting the core, stems from *Bleistein*. Indeed, Holmes, in *Bleistein*, extended the margins of copyright in the name of defending what he conceived of as copyright's core, when he held that copyright protected circus advertisements, in the name of protecting Goya and Manet.

110 *See supra* note 94 and accompanying text.

111 *See* Tennessee Fabricating Co. v. Moultrie Mfg. Co., 421 F.2d 279, 280 (5th Cir. 1970) (holding that the copyright registration for "a [twelve-inch square] architectural metal casting unit intended for use . . . [as] a decorative screen or room divider" was valid and copyright was infringed by defendants who had plugmolded and marketed an identical product); Hub Floral Corp. v. Royal Brass Corp., 454 F.2d 1226, 1227 (2d Cir. 1972) (an "octagonal planter, which is a stylized container" was copyrightable within § 5(g) of the 1909 Act).

112 *See* Register's Draft Report 1975, ch. VII, at 12 ("[A]ll original two-dimensional designs for useful articles . . . were subject to copyright registration. The same was true of those three-dimensional designs that can be conceptually separated and are capable of existing independently of the utilitarian aspects of the article embodying them.").

113 *See, e.g.*, SCOA Indus. v. Famolare, Inc., 192 U.S.P.Q. (BNA) 216, 218 (S.D.N.Y. 1976) ("There can be no valid copyright in troughs in the sole or wavy lines on the sides

7. Compromise and Contradiction

a. Deletion of Title II from the Copyright Act of 1976

Several strands of the applied art/industrial design problem came together in 1976. After more than seventeen years of congressional debate, the Copyright Act of 1976[114] was finally passed late in the year, with a *sui generis* design protection component removed from the Act at the eleventh hour.[115] Although *Esquire, Inc. v. Ringer*[116] arose under the 1909 Copyright Act,[117] which was still in effect during congressional debate on the 1976 Copyright Act, the case would have an important effect on subsequent interpretations of the 1976 Act.

The Copyright Office was apparently influential in getting the House Committee on the Judiciary to amend the pending copyright bill. The separability language of Copyright Office regulation section 202.10(c)[118] was engrafted onto the legislative definition of "pictorial, graphic, and sculptural works" in section 101 of the then pending Copyright Revision Bill.[119] The lan-

---

These have no existence as works of art and if they did have, lack even the minimum originality needed for copyright."); Eltra Corp. v. Ringer, 194 U.S.P.Q. (BNA) 198, 200-01 (E.D. Va. 1976) (typeface design not separable); Esquire, Inc. v. Ringer, 414 F. Supp. 939, 941 (D.D.C. 1976), *rev'd*, 591 F.2d 796 (D.C. Cir. 1978), *cert. denied*, 440 U.S. 908 (1979) (design of an outdoor lamp not separable). *But c.f.* L & L White Metal Casings Corp. v. Cornell Metal Corp., 353 F. Supp. 1170, 1171 (E.D.N.Y. 1972) (copyright registrations held valid for "castings for fixtures, pedestals, lamps and furniture"); S.K. Potteries & Mold Co. v. Sipes, 192 U.S.P.Q. (BNA) 537 (N.D. Ind. 1976) (ornamental ceramic molds of Christmas decorations copyrightable).

114 17 U.S.C. §§ 101-810 (1988).

115 *See* H.R. REP. No. 1476, 94th Cong., 2d Sess. 5, *reprinted in* 1976 U.S. CODE CONG. & ADMIN. NEWS 5659, 5663 [hereinafter H.R. REP. No. 1476].

116 414 F. Supp. 939 (D.D.C. 1976), *rev'd*, 591 F.2d 796 (D.C. Cir. 1978), *cert. denied*, 440 U.S. 908 (1979).

117 1909 Act, *supra* note 13.

118 37 C.F.R. § 202.10 (1990).

119 *Compare* S.22, 94th Cong., 1st Sess. tit. I (1975) *reprinted in* S. REP No. 473, 94th Cong., 1st Sess. § 101, at 2 (Comm. Print 1975) (no separability language) *with* 17 U.S.C. § 101 (1976) (separability language in definition of "pictorial, graphic, and sculptural works"). Note also the congressional explanation of separability:

> In adopting this amendatory language [based on Regulation 202.10 (c)], the Committee is seeking to draw as clear a line as possible between copyrightable works of applied art and uncopyrighted works of industrial design. . . . Unless the shape of an automobile, airplane, ladies' dress, food processor, television set, or any other industrial product contains some element that, *PHYSICALLY OR CONCEPTUALLY*, can be identified as separable from the utilitarian aspects of that article, the design would not be copyrighted under the bill. The test of separability and independence from 'the utilitarian aspects of the article' does not depend upon the nature of the design—that is, even if the appearance of an article is determined by esthetic (as opposed to functional) considerations, only elements, if any, which can be identified separately from the useful article as such are copyrightable. And, even if the three-dimensional design contains some such element (for example, a carving on the back of a chair or a floral relief design on silver flat-

guage of section 202.10(c) which referred to "*sole* intrinsic function" was changed to "*an* intrinsic utilitarian function" in the 1976 Act.[120] By changing "*sole* intrinsic function" to "*an* intrinsic utilitarian function," virtually all "ornamental designs of useful articles" were now subject to the separability test. At this time, however, the *sui generis* design protection of Title II was still in place,[121] providing a theoretical safety net for industrial designs extruded from copyright protection under the new Act.

At the last minute, the House Judiciary Subcommittee on Courts, Civil Liberties, and the Administration of Justice struck Title II from the Senate version of the General Copyright Revision Bill.[122] Title II was therefore excluded from the final Act, enacted in October 1976 by the Copyright Revision.[123]The

---

> ware), copyright protection would extend only to that element, and would not cover the over-all configuration of the utilitarian article as such.

H.R. REP. No. 1476, *supra* note 115, at 5668 (emphasis added).

120 17 U.S.C. § 101 (1988) (emphasis added).

121 *See* S.22, 94th Cong., 1st Sess. tit. II (1975), *reprinted in* S. REP. No. 473, 94th Cong., 1st Sess. § 205, at 162 (Comm. Print 1975); SENATE COMM. ON THE JUDICIARY, S. REP. No. 473, COPYRIGHT LAW REVISION, 94th Cong., 2nd Sess. 5 (1975), *reprinted in* 1976 U.S. CODE CONG. & ADMIN. NEWS 5659. Title II would have granted a five year term of protection, with an option for a five year renewal, for a total of ten years. However, it would have excluded ornamental designs of useful articles if they were " ' staple or commonplace, such as a standard geometric figure, familiar symbol, emblem or motif, or other shape, pattern or configuration which has become common, prevalent or ordinary,' " which could be read as a watered down non-obviousness test as well as requiring independent creation. Reichman I, *supra* note 1, at 1252. Professor Reichman notes that other sources suggest that there was "informal opposition behind the scenes from major industries, including sectors of the automobile industry, and from the manufacturers of spare parts." Furthermore, there is evidence in foreign literature that "big business" might have favored a patent model of protection, and that small industry would favor a copyright approach. *Id.* at 1251 n.577. *See also Hearings on H.R.2223 Before the Subcomm. on Courts, Civil Liberties, and the Administration of Justice of the House Comm. on the Judiciary*, 94th Cong., 1st Sess. (1975) (testimony of Irwin Goldbloom for the Justice Dept.), *reprinted in* 14 OMNIBUS COPYRIGHT REVISION LEGISLATIVE HISTORY, at 139-49:

> A threshold consideration before finding that the needs are such that this new type of protection should be available is whether the benefits to the public of such protection outweigh the burdens. We believe that insufficient need has been shown to date to justify removing from the public domain and possible use by others of the rights and benefits proposed under the present bill for such ornamental designs. . . . [D]esign patents . . . are as far as the public should go to grant exclusive rights for ornamental designs of useful articles in the absence of an adequate showing that the new protection will provide substantial benefits to the general public which outweigh removing such designs from free public use.
>
> . . . .
>
> If the contribution made to the public by the creation of an ornamental design of a useful article is insufficient to rise to patentable novelty, the design should not be protected by the law.

Id. at 139-40.

122 *See* H.R. REP. No. 1476, *supra* note 115, at 5663.

123 *See* HOUSE COMM. OF CONFERENCE, GENERAL REVISION OF THE COPYRIGHT LAW, TITLE 17 OF THE UNITED STATES CODE, H.R. CONF. REP. No. 1733, 94th Cong., 2d Sess. 82 (1976), *reprinted in*, 1976 U.S. CODE CONG. & ADMIN. NEWS 5810. Deletion of Title II

Copyright Revision Act of 1976 was thus a mangled version of a partial cumulation regime,[124] without the safety net of design protection for articles failing to meet the threshold of copyrightability, but retaining a broad definition of separability applicable to "useful article[s]"[125] with "an intrinsic utilitarian function".[126] Thus, the 1976 Copyright Act retained effective filters, but lacked a receptacle for the filtered material that would have given meaning to the filters' existence.

b. *Esquire, Inc. v. Ringer*

In *Esquire Inc. v. Ringer*,[127] the Copyright Office refused copyright registration to a three-dimensional modernist outdoor lighting fixture, devoid of ornamentation, as a sculptural "work of art" under the 1909 Act. The manufacturer sued the Copyright Register in a *mandamus* action to compel registration of the fixture. *Esquire* claimed the fixture was made with the intent of creating " 'works of modernistic form sculpture.' "[128] The Copy-

---

was supposedly to enable the House Judiciary Committee to give it "further study." However, Chairman Kastenmeier stated:

> The final major area of controversy is title II of the Senate bill which provides for a new form of protection for ornamental designs which cannot be identified separately from the useful articles of which they are part. This 'no mans land' [sic] between copyright and patent law presents difficult public policy questions. The Department of Justice strongly opposed the creation of this new form of intellectual property on the grounds that no need for it had been demonstrated. Because sufficient information was not available to enable the subcommittee to resolve the issue at this time, we deleted title II from the bill with the understanding that the subject would be considered in depth during the next Congress.

122 Cong. Rec. 31979 (1976) (cited in Norris Indus. v. ITT, 212 U.S.P.Q. (BNA) 754, 756 (N.D. Fla. 1981), *aff'd*, 696 F.2d 918 (11th Cir. 1983).

124 *See supra* note 9.

125 "A 'useful article' is an article having an intrinsic utilitarian function that is not merely to portray the appearance of the article or to convey information. An article that is normally part of a useful article is considered a 'useful article.' " 17 U.S.C. § 101 (1988). However, the word "useful" is subject to several constrictions. The district court in Gay Toys, Inc. v. Buddy L Corp., 522 F. Supp. 622 (E.D. Mich 1981), held that a toy airplane was "useful" because a toy plane "is a thing to play with. Play is an integral part of growing up. Children need toys. A toy airplane is useful and possesses utilitarian and functional characteristics in that it permits a child to dream and to let his or her imagination soar." *Id.* at 625. The Court of Appeals reversed, finding that the district court's rationale as to what is "useful" could swallow the general rule. *Gay Toys*, 703 F.2d 970 (6th Cir. 1983). "A painting of Lindbergh's Spirit of St. Louis invites the viewer 'to dream and to let his or her imagination soar,' and would not be copyrightable under the district court's approach." *Id.* at 973. In that sense, every work of art becomes a "useful article."

126 17 U.S.C. § 101.

127 414 F. Supp. 939 (D.D.C. 1976), *rev'd*, 591 F.2d 796 (D.C. Cir. 1978), *cert. denied*, 440 U.S. 908 (1979).

128 *Esquire*, 591 F.2d at 800 (quoting appellee's brief at 5). Esquire described the fixtures as follows: " 'The ELLIPTRA I and ELLIPTRA II fixtures include oblate housings having a rounded upper portion, a cylindrical band between the upper and lower por-

right Office relied on section 202.10(c) in rejecting the lighting fixture design, and thus "kept with the practice of denying copyright to utilitarian objects followed since 1910."[129] The Office indicated that because the fixture's aesthetically appealing features could not be identified separately as a work of art distinct from the entire shape of the article,[130] it could not be copyrighted. The manufacturer responded that section 5(g) of the 1909 Act qualified the lighting fixture as a "work of art," and that the Copyright Office had wrongfully refused registration because of the article's utilitarian purpose, in violation of *Mazer v. Stein.*[131] The D.C. Circuit in 1978 reversed the *Esquire* district court,[132] providing a foothold for the non-cumulation approach initially

---

tions, and a cylindrical lower edge portion. The ELLIPTRA III design utilizes a generally cup-shaped housing having a generally elliptical cross section tapering into a rounded rear portion.' " *Id.* at 798 n.2 (quoting plaintiff's brief at 4).

129 *Esquire,* 414 F. Supp. at 940-41.

130 *Id.* at 941.

131 374 U.S. 201 (1954).

132 Judge Gessell, for the district court, dismissed the Copyright Office's idea of separability as an "elusive semantic dispute" and challenged the Register to articulate the policies, purposes and principles underlying separability. *Esquire,* 414 F. Supp. at 941. In response, the Copyright Office referred back to the old 1910-1948 standard of copyrightability, modified by the Copyright Office itself, which used "art in the historical and ordinary sense" as its organizing principle. *See* Rosenthal v. Stein, 205 F.2d 633, 635 (9th Cir. 1953) ("A thing is a work of art if it appears to be within the historical and ordinary conception of the term art."). Supposedly, this standard accounted for the exclusion of "shapes and forms of . . . useful articles," and avoided trade restraints of up to 56 years in "industrial designs of everything from automobiles to bathtubs to dresses." *Esquire,* 414 F. Supp. at 940, 941.

Not surprisingly, the Copyright Register was hard pressed to come up with a defensible, uncontradicted rationale for excluding Esquire's lighting fixture. *Id.* Exclusion based on the fact that the fixture was destined for a utilitarian purpose was proscribed by *Mazer.* Exclusion on the basis of insufficiently conceptually separable artistic value was contradicted by the granting of copyright protection to other designs equally inseparable. Such a contradiction amounted to a conclusive presumption against protecting modernist design, and a privileging of baroque ornamental decoration. The Copyright Office's attempt to distinguish the Esquire lighting fixture from other copyrighted items such as geometric flowerpots, rectangular architectural fixtures, and castings for plumbing fixtures, raised a strong suspicion that impermissible subjective pre-biases and values were the driving force behind the Copyright Office's decisions. The Copyright Office was acutely aware of the anomaly of articles such as "textile designs, wallpaper, floor tiles, painted or printed decorations, 'certain' lamp bases, carvings on furniture, costume jewelry, [and] decorator items" getting copyright protection while modern functional designs were only getting shorter term design protection or were being left unprotected. The Copyright Office was being somewhat disingenuous by pointing to this discrepancy, since its explicit policy since 1956 had been precisely to exclude functional designs, while allowing in the anomalies. *See* Register's Draft Report 1975, ch. VII, at 12 (1975).

Judge Gessell used the 1959 regulation's "sole intrinsic function" language to undermine the Copyright Office's position. See *supra* note 67 and accompanying text for the provision. Because the "outdoor lights serve both to decorate and illuminate" and were "exclusively decorative" during the daytime, the fixture's "sole intrinsic function" could not be its utility. *Esquire,* 414 F. Supp. at 941. Using this reasoning, there could be no copyright denial for any attractively shaped utilitarian object under a "sole intrin-

advanced by the Copyright Office in 1959.[133] Judge Bazelon, speaking for the D.C. Circuit, rebutted the suggestion that the new separability criteria offended the *Bleistein* non-discrimination principle[134] because it excluded modern functional designs from copyright protection. Bazelon narrowly interpreted *Bleistein*'s non-discrimination principle as "concerned only with conscious bias against one form of art—in that case the popular art reflected in circus posters."[135] The court saw no justification "for extending the nondiscrimination principle of *Bleistein* to include action having an unintentional, disproportionate impact on one style of artistic expression."[136] The Court stated that a further extension of *Bleistein* into this area would undermine the legitimate congressional directive "that copyright protection should not be afforded to industrial designs."[137] Therefore, a broad reading of *Bleistein* was trumped by congressional policy.

The court reasoned that by deleting Title II from the 1976 Copyright Act,[138] Congress exhibited concern for the "obvious and anti-competitive effects" which would result from the grant of a "new monopoly" to industrial design[139] if the overall shape

---

sic function test" because there would always be an added decorative function. *See* NIMMER ON COPYRIGHT, supra note 37, at 2-91.

After skewering the Copyright Office's restrictive position, Judge Gessell attempted to excavate an expansive interpretation of *Mazer v. Stein*:

> The forms represented by Esquire's fixtures emphasize line and shape rather than the realistic or the ornate but it is not for the Register to reject them on artistic grounds or because the form is accommodated to a utilitarian purpose. There cannot be and there should not be any national standard of what constitutes art and the pleasing forms of the Esquire fixtures are entitled to the same recognition afforded more traditional sculpture.

Esquire, 414 F. Supp. at 941 (citations omitted).

The *Esquire* District Court recognized the type of covert aesthetic privileging in which the Copyright Office was engaged, and in the name of *Bleistein* and *Mazer*, attempted once again to expand the margins of copyright. What the court failed to realize, though, was the fundamental lack of any non-controversial value-free baseline from which to begin making coherent decisions in this confused area.

133 *See supra* notes 66-68.

134 *See supra* notes 11-21 and accompanying text.

135 *Esquire*, 591 F.2d at 805.

136 *Id.*

137 *Id.*

138 *See supra* notes 121-23 and accompanying text.

139 *Esquire*, 591 F.2d at 801 (quoting the Copyright Register's brief):

> 'First, in the case of some utilitarian objects, like scissors or paper clips, shape is mandated by function. If one manufacturer were given the copyright to the design of such an article, it could completely prevent others from producing the same article. Second, consumer preference sometimes demands uniformity of shape for certain utilitarian articles, like stoves . . . . People simply expect and desire certain everyday useful articles to look the same particular way. . . . Third, insofar as geometric shapes are concerned, there are only a limited amount of basic shapes, . . . [and] [t]hese shapes are obviously in the public domain.'

Id. at 801 n.15.

of useful articles were to be copyrighted. The Register feared that "the whole realm of consumer products—garments, toasters, refrigerators, furniture, bathtubs, automobiles, etc.—and industrial products designed to have aesthetic appeal—subway cars, computers, photocopying machines, typewriters, adding machines, etc.,"[140] would qualify for copyright protection as "works of art" if the floodgates to industrial design protection were opened. Judge Leventhal, in a concurring opinion, noted:

> Form follows function, in the credo of one school of art. Yet the overall legislative policy against monopoly for industrial design sustains the Copyright Office in its effort to distinguish between the instances where the aesthetic element is conceptually severable and the instances where the aesthetic element is inextricably interwoven with the utilitarian aspect of the article.[141]

The *Esquire* opinion gave dispositive weight to the "intent" of Congress to exclude industrial design from the scope of the 1976 Act (even though the *Esquire* case was subject to the 1909 Act). The legislative history, however, could also be read to intend protection for applied art under the category of "pictorial, graphic and sculptural works" in section 101 of the 1976 Copyright Act.[142] The argument that congressional intent justified *per se* exclusion of industrial design was ambiguous at best, and revolved around the significance of the last-minute deletion of Title II from the 1976 Copyright Act.[143] Thus, the D.C. Circuit took the ambiguous legislative his-

---

140 *Id.* at 801.

141 *Id.* at 807 (Leventhal, J., concurring). *But cf.* NIMMER ON COPYRIGHT, *supra* note 37 at 2-96.2, n.115.1. The Esquire design was *not* a shape dictated by function, but a combination of various geometric abstract three-dimensional shapes and at odds with established copyright protection for two-dimensional designs utilizing combinations of geometric shapes. If Judge Leventhal assumed that the Esquire fixture was a form dictated by function, one wonders what he would make of an ordinary street lamp.

142 *See* H.R. REP. No. 1476, *supra* note 115, at 54.

> [T]he definition of 'pictorial, graphic, and sculptural works' carries with it no implied criterion of artistic taste, aesthetic value, or intrinsic quality. The term is intended to comprise not only 'works of art' in the traditional sense but also . . . works of 'applied art.' . . .
>
> In accordance with . . . *Mazer v. Stein*, works of 'applied art' encompass all original pictorial, graphic, and sculptural works that are intended to be or have been embodied in useful articles, regardless of factors such as mass production, commercial exploitation, and the potential availability of design patent protection. . . .
>
> The Committee has added language to the definition of 'pictorial, graphic, and sculptural works' in an effort to make clearer the distinction between works of applied art protectable under the bill and industrial designs not subject to copyright protection.

Id. (citation omitted).

143 If design protection was excised from the 1976 Act, an equally plausible assump-

tory of the 1976 Act, applied it to a case arising under the 1909 Act, and in so doing, established a form of strict separability. This created a *de facto* presumption against modern industrial design, justified by both the *Bleistein* non-discrimination principle and deference to congressional intent. These high-level justifications, at such an extremely indeterminate level of generality, allowed for wildly erratic judicial results in the years following the passage of the Copyright Act of 1976.[144]

c. The History of the Second Circuit

Against the background of growing instability in copyright law regarding the protection of industrial design in the early 1970s, the Second Circuit sought to invigorate design patent law by lowering the non-obviousness threshold.[145] Simultaneously, the Second Circuit raised the copyright originality threshold so as to steer noncopyrightable articles into the design patent fold.[146]

In *Alfred Bell & Co. v. Catalda Fine Arts, Inc.*,[147] the court contemplated the originality requirement of copyright law, considering whether a mezzotint copy of a work in the public domain could be copyrighted. The court found the reproduction to be copyrightable, saying that "[n]o matter how poor artistically the 'author's' addition, it is enough if it be his own."[148] The court

---

tion could be made that Congress intended manufacturers who had invested in successful industrial designs to seek protection under trademark, unfair competition, or design patent law. Foreclosure of these three alternative avenues, either through a high threshold of entry (design patent), pre-emption under section 301 of the 1976 Act (state unfair competition law), or reluctance to allow potentially unlimited protection (federal trademark law), would then mean that Congress intended to send industrial designs into the public domain, regardless of the creative content they possessed. However, this result would contradict *Mazer v. Stein*, the language of the H.R. REP. No. 1476, *supra* note 115, and the protection of applied art in the 1976 Act.

144 *See infra* notes 179-283 and accompanying text.

145 For a discussion of the non-obviousness threshold of patent law, see *supra* notes 90-93. The lowered threshold for design patent protection can be conceived of as a quantitative creativity requirement, that is, a requirement of distance from material in the public domain or "prior art."

By the mid-1970s, there was a clear split between the appellate and district courts in the Second Circuit regarding the appropriate threshold for copyright protection for industrial designs. The district courts insisted on a patent-like approach requiring a certain distance from prior art, while the Second Circuit insisted on an opposed copyright model with minimal thresholds for creativity and originality. *See generally* Reichman, *Design Protection After the Copyright Act of 1976: A Comparative View of the Emerging Interim Models*, 31 J. COPYRIGHT SOC'Y 267, 298-303 (1984) [hereinafter Reichman II] (contrasting the French, German, Dutch, and English systems of intellectual industrial property protection with the American system).

146 *See infra* notes 151-220 and accompaying text. The heightened copyrightability threshold can be considered a qualitative creativity requirement.

147 191 F.2d 99 (2d Cir. 1951).

148 *Id.* at 103 (citing *Bleistein*, 188 U.S. at 239).

went so far as to include "unintentional" variations of works in the public domain within copyright protection.[149] Thus, *Catalda* and *Bleistein* respectively stand for extremely minimal copyright thresholds for both originality and creativity.[150]

In the late 1960s, courts in the Second Circuit began manifesting dissatisfaction with the *de minimis* threshold for originality established in *Catalda*. In *Gardenia Flowers, Inc. v. Joseph Markovits, Inc.*,[151] the District Court for the Southern District of New York struck down copyrights in corsage designs of artificial flowers for their failure to meet minimum requirements of originality and creativity set forth by the Copyright Office. The court held that the creativity requirement in the Copyright Office regulation[152] was "separate and distinct from authorship or originality," and, furthermore, the corsage designs lacked the sufficient quantitative creativity necessary to distinguish them from patterns "common and traditional in the trade."[153] At odds with the prevailing rationale of *Catalda*—that the translation of something in the public domain into a new medium was copyrightable expression—the court in *Gardenia Flowers* asserted that " '[t]he purpose of copyright law is to protect creation, not mechanical skill.' "[154]

The holding of the district court in *Gardenia Flowers* was contradicted two years later in *Thomas Wilson & Co. v. Irving J. Dorfman Co.*[155] In this case, the Second Circuit held that any

---

149 *Id.* at 105. ("A copyist's bad eyesight or defective musculature, or a shock caused by a clap of thunder, may yield sufficiently distinguishable variations. Having hit upon such a variation unintentionally, the 'author' may adopt it as his and copyright it.") *See* International News Serv. v. Associated Press, 248 U.S. 215 (1918); J.L. Mott Iron Works v. Clow, 82 Fed. 316 (7th Cir. 1897) (Copyright protection requires a modicum of intellectual creativity, however minimal); Baker v. Selden, 101 U.S. 99 (1879); The Trade-mark Cases, 100 U.S. 82 (1879).

150 *See* NIMMER ON COPYRIGHT, *supra* note 37, at 2-84 n.59 ("Where creativity refers to the nature of the work itself, originality refers to the nature of the author's contribution to the work.").

These modest requirements for copyright should be juxtaposed against the more stringent requirements for design patent protection. Under design patent law, there is a strictly observed "non-obviousness" requirement. *See* 35 U.S.C. §§ 103, 171; *see also* Graham v. John Deere, 383 U.S. 1 (1965) (patents dependent on novelty, utility, and "non-obvious" nature of "subject matter sought to be patented").

Industrial design falls into the interstices between these two very separate regimes and its anomalous nature highlights the contradictions of both approaches.

151 280 F. Supp. 776 (S.D.N.Y. 1968). *See also* Oppenheimer, *Originality in Art Reproductions: "Variations" in Search of a Theme*, 27 ASCAP COPYRIGHT L. SYMP. 207, 218-21 (1982) (examining the contradictory treatment given reproductions of works of art in the public domain under copyright law).

152 37 C.F.R. § 202.10(b) (1959), as amended June 18, 1959 (repealed Jan 1, 1978, 43 Fed. Reg. 966 (1978)).

153 *Gardenia Flowers*, 280 F. Supp. at 781, 783.

154 *Id.* at 783 (citation omitted).

155 433 F.2d 409 (2d Cir. 1970).

requirement of quantitative creativity, in the sense of patent-like "distance from prior art," was without both constitutional and statutory support: "[I]n sharp contrast to a patent, the requirement of originality in the creative sense does not appear in [the 1909] statute."[156] Despite the fact that the court felt compelled to state that it was "not overwhelmed by 'the creative activity' embodied in" a floral pattern used in lingerie, it nonetheless upheld the copyright.[157]

In *Puddu v. Buonamici Statuary, Inc.*,[158] the Second Circuit reaffirmed the modesty of the creativity and originality requirements. Invoking both *Catalda* and *Bleistein*, the court reversed the district court's requirement of quantitative creativity. By 1974, the Second Circuit in *Soptra Fabrics Corp. v. Stafford Knitting Mills, Inc.*[159] went so far as to hold that the placement of an otherwise uncopyrightable textile design in a repetitive pattern copyrightable.

In *Kuddle Toy, Inc. v. Pussycat-Toy Co.*,[160] the District Court for the Eastern District of New York defended the "patent-like" approach to copyright in industrial designs, and challenged the copyrightability of minute details. *Kuddle Toy* involved minuscule variations from a sequence of copyrighted teddy bears going back more than a century. Striking down the plaintiff's copyrights on the teddy bears, the court found that the string of copyrights based on trivial variations, in effect, gave the manufacturer a perpetual lock on the commonplace, traditional teddy bear. The court determined that by "magnifying mere difference[s] into intended design change[s]," the manufacturer sought *de facto* appropriation from the public domain.[161] In essence, the *Kuddle Toy* court warned manufacturers embarking on small variations of works in the public domain that they did so at their own risk.

The *Kuddle Toy* court evinced the deep contradictions into which copyright and design patent law had fallen.[162] Copyright

---

156 *Id.* at 411 (citation omitted).

157 *Id.* at 411 n.4.

158 450 F.2d 401, 402 (2d Cir. 1971) ("[T]he differences suffice to satisfy the modest requirement of originality laid down by the Supreme Court in Bleistein v. Donaldson Lithographing Co., and by this Court in Alfred Bell & Co. v. Catalda Fine Arts.") (citations omitted).

159 490 F.2d 1092 (2d Cir. 1974).

160 183 U.S.P.Q. (BNA) 642 (E.D.N.Y. 1974).

161 *Id.* at 654, 657 "[N]o publication with copyright notice can take anything in the public domain out of the public domain, or in any way dissolve or subordinate an earlier author's subsisting rights of copyright in the same aggregate." *But cf.* Doran v. Sunset House Distrib. Corp., 197 F. Supp. 940 (S.D. Cal. 1961).

162 *Kuddle Toy*, 183 U.S.P.Q. at 656-59.

law, by way of its insistence on an almost complete lack of evaluative criteria, was granting long-term protection for all types of designs with little or no creative content. By contrast, design patent law, the purpose of which was supposedly to stimulate design innovation, was excluding designs from its short-term protection through its high threshold of non-obviousness.[163]

In 1974, the Second Circuit tentatively began to refashion the non-obviousness barrier in *Lancaster Colony Corp. v. Aldon Accessories, Ltd.*,[164] holding that a design patent in a modernistic ashtray was both valid and had been infringed. The court held that the "aesthetically pleasing design" of the ashtray and its "neatness, simplicity, functional style and general air of contemporary solidity," were non-obvious.[165] The court determined that the ashtray was exactly the type of article the design patent statute meant to encourage.[166] This holding created the possibility for a lower non-obviousness threshold for industrial designs in the Second Circuit, at least at the infringement stage.[167]

In *L. Batlin & Son, Inc. v. Snyder*,[168] the Second Circuit formulated the doctrine of "substantial originality,"[169] which served to elevate the threshold of copyrightability. *Batlin* involved plastic reproductions of an Uncle Sam cast iron bank in the public domain. An importer registered its reproductions as "sculpture" with the Copyright Office on the basis of small variations it had incorporated between the public domain original and the plastic replica.[170] A second importer was also producing Uncle Sam banks in cast iron, and after becoming aware of the first im-

---

163 *See supra* note 150 and accompanying text.

164 506 F.2d 1197 (2d Cir. 1974). *Lancaster Colony* was significant because between 1922 and 1974, the Second Circuit only upheld two design patents, which led to an almost conclusive presumption against their validity. *See, e.g.*, Rains v. Niaqua, Inc., 406 F.2d 275 (2d Cir. 1969); *see also* Schnadig Corp. v. Gaines Mfg. Co., 620 F.2d 1166, 1167 (6th Cir. 1980) ("[D]esign patents perform a distinct function in the federal scheme of legal protection for creative works.").

165 *Lancaster Colony*, 506 F.2d at 1198.

166 *Id.* at 1199, 1200.

167 This lowered standard of non-obviousness was not extended to the registration stage, substantially reducing its effectiveness in filtering out articles which might be excluded under a higher copyright originality threshold. Other disadvantages of design patent protection include the expense, length, and cumbersomeness of the application process, and the uncertainty of the results of bringing a suit for infringement. *See* Brown, *Design Protection: An Overview*, 34 U.C.L.A. L. REV. 1341, 1356 (1989) [hereinafter *Design Protection: An Overview*]; *see also infra* notes 289-92 (discussing design patent drawbacks).

168 394 F. Supp. 1389 (S.D.N.Y. 1975), *rev'd*, 536 F.2d 486 (2d Cir. 1976). *Cf.* Durham Indus. v. Tomy Corp., 630 F.2d 905 (1980) (originality requirement of copyright law cannot be satisfied by the mere reproduction of a work of art in another medium); Eden Toys, Inc. v. Marshall Field & Co., 675 F.2d 498 (2d Cir. 1982).

169 *Batlin*, 536 F.2d at 490-92.

170 *Id.* at 488.

porter's efforts, began producing plastic copies of the copyrighted plastic replicas as well.

Despite *Catalda*'s holding that barely distinguishable variations are copyrightable,[171] the court decided that the variations in the registered plastic replica and the public domain cast iron bank were insufficient for copyright protection.[172] The court opined that unless the new article represented a "minimal element of creativity"[173]—originality in the sense of independent effort—allowing copyright protection would thwart the constitutional and statutory policies, purposes, and principles underlying copyright law.[174] The court believed that to grant such protection would "put a weapon for harassment in the hands of mischievous copiers"[175] and would allow them to bar others from gaining legitimate access to subject matter in the public domain.[176]

Three dissenting judges in *Batlin* feared the reinstitution of a "purpose" test in the guise of a "physical" versus "true artistic" skill characterization that *Mazer v. Stein* had expressly overruled.[177] The dissent also criticized the creation of legal tests masking covert judicial value judgments and noted the disastrous impact that the decision would have on investment.[178]

Thus, as the Copyright Act of 1976 was headed toward passage, the Second Circuit, in marked contrast to the D.C. Circuit,[179] was poised to implement a regime of partial cumulation.[180] The Second Circuit had begun lowering the threshold of design patent non-obviousness and had elevated the copyright threshold for applied art to "substantial originality."

---

171 *See supra* note 150 and accompanying text.

172 There was a latent recognition in *Batlin* that by changing the medium from the public domain cast iron original into a plastic replica, the manufacturer had overriding exigencies of functional purpose which limited the scope for creative content, insofar as transforming the original. *Batlin*, 536 F.2d at 489. "[T]here were no elements of difference that amounted to significant alteration or that had any purpose other than the functional one of making a more suitable (and probably less expensive) figure in the plastic medium." *Id.* "Nor can the requirement of originality be satisfied simply by the demonstration of 'physical skill' or 'special training.' . . . A considerably *higher* degree of skill is required, true artistic skill, to make the reproduction copyrightable." *Id.* at 491.

173 *Id.* at 490 (quoting 1 M. NIMMER, THE LAW OF COPYRIGHT § 10.2, at 36 (1975)).

174 *Id.*

175 *Id.* at 492.

176 *Id.*

177 *Id.* at 492-94 (quoting 1 M. NIMMER, THE LAW OF COPYRIGHT § 10.2, at 36 (1975)). "[T]he author's reasons for making changes should be irrelevant to a determination of whether the differences are trivial." *Id.* at 493. (Meskill, J., Timbers, J., Van Graafeiland, J., dissenting).

178 *Id.* at 492.

179 *See supra* notes 127-41 and accompanying text.

180 See *supra* note 9 for a definition of partial cumulation.

Coupled with the anticipated passage of Title II,[181] the Second Circuit would have had the tools to keep most industrial designs out of copyright, steering them to either design patent protection or short term *sui generis* design protection. However, because Title II was eventually deleted[182] from the 1976 Copyright Act, the court's decision not to follow *Catalda* and *Bleistein* lacked the clear legislative pretext that Title II's passage and implementation would have provided, leaving the Second Circuit in an embarrassing position.

d. *Kieselstein-Cord v. Accessories by Pearl, Inc.*

Between 1976 and 1980, the Second Circuit was faced with a choice. Either it could adopt the legal theory of non-cumulation and exclude all industrial design from copyright protection, as the D.C. Circuit was doing,[183] or it could try to implement the *Batlin* partial cumulation approach[184] without the design protection component. In *Kieselstein-Cord v. Accessories by Pearl, Inc.*,[185] the Second Circuit confronted these choices and surreptitiously introduced a qualitative originality standard into copyright law, using conceptual separability to mediate the contradictions engendered by the failure to pass a design protection law.[186]

Kieselstein involved two gold and silver designer belt buckles marketed to "high fashion stores and jewelry stores."[187] At issue was an unauthorized copy of the belts cast in cheap metal. Because Kieselstein-Cord, the designer, had registered the buckles as "original sculpture and design"[188] with the Copyright Office, he was able to bring suit against the infringer.

Under the 1976 Act,[189] the utilitarian function of the belt buckles did not automatically exclude them from copyright protection. If the buckles were to be protected pieces of "applied art" under the definition of "pictorial, graphic, and sculptural works" in section 101, they would also be within the definition of a "useful article."[190] Their copyright status thus depended on

---

[181] *See supra* note 122.
[182] *See supra* notes 122-23 and accompanying text.
[183] *See supra* notes 127-44 and accompanying text.
[184] *See supra* notes 168-76 and accompanying text.
[185] 632 F.2d 989 (2d Cir. 1980).
[186] *Id.*
[187] *Id.* at 991.
[188] *Id.* at 990-91.
[189] 17 U.S.C. § 101 (1988).
[190] *Id.*

the section 101 separability standard.[191] If the Second Circuit had chosen to follow the D.C. Circuit, it could have applied *Esquire*'s strict separability criterion.[192] Under this criterion, it could be argued that the design was incapable of separate existence and the belt buckles were an instance "where the aesthetic element is inextricably interwoven with the utilitarian aspect of the article."[193] Contrary to *Esquire*, however, the Copyright Office had already accepted the article for registration, causing the Second Circuit to attempt to distinguish between the non-copyrightable *Esquire* lighting fixture and the designer belt buckles. To accomplish this, the court turned to the only separability exception that Congress had provided—if "some element that, physically or conceptually, can be identified as separable from the utilitarian aspects" of an article, that element would be copyrightable.[194]

Judge Oakes, writing for the Second Circuit, began his opinion by invoking *Batlin*'s "substantial originality" criterion,[195] but found it a barrier to the Kieselstein-Cord belt buckle design. Citing Nimmer, the court said that none of the pertinent authorities—*Mazer*, the old regulations, the 1976 statute—offered any solution to the "line-drawing problem inherent in delineating the extent of copyright protection available for works of applied art."[196] The *Kieselstein* court interpreted the legislative intent of the House Report relied upon by the *Esquire* court[197] as inveighing against any inherently uncopyrightable category of articles called "industrial design."[198]

By using the "physically or conceptually separable" language in the House Report,[199] the court reasoned that even in-

---

191 'Pictorial, graphic, and sculptural works' include two-dimensional and three-dimensional works of fine, graphic, and applied art, photographs, prints and art reproductions, maps, globes, charts, diagrams, models, and technical drawings, including architectural plans. Such works shall include works of artistic craftsmanship insofar as their form but not their mechanical or utilitarian aspects are concerned; the design of a useful article, as defined in this section, shall be considered a pictorial, graphic, or sculptural work only if, and only to the extent that, such design incorporates pictorial, graphic, or sculptural features *that can be identified separately from, and are capable of existing independently of*, the utilitarian aspects of the article.

Id. (emphasis added).

192 For a discussion of *Esquire*, see *supra* notes 127-44 and accompanying text.

193 Esquire, Inc. v. Ringer, 591 F.2d 796, 807 (Leventhal, J., concurring).

194 *See* H.R. Rep. No. 1476, *supra* note 115, at 55.

195 *See supra* notes 168-76 and accompanying text.

196 *Kieselstein*, 632 F.2d at 992-93 (citing Nimmer On Copyright, *supra* note 37, at 2-89 (1980)).

197 H.R. Rep. No. 1476, *supra* note 115. *See Esquire*, 591 F.2d at 796.

198 *Kieselstein*, 632 F.2d at 993.

199 H.R. Rep. No. 1476, *supra* note 115, at 5668.

dustrial design may have conceptually separable elements which could be copyrightable as applied art.[200] In order to make this determination, the court asked whether the belt buckles "[rose] to the level of creative art,"[201] and found that they did.[202] The court also utilized a primary/subsidiary purpose test, and determined that "[t]he primary ornamental aspect of the Vaquero and Winchester buckles is conceptually separable from their subsidiary utilitarian function."[203] The court reaffirmed the elevated "substantial originality" requirement of *Batlin* and instituted a parallel, though covert, substantial creativity requirement for copyrightability under the guise of conceptual separability.[204]

Finally, the court indicated that Copyright Office registration would not be dispositive, and "[i]t will . . . always be necessary to determine whether in a given case there is a physically or conceptually separable artistic sculpture or carving capable of existing independently as a work of art."[205] By implying that the Copyright Office had engaged in an impermissible exercise of aesthetic discretion and needed to be supervised by the courts, the Second Circuit appeared to be trying to distract attention from its own judicial departure from *Bleistein*'s non-discrimination principles.[206]

The elements the court considered relevant to its decision to uphold Kieselstein's copyright in the belt buckles were the buckles' marketplace success,[207] multiple ornamental uses different than that of an ordinary buckle,[208] institutional recognition, direct evidence of copying,[209] and the fact that the buckles were hand-manufactured from precious materials.[210] Within these relevant factors, many contradictory undercurrents emerge. Primary is the desire to "launder" subjective assessments of aesthetic value through the objective marketplace. In the *Kieselstein* opinion, the marketplace takes on the aspect of an objective,

---

200 *Kieselstein*, 632 F.2d at 993-94.

201 *Id.* at 994.

202 *Id.*

203 *Id.* at 993. In applying this test of qualitative creativity, the Second Circuit cited ancient Egyptian and Scythian art in support of classifying Kieselstein's belt buckles as an art form. *Id.* at 994.

204 *Id.* "The basic requirements of originality and creativity, which the two buckles satisfy and which all works of art must meet to be copyrighted, would take the vast majority of belt buckles wholly out of copyrightability." *Id.*

205 *Id.*

206 *Id.* The opinion does not mention *Bleistein*.

207 Over 4,000 buckles were sold. *Id.* at 991.

208 *Id.* at 993-94.

209 The infringer called his buckle the "Barry Kieselstein Knock-off." *Id.*

210 *Id.* at 990-91, 994.

neutral indicator of aesthetic value, when under other accounts, the market is nothing more than an aggregate of subjective, mixed-motive individual choices that are ambiguous at best. By depending on institutional validation, a similar "laundering" of the subjective into the objective occurs. In this privileging of handmade goods over manufactured goods, questionable assumptions about "art" as opposed to "design," and commonplace materials as opposed to precious materials, are made.

While acknowledging Kieselstein's success at creating "admirable aesthetically pleasing examples of modern design,"[211] Judge Weinstein in his dissent found the form of the belt buckles inseparable from their function of "keep[ing] the tops of trousers at waist level."[212] Referring to the legislative history of the 1976 Copyright Act,[213] Judge Weinstein argued that, contrary to the majority's opinion, there is certainty in the law regarding applied art, namely that "ornamental or superfluous designs contained within useful objects"[214] are protected, and "artistically designed functional components of useful [(non-representational)] objects" are not.[215] Judge Weinstein further argued that this certainty required the denial of copyright protection for Kieselstein's belt buckles, even at the acknowledged cost of allowing the proliferation of cheap "knock-offs" by commercial pirates.[216] Congressional policy determinations favoring "commerce and the masses rather than the artists, designers and the well-to-do" required this result.[217]

To Judge Weinstein, the majority's opinion intolerably twisted the separability doctrine to produce and justify the results it sought. The majority's decision ignored clear congressional directives, thereby privileging elite, high fashion designers and consumers at the expense of the "less affluent," [218] charging "the

---

211 *Id.* at 994 (Weinstein, J., dissenting).

212 *Id.*

213 *Id.* at 996-98.

214 *Id.* at 996.

215 *Id.*

216 *Id.* at 994 (reminiscent of Holmes' concurrence in International News Serv. v. Associated Press, 248 U.S. 215, 246 (1918) (Holmes, J., concurring) ("Property, a creation of law, does not arise from value, although exchangeable—a matter of fact. Many exchangeable values may be destroyed intentionally without compensation.")).

217 *Id.* at 999. (Judge Weinstein analogized the concerns about promoting competition, widespread availability of quality products and advances in copying technology in the area of applied art/industrial design to the "similar need to balance societal interest in the availability of literary and dramatic works against the copyright holders' interest in their exclusive enjoyment . . . reflected in the fair use provisions of the Copyright Act of 1976."). *Id.*

218 *Id.*

public a fee for the use of improved and pleasing new designs and styles in useful articles."[219]

De facto standards of both quantitative creativity and qualitative creativity emerged in the Second Circuit by 1980.[220] As *Kieselstein* made clear, the "substantial originality" inquiry preceded any questions of separability, and together these doctrines provided effective screens to filter out industrial design from copyright. However, this development was in acute tension with the *Bleistein* non-discrimination principle, earlier cases, and sharply divided, inconsistent opinions within the Second Circuit itself.

B. The Profound Incoherence of "Conceptual Separability"

1. *Carol Barnhart, Inc. v. Economy Cover Corp.*

By 1985, the ambiguity of the *Kieselstein* opinion[221] became manifest. In *Carol Barnhart, Inc. v. Economy Cover Corp.*[222] "conceptual separability" was reappraised by the Second Circuit and given a severely restricted reading.[223] At issue in *Carol Barnhart* was the copyrightability of four male and female polystyrene mannequin torsos (two nude and two clothed), which the Copyright Office had accepted for registration as "sculpture."[224] The torsos were anatomically correct, life-size, armless, headless, and their backs were hollow. The designer had initially modeled the torsos in clay,[225] which were then used to create a mold from which the polystyrene models were made.[226] Barnhart's ads stressed that the models could be used to display "sweaters, blouses, and dress shirts, . . . and [were] sold in multiples of twelve."[227]

A competitor began marketing four upper torsos which admittedly had been copied from Barnhart's models.[228] Barnhart sued his competitor for infringement of the copyright in his

---

219 *Id.* at 998.

220 Quantitative creativity refers to *Batlin*'s "substantial originality" requirement. *See supra* notes 168-76 and accompanying text. Qualitative creativity refers to *Kieselstein*'s "conceptual separability." *See supra* notes 199-204 and accompanying text.

221 *See supra* notes 183-220 and accompanying text.

222 773 F.2d 411 (1985).

223 This restrictive reading was close in spirit to Judge Weinstein's dissent in *Kieselstein*. *See supra* notes 211-19.

224 *Carol Barnhart*, 773 F.2d at 412.

225 *Id.*

226 *Id.*

227 *Id.*

228 *Id.* at 413.

"sculpture."[229] Judge Mansfield, for the Second Circuit, reviewed the voluminous legislative history of the 1976 Act (including the deletion of Title II), the 1976 Act itself, the cases, the Copyright Office regulations, the 1909 Act, and *Bleistein*,[230] before concluding that "Congress has explicitly refused copyright protection for works of applied art or industrial design which have aesthetic or artistic features that cannot be identified separately from the useful article."[231]

The court dismissed the claim asserted by the Barnhart manufacturer that the torsos fell within a traditional art form and were therefore entitled to a lower level of copyright scrutiny.[232] In making its decision, the court ignored that Justice Holmes invoked the non-discrimination principle in *Bleistein* in order to expand the scope of copyright protection. In a sense, Justice Holmes created a presumption in favor of copyright protection when an article's aesthetic qualities are in doubt. [233] By 1985, this principle had become so indeterminate, however, that it could be invoked to exclude articles with clearly "aesthetically satisfying and valuable" qualities under the cloak of conceptual separability, and was also used to justify a high, rather than a low, standard of copyrightability.[234]

The court unsuccessfully attempted to distinguish the *Kieselstein* belt buckles from the partial torsos, stating that "the ornamented surfaces of the buckles were not in any respect required by their utilitarian functions; the artistic and aesthetic features could thus be conceived of as having been added to, or superimposed upon, an otherwise utilitarian article."[235] The court, however, claimed that the artistic features in the *Carol Barnhart* torsos, such as "the life-size configuration of the breasts and the width of the shoulders, are inextricably intertwined with the utilitarian feature, the display of clothes."[236] The opinion concluded with a

---

229 *Id.* The district court granted summary judgment against Barnhart because the "Barnhart forms possessed no aesthetic features that could exist, either physically or conceptually, separate from the forms as utilitarian articles, [and] they were not copyrightable." *Id.* at 414.

230 It seems consistent that whenever the *Bleistein* non-discrimination principle is invoked, it inevitably serves as a justification for precisely the type of blatant judicial value discriminations that *Bleistein* warned against.

231 *Carol Barnhart*, 773 F.2d at 418.

232 *Id.*

233 *See supra* notes 12-19.

234 *Carol Barnhart*, 773 F.2d at 418.

235 *Id.* at 419.

236 *Id. But see* Ted Arnold Ltd. v. Silvercraft Co., 259 F. Supp. 733, 736 (S.D.N.Y. 1966). In defending a physical separability analysis "we would not agree with defendant that [the products'] 'sole intrinsic function . . . is its utility.' Customers are paying fifteen

confused reference to modern art:

> Almost any utilitarian article may be viewed by some separately as art, depending on how it is displayed (e.g., a can of Campbell Soup[237] or a pair of ornate scissors affixed to the wall of a museum of modern art). *But it is the object, not the form of display, for which copyright protection is sought.*[238]

The *Carol Barnhart* opinion is full of epistemologically weak assumptions about the nature of art, industry, and law. Moreover, it failed to address the twentieth century conundrum: What is meaning if it is not context?[239] The court seems to have believed in some *a priori* fundamental, intrinsic utilitarian function which, once inhered in an object, could not be expunged. As a result, conceptual separability became a very high hurdle, if not a conclusive presumption, against copyright protection for industrial design.

In his dissent, Judge Newman pushed the *Kieselstein* rationale of separability[240] to the point where it vanished into a puff of abstract generalizations. The dissent began by distinguishing the conceptual separability of functional design elements in copyright from the functionality defense in federal trademark law.[241] It then attempted a paradigmatic definition by first reviewing four models of conceptual separability.[242] After surveying these four models, Judge New-

---

dollars for it, not because it sharpens pencils uncommonly well, but because it is also a decorative conversation piece." (citation omitted). Similarly, customers would not pay $165 for a mere belt buckle.

237 Undoubtedly, Judge Mansfield is referring to the Pop artist, Andy Warhol, and his silk-screened paintings of Campbell's Soup can labels. Warhol, however, was painting the label of the soup can, not putting an actual soup can on display. Mansfield seems to have confused a representation of an item with the item itself.

238 *Carol Barnhart*, 773 F.2d at 419 n.5 (emphasis added) (author's footnote). This statement directly contradicts the relevance that the *Kieselstein* court attached to alternate display contexts in which the designer's belt buckles were utilized. *See supra* notes 199-200 and accompanying text.

239 *See supra* Part II.

240 *See supra* notes 199-200 and accompanying text.

241 *Carol Barnhart*, 773 F.2d at 420 n.1 (Newman, J., dissenting). A design feature may not serve as a trademark if it is functional. A feature is functional if it is " 'essential to the use or purpose of the article' or 'affects the cost or quality of the article.' " (citing Inwood Laboratories, Inc. v. Ives Laboratories, Inc., 456 U.S. 844, 850 n.10 (1982) (discussing Lanham Act, ch. 540, § 43(a), 60 Stat. 427, 441 (1946) (codified at 15 U.S.C. § 1125(a)(1988))). *See* LeSportsac, Inc. v. K Mart Corp., 754 F.2d 71 (2d Cir. 1985) (Newman, J.); Stormy Clime Ltd. v. Progroup, Inc., 809 F.2d 971 (2d Cir. 1987). *Cf.* W.T. Rogers Co. v. Keene, 778 F.2d 334 (7th Cir. 1985) (Posner, J.); Vaughn Mfg. Co. v. Brikam Int'l, 814 F.2d 346 (7th Cir. 1987); American Greetings Corp. v. Dan-Dee Imports, 807 F.2d 1136 (3d Cir. 1986); Standard Terry Mills v. Shen Mfg. Co., 803 F.2d 778, 781 (3d Cir. 1986). *But cf.* Ideal Toy Corp. v. Plawner Toy Mfg. Co., 685 F.2d 78 (3d Cir. 1982).

242 The first model focused on use. "An article used primarily to serve its utilitarian function might be regarded as lacking 'conceptually separable' design elements even though those design elements rendered it usable secondarily solely as an artistic work." *Carol Barnhart*, 773 F.2d at 421. In a sense, Judge Newman accused the majority of sur-

man produced a fifth one, his own "temporal displacement"[243] model, which the majority called a "bottomless pit."[244] According to this test, conceptual separability would be found, if and only if the non-utilitarian impression of an article could be successively and completely displaced by a non-utilitarian impression of the same article. Judge Newman, in an understatement, acknowledged that "courts will inevitably be drawn into some minimal inquiry as to the nature of art."[245] Somewhat disingenuously, Judge Newman went on to say that "[o]f course, courts must not assess the *quality* of art," even though in his test "the separate concept that will satisfy the test of 'conceptual separability' will often be the concept of a work of art."[246]

Conceptual separability is, at the very least, a mercurial idea. By comparing the analyses of the *Esquire* and *Carol Barnhart* courts, the paradoxes and ironies of conceptual separability become evident. The courts used conceptual separability to exclude from copyright protection both an abstract lighting fixture, in which

---

reptitiously depending on the context to deny the styrene replicas of the torsos copyrightability, when he said that a "copyrightable design of a life-size sculpture of the human body should not lose its copyright protection simply because mannequin manufacturers copy it, replicate it in cheap materials, and sell it in large quantities to department stores to display clothing." *Id.* The second model focused on determining what the primary and subsidiary functions of the article are. A third model, the "market" approach, suggested by Professor Nimmer, asserted that " 'conceptual separability exists where there is any substantial likelihood that even if the article had no utilitarian use it would still be marketable to some significant segment of the community simply because of its aesthetic qualities.' " *Id.* The fourth model found conceptual separability "whenever the design of a form has sufficient aesthetic appeal to be appreciated for its artistic qualities." *Id.* at 422. Judge Newman gave the example of an uncopyrightable artistically designed chair whose good design can be appreciated but is not conceptually separable from the functional purpose of an object on which people sit. *Id.*

243 W. Patry gave this name to Judge Newman's test. LATMAN'S THE COPYRIGHT LAW 43-45 (1986). The "temporal displacement" test of conceptual separability consisted of ascertaining whether the article stimulates "in the mind of the ordinary observer any concept that is distinct from the concept of the form's utilitarian function" and whether this "non-utilitarian concept can be entertained in the mind of the ordinary observer without at the same time contemplating the utilitarian function." *Carol Barnhart*, 773 F.2d at 423.

To Judge Newman, as to the *Kieselstein* majority, factors such as display or use apart from utilitarian function, expert opinion, and survey evidence bearing on the context of an article would be relevant. This evidence would further modify the "temporal displacement" test by gauging the ordinary observer's response only after visual inspection and consideration of the contextual evidence, to see whether it would engender a separate non-utilitarian concept that would displace the utilitarian concept. *Id.* The abstraction of Judge Newman's test is apparent in that he found the two nude torsos copyrightable. Regarding the other two clothed torsos, he was "uncertain what concept or concepts would be engendered in the mind of an ordinary observer." *Id.* at 426.

244 *Carol Barnhart*, 773 F.2d at 419 n.5. The majority also calls it a "standard so ethereal as to amount to a 'nontest' that would be extremely difficult, if not impossible, to administer or apply." *Id.*

245 *Id.* at 423.

246 *Id.*

"form and function" were supposedly so intertwined that they were inseparable,[247] and realistic representations of the human torso, because the representation was so intertwined with its utilitarian use as a clothing display.[248]

In contrasting *Kieselstein* and *Carol Barnhart,* the equivocation between an insistence on the dispositive relevance of context[249] and the irrelevance of its form of display[250] cannot be reconciled. The inconsistencies are readily apparent. *Bleistein* and *Mazer* insisted on the irrelevance of the ultimate commercial origination or destination of an artifact.[251] *Esquire* used a "commercial destination" test in the guise of conceptual separability.[252] In *Kieselstein*, the commercial destination confirmed an artifact's separability.[253] *Carol Barnhart* used conceptual separability to deny an article protection because of its inherently utilitarian qualities.[254] As these cases illustrate, the almost free-floating, ever-changing level of abstraction and generality engaged in by the courts generated contradiction across cases, and indeed, within the cases themselves. Conceptual separability might thus be analogized to an onion — a series of thin layers that ultimately has no core.

2. *Brandir International, Inc. v. Cascade Pacific Lumber Co.*

In *Brandir International, Inc. v. Cascade Pacific Lumber Co.*,[255] the Second Circuit considered the copyrightability of a one-piece undulating bicycle rack made of bent tubing which originated from a minimalist wire sculpture. In the period between 1980 and 1987, Judge Oakes, the author of the *Kieselstein* majority opinion,[256] modified his earlier interpretation of conceptual separability. He seemed to have fallen prey to doubts about the possibility of Congress establishing a clear line between applied art and industrial design through use of a separability test, while

247 *See* Esquire, Inc. v. Ringer, 591 F.2d 796, 807 (1978) (Leventhal, J., concurring); see *supra* notes 127-44 and accompanying text for a discussion of the case.

248 *See Carol Barnhart*, 773 F.2d at 418. These doctrinal contortions are partially a result of the mangling of the 1976 Copyright Act caused by the last-minute deletion of Title II. *See supra* notes 122-26 and accompanying text.

249 Kieselstein-Cord v. Accessories by Pearl, Inc., 632 F.2d 989, 990-91, 994 (2d Cir. 1980).

250 *Carol Barnhart*, 773 F.2d at 419 n.5. "But it is the object, not the form of display, for which copyright protection is sought."

251 *See supra* notes 11-21, 34-41 and accompanying text.

252 Esquire, Inc. v. Ringer, 591 F.2d 796, 801 (1978). *See supra* notes 127-44 and accompanying text.

253 *Kieselstein*, 632 F.2d at 990-91, 994.

254 *See supra* note 234 and accompanying text.

255 834 F.2d 1142 (2d Cir. 1987).

256 *See supra* note 185.

realizing that "the line Congress attempted to draw between copyrightable art and noncopyrightable design 'was neither clear nor new.' "[257] Surveying the cases which had arisen, including *Carol Barnhart*,[258] Judge Oakes proclaimed that " '[c]onceptual separability' is thus alive and well, at least in this circuit."[259]

Judge Oakes began by flagging the deep tension between the effort of the Copyright Act of 1976 to draw as clear a line as possible between applied art and industrial design, and the fact that " 'there is no line, but merely a spectrum of forms and shapes responsive in varying degrees to utilitarian concerns.' "[260] The legislative limitation of separability as applied to industrial design was " 'an attempt to identify elements whose form and appearance reflect the unconstrained perspective of the artist' "; these elements would not be by-products of the industrial design process, and " '[c]opyrightability, therefore, should turn on the relationship between the proferred work and the process of industrial design.' "[261] If Judge Oakes in *Kieselstein* surreptitiously sought to derogate from the *Bleistein* non-discrimination principle, in *Brandir* he seemed to implicitly deviate from the holding in *Mazer* that production of a work of art intended for mass-production does not preclude copyrightability.[262] This is similar to the attention Judge Oakes gave to the origination process of the belt buckles in *Kieselstein*,[263] and begs the fundamental question at the core of all these cases: Is industrial design art, and if not, then what is it, and what are we going to do about it?

Judge Oakes' re-definition of conceptual separability focused

---

257 *Brandir*, 834 F.2d at 1143 (quoting Denicola, *Applied Art and Industrial Design: A Suggested Approach to Copyright in Useful Articles*, 67 MINN. L. REV. 707, 720 (1983) [hereinafter Denicola]).

258 *See supra* notes 222-46 and accompanying text.

259 *Brandir*, 834 F.2d at 1144. Other cases cited by Judge Oakes were Norris Indus. v. ITT, 696 F.2d 918, 923-24 (11th Cir. 1983) (Copyright Register's refusal to accept wire wheel hub caps as art upheld because there was no "conceptually separable" work of art); Transworld Mfg. Corp. v. Al Nyman & Sons, 95 F.R.D. 95 (D. Del. 1982) (insufficient conceptual separability in an eyeglass display case to support denying summary judgment on copyrightability); Animal Fair, Inc. v. Amfesco Indus., Inc., 620 F. Supp. 175, 187 (D. Minn. 1985) (bear paw design features were "conceptually separate from the utilitarian aspects of its slipper").

260 *Brandir*, 834 F.2d at 1145 (quoting Denicola, *supra* note 257, at 720).

261 *Id.* at 1145 (citing Denicola, *supra* note 257, at 741, 742).

262 Mazer v. Stein, 347 U.S. 201, 204, 218 (1954) (" 'A subsequent utilization of a work of art in an article of manufacture in no way affects the right of the copyright owner to be protected against infringement of the work of art itself.' "). "We find nothing in the copyright statute to support the argument that the intended use or use in industry of an article eligible for copyright bars or invalidates its registration. We do not read such a limitation into the copyright law." (quoting Stein v. Mazer, 204 F.2d 472, 477 (4th Cir. 1953)).

263 Kieselstein-Cord v. Accessories by Pearl, Inc., 632 F.2d 989, 990 (2d Cir. 1980) (describing belt buckles which were hand-manufactured from precious metals).

on the context of the article's origin: "[I]f design elements reflect a merger of aesthetic and functional considerations, the artistic aspects of a work cannot be said to be conceptually separable from the utilitarian elements."[264] Judge Oakes sentimentally idealized the "pure" artist as opposed to the designer. Copyright protection " 'ultimately should depend on the extent to which the work reflects artistic expression uninhibited by functional considerations,' . . . [and] where design elements can be identified as reflecting the designer's artistic judgment exercised independently of functional influences, conceptual separability exists."[265]

Several latent dichotomies, such as art and utility, idea and expression, public and private, and subjective and objective, which copyright law has repeatedly sought to contain and suppress, lurk immediately below the surface of Oakes' valorization of the artist and implicit derogation of the designer. In some ways, *Brandir* is similar to the *Esquire* concurrence and the *Kieselstein* dissent.[266] In both of those minority opinions, it was precisely because of the success with which artistic form was merged with utilitarian function that copyright protection was denied.[267]

Judge Oakes attempted to reconcile this new separability test with past Second Circuit cases. *Kieselstein*'s buckle designs were copyrightable because "the artistic aspects of the belt buckles reflected purely aesthetic choices, independent of the buckles' function, while in *Carol Barnhart* the distinctive features of the torsos—the accurate anatomical design and the sculpted shirts and collars—showed clearly the influence of functional concerns."[268] Furthermore, evidence of the design process is essential to establishing whether aesthetic or utilitarian considerations predominate.[269] Thus, Judge Oakes chose to focus not on the

---

264 *Brandir*, 834 F.2d at 1145.

265 *Id.*

266 See *supra* notes 211-219 for a discussion of the *Kieselstein* dissent. In his concurring opinion in *Esquire*, Judge Leventhal opined: "*Esquire* contends that the restrictive passage . . . where 'the sole intrinsic function of an article is its utility,' must be read narrowly . . . . I join in the rejection of that contention." Esquire, Inc. v. Ringer, 591 F.2d 796, 807 (D.C. Cir. 1978) (Leventhal, J., concurring).

267 *See Esquire*, 591 F.2d at 807 (Leventhal, J., concurring) ("Form follows function, in the credo of one school of art. Yet the overall legislative policy against monopoly for industrial design sustains the Copyright Office in its effort to distinguish between the instances where the aesthetic element is conceptually severable and the instances where the aesthetic element is inextricably interwoven with the utilitarian aspect of the article."); *Kieselstein*, 632 F.2d at 994 (Weinstein, J., dissenting) ("It is the originator's success in completely integrating the artistic designs and the functional aspects of the buckles that preclude copyright.").

268 *Brandir*, 834 F.2d at 1145.

269 *Id.* at 1145-46.

context of display or the intrinsic qualities of the article, but on the context of creation or manufacture. Citing *Bleistein*, Judge Oakes claimed that this focus on the manufacturing process resolved the recurrent problem of judges allowing aesthetic biases to influence their decisions. This focus would " 'alleviate the de facto discrimination against nonrepresentational art that has regrettably accompanied much of the current analysis.' "[270]

In the context-focused inquiry of *Brandir*, the sculptor, Levine, who created the wire model for the bike rack, stumbled across its utilitarian application. While Levine had never sold or exhibited the wire sculpture as art, he had received architectural and design awards for the bike rack design which he exhibited in an industrial design show.[271] Three years after putting the bike rack on the market, Levine discovered that the Cascade Pacific Lumber Co. was selling a similar product, so he sought to copyright the bike rack.[272] The Copyright Office denied registration because the bike rack lacked any element that was " 'capable of independent existence as a copyrightable pictorial, graphic, or sculptural work apart from the shape of the useful article.' "[273] In spite of the registration denial, Levine went ahead and attached a copyright notice to the bike racks.[274]

The court determined that the bike rack, being manufactured from industrial materials (2 3/8" standard steam pipe), "remains . . . the product of industrial design. Form and function are inextricably intertwined in the rack, its ultimate design being as much the result of utilitarian pressures as aesthetic choices,"[275] and therefore not copyrightable.[276]

---

270 *Id.* at 1145 (quoting Denicola, *supra* note 257, at 745). An important contradiction which Judge Oakes did not openly acknowledge is buried in one of his footnotes. Judge Oakes made the point that form does not follow function in much of modern design and is merely an alternate aesthetic choice. "[T]he shape of a Mickey Mouse telephone is copyrightable because its form is independent of function, and '[a] telephone shape owing more to Arp, Brancusi, or Moore than Disney may be equally divorced from utilitarian influence.' " *Id.* at 1145 n.3 (quoting Denicola, *supra* note 257, at 746). Judge Oakes did not explain exactly how his hypothetical telephone design is distinguished from the *Brandir* bike rack. This is at odds with Oakes' approval of *Esquire*'s denial of copyright to a modernist lighting fixture precisely because of its successful merger of form and function.

271 *Id.* at 1146.

272 *Id.*

273 *Id.*

274 *Id.*

275 *Id.* at 1147.

276 By reversing the district court on the issue of summary judgment on the trade dress infringement claim, the Second Circuit seemed as though it wished to leave the door open for possible Lanham Act protection for industrial design extruded from copyright under Judge Oakes' new "design process" test of separability, thus implementing a scheme of partial cumulation. The *Brandir* court distinguished the functionality criteria

Judge Winter, in his dissent, criticized the majority's opinion, stating that it "diminishes the statutory concept of 'conceptual separability' to the vanishing point," and, by focusing on process, "makes copyright protection depend upon largely fortuitous circumstances concerning the creation of the design in issue."[277] Sensing the deep contradictions that pervade this area, and speaking of *Kieselstein* and *Carol Barnhart* in particular, Judge Winter believed that "these cases [were] not reconcilable" and that "*Carol Barnhart* paid only lip service" to conceptual separability while actually "appl[ying] a test of physical separability."[278]

Judge Winter formulated yet another separability test, similar to the one in Judge Newman's dissent in *Carol Barnhart*: "[W]hether the design of a useful article, however intertwined with the article's utilitarian aspects, causes an ordinary reasonable observer to perceive an aesthetic concept not related to the article's use."[279] Judge Winter correctly pointed to the inherently unknowable and subjective choices[280] made by the designer as a fallacious basis on which to make copyright protection pivot, thereby collapsing the supposedly objective into the subjective. However, Judge Winter's test seems equally ethereal and manipulable, as he conjured the images of the bike rack sitting on a desert island or surrounded by a barrier in a park—virtually any article could be envisioned in a context which would make "its status as a work of art . . . beyond dispute."[281]

In the Second Circuit alone, there are at least six contradictory formulations of conceptual separability.[282] Despite repeated

---

necessary to show trade dress infringement from copyright functionality, which precludes protection. "[T]he true test of functionality is not whether the feature in question performs a function, but whether the feature 'is dictated by the functions to be performed.' " *Id.* at 1148 (*quoted in*, LeSportsac, Inc. v. K Mart Corp., 754 F.2d 71, 76 (2d Cir. 1985) (citing Warner Bros. Inc., 724 F.2d 327, 331 (2d Cir. 1983))). This definition of functionality for trade dress infringement indicates that evidence of alternate constructions, which would perform the same function, inveighs against a finding of functionality.

277 *Id.* at 1151 (Winter, J., concurring in part and dissenting in part).

278 *Id.*

279 *Id.*

280 *Id.* at 1152 ("I cannot agree that copyright protection . . . turns on whether Levine serendipitously chose the final design . . . during his initial sculptural musings or whether the original design had to be slightly modified to accommodate bicycles.").

281 *Id.*

282 The following is a listing, by circuit, of significant cases which discuss conceptual separability. Third Circuit: Trans-World Mfg. Corp. V. Al Nyman & Sons, 95 F.R.D. 95 (D. Del. 1982), *later proceeding*, 750 F.2d 989 (Fed. Cir. 1984) (adopting the *Kieselstein* approach to conceptual separability); Sixth Circuit: Gay Toys, Inc. v. Buddy L Corp., 522 F. Supp. 622 (E.D. Mich. 1981), *vacated*, 703 F.2d 970, 973 (6th Cir. 1983) (holding that the function of a toy plane is closer to "works of art" than to the "intrinsic utilitarian function" of industrial products); Eighth Circuit: Animal Fair, Inc. v. Amfesco Indus., 620 F. Supp. 175 (D. Minn. 1985), *aff'd without opinion*, 794 F.2d 678 (8th Cir. 1986)

attempts to reconcile the statutes, cases, regulations, and legislative history, the doctrine of conceptual separability has exacerbated, rather than moderated, some of the deepest conflicts in copyright law.[283]

(all of the design elements of a bear's paw slipper can be copyrighted, agreeing with the *Kieselstein* approach); Ninth Circuit: National Theme Prods., Inc. v. Jerry B. Beck, Inc., 696 F. Supp. 1348, 1353 (S.D. Cal. 1988) (concurring in the Second Circuit's adoption of Professor Denicola's focus on the designer's creative process in creating a useful article, but "[t]o the extent that . . . *Brandir* relies upon the sequences of actions . . . made in putting together an article, the court believes the Second Circuit improperly applied the Denicola test" because the results will turn on "largely fortuitous circumstances," and holding that costumes are copyrightable if their artistic features can be conceptually separated from the costume's useful function); Poe v. Missing Persons, 745 F.2d 1238 (9th Cir. 1984) (in determining whether a swimsuit was a useful article or a copyrightable work of conceptual art, relevant factors bearing on conceptual separability included: expert testimony; creator's intent; custom and usage in the art world and clothing trade and marketability as a work of art—the court held that the artist/designer had attempted to create a work of art that portrayed a swimsuit); Fabrica, Inc. v. El Dorado Corp., 697 F.2d 890, 890 (9th Cir. 1983) (display folders containing carpet samples were held to be "useful objects" with no features capable of conceptual separability; following *Esquire*, upholding a claim of unfair competition based on copying of trade dress). Eleventh Circuit: Norris Indus., Inc. v. ITT, 696 F.2d 918, 924 (11th Cir. 1983) (wire wheel hubcaps for cars held to be uncopyrightable because they are "useful articles containing no physically or conceptually separable works of art" with no features that meet the requirements of independent existence and separate identity).

[283] *See* Kennedy, *The Stages of the Decline of the Public/Private Distinction*, 130 U. PA. L. REV. 1349 (1982). Professor Kennedy suggests six loose stages that have more than glancing relevance to a discussion of the art/utility distinction as well:

> Success for a legal distinction has two facets. First, it must be possible to make the distinction: people must feel that it is intuitively sensible to divide something between its poles, and that the division will come out pretty much the same way regardless of who is doing it. Second, the distinction must make a difference: a distinction without a difference is a failure even if it is possible for everyone to agree every time on how to make it. Making a difference means that it seems plain that situations should be treated differently depending on which category of distinction they fall into.
>
> . . . .
>
> 1. *Hard Cases with Large Stakes*
>
> While a distinction is still in its heyday, there arise cases about which people disagree passionately, and on whose resolution those same people believe a great deal turns. . . .
>
> Hard cases with large stakes engage peoples' energies in the task of manipulating the distinction, analyzing it, fretting about it. Hard cases are a sign of health, but they are also an indication that there may be trouble ahead. The trouble begins with:
>
> 2. *The Development of Intermediate Terms*
>
> . . . .
>
> The development of intermediate terms . . . probably represents the emergence of serious conflict about how to characterize a large number of hard cases with large stakes, as well as a sense on the part of the deciding people that they can't just come down cleanly on one side or the other. Consensus about categorization begins to break down. Second, it probably means that it is becoming more difficult to decide what difference it makes how we categorize a situation. The intermediate entity gets treated 'as though' it were public for some purposes, and 'as though' it were private for other purposes. This means not only that the institution in question 'falls on the line,' but also that the responses that used to follow, à la Pavlov, when I

3. Alternative Approaches of the Circuits in the 1990s

a. Design Patent

Insofar as conceptual separability is alive, but not well,[284] the alternatives available for protection of industrial design in the absence of a *sui generis* design protection law must be examined.[285] Design patents for "any new, original and ornamental design for an article of manufacture"[286] have been available since 1842,

---

said public or you said private, begin to lose their all-or-nothing, set-like quality.

3. Collapse

An important . . . moment in the history of a distinction arrives when troublemakers begin to argue that the distinction is incoherent because, no matter how you try to apply it, you end up in a situation of hopeless contradiction.

. . . .

4. *Continuumization*

. . . .

Continuumization seems to go along with the disaggregation of the package of legal responses that once seemed to follow 'logically' from the choice to categorize an institution one way or another. . . . In continuum consciousness, the ideal is a range of legal responses exactly calibrated to the range of fact situations: an overlay of one continuum on the other.

. . . .

5. *Stereotypification*

. . . .

. . . [S]tereotypification is the working out, in the reassuring context of continua, of the practical implications of Collapse. 'Legal' arguments prove too much: it just can't be the force of the formulae we use that causes our conviction that one side or the other is right, since we reject the identical arguments in the next case. And we have no meta-principle of appropriateness that will tell us when argument *A* is right or when, on the contrary, it is flat wrong and *B* is right. When a distinction reaches this stage, using it in legal argument seems a mere exercise: we can do it so well we can't believe in it any more.

6. *Loopification*

. . . One's consciousness is loopified when the ends of the continuum seem closer to one another, in some moods . . . , than either end seems to the middle. Otherwise stated, one's consciousness is loopifed when one seems to be able to move by a steady series of steps *around* the whole distinction, ending up where one started without ever reversing direction.

Id. at 1349-54. *But cf.* Shapiro, *The Death of the Up/Down Distinction*, 36 STAN. L. REV. 465 (1984) (parodying Professor Kennedy's musings on the Public/Private distinction).

284 *See supra* note 3.

285 NIMMER ON COPYRIGHT, *supra* note 37, § 2.08[B][3], at 2-104. "[U]nless and until special design legislation is adopted, if the choice is full copyright protection or none at all, it may be that the former alternative is preferable to the latter." *Id.*

286 35 U.S.C. § 171 (1988). *See also* Act of Aug. 29, 1842, ch. 2633, 5 Stat. 543-44 (1842) ("any citizen . . . who by his . . . own industry . . . may have invented or produced any new and original design for a manufacture . . . may make appplication . . . to the Commissioner of Patents . . .[who] may grant a patent therefor"); Graham v. John Deere Co., 383 U.S. 1 (1966). *But see* Michaelson, *Design Patents and Obviousness—Obviousness to Whom?*, 52 J. PAT. OFF. SOC'Y 620 (1970) (discussing the rationale of the CCPA case holding that the test for obviousness is whether the design would have been obvious to the "ordinary, intelligent observer," and cases in opposition).

though until recently they have been relatively moribund.[287] While Professor Reichman thought in the 1980s that design patents were on the verge of being reinvigorated,[288] there has been much countervailing pressure against utilizing them to protect industrial design.

First, certification is lengthy and expensive.[289] Second, even if one managed to secure a design patent, after a typical wait of two or more years, (during which time a patent attorney would necessarily have been retained at considerable expense), the patent would be found invalid by the court.[290] Third, in the minority of cases where patents were found to be valid after a challenge, only about half would be held to have been infringed.[291] Additionally, courts have been extremely skeptical of design patents that appear to capture the primarily functional features of an item under the guise of ornamentation, a skepticism reminiscent of copyright law's antipathy to protection of utilitarian features of manufactured articles.[292]

Even with a lowered non-obviousness standard, design patent protection for a period of fourteen years[293] is not the solution to the conundrum of protection for industrial design. Insofar as the patent requirement of non-obviousness was relaxed, it could not be lowered to meet the raised "substantial originality" copyright requirement established in *Batlin*.[294] If it were, it would then confer on noncopyrightable industrial designs "absolute" patent protection.[295] If the anxieties about the undesirable anti-

---

287 *See* Reichman II, *supra* note 145, at 308-12.

288 *See* Reichman I, *supra* note 1.

289 Lindgren, *The Sanctity of the Design Patent: Illusion or Reality? 20 Years of Design Patent Litigation Since Compco v. Day-Brite Lighting, Inc., and Sears, Roebuck & Co. v. Stiffel Co.*, 10 OKLA. CITY U. L. REV. 195, 261, app. II (1985).

290 *See Design Protection: An Overview*, *supra* note 167, at 1355-59. Examples of judicial hostility to design patent validity include Hadco Prods. v. Walter Kidde & Co., 462 F.2d 1265, 1273 (3d Cir. 1972) (patented designs dissembled into component parts, then attacked on grounds of obviousness by applying prior art in piecemeal fashion); G.B. Lewis & Co. v. Gould Prods., 436 F.2d 1176, 1178 (2d Cir. 1971) (virtually conclusive presumption that design patents are invalid as a matter of law); Barofsky v. General Elec. Co., 396 F.2d 340, 344-45 (9th Cir. 1968) (modern functional design found wanting in ornamentality and excessively influenced by technical factors).

291 *See Design Protection: An Overview*, *supra* note 167, at 1355-57.

292 *See, e.g.*, Power Controls Corp. v. Hybrinetics, Inc., 806 F.2d 234 (Fed. Cir. 1986); C & M Fiberglass Septic Tanks, Inc. v. T & N Fiberglass Mfg., 214 U.S.P.Q. (BNA) 159 (D.C. Cir. 1981); *In re* Nalbandian, 661 F.2d 1214, 1216 (C.C.P.A. 1981); Schandig Corp. v. Gaines Mfg. Co., 620 F.2d 1166 (6th Cir. 1980); Lancaster Colony Corp. v. Aldon Accessories, Ltd., 506 F.2d 1197 (2d Cir. 1974); Rains v. Niaqua, Inc., 406 F.2d 275 (2d Cir. 1969); Barofsky v. General Elec. Corp., 396 F.2d 340 (9th Cir. 1968).

293 35 U.S.C. § 171 (1988).

294 L. Batlin & Son, Inc. v. Snyder, 536 F.2d 486 (2d Cir. 1976).

295 Independent creation is not a defense to patent infringement. However, copyright is not a bar to a design patent, but a design patent is a bar to copyright registration. *See*

competitive effects of copyright protection for designs[296] are taken seriously, then design patent protection would be inappropriate at best. At worst, rather than encouraging innovation, design patent protection would turn industrial design into a liability mine field into which designers, investors, manufacturers, and consumers ventured at their own risk.

b. Unfair Competition

Congress' failure to pass Title II as part of the 1976 Copyright Revision Act[297] destabilized intellectual property law. The issue of a demarcation between applied art and industrial design can be seen as occurring at the margins of copyright, and of little significance to core concerns of intellectual property protection. The implications, however, of the continually growing sense of incoherence in the law have corroded fundamental legal principles and assumptions. As copyright sought to exclude industrial designs through use of conceptual separability, increased pressure was placed on design patent and unfair competition laws to provide a haven for these excluded articles. The following is an examination of the leading unfair competition cases and an analysis of their countervailing tensions.[298]

The question of whether the normative baseline is competition, with protection the exception, or whether the baseline is protection with competition the exception, cannot be evaded. Copyright, patent, and unfair competition law all provide different and conflicting answers.[299] If competition is the baseline, the

---

In re Yardley, 493 F.2d 1389, 1394 (C.C.P.A. 1974); 37 C.F.R. § 202.10(a) (1986); *see also* Milch, *Protection for Utilitarian Works of Art: The Design Patent/Copyright Conundrum*, 10 COLUM.-VLA J.L. & ARTS 211 (1986) (examining the conceptual and procedural inadequacies of both design patent and copyright law with respect to works of art which may also fulfill a useful function).

296 We do not believe, however, that it would be appropriate to extend the copyright law to industrial designs as such. In this area there is a delicate balance between the need for protection on the part of those who originate and invest in a design, and the possible effect of protection, if over-extended, in restraining competition.

STAFF OF HOUSE COMM. ON THE JUDICIARY, 87TH CONG., 1ST SESS., REPORT OF THE REGISTER OF COPYRIGHT ON THE GENERAL REVISION OF THE U.S. COPYRIGHT LAW 13 (Comm. Print 1961).

297 *See supra* note 122-23 and accompanying text.

298 Design patent protection has several drawbacks and the potential to undermine the policies, such as rewarding innovation, that it was meant to encourage. *See supra* notes 293-96 and acccompanying text.

299 *See* The Trademark Cases, 100 U.S. 82, 94 (1879) (writings must constitute "the fruits of intellectual labor" to receive copyright protection, therefore a trademark did not constitute a writing and could not claim copyright protection). *Cf.* International News Serv. v. Associated Press, 248 U.S. 215, 236 (1918) (While news itself is not copyrightable, a person who through his own pain and expense, gathers news to publish for

imitation and reproduction of someone else's product is not a legal wrong unless the legal system has conferred a property right and a corresponding duty of non-interference on competitors. If there is no corresponding duty of non-interference, then there could be injury to the legal right without legal remedy through privileged competition.[300] Thus, the conflict gets restated as competition versus property, and if competition is privileged, then noncompensable economic harm can occur.[301] If property is privileged, then boundary-crossings that violate property rights will trump competition. Intellectual property is particularly troublesome, however, because it is a form of property insusceptible, except by weak analogy, to traditional boundary crossing analysis.[302]

Ideally, under unfair competition law, a first seller has a right of action against competitors who create an object that is so similar to those of the first seller[303] that there is a likelihood of confusing the two.[304] To obtain trademark protection, a design must become distinctive of the producer, having acquired a secondary meaning in the mind of the consumer.[305] "Trade dress," tradi-

---

profit can have a quasi-property right in what he has created. This right can be asserted against a rival in the same business who appropriated the results at the expense of the original party.).

300 *See* Industria Arredamenti Fratelli Saporiti v. Charles Craig, Ltd., 725 F.2d 18, 20 (2d Cir. 1984) ("[B]eyond the protection of the patent laws, the general policy of our law is to favor competition. Early comers may not exclude latecomers. One may not welcome new competition, but one may not legally complain of it. . . . The newcomer may produce and sell identical goods, so long as he does not use another's figurative label.").

301 *See* Singer, *The Legal Rights Debate in Analytical Jurisprudence From Bentham to Hohfeld*, 1982 WIS. L. REV. 975 (1982) (discussing proto-legal realist Wesley Hohfeld's analytic system of "rights/no rights" and the extent to which the legal regime allows noncompensible economic harm); Gordon, *An Inquiry into the Merits of Copyright: The Challenges of Consistency, Consent, and Encouragement Theory*, 41 STAN. L. REV. 1343 (1989) (examining Bentham-derived incentive-based rationalizations offered for copyright law).

302 *See* Vandevelde, *The New Property of the Nineteenth Century: The Development of the Modern Concept of Property*, 29 BUFFALO L. REV. 325 (1980) (discussing the dematerialization of property in nineteenth century trademark cases and the rise of intangible property interests in commerce, such as "good will"); *see also* Cohen, *Transcendental Nonsense and the Functional Approach*, 35 COLUM. L. REV. 809 (1935); Cohen, *Property and Sovereignity*, 13 CORNELL L.Q. 8 (1927) (two seminal legal realist critiques examining the tautology of property as a social construct, *i.e.*, as something protected because it is valuable or as valuable precisely because it is protected).

303 Lanham Act § 43(a), 15 U.S.C. § 1125(a) (1988). Section 43(a) provides in part:

> Any person who [shall] . . . [use] in connection with any goods or services, or any container for goods . . . [any] false or misleading representation of fact . . . shall be liable in a civil action by any person who believes that he or she is or is likely to be damaged by [the use of any such false description or representation].

See also 2 P. GOLDSTEIN, COPYRIGHT § 15.14 (1989) (a creator may assert claims for passing off, misrepresentation, or misappropriation).

304 15 U.S.C. § 1125(a).

305 *Id.* § 1052(f).

tionally has referred to close similarities in the labeling or packaging of a good.[306]

In the area of trade dress protection and infringement, three general types of mediators have emerged to deal with the contradictions arising from attempts to demarcate a clear line between protected expression and unprotected ideas: (1) relaxed judicial interpretations of what constitutes a non-functional, and therefore protectable feature; (2) slack secondary meaning requirements for design and trade dress; and (3) expansive readings of section 43(a) of the Lanham Act.[307]

In the *Sears-Compco* decisions,[308] the Supreme Court held that states could not ban the copying of articles unprotected by

---

306 With Title II's collapse, and the subsequent development of conceptual separability, pressure on unfair competition law to accommodate designs excluded from copyright has caused an expansion of the idea of "trade dress" to also encompass the configuration and design of market goods. Configuration and design are roughly equivalent to "overall shape" and "ornamentation" in copyright law. *See Design Protection: An Overview*, *supra* note 167, at 1358. To qualify for protection as trade dress, the overall configuration and design of a product must be distinctive of a particular source. Mere similarity of appearance is insufficient for trade dress infringement. *See* Note, *Trademark Protection of Objects and Configurations: A Critical Analysis*, 59 MINN. L. REV. 541 (1975). To gain protection, overall configuration and design must also acquire "secondary meaning," which is a "connection in the consumer's mind between the mark and the product's producer, whether that producer is known or unknown." Ambrit, Inc. v. Kraft, 805 F.2d 974, 979 n.14 (11th Cir. 1986). Non-functional features must be separated from functional features, because functional features of a product cannot qualify for trade dress protection.

The Eleventh Circuit has interpreted § 43(a) as creating a federal cause of action for trade dress infringement. *See, e.g.*, John H. Harland Co. v. Clarke Checks, Inc., 711 F.2d 966, 980 (11th Cir. 1983); Original Appalachian Artworks, Inc. v. Toy Loft, Inc., 684 F.2d 821, 830-32 (11th Cir. 1982). "Trade dress" involves the total image of a product and may include features such as size, shape, color or color combinations, texture, graphics, or even particular sales techniques. *Harland*, 711 F.2d at 980. Although most trade dress infringement actions involve the packaging or labeling of goods, recently the "courts have recognized that the design of a product itself may constitute protectable trade dress under § 43(a) of the Lanham Act." *Id.* A plaintiff must show the following three elements to prevail on a claim for trade dress infringement under § 43(a): 1) that the trade dress of two products is confusingly similar; 2) that the features of the trade dress are primarily non-functional; and 3) that the trade dress has acquired secondary meaning. *See, e.g.*, Black & Decker Co. v. Ever-Ready Appliance Mfg. Co., 518 F. Supp. 607, 616 (E.D. Mo. 1981), *aff'd*, 684 F.2d 546 (8th Cir. 1988).

307 Lanham Act § 43(a), 15 U.S.C. § 1125(a).

308 Sears, Roebuck & Co. v. Stiffel Co., 376 U.S. 225 (1964); Compco Corp. v. Day-Brite Lighting, Inc., 376 U.S. 234 (1964). *See also* Inwood Laboratories, Inc. v. Ives Laboratories, Inc., 456 U.S. 844, 863 (1982) (White, J., concurring) ("A functional characteristic is 'an important ingredient in the commercial success of the product,' and, after expiration of a patent, it is no more the property of the originator than the product itself. . . . Reproduction of a functional attribute is legitimate competitive activity." (quoting a pre-*Mazer* case, Pagliero v. Wallace China Co., 198 F.2d 339, 343 (9th Cir. 1952) (establishing the 9th Circuit doctrine of "aesthetic functionality," which precluded trademark protection for china designs)). *Cf.* Truck Equip. Serv. Co. v. Freuhauf Corp., 536 F.2d 1210 (8th Cir. 1976), *cert. denied*, 429 U.S. 861 (1976) (profile of a hopper truck not functional and signified design originator as the source).

copyright or patent law under the guise of regulating unfair competition:

> That an article copied from an unpatented article could be made in some other way, that the design is 'nonfunctional' and not essential to the use of either article, that the configuration of the article copied may have a 'secondary meaning' which identifies the maker to the trade, or that there may be 'confusion' among purchasers as to which article is which or as to who is the maker, may be relevant evidence in applying a State's law requiring such precautions as labeling; however, and regardless of the copier's motives, neither these facts nor any others can furnish a basis for imposing liability for or prohibiting the actual acts of copying or selling.[309]

In *LeSportsac, Inc. v. K Mart Corp.*,[310] the Second Circuit held that the "design of a product itself may function as its packaging, serving to distinguish it from other products, and hence be protectable trade dress under § 43(a)."[311] In response to K Mart's argument that the LeSportsac design it had copied was functional because it was " 'an important ingredient in the commercial success of the product,' "[312] the court found that while it might be possible that "aesthetic appeal" is an "essential feature," if consumers buy the product because the design identifies and distinguishes the goods as genuine, then the design "primarily serves a legitimate trademark purpose—identifying the source of the product—and should be eligible for protection even though it is also an 'important ingredient' in the product's commercial success."[313]

In a Seventh Circuit case, *W.T. Rogers Co. v. Keene*,[314] Judge Posner attempted to reconcile the opposing uses of a design's appearance as function and identification. *Keene* involved a section 43(a) action by a manufacturer against a former employee over the shape of stacking plastic letter trays, copies of which the ex-employee had

---

309 *Compco Corp.*, 376 U.S. at 238 (Black, J.).

310 754 F.2d 71, 74 (2d Cir. 1985) (K Mart admitted copying the general design of lightweight luggage made of parachute nylon, carpet tape, and color coordinated zippers). *But cf.* Stormy Clime Ltd. v. Progroup, Inc., 809 F.2d 971, 977-78 (2d Cir. 1987) (endorsing *LeSportsac* but warning that unlimited trademark protection could "undermine the objectives of the patent laws"); Industria Arredamenti Fratelli Saporiti v. Charles Craig, Ltd., 725 F.2d 18 (2d Cir. 1984) (holding that a sofa's design was not just a label but "a principal characteristic of the sofa"). *See also* Warner Bros. v. Gay Toys, Inc., 658 F.2d 76 (2d Cir. 1981) (design of toy cars was trade dress); Harlequin Enters. Ltd. v. Gulf & Western Corp., 644 F.2d 946 (2d Cir. 1981) (paperback book cover design was trade dress).

311 *LeSportsac*, 754 F.2d at 75.

312 *Id.* at 77 (quoting *Fratelli*, 725 F.2d at 18).

313 *Id.* at 78.

314 778 F.2d 334 (7th Cir. 1985).

begun manufacturing. The court defined functionality as "something that other producers of the product in question would have to have as part of the product in order to be able to compete effectively in the market."[315] Under this analysis, a feature can be trademarked if it is non-functional, that is, if competitors can still "compete effectively" without using it.[316]

The court was careful to separate legitimate section 43(a) interests from other interests trying to bootstrap their way into unfair competition law: "What Rogers may fear . . . is not the loss of an identifying mark but the loss of a competitive advantage stemming from the exclusive possession of a popular design . . . ."[317] Judge Posner tried to maintain the integrity of strict categories by insisting that the issue was not protection of an "identifying mark," but a "pleasing design" and that the "manufacturer must seek the aid of the design-patent law, with its stringent requirements and its 14-year limitation, and not the aid of the trademark laws."[318]

In the Ninth Circuit, the invocation of "aesthetic functionality"[319] as a bar to trademark protection stems from *Pagliero v. Wallace China Co.*,[320] decided in 1952. In *Pagliero*, a manufacturer of china tried unsuccessfully to keep a competitor from copying its designs. The court held that even if secondary meaning could be shown, the china's appearance could still be functional and imitable.[321]

In 1981, the limits of *Pagliero* were reached in *Vuitton et Fils, S.A. v. J. Young Enterprises.*[322] In *Vuitton*, a competitor asserted that the Vuitton fleur-de-lis was an invalid trademark because it was functional and a national insignia, and therefore, the competitor was free to utilize the imprint on his own luggage.[323] The court upheld the Vuitton trademark, stating that its decision was "aimed at avoiding the use of a trademark to monopolize a design feature which, in it-

---

315 *Id.* at 346.

316 *Id.* at 343.

317 *Id.* at 348.

318 *Id.* Contrast *Keene* with the much more open-ended approach to functionality that the Second Circuit used. Judge Posner's opinion in *Keene* implicitly criticized the Second Circuit's blurring of the boundaries between copyright, design patent, and unfair competition. For a discussion of Second Circuit cases in this area, see *supra* notes 145-283 and accompanying text.

319 "When goods are bought largely for their aesthetic value, their features may be functional because they definitely contribute to that value and thus aid the performance of an object for which the goods are intended." RESTATEMENT OF TORTS § 742 comment a. (1938).

320 198 F.2d 339 (9th Cir. 1952).

321 *Id.* at 343-44.

322 644 F.2d 769 (9th Cir. 1981).

323 *Id.* at 771.

self and apart from its identification of source, improves the usefulness or appeal of the object it adorns."[324] The appeals court also disapproved of the lower court's holding that any feature of a product which contributes to its consumer appeal and salability is, as a matter of law, a functional element of that product.[325]

The Ninth Circuit was divided, however, when it came to excluding nontraditional utilitarian designs from copyright, but did allow the excluded designs to be protected under expanded unfair competition law. In *Fabrica, Inc. v. El Dorado Corp.*,[326] the court denied copyright protection to display folders containing carpet samples, finding that they were "useful articles" with no features capable of conceptual separability.[327] The court, however, upheld a section 43(a) claim for trade dress infringement, without finding tension between expansion of trade dress protection and the limiting force of aesthetic functionality.[328]

In a case involving stuffed teddy bears with sentimental messages on their bellies, the Third Circuit upheld the theory that aspects of a product's appearance could be functional and were, therefore, incapable of being unfairly appropriated by a competitor.[329] The court found that the originator was entitled to a certain level of protection against confusion as to functional features but that the competitor, Dan-Dee, "may not be prohibited from marketing a teddy bear with tummy graphics, but . . . may be required to take reasonable steps to minimize the confusion."[330] In *Keene Corporation v. Paraflex Industries, Inc.*,[331] the Third Circuit considered aesthetic functionality as applied to a modernistic outdoor lighting fixture called the "Wall Cube," contrasting the copyright treatment of a similar outdoor lighting fixture in *Esquire*.[332] Judge Sloviter re-

---

324 *Id.* at 774.

325 *Id.* at 773.

326 697 F.2d 890 (9th Cir. 1983). *But see* First Brands Corp. v. Fred Meyer, Inc., 809 F.2d 1378, 1382 n.3 (9th Cir. 1987) (in dicta, the court stated that the " 'aesthetic' functionality test has been limited, *Vuitton*, 644 F.2d at 773, if not rejected, *Fabrica*, 697 F.2d at 895").

327 *Fabrica*, 697 F.2d at 893. "There is no element of the folders that can be separated out and exist independently of their utilitarian aspects." *Id.*

328 *Id.* at 895.

329 American Greetings Corp. v. Dan-Dee Imports, Inc., 807 F.2d 1136, 1143-44 (3d Cir. 1986). *See also* Standard Terry Mills v. Shen Mfg. Co., 803 F.2d 778 (3d Cir. 1986) (finding aesthetic functionality in window-pane weave design of dish towel, making copying by competitor permissible).

330 *American Greetings*, 807 F.2d at 1149.

331 653 F.2d 822 (3d Cir. 1981).

332 *Esquire, Inc. v. Ringer*, 414 F. Supp. 939 (D.D.C. 1976), *rev'd*, 591 F.2d 796 (D.C. Cir. 1978), *cert. denied*, 440 U.S. 908 (1979); *see supra* notes 127-45 and accompanying text.

fused to enjoin the copying of the modernistic fixture,[333] but sought to distance the court's approach from the Ninth Circuit's broad view of aesthetic functionality which the court felt "provide[d] a disincentive for development of imaginative and attractive design [because t]he more appealing the design, the less protection it would receive."[334]

In a confused fashion, the court tried to tie aesthetic functionality to utilitarian function, holding that "[w]hen the design itself is not significantly related to the utilitarian function of the product, but is merely arbitrary, then it is entitled to protection as a design trademark if it has acquired the distinctiveness necessary to achieve a secondary meaning."[335] This holding that the "arbitrary" component in design is protected by trademark, but that the aesthetic one is not, is strikingly parallel to the contradictory and incoherent results that various formulations of conceptual separability have produced in copyright law.[336]

The Court of Appeals for the Federal Circuit is aligned more closely to the Third and Sixth Circuits' approach than to the expansive interpretations of non-functionality of the Second Circuit, or the restrictive aesthetic functionality criterion of the Ninth Circuit. Judge Rich has held that the "public policy involved in this area of the law [is] not the *right* to slavishly copy articles which are not protected by patent or copyright, but the *need* to copy those articles, which is more properly termed the right to compete *effectively*."[337] Judge Rich's statement reveals the problem of establishing a coherent baseline from which to measure the privileges, duties, and rights involved. To Judge Rich, the baseline is the need to insure competitive markets, and the privilege to copy is an instrumental means to that end. In the Second Circuit, protecting the integrity of the design originator's bundle of rights is apparently the baseline. In the Ninth Circuit, the baseline interest in free competition is implemented through using aesthetic functionality as a *de facto* privilege to copy designs not explicitly shielded by copyright or patent law.[338]

The copyright regime of separability, with heightened qualita-

333 *Keene*, 653 F.2d at 826-27.

334 *Id.* at 825.

335 *Id.*

336 *See supra* notes 94, 189-94 and accompanying text.

337 *In re* Morton-Norwich Prods. Inc., 671 F.2d 1332, 1339 (C.C.P.A. 1982) (emphasis in original). *Cf. In re* DC Comics Inc., 689 F.2d 1042, 1045 (C.C.P.A. 1982) (trademark registrations allowed for drawings of Batman and Superman as trademarks for dolls representing the same super heroes); *see* Oddi, *The Functions of "Functionality" in Trademark Law*, 22 Hous. L. Rev. 925, 943-49 (1985).

338 Pagliero v. Wallace China Co., 198 F.2d 339, 343-44 (9th Cir. 1952) ("If the particular feature is an important ingredient in the commercial success of the product, the

tive criteria of creativity and originality, dependent on either unfair competition law or design patent law to pick up excluded industrial designs, is deeply problematic. Unfair competition law is beset by the same internally contradictory dichotomies plaguing copyright, only the names of the particular dichotomies are different. Multiple, inconsistent, and irreconcilable tests abound, seeking to establish a clear line of demarcation between the functional and the aesthetic. An uncopyrightable industrial design seeking refuge under section 43(a) will be ground through the same defective machinery, only with different labels.

Design patent law is ideally a more attractive vehicle for the protection and encouragement of innovation in industrial design. It suffers, however, from institutional arteriosclerosis due to procedural and doctrinal encrustations.[339] These problems have to be purged before design patent can become a realistic alternative to design protection.[340] These respective regimes suffer from leakage into the law of unarticulated judicial, administrative, and legislative bias, and are characterized by preconception and judicial desperation not to betray *Bleistein*'s impossible neutrality[341]—which is exactly what occurs.

III. Context—A Story About the Origins of Industrial Design and Copyright Law

Before embarking on this truncated account, a few caveats are in order. A history of design will necessarily overlap with social, cultural, political, and economic histories, because design is an expression of the culture in which it was commissioned, conceived, produced, distributed, and consumed. Accounts of this sort will be heavily skewed towards the tastes, appetites, and habits of the wealthy since the powerful elites were the primary subsidizers and consumers of design until well after the Industrial Revolution, and indeed, are a powerful force fueling contemporary art and design innovation at the present.

As with any history, there are a plethora of tendencies, ideas, and movements occurring simultaneously, and a certain reductionism is essential to narrative coherence. This drive toward reduction deeply conflicts with the countervailing need to evoke

---

interest in free competition permits its imitation in the absence of a patent or copyright.").

339 *See supra* notes 289-96 and accompanying text.

340 *See Design Protection: An Overview*, *supra* note 167, at 1356-57; Comment, *Design Protection — Time to Replace the Design Patent*, 51 Minn. L. Rev. 942 (1967).

341 188 U.S. 239 (1903). *See supra* notes 11-21 and accompanying text.

the diversity, contradiction, and complexity of a particular strand followed through successive periods of history. This section admittedly paints with a very broad brush.

Some of the background stylistic analysis of industrial design, according to movements such as Rococco, Neoclassicism, Romanticism, and Modernism,[342] are rooted in relatively conventional art history notions, which are, at best, lenses with limited scope. However, the main thrust of this section is not to explicate clear stylistic categories, but to sketch a plausible story of how art and industry emerged from a common source and were constituted by nineteenth century consciousness into separate spheres. Furthermore, with the collapse of the nineteenth century world-view, art and industry were transformed, moving toward potential merger once again.

In the late twentieth century, industrial design is an integral part of the vast array of goods manufactured by serial or mass-production methods. Industrial design has been professionalized and has emerged in the twentieth century as part of the trend toward specialization in large-scale modern industry. Generally, today, the industrial designer is either a direct employee of an organization or an independent consultant working on a commission basis for a variety of clients. Part of the task of industrial design is translating technological or scientific developments into products which will attract a mass-audience of consumers, having a major impact on a company's overall performance.

A crucial aspect of industrial design is acknowledgement of the manufacturing context for which designs are created. Industrial designers must produce a plan of a form for mass production, which involves separating the process of conception from the actual manufacturing process. Industrial design is not confined to any one material or to a particular category of artifact or environment. Indeed, the very pervasiveness of industrial products has caused them to become invisible despite the crucial role they play in shaping the material framework of our lives.

Industrial design's simultaneous ubiquity and diversity[343] have proved to be extremely problematic in the area of intellectual property law. While industrial designs may have been conceived to serve certain useful purposes and reflect certain values,

---

[342] For a discussion of Neoclassicism and Romanticism, see 2 F. HARTT, ART: A HISTORY OF PAINTING, SCULPTURE, ARCHITECTURE 302-13, 315-31 (1976) [hereinafter HARTT]. For a discussion of Rococco, see H. GARDNER, ART THROUGH THE AGES 819-31 (9th ed. 1991) [hereinafter ART THROUGH THE AGES].

[343] *See* J. HESKETT, INDUSTRIAL DESIGN 119 (1980) [hereinafter HESKETT].

they are also undeniably works of the creative intellect,[344] embodying and contradicting the paradigm of intellectual property. This duality of utilitarian function and aesthetic value has resulted in an internally inconsistent set of congressional, administrative, and judicial decisions,[345] which repeatedly demonstrate the metaphysical nature of copyright law.

To understand the contemporary meaning or meanings of industrial design, it is necessary to examine the nature of the art/utility dichotomy and the historical context in which it developed. The art/utility split is part and parcel of the pervasive cleavage of the universe into mutually exclusive, dichotomous spheres of experience which occurred in Western thought during the eighteenth and nineteenth centuries.[346]

In this account, the twentieth century can be seen as an era in which these once clear dichotomies began disintegrating at an ever increasing rate, due to internal contradictions and external historical contingencies. What we are left with in the late twentieth century is a fragmentation of earlier world-views. These fragments prove tantalizing because they promise illusory

---

[344] Chafee, *Reflections on the Law of Copyright*, 45 COLUM. L. REV. 503, 506-11 (1945). (" '[I]ntellectual property is, after all, the only absolute possession in the world. . . . The man who brings out of nothingness some child of his thought has rights therein which cannot belong to any other sort of property.' " *Id.* at 506-07 (citing Solberg, *Copyright Reform*, 14 NOTRE DAME LAW. 343, 358 (1939) (quoting Harvard geologist Nathaniel S. Shaler, in 1878))). *See also* White-Smith Music Publishing Co. v. Apollo Co., 209 U.S. 1 (1908) (Holmes, J., concurring).

> The notion of property starts, I suppose, from confirmed possession of a tangible object and consists in the right to exclude others from interference with the more or less free doing with it as one wills. But in copyright property has reached a more abstract expression. The right to exclude is not directed to an object in possession or owned, but is *in vacuo*, so to speak. It restrains the spontaneity of men where but for it there would be nothing of any kind to hinder their doing as they saw fit. It is a prohibition of conduct remote from the persons or tangibles of the party having the right. It may be infringed a thousand miles from the owner and without his ever becoming aware of the wrong.

Id. at 19.

[345] *See supra* Part II, CONTRADICTION IN THE CASES, THE COPYRIGHT OFFICE, AND CONGRESS.

[346] This cleavage manifested itself in many different guises: the split between public and private; fact and value; conceptions of separate spheres of state coercion and individual liberty; law and politics; theory and practice; idea and expression; and art and industry. *See, e.g.*, Frug, *The City as a Legal Concept*, 93 HARV. L. REV. 1051, 1099-1105 (1980) (discussing the emergence of the Public/Private distinction in the municipal law of corporations); K. Marx, *On the Jewish Question*, in WRITINGS OF THE YOUNG MARX ON PHILOSOPHY AND SOCIETY 216 (L. Easton & K. Guddot eds. 1967) (discussing the split between civil society and the state characteristic of nineteenth century American society); Olsen, The Family and the Market; A Study of Ideology and Legal Reform, 96 Harv. L. Rev. 503, 1501, 1563-64 (1983) (criticizing traditional liberalism's market/family dichotomy). *See also* Kennedy, *The Structure of Blackstone's Commentaries*, *infra* note 454 (discussing the way eighteenth century liberal thought relentlessly split the world into polar dichotomies).

rationalization and order in the face of a world which has grown increasingly contradictory and complex.[347] Insofar as the art/industry dichotomy is analogous to, and implicated by the public/private split, it is useful to try to analyze its rise and fall.[348]

A. Origins

Some past civilizations have defined *art* as skill developed by practice.[349] The Romans used the word *ars*, the root of which signified manual skills achieved in large measure by imitating the works of one's predecessors.[350] As recently as the end of the nineteenth century, Western art in the academies was taught through intensive copying of existing contemporary and ancient

---

[347] *See* T. Kuhn, *The Structure of Scientific Revolutions*, in INTERNATIONAL ENCYCLOPEDIA OF UNIFIED SCIENCE (1962) (During the twentieth century, a shift occurred in Western thought from an epistemology of certainty premised on a permanent, neutral framework ("essentialism") to a new epistemology (called variously "historicism," "hermeneutics," "post-modernism," "contextualism") which has as one of its thematic obsessions the critique of absolutes and the acknowledgement of context-bound local knowledge. Seminal works seeking to explain the phenomenological world in the context of a universe where there are no transparent, universal, and neutral frameworks include Kuhn's discussion of the effects of generational paradigm shifts in scientific thought.). Others include: C. GEERTZ, THE INTERPRETATION OF CULTURES (1973) (suggesting that social contextualization is a way to understand culture as a symbolic system and how signifiers signify in a local, non-absolutist context); P. BERGER & T. LUCKMANN, THE SOCIAL CONSTRUCTION OF REALITY: A TREATISE IN THE SOCIOLOGY OF KNOWLEDGE (1966) (approaching the concepts of meaning, understanding, nationality, and certainty as referring to a sense of compelledness felt characteristically within a particular culture); J. POCOCK, POLITICS, LANGUAGE, AND TIME: ESSAYS ON POLITICAL THOUGHT AND HISTORY (1971) (extension of Kuhn's notion of successive controlling intellectual paradigms to the history of political thought); Williams, *Critical Legal Studies: The Death of Transcendence and the Rise of the New Langdells*, 62 N.Y.U. L. REV. 429 (1987) (discussing the new epistemology in terms of an approach to law and legal history).

[348] This admittedly cursory sketch of design history is meant to focus on the development of the strand which eventually came to be associated with the rhetorical slogan, "Form follows function." *See* ART THROUGH THE AGES, *supra* note 342, at 947-48. While this slogan was coined by the American architect Louis Sullivan (1856-1924), it has become associated with the Bauhaus, the International School, and Modernism in general. In the process, it has become devoid of any significant meaning. For example, this phrase was used by the *Esquire* court to deny copyright protection to a light fixture, in which, emphatically, form certainly did not follow function. Esquire, Inc. v. Ringer, 591 F.2d 796, 807 (D.C. Cir. 1978). For a discussion of *Esquire*, see *supra* notes 127-44 and accompanying text.

[349] For a definition of the Greek *techne*, see 1 J. MERRYMAN & A. ELSEN, LAW, ETHICS AND THE VISUAL ARTS 3-1 (1981) [hereinafter MERRYMAN]. *See also* PLATO, POLITICUS 258, *quoted in* Esquire, Inc. v. Ringer, 414 F. Supp. 939, 941 n.* (D.C. 1976), *rev'd*, 591 F.2d 796 (D.C. Cir. 1978), *cert. denied*, 440 U.S. 908 (1979) ("All the handicrafts possess a scientific content which has grown up along with them and is embodied in their practice. The manufactured article is the joint product of the science and the practice which are combined in the handicraft."); PLATO, THE REPUBLIC II 149 (P. Shorey trans.) (Plato assigned craftsmen and practitioners of the useful arts to the lowest stratum of his ideal republic. Craftsmen and citizens were to be separated by law because the duties of citizens were time consuming, and all the arts, except philosophy, were base and mechanical.).

[350] MERRYMAN, *supra* note 349, at 3-1.

two- and three-dimensional works.[351]

During the Middle Ages, artists formed guilds similar to apothecaries, saddlemakers, and other craftsmen. These professions were considered the mechanical arts, and their practitioners were producers who worked manually for payment.[352] During this period the separation of art from industry began. There is no precise historical point at which the idea of craft separated into expressive conceptual and labor components. Instead, this separation can be viewed as an historical tendency. Prior to the Industrial Revolution, processes of social change occurred at a slower pace, and craftsmen were not innovators, but rather made minor adaptations to forms developed by earlier craftsmen.

During the late Medieval period and early Renaissance, there was a growth of trade in cities such as Florence, Venice, and Nuremberg. This growth in trade spurred the formation of large workshops which catered to the tastes of churches, monarchs, and wealthy merchants.[353] These workshops utilized traditional techniques of hand-manufacture in which the border between artistry and craftsmanship was extremely fluid. Often, multiple objects of the same type were made. A rise in commercial competition that threatened the fifteenth century led to a demand for innovation, which threatened the artisan's emphasis on maintaining established forms.[354]

---

[351] *Id.*

[352] *See* ART THROUGH THE AGES, *supra* note 342, at 317 ("The invention and development of tools and mechanisms that extended humanity's powers over the environment and that facilitated manufacture were encouraged in part by the new dignity that the Church's disapproval of slavery conferred on manual labor and skills. Free craftsmen—not slaves as in the ancient world—were the Medieval agents of production; organized in guilds, they constituted the firm foundation of the Medieval urban economy."); B. BUGBEE, THE EARLY AMERICAN LAW OF INTELLECTUAL PROPERTY: THE HISTORICAL FOUNDATIONS OF THE U.S. PATENT AND COPYRIGHT SYSTEMS 49-50 (1961) [hereinafter BUGBEE].

> The legal protection of the products of creative thought appears to have been virtually ignored in ancient and medieval times. In classical civilizations, society evidently looked down upon the practice of useful arts, and regarded inventions, despite the work of Archimedes and others, as playthings beneath the dignity of a true thinker.

[353]
> The Renaissance was an orientation of the European mind towards the forms of Roman and Greek civilization, and towards the meaning of classical culture. On the latter side its impulse was plainly a liberating one . . . . Classical civilization, on the other hand, was not an unmixed good: for it served all too quickly to stereotype in old forms a spirit which had been freshly reborn, and it set up a servile principle in the arts . . . .

L. MUMFORD, STICKS AND STONES: A STUDY OF AMERICAN ARCHITECTURE AND CIVILIZATION 13 (2d ed. 1958) [hereinafter MUMFORD].

[354] *See* BUGBEE, *supra* note 352. Bugbee places the "origination of State protection for intellectual property in Renaissance Italy." *Id.* at 61. Bugbee sees fourteenth century

At this point design innovation did not necessarily mean the creation of new forms, but rather the addition of fashionable decoration and ornamentation. By the early sixteenth century, following the invention and dissemination of the printing press by Gutenberg in the 1450s, the first pattern books began to appear.[355] The appearance of pattern books signified the divorce of a designer from the application of his designs. At approximately this point in the sixteenth century, the word "design" emerged, which recognized a separation of what had previously been a unitary idea of craft into intellectual and manual work.[356]

> [Gardner stresses] the high value that Renaissance artists placed on *theory*. . . . [I]f any occupation or profession were to have dignity and be worthy of honor, it must have an intellectual basis. . . . [F]or somewhat similar reasons, 'fine' artists today are likely to consider their pursuits superior to those of 'commercial' artists. Renaissance artists strove to make themselves scholars and gentlemen, to associate with princes and the learned, and to rise above the long-standing ancient and medieval prejudice that saw them as mere handicraftsmen.[357]

As "design" was splitting off from craft, so too was "high" art.

---

grants of monopolies to stimulate commerce (*i.e.*, mill-building and importation, new methods of carding wool and water transport), reward favorites, and increase the state treasury by their sale as the basis for modern copyright and patent protection.

> These grants, while apparently lacking elements essential to a patent for invention, reflect State and municipal efforts to develop domestic industry by means of importation franchises and monopolies and 'such encouragements' as bounties, loans, exemptions, and various forms of protection and assistance. Utility was the central consideration . . . . This policy of industrial stimulation by the State in the later Middle Ages and early Renaissance, while unconcerned with originality, probably facilitated the protection of intellectual property later, as did the accumulation of private capital for investment and the growing importance of the individual.

Id. at 66.

355 Pattern books were mechanically reproduced collections of engravings containing illustrations of decorative and ornamental patterns and motifs which could be utilized repetitively in the textile or furniture-making trades.

356 Cooley, *From Brunelleschi to CAD-CAM*, in DESIGN AFTER MODERNISM 197 (J. Thackara ed. 1988) [hereinafter Cooley].

357 ART THROUGH THE AGES, *supra* note 342, at 608-09 (discussing the effect of the 1453 Turkish conquest of Constantinople which precipitated an influx of Greek scholars into the Italian city-states. This helped fuel an appetite for classical art and philosophy, which in turn fueled the further development of humanism). *See also* N. PEVSNER, PIONEERS OF THE MODERN MOVEMENT: FROM WILLIAM MORRIS TO WALTER GROPIUS 21 (1937) [hereinafter PEVSNER] ("Leonardo da Vinci wanted the artist to be a scientist and a humanist, but by no means a craftsman. . . . However, this attitude of artistic presumption remained exceptional until the end of the eighteenth century."); Cooley, *supra* note 356 (describing Brunelleschi's discovery in 1413 of the optical "truth" of linear perspective as the turning point in design methodology and the history of design, when "theoretical forms of knowledge" began to separate from practice, or "things we know but cannot tell").

However, between "art" and "design" there was still much fluidity, undoubtedly due in part to their common sources of royal or state subsidy and patronage, and their common split between theory and practice.

Threaded through this period is the theme of state censorship. The origins of copyright involve the double-edged state grant, which subsidized approved content and suppressed the disapproved.[358]

---

[358] B. KAPLAN, AN UNHURRIED VIEW OF COPYRIGHT 3-4 (1967) [hereinafter KAPLAN]. The monopoly granted by the Crown was the stationer's, not the author's. Kaplan also states that "copyright has the look of being gradually secreted in the interstices of the censorship," referring to the Elizabethan grants of patents for specific works, confining printing to authorized press, pre-publication licensing of books, and use of trade organizations and government agencies for enforcement. Kaplan's copyright chronology potentially bridges two paradigms of intellectual property (group protection of a craftsman's guild and protection of the individual "artistic spark") *Id.*:

> 1476: Caxton founds press in Westminster.
>
> 1485-1518: Royal printer appears.
>
> 1534: Upheaval of Act of Supremacy (censorship through licensing).
>
> 1557: Queen Mary charters stationers as "literary constables."
>
> 1695: Emancipation of English press (through non-renewal of stationers' patent which was granted post-restoration in 1662).
>
> 1710: Statute of Anne (Kaplan suggests that stationers strategically piggybacked their claims in the name of authors).
>
> 1720: Case that tried to stop an English translation of a Latin book (translation allowed).
>
> 1740: Abridgement cases (cartographers sought to avoid infringement by adding something intellectual and new to maps).
>
> 1774: Donaldson v. Beckett: perpetual copyright denied
>
> 1785: Sayre v. Moore: maps analogized to, but distinct from dictionaries and histories, copying allowed because of the usefulness of maps; danger apprehended if every map maker had to introduce variation
>
> 1809: Longman v. Winchester, 16 Ves. Jun. 269, 33 Eng. Rep. 987 (Ch. 1809) Chancellor Eldon went after a copier's "imperial Calender" which absorbed information from original calender but added material and corrections—Eldon came down on the copier because he availed himself of the originator's labor; and had not "replowed the field".

Id. at 3-21.

Kaplan sees *Longman* in 1809 as the turning point away from *Sayre* and notes the move away from Mansfield's "higher" threshold for protection to broader protection in the translation and abridgement cases. This was not spun out of logic but out of socio-economic-cultural changes such as the rise of the market economy in the late eighteenth century. One of Kaplan's key points is that the initial patents were extended to the publishers as a group and *not* to individual authors. This movement appears to converge with emerging literary markets and the Enlightenment focus on possessive individualism (a very early incarnation of the idea of "rights as trumps"). Note that copyright is distinguished from a pre-political right because the monopoly grant is limited, not perpetual, and derives from the sovereign. Somewhere in the concept is also the Lockean notion of mixing one's labor with nature and thereby gaining a natural right in the outcome. *Id.* at 19-22.

> An indulgent attitude toward using other people's works seemed increasingly out of keeping with the realities of the market. The business of publishing and distributing books had become bigger, more competitive, more impersonal; the stakes were higher, the risks more serious. In this atmosphere there would be ever greater anxiety about marking out metes and bounds of literary ownership, and courts might be expected to respond to arguments about protection of investment.

By the seventeenth century, the trade centers of Europe shifted from the Mediterranean to such centralized nation-states as France, which border the North Atlantic.[359] The lavish courts of these absolute monarchies provided patronage for artisans and skilled craftsmen, with the establishment of large crown-controlled manufactories.[360] These manufactories produced for royal consumption fine tapestries, furniture, metal work, and porcelains, with designs supplied to the artisans by the court artist.[361]

Simultaneously, a profound split between "pure" art and industry emerged, with "design" ironically falling on the "pure" art side of the division. While the "third estate," composed of the increasingly wealthy and influential middle-class,[362] was ascending to greater power, the aristocracy still remained the patrons of the arts, and the arts reflected the decadence of the ruling class taste in decline. "The art that won aristocratic favor was luxurious, frivolous, sensual, and clever. . . . Intricate and witty artifice now became the objective in all the arts . . . ."[363]

By the middle of the eighteenth century in France, the designer, in addition to being a discrete specialist for the royal manufactories, also worked with commercial companies. These companies desired high-quality surface pattern designs, including those produced by wallpaper and textile manufacturers. Following the French Revolution, and the collapse of the absolute monarchy these royal manu-

---

Id. at 22.

359 *See* ART THROUGH THE AGES, *supra* note 342, at 809.

> As a symbol of the power of absolutism, Versailles is unsurpassed. It also expresses, in the most monumental terms of its age, the rationalistic creed, based on the mathematical philosophy of Descartes, that all knowledge must be systematic and all science must be the consequence of the imposition of the intellect on matter. The whole stupendous design of Versailles proudly proclaims the mastery of human intelligence over the disorderliness of nature.

Id.

360 *See* HESKETT, *supra* note 343, at 11.

361 *Id.* at 11-12. Heskett gives the example of the introduction of porcelain to Europe in the seventeenth century to illustrate the complex interaction between expanding commerce, royal investment, innovation, and the fluidity of the roles of designer, artist, and craftsman. Once the Meissen manufactory had uncovered the secret of producing porcelain in Saxony, court artists began designing vessels and figurines, as well as decorative motifs. Maintainance of these porcelain manufactories, created solely for use of the Royal court, required massive subsidies. By the middle of the eighteenth century, the Royal manufactories entered some of the newly opened commercial markets in order to offset these large operation costs. As the enlarged export markets increased demand, traditional craft methods of hand production continued, but with a concomitant drop in quality of workmanship. *Id.* at 12-13.

362 *See* R. UNGER, LAW IN MODERN SOCIETY 72 (1976) (comparative study of the place of law in different societies examining the conditions under which "modern" society emerged).

363 ART THROUGH THE AGES, *supra* note 342, at 818.

factories had to adapt to marketplace competition. Their designers became employees, instead of royal functionaries. Guilds were dissolved in 1791 as vestiges of medieval hierarchy, industry came to be identified with the bourgeoisie, as opposed to the church and nobility. A plutocracy of wealthy merchants replaced the fallen aristocracy in France and the market then catered to the emerging bourgeoise.[364]

During the eighteenth century, the absence of an absolute monarchy in England in the model of Louis XIV in France, forced English designers to expand earlier and more extensively into the commercial marketplace. By the mid-eighteenth century, rapid technological growth and applied science generated new processes and products.[365] Names like Chippendale, Wedgewood, and Boulton belonged to commercial entrepreneurs, not artists.[366] These innovators produced "competitively priced fashionable objects" and developed new methods of manufacture to serve the newly emergent merchant class.[367] Eclecticism and innovation were the corner-

---

364 *See* J. LOCKE, *The Second Treatise of Civil Government*, in TWO TREATISES OF GOVERNMENT (1789) (P. Laslett ed. 1970) (emphasizing the natural rights of individuals to property and liberty and the contingent nature of political obligation); 1 BLACKSTONE, COMMENTARIES ON THE LAWS OF ENGLAND 32-92, 117-41 (G. Tucker ed. 1969); P. ATIYAH, THE RISE AND FALL OF FREEDOM OF CONTRACT (1979). For a discussion of the Scottish Enlightenment vision of freeholders unbound from feudal shackles and superstition, see A. SMITH, LECTURES ON JURISPRUDENCE 86 (R. Meek, D. Raphael & P. Stein eds. 1978).

> It is found that society must be pretty far advanced before the different trades can all find subsistence, that is, before those trades which do not immediately procure food of some sort . . . can be depended on for a subsistence. . . . To bring about therefore the separation of trades sooner than the progress of society would naturally effect, and prevent the uncertainty of all those who had taken themselves to one trade, it was found necessary to give them a certainty of a comfortable subsistence.—And for this purpose the legislature determined that they should have the priviledge [sic] of exercising their seperate [sic] trades without the fear of being cut out of their liveleyhood [sic] by the increase of their rivalls [sic]. That this was necessary therefore in the [first] stages of the arts to bring them to their proper perfection, appears very reasonable and is confirmed by this, that it has been the generall [sic] practise [sic] of all the nations in Europe. But as this end is now fully answered, it were much to [be] wished that these as well as many other remains of the old jurisprudence should be removed.

Id. See also J.W. BURROW, A LIBERAL DESCENT: VICTORIAN HISTORIANS AND THE ENGLISH PAST 21-35 (1981) (discussing the variety of Whiggisms and Human Challenge); Horwitz, *Republicanism and Liberalism in American Constitutional Thought*, 29 WM. & MARY L. REV. 57 (1987) (reinterpreting eighteenth century Scottish humanist philosophers such as Adam Smith through the lense of civic republican ideology, rather than traditional *laissez-faire* liberalism).

365 Examples of such new processes include cast iron (Darby, 1735), the crucible process of melting steel (Huntsman, 1740), the steam engine and steam boiler (Watt, 1765, 1781), a water-frame for spinning (Arkwright, 1769), and the power loom (Cartwright, 1784).

366 *See* HESKETT, *supra* note 343, at 13.

367 *Id.* For example, the Sheffield plating process, which used "an inexpensive method of plating silver to a copper base," was exploited by Matthew Boulton in the

stones of design during this period.[368] " 'Fashion hath much to do in these things,' . . . 'and that of the present age distinguishes itself by adopting the most Elegant ornaments without presuming to invent new ones.' "[369]

B. Developments

The separation of "beauty" and "utility," rooted in Enlightenment ideas and refracted through the prism of nascent Romanticism,[370] was very much at odds with the profoundly democratizing effects of mass production. The sharp separation between art and utility, which can be traced to the Renaissance, emphasized theory divorced from practice and art over its applications. Ironically, at the very moment of the Industrial Revolution when it was plausible for their integration, art and utility split into mutually exclusive intellectual and aesthetic realms.

---

production of ornamental and decorative metal works such as buttons, buckles, clasps, and mountings. *Id.* at 13-14.

368 *Id.* at 14-17. Boulton's pattern books were kept current through a network of agents who supplied a stream of objects, casts, drawings, books, and sketches from which he drew, as well as commissioned drawings from prominent artists. *See id.* at 18. Because of the simplicity and repetitive motifs which were conducive to mass replication, Boulton's neo-classical designs were a link between the older crafts tradition and the newer mass-production technology of molds and casts. While expanding mass-production, Boulton also continued producing hand-crafted high-quality items for an elite clientele.

Josiah Wedgwood, a contemporary of Boulton's, divided his ceramic work into categories of " 'ornamental' " and " 'useful wares,' " equivalent to Boulton's distinction between high-quality and mass-produced items. *Id.* at 15. Wedgwood's "ornamental" ware garnered acclaim and kudos among the wealthy, in turn fueling the appetite for his mass-produced ceramics. Wedgwood succeeded in casting clay in molds, allowing him to create and exploit a market for inexpensive, quality ceramic tableware. The process of wet molding ceramics further removed control from the workers and placed it in the hands of the designer of the prototype. To this development, Wedgwood added techniques of mechanical printing transfer, replacing laborious hand-painting, which facilitated rapid production. In 1773, he built a factory set up for mechanical casting, incorporating division of labor and mass production. Catalogs advertising Wedgwood products were issued. *Id.* at 17.

While Boulton catered to swiftly changing tastes in a fashion market for decoration, and Wedgwood attended to a middle-class domestic market with requirements of utility and durability which had to be reconciled with the ornamental impulse, both shared the notion that aesthetic values were subordinate to market and manufacturing contingencies. *Id.* at 18. Both men also primarily utilized designs that came from outside of the factory. *Id.* Design was beginning to be something that was applied to the manufacturing process, not a derivation from it.

369 *Id.* at 14 (quoting Charles Boulton).

370 "In France, the period of separation between the fine arts or 'pure arts' and industry was most marked in the seventeenth and eighteenth centuries, when 'industry was considered the worst enemy of art.' " Reichman I, *supra* note 1, at 1145 n.3 (quoting C. Carreau, Merite et Droit D'Auteur 191 (1981)); Art Through the Ages, *supra* note 342, at 818-19 (discussing Rousseau's doctrine of the free quest for identity and search for the "natural" man, who has been obscured by society). *See generally* Kennedy, *The Structure of Blackstone's Commentaries*, 28 Buffalo L. Rev. 205 (1979) (on the relationship between Enlightenment liberal political philosophy and the English common law).

With Romanticism sweeping the so-called "fine" arts, the Renaissance paradigm of the artist as the "universal" man became transmogrified into the tragic Promethean individual artist apart from society, seeking to transcend and escape traditional values and conventional history.[371]

By the end of the eighteenth century, the term "fine" art had emerged, contemporaneous with the change of the name of the French Royal Academy to the *Academie Ecol des Beaux-Arts* in 1795. The *Academie Ecol des Beaux-Arts* sanctioned painting, sculpture, and architecture as "superior to the crafts."[372] The new academicians, with a focus on science, theory, and history, regarded themselves as being dedicated to the gratification of taste and the pursuit of "pure" beauty, apart from and above mere craftsmen who produced useful objects. This split between "high" art and industry further reproduced itself within manufacturing, where there were now "designers" and "workers."

Prior to the nineteenth century and the arrival of the Industrial Revolution, ornamentation and decoration had been the expression of a craftsman's skill in working precious materials, having both aesthetic and economic value. Design had largely been integrated with craft, but now, prodded by industrialization, it shifted to imitating the "pure" arts. It attempted to legitimize its new status by aping the forms, but not the substance, of luxurious ornament.[373] As was the case with the social sciences a century later, design was starting to become professionalized as a discrete specialty, completely separate from the manual trades.[374] The new manufacturing technologies and materials of the Industrial Revolution, such as stamping, molding, plating, and veneering, were capable of simulating the look of traditional high quality craftwork at a much lower cost.[375] The appearance of intricate texture and elegant design, which were once the preserve

371 Romanticism, as a cultural and social movement, is beyond the scope of this Article. For our purposes, it can be seen on one level as a revolt against the Rationalist tradition of the Enlightenment and its emphasis on balance and proportion. On another level, Romanticism can be seen as introducing the notion that art yields concrete insight into reality and that reason can be present only in the guise of abstract concepts. Romanticism views art as an end in itself. It should be judged solely by aesthetic, and not utilitarian or ornamental criteria.

372 MERRYMAN, *supra* note 349, at 3-1.

373 *See* HESKETT, *supra* note 343, at 19.

374 For a detailed account of the professionalization of the social sciences in the late nineteenth and early twentieth centuries, see E. PURCELL, THE CRISIS OF DEMOCRATIC THEORY (1973).

375 *See* HESKETT, *supra* note 343, at 19.

of luxury and aristocracy, became accessible to the middle class at a significantly lower cost.

The design criteria and standards of these newly emergent industries were derived from an earlier period when elaborate form, ornate decoration, and costly materials symbolized wealth and power. The lower cost and quality of these products fed the voracious appetites of the growing middle class for products signifying status, taste, prestige, standing, and culture.[376] Unfortunately, decoration and ornament were used indiscriminately, resulting in a baroque mockery of vanished elegance, insensitive to new, industrial realities.[377] Manufacturers hastened to ornament simple articles in order to raise the market price for their products, realizing that a useful item with ostentatious decoration would sell for more than a similar, but unadorned, item.

Generally, the nineteenth century had an intense fixation with earlier historical periods. Regarding design, this historical obsession further expanded the vernacular of available stylistic forms and sources. These expanded sources were primarily evaluated according to their decorative, rather than their structural qualities. Out of these new resources, manufacturers ransacked and pillaged history, in search of novelty which could be transformed into marketable ornamentation and decorative features for the insatiable appetite of the *noveau riche*. Often the results were a grotesque pastiche of historical forms slapped onto articles with little thought of the inter-relationship between the past or present, or the nature of the articles themselves.[378]

Writing in the 1930s, Nikolaus Pevsner described a picture of the early- to mid-nineteenth century:

> [M]anufacturers were, by means of new machinery, enabled to turn out thousands of cheap articles in the same time and at the same cost as were formerly required for the production of one well-made object. Sham materials and sham technique were dominant all through industry. Skilled craftsmanship,

---

376 *Id.*

377 *See generally* E.P. THOMPSON, THE MAKING OF THE ENGLISH WORKING CLASS (1968) (examining the complex and contradictory relationships among culture, class, and consciousness in early industrial England).

378 *See* V. PAPANEK, DESIGN FOR THE REAL WORLD 22-23 (1971). Initially, industrial design was little more than a belated attempt to conceal the patent ugliness proliferated by developing technologies. "Looking at the machine, they saw a new thing, a thing that seemed to cry out for decorative embellishments. These decorations were usually garnered from classical ornaments and from major raids into the animal and vegetable kingdoms. Thus, giant hydraulic presses dripped with acanthus leaves, pineapples, stylized wheat sheaves." *Id.* at 23. However, ugliness is not intrinsic. It is a social creation—loaded with all kinds of ideological and psychological baggage.

> still so admirable when Chippendale and Wedgwood were at work, was replaced by mechanical routine. Demand was increasing from year to year, but demand from an uneducated and debased population, living a slave-life in filth and penury.[379]

During the mid-Victorian period, discourse regarding the relation of an object to its function centered around the question of the appropriateness of its decorative style, which often was a melange of various historic stylistic flourishes.[380]

Reformers and critics who attacked "art for art's sake"[381] as an elitist slogan, pointed to Cellini saltcellars, Raphael candelabra, and other *objets d'art* as proof that art was still art even when attached to useful objects.[382] However, evoking images of Renaissance saltcellars minimized the economic aims of industrial design—which had hit its stride by the mid-nineteenth century. William Morris spearheaded the attack on industrialization in Victorian England. With the Arts and Crafts movement, he sought to bring art back in touch with life.[383] To Morris, Victorian "fine" artists and designers " 'wrap[ed] themselves up in dreams of Greece and Italy . . . which only a very few people even pretend to understand or be moved by.' "[384] Morris sought to revive the handicraft tradition, denouncing the elitism and irrelevance of the "art for art's sake" movement. To him, art was "the expression by man of his pleasure in labour," and the Romantic emphasis on artistic inspiration as a conduit to underlying reality was mystifying nonsense. " '[T]here is no such thing; it is a mere matter of craftsmanship.' "[385]

---

379 PEVSNER, *supra* note 357, at 21.

380 Originally the contextual integration of art in tradition found its expression in the cult. We know that the earliest art works originated in the service of a ritual—first the magical, then the religious kind. . . . The secular cult of beauty, developed during the Renaissance and prevailing for three centuries, clearly showed that ritualistic basis in its decline and the first deep crisis which befell it. With the advent of the first truly revolutionary means of reproduction, photography, simultaneously with the rise of socialism, art sensed the approaching crisis which has become evident a century later. At the time, art reacted with the doctrine of *l'art pour l'art*, that is, with a theology of art. This gave rise to what might be called a negative theology in the form of the idea of 'pure' art, which not only denied any social function of art but also any categorizing by subject matter.

Benjamin, *The Work of Art in the Age of Mechanical Reproduction* (1936), in MODERN ART AND MODERNISM: A CRITICAL ANTHOLOGY 220 (F. Frascina & C. Harrison ed. 1982).

381 *See infra* note 388.

382 2 S. LADAS, PATENTS, TRADEMARKS AND RELATED RIGHTS: NATIONAL AND INTERNATIONAL PROTECTION 831 (1975).

383 *See* PEVSNER, *supra* note 357, at 23 (Morris' firm was named "Morris, Marshall & Faulkner, Fine Art Workmen in Painting, Carving, Furniture and the Metals.").

384 *Id.* at 23.

385 *Id.*

William Morris was a contradictory figure. While he abhorred the industrialization of the nineteenth century and its concomitant degradation of life and labor, he accepted the skewed historicism of the Victorian era.[386] Looking backward to the time of cathedrals and craft guilds, but without considering the effect of the rigid religious and social hierarchies, Morris proclaimed, " '[I]t is not possible to dissociate art from morality, politics and religion.' "[387] He denounced "art for art's sake" as dangerous elitism, proclaiming, " 'I don't want art for a few, any more than education for a few, or freedom for a few.' "[388] Yet, when workers rioted in London, aroused in part by Morris' own romantic socialist polemics, he withdrew into his own private world of Pre-Raphaelite beauty and poetry.[389] "While Morris wanted an art 'by the people for the people,' "[390] his handcrafted pieces of applied art were exorbitantly priced.[391] To use his own pejorative which he had hurled at advocates of "art for art's sake," his work ended up becoming art "for 'the swinish luxury of the rich.' "[392]

Morris was appalled by Victorian industry's treatment of its workers as depersonalized adjuncts of machines, precluded from producing skillful, meaningful, and creative work. To Morris, such work was an essential element of their humanity.[393] The Arts and Crafts movement put forward a profoundly nostalgic, sentimentalized and idealistic program of Medieval values.[394] With these values, Morris sought to recreate a harmonious, non-industrial society—a society in which human life was dignified and given meaning by the skills and creativity of handcraftsmanship.[395]

---

386 *Id.* at 21-22.

> During the Renaissance, artists had first learnt to consider themselves superior beings, bearers of a great message. . . . Schiller was the first to form a philosophy of art which made the artist the most venerable of men. . . . Coleridge, Shelley, [and] Keats followed in England. The artist is now no longer a craftsman, no longer a servant, he is a priest. . . . The artist began to despise utility and the public, . . . [to]shut himself off from the real life of his time, withdrawing into his sacred circle and creating art for art's, art for the artist's, sake. Concurrently the public lost understanding of his personal, outwardly useless utterances. . . . [H]e was ridiculed by the vast majority of his contemporaries, and extolled only by a small set of critics and wealthy connoisseurs.

387 *Id.* at 24.

388 *Id.* at 23.

389 *Id.* at 25.

390 *Id.* at 25-26.

391 *Id.* at 27. (A disciple of Morris', Walter Crane, wrote " 'cheapness as a rule . . . can only be obtained at the cost of the . . . cheapening of human life and labour.' ").

392 *Id.* at 26.

393 *Id.* (" 'As a condition of life, production by machinery is altogether an evil.' ").

394 *See* HESKETT, *supra* note 343, at 85, 87.

395 *See id.* at 19-20 ("Morris . . . shared Pugin's admiration of medieval society and art, but expanded his equation of aesthetic and ethical values in [his] sweeping condemna-

The importance of Morris and his followers in the Arts and Crafts movement was two-fold. Their first contribution was the complete rejection of decoration and ornamentation as a symbol of past decadence and excess. Second, they placed a new stress on the structure and function of objects as an emblem of moral, social, and aesthetic renewal. It was this strand that was absorbed and transformed during the late nineteenth century in the United States and Europe. This approach developed into a glorification and celebration of modern industry and the machine age, an approach which came to be known as "functionalism."[396]

The Belgian architect Henri Van de Velde gathered up the strands of the Arts and Crafts movement, discarding some and emphasizing others. Van de Velde wrote, " 'The seeds that fertilised our spirit, evoked our activities, and originated the complete renewal of ornamentation and form in the decorative arts, were undoubtedly the work and the influence of John Ruskin and William Morris.' "[397] Van de Velde, one of the originators of *Art Nouveau,* decisively broke with Morris' anti-machine ideology. In lectures given in 1894, Van de Velde's fundamental starting point was the machine, " 'Why should artists who build palaces in stone rank any higher than artists who build them in metal?' Engineers are 'the architects of the present day.' . . . What we need is 'a logical structure of the products, uncompromising logic in the use of materials, proud and frank exhibition of working processes.' "[398]

Van de Velde continued to develop Morris' moral and social principles, arguing that objects could not be considered separate from their method of production and context of use.[399] He felt that artists and designers should be controlling influences, guardians insuring predominance of human needs.[400] Van de Velde stressed the importance of linking theory and practice. If designers exclusively concerned themselves with the quest for new forms, these newly discovered forms could later be exploited out of context, thereby mangling the theory by distorting its application. This is, however, what happened to *Art Nouveau* as it became yet another ornamental style applied to products, severed from its origins.

---

tion of industry and its products, pointing to the human cost and sacrifice involved in a social system that required and produced such goods.").

396 *See generally* P. JOHNSON, MODERN ARCHITECTURE INTERNATIONAL EXHIBITION (1931) (introducing European "functionalists" to American audiences and draining the social agenda from the "functionalist" program).

397 PEVSNER, *supra* note 357, at 30.

398 *Id.* at 31.

399 *See id.* at 31.

400 *See* HESKETT, *supra* note 343, at 88.

Van de Velde and *Art Nouveau* stand at the end of the nineteenth century "craftsman" tradition,[401] drawing upon curvilinear natural forms for inspiration, while beginning a new tradition by exploiting light metal structures.[402] This use was made possible by developments in engineering and fabrication technology in the late nineteenth and early twentieth centuries.[403] In *Art Nouveau*, the structure itself was transformed into its own ornament. This attempt "to create a new, universal style which would harmonize all aspects of the visual environment into a total entity, a complete work of art that would be the embodiment of cultural and social unity" carried the Arts and Crafts strand of moral didacticism forward into the twentieth century.[404]

The writings and works of John Ruskin[405] and William Morris were important influences in the United States, particularly on the work of Henry H. Richardson.[406] Richardson sought to revive the Romanesque style by using "heavy round arches and massive masonry walls," but with original ornament drawn from natural forms.[407] He managed to integrate these elements, using new building technologies, without degenerating into historical pastiche.

Richardson's protege, Louis Sullivan, who has been called "the first truly modern architect,"[408] felt that the traditional preoccupation with historical styles impeded the development of an architec-

---

401 Notwithstanding the approaching reformulation of the "craftsman" tradition, one of Van de Velde's followers wrote in 1906, " 'In the craftsman three activities, of artist, producer and salesman, are combined.' " Because these functions had become separated, mechanically reproducing hand-made designs, and a new aesthetic found, " 'the machine must be spiritualized.' " *Id.*

402 *See* HARTT, *supra* note 342, at 430.

403 *See* Fisher, *Reconstructing the Fair Use Doctrine*, 101 HARV. L. REV. 1659, 1747 (1988) [hereinafter FISHER, FAIR USE]. Fisher's article discusses the impact of industrialization in the United States in the nineteenth century: "Prior to the onset of industrialization, many artisans also cherished a version of this ideal and to some degree realized it." *Id.* "Meaningful work requires skill and concentration, presents the laborer with challenges and problems he can overcome only through the exercise of initiative and creativity, and is part of a larger project he considers socially valuable and must take into account in making his decisions." *Id.* For detailed studies of cultural, social, and legal developments in nineteenth century America, see generally A. DAWLEY, CLASS AND COMMUNITY: THE INDUSTRIAL REVOLUTION IN LYNN (1976); S. ROSS, WORKERS ON THE EDGE: WORK, LEISURE AND POLITICS IN INDUSTRIALIZING CINCINNATI, 1788-1850 (1984) (on the ways the spread of industrial capitalism deprived an ever-larger portion of the population of meaningful work, causing changes in the consciousness of the average worker, including a sense of separation from the goods and institutions that a person has created and causing passivity and divisions into avenues of over consumption).

404 HESKETT, *supra* note 351, at 86.

405 *See, e.g.*, RUSKIN, THE STONES OF VENICE (J.G. Links ed. 1960) (in particular, Ruskin's description and theory of the virtues of the "Gothic mode").

406 Among other notable structures, Richardson designed Austin Hall on the Harvard Law School campus.

407 ART THROUGH THE AGES, *supra* note 342, at 947.

408 *Id.* at 948.

ture in which "form follows function."[409] Sullivan wanted the exteriors of his buildings to reflect their inner structure, which by the late nineteenth century included a considerably expanded vocabulary of new forms and building technologies.[410] Standardization, prefabrication, and other new technologies and materials allowed innovative designs involving vast enclosed spaces and densities. Somewhere between the works of John Roebling, designer of the Brooklyn Bridge,[411] and Louis Sullivan, the "modern" engineering aesthetic became elevated over earlier impulses to historicist ornamentation and design.

One must consider the socialist, humanist, and moral underpinnings of William Morris in order to fully appreciate Sullivan's slogan that "form follows function." While this expression might be "misinterpreted as expressing a somewhat crude structural and aesthetic determinism," Sullivan "attempt[ed] to formulate a concept of organic unity in architecture [and design] in which function, structure and appropriate decoration could be fused."[412] Past architecture and design had been inextricably linked to the cultural refinements and indulgences of the aristocracy. In the late nineteenth century, the emerging industrial city, the rise of the working classes, and the urgent need for housing to accommodate an ever increasing population led to an expanded concept of social responsibility. Frank Lloyd Wright, who had worked under Sullivan, understood the ideological imperatives latent in a commitment to the organic and natu-

---

409 *Id.* Consider the parallels between Louis Sullivan's polemical "form follows function" and Christopher Langdell's equally polemical "Law is a science." They both originated in the last quarter of the nineteenth century and placed an emphasis and faith in the deducibility of certain universal truths, valid at all times and all places. Ironically, Langdell is now seen as the antithesis of modernity in legal thought. The heirs to functionalism in art, design, and architecture (the "International" style, a universalist name that would have pleased Langdell), until recently, continued to rule the roost. Indeed, if one looks at an opinion like Esquire, Inc. v. Ringer, 414 F. Supp. 939 (D.D.C. 1976), *rev'd*, 591 F.2d 796 (D.C. Cir. 1978), *cert. denied*, 440 U.S. 908 (1979), it is surprising to discover that judges are still incanting the phrase "form follows function" as though it really determined something, that all of its historical baggage did not hopelessly muddle whatever clarity it may have originally held. *See*, Kennedy, *Toward an Historical Understanding of Legal Consciousness: The Case of Classical Legal Thought in America, 1850 - 1940*, 3 RESEARCH IN LAW AND SOCIOLOGY 3 (1980) (discussing the shift of the late nineteenth and early twentieth century "classical" style of legal thought and rhetoric); Grey, *Langdell's Orthodoxy*, 45 U. PA. L. REV. 1 (1983) (discussing "classical" legal thought and its paradigmatic expositor, Christopher Columbus Langdell, and his re-creation of contract law in his own image).

410 For example, electricity, elevator technology, and skyscrapers built on steel grids with poured concrete slabs. *See* ART THROUGH THE AGES, *supra* note 342, at 714.

411 "All that the age had just cause for pride in—its advances in science, its skill in handling iron, its personal heroism in the face of dangerous industrial processes, its willingness to attempt the untried and the impossible—came to a head in the Brooklyn Bridge." MUMFORD, *supra* note 353, at 52.

412 HESKETT, *supra* note 343, at 62.

ral in architecture and design, as opposed to the ornamental and historical. "Classic architecture was all fixation-of-the-fixture. . . . Now why not let walls, ceilings, floors become seen as component parts of each other, their surfaces flowing into each other. . . ."[413] "You may see the appearance . . . in the surface of your hand contrasted with the articulation of the bony skeleton itself. This ideal, profound in its architectural implications . . . I called . . . *continuity*."[414]

Wright's early independent work included designs for furniture, intended to be an integral part of the houses he designed. Similar to Henri Van de Velde, Wright "came to realize, however, that the clean, straight lines of his furniture could be better achieved by the precision of machines than by hand."[415] While not denying that machines could be used to produce "butchered forms," he also saw the potential to emancipate what he felt was the true nature and beauty of materials. Wright once wrote that

> 'machines have undoubtedly placed within reach of the designer a technique enabling him to realize the true nature of wood in his designs harmoniously with man's sense of beauty, satisfying his material needs with such economy as to put this beauty of wood in use within the reach of everyone.'[416]

From out of *Art Nouveau*, Louis Sullivan, Frank Lloyd Wright, and others the principle of structure emerged, which, when coupled with new building technologies,[417] freed architecture from traditional concerns of stability and support. With traditional design concerns subordinated, issues of aesthetics and utility of the structure were thrust into the forefront. Le Corbusier described "functional" houses as "machines for living in."[418] Adolph Loos equated

---

[413] F.L. WRIGHT, AN AMERICAN ARCHITECTURE 205 (E. Kaufman ed. 1955) (Wright sought to implement this continuity in his buildings by stressing the space, not the mass. "I came to realize that the reality of a building was not the container but the space within". *Id.*).

[414] *Id.* at 208.

[415] HESKETT, *supra* note 343, at 62-64.

[416] *Id.* at 64. But Wright's claims also suffered from deep contradictions. First, his claims of inevitability for simple geometric forms ignored vast capabilities of technology to create virtually any form. No form is inevitable. Second, Wright did not seem to acknowledge the human costs of rapidly progressing technology which caused the complete rejection of the craft concept of work. These costs are embodied by "scientific management" and the assembly line, with their ensuing focus on squeezing every last drop out of workers in the name of efficiency.

[417] For example, the steel grid and reinforced concrete eliminated the need for bracing thrust pressures with resisting mass, making a heavy load bearing wall unnecessary. Therefore walls potentially became "screens". Similarly, cantilevering allowed spatial reach with support at one end only.

[418] *See* HARTT, *supra* note 342, at 438; ART THROUGH THE AGES, *supra* note 342, at 1002. Lewis Mumford observed that

ornament with "crime." The early European functionalists prescribed a severe and dogmatic insistence on planar rectilinearity and non-ornamentation, at odds even with the proto-functionalist designs of Wright. The European "functionalists" eschewed naturalism and the organic in favor of machined-planed severity.[419]

In the early twentieth century, artistic and architectural movements proliferated feverishly.[420] Prior to the Modern Movement[421] in design, the fundamental purpose of an architectural treatise was to identify an aesthetic canon to help future practitioners avoid errors of symmetry, measure, and style. Although all architectural

---

> in the first stages of industrial development the factory affected the environment of architecture, in its latest state the factory has become the environment. A modern building is an establishment devoted to the manufacture of light, the circulation of air, the maintenance of a uniform temperature, and the vertical transportation of its occupants.

MUMFORD, *supra* note 353, at 75.

419 *See* HARTT, *supra* note 342, at 437.

420 Among these late nineteenth and early twentieth century movements were Realism, Impressionism, Post-Impressionism, Symbolism, Cubism, Constructivism, Futurism, Suprematism, Dadaism, and Surrealism. Of special significance is Cubism, which fractured the traditional integral picture plane, dislocating and disintegrating natural form into its aesthetic components. Art historians traditionally cite Pablo Picasso and Georges Braque as the progenitors of Cubism, and often draw parallels to architectural functionalism's use of glass wall and cubic spaces as a translation of cubism's vernacular into the architectural realm. *See* ART THROUGH THE AGES, *supra* note 342, at 959, 960-61 (on the impact of European cubism); HESKETT, *supra* note 343, at 92-93. *See generally* READINGS IN AMERICAN ART SINCE 1900; A DOCUMENTARY SURVEY (B. Rose ed. 1968) (on the impact of European *avant-garde* on American Art in the twentieth century); MODERN ART AND MODERNISM: A CRITICAL ANTHOLOGY 220 (F. Frascina & C. Harrison ed. 1982) (critical writings by leaders of Cubism, Fauvism, Futurism, and other modernist movements of the early twentieth century); MODERN ARTISTS ON ART: TEN UNABRIDGED ESSAYS (R. Herbert ed. 1964) (manifestos by Kandinsky (1913), Malevich (1927), Gabo (1937), Mondrian (1937), Le Corbusier (1920), Metzinger (1912), Boccioni (1913), Klee (1924), Beckmann (1938) and Moore (1934)); R. VENTURI, COMPLEXITY AND CONTRADICTION IN ARCHITECTURE (1966) (critique of modernist architecture); S. ABERCROMBIE, ARCHITECHURE AS ART (1984) (discussing the split between "building" and "architecture"); K. FRAMPTON, MODERN ARCHITECHURE: A CRITICAL HISTORY (1985) (surveying of different schools of architectural modernism in the twentieth century) [hereinafter FRAMPTON]; M. BROWN, S. HUNTER, J. JACOBUS, N. ROSENBLUM & D. SOKOL, AMERICAN ART (1979) (focusing on American Pop, Minimalist, and Performance Art of the 1960s and 1970s); H. ROSENBERG, THE ANXIOUS OBJECT (1964) (a critical analysis of 1950s and early 1960s abstract expressionism); L. NOCHLIN, REALISM (1971) (re-examining the French Realist painters of the mid-nineteenth century); R. POGGIOLI, THE THEORY OF THE AVANT-GARDE (1968) (discussing modernism and polemics); THE NEW ART HISTORY (A. Rees & F. Borzello ed. 1988) (a post-modern analysis of modernism).

421 The Modern movement in design should be distinguished from Modernism in general. Design "Moderns," while sharing an antipathy to traditional "bourgeoisie" culture, values, and forms, pursued a profound essentialist idealism, searching for universal truth with which to transform and order the world, generating an Apollonian and classical pole. By contrast, much of the development of modernism in the other areas has been obsessively concerned with relentlessly pulverizing categories, profoundly skeptical about essentialist claims, generating contradiction gleefully, and playing out the inherited Romantic strand of rebellion, chaos and disorder, the Dionysian pole. These deep tensions existing within the same movement, indeed, within the same individual, indicate the deeply felt need for mediators like "form follows function," yet simultaneously, serve to make its mediation unpalatable, ambiguous and unstable.

manifestos of the early twentieth century claimed to reflect the functional and aesthetic needs of society, their actual content was not characterized by flexibility or sensitivity to these needs.[422] Particularly during the period from 1910 to 1940, these architectural manifesto writers took an imperious view of civilization's working and living requirements, structuring their designs with an almost fascistic dedication to system, efficiency, and order. One could hear, repeated with religious fervor, the themes that technology was a panacea for society's troubles, the house was a typological form, the building was a statement of social responsibility, formalism should be the overriding aesthetic, and that function should be the ultimate goal.[423]

In 1919, Henry Van de Velde appointed Walter Gropius as his successor to the Weimar School of Arts and Crafts,[424] founded by Van de Velde in 1906.[425] Gropius promptly renamed the school *Das Staatliche Bauhaus* and redesigned its curriculum into one with a strong utopian bent, which stressed that "functional" design was the solution to urgent problems in the areas of housing, urban planning, and mass-production.[426] Gropius de-emphasized the verbal disciplines, focusing on handicraft training as the natural base for models leading to industrial products.[427] The Bauhaus aesthetic glorified the machine form as natural and took as its classic paradigm the cubic unit—a box.[428] In 1919, Gropius proclaimed: " 'To-

---

422 *See* T. WOLFE, FROM BAUHAUS TO OUR HOUSE 16-17 (1981) [hereinafter WOLFE]; FRAMPTON, *supra* note 420, at 116-29.

423 *See* FRAMPTON, *supra* note 420, at 116-29.

424 Following the German defeat in World War I and the Russian Revolution, the economy was in shambles, and Gropius, Lazlo Moholy Nagy and others who were soon to form the Bauhaus, issued the following manifesto:

> 'Painters, Architects, Sculptors, you whom the bourgeoisie pays with high rewards for your work—out of vanity, snobbery, and boredom—Hear! To this money there clings the sweat and blood and nervous energy of thousands of poor hounded human beings—Hear! It is an unclean profit . . . we must be true socialists—we must kindle the highest socialist virtue: the brotherhood of man.'

WOLFE, *supra* note 422, at 16 (quoting the *Novembergruppe Arbeitstrat fur Kunst* (Working Council for Art) 1919 Manifesto).

425 SIR BANISTER FLETCHER, A HISTORY OF ARCHITECTURE 1323 (19th ed. 1987) [hereinafter A HISTORY OF ARCHITECTURE].

426 "In architecture, the school stood for the promotion of functionalism, a characteristic not easily accepted in the 1920s, even by architects who might now be thought of as functionalists." *Id.* at 1324.

427 J. WINES, DE-ARCHITECTURE at 23 (1987) [hereinafter WINES]. " 'Bauhaus architects saw the function of their architecture as the creation of a language of 'its' own. This language was liberalist—antirhetorical, antisymbolic and (supposedly) free from ideological contamination, a utopian language of pure function and pure mentality.' " (quoting D. Graham).

428 *See, e.g.*, WOLFE, *supra* note 422; ESSAYS IN ARCHITECTURAL CRITICISM: MODERN ARCHITECURE AND HISTORICAL CHANGE (A. Colquhoun ed. 1981); FRAMPTON, *supra* note 420.

gether let us desire, conceive, and create the new structure of the future, which will embrace architecture and sculpture and painting in one unity and which will one day rise toward the heavens from the hands of a million workers like the crystal symbol of a new faith.' "[429]

In 1924, Ludwig Mies van der Rohe, one of the Bauhaus' master polemicists, said, " 'industrialization [is] the central problem of building in our time. If we succeed in carrying out this industrialization, the social, economic, and also the artistic problems will be readily solved.' "[430] This explicit utopianism readily manifested itself in an exuberant optimistic scientism. In 1926, stressing technical objectivity, efficiency, and geometric form, Gropius wrote:

> 'The Bauhaus workshops are essentially laboratories . . . .
>
> In these laboratories the Bauhaus wants to train a new kind of collaborator for industry and the crafts, who has an equal command of both technology and form. To reach the objective of creating a set of standard prototypes . . . requires the selection of the best . . . men . . . who are imbued with an exact knowledge of the design elements of form and mechanics and their underlying laws.'[431]

There was a gross shortfall between the Bauhaus' grand claims of design's transformative power and the number of Bauhaus prototypes actually put into production. However, Gropius and his cadre of followers proved tremendously influential in redesigning the curriculum of architecture, art, and design education, particularly following the Bauhaus' closure by the Nazis in 1933.[432] It was subsequently reborn in the United States with the appointment of Gropius at the Harvard Design School in 1934,[433] and the founding of the New Bauhaus in Illinois in 1937.[434]

The onset of the Great Depression in the United States created intense economic and competitive pressures among the firms which had survived the 1929 Wall Street crash.[435] Against the background of Bauhaus rhetoric proclaiming the apotheosis of functionalism, the professionalization of design occurred. The grafting of Bauhaus essentialism onto commercial contexts confronted a modernist paradox of the market: Do consumer expectations create demand for

---

429 WINES, *supra* note 427, at 22.
430 *Id.* at 23.
431 HESKETT, *supra* note 343, at 101.
432 *See* A HISTORY OF ARCHITECTURE, *supra* note 425, at 1324.
433 *Id.*
434 *See* HESKETT, *supra* note 343, at 103.
435 *Id.* at 105.

designs or do designs create consumer expectations? The ideological function of design, in projecting the images of dynamism, progress, and intimations that technical progress would bring a materially improved, infinitely expanding and aesthetically brighter future, was a marketplace translation and mutation of the socialist, utopian content of the European Bauhaus into the vernacular of the United States.[436]

During the 1930s, 1940s, and 1950s, in the United States, distribution of mass-consumer products became pervasive, created images of increasing material affluence and progress.[437] Stoves, lamps, refrigerators, washing machines, vacuum cleaners, and electric irons were introduced under the banners of "labor saving" and "convenience," conditioning Americans to rapid style changes and growing consumerism. These streamlined[438] refrigerators and vacuum cleaners were heralded as logical and necessary results of the

---

436 *See id.* at 104.

437 *Cf.* Kennedy, *Radical Intellectuals in American Culture and Politics, or My Talk at the Gramsci Institute*, 1 RETHINKING MARXISM 100, 102-03 (Fall 1988).

> American culture . . . is both the product and cause of economic development: endless economic expansion and the opportunities for advancement it offers breed the individualism, materialism, and philistinism that in turn provide the spiritual fuel, the true 'spirit of capitalism' the system needs to keep going.
>
> But this is also a culture of false consciousness in the service of capitalist stability. The main costs of American-style development are grotesquely exaggerated disparities between rich and poor—rendered particularly repulsive by the vulgarity of the self-made economic elites . . .
>
> [Individualism, materialism, and philistinism] all bolster fantasies in the mass of workers that they too will one day become millionaires, or at least escape economic marginality. These fantasies pacify them in the face of the conspicuous consumption of the rich, and reconcile them to the dreary, culturally empty quality of everyday existence in America.
>
> . . . .
>
> America is thus the land of Gramsci. Civil society is not just strong, it is forged of steel.

438 Streamlining, during the 1930s and 1940s was an example of assorted products parading under the guise of "functionality," when in actuality their "streamlining" had little, if anything, to do with their function. *See* HESKETT, *supra* note 343, at 120. A teardrop-shaped stapler, designed by Orlo Heller in 1936 as "a piece of pure styling, of mannerism imposed with little attention to mechanical function" is a good example. *Id.* (Also note the outer limits of streamlining, as defined by consumer taste, are illustrated by the failure of R. Buckminster Fuller's three-wheeled, teardrop shaped Dymaxion car of 1934.). Thus, the meaning of "functionalism" became distorted, becoming a synonym for modernity and speed, acting as a pure marketing device for the useful articles embodied in the design. *See id.* The contradictions of streamlining arise from the way in which streamlining, originally derived from scientific aerodynamic wind tunnel testing of aircraft, became a decorative style when applied to objects having no need for aerodynamic design. *Id.* at 121-22. The gratuitously applied style affected the entire shape and configuration of the article, and could not be "conceptually separated" without reference to some "platonic" paradigm. This arbitrary appropriation of a style for its latent ideologic content is the inescapable conundrum which the "form follows function" movement unsuccessfully sought to evade. *See* ART THROUGH THE AGES, *supra* note 342, at 948.

application of the "form follows function" credo.[439] Yet, it is hard to reconcile constant product changes and modifications with the attainment of a universal result, unless planned obsolescence and rapid style turnover can be considered a "function."[440] Additionally, cost constraints influenced designers. For example, in the early refrigerators, metal stamping processes could only form large pieces of sheet metal into wide curves and corners, and sharp angles were too expensive and time-consuming to achieve. Therefore, the curved, convex outline was imposed on the designer because of the need to obtain low cost through high-speed production.

At the other end of the spectrum, technological advances freed designers by reducing functional elements.[441] Style, from blatant stylistic fantasy to geometric "*moderne*," became a matter of designer choice, unconstrained by function. The development of synthetic plastics furthered this phenomenon by liberating designers from more external constraints imposed by materials. Consumer expectations, corporate identity, seasonal product style changes, advertising, and variable market forces were packed into the "form follows function" slogan, which had become stretched so thin as to become virtually meaningless. If everything was, or could be, "functional," then any or all forms could be dictated by indeterminate and general function.

By the late 1930s, Le Corbusier, Gropius, and the Bauhaus were firmly professionalized and entrenched in the consciousness of architecture and industrial design.[442] However, during the 1940s and 1950s, it was becoming evident that only the means, and not the meanings, of the original Modernist movement remained. There was a growing disenchantment with the "promise of technology." Industrial growth was beginning to be seen more as a source of oppression rather than liberation—as a force creating numbing conformity, alienation, depersonalization, which stultified consumers.

The "glass and steel box" had not led to utopia. The Bauhaus had gone from being a socialist utopian visionary movement with a paradigmatic aspiration to design a brave new world of humanized worker's housing and work places, to a style associated with multinational mega-corporate firms. The so-called "International" style became synonymous with corporate power, culture, and values.[443]

---

439 *See supra* note 409.

440 HESKETT, *supra* note 343, at 143-56.

441 This trend continues today as increasing miniaturization makes claims that a form follows an object's function increasingly implausible, particularly so if the essential "functional" component can be embodied on a tiny microchip.

442 *See* A HISTORY OF ARCHITECTURE, *supra* note 425, at 1324.

443 *See* H.W. Janson, 19TH AND 20TH CENTURY ART 339-40.

The entire content of "form follows function" became drained, its meanings hopelessly scattered, distorted, and lost. Designers were now firmly professionalized and entrenched in corporate institutions, designing products not for a socialist utopia, but in order to maximize profits, in the name of function and modernity. This is the same irony which befell William Morris' Arts and Crafts movement a generation earlier, when his anti-industrial rhetoric was transmuted into a valorization of industry and the machine age.[444]

By 1949, against mounting attacks, Gropius defended the dogma of the International style:

> 'The fear that individuality will be crushed out by the growing "tyranny" of standardization is the sort of myth which cannot sustain the briefest examination. In all great epochs of history the existence of standards—that is the conscious adoption of typeforms—has been the criterion of a polite and well-ordered society; for it is a commonplace that repetition of the same things for the same purposes exercises a settling and civilizing influence on men's minds.'[445]

The core problem was that a "polite and well-ordered society" was growing increasingly irrelevant in a hopelessly complex, pluralistic, chaotic, and disordered world. Ironically, the pursuit of unity between theory and practice, for an indissoluble fusion between the aesthetic and the useful, produced its exact antithesis: the degeneration of "unity" into just another style, among thousands, to be applied much like kitsch Victorian floral appliques, with little regard for social contexts of creation, use, or history.

It is also ironic that at the very moment of the Bauhaus' crisis of belief in "form follows function," the Supreme Court, in *Mazer v. Stein*,[446] recognized applied art and design as protectable intellectual property.[447] Both the Balinese figurine in *Mazer* and the

---

444 *See supra* notes 383-96 and accompanying text.

445 Wines, *supra* note 427, at 23. *See also* E. Purcell, The Crisis of Democratic Theory (1971) (During the 1940s and 1950s the most potent accusation or rebuttal one could throw against an intellectual opponent was that their position led inevitably to totalitarianism.).

Parallels to the Legal Realists should be mentioned because of their entrenchment in power during the New Deal and their subsequent apologetics for ramshackle compromises and attempts at historical revision to show the necessity and inevitability of the rise of the administrative welfare state in the 1950s and 1960s through ideas like consensus, or Llewellyn's collapse of the descriptive into the prescriptive in the formulation of the U.C.C.

446 347 U.S. 201 (1954); *see supra* notes 30-39 and accompanying text.

447 In a sense, the Supreme Court's encounter with the notion of "form follows function" has the strange quality of twins separated at birth, being reacquainted years later. The genesis of the Classical Legal Thought and the "Functionalist" movement in design and architecture share their deductive methodologies, scientism, choate yearnings for

Bauhaus geometric design shared a genesis in industrial design. The ceramic casting of the Balinese dancer, inserted with electric wiring and fixtures, captured the essense of the Bauhaus' dilemma. Technology and industry freed designers from "functional" constraints, but cast designers back into the dreaded ocean of arbitrary subjective ornamentation, denying them an objective "functional" design criterion. It is not surprising that the cases decided after *Mazer* have often reached confused holdings.[448] It is on that edge of art and industry, the subjective and objective, the functional and the aesthetic, that our inherited and contingent mediators have failed to work.

The International style took a turn toward the subjective and metaphysical in the 1950s. Le Corbusier, in 1953, wrote that architecture is a condition in which " 'a fathomless depth gapes open, all walls are broken down, every other presence is put to flight, and the miracle of inexpressible space is achieved.' "[449] The Social Engineers claimed consensus, but on closer examination, deep conflicts and controversies over fundamental values and assumptions had emerged. The realization was dawning that Modernist formalism had squeezed out the possibilities of aesthetic experience in the creation of self-voiding empty space, trimmed of all eclectic historical influences. The limits of "functionalism" were being reached in architecture and design; the constraints of "form follows function" could be seen as nothing more than a standardized, conformist, and superficial concept.

The empiricism, optimism, and false consensus that characterized much of the 1950s tragically played itself out in the Vietnam War. All the previously suppressed cultural contradictions erupted. By the mid-1960s, the former either black or white choices, had begun mutating into a philosophical system based on the acceptance of contradiction. The sciences had long dealt with the concepts of indeterminacy and relativity, and it was only a matter of time before these abstract considerations penetrated the world of architecture. Art could not be coherently separated from industry, yet it could not be coherently integrated with it either. For every theory purporting to rationalize a clear dividing line, dissonant anomalies could be found. Theories of universal harmonies, proclaiming the melding of the "aesthetic" and "useful" only sowed the seeds of their self-

---

essentialist, true-at-all-times-and-all places universal principles in the 1880s, and their subsequent professionalization and distortion, but tenacious survival.

448 *See, e.g.*, notes 49-64 and accompanying text.

449 WINES, *supra* note 427, at 24.

destruction. In 1966, Robert Venturi published *Complexity and Contradiction in Architecture*, a chastened manifesto, wherein he stated,

> Everywhere, except in architecture, complexity and contradiction have been acknowledged, from Gödel's proof of ultimate inconsistency in mathematics to T.S. Eliot's analysis of 'difficult' poetry and Joseph Albers' definition of the paradoxical quality of painting.
>
> . . . .
>
> I am for richness of meaning rather than clarity of meaning; for the implicit function as well as the explicit function. I prefer 'both-and' to 'either-or,' black and white, and sometimes gray, to black or white.[450]

C. Ironies

This recitation of the history of design illustrates that "form follows function" is nothing more or less than an extreme historically contingent polemic whose meaning has shifted considerably over time. Insistence on the stability of meaning, over time serves to obscure the nature of judicial prejudice. There seems to be an implicit acknowledgement of an aesthetic hierarchy, with "functional" design at the top, mixed with a curious judicial self-abnegation. It is as though the judges are saying, "I know this stuff's supposed to be 'good', but I *can't* legally recognize it."[451] Holmes' admonition in *Bleistein v. Donaldson Lithographing Co.*[452] regarding aesthetic judicial restraint[453] is invoked at such a high level of generality, that it becomes pathologically indeterminate, capable of providing potentially broad protection, or complete denial of protection, to industrial design.

This account is meant as a reminder of how prone to self-delusion we are in announcing the discovery of universally valid principles. Indeed, courts and legal commentators often do so, on the eve of the very collapse of these newly announced "universals."[454] The judges in these cases seem to speak from some historically privileged vantage point. They assume that other areas of culture, industry, and society have a similar per-

---

450 R. Venturi, Complexity and Contradiction in Architecture 16 (1966).

451 *See* R. Cover, Justice Accused 119-23 (1975) (discussing the self-abnegating judicial "can't" in the context of anti-slavery judges reaching pro-slavery decisions in particular cases).

452 188 U.S. 239 (1903).

453 *See supra* text accompanying note 12.

454 *See, e.g.*, Kennedy, *The Structure of Blackstone's Commentaries*, 28 Buffalo L. Rev. 205, 237, 244-49 (1979) (pointing out Blackstone's belief that the soon-defunct writ system was essential to preservation of English liberty).

ception of the underlying essential stability of fundamental principles that they think the law possesses or should possess.

Cases in this area present judges with complex and contingent situations which do not offer easy choices.[455] Seeking to mediate the contradictory tensions infesting the boundary between aesthetics and utility, judges, administrators, and legislators have resorted to ever more incoherent and abstract tests to deny that they engaged in aesthetic value judgements proscribed by *Bleistein*. *Bleistein* demands aesthetic value-neutrality from the judiciary, yet simultaneously commands them to make value-laden decisions, after having stripped them of the essential tools with which to make those difficult choices.[456]

This Article has used an historical analysis to suggest that this area of law is defined more by its basic contradictions than by any single truthful answer, and that the answers which are achieved are partial, contradictory, oscillating, contingent, and provisional.[457] As icons, signs, symbols, and products accumulate, and infernally proliferate, courts have abdicated any responsibility for clearing a path through the morass, deferring to Congress. Congress hatches mutilated compromises that reflect little more than confused deals cut behind the scenes with the various interest groups they are supposed to be regulating. *Bleistein* offers no indicia or guideposts, except to remain a font of paralysis and confusion, and the decisions flowing from it are nothing but factional compromises at odds with the professed ideals of society.

IV. Conclusion

Many of the courts which have grappled with the question of conferring intellectual property rights on the products of the industrial design process have focused on the aesthetic/utilitarian qualities of the object itself, producing an increasingly unintel-

---

455 *See* Fisher, Fair Use, *supra* note 403, at 1775. Fisher discusses the extraordinary difficulty of obtaining information to ascertain the economically optimal package of entitlements for a given type of copyrighted work. Even determining popular tastes for different types of intellectual products and their uses would be difficult. Gathering reliable data with regard to such crucial variables as the sensitivity of various producers to fluctuations in anticipated incomes and the mutability of each of the relevant sets of preferences would be impossible. *See* Breyer, *The Uneasy Case For Copyright: A Study of Copyright in Books, Photocopies, and Computer Programs*, 84 Harv. L. Rev. 281 (1970).

456 *See supra* notes 11-21 and accompanying text.

457 *See* Gordon, *Critical Legal Histories*, 36 Stan. L. Rev. 57, 116 (1984) ("[I]f it turns out to be true that law is founded upon contradictions, it cannot also be true that any particular legal form is required by, or a condition of, any particular set of social practices.").

ligible body of law that focuses on the issue of "conceptual separability." Courts have clung to incoherent distinctions which have grown increasingly abstract with each new case, religiously invoking the phrase "form follows function."[458]

Courts need to use a broader analysis focusing on questions which look at the reach and meaning of industrial design, including: (1) how the artifacts came into existence;[459] (2) the application of the artifact; and (3) the historical context, both general and particular, from which industrial design arose.[460] At the very least, courts need to acknowledge that while designers may create forms with defined purposes, the perception of those forms, and the functional or symbolic values that get attributed to them, are contingent, influenced by attitudes towards the underlying purposes of application. Courts need to shift the emphasis downward from the abstract level of enclosed, hermetic legal values, to a much lower level of relative interpretation, placing their analysis in complex and contradictory cultural experience.

The scope of industrial design is intimately linked with the development of industrialization. As long as our inherited, but ultimately incoherent categories of nineteenth century liberalism continue to confuse and obscure the actual issues, copyright law will continue in its vicious cycle of inconsistent decisions. Industrial design has been concerned with the complicated and at times, contradictory interplay between aesthetics, commerce, technology, language, ideology, and democratization. Legal thought, reluctant and fearful to face contemporary society, let alone implications for the future, has held tightly to archaic, abstract, and incoherent distinctions, which technological change has rendered inappropriate and dangerous—ethereal distinctions between the utilitarian and the aesthetic, divisions between content and the container, dichotomies between the public and the private.

---

458 *See supra* note 409, and text accompanying note 439.

459 The beginnings of this contextual approach can be seen in Brandir Int'l, Inc. v. Cascade Pacific Lumber Co., 834 F.2d 1142 (2d Cir. 1987), and Professor Denicola's article. *See* Denicola, *supra* note 257. However, both of these sources stop far short of the reimagination of the historical and social contexts of industrial design. *Brandir* in particular is pernicious for its idealized, sentimental image of the "unconstrained perspective of the artist" as opposed to the corporate team player of industrial designs. That both of these stereotypes do more harm than good should be self-evident. For example, see HESKETT, *supra* note 343, at 113-14, describing the changing contexts of the Volkswagen—from symbol of the Third Reich to fun object of the 1950s.

460 The contradictory nature of history in general, and design history in particular should give a judge pause before invoking a phrase like "form follows function" as though it reflected an eternal verity and not a contingent, unstable set of culturally bound associations.

The question should not be how to draw the line between industrial design and applied art, but whether these inherited unstable distinctions are: (1) applicable at all in the late twentieth century *vis a vis* interdependence, contradiction, and complexity, and (2) deserve to be rejected because they are simply based on bad values.[461] The conventional story about applied art and industrial design has led us into a legal universe in which "rights are trumps,"[462] the "neutral state"[463] rules, and the impoverished "voluntarist self"[464] are the only games in town—the debate as to what might be the conditions for democracy, self-governance, and an "objective" substantive public interest[465]

---

461 In the context of normative bases from which to reconstruct the Fair Use Doctrine, Professor Fisher sets out a tentative sketch of the good life, as distinguished from the tradition of utilitarianism and Kantian liberalism:

> The good life is a life of self-determination, commitment, moderate risk, and meaningful work. The activities, bonds, and communities through which a person defines himself are freely chosen; the person is engaged in projects and relationships that carry with them a chance of failure; work is important and, for the most part, creative.

FISHER, FAIR USE, *supra* 403, at 1746-47 (citation omitted).

462 *See* I. SHAPIRO, THE EVOLUTION OF RIGHTS IN LIBERAL THEORY (1986); Horwitz, *Rights*, 23 HARV. C.R.-C.L. L. REV. 393, 400 (1988) ("natural rights philosophy is rooted historically in an adversarial vision of human freedom as the absence of external restraint"); *see, e.g.*, R. Unger, KNOWLEDGE AND POLITICS (1976).

463 *See, e.g.*, Bork, *Neutral Principles and Some First Amendment Problems*, 47 IND. L.J. 1 (1971) (a right-wing defense of "neutrality" and an attack on "contextualism"); BASIC PROBLEMS IN THE MAKING AND APPLICATION OF LAW, *supra* note 62; Wechsler, *Toward Neutral Principles of Constitutional Law*, 73 HARV. L. REV. 1 (1959) (Wechsler applied "legal process" theory to constitutional law and denounced those who he thought sought to politicize law); *see also supra* note 63 and accompanying text.

464 *See, e.g.*, J. Rawls, A THEORY OF JUSTICE (1971); R. DWORKIN, TAKING RIGHTS SERIOUSLY (1977). *But cf.* M. SANDEL, LIBERALISM AND THE LIMITS OF JUSTICE (1982); A. MacIntyre, *After Virtue* (1981), in LIBERALISM AND ITS CRITICS 125 (M. Sandel, ed. 1984)

> [S]ocial obstacles derive from the way in which modernity partitions each human life into a variety of segments, each with its own norms and modes of behaviour. . . . [W]ork is divided from leisure, private life from public, the corporate from the personal.
>
> . . . .
>
> [T]he unity of a human life becomes invisible to us when a sharp separation is made . . . between the individual and the roles that he or she plays . . . A social setting may be an institution . . . a setting has a history, a history within which the histories of individual agents not only are, but have to be situated, just because without the setting and its changes through time the history of the individual agent and his changes through time will be unintelligible.

Id. (Sandel and MacIntyre may be considered "civic republicans" or "communitarians" with underlying philosophical differences which are in opposition to rights-based Rawsian liberalism).

465 For instance, a search for decentralized economic forms to accompany decentralized political power. *See* FISHER, FAIR USE, *supra* note 403, at 1761-62 (citation omitted) (comparison of a possible, but chastened, utopian society to the contemporary United States).

> [C]ompared to the United States today, the creativity and challenge of persons' jobs would be greater and more equal; the material resources at each person's disposal would be somewhat less (on average) and much more

have seemingly dropped out of the national discourse. Shallow instrumental concerns get mouthed, implausible stereotypes get raised, and the real issues pass by unnoticed, not even part of the discourse.

> equal; and the state would be more extensively involved in fostering artistic innovation and providing people decent food, clothing, housing, and medical care and more-than-decent educations. . . . More fundamentally, by celebrating such a life and by inculcating the habits, moods, and motivations crucial to it, the society would induce persons to seek and share it.

Id.

ON THE AUTHOR EFFECT: CONTEMPORARY COPYRIGHT AND COLLECTIVE CREATIVITY

PETER JASZI*

> Are there influences at work that will in time abate feelings of proprietorship and thus modify conceptions of copyright, especially those bearing on plagiarism? Probably so.
>
> Much intellectual work including the distinctively imaginative is now being done by teams, a practice apt to continue and grow. The French have a name for it—*traveau d'équipe*. Such collaboration, I fancy, may diffuse and diminish emotions of original discovery and exclusive ownership.
>
> —Benjamin Kaplan, *An Unhurried View of Copyright*[1]

As exemplified by the articles in this volume, recent scholarship on "authorship" reflects various influences. Among the most important are Michel Foucault's article, *What is an Author?*,[2] and Benjamin Kaplan's book, *An Unhurried View of Copyright*. Since the late 1960s, these two texts have influenced work in literary and legal studies respectively. Only recently, however, have the lines of inquiry that Foucault and Kaplan helped to initiate begun to converge.

Foucault asked literary critics and historians to question the received modern idea of "authorship," and to reimagine its future by reunderstanding its past. For the first time, he located the emergence of the "author" in the cultural context of the eighteenth century, arguing that "[t]he coming into being of the notion of the 'author' constitutes a privileged moment of *individualization* in the history of ideas."[3] Moreover, he emphasized that the idea of "authorship" was neither natural nor inevitable, but represented only one possible means to the end of constraining the "proliferation of meaning."[4] In so doing, Foucault suggested

---

* Professor of Law, Washington College of Law, The American University. B.A., 1968, Havard College; J.D., 1971, Harvard Law School. This article is a small part of a larger collaborative project, and I gratefully acknowledge Martha Woodmansee's contribution to both.

1 BENJAMIN KAPLAN, AN UNHURRIED VIEW OF COPYRIGHT 117 (1967).

2 The essay first appeared in English a decade later. *See* Michel Foucault, *What is an Author?*, *in* TEXTUAL STRATEGIES: PERSPECTIVES IN POST-STRUCTURALIST CRITICISM 141 (J. Harari ed., 1979).

3 *Id.* at 141.

4 *Id.* at 159.

(in general terms) the potential for research into how practices of writing and reading have been organized around the idea of the "author."[5]

Kaplan, for his part, expressed an invigorating skepticism about the inevitability of the legal rules that define copyright, pointing out the transformational changes to this field of law over its few centuries of history. He argued that, by demythologizing copyright doctrine, the legal community could make space for reasoned development of the law in a time of rapid technological change. Although he did not specifically anatomize the notion of the "author" around which copyright is organized, Kaplan noted certain corollaries of that notion. He called on lawyers to reconsider the trend in Anglo-American copyright toward ever-greater protection against unlicensed imitation,[6] the origins of which he located in the obsession with "originality," which marked Romantic literary criticism.

Over the past twenty five years, Kaplan's critique of basic copyright concepts has been influential in practical discussion of legal policy, while followers of Foucault have investigated the "construction of authorship" in the domain of literary culture. In retrospect, however, it is surprising how recently scholars have begun to attend to the ways in which the cultural figuration of the "author," as the inspired creator of unique works of art, has interacted with the legal notion of the "author" as the bearer of the portable rights in literary and artistic property.

In 1984, Martha Woodmansee began to construct the bridge to join literary and legal perspectives. She demonstrated how a new class of professional writers in eighteenth-century Germany, seeking to justify legal protection for their labors, "set about redefining the nature of writing," and thus helped to "give the

---

5

> Certainly it would be worth examining how the author became individualized in a culture like ours, what status he has been given, at what moment studies of authenticity and attribution began, in what kind of system of valorization the author was involved, at what point we began to recount the lives of authors rather than of heroes, and how this fundamental category of "the-man-and-his-work criticism" began.

Id. at 141.

6

> [I]f man has any "natural" rights, not the least must be a right to imitate his fellows, and thus to reap where he has not sown. Education, after all, proceeds from a kind of mimicry, and "progress," if it is not entirely an illusion, depends on generous indulgence of copying.

KAPLAN, *supra* note 1, at 2.

concept of authorship its modern form."[7] More recently, Mark Rose has explored the ways in which debates over the extent of rights in literary property in eighteenth-century England both fed and fed upon developments in literary theory. He has concluded that the reception of German romanticism in England came only after "the ground had been prepared by the long debate over copyright," and that "the romantic elaboration of such notions as originality, organic form, and the work of art as the expression of the unique personality of the artist was in a sense the necessary completion of the legal and economic transformation that occurred during the copyright struggle."[8] And Carla Hesse has shown that in France, the idea of the individualistic "author" as the bearer of literary property rights was introduced as an instrument of monarchist repression—a "legal instrument for the regulation of knowledge"—and that the French revolutionaries later sought to "dethrone the absolute author . . . and recast him, not as a *private* individual (the absolute bourgeois), but rather as a *public* servant, as the model citizen."[9]

For my part, I have begun to trace some of the specific linkages between the ideology of "authorship" and the formation of particular doctrinal structures in the law of copyright.[10] In the quotation I chose to introduce this essay, Professor Kaplan looks forward to a reconfiguration of copyright to take fuller account of collaborative creative practices. In her contribution to this volume, Martha Woodmansee demonstrates that the Romantic notion of "author" handed down to us from the eighteenth century never has been particularly apt to the realities of the writing process.[11] In what follows, I have sought to demonstrate how the persistence of the notion of "authorship" in American copyright law makes it difficult for any new legal synthesis, which would focus on the reality of collective creativity, to emerge.

First, however, it may be useful to review how a particular

---

[7] Martha Woodmansee, *The Genius and the Copyright: Economic and Legal Conditions of the Emergence of the 'Author'*, 17 EIGHTEENTH-CENTURY STUD. 425, 426 (1984).

[8] Mark Rose, *The Author as Proprietor:* Donaldson v. Becket *and the Geneology of Modern Authorship*, 23 REPRESENTATIONS 51 (1988).

[9] Carla Hesse, *Enlightenment Epistemology and the Law of Authorship in Revolutionary France, 1777-1793*, 30 REPRESENTATIONS 109 (1990).

[10] *See* Peter Jaszi, *Toward a Theory of Copyright: The Metamorphoses of "Authorship,"* 1991 DUKE L.J. 455 [hereinafter *Metamorphoses*]. Other writers have expanded the discussion by analyzing the significance of the "authorship" concept in domains of law other than copyright. *See* James Boyle, *The Search for an Author: Shakespeare and the Framers*, 37 AM. U. L. REV. 625 (1988); James Boyle, *A Theory of Law and Information: Copyright, Spleens, Blackmail, and Insider Trading*, 80 CAL. L. REV. (forthcoming 1992).

[11] *See generally* Martha Woodmansee, *On The Author Effect: Recovering Collectivity*, 10 CARDOZO ARTS & ENT. L.J. 279 (1992).

version of the idealogy of "authorship" informed English—and ultimately American—copyright doctrine. Unlike the events in late eighteenth-century Germany, the first introduction of the "author" into English law had not been the outcome of any philosophically-grounded argument for "authors' rights" as such. In fact, late seventeenth- and early eighteenth-century efforts to establish copyright reflected no concern whatsoever about the situation of working writers: the Statute of Anne of 1710 was the result of lobbying by and for established London-based publishers and booksellers seeking new legal weapons against down-market competition spawned by the proliferation of print technology. Even in its incomplete, pre-Romantic form, "authorship" had positive connotations as a designation for literary activity of special merit, and the booksellers co-opted the term to create a stable legal foundation for a market in texts as commodities.[12]

After its introduction into the law of copyright, even as it received new content from developments outside legal culture, "authorship" remained a malleable concept, generally deployed on behalf of publishers rather than writers.[13] Indeed, the interests most directly at stake in disputes over the content of copyright law usually are those of firms and individuals with capital

---

[12] In practice the rights thus created were unlikely to remain with the individual "author" for long. Long after the first copyright laws, writers generally continued to sell their rights, bundled with the manuscripts to which they pertained, to publishers for lump sum payments. *See* 1 VICTOR BONHAM-CARTER, AUTHORS BY PROFESSION 17-25 (1978). For the subsequent development of publishing practices and the market in commodity texts, see N.N. FELTES, MODES OF PRODUCTION OF VICTORIAN NOVELS (1986).

[13] Publishers' invocations of "authorship" as a rationale for the extension of their own effective monopolies did not always succeed: the idea of the "author" did not acquire its full cultural charge for some years after 1710, and (as Mark Rose has documented) in 1774 the London publishers lost their hard-waged battle to establish perpetual copyright as a kind of "natural right" of "authorship," though only barely. *See* Rose, *supra* note 8. A majority of the common law judges who advised the House of Lords in the case of Donaldson v. Becket, 2 Bro P.C. 129, 1 Eng. Rep. 637, 4 Burr. 2408, 98 Eng. Rep. 257 (1774) seem to have accepted the ahistorical proposition that there *had been* a perpetual common law copyright prior to the enactment of the Statute of Anne; however, a majority of the judges (and presumably of the law lords who took the final decision) appear to have believed that this common law right was superceded by that enactment. *See* GAVIN MCFARLANE, COPYRIGHT THROUGH THE CASES 15-16 (1986). For an alternate interpretation of the "holding" of *Donaldson*, see Howard B. Abrams, *The Historic Foundation of American Copyright Law*, 29 WAYNE L. REV. 1119, 1128-29 (1983). For additional discussion of the case and its implications, see Rose, *supra* note 8, at 51. In particular, Rose notes that as of the time of the debate over perpetual copyright, the "mystification of original poetic creation and the concept of the creative process as organic rather than mechanical . . . anticipated in [Edward] Young's *Conjectures on Original Composition*" enjoyed greater currency in Germany than in England. *Id.* at 75-76. Had the case been decided after the popularization of these ideas in England by Wordsworth, Coleridge and others, the outcome on the issue of perpetual copyright might well have been different.

investments in the means by which the productions of creative workers are distributed to consumers.[14] These distributors have reaped most of the benefits of copyright's cultivation of Romantic "authorship."

The story of "authorship's" instrumental role in the development of eighteenth-, nineteenth- and much of twentieth-century Anglo-American copyright doctrine has been told elsewhere.[15] It includes such notable episodes as a court's justification of copyright protection for commercial photography in the form of a studio portrait of Oscar Wilde. In that case, *Burrow-Giles Lithographic Co. v. Sarony*,[16] the Supreme Court concluded that such photographs should be viewed as "representatives of the original intellectual conceptions of the author."[17] Far more recently, lawyers and judges have invoked the vision of the Romantic "author-genius" in rationalizing the extension of copyright protection to computer software. The conceptual challenge to copyright posed by computer technology has been submerged in an insistence that programs are no less inspired than traditional literary works, and that the imaginative processes of the

---

[14] *See* CRAIG JOYCE ET AL., COPYRIGHT LAW § 1.05, at 19-20 (2d ed. 1991) [hereinafter COPYRIGHT LAW]. This is true despite the fact that doctrinal and policy conflicts in copyright law have come to be cast in terms of the notionally opposed interests of "authors" and "users," a binary approach to identifying the interests at stake is typical of the Supreme Court's copyright jurisprudence. Justice Stewart, in Twentieth Century Music Corp. v. Aiken, 422 U.S. 151 (1975), put the matter this way:

> The immediate effect of our copyright law is to secure a fair return for an "author's" creative labor. But the ultimate aim is, by this incentive, to stimulate artistic creativity for the general public good.

Id. at 156.

[15] *See Metamorphoses*, *supra* note 10.

[16] 111 U.S. 53 (1884). In the first line of its opinion, the Supreme Court tellingly describes the defendant as "a photographer, with [a] large business in those lines in the city of New York." *Id.* In fact, that business entailed not only the taking of photographs, but the sale and distribution of copies to the public, and it was on this latter aspect of the business that the activities of the defendant company impinged.

[17] *Id.* at 58. Photography had perplexed nineteenth-century lawyers who saw the machine, rather than human agency, as the source of the photographic image. *See* BERNARD EDELMAN, OWNERSHIP OF THE IMAGE: ELEMENTS FOR A MARXIST THEORY OF LAW 43-47 (Elizabeth Kingdom trans., 1979). In *Burrow-Giles Lithographic Co. v. Sarony*, the court resolved the dilemma by stressing the analogies between photography and more traditional forms of creative enterprise. The court found that the image involved there was a

> useful, new, harmonious, characteristic, and graceful picture, and that said plaintiff made the same . . . entirely from his own original mental conception, to which he gave visible form by posing [the subject] in front of the camera, selecting and arranging the costume, draperies, and other various accessories in said photograph, arranging the subject so as to present graceful outlines, arranging and disposing the light and shade, suggesting and evoking the desired expression, and from such disposition, arrangement, or representation, made entirely by the plaintiff, he produced the picture in suit . . . .

Burrow-Giles, 111 U.S. at 54-55.

programmer are analogous to those of the literary "author."[18]

The so-called "work-for-hire" doctrine provides an even more dramatic example of the ways in which the ideology of "authorship" has been manipulated. This rule, which is most commonly part of the jurisprudence of countries which trace their laws of intellectual property back to Britain, awards ownership of a work produced within the scope of employment to the employer—as its "author-in law," so to speak. Although it is somewhat unusual in comparative law context,[19] this identification of employer as author is more than a crude, instrumental fiction—rather, it is a logical (if perverse) working out of the underlying assumption that the essence of "authorship" lies in original, inspired creative genius. Judicial opinions in these cases incorporate a characteristic move: If the essence of "authorship" is inspiration, then it is the "employer's" contribution as the "motivating factor" behind that work (in the words of one decision)[20] that matters, rather than the mere drudgery of the "employee."[21] The United States Supreme Court's most recent pronouncement on the subject makes the same point, although in different terms: In "work-for-hire" cases, the crucial inquiry is into "the hiring party's right to control the manner and means by which the product is accomplished."[22]

Over the history of Anglo-American copyright, Romantic "authorship" has served the interests of publishers and other distributors surprisingly well. Recently, however, it played a more unpredictable role in shaping legal doctrine, as is apparent from the recent upsurge in interest in "moral rights"—long a feature of continental legal culture with its unabashed adherence to the cause of "authors' rights,"[23] but a recent arrival on the scene in most common law countries.[24] As might be expected, publishers,

---

[18] *See* Anthony Clapes et al., *Silicon Epics and Binary Bards: Determining the Proper Scope of Copyright Protection for Computer Programs*, 34 UCLA L. REV. 1493, 1510-45 (1987). The argument caters to firms that employ individuals to engage in this sort of "authorship." Ultimately, this appeal to notions of "authorial genius" may do more to obscure than to clarify the stakes in decisions about software protection. *See* Pamela Samuelson, *Creating a New Kind of Intellectual Property: Applying the Lessons of the Chip Law to Computer Programs*, 70 MINN. L. REV. 471 (1985).

[19] SAM RICKETSON, THE BERNE CONVENTION FOR THE PROTECTION OF LITERARY AND ARTISTIC WORKS 1886-1986, at 158-59 (1987).

[20] *See* Picture Music, Inc. v. Bourne, Inc., 457 F.2d 1213, 1214 (2d Cir.), *cert. denied*, 409 U.S. 997 (1972).

[21] *See Metamorphoses*, *supra* note 10, at 485-91.

[22] Community for Creative Non-Violence v. Reid, 490 U.S. 730, 751 (1989).

[23] *See* Frederic Pollaud-Dulian, *Le Droit Moral en France, a Travers la Jurisprudence Recente*, [*Moral Rights in France, Through Recent Case Law*], 145 REVUE INTERNATIONALE DU DROIT D'AUTEUR 126, 126-32 (1990).

[24] *See, e.g.*, Copyright, Designs and Patents Act, 1988, ch. 48, §§ 77-89 (Eng.), *re-*

software manufacturers, and motion picture companies have been less than enthusiastic about new legal rules which would give "authors" the inalienable rights to insist on proper attribution of their works and to object when those works are modified or destroyed in connection with (or subsequent to) their commercial exploitation. But despite organized resistance from the latter-day counterparts of the eighteenth-century London booksellers, the idea of "moral rights" has gained a toe-hold even in the United States, though not yet with respect to literary works.[25] The development of "moral rights" is best understood in strictly ideological terms, and it should come as no surprise that legislators arguing in support of "moral rights" should unconsciously echo the rhetoric of William Wordsworth:[26]

> Artists in this country play a very important role in capturing the essence of culture and recording it for future generations. It is often through art that we are able to see truths, both beautiful and ugly.
>
> Therefore, I believe it is paramount to the integrity of our culture that we preserve the integrity of our artworks as expressions of the creativity of the artist.[27]

The instance of "moral rights" is but one example of how the Romantic conception of "authorship" is displaying a literally unprecedented measure of ideological autonomy in legal context.[28] Recent copyright decisions show that even as scholars in literary studies elaborate a far-reaching critique of the received

---

printed in 3 COPYRIGHT LAWS AND TREATIES OF THE WORLD (BNA) [hereinafter CLTW]; Copyright Act, R.S.C., ch. C42, §§ 12.1-.2 and 18.1-.2 (1985) (Can.), *reprinted in* 1 CLTW, *supra* (Canadian provisions adopted in 1988). "Moral rights" reasoning probably failed to penetrate the common law countries earlier because of the existence of a counter-motif, in tension with that of "authors' rights." The common law countries rationalized copyright to be a limited monopoly designed to serve the public interest by promoting investment in the creation and distribution of works of the imagination. This "incentive" theory—probably the most commonly articulated public policy underlying copyright—draws into question any proposal that would enhance protection at the public users' expense, including the restrictions on re-use of copyright works implied in any "moral rights" scheme. For the various rationales underlying copyright legislation, see COPYRIGHT LAW, *supra* note 14, at 14-21.

25 Visual Artists Rights Act of 1990 § 603(a)(codified at 17 U.S.C.A. § 106A (West Supp. 1992)). For a discussion of this legislation, see COPYRIGHT LAW, *supra* note 14, at 621-27.

26 *See* Woodmansee, *supra* note 7, at 280.

27 135 CONG. REC. E2227 (daily ed. June 20, 1989) (statement of Rep. Markey), *quoted in* Visual Artists Rights Act of 1990, H.R. 514, 101st Cong., 2d Sess. 1, 6 (1990).

28 We can expect more jurisprudential developments to reflect uncritical faith in the concept of "authorship" in years and decades to come; the 1988 adherence of the United States to the Berne Convention inevitably will produce further assimilation of U.S. copyright culture to that of the Berne Union. *See* Peter Jaszi, *A Garland of Reflections on Three International Copyright Topics*, 8 CARDOZO ARTS & ENT. L.J. 47, 58 (1989).

Romantic concept of "authorship," American lawyers are reaching out to embrace the full range of its implications.

The latest copyright decision of the United States Supreme Court, *Feist Publications, Inc. v. Rural Telephone Service*,[29] decided in March 1991, is a striking manifestation of this ideological entrenchment. The numbingly mundane facts of the underlying dispute serve to display the legal issues in higher relief: Feist, a firm that specialized in publishing regional telephone directories, was refused by Rural Telephone Service to license Rural's "white pages" directory, which covered a small part of the larger geographic area to be encompassed in Feist's projected directory. Feist went ahead and copied Rural's alphabetically-organized listings and Rural sued for copyright infringement. The case raised questions about how much copyright protection a telephone book should receive—or whether it should receive any protection at all. Before the Supreme Court weighed in, most lawyers assumed that some degree of copyright protection was available to safeguard capital investments in comprehensive, predictably-organized compilations of uncopyrightable data, such as phonebooks, price lists, and legal databases. Courts and commentators had reasoned that the "skill and effort" or "sweat of the brow" that went into preparing such compilations was enough in the way of "authorship" to justify protection.[30] To the consternation of many, the Supreme Court held otherwise by a unanimous vote,[31] reasoning that, to pass the constitutional threshold, copyrightable works must possess "some minimal degree of *creativity*," and that, in producing its local telephone directory, Rural Telephone Service had "expended sufficient effort to make the white pages directory useful, but insufficient *creativity* to make it *original*."[32] Reaching back into the Court's store of

---

[29] 111 S. Ct. 1282 (1991).

[30] Before *Feist Publications, Inc. v. Rural Telephone Service*, the leading cases on the subject were Leon v. Pacific Tel. & Tel. Co., 91 F.2d 484 (9th Cir. 1937), and Jeweler's Circular Publishing Co. v. Keystone Publishing Co., 281 F. 83 (2d Cir.) (L. Hand, J.), *cert. denied*, 259 U.S. 581 (1922). These cases endorsed copyright protection based on capital investment in compiling "facts." In *Feist*, Justice O'Connor asserted that these earlier courts "misunderstood" the copyright statute. *See Feist*, 111 S. Ct. at 1291. Prior to *Feist*, copyright scholars were divided on the issue. *Compare* Robert C. Denicola, *Copyright in Collections of Facts: A Theory for the Protection of Non-fiction Literary Works*, 81 COLUM. L. REV. 516 (1981) *with* William Patry, *Copyright in Compilations of Facts (or Why the "White Pages" Are Not Copyrightable)*, 12 COMM. & THE LAW 37 (1990). For an extremely sophisticated discussion, ultimately favoring "sweat of the brow" protection, see Jane C. Ginsburg, *Creation and Commercial Value: Copyright Protection of Works of Information*," 90 COLUM. L. REV. 1865 (1990).

[31] Only Justice Blackmun declined to join in Justice O'Connor's opinion, concurring in the judgment without a stated rationale.

[32] *Feist*, 111 S. Ct. at 1296 (emphasis added).

historical precedents, Justice O'Connor recalled the language of *The Trade-Mark Cases* of 1879: Copyright should extend only to works that "are *original*, and are founded in the creative powers of the mind. The writings which are to be protected are *the fruits of intellectual labor*, embodied in the form of books, prints, engravings, and the like."[33]

The *Feist* decision raises more questions than it answers; it will take time to determine exactly what kind of intellectual steel will suffice to strike "the minimal creative spark required by the Copyright Act and the Constitution."[34] The likely answers, in turn, may depend on the values and beliefs underlying the Court's decision. Unlike many important copyright decisions, *Feist* cannot be explained as a more or less transparent concession to the interests of publishers and other distributors. Indeed, the decision runs directly counter to those interests, leaving valuable and vulnerable "information products," which represent considerable capital investments, without clear protection against misappropriation.

As a matter of information policy, the Court may have been right to cut back on available grounds of legal protection for compilations of data;[35] perhaps the social benefits of making information more generally available outweigh the private costs of denying it protection. There is no indication, however, that members of the Court gave this rationale any consideration, let alone embraced it. So far as Justice O'Connor's opinion reveals, the Court was moved solely by its adherence to a vision of originality "distilled [in earlier opinions] from the Constitution's use of the word 'authors' "; an "author" being defined "to mean 'he to whom anything owes its origin; originator; maker.' "[36] The obvious criticism of *Feist*—that it embodies a barren jurispru-

---

33 100 U.S. 82, 94 (1879).

34 *Feist*, 111 S. Ct. at 1297. Early articles discussing the implications of *Feist* include Michael Schwartz, *Copyright in Compilations of Facts: Feist Publications, Inc. v. Rural Telephone Service*, 13 Eur. Intell. Prop. Rev. 178 (1991); Michael R. Klipper & Meredith S. Senter, Jr., *The Facts After Feist: The Supreme Court Addressses the Issue of the Copyrightability of Factual Compilations*, in Fact and Data Protection After *Feist* 343 (Jon A. Baumgarten ed., 1991); and David Goldberg & Robert J. Bernstein, *The Fallout from "Feist": (Copyrightability of Telephone Listings)*, 206 N.Y. L.J. 3 (1991).

35 *See* L. Ray Patterson & Craig Joyce, *Monopolizing the Law: The Scope of Copyright Protection for Law Reports and Statutory Compilations*, 36 UCLA L. Rev. 719 (1989). Other recent Supreme Court intellectual property decisions have reflected concern over the potential of legal protection to restrict vigorous competition. *See, e.g.*, Bonito Boats, Inc. v. Thunder Craft Boats, Inc., 489 U.S. 141 (1989).

36 *Feist*, 111 S. Ct. at 1288, (citing Burrow-Giles Lithographic Co. v. Sarony, 111 U.S. 53, 58 (1884)). The constitutional reference is to article I, Section 8, clause 8—authorizing congressional intellectual property legislation.

dence of rule formalism—is ultimately inapposite. In fact, the opinion wears its values on its sleeve; from first to last, its rhetoric proceeds from unreconstructed faith in the gospel of Romantic "authorship."

That Romantic "authorship" is alive and well in late twentieth-century American legal culture has consequences for the law's engagement with (or failure to engage) the realities of contemporary polyvocal writing practice—which increasingly is collective, corporate, and collaborative. In practice, the law often proves ungenerous to non-individualistic cultural productions, like "folkloric" works, which cannot be reimagined as products of solitary, originary "authorship" on the part of one or more discrete and identifiable "authors."[37] By the same token, the extension of copyright protection to new categories of works may entail reimagining them so as to suppress complicating details about their modes of production.[38] At base, however, the law is not so much systematically hostile to works that do not fit the individualistic model of Romantic "authorship" as it is uncomprehending of them. Such works are marginalized or become literally invisible within the prevailing ideological framework of discourse in copyright—even to the point of literal invisibility.

Feist, once again, provides an example of this process of marginalization. The Court's discussion of copyright in telephone directories takes off from what is, from the perspective of copyright doctrine, a non-controversial premise: "Facts" are natural and uncreated; they are not protectable in themselves:

> Census-takers, for example, do not "create" the population figures that emerge from their efforts; in a sense, they copy these figures from the world around them. Census data therefore do not trigger copyright because these data are not "original" in the constitutional sense. The same is true of all facts—scientific, historical, biographical, and news of the

---

[37] The more obvious case in point is "folkloric" works. These corporate works have no identifiable author(s), and their continual re-production through transmission within a cultural group makes it difficult to locate the moment at which any hypothesized individual can have made an "original," "authorial" contribution. *See* Marie Niedzielska, *The Intellectual Property Aspects of Folklore Protection*, 1980 COPYRIGHT 339.

[38] Thus, the extension of copyright to photographs both glorifies the camera operator as an "artist-genius" and suppresses the claims of the photographic subject to merely a part in the production of the image. *See Metamorphoses*, *supra* note 10, at 480-81 n.97. Jane Gaines recently has identified the ways in which the courts minimized or suppressed the "authorship" claims of photographic subjects—including those of Oscar Wilde in the *Burrow-Giles Lithographic Co. v. Sarony* decision. *See* JANE GAINES, CONTESTED CULTURE: THE IMAGE, THE VOICE, AND THE LAW 74-83 (1991). For a discussion of *Burrow-Giles*, see *supra* notes 16-17 and accompanying text.

day.[39]

Thus, any "authorship" in the "white pages" must be sought in the acts of collecting and (especially) presenting the unprotected data which make up the individual directory entries in which individuals' given (or self-elected) names are associated with their chosen addresses and assigned telephone numbers.

From another perspective the distinction between uncreated "facts" and created "works" is purely fictitious. As Stanley Fish has pointed out, no so-called "fact" is interpretation-free—ultimately they are products rather than predicates of interpretation.[40] To revert to the Court's example in *Feist*, the preordained categories of the census form define the "data" to be reported, not the reverse. If we seek non-circular justifications for the law's refusal to extend protection to such information collections, we must look beyond the naive distinction between the pre-existent and the "original."

Thus, the real problem with the "facts" involved in *Feist* is not that they fail to reflect human agency, but that they have—in fact—an embarrassment of very human sources. A telephone directory listing sums up a complex amalgam of choices, to which the subject of a given entry, as well as her parents, friends, teachers, and others—such as various real estate developers and government employees—have made contributions over time. And to complicate matters further, all these have interacted in complex, webbed relational patterns in making their contributions.

There may be sufficient reasons why such data should be placed firmly and irrevocably in the "public domain." Indeed, the very multiplicity and interdependency of their "authors" may explain why we should treat name/address listings as common property.[41] But rather than engaging in a critical assessment of the utility or disutility of copyright protection for "facts," the

---

39 *Feist*, 111 S. Ct. at 1288-89 (citations omitted).

40 STANLEY FISH, DOING WHAT COMES NATURALLY: CHANGE, RHETORIC AND THE PRACTICE OF THEORY IN LITERARY AND LEGAL STUDIES 61 (1989). In the context of copyright, Jane Ginsburg has charcterized—and criticized—the argument that "facts and theories" simply "are" as "the Platonic fact precept":

> If an historical "truth" in the Platonic sense exists, it can never be discovered, because the same diversity of understanding, approach, and predilection which makes every personality unique precludes a unity of historical interpretation.

Jane C. Ginsburg, *Sabotaging and Reconstructing History: A Comment on the Scope of Copyright Protection in Works of History after* Hoeling v. Universal City Studios, 29 BULL. COPYRIGHT SOC'Y OF THE U.S.A. 647, 658 (1982).

41 For the values associated with common rights in the real property context, and their gradual extinction through the rise of a strictly proprietary model of property law, see E.P. THOMPSON, CUSTOMS IN COMMON 97-184 (1991).

Court in *Feist*, like other courts in prior cases, put its wholly uncritical faith in one vision of the creative process—the Romantic ideal of "authorship."

In other doctrinal settings, faith in solitary, originary Romanic "authorship" blinds decision-makers to the advantages of non-conforming cultural production. Copyright law, with its emphasis on rewarding and safeguarding "originality," has lost sight of the cultural value of what might be called "serial collaborations"—works resulting from successive elaborations of an idea or text by a series of creative workers, occurring perhaps over years or decades. Before copyright law's acceptance of Romantic "authorship" was complete, for example, copyright actually encouraged the creation of popular adaptations of preexisting works, on the ground that "[a]n abridgment preserving 'the whole' of a work 'in its sense' is 'an act of understanding,' 'in the nature of a new and meritorious work.' "[42] But where the law formerly envisioned the possibility of improving existing works by redaction or expansion, modern copyright is more myopic, focussing exclusively on the potential for harm to the interests of the original "author." Today, the privilege of producing "derivative works" that re-work or incorporate protected pre-existing texts generally is reserved to those who have obtained copyright permission.[43]

Among the array of doctrines that make up contemporary copyright law, however, there remain several which can be deployed to legitimate unauthorized borrowings from protected works by subsequent "authors." One of these teaches that in order to constitute an infringement of copyright, a new work must be "substantially similar" to that from which its "author" copied; where the material copied is itself in the public domain, or is too insignificant in quantity, or is altered beyond recognition, there can be no liability. In practice, the crucial question is how the courts will interpret "substantial similarity." Here, recent case law had tended toward what may be called "totality" analysis, which has had the effect of further restricting re-use of existing textual materials.[44]

---

[42] KAPLAN, *supra* note 1, at 12 (quoting Newberry's Case, Lofft 775, 98 Eng. Rep. 913 (Ch. 1773)). *See also Metamorphoses*, *supra* note 10, at 472.

[43] *See, e.g.*, 17 U.S.C. § 106(2) (1988). Where a "derivative work" has been produced with the permission of the owner of a copyrighted underlying work, contemporary copyright law favors the owner of the underlying work. *See Metamorphoses*, *supra* note 10, at 492-96 (discussing reversionary rights and the Supreme Court decision in Stewart v. Abend, 495 U.S. 207 (1990)).

[44] "Totality" analysis began in earnest with Sid & Marty Krofft Tel. v. McDonald's

"Totality" analysis is yet another doctrinal reflection of the ideology of Romantic "authorship." In this interpretation of copyright doctrine, "authors'" rights in their "works" extend not only to the content of their own devising, but also to what they have themselves borrowed from the intellectual "commons"—presumably because they subsequently have impressed their artistic personalities on these borrowed materials. This vision marginalizes yet other "authors," who arrive still later on the scene, and denies that they might have an equally important role to play in the continuing process of cultural transmission by which texts are reformulated and elaborated. In effect, "totality" analysis converts copyright into a textual Homestead Act.

A recent example of this tendency in copyright is provided by the recent trial and appellate court decisions in *Rogers v. Koons*.[45] The plaintiff, Art Rogers, had photographed a couple holding a litter of German Shepherd puppies. That black-and-white image had first appeared in Rogers's newspaper photography column. It was undisputed that the defendant, Jeff Koons, had employed the image as the basis for a large three-dimensional wood sculpture with a non-naturalistic color scheme. Indeed, Koons argued that his choice of that image was self-conscious: The theme of the exhibition in which the sculpture was displayed (the "Banality Show") necessarily entailed the re-use of images already in cultural circulation.

The district court granted summary judgment for the plaintiff on the issue of the defendant's liability for copyright infringement, and thereafter this ruling was upheld by the Second Circuit Court of Appeals. In each instance, the court's opinion reflects its writer's faith in the ideology of Romantic "authorship." Indeed, the outcome of Judge Cardamone's opinion on appeal could hardly be in doubt after the opening paragraph:

> The key to this copyright infringement suit, brought by a

Corp., 562 F.2d 1157 (9th Cir. 1977), which proved (for better or worse) to be the most influential copyright infringement decision of recent times. The court's copyright infringement analysis was summarized in a phrase: "[The defendants] have captured the 'total concept and feel' of the [plaintiffs'] show." *Id.* at 1167. Traditional copyright limitations, such as the rule that protection attaches only to "expressions" and not to "ideas," are inherently at odds with "totality" analysis; nonetheless, it has enjoyed considerable favor in the courts. For the subsequent rise of this approach to assessing "substantial similarity," as well as some indications that its validity is now being called into question, see COPYRIGHT LAW, *supra* note 14, at 687-91 and *Metamorphoses*, *supra* note 10, at 491 n.138.

45 751 F. Supp. 474 (S.D.N.Y. 1990), *modified*, 777 F. Supp. 1 (S.D.N.Y. 1991), *and aff'd*, 960 F.2d 301 (2d Cir. 1992). The Second Circuit affirmed summary judgment in favor of the plaintiff on the issue of liability.

> plaintiff photographer against a defendant sculptor and the gallery representing him, is defendants' borrowing of plaintiff's expression of a typical American scene—a smiling husband and wife holding a litter of charming puppies. The copying was so deliberate as to suggest that defendants resolved so long as they were significant players in the art business, and the copies they produced bettered the price of the copied work by a thousand to one, their piracy of a less well-known artist's work would escape being sullied by an accusation of plagiarism.[46]

In this telling summary account, the conflict posed is not between the competing claims of two cultural workers, pursuing different objectives in different media, but between a pure "artist," on the one hand, and corrupt "players in the art business," on the other.[47]

---

[46] *Koons*, 960 F.2d at 303.

[47] Later in the opinion, in introducing basic concepts of copyright, Judge Cardamone notes that James Madison had supported a constitutional grant of congressional power to enact copyright laws on the basis that authors had enjoyed such a right at common law, citing to *The Federalist* and to Blackstone's *Commentaries on the Laws of England*. *See id.* at 306. In fact, the question of what rights British authors enjoyed before the enactment of the Statute of Anne is not free from doubt, and the content and context of the cited passage from Blackstone is revealing. In the *Commentaries on the Laws of England*, Blackstone argues not that English common law *did* recognize the common law rights of individual "authors" but that it *should* (or should have) done so, because copyright should be regarded as a species of natural rights based (like property in land) on "occupancy":

> When a man by the exertion of his rational powers has produced an original work, he has clearly a right to dispose of that identical work as he pleases, and any attempt to take it from him, or vary the disposition he has made of it, is an invasion of his right of property. Now the identity of a literary composition consists intirely in the *sentiment* and the *language*; the same conceptions, cloathed in the same words, must necessarily be the same composition: and whatever method be taken of conveying that composition to the ear or the eye of another, by recital, by writing, or by printing, it is always the identical work of the author which is so conveyed.

2 COMMENTARIES ON THE LAWS OF ENGLAND 405-06 (Photo reprint 1979) (1766). *See* the discussion of Blackstone in Rose, *supra* note 8, at 63-64. Blackstone was a near-contemporary of Edward Young, Woodmansee, *supra* note 7, at 280, and his vision of the source of authorial entitlements is bound up with the Romantic ideology of "authorship" of which Young was an early exponent.

The district court opinion in *Koons* also displayed an affinity for the vision of copyright as a natural or inherent right. In his introduction to copyright concepts, Judge Haight quoted at some length from a 1924 decision of the Second Circuit Court of Appeals, King Features Syndicate v. Fleischer, 299 F. 533 (2d Cir. 1924). *King Features* involved a three-dimensional reproduction of a two-dimensional work of graphic art in the context of commercial, (rather than fine) art—the imitation of a cartoon character in the design of a mass-produced children's toy. The appellate panel concluded that "[d]oing this is omitting the work of the artisan, but appropriating the genius of the artist," *id.* at 535, and had expressed the view that:

> A piece of statuary may be infringed by the picture of the statuary for the Copyright Act *secured to the author* the *original and natural rights*, and it is the intendment of the law of copyrights that they shall have a liberal construction in order to give effect to what may be considered as an *inherent right of the author* in his work.

The invidious comparison is reinforced in succeeding paragraphs that further characterize the parties: Rogers is presented as a generally acclaimed "artist-photographer,"[48] widely published and exhibited, whose photograph "Puppies" had come to the defendant's attention as the result of a notecard issued by a firm specializing in "high quality reproductions of photographs by well-respected American photographers including, for example, Ansel Adams."[49] Koons, although finally conceded the designation of "artist," is portrayed as a controversial figure, whose claims to artistry are tainted by acquisitiveness. Although the information may be legally irrelevant, strictly speaking, Judge Cardamone notes that "[w]hile pursuing his career as an artist, he also worked until 1984 as a mutual funds salesman, a registered commodities salesman and broker, and a commodities futures broker," and concludes the description by quoting a newspaper critic's assessment that "Koons is pushing the relationship between art and money so far that everyone involved comes out looking slightly absurd."[50] Clearly enough,

---

Id. at 536 (emphasis added). That Judge Haight, writing almost sixty years after the *King Feeatures* case, chose to ground his analysis in the quoted language is representative of copyright law's general devaluation of later-created "derivative" works in the ideology of Romantic "authorship."

[48] *Koons*, 960 F.2d at 303.

[49] *Id.* at 304.

[50] *Id.* The comment (attributed only to an unamed "New York Times Critic"), which concludes the introductory section of Judge Cardamone's opinion headed "Koons," can be found in Michael Brenson, *Greed Plus Glitz, With a Dollup of Innocence*, N.Y. Times, Dec. 18, 1988, § 2, at 41. The article, which, like the opinion, emphasizes Koons's background in financial markets, is generally critical of the sculptor and his productions, characterizing Koons as "wanting more money than any artist his age has ever made from art" and his works as "[f]antasies of American youth and adolescence [which] are embalmed, frozen into glamorous and deathless products." *Id.* at 44. Other passages help to illuminate Judge Cardamone's skepticism about artistic Koons:

> His art is largely strategic. Images have been appropriated from photographs of popular culture and then collaged together into spanking new commodities. *They were made collectively, even anonymously, by workshops in northern Italy. What seems to matter is not the originality of the artist, but rather images that belong to an entire culture and that everyone in that culture can use.*

Id. (emphasis added).

Koons certainly does not fit the stereotype of a Romantic "author," as the following comparison with another artistic rebel makes clear:

> In medium, method and response to the past, however, the Koons and the Manet could not be further apart. While Manet painted his work, Koons supervised the production of his statue. While Manet was making art that he hoped would speak on equal terms with Titian and Goya, Koons makes art that he hopes can speak on equal terms with Michael Jackson.

Id.

Judge Cardamone does not refer to the final paragraph of the article, which grants Koons the epithets "smart and inventive," and indicates that his work "helps define some of the deeper tensions within the contemporary art world." *Id.*

A subsequent journalistic treatment of Koons and his works, argues that the controversy surrounding the sculptor stems (at least in part) from the challenge he poses to the

Koons's worldliness in money matters does not weigh in his favor.

Nor does his way of working. Before comparing the two works at issue in the case, Judge Cardamone's appellate opinion emphasizes the differences between the working methods of the individuals who created them. Rogers is a complete artist, whose personal life and art are fully integrated: "[He] has a studio and home at Point Reyes, California, where he makes his living by creating, exhibiting, publishing and otherwise making use of his rights in his photographic works."[51] By contrast, Koons's production is characterized by extreme division of labor. Not only is he "represented" by sales galleries in various parts of the world, but he does not personally execute the projects he conceives for ultimate sale: In preparation for the Banality Show, "[c]ertain European studios were chosen to execute his porcelain works, other studios chosen for the mirror pieces, and the small Demetz Studio, located in the northern hill country town of Ortessi, Italy, was selected to carve the wood sculptures."[52]

Finally, in the treatment of the issue of "substantial similarity," judicial attitudes toward the competing visions of creativity represented by Rogers and Koons are brought to bear on the issue of liability.[53] The courts may well have been right to reject

---

vision of artistic purity, which is closely associated with the ideology of Romantic "authorship":

> But to many of the artists who toy with advertising, Jeff Koons among them, "selling out" is a virtue, a backhanded way of stirring artistic rebellion. It is a post-Pop, post-punk pose that defies the traditional notion of what artists and art should be—poor and unknown. Peddling an image of themselves in the the manner of a movie star not only promises to make artists famous; it also allows them to thumb their noses at the assumption that art is somehow above the marketplace.

Paul Taylor, *The Art of P.R., and Vice Versa*, N.Y. TIMES, Oct. 27, 1991, § 2, at 1, 35.

[51] *Koons*, 960 F.2d at 303.

[52] *Id.* at 304-05. Koons's working relationship with the Demetz Studio was independently relevant to the analysis of the liability issue, and Judge Cardamone's opinion emphasizes how Koons directed "his artisans" by specifying that various details of the sculpture were to be "like [the] photo" or "as per photo." *Id.* at 305. At the same time, however, the implicit contrast drawn between Koons's and Rogers's methods belies Judge Cardamone's biases, as does the passage in Judge Haight's district court opinion, which emphasizes that "[q]uestions of size and color aside, the sculpture is as exact a copy of the photograph as [Koons's] hired artisans could fashion, which is precisely what [he] told them to do." *Koons*, 751 F. Supp. at 478.

In Romantic theory, the "true" artist was one who had escaped the division of labor, which characterized modern life generally, and who united "head and heart, shrewdness and ingenuity, reason and imagination in a harmonious alliance, that so to speak restores the *whole person* in us." FRIEDRICH SCHILLER, ON BÜRGER'S POEMS (1791), *quoted in* MARTHA WOODMANSEE, *"Art" as a Weapon in Cultural Politics: Rereading Schiller's "Aesthetic Letters," in* AESTHETICS IN THE MARKETPLACE (forthcoming 1993).

[53] *Rogers v. Koons* also involved a "fair use" issue, and the characterization of Koons's artistic activities as "commercial" figured significantly there: "[W]e note that Koons'[s]

the main lines of the sculptor's defense: that, in assimilating the image of the photograph, Koons had taken no more than unprotected factual information concerning the existence and appearance of the photographic subjects;[54] and that, at the same time, he had altered and embellished the image (by, among other things, inserting flowers in the hair of the human figures and providing the puppies with grotesque bulbous noses). After all, the arrangement of the furniture and figures, *was* reproduced in the sculpture from the photograph. If it represented Rogers's copyrightable "authorship," then a legally significant taking of protected material probably *did* occur. For the purposes of the present discussion, however, the correctness of the outcome is less significant than the technique of decision.

Certainly, Judge Cardamone's opinion eschews naive "totality" analysis, acknowledging that "ideas, concepts, and the like found in the common domain are the inheritance of everyone," so that "in looking at these two works of art to determine whether they are substantially similar, focus must be on the similarity of the *expression* of an idea or fact, not on the similarity of the facts, ideas, or concepts themselves."[55] Despite its apparent sophistication,[56] however, Judge Cardamone's approach to sub-

---

substantial profit from his intentionally exploitive use of Rogers's work also militates against a finding of fair use . . . ." *Koons*, 960 F.2d at 309.

54 In the district court opinion, Judge Haight stated that "Koons does not articulate what non-protectible factual expression he regards himself as having used." 751 F. Supp. at 477. Perhaps the sculptor also relied on the seemingly unpromising (and ultimately ill-fated) argument that "Rogers' copyright protection 'is strictly limited to the work *as a photograph*.' " *Id.* (quoting trial brief submitted by Koons). Koons could have argued, however, that Rogers did not "create" or "originate" the physical appearance of the photographic subjects, and that he had not borrowed elements of the photograph for which Rogers was responsible: the lighting scheme employed when the photograph was taken, for example, or the balance of tones achieved when it was processed.

55 *Koons*, 960 F.2d at 308. It is less clear whether Judge Haight in the district court appreciated the importance of discounting copying of mere unprotected ideas in the course of substantial similarity analysis.

56 In most respects, Judge Cardamone's opinion merely expands upon the analysis of the district court, as reflected in the following passage:

> [T]he present test of substantial similarity in the Second Circuit is "whether an average lay observer would recognize the alleged copy as having been appropriated from the copyrighted work."
>
> There is no question in the case at bar that "an average lay observer" would recognize the sculpture "String of Puppies" as "having been appropriated from" the photograph "Puppies." Questions of size and color aside, the sculpture is as exact a copy of the photograph as [the sculptor's] hired artisans could fashion, which is precisely what [he] told them to do. Indeed, [the puppies's owner's] friend, having observed a newspaper picture of the sculpture, assumed that it was [the original] photograph, having been "colorized."

Koons, 751 F. Supp. at 478 (citing and quoting Ideal Toy Corp. v. Fab-Lu Ltd., 360 F.2d 1021, 1022 (2d Cir. 1966)).

This passage incorporates the ideology of "authorship" and the cult of "originality" in a number of reinforcing ways. For one, the totalizing tendencies of the quoted "stan-

stantial similarity analysis still reflects the tendency to lump together the clearly protected, arguably protected, and certainly even unprotected elements of a copyrighted work in comparing it to another, allegedly infringing work. In characterizing the protected elements of the photograph, Judge Cardamone notes that it is the "expression" that Rogers "caught in the placement, in the particular light, and in the expressions of the subjects—that gives the photograph its charming and unique character, that is to say, makes it original and copyrightable."[57] In the following paragraph, Judge Cardamone asserts that Koons overstepped the line when he used "the identical expression of the idea that Rogers created; the composition, the poses, and the expressions . . . ."[58]

It is instructive to set these two lists of elements—protected and copied—side by side. Notably, Judge Cardamone does not rely on the difficult notion that the "particular light" of the photograph somehow was reproduced in the sculpture. But, while this protected element drops out of the comparison, the element of "placement" is subdivided into "composition" and "poses" in the itemization of Koons's borrowings—although the distinction between the two is not specified. Finally, both lists refer to the

---

dard," with its emphasis on "recognition" of "appropriation," necessarily privilege prior works over subsequent ones. The same language, which is drawn from Ideal Toy Corp. v. Fab-Lu Ltd., 360 F.2d 1021, 1022 (2d Cir. 1966), is identified by Judge Cardamone as a source of precedential guidance on the substantial similarity issue. Slip op. at 12. Judge Haight dismisses in passing the claimed differences (matters of "size and color") between the two works, implicitly applying Judge Learned Hand's famous observation that "no plagiarist can excuse the wrong by showing how much of his work he did not pirate." Sheldon v. Metro-Goldwyn Pictures Corp., 81 F.2d 49, 56 (2d Cir.), *cert. denied*, 298 U.S. 669 (1936). This *dictum* uncovers the preconception that the truly "original" is superior to the merely "derivative," which has its source in the ideology of "authorship." Notably, it is cited explicitly by Judge Cardamone. Slip op. at 14. (In other contexts, it should be noted, Hand's superficially attractive principle has proved difficult to uphold consistently. In Warner Bros. v. American Broadcasting Cos., 720 F.2d 231 (2d Cir. 1983), for example, Judge Jon Newman reconsiders the validity of the Hand *dictum* and concludes that differences may matter more where substantial similarity determinations involving "graphic or three-dimensional" works are involved. *Id.* at 241.)

As already noted, *see supra* note 52, Judge Haight makes much of the point that the sculpture was not executed by the sculptor who affixed his signature to it, but by mere "hired artisans"—thus marginalizing the sculptor's contribution and undercutting the claims of his work to independent legitimacy as a product of "authorship." In this, too, Judge Cardamone's opinion follows.

One important move in the passage just quoted from the district court opinion, however, is not reproduced in that of the court of appeals. Judge Haight trivializes the inquiry into substantial similarity by invoking the subjectivity of an individual (the "friend") who is in no sense representative of any real or hypothetical audience group. The absence of any equivalent passage in Judge Cardamone's opinion is a mark of its greater sophistication, but not necessarily of any basic difference in its orientation.

[57] *Koons*, 960 F.2d at 308.

[58] *Id.* at 308.

"expressions" of the subjects, but nowhere is it indicated to what extent or in what way these reflected Rogers's agency, rather than that of the subjects themselves.[59] In effect, the case for substantial similarity is strengthened by a systematic inflation of the claims of "authorship." If this is not "totality" analysis in its pure form, it is the next best thing.

On the particular facts, Judge Cardamone may well have been correct to conclude that "no reasonable jury could have differed on the issue of substantial similarity."[60] Nevertheless, his opinion effectively embraces an approach to substantial similarity analysis that is structurally biased in favor of the claims of the "author" whose work has temporal priority—a standard that cannot account fully for the possibility that "recognizable" borrowings incorporated from preexisting works into new ones may be of elements that are in the public domain.

The Romantic vision of "authorship," in which this approach to "substantial similarity" analysis is rooted, informs other critical passages of the court of appeals opinion in *Rogers v. Koons*. Thus, Judge Cardamone finds a fatal flaw in Koons' defense that the sculpture was a satire or parody qualifying as a privileged "fair use": The "fair use" doctrine applies only when the copied work itself is, "at least in part, an object of the parody . . . ."[61] This limitation, he insists, is needed if we are to ensure "public awareness of the original work" in cases of "fair use" parody:

> By requiring that the copied work be an object of the parody, we merely insist that the audience be aware that underlying the parody there is an original and separate expression, attributable to a different artist.[62]

In this reasoning, parody can qualify as "fair use" only so long as it acknowledges its subordinate position in the hierarchy of works, and, by extension, the subordinate position of its creator in the hierarchy of "authors." This limit is required, Judge

---

59 For the general tendency of copyright law to efface the role of the photographic subject in the production of images incorporating his or her likeness, see *supra* note 16.

60 *Koons*, 960 F.2d at 308.

61 *Id.* at 310 (citing MCA, Inc. v. Wilson, 677 F.2d 180, 185 (2d Cir. 1981)).

62 *Id.* The passage continues: "This awareness may come from the fact that the copied work is publicly known or because its existence is in some manner acknowledged by the parodist in connection with the parody." *Id.* at 310. Of course, it is not self-evident that had Koons acknowledged Rogers in connection with his sculpture, the outcome would have been different. Finally, Judge Cardamone's views on "fair use" are shaped in large part by his perception that the defendant's "commercial" exploitation of Rogers' photograph was a use of a kind which could prejudice the potential market for that work if it became "widespread."

Cardamone indicates, because "otherwise there would be no real limitation on the copier's use of another's copyrighted work to make a statement about some aspect of society at large."[63] Like other features of the doctrine applied in *Rogers v. Koons*, this one operates to discourage artists whose methods entail reworking preexisting materials, while rewarding those whose dedication to "originality" qualfies them as true "authors" in the Romantic sense.

The outcome in *Rogers v. Koons* notwithstanding, an otherwise actionable appropriation of material from a preexisting work may be excused on the ground that it represents a privileged "fair use" rather than (as is usually the case) an "unfair" one. One persuasive ground on which a defense of "fair use" may be premised is a claim that the defendant not only took protected material, but somehow transformed it in the taking. Thus, in her recent decision in *Basic Books, Inc. v. Kinko's Graphics Corp.*,[64] District Judge Constance Baker Motley wrote:

> [T]he Supreme Court has found that "the distinction between 'productive' and 'unproductive' uses may be helpful in calibrating the balance [of interests]."[65]

The opinion continued, under the heading "Transformative use":

> It has been argued that the essence of "character and purpose" [one of the four considerations itemized in 17 U.S.C. § 107, which codifies the fair use doctrine] is the transformative value, that is, productive use, of the secondary work compared to the original. District Court Judge Leval has noted that, "[t]he use . . . must employ the quoted matter in a different manner or for a different purpose from the original."[66]

Where "fair use" is concerned, it seems, mere "users" need not apply. The doctrine may be invoked only by those who have special claims to "authorship" in their own work.

The *Basic Books* litigation involved another form of "serial collaboration"[67]—making anthologies of selections from published writings for use as textbooks in college courses. The suit

---

63 *Id.* at 310.

64 758 F. Supp. 1522 (S.D.N.Y. 1991).

65 *Id.* at 1530 (quoting Sony Corp. v. Universal City Studios, Inc., 464 U.S. 417, 455 n.40 (1984) (alteration in original)).

66 *Id.* (quoting Pierre Leval, *Toward a Fair Use Standard*, 103 HARV. L. REV. 1105, 1111 (1990)).

67 For a definition and discussion of serial collaborations, see *supra* text accompanying note 41.

was brought by publishers against a commercial photocopying service that had prepared anthologies including unauthorized excerpts from copyrighted works; the materials in these compilations had been chosen by instructors to suit their own courses, culled from books and various other publications which totalled (in each case) thousands of pages. The litigation turned on the photocopying company's defense of "fair use," and the finding for the publishers was justified, in significant part, on the grounds that the use in question was a mere "non-transformative repackaging":

> In this case, there was absolutely no literary effort made by Kinko's to expand upon or contextualize the materials copied. The excerpts in suit were merely copied, bound into a new form, and sold. . . . The copying in suit had productive value only to the extent that it put an entire semester's resources in one bound volume for students. It required the judgment of the professors to compile it, though none of Kinko's.[68]

This puzzling passage is open to two distinct interpretations. It may be that "literary effort" and mere "judgment" are two different things, and that selecting and collating the excerpts to be included in an anthology is not the kind of new "authorship" that Judge Motley believes deserves recognition.[69] Or perhaps the photocopying company should not have been given credit for any "literary effort" invested in the design of anthologies by others.[70] One way or another, the value added to the preexisting materials by the act of compiling them is lost in the economy of this decision. Either way, the intellectual contribution that went into the creation of the "secondary" works goes unacknowledged in the *Basic Books* case, and its significance remains unanalyzed. Certainly, the value of such compilations cannot be accounted for

68 *Basic Books*, 758 F. Supp. at 1530-31 (citations omitted).

69 Notwithstanding the language of the decision, the "selection, coordination and arrangement" of preexisting materials is considered a form of "authorship" where those materials are not copyrighted or are used with permission. *See* 17 U.S.C. § 101 (1988) (defining "compilation" as "a work formed by the collection and assembling of preexisting materials or of data that are selected, coordinated, or arranged in such a way that the resulting work as a whole constitutes an original work of authorship"); *see also* Feist Publications, Inc. v. Rural Tel. Serv., 111 S. Ct. 1282, 1289 (1991). Is there a double standard at work in *Basic Books* with one level of "authorship" being sufficient to form the basis of a claim to copyright, and another, higher level being necessary to avoid liability for infringement?

70 The professors who used the "anthologies" involved in the *Basic Books* litigation were not defendants in the litigation. The defendant company's efforts to claim that its use was privileged—for educational purposes—were rejected by the court: "The extent of its insistence that theirs are educational concerns and not profitmaking ones boggles the mind." *Basic Books*, 758 F. Supp. at 1532.

within the framework imposed by the ideology of "authorship."[71]

In *Feist*, the Supreme Court failed to recognize that "factual" data, like name/address listings in a directory, are themselves the products of complex processes of corporate writing. Similarly, the opinions in *Rogers v. Koons* and *Basic Books* came to their conclusions by marginalizing the cultural significance of what I have called "serial collaboration"—a writing practice that cannot easily be accommodated within the Romantic conception of "authorship."

We should also note that copyright fails to come to terms with the reality of even more obvious forms of literary and artistic collaboration. Although copyright law has a category for works created by several writers working together on a preconcerted basis, the consequences that flow from the categorization of a work as one of "joint authorship" reflect the individualistic bias of American copyright doctrine. In effect, "a joint work" has several individual "authors": Each "joint author" must possess the legal attributes and should retain the legal prerogatives associ-

---

[71] The dependence on Romantic ideas of "authorship" by copyright law limits the availability of the "fair use" defense in such a case as *Basic Books*. The same conception of "authorship," however, has been invoked to justify "fair use." In Wright v. Warner Books, Inc., 953 F.2d 731 (2d Cir. 1991), the most recent in a series of Second Circuit decisions involving the applicability of "fair use" to quotations from unpublished manuscripts, the court concluded that the defendant's unauthorized takings from the unpublished letters and diaries of the writer, Richard Wright, were privileged. One factor that a "fair use" analysis must address, according to section 107 of the Copyright Act, is "the amount and substantiality of the portion used." In setting the stage for the discussion of this factor in the *Wright* decision, Judge Meskill observed that not all the passages quoted by the defendant were the subject matter of copyright: "Of the ten quoted sections [from the letters], four bear Wright's stamp of creativity and meet the threshold test of copyright protection. The other six tersely convey mundane details of Wright's life . . . ." *Id.* at 736. This remarkable invocation of the concept of "authorship" to deny protection to merely "mundane" passages is echoed later in the opinion, in the discussion addressing "fair use." *See id.* at 736-40. In the "fair use" section of the opinion, Judge Meskill considered a fifty-five word quotation from an unpublished letter. Judge Meskill states that "[t]he quoted passage is indeed stylistic. However, it is the only quoted piece of expression that represents anything close to the central point communicated in any of the letters." *Id.* at 738.

In its early decision in Bleistein v. Donaldson Lithographing Co., 188 U.S. 239 (1903), the United States Supreme Court disclaimed any role for the judiciary in assessing the "worth" of works for which copyright protection is claimed, "outside of the narrowest and most obvious limits." *Id.* at 251. If the issue in Wright had been posed as a choice between characterizations of the passages in question as meritorious or meritless writing, conflict with the *Bleistein* principle would have been inevitable. By presenting the choice as being between the characterizations "stylistic" and "non-stylistic" writing, however, the conflict is avoided. The issue, as the court presents it, is not whether the passages are worthwhile, but whether they are the outcome of "authorship" in the first instance. In one respect, this treatment of the issue may represent a mere sleight of hand; in another, however, it accurately reflects the underlying assumptions of the copyright system. If a glorified vision of "authorship" animates our law of copyright, we should expect to find that works deficient in "authorship" are denied all protection or (at least) rendered particularly vulnerable to "fair use."

ated with solitary, originary "authorship." Thus, only identified or identifiable individuals can receive legal recognition for their contribution to a "joint work,"[72] while the duration of protection for a "joint work" is measured in terms of the longest-surviving of its several "authors." Perhaps most critically, each of those "authors" is entitled to use and authorize the use of the work as though he or she were solely responsible for its creation.[73] Far from acknowledging the extent to which participation in a corporate, creative enterprise entails the surrender of individual prerogative, copyright law implicitly assumes the continued relevance of the Romantic vision of "authorship" to this domain.

The Copyright Act and case law thus tend to treat "joint authorship" as a deviant form of individual "authorship." Indeed, in many particular instances copyright refuses to acknowledge the existence of "joint authorship," or does so only grudgingly. Indeed, one of the significant innovations of the major statutory revision of American copyright law, completed in 1976, was its substantial narrowing of the range of circumstances in which what might be termed a "collaboration" in the lay sense is recog-

---

[72] American copyright law provides for anonymous works, "of which no natural person is identified as author." 17 U.S.C. § 101 (1988). However, the statute assumes that in such instances one or more potentially identifiable individuals created the work, and includes special provisions allowing them to come forward and declare their identities. *See* 17 U.S.C. § 302(c) (1988).

[73] The "joint author's" right to use or authorize use is subject to a duty to account to his or her collaborator(s) for the financial proceeds. It also is subject to a limited and ill-defined exception, derived from the general law of co-tenancy: uses of the work that are deemed "destructive" require the general consent of all "joint authors" of the work. There was early support for the view that a transfer of rights by one joint owner which "practically precludes the other from a like use" should fall within the bar. *See* Shapiro, Bernstein & Co. v. Jerry Vogel Music Co., 73 F. Supp. 265 (S.D.N.Y. 1947). *But see* Herbert v. Fields, 152 N.Y.S. 487 (1915). But recent commentators have stated that "as a general matter [courts should] confine relief to situations in which a co-owner's conduct may place the work in the public domain." PAUL GOLDSTEIN, 1 COPYRIGHT § 4.2.2.2 (1989). Others have noted that "only in those limited circumstance [sic] where by its nature the work can be exploited in one and only one medium and that medium customarily does not use competitive versions of the same work . . . a most rare type of situation." MELVILLE B. NIMMER & DAVID NIMMER, NIMMER ON COPYRIGHT § 6.10[A], at 6-28 (1991).

Since American copyright traditionally has provided only for "economic" as distinct from "moral" rights, we have no guidance on the problems that could arise, under the recently-enacted Visual Artists Rights Act of 1990. Although the Visual Artists Rights Act, which is codified at 17 U.S.C. § 106A, does provide for joint ownership of moral rights, nothing in the statute or the legislative history specifies the result when one "joint author" of a qualifying work objects to a use proposed or undertaken by another on non-economic grounds. Although it states that "authors" of a joint work of visual art are co-owners of the rights to claim authorship and object to the distortion, mutilation, or other prejudicial modification of the work, the statute gives no guidance concerning how that right would be exercised between the "joint authors"—nor does the legislative history. If the treatment of "economic" rights is any guide, we may presume that when one "joint author" has authorized a particular use, the scope of another right to object will be limited.

nized as a "joint work" in the legal one. Before 1976, courts were content to hold that a work of "joint authorship" need not be the result of face-to-face collaboration: as when, for example, lyrics were added to an already-completed tune.[74] By contrast, Section 101 of the 1976 Copyright Act defines "joint authorship" so to require "the intention, *at the time the writing is done*, that the parts be absorbed or combined into an integrated unit."[75]

Law's insistence on formally disaggregating collaborative productions, rather than categorizing them as "joint works," is apparent in recent decisions concerning the vexed question of whether the contribution of each "joint author" must be one which would be considered a copyrightable "work" in itself.[76] Although many courts have dealt with this issue in recent years,[77]

---

74 *See* Shapiro, Bernstein & Co. v. Jerry Vogel Music Co, Inc., 221 F.2d 569 (2d Cir.), *modified*, 223 F.2d 252 (1955) (the "Twelfth Street Rag" decision.)

75 H.R. Rep. No. 1476, 94th Cong., 2d Sess. 103, 120, *reprinted in* 1976 U.S.C.C.A.N. 5659, 5736 (emphasis added) (glossing the definition of "joint work" in Section 101 of the 1976 Copyright Act). All questions of temporality aside, the requirement that contributions to a "joint work" be ones intended to be "merged into inseparable or interdependent parts of a unitary whole," *id.*, is notably restrictive in itself, although it is nothing new. Here, the hyperbolic language of a 1944 opinion of Judge Learned Hand is instructive. A work of "joint authorship" comes into being, he stated, because "when [both "authors"] plan an undivided whole . . . , their separate interests will be as inextricably involved, as are the threads out of which they have woven the seamless fabric of the work." Edward B. Marks Music Corp. v. Jerry Vogel Music Co., 140 F.2d 266, 267 (2d Cir. 1944). The continuing tendency of courts to disaggregate creative contributions wherever possible, on the grounds that the resultant product is not "unitary," or "integrated," or "undivided," is exemplified by such decisions as Weissman v. Freeman, 868 F.2d 1313 (2d Cir.), *cert. denied*, 110 S. Ct. 219 (1989).

76 As detailed below, this problem usually arises when one collaborator is responsible for the basic idea of a project, while another has undertaken its actual execution. But it could arise in other contexts as well. Copyright law does not extend protection to words, individual musical notes or short phrases. Stratchborneo v. ARC Music Corp., 357 F. Supp. 1393, 1405 (S.D.N.Y. 1973); Shapiro, Bernstein & Co. v. Jerry Vogel Music, 161 F.2d 406, 409 (2d Cir. 1947). Obviously, however, we can imagine a literary or musical project realized by inviting large numbers of individuals to make separate, sequential, contributions, each consisting of sub-copyrightable expression. It seems unlikely that the whole would be considered more than the sum of the parts under prevailing copyright doctrine. (For this example, though not necessarily for the conclusion I draw from it, I am indebted to Bruce Joseph, Esq.).

77 *See, e.g.*, S.O.S., Inc. v. Payday, Inc., 886 F.2d 1081 (9th Cir. 1989); Olan Mills, Inc. v. Eckerd Drug of Texas, Inc., 1989 Copyright L. Dec. (CCH) ¶ 26,420 (N.D. Tex. 1989); Ashton-Tate Corp. v. Ross, 728 F. Supp. 597 (N.D.Cal. 1989); Boggs v. Japp, 1988 Copyright L. Dec. (CCH) ¶ 26,347 (E.D. Va. 1988); Whelan Assocs., Inc. v. Jaslow Dental Lab., Inc., 609 F. Supp. 1307 (E.D.Pa. 1985), *aff'd*, 797 F.2d. 1222 (3d Cir. 1986), *and cert. denied*, 479 U.S. 1031 (1987); Meltzer v. Zoller, 520 F. Supp. 847 (D.N.J. 1981). The Ninth Circuit Court of Appeals summarized the prevailing view in *S.O.S.*:

> A person who merely describes to an author what the commissioned work should do or look like is not a joint author for purposes of the Copyright Act . . . . To be an author, one must supply more than mere direction or ideas: one must "translate[] an idea into a fixed, tangible expression entitled to copyright protection." [citing CCNV v. Reid, 846 F.2d 1485 (D.C. Cir. 1988), *modified on other grounds*, 490 U.S. 730 (1989)]. The supplier of an idea is no

and most have answered in the affirmative,[78] the most important precedent in the area is the recent decision in *Childress v. Taylor*.[79] *Childress* involved a dispute over ownership in a play about the legendary black entertainer "Moms" Mabley. Alice Childress was a veteran stage performer, who had conceived the idea of such a play as a vehicle for herself and had assembled extensive documentation of Mabley's life and career. Childress then persuaded a playwright, Clarice Taylor, to prepare a script embodying her ideas and incorporating her research.

After Taylor's script had been completed, Childress allegedly misappropriated its contents as the basis for a "Moms" Mabley play of her own, and Taylor brought suit. The issue of "joint authorship" was squarely presented—only if Taylor was found to be the sole "author" of the play did Taylor have a claim against Childress. The trial court ruled in favor of Taylor, on the ground that Childress's "ideas and research" did not represent a copyrightable, and thus legally significant, contribution. The court of appeals revisited the issue in an opinion which conceded that the issue posed was "open in this Circuit" and "troublesome,"[80] both because it is one to which the statute does not speak in so many words[81] and because conventional policy justifications for

---

> more an "author" of a program than is the supplier of the disk on which the program is stored.

886 F.2d at 1087 (alteration in original).

[78] The most important exception is the *dictum* in Judge Ruth Ginsberg's opinion in Community for Creative Non-Violence v. Reid, 846 F.2d 1485, 1497 (D.C. Cir. 1988), *modified on other grounds*, 490 U.S. 730 (1989). After disposing of the "work for hire" issue, Judge Ginsberg noted that the question of whether the statute at issue had been a "joint work" hadn't been before the court, but suggested that it "might qualify as a textbook example of a jointly-authored work," and that merely supplying the general idea or concept for the work might count toward a finding of "authorship" on the part of one of the claimants to ownership rights. *Id.* at 1497. She continued: "Its contribution to the steam grate pedestal *added to its initial conceptualization and ongoing direction of the realization [of the work]*." *Id.* (emphasis added). The emphasized contributions, of course, are not ones which conventionally would be regarded as copyrightable in themselves.

More recently, another federal appellate court has explicitly held that the issue is an open one. *See* Andrien v. Southern Ocean County Chamber of Commerce, 927 F.2d 132, 136 (3d Cir. 1991) (en banc). *See also* Steve Altman Photography v. United States, 18 Cl. Ct. 267 (1989) (suggesting that "conceiving the idea" for a photograph may be a legally relevant authorial contribution).

[79] 945 F.2d 500 (1991).

[80] *Id.* at 506.

[81] Judge Newman's opinion for the curcuit court notes that

> [t]he textual argument from the statute is not convincing. The Act surely does not say that each contribution to a joint work must be copyrightable, and the specification that there be "authors" does not necessarily require a copyrightable contribution. "Author" is not defined in the Act and appears to be used only in its ordinary sense of an originator. The "author" of an uncopyrightable idea is nonetheless its author even though, for entirely valid reasons, the law properly denies him a copyright on the result.

Id. Although the passage demystifies the statutory terminology, its vision of the "ordi-

copyright protection do not dictate a clear answer:

> If the focus is solely on the objective of copyright law to encourage the production of creative works, it is difficult to see why the contributions of all joint authors need be copyrightable. An individual creates a copyrightable work by combining a non-copyrightable idea with a copyrightable form of expression; the resulting work is no less a valuable result of the creative process simply because the idea and the expression came from two different individuals. Indeed, it is not unimaginable that there exists a skilled writer who might never have produced a significant work until some other person supplied the idea.[82]

Indeed, such working relationships are more than "not unimaginable." Our knowledge of contemporary writing practice, to say nothing of our reconstructions of historical instances like Samuel Johnson's various "secret collaborations,"[83] suggests they are common—if not typical—among collaborators.

The above quoted passage comes as close as anything in copyright jurisprudence to acknowledging the complexities of collaboration, and the difficulties inherent in a legal framework shaped by the individualistic assumptions of Romantic "authorship." Unfortunately, having achieved this insight, Judge Jon Newman, who wrote the opinion for the ciruit court, turns away from it. He discusses, instead, the various pragmatic justifications for insisting on copyrightable contributions from all "joint authors,"[84] concluding, somewhat vaguely, that such a rule embodying such insistence "seems more consistent with the spirit of copyright law."[85]

Ultimately, the *Childress* court fails to confront the issues it identifies so clearly. Instead, it retreats into a restrictive vision of "joint authorship," aligning itself with the general tendency of American statute and case law. Once again, copyright law has been baffled by its inherited vision of Romantic "authorship," and reconsideration of the law's uncomprehending treatment of corporate creativity has been deferred. Rather than confronting the reality of prevailing writing practice, another court has be-

---

nary sense" of the word "author" is dependent upon a set of assumptions inherited by law from Romantic aesthetics.

82 *Id.*

83 *See* Woodmansee, *supra* note 7, at 281-88.

84 These include the discouragement of fraudulent claims and the striking of "an appropriate balance in the domains of both copyright and contract law." *Id.* at 507.

85 *Id.*

come an active participant in the ongoing process of its mystification.

The revision of copyright concepts to take fuller account of collaborative cultural production, forseen by Professor Kaplan, has yet to occur. But what, one might fairly ask, are the implications of copyright's recursive insistence on forcing all writing into to the Procrustean doctrinal model shaped by the individualistic, Romantic concept of "authorship"? In closing, let me suggest one area (among many) in which the continuing failure of copyright to comprehend collective creativity may soon have real, adverse consequences.

As Martha Woodmansee has noted, electronic technology is playing a crucial role in promoting writing practices in which the identities of individual contributors to shared dynamic texts are deemphasized, and their useful contributions effectively merged.[86] One environment in which this trend is notable is that of the many loosely connected national and international computer networks that form, collectively, the so-called "Internet." To date, the Internet (with its bewildering array of available "bulletin boards," "newsgroups," and "electronic texts") has developed as a spontaneous, cooperative, non-governmental response to the potential of new technologies. Thus, activities in the Internet environment have been free (for the most part) from legal regulation.[87] Among other things, the Internet environment has fostered a class of new "infopreneurs," who gather available data from the network, augmenting and repackaging it for further distribution.[88]

Obviously, there are tensions between some practices the Internet facilitates and traditional notions of proprietary rights in writing. As one commentator has noted, "In this informal and often unpredictable intellectual collaboration, authorship is frequently unrecorded"[89]—not to say uncompensated! In many respects, the conditions of the Internet environment today resemble those which prevailed at other moments of polymorphous collaboration, unrestrained plagiarism, and extraordinary cultural productivity—such as the Elizabethan stage or Hollywood before 1915.

---

86 *See* Woodmansee, *supra* note 7, at 289-91.

87 *See generally Information Policy: Superhighway Bill Sketches Outline of Ubiquitous Computer Network*, DAILY REP. FOR EXECS. (BNA), § C-1, Nov. 26, 1991.

88 *See* Bruce L. Flanders, *Barbarians at the Gate: New Technologies for Handling Information Pose a Crisis Over Intellectual Property*, 22 AM. LIBRARIES 668 (July 1991).

89 *Id.*

These conditions, however, may not prevail for long. Last year's congressional enactment of the so-called "Information Superhighway" legislation, which calls for the creation of a new, federally-funded, high-speed network within the Internet (the National Research and Education Network, or NREN), may serve as the catalyst for bringing the electronic network environment as a whole under firmer legal control, through (among other means) the extension of copyright regulation to the activities of network users.

A battle is shaping over the future of the Internet. On the one side are those who see its potential as a threat to traditional notions of individual properietorship in information, and who perceive the vigorous extension of traditional copyright principles as the solution.[90] On the other side are those who argue that the network environment may become a new cultural "commons," which excessive or premature legal control may stifle.[91]

There will certainly be some need for regulation as the network environment evolves and copyright will most definitely have a role to play.[92] The ideology of Romantic "authorship," however, has greater potential to mislead than to guide the decision-makers who will shape the the legal regime for this new and promising communications technology.

---

[90] *See, e.g.*, *id.* (predicting "an information anarchy where current copyright law and policy is, to put it politely, ineffectual and outdated").

[91] The position is typified by the views of Mitchell Kapor, president of the Electronic Frontier Foundation, Inc., and Jerry Berman, director of the American Civil Liberties Union Information Technology Project, who argue for "open network architecture," and stress that

> [w]e know from past demand on the Internet and commercial personal computer networks that the network will be used for electronic assembly—virtual town halls, village greens, and coffee houses, again taking place not just through shared text (as in today's computer networks), but through multimedia transmissions, including images, voice and video. Unlike the telephone, this network will also be a publications medium, distributing electronic newsletters, video clips and interpreted reports.

Mitchell Kapor & Jerry Berman, Building The Open Road: The NREN as a Test-Bed for the National Public Network (1991) (on file with the Electronic Frontier Foundation, Inc.).

[92] *See, e.g.*, John R. Garrett, *Text to Screen Revisited: Copyright in the Electronic Age*, ONLINE, Apr. 1991, at 22 (describing activities of the Copyright Clearance Center in clearing rights for the distribution of copyrighted texts by electronic means).

AUTHOR/IZING THE CELEBRITY: PUBLICITY RIGHTS, POSTMODERN POLITICS, AND UNAUTHORIZED GENDERS

ROSEMARY J. COOMBE*

Who authors the celebrity? Where does identity receive its authorization? I shall argue that the law constructs and maintains fixed, stable identities authorized by the celebrity subject. In so doing, however, the law also produces the possibility of the celebrity signifier's polysemy. The celebrity image[1] is a cultural lode of multiple meanings, mined for its symbolic resonances and, simultaneously, a floating signifier, invested with libidinal energies, social longings, and political aspirations.

Focusing upon cultural practices that engage, reproduce, ironize and transform the meaning and value of celebrity personas to assert alternative gender identities, I shall argue that the celebrity is authored in a multiplicity of sites of discursive practice, and that in the process, unauthorized identities are produced, both for the celebrity and for her diverse authors. Through its prohibitions, the law produces the means by which unauthorized identities are both engendered and endangered.

I will very briefly summarize the legal doctrine of personality rights[2] and argue that the rationales traditionally offered for recognizing and protecting rights to the celebrity persona cannot be supported and do not justify the extent of the protections legally afforded celebrities, their estates, or their assignees. The social

---

* Assistant Professor of Law, University of Toronto. B.A., 1981, LL.B., 1984, University of Western Ontario; J.S.M., 1988, J.S.D., 1992, Stanford University. This paper was presented at the Society for Critical Exchange Conference, "Intellectual Property and the Construction of Authorship," April 19-21, 1991, as one of the Loewenstein Lectures on Law, Power, and Representation, at Amherst College, April 22, 1991 and at the Culture and Consumption Lecture Series sponsored by the Humanities Doctoral Programme at Concordia University, October 1, 1991. The author would like to thank Peter Jaszi, Martha Woodmansee, Austin Sarat and David Howes for enabling the critical participation of diverse audiences in the authorship of this paper.

[1] I will use the term "celebrity image" to designate not only the celebrity's visual likeness, but rather, all elements of the complex constellation of visual, verbal, and aural signs that circulate in society and constitute the celebrity's recognition value. The term "persona" will also refer to this configuration of significations. I will also use the terms "celebrity" and "star" interchangeably.

[2] I use the umbrella term, "personality rights," to encompass the tort of appropriation of personality as it has developed at common law, the proprietary right of publicity that has developed in American law, and rights to prevent the appropriation of, *inter alia*, names and likenesses that have been enacted in provincial and state statutes as well as federal trademark legislation.

and cultural value of the celebrity image will then be situated in the larger historical context of late capitalism and the related cultural conditions of postmodernism.

Popular cultural practices that engage celebrity images in innovative fashions will then be explored to demonstrate the vibrant role played by these cultural icons in the self-authorings of subaltern social groups. Gay male appropriations of female stars in camp subculture, lesbian reworkings of James Dean, and middle class women's use of the *Star Trek* characters in the creation of fan magazines (fanzines) are practices that rewrite media imagery in subversive but politically expressive fashions. Investing celebrity personas with new and often oppositional meanings, these subordinate groups assert unauthorized gender identities. They thereby affirm both community solidarity and the legitimacy of their social difference by empowering themselves with cultural resources that the law deems the properties of others.

Liberal notions of freedom of expression fail to grasp the nature of contemporary cultural politics of postmodernism, I suggest, because they are held hostage by the philosophical conceits of the Enlightenment. In conclusion, I propose that we situate these practices in an enlarged vision of contemporary democracy that recognizes—as political practice—dialogic cultural activities of articulating the social world and authoring politically salient forms of difference. In this context, we can begin to consider the political costs of granting the celebrity exclusive rights to authorize her (own) image.

I. The Legal Protection of the Celebrity Persona

Anglo-American legal jurisdictions recognize the right of individuals to protect publicly identifiable attributes from unauthorized and unremunerated appropriation by others for commercial purposes or economic benefit.[3] Originally developed primarily to deal with an unauthorized use of a person's name or picture in advertising that suggested the individual's en-

[3] In Canada and Britain this right developed at common law into a distinct cause of action known as the tort of appropriation of personality. In the United States, the right of publicity arose as a category of the right of privacy which protects the individual against misappropriations of her name or likeness, and is recognized as a common law tort. Various states have also incorporated these rights in privacy statutes and state constitutional provisions. The literature detailing the origins and developing scope of these rights is so voluminous that a 256 page bibliography of relevant American literature was published in 1987. *See* Lisa Lawrence, *The Right of Publicity: A Research Guide*, 10 Hastings Comm. & Ent. L.J. 143 (1987). Today the literature is even more extensive, and I make no effort to summarize all the nuances of the field here.

dorsement of a product, the right of publicity has been greatly expanded in the twentieth century. It is no longer limited to the name or likeness of an individual, but now extends to a person's nickname, signature, physical pose, characterizations, singing style, vocal characteristics, body parts, frequently used phrases, car, performance style, mannerisms, and gestures, provided that these are distinctive and publicly identified with the person claiming the right. Although most cases still involve the unauthorized advertising of commodities, rights of publicity have been evoked to prohibit the distribution of memorial posters, novelty souvenirs, magazine parodies, and the presentation of nostalgic musical reviews, television docudramas, and satirical theatrical performances. Increasingly it seems that any publicly recognizable characteristic will be legally recognized as having a commercial value that is likely to be diminished by its unauthorized or unremunerated appropriation by others.

The right is recognized as proprietary in nature and may therefore be assigned, and the various components of an individual's persona may be independently licensed. A celebrity could, theoretically at least, license her signature for use on fashion scarves, grant exclusive rights to reproduce her face to a perfume manufacturer, her voice to a charitable organization, her legs to a pantyhose company, particular publicity stills for distribution as posters or postcards, and continue to market her services as a singer, actor, and composer. The human persona is capable of almost infinite commodification, because exclusive, non-exclusive, and temporally, spatially, and functionally limited licenses may be granted for the use of any aspect of the celebrity's public presence. Furthermore, the right of publicity has been extended beyond the celebrity, her licensees, and assignees, to protect the celebrity's descendants and their assignees and licensees.[4]

---

[4] American courts are divided on the issue of whether a right of publicity survives the individual's death and in what circumstances. Some courts have refused recovery for the relatives or assignees of a decedent where the name or likeness has been appropriated for commercial purposes on the grounds that an individual's personal right of privacy does not survive his death. Others have allowed recovery for invasion of privacy in similar circumstances. Decisions predicated upon rights of publicity range from those that hold that the right survives death in all circumstances, those that require the celebrity to have engaged in some form of commercial exploitation during her life before the right will be descendible, and those which unconditionally oppose descendibility in any circumstances. The tendency, however, has been towards greater recognition of the descendibility of publicity rights, and state legislatures have also inclined towards statutory recognition of the descendibility of such rights. The issue has yet to be determined or even seriously addressed in Canadian or British courts because the right is still considered a personal rather than a proprietary one.

II. The Value of the Celebrity Image

It is impossible to deny the potential value of the celebrity persona in an age of mass production and communications technologies. The aura of the celebrity is a potent force in an era in which standardization, rationalization and the controlled programming of production characterize the creation and distribution of goods and the capacity of mass media communications to convey imagery and information across vast distances is harnessed to ensure consumer demand. As mass market products become functionally indistinguishable, manufacturers must increasingly sell them by symbolically associating them with the aura of the celebrity—which may be the quickest way to establish a share of the market. It is suggested that fame has become the most valuable (and also the most perishable) of commodities and that celebrity will be the greatest growth industry in the nineties.[5] "With its alchemical power to turn the least promising of raw material[s] into alluring and desirable artefacts" such as designer jeans, sunglasses, deodorants, architect's tea kettles, and coffee mugs, "[f]ame's economic applications are limitless."[6] The value that a famous name adds to a product may be astronomical; London outworkers knit pullovers for £6—with a Ralph Lauren tag they sell for $245 in New York—but Lauren does have a $17 million annual advertising budget to cover.[7]

Celebrities, then, have an interest in policing the use of their personas to insure that they do not become tainted with associations that would prematurely tarnish the patina they might license to diverse enterprises. This potential commercial value is generally offered as reason in itself to protect the star's control over his identity through the allocation of exclusive property rights; because such interests have market value, they deserve protection. Others, like myself, see this as "a massive exercise in question-begging."[8] Market values arise only after property rights have been established and enforced; the decision to allocate particular property rights is a prior question of social policy that requires philosophical and moral deliberations[9] and a consideration of social costs and benefits.

---

5 Deyan Sudjic, Cult Heroes: How to be Famous for More than Fifteen Minutes (1989).

6 *Id.* at 19.

7 *Id.* at 83.

8 David Lange, *Recognizing the Public Domain*, 44 Law & Contemp. Probs. 147, 156 (1981).

9 See Margaret Radin, *Market Inalienability*, 100 Harv. L. Rev. 1859 (1987) and Elizabeth S. Anderson, *Is Women's Labor a Commodity?* 19 Phil. & Pub. Aff. 71 (1990) for

In determining whether to grant a property right in a celebrity's persona, we might consider traditional liberal justifications in support of private property. The idea that people are entitled to the fruits of their own labor, and that property rights in one's body and its labor entail property rights in the products of that labor, derives from John Locke[10] and is persuasive as a point of departure. It does not, however, advance the argument in favor of exclusive property rights very far. As Edwin Hettinger remarks, "assuming that labor's fruits are valuable, and that laboring gives the laborer a property right in this value, this would entitle the laborer only to the value she added, and not to the *total* value of the resulting product."[11]

Publicity rights are justified on the basis of the celebrity's authorship—her investment of time, effort, skill, and money in the development of the image. Such claims, however rhetorically persuasive, are rarely supported by any empirical data. How much of a star's celebrity and its value is due to the individual's own efforts and investments? Clearly, individual labor is necessary if the persona is to have value and we could not appreciate stars without their expenditure of effort. However, as Hettinger argues, "it does not follow from this that all of their value is attributable to that labor."[12]

Star images must be made, and, like other cultural products, their creation occurs in social contexts and draws upon other resources, institutions, and technologies. Star images are authored by studios, the mass media, public relations agencies, fan clubs, gossip columnists, photographers, hairdressers, body-building coaches, athletic trainers, teachers, screenwriters, ghostwriters, directors, lawyers, and doctors. Even if we only consider the production and dissemination of the star image, and see its value as solely the result of human labor, this value cannot be entirely attributed to the efforts of a single author.

Moreover, as Richard Dyer shows, the star image is authored by its consumers as well as its producers; the audience makes the celebrity image the unique phenomenon that it is.[13] Selecting from the complexities of the images and texts they encounter,

---

philosophical discussions of the factors we need to weigh in determining if commodification is an appropriate mode of valuation.

[10] JOHN LOCKE, SECOND TREATISE OF CIVIL GOVERNMENT, ch. 5 (Wm. B. Eerdmans Publishing Co. 1978) (1690).

[11] Edwin Hettinger, *Justifying Intellectual Property*, 18 PHIL. & PUB. AFF. 37 (1989).

[12] *Id.*

[13] *See* RICHARD DYER, HEAVENLY BODIES: FILM STARS AND SOCIETY (1986); RICHARD DYER, STARS (1979).

they produce new values for the celebrity and find in stars sources of significance that speak to their own experience. These new meanings of the star's image are freely mined by media producers to further enhance its market value. As Marilyn Monroe said in her last recorded words in public, "I want to say that the people—if I am a star—the people made me a star, no studio, no person, but the people did."[14]

The star image is authored by multitudes of persons engaged in diverse activities. Moreover, stars and their fame are never manufactured from whole cloth—the successful image is frequently a form of cultural *bricolage* that improvises with a social history of symbolic forms. Consider the Marx Brothers. Clearly their characterizations involved creative activity, but, as David Lange points out,

> what we cannot know in fact . . . is how much the characters created by the Marx Brothers owe to the work of tens, scores, perhaps hundreds of other vaudeville and burlesque performers with whom they came into contact . . . . What we do not know, in short, is how much of these characters the Marx Brothers themselves appropriated from others. All that is certain is that they created themselves, individually and collectively, as a kind of living derivative work. That much Groucho himself has told us . . . . To be sure, the Marx Brothers became celebrities as most vaudevillians did not. But surely we are not rewarding them on that ground alone.[15]

Publicity rights enable stars to "establish dynasties on the memory of fame."[16] In *Groucho Marx Productions, Inc. v. Day and Night Co.*,[17] those who held rights in the Marx Brothers made a successful publicity rights claim against the creators of the play *A Day in Hollywood, A Night in the Ukraine*. The play's authors intended to satirize the excesses of Hollywood in the thirties and invoked the Marx Brothers as characters playfully imagined interpreting a Chekhov drama. The defendants were found liable, and their First Amendment claim was dismissed on the ground that the play was an imitative work.

The Marx Brothers themselves might be seen as imitative or derivative works, whose creation and success as icons in popular culture derive from their own creative reworkings of the signifying repertoire of the vaudeville community. Contemporary stars

---

14 Dean MacCannell, *Marilyn Monroe Was Not a Man*, 17 DIACRITICS 114, 115 (1987).
15 Lange, *supra* note 8, at 161-62.
16 *Id.* at 162.
17 523 F. Supp. 485 (S.D.N.Y. 1981), *rev'd*, 689 F.2d 317 (2d Cir. 1982).

are authored in a similar fashion. How much does Elvis Costello owe to Buddy Holly, Prince to Jimi Hendrix, or Michael Jackson to Diana Ross? Take the image of Madonna, an icon whose meaning and value lie partially in its evocation and ironic reconfiguration of several twentieth-century sex-goddesses and ice-queens (Marilyn Monroe obviously, but also Jean Harlow, Greta Garbo, and Marlene Dietrich) that speaks with multiple tongues to diverse audiences. Descriptions of the Madonna image as semiotic montage abound,[18] but this extract from the *Village Voice* is my favorite:

> What Madonna served up in the name of sexuality was not liberation as I'd known it, but a strange brew of fetishism and femininism. Only later would I understand that the source of her power is precisely this ambiguity. It's a mistake to think of any pop icon as an individual . . . . Madonna is a cluster of signs, and what they add up to is precisely the state of sex in the culture now: torn between need and rage and unable to express one without the other.
>
> . . . .
>
> Madonna raids the image bank of American femininity, melding every fantasy ever thrown onto the silver screen and implanting them in the body and voice of every-babe.[19]

In an era characterized by nostalgia for the golden age of the silver screen and an aging baby boom generation's fascination with the television culture of its youth, successful images are often those which mine media history for evocative signifiers from our past. This is not to deny that such appropriations are creative endeavours; it is to stress emphatically that they are and to assert that such authorial processes ought not to be frozen, limited, or circumscribed by the whims of celebrities or the commercial caprice of their assignees.

If the Madonna image appropriates the likenesses of earlier screen goddesses, religious symbolism, feminist rhetoric, and sadomasochistic fantasy to speak to contemporary sexual aspira-

---

[18] For one example, see Teresa Podlesney, *Blondes*, *in* THE HYSTERICAL MALE: NEW FEMINIST THEORY 82 (Arthur & Marilouise Kroker eds., 1991), where the author argues that "the blonde" is the perfect post-WWII product and the ultimate sign of U.S. global supremacy, white patriarchy and the triumph of American mass media and mass production. Madonna, she suggests, is the "blondest blonde ever . . . with forty years of the blonde phenomenon informing her every move." As Podlesney also notes, Madonna has frequently been "heralded for (mis)(re)appropriating the iconography of the blonde bombshell in a cynical defiance of the rules of sexuality codified by patriarchy." *Id.* at 84.

[19] Richard Goldstein, *We So Horny: Sado Studs and Super Sluts: America's New Sex'Tude*, VILLAGE VOICE, Oct. 16, 1990, at 36.

tions and anxieties, then the value of the image derives as much, perhaps, from the collective cultural heritage on which she draws as from her individual efforts. But if we grant Madonna exclusive property rights in her image, we simultaneously make it difficult for others to appropriate those same resources for new ends, and we freeze the Madonna constellation itself. Future artists, writers, and performers will be unable to draw creatively upon the cultural and historical significance of the Madonna montage without seeking the consent of the celebrity, her estate, or its assigns, who may well deny such consent or demand exorbitant royalties. As Lange argues, the proliferation of successful publicity rights claims occurs at the expense of our rights to the public domain.[20] Consequentially, access to the public domain is choked, or closed off, and the public "loses the rich heritage of its culture, the rich presence of new works derived from that culture, and the rich promise of works to come."[21]

Some celebrity images seem significant to the North American social imagination that they might be said to constitute parts of a collective cultural heritage. Such images should not be subject to control by the parochial interests of celebrity's estates. Elvis Presley provides an apt example. In the recent film *Mystery Train*, director and producer Jim Jarmusch explores the cultural and psychological significance of Presley in the depressed economy of Memphis, Tennessee and in the consciousness of those who live on its social margins. The film also addresses his charisma for those in other countries whose fascination with American media images manifests itself in pilgrimages that have turned Memphis into a late twentieth-century mecca. The possibility that Elvis Presley's estate might seek to prohibit the production and/or distribution of a film such as this,[22] while simultaneously arranging to market cologne designed "for all the King's men,"[23]

---

20 Lange, *supra* note 8, at 163.

21 *Id.* at 165.

22 I have no idea whether Jarmusch sought the consent of the Presley estate or the corporate owners of his publicity rights and, if so, what royalties he agreed to pay. Nor do I know whether the Presley estate ever sought to enjoin the film's production or to demand royalties. The very possibility of such an injunction and its desirability is what is at issue here. Celebrities or their estates are not obliged to grant licenses for the use of their image regardless of the artistic or social merit of the work in which they are employed, and may withhold consent on any pretext. In this hypothetical scenario, *Mystery Train* might be privileged under the First Amendment, but then again, it might not. For a discussion of some of the problems with the concept of freedom of speech in the postmodern era, see *infra* at Part V. See also my extended discussion in *Publicity Rights and Political Aspiration: Mass Culture, Gender Identity, and Democracy* 26 NEW ENG. L. REV. (forthcoming 1992) [hereinafter *Publicity Rights*].

23 A party launching the Elvis Presley cologne was held at the New York club Hot

indicates the parameters of the problem. The opportunity for the celebrity's assignees to behave this way has, in fact, been seized. When the City of Memphis decided to erect a bronze statue to memorialize Elvis as part of a city redevelopment scheme, a nonprofit city corporation offered pewter replicas of the King in return for donations to finance the monument. Owners of rights to commercially exploit the Presley likeness were quick to seek and obtain an injunction.[24]

A Lockean labor theory justifying property rights in the celebrity image is inadequate to establish a right to receive the full market value of the star persona or to support exclusive rights to control its circulation and reproduction in society. Liberal values protecting individual freedom guarantee the possession and use only of the product of one's personal labors and only insofar as the exercise of this right does not harm the rights of others. Enabling celebrities and their estates and assigns to exercise absolute rights to authorize the circulation of the celebrity image may have adverse consequences, both for the preservation of our collective cultural heritage and for our future cultural development.

The social value and cultural meaning of the celebrity image has its genesis in the same historical conditions that created the possibility of its economic value. In his illuminating essay "The Work of Art in the Age of Mechanical Reproduction," Walter Benjamin suggests that technologies of mechanical reproduction and systems of mass production changed modes of human perception and evaluation, fundamentally altering our aesthetic responses. These changes, I argue, are integrally related to the cultural value of the celebrity image in contemporary social life.

To reiterate Benjamin's central argument—the work of art traditionally had a tangible individuated presence in time and space, a singular history, and a situation in a cultural tradition. This notion of the original, necessary to the idea of authenticity and to the work's authority, increasingly becomes irrelevant in an age of technical reproduction. Mass reproduction creates copies that possess an independence from the original; they can tran-

---

Rod in early October 1990. Michael Musto, *La Dolce Musto*, VILLAGE VOICE, Oct. 26, 1990, at 44.

[24] Memphis Dev. Found. v. Factors Etc., Inc., 441 F. Supp. 1323 (W.D. Tenn. 1977). Presley's relatives, however, are not necessarily realizing the profit or controlling the uses to which the image is put. Prior to his death, Presley had conveyed the exclusive right to exploit his name and likeness to a corporation controlled by Colonel Tom Parker, his manager, in exchange for royalties. Factors Etc., Inc. is an assignee corporation controlled by Parker who is presumably free to exploit the Presley image in any manner. Once exclusive rights to attributes of the persona are assigned, they may be utilized without regard for the sentiments and sensibilities of heirs.

scend the limitations of the original's physical tangibility and susceptibility to age and deterioration. As the art work's substantive duration ceases to matter, the art object loses its authority or its aura—"[the] unique phenomenon of a distance however close it may be."[25] The aura embodies the work's value by engaging the beholder's affective, reflexive relationship to the cultural tradition in which the work is situated. The artwork is unapproachable; both in its physically unique embodiment, and in its tangible history in a cultural tradition, it resists too intimate an appropriation by the beholder into his own physical and cultural lifeworlds.

The work of art's aura is lost in the age of mechanical reproduction because "the technique of reproduction detaches the reproduced object from the domain of tradition."[26] By substituting a plurality of copies for a unique existence, it enables the consumer to position the reproduction in his own lifeworld without any necessary awareness of an original or its historical situation. The photograph and the film represent the culmination of the destruction of the aura because they are designed for reproducibility. "From a photographic negative, for example, one can make any number of prints; to ask for the 'authentic' print makes no sense."[27] The criterion of authenticity ceases to be applicable to artistic reproduction. The uniqueness of a work of art was due to the work's situation in a traditional ritual context that defined its use value. Technologies of mass reproduction enabled copies to transcend the work's historical use value in social cults of ritual and become pure objects of exchange value or commodities.

Benjamin's reflections on the work of art and the decline of its aura may help us to understand the cultural significance of the celebrity image. Here I want to go beyond Benjamin's own disjointed observations of the screen actor as one who has his performance fragmented by the camera, is alienated from his audience, deprived of his corporeality, and dissolved into flickering images and disembodied sounds.[28] He sees the effect of film as engaging the whole living person but destroying its aura and replacing the actor's aura with an artificially produced "personal-

---

[25] Walter Benjamin, *The Work of Art in the Age of Mechanical Reproduction*, *in* ILLUMINATIONS 243 n.5 (Hannah Arendt ed. & Harry Zohn trans., 1968).

[26] *Id.* at 221.

[27] *Id.* at 224.

[28] *Id.* at 228-29.

ity" that is only the "phony spell of [the] commodity."[29] Benjamin alludes to the possibility of another, alternative understanding of the celebrity with his reference to "the cult of the movie star"[30]—one that suggests that celebrities may represent residual vestiges of the "auratic" in contemporary mass culture.

If the work of art's aura derives from its unique, embodied or tangible presence in time and space, an individual history, and a situation in a cultural tradition, then it is difficult to deny the aura of the celebrity. However often a celebrity's likeness is reproduced, there remains a social knowledge of the celebrity as an individual human being with an unapproachable or distant existence elsewhere, a life history, and a mortal susceptibility to the processes of heartache, illness, aging, and ultimately, death. It is difficult to envisage Elvis Presley without conjuring up images of health, vibrancy, and sexual energy followed by injury, gluttony, corpulence, and decay. Arguably, the celebrity evokes the fascination she does because however endlessly her image is reproduced, her substantive duration, that is, her life, never becomes wholly irrelevant. She never loses her autonomy from the objects that circulate in her likeness.

Moreover, the star is historically situated and lives her life in historical and social conditions that give her image its meaning, resonance, and authority. The celebrity image's value might also be seen to reside in its character as a particular human embodiment of a connection to a social history that provokes its beholder to reflect upon her own relationship to the cultural tradition in which the star's popularity is embedded. We all consider celebrities from different social positions. As a feminist and social democrat, for example, I cannot perceive Marilyn Monroe without reflecting upon my own troubled relationship to male definitions of female sexuality, the femininity of sexual innocence, the Playboy tradition, the Cold War and Monroe's own left wing politics.[31] Celebrity images, I would contend, always maintain their aura because they bind subjects in affective and

---

29 *Id.* at 231.

30 *Id.*

31 See Graham McCann, Marilyn Monroe (1988) for an extended elaboration of a male feminist's reflections on his relationship to the Monroe persona, and Dyer, *supra* note 13, for an insightful discussion of her position in newly emergent discourses of sexuality in the 1950s. Monroe's ongoing dynamic presence in contemporary sexual politics is addressed in MacCannell, *supra* note 14, a perceptive and scathing review of biographies written by Norman Mailer, Gloria Steinem, Anthony Summers, and Roger G. Taylor.

historically mediated relationships that preclude their appropriation as pure objects.[32]

Stewart Ewen sees the power of the celebrity image as rooted in photography's simultaneous affinity to reality and fantasy,[33] and as a cultural response to modern social experiences of alienation, and anomie. The celebrity is an icon of the significance of the personal and the individual in a world of standardization and conformity—embodying the possibility of upward mobility from the mass, "[c]elebrity forms a symbolic pathway, connecting each aspiring individual to a universal image of fulfillment: to be someone, when 'being no one' is the norm."[34]

The seductive power of celebrity auras and their ubiquity in contemporary social life make the celebrity persona a compelling and powerful set of signifiers in our cultural fields of representation. Simultaneously embodying the fantastic and the real, utopian ideals and quotidian practices, and the realization of popular aspirations for recognition and legitimacy, the celebrity form attracts the authorial energies of those for whom identity is a salient issue and community an ongoing dilemma.

III. "Doing Gender": The Celebrity Form and the Politics of Postmodernism

What meaning do particular celebrities have in people's own social experiences? It is necessary to make philosophical arguments about the cultural losses contingent upon the commodification of the celebrity image socially concrete. In so doing, the political dimensions of this foreclosure on the use of cultural resources comes into relief. Marginal social groups are continually engaged in nascent constructions of alternative identities. The celebrity image plays a central role in many of these cultural practices.

The practices I will examine are those of gay male camp subculture in the pre-liberation era, lesbian refashionings of pop icons, and, finally, middle class women's engagement in the reading, writing, and circulation of *Star Trek* fanzines. These practices involve the redeployment of celebrity images—an aspect of that rearticulation of commodified media texts that has been defined as the essence of popular culture.[35] Theorists of postmodernism

---

32 I am grateful to Kathleen Robertson for clarifying this point.

33 Stuart Ewen, All Consuming Images: The Politics of Style in Contemporary Culture 90 (1988).

34 *Id.* at 95-96.

35 Hal Foster, Recodings: Art, Spectacle, Cultural Politics (1985).

assert that contemporary cultural theory must come to terms with "the textual *thickness* and the visual *density* of everyday life . . ."[36] in societies characterized by pervasive media imagery and commodified forms of cultural representation. A central dimension of the study of postmodernism has therefore been a concern with the ways in which people "live and negotiate the everyday life of consumer capitalism"[37] and use mass culture in their quotidian practices. Cultural consumption is increasingly understood as an active use rather than a passive dependence upon dominant forms of signification. As Michel de Certeau and Paul Willis argue, consumption is always a form of production and people continually engage in cultural practices of *bricolage*—resignifying media meanings, consumer objects, and cultural texts in order to adapt them to their own interests and make them fulfill their own purposes.[38] These practices are central to the political practices of those in marginal or subordinated social groups who forge "subcultures" with resources foraged from the mediascape.[39]

Subcultural practices involve improvisational cultural appropriations that affirm emergent cultural identities for those in subordinate social groups.[40] Angela McRobbie argues that the frenzied expansion of mass media enables new alliances and solidarities across traditional spatial, racial, and cultural boundaries and resources for producing new meanings and new identities:

> Sontag's linking [of camp] with . . . gay men, is instructive because she shows how a relationship evolved around a social

---

36 Angela McRobbie, *Postmodernism and Popular Culture*, *in* POSTMODERNISM: ICA DOCUMENTS 165 (Lisa Appignanesi ed., 1989).

37 Andrew Ross, *Introduction* to UNIVERSAL ABANDON? THE POLITICS OF POSTMODERNISM at xv (1988). *See also* Rosemary J. Coombe, *Encountering the Postmodern: New Directions in Cultural Anthropology*, 28 CANADIAN REV. OF SOC. & ANTHROPOLOGY 188 (1991); Rosemary J. Coombe, *Beyond Modernity's Meanings: Engaging the Postmodern in Cultural Anthropology*, 11 CULTURE 111 (1991); Rosemary J. Coombe, *Postmodernity and the Rumor: Late Capitalism and the Fetishism of the Commodity/Sign*, *in* JEAN BAUDRILLARD: THE DISAPPEARANCE OF ART AND POLITICS (1991); LINDA HUTCHEON, THE POLITICS OF POSTMODERNISM (1989); PAUL WILLIS, COMMON CULTURE (1990).

38 Ross, *supra* note 37, at xv; MICHEL DE CERTEAU, THE PRACTICE OF EVERYDAY LIFE (1984).

39 The concept of the mediascape is borrowed from Arjun Appadurai, *Disjuncture and Difference in the Global Cultural Economy*, *in* GLOBAL CULTURE: NATIONALISM, GLOBALIZATION, AND MODERNITY 295 (Mike Featherstone ed., 1990). He asserts that we need to consider the complexity of the global flow of cultural imagery as producing new fields he defines as ethnoscapes, technoscapes, finanscapes, mediascapes, and ideascapes.

40 STEVEN CONNOR, POSTMODERNIST CULTURE: AN INTRODUCTION TO THEORIES OF THE CONTEMPORARY 186 (1989). Dick Hebdige, for example, describes the manner in which music styles like rap and hip hop deploy existing cultural forms using principles of parody, pastiche, and irony to articulate and negotiate mixed, plural, or transitional identities for social groups at the margins of national or dominant cultures. *See* DICK HEBDIGE, CUT 'N' MIX: CULTURE, IDENTITY, AND CARIBBEAN MUSIC (1987).

> minority making a bid for a cultural form in which they felt they could stake some of their fragmented and sexually deviant identity. The insistence, on the way, on both style and pleasure made the product attractive to those outside as well as inside . . . she is describing how forms can be taken over, and re-assembled . . . [which] often means outstripping their ostensible meaning. . . . And if media forms are so inescapable . . . then there is no reason to assume that consumption of pastiche, parody or high camp is, by definition, without subversive or critical potential. Glamour, glitter, and gloss, should not so easily be relegated to the sphere of the insistently apolitical.[41]

Mass media imagery provides people who share similar social experiences with the opportunity to express their similarity by imbuing with emotional energy a range of cultural referents to which media communications have afforded them shared access. It also enables them to author/ize their difference by improvising with those images to make them relevant to their social experiences and aspirations.

If the celebrity is an image that is both fantastic and real, embodying the realization of widespread aspirations for public affirmation, it is especially likely to attract the authorial energies of those in marginal groups for whom recognition, legitimacy, and positively evaluated identity are compelling issues. Although the "recoding" of celebrity images is in no way limited to a concern with gender identity, I will focus upon practices which question traditional formulations of gender and express desires to construct alternatives.

The concept of alternative gender identities is borrowed from Judith Butler's ovarian work, *Gender Trouble*, in which she suggests that a feminist politics requires an inquiry into the political construction and regulation of gendered identities, a radical critique of the limitations of existing categories of identity, and an exploration of practices in which alternatively gendered worlds are imagined. The practices I will be exploring are active performances of gender "that disrupt the categories of the body, sex, gender, and sexuality and occasion their subversive resignification and proliferation beyond the binary frame."[42]

Feminist theory recognizes a distinction between sex and gender, asserting "that whatever biological intractability sex ap-

---

[41] McRobbie, *supra* note 36, at 174-75.

[42] Judith P. Butler, Gender Trouble: Feminism and the Subversion of Identity at xii (1990).

pears to have, gender is culturally constructed."[43] As Butler suggests, the inevitability or objective facticity of the relationship between sex, gender, desire, and sexual practice is potentially contested by the idea of gender as an undetermined interpretation of sex. The recognition of gender as a cultural construct enables the possibility of a multiplicity of genders, and also raises the question of whether sex itself may not be produced through the limitations that restrict the performance of gender to a binary economy. Regimes of power institute, maintain, and try to stabilize naturalistic and causal relations of coherence among and between sex, gender, sexual desire, and sexual practice, but such correspondences are neither "natural" nor inevitable.[44] Other identities that express discontinuous relations between biological sex, cultural gender, and the "expression" or "effect" of these in sexual desire and practice are persistent and provide critical opportunities for contesting the dominant sexual economy.[45]

Identity is always a practice of articulation from within existing cultural forms; gender is performative, a doing and constituting of the identity it is purported to be. These performances are always constructed within the terms of discourse and power, and thus engage heterosexual cultural conventions.[46] Butler is interested in modes of "doing" gender that evoke, but do not constitute, simple reproductions of the terms of power that subvert the very constructs they mobilize, "displacing those naturalized and reified notions of gender that support masculine hegemony and heterosexist power."[47] For example, "numerous lesbian and gay discourses . . .[position themselves in] resignificatory relationships to heterosexual cultural configurations."[48] This repetition of heterosexual cultural forms may be the site of their denaturalization, bringing "into relief the utterly constructed status of the so-called heterosexual original."[49]

Celebrity images provide important cultural resources for many practices of "doing" gender that subvert and reconstruct

---

[43] *Id.* at 6.

[44] *Id.* at 17.

[45] *Id.* at 17-23.

[46] *Id.* at 25-30. Butler's position here is congruent with my stance in Rosemary J. Coombe, *Room for Manoeuver: Toward a Theory of Practice in Critical Legal Studies*, 14 LAW & SOC. INQUIRY 69 (1989), where I argue that subjectivity is always constructed within the discursive forms of prevailing structures of power, through the creative process of *bricolage*—cultural practices that deploy existing cultural forms in ever emergent new fashions that may transform structures of power even as they evoke its significations.

[47] BUTLER, *supra* note 42, at 33-34.

[48] *Id.* at 121.

[49] *Id.* at 31.

dominant forms of gender identity. The denaturalization of heterosexual cultural forms is readily apparent in gay camp subculture, a phenomenon I have already alluded to as involving an engagement with media-disseminated celebrity images. Andrew Ross argues that gay camp has had a significant influence on changing social definitions of masculinity and femininity from the late fifties, working "to destabilize, reshape and transform the existing balance of accepted sexual roles and sexual identities."[50] Whatever its ultimate cultural effects, however, its origins must be understood in the context of gay urban life in the pre-liberation period. In the 1950s and 1960s a sophisticated gay male subculture evolved around a fascination with classical Hollywood film stars like Judy Garland, Bette Davis, Mae West, Greta Garbo, and Marlene Dietrich. In an age when their ability to be open about the fact that they were gay was circumscribed, gay men's use of certain star images constituted a kind of "going public" or "coming out." Camp contained a kind of commentary on the ongoing feat "of *survival* in a world dominated by the tastes, interests, and definitions of others."[51]

This is explicated by Esther Newton, whose ethnographic study of drag queens and urban camp subculture in the late 1960s indicates that camp humor grew out of the incongruities of living gay and male in a patriarchal and heterosexist society during a period when the stigma of being gay was largely accepted and internalized rather than rejected as illegitimate.[52] Drag queens were homosexual men performing the social character of "women" (that is, the signs and symbols of a socially defined American category) by artificially creating the image of glamorous women. Drag performs a subtle social critique:

> The effect of the drag system is to wrench the sex roles loose from that which supposedly determines them, that is, genital sex. Gay people know that sex-typed behavior can be achieved, contrary to what is popularly believed. They know that the possession of one type of genital equipment by no means guarantees the "naturally appropriate" behavior.
>
> . . . .
>
> [One of the] symbolic statement[s] of drag questions the "naturalness" of the sex-role system *in toto*; if sex-role behavior can be achieved by the "wrong" sex, it logically follows that it is in reality also achieved, not inherited, by the "right"

---

50 Andrew Ross, No Respect: Intellectuals and Popular Culture 159 (1989).

51 *Id.* at 144.

52 Esther Newton, Mother Camp: Female Impersonators in America 3 (1979).

> sex. . . . [It] says that sex-role behavior is an appearance [or performance].[53]

The most popular stars in the camp pantheon, subject of most frequent impersonation, were "glamorous" in highly mannered ways that indicated an awareness of the artifice in which they were engaged. This celebration of the personas of those who subtly mocked the corny flamboyance of femaleness "defetishize[d] the erotic scenario of woman-as-spectacle."[54] Thus, they explored the relation between artifice and nature in the construction of sexuality and gender long before these issues were recognized as part of the political agenda.

Camp lost its appeal with the arrival of a militant gay politics that asserted the "natural" quality of homosexuality, revived "masculine" styles, and sought to undermine the "effeminacy" of the stereotypical gay image. The finale of Michel Tremblay's acclaimed 1974 play *Hosanna*[55] well illustrates the new attitude towards camp. Hosanna, an aging drag queen who identifies with, and projects her identity upon, Elizabeth Taylor, is humiliated and forced to renounce her attachment to the star, and disarm herself of her Taylor impersonation. Stripped naked, he declares, "I'm a man," and (at long last, it is implied), allows his lover to embrace his "true" "masculine" self. Camp has, however, enjoyed something of a resurgence in the 1980's, confluent, perhaps, with the influence of Foucault, poststructuralism, and a revival of the credibility of the notion of the socially constructed subject.

Lesbian engagement with celebrity images is a less documented and more recent phenomenon. One lesbian challenge to the "truth" of sex, gender, and desire and the restrictions of a binary sexual economy is given voice and celebrated by Sue Golding in her discussion of a performative gender identity she calls lesbian hermaphrodism. This "erotic sensibility,"[56] worn, felt, and enacted by a number of lesbians, is a "fictionalized sexuality"[57] that finds its performative significations in mass media icons which it replicates in ironic, playful, and assertive reconfigurations:

---

53 *Id.* at 103.

54 Ross, *supra* note 50, at 159.

55 Michel Tremblay, Hosanna (John Van Burek & Bill Glassco trans., Vancouver 1974).

56 Sue Golding, *James Dean: The Almost Perfect Lesbian Hermaphrodite*, *in* Sight Specific: Lesbians and Representation 49 (Dionne Brand ed., 1988).

57 *Id.* at 50.

> I know you've seen the type: no tits, no cock, oozing with a kind of vulnerable "masculinity," sheathed in a 50s style black-leather motorcycle jacket. Or to put it slightly differently, it's James Dean, with a clit . . . . What emerges is the 'virile girl', the butch baby, full of attitude but not of scorn, lots of street smarts and a bit of muscle. This new hermaphrodite embodies forever the image of the destructive adolescent dramatically and in one being, teeming with a creative, raw energy, and beckoning with the possibility of a new era. But she's public . . . [not] simply "out of the closet". . . . [S]he is the orphan of a people's imaginary . . .[including] that kind of feminism which knew above all that sexual difference was ever only a political and not biological category. She is public in the most profound sense of the term: a composite copy of a mass invention, a replica of our own societal icons which are themselves never anything other than a public fiction. She is James Dean over and over again: James Dean with his arrogant hair, James Dean with his tight black denims, James Dean with the bitter brat look, James Dean with the morbid leather boots, James Dean against the whole boring suburban middle class.[58]

As Golding makes clear, this is an erotic sensibility or sexual identity that rejects the truth of anatomical sex and goes well beyond the idea of gender as a cultural construction built upon a prediscursive or naturally sexed body that provides a politically neutral surface for multiple significations. Demonstrating that gender identity (construed as a causal or natural relationship among sex, gender, sexual practice, and desire) is the effect of a regime of power, this gender rebel without a cause also rejects those prior forms of "gender trouble" that accepted and worked within the terms of the natural sex/cultural gender dichotomy. This hermaphrodism bears no relation to biological chromosome content, nor is it a '60s "androgyny" that built a sexual aesthetic around an "absence" of the sexual organs, or a '70s sexual aesthetic that ironized the ways in which society enforces gender specific clothing.[59] Rather, this gender rebel performs with her body an erotic identity that is an embodied performative—"the defiant aesthetic of the erotic masculine shot through with the voluptuousness of the female sexual organs."[60]

An "erotic mutant," "a fractured playfulness of social icons (like the Dean image, although Elvis Presley offers other pos-

---

58 *Id.* at 52.

59 *Id.*

60 *Id.*

sibilities) copied over and over,"[61] by the lesbian hermaphrodite exemplifies the sex/gender/desire/practice matrix as a performatively enacted signification that parodies, proliferates, and subverts gendered meanings. "Doing gender," however, is not the exclusive preserve of gays and lesbians, however more likely the social conditions of their existence are to incline them to contest hegemonic norms of gender identity. This is illustrated by the authorial activities of *Star Trek* fanziners, who construct communities and articulate new gender identities by literally re-writing their favorite television series characters.

Star Trek fans constitute a social and cultural network that is international in scope. Within this community, there are distinct groups of fans that organize around the production, circulation, and consumption of fanzines.[62] This subculture is explored with great sensitivity by Camille Bacon-Smith in her sparkling ethnography, *Enterprising Women*. The fanzine community is almost exclusively female and predominantly heterosexual. It involves middle class women who work as housewives and in nursing, teaching, clerical, and service occupations.[63] Fans exchange letters, distribute newsletters, create artwork, make videotapes, and produce and circulate fanzines that contain original fiction, poetry, and illustrations by women across North America, Britain, and Australia.[64] In 1988, it was estimated that there were 300 publications that enabled fans to explore aspects of television series; 120 of them centered on *Star Trek*,[65] a number which no doubt underestimates the production of fan literature because it does not include literature circulated only in photocopy circuits or more covertly circulated publications.[66]

---

61 *Id.*

62 For a discussion of the social and institutional structures of fan communities see, CAMILLE BACON-SMITH, ENTERPRISING WOMEN: TELEVISION, FOLKLORE, AND COMMUNITY at ch. 2 (1992).

63 *Id.*; Henry Jenkins, *Star Trek Rerun, Reread, Rewritten: Fan Writing as Textual Poaching*, 5 CRITICAL STUD. IN MASS COMM. 85 (1988); Constance Penley, To Boldly Go Where No Woman Has Gone Before: Feminism, Psychoanalysis, and Popular Culture, Public lecture delivered at the Public Access series "Capital/Culture," Toronto (Apr. 24, 1990) and at the conference, "Cultural Studies Now and in the Future" sponsored by the Unit for Criticism and Interpretive Theory, University of Illinois at Urbana-Champaign (Apr. 5-9, 1990).

64 Usually produced out of women's homes, fanzines are generally mimeographed or photocopied reproductions, but some have become more sophisticated with the introduction of computerized desktop publication technology; few issues are less than a hundred pages long.

65 Jenkins, *supra* note 63, at 89.

66 Penley, *supra* note 63, estimates that there are three to five hundred publishers of homoerotic fanzines alone (which would include those featuring characters from *Miami Vice, Simon and Simon, Starsky and Hutch*, as well as the *Star Trek* characters). These publications are sold at cost, relying upon subscriptions and often pre-payment to finance

In their creative endeavors, fanzine contributors employ images, themes, and characters from a canonized set of mass culture texts (the *Star Trek* television series episodes, films, and commercially produced novels), to explore their own subordinate status, voice frustration and anger with existing social conditions, envision and construct alternatives, share new understandings, and express utopian aspirations. In so doing, they force media texts to accommodate their interests, to become relevant to their needs, and thereby empower themselves with mass culture images. Issues of gender roles, sexuality, and the tension between family obligations and professional ambition are explored in the *Star Trek* future world—one which holds out the promise of opportunities for nontraditional female pleasures, active involvement in central decision making roles, and a state of sexual equality in which emotional needs and professional responsibilities are taken seriously by men and women alike.[67]

In most stories, women are engaged in rewriting the masculine gender rather than in imagining alternative feminine ones.[68] Many stories involve male friendships: and two significant genres of fanzine fiction are "Slash" (or homoerotic) and "Hurt-Comfort"[69] stories, both of which center on relationships between the male characters. In all of these stories, the links between anatomy, gender, desire, and sexual practice are sundered. In the male friendship stories, the male characters are alternatively engendered. Stripping them of a rationalist, ego-centered individualism, the fans imbue them with emotionality and empathy, knitting them into close family and community relationships as well as intimate caring friendships which nurture and support them in their adventures.[70]

In "Slash" fiction, women write erotic stories and draw illustrations depicting a love relationship between Kirk and Spock.[71] Fearing social ridicule, loss of employment, and possibly legal

---

production and distribution costs. BACON-SMITH, *supra* note 62, at 3; producers are motivated more by the desire to express identity and establish community than any monetary interest and often operate at a loss.

67 Jenkins, *supra* note 63, at 93-97.

68 It appears that stories focusing on women represent less than a quarter of the stories fanziners read, according to a 1990 survey reported in *Enterprising Women*. BACON-SMITH, *supra* note 62, at 157.

69 Hurt/Comfort stories are those in which one male character is hurt and suffers and the other comforts and nurses him. For a more in depth discussion of Hurt/Comfort stories, see BACON-SMITH, *supra* note 62, at Chapter 10.

70 *Id.* at 212-18.

71 Erotic fiction is also written about the characters in *Starsky and Hutch*, *Blake 7*, and *The Professionals*. For a longer discussion of Slash fiction writing, see Constance Penley, *Brownian Motion: Women, Tactics, and Technology?*, *in* TECHNOCULTURE 135 (1991) and

repercussions[72] fanzine writers often write such stories under pseudonyms. Much of this literature circulates only through complex subterranean photocopying networks in order to evade exposure outside of the group.[73] So well-hidden is the circuit that only the most experienced readers and writers have access to it. Bacon-Smith describes a number of tasks performed by the homoerotic romance and rejects the idea that the male characters are surrogate women—an idea popularized by Joanna Russ when she argued that because of the overriding importance of touch, to the slow thoroughness and sensitization of the whole body, the sexuality expressed is female.[74] Bacon-Smith, however, asserts that these women are writing consciously and deliberately about men, exploring who men are and reconstructing them into people with whom it might be more comfortable to share life, love, and sexual relationships. These women want to explore relationships between powerful equals while tearing "down the very institution of hierarchical power that constructs men as individuals"—reconstructing power itself as an integrated union of mutuality with full and open communication.[75]

In all of these stories the "male" characters are given a combination of gender traits—Kirk's "feminine" traits are matched to Spock's "masculine" ones and vice-versa. Each shares aspects of traditional gender roles. In this way, new genders are inscribed on "male" bodies, and new desires, experiences, feelings, and practices may therefore proliferate.[76] As well as being alternatively engendered, the male characters are freshly embodied; their bodies are inscribed with ranges of sensitivity, expanded zones of erogeneity and a heightened receptivity to tactile

Constance Penley, *Feminism, Psychoanalysis and the Study of Popular Culture, in* CULTURAL STUDIES (1991).

72 Constance Penley told me in conversation that Lucasfilm threatened legal action—most likely an injunction on copyright grounds—when they discovered that fanzine writers had depicted Luke Skywalker and Han Solo in an erotic relationship. BACON-SMITH, *supra* note 62, at 251 n. 6, also notes that the fandom has had an uneasy relationship with Lucasfilm but does not elaborate.

73 *Id.* at 314. Not all *Star Trek* fans share the same attitudes about this fiction. Some fans oppose these stories on religious or moral grounds, others find them "untrue" to the source or canon, some find them too explicit, and others worry about exposing the original actors to ridicule. *Id.* at 334-37.

74 *See* BACON-SMITH, *supra* note 62, at 371.

75 *Id.* at 379-81.

76 This would help to explain why fans do not necessarily see the sexual relationship between Kirk and Spock as a homosexual one. Penley, *supra* note 63. As some fans see it, there are forms of love that defy description; the sexual orientation of Kirk and Spock is irrelevant because their love is a matter of cosmic destiny. *Id.* For similar reasons, fans don't see even the most sexually graphic material as pornographic. BACON-SMITH, *supra* note 62, at 369. Such categories are simply inappropriate in these alternative universes.

pleasures and physical comfort. Their heroes' pain, decontextualized in the mass media, is re-united by fanzine writers with both physical and psychological suffering. The male characters then, are reconstructed as fully emotional and sentient beings. Arguably, the fanzine writers perform the most thorough practices of "doing gender" that have been examined. Constructing new connections between novel (male?) bodies, new (masculinities?), erotic desires, and sexual practices, they simultaneously situate these newly engendered creatures in personal and social relationships, empowering themselves and their community as they do so.

IV. Juridical Productions of Cultural Space(s)

Superficially, these subcultural practices seem distant, if not utterly divorced from the legal regime of personality rights, but they occupy a space intersected by a multiplicity of relations between law and cultural form. I am concerned here, not simply with law as a set of prohibitions, but with law as it is imbricated in the everyday life of cultural practice.[77] The risks these people run under legal regimes of prohibition are real ones—so are the ethical risks of writing about their practices. Bacon-Smith, Jenkins, and Penley have been very careful not to reveal details about, or examples of, particular fanzine writing, filming, and drawing practices or the identities of practitioners. I respect their circumspection and similarly will not, as a matter of ethical principle, delineate the precise ways in which fanzines or performers in gay and lesbian subcultures could be held to violate personality rights (as well as the copyright and trademark rights held by the commercial producers of the media products on which they draw). To do so would be to provide the legal resources with which to prosecute them, or with which they might be threatened with potential legal action.

Juridical powers, however, are productive as well as prohibitive; the law is generative of knowledges, spaces, categories, identities, and subjectivities.[78] The law of publicity rights, by

[77] For longer discussions of this approach to thinking about law, see Robert Gordon, *Critical Legal Histories*, 36 Stan. L. Rev. 57 (1984) and Coombe, *supra* note 46.

[78] In *History of Sexuality Volume I: An Introduction*, Michel Foucault argued that juridical regimes must be understood as productive rather than merely prohibitive—producing what they purport merely to represent. Michel Foucault, History of Sexuality Volume I: An Introduction (Robert Hurley trans., Vintage Books 1980)(1976). For a general discussion of the socially constitutive character of law, see Christine Harrington & Barbara Yngvesson, *Interpretive Social Research*, 15 Law & Soc. Inquiry 135 (1990). For a discussion of the juridical production of class and gender subjectivities in the transition

prohibiting reproductions of the celebrity image for another's advantage, promotes the mass circulation of celebrity signifiers by ensuring that they will have a market value. If the image were freely available for mass reproduction, there would, presumably, be less of an incentive to engage in the investments necessary to disseminate it through media channels. Ironically, then, the law creates the cultural spaces of postmodernism in which mass media images become available for signifying practices. It produces fixed, stable identities authored by the celebrity subject, but simultaneously creates the possibility of places of transgression in which the signifier's fixity and the celebrity's authority may be contested and resisted. Authorized and unauthorized identities are both, therefore, engendered in relation to this juridical regime. The law, however, lends its authority only to those meanings that the celebrity wishes to appropriate, attributing these to her own efforts, and implicitly denies that any cultural value is being produced elsewhere.

Power may produce resistance in the Foucauldian sense, but it does not determine the form or the content of the practices that transgress its strictures. Through its prohibitions, the law may produce the means by which unauthorized identities are both engendered and endangered, but these practices are not simply effects or consequences of juridical regimes. People's interests and inclinations to engage in the construction of alternative gender identities are shaped by multiple hegemonies. Performative enactments of erotic identity are unlikely to be univocal direct statements of opposition to any singular structure of power; more often they may engage multiple forms of cultural "resistance" to multiple instances of power. Through irony, mockery, parody, pastiche, and alternative modes of appreciation, activities of creative appropriation enable fans to comment indirectly on gender ideology, law, and the commodity form.

Such commentary is especially cogent in the fanzine context. Fans don't see *Star Trek* as something that can be reread, but as something that must be rewritten in order to make it more responsive to their needs and a better producer of personal and community meanings.[79] According to Henry Jenkins, fans expressly reject the idea that the *Star Trek* texts or the Kirk/Spock characters are a privileged form of exclusive property but at the

---

to industrial capitalism, see Rosemary J. Coombe, *Contesting the Self: Negotiating Subjectivities in Nineteenth Century Ontario Defamation Trials*, 11 STUD. L., POL. & SOC. 3 (1991).

[79] Jenkins, *supra* note 63, at 87.

same time they have developed a complex moral economy[80] in which they legitimize their unorthodox appropriation of the media texts, characters, and personas. Despite the potential for legal prosecution, they see themselves as loyalists, fulfilling the inherent promise and potential of the series—a potential unrealized or betrayed by those who "own" the intellectual property rights in it. Fans respect the original texts and regularly police each other for abuses of interpretive license, but they also see themselves as the legitimate guardians of these materials, which have too often been manhandled by the producers and their licensees for easy profits.[81] As one fan writes: "[W]e have made [Star Trek] uniquely our own, so we do have all the right in the world . . . to try to change it for the better when the gang at Paramount starts worshipping the almighty dollar, as they are wont to do."[82] Fan writers exercise an ethic of care with regard to the characters—a care they fear commercially motivated parties frequently do not share.[83]

Although fanziners, gay camps, and lesbian hermaphrodites are not engaged in practices in direct opposition to the law (however they may unintentionally violate it), the law of publicity rights informs their performative activities. The knowledge that the cultural icons with which they express themselves do not belong to them, however affectionately they are adopted, is constitutive of these practices. The relationship of fans to the commodification of the signifiers whose meanings they create may be one of admiration or antagonism, irony, parody, fear, or complicitous critique.[84] In any case, the law generates the space for a proliferation of politics as well as identities, and polities as

---

[80] The term is borrowed from E.P. Thompson, *The Moral Economy of the English Crowd in the Eighteenth Century*, PAST AND PRESENT, Feb. 1971, at 76.

[81] Jenkins, *supra* note 63, at 100.

[82] *Id.*

[83] In ENTERPRISING WOMEN, Bacon-Smith also illuminates the complexities of the attitudes fanwriters hold with regard to the legal status of the source product. On the one hand they are aware that the characters, plots, films, television episodes, videos, logos, and dialogues with which they work are the properties of others. On the other hand, they take quite seriously the philosophy of "IDIC" (Infinite Diversity in Infinite Combination), propagated by Gene Roddenberry, the originator of *Star Trek*. They respect the legal prohibition against profiting from their writing, tape-making, and artistic activities, but the possibility that their activities might still be enjoined on copyright, trademark, or publicity rights grounds does not appear to operate as a serious deterrent. These women know they assume risks of legal prosecution, but legal risks are only very few and possibly the most distant of the risks they face; indeed, Bacon-Smith implies that the assumption, management, and shared exploration of risk is the central ethos of the community, and constitutive of the construction and reconstruction of culture in which they engage. BACON-SMITH, *supra* note 62, at 302-452.

[84] For a discussion of complicitous critique as an attitude symptomatic of postmodernism, see LINDA HUTCHEON, THE POLITICS OF POSTMODERNISM (1989).

well as genders, as people create their own ethical distinctions between expression and theft. Communication always involves borrowing the images of alterity. Only recently has it become a form of trespass.

V. Infinite Diversity in Infinite Combination: Democracy as Dialogic Practice

The cultural politics of constructing alternative gender identities, through improvisations upon the celebrity image, are not readily appreciated using current juridical concepts or easily encompassed by the liberal premises upon which legal categories are grounded. The reasons for these difficulties, I believe, can be located within the contradictions, instabilities, and ambiguities of liberal legal discourse itself—contradictions that are becoming increasingly apparent in the condition of postmodernity.[85]

Liberal legal discourse addresses the expression of identity, community, and political aspiration under the rubric of free speech or freedom of expression, a field of doctrine that clings tenaciously to Enlightenment concepts in the face of late capitalist realities. As Owen Fiss notes, the constitutional protections of freedom of speech rest on increasingly anachronistic premises that do not address the salient characteristics or challenges of capitalist mass communications systems in North America.[86] Presupposing that the biggest threat to public discourse is the silencing of the individual speaker by the state, "the Free Speech Tradition can be understood as a protection of the street corner speaker."[87] Assuming a natural division between public and private actors, free speech simply protects all "private" actors, regardless of their power, against the evils of state intervention, notwithstanding that in an age of mass media conglomerates, threats to the autonomy of speech and public debate are more likely to come from extremely powerful "private" actors who control the most influential circuits and contents of communication.[88] Increasingly, a person's right to political speech may encroach upon another's rights of property (the need to picket in shopping malls, for example) and property rights generally prevail unless the property holding citizen is understood to hold the

---

[85] I explore these contradictions in more detail in *Publicity Rights*, *supra* note 22.

[86] Owen Fiss, *Free Speech and Social Structure*, 71 Iowa L. Rev. 1405 (1986).

[87] *Id.* at 1408.

[88] *Id.* at 1410-13.

property for public use (and thus to exercise a "governmental" function so that she must be treated like a state).

Critics on the left argue that the public/private and state/citizen dichotomies of freedom of speech law mystify and distort our understanding of contemporary political life

> because government is implicated in all activity that occurs within its territorial jurisdiction. As sovereign, the government is as responsible for its active decisions not to intervene and regulate as it is for its decisions to act affirmatively. . . . [T]he retention of an existing situation is also due to the efforts and actions of the state. . . . The protection of private property and the enforcement of private contracts by the government attests to the strong and necessary presence of government in private transactions. . . . Property and contract are creatures of the state and support for these allocative regimes is neither more nor less politically neutral or activist than opposition to them. The question is not whether government should intervene, but when and how . . . .[89]

When "public" speech interests come up against "private" property interests, the latter almost invariably triumph, ensuring that "the law insulates vast sectors of the social hierarchy from official scrutiny and public accountability."[90] Those who hold "private" property are not required to consider the "public" interest in free speech in their exercise of exclusive property rights. Once we break down this untenable distinction, however, and recognize the state's role in creating and enforcing property rights, "the question of whose entitlements are to be protected from whose interference becomes a contested matter of political choice rather than the correct application of abstract principle."[91]

Laws commodifying the celebrity image inevitably come up against concerns about freedom of expression, but they do so sporadically, yielding inconsistent and confused rationales that reveal the inadequacies of liberal discourse in the cultural conditions of postmodernism. It is generally accepted that rights of publicity must yield to social interests in freedom of expression, "when first amendment principles outweigh the celebrity's interest in compensation."[92] But when will this be the case?

---

89 Alan Hutchinson, *Talking the Good Life from Free Speech to Democratic Dialogue*, 1 YALE J.L. & LIB. 17, 21 (1989).

90 *Id.* at 22.

91 *Id.*

92 Lawrence, *supra* note 3, at 332.

Courts routinely assert that the First Amendment protects publication of news of a celebrity but does not protect commercial uses of celebrity images.[93] Often this is premised on a distinction between fact and fiction—factual accounts about celebrity behavior do not violate their publicity rights because celebrities are the subject of legitimate news.[94] Newspapers, films, and documentaries are not understood to be engaged in commercial purposes when they publish news, notwithstanding that their production, distribution, and exhibition is a large commercial enterprise carried on for private profit.[95] Distinctions between fact and fiction, publishing news about a celebrity and commercially exploiting her image, are notoriously difficult to maintain in the promotional culture[96] of postmodernity. The courts' efforts to employ and maintain such distinctions yield contradictory and sometimes ludicrous results, as the following cases, drawn from the same jurisdiction, illustrate.

Ann-Margret sued *High Society* magazine for a violation of publicity rights for the unauthorized use of a semi-nude photograph taken from one of her films. The court dismissed the action on the basis that the photograph was newsworthy and its use protected.[97] The same year, a model brought legal action for the unauthorized use of a nude photograph in the same magazine. The court rejected the defendant's claim that the First Amendment protected use of the photos because the model was not shown participating in a newsworthy event; the photographs, therefore, were not a matter of public interest.[98] When a couple found their nude photographs in a commercially distributed mass market guide to nude beaches, however, a court denied them relief and upheld the publisher's right to disseminate information of public interest; the photographs were not being used for commercial purposes.[99]

---

[93] *See, e.g.*, Grant v. Esquire, Inc., 367 F. Supp. 876 (S.D.N.Y. 1973); Rinaldi v. Village Voice, 359 N.Y.S.2d 176 (Sup. Ct. 1974), *cert. denied*, 423 U.S. 883 (1975); Garner v. Triangle Publications, 97 F. Supp. 546 (S.D.N.Y. 1951).

[94] *Garner*, 97 F. Supp. at 549.

[95] University of Notre Dame du Lac v. Twentieth Century-Fox Film Corp., 256 N.Y.S.2d 301 (Sup. Ct.), *aff'd*, 259 N.Y.S.2d 832 (1965).

[96] The concept of promotional culture is developed by Andrew Wernick, *Promotional Culture*, 15 CAN. J. POL. & SOC. THEORY 260 (1991). He contends that North American culture has come to present itself at every level as an endless series of promotional messages. Advertising, besides having become a most powerful institution in its own right, has been effectively universalised as a signifying mode.

[97] Ann-Margret v. High Soc'y Magazine, 498 F. Supp. 401 (S.D.N.Y. 1980).

[98] Hansen v. High Soc'y Magazine, Inc., 5 Media L. Rep. (BNA) 2398 (Sup. Ct.), *rev'd on other grounds*, 76 A.D.2d 812, 429 N.Y.S.2d 552 (1980).

[99] Creel v. Crown Publishers, 115 A.D.2d 414, 496 N.Y.S.2d 219 (1985).

Law students are trained to rationalize and distinguish such cases to show how categories like disseminating information in the public interest and commercial exploitation of another's name and likeness are rational, desirable, and necessary. Celebrities and the media industries reward them handsomely for their efforts. Even the most determined law student, however, might have difficulty supporting a decision which held that the unauthorized use of "before and after" photos of a girl in a teen magazine—replete with the brand names of the products used to effect the transformation—was a newsworthy use of her name and likeness rather than a commerical exploitation.[100]

The underlying distinction between fact and fiction that must provide the scaffolding for this conceptual structure becomes increasingly fragile in postmodernity as societies become saturated with signification and the value of the "hyperreal" accelerates.[101] Courts have found it increasingly difficult to distinguish truth from falsity, and fact from fiction, or to limit First Amendment protection to objective renderings that correspond to some knowable reality. They maintain, however, the philosophical edifice of "the mirror of nature"[102] by developing ever more distinctions within distinctions to keep its structure intact.

A defendant is held to forfeit the privilege of disseminating newsworthy information if her use is materially and substantially false and she has recklessly disregarded its falsity.[103] When a comedian ran a mock campaign for President as a publicity stunt, however, he was unable to prevent an entrepreneur from distributing a poster bearing his photograph with the caption, "For President."[104] The court determined that the poster was newsworthy and thus that the defendant was engaged in spreading information rather than in commercial exploitation. It did not address the issue of whether the "information" defendant disseminated was to be characterized as materially false (the comedian was not running "For President") or factual information about a fictitious candidacy (a true account of a falsity). When Elvis Presley died, however, those who held his publicity rights

---

100 Lopez v. Triangle Communications, Inc., 421 N.Y.S.2d 57 (1979).

101 For discussions of "hyperreality," see UMBERTO ECO, TRAVELS IN HYPERREALITY (1989) and JEAN BAUDRILLARD, SIMULATIONS (1983). *See also* JEAN BAUDRILLARD, SELECTED WRITINGS 166-84 (Mark Poster ed., 1988); DOUGLAS KELLNER, JEAN FROM MARXISM TO POSTMODERNISM AND BEYOND 60-92 (1989).

102 The phrase, of course, is borrowed from RICHARD RORTY, PHILOSOPHY AND THE MIRROR OF NATURE (1979).

103 Lerman v. Flynt Distrib. Co., 745 F.2d 123 (2d Cir.), *cert. denied,* 471 U.S. 1054 (1984).

104 Paulsen v. Personality Posters, Inc., 299 N.Y.S.2d 501 (Sup. Ct. Spec. Term 1968).

successfully stopped an entreprenuer from marketing a picture of Presley "In Memorium."[105] Perhaps the New York courts, like the weekly tabloids, doubt that "the King" has truly departed.

Accomodating the immense potential value in fictionalizing the lifestyles of the rich and famous has provoked courts to articulate new distinctions within the fact and fiction dichotomy. A New York court held that a right of publicity will not be recognized where a fictionalized account of a public figure's life is depicted in such a way that the audience knows (truly?) that the events are falsely represented.[106] Another New York bench, however, decided that allowing the publication of a known fictional bibliography of a (factual) baseball player would take freedom of expression too far given the defendant's limited research efforts to verify his story.[107] The book was seen as a clear case of "a commercial exploitation."

The efforts of a film producer to verify his findings, however, were not investigated when he represented a deceased pilot's alleged reappearance as a ghost in his mass marketed movie. The pilot served as captain aboard an Eastern Airlines flight that crashed in 1972. After the crash, people reported that the captain and crew of the fated flight appeared as ghosts aboard other Eastern planes. Relatives of the deceased brought action for unauthorized commercial use of name and likeness against the maker of the film that reconstructed these events.[108] The filmmaker prevailed because of his right to disseminate information "of current and legitimate public interest" under the "newsworthiness" section of the Florida statute.[109] If the case were considered in New York, the following questions might have been addressed: Was the information "true"? Was it substantially "false"? Did the filmmaker recklessly disregard its falsity, or was he providing a fictionalized account of a real person's activities? Will a fictionalized version of a real person's activities, as imagined by other people, be protected? Perhaps it depends how carefully you've verified the falsity of your fabrication and how easily the audience can identify the activities as fictional. But what if most of them believe in ghosts? In any case, there is a

---

105 Factors Etc., Inc. v. Creative Card Co., 444 F. Supp. 279 (S.D.N.Y. 1977), *aff'd sub nom.* Factors Etc., Inc. v. Pro Arts, Inc., 579 F.2d 215 (2d Cir.), *cert. denied*, 440 U.S. 908 (1978).

106 Hicks v. Casablanca Records, 464 F. Supp. 426 (S.D.N.Y. 1978).

107 Spahn v. Julian Messner, Inc., 250 N.Y.S.2d 529 (Sup. Ct. Spec. Term 1964), *vacated*, 387 U.S. 239 (1967).

108 Loft v. Fuller, 408 So. 2d 619 (Fla. Dist. Ct. App. 1981).

109 FLA. STAT. ch. 540.08 (1990).

legitimate public interest in disseminating (true?) information about (actual) ghost sightings in the state of Florida.

Attempting to limit freedom of speech defenses in publicity rights claims to the dissemination of factual information in the name of newsworthiness is conceptually boggling, culturally untenable, and politically pernicious. We value freedom of expression not as a means of spreading verifiable information about a world of brute fact, but as the activity with which we culturally construct worlds, create social knowledges, forge ethics, and negotiate intersubjective moral truths whose credence is never established by a measurable correspondence to an objective reality. Self, society, and identity are realized only through the expressive cultural activity that reworks those cultural forms that occupy the space of the social imaginary.[110]

Political theorists of the postmodern condition point to the necessarily cultural character of contemporary politics. The social and political orders in which we live are contingent creations that we ourselves discursively construct. It is through creative cultural practices of articulation that the social world is given meaning, and, hence, it is always contestable and open to re-articulations. Ernesto Laclau and Chantal Mouffe, in particular, see practices of articulating social difference as central to democratic politics.[111]

All knowledges of social identity are symbolic systems of difference, and representational structures of difference are, by their very nature, incapable of achieving closure. No structure of differential identity is ever final; new forms of difference are always emergent, and new social identities continually assert their legitimacy and presence. Indeed, advances in the democratization of Western societies are dependent upon "autonomous initiatives starting from different points within the social fabric,"[112] as new groups constitute themselves politically. Laclau and

---

110 The concept of the social imaginary is developed in CORNELIUS CASTORIADIS, THE IMAGINARY INSTITUTION OF SOCIETY (Kathleen Blamey trans., MIT Press 1987) (1975).

111 *See* ERNESTO LACLAU & CHANTAL MOUFFE, HEGEMONY AND SOCIALIST STRATEGY: TOWARDS A RADICAL DEMOCRATIC POLITICS (Winston Moore & Paul Cammack trans., 1985); Ernesto Laclau & Chantal Mouffe, *Post Marxism Without Apologies*, NEW LEFT REV., Nov./ Dec. 1987, at 79 [hereinafter *Post-Marxism*]; Chantal Mouffe, *Radical Democracy: Modern or Postmodern?*, *in* UNIVERSAL ABANDON? THE POLITICS OF POSTMODERNISM 31 (Andrew Ross ed., 1988); *see also*, Fred Dallmayr, *Hegemony and Democracy: On Laclau and Mouffe*, 1 STRATEGIES: J. THEORY, CULTURE, & POL. 29 (1988); FRED DALLMAYR, MARGINS OF POLITICAL DISCOURSE (1989); Bradley Macdonald, *Towards a Redemption of Politics: An Introduction to the Political Theory of Ernesto Laclau*, 1 STRATEGIES: J. THEORY, CULTURE, & POL. 5 (1988).

112 *Post-Marxism*, *supra* note 110, at 105.

Mouffe refuse to privilege any particular subject positions, seeing the contemporary political world as one of multifaceted struggles amongst peoples continually articulating new social identities from discursive resources. Democratic politics is essentially a dialogic process whereby social identities are continually emergent in political articulation. A radical and plural democracy must maintain optimal conditions for encouraging such articulations.

Articulations of identity are possible only in conditions of polysemy, symbolic ambiguity, and a surplus of meaning, where the necessary cultural resources for contesting meaning and asserting identity are freely accessible. In the condition of postmodernity, our cultural resources are increasingly the properties of others, and meaning is the monopoly of an elite who control the commodified texts that pervade our social lives.[113] These are the cultural images with which politically salient forms of difference may increasingly be shaped. Whose identities will be authorized and whose authorship will be recognized? As the cultural cosmos in which we live becomes increasingly commodified, we will need to define and defend the cultural practices of articulation with which we author the social world and construct the identities we occupy within it.

---

[113] An extended version of this argument that draws its examples from the fields of copyright and trademark law may be found in Rosemary J. Coombe, *Objects of Property and Subjects of Politics: Intellectual Property Laws and Democratic Dialogue*, 69 TEX. L. REV. 1853 (1991).

THE INTERDISCIPLINARY FUTURE OF COPYRIGHT THEORY

ALFRED C. YEN*

I. INTRODUCTION

The proper scope of an author's property has long troubled copyright analysts. Most agree that authors should (and do) own the right to prevent others from literally duplicating original copyrighted material. Beyond that, the reach of an author's rights becomes very hazy. Can an author prevent the use of her plot or characters? What about the general appearance of sculpture, a painter's style or a photographer's perspective and choice of subject matter? One hundred and fifty years ago all of these items were part of the public domain.[1] Recent decisions, however, suggest that these items have now become private property.[2]

At first glance, extending authors' rights beyond literal reproduction seems like a good idea. As Judge Learned Hand stated, "It is of course essential to any protection of literary property . . . that the right cannot be limited literally to the text, else a plagiarist would escape by immaterial variations."[3] However, sober reflection indicates that too much of this good thing is undesirable. Authorship is possible only when future authors have the ability to borrow from those who have created before them.[4] If too much of each work is reserved as private property

* Associate Professor of Law, Boston College Law School. B.S., M.S., 1980, Stanford University; J.D., 1983, Harvard Law School. The author would like to thank Tracy Tanaka, Boston College Law School class of 1991, for her able research assistance. Some of the research reflected in this essay was supported by research grants from Boston College, Boston College Law School and the Boston College Law School Fellows.

1 Early copyright decisions reflect a very narrow view of the kinds of appropriation which constitute infringement. *See* Stowe v. Thomas, 23 F. Cas. 201 (C.C.E.D. Pa. 1853) (No. 13,514) (refusing to find defendant's German translation an infringement of Harriet Beecher Stowe's Uncle Tom's Cabin).

2 *See* Sid & Marty Krofft Television Prods., Inc. v. McDonald's Corp., 562 F.2d 1157, 1167 (9th Cir. 1977) (protecting "total concept and feel" of plaintiff's costumed characters and television series); Sheldon v. Metro-Goldwyn Pictures Corp., 81 F.2d 49 (2d Cir. 1936) (protecting plot of play); Steinberg v. Columbia Pictures, Inc., 663 F. Supp. 706, 709 (S.D.N.Y. 1987) (protecting plaintiff's perspective and style in illustration referred to as "a parochial New Yorker's view of the world"); Kisch v. Ammirati & Puris, Inc., 657 F. Supp. 380 (S.D.N.Y. 1987) (denying defendant's motion to dismiss copyright claim based in part on plaintiff's choice of camera angle, lighting, and subject matter).

3 Nichols v. Universal Pictures Corp., 45 F.2d 119, 121 (2d Cir. 1930).

4 *See, e.g.*, Emerson v. Davies, 8 F. Cas. 615, 619 (C.C.D. Mass. 1845) (No. 4,436):

through copyright, future would-be authors will find it impossible to create. Society would presumably suffer from the decreased production of creative works. Proper construction of our copyright law therefore depends on striking a socially acceptable balance between the interests of authors and the public.

From a purely intuitive point of view, two issues certainly seem relevant. First, society would like to ensure the promotion of social welfare through the production of creative works. Second, society would also want to strike a just and fair compromise between authors and consumers of creative works. If we are to believe various statements made by the Supreme Court, however, the first issue is the only one which may be considered when interpreting American copyright law. For example, in *Sony Corp. of America v. Universal City Studios Inc.*, the Supreme Court wrote:

> The monopoly privileges that Congress may authorize are neither unlimited nor primarily designed to provide a special private benefit. Rather, the limited grant is a means by which an important public purpose may be achieved. It is intended to motivate the creative activity of authors and inventors by the provision of a special reward, and to allow the public access to the products of their genius after the limited period of exclusive control has expired.[5]

In my view, this one-sided approach to copyright cultivates an obviously cramped view of an area which is assuming ever-increasing importance for our society. After all, justice and fairness are key considerations in most areas of the law, especially property law.[6] Why should copyright be any different?

This Essay will briefly, but critically, examine the major reasons which have been given for why copyright should be different from other areas of the law. Part II will begin by sketching two copyright theories which follow the intuitions outlined above. The first theory justifies copyright as an economic incentive which advances social welfare. The second justifies copyright as

---

> In truth, in literature, in science and in art, there are, and can be, few, if any, things, which, in an abstract sense, are strictly new and original throughout. Every book in literature, science and art, borrows, and must necessarily borrow, and use much which was well known and used before. . . . No man writes exclusively from his own thoughts, unaided and uninstructed by the thoughts of others. The thoughts of every man are, more or less, a combination of what other men have thought and expressed, although they may be modified, exalted, or improved by his own genius or reflection.

[5] Sony Corp. of Am. v. Universal City Studios, Inc., 464 U.S. 417, 429, *reh'g denied*, 465 U.S. 1112 (1984).

[6] For an overview of various philosophies of property, see LAWRENCE C. BECKER, PROPERTY RIGHTS: PHILOSOPHICAL FOUNDATIONS (1977).

the legal vindication of a person's moral right to property in the fruits of her labor. Part III will study the reasons for suppressing the discussion of justice and fairness in copyright jurisprudence. This Essay will show that these reasons are insufficient to support the suppression, and goes on to outline arguments which demonstrate that considerations of justice and fairness are essential to a complete copyright theory. The Essay concludes with some remarks about the future of copyright theory.

II. Two Models of Copyright

Modern American copyright scholars recognize two apparently conflicting copyright theories. The first, and dominant, theory states that copyright exists solely to provide necessary economic incentives for the production of creative work. Under this view, copyright is necessary because in its absence those interested in using the author's work would simply copy the work instead of buying it from the author. Authors would then find their economic returns too small to justify the costs of authorship. In such a situation authors might not produce and social welfare would presumably suffer.[7] To remedy this problem, economic theory supports granting authors copyright in their works. However, those rights are necessarily limited in scope, because copyright imposes costs on society in exchange for the benefits of induced creative activity. First, the owner of copyright will charge a monopoly price for her work. The number of people who gain access to the work will therefore decrease.[8] Second, copyright raises the production cost of future works, because prohibiting borrowing from existing works makes it more difficult for future authors to create.[9] Thus, the proper degree of copyright protection is that which maximizes the difference between the benefits of induced creative activity and the costs of increased authors' rights.[10]

The second, and generally less well explored "natural law theory" considers copyright as the legal vindication of a person's

---

[7] *See* William M. Landes & Richard A. Posner, *An Economic Analysis of Copyright Law*, 18 J. Legal Stud. 325, 328 (1989). In economic terms, an inefficiency, or "market failure," has occurred.

[8] William W. Fisher III, *Reconstructing the Fair Use Doctrine*, 101 Harv. L. Rev. 1659, 1700-02 (1988).

[9] Landes & Posner, *supra* note 7, at 332.

[10] Fisher, *supra* note 8, at 1717. *See also* Landes & Posner, *supra* note 7, at 326. This economic statement captures the conventional adage that copyright balances incentives for production against the need for free access to works.

moral right to property in the fruits of her labor.[11] Under this theory, copyright's justification does not rest upon any showing of economic necessity. Instead, copyright exists because society's failure to protect authors' property interests would result in the denial of a basic human right. Thus, the author rightfully gains copyright in her work to the extent that she can claim sole credit for the work's creation.

A. *The American Choice*

Although both of the above described theories support copyright's existence and suggest its boundaries, American analysts generally insist that copyright rests solely on economics. Both the United States Supreme Court and Congress have stated that copyright exists only for the purpose of advancing social welfare through economic incentives for authorship.[12] Moreover, the Supreme Court has explicitly rejected natural law copyright arguments.[13] Analysts generally follow this lead by explaining copyright's basic doctrines such as originality and the idea/expression dichotomy in economic terms.[14] Two separate lines of thinking support this choice.

---

11 This theory descends from eighteenth-century concepts of property. These concepts are reflected in the writings of William Blackstone and John Locke. *See* 2 WILLIAM BLACKSTONE, COMMENTARIES *8; JOHN LOCKE, TWO TREATISES OF GOVERNMENT at § 27 (Peter Laslett ed., 1970) (3d ed. 1698).

12 *See supra* text accompanying note 5. *See also* H.R. REP. No. 2222, 60th Cong., 2d Sess. 7 (1909), *reprinted in* 6 LEGISLATIVE HISTORY OF THE 1909 COPYRIGHT ACT, at S7 (1976).

> The enactment of copyright legislation . . . is not based upon any natural right that the author has in his writings . . . but upon the ground that the welfare of the public will be served and progress of science and useful arts will be promoted by securing to authors for limited periods the exclusive rights to their writings.

13 *See* Wheaton v. Peters, 33 U.S. (8 Pet.) 591, 654-68 (1834).

14 These concepts are embodied in our present copyright code at 17 U.S.C. § 102 (1988). Together they define the existence and scope of copyright in a given work. Originality provides the basic requirement for copyrightability by providing that only "original works of authorship" are eligible for protection. 17 U.S.C. § 102(a). Copyright therefore does not protect works which lack minimal creativity or are simply copies of other preexisting works. *See* Toro Co. v. R & R Prods. Co., 787 F.2d 1208, 1213 (8th Cir. 1986) (denying protection to manufacturer's parts numbering system because of lack of originality); L. Batlin & Son, Inc. v. Snyder, 536 F.2d 486 (2d Cir.) (holding that a copy of preexisting work in public domain lacks sufficient originality), *cert. denied*, 429 U.S. 857 (1976); Magic Mktg., Inc. v. Mailing Servs. of Pittsburgh, Inc., 634 F. Supp. 769 (W.D. Pa. 1986) (advertising phrases on envelope lack originality).

However, the mere fact that a work is "original" does not mean that copyright prohibits all borrowing from that work. Instead, the idea/expression dichotomy permits some borrowing from every copyrighted work by specifically excluding ideas from an author's property. 17 U.S.C. § 102(b). Thus, even though a book is protected by copyright, a future author is free to borrow the ideas embodied in the book. Only the book's expression remains protected from copying. Landsberg v. Scrabble Crossword Game Players, Inc., 736 F.2d 485 (9th Cir.) (denying protection for instructions on how to play

The first rests on the descriptive claim that Americans have always viewed copyright as a matter of economics, and not a basic matter of fairness and justice. Proponents of this argument base their position on statements such as those noted in the preceding paragraph. They also point out that the Constitution explicitly contemplated an economic basis for copyright by authorizing Congress to "promote the progress of . . . the useful arts."[15] Departure from economic copyright theory therefore represents an unwarranted, and perhaps unconstitutional, change from established practice.

The second line of thinking rests on the normative claim that natural law copyright theory leads to dire consequences. As an initial matter, proponents of this view note that copyright lasts for only a limited duration.[16] By contrast, natural law principles would allow copyrights of unlimited duration. Furthermore, copyright sometimes allows individuals to borrow original material created by other authors.[17] They contend that a serious re-

---

Scrabble), *cert. denied*, 469 U.S. 1037 (1984); Baker v. Selden, 101 U.S. 99 (1879) (idea of a double-entry bookkeeping system not protected by copyright).

For example, since originality defines the works eligible for copyright protection, its economic interpretation becomes an exercise in determining whether extending copyright to a given work promotes social welfare. Similarly, application of the idea/expression dichotomy becomes an economic cost-benefit calculation. If authors need more incentive to produce creative works, then fewer facets of works should be considered ideas, and more facets should be considered expressions. If society needs greater access to works, the converse is true. This vision suggests the use of economic analysis to strike the required balance between the interests of authors and the interests of society. *See* Whelan Assocs., Inc. v. Jaslow Dental Lab., Inc., 797 F.2d 1222, 1235 (3rd Cir. 1986).

> [P]recisely because the line between idea and expression is elusive, we must pay particular attention to the pragmatic considerations that underlie the distinction and copyright law generally. In this regard, we must remember that the purpose of the copyright law is to create the most efficient and productive balance between protection (incentive) and dissemination of information, to promote learning, culture and development.

cert. denied, 479 U.S. 1031 (1987).

Major articles which adopt a primarily economic view of copyright include Stephen Breyer, *The Uneasy Case for Copyright: A Study of Copyright in Books, Photocopies, and Computer Programs*, 84 HARV. L. REV. 281 (1970); Wendy J. Gordon, *Fair Use as Market Failure: A Structural and Economic Analysis of the Betamax Case and its Predecessors*, 82 COLUM. L. REV. 1600 (1982); Robert M. Hurt & Robert M. Schuchman, *The Economic Rationale of Copyright*, 56 AM. ECON. REV. 421 (1966); Landes & Posner, *supra* note 7; Peter S. Menell, *An Analysis of the Scope of Copyright Protection for Application Programs*, 41 STAN. L. REV. 1045 (1989). A recently published treatise by a leading copyright scholar, Professor Paul Goldstein, also reflects the current primacy of economic theories of copyright. PAUL GOLDSTEIN, COPYRIGHT: PRINCIPLES, LAW AND PRACTICE (1989). Although Professor Goldstein does not exclusively use economic terms to explain copyright principles, they certainly play a major role in many key areas of his work.

15 U.S. CONST. art. 1, § 8, cl. 8.

16 Copyright terms presently last for the life of the author plus fifty years. *See* 17 U.S.C. § 302 (1988). Additionally, the Constitution requires Congress to secure an author's copyright for only a limited period of time. U.S. CONST. art. 1, § 8, cl. 8.

17 For a description of the so-called idea/expression dichotomy, see *supra* note 14.

gime of property in the fruits of an author's labor would never allow such a result. Thus, adherents to the second justification state that recognition of copyright's natural law basis destroys any balance between the interests of authors and the public.[18]

1. Evaluation of the Descriptive Claim

As noted previously, the descriptive claim for suppression of copyright's natural law facets rests on constitutional language and a long string of statements which purportedly restrict copyright analysis to economics. Closer examination of the record shows, however, that the case for suppression is far from air tight. If nothing else, early Americans did not view copyright as a purely economic instrument. Instead, they referred explicitly to copyright's support in both economics and natural law. For example, no fewer than seven state copyright statutes contained preambles such as New Hampshire's, which read:

> As the improvement of knowledge, the progress of civilization, and the advancement of human happiness, greatly depend on the efforts of learned and ingenious persons in the various arts and sciences; as the principal encouragement such persons can have to make great and beneficial exertions of this nature, must consist in the legal security of the fruits of their study and industry to themselves; and as such security is one of the natural rights of all men, there being no property more peculiarly a man's own than that which is produced by the labor of his mind . . . .[19]

---

18 See Howard B. Abrams, *The Historic Foundation of American Copyright Law: Exploding the Myth of Common Law Copyright*, 29 WAYNE L. REV. 1119, 1185-87 (1983); Lyman Ray Patterson, *Private Copyright and Public Communication: Free Speech Endangered*, 28 VAND. L. REV. 1161, 1210 (1975).

19 Act of Nov. 7, 1783, 1783 N.H. Laws 305. The copyright statutes of Massachusetts and Rhode Island contained essentially identical preambles. *See* An Act for the Purpose of Securing to Authors the Exclusive Right and Benefit of Publishing their Literary Productions, for Twenty-One Years, ch. 26, 1783 Mass. Acts 236; An Act for the Purpose of Securing to Authors the Exclusive Right and Benefit of Publishing their Literary Productions, for Twenty-One Years, 1783 R.I. Acts & Resolves 6. Furthermore, the Connecticut statute provided:

> Whereas it is perfectly agreeable to the Principles of natural Equity and Justice, that every Author should be secured in receiving the profits that may arise from the Sale of his Works, and such Security may encourage Men of Learning and Genius to publish their Writings which may do Honor to their Country, and Service to Mankind . . . .

Act of Jan. 8, 1783, 1783 Conn. Pub. Acts 617. The New York statute is substantially identical. An Act to Promote Literature, ch. 54, 1786 N.Y. Laws 298. The New Jersey statute contained the following preamble:

> Whereas Learning tends to the Embellishment of Human Nature, the Honor of the Nation, and the general Good of Mankind; and as it is perfectly agreeable to the Principles of Equity, that Men of Learning who devote their Time

This thinking was echoed in Madison's support for the Federal Constitution's grant of congressional authority to enact copyright legislation:

> The utility of [the copyright power] will scarcely be questioned. The copyright of authors has been solemnly adjudged in Great Britain to be a right of common law. The right to useful inventions seems with equal reason to belong to the inventors. The public good fully coincides in both cases with the claims of individuals.[20]

Evidence of copyright's non-economic heritage exists in modern copyright as well. Despite ostensibly relying on a purely economic outlook, the Supreme Court occasionally adopts statements which reflect copyright's roots in fairness and justice.[21] From statements like these we can conclude that natural law actually motivates courts, despite protestations to the contrary. Furthermore, it has been suggested that modern copyright doctrine is entirely consistent with a regime constructed from natural law principles, and that economically interpreted concepts such as the idea/expression dichotomy actually owe their ancestry to natural law.[22] Finally, when one considers the existence of copyright protection for works which do not require economic incentives for production,[23] it is hard to believe that the repeated state-

---

> and Talents to the preparing of Treatises for Publication should have the profits that may arise from the Sale of their Works secured to them . . . .

An Act for the Promotion and Encouragement of Literature, ch. 21, 1783 N.J. Laws 47. Finally, the North Carolina statute provided:

> Whereas nothing is more strictly a man's own than the fruit of his study, and it is proper that men should be encouraged to pursue useful knowledge by the hope of reward; and as the security of literary property must greatly tend to extension of arts and commerce . . . .

Act of Dec. 29, 1785, ch. 26, 1785 N.C. Laws 22.

For a more complete analysis of evidence that early Americans viewed copyright as a matter of natural law, see Gary Kauffman, *Exposing the Suspicious Foundation of Society's Primacy in Copyright Law: Five Accidents*, 10 COLUM.—VLA J.L. & ARTS 381, 403-08 (1986).

20 THE FEDERALIST No. 43, at 279 (James Madison) (E.M. Earle ed., 1976). Madison's reference to common law copyright in Great Britain approvingly refers to the famous case of Millar v. Taylor, 4 Burr. 2303, 98 Eng. Rep. 201 (1769), which explicitly recognized and enforced a natural law copyright claim. Although *Millar v. Taylor* was overruled in 1774, Madison's reference still stands as an endorsement of its result and reasoning. For a discussion of common law copyright, see LYMAN RAY PATTERSON, COPYRIGHT IN PERSPECTIVE (1968); Abrams, *supra* note 18, at 1119.

21 *See* Mazer v. Stein, 347 U.S. 201, 219 ("Sacrificial days devoted to such creative activities deserve reward commensurate with the services rendered."), *reh'g denied*, 347 U.S. 949 (1954).

22 See Alfred C. Yen, *Restoring the Natural Law: Copyright as Labor and Possession*, 51 OHIO ST. L.J. 517, 529-39 (1990).

23 For example, copyright protects theses papers written by graduate students in fulfillment of degree requirements. These works would be produced with or without copyright law. Thus, it is hard to see how copyright protection for such works increases the

ments which restrict copyright theory to economics provide an accurate description of actual copyright thinking. The claim that courts and legislatures never associate natural law principles with copyright is simply untrue. We should therefore criticize the extant purely economic copyright regime for its failure to recognize copyright's roots in both economics and natural law.

2. Evaluation of the Normative Claim

The second reason for suppressing copyright's natural law roots is the belief that consideration of natural law will destroy any balance between the interests of authors and consumers. This concern is certainly understandable. The idea that a person should have a property interest in the fruits of her labor is powerful. Since a copyrighted work is surely the product of an author's labor, it would seem that all borrowing from a copyrighted work violates the author's property in the fruits of her labor. Copyright would therefore necessarily have to prohibit any unauthorized use of a copyrighted work. Future authors would find no public domain from which to draw because everything (including language) would owe its existence to other human beings.

This fear is unjustified, for the notion that authors can claim creative responsibility for (and therefore property in) an entire work is simply false. Any frank appraisal of authorship must conclude that each author's work contains both the author's original creations and material drawn from other authors[24] and the society in which the author lives.[25] Authorship is therefore not the creation of works which spring like Athena from the head of Zeus, but the conscious and unconscious intake, digestion, and transformation of input gained from the author's experience within a broader society. This realization provides the factual basis from which the natural law theorist justifies a strong public domain.

---

production of creative works. Their protection must therefore rest on something other than economic theory.

[24] *See supra* note 4; Jessica Litman, *The Public Domain*, 39 EMORY L.J. 965, 1010-11 (1990). Brief consideration of one's own work should prove the essential truth of this proposition. The honest legal scholar must admit that his arguments, conceptions, methods of analysis, writing style, and terminology are heavily influenced, if not directly formed, by the writings of others. Similarly, composers use sounds they have heard before, writers recycle plots, and computer programmers use logic and techniques that they have seen before.

[25] A good example of this is our recognition of Mozart's music as both "Mozartean" and German in its personality. Similarly, the work of Renoir and Monet can be identified both individually and as French.

The easiest case occurs when authors borrow material from society without restatement. In this situation, the natural law implication is clear. Since the author did not create the borrowed material, the author has no moral claim to property in it. Indeed, granting an author property in the material by prohibiting its use in future works would be unjust, for society would be deprived of material that it had created. Thus, to the extent that borrowed material already belongs to society, it should remain in the public domain.

When material is borrowed and restated, the case for a public domain is less clear, but equally sound. Consider a work in which an innocent person is convicted of a crime and imprisoned. Even if the work is fictional, it is not solely the product of the author's labor. Rather, the work captures the products of society (the plot) and the author (the rewriting of the plot). In effect, society and the author are jointly responsible for the work's creation, and both should own some property rights in the work. This implies putting part of the work into the public domain while allowing the author property rights in other parts through some sort of equitable division.[26] Thus, certain aspects of this material become the author's property even though some public property will be lost. More important, other aspects of the material become public property even though the author will lose property rights in some of her original creations. The point is that society and authors must each get a fair share of works for which they are jointly responsible.

Of course, the foregoing analysis leaves open the question of how copyright should treat material which can be separately identified as solely that of the author. A superficial natural law analysis might conclude that copyright protects all of this material. After all, if society did not create the material, it must have been created by the author, and she should be able to claim her property rights.

---

[26] In other words, others have the right to copy some portions of the author's work. In defining the scope of borrowing, courts must remain cognizant of the possibility that the author's original material may be inseparable from public domain material. In these cases, the so-called doctrine of merger should be applied so that the public domain is not privately appropriated through copyright. The public domain is actually augmented by denying property rights in original material. *See* Herbert Rosenthal Jewelry Corp. v. Kalpakian, 446 F.2d 738, 742 (9th Cir. 1971) (holding that defendants did not copy plaintiff's jeweled bee pin because it was not "an 'idea' that defendants were free to copy"). Additional natural law support for this proposition comes from the famous Lockean proviso. In that passage, Locke denies the existence of property in the fruits of a person's labor where the appropriation fails to leave "enough and as good" for others. LOCKE, *supra* note 11.

A closer examination, however, shows that this position actually understates the extent of a natural law public domain, which prefers including original creations rather than excluding them.

If the public domain only contained material for which no person could claim creative credit, authors would receive compensation from all who borrowed their original material. Concurrently, all authors who wanted to borrow from their predecessors would have to pay for the privilege of doing so. Although such a scheme seemingly gives each person the fruits of her labor, it would in fact create an unjustified windfall to authors fortunate enough to have already created copyrighted material.

If existing authors gained the power to prohibit all borrowing from their works, they would reap huge benefits from subsequent authors who borrowed from them. At the same time, however, they would probably never be forced to compensate prior authors from whom they had borrowed. In some cases the prior authors (and their heirs) may be dead. In other cases the prior works may never have been copyrighted. Worse yet, in some cases the prior authors might not be aware that borrowing had even occurred. Thus, present day authors would gain the fruits of their labors while never paying for their use of the labor of others.

By contrast, a vigorous public domain that contains original material avoids the problem of unjust enrichment. Since practically every author would both owe and be owed compensation under a complete property rights scheme, it would seem eminently fair to simply abandon the futile task of trying to reach a perfect accounting of compensation among all authors. Instead, society could "balance the books" in a more equitable manner by forgiving many of the "debts" owed by modern authors to their predecessors. In return for this windfall, modern authors should forgive similar debts to future authors by dedicating some of their material to the public domain. In other words, the public domain would be used as a device through which authors could both borrow from and compensate one another. The effect of such a scheme would be to place even original material into a public domain.[27]

---

[27] The equitable contribution of authors to the public domain could be achieved in two ways. First, portions of every work should be dedicated to the public domain immediately upon creation. These portions should include those which are both likely to have been borrowed (and therefore not original) and likely to be borrowed in the future. A good example in modern copyright is the doctrine of *scenes a faire*, which places trite

III. The Necessary Consideration of Fairness and Justice

So far this Essay has shown that the primary reasons for suppressing natural law theories of copyright are not compelling. Indeed, it seems that the use of a natural law theory would be consistent with present doctrine and would justify the existence of a healthy public domain which complements the property rights of authors. However, die-hard economic theorists will surely not give up so easily. They may contend that economics alone provides the best way to construct any system of rights, including copyright.[28] In my view, however, any attempt to construct a copyright regime solely on economics is likely to fail. The relevant problems can best be exposed by briefly setting forth the premises on which an economic copyright regime would stand.

As the reader is undoubtedly aware, a fundamental proposition of modern economics is that, under perfect conditions, the unregulated self-interested transactions of individuals maximize social welfare.[29] Of course, perfect conditions never exist. Government should therefore use the legal system to correct the misallocation of resources caused by the lack of perfect conditions. If one assumes that social welfare can be expressed in dollar terms, we should then select the copyright regime which maximizes society's wealth, where wealth is defined as "the value in

---

plots, scenes, and sequences into the public domain. *See, e.g.*, Schwartz v. Universal Pictures Co., 85 F. Supp. 270, 275 (S.D. Cal. 1945); Cain v. Universal Pictures Co., 47 F. Supp. 1013, 1017 (S.D. Cal. 1942). Although these trite devices may sometimes be original, the likelihood of their having been borrowed and their use by future authors makes their immediate inclusion in the public domain fair. Second, all works should receive copyright protection for a limited time only, thereby ensuring eventual dedication to the public domain while providing a fair vindication of the author's creative labor. Such a result presently exists under 17 U.S.C. § 302 (1988), which terminates copyright fifty years after the death of the author.

28 The pros and cons of such a proposition require a lengthy ethical and economic discussion which space will not permit. Suffice it to say that such theorists have grown numerous in recent years through the proliferation of the "Chicago School" of the law and economics movement. It should also be stated that not all economic analysts agree with the strong normative claims of the Chicago School. For defenses of an economics only approach to all of law, see A. Mitchell Polinsky, An Introduction to Law and Economics (1989); Richard A. Posner, *Utilitarianism, Economics, and Legal Theory*, 8 J. Legal Stud. 103 (1979). For criticisms of these defenses, see Jules Coleman, Markets, Morals and the Law (1988); Robert Cooter & Thomas Ulen, Law and Economics 10 n.8 (1988):

> The claim that law can be reduced to economics is similar to the claim that used to be made in psychology that mind can be reduced to behavior. This proposition, called "reductivism" in philosophy, is dead in psychology, and it ought to be laid to rest in the economic analysis of law, too.

Id.; Ronald M. Dworkin, *Is Wealth a Value?*, 9 J. Legal Stud. 191 (1980).

29 Cooter & Ulen, *supra* note 28, at 44-49 (describing economic efficiency theorems and defining conditions necessary for efficient operations of markets).

dollars or dollar equivalents . . . of everything in society. It is measured by what people are willing to pay for something or, if they already own it, what they demand in money to give it up."[30]

In other words, government should correct misallocations of property rights by 1) determining the price each person sets for her property; and 2) reassigning each person's property to others whenever the amount others are willing to pay for the property exceeds the amount for which the individual is willing to sell that property.

Although quite brief, the foregoing is sufficient to expose two practical problems which make reliance on a purely economic copyright model highly questionable. First, the necessity of ascertaining prices means that courts require information they simply do not have. This lack of information causes two related problems for the economist. If economists do not have reliable data on individual preferences, their calculations are necessarily estimates. In an area such as copyright, the lack of information is so severe that economic recommendations become little more than random guesses about whether certain interpretations of copyright actually stimulate creativity.[31] Moreover, even if information related to copyright were available, the lack of information for other sectors of the economy would mean that recommendations that appear to increase welfare through copyright may in fact decrease social welfare overall.[32]

Even if these information problems could be overcome, sole reliance on economics to assign copyright rights would remain a highly dubious proposition, for economics is sometimes incapable of choosing among conflicting alternatives. For example, it is

---

30 Posner, *supra* note 28, at 119.

31 *See* George L. Priest, *What Economists Can Tell Lawyers About Intellectual Property: Comment on Cheung*, *in* 8 RESEARCH IN LAW AND ECONOMICS: THE ECONOMICS OF PATENTS AND COPYRIGHT 19, 21 (John Palmer & Richard O. Zerbe, Jr. eds., 1986).

> The inability of economists to resolve the question of whether activity stimulated by the patent system or other forms of protection of intellectual property enhances or diminishes social welfare implies, unfortunately, that economists can tell lawyers ultimately very little about how to enforce or interpret the law of intellectual property.

32 *See* E.J. MISHAN, COST-BENEFIT ANALYSIS 98-101 (1976) (describing the problem of second best). This problem may be illustrated by the following example. Suppose that the available information suggests that an increase in copyright incentives would cause a net increase in productive works of $100 million. At first blush, such a change seems presumptively desirable. The net increase, however, occurs only by diverting capital and human labor from other sectors of the economy to the production of copyrightable works. The losses incurred in those other sectors must therefore be weighed against the gains in the copyright area before one can consider the change wealth maximizing. The difficulty of identifying all of the affected sectors and gathering the necessary information makes it extremely difficult, if not impossible, for the economist to make an unequivocal welfare maximizing recommendation.

a well known fact that the price a person is willing to pay for a resource depends on what the person already owns. If a person owns very little, then she is unable to offer more than a small amount for a resource no matter how badly she desires it. By contrast, if she is wealthy, she is able to offer a lot.[33] Furthermore, the price a person is willing to pay for an entitlement is generally less than what she will sell the entitlement for once she owns it.[34] Since those who own entitlements such as copyrights are likely to value them more than those who do not, the wealth maximizer naturally prefers to assign rights according to the status quo. This turns wealth maximization into a normative principle which justifies whatever assignment of property rights is proposed.[35] The only way out of such a dilemma is to consider other reasons (such as fairness and justice) for assigning property rights to an individual.

V. The Interdisciplinary Future of Copyright Theory

American copyright theory should thus be expanded to include the natural law model which has long been suppressed. This does not mean that we should discard the economic model. Copyright obviously functions as an economic instrument in our society, and we should continue to analyze it from that perspective. At the same time, however, we must realize that we cannot find all the answers to copyright's riddles in the discipline of economics. By restoring natural law thinking to copyright jurispru-

---

33 One might be tempted to consider how much those who are not wealthy would pay for rights if they were. Economists ignore hypothetical preferences, however, based on unowned wealth. As Judge Posner states, "[t]he only kind of preference that counts in a system of wealth maximization is thus one that is backed up by money—in other words, that is registered in a market." Posner, *supra* note 28, at 119.

34 MISHAN, *supra* note 32, at 133-134 (1976); Cass R. Sunstein, *Legal Interference with Private Preferences*, 53 U. CHI. L. REV. 1129, 1151 (1986).

35 MISHAN, *supra* note 32, at 140-141, 398-401. A similar problem is raised by the so-called Scitovsky Paradox. *See* Tibor Scitovsky, *A Note on Welfare Propositions in Economics*, 9 REV. ECON. STUD. 77 (1941). The problem noted in the text can be illustrated by the following example. Consider proposal A. If proposal A is adopted, the producers of records own the right to make cassette tapes from the records they produce. Producers value this right at $200 because this is the additional revenue that they can gain by making and selling cassette tapes to consumers. Suppose further that consumers would be willing to buy the rights of making cassette tapes, but only if the price were $190 or less. In this hypothesized situation, proposal A seems clearly wealth maximizing and should be adopted. Since producers value the right more than consumers do, wealth is maximized by assigning the right to producers.

For purposes of comparison, now consider proposal B, which is the opposite of proposal A. Consumers now have the right to freely make cassette tapes from records. Since they now own the right in question, consumers in situation B value the entitlement more than they did in situation A. Suppose that they consequently will not part with the right for anything less than $203. Under these facts, proposal B is preferable to proposal A, and should be adopted.

dence, we simply recognize that copyright exists not only to promote social welfare, but also to secure to each person a basic human right.[36] Proper construction of our copyright law therefore depends on two separate inquiries. First, we must decide just how much property we think authors deserve. Second, we must decide how to structure the laws which secure those rights to take advantage of our economic system's ability to stimulate creative activity for our mutual benefit. The study of these questions forecasts a broad and interesting cross-disciplinary future for copyright theory.

For example, the question of how much property authors deserve starts with an attempt to separate original material from borrowed material in each work. Of course, the nature of authorship makes it likely that this attempt will only be partially successful in giving authors and society their just desserts. Borrowed material is often recast and reshaped to the extent that its identification or separation is impossible. Even seemingly original creations sometimes depend on borrowing which is not readily apparent. When this happens, society must construct an equitable division of property between the author and the public. Brief reflection shows how the legal theorist's conception of this division would benefit from cross-disciplinary inquiry. First, any separation of original material from borrowed material requires sophisticated notions of creativity and borrowing. Second, if we are serious about making an equitable division between authors and society on the basis of the author's debt to her predecessors, society's belief about the size of this debt becomes vitally important. Art historians, literary critics and authors themselves will undoubtedly have valuable insights to contribute to this debate.

Similarly, the question of how to structure legal entitlements to take advantage of our economic system also requires competence in areas often outside a lawyer's training. Regardless of how much property society thinks an author deserves, a wide range of legal tools will become available to secure the necessary rights. The obvious tool is the "breadth" of copyright's reach. If authors deserve a lot, even very faint borrowings might become actionable. However, other tools may secure for authors their just desserts equally as well. Changing the length of copyright's term, creating licensing schemes, or even making cash payments

36 This view is reflected in the Universal Declaration of Human Rights, G.A. Res. 217 [III], U.N. Doc. A/810, at 76 (1948), which states, "[e]veryone has the right to the protection of the moral and material interests resulting from any scientific, literary or artistic production of which he is the author."

to authors would all affect the size of authorship's rewards. If society wants to structure its copyright rewards to take advantage of our capitalist system, economists will undoubtedly have helpful recommendations for choosing among the various alternatives. Since capitalism in turn depends on the cooperative behavior of individuals, psychologists may be able to suggest legal arrangements which facilitate bargaining.[37]

Without question, the future sketched out above will be difficult to explore. Few persons can claim expertise in all the disciplines relevant to copyright's construction. This problem may deter some from changing the monolithic economic inquiry which presently dominates copyright jurisprudence. Perhaps too many cooks will ultimately spoil copyright's broth. Although such a fear is perfectly understandable, I believe that we should nevertheless expand our copyright discourse. Copyright law gives individuals the power to control the future use of texts, paintings, compositions, and other forms of communication. It therefore fundamentally affects the kind of intellectual life each of us is able to lead. Everyone, regardless of perspective, should therefore be encouraged to participate in the ordering of that life.

---

[37] For example, economists often suggest that property rights exist for the purpose of facilitating the private bargaining which promotes social welfare. Since empirical research shows that bargaining is more likely to occur when the parties' rights are clear, it seems that a judge or legislature interested in using copyright to advance social welfare would select the least ambiguous rules possible. *See* COOTER & ULEN, *supra* note 28, at 99-100. This insight is noteworthy because the present trend permits plaintiffs to claim copyright in increasingly vague facets of their works. *See* Fisher, *supra* note 8, at 1659 (criticizing fair use doctrine as vague and uncertain); Alfred C. Yen, *A First Amendment Perspective on the Idea/Expression Dichotomy and Copyright in a Work's "Total Concept and Feel,"* 38 EMORY L. J. 393 (1989) (criticizing modern interpretation of the idea/expression dichotomy as vague). To the extent that these decisions are justified as welfare maximizing economic incentives for authors, the potential welfare benefits may be offset by the difficulty authors and potential consumers will face in bargaining over exploitation of these vague rights.

COMPARING BROADCAST STRUCTURES: TRANSNATIONAL PERSPECTVES AND POST-COMMUNIST EXAMPLES

MONROE E. PRICE*

I. THINKING TRANSNATIONALLY

Enough activity is taking place, in terms of research and advice on broadcasting structures in Central and Eastern Europe and the former Soviet Union, that it is worthwhile to step back and think about the formidable process of shaping transnational perspectives. What is in the wardrobe of public or private concerns that motivates cross-cultural communications studies? In these extraordinary times of trying to manufacture liberal democracies from national pasts and the detritus of command economies, are these advising activities productive? How should one measure effectiveness? Who are the interested parties and what is the basis of their interests?

Governments, including those of the United States, the United Kingdom, and France, provide financial support for travel, research, and the interaction of journalists and scholars;[1] American foundations and universities provide critical encouragement. The outline of a small industry, made up partly of communications scholars from the West and academics and broadcasters from the East, is taking shape. It will be possible—maybe not now, but certainly at some future time—to establish a production chart: who are the manufacturers of new laws?; who are those engaged in research and development?; who are the retailers?; who are the installers and repairmen?[2] And finally, if

---

* © 1993 Monroe E. Price, Danciger Professor of Law and Director, Squadron Program on Law, Media, and Society, Benjamin N. Cardozo School of Law, Yeshiva University. B.A. 1960, LL.B. 1964, Yale University. This essay is part of a larger project on television and national identity under a grant from the John and Mary Markle R. Foundation. I wish to thank Professor Andrei Richter, Moscow State University and Professor Peter Krug, University of Oklahoma for reading and contributing to the manuscript; and Ellen Mickiewicz, Professor of Political Science and Fellow of the Carter Presidential Center at Emory University, Professor Andras Sajo, Central European University, and Professor Eric Barendt, University College, London for their comments on various parts of the essay. The Institute for International Communications allowed me to explore a number of related questions as guest editor of InterMedia. I have benefitted from being a member of the Commission on Radio and Television Policy, based at the Carter Presidential Center, but the opinions and errors in this essay are my own.

1 *See, e.g.*, *Expanding the Boundaries of Freedom: The Balkans to the Baltics*, Report of the International Media Fund, Washington, D.C. 1992.

2 A number of American legal scholars have assisted in the construction of new con-

things do not work out, who will collect the debris?

At this nascent industry's most basic level, there is the project of chronicling specific statutory drafts and laws country by country, organizing them by category, and engaging in a textual analysis that compares the proposed and achieved shifts in one state to those in another.[3] Various categories for analysis and archiving automatically come to mind; e.g., prior censorship, frequency allocation, extent of privatization, journalists' rights, viewers' rights, appointment of chief executive officers of public service broadcasters, composition and appointment of supervisory or regulatory bodies, and judicial review of regulatory decisions. Yet, in the post-modern, post-critical, post-legal-realist world we are more than naturalists with stuffed cabinets of statutes pinned like butterflies under glass. The mere text of laws, and certainly drafts, can be misleading, especially if the purpose of examining these is to reveal the evolution of the relationship between broadcasting structures and society. Without a sense of context, these drafts and statutes are evidence not of broadcasting practices, but of political divisions, possible aspirations, societal compromises, local confusions, or international fashions. The purpose of this essay and the collection of essays and appendices that follows is to provide that context, which will facilitate examination of the evolution in this relationship.

To measure actually the expansion of democratic values, the

stitutions and statutes. These include, among many others, Professor Herman Schwartz, American University; Professor A.E. Dick Howard, University of Virginia; Professor Lawrence Tribe, Harvard University; Professor Peter Tillers, Benjamin N. Cardozo School of Law; and Professor Ruti Teitel, New York Law School. In Washington D.C., David Webster has convened the Trans-Atlantic Dialogue, a group of experts specially brought together to advise on press and media issues. The Central and Eastern European Law Initiative, an ambitious project of the American Bar Association, has provided small technical advisory missions of lawyers and academics on a wide variety of subjects, including the press and broadcasting laws of the newly emerging states. The International Media Fund, started with government financing, has paired journalism schools in the United States with counterparts in Central and Eastern Europe, and has hosted sessions designed to encourage revisions in structural thinking about the relationship between the press and the state. Internews, an organization that pioneered "space bridges" (satellite links) between the Soviet Union and the United States, has conducted intensive training sessions for journalists in independent reporting and has been instrumental in forging connections among such journalists in different Republics. The Carter Presidential Center in Atlanta, part of Emory University, has spawned the Commission on Radio and Television Policy—directed by Professor Ellen Mickiewicz—which has helped develop a model broadcasting statute for the Republics of the former Soviet Union. The author of this essay is a member of the Commission and participated in developing the draft. A complete list of those involved is too long to set forth here.

3 The International Association of Mass Communications Research ("IAMCR") has established an entity called BLER (Broadcasting Laws of Eastern Europe and Russia), with a timetable for reports and analyses. The *rapporteur* is Professor Wolfgang Kleinwachter.

mere examination of documents is far from sufficient. Travel, meetings, and discourse must take place. There is a kind of odd intercourse here, reminiscent of European exploration of exotic lands. Western journalists and scholars travel to Central Europe or the former Soviet Union, where they spend time conducting interviews; a mosaic of their impressions provides some insight into what is taking place. Czechs, Poles, Russians, and Slovenians are flown to London, Washington, and Paris, like Native exemplars of a distant past; they perform and are studied to provide a basis for Western academics, governments, and businesses to determine the lay of the land. Meetings take place in castles and conference centers, or by fax and phone.

But what is communicated, even face-to-face? The problems of communication are probably similar to those that plagued eighteenth- and nineteenth-century scholars and civil servants. Formal language difficulties aside, a fundamental hurdle is the uncertainty about transferability of concepts. We cannot really know how rooted in a particular history and flow of experiences a set of practices might be. No matter how sophisticated we are, how schooled in the relativism of anthropology and sociology, it is too easy to conclude that laws and institutions come in ready-made, almost modular packages (though sometimes they must). What we must take into account is not merely the translation of words, or even of concepts, but the translation of deeply ingrained administrative environments. One cannot talk of "judges," of "neutral principles," or of "accountability of government officials to the rule of law" without sensitivity to the complexities of adjustment. Dynastic memory makes some forms of power and hierarchy more acceptable in the East than in the West. Even simple concepts, such as those involved in the implementation of broadcasting alternatives, may have complex counterparts.[4] On the other hand, tacit acceptance of the limitations that bar modular transformations will render the Western observer almost useless, for the implementation of Western ideals is critical to the development of liberal democracies. What should be sought, but is difficult to achieve, is the project of interpretation. Such interpretation comprises a critical study of the statutes and laws drafted in the transitional states, the construc-

---

4 Such concepts include industry self-regulation of indecent programming, the structure of public service broadcasters, libel laws, rights of reply, immunity for journalists, and policies with respect to political advertising. *See* PNINA LAHAV, PRESS LAW IN MODERN DEMOCRACIES: A COMPARATIVE STUDY (1985).

tion of a set of narratives about the reshaping of broadcasting systems, and a journey into the dark forest of hermeneutics.

Only through the lens of differences—differences which have their origins in disparate internal histories—can the transferability of concepts be perceived; and the quintessential example of central historical differences is in the meaning attached in a given society to "freedom of expression"—the relationship between the political state and the media—the bellwether of differences in how states regulate the distribution of information.[5] Internal histories of free speech are hardly laboratory-pure, however. They are made through the absorption of other histories: histories of violence and war, of idealism and cynicism; histories that have become more complex with the expansion of international trade. It is this trade, not only in images and in goods but in the very concept of how pictures, thoughts, and words are regulated, that underscores the importance of the search for national identity in the transition states.[6] The tasks of interpreting new statutes and constructing a new broadcasting system are rendered more coherent by trying to locate, in each instance, the role of the state as a shaper of national identity.

In a world trained to think of itself as immersed in the "information era," the relationship between the nature of any given political system and the structure of its communication systems is of great importance. For the political scientist Karl Deutsch, one way of understanding the political essence of a society is to examine and calibrate its internal web of message-sending.[7] He offers what he calls a "functional definition of nationality,"[8] a predictive model for the behaviors of nations that relies on gauging the coherence of its communication systems. For Deutsch, "the range and effectiveness of social communication . . . may tell us how effectively [a community] has become integrated, and how far it has advanced, in this respect, toward becoming a na-

---

5 Much has been written on this question. Two interesting recent books are LEE BOLLINGER, IMAGES OF A FREE PRESS (1991) and STEVEN SHIFFRIN, THE FIRST AMENDMENT, DEMOCRACY, AND ROMANCE (1990).

6 This search is partly in response to threats to the permeability of their boundaries. What constitutes permeability is a function of borders and definitions of national cultures. The vast reach of the former Soviet Union's central television signals did not present a formal issue of permeability when the boundaries of the U.S.S.R. existed. With the Union dissolved, the presence of these signals in Ukraine or Lithuania is now differently defined. As to the complex issues of permeability in Western Europe, see ELI NOAM, TELEVISION IN EUROPE (1991).

7 KARL W. DEUTSCH, NATIONALISM AND SOCIAL COMMUNICATION, AN INQUIRY INTO THE FOUNDATIONS OF NATIONALITY (2d ed. 1966).

8 *Id.* at 97.

tion."[9] He added that the limits of selfhood of a group of people "will be the limits of its effectiveness in transmitting and circulating information."[10]

Conversely, any study about the regulation of television must be more comprehensive, not focusing on just a single aspect of a general system, but touching questions concerning the nature of the entire communications and political structure. Of course, this is a difficult task. Television itself is mesmerizing, powerful, and ubiquitous, with an immediate glamour and presence that makes it the first, and strangely isolated, object of interest and study—a kind of demon of modern life. Indeed, the role of television may be shifting in its relationship to other media, including computers and radio. For example, the increase of global programming, partly a consequence of the improved capacity of satellite transmission and cable distribution, may mean that television is a progressively weaker instrument for the making of national identities. Regardless, the regulation of television receives enormous attention. It may not, however, be the kind of attention that fully takes into account all the necessary factors to be considered in defining the relationship between the media and society.

Part of the problem is that scholars are condemned to compare societies that have had almost opposite histories of communications structures—some moving toward liberal democracy from autocratic command approaches, some seeking to increase the diversity of content and the ease of access in an already relatively-free communications structure. Some societies have asserted the power to use communications networks totally to shape or control loyalties, while others have encouraged competition against the state and have also limited the state's role. There is a spectrum here, not necessarily of democracy versus authoritarianism, but of active state involvement in the construction of a public sphere and of sustaining a national identity on the one hand, or pretending to leave these questions to the mar-

---

9 *Id.* at 99.

10 *Id.* at 167. The pursuit of Karl Deutsch's almost quantitative approach to definition coexists with another kind of elaboration; namely, the study of how the origins of any particular modern nationhood have been created, invented, or imagined. *See, e.g.*, Benedict Anderson, Imagined Communities: Reflections on the Origin and Spread of Nationalism (1991); The Invention of Tradition (Eric J. Hobsbawm and Terence Ranger eds., 1983). While it is true that the circulation of information and access to outward messages indicate the health and durability of an organism (as Deutsch makes clear), it is also important to study how the state, or the political elite, participates in that zone of communication, frequently using its participation to create a representation of the state that functions as a reinforcing instrument of its own power.

ket on the other. Only by being reflective about these more complex issues—and not focusing solely on a single model of the democratic state—can Western observers and counselors constructively participate in the task of attempting to democratize and provide greater freedom for broadcasting structures in former socialist states.[11]

II. Speech, Political, and Economic Structures

An obvious and critical element in reviewing the patterns of a restructured media involves sources of financial support, the essence of the relationship with the state. In the Soviet *ancien regime*, the goal of the monopoly broadcasters, as instruments of the state, was relatively clear, and the source of financing to perform the prescribed functions was also clearly established.[12] The transformation of the once-formidable First Channel of the Soviet Union, virtually the official voice of the Soviet Union, provides an example. Secure in its financing, it was secure in its purpose. In the post-Soviet world, however, it suddenly had an ambiguous status and mandate, and that ambiguity was reflected in the insecurity of financing. With the loosening of the imperial ties, the Channel was seeking to be pan-Republican, the soft unifier of the "Commonwealth of Independent States," of the "Newly Independent States," of the territories of the former Soviet Union, or of some other geo-political mass.[13] This alternative was not necessarily consistent with the political goals of the new Republics, and ambiguity in role leads to ambiguity in financing. An informal agreement among the presidents of the Republics to maintain and finance the Channel provided shaky assurance. It was not clear whether the First Channel's purpose

---

[11] The problem of expression is closely bound with specific pasts. In Bulgaria, for example, in early 1992, a fervent group—calling itself the "Ten Words Are Enough Movement"—sought to adopt a minimalist approach to the role of the state in defining a broadcasting system. Ten words, declaring that the media must be free, were believed sufficient to lead a new liberal democratic world. Perhaps this movement should have been embraced. However, the group was attacked as reactionary, linked to the Communist past, and as championing the *status quo ante.* The portability of the words of the First Amendment of the United States Constitution is a perilous matter, both for scholars and policy makers. *See* Verginia Jordanova, *The Politics of Change in Bulgaria*, 20 InterMedia No.3, at 16 (1992).

[12] *See* Peter Krug, *The Abandonment of the State Radio-Television Monopoly in the Soviet Union: A First Step Toward Broadcasting Pluralism?*, 9 Wisc. Int'l L.J. 377 (1991); Anna G. Kachkaeva and Andrei G. Richter, *The Emergence of Non-State TV in the Ukraine*, 17 Canadian J. Comm. 511 (1992).

[13] The very confusion over nomenclature, depending on whether adherents to the Commonwealth, former Republics, the Balkans, or other areas are included in a political grouping, underscores the problem of ambiguity of purpose and financing.

was to provide a Russian language signal to the large numbers of Russian nationals who inhabited the new states, to provide a common information sphere, to establish a new sense of linkage between a different center and a different periphery, or merely to maintain a flow of entertainment at a difficult economic period while the several state television networks were still weak and inexperienced.

To determine whether there is a model for a pan-Republic service is to assume important questions about what cultural, communications, and economic links there will be among the component parts of the Union. Ukrainian officials and others complain that the Channel maintains the tradition of Russification, and that it continues to be a voice of the Russian empire, though perhaps more subtly. What should the policy of the First Channel be? Who should appoint its chief? How are these questions considered from the perspective of free speech ideas? Programming changes were evident in the early 1990s as the First Channel sought to attract an audience with demographic features attractive to advertisers. Consequently, programming content that would not insult its now more diverse political constituency was necessary. An MTV look replaced the more somber presidium aesthetic. In what would probably be a temporary compromise, the Russian Federation seemed to underwrite the Channel's program costs prior to 1993 (though trying to decentralize transmission costs), partly as a reflection of the view in other Republics that the Channel espouses a Russian, not a regional, perspective.

Patterns of financing are more commonly a matter of concern in development of the print media than they are in television. An official state television network, financed by the state, is taken for granted in ways that a state-financed newspaper is not. As a result, questions involving the allocation and subsidization of newsprint are ubiquitous. Perhaps, in many of these structures, the state must underwrite civil society and its zone of discourse. Nonetheless, withdrawing subsidies from television may mean a steady decline to a diet of the shabbiest programming and the elimination of television as a source of culture, information, and discourse, just as it may mean a deterioration of the supply of information through newspapers. Transaction costs, including obstacles imposed by the assertion of intellectual property rights, can impede the growth of strong public service or independent broadcasters. Indeed, in some contexts, the adoption of a copyright regime may protect better-heeled state television monopolies from the competition of non-state broadcasters.[14] Non-enforcement or slack enforcement of copyright can be seen as a kind of subsidy that discriminates in favor of independent broadcasters. Almost universally, advertising has become an acceptable, if not mandatory, source of revenue.[15] In societies where people are trying to be consumers, but where demand for consumer goods is not high and the supply is problematic, developing a market for advertising is quite difficult. Much advertising (off, more than on, television) is used to develop brand identification so that when the market matures particular competitors will have built a franchise for themselves.[16]

Redefinition of concepts of "independence," (as in "independent broadcaster") is a frequent aspect of the narratives of transformation. Westerners are always looking for "independent" journalists or "independent" producers, rarely stopping to examine the context of independence. In Ukraine, for example, where "independent" television services are beginning, they not only use the state transmitter and the state studio facilities, but they broadcast pursuant to rights that seem to be governed by the state television service itself.[17] One can see the hazards looming, but whether outside experts can merely fit the proper piece into the machinery of regulation is unclear. A sign of the difficult passage to independence could be witnessed during the early 1990s in Kiev as the state television service physically manifested its endurance.[18] A gleaming new television facility, started

---

[14] The policy of the United States is to assure that the copyrights in motion pictures are respected and that films are not pirated. But most so-called infant "independent" television stations in the transition societies (primarily the Newly Independent States) were reliant on bootlegged films and similar product for a competitive edge. In some markets, these pirate-based independents were accounting for almost fifty percent of the audience market. Thus, it may be in the interest of the state broadcasters to choke off the supply of product to these competitors by joining in the insistence on compliance with copyright law.

[15] For a brilliant article on the impact of advertising support on content in the American context, see C. Edwin Baker, *Advertising and a Democratic Press*, 140 U. PA. L. REV. 2097 (1992).

[16] See Andrei G. Richter, *Broadcasting Law in the Ukraine,* BROADCASTING IN TRANSITION, NETCOM PAPERS No. 3, at 60-61 (Leipzig 1993) for a discussion of the role of advertising on Ukrainian television.

[17] In early 1993, the Commission on Radio and Television Policy (based at the Carter Center in Atlanta with a membership of American broadcasting professionals and professionals from across the former CIS) helped prepare a Charter of Media Independence for use by non-state broadcasting entities in the former Soviet Union. The Charter provides that subscribing stations "adopt ethical guidelines that assure independence from government and other entities that might compromise journalistic objectivity."

[18] The overwhelming majority of radio and television channels in Ukraine are state owned; regional companies, theoretically autonomous, are very much under Kiev's administration. The state company is headed by a president appointed by the Cabinet of

as a monument during the statist days of a decade ago, was prepared for occupancy. Perhaps architecture, not legislation, demonstrates the role of the state in broadcasting—a physical symbol of the continuing relationship of state interest to non-state originated communications. Often things are not as they appear to be to the foreign observer; this makes long-distance reliance on formal language, or even casual narrative, extremely perilous as a guide to transformations.

III. Interpreting Texts

A substantial distinction still exists between approaches to broadcasting structures in post-Communist and Western societies. In the transitional societies, perhaps primarily in the former Republics of the Soviet Union, the state's role in both establishing national identity and rendering the idea of the state more coherent has continued. The background factors—the social, economic, and political contexts—are clear. But what about text? Do the emerging texts of press and broadcasting laws reflect these differences? In the United States, Great Britain, and in Europe, the modern state appears—with some cyclical moves—to cope with competing demands for the loyalty of its citizens through the vocabulary of deregulation; i.e., the appearance of as little governmental intervention as possible and, to the extent possible, a continuing diminution in that intervention. For example, in the summer of 1992, President Mitterand of France was precluded from establishing a publicly-funded television advertising campaign to convince French voters to ratify the Maastricht

---

Ministers with the consent of the Committee on Mass Media of Ukraine's Supreme Soviet. Nikolai F. Okhmakevish, the head of the company in 1992, was head of its predecessor during the Soviet era. All three vice-presidents are also appointed by the Cabinet. There is one full-time channel administered by Ukranian state television (UT-1), which includes political programs and official information. Two other efforts are three-hour daily preemptions of the Russian channel from Moscow: UT-2 is less politicized, and UT-3, born in 1992, is mainly experimental, broadcasting movies and dramas from the West, dubbed into Ukranian.

The basic languages on the Ukranian channels are Ukranian and Russian. In early 1993, the balance between the two was almost fifty-fifty, although the Russian programming is dwindling since no new programs are produced in the Russian language. Non-state television entities broadcast primarily in Russian. Dish antennas were prohibited for private use at the end of the 1980s. Kachkaeva and Richter, *supra* note 12, at 511-523.

Kachkaeva and Richter identify three stages in the evolution of "alternate television" in the former Soviet Union. In its first stage (1988-89), these were seen as in opposition to the "rearguard actions of [state] bureaucrats during the *glasnost* drive." *Id.* at 512. The second stage, during the disintegration of Gostelradio in 1990-91, involved use by the alternative institutional structures of state facilities and joint ventures with state television. The third phase began after the failed coup d'etat of August 1991. *Id.*

Treaty on European Union. Government use of its resources for the overt shaping of national identities through the media is considered less and less acceptable, and to the extent it takes place, it should be openly articulated and its structure should be transparent.[19] During the early 1990s, the situation was otherwise in the republics of the former Soviet Union and the states of Central and Eastern Europe. War (or the threat of war), irredentism, fierce immigration debates, and the general instability of economic transformations, meant that the competition for loyalties was extraordinary. The very definition of the state was often at issue. Therefore, government intervention in the cultivation of national identity was developing at a fevered pitch.

Of course, there is much—perhaps too much—that the formal statutory language, and even the process leading to enactment of the statute, does not disclose. Where does technology come in?; how much is regulable?; and how much is determined by the entry of satellite and cable technology rather than by the articulated desires of lawmakers? The formal language does not disclose the power of the audience, nor how it reads what is on the screen, nor what changes in its viewing patterns ensued from the entry of new competitors who are often outside the formal framework. Nor does the formal wording indicate patterns of conformity between the aspirations of law and the action of officials, much of what is called the "rule of law." And aside from verbal aspirations, which mirror some adopted notion of democracy, the infrastructure for transformation (i.e., existence of a consumer market, availability of capital, and incentives for investment) may be wildly out of kilter with the established model. The language of statutes may have the purpose of camouflage, or may be designed to placate an international community rather than to guide conduct. The purpose here is not to determine what the law "is" or what conduct is proscribed or permitted; rather, it is to look at statutes in the same way that an archaeologist looks at shards to help decipher, decode, and explain an ancient civilization—as narrative text about the society.

All this said, studying the language of legislative provisions, proposed and enacted, that deal with the relationship between the media and the state is a way to search for the vocabulary of change. Laws and lawmaking are clues as to the nature of the

[19] How and whether these goals have been achieved or whether it is, in fact, an objective, is the subject of a larger project which touches upon such complex issues as funding for public broadcasting, subsidy policy with respect to the arts, and structures of access during political debates.

transformations—whether, for example, they represent a revolution of rights, or as Andras Sajo has argued, an attempt to restore some hard-to-locate pre-Socialist order of an imagined national past. Broadcasting legislation might be the actual working out of conflicts, or it may be evidence of inexorable anxieties that plague the society. Some parts of the new broadcasting laws may be drafted not as a reflection of internal realities, but rather of the compulsion, inducement, or idealized hopes of outside models—a mirror pointed outside toward the face of the West. Some parts show the scars of the past; they can be read mainly as articulated triumphs over some seemingly rejected torturous practice, retained in the very act of forceful repression. Broadcasting statutes reflect the definition of power in the new societies and the competition between assertions of legislative, executive, judicial, and personal authority. As they reveal the ambivalence toward the shift in ownership from public to private, the statutes and the statutory process involve the debate over the state monopoly for loyalties. There are residual prohibitions on those outside the state: *glasnost* with limitations, restrictions on ownership, and limitations on the range in which hostility to the very idea of the state can be expressed. During the current period of change, these new legal texts provide some insight into the new conceptions of the state, of government, and of democracy that their drafters hold. In the remainder of this essay, I examine several such transitional statutes or drafts of broadcasting laws.

A. *The Russian Federation Law on Mass Media of 1991*

Convoluted and complex by American standards, the Russian Federation Law on Mass Media of 1991 was one of the first and most comprehensive media statutes to emerge in the post-Communist era.[20] Intrigue, xenophobia, a search for modernity,

---

20 At the time this article was going to press, the Russian Federation Law on Mass Media of 1991 ("Russian Media Law") was embroiled in the fierce contest between President Yeltsin and the Congress of People's Deputies. On March 28, 1993, the Congress passed a decree that required the heads of state television and radio broadcasting companies to be appointed and dismissed by a new entity called the "Federation Observation Council for the Ensurance of the Freedom of Speech at State Television and Radio Broadcasting," though only with the consent of the Supreme Soviet of the Russian Federation. Concluding that "unequal granting of time on tv and on the air to expressions of different political views" amounted to political censorship, the Congress decreed that "the activity of organs of management unenvisaged by law . . . should stop." Tass Reports, Mar. 28, 1993.

Just prior to the above-mentioned congressional decree, Boris Yeltsin issued a special decree on March 20, 1993, in view "of the real threat to the freedom of information . . . and in order to avert the monopolization of the mass information media and unlawful interference in their activity." He placed the mass media "under the protection of

compliance with international pressures, the "solutions" proposed by advisors parachuted in from the United States and elsewhere—all this is part of the mix that produced the infant legislative drafts in Russia and other beleaguered new states. Everywhere was the blanket of the past—with its purposive, penetrating, stifling controls—a complex backdrop for the evaluation of any proposed approach.

The Russian Media Law can only be understood as an evolution from the preceding order, not as a comparison to some distant and culturally ill-fitting parallel.[21] Looking at the media law may be like examining the wrists of a recently-freed prisoner where the marks of the chains are still present. Drafted by a group of journalists and academics as an ideal, almost apolitical, formulation of the relationship between the media and the state, the statute is organized into seven chapters, the first of which, by honored position, sets forth a basic guarantee of freedom from censorship for "mass information."[22] The second chapter provides a form of regulation relatively unknown in the United States: a detailed concern with the internal organization of the media activities, including meticulous concern with the organization of ventures, the agreement between founder and editor, and the arrangements, both editorial and functional, between the editor-in-chief and the journalists.[23] The third chapter includes a guarantee of physical distribution of newspapers and magazines that reflects a remembered fear of the perils of state control over the machinery of distribution.[24] This chapter also deals with the issuance, regulation, and annulment of television and radio broadcast licenses,[25] as well as familiar aspects of content con-

---

the law *and the president of the Russian Federation as the supreme official personage of the state.*" BBC Summary of World Broadcasts, Mar. 24, 1993 (emphasis added). The Ministry of Internal Affairs was charged with the responsibility of guarding state television and radio companies, presumably from interference by perceived enemies of the state. *Id. See also Yeltsin Decree on Information Stability,* BBC Summary of World Broadcasts, Mar. 25, 1993 (establishing minimum standards which include the guidance of the declaration on the media and human rights of the consultative assembly of the Council of Europe).

21 *See* Brian McNair, Glasnost, Perestroika and the Soviet Media (1991) and Ellen Mickiewicz, Split Signals: Television and Politics in the Soviet Union (1988) for a history of media in the Soviet Union.

22 It is more than interesting that what the legislation purports to cover is described as "mass information." This term has the flavor of the model of society in which there is a largely undifferentiated class-constant population with a vertical relationship between the publisher and the reader. Already, the law reveals a valuable conceptual relic of the past.

23 Russian Media Law art. 22.

24 *Id.* art. 25.

25 *Id.* art. 31-32.

trol.[26] The fourth chapter demonstrates the synergetic nature of freedoms. Not only must there be the abolition of censorship, and not only must the finished product of the editorial process receive guaranteed distribution, but the citizens' right to receive information must also be assured.[27] The fifth chapter reminds the journalist of the occupation's double-edged sword. The state affords a journalist power, but he or she must be responsible. Thus, there is an ornate and important set of regulations describing the rights and responsibilities of journalists,[28] a section that is rich in its reverberations of past into future. Other sections deal with foreign publications and foreign correspondents,[29] the imposition of sanctions for statutory violations,[30] immunities for journalists and editors,[31] and citizen access to the courts.[32] The sixth and seventh chapters pertain to interstate agreements and other foreign matters, and placing responsibility for violation of the statute, respectively.

The outline of the statute tells us something about the drafters' consciousness in terms of the national goals for a broadcasting system. This is not a statute that begins with language glorifying the state, or in which the state is even the central actor. The idea—the very organization—of the statute is to involve the state as little as possible, to construct autonomous broadcasting entities that have rights against the state, rather than the other way around. But it requires a more meticulous examination of the statute's provisions to determine the extent to which the state creeps back in. As an embodiment of Western traditions of independence, the statute might be an emblem of democratization—an ingredient, like a new flag, of a new national identity—rather than the means to implement or require aspects of loyalty.

The censorship provisions have such significance and scope that they become an important starting point in examining the statute for its narrative import. Obviously, a broad prohibition of censorship was important to proclaim, as the statute begins with

---

26 *Id.* art. 36 (addressing advertising) and art. 37 (regarding erotic publications).

27 *Id.* art. 38.

28 *Id.* art. 47, 49.

29 *Id.* ch. VI. Entitled *Interstate Cooperation,* chapter six encompasses art. 53-55.

30 *Id.* art. 56, 59-60.

31 *Id.* art. 57.

32 *Id.* art. 61. One appealing aspect of the draft statute, from the archaeological perspective, is that it appears to be almost wholly home-grown. It has the charm of aspiration, seeking to absorb the style of democratic societies without the support or context, and with a need to extend the tools and the vocabulary. In that sense it is also an interesting baseline against which to look at later developments and at statutes where the intervention of foreign scribes is more evident.

a general prohibition on governmental and some non-governmental intervention in editorial policy.[33] More interesting, however, is what was omitted from the sweep of anti-censorial zeal: Article 4 lists the permissible content prohibitions and thereby somehow defines the proper zone of national concern with the shaping of public consciousness.[34] For example, the statute prohibits instruments of mass information from calling for a change in the existing constitutional order by force; from arousing religious animosities; from fomenting social, class, or national intolerance; or from proliferating war propaganda.[35]

These exceptions, these nodes of sensitivity, are extraordinarily expressive of the overriding concerns of an insecure young state—as they were of an insecure older state before it. To prohibit a call for revolution in the existing constitutional structure suggests an institutional aspiration for stability, for the preservation of basic elements of the status quo, for a political debate that has important bounds. The exception is a sign of concern, perhaps justified, that some speech, by representatives of the Soviet *ancien regime* for example, is potentially very dangerous, and that the state has a duty to defend against the promulgation of messages that could be destructive to the process of openness. Prohibiting the arousal of religious animosities suggests a role for the nation in fostering, preserving, or perhaps strengthening the position of religious organizations. This exception from the ban on censorship foretells a society in which these specific wounds to an important institution cannot be permitted again. An exception prohibiting speech that foments social, class, or national intolerance denotes an important role for the state in ameliorating the harsh schisms and ancient hatreds between ethnic groups—breaking with a tradition that sometimes required the denial that these and other conflicts existed. The prohibition against "war propaganda" is also a reminder of past beliefs (founded or not) that a private, capitalist press can stir the people into unwarranted aggression, against the interest of the state. Here, as in all of the exceptions, the state is positioned as separate, authoritative, and capable of having a proper sense of what is a just war and what is not.

---

[33] *Id.* art. 3.

[34] *Id.* art. 4.

[35] *Id.* The law prohibits the divulgence of official secrets, the use of the mass media to perform criminal acts, and the use of hidden or subliminal advertising. Some of these prohibitions may be based on Article 20 of the International Covenant on Civil and Political Rights, which prohibits propaganda for war and advocacy of national, racial or religious hatred.

Censorship is the negative aspect of government power. A media act can also be revealing in terms of its implications for the resulting structure of a press sector. Will there be an all-powerful state broadcasting authority with private entities only at the margin? Can government assure "diversity" in terms of an imposed outcome in which many voices are guaranteed to be heard? Or will the solution be market-oriented, in which the state withdraws and has little assurance as to the organic composition of the resulting economic circumstance? The law that I am examining, like many media statutes, is tantalizing concerning these questions, but not sufficiently detailed to allow the archaeologist to know what actually was intended or what might have grown from the draft.[36]

I have mentioned the provisions for the registration and internal management of mass media.[37] A statute that requires prepublication registration with discretionary approval makes some statement about the potential role of the state. A registration scheme can be non-threatening by limiting the discretion of the registration authority. The Russian Media Law of 1991 tries to accomplish this by limiting the power of the registering authority to grant registration. Because there are limits on who can establish the mass media, a registration could be refused if the ownership or structure is improper. More troublesome is the power to deny a registration of the applicant where the registering authority knows that the content to be produced would violate the law (for example, that it would foment class or national intolerance).[38] A registration scheme often conditions permission to publish on the proper kind of ownership, and ownership restrictions provide one of the most important insights into the national

---

[36] Earlier drafts dealt with monopoly aspects. Article 4 empowered the government to set standards to assure that instruments of mass information were not so concentrated as to constitute a monopoly. Article 28 stated that for printed periodicals, no group of such periodicals should have a combined circulation exceeding 30 percent of the printed periodicals within a specific territory. The exact implications for the structure of a television and radio industry were left for another law. So long as the reader does not know how extensive, how much of a market share, or how pervasive state broadcasting will be (or whether a state-controlled newspaper will be subsidized and have favorable access to newsprint), the power of government officials to shape loyalties and to impose an idea of the state cannot be ascertained.

[37] Russian Media Law, ch. II (encompasses art. 7-24).

[38] *Id.* art. 13. The registration authority could have established separate fees for registrants based on the following: (1) fees for instruments of mass information that specialize in the production of advertising or erotic material could be higher, while; (2) publications for children, youths, invalids, and for education and culture could be lower. This power is an important one because it would give an agency the need to decide on a discriminatory fee structure and some authority to decide what constitutes a publication in each category.

tendencies of a media law. In the Russian statute, which has a category called "founder,"[39] foreign citizens cannot establish the mass media,[40] nor can persons without citizenship who do not live continuously within the boundaries of the Russian Federation.[41]

Ownership is a clue, in another vital way, to analyzing the effect of the media in shaping national identity. Should the government, directly or indirectly, be able to establish and operate an instrument of mass information? One could conceive the answer to this question as a hallmark determinant about the nature of the state and its potential for shaping public opinion and fostering loyalties. Most Western democracies have had state-controlled, or heavily state-influenced broadcasters; in a sense, that is what public service broadcasting has been. The United States has been relatively unique in its historic policy of ambivalence toward all but the private.[42] The Russian law would permit, in Article 7, any "state organ" to found a mass media.[43] The statute denotes continuity with the environment of the past, a situation in which great powers in the society—Ministries, Unions, even Parliament—can be founders of newspapers.

National power to register—to legitimate—implies a power to deregister, to close, to delegitimate. The relationship between a publication and the state, and the capacity of the state to influence content (often not so subtly) is a function of this harshest of sanctions: the power of the government to actually close a newspaper down. One could conceive of a statutory scheme that had no such power, relying, if necessary, on the ordinary authority of the state to punish individuals for criminal acts, or to collect taxes, or to impose damages for injury inflicted. The Russian law has the beguiling appearance of liberalization, but also an implied sense that the government can step in when something is dreadfully wrong. Article 16 governs the power to close down the mass media.[44] The article speaks in the language of limita-

---

39 *See infra* note 48.

40 Russian Media Law, art. 7. In the United States, newspapers and magazines can be founded by anyone, and so can broadcasting entities, though there is a percentage limitation on the degree of ownership by noncitizens.

41 *Id.* This does not prevent foreigners from circulating their foreign-published mass media. That is governed by Article 54.

42 I include the nonprofit public broadcasting stations within the realm of the ambivalence.

43 Article 7 of the Russian Media Law, entitled *Founder,* reads as follows: "[t]he founder (cofounder) of a mass media may be a citizen, an association of citizens, an enterprise, institution, organization, or state organ."

44 Article 16 of the Russian Media Law is entitled *Termination and cessation of activity.*

tions. Only in certain circumstances can the founder himself cease publication. Furthermore, the Ministry of Press and Information can force closure only if the publication, after warning, persists in violating the prohibitions discussed above (fomenting conflict,[45] etc.), and then only after a court order.[46]

The statute, because it undertakes to regulate the internal working of the press and because it would confer special privileges on the press, must define the press. This leads to a hypothesis worth testing in construing draft media legislation: from a statute's definition of the press, one can infer a definition of the state. There could be a corollary: from a statute's definition of the powers of the state, one can infer the nature of the press. In the United States, one unusual and intriguing aspect of First Amendment jurisprudence is that, over time, definitions of "the press" have almost disappeared, even though the amendment specifically prohibits Congress from abridging "freedom of speech, or of the press." There has been an understanding that the press is freer if it has the rights of mere speakers in society than if it has more specific rights that come from a defined status.[47] Under the Russian law, the "press," referred to as a "mass media," has a defined status; each publication has a stated purpose and a stated range of publication, each registers, and each has an announced internal structure.

The 1991 Russian Federation Law on Mass Media specifies a

During the run-up to the April 25, 1993 referendum, the Ministry of Information sought closure of a newspaper for "collective fabricated hooliganisms." *Moscow Evening News* (Apr. 20, 1993).

[45] The then-Minister of Information, Mikhail Poltoranin, issued a warning to *Sovetskaya Rossiya,* which the newspaper was required to carry in its June 27, 1992 edition. The minister quoted an article about picketing at Ostankino. "Russia's government has launched a bloody war against its own people . . . blood is being shed in Moscow's streets . . . . More than two hundred people were injured. There are fatalities . . . ." The minister pointed out that the reports "have been officially denied as not corresponding to the facts." Russian Press Digest, RusData DiaLine, June 27, 1992.

Subsequently, at the time of the spring 1993 crisis, the Minister of Press and Information initiated court action to close down *Sovetskaya Rossiya* and another paper, *Den.* Press Conference of Minister of Information, Mikhail Fedotov, Mar. 23, 1992, Fed. Info. Sys. Corp., Official Kremlin Int'l New Broadcast.

[46] *See* Russian Media Law, art. 43-46 (public remedies) and art. 60 (possible additional private remedies). Article 15 renders registrations possibly "invalid" if, among other reasons, the registration was obtained deceptively, or if the instrument of mass information has not been published for a year, or if the statute of editorship has not been accepted.

[47] Hence, debates in the United States over whether reporters should have special rights of access, whether newspapers should have libel defenses greater than those of citizens, and whether journalists should have special shield laws. *See infra* note 64. Of course, there are some definitions, including those for special mailing privileges (but these are for printed matter, not press). In addition, regulatory bodies, such as the FCC, must determine who comes within their sway.

set of rules setting forth the relationship between the "founder"[48] and the staff for most "mass media."[49] The law accords the journalists' collective the right to approve the regulations by a majority vote, provided that no less than two-thirds of its membership is present and that the regulations are also approved by the founder.[50] These regulations would cover the manner of appointing the editor-in-chief,[51] the manner for ceasing operation,[52] and the manner by which founders or publishers could be changed.[53] Article 26 of the law seems to mandate that a publication could only be distributed after the editor has given permission.[54] Journalists, in their capacity as journalists, are provided special rights of access, including a kind of post-Chernobyl right to visit calamities, catastrophes, and "mass unrest and mass gatherings of citizens, as well as areas in which a state of emergency has been declared."[55] Somewhat chillingly, they are burdened with responsibilities as well.[56] If journalists "fail" (e.g., if they distribute false information that impugns the honor and dignity of a state organ),[57] they can be stripped of accreditation by that agency. If they are "good," the government "guarantees the journalist protection of his honor, dignity, health, life and property."[58] The inverse is troubling because it infers that one who is not "good" is not guaranteed these protections. The Russian law, perhaps revealing fears from the past, seeks to guarantee, in some detail, the freedom to distribute mass media, and to specifically enjoin the government, unions, and citizens from harming the process of disseminating information. The law imposes a

48 The concept of "founder" is itself an interesting artifact of free speech theory. All mass media were organs of the government or of the Party; the transition to another form of collective ownership had to take place through the creation of sponsoring organizations, not private publishers. Consequently, the device of "founder" was invented, a kind of intermediary between government and Party on the one hand, and journalists on the other. Interview with Professor Yuri Baturin, author of the Union Press Law, in Moscow (Feb. 3, 1993).

49 Russian Federation Law on Mass Media of 1991, art. 18-22.

50 *Id.* art. 20.

51 *Id.* art. 20, ¶ 3.

52 *Id.* art. 20, ¶ 4.

53 *Id.* art. 18, ¶ 5. The decree of the Russian Congress of People's Deputies, March 28, 1993, "On Measures to Ensure the Freedom of Speech at State Television and Radio Broadcasting and in News Organizations" included a provision stipulating that organs of executive authorities and their officials "cannot be founders of state television and radio broadcasting companies and news organizations, and that their powers pass on to representative authorities and local government authorities." Tass Reports.

54 "The distribution of the mass media product is permitted only after the editor-in-chief gives permission for publication (airing)." Russian Media Law, art. 26.

55 *Id.* art. 47.

56 *Id.* art. 49.

57 *Id.* art. 48.

58 *Id.* art. 49.

duty on government, unions, and certain official entities to furnish information about their activities to newspapers, television, and other mass media.[59] The Bulgarian draft seems to have a similar provision.[60]

In the American context, we do not ordinarily think of government as ordering a particular design for the internal structure of a newspaper organization or a television network. There is no guarantee in American law that an editor will be "independent" of the publisher. To the extent that an editor is independent, it is a result of tradition, not a constitutional or statutory right. It is also rare, unless reflected in the ownership structure, for journalists, as a body, to have rights independent of collective bargaining agreements.[61]

From this perspective, looking at the shards of the Russian law, a perverse statism appears. The architects seem to overdefine freedom, stamping out any interference with the journalist, whether by the government or by the publisher. Accordingly, the legislation must posit how an instrument of mass information should be organized by imposing limits on how the editor is hired and fired, as well as by providing both the journalists and the editor with specific rights concerning the financial and editorial management of the publication.[62] The authors of the law—the architects of the building we are trying to reconstruct—considered these provisions as additional guarantors of freedom. But the law is strangely limiting. It discourages foreign investment and is dependent on the state to sanction internal agreements. Consequently, it is likely to lead to less diversity and

---

59 *Id.* art. 35, 38.

60 *See* Jordanova, *supra* note 11, at 16.

61 Such agreements usually deal with the economic terms and conditions of employment.

62 The Russian law presupposes a formal arrangement. Every mass media product would include three distinct components: a founder, an editor-in-chief, and a journalists' collective. Together, the editor-in-chief and the journalists' collective are known as "the editorship." Article 19 states that the editorship performs its tasks "on the basis of professional independence," and Article 18 states that the founder cannot interfere with the editorship except as the founder and the editorship have agreed. A status agreement is required to cover a number of extremely important points (Articles 16 and 20). For example, it sets forth the circumstances under which the owner may close the newspaper. The document must also set forth how the editor-in-chief is appointed and, presumably, how he or she is removed. The agreement would specify what powers the journalists' collective possesses and what happens if there is a proposed change in ownership or constituency. It would be interesting to know if there is a European or other model for this kind of document. Under Article 22, the founder and the editor are also to agree as to the very important financial side of producing an instrument of mass information. For example, they should agree on "ensuring proper education and social domestic living conditions and labor conditions for the editorial office associates." Russian Media Law, art. 22.

innovation than might otherwise be the case. The greater the opportunities for disputatious friction between publisher and editor, the more likely the state will be called in as arbiter.[63] Article 47 provides journalists with a right of access,[64] and, as with the definition of "the press," one question is whether there should be an official category of "journalist" who has more of a right than anyone else to enter prisons, to rummage through government files, or to see what is going on in defense installations. The law seems to resolve this question quite firmly. The journalist has rights *as a journalist.* These rights of access include the right to look for information, to visit government organs, to copy papers, and to take photographs.

Privileges yield responsibilities, as Vaclav Havel learned from his frankness with Western press notables. Asserting such responsibilities, however, raises fears that an alternative framework for censorship is being structured. For example, Article 49 provides a virtual Boy Scout Code: the journalist is supposed to verify information, protect confidential sources, honor those who should be cited, get prior permission when it appears that a news report will be an invasion of privacy, notify those persons whose pictures have been taken, keep superiors informed of possible law suits, and refuse assignments that might entail breaking the law.[65] If a journalist does all this, the government then "guarantees the journalist protection of his honor, dignity, health, life and property" as a person who performs a public duty.[66] As meritorious as these goals appear, the imposition of such government standards suggests a relationship between journalist and government that is reminiscent of the sometimes velvet, sometimes steel prison of the past.[67]

---

63 In an earlier draft of the statute, the broadcast licensing authority could require at least a statement of how much time will be devoted to foreign programs and to transmissions from any Commonwealth-wide entity. Article 33(f) would have allowed a requirement that the licensee distribute "information and materials of organs of government power and leadership."

64 There is complex case law on this question in the United States which leans toward a principle that there is no higher right of access for journalists than for citizens. *See* Richmond Newspapers, Inc. v. Virginia, 448 U.S. 555 (1980) (validating the proposition that the media acts as a surrogate for the public); Saxbe v. Washington Post Co., 417 U.S. 843 (1974); Pell v. Procunier, 417 U.S. 817 (1974).

65 The law also provides that a journalist should "respect the rights, legal interests, honor, and dignity of citizens and organizations." Russian Media Law, art. 49.

66 *Id.* Journalists can be excluded from events "when the decision has been made to hold a closed meeting." *Id.* art. 48. A government organization can also strip a journalist of his or her accreditation, though only with court approval, if the rules are broken or if the journalist distributes false information that impugns the honor and dignity of the government organization. *Id.* This seems like an invitation to harass the journalist.

67 Article 51 provides that the journalist is forbidden to use his or her privileged

Finally, one important measure of a media statute's treatment is the openness of a society to foreign sources of information. The Russian Media Law demonstrates the desire for a state with permeable boundaries; indeed, Article 54 asserts that the citizens of the Russian Federation are "guaranteed unhindered access to reports and materials of the foreign mass media." But, with its vestiges of statism, the law must define freedom, and, in so doing, suggests the potential for state intervention and control. For example, Article 53 authorizes "interstate agreements" with respect to foreign mass media. The circumstances of distributing such foreign publications can be decided by "interstate agreement," a phrase of complex ambiguity. In the 1950s and 1960s, the United States and the Soviet Union had an agreement in which the Soviet Union had the right to distribute a limited number of copies of *Soviet Life* in the United States and the United States was permitted to distribute limited numbers of like publications in the Soviet Union.[68]

The Russian Media Law of 1991 was drafted under the auspices of journalists, and it reflected their view of mass media. It was also a monument to the idea of new freedoms, of a transformation. The legislation was deemed an idealistic construct and was celebrated as an artifact of the new order. In the brutal year of Soviet dissolution and the inchoate adjustment to new realities, perspectives on the nature and function of law were substantially altered. The 1991 law was largely about press immunity from government intervention; major provisions dealt with the rights of journalists against their publishers and editors, and with the rights of citizens and journalists against the state.[69] Little in the law touched upon the role of legislative bodies, as opposed to

---

position to cover up falsification of information, distribute rumors under the guise of truth, collect information for unauthorized persons or organizations, or distribute information "for the purpose of defaming a citizen or individual categories of citizens exclusively on the basis of sex, age, racial or national affiliation, language, attitude toward religion, profession, place of residence and work, or in connection with their political convictions." Articles 59 and 60 provide a list of potential sanctions for journalists who are not true to these responsibilities. Again, these may be meritorious goals, but the existence of a "journalist" status—with standards to be enforced and sanctions that can be imposed—provides substantial state leverage.

68 For a discussion of these agreements and restrictions on the export and import of film, as well as other attributes of the Cold War, see ELIZABETH HULL, TAKING LIBERTIES (1990). *See also* Monroe E. Price, *The First Amendment and Television Broadcasting by Satellites*, 23 UCLA L. REV. 879 (1976). Under the Russian Media Law, where there is no such agreement, the foreign publication would apply to the Ministry of Press and Information. Article 54 singles out direct television broadcasting for special protection. No limitations are allowed for such programs except by prior inter-governmental treaties.

69 *See* Russian Media Law, art. 38, 39, 47 (journalists' rights) and art. 43-46, 49, 51, 59, and 62 (citizens' rights against the media).

the powers of the president or his Ministry of Press and Information. That would soon change. From the summer of 1992 through the spring of 1993, deliberations in the Congress of People's Deputies reflected political competition, arguments over control, and a focused sense that the future structure of the media should be a matter of keen debate.[70]

Within the scope of the debates leading to a 1992 parliamentary draft, the idea of a commission established to ensure that all power would not be established by the president was discussed.[71] According to the proposal, the director general of any government-controlled mass media (which could include some newspapers as well as radio and television) would be appointed only after approval by such a commission. The pattern of ministerial subsidies for mass media would be subjected to scrutiny, and a legislative standard regarding the amount of circulation would be established for such subsidies. Also implicated was the status of the major newspaper *Izvestia.* Although founded by the Soviet Parliament, journalists claimed the paper for themselves after the approval of the all-senior Soviet in August of 1991. By 1992, the Russian Parliament, through its speaker, was asserting that it was, in effect, the publisher, with some rights over editorial policy. "Freedom of the Press," became a rallying cry, particularly for President Boris Yeltsin, in opposing greater parliamentary power. Almost all legislation, whether having to do with *Izvestia* or with radio and television, was pigeonholed as an interference with freedom of the press. Undoubtedly, a less encumbered press was an objective, but the statutory debate was also about which political forces would have more or less leverage in defining the new Russia. For those who favored a faster turn to the West and a more dramatic commitment to a market economy, resistance to parliamentary intervention had political as well as ideological advantages. A "free press" was more likely to side with the president than with Parliament, at least in the short run.[72]

b. *Other Attempts at Transformation*

With regard to broadcasting structures, somewhat similar agonies affected almost all of the other states in the former so-

---

70 The intensity of the struggle over the press between the president and the Parliament became extraordinary in the crisis of the spring of 1993.

71 This commission was never established in the draft law.

72 For an extremely detailed account of the *Izvestia* controversy, see Jamey Gambrell, *Moscow: The Front Page,* N.Y. Rev. Books, Oct. 8, 1992, at 56.

cialist bloc. In each, the problem of defining the new state and fashioning identities coexisted with the tasks of transformation, economic change, and reordering of the media. Sharp differences, of course, existed. In Ukraine, for example, where arbitrary borders, a sizeable ethnic minority, and an unsure set of past imaginings existed, the creation of a new identity was a formidable undertaking. The task of accommodating transition was perhaps less difficult in a locus like Hungary, whose history of a separate existence was richer and more stable than elsewhere. Even in Hungary, though, a history and narrative had to be found that would satisfactorily come to terms with the Communist period, with the Nazi period, with the claims of the Church, with attitudes toward Jews, and with the relationship between Hungary and the Hungarian communities in Romania, Slovakia, and elsewhere. Control of this process—power over the narrative—became a central element in the restructuring of the media.

Rhythms of adjustment and similarities in approaches to transition became relatively obvious. Almost everywhere, there was a struggle over the direction of the state television and radio stations. Almost everywhere, newly energized political parties sought a process of change that would, they thought, favor their outlooks. Competition for control was also institutional, with the question of the appropriate balance between parliamentary control, independence, and executive direction always an issue. Almost everywhere, men and women of the past were trying to shake or modify the persona of state television as an instrument of power, seeming to become critics of government—watchdogs enforcing some mythical right to know. Almost everywhere, there were politicians who, having come to power democratically, now claimed that the historic capacity to use broadcasting as an instrument of the state belonged legitimately to them.

As mentioned earlier, in most of these societies the struggle for power focused on the capacity to name the senior officials of radio and television. Competition over loyalties was a hallmark of the debate surrounding the Hungarian media law. The debate in Hungary took place against the backdrop of a Parliament in which the majority, but not a super-majority, represented the Magyar Democratic Forum ("MDF"), a coalition of somewhat rightist factions, more or less nationalistic organizations, and religious groups. The second party, the Free Democrats, represented more of a liberal, cosmopolitan, European tradition. Under an agreement dating from the formation of the government, a super-majority, requiring approval outside the ruling coalition, was required for passage of the legislation. Given this sharp struggle for power, governance of the media was of utmost importance because it had the potential to define not only a vision of the future (and the past), but also an ideology that might influence forthcoming elections. The drama of competition for loyalties was underscored in the debate over governance of state radio and television. Each of the two major sides in the Parliament drafted an alternative form of governance. The Free Democrats proposed that the presidents of radio and television be elected and discharged by Parliament (after a hearing by its Cultural and Press Committee), with a two-thirds vote required. The MDF proposed that the heads of radio and television be appointed by the president upon the initiative of the prime minister, thereby more firmly lodging power in the government. Prior to passage of the legislation, a dispute concerning the power to discharge senior broadcasting officials almost caused a constitutional crisis in Hungary. The prime minister instructed the president of Hungary, Arpad Goncz, to dismiss the heads of radio and television, partly in response to a concern among the government officials that state broadcasters were biased against them. The president refused to be bound by the prime minister's request, and the issue was pursued in Hungary's Constitutional Court, which decided in favor of the president.[73] The situation was eased by the president's announcement that he would follow the procedure set forth under the new legislation, including a commitment to recognize the prime minister's power to hire and fire, and ultimately by the decision of the heads of television and radio to resign.

What was significant in both the drafting process and the arguing of the constitutional case was the shift between the language of law and the language of politics. At the grand level, this was a debate about institutions: how ceremonial was the role of the president of Hungary to be?; what was the nature of the power in a parliamentary government when the prime minister has majority support? Also at the grand level, it was a debate in which "freedom of the press" was invoked. Those who sought to maintain the heads of television and radio in power represented their position not as a struggle between two parties, or even between the president and the prime minister, but as a question of the government's power to intervene in the management of the media. In that respect, the debate represented a test of the pace

---

73 MK. 48/1991 (X.26) [Magyar Közlöny].

of transformation, of the rate of adoption of Western (perhaps American) ideas. Immunity from intervention, the kind of immunity that would not lead even to subtle government pressure, would be a better token of a shift towards the West. On the other hand, the debate could also be read as almost purely political—an important battleground among the skirmishes leading to the next Hungarian elections, sometimes represented as keeping state television and radio neutral, sometimes as a contest over the nature and form that control and bias would take. How one mediates between the discourse of the law and the discourse of politics remains unclear. From the outside—from what is thought to be an Archimedal point of observation, but is, perhaps inevitably, an American perspective—maximizing immunity from governmental intervention is devoutly to be desired. Yet the difficulties involved in enshrining and enforcing the principle suggest that its invocation masks the competition for loyalties within the transition societies.

Poland provides another example. After Solidarity came to power in September 1989, Prime Minister Tadeusz Mazowiecki, in his maiden speech to Parliament, announced that the government would maintain control over state television and radio, in part to promote beneficial change during a period of severe economic constraints and austerity measures.[74] In Poland, as in Hungary, there had been a struggle between government and the president for control of television, though for quite different reasons, given that in Poland the position of the president was far more powerful and the prime ministers were dependent on the president for patronage. Accordingly, the prime ministers followed the president's wishes regarding appointments to the top positions in Polish state broadcasting. In Poland, as Karol Jakubowicz has put it, "there is little real belief in the ideal of autonomous, impartial and politically neutral public service broadcasting."[75] Indeed, "it is quietly assumed that every government will seek to bring pressure to bear"[76] on the state media in any way it can.

In political terms, . . . PRTV is poised between the govern-

---

[74] Prior to September 1989, Solidarity had obtained the right of opposition parties to broadcast weekly programs on radio and television; the Roman Catholic Church also had rights to air time and, more importantly, to establish its own radio and television stations. In this early period, Solidarity also had its own department within Polish Radio and Television, which was dissolved upon Solidarity's ascendancy to power.

[75] Karol Jakubowicz, The Restructuring of Television in East-Central Europe (paper given at the CCIS, University of Westminster) (May, 1992).

[76] *Id.*

> ment and the president. There is direct political intervention in the running of television, especially as regards news and current affairs. This takes the form both of securing the appointment of ranking executives (like the head of the news department) known to support either the president or the prime minister, and of residual day-to-day "manual steering," with government officials influencing coverage of particular stories or making their displeasure known if news or current affairs departments dealt with issues in a way they do not accept.[77]

The mechanisms for structuring the broadcasting councils—bodies that supervise the public service or state broadcasting companies and sometimes allocate frequencies for private broadcasters—also reflect the struggle for power. Often, the German system of a *Rundfunkrat,* which provides for broad representation by officials, parliamentarians, and citizens, was taken as a model, though revised substantially to reflect local political exigencies. The working draft of a Polish broadcasting bill, later enacted, envisaged a National Broadcasting Council that would be, in theory, relatively autonomous, outside the government, subordinate neither to the Council of Ministers nor to the Parliament, and, hopefully, immune from political pressures. The president would nominate the head of the Council, who might or might not have considerable powers as chief. The Council would consist of nine members: three nominated by the Sejm, three by the Senate (the two chambers of the Parliament), and three nominated by the president. In Romania, the National Audio-Visual Council consisted of two members nominated by the president, three by the government, and six by the Parliament. In Russia, a new Federal Broadcasting Commission would have three members nominated by the president, three by the Constitutional Court, and six by the chambers of Parliament.[78]

A more elaborate articulation of the representational issues was present in the Hungarian draft legislation. The legislation would establish a Supervisory Committee of Hungarian Radio and Television that would function only at a policy level and not intervene in the quotidian activities of the state companies. About half of the committee would be composed of appointees from government and Parliament, but parliamentary members would represent not the body as a whole, but rather the political parties represented in the Parliament. In addition to sitting

---

[77] *Id.*

[78] *See* Wolfgang Kleinwachter, *Out with the Cold, in with the New?*, 20 InterMedia No. 3, at 12-13 (1992).

members, each political faction would appoint a public member. From a prescribed list, selected organizations would delegate a member. These organizations included national and ethnic minorities in Hungary, nationalities outside Hungary, religious organizations, and organizations of journalists, environmentalists, and employees. A substitute version would have provided rotating membership for organizations within the following classes: (a) the historic churches of Hungary; (b) the nationalities of Hungary; (c) trade unions; (d) youth organizations; (e) pensioners' organizations; (f) environmentalists and conservationists; and (g) women's organizations.[79]

The debate in Hungary over a new media act showed other problems in fusing the old vocabulary with the novel technological and political context. A statute was drafted that embraced aspects of the European Community Broadcasting Directive of October 3, 1989 ("Television Without Frontiers Directive),[80] but also maintained emblems of national identity (e.g., high quotas for Hungarian-made programs—primarily on the public systems, but also on the private systems). It included exhortations that public broadcasters pay special attention to the values of national and ethnic minorities in Hungary, as well as the values of Hungarian and general culture. The draft statute obligated them to provide "extensive, comprehensive, objective and unbiased information about Hungarian . . . events . . . which are of interest to the general public." Further, the draft statute required substantial ownership by Hungarians, or Hungarian-based entities, of the private television distribution systems.[81]

Another draft, for the law on public media in Slovenia,[82] is equally fascinating in terms of providing insight into the structures of transformation. Like the Russian statute, the Slovenian draft encompasses print and broadcast media. The definition of mass media includes "daily and periodical publications (newspa-

---

79 Draft Media Act, Ministry of Justice, 20.053/1991 IM.VII (Second Draft), including alternate A and B versions.

80 Council Directive 89/552, 1989 O.J. (L298) 23 [hereinafter Television Without Frontiers Directive]. For further information on the Directive and the Convention of the Council of Europe, see TRANSFRONTIER TELEVISION IN EUROPE: THE HUMAN RIGHTS DIMENSION (Cassese & Clapham eds., 1990).

81 The regionalist tendencies in the draft are clearly toward Europe. Hungary, on the fast track for full membership in the European Community, has seen bringing its broadcasting structure into conformity with the requirements of the Community as a relatively easy step. Consequently, the drafts included a European quota for programs as well as a Hungarian one, and many of the prohibitions (on advertising and sponsorship) are similar to those in the Television Without Frontiers Directive, though with some exceptions.

82 Slovenia Draft Law on Public Media, Dec. 19, 1991.

pers and magazines) radio and television channels . . . as well as other forms of daily or periodically issued information through print, voice or picture and in a way which is accessible to the public."[83] Also extremely important is Article 2, which rather singularly among the draft statutes explicitly recognizes a national identity role. The draft provides that the Republic of Slovenia is responsible for the development of public media "important for the fulfillment of the rights of Slovenian citizens to be informed and for the preservation of Slovenian national identity."[84] The draft also creates an obligation for the government to provide information to the Italian and Hungarian nationalities in Slovenia and the Slovenian nationalities in Italy, Austria, and Hungary. The relationship between the government and the national minorities recurs throughout the legislation. For example, if a newspaper or television station is founded to provide information for the Italian or Hungarian nationalities, the relevant community must be consulted regarding not only content, but also the appointment and dismissal of the editor, unless the newspaper or television station is founded by the national community itself.[85] Further, as a kind of substantive fairness, Slovene-language national radio and television programs must contain information about the life and work of the Italian and Hungarian nationalities.[86]

Remnants of the search for identity are also reflected in the legislation's nostalgia for institutional originators of mass publications—institutions that provide a program, a purpose, and a link with a collective self. Like the Russian statute, the draft Slovenian media act preserves the idea of a "founder" (an institution or individual that "defines the contextual basis" of the publication) and ensures that the financial and material conditions exist for implementing the founder's vision.[87] The founder is empowered to appoint or dismiss the editor, though the draft statute provides some notion of a check by the journalists.[88] The founder is obliged to appoint a public council that would evaluate its editorial product, determine whether journalistic codes of ethics have been upheld, and discuss the proposals and comments of journalists, listeners, viewers, or readers, as the case

---

83 *Id.* art. 1.
84 *Id.* art. 2.
85 *Id.* art. 8.
86 *Id.* art. 16.
87 *Id.* art. 8.
88 A "consensus" or some other vote of the journalists might be necessary for either the appointment or the dismissal. *Id.*

may be. The members of these councils would be drawn from viewers or listeners, prominent experts, and organizations related to the media. Public officials or members of the founder's family would not be permitted to be members of the council.

The Slovenian draft also shows vestigial efforts to prescribe a public sphere by constructing a framework for discourse that is neither a monopoly of the state nor the precinct of the owners of publications or radio and television stations. The mandating of councils advisory to the founder is an indicator of the search for a public sphere. One function of these councils would be to determine "the influence the public has on the realization of the content and editorial policies of a public medium."[89] Also indicative of these efforts is the detail in which the draft statute describes a citizen's right to access for the purpose of replying to damaging published information. To ensure that the right is effective, the draft statute requires that the editor responsible for the whole of a publication (or for parts, where there is more than one) be clearly identified. Intriguingly, both the Russian Media Law and the Slovenian draft place great emphasis, and provide enormous detail, on a right to reply. Emerging from a context in which accusations could go unanswered, the revisionists seize on the right of reply as providing the model of a better society.

The Slovenian draft statute, like the Russian Media Law, establishes journalists as a specialized professional class with rights and accompanying responsibilities. The Slovenian model creates, at least as one alternative, a collegial entity called the Chamber of Journalists.[90] The Chamber, a separate and presumably independent entity, would examine and license journalists "who fulfill the conditions defined by the Chamber . . . and successfully pass its professional examination."[91] The Slovenian draft, while asserting responsibilities of journalists,[92] is not as comprehensive and, as a result, is not as potentially intimidating as the Russian Media Law. Defining journalists as an entity seems to be the professionalization of the public sphere: taking what is a desire for a Republic of Letters and locating it in a specialized social entity charged with important general obligations (such as pro-

[89] *Id.* art. 9.

[90] *Id.* art. 12.

[91] *Id.* art. 13. The Chamber also determines when a journalist's license may be revoked. The draft included the possibility of omitting the licensing scheme and not establishing such a Chamber.

[92] *Id.* art. 15.

viding for the free flow of information and the openness of public media to a variety of opinions).

IV. Conclusion: Searching for Standards

Given the bewildering complexities inherent in evaluation, one might ask whether absolute norms can be expressed, or whether Western observers are doomed to come to the task of advice and evaluation with their objectives wholly suppressed or only half-articulated. An effort to make more transparent the standards used by those who are engaged in the process of change could be useful. Some obvious formal norms are Article 19 of the Universal Declaration of Human Rights, Article 10 of the European Convention on Human Rights, Articles 19 and 20 of the International Covenant on Civil and Political Rights[93] and the First Amendment to the United States Constitution. These norms, part of the consensus for the new discourse, are superficially advocated, transferred, and transported—even enforced—as a condition of providing financial assistance. But what motivations provide the underpinnings of this consensus? Why do the messengers from the West seem so committed to particular free-speech practices, which are familiar to them but are sometimes difficult to translate in exact terms across formerly impenetrable borders? We need to unpack the surface ideas of these concepts and determine what bases exist for giving individual and governmental support to advocacy of the vital speech aspects of liberal transformations. Given the basic context of this discussion—namely, that of Western observers studying transformations said to be *from* authoritarianism *to* greater political involvement—measuring the formal adoption of Western words in media statutes and in constitutional forms ought not be considered sufficient. In thinking about transformations in these transitional societies, it is useful to ask whether the same objectives exist for Western intervenors that consciously or unconsciously underlie their appraisal of speech regulation in their own countries. Are these champions of arguments grounded in domestic political theory, in self-realization, and in the protection of dissent at home restricted to similar arguments in considering reform

[93] The former USSR, the former Czechoslovakia, the former Yugoslavia, Poland, Hungary, Bulgaria and Romania were parties to the International Covenant. As to whether the Russian Federation succeeded to the Soviet Union's human rights treaties, see van den Berg, *Human Rights in the Legislation and the Draft Constitution of the Russian Federation*, 18 Rev. Cent. & E. Eur. L. 197, 199-203 (1992) (formerly Rev. Socialist L.).

abroad?[94] Is it enough to say that the desired restructuring of the broadcasting system contributes in fact to a more pluralistic, democratic society? If the motivation of the Western advisors is not merely to replicate their home ambitions, how can their goals be articulated? Several sources of motivation can be contemplated, if not for those who advise, then for those who recruit and dispatch the advisors.

What might be called the "missionary basis" is altruistic. Its source is a profound moral and political belief in human dignity, and a concurrent duty, philosophical and almost religious in origin, to ensure that others see the light. It is the understandable desire to make a common bond with people similarly situated who can be assisted in reaching shared goals. Academics devote their time to writing and advising about the transformation of broadcasting structures because they fundamentally believe in freedom and want to extend its reach. Like many of their fellows in and out of government, academics may be caught up with the hope for an ideal that is unrealized in their own countries. Free speech is fundamental to a democratic society; in some respects it is the centerpiece of a secular religion with a strong and productive priesthood. There are variants on this missionary theme. Some find it more congenial to preach their doctrine abroad than at home. There is a romantic illusion that in a transforming society, hurdles that seem insurmountable in the structured home environment might be overcome elsewhere. To the extent that free speech is the celebration of dissent against authority, the advocacy of broadcasting reform abroad can be the consequence of frustration with battling against an entrenched establishment at home. This time, they hope, a society will get it right.

Even if change, in text and practice, appears to contribute little to these goals in the short run, an iron variant can be articulated: broadcasting reform is designed to create a safety net for democratic political change. By placing talent trained outside the government's immediate control together with a kind of technology of independence, the sustainability of democratic dissent is perpetuated. The immediate historical setting for this argument is the famed August 1991 coup in Moscow. The inability of its perpetrators to gain immediate control of radio and other means of communication was said to be an important element in its downfall. Permeable information frontiers, including a network of domestic independent transmitters (in both senses of the

94 *See* Shiffrin, The First Amendment, Democracy and Romance 3 (1990).

term), provide a resource for continued discourse and criticism. In times of emergency, they provide an alternate source for representations of truth and calls to action.

Of course, even this standard is full of complexity—since pluralism and democracy can be at odds—and much of the debate (or lack of debate) in the region is about the pace of change itself. "Progress" against this standard seems to involve three sub-tests: (1) is there a greater flow of information to the citizenry than before?; (2) is there a larger zone for public discourse than before?; and (3) is there a capacity for a broad diversity of views, including the unfettered opportunity to criticize the government? The relationship between this cluster of standards and the new and proposed broadcasting structures is a difficult one. That the absence of censorship increases the availability of information and affords a greater diversity of views is axiomatic.[95] But in what distribution? Though other segments of the population now have quicker access to greater quantities of the world's information store, are there large segments that are more deprived of information now than before? Assumptions about how much news (biased and unbiased) was available under the *ancien regimes* of the newly emerging states may be far wide of the mark. In the absence of competition, news programs may have been watched more consistently by a greater range of the population. New economic differentiation may mean greater access to information by the rich or middle class, and less access by the working class. This will be particularly true if state broadcasting diminishes or if its subsidies and quality decline. The modern trend in the West is to move away from requirements that a substantial percentage of time be devoted to news and documentary programming. Arguably, in the transformed, advertising-supported structure of the media, the zone of public discourse—of argumentation and establishment of opinion outside the umbrella of government—is far more likely to exist in newspapers than in television (with radio falling somewhere in between). With regard to minorities, television may become a place for the mere parading of diversity—a pluralism structured by the state, as opposed to a forum for a sharp diversity of views or sources of information. Those rendering advice are thus often involved in an odd cultural bind: either recommending a free-market approach in which increased entertainment crowds out news and cultural programming, or

---

95 More than anecdotal accounts of persistent censorship exist, but the pace of movement is beyond the scope of this article.

recommending output-based structures (more news, more education) that are superficially inconsistent with trends in their own countries. Most proposed broadcast structures seem to have more substantial public service requirements than is currently fashionable in the market-based structures of the West.[96]

A frequently articulated national defense argument is related, but problematic: i.e., free speech yields a democratic state, and democratic neighbors are less likely to engage in war; reason prevails where discourse is open and unencumbered. Nevertheless, free speech can also subvert governments and destroy, as well as promote, democratic forms. For American foreign policy, piping truth behind the Iron Curtain was sometimes considered therapeutically destabilizing. Among the shaky neophyte republics (now friends), the destabilizing aspects of truth may not continue to be of such high priority. From a defense perspective, then, free speech becomes double-edged. The time may come when Western passions no longer demand the adoption of speech codes that tolerate the widest range of criticism and diversity. Destabilizing speech can come from neo-Nazis, fundamental religionists, ethnic separatists, or advocates of the old totalitarian way of life.

Altruism, commitment to democracy, and the creation of stable democratic societies—these are the major tropes of reform. But other motivations can be briefly canvassed. One is that an enhanced world market relies on the expansion of efficient national markets, and that both require broadly available uncensored information. The capacity to distribute information to potential consumers, whether retail or manufacturing, is vital to nurturing demand. Moreover, unencumbered access to information concerning societal activities—whether it is the plans of government, the political tendencies of the citizenry, or aspects of behavioral change—is profoundly important for those who take risks (e.g., entrepreneurs and producers). Late twentieth-century ideas of free speech include substantial opportunities for advertising and commercial messages, as well as for corporate influence over the structure of taste and consumption. Accordingly, the West is a net exporter of the products that accompany free

---

96 There is also the question of differing determinations of what constitutes "news." In some instances, such as the Hungarian draft, there is a requirement that the news be objective. What constitutes "news" is a politically charged subject and is substantially affected, in most of these loci of transformation, by government policies. "News," as the consequence of a command structure, will differ, it is assumed, from "news" that is the product of a market; but how—other than in terms of the potential for criticism of the government—is rarely clear.

speech—its paraphernalia and programming. Enhanced networks of communication become the infrastructure for substantial developments in trade.[97] In these terms, a standard to be applied in evaluating reform is whether the broadcasting transformation contributes to the strengthening of a market economy, both by enhancing the market for information and ideas, and by enhancing the market for other goods and services. Privatization of the broadcast media is often put forward as a measure for acceptable movement, but this point must be analyzed further. In most of the countries, the pace of privatization of television—in the sense of taking state services and turning them over to private entities—has been quite slow, although the process is speedier for newspapers and radio. There are few, if any, examples of fully privatizing a major television service (i.e., sale to a private entity unconnected with the government).

Another standard not often articulated by Western observers—and possibly in conflict with those more frequently stated—is whether a transformation contributes to establishing a more secure and enduring national identity. Some draft statutes (e.g., Slovenia's and Bulgaria's)[98] reinforce the new national identity and duty of the broadcasting enterprise. There is no objective national identity, however, and it thus falls to the government or to the broadcaster (as a surrogate) to define which national identity should be projected. Certainly, unstable regimes rely on the state-controlled media to help strengthen their power. These are often states in the process of being "invented," to use Hobsbawm's term,[99] or "imagined," to use Benedict Anderson's term.[100] The role of the broadcasting system in this process is an important priority. In Kiev, a special effort has been made to find and promulgate a Ukrainian national identity.[101] Perhaps it is no accident that the Crimean Parliament, largely Russian, declared that the substitution of its channel for the Russian Channel from Moscow was one ground for its short-lived declaration of inde-

---

97 There is a more cynical view of the link between the messengers of democratic reform and developments in trade. The patina of democracy, including the freedom associated with broadcasting reform, compensates for injurious developments in the economic sphere. In some transforming societies, according to this view, chaos, flights of capital, disappearance of natural resources, and declining quality in the fundamentals of the standard of living are articulated as transitional, with the new freedoms serving as partial, and perhaps sufficient, compensation.

98 *See* Breda Luther, *Slovenia Struggles with the Reithian Ethos,* 20 INTERMEDIA No. 4-5, at 33 (1992); Jordanova, *supra* note 11, at 16.

99 THE INVENTION OF TRADITION, *supra* note 10.

100 ANDERSON, *supra* note 10.

101 *See* Richter, *supra* note 16, at 60-61.

pendence.[102] But certainly, a fundamental problem in the translation of concepts concerns the way in which the state defines the role of the broadcasting system. National quota provisions and statutory obligations to reflect the cultures of specific national minorities are frequent characteristics of the new identity-oriented legislation that is typical of our time. More important than these formal provisions, however, is the internalized idea of the broadcasting system. Perhaps by definition, the *ancien regime* treated the mass media as an instrument of the state, dedicated to its own perception of what was needed to strengthen the public cause. Even now, it is hard for this concept to disappear, and for those who try to cross the borders of understanding, comprehending this concept may be important.

We have come to think of broadcasting as part of "the press" or part of "speech" and, therefore, specially privileged. But in terms of generating images of national identity, broadcasting institutions have to be seen among other media that perform similar functions. Educational systems are the prime example. Many of the debates about the purpose and content of public education (or the public financing of private education) turn on the state's role in reproducing itself, in delineating itself, and in projecting itself in certain ways. In some countries—England among them—the connections between the role of the state in education and its role in broadcasting have been quite evident. Perhaps what is occurring in Central and Eastern Europe and the former Soviet Union is the formation of a complex market for individual and group loyalties—a market that can be defined in the same manner as the market for capital, labor, automobiles, or sugar. If there is such a market, the government certainly plays a role both as a creator and as a participant. One can look at proposed structures in these countries (or at international conventions and existing structures) as methods of articulating the particular rules that apply to this competitive marketplace. These rules, by measuring out the rights of individuals to receive and impart information, delimit the state's power to coerce an unfair advantage in the competition for loyalties. Most Western structures similarly impose constitutional norms that deny government the power to monopolize the market for national identities. What they do not do, however, is preclude the state from acting as one of the competitors. For example, the First Amendment to the Constitution

---

102 The complexity of the new literature on national identity is extraordinary, and this is not the place to parse it. See addendum for a bibliographic listing of such literature.

of the United States, which precludes Congress from abridging the freedom of speech and the press, forbids the government from using the force of law to block competition in the market for loyalty and national identity. The First Amendment does not disable the government from participating as a seller in the market for loyalties, except in one particular way—by establishing a church. The European Convention on Human Rights also provides for an open market for loyalties in Article 10, but it provides very specific and relevant exceptions. Governments may restrict their competitors when regulation "is necessary in a democratic society in the interests of national security, territorial integrity or public safety."[103]

As the struggling governments of Central and Eastern Europe enter this market for loyalties, one can look at their statutory drafts from this analytical framework. What competition for loyalties is permitted? Does the state have a monopoly both in broadcasting and the press? Does a competitive and vital newspaper market make a concentrated and government-oriented broadcasting structure more tolerable? Does the march toward privatization and commercialization mean that broadcasting will be less of a forum for public discourse and competition than might otherwise be the case? Additionally, as these countries are dedicating themselves to transforming broadcasting structures, important global transformations come into play that may render a viable and effective national system impossible. The increasing permeability of borders to signals and information from abroad means that purposive efforts to control discourse may be increasingly ineffective. Besides, given the depth and persistence of basic ideas of identity held by national subgroups (as we see bursting forth everywhere: the Slovaks out of Czechoslovakia, the Russians in the Ukraine, the Germans in Kazakhstan, the dismemberment of Yugoslavia), it is not clear that the talent, skill, and insight involved in using broadcasting to build counter-identities—identities of cohesiveness—can be effective. Perhaps broadcasting can reinforce and inflame, but not shift, deep-

---

[103] The state may also restrict (or impose conditions or penalties) for the protection of health or morals, for the protection of the reputation or rights of others, for preventing the disclosure of information received in confidence, or for maintaining the authority and impartiality of the judiciary. The British government, in a case that was arguably about national identity, cited the confidentiality protection provision in seeking an injunction against a former member of the British Security Services. *See* Sunday Times v. United Kingdom (no. 2), 50 Eur. Ct. H. R. 241/312 (1991). For a discussion of the case see *Violation of Article 10 ECHR on Account of Interlocutory Injunctions Imposed on the Publication of Details in the Book "Spycatcher" Alleging Unlawful Conduct by the British Security Service*, 13 HUM. RTS. L.J. No. 1-2, at 30.

seated popular identities. Finally, the entry of advertising creates new, and potentially more effective, competitors for loyalty. These are forces that shift individual identities from those of citizens to a new status as consumers, who believe not in their flag, but in their commercial hopes and fantasies. The Western observer comes on the scene of Eastern transformations at a time when, for him, the positive function of the state in preserving and communicating the idea of the center has diminished. Both the BBC in Great Britain and the Public Broadcasting Service in the United States have been under fire recently because of doubts about whether government should generate (or subsidize the generation of) images of national identity. If allowed, what images they should be permitted to so generate?[104]

Every state[105] holds a conversation with its subjects as to the legitimacy of its existence. In this conversation, the state is engaged in self-justification, in making the case for the continuation and improvement of the state, and in seeking the loyalty of its citizens. Governments generate images that reinforce the relationship between its subjects and itself for many reasons. Indeed, national identity, so theatrical and compelling a concept, may be nothing more than that collection of images that the government (or a series of interest groups) manufactures or encourages to keep itself in power. The state may claim to intervene in defense of its culture, and that may be a valid and relevant ground for the intervention. But those in power may use the machinery of the state to encourage a world outlook—grounded components of a "national identity"—which, to reinforce their dominance, is consonant with their political status. Some states may have so weak a franchise (absent force and fiction), that the creation and propagation of a narrative of legitimacy is all-consuming, pervasive, and devastatingly revealing of the regime. Even in democratic societies, however, the necessity for generat-

---

104 *See, e.g.*, CULTURE WARS: DOCUMENTS FROM THE RECENT CONTROVERSIES IN THE ARTS (R. Bolton ed., 1992) (focusing on the National Endowment for the Arts). One might wonder whether there is or should be a jurisprudence of transformations; whether there is a way of looking at the process of restructuring of legal systems at the time of paradigm shifts—from capitalism to socialism, from feudalism to the modern state, from an authoritarian society to a democratic one. Looking across examples of these vast changes, are there similarities from which we can predict the process of change? What might be interesting would be to ask this question: if there were such a jurisprudence of transformation, what would it tell us about the complexities of restructuring broadcasting systems? Or, put differently, given the experience that is accumulating in the process of restructuring, what can we infer from it that will help articulate or foreshadow such a jurisprudence of transformation?

105 Perhaps it is more accurate to say the ruling elite in every state.

ing and maintaining a narrative of community is an important occupation. What is significant is that these ideas and images are part of every state's definition.

Addendum

See e.g., BENEDICT ANDERSON, IMAGINED COMMUNITIES: REFLECTIONS ON THE ORIGIN AND SPREAD OF NATIONALISM (1991); ARJUN APPADURAL, IMPLODING WORLDS: IMAGINATIONS AND DISJUNCTURE IN THE GLOBAL CULTURAL ECONOMY; JAY G. BLUMLER, TELEVISION AND THE PUBLIC INTEREST (1992); JAY G. BLUMLER ET AL., COMPARATIVELY SPEAKING: COMMUNICATION AND CULTURE ACROSS SPACE AND TIME (1992); RICHARD COLLINS, CULTURE, COMMUNICATION AND NATIONAL IDENTITY: THE CASE STUDY OF CANADIAN TELEVISION (1990); RICHARD COLLINS, TELEVISION, POLICY AND CULTURE (1990); DANIEL DAYAN AND ELIHU KATAZ, MEDIA EVENTS: THE LIVE BROADCASTING OF HISTORY (1992); LAWRENCE GROSSBERG ET AL., CULTURAL STUDIES (1992); ERIC J. HOBSBAWM, NATIONS AND NATIONALISM SINCE 1987 (1990); THE INVENTION OF TRADITION (Eric J. Hobsbawn & Terence Ranger eds., 1983); CONRAD P. KOTTAK, PRIME TIME SOCIETY: AN ANTHROPOLOGICAL ANALYSIS OF TELEVISION AND CULTURE (1990); JAMES LULL, CHINA TURNED ON: TELEVISION, REFORM AND RESISTANCE (1991); BRIAN MCNAIR, GLASNOST, PERESTROIKA AND THE SOVIET MEDIA (1991); DAVID MORLEY, TELEVISION, AUDIENCES AND CULTURAL STUDIES (1992); RALPH NEGRINE AND STYLAINOS PAPATHANASSOPOULOUS, THE INTERNATIONALISATION OF TELEVISION (1990); ELI NOAM, TELEVISION IN EUROPE (1992); J. PINES, BLACK AND WHITE IN COLOUR: BLACK PEOPLE IN BRITISH TELEVISION SINCE 1936 (1992); VICTOR PORTER AND SUSAN HASSELBACH, PLURALISM, POLITICS AND THE MARKETPLACE: THE REGULATION OF GERMAN BROADCASTING (1991); MARC RABOY AND BERNARD DAGENAIS, MEDIA, CRISIS AND DEMOCRACY; MASS COMMUNICATION AND THE DISRUPTION OF SOCIAL ORDER (1992); PHILIP SCHLESINGER, MEDIA, STATE AND NATION: POLITICAL VIOLENCE AND COLLECTIVE IDENTITIES (1991); MICHAEL SKOVMAND AND KIM C. SCHRODER, MEDIA CULTURES: REAPPRAISING TRANSNATIONAL MEDIA (1992); ANTHONY D. SMITH, NATIONAL IDENTITY (1991).

FAIR USE MISCONSTRUED: PROFIT, PRESUMPTIONS, AND PARODY

WILLIAM F. PATRY* AND SHIRA PERLMUTTER**

I. INTRODUCTION

In the first fair use case decided in the United States, *Folsom v. Marsh*,[1] Justice Joseph Story began his opinion by expressing a healthy respect for the difficulties such cases pose:

> This is one of those intricate and embarrassing questions, arising in the administration of civil justice, in which it is not, from the peculiar nature and character of the controversy, easy to arrive at any satisfactory conclusion, or to lay down any general principles applicable to all cases.[2]

A century later, a panel of the Second Circuit that included both Judges Hand described fair use as "the most troublesome [issue] in the whole law of copyright."[3] The Supreme Court's experience with the doctrine bears out this assessment. The Court's first two encounters with fair use resulted in affirmances by an equally divided vote.[4] The Court's third attempt, in *Sony Corporation of America v. Universal City Studios*,[5] resulted in a 5-4 decision handed down only after the case had been reargued.

The thorniness of fair use is not due to any failure on the part of the legislature or the judiciary. To the contrary, it is inherent in the common law nature of the doctrine as a mul-

---

* Counsel, U.S. House of Representatives, Committee on the Judiciary, Subcommittee on Intellectual Property and Judicial Administration.

** Assistant Professor, The Catholic University of America, Columbus School of Law.

The authors acknowledge their debt to United States District Judge Pierre N. Leval, whose speech to the Washington Chapter of the Copyright Society of the U.S.A. on April 13, 1993, inspired some of the ideas in this article. We also thank Paul Riley, Class of 1994 at the Columbus School of Law, for his research assistance.

1 9 F. Cas. 342 (C.C.D. Mass. 1841) (No. 4,901). Two years before *Folsom*, Justice Story decided Gray v. Russell, 10 F. Cas. 1035 (C.C.D. Mass. 1839) (No. 5,728), which raised many of the same issues. While *Folsom* owed much to earlier English cases, Justice Story synthesized and articulated the doctrine so well that later English courts cited to his formulation. *See, e.g.*, Scott v. Stanford, L.R. 3 Eq. 718, 722 (1867). *See generally* WILLIAM F. PATRY, THE FAIR USE PRIVILEGE IN COPYRIGHT LAW 6-17 (reviewing early English cases), and 19-25 (reviewing *Folsom v. Marsh*) (1985) ("THE FAIR USE PRIVILEGE"). The fair use provision of the current U.S. copyright statute is substantially derived from *Folsom*. *See id.* at 24-25.

2 9 F. Cas. at 344.

3 Dellar v. Samuel Goldwyn Inc., 104 F.2d 661, 662 (2d Cir. 1939) (per curiam).

4 Columbia Broadcasting System, Inc. v. Loew's, Inc., 356 U.S. 43 (1958); Williams & Wilkins Co. v. United States, 420 U.S. 376 (1975).

5 464 U.S. 417 (1984).

tifaceted process by which courts can finely calibrate not only the equities between the parties in a given case, but also the fundamental public policies at stake in drawing the line between private property and free use. Fair use is one of the principal mechanisms by which the constitutional goal to "promote the Progress of Science . . . , by securing for limited Times to Authors . . . the exclusive Right to their . . . Writings"[6] is achieved. As the Supreme Court has explained, fair use is "an 'equitable rule of reason,' which 'permits courts to avoid rigid application of the copyright statute when, on occasion, it would stifle the very creativity which that law is designed to foster.' "[7] In brief, fair use is a critical safety valve of copyright.[8] Flexibility and sensitivity in application are essential to its successful functioning.[9]

The origins of fair use date back to judicial opinions of the nineteenth century.[10] As developed by the courts, it was a privilege granted to one author to make unauthorized use of the copyrighted material of another for purposes such as criticism and comment. Entitlement to the privilege was based on a case-

---

6 U.S. CONST. art. I, § 8, cl. 8.

7 Stewart v. Abend, 495 U.S. 207, 236 (1990) (quoting Sony Corp. of America v. Universal City Studios, Inc., 464 U.S. 417, 448 (1984), and Iowa State University Research Foundation, Inc. v. American Broadcasting Cos., 621 F.2d 57, 60 (2d Cir. 1980)). In the words of Justice Blackmun in his dissent in *Sony*, 464 U.S. at 477-78: "[T]he fair use doctrine plays a crucial role in the law of copyright. . . . There are situations . . . in which strict enforcement of [the copyright] monopoly would inhibit the very 'Progress of Science and useful Arts' that copyright is intended to promote. . . . In such a case, the fair use doctrine acts as a form of subsidy—albeit at the first author's expense—to permit the second author to make limited use of the first author's work for the public good." *See also* Horace G. Ball, LAW OF COPYRIGHT AND LITERARY PROPERTY 260 (1944), *quoted in* Harper & Row, Publishers, Inc. v. Nation Enterprises, 471 U.S. 539, 549 (1985):

> [T]he author's consent to a reasonable use of his copyrighted works ha[d] always been implied by the courts as a necessary incident of the constitutional policy of promoting the progress of science and the useful arts, since a prohibition of such use would inhibit subsequent writers from attempting to improve upon prior works and thus . . . frustrate the very ends sought to be attained.

8 Other safety valves incorporated in the copyright law include the prohibition of copyright protection for ideas, facts, systems, etc., 17 U.S.C. § 102(b) (1978), and the rule that infringement may be found only when the defendant has appropriated a substantial amount of expressive material, thereby permitting the unauthorized appropriation of *de minimis* amounts of expression. *See, e.g.*, Original Appalachian Artworks, Inc. v. Toy Loft, Inc., 684 F.2d 821 (11th Cir. 1982).

9 This point was brought home last year when Congress, concerned that the Second Circuit had adopted a *per se* rule barring fair use of unpublished works, amended the fair use provision of the Copyright Act. Act of October 24, 1992, Pub. L. No. 102-492, § 107, 106 Stat. 3145. The Act added the following sentence at the end of section 107: "The fact that a work is unpublished shall not itself bar a finding of fair use if such finding is made upon consideration of all the above factors." The amendment was designed to ensure that "[a]ll claims of fair use . . . be judged on the totality of the facts in the particular case by balancing all the factors." *See* H.R. REP. NO. 102-836, 102d Cong., 2d Sess. 3 (1992).

10 *See* THE FAIR USE PRIVILEGE, *supra* note 1, at 6-64.

specific analysis of all the relevant circumstances, taking into account the entire complex of facts and equities presented.

The fair use doctrine remained entirely judge-made until enactment of the Copyright Act of 1976.[11] In replacing the 1909 Act with a new and comprehensive statute, Congress for the first time included fair use, in recognition of its role as an important limitation on the copyright owner's rights.[12] Although the precise wording of the provision went through a number of revisions, its purpose was clear: Congress intended the provision "to restate the present judicial doctrine of fair use, not to change, narrow, or enlarge it in any way,"[13] and to entrust its future development to the courts.[14]

This intent was reflected in the drafting of the fair use provision, section 107. Unlike other sections of the statute that provide specific, detailed exemptions from or limitations on the copyright owner's exclusive rights, section 107 is open-ended and flexible. Its operative language states simply that "the fair use of a copyrighted work . . . is not an infringement of copyright." The statute does not define the term "fair use," but instead gives examples of types of use that might be considered fair,[15] as well as four illustrative factors to be considered, each derived nearly verbatim from the language of prior judicial opinions.[16]

The decision to include fair use in the new statute was understandable. The form that the reference took, however, going beyond a bare-bones statement that "fair use is not infringement," and instead delineating this quintessential common law process in statutory terms, has led some courts to misinterpret Congressional intent.[17] There is a natural tendency to treat stat-

---

[11] 17 U.S.C. §§ 101 *et seq.* (1978).

[12] *See infra* text at notes 24-33.

[13] H.R. REP. No. 94-1476, 94th Cong., 2d Sess. 66 (1976); S. REP. No. 94-473, 94th Cong., 1st Sess. 62 (1975).

[14] *See infra* text at notes 29-33.

[15] The statute lists in the first sentence "purposes such as criticism, comment, news reporting, teaching (including multiple copies for classroom use), scholarship, or research." 17 U.S.C. § 107.

[16] *See infra* text at notes 50-51.

[17] During the revision process that led to passage of the 1976 Act, some objected to any codification of fair use, fearing that it would lose its essential character as evolving, judge-made law. *See* COPYRIGHT LAW REVISION PART 2: DISCUSSION AND COMMENTS ON REPORT OF THE REGISTER OF COPYRIGHTS ON THE GENERAL REVISION OF THE U.S. COPYRIGHT LAW, 88th Cong., 1st Sess. 25, 28, 261, 284, 315, 350 (House Comm. Print 1963), *discussed in* THE FAIR USE PRIVILEGE, *supra* note 1, at 218-21 (reporting opposition by NBC, music publishers, the Authors League of America, ASCAP, and the Motion Picture Association of America). A majority of those commenting on drafts of the bill, however, saw a benefit in affirming the existence of the doctrine in the new statute. COPYRIGHT

utory language as carved in stone, as rigid rules rather than broad guidelines. Despite Congress's desire that the courts continue to chart their own development of fair use, the very presence of the statutory provision has inhibited many from doing so. Rather than looking to the plain language of section 107 in its entirety in light of its purpose as a confirmation of judge-made law, courts have isolated and overemphasized individual words and phrases, taking as limitations on their power language intended as guidance.

This tendency has been exacerbated by the exoticism of fair use to most courts. Even in those jurisdictions with heavy diets of copyright, such as the Southern District of New York, most judges do not regularly try fair use claims, and thus do not have the opportunity to develop familiarity with the area. Given the open-endedness of the doctrine, and the frequency of disagreement by appellate courts, deciding fair use cases may be an intimidating experience.[18] Accordingly, there is an understandable desire to find bright-line rules, whether in the language of the statute or in broad statements in prior opinions. With the illusion of certainty such rules provide, decision-making becomes easier.

Whatever the reasons, the result has been mechanistic, formulaic decisions—opinions that recite sonorous phrases drawn from statute and case law rather than engage in the sensitive balancing of factors that is the essence of fair use. The negative impact of such cases on the law may not be immediately obvious because their resolutions are frequently subject to reasonable debate. But the conceptual damage done to the fair use doctrine is real, and reflected dramatically in those cases that do go wrong.

The damage to fair use extends to every aspect of the doctrine. The most serious problems, however, have been manifested in application of the first and fourth factors set out in section 107: "the purpose and character of the use" and "the effect of the use upon the potential market for or value of the copyrighted work."[19] By misinterpreting the language of the

---

LAW REVISION PART 3: PRELIMINARY DRAFT FOR REVISED U.S. COPYRIGHT LAW AND DISCUSSIONS AND COMMENTS ON THE DRAFT BILL at 158 (1964). As to the form which this affirmation should take, a consensus emerged that "favor[ed] either no definition at all or else a very, very broad one—so broad that it would not, as some said, 'freeze the doctrine as it stands today.' " *Id.*

[18] United States District Judge Pierre Leval has colorfully described this experience: "It has been exhilarating to find myself present at the cutting edge of the law, even though in the role of the salami." Pierre N. Leval, *Fair Use or Foul? The Nineteenth Donald C. Brace Memorial Lecture*, 36 J. COPR. SOC'Y 167, 168 (1989).

[19] Much controversy was generated in the late 1980s by the Second Circuit's treat-

statute and reading too much into dicta from the two major Supreme Court opinions on fair use,[20] some courts have altered radically the traditional approach to the doctrine. Rather than examining all of the circumstances bearing on these two factors as well as the fair use inquiry as a whole, they have resorted to a simplistic judgment call turning on a characterization of the use as either commercial or not.[21] In the process, they have adopted a series of presumptions and rules of thumb—a method of analysis antithetical to the very nature of fair use.

This year, the damage may be reversed. The Supreme Court has agreed to hear in the October 1993 term a copyright case involving a parody of a popular song, *Acuff-Rose Music, Inc. v. Campbell.*[22] As an extreme example of a misreading of the statute and the Supreme Court fair use decisions, the Sixth Circuit's opinion in *Acuff-Rose* provides the Court with an excellent vehicle to clarify the meaning of its own statements on the issue of commercial use. The Court will also have the opportunity to address for the first time copyright parody, a type of use that presents some unique fair use issues.[23]

---

ment of the second statutory factor, "the nature of the copyrighted work." Starting with the Supreme Court's decision in Harper & Row, Publishers, Inc. v. Nation Enterprises, 471 U.S. 539 (1985), courts had treated the unpublished nature of a plaintiff's work as an important element weighing against fair use in applying section 107. In two opinions dealing with the use by biographers of unpublished letters and diaries of the subjects of the biographies, the Second Circuit arguably went further, making statements suggesting that it would be extremely difficult ever to establish fair use of unpublished works. *See* New Era Publications Int'l, ApS v. Henry Holt and Co., 873 F.2d 576 (2d Cir.), *reh'g denied en banc,* 884 F.2d 659 (2d Cir. 1989), *cert. denied,* 493 U.S. 1094 (1990); Salinger v. Random House, Inc., 811 F.2d 90 (2d Cir.), *cert. denied,* 484 U.S. 890 (1987). The resulting strong reaction from the publishing community ultimately led to the enactment in 1992 of legislation amending section 107. *See infra* note 25 and accompanying text. The legislation was intended to leave Justice O'Connor's comprehensive opinion in *Harper & Row* unaffected in any way. *See* H.R. Rep. No. 102-836, 102d Cong., 2d Sess. 9 (1992); 138 Cong. Rec. H7991 (August 11, 1992) (remarks of Mr. Hughes).

The problems that have developed with the first and fourth factors have not been as noticeable, primarily because they do not impact any one particular industry. Nevertheless, they are considerably more pernicious, as they threaten to skew the analysis in every fair use case.

20 *Harper & Row,* 471 U.S. 539; Sony Corp. of America v. Universal City Studios, Inc., 464 U.S. 417 (1984). The only other opinion by the Supreme Court addressing the topic of fair use is Stewart v. Abend, 495 U.S. 207 (1990), which discusses the doctrine briefly in the course of analyzing the impact of a reversion of renewal rights on the continued use of a derivative work prepared under a grant during the initial copyright term.

21 *See infra* text at notes 60-65.

22 972 F.2d 1429 (6th Cir. 1992), *cert. granted,* 113 S. Ct. 1642 (1993).

23 The Court once before granted *certiorari* in a copyright parody case, but has not yet provided any guidance on the subject. In 1957, a case involving a parody by the comedian Jack Benny of the movie "Gaslight," entitled "Autolight," was argued before the Court. In 1958, an equally divided Court affirmed the Ninth Circuit's opinion rejecting the parody defense. Columbia Broadcasting System, Inc. v. Loew's, Inc., 356 U.S. 43 (1958), *aff'g* 239 F.2d 532 (9th Cir. 1956).

II. Discussion

A. *The 1976 Act's Recognition of Fair Use*

The proper place to begin, as indicated by the Court's statement of the question for review,[24] is with the statute. The fair use provision of the Copyright Act reads as follows:

> § 107. Limitations on exclusive rights: Fair use
>
> Notwithstanding the provisions of sections 106 and 106A, the fair use of a copyrighted work, including such use by reproduction in copies or phonorecords or by any other means specified by that section, for purposes such as criticism, comment, news reporting, teaching (including multiple copies for classroom use), scholarship, or research, is not an infringement of copyright. In determining whether the use made of a work in any particular case is a fair use the factors to be considered shall include-
>
> (1) the purpose and character of the use, including whether such use is of a commercial nature or is for nonprofit educational purposes;
> (2) the nature of the copyrighted work;
> (3) the amount and substantiality of the portion used in relation to the copyrighted work as a whole;
> (4) the effect of the use upon the potential market for or value of the copyrighted work.
>
> The fact that a work is unpublished shall not itself bar a finding of fair use if such finding is made upon consideration of all the above factors.[25]

The plain words of section 107 rule out application of bright line tests or conclusive presumptions. Rather than setting forth a test or definition for fair use,[26] the provision simply states the

---

[24] The Supreme Court phrased the question "Whether petitioners' commercial parody was a 'fair use' within the meaning of 17 U.S.C. Section 107." 113 S. Ct. at 1642. The Court substituted this single question for the four originally presented in the petition for *certiorari*.

[25] 17 U.S.C. § 107. Since the statute's enactment in 1976 (effective January 1, 1978), section 107 has been amended twice. In 1990, "and section 106A" was added to the opening phrase, in order to make subject to fair use the moral rights granted to visual artists by the Visual Artists Rights Act of 1990, Pub. L. No. 101-650, title VI, 104 Stat. 5089, 5128, 5132 (effective June 1, 1991). In 1992, the final sentence was added, dealing with fair use of unpublished works. Act of October 24, 1992, Pub. L. No. 102-492, 106 Stat. 3145.

[26] As explained in the legislative reports accompanying the 1976 Act:

> Although the courts have considered and ruled upon the fair use doctrine over and over again, no real definition of the concept has ever emerged. Indeed, since the doctrine is an equitable rule of reason, no generally applicable definition is possible, and each case raising the question must be decided on its own facts.

H.R. Rep. No. 94-1476, 94th Cong., 2d Sess. 65 (1976); S. Rep. No. 94-473, 94th Cong.,

general principle of the doctrine and lists four factors to be considered. It does not ascribe relative weight to any individual factor,[27] and the factors are by definition made illustrative only.[28]

As Justice Blackmun has remarked, section 107 constitutes "statutory recognition" of the fair use doctrine[29] in a form that incorporates a number of criteria previously developed by the courts.[30] This is explicitly stated in the legislative reports:

> *General intention behind the provision*
>
> The statement of the fair use doctrine in section 107 offers some guidance to users in determining when the principles of the doctrine apply. However, the endless variety of situations and combinations of circumstances that can arise in particular cases precludes the formulation of exact rules in the statute. The bill endorses the purpose and general scope of the judicial doctrine of fair use, but there is no disposition to freeze the doctrine in the statute, especially during a period of rapid technological change. Beyond a very broad statutory explanation of what fair use is and some of the criteria applicable to it, the courts must be free to adapt the doctrine to particular situations on a case-by-case basis. Section 107 is intended to restate the present judicial doctrine of fair use, not to change, narrow, or enlarge it in any way.[31]

1st Sess. 62 (1975). *See also* Sony Corp. of America v. Universal City Studios, Inc., 464 U.S. 417, 476 (1984) (Blackmun, J., dissenting): "Nor did Congress provide definitive rules when it codified the fair use doctrine in the 1976 Act; it simply incorporated a list of factors 'to be considered'. . . ."

27 *See Sony*, 464 U.S. at 476 (1984) (Blackmun, J., dissenting) ("No particular weight . . . was assigned to any of th[e] [factors]"); Lewis Galoob Toys, Inc. v. Nintendo of America, Inc., 964 F.2d 965, 970 (9th Cir. 1992) ("Section 107 does not indicate how much weight should be ascribed to each [factor]."), *cert. denied*, 113 S. Ct. 1582 (1993).

28 This is accomplished through the section's repeated use of the terms "including" and "such as," terms defined in the general definitional section of the Act. *See* 17 U.S.C. § 101 (1978) ("The terms 'including' and 'such as' are illustrative and not limitative."). *See also* H.R. Rep. No. 94-1476, 94th Cong., 2d Sess. 65 (1976) (the four factors are "in no case definitive or determinative, [but] provide some guage [sic] for balancing the equities"); H.R. Rep. No. 102-836, 102d Cong., 2d Sess. 9-10 (1992) (Use of the phrase "all the above factors" in the 1992 amendment to section 107 was intended to "encompass the terms 'including' and 'such as' embodied in the preamble to Section 107, terms that are defined in Section 101 of title 17 as being 'illustrative and not limitative.' Thus, for unpublished works as for all other copyrighted works, the courts must consider all four statutory factors, but they may, at their discretion, consider any other factors they deem relevant.").

29 *Sony*, 464 U.S. at 476 (Blackmun, J., dissenting).

30 The first, third, and fourth factors were derived from Justice Story's opinion in Folsom v. Marsh, 9 F. Cas. 342 (C.C.D. Mass. 1841) (No. 4,901). *See* The Fair Use Privilege, *supra* note 1, at 24-25.

31 H.R. Rep. No. 94-1476, 94th Cong., 2d Sess. 66 (1976); S. Rep. No. 94-473, 94th Cong., 1st Sess. 62 (1975). There is one respect, however, in which courts are more restricted than before enactment of section 107: the statute altered the process of decision-making to the extent that it directs courts to consider at least the four factors specified. *See* Pacific & Southern Co. v. Duncan, 744 F.2d 1490, 1495 n.7 (11th Cir. 1984),

Thus, section 107 is not a typical statutory provision representing Congress's creation of new law and establishment of rules for the courts to apply. It is instead a direction to the courts to continue to develop the common law.[32] It is therefore misleading to characterize section 107 as a "codification" of the doctine. Fair use would not have been embodied in statutory language at all but for Congress's omnibus revision in 1976 of the antiquated 1909 Act. Given the importance and frequency of fair use claims in copyright litigation, Congress believed it would be misleading not to mention the defense as part of the comprehensive new law.[33] The failure of some courts to recognize section 107's unique nature as statutory recognition of a judge-made rule of reason is responsible for much of the damage to the doctrine. We shall focus on two areas of particular concern: the adoption of presumptions for or against entire categories of uses, and the proper interpretation of the fourth statutory factor, the harm to the market for the copyrighted work.

B. *The Preamble to Section 107*

The preamble to section 107 lists six illustrative types of purposes that may qualify for fair use consideration:

> Notwithstanding the provisions of sections 106 and 106A, the fair use of a copyrighted work, including such use by reproduction in copies or phonorecords or by any other means specified by that section, for purposes such as *criticism, comment, news reporting, teaching (including multiple copies for classroom use), scholarship, or research,* is not an infringement of copyright.[34]

One issue that has bedeviled the courts is the significance to be given to this list. Explicit in the language of the statute is the list's nonexclusivity;[35] the uses enumerated are only examples, and uses that are not mentioned may also qualify as fair.[36] There

---

cert. denied, 471 U.S. 1004 (1985). In contrast, earlier cases occasionally resolved the fair use defense based on only some of these factors. *See infra* text at notes 119-23.

[32] *See* Fisher v. Dees, 794 F.2d 432, 435 (9th Cir. 1986) (Section 107 "did not freeze the fair use doctrine in stone. Rather, Congress expressly sought to preserve the doctrine's common law character."); Triangle Pub., Inc. v. Knight-Ridder Newspapers, Inc., 626 F.2d 1171, 1174 (5th Cir. 1980) ("Congress made clear that it in no way intended to depart from Court-created principles or to short-circuit further judicial development.").

[33] *See* REPORT OF THE REGISTER OF COPYRIGHTS ON THE GENERAL REVISION OF THE U.S. COPYRIGHT LAW, 87th Cong., 1st Sess. 25 (House Comm. Print 1961), *quoted in* THE FAIR USE PRIVILEGE, *supra* note 1, at 215.

[34] 17 U.S.C. § 107 (1978) (emphasis added).

[35] This nonexclusivity is communicated by the preamble's use of the defined terms "including" and "such as." *See supra* note 28.

[36] *See* Weissmann v. Freeman, 868 F.2d 1313, 1323 (2d Cir. 1989) ("Analysis begins

is a common thread to most of these examples: they represent productive uses—uses that produce some benefit to the public beyond the value of the copyrighted work.[37] The one exception is the reference to multiple copies for classroom use—more a substitute for purchasing the original work than the creation of new value. Yet, while the list suggests that productive uses may be worthy candidates for fair use treatment, its nonexclusive nature and the inclusion of classroom copying indicate that in appropriate cases the privilege may also be extended to nonproductive uses.[38]

What status is then to be given to particular uses that fall within the statutory examples? Some decisions by the Second Circuit have held that where a use is for one of the enumerated purposes (*e.g.*, criticism), the first statutory factor—the purpose and character of the use—should be weighed in favor of the party asserting the fair use defense.[39] This approach pays too much respect to terms intended merely as examples,[40] and overlooks the language and structural purpose of the preamble. The preamble merely states the principle that fair use is not infringement; whether a particular use is fair will depend on evaluation of the four factors that follow. Adoption of the Second Circuit's ap-

---

not by elevating the statutory guides into inflexible rules, but with a review of the underlying equities.").

37 *See* Sony Corp. of America v. Universal City Studios, Inc., 464 U.S. 417, 478-80 (1984) (Blackmun, J., dissenting).

38 Based on similar reasoning, the majority in *Sony* rejected the argument that a nonproductive use could not qualify as fair. 464 U.S. at 455 n.40. The Court held that an unproductive use, video tape recorder time-shifting of over-the-air broadcasts of audiovisual works, constituted fair use, where the copyright owners had not demonstrated harm to their potential market. *See also* THE FAIR USE PRIVILEGE, *supra* note 1, at 362-64.

39 *See* Wright v. Warner Books, Inc., 953 F.2d 731, 736 (2d Cir. 1991) ("There is a strong presumption that factor one favors the defendant if the allegedly infringing work fits the description of uses described in § 107."); New Era Pub. Int'l, ApS v. Carol Pub. Group, 904 F.2d 152, 156 (2d Cir.) ("If a book falls into one of these categories, assessment of the first fair use factor should be at an end."), *cert. denied*, 498 U.S. 921 (1990). *See also* Arica Institute, Inc. v. Palmer, 970 F.2d 1067, 1077 (2d Cir. 1992); New Era Pub. Int'l, ApS v. Henry Holt & Co., 873 F.2d 576, 583 (2d Cir.), *reh'g denied en banc*, 884 F.2d 659 (2d Cir. 1989), *cert. denied*, 493 U.S. 1094 (1990); Maxtone-Graham v. Burtchaell, 803 F.2d 1253, 1260 (2d Cir. 1986), *cert. denied*, 481 U.S. 1059 (1987); Lish v. Harper's Magazine Foundation, 807 F. Supp. 1090, 1097-98 (S.D.N.Y. 1992). *But see* Twin Peaks Prods., Inc. v. Publications Int'l, Ltd., Nos. 92-7933, 92-7985, slip op. at 13 (2d Cir. June 7, 1993 *as amended* July 6, 1993) (seemingly adopting an approach more consistent with the statute by referring to preamble examples as "non-exclusive purposes for which a protected fair use may be made").

40 "[W]hether a use referred to in the first sentence of section 107 is a fair use in a particular case will depend upon the application of the determinative factors, including those mentioned in the second sentence." S. REP. No. 94-473, 94th Cong., 1st Sess. 62 (1975). *See also* H. REP. No. 94-1476, 94th Cong., 2d Sess. 66 (1976) (emphasis added): "[The] reference to 'multiple copies for classroom use' is a recognition that, *under the proper circumstances of fairness*, the doctrine can be applied to reproductions of multiple copies for the members of a class."

proach would come close to rendering the first factor superfluous.[41]

The Supreme Court has previously rejected an effort to ascribe undue weight to uses mentioned in the preamble. In *Harper & Row, Publishers, Inc. v. Nation Enterprises*, the Court rejected a similar claim by *The Nation* magazine that its news reporting purpose automatically entitled it to have the first factor resolved in its favor. As the Court explained:

> [T]he examples enumerated in § 107 . . . "give some idea of the sort of activities the courts might regard as fair use under the circumstances." This listing was not intended to be exhaustive, or to single out any particular use as presumptively a 'fair' use. The drafters [of the 1976 Act] resisted pressures from special interest groups to create presumptive categories of fair use, but structured the provision as an affirmative defense requiring a case by case analysis. The fact that an article arguably is 'news' and therefore a productive use is simply one factor in a fair use analysis.[42]

C. *The First Statutory Factor: The Purpose and Character of the Use*

1. General

As the first enumerated factor, the statute directs courts to consider "the purpose and character of the use, including whether such use is of a commercial nature or is for nonprofit educational purposes."[43] This language is instructive in several respects. First, it focuses the court's inquiry on the type of use being made, rather than the type of entity making the use. While not unrelated, they do not necessarily coincide. A profit-making company may on occasion engage in a noncommercial use; a nonprofit organization may use a work in a way that is blatantly commercial.[44]

---

41 *See* Astoria Federal Savings & Loan Assoc. v. Solimino, 111 S. Ct. 2166, 2171-72 (1991) (Souter, J.) ("[O]f course we construe statutes, where possible, so as to avoid rendering superfluous any parts thereof.").

42 471 U.S. 539, 561 (1985) (citations omitted).

43 17 U.S.C. § 107(1) (1978).

44 *See* Lish v. Harper's Magazine Foundation, 807 F. Supp. 1090, 1101 (S.D.N.Y. 1992) ("[T]he mere fact that Harper's is a non-profit organization that operates at a loss does not preclude a finding of 'commercial use'; non-profit organizations enjoy no special immunity from determinations of copyright violation. The question under factor one is the purpose and character of the use, not of the alleged infringer."), *later op.*, COPR. L. REP. (CCH) ¶ 27,048 (S.D.N.Y. 1993).

The courts have also properly rejected attempts by for-profit users to stand in the shoes of their customers making non-profit or noncommercial uses. *See* Educational Testing Service v. Katzman, 793 F.2d 533, 543 (3d Cir. 1986); Pacific & Southern Co. v.

Second, the statutory language indicates that the commercial character of the use alone does not end the inquiry on the first factor. The use of the defined term "including" makes clear that the use's commercial or non-profit educational nature is not the only relevant consideration.[45] Unfortunately, some courts have forgotten the "fundamental principle of statutory construction (and indeed, of language itself) that the meaning of a word cannot be determined in isolation, but must be drawn from the context in which it is used."[46] The context of the "commercial nature" phrase as merely a subsidiary part of the first factor indicates that the commercial or nonprofit educational element of a given use is but one aspect of its more general purpose and character. Courts may therefore go beyond such categorization and examine other aspects of the purpose and character of the use[47]—for example, whether the copyrighted material was used for purposes of criticism or comment.[48] While one aspect of the use's purpose may be the purpose of the defendant's work as a whole, the focus should be on the purpose of each specific use of the plaintiff's expression.[49]

Finally, a reading of the text itself leads to the conclusion that it does not establish an either-or choice, with commercial uses banished to copyright purgatory and nonprofit educational uses admitted to the promised land of privilege. Not all uses can be classified as either "commercial" or "nonprofit educational"; some nonprofit uses, for example, are not educational. Perhaps for this reason, it has become common to substitute the contrast-

---

Duncan, 744 F.2d 1490, 1496 (11th Cir. 1984), *cert. denied*, 471 U.S. 1004 (1985); Basic Books, Inc. v. Kinko's Graphic Corp., 758 F. Supp. 1522, 1531-32 (S.D.N.Y. 1991); Association of American Medical Colleges v. Mikaelian, 571 F. Supp. 144, 152-53 (E.D. Pa. 1983), *aff'd per curiam*, 734 F.2d 3 (3d Cir. 1984).

45 *See supra* text at note 28.

46 Deal v. United States, No. 91-8199, 1993 U.S. LEXIS 3134, at *6-7 (1993). *See also* Smith v. United States, 61 U.S.L.W. 4503, 4505 (1993) (O'Connor, J.): "Language, of course, cannot be interpreted apart from context. The meaning of a word that appears ambiguous if viewed in isolation may become clear when the word is analyzed in light of the terms that surround it."

47 *See* Consumers Union of United States, Inc. v. General Signal Corp., 724 F.2d 1044, 1049 (2d Cir. 1983) ("The distinction between 'commercial nature' and 'nonprofit educational purposes' is merely illustrative of what is included in assessing the core of the criterion, which is the purpose of and character of the use."), *reh'g denied en banc*, 730 F.2d 47 (2d Cir.) (Oakes, J., dissenting), *cert. denied sub nom.* Consumers Union of United States, Inc. v. New Regina Corp., 469 U.S. 823 (1984), *on remand*, 664 F. Supp. 753 (S.D.N.Y. 1987).

48 *See infra* text at notes 81-89.

49 *See* Pierre N. Leval, *Toward a Fair Use Standard*, 103 HARV. L. REV. 1105, 1112-13 (1990): "Courts must consider the question of fair use for each challenged passage and not merely for the secondary work overall. . . . Simply to appraise the overall character of the challenged work tells little about whether the various quotations of the original author's writings have a fair use purpose or merely supersede."

ing "commercial or noncommercial" formulation for the statutory "commercial or nonprofit educational."

The import of the statutory language is underlined by the history of the first factor, which can be traced back to Justice Story's opinion in *Folsom v. Marsh*.[50] Justice Story phrased his version of the factor as "the nature and objects of the selections made."[51] In 1963, early in the revision process leading up to the 1976 Act, the Copyright Office circulated a preliminary draft bill which described the first factor as "the purpose and character of the use," without referring to commerciality or indicating any particular aspect of purpose and character as relevant.[52] Subsequent drafts of the bill either omitted any mention of specific factors[53] or retained the Copyright Office's language unchanged.

It was not until September 1976, one month before passage of the revision bill, that the phrase "including whether such use is of a commercial nature or is for nonprofit educational purposes" was added by the House Judiciary Committee, in order to mollify educators who had lobbied unsuccessfully for an across-the-board exemption for nonprofit educational uses.[54] The Judiciary Committee Report explained:

> This amendment is not intended to be interpreted as any sort of not-for-profit limitation on educational uses of copyrighted works. It is an express recognition that, as under the present law, the commercial or non-profit character of an activity, while not conclusive with respect to fair use, can and should be weighed along with other factors in fair use decisions.[55]

In other words, this final phrase of the first factor was intended not to affect the substance of fair use but to serve as a sop to an

---

50 9 F. Cas. 342 (C.C.D. Mass. 1841) (No. 4,901).

51 *Id.* at 348. The full quote reads: "In short, we must often, in deciding questions of this sort, look to the nature and objects of the selections made, the quantity and value of the materials used, and the degree in which the use may prejudice the sale, or diminish the profits, or supersede the objects, of the original work." Some of the same factors were identified as relevant by Justice Story two years earlier in Gray v. Russell, 10 F. Cas. 1035, 1038-39 (C.C.D. Mass. 1839) (No. 5,728).

52 *See* Copyright Law Revision Part 3: Preliminary Draft for Revised U.S. Copyright Law and Discussions and Comments on the Draft at 6, § 6 (September 1964). The full statutory evolution of section 107 is described in The Fair Use Privilege, *supra* note 1, at 482-85. Sections from the various legislative reports discussing fair use are reproduced *id.* at 486-513.

53 Identical bills introduced in the House and the Senate in 1965 contained a minimalist fair use provision reading in its entirety as follows: "Notwithstanding the provisions of section 106, the fair use of a copyrighted work is not an infringement of copyright." H.R. 4347 and S. 1006, 89th Cong., 1st Sess. (1965).

54 *See* The Fair Use Privilege, *supra* note 1, at 296-304.

55 H.R. Rep. No. 94-1476, 94th Cong., 2d Sess. 67 (1976).

unhappy interest group, by recognizing in the statute itself that their type of use was one that might be fair in appropriate circumstances.

It should also be noted in this connection that one of the major distinctions between the 1909 and 1976 Acts is the new Act's rejection of the prior across-the-board nonprofit exemptions. This rejection is implemented in a number of ways. To begin with, it is reflected in the very structure of the 1976 Act: a broad grant of exclusive rights in section 106, limited only by the privileges, exemptions, and compulsory licenses contained in sections 107 to 120.[56] In contrast, the 1909 Act placed the restrictions on the copyright owner's rights within the grant of rights.[57] In 1976, Congress expressly rejected the continuation of the former nonprofit exemptions based on concerns that the "line between commercial and 'nonprofit' organizations is increasingly difficult" to draw, and that a broad nonprofit exemption might result in supplanting the market for many works.[58] This fundamental change was also reflected in Congress's refusal to accede to educators' request for blanket statutory fair use privileges.[59]

2. The Meaning of "Commercial"

In the overall context of an equitable rule of reason, it may not make sense to classify any particular use as either commercial or noncommercial. Few uses will qualify as purely one or the other; most involve some degree of monetary gain, whether direct or indirect. In evaluating this aspect of the nature of the use,

---

56 *See* H.R. REP. No. 94-1476, 94th Cong., 2d Sess. 61 (1976); S. REP. No. 94-473, 94th Cong., 1st Sess. 57 (1975).

57 *See* 17 U.S.C. §§ 1(b)-(e) (1909).

58 H.R. REP. No. 94-1476, 94th Cong., 2d Sess. 62-63 (1976).

59 *See id.* at 66-67. "The Committee . . . adheres to its earlier conclusion that a specific exemption freeing certain reproductions of copyrighted works for educational and scholarly purposes from copyright control is not justified." The report also stated:

> The specific wording of section 107 as it now stands is the result of a process of accretion, resulting from the long controversy over the related problems of fair use and the reproduction (mostly by photocopying) of copyrighted material for educational and scholarly purposes. For example, the reference to fair use 'by reproduction in copies or phonorecords or by any other means' is mainly intended to make clear that the doctrine has as much application to photocopying and taping as to older forms of use; it is not intended to give these kinds of reproduction any special status under the fair use provision or to sanction any reproduction beyond the normal and reasonable limits of fair use. Similarly, the newly-added reference to 'multiple copies for classroom use' is a recognition that, under the proper circumstances of fairness, the doctrine can be applied to reproductions of multiple copies for the members of a class.

Id. at 66.

some have proposed placing the commercial nature of a use on a continuum, with commerciality viewed as a matter of degree.

The continuum approach is appealing, as it avoids the artificiality of an either/or choice, instead reflecting the reality of the wide range of possible uses. As the Second Circuit has pointed out:

> We do not read Section 107(1) as requiring us to make a clear-cut choice between two polar characterizations, "commercial" and "non-profit." Were that the case, fair use would be virtually obliterated, for "all publications presumably are operated for profit . . . ." The commercial nature of a use is a matter of degree, not an absolute . . . .[60]

At one extreme of the continuum (the most favorable for the defense) would be a use for educational purposes in a nonprofit institution not charging any fee.[61] At the other extreme would be the use of a copyrighted work to promote or sell a commercial product or service.[62] The intermediate uses are the ones that

---

60 Maxtone-Graham v. Burtchaell, 803 F.2d 1253, 1262 (2d Cir. 1986) (quoting Koussevitzky v. Allen, Towne & Heath, 68 N.Y.S.2d 779, 783, *aff'd*, 69 N.Y.S.2d 432 (1st Dept. 1947), *as quoted in* Rosemont Enterprises, Inc. v. Random House, Inc., 366 F.2d 303, 307 (2d Cir. 1966), *cert. denied*, 385 U.S. 1009 (1967)), *cert. denied*, 481 U.S. 1059 (1987). *Accord*, Sega Enters. Ltd. v. Accolade, Inc., 977 F.2d 1510, 1522 (9th Cir. 1992). *See also* New Era Pubs. Int'l, ApS v. Henry Holt & Co., 695 F. Supp. 1493, 1506-07 (S.D.N.Y. 1988) (citing *Maxtone-Graham*: "Scholars and critics do not lose their license to make fair use by earning their bread from their writing."), *aff'd on other grounds*, 873 F.2d 576 (2d Cir.), *reh'g denied en banc*, 884 F.2d 659 (2d Cir. 1989), *cert. denied*, 493 U.S. 1094 (1990).

61 *See, e.g.*, Williams & Wilkins Co. v. United States, 487 F.2d 1345 (Ct. Cl. 1973), *aff'd by an equally divided Court*, 420 U.S. 376 (1975). It is not surprising that few of the reported cases involve this type of use.

62 Even at this extreme, there will be differences in the degree of commerciality. A use may be seen as less commercial where the product sold is completely separate from the copyrighted work than where the product sold itself incorporates portions of the work. *Compare* Eveready Battery Co. v. Adolph Coors Co., 765 F. Supp. 440 (N.D. Ill. 1991) (advertisement for beer copying and satirizing copyrighted advertisement for batteries); Tin Pan Apple, Inc. v. Miller Brewing Co., 737 F. Supp. 826 (S.D.N.Y. 1990) (advertisement for beer copying rap group's performance); Consumers Union of U.S., Inc. v. New Regina Corp., 664 F. Supp. 753 (S.D.N.Y. 1987) (advertisement for vacuum cleaners quoting from copyrighted publication evaluating quality of vacuum cleaners) *and* Steinberg v. Columbia Pictures Industries, Inc., 663 F. Supp. 706 (S.D.N.Y. 1987) (promotional poster for movie) *with* Dallas Cowboy Cheerleaders, Inc. v. Scoreboard Posters, Inc., 600 F.2d 1184 (5th Cir. 1979) (posters of cheerleaders substantially similar to plaintiff's cheerleaders poster); Original Appalachian Artworks, Inc. v. Topps Chewing Gum, Inc., 642 F. Supp. 1031 (N.D. Ga. 1986) (stickers with satirical versions of plaintiff's wholesome dolls) *and* DC Comics Inc. v. Unlimited Monkey Business, Inc., 598 F. Supp. 110 (N.D. Ga. 1984) (use of copyrighted characters in providing singing telegram services). *See also* Triangle Publications, Inc. v. Knight-Ridder Newspapers, Inc., 626 F.2d 1171, 1176 (5th Cir. 1980) ("[T]he precise characteristics of the commercial use in this case caution against too much weight being given to the fact that the use is commercial"; copyrighted work used in comparative advertising, rather than in an attempt to palm off).

have led to mixed results: the use of the copyrighted work in literary or artistic expression created by the defendant that is sold in the marketplace. Such uses may include news reporting, critical commentary and scholarship published in book or journal form, and parody—indeed, many of the uses listed as examples in the preamble to section 107. Within this intermediate category, commerciality may come in degrees. The defendant's active marketing of the plaintiff's work, such as the use of copyrighted material on the cover of a larger work to attract buyers, should be considered more commercial than the use of portions of a copyrighted work as only part of another work, such as an article or photograph included within a magazine.[63]

In assessing the first factor balance, courts should examine the manner in which particular material from the plaintiff's work is used. Did the defendant reproduce the copyright owner's expression for the purpose of marketing the precise form of that expression, or for the purpose of making his own additional statement? Other aspects of the use's "purpose and character," such as its critical function, should not be confused with the question of its degree of commerciality. The question of whether the use is entertainment or scholarship should be separated from the different question of whether it brings in profit, allowing courts to focus on the degree of social benefit fostered by that type of use.[64]

Even within a single work, the "purpose and character" of a defendant's use of material from the plaintiff's work may vary, with some uses by the defendant weighing against fair use while others do not. For example, a biographer's reproduction of a passage from a famous writer's book to illustrate the particular technique she used may be fair use, while the reproduction of "juicy" excerpts from one of the writer's personal letters on the dust jacket of the biography in order to lure people to buy it might not be. Although in both cases the biography is "commercial" in the sense that it is sold for money, and in both it constitutes a form of scholarship, only the former use of the writer's

---

[63] *See* Haberman v. Hustler Magazine, Inc., 626 F. Supp. 201 (D. Mass. 1986) (plaintiff's photographs reproduced within magazine, not on cover). *Cf.* L.L. Bean, Inc. v. Drake Publishers, Inc., 811 F.2d 26 (1st Cir.) (holding trademark parody protected by First Amendment in part because parody was internal article, not used on cover to sell magazine), *cert. denied*, 483 U.S. 1013 (1987).

[64] The relevant value to society is that of the work's genre or category, not of that work in particular. Courts should not be engaged in evaluating aesthetic or scholarly quality. *See* Twin Peaks Prods., Inc. v. Publications Int'l, Ltd., Nos. 92-7933, 92-7985, slip op. at 13 (2d Cir. June 7, 1993 *as amended* July 6, 1993).

work adds to the public discourse in a manner that should cause the first statutory factor to weigh in the defendant's favor.

Finally, it should not matter how successful the defendant's marketing of its work has been. If a use is made for financial gain, the fact that the defendant has sold one hundred copies rather than 100,000 makes the nature of the use—as opposed to its extent—no less commercial. The converse is also true; a best-selling use is no more commercial than a work that ends up in the remainder bin.[65]

3. The Supreme Court's Gloss on "Commercial" Use

Each of the Supreme Court's three fair use opinions refers to the application of the doctrine to commercial uses, although none has analyzed in depth the meaning of "commercial."

a. Sony Corp. of America v. Universal City Studios, Inc.[66]

In *Sony*, the Supreme Court did not attempt to define when a use is commercial, concluding without difficulty that the use at issue, time-shifting by consumers in their homes of audiovisual works broadcast over the air, was nonprofit.[67] Nevertheless, as discussed below,[68] *Sony* contains important language on the consequences of a use being deemed "commercial."

b. Harper & Row, Publishers, Inc. v. Nation Enterprises[69]

In *Harper & Row*, a purported "news reporting" use of President Ford's then-unpublished memoirs was found to have "not merely the incidental effect but the *intended purpose* of supplanting the copyright holder's commercially valuable right of first publication."[70] The Court observed that *The Nation*, "like its competitor newsweekly . . . was free to bid for the right of abstracting excerpts from [the book]."[71] *The Nation*'s failure to do so led the Court to draw the following distinction:

> The crux of the profit/nonprofit distinction is not whether the sole motive of the use is monetary gain but whether the user stands to profit from exploitation of the copyrighted ma-

---

65 This is not to say that the amount of the defendant's sales is irrelevant to the fair use inquiry; it may enter the equation when the fourth factor is considered, in determining the impact on the value of and potential market for the copyrighted work.

66 464 U.S. 417 (1984).

67 *Id.* at 449.

68 *See infra* text at notes 145-70.

69 471 U.S. 539 (1985).

70 *Id.* at 562.

71 *Id.* at 563.

terial without paying the customary price.[72]

This statement, resonant and often-quoted, has much to recommend it. It captures the core of commerciality: not just the receipt of income from sales of the defendant's work, but also the financial benefit obtained by avoiding an otherwise-due payment for the use of the copyrighted work.

Harper & Row's "crux" standard may be apt in cases such as *American Geophysical Union v. Texaco, Inc.*,[73] where copyright owners had established a licensing fee arrangement through the Copyright Clearance Center for the reproduction of scientific journal articles, not in order to prevent the reproduction of their works, but to make reproduction easy and inexpensive.[74] Other courts have also rejected fair use claims where a customary fee was available but unpaid.[75]

On the other side, the *Harper & Row* "crux" standard might be applied to say that a defendant's willingness to pay a customary fee should weigh *against* a finding of commercial use. In *Acuff-Rose*, for example, application of the standard could result in a finding that 2 Live Crew's use of "Oh, Pretty Woman" was noncommercial since the group *did* offer to pay such a fee.[76] But the

---

72 *Id.* at 562.

73 802 F. Supp. 1 (S.D.N.Y. 1992) (Leval, J.), *appeal argued* No. 92-9341 (2d Cir. May 20, 1993). Judge Leval found a commercial purpose in Texaco's photocopying, since the copying was done "to improve Texaco's commercial performance." *Id.* at 16.

74 A concern over possible harm to scientific research or excessive burdens on users due to the lack of such easily available licensing may have been responsible for the splintered vote by the Supreme Court in the *Williams & Wilkins* case, which also involved photocopying from scientific journals, but in the days before a pre-approved clearance mechanism for photocopying had been established. *See* Williams & Wilkins Co. v. United States, 420 U.S. 376 (1975), *aff'g by equally divided vote* 487 F.2d 1345 (Ct. Cl. 1973).

75 *See* Telerate Systems, Inc. v. Caro, 689 F. Supp. 221, 229 (S.D.N.Y. 1988) (citing *Harper & Row* and finding plaintiff had established a customary licensing fee for copying portions of its computer data base); New Line Cinema Corp. v. Bertlesman Music Group, Inc., 693 F. Supp. 1517, 1526 (S.D.N.Y. 1988) (citing *Harper & Row* and finding plaintiff had established a usual licensing fee for use of its songs in music videos). *See also* Cable/Home Communication Corp. v. Network Prods., Inc., 902 F.2d 829, 844 (11th Cir. 1990).

76 The amount 2 Live Crew offered to Acuff-Rose was the rate for the mechanical compulsory license set forth in section 115 of title 17, as adjusted by the Copyright Royalty Tribunal. *See* 17 U.S.C. § 115 (1978); 37 C.F.R. § 307. (Currently, the rate is 6.25 cents per song or 1.2 cents per minute of playing time or fraction thereof, whichever is larger.)

The compulsory license itself was not available to 2 Live Crew because it does not extend to parodies. Section 115(a)(2) permits an arrangement of the song only "to the extent necessary to conform it to the style or manner of interpretation of the performance involved, but the arrangement shall not change the basic melody or fundamental character of the work. . . ." A license for a parody therefore can only be obtained from the copyright owner.

The compulsory license rate is nevertheless a convenient reference point for the value of similar licenses. While the lower courts did not resolve the issue of whether the

resonance of the "crux" passage obscures a fundamental problem. The standard is ultimately circular, given its reference to the failure to pay "the customary price." By definition, if the defendant's use is fair, no fee, customary or not, is due. A finding of fair use represents a determination that the use should require neither consent nor fee.

c. Stewart v. Abend[77]

This most unlikely of fair use claims—by the motion picture company interests that produced the movie "Rear Window," involving their use in the movie of the short story "It Had to be Murder"—was quickly dispatched by the Supreme Court. The Court resolved the first factor against the defendants, on the grounds that the use did not fit into any of the section 107 preamble examples, had brought in 12 million dollars when the movie was re-released, and was hardly educational (as the defendants asserted).[78]

Given the factual contexts of the Court's three fair use cases, it has yet to confront the core of the first factor. The contributory infringement claim in *Sony* concerned noncommercial uses; in *Stewart*, the use was plainly commercial. *Harper & Row* involved the deliberate conversion of a planned use of copyrighted material to make a news event of the very act of infringement. *Acuff-Rose* presents a less obvious array of facts, requiring careful examination of the purpose and character of the use.

4. Other Aspects of a Use's "Purpose and Character"

Fully evaluating the first statutory factor requires more than just examining the use's degree of commerciality. The first factor entails a multifaceted inquiry, looking at all aspects of the use's "purpose and character." We have already discussed the aspects of productive use and of the use's social value: is the user engaged in entertainment, scholarship, or criticism? Where the defendant's use could be characterized as entertainment, courts have tended to find that its commercial nature weighs the first factor against fair use.[79] Where, on the other hand, the use may be viewed as serious scholarship, the fact that it is sold for money

---

compulsory license rate offered by 2 Live Crew was adequate, *see* 754 F. Supp. at 1152, it may have been a reasonable benchmark for the *Harper & Row* "customary fee."

[77] 495 U.S. 207 (1990).

[78] *Id.* at 237.

[79] *See, e.g.*, Stewart v. Abend, 495 U.S. 207, 237 (1990) (upholding finding that movie "Rear Window" by Alfred Hitchcock was commercial rather than educational).

has often been eclipsed in evaluating the first factor.[80]

Other aspects of the use's "purpose and character" considered by the courts have included the user's bad faith,[81] distortion of the copyright owner's work,[82] and the user's interest in responding to a personal attack.[83] This list is not exclusive; in appropriate circumstances, courts may examine the public interest, the First Amendment, privacy concerns, or additional equitable factors.[84] While many of these considerations are appropriately addressed under the rubric of the first statutory factor, they may also be treated as separate and distinct factors beyond the four illustrative ones.

Nor need the first factor simply be resolved as "pro" or "con" fair use, depending on which aspect of the use predominates, its profit-making purpose or its scholarly character. Before fair use was incorporated in the statute, courts did not treat the factors as a checklist, with each factor reduced to a plus or minus. The mere listing of four factors in the 1976 Act, however, has led some courts improperly to take this approach.[85] Certainly as a whole does not support it.

---

80 *See, e.g.*, Sega Enters. Ltd. v. Accolade, Inc., 977 F.2d 1510, 1522 (9th Cir. 1992) (reverse compilation of computer program to gain access to its unprotectible components); Arica Institute, Inc. v. Palmer, 970 F.2d 1067 (2d Cir. 1992) (psychology self-help book); Wright v. Warner Books, Inc., 953 F.2d 731 (2d Cir. 1991) (biography).

81 *See Harper & Row*, 471 U.S. at 562 (finding bad faith in knowing exploitation of purloined manuscript): "Also relevant to the 'character' of the use is the 'propriety of the defendant's conduct.' 3 Nimmer § 13.05[A], at 13-72. 'Fair use presupposes good faith and fair dealing.' " Time, Inc. v. Bernard Geis Associates, 293 F. Supp. 130, 146 (S.D.N.Y. 1968) (citation omitted). *See also* Rogers v. Koons, 960 F.2d 301, 310 (2d Cir.) (deliberate removal of copyright notice from plaintiff's work), *cert. denied*, 113 S. Ct. 365 (1992); Weissmann v. Freeman, 868 F.2d 1313, 1323-24 (2d Cir. 1989) (attempt to pass off plaintiff's work as defendant's); Marcus v. Rowley, 695 F.2d 1171, 1175-76 (9th Cir. 1983) (verbatim copying from the plaintiff's work without giving credit). These types of conduct should be distinguished from the decision to proceed with the use after denial of permission from the defendant, which should not be considered to evidence bad faith. *See* Wright v. Warner Books, Inc., 953 F.2d 731, 737 (2d Cir. 1991); Maxtone-Graham v. Burtchaell, 803 F.2d 1253, 1264 (2d Cir. 1986), *cert. denied*, 481 U.S. 1059 (1987); and parody cases discussed in *infra* note 193.

82 *See* Maxtone-Graham v. Burtchaell, 803 F.2d 1253, 1261 (2d Cir. 1986) (recognizing relevance of issue but finding no sufficient distortion to consider), *cert. denied*, 481 U.S. 1059 (1987); Lish v. Harper's Magazine Foundation, 807 F. Supp. 1090, 1096-97 (S.D.N.Y. 1992) (same).

83 *See, e.g.*, Hustler Magazine, Inc. v. Moral Majority, Inc., 796 F.2d 1148 (9th Cir. 1986).

84 *See, e.g.*, Rosemont Enters., Inc. v. Random House, Inc., 366 F.2d 303, 311-312 (2d Cir. 1966) (Lumbard & Hays, JJ., concurring) (censorship), *cert. denied*, 385 U.S. 1009 (1967); Time, Inc. v. Bernard Geis Associates, 293 F. Supp. 130, 146 (S.D.N.Y. 1968) (public interest).

85 *But see* Twin Peaks, Inc. v. Publications Int'l, Ltd., Nos. 92-7933, 92-7985, slip op. at 14 (2d Cir. June 7, 1993 *as amended* July 6, 1993): " 'Purpose' in fair use analysis is not an all-or-nothing matter. The issue is not simply whether a challenged work serves one of the non-exclusive purposes identified in section 107, but whether it does so to an insignificant or a substantial extent. The weight ascribed to the 'purpose' factor involves

As the Second Circuit pointed out a decade before enactment of the 1976 Act,

> Whether an author or publisher reaps economic benefits from the sale of a biographical work, or whether its publication is motivated in part by a desire for commercial gain, or whether it is designed for the popular market, i.e., the average citizen rather than the college professor, has no bearing on whether a public benefit may be derived from such a work. Moreover, the district court in emphasizing the commercial aspects of the [defendant's] biography failed to recognize that "[a]ll publications presumably are operated for profit . . . ." and that 'both commercial and artistic elements are involved in almost every [work] . . ." Thus, we conclude that whether an author or publisher has a commercial motive or writes in a popular style is irrelevant to a determination of whether a particular use of copyrighted material in a work which offers some benefit to the public constitutes a fair use.[86]

Of course, even where the first factor on balance favors the copyright owner, fair use may be found based on other factors in the case—both the three listed in the statute and any other circumstances the court finds relevant.[87] There is no easy formula, however. One cannot simply calculate that a plus on three or more factors adds up to fair use, while a plus on only two adds up as a draw and therefore does not fulfill the defendant's burden of persuasion on the affirmative defense.[88] Fair use is not the copy-

---

a more refined assessment than the initial, fairly easy decision that a work serves a purpose illustrated by the categories listed in section 107."

[86] Rosemont Enters. Inc. v. Random House, Inc., 366 F.2d 303, 307 (2d Cir. 1966) (citations omitted), *cert. denied*, 385 U.S. 1009 (1967). More recently, the same court explained, "[W]hether the profit element of the fair use calculus affects the ultimate determination of whether there is a fair use depends on the totality of the factors considered; it is not controlling." Rogers v. Koons, 960 F.2d 301, 309 (2d Cir.), *cert. denied*, 113 S. Ct. 365 (1992).

[87] The converse may also be true: even a nonprofit educational use may not qualify as fair. *See, e.g.*, the following cases finding educational uses not to be fair use even though no profit was made from the unauthorized reproduction of the copyrighted material: Marcus v. Rowley, 695 F.2d 1171 (9th Cir. 1983); Encyclopaedia Britannica Educ. Corp. v. Crooks, 447 F. Supp. 243 (W.D.N.Y. 1978), 542 F. Supp. 1156 (W.D.N.Y. 1982); Wihtol v. Crow, 309 F.2d 777 (8th Cir. 1962); Macmillan Co. v. King, 223 F. 862 (D. Mass. 1914).

[88] As expressed by the Second Circuit in Wright v. Warner Books, Inc., 953 F.2d 731, 740 (2d Cir. 1991), "The fair use test remains a totality inquiry, tailored to the particular facts of each case. Because this is not a mechanical determination, a party need not 'shut out' her opponent on the four factor tally to prevail." *Cf.* College Entrance Exam. Bd. v. Cuomo, 788 F. Supp. 134, 140 (N.D.N.Y. 1992) (two-to-two tie on fair use factors resolved in defendant's favor based on holding that burden of proof is borne by plaintiff in preliminary injunction context). *See also* Leval, *supra* note 49, at 1110 ("The factors do not represent a score card that promises victory to the winner of the majority.").

right equivalent of a political election, in which courts tally up the factors, and the winner takes all. Individual factors may be evenly weighed, strongly or weakly favor one side, or even be unresolved. A weakness in one factor may be marginally offset by a strength on a different factor. Fair use is a weighing process involving nonexclusive and multifaceted factors,[89] not an exercise in computation.

D. *The Fourth Statutory Factor*

The fourth statutory factor, "the effect of the use on the potential market for or value of the copyrighted work," raises difficult issues of theory and proof. How should the potential market be defined? What type of harm to the value of the work should be considered? How should the burdens of production and of proof be allocated?

1. Identifying the Relevant Potential Market

As a preliminary matter, it is obvious that the potential market must be confined to those uses that can reasonably be construed to be within the Copyright Act's grant of rights in sections 106 and 106A, as limited by sections 107-120. As Justice Stevens observed in *Sony*, "An unlicensed use of the copyright is not an infringement unless it conflicts with one of the specific rights granted by the copyright statute."[90]

In an era when licensing and subsidiary rights have taken on increasing importance, the potential market for the copyrighted work goes well beyond the sale of copies of the work in its original form. Today, the market for derivative works is an economically important part of the copyright owner's market, and therefore an important part of the incentive that drives the copyright system. Recognizing this fact, courts have appropriately included in their consideration of the fourth factor the effect of the defendant's use on the copyright owner's ability to license the preparation of derivative works.[91] Many cases have examined the

89 The Supreme Court's opinion in *Harper & Row* provides a good illustration of the multifaceted nature of each statutory factor. On the second factor, the Court examined the degree of creativity of the copyrighted work and whether the work was published or unpublished. 471 U.S. at 563-64. Its analysis of the third factor focused on both the quantitative and the qualitative significance of the amount taken, in relation to both the copyrighted work as a whole and the infringing work. 471 U.S. at 564-66. Finally, on the fourth factor, the Court looked to evidence of actual damage as well as proof of harm to the potential market for derivative works. 471 U.S. at 566-69.

90 464 U.S. 417, 447 (1984).

91 *See* Harper & Row, Publishers, Inc. v. Nation Enterprises, 471 U.S. 539, 568 (1985)

economic impact of the plaintiff's loss of an opportunity to sell a literary work for publication in a different form, such as a serialization of excerpts or a collection of letters.[92] In the context of the visual arts, the copyright owner's potential market has been interpreted to include the right to prepare a three-dimensional version of a two-dimensional work of art.[93]

Too broad an interpretation of the potential market, however, presents its own dangers. If taken to a logical extreme, the fourth factor would always weigh against fair use, since there is always a *potential* market that the copyright owner could in theory license. By definition, once the affirmative defense of fair use is invoked, there has already been a finding of infringement. Accordingly, the defendant's use necessarily falls within the area of the copyright owner's exclusive rights and therefore could have been licensed.

For example, a copyright owner could theoretically could license book reviews as well as serializations. But while a serialization may satisfy some readers' desire to purchase the book, few interested in reading a novel are likely to be satisfied by a review. Including in the potential market uses such as book reviews is therefore inappropriate.

The problem of defining the market is particularly acute where the use is one that the copyright owner disapproves of and is unlikely to exploit or authorize at any price, such as parody. As a derivative work, parody could be viewed as a potential market available for licensing. Because it is almost unheard of for a copyright owner to welcome or even willingly tolerate mockery, however, allowing him or her to retain a veto over such uses raises a real threat of censorship.[94] The result would be the loss

---

("Th[e] inquiry [on the fourth factor] must take account not only of harm to the original but also of harm to the market for derivative works.").

92 *See, e.g., id.* at 568 and cases cited therein; Salinger v. Random House, Inc., 811 F.2d 90 (2d Cir. 1987).

93 *See* Rogers v. Koons, 960 F.2d 301, 312 (2d Cir.), *cert. denied*, 113 S. Ct. 365 (1992); United Feature Syndicate, Inc. v. Koons, 817 F. Supp. 370 (S.D.N.Y. 1993); Campbell v. Koons, 1993 U.S. Dist. LEXIS 3957 (S.D.N.Y. filed April 1, 1993).

94 The Ninth Circuit has recognized that "[p]arodists will seldom get permission from those whose works are parodied. Self-esteem is seldom strong enough to permit the granting of permission even in exchange for a reasonable fee." Fisher v. Dees, 794 F.2d 432, 437 (9th Cir. 1986). The attitude of many copyright owners toward parody was recently illustrated vividly in Lawrence O'Toole, *Ego, Paranoia and Power in the Land of Musical Rights*, N.Y. TIMES, May 30, 1993, Section 2, at 1: "Requests for comedy uses of 'You'll Never Walk Alone' and 'Climb Ev'ry Mountain' are always turned down, according to Ted Chapin, executive director of the Rodgers and Hammerstein Organization: 'For better or worse, those are our hymns. If we start making fun of them, then that's a problem.' Parody can literally place you in court."

In *Acuff-Rose* itself, 2 Live Crew's request for a license was turned down by Acuff-

of the public interest and First Amendment values in informative criticism and humorous comment.[95] In the words of the Ninth Circuit, "The parody defense to copyright infringement exists precisely to make possible a use that generally cannot be bought."[96]

Judicial response to parody has been inconsistent, with courts struggling with issues of what is a legitimate parody, how closely a parodist can imitate the original, and whether distasteful or obscene parodies can be fair use.[97] While its social value is obvious to most, parody by its nature requires a greater amount of copying than a book review to make its point. Moreover, a parody of a song is still a song, sold in the same record stores as the copyrighted work. It is therefore critical that the potential market for the copyrighted work not be defined so broadly as to sweep within it every conceivable use.[98]

The question remains how to circumscribe the scope of the relevant potential market so as to ensure that the fourth factor has independent meaning and does not become circular, while still protecting the core economic interests of the copyright owner. One possibility would be to include only those uses that the copyright owner has actually licensed, or is negotiating to license.[99] This approach would not only avoid the censorship problem, but would have the advantage of ruling out speculative harm that may never occur.[100] But it seems overly restrictive to

---

Rose not on the basis of the nature of 2 Live Crew's parody, but on the categorical ground that "we cannot permit the use of a parody of 'Oh, Pretty Woman.'" *See* 972 F.2d at 1432.

[95] It has also been argued that the copyright owner in these circumstances is seeking to exploit moral rights rather than economic rights, and that such an interest is not cognizable under U.S. law. *See, e.g.*, Melanie A. Clemmons, *Author v. Parodist: Striking a Compromise*, 46 OHIO ST. L.J. 3, 8 (1985).

[96] Fisher v. Dees, 794 F.2d at 437.

Judge Leval has decried what he calls the "widow censor" who vetoes the use of a spouse's writings in historical works that may not be deemed flattering. Leval, *supra* note 49, at 1118. *See also* O'Toole, *supra* n. 94:

> The families, heirs and trustees of departed musical geniuses have their own agendas. . . . A musical estate can argue that a stylized version of a song strays from a composer's intentions, and songwriters are no longer around to give their yea or nay. . . . In keeping a talonlike grip on the rights to music and lyrics, estates—normally run by a small committee of heirs and executors—can be overly protective. Many of them make it their mission to be keepers of the creative flames.

[97] These issues are discussed at *infra* text accompanying notes 224-25.

[98] *See* Twin Peaks Prods., Inc. v. Publications Int'l, Ltd., Nos. 92-7933, 92-7985 slip op. at 22 (2d Cir. June 7, 1993 *as amended* July 6, 1993).

[99] Under this approach, the potential market would include such items as the lost contract for the prepublication rights for President Ford's memoirs in *Harper & Row*.

[100] *Cf.* Lewis Galoob Toys, Inc. v. Nintendo of America, Inc., 964 F.2d 965 (9th Cir. 1992) (insufficient proof of harm to potential market for derivative works where the

limit the copyright owner to markets already in the process of exploitation at the time the infringement takes place. It should not be necessary, for example, for a photographer to have begun to negotiate rights to make a three-dimensional version of his photograph in order to claim that his potential market is hurt by the unauthorized creation of such a work.[101] As the Eleventh Circuit has noted, "Copyrights protect owners who immediately market a work no more stringently than owners who delay before entering the market."[102]

A preferable approach would be to give effect to the plain meaning of the term "potential," interpreting the fourth factor to include not only uses currently being exploited, but also uses which the copyright owner might have an interest in exploiting in the future.[103] If the copyright owner were required to demonstrate that such an interest already existed, many potential sources of income would be excluded from the analysis. Few photographers may have thought of the possibility of licensing three-dimensional rights to their photographs.

On the other hand, the potential market should not be deemed to include uses that the plaintiff has an affirmative desire *not* to license—the situation where the plaintiff would prefer that type of use not to be made at all.[104] This would exclude as not

---

plaintiff had not yet issued or considered issuing altered versions of existing video games or showed reasonable likelihood of such a market), *cert. denied*, 113 S. Ct. 1582 (1993); Wright v. Warner Books, Inc., 953 F.2d 731, 739 (2d Cir. 1991) (noting lack of evidence that allegedly planned project to publish collection of letters would go forward); Narell v. Freeman, 872 F.2d 907, 914 (9th Cir. 1989) (dismissing plaintiff's arguments as to possible licensing and adaptation of historical book as "purely speculative, . . . [in] the absence of any such offers").

101 *See* Rogers v. Koons, 960 F.2d 301 (2d Cir. 1992), *cert. denied*, 113 S. Ct. 365 (1992).

102 Pacific & Southern Co. v. Duncan, 744 F.2d 1490, 1496 (11th Cir.), *reh'g denied en banc*, 749 F.2d 733 (11th Cir. 1984), *cert. denied*, 471 U.S. 1004 (1985).

103 *Cf.* Twin Peaks Prods., Inc. v. Publications Int'l, Ltd., Nos. 92-7933, 92-7985 slip op. at 21 (2d Cir. June 7, 1993 *as amended* July 6, 1993) ("in the cases where we have found the fourth factor to favor a defendant, the defendant's work filled a market niche that the plaintiff simply had no interest in occupying," such as parody).

104 Professor Wendy Gordon has referred to such "anti-dissemination motives" as presenting a situation where ordinary market mechanisms for licensing may break down, justifying in part a finding of fair use. Wendy J. Gordon, *Fair Use as Market Failure: A Structural and Economic Analysis of the* Betamax *Case and its Predecessors*, 82 COLUM. L. REV. 1600, 1632 (1982). Economic analyses of fair use have also been proposed by other commentators, including Richard A. Posner, *When is Parody Fair Use?*, 21 J. LEGAL STUD. 67 (1992) and William W. Fisher, *Reconstructing the Fair Use Doctrine*, 101 HARV. L. REV. 1661 (1988).

The central flaw in these economic models is that the ultimate goal of copyright is to reward creativity, not efficiency. The two may not and need not lead to the same results. See critiques of the economic approach in Alfred C. Yen, *When Authors Won't Sell: Parody, Fair Use, and Efficiency in Copyright Law*, 62 U. COLO. L. REV. 79 (1991); Ralph S. Brown, *Eligibility for Copyright Protection: A Search for Principled Standards*, 70 MINN. L.

"potential" in any meaningful sense uses such as publication of private papers that the plaintiff has sought to keep from the public eye,[105] or a parody that ridicules the copyrighted work or connects it to themes the plaintiff finds distasteful. To the extent, however, that a plaintiff's decision not to exploit a market is based not on censorship but on the judgment that the economic value of the copyrighted work will be greater without such use, that market should be included. In this situation, the plaintiff in essence *is* interested in that market—it just finds it more lucrative to exploit other markets if it withholds a license.[106] Similarly, refraining from exploitation because of long-term business goals should not make the deliberately bypassed market fair game for copiers.[107]

2. What Type of Harm to the Value of the Work?

Similar questions arise as to the type of harm to the value of the work that should be cognizable in examining the fourth factor. The central focus should be harm arising from the ability of

---

REV. 579 (1985). In addition, any economic model is necessarily highly subjective, requiring numerous assumptions and judgments that courts are ill-equipped to make.

Most fundamentally, however, fair use is not about optimal allocation of resources or predictability. Where Congress wanted predictability, or believed that transactional costs imposed too high a burden on copyright owners or users, it created specific exemptions or compulsory licenses. (Even in the area of compulsory licenses, Congress refused to permit the Copyright Royalty Tribunal to set a market rate for cable television retransmissions, and carefully circumscribed the factors that the Tribunal can consider. *See* 17 U.S.C. § 801(b)(2) (1978)). If Congress had wished fair use to serve as a tool in the cause of economic theory, it would not have provided a general provision intended to continue the common law.

105 *Cf.* Salinger v. Random House, Inc., 811 F.2d 90, 99 (2d Cir.) (including in potential market under fourth fair use factor the market for a collection of J.D. Salinger's unpublished letters, despite Salinger's notorious desire for privacy, based on the rationale that he might someday change his mind), *cert. denied*, 484 U.S. 890 (1987).

Although evaluation of the fourth factor should not include harm to a potential market that the copyright owner will not exploit, the copyright owner's desire to keep his work private may be relevant to the fair use analysis in another respect. Under the second statutory factor, the right of first publication means that the unpublished nature of the work will weigh against fair use. *See Harper & Row*, 471 U.S. at 550-51 and 564.

106 *See* Consumers Union of United States, Inc. v. General Signal Corp., 730 F.2d 47, 49 (2d Cir. 1984) (Oakes, J., dissenting from denial of petition for rehearing) (potential markets that copyright owner refuses to license because it believes refusal will give copyrighted work greater value should be included in evaluating fourth factor), *cert. denied sub nom.* Consumers Union of United States, Inc. v. New Regina Corp., 469 U.S. 823 (1984), *on remand*, 664 F. Supp. 753 (S.D.N.Y. 1987). Other legitimate economically-based reasons might include a fear of over-saturating the market.

107 *See* Dr. Pepper Co. v. Sambo's Restaurants, Inc., 517 F. Supp. 1202 (N.D. Tex. 1981) (concern for loss of business goodwill); Steinberg v. Columbia Pictures Indus., 663 F. Supp. 706 (S.D.N.Y. 1987) (copyright owner's interest in maintaining reputation as noncommercial artist). One commentator has referred to such bypassed derivative markets as uses that the public might view as "having the stamp of [the author's] approval." A. Hunter Farrell, *Fair Use of Copyrighted Material in Advertisement Parodies*, 92 COLUM. L. REV. 1550, 1576 (1992).

the defendant's use to substitute for the plaintiff's work in the marketplace.[108]

There are many ways in which the unauthorized use of a copyrighted work may damage its value. Not all of them are relevant to the issue of fair use. While the copying of unprotectible material from a work, such as an important idea,[109] facts,[110] or the work's overall style,[111] may result in competition in the marketplace and lower the number of sales, such loss should not be considered. The harm must be caused by the use of copyrightable expression from the plaintiff's work.[112] Accordingly, courts have held that harm caused solely by the fact that the two works compete in the same general market does not fall within the scope of section 107(4).[113]

Indirect harm caused to the value of the work by the taking of expression may also be eliminated from consideration. For example, while the use of expression to criticize or ridicule the copyrighted work may indeed diminish consumers' desire to purchase it, that is a risk inherent in making the work public, and not the kind of harm to its value that lessens the likelihood of fair use.[114]

In the context of parody, the Ninth Circuit has explained:

---

108 *See* Consumers Union of United States, Inc. v. General Signal Corp., 724 F.2d 1044, 1050 (2d Cir. 1983), *petition for reh'g denied*, 730 F.2d 47 (2d Cir.), *cert. denied sub nom.* Consumers Union of United States, Inc. v. New Regina Corp., 469 U.S. 823 (1984), *on remand*, 664 F. Supp. 753, 758 (S.D.N.Y. 1987) ("The fourth factor is aimed at the copier who attempts to usurp the demand for the original work"). *See also* Wright v. Warner Books, Inc., 953 F.2d 731, 739 (2d Cir. 1991); Maxtone-Graham v. Burtchaell, 803 F.2d 1253, 1264 (2d Cir. 1986), *cert. denied*, 481 U.S. 1059 (1987); Hustler Magazine, Inc. v. Moral Majority, Inc., 796 F.2d 1148, 1155-56 (9th Cir. 1986) (each focusing on whether the plaintiff's work would be supplanted in the marketplace, and reaching a negative conclusion).

109 *See* Baker v. Selden, 101 U.S. 99 (1880).

110 *See* Feist Publications, Inc. v. Rural Telephone Service Co., 111 S. Ct. 1282 (1991).

111 *Cf.* Steinberg v. Columbia Pictures Indus., 663 F. Supp. 706 (S.D.N.Y. 1987).

112 *See* Wright v. Warner Books, Inc., 953 F.2d 731, 739 (2d Cir. 1991).

113 *See* Sega Enters. Ltd. v. Accolade, Inc., 977 F.2d 1510, 1523 (9th Cir. 1992) (harm to market on fourth statutory factor does not include harm from "use which simply enables the copier to enter the market for works of the same type as the copied work"); Arica Inst., Inc. v. Palmer, 970 F.2d 1067, 1078 (2d Cir. 1992) ("defendant, after all, is perfectly entitled to create a competing work").

114 *See* Association of Am. Medical Colleges v. Cuomo, 928 F.2d 519, 525 (2d Cir.) ("Adverse impact that results from criticism or unfavorable comment on the copyrighted work is not considered in evaluating [the fourth statutory] factor"), *cert. denied*, 112 S. Ct. 184 (1991); Fisher v. Dees, 794 F.2d 432, 437-38 (9th Cir. 1986); Consumers Union of United States, Inc. v. General Signal Corp., 724 F.2d 1044, 1050 (2d Cir. 1983), *petition for reh'g denied*, 730 F.2d 47 (2d Cir.), *cert. denied sub nom.* Consumers Union of United States, Inc. v. New Regina Corp., 469 U.S. 823 (1984), *on remand*, 664 F. Supp. 753 (S.D.N.Y. 1987) ("The Copyright Act was not designed to prevent . . . indirect negative effects of copying. . . . The copyright laws are intended to prevent copiers from taking the owner's intellectual property, and are not aimed at recompensing damages which may flow indirectly from copying").

> In assessing the economic effect of the parody, the parody's critical impact must be excluded. Through its critical function, "a parody may quite legitimately aim at garroting the original, destroying it commercially as well as artistically." Copyright law is not designed to stifle critics. . . . [T]he economic effect of a parody with which we are concerned [in assessing the fourth factor] is not its potential to destroy or diminish the market for the original—any bad review can have that effect—but rather whether it *fulfills the demand* for the original. Biting criticism suppresses demand; copyright infringement usurps it. Thus, infringement occurs when a parody supplants the original in markets the original is aimed at, or in which the original is, or has reasonable potential to become, commercially valuable.[115]

It is rare for true parody to perform this function; few fans of a classic song or movie will buy the parody instead, or vice versa. As a result, in most parody cases, the fourth factor will tend to weigh in favor of fair use.[116]

Finally, some parodies may be in an artistic genre different from the original, giving rise to the claim that the potential market for that particular genre is injured by the defendant's use. For example, in *Acuff-Rose*, because 2 Live Crew's work was not just a parody but a rap parody, the plaintiff might argue that its ability to license rap versions of "Oh, Pretty Woman" had been harmed. Leaving aside the question of the inherent plausibility of the idea that Acuff-Rose would ever license a rap version of the song, such an argument obscures the nature of the relevant market. For a potential derivative market to be harmed in this manner, the defendant's parody must make less likely an authorized non-parody version in the *same* genre. It is not enough to assert that the genre itself represents a potential derivative market; there is no more reason to assume that other rap versions of "Oh, Pretty Woman" will be deterred by 2 Live Crew's rap parody than to assume that any parody will deter the creation of non-parody derivative works.

3. *Harper & Row*'s Elevation of the Fourth Factor to Preeminence

In *Harper & Row*, the Court characterized the fourth statu-

---

115 Fisher v. Dees, 794 F.2d at 437-38 (quoting Professor Benjamin Kaplan, An Unhurried View of Copyright 69 (1967)) (holding parody of song "When Sunny Gets Blue," entitled "When Sonny Sniffs Glue," to be a fair use).

116 *See infra* discussion at text accompanying notes 214-15.

tory fair use factor, "the effect of the use upon the potential market for or value of the copyrighted work," as "undoubtedly the single most important element of fair use."[117] This phrase has taken on tremendous weight, becoming a lodestar to lower courts.[118] Yet its significance has been overstated.

Cases applying the fair use doctrine prior to the 1976 Act did not order the various factors according to importance, nor was there a consensus that the fourth factor was to be given more weight than the others. Indeed, prior to the incorporation in the statute of fair use, courts were free not to analyze the fourth factor at all.[119] A number of cases rejected fair use where no harm to the market had been established,[120] or resolved the defense according to one or more of the first three factors.[121] Justice Story's opinion in the seminal American fair use case, *Folsom v. Marsh*,[122] rejected the defense despite the lack of any evidence showing harm to the plaintiff's market; to the contrary, the in-

---

[117] 471 U.S. 539, 566 (1985), *citing* 3 M. NIMMER ON COPYRIGHT § 13.05[A] at 13-76 (1985). This language was repeated in the Supreme Court's third and most recent fair use opinion, Stewart v. Abend, 495 U.S. 207, 238 (1990) (again citing only Nimmer).

[118] The phrase is quoted or paraphrased in almost every fair use case. *See, e.g.*, Arica Inst., Inc. v. Palmer, 970 F.2d 1067, 1078 (2d Cir. 1992); Los Angeles News Serv. v. Tullo, 973 F.2d 791, 798 (9th Cir. 1992); Cable/Home Communication Corp. v. Network Prods., Inc., 902 F.2d 829, 845 (11th Cir. 1990).

[119] *See* Pacific & Southern Co. v. Duncan, 744 F.2d 1490, 1495 n.7 (11th Cir.), *reh'g denied en banc*, 749 F.2d 733 (11th Cir. 1984), *cert. denied*, 471 U.S. 1004 (1985).

[120] *See, e.g.*, Walt Disney Prods. v. Air Pirates, 581 F.2d 751, 758 (9th Cir. 1978), *cert. denied sub nom.*, O'Neill v. Walt Disney Prods., 439 U.S. 1132 (1979); Warner Bros., Inc. v. American Broadcasting Cos., 720 F.2d 231, 242 (2d Cir. 1983); Amana Refrig., Inc. v. Consumers Union of United States, Inc., 431 F. Supp. 324, 326 (N.D. Iowa 1977); Time, Inc. v. Bernard Geis Assoc., 293 F. Supp. 130, 146 (S.D.N.Y. 1968); Phillips v. Constitution Pub. Co., 72 U.S.P.Q. 69 (N.D. Ga. 1947); Macmillan Co. v. King, 223 F. 862, 866 (D. Mass. 1914); West Pub. Co. v. Lawyers' Co-op. Pub. Co., 79 F. 756, 770-773 (2d Cir. 1897); Farmer v. Elstner, 33 F. 494, 497 (C.C.E.D. Mich. 1888).

[121] *See* Wihtol v. Crow, 309 F.2d 777, 780 (8th Cir. 1962) (extensive copying; no fair use despite nonprofit use); Eisenschiml v. Fawcett Pubs., Inc., 246 F.2d 598, 604 (7th Cir. 1957) (*de minimis* taking); Toksvig v. Bruce Pub. Co., 181 F.2d 664, 667 (7th Cir. 1950) (lack of a productive use); List Pub. Co. v. Keller, 30 F. 772 (C.C.S.D.N.Y. 1887) (extensive copying); Social Register Ass'n v. Murphy, 128 F. 116 (C.C.R.I. 1904) (lack of a productive use); Italian Book Corp. v. American Broadcasting Cos. 458 F. Supp. 65, 70-71 (S.D.N.Y. 1978) (incidental use); Holdredge v. Knight Pub. Corp., 214 F. Supp. 921, 924 (S.D. Cal. 1963) (extensive copying); Toulmin v. Rike-Kumler Co., 137 U.S.P.Q. 533 (S.D. Ohio 1962), *aff'd*, 316 F.2d 232 (6th Cir. 1963) (*de minimis* taking); Loew's, Inc. v. Columbia Broadcasting System, Inc., 131 F. Supp. 165 (S.D. Cal. 1955), *aff'd sub nom.* Benny v. Loew's, Inc., 239 F.2d 532 (9th Cir. 1956) (wholesale copying), *aff'd by an equally divided Court*, 356 U.S. 43 (1958); Karll v. Curtis Pub. Co., 39 F. Supp. 836, 837 (E.D. Wis. 1941) (incidental use and implied consent); Broadway Music Corp. v. F-R Pub. Corp., 31 F. Supp. 817, 818 (S.D.N.Y. 1940) (incidental use); Shapiro, Bernstein & Co. v. P.F. Collier & Son Co., 26 U.S.P.Q. 40, 43 (S.D.N.Y. 1934); Sayers v. Spaeth, 20 COPYRIGHT OFFICE DECISIONS 625, 626 (S.D.N.Y. 1932) (extensive copying; fair use denied even though defendant had obtained, in good faith, permission from an assignee of plaintiff it mistakenly believed was the copyright owner); Estate of Hemingway v. Random House, Inc., 23 N.Y.2d 341 (1968) (*de minimis* taking).

[122] 9 F. Cas. 342 (C.C.D. Mass. 1841) (No. 4,901).

tended markets for the parties' works were quite different.[123]

Nor does the statutory language give special emphasis to the fourth factor. On its face, section 107 does not favor any listed factor over any other.[124] Assigning predetermined weights to individual factors is inconsistent with Congress's recognition that, in applying fair use as an equitable rule of reason, "the relative weight to be given [the statutory factors] will differ from case to case."[125] Courts should be free to weigh each factor as appropriate on the facts of a given case.

What is the source, then, of this emphasis on the fourth factor? The *Harper & Row* Court did not provide any explanation for the proposition that this factor is the most important, citing only a single commentator, the late Professor Melville Nimmer.[126] But the handful of cases cited by Professor Nimmer do not bear out the proposition.[127] Nimmer himself hedged the

---

123 Justice Story expressed regret that his finding of infringement would interfere "with the very meritorious labors of the defendants, in their great undertaking of a series of works adapted to school libraries." 9 F. Cas. at 349.

124 As Justice Blackmun has noted, "No particular weight . . . was assigned to any of th[e] [factors]." Sony Corp. of Am. v. Universal City Studios, Inc., 464 U.S. 417, 476 (1984) (Blackmun, J., dissenting).

125 H.R. Rep. No. 94-1476, 94th Cong., 2d Sess. 72 (1976); S. Rep. No. 94-473, 94th Cong., 1st Sess. 65 (1975).

126 3 M. Nimmer, Nimmer on Copyright § 13.05[A] at 13-76 (1985).

127 The cases (in the edition cited by *Harper & Row*) were: Triangle Publications, Inc. v. Knight-Ridder Newspapers, Inc., 626 F.2d 1171, 1174 (5th Cir. 1980); Dow Jones & Co. v. Board of Trade, 546 F. Supp. 113 (S.D.N.Y. 1982); Time, Inc. v. Bernard Geis Assoc., 293 F. Supp. 130 (S.D.N.Y. 1968); Trebonik v. Grossman Music Corp., 305 F. Supp. 339 (N.D. Ohio 1969); H.C. Wainwright & Co. v. Wall Street Transcript Corp., 418 F. Supp. 620 (S.D.N.Y. 1976), *aff'd sub nom.* Wainwright Securities, Inc. v. Wall Street Transcript Corp., 558 F.2d 91 (2d Cir. 1977); Williams & Wilkins Co. v. United States, 487 F.2d 1345 (Ct. Cl. 1973), *aff'd by an equally divided Court*, 420 U.S. 376 (1975); Public Affairs Assocs. v. Rickover, 284 F.2d 262 (D.C. Cir. 1960), *vacated for an insufficient record*, 369 U.S. 111 (1962); and Hill v. Whalen & Martell, 220 F. 359 (S.D.N.Y. 1914).

Taking these cases one by one, *Public Affairs Associates* did not even discuss market effect, and instead turned on the ground that the declaratory judgment plaintiff planned to take too much of the work, an issue covered by the third factor. *Triangle* merely stated that courts "generally" had placed "most emphasis" on the fourth factor, not that it was *per se* the "single most important element." *Triangle*'s support for even this more limited proposition was weak. The opinion lists two authorities: an earlier edition of Nimmer (in the edition cited in *Harper & Row*, Nimmer then cited *Triangle* as support for the same proposition for which *Triangle* had cited Nimmer), and Time, Inc. v. Bernard Geis Assoc., 293 F. Supp. 130 (S.D.N.Y. 1968). *Time*, which involved unauthorized reproductions of the Zapruder photographs of President Kennedy's assassination, did not treat the fourth factor as the most important. Although the court cited to a passage from *Folsom v. Marsh* on the subject of injury to the plaintiff, 293 F. Supp. at 144, it was referring to Justice Story's conclusion. In finding fair use, the court rested principally on the ground that "[t]here is a public interest in having the fullest information available on the murder of President Kennedy." 293 F. Supp. at 146.

Dow Jones cites Nimmer, *Triangle Publications*, and one other case, Meeropol v. Nizer, 560 F.2d 1061, 1070 (2d Cir. 1977), *cert. denied*, 434 U.S. 1013 (1978). *Trebonik v. Grossman* listed a number of factors, including good faith. No one factor was treated as determinative, and no statement was made at all about the relative importance of the fourth

proposition's strength by declaring that one had to look beyond the cases' "stated rationale," and undercut his conclusion by citing a number of cases to the contrary.[128]

The fourth factor may be quite important in many cases. Certainly where there is proof of actual harm to the market, as in *Harper & Row*, this factor should weigh heavily in the balance.[129] In such circumstances, the damage to the copyright owner's incentives may outweigh the loss to the public from forbidding the use.

In any given case, however, other factors may be of equal or greater significance. A use may be fair despite some harm to the potential market if its social value is high; a use may not be fair despite a lack of harm if it takes extensively for no socially valuable type of purpose. Resolution of the fourth factor in the plaintiff's favor should not be a prerequisite for the plaintiff to prevail.[130] As Justice Story recognized more than a century ago, a plaintiff should not be required to show harm in order to defeat a fair use defense; if a use is excused for lack of such proof, many small uses, innocuous in themselves, may have a cumulative impact of destroying the market.[131]

Moreover, requiring proof of harm on the fourth factor for a plaintiff to prevail is inconsistent with the fact that such proof is not necessary either to establish a prima facie case of infringe-

---

factor. *Wainwright v. Wall Street Transcript* focused principally on defendant's extensive taking. *Willams & Wilkins v. United States* discusses many fair use factors. If one had to choose one factor as the most important to the disposition of that case, it would not, in our opinion, be the potential harm to the copyright owner's market (which seems obvious although unpersuasive to the majority), but the Court of Claims' concern for the public interest in the scientific research conducted by the National Institutes of Health. *Hill v. Whalen & Martell* does emphasize the importance of an adverse market impact, describing it as "ordinarily decisive."

128 The same edition of Nimmer cites the following cases as "*cf.*": Loew's, Inc. v. Columbia Broadcasting System, Inc., 131 F. Supp. 165 (S.D. Cal. 1955), *aff'd sub nom.* Benny v. Loew's, Inc., 239 F.2d 532 (9th Cir. 1956), *aff'd by an equally divided Court sub nom.* Columbia Broadcasting System, Inc. v. Loews, Inc., 356 U.S. 43 (1958); Associated Music Pub., Inc. v. Debs Memorial Radio Fund, Inc., 141 F.2d 852 (2d Cir. 1944); and Toulmin v. Rike-Kumler Co., 137 U.S.P.Q. 533 (S.D. Ohio 1962), *aff'd*, 316 F.2d 232 (6th Cir. 1963). *Benny* was decided on the ground of wholesale copying. *Associated Music* was decided on the grounds of substantial copying and the defendant nonprofit radio station's purpose of boosting its audience. *Toulmin* was decided on the ground of *de minimis* copying.

129 471 U.S. 539, 567 (1985). As the Court observed, "Rarely will a case of copyright infringement present such clear-cut evidence of actual damage."

130 The converse is also true: a defendant need not prove lack of harm to the plaintiff's market to establish fair use. No single factor is essential.

131 9 F. Cas. at 349. *See also Harper & Row*, 471 U.S. at 569, quoting S. REP. No. 94-473, 94th Cong., 1st Sess. 65 (1975): "Isolated instances of minor infringements, when multiplied many times, become in the aggregate a major inroad on copyright that must be prevented."

ment or to obtain damages. If the fourth factor is to be given extra weight not only in cases where there is proof of actual or potential harm, but also in cases where there is not, a finding of fair use would come dangerously close to judicial rewriting of a statute that deliberately departed from prior law requiring the copyright owner to prove the defendant's use was for profit.[132]

The proposition that the fourth factor is "the single most important element" is also difficult practically to apply. How are courts (or juries)[133] to weigh all four factors in light of the importance of the fourth? Is the fourth factor to be given 51% of the total fair use weight? If so, fair use effectively becomes a one-factor doctrine. Is the fourth factor instead to be given more weight individually than each of the other three factors—*i.e.*, 26% or more? And what happens when factors beyond the four set forth in the statute are added to the mix? The common law character of fair use, the plain language of the statute, and *Harper & Row's* general approach to fair use argue against such a mechanistic reading.

4. Evaluating the Fourth Factor

The preeminence given to the fourth factor by *Harper & Row* has been particularly troublesome in light of the tendency of the courts to treat that factor as an either-or proposition: if any harm is established, the factor is deemed to favor the plaintiff; if not, to favor the defendant. Like the first factor issue of commerciality, however, harm to the potential market is a matter of degree. A finding of harm therefore should not necessarily lead to rejection of the fair use defense.[134]

In some circumstances, the defendant's use will cause only minor harm to the plaintiff's potential market, which when weighed in the balance with the other relevant factors, including the public benefit from that type of use, may lead to a finding that the use is fair. An all-or-nothing approach to the fourth factor, combined with a broad definition of the potential market and strengthened by the extra weight conferred by *Harper & Row*, would mean that the defendant loses whenever there is a possi-

---

132 *See supra* text accompanying notes 56-59.

133 *See* Jartech, Inc. v. Clancy, 666 F.2d 403 (9th Cir.), *cert. denied*, 459 U.S. 826 (1982).

134 Indeed, even a use that *benefits* the market for the copyrighted work may not be fair. *See* Lloyd L. Weinreb, *Fair's Fair: A Comment on the Fair Use Doctrine*, 103 HARV. L. REV. 1137, 1146-47 (1990) (pointing out that the movie *Rear Window* was held not to be a fair use of the underlying story by Cornell Woolrich, despite that fact that it "became a selling point for anthologies containing the . . . story").

bility that the plaintiff might license a similar use. As Judge Leval has pointed out,

> [I]f an insubstantial loss of revenue turned the fourth factor in favor of the copyright holder, this factor would never weigh in favor of the secondary user. And if we then gave serious deference to the proposition that it is "undoubtedly the single most important element of fair use," fair use would become defunct. The market impairment should not turn the fourth factor unless it is reasonably substantial.[135]

E. *Presumptions and Burdens of Proof*

1. Burdens of Proof

In an infringement suit, the copyright owner bears the burden of proof in making out her *prima facie* case: ownership of a valid copyright and unauthorized copying by the defendant of substantial expression from the copyrighted work. There is no infringement if the copying involves only unprotectible elements, such as ideas, processes or facts,[136] or if only insubstantial similarities exist between the expression of the two works.[137] Once a *prima facie* case has been established, the defendant bears the burden of proof on any affirmative defenses.

In *Harper & Row, Pub., Inc. v. Nation Enterprises*, the Supreme Court held that fair use is an affirmative defense.[138] The party asserting fair use[139] thus bears the burden of production as well as the ultimate burden of persuasion. Since fair use is established by weighing all the relevant factors, this means that the proponent of the defense must persuade the court that the factors, taken together, balance in its favor.

If *Harper & Row* had been the Supreme Court's first fair use opinion, fair use analysis today might be considerably simpler. The year before, however, the Court had handed down its opinion in *Sony Corporation of America v. Universal City Studios, Inc.*[140]

---

135 Leval, *supra* note 49, at 1124-25.

136 *See* Feist Pub., Inc. v. Rural Telephone Serv. Co., 111 S. Ct. 1282 (1991); Salinger v. Random House, Inc., 811 F.2d 90, 97 (2d Cir.), *cert. denied*, 484 U.S. 890 (1987).

137 Rogers v. Koons, 960 F.2d 301, 308 (2d Cir.), *cert. denied*, 113 S. Ct. 365 (1992).

138 471 U.S. 539, 561 (1985). *See also* Sega Enters. Ltd. v. Accolade, Inc., 977 F.2d 1510, 1521 (9th Cir. 1992) (contrasting fair use with the section 117 exemption from the copyright owner's grant of rights).

139 Depending on the procedural context of the litigation, the fair use defense may be asserted by any party. In the typical lawsuit, however, it will be the defendant who relies on fair use. Accordingly, we will for the sake of simplicity refer to the party asserting the defense as "the defendant."

140 464 U.S. 417 (1984).

Because *Sony* involved complex issues far removed from the traditional arena of fair use, it complicated the Court's effort to formulate general principles.[141] In particular, the claim of contributory infringement by marketing a mass-produced consumer article (the Betamax video tape recorder)[142] used for home time-shifting of over-the-air free broadcast programming forced the Court to focus on issues ancillary—if not foreign—to the core of fair use.[143]

The contributory infringement claim arguably could have been dismissed without reaching fair use. Instead, fair use was subsumed as part of the contributory infringement analysis, as a basis for concluding that the Betamax was capable of commercially significant noninfringing uses.[144] In addressing fair use in this specific context, certain references to "presumptions" were made in the majority opinion that have since been applied in widely divergent contexts, giving them a heightened meaning beyond the Court's apparent intent.

---

141 *See* American Geophysical Union v. Texaco, Inc., 802 F. Supp. 1, 22 (S.D.N.Y. 1992), *appeal argued* No. 92-9341 (2d Cir. May 20, 1993) ("*Sony* and *Williams & Wilkins* do not purport to define the heartland of fair use. To the contrary, they present themselves as defining its remote extremities").

142 Although contributory infringement was a well-established doctrine in copyright law by the time of *Sony*, and had been applied by the Supreme Court in Kalem Co. v. Harper Bros., 222 U.S. 55 (1911) (holding the producer of a motion picture that constituted an unauthorized dramatization of the novel *Ben Hur* liable for sale of copies of picture to jobbers who in turn arranged for theatrical exhibition of the movie), the producer in *Kalem Co.* who was found contributorily liable had personally caused the copyright owner's work to be copied and distributed. *Kalem Co.* was thus quite similar to the traditional "dance hall" contributory infringement cases. *See, e.g.*, Dreamland Ball Room, Inc. v. Shapiro, Bernstein & Co., 36 F.2d 354 (7th Cir. 1929); Gershwin Pub. Corp. v. Columbia Artists Mgt., Inc., 443 F.2d 1159 (2d Cir. 1971); Famous Music Corp. v. Bay State Harness Horse Racing & Breeding Ass'n, Inc., 554 F.2d 1213 (1st Cir. 1977); KECA Music, Inc. v. Dingus McGee's Co., 432 F. Supp. 72 (W.D. Mo. 1977).

143 These issues included the meaning of the legislative history of the 1971 Sound Recording Amendment and its relationship to section 107 of the 1976 Act, the manner in which harm to the market might be demonstrated in the case of new technologies, the appropriate remedy in a contributory infringement case brought against the manufacturer of a consumer article such as the Betamax (including the controversial issue of judicially-imposed compulsory licensing), copying for private use, productive versus nonproductive uses, and the question of single versus multiple copying.

144 This subordination of the fair use issue is evident from the structure of the Court's opinion. The discussion of fair use occurs in Part IV, which begins:

> The question is whether the Betamax is capable of commercially significant noninfringing uses. In order to resolve that question, we need not explore *all* the different potential uses of the machine and determine whether or not they would constitute infringement. Rather, we need only consider whether on the basis of the facts as found by the district court a significant number of them would be non-infringing.

464 U.S. at 442. Two types of potential uses were examined, authorized and unauthorized time-shifting. Part IVA contains the Court's discussion of authorized time-shifting; Part IVB contains the Court's discussion of unauthorized time-shifting, and its analysis of fair use.

2. The *Sony* "Presumptions"

a. *The First Factor "Presumption"*

Ironically, the last-minute addition to the first statutory factor of the phrase, "including whether such use is of a commercial nature or is for nonprofit educational purposes," intended to give solace to nonprofit educators,[145] has been applied vigorously against commercial users. This surprising twist has come about because of later interpretations of the following statement made in *Sony*, in the context of finding the use of the Betamax tape recorder for time-shifting purposes to be fair use: "[E]very commercial use of copyrighted material is presumptively an unfair exploitation of the monopoly privilege that belongs to the owner of copyright."[146]

This passage has haunted fair use ever since, appearing in some form in virtually every commercial use case of the past decade. Absent from these subsequent opinions, however, has been serious analysis of what the statement means.[147] The conclusion is inescapable from both the textual and the historical context that the Court did not intend to establish a true presumption in the technical sense, shifting burdens of production or proof.[148] Nor would such a presumption be appropriate as a method of determining the affirmative defense of fair use.

Most basic is the seldom-noted fact that since the use before the Court in *Sony* was found to be noncommercial, the statement is pure dictum. It was made in passing, without any explanation of what such a presumption might mean or how it was to be applied. Other language in the opinion makes clear that what was intended was not a technical presumption (let alone a near-con-

---

145 *See supra* text accompanying notes 54-59.

146 464 U.S. at 451. *See also id.* at 449: "If the Betamax were used to make copies for a commercial or profit-making purpose, such use would presumptively be unfair."

147 Two notable exceptions are the Second Circuit's opinion in Maxtone-Graham v. Burtchaell, 803 F.2d 1253, 1262 (2d Cir. 1986), *cert. denied*, 481 U.S. 1059 (1987), which concluded, "[W]e do not read [the sentence from *Sony*] as altering the traditional multifactor fair use inquiry. . . . Only an unduly narrow reading of the language in *Sony Corp.* and an inattention to the context could lead to the conclusion that the Court intended to attach heightened significance to the element of commerciality," and Judge Leval's opinion in American Geophysical Union v. Texaco, Inc., 802 F. Supp. 1, 12-13 (S.D.N.Y. 1992), *appeal argued* No. 92-9341 (2d Cir. May 20, 1993).

148 *Cf.* Fed. R. Evid. 301:

> In all civil actions and proceedings not otherwise provided for by Act of Congress or by these rules, a presumption imposes on the party against whom it is directed the burden of going forward with evidence to rebut or meet the presumption, but does not shift to such party the burden of proof in the sense of the risk of nonpersuasion, which remains throughout the trial upon the party on whom it was originally cast.

clusive one), but simply a recognition that the commercial nature of a use should be considered in the fair use balance, and would tend to weigh against a finding of fair use. In an earlier paragraph, the Court stated, "Although not conclusive, the first factor requires that 'the commercial or nonprofit character of an activity' be weighed in any fair use decision," quoting the statement in the House Report that this aspect of a use "can and should be weighed along with other factors."[149]

Sony's entire approach to fair use belies an intent to establish any system of presumptions. The Court stressed the nature of the doctrine as "an equitable rule of reason," quoting language from the House Report recognizing that no general definition of fair use was possible, and that each case must be decided on its own particular facts.[150] The opinion noted that the Senate Committee too had "eschewed a rigid, bright line approach to fair use."[151] Finally, in rejecting the Court of Appeals' holding that non-productive uses could never be fair, the Court criticized the lower court for not having engaged in any "equitable rule of reason" analysis, but instead applying a "rigid" requirement that every fair use must be productive. Explaining that this understanding of fair use was erroneous, the Court stated:

> Congress has plainly instructed us that fair use analysis calls for a sensitive balancing of interests. The distinction between "productive" and "unproductive" uses may be helpful in calibrating the balance, but it cannot be wholly determinative. Although copying to promote a scholarly endeavor certainly has a stronger claim to fair use than copying to avoid interrupting a poker game, the question is not simply two-dimensional.[152]

The same reasoning applies equally to artificial distinctions between "commercial" and "noncommercial" uses.

The Supreme Court has subsequently interpreted the *Sony* first factor "presumption" as an element in the fair use balance rather than as a true presumption. In *Harper & Row, Pub., Inc. v.*

---

[149] 464 U.S. at 448-49 and n.32, quoting H.R. Rep. No. 94-1476, 94th Cong., 2d Sess. 66 (1976). In addition, if the Court had intended a technical presumption of unfair use to follow from a finding of commerciality, there would have been no need to provide an additional presumption of harm to the market on the fourth factor. *See infra* discussion at text accompanying notes 158-70.

[150] 464 U.S. at 448-49 n.31, quoting H.R. Rep. No. 94-1476, 94th Cong., 2d Sess. 65-66.

[151] 464 U.S. at 449 n.31, citing S. Rep. No. 94-473, 94th Cong., 1st Sess. 65-66 (1975).

[152] 464 U.S. at 455 n.40.

Nation Enterprises,[153] the Court quoted the famous sentence from *Sony*, but prefaced it with the following: "The fact that a publication was commercial as opposed to nonprofit is a separate factor that *tends to weigh* against a finding of fair use."[154] *Harper & Row*'s approach is consistent with the pre-1976 Act case law—case law that Congress intended section 107 to confirm.[155]

The same result should follow as a matter of policy. Not only are presumptions as an analytical technique antithetical to the nature of fair use, a presumption of unfairness based on commerciality is inappropriate. No use should be considered presumptively either fair or unfair based solely on the user's financial benefit; the determination can only be made based on all the facts. Even uses for nonprofit educational purposes may easily fail to qualify as fair—for example, a teacher's preparation and distribution of an anthology from numerous copyrighted works to her class as a substitute for purchase of those works.[156] Finally, in the Supreme Court's next foray into the turbulent waters of fair use, *Harper & Row*, the Court rejected an argument that particular uses were presumptively fair,[157] a holding that should equally apply to particular uses being presumptively unfair.

b. *The Fourth Factor "Presumption"*

The majority opinion in *Sony* contains yet another reference to "presumptions" in its analysis of the fourth statutory factor. The Court stated:

> A challenge to a noncommercial use of a copyrighted work requires proof either that the particular use is harmful, or that if it should become widespread, it would adversely affect the potential market for the copyrighted work. Actual present harm need not be shown; such a requirement would leave the copyright holder with no defense against predictable damage. Nor is it necessary to show with certainty that future harm will result. What is necessary is a showing by a preponderance of the evidence that *some* meaningful likelihood of fu-

---

153 471 U.S. 539 (1985).

154 *Id.* at 562 (1985) (emphasis added). *See also* Stewart v. Abend, 495 U.S. 207, 237 (1990).

155 *See supra* text accompanying note 31.

156 *See* Marcus v. Rowley, 695 F.2d 1171 (9th Cir. 1983); *Agreement on Guidelines for Classroom Copying in Not-for-Profit Educational Institutions and Guidelines for Educational Uses of Music*, contained in H.R. REP. No. 94-1476, 94th Cong., 2d Sess. 68-71 (1976), reproduced in THE FAIR USE PRIVILEGE, *supra* note 1, at 507-11.

157 The drafters of the 1976 Act "resisted pressures from special interest groups to create presumptive categories of fair use." 471 U.S. at 561.

> ture harm exists. *If the intended use is for commercial gain, that likelihood may be presumed.* But if it is for a noncommercial purpose, the likelihood must be demonstrated.[158]

This language too has caused problems in fair use analysis. Again, the central question is whether the Court intended to create a technical presumption. Does *Sony* shift the burden of production on the fourth statutory factor depending on the commerciality of the use in each case? As with the first factor presumption, it must be noted that the statement is dictum, made without a full exposition in the context of examining a noncommercial use. Moreover, the Court tells us the likelihood of harm "may" be presumed, not that it must be—the language of permissible inference rather than mandatory burden-shifting. Nevertheless, the statement's context is quite different from that of the first factor presumption. It occurs not in passing in the course of a general discussion of the fourth factor, but as part of a specific analysis of burdens of proof.

There is a certain logic to the idea of presuming harm where the use is commercial. All things being equal, a commercial use, by virtue of its nexus to the marketplace, may be more *likely* to cause economic harm than a nonprofit use.[159] But this will not always be the case. Some commercial uses may cause no harm at all; some nonprofit uses may have a far more devastating impact than a commercial use. For example, the market may be entirely destroyed when a nonprofit organization distributes material portions of a copyrighted work, without charge, to those individuals who constitute the principal audience for the work.

Since harm to the copyright owner's market from a commercial use is far from inevitable, it should not be presumed without evidence. Doing so collapses the first and fourth factors, making the commercial nature of the use so powerful as to be nearly conclusive. This is an inappropriate result for several reasons. First, it virtually eliminates one factor from the fair use balance. Sec-

---

[158] 464 U.S. at 451 (emphasis added).

[159] The 1976 House Judiciary Committee report demonstrates similar reasoning in the context of newsletters:

> Whether the copying of portions of a newsletter is an act of infringement or a fair use will necessarily turn on the facts of the individual case. However, as a general principle, it seems clear that the scope of the fair use doctrine should be considerably narrower in the case of newsletters than in that of either mass-circulation periodicals or scientific journals. The commercial nature of the user is a significant factor *in such cases*: Copying by a profit-making user of even a small portion of a newsletter *may* have a significant impact on the commercial market for the work.

H.R. REP. No. 94-1476, 94th Cong., 2d Sess. 73-74 (1976) (emphasis added).

ond, it raises anew the difficulty of defining what uses are "commercial" and to what extent.[160] In addition, any logical basis for the presumption disappears once one acknowledges that the commerciality of the use is but one aspect of its "purpose and character."[161] For certain commercial works, such as parody, it is more likely than not that the defendant's use will *not* affect the plaintiff's potential market in a manner cognizable under section 107—that is, by serving as a substitute for the original.[162]

Given the *Sony* Court's permissive rather than mandatory language, it may have meant no more than that a commercial use will tend to harm the potential market more readily than a nonprofit use. It seems unlikely that the Court meant to direct lower courts to regard all commercial use as resulting in harm to the potential market for the work unless the defendant proves otherwise.

The key to understanding the *Sony* "presumptions" and burden-shifting may be found in two assumptions under which the majority may have operated.

The first assumption is manifested in the majority's apparent search for a discrete "right to prohibit time-shifting," and its treatment of that right as not included in the bundle of exclusive rights granted to the copyright owner under section 106. The district court expressly so held.[163] The Ninth Circuit began its opinion by rejecting this conclusion, recognizing that the 1976 Act was structured so as to provide a broad grant of rights, subject to specific privileges, exemptions, and compulsory licenses.[164] To the court of appeals, time-shifting was an infringement of the copyright owner's exclusive right to reproduce the work in copies unless excused by fair use.[165]

Although the Supreme Court did not directly rule on this point, there is language in the majority opinion supporting the district court's interpretation. For example, the opinion concludes as follows:

---

160 *See supra* text accompanying notes 60-78.

161 *See supra* text accompanying notes 79-80.

162 *See supra* text accompanying notes 115-16.

163 480 F. Supp. 429, 443 (C.D. Cal. 1979): "The broad language of the New Act suggests that copyright holders have monopoly power over all reproductions of their works. Legislative history, however, shows that Congress did not intend this broad statement to include reproductions of sound recordings for home use. The central question here is whether Congress intended the same language to give copyright holders of audiovisual works monopoly power over off-the-air recording of their works for home use. Legislative history does not show this intent."

164 *See supra* text accompanying notes 56-59.

165 659 F.2d 963, 965-69 (9th Cir. 1981).

> One may search the Copyright Act in vain for any sign that the elected representatives of the millions of people who watch television every day have made it unlawful to copy a program for later viewing at home, or have enacted a flat prohibition against the sale of machines that make such copying possible.[166]

Yet section 106 on its face imposes just such a prohibition. The Ninth Circuit was therefore correct on this point. The importance of the Supreme Court's lack of clarity as to whether time-shifting was outside of the copyright owner's rights, or within those rights but excused, was carried over into the second assumption, which concerns the procedural posture of fair use.

The carry-over is reflected in the following passage in the *Sony* majority opinion, which appears to mix the issues of scope of rights and of fair use: "All reproductions of the work, however, are not within the exclusive domain of the copyright owner; some are in the public domain. Any individual may reproduce a copyrighted work for a fair use; the copyright owner does not possess the exclusive right to such a use."[167] While not free of ambiguity, this passage suggests that the *Sony* majority, writing a year before *Harper & Row*, did not regard fair use as an affirmative defense. If so, this may explain why the Court felt free to treat commercial and noncommercial uses differently.[168]

Under *Sony*, if the use is deemed commercial, the burden of proving fair use appears to be placed on the defendant.[169] If the use is deemed noncommercial, at least a portion of the burden shifts: the burden of proving harm to the market under the fourth factor is placed on the copyright owner, becoming part of the copyright owner's case-in-chief.[170] If, however, fair use is an affirmative defense, as *Harper & Row* now instructs, this disparate treatment of commercial and noncommercial uses does not make sense: the burden of proving the defense should remain throughout on the party asserting it.

The Court's two fair use decisions after *Sony* indicate that no technical presumption was intended. Both involved uses found to be commercial on the first factor; neither applied a presump-

---

166 464 U.S. at 456.

167 *Id.* at 433.

168 Even portions of Justice Blackmun's dissent may be read to treat fair use considerations as part of the copyright owner's case-in-chief, *see* 464 U.S. at 462-63, 482 (proposing to place certain burdens on the copyright owner in fair use claims), although on balance the dissent appears to regard fair use as an affirmative defense.

169 *Id.* at 451.

170 *Id.*

tion of harm on the fourth factor, or even discussed the possibility of doing so. Rather, each examined evidence showing harm to the plaintiff's actual or potential market.[171]

Equally as important, *Harper & Row* clarified the status of fair use as an affirmative defense.[172] The *Sony* "presumptions" must therefore be reexamined from a new procedural perspective: the burden of proving the defense (including logically all elements of the defense) remains on the party asserting it. If no evidence is produced on the question of harm to the market, the fourth factor should not be resolved in either side's favor. Since the ultimate burden of proof on the defense rests with the defendant whether the use is commercial or not, the defendant will have to convince the court that the other factors on balance establish fair use.

F. *The* Sony/Harper & Row *"Double Whammy" for Commercial Uses*

Unfortunately, the dangers inherent in treating the *Sony* language as creating true presumptions, rather than as *Harper & Row*'s weighted consideration, have been realized in a number of subsequent decisions. Although not all courts have been led astray, some have. Many courts still examine all the circumstances, and engage in the sensitive balancing fair use demands.[173] But others have been less thoughtful, citing the *Sony* presumptions and the preeminence of the fourth factor, and concluding after only superficial analysis of the facts that a commercial use is plainly unfair.[174] At its worst, the analysis proceeds via the following chain of logic: (1) defendant's use is commercial; (2) commercial uses are presumptively unfair and presumptively

---

[171] *See* Stewart v. Abend, 495 U.S. 207, 236-38 (1990); *Harper & Row*, 471 U.S. 539, 566-69 (1985).

[172] *See supra* text accompanying notes 138-39.

[173] One good example is the district court's opinion in *Acuff-Rose*, 754 F. Supp. 1150 (M.D. Tenn. 1991). *See also* Rogers v. Koons, 960 F.2d 301 (2d Cir.), *cert. denied*, 113 S. Ct. 365 (1992); American Geophysical Union v. Texaco, Inc., 802 F. Supp. 1 (S.D.N.Y. 1992), *appeal argued* No. 92-9341 (2d Cir. May 20, 1993); Caratzas v. Time Life, Inc., Copyr. L. Rep. (CCH) ¶ 27,012 (S.D.N.Y. 1992).

[174] *See, e.g.*, Financial Info., Inc. v. Moody's Investors Serv., Inc., 751 F.2d 501, 508-09 (2d Cir. 1984) ("*Sony* repeatedly stresses that the 'first factor'—whether the use is commercial or nonprofit—not only must necessarily be a part of a court's analysis, but *must* also, if the use proves commercial, give rise to a presumption of unfair use. The Court could hardly have been more lucid on this point. . . . *Sony* requires that we recognize a presumption of unfair use by Moody's arising from its commercial use of the copyrighted material"); Kepner-Tregoe, Inc. v. Leadership Software, Inc., 22 U.S.P.Q.2d 1788 (S.D. Tex. 1992); Paramount Pictures Corp. v. Labus, 16 U.S.P.Q.2d 1142 (W.D. Wis. 1990); Hutchinson Tel. Co. v. Fronteer Directory Co., 640 F. Supp. 386, 390 (D. Minn. 1986).

result in harm to the potential market for the copyrighted work; (3) harm to the market is the single most important fair use factor; (4) defendant's use is therefore not fair use. In sum, the two *Sony* "presumptions," magnified by *Harper & Row*'s elevation of the fourth factor, have the potential to become a nearly invincible double whammy, transforming what should be only one part of a single fair use factor into a *per se* disqualification.

The Sixth Circuit's majority opinion in *Acuff-Rose* is a graphic illustration of this type of decision making.[175] On the first fair use factor, the majority cited *Sony* for the proposition that "[t]he use of a copyrighted work primarily for commercial purposes has been held by the Supreme Court to be presumptively unfair."[176] Rejecting the district court's weighing of the value of parody in the first factor balance,[177] the court of appeals tied the first factor to the fourth, stating that it was 2 Live Crew's burden to rebut the *Sony* presumption of unfairness by convincing the court that "the parody does not unfairly diminish the economic value of the original."[178]

The majority opened its fourth factor analysis with *Harper & Row*'s "single most important element" statement.[179] Quoting *Sony*'s fourth factor "presumption" language, it concluded: "In the instant case, the use of the copyrighted work is wholly commercial, so that we presume a likelihood of future harm to Acuff-Rose exists."[180] Criticizing the district court for "refus[ing] to indulge the presumption," the court rejected its finding, based on evidence in the record, that 2 Live Crew's version of the song is extremely unlikely to affect the market for the Acuff-Rose original, because the audiences for the two works are entirely different.[181] The brand of presumption applied here was strong

175 The Sixth Circuit majority did not cite the only other Sixth Circuit fair use case decided under the 1976 Act—a case that differs sharply in both result and analysis. *See* Pro Arts, Inc. v. Hustler Magazine, Inc., 787 F.2d 592 (6th Cir. 1986) (table), Nos. 85-3022, 85-3041 (unpublished *per curiam* opinion, filed March 25, 1986), discussed at *infra* note 201.

176 972 F.2d at 1436.

177 *See infra* text accompanying notes 221-23.

178 972 F.2d at 1437 (quoting Fisher v. Dees, 794 F.2d 432, 437 (9th Cir. 1986)).

179 972 F.2d at 1438.

180 *Id.*

181 *Id.* at 1439. The district court's findings are reported at 754 F. Supp. at 1158. The majority explained that the evidence in the record was "irrelevant" because it did not take into account harm to the potential market for derivative works. 972 F.2d at 1439. The court did not, however, explain what type of derivative works should have been considered. If what it had in mind was the potential market for licensing parodies, such a market should not have been considered in the fourth factor analysis, given the censorship danger. *See supra* text accompanying notes 94-96.

indeed, if not conclusive.[182]

Cases like *Acuff-Rose* thus demonstrate that following *Sony* and *Harper & Row*, fair use analysis has come to embody the phenomenon identified by Professor Phillip Areeda in the context of antitrust law:

> As with most instances of judging by catch-phrase, the law evolves in three stages: (1) An extreme case arises to which a court responds.[183] (2) The language of that response is then applied—often mechanically, sometimes cleverly—to expand the application. With too few judges experienced enough with the subject to resist, the doctrine expands to the limits of its language, with little regard to policy. (3) Such expansions ultimately become ridiculous, and the process of cutting back begins.[184]

The Supreme Court's review of *Acuff-Rose* will hopefully begin a salutary cutting back process.

G. *Fair Use and Parody*

1. Parody As a Favored Use

The Sixth Circuit's analysis in *Acuff-Rose* is particularly disturbing in light of the humorous nature of the work involved. Parody is a type of use that has elicited generous fair use treatment in recent years.[185] This generosity stems from the recogni-

[182] At one point in the opinion, the majority stated: "We have already determined that harm for purposes of the fair use analysis *has been established* by the presumption attaching to commercial uses." 972 F.2d at 1439 (emphasis added).

[183] In the case of fair use, the initial extreme case to which the Supreme Court responded was Sony Corp. of Am. v. Universal City Studios, Inc., 464 U.S. 417 (1984). *See supra* discussion in text at notes 140-70.

[184] Phillip Areeda, *Essential Facilities: An Epithet in Need of Limiting Principles*, 58 ANTITRUST L.J. 841, 841 (1989).

[185] The following is a partial list of the fair use opinions involving parody decided under the 1976 Act: Acuff-Rose Music, Inc. v. Campbell, 972 F.2d 1429 (6th Cir. 1992), *cert. granted*, 113 S. Ct. 1642 (1993); Rogers v. Koons, 960 F.2d 301 (2d Cir.), *cert. denied*, 113 S. Ct. 365 (1992); Fisher v. Dees, 794 F.2d 432 (9th Cir. 1986); Pro Arts, Inc. v. Hustler Magazine, Inc., 787 F.2d 592 (6th Cir. 1986) (table), Nos. 85-3022, 85-3041 (unpublished per curiam opinion, filed March 25, 1986); Warner Bros., Inc. v. American Broadcasting Cos., 720 F.2d 231 (2d Cir. 1983); DC Comics Inc. v. Reel Fantasy, Inc., 696 F.2d 24 (2d Cir. 1982); MCA, Inc. v. Wilson, 677 F.2d 180 (2d Cir. 1981); Elsmere Music, Inc. v. National Broadcasting Co., 623 F.2d 252 (2d Cir. 1980) (per curiam); Dallas Cowboys Cheerleaders, Inc. v. Scoreboard Posters, Inc., 600 F.2d 1184 (5th Cir. 1979); Walt Disney Prods. v. Air Pirates, 581 F.2d 751 (9th Cir. 1978), *cert. denied sub nom.* O'Neill v. Walt Disney Prods., 439 U.S. 1132 (1979); United Feature Syndicate, Inc. v. Koons, 817 F. Supp. 370 (S.D.N.Y. 1993); Campbell v. Koons, 1993 U.S. Dist. LEXIS 3957 (S.D.N.Y. filed April 1, 1993); Eveready Battery Co. v. Adolph Coors Co., 765 F. Supp. 440 (N.D. Ill. 1991); Tin Pan Apple, Inc. v. Miller Brewing Co., 737 F. Supp. 826 (S.D.N.Y. 1990); New Line Cinema Corp. v. Bertlesman Music Group, Inc., 693 F. Supp. 1517 (S.D.N.Y. 1988); Original Appalachian Artworks, Inc. v. Topps Chewing Gum, Inc., 642 F. Supp. 1031 (N.D. Ga. 1986); Update Art, Inc. v. Maariv Israel Newspaper,

tion of parody as a use that confers a real public benefit, comparable to the uses listed in the preamble to section 107.[186] In the words of the Second Circuit, "[P]arody and satire are valued forms of criticism, encouraged because this sort of criticism itself fosters the creativity protected by the copyright law."[187] Commentators too have noted that parody furthers First Amendment values as well as copyright values.[188]

The Supreme Court has yet to address the subject of parody in a written opinion. Its sole venture into the field occurred thirty-five years ago, when it affirmed by an equally divided vote a decision by the Ninth Circuit holding that a television parody by the comedian Jack Benny of the movie "Gaslight" (starring Charles Boyer, Ingrid Bergman and Joseph Cotton), entitled

---

Inc., 635 F. Supp. 228 (S.D.N.Y. 1986); DC Comics Inc. v. Unlimited Monkey Business, Inc. 598 F. Supp. 110 (N.D. Ga. 1984); Dr. Pepper Co. v. Sambo's Restaurants, Inc., 517 F. Supp. 1202 (N.D. Tex. 1981); Pillsbury Co. v. Milky Way Prods., Inc., 215 U.S.P.Q. 124, 131 (N.D. Ga. 1981); DC Comics, Inc. v. Crazy Eddie, Inc., 205 U.S.P.Q. 1177 (S.D.N.Y. 1979); Metro-Goldwyn-Mayer, Inc. v. Showcase Atlanta Coop Prods., Inc., 479 F. Supp. 351 (N.D. Ga. 1979).

186 While not included in the language of section 107 itself, parody is mentioned in the legislative reports as an example of possible fair use. *See* H.R. REP. No. 94-1476, 94th Cong., 2d Sess. 65 (1976); S. REP. No. 94-473, 94th Cong., 1st Sess. 61 (1975) (listing "use in a parody of some of the content of the work parodied" as a type of activity that might be regarded as fair use "under the circumstances"). In an oblique statement during the revision process leading up to the 1976 Act, the Copyright Office expressed the hope that reference to parody in the legislative reports would give wider latitude to the courts to find fair use than would a specific statutory reference. *See* COPYRIGHT LAW REVISION PART 5: 1964 REVISION BILL WITH DISCUSSIONS AND COMMENTS, 89th Cong., 1st Sess. 101 (House Comm. Print 1965), quoted and discussed in THE FAIR USE PRIVILEGE, *supra* note 1, at 234-235.

187 Rogers v. Koons, 960 F.2d 301, 310 (2d Cir.), *cert. denied*, 113 S. Ct. 365 (1992). *See also* Warner Bros., Inc. v. American Broadcasting Cos., 720 F.2d 231, 242 (2d Cir. 1983) ("It is decidedly in the interests of creativity, not piracy, to permit authors to take well-known phrases and fragments from copyrighted works and add their own contributions of commentary or humor"); Elsmere Music, Inc. v. National Broadcasting Co., 623 F.2d 252, 253 (2d Cir. 1980) (per curiam) ("[I]n today's world of often unrelieved solemnity, copyright law should be hospitable to the humor of parody"); Berlin v. E.C. Publications, Inc., 329 F.2d 541, 545 (2d Cir.) ("[A]s a general proposition, we believe that parody and satire *are* deserving of substantial freedom—both as entertainment and as a form of social and literary criticism"), *cert. denied*, 379 U.S. 822 (1964). *Cf.* Cliffs Notes, Inc. v. Bantam Doubleday Dell Publishing Group, Inc., 886 F.2d 490, 493 (2d Cir. 1989) ("parody is a form of artistic expression" protected by the First Amendment); L.L. Bean, Inc. v. Drake Publishers, Inc., 811 F.2d 26, 33 (1st Cir.) (recognizing "the vital importance of parody," despite fact that it is "often offensive"), *cert. denied*, 483 U.S. 1013 (1987).

188 Among the numerous articles addressing the topic of fair use and parody, particularly eloquent encomiums to parody can be found in M. Chagares, *Parody or Piracy: The Protective Scope of the Fair Use Defense to Copyright Infringement Actions Regarding Parodies*, 12 COL. J. L. & ARTS 229, 230-31 (1988); Julie Bisceglia, *Parody and Copyright Protection: Turning the Balancing Act Into a Juggling Act*, 34 COPYRIGHT L. SYMP. (ASCAP) 1, 4-6 and 33-36 (1987); Harriette K. Dorsen, *Satiric Appropriation and the Law of Libel, Trademark, and Copyright: Remedies Without Wrongs*, 65 B.U. L. REV. 923, 923-24 (1985); Charles C. Goetsch, *Parody as Free Speech—The Replacement of the Fair Use Doctrine by First Amendment Protection*, 3 W. NEW ENG. L. REV. 39, 40-42 (1980).

"Autolight," was an infringement not excused by the defense of fair use.[189] The Ninth Circuit's conclusion was based on both the extensive degree of copying,[190] and the refusal to offer parody treatment more lenient than that accorded to the ordinary act of appropriation.[191] Much has changed since then. Later cases, particularly in the Ninth and Second Circuits, have significantly refined the application of fair use to parody.

It is now generally accepted that, while there is no absolute parody defense, parody may qualify as fair use in appropriate circumstances.[192] Moreover, the courts have accorded parody more favorable fair use treatment than the ordinary use in several respects. The most meaningful differences have emerged in the analysis of the first and fourth statutory factors.[193]

---

189 Columbia Broadcasting System, Inc. v. Loew's, Inc., 356 U.S. 43 (1958), *aff'g* 239 F.2d 532 (9th Cir. 1956). This case is discussed in THE FAIR USE PRIVILEGE, *supra* note 1, at 153-58.

190 The court stated: "The fact that a serious dramatic work is copied practically verbatim, and then presented with actors walking on their hands or with other grotesqueries, does not avoid infringement of the copyright . . . . If the material taken by appellants from 'Gas Light' [sic] is eliminated, there are left only a few gags, and some disconnected and incoherent dialogue." 239 F.2d at 536.

191 239 F.2d at 537 (accepting the district court's holding that "parodized or burlesqued taking is to be treated no differently from any other appropriation").

192 *See* Fisher v. Dees, 794 F.2d 432, 435-36 (9th Cir. 1986) (describing the *Benny v. Loew's* decision as "essentially repudiated by Congress's recognition of parody in the notes to the Copyright Act of 1976," and stating that "in *Walt Disney Productions v. Air Pirates*, 581 F.2d 751 (9th Cir. 1978), *cert. denied*, 439 U.S. 1132 (1979), we gave the Benny opinion a narrow interpretation and acknowledged that parody is a potential fair use subject to the multi-factor analysis codified in section 107").

193 Parody also benefits incidentally from two other aspects of fair use analysis, relating to the first and fourth statutory factors. On the first factor, in dealing with claims of bad faith based on the decision to proceed with the use after denial of permission by the copyright owner, courts may take into account the fact that copyright owners rarely consent to parody. *See* Fisher v. Dees, 794 F.2d at 437 ("To consider [the parodist] blameworthy because he asked permission would penalize him for this modest show of consideration. Even though such gestures are predictably futile, we refuse to discourage them"); Pro Arts, Inc. v. Hustler Magazine, Inc., 787 F.2d 592 (6th Cir. 1986) (table), Nos. 85-3022, 85-3041 (unpublished per curiam opinion, filed March 25, 1986) ("The district court further erred in considering the fact that plaintiff would not consent to defendants' use relevant to the fair use determination. Fair use does not require the copyright owner's consent. Rather, fair use, as a statutory defense, anticipates that consent will not be forthcoming.") (citations omitted).

On the fourth factor, a true parody is highly unlikely to fulfill the same demand in the market as the original, or even a licensed derivative work. *See supra* text accompanying notes 88-97. Accordingly, this factor is likely to weigh in favor of fair use in most parody cases. *Compare Pro Arts*, 787 F.2d 592 *with Acuff-Rose*, 972 F.2d at 1438-39. *Acuff-Rose*'s presumption of harm to the market is therefore even more inappropriate. *See supra* text at notes 175-84.

The remaining statutory factor, "the nature of the copyrighted work," typically weighs against fair use in the context of parody. Most works parodied are entertainment properties, works that are highly creative. Moreover, they are virtually always publicly disseminated, as parodists almost by definition aim at well-known targets. Again, however, this is just one factor in the analysis; if given too much weight, few parodies could qualify as fair use.

In assessing the first factor, parody has been recognized as a productive use, providing a benefit to society—an aspect of the "purpose and character of the use" that weighs in favor of a finding of fair use.[194] Indeed, most courts examining parody fair use claims have found that the satiric purpose outweighed the commercial aspects of the use in evaluating the first factor, and have either refrained from applying the *Sony* "presumption" or have held it to be rebutted.[195]

An exception to this approach is the Sixth Circuit's opinion in *Acuff-Rose*. The district court had granted summary judgment to 2 Live Crew, finding that it was entitled to the fair use defense as a matter of law.[196] In examining the first statutory factor, the court had cited *Harper & Row*'s statement that a commercial purpose merely "tends to weigh against a finding of fair use,"[197] and noted that parody was a favored use, with many parodies more in the nature of commentary than commercial exploitation.[198]

In its opinion reversing the district court and finding that 2 Live Crew's use was not fair, the Sixth Circuit reprimanded the district court for its lenient approach to parody:

> We agree that commercial purpose is not itself controlling on the issue of fair use, but find that the district court placed insufficient emphasis on the command of *Harper & Row*, wherein the Supreme Court expressly reaffirmed its earlier holding that "[E]very commercial use of copyrighted material is presumptively an unfair exploitation of the monopoly privilege that belongs to the owner of the copyright." Therefore, in analyzing the purpose and character of 2 Live Crew's use of the copyrighted song, the facts in the record require that we start from the position that the use is unfair. . . . Although in this case we do not set aside the district court's conclusion that 2 Live Crew's song is a criticism in the nature of a parody in the popular sense, we nevertheless find that the district court

---

194 *See* Leval, *supra* note 49, at 1111 (characterizing parody as one type of "transformative" use).

195 *See, e.g.*, Fisher v. Dees, 794 F.2d 432, 437 (9th Cir. 1986); Pillsbury Co. v. Milky Way Prods., Inc., 215 U.S.P.Q. 124, 131 (N.D. Ga. 1981). *See also* Note, *The Parody Defense to Copyright Infringement: Productive Fair Use After* Betamax, 97 HARV. L. REV. 1395, 1408 (1984). In the above cases, the commercial aspect was the sale of the parody for money. The first factor balance may differ in situations where the degree of commerciality is greater, for example, where the parody is used to advertise a commercial product. *See, e.g.*, Tin Pan Apple, Inc. v. Miller Brewing Co., 737 F. Supp. 826 (S.D.N.Y. 1990); Original Appalachian Artworks, Inc. v. Topps Chewing Gum, Inc., 642 F. Supp. 1031, 1034 (N.D. Ga. 1986).

196 Acuff-Rose Music, Inc. v. Campbell, 754 F. Supp. 1150 (M.D. Tenn. 1991).

197 754 F. Supp. at 1154 (quoting *Harper & Row*, 471 U.S. at 562).

198 754 F. Supp. at 1154.

> erred in the process of determining that the criticism constituted a fair use of the copyrighted work. We find that the admittedly commercial nature of the derivative work—the *purpose* of the work being no less important than its *character* in the Act's formulation—requires the conclusion that the first factor weighs against a finding of fair use.[199]

Under the Sixth Circuit's reasoning, parody is treated no differently from any ordinary use. If sold for money, it will be deemed commercial and presumptively unfair, with the first factor resolved against the parodist. Indeed, the majority opinion goes beyond any reasonable interpretation of *Sony* by holding that the first factor not only *may* but *must* be resolved against fair use where the use is commercial. This result ignores the value of parody as recognized by Congress, commentators and other courts (including the only other Sixth Circuit fair use opinion under the 1976 Act).[200]

The other advantage given to parody by the courts is in the treatment of the third statutory factor, "the amount and substantiality of the portion used in relation to the copyrighted work as a whole."[201] After some uncertainty in the early

---

199 972 F.2d at 1436-37 (citations omitted).

200 *See* Pro Arts, Inc. v. Hustler Magazine, Inc., 787 F.2d 592 (6th Cir. 1986) (table), Nos. 85-3022, 85-3041 (unpublished per curiam opinion, filed March 25, 1986). In *Pro Arts*, the Sixth Circuit reversed a finding of copyright infringement, holding that the reproduction of the plaintiff's poster in the background of a photograph used in the defendant's advertisement constituted fair use. In an approach diametrically opposed to that in *Acuff-Rose*, the court of appeals stated:

> [C]ommercial motivation, while relevant to the fair use inquiry, is not conclusive. . . . The commercial character of defendants' use must be weighed along with the other factors relevant to the fair use issue. The facts of the instant case caution against according too much weight to this factor. While the primary purpose of defendants' use . . . was commercial gain, it is apparent that a secondary purpose . . . was to parody the culture of the seventies.

Id. The court concluded, "In viewing 'the general commercial nature of defendants' use' as dispositive of the question of fair use, the district court incorrectly applied 17 U.S.C. § 107." *Id.*

201 The majority in *Acuff-Rose* agreed with Fisher v. Dees, 794 F.2d 432, 438 n.4 (9th Cir. 1986), that "[t]he amount of the original work which is appropriated is a factual issue, but the question whether the taking is excessive under the circumstances is one of law." 972 F.2d at 1438. This holding misconstrues the nature of the inquiry under the third factor. As part of its *prima facie* case, the copyright owner must prove the defendant appropriated a substantial amount of protected material. *De minimis* uses do not rise to this level. Thus, at one end of the spectrum, we have a *de minimis* amount of copying or less, resulting in a directed verdict for the defendant. In the middle of the spectrum is the defendant's copying of a substantial amount, an issue that is routinely decided by juries. As an affirmative defense, fair use deals with the middle to upper end of the spectrum: a taking so substantial that, absent the defense, judgment for the copyright owner results. Analysis of the third fair use factor is but a continuation of the substantial similarity inquiry. *See* Narell v. Freeman, 872 F.2d 907, 914 (9th Cir. 1989). There is thus no reason why the third factor should be one solely for the court. Indeed, since fair use may be decided by a jury, Jartech, Inc. v. Clancy, 666 F.2d 403 (9th Cir.), *cert. denied*,

cases,[202] the Second and Ninth Circuits have concluded that parody, in order to be effective, needs extra breathing room. Accordingly, they have held that parodists should be given additional leeway to use more of the copyrighted work than would be permitted the ordinary copier.[203]

Exactly how much more is a question no one has been able to answer, and perhaps no one can, given the fact-specific nature of fair use.[204] Plainly there must be limits; not anything goes.[205]

---

459 U.S. 826 (1982), it is difficult to see how the *Fisher/Acuff-Rose* approach could work. The jury would be given the first, second, and fourth factors to decide, but not the third. The court would decide the third factor, and presumably then direct the jury to balance all the factors, taking into account the court's ruling.

202 These early cases suggested a test allowing the parodist to take just enough to recall or conjure up the work parodied. *See* Walt Disney Prods. v. Air Pirates, 581 F.2d 751, 757 (9th Cir. 1978), *cert. denied sub nom.* O'Neill v. Walt Disney Prods., 439 U.S. 1132 (1979) ("courts have analyzed the substantiality of copying by a parodist by asking whether the parodist has appropriated a greater amount of the original work than is necessary to 'recall or conjure up' the object of his satire"); Berlin v. E.C. Publications, Inc., 329 F.2d 541, 545 (2d Cir.) ("[W]here, as here, it is clear that the parody has neither the intent nor the effect of fulfilling the demand for the original, and where the parodist does not appropriate a greater amount of the original work than is necessary to 'recall or conjure up' the object of his satire, a finding of infringement would be improper.") (dictum), *cert. denied,* 379 U.S. 822 (1964); Columbia Pictures Corp. v. National Broadcasting Co., 137 F. Supp. 348, 350 (S.D. Cal. 1955) ("In historical burlesque a part of the content is used to conjure up, at least the general image, of the original. Some limited taking should be permitted under the doctrine of fair use, in the case of burlesque, to bring about this recalling or conjuring up of the original.").

203 *See* Rogers v. Koons, 960 F.2d 301, 311 (2d Cir.), *cert. denied,* 113 S. Ct. 365 (1992); Fisher v. Dees, 794 F.2d 432, 438-39 (9th Cir. 1986); Elsmere Music, Inc. v. National Broadcasting Co., 623 F.2d 252, 253 n.1 (2d Cir. 1980) (per curiam) ("[T]he concept of 'conjuring up' an original came into the copyright law not as a limitation on how much of an original may be used, but as a recognition that a parody frequently needs to be more than a fleeting evocation of an original in order to make its humorous point. A parody is entitled at least to 'conjure up' the original.").

204 *Cf.* Judge Learned Hand's observation in Nichols v. Universal Pictures Corp., 45 F.2d 119, 121 (2d Cir. 1930), *cert. denied,* 282 U.S. 902 (1931), referring to his "abstractions" test for separating idea from expression: "Nobody has ever been able to fix that boundary, and nobody ever can."

205 The Ninth Circuit has suggested that the amount permitted to be taken should depend on various factors, among them "the degree of public recognition of the original work, the ease of conjuring up the original work in the chosen medium, and the focus of the parody." Fisher v. Dees, 794 F.2d at 439. In the case of a song, greater leeway would be given than in the case of other works, such as the graphic arts. The court explained:

> Like a speech, a song is difficult to parody effectively without exact or near-exact copying. If the would-be parodist varies the music or meter of the original substantially, it simply will not be recognizable to the general audience. This 'special need for accuracy' provides some license for 'closer' parody. . . . To be sure, that license is not limitless: the parodist's desire to make the best parody must be 'balanced against the rights of the copyright owner in his original expressions.'

Id. (quoting Walt Disney Prods. v. Air Pirates, 581 F.2d 751, 758 (9th Cir. 1978), *cert. denied sub nom.* O'Neill v. Walt Disney Prods., 439 U.S. 1132 (1979)). *See also* Berlin v. E.C. Publications, Inc., 329 F.2d 541, 545 (2d Cir.), *cert. denied,* 379 U.S. 822 (1964) ("the fact that defendants' parodies were written in the same meter as plaintiffs' compositions would seem inevitable if the original was to be recognized"); Original Appalachian Artworks, Inc. v. Topps Chewing Gum, Inc., 642 F. Supp. 1031, 1035-36 (N.D. Ga.

Yet as long as the parody is different enough from the original to be identifiable as a separate work, one that would not serve as a satisfactory substitute for the original, substantial leeway should be given. Up to a point (probably the point where the works are no longer clearly differentiated),[206] the more that is copied, the funnier the parody, providing multiple shocks of recognition in an incongruous context. Maybe a parodist should not be entitled to make the best parody possible,[207] but the public also loses if only mediocre parodies can qualify as fair use.

2. What Is a Fair Use Parody?

Given these major advantages in the fair use analysis, the characterization of a use as parody is often quite significant. It is therefore critical to determine what qualifies a use as a parody for fair use purposes. A number of subsidiary questions may be raised.

First, what is the satirical target of the parody? Is it a comment on the plaintiff's work in particular, or a use of the plaintiff's work as a vehicle to make a humorous statement about society generally? A number of courts have held that the plaintiff's work must be at least in part an object of the parody for the parody to qualify for special fair use status.[208] As long as it is liberally interpreted, this conclusion is appropriate. If the defendant is commenting on something that has nothing to do with the plaintiff's work, he has no need to use the plaintiff's work to make that comment. He can equally well create his own expression, or use material in the public domain.[209] Without such a limitation on the parody defense, anyone's expression would be

---

1986) (in rejecting fair use defense for satirical version of popular soft-sculptured dolls, distinguishing *Fisher v. Dees* in part on ground that graphic arts require less close copying than musical works).

[206] *Cf.* Cliffs Notes, Inc. v. Bantam Doubleday Dell Publishing Group, Inc., 886 F.2d 490, 494 (2d Cir. 1989): "[T]he keystone of parody is imitation. . . . A parody must convey two simultaneous—and contradictory—messages: that it is the original, but also that it is *not* the original and is instead a parody. To the extent that it does only the former but not the latter, it is not only a poor parody but also vulnerable under trademark law, since the consumer will be confused."

[207] *See* Walt Disney Prods. v. Air Pirates, 581 F.2d at 758.

[208] *See* Rogers v. Koons, 960 F.2d 301, 310 (2d Cir.), *cert. denied*, 113 S. Ct. 365 (1992); Fisher v. Dees, 794 F.2d at 439 n.5; MCA, Inc. v. Wilson, 677 F.2d 180, 183-85 (2d Cir. 1981).

[209] Fair use should not excuse the copying of a melody just because it is familiar or tuneful, to use as a vehicle for unrelated lyrics that will make people laugh. *See* Fisher v. Dees, 794 F.2d at 439 n.5 (describing purpose of defendant's copying in MCA, Inc. v. Wilson, 677 F.2d 180 (2d Cir. 1981), as "simply to reap the advantages of a well-known tune and short-cut the rigors of composing original music"). *Cf.* Berlin v. E.C. Publications, Inc., 329 F.2d 541 (2d Cir.), *cert. denied*, 379 U.S. 822 (1964) (defendants created words to be sung to famous tunes; melodies referred to by title rather than copied).

fair game as a vehicle to make an unrelated statement.[210] In the absence of a need to use that particular work, there is inadequate justification for carving out a substantial chunk of the copyright owner's exclusive rights.

On the other hand, the relationship between the parody and the original need not be consanguineal. The parody could legitimately comment on other aspects of society as well if the plaintiff's work is lampooned in the process. It should also be sufficient if the plaintiff's work is associated in the public mind with the aspect of society commented on.[211] Otherwise parodists would be severely constrained in their ability to satirize a distinct era or style. Nor does the parody have to be subtle, clever, or sophisticated. Even broad caricature or a simplistic poking of fun may merit treatment as parody;[212] it is not for judges to impose on the public their own views of what constitutes good humor, any more than good art.[213]

---

210 The Second Circuit has concluded that

> this is a necessary rule, as were it otherwise there would be no real limitation on the copier's use of another's copyrighted work to make a statement on some aspect of society at large. If an infringement of copyrightable expression could be justified as fair use solely on the basis of the infringer's claim to a higher or different artistic use—without ensuring public awareness of the original work—there would be no practicable boundary to the fair use defense. . . . The rule's function is to insure that credit is given where credit is due. By requiring that the copied work be an object of the parody, we merely insist that the audience be aware that underlying the parody there is an original and separate expression, attributable to a different artist. This awareness may come from the fact that the copied work is publicly known or because its existence is in some manner acknowledged by the parodist in connection with the parody.

Rogers v. Koons, 960 F.2d at 310.

Of course, the defendant's use might still qualify as fair upon a full analysis; it simply would not be afforded the more lenient treatment given parody. *See* Rogers v. Koons, 960 F.2d 301; Pillsbury Co. v. Milky Way Prods., Inc., 215 U.S.P.Q. 124 (N.D. Ga. 1981) (rejecting defendant's claim that work was a parody, but evaluating the fair use defense).

211 For example, the Capitol Steps, a political satire musical group, has recorded a song, "Like a Suburban Drone," that cleverly uses Bob Dylan's famous song "Like a Rolling Stone." By substituting lyrics that describe the bourgeois, middle-class life now led by the people who may have associated themselves in the 1960s with Dylan's lyrics, the song lampoons those individuals precisely by its use of the original song. This type of use should be considered a parody for fair use purposes.

On the other hand, where a political satire group reproduces the music to a song that has no connection to the lyrics it creates, fair use is unlikely. There is not and should not be a *per se* rule favoring parody merely because the parodist's message is political. Each use must be evaluated on its own.

212 *Cf.* Cliffs Notes, Inc. v. Bantam Doubleday Dell Publishing Group, Inc., 886 F.2d 490, 495-96 (2d Cir. 1989) ("[P]arody may be sophisticated as well as slapstick; a . . . work is a parody if, taken as a whole, it pokes fun at its subject.").

213 In the famous words of Justice Holmes:

> It would be a dangerous undertaking for persons trained only to the law to constitute themselves final judges of the worth of pictorial illustrations, outside of the narrowest and most obvious limits. At the one extreme some

While it should not be necessary for the plaintiff's work to be well-known, its degree of notoriety will bear on the credibility of a claim that the defendant's use is a parody.[214] Although it is theoretically possible that one would wish to satirize an unknown work, it is unlikely. The market for such a satire would be small indeed; rather, most purchasers would buy ignorant of the parody, unaware that there were two separate works involved, the plaintiff's and the defendant's.[215]

Facts extrinsic to the nature of the defendant's work itself should not be considered. Thus, it is irrelevant whether the defendant's work is embodied in a traditional medium for parody, such as a satirical revue[216] or a comedy album,[217] as opposed to a single song on a non-comic album, or a single illustration or article in a serious magazine.[218] Nor should it matter whether the

---

> works of genius would be sure to miss appreciation. Their very novelty would make them repulsive until the public had learned the new language in which their author spoke. It may be more than doubted, for instance, whether the etchings of Goya or the paintings of Manet would have been sure of protection when seen for the first time. At the other end, copyright would be denied to pictures which appealed to a public less educated than the judge. Yet if they command the interest of any public, they have a commercial value—it would be bold to say that they have not an aesthetic and educational value—and the taste of any public is not to be treated with contempt.

Bleistein v. Donaldson Lithographing Co., 188 U.S. 239, 251-52 (1903). The same principle applied in the context of parody was well expressed in University of Notre Dame Du Lac v. Twentieth Century-Fox Film Corp., 256 N.Y.S.2d 301, 307 (App. Div. 1965): "Whether [the defendant's work] is good burlesque or bad, penetrating satire or blundering buffoonery, is not for us to decide. It is fundamental that courts may not muffle expression by passing judgment on its skill or clumsiness, its sensitivity or coarseness; nor on whether it pains or pleases." *See also* Berlin v. E.C. Publications, Inc., 329 F.2d 541, 545 (2d Cir.), *cert. denied*, 379 U.S. 822 (1964) ("While the social interest in encouraging the broad-gauged burlesques of Mad Magazine is admittedly not readily apparent, and our individual tastes may prefer a more subtle brand of humor, this can hardly be dispositive here") (citing *Bleistein*, 188 U.S. at 239).

[214] *See* United Feature Syndicate, Inc. v. Koons, 817 F. Supp. 370 (S.D.N.Y. 1993) (defendant artist's parody claim unconvincing where he testified that he was not familiar with subject of claimed parody); Campbell v. Koons, 1993 U.S. Dist. LEXIS 3957 (S.D.N.Y. filed April 1, 1993); Yankee Publishing Inc. v. News Am. Publishing Inc., 809 F. Supp. 267, 281 (S.D.N.Y. 1992) (distinguishing Rogers v. Koons, 960 F.2d 301 (2d Cir.), *cert. denied*, 113 S. Ct. 365 (1992), as involving a finding of lack of veracity as to whether defendant was engaging in parody where parody treatment of original difficult to discern, object of parody not known to intended audience, and copying done in bad faith).

[215] *Cf.* definition in Clemmons, *supra* note 95, at 12:

> A parody is a work that transforms all or a significant part of an original work of authorship into a derivative work by distorting it or closely imitating it, for comic effect, in a manner such that both the original work of authorship and the independent effort of the parodist are recognizable.

[216] *See, e.g.*, Elsmere Music, Inc. v. National Broadcasting Co., 623 F.2d 252 (2d Cir. 1980) (per curiam) (song used as part of "Saturday Night Live" television show).

[217] *See, e.g.*, Fisher v. Dees, 794 F.2d 432 (9th Cir. 1986) (song on comedy album entitled, "Put It Where the Moon Don't Shine").

[218] *Cf.* L.L. Bean, Inc. v. Drake Publishers, Inc.. 811 F.2d 26 (1st Cir.), *cert. denied*, 483

defendant has a track record as a parodist.[219] First-time parody is equally as deserving of protection as the parody of experience, and even a serious artist is entitled to an occasional foray into humor.[220] Parodists must get their start somewhere, and the public benefits in exactly the same way.

The treatment of the question of the work's status as parody by the Sixth Circuit in *Acuff-Rose* can best be described as schizophrenic. The majority began its fair use discussion by announcing that, for purposes of the opinion, it would accept the district court's finding that 2 Live Crew's song was a parody of "Oh, Pretty Woman."[221] It immediately undercut this statement, however, with a lengthy footnote explaining that it did so "with considerable reservation, as the district court's parody analysis [did] not, in our view, comport with proper analysis of that term."[222]

U.S. 1013 (1987) (parody of plaintiff's catalogue within otherwise non-humorous adult magazine).

219 *Cf.* Original Appalachian Artworks, Inc. v. Topps Chewing Gum, Inc., 642 F. Supp. 1031, 1034 (N.D. Ga. 1986) ("Neither are the Garbage Pail Kid stickers merely one of a series of spoofs of various different products, as defendant has produced in the past, nor a single cartoon or editorial in a broader satirical product such as Mad Magazine.").

220 Many serious and well-known writers have been known to "tr[y] their hand at parody." Dorsen, *supra* note 188, at 952-53 and n.141 (listing as examples Shakespeare, Pope, Fielding, Austen, Hemingway, and Faulkner).

221 972 F.2d at 1435. The district court's parody finding, as explicitly accepted by the court of appeals, extended to both the work's character and its purpose. *Id.*

222 *Id.* n.8. The basis for the disagreement was the Sixth Circuit's inability to "discern any parody of the original song." The Court explained:

> In our opinion, this is not a new work which makes ridiculous the style and expression of the original, although there is plainly an element of the ridiculous to the new work. We cannot see any thematic relationship between the copyrighted song and the alleged parody. The mere fact that both songs have a woman as their central theme is too tenuous a connection to be viewed as critical comment on the original.

Id. at 1436 n.8. In a persuasive dissenting opinion, Judge Nelson took the opposite view, concluding that

> the 2 Live Crew song is a quintessential parody. . . . [It] both imitates and distorts the original work for comic or satiric effect, and does so in such a way that both the original work and the work of the parodist are readily recognizable. The parody (done in an African-American dialect) was clearly intended to ridicule the white-bread original—and if a higher criticism is necessary to qualify the derivative work as true parody, such criticism is readily discernible.

Id. at 1441-42. Indeed, the majority's inability to see 2 Live Crew's version of the song as parody is difficult to understand. It suggests a certain myopia when faced with crude satire or the humorous perspective of a different culture.

It is also interesting to note that *Acuff-Rose* presents the relatively rare situation of a song parody where the music is parodied as well as the words. As described by the district court, "[t]he parody also employs a number of musical devices that exaggerate the original and help to create a comic effect," including a heavily distorted "scraper" sound, vocalists singing simultaneously in different keys, and an annoyingly repetitious use of the original's distinctive bass riff. 754 F. Supp. at 1155. In the handful of existing song parody cases, the humor has generally focused on the lyrics. *See* Fisher v. Dees, 794 F.2d 432 (9th Cir. 1986); MCA, Inc. v. Wilson, 677 F.2d 180 (2d Cir. 1981); Elsmere

And the court's analysis of the fair use defense treated the defendants' work as a typical commercial use, refusing to give any consideration to its status as parody.[223]

An additional question that has been raised in analyzing parody is whether the defendant's work is *dis*qualified for special treatment by pornographic, vulgar or otherwise offensive content? Arguably such content might be viewed as one aspect of the "character" of the work. Some courts appear to have concluded, at least implicitly, that the answer is yes.[224] Again, such a conclusion impermissibly involves the court in evaluating aesthetic content. Copyright law should be applied to further copyright values, not unrelated values that may be protected, if at all,

---

Music, Inc. v. National Broadcasting Co., 623 F.2d 252 (2d Cir. 1980) (per curiam). Of course, satirizing the lyrics alone would be enough to make the resulting work a parody of the entire song. *See* 17 U.S.C. § 102(a)(2) (1978) (category of "musical works" subject to copyright protection includes "any accompanying words").

[223] Thus, the Sixth Circuit found that the first statutory factor weighed against fair use because of the commercial nature of the use, without giving the customary weight to the character of the work as parody. *See supra* text accompanying note 200. On the third factor, the court gave the defendants no extra leeway. Noting the district court's finding that no more was taken than necessary to accomplish the defendants' parodic purpose, the court of appeals stated, "Near verbatim taking of the music and meter of a copyrighted work without the creation of a parody is excessive taking," 972 F.2d at 1438, an odd statement in the context of its previously stated acceptance of the finding that the work was a parody. The sole explanation given for rejecting the district court's finding on this factor was the cryptic and inaccurate statement that "the [district] court was using the term parody in its popular [as opposed to legal] sense." *Id. See also id.* at 1435 (positing a distinction between the popular definition of "parody" and its "statutory definition"). The district court clearly held that the use was a parody in the legal sense. *See* 754 F. Supp. at 1154-55.

[224] *See* MCA, Inc. v. Wilson, 677 F.2d 180 (2d Cir. 1981); Dallas Cowboys Cheerleaders, Inc. v. Scoreboard Posters, Inc., 600 F.2d 1184 (5th Cir. 1979); Walt Disney Prods. v. Air Pirates, 581 F.2d 751 (9th Cir. 1978), *cert. denied sub nom.* O'Neill v. Walt Disney Prods., 439 U.S. 1132 (1979); Original Appalachian Artworks, Inc. v. Topps Chewing Gum, Inc., 642 F. Supp. 1031 (N.D. Ga. 1986); DC Comics Inc. v. Unlimited Monkey Business, Inc. 598 F. Supp. 110 (N.D. Ga. 1984); Walt Disney Prods. v. Mature Pictures Corp., 389 F. Supp. 1397 (S.D.N.Y. 1975). *But see* Pillsbury Co. v. Milky Way Prods., Inc., 215 U.S.P.Q. 124, 131 (N.D. Ga. 1981) ("The Copyright Act . . . does not expressly exclude pornographic materials from the parameters of the fair use defense . . . . The character of the unauthorized use is relevant, but, in the court's judgment, the fact that this use is pornographic in nature does not militate against a finding of fair use."). It is arguable that the Sixth Circuit was influenced by similar reasoning in examining the undeniably crude lyrics in *Acuff-Rose*, despite the district court's finding that "2 Live Crew's version is neither obscene nor pornographic." 754 F. Supp. at 1155 n.4. (By 2 Live Crew's standards, they may have been, as the title of their album suggests, "As Clean As They Wanna Be.")

The Second and Ninth Circuits have so far both declined to take an explicit position on this issue. *See* Fisher v. Dees, 794 F.2d 432, 437 ("Assuming without deciding that an obscene use is not a fair use, . . . we conclude, after listening to it, that the parody is innocuous—silly perhaps, but surely not obscene or immoral."); Warner Bros., Inc. v. American Broadcasting Cos., 720 F.2d 231, 242 n.8 (2d Cir. 1983) ("We have no occasion in this case to consider the limiting principle that arises when attempts at parody take the form of scatological humor."). *Cf.* L.L. Bean, Inc. v. Drake Publishers, Inc., 811 F.2d 26 (1st Cir.), *cert. denied*, 483 U.S. 1013 (1987) (repudiating similar principle in the context of trademark parody).

through other bodies of law.[225]

In light of the acceptance of parody as a type of use to be encouraged, the Sixth Circuit's use of the "double whammy" in *Acuff-Rose* is doubly destructive. Not only does it perpetuate a disturbing development in fair use analysis generally, it also distorts the evolving body of parody law.

III. Conclusion

As difficult as it is to apply, fair use must remain a sensitive, flexible doctrine, responsive to the facts of each individual case. Presumptions, formulas and rigid rules are foreign both to the doctrine's traditional nature and to its statutory formulation.

It might be argued that this approach leaves courts free simply to follow their gut instincts, legitimized by the recitation of statutory terminology. Some might prefer a more objective framework, governed by fixed criteria. Such a preference is entirely rational; greater predictability would unquestionably assist second authors in creating and lawyers in advising them.[226]

But equity and reasonableness, the essence of fair use, cannot be cast in stone, and Congress has wisely eschewed such an approach. Within the guidance of the statutory factors, and judicial precedent applying those factors, Congress has instructed that the courts are to continue a common law, fact-specific approach. The desired open-endedness is necessary if the fair use doctrine is to preserve its function of calibrating the optimal balance of public interests on both sides of the copyright scale.

---

225 *Cf.* Feist Publications, Inc. v. Rural Tel. Serv. Co., 111 S. Ct. 1282, 1289-90 (1991) (perceived unfairness of allowing free rides through copying of material collected through great effort and investment cannot be remedied under copyright law, which implements values of creativity, not fairness). Concerns over the content of a parody may be addressed through the invocation of obscenity laws, or an action for defamation, disparagement or tarnishment.

226 The negative effects of the doctrine's lack of predictability have been noted by a number of commentators. *See, e.g.*, Leval, *supra* note 49, at 1106-07.

ALIENABILITY RESTRICTIONS AND THE ENHANCEMENT OF AUTHOR AUTONOMY IN UNITED STATES AND CONTINENTAL COPYRIGHT LAW

NEIL NETANEL*

I. INTRODUCTION

A cardinal incident of what we commonly call ownership is the right to relinquish title to the object of ownership and to direct to whom, if anyone, that title is to be transferred.[1] The owner of a shoe or the holder of a right to receive the winnings of the New York State Lottery may freely sell, give away, or bequeath the shoe or right, or may abandon the shoe or waive the right to the lottery winnings.[2]

American law has traditionally treated authors' creations as objects of ownership. In enacting the Copyright Act of 1976, Congress declared its adherence to "the principle of unlimited alienability of copyright."[3] The Copyright Act accords authors a bundle of exclusive rights to exploit their work, including: the right to reproduce, publicly exhibit, distribute copies, and make adaptations.[4] The principle of unlimited alienability requires that an author be free to assign, license, and waive each of these exploitation rights, much like the owner of a shoe, car, or home. It also means that the author's assignee becomes the new sovereign owner of those rights. Thus, absent an express contractual obligation to the contrary, the assignee is entitled to exploit or dispense with the work as the assignee sees fit, without further need to obtain author consent.

---

* © 1992 Neil Netanel, J.S.D. Candidate, Stanford Law School. B.A. 1976, Yale University; J.D. 1980, Boalt Hall School of Law, University of California at Berkeley. The author wishes to thank Paul Goldstein, Axel Aus der Mühlen, Joël Dorkam, David Nimmer, Margaret Jane Radin, Barbara Weinstock and Joshua Weisman for their helpful comments and suggestions.

[1] A. M. Honore, *Ownership*, *in* OXFORD ESSAYS IN JURISPRUDENCE 107, 118-19 (A.G. Guest ed., 1st ser. 1961). *But see* Margaret J. Radin, *Market-Inalienability*, 100 HARV. L. REV. 1849, 1909-21 (1987) (arguing that where property is necessary for self-constitution and personal development, it should be subject to alienability restrictions).

[2] *See* N.Y. TAX LAW §§ 1600-16 (McKinney 1987). *But see* CAL. GOV'T CODE § 8880.32(g) (West 1992) (providing that the right of any person to a California State Lottery prize shall not be assignable, except to his estate or by appropriate judicial order).

[3] H.R. REP. No. 1476, 94th Cong., 2d Sess. 21, 123 (1976) [hereinafter 1976 HOUSE REPORT].

[4] 17 U.S.C. § 106 (1988).

The application of traditional property concepts to copyright, as expressed in the Copyright Act's principle of unlimited alienability, contrasts with Continental European copyright doctrine.[5] Continental doctrine regards literary and artistic works as inalienable extensions of the author's personality. This view finds expression in restrictions on the market transfer and waiver of copyright. These restrictions are designed, in large part, to protect the author's personal interest in determining whether, when, by whom, and in what manner his work is presented to the public. The alienability restrictions under Continental doctrine include those arising from the author's so-called "moral right."[6] With certain limitations, the moral right entitles an author—even after granting to another the exclusive right to market his work—to block publication, determine how authorship is attributed, and prevent material changes in, or uses of, the work that are repugnant to the author's artistic conception. An author's control over the communication of his work is further enhanced under Continental doctrine through several additional barriers to copyright commodification, which operate in synergy with the moral right. These barriers include: unwaivable transferee obligations to disseminate the work, restrictions on retransfers, rules of contract interpretation that require authors' copyright grants to be narrowly construed, and limitations on author ability to convey rights in works not yet created. Finally, in some European countries copyright is simply non-assignable, although authors may grant licenses to exploit their work.

While essentially foreign to American jurisprudence, the Continental conception of creative works as inalienable extensions of personality has established a beachhead in this country. A number of U.S. courts have attempted to fashion analogues to certain Continental copyright inalienability restrictions out of American unfair competition, tort, and contract law.[7] The Supreme Court has noted that the U.S. Copyright Act's right of publication implicates authors' personal interest in creative control in addition to their

---

[5] It is preferable to refer to Continental doctrine as "authors' rights," rather than "copyright," in order to translate Continental nomenclature more accurately and reflect Continental concerns for the interest of natural authors more precisely. Nevertheless, for the sake of stylistic simplicity, this Article generally refers to both Continental and United States doctrine as "copyright."

[6] The term "moral right" is a translation of the French "*droit moral*." The German "Urheberpersönlichkeitsrecht," meaning "author's rights of personality," describes the nature of the rights more accurately, but the commonly-used terms "moral right" and "moral rights" will be employed here.

[7] *See infra* notes 203-10 and accompanying text.

proprietary interest in the work's exploitation.[8] In addition, several state legislatures and, most recently, Congress have accorded a measure of moral rights protection to creators of fine art.[9] Finally, numerous commentators have called for expanded recognition of authors' personal rights in their work.[10]

The United States' accession to the Berne Convention for the Protection of Literary and Artistic Works, effective March 1, 1989, has given considerable impetus to this tentative movement toward Europeanization. The Convention's provisions are largely reflective of Continental copyright doctrine and contain requirements concerning authors' moral right to be identified with and to prevent distortions of their works even after the right to exploit the work has been sold or licensed.[11] After years of debate over the extent to which these requirements would upset the equilibrium of U.S. copyright law and run counter to traditional property doctrine in this country,[12] Congress laid the groundwork for accession by enacting the Berne Convention Implementation Act of 1988.[13] The Implementation Act provided for the minimal amount of change in domestic law thought necessary to bring the United States into compliance with the Convention's provisions, and did not provide for explicit recognition of moral rights or any other

---

8 Harper & Row v. Nation Enterprises, 471 U.S. 539, 555 (1984).

9 *See infra* note 227.

10 *See, e.g.*, Phyllis Amarnick, *American Recognition of the Moral Right: Issues and Options*, 29 COPYRIGHT L. SYMP. (ASCAP) 31 (1983); Edward J. Damich, *The Right of Personality: A Common-Law Basis for Protection of the Moral Rights of Authors*, 23 GA. L. REV. 1 (1988); Roberta R. Kwall, *Copyright and the Moral Right: Is an American Marriage Possible?*, 38 VAND. L. REV. 1 (1985); John H. Merryman, *The Refrigerator of Bernard Buffet*, 27 HASTINGS L.J. 1023 (1976); Michael E. Horowitz, Note, *Artists' Rights in the United States: Toward Federal Legislation*, 25 HARV. J. ON LEGIS. 153 (1988).

11 The Berne Convention for the Protection of Literary and Artistic Works, art. 6*bis*, S. TREATY DOC. NO. 27, 99th Cong., 2d Sess. 3706 (1986) [hereinafter Berne Convention].

12 *See* MELVILLE B. NIMMER & DAVID NIMMER, NIMMER ON COPYRIGHT § 8.21[2][a], at 8-279 to 8-280 (1993) (discussing the "avalanche of opposition to moral rights" in Congressional debates concerning adherence to the Berne Convention); *Berne Convention Implementation: Hearings on H.R. 4262 Before the Subcomm. on Courts, Civil Liberties, and the Administration of Justice of the House Comm. on the Judiciary*, 100th Cong., 1st & 2d Sess. 345-48 (1987-88) [hereinafter *Berne Hearings*] (statement of the Coalition to Preserve the American Copyright Tradition) (arguing that the concept of the moral right is outside the U.S. Copyright tradition and purpose of providing an economic incentive for the creation and dissemination of works of authorship); Stephen L. Carter, *Owning What Doesn't Exist*, 13 HARV. J.L. & PUB. POL'Y 99, 101 (1991) (asserting that the moral right doctrine means that owners of paintings, films and other cultural works "should not have the right to do with their possessions as they wish"); Lawrence A. Beyer, *Intentionalism, Art and the Suppression of Innovation: Film Colorization and the Philosophy of Moral Rights*, 82 NW. U. L. REV. 1011, 1047, 1052-54 (1988) (arguing that the moral right of integrity runs counter to traditional notions of freedom of choice in market transactions).

13 Berne Convention Implementation Act of 1988, Pub. L. No. 100-568, 102 Stat. 2853 (codified as amended in scattered sections of 17 U.S.C.).

Continental restriction on copyright alienability.[14] Despite this ostensibly minimalist approach, in the view of many commentators adherence to Berne will work a gradual but appreciable change in the American copyright system by exposing it to the continuing influence of Continental copyright doctrine.

The Visual Artists Rights Act of 1990 exemplifies this influence, as well as Congressional efforts to contain it.[15] According to the House Report, the Act is designed to bring "U.S. law into greater harmony with laws of other Berne countries."[16] The Act accords creators of original works of fine art certain narrowly circumscribed non-transferable and only partially waivable moral rights.[17] Unlike traditional American copyright, these newly enacted rights are non-transferable and only partially waivable.[18] Moreover, the Act requires that the Register of Copyrights conduct a study to determine whether the rights should be waivable at all.[19]

This Article examines the Continental copyright alienability limitations described above and the extent to which they may be compatible with American legal norms. Throughout this Article

---

14 The House Committee report accompanying the Berne Convention Implementation Act bill noted that the proposed legislation adopted the "minimalist approach" of "amending the Copyright Act only where there is a clear conflict with the express provisions of the Berne Convention (Paris Act of 1971); and further, . . . only insofar as it is necessary to resolve the conflict in a manner compatible with the public interest, respecting the preexisting balance of rights and limitations in the Copyright Act as a whole." H.R. Rep. No. 609, 100th Cong., 2d Sess. 20 (1988). With regard to moral rights, the Berne Convention Implementation Act provides:

> (b) Certain Rights Not Affected. The provisions of the Berne Convention, the adherence of the United States, thereto, and satisfaction of the United States obligations thereunder, do not expand or reduce any right of an author of a work—
>
> (1) to claim authorship of the work; or (2) to object to any distortion, mutilation, or other modifications of, or other derogatory action in relation to, the work, that would prejudice the author's honor or reputation.

Berne Convention Implementation Act, *supra* note 13, § 3.

15 Visual Rights Act of 1990, Pub. L. No. 101-650, 104 Stat. 5128 (codified as 17 U.S.C. § 106A (Supp. II 1990)). Ironically, the ultimate effect of the Visual Artists Rights Act may actually be to limit artists' moral rights by preempting state statutory provisions that accorded broader protection. *See* Nimmer & Nimmer, *supra* note 12, § 8.21 [B][2], at 8-282.6 to 8-292; *see infra* note 227. For a further discussion of the Visual Artists Rights Act see *infra* text accompanying notes 227-53.

16 H. Rep. No. 253, 101st Cong., 2nd Sess. 10 (1990) (quoting *The Visual Rights Act of 1989: Hearings on H.R. 2690 Before the Subcomm. on the Courts, Intellectual Property, and the Admin. of Justice*, 101st Cong., 1st Sess. 37 (1989) (statement of Ralph Oman, Register of Copyrights), reprinted in 1990 U.S.C.C.A.N. 6915, 6920 [hereinafter Visual Artists House Report].

17 *See infra* text accompanying notes 235-40.

18 Visual Rights Act of 1990, Pub. L. No. 101-650, §§ 603(e), 608(a), 104 Stat. 5128 (codified at 17 U.S.C. § 106A(e) (Supp. II 1990)). A waiver of the rights is effective only as to the works and the uses of such works that are specifically identified in a written instrument signed by the author. *Id.* § 603(e)(1). Moreover, the waiver is effective only as to the transferee to whom it is made. Visual Artists House Report, *supra* note 16, at 18-19.

19 *See infra* text accompanying notes 247-53.

the limitations are referred to as "autonomy inalienabilities": "inalienabilities" because they severely circumscribe author ability to alienate copyright entitlements by transfer or waiver, and "autonomy" because, although they limit authors' contractual freedom, they are designed ultimately to enhance authors' independent control of expression and communication *vis-à-vis* publishers, producers, and other persons who have obtained economic exploitation rights in creative works. In this Article the French and German copyright traditions will be exclusively relied on to represent Continental doctrine. These two traditions reflect, respectively, the Hegelian and Kantian schools of copyright thought, which have exerted a predominant influence on jurists and lawmakers throughout the civil law world.

Prior comparative scholarship in this area has suffered from three principal shortcomings, which this Article seeks to address. First, the commentary has centered on the moral right to the exclusion of other Continental copyright alienability restrictions. This narrow focus takes the moral right out of its context in Continental doctrine and fails to account for the synergistic effects of its operation with other autonomy inalienabilites.

Second, only passing consideration has been given to the troublesome question of the extent to which the moral right is actually inalienable, as Continental doctrine purports it to be. Commentators seeking to minimize the inconsistencies between United States and Continental doctrine have argued that the moral right is inalienable only in theory. This position confuses statutory limitations on the scope and exercise of the moral right with the author's waiver of the right. This Article examines the moral right alienability question in some detail and concludes that the moral right, together with other Continental doctrine, constitutes a significant restraint on copyright alienability.

Third, in assessing the extent to which the moral right finds American law parallels, the commentary tends to concentrate on statutory provisions and individual case holdings without considering their rhetorical underpinnings or practical effect. In failing to consider the rhetorical foundations, some commentators have exaggerated the extent to which American and Continental law converge. To the extent that American law contains approximate parallels to Continental autonomy inalienabilities, the parallels result from a patchwork of rules and policies designed to protect a variety of economic, public, and personal interests. But as this Article will show, Continental moral rights, together with other autonomy inalienabilities, form a cohesive legal doctrine, backed by a longstanding theoretical tradition that espouses an inseverable personal connection between authors and their creations. It is a thesis of this Article that the theoretical and doctrinal rationales for legal rules make a difference in their import. The rhetoric of Continental commentators, together with the matrix of rules that are seen to act in concert to protect author autonomy, promote a very different conception of creative expression than does American law. As we shall see, Continental authors' rights ideology has supported judicial applications of autonomy inalienability rules that far exceed the scope of American analogues. In addition, one must presume that the ideology informs the attitudes and practices of Continental authors and publishers even beyond its expression in case law.

At the same time, and somewhat contradictorily, some commentators have overestimated the significance of the moral right by giving undue weight to black letter law and insufficient consideration to industry practice.[20] The exigencies of the market may vitiate Continental law protection of author autonomy in some sectors. For example, independent scriptwriters and directors, who generaly rely on an ongoing relationship with producers for their livelihood, may be reluctant to exert their autonomy rights in the face of producer opposition. To the extent that autonomy alienability rules are ignored in practice, their import on the Continent and their divergence from American law may be reduced. On the other hand, Continental case law evinces considerable author willingness to counter egregious violations of their autonomy rights in most areas, including television and film production. This suggests that, even if moral rights and other autonomy inalienability rules do not fully inform industry practice, they do afford authors with additional leverage in determining the manner in which authors' works are disseminated.

With these points in mind, Part I of this Article examines the theoretical bases for the divergent treatment of copyright and alienability in American and Continental doctrine. Part II discusses the substantive similarities and differences between the Continental moral rights doctrine and its American analogues. Part III examines the inalienability of the moral right. Part IV discusses and compares the lesser known, but equally important, Continental autonomy inalienabilities and their American counterparts. Together with the moral right, these alienability restrictions provide

[20] The author is indebted to Paul Goldstein for raising this issue and for the insights gained from discussions with him concerning it.

for a measure of continuing author sovereignty over creative works, and a correlative restriction on transferees' free exploitation and disposition of such work that is unknown in the United States.

II. Comparative Copyright Theory

United States copyright law differs fundamentally from its Continental counterpart. U.S. copyright doctrine applies traditional property principles to the field of copyright, and treats authors' works as the subject of proprietary, quasi-ownership rights.[21] In contrast, Continental copyright law and doctrine focuses on the author and his personal relationship to his work.[22] Continental doctrine views copyright essentially as the protection of the author's individual character and spirit as expressed in his literary or artistic creation.[23] Although a work may be commercially exploited, it is not simply a commodity—and many commentators would say that it is not a commodity at all.[24] Instead, the work is seen, partially or wholly, as an extension of the author's personality, the means by which he seeks to communicate to the public. "When an artist creates, . . . he does more than bring into the world a unique object having only exploitive possibilities; he projects into the world part of his personality and subjects it to the ravages of public use."[25]

---

21 *See generally* Wendy J. Gordon, *An Inquiry into the Merits of Copyright: The Challenges of Consistency, Consent and Encouragement Theory*, 41 Stan. L. Rev. 1343 (1989).

The non-recognition of any inherent, personal connection between the author and his work has also been suggested by the formal requirements and work-for-hire provisions of the U.S. Copyright Act. Under the Act, an author's work is protected only when and if it is "fixed in any tangible medium of expression." 17 U.S.C. § 102(a) (1988). In addition, until recent amendments designed in large part to bring the U.S. into compliance with the Berne Convention, protection has been conditional compliance with statutory requirements of notice and registration. For a thorough discussion of the statutory formalities and their gradual and incomplete elimination under the Copyright Act of 1909, the Copyright Act of 1976, and the Berne Convention Implementation Act, see Nimmer & Nimmer, *supra* note 12, ch. 7.

Under the work-for-hire provisions, when an employee creates a work in the course of employment, the employer—and not the employee—is deemed to be the "author" of the work for purposes of the Copyright Act. The employer is also the first copyright owner, unless the parties have agreed otherwise. 17 U.S.C. § 201(b) (1988).

22 For example, the German Copyright Statute provides: "Copyright shall protect the author with respect to his intellectual and personal relations to the work, and also with respect to the utilization of the work." Gesetz über Urheberrecht und verwandte Schutz rechte, 1965 Bundesgesetzblatt [BGB1.] I art. II (F.R.G.) [hereinafter German Act] (translated in UNESCO, 2 Copyright Laws and Treaties of the World art. II (1987)).

23 *See* Stig Strömholm, *Droit Moral—The International and Comparative Scene from a Scandinavian Viewpoint*, 14 Int'l Rev. Indus. Prop. & Copyright L. [I.I.C.] 1, 13 (1983) ("'The expression of individuality' has in fact become the central formula around which all Continental European copyright law . . . is organized.").

24 *Id.*

25 Martin A. Roeder, *The Doctrine of Moral Right: A Study in the Law of Artists, Authors and Creators*, 53 Harv. L. Rev. 554, 557 (1940) (summarizing the Continental perspective on

The contrasting approaches of United States and Continental copyright laws are reflected in the treatment of the alienability of authors' rights in each system. In the United States, copyright inalienabilities are an anomaly. Until the recent enactment of the Visual Artists Rights Act of 1990, the single substantive alienability restriction found in the Copyright Act—the right of authors and their heirs to terminate copyright grants after thirty-five years—served solely to improve the bargaining position of the author so that he could achieve a greater return on the exploitation of his work.[26] Continental copyright law, on the other hand, has long contained pervasive restrictions on alienability. In essence, these restrictions reflect the idea that the author's transfer of his exploitation rights does not disengage him from his work.

The fundamental differences between United States and Continental copyright law originate in the divergent influences of Anglo-American and Continental liberalism, particularly, in the varying classification and treatment of authors' works within these traditions as subject or object, person or property. United States copyright law has been molded principally by classical utilitarianism and, to a lesser extent, by Lockean natural right theory.[27] Con-

---

moral rights). Continental copyright provides for "patrimonial" or "pecuniary" rights, similar to those in the United States, that enable the author to commercially exploit his work. As in the United States, the author in France or Germany has the exclusive right for a limited number of years to reproduce, distribute, exhibit and publicly communicate his work and to exploit adaptations of his work. GERMAN ACT, *supra* note 22, arts. 15-22; Loi du 11 mars 1957 Sur la Propriete Litteraire et Artistique, arts. 26-28, 1957 J.O. 2733, 1957 D.L. 102 (Fr.) [hereinafter FRENCH ACT] (translated in UNESCO, 1 COPYRIGHT LAWS AND TREATIES OF THE WORLD (1987)). But in contrast to U.S. law, the exploitation rights are vested only in the natural person who created the work (except rights in computer software under the French Act). André Lucas & Robert Plaisant, *France*, *in* 1 INTERNATIONAL COPYRIGHT LAW AND PRACTICE FRA-1, FRA-42 (Melville B. Nimmer & P. Geller eds., 1992); Adolf Dietz, *Germany*, *in* 1 INTERNATIONAL COPYRIGHT LAW AND PRACTICE, *supra*, at FRG-1, FRG-44 to FRG-45. They also take effect immediately upon the work's completion, without any requirement of fixation or registration. Lucas & Plaisant, *supra*, at FRA-11 to FRA-12; Dietz, *supra*, at FRG-16 to FRG-17. Moreover, the exploitation rights are said to be intertwined with and subordinate to the author's various personal rights in his work.

26 17 U.S.C. §§ 203, 304 (1988). According to the House Report accompanying the 1976 Copyright Act, the termination provision was "needed because of the unequal bargaining position of authors, resulting from the impossibility of determining a work's value until it has been exploited." H.R. REP. No. 1476, 94th Cong., 2d Sess. 124 (1976). In addition to its restriction on inter vivos transfers, 17 U.S.C. § 203 specifies which persons are to hold the author's termination interest in the event of his death. Similarly, the Copyright Act of 1909, which provided for a two-term renewable copyright, enumerated mandatory heirs to the author's renewal interest. It was held that, under the 1909 Act, an author could prospectively assign his own renewal interest during the first copyright term, but not that of the statuory heirs. For an insightful discussion of these copyright-law restraints on authors' freedom to devise the termination and renewal interests, see Francis M. Nevins, Jr., *The Magic Kingdom of Will-Bumping: Where Estates Law and Copyright Law Collide*, 35 J. COPYRIGHT SOC'Y 77 (1988).

27 The Supreme Court has also given credence to the idea that the right to control the first public distribution of an author's work implicates the author's "personal interest in

tinental copyright law, on the other hand, is a combination of natural rights concepts and German idealism. An examination of these contrasting theoretical underpinnings is the key to understanding the disparate treatment of alienability in the two systems.

A. *Anglo-American Liberalism and Authors' Works as Alienable Goods*

The fundamental overriding purpose of U.S. copyright law is social utility. The U.S. Supreme Court has repeatedly stated that the limited "monopoly privileges" granted to authors by the Copyright Act are designed to advance the public welfare by providing economic incentives for creative effort, while at the same time making the fruits of such effort available to as many people as possible, as cheaply as possible.[28] Authors are granted exclusive rights in order to spur the creation and dissemination of their work. Copyright is a privilege designed to serve the public interest, not an entitlement arising from the fact of creation.[29]

Lockean labor-desert theory enjoyed a prominent role in early Anglo-American doctrine, but has since provided a distinctly secondary rationale for copyright protection.[30] Recent Supreme Court

---

creative control," as well as the "property interest" of "exploitation of prepublication rights." Harper & Row v. Nation Enterprises, 471 U.S. 539, 555 (1984). The common law right of authors to prevent public dissemination of their works was also enlisted in support of the state law right of privacy. Louis D. Brandeis & Samuel D. Warren, *The Right to Privacy*, 4 HARV. L. REV. 193, 198-99 (1890).

28 *See, e.g.*, Sony Corp. of America v. Universal City Studios, Inc., 464 U.S. 417, 429 (1984); Twentieth Century Music Corp. v. Aiken, 422 U.S. 151, 156 (1975).

29 The utilitarian view of copyright has a venerable historic tradition. It finds its statutory antecedent in the first copyright statute, the English Statute of Anne of 1710. 8 Anne, c. 19 (1710). This statute is entitled "An Act for the Encouragement of Learning" and recited that it was enacted to enable learned men to write useful books. *Id.* It accorded authors and their assigns the sole right to print and reprint the authors' books for a period of fourteen years from first publication, upon compliance with registration and deposit requirements and subject to the power of various authorities to fix a fair price for copies of the book if they determined that price sought by the publisher was unreasonably high. *Id.* *See also* AUGUSTINE BIRRELL, SEVEN LECTURES ON THE LAW AND HISTORY OF COPYRIGHT IN BOOKS 21 (1899). The focus on copyright as a means to promote the general public good was incorporated in the intellectual property clause of the Constitution, which empowers Congress "[t]o promote the Progress of Science and useful Arts, by securing for limited Times to Authors and Inventors the exclusive Right to their respective Writings and Discoveries." U.S. CONST. art. I, § 8, cl. 8. Similarly, the first federal copyright statute, like the Statute of Anne, was entitled "An act for the encouragement of learning" and, like subsequent federal copyright statutes until the Copyright Act of 1976, required publication and compliance with deposit and notice requirements as a condition to protection. Act of May 31, 1790, ch. XV, 1 Stat. 124.

30 *See* William F. Fisher III, *Reconstructing the Fair Use Doctrine*, 100 HARV. L. REV. 1661, 1688-89 (1988) (noting that early American commentary on copyright law frequently invoked labor-desert theories). Moreover, several state copyright statutes enacted prior to the first federal copyright statute invoked Lockean natural rights doctrine, as well as public benefit rationale, to support the granting of exclusive rights in literary works. The preamble to the Massachusetts Act of March 17, 1783, stated, for example, that " 'the legal security of the fruits of their study and industry . . . is one of the natural rights of all men, there

opinions have reiterated that rewarding the author is a secondary consideration of copyright law and that the author has no natural right to such a reward.[31]

The labor-desert theory rests upon the idea that authors acquire a natural property right in their work by virtue of having exerted the effort to create it. At its foundation, this concept likens the author's original expression of an idea to a material object transformed by human labor. In Locke's theory, one earns the right to appropriate a material object by "mingling" it with one's physical labor and improving it to create a value-added version of the object, in essence a new object, that did not exist previously.[32] For Lockean proponents of a natural law copyright, the author's expression is an ideal object, a "product of the mind" which the author has procured the right to hold as his property by having created it with his mental labor.[33]

Eighteenth- and nineteenth-century advocates of the labor-desert theory argued that products of the mind are properly the subject of a perpetual property right that stands independently of any statutory grant or privilege.[34] Modern-day proponents of this the-

being no property more peculiarly a man's own than that which is procured by the labor of his mind.' " Massachusetts Act of March 17, 1783, *quoted in* Jane C. Ginsburg, *A Tale of Two Copyrights: Literary Property in Revolutionary France and America*, 147 R.I.D.A. 125, 145-47 (1991). Republican ideology also played a prominent role in early American copyright law. For a discussion of this influence, see *id.*

31 *See, e.g.*, Sony Corp. of America v. Universal City Studios, Inc., 464 U.S. 417, 429 (1984). *See also* Ralph S. Brown, *Eligibility for Copyright Protection: A Search for Principled Standards*, 70 MINN. L. REV. 579, 593 (1985) (citing "the deeply rooted understanding that copyright flows from acts of Congress and not from natural right").

32 *See* JOHN LOCKE, THE SECOND TREATISE OF GOVERNMENT §§ 27-28, at 17-18 (Thomas Pearson ed., 1952) (1689).

33 AYN RAND, *Patents and Copyrights*, *in* CAPITALISM: THE UNKNOWN IDEAL 126, 130 (1967). *See also* Millar v. Taylor, 98 Eng. Rep. 201, 221 (K.B. 1769) (Austin, J.). Although Lockean labor-desert theory and the utilitarian incentive theory both award productive labor, their emphasis is completely different. Under the former the laborer has a God-given natural right in the product of his labor, prior to any social order. Under the latter the producer's right is entirely a matter of social convention. It is actually more a benefit than a right, and that benefit is entirely subject to the will of the sovereign.

34 *See, e.g.*, *Millar*, 98 Eng. Rep. at 250-54 (L. Mansfield). The debate over whether authors enjoy a perpetual, common law, proprietary copyright that survives the enactment of limited statutory protection involved many of the most prominent legal and literary figures of the time. As noted by Justice M'Lean: "Perhaps no topic in England has excited more discussion, among literary and talented men, than that of the literary property of authors. So engrossing was the subject, for a long time, as to leave few neutrals, among those who were distinguished for their learning and ability." Wheaton v. Peters, 33 U.S. (8 Pet.) 591, 654-55 (1834).

Proponents of a perpetual common law right included William Blackstone, Lord Mansfield, John Milton, and Mark Twain; opponents included Samuel Johnson and David Hume. The debate and litigation concerning this issue is discussed in: MARK ROSE, AUTHORS AND OWNERS: THE INVENTION OF COPYRIGHT 67-112 (1993), BENJAMIN KAPLAN, AN UNHURRIED VIEW OF COPYRIGHT 12-16, 26-27 (1968), and BIRRELL, *supra* note 29, at 99-138. Mark Twain's cogent and entertaining argument in support of a perpetual property right

ory generally concede that the authors' rights must be limited in time and scope, provided that authors receive a fair return for their labors.[35] Even so, they continue to employ the property analogy in defense of the copyright system[36] and to couch the relation between authors and their work as "absolute possession" and the "exclusive right of use and disposal,"[37] classical liberal terminology for people's dominion over external things.

Significantly, both the utilitarian and natural rights models assume and require the free alienability of copyright. Under the utilitarian model, the widespread dissemination of intellectual works is as important a goal of copyright as is their creation. Since dissemination is accomplished by publishers and distributors, rather than authors, copyright is designed as much to protect the publisher's investment in bringing a work to market as it is to give the author an incentive to produce.[38] Thus, since the Statute of Anne of 1710, the English predecessor to U.S. copyright law, statutory copyright privileges have been accorded to authors' assigns as well as to authors themselves.[39]

Moreover, the utilitarian model of economic incentive to stimulate author production and publisher dissemination presupposes a private-property based milieu in which authors' and publishers'

---

in literary works is presented in MARK TWAIN, *Petition Concerning Copyright, in* THE COMPLETE HUMOROUS SKETCHES AND TALES OF MARK TWAIN 1875 (C. Naider ed., 1961).

35 This is much more modest than the historical claim for perpetual property right, since it introduces the question of what is a fair return. *See* Stephen Breyer, *The Uneasy Case for Copyright: A Study of Copyright in Books, Photocopies, and Computer Programs*, 84 HARV. L. REV. 281, 284-85 (1970). Earlier proponents of the natural rights theory of copyright maintained that an author is entitled to whatever profits his mental products produce, without limit in amount or time. *See, e.g., Millar*, 98 Eng. Rep. at 231 (Yates, describing the argument of William Blackstone before the court). Advocates of a fair return contend that the securing of this entitlement is an independent and proper goal of the U.S. Copyright Act. *See* Fisher, *supra* note 30, at 1688-89 (arguing that the Supreme Court has alluded to a right of fair return that is independent of considerations of social utility); David Ladd, *The Harm of the Concept of Harm in Copyright*, 30 J. COPYRIGHT SOC'Y 421, 425-27 (1982-83) (asserting that the basis of U.S. copyright is "a felt sense of what is right and just"). *See also* Alfred C. Yen, *Restoring the Natural Law: Copyright as Labor and Possession*, 51 OHIO ST. L.J. 517, 546-47 (1990) (arguing that the limits to the scope of copyright protection can be found in a careful use of natural law principles).

36 *See generally* Gordon, *supra* note 21.

37 *See* Ladd, *supra* note 35, at 426 (quoting from statement of Professor Nathan Shaler presented to Congress in 1936 by then Register of Copyrights Throvald Solberg); RAND, *supra* note 33, at 130.

38 *See* Breyer, *supra* note 35, at 292, 293-94.

39 *See, e.g.*, 8 Anne, c. 19 (1710); 17 U.S.C. § 106 (1988) (according exclusive rights to the "owner of copyright"). Prior to the Statute of Anne, state grants of exclusive printing rights were accorded solely to publishers, not to authors. They were designed to encourage and regulate the printing trade, rather than give incentives to authors. Herman Finkelstein, *The Copyright Law—A Reappraisal*, 104 U. PA. L. REV. 1025, 1033-35 (1956). Publishers, not authors, were the prime beneficiaries of the Statute of Anne as well, since it was the practice at the time for publishers to take assignment of all rights in a work upon purchase of the manuscript. KAPLAN, *supra* note 34, at 7-9.

rewards are determined in the marketplace. This model necessarily views intellectual works as commodities. Their social utility and value to the author is measured by the amount the public will pay for them. Thus Adam Smith, although generally critical of monopoly privileges, lauded the temporary monopoly granted to authors and their assigns under the Statute of Anne as an efficient means of stimulating book production: "[I]f the book be a valuable one the demand for it in [the copyright period] will probably be a considerable addition to [the author's] fortune. But if it is of no value the advantage he can reap from it will be very small."[40] Modern proponents of Smith's functionalist, economic analysis view the creation of works of authorship much like the production of fungible consumer goods. They minimize non-economic inducements for such creation, such as prestige and the simple desire to create, and propose fine-tuning the copyright system to provide just the right amount of incentive for creative activity, without leading to under- or over-stimulation of production.[41]

For proponents of the natural rights theory of copyright, alienability follows from the analogization of copyright to the liberal prototype of property. The products of mental labor are their creator's property, just like the fruits of physical labor. And since alienability is an essential characteristic of property, products of mental labor, like corporeal property, must be fully "saleable."[42]

---

40 ADAM SMITH, LECTURES ON JURISPRUDENCE 83 (R.L. Meek, D.D. Raphael, P.G. Stein eds., Glasgow ed. 1978). Smith's intellectual descendants have not been so benign in their treatment of copyright. Encouraged in part by the Supreme Court utilitarian orientation to copyright, several commentators have questioned to what extent, if any, the exclusive privileges granted to authors and their assigns can be justified on economic grounds. *See* Fisher, *supra* note 30, at 1723-26 (calling for the replacement of copyright entitlements with liability rules and compulsory licensing systems on "economic efficiency" grounds); Stephen Breyer, *supra* note 35, at 281 (casting doubt on whether copyright is the most efficient means to encourage production of works of authorship and concluding that, at the very least, copyright protection should not be extended or strengthened); Hurt & Schuchman, *The Economic Rationale of Copyright*, 56 AM. ECON. REV. 421, 439 (1966) (arguing that "the traditional assumption that copyrights enhance the general welfare is at least subject to attack on theoretical [economic] grounds"). *But cf.* William M. Landes & Richard A. Posner, *An Economic Analysis of Copyright Law*, 18 J. OF LEGAL STUD. 325 (1989) (seeking to explain basic tenets of copyright doctrine on economic efficiency grounds). Functionalist criticism of copyright has a long history. In debates over the Literary Copyright Act of 1842, Lord Macauley attacked copyright as an undesirable monopoly that could be justified only to the extent that it achieved its objective of encouraging authors to write. *See* T. MACAULEY, SPEECHES ON COPYRIGHT (C. Gaston ed., 1914).

41 *See, e.g.*, John Cirace, *When Does Complete Copying of Copyrighted Works for Purposes Other Than for Profit or Sale Constitute Fair Use? An Economic Analysis of the Sony Betamax and Williams & Williams Cases*, 28 ST. LOUIS U. L.J. 647, 681 (1984) (arguing that overcompensation to copyright owners "may overstimulate production of their works"); Landes & Posner, *supra* note 40, at 327-28 (stating that works will be created "only if the difference between expected revenues and the cost of making copies equals or exceeds the cost of expression").

42 Millar v. Taylor, 98 Eng. Rep. 201, 221 (K.B. 1769) (Aston, J.).

Alienability has also traditionally been required to enable the author to "reap the pecuniary profits of his own ingenuity and labour."[43] At the time of the enactment of the Statute of Anne, like today, the principal means by which authors could earn a return from their labor was to bring their works to the market by selling or licensing the copyright to a publisher.[44] In addition, alienability was seized upon as a mechanism for limiting the duration of the author's property right. In 1834, in its seminal decision on the issue of the perpetual copyright, the United States Supreme Court accepted the Lockean argument that "a literary man is as much entitled to the product of his labour as any other member of society."[45] The Court ruled, however, that the author "realises this product by the transfer of his manuscripts, or in the sale of his works, when first published."[46] The author's natural law property right is either assigned to the transferee of the unpublished manuscript or extinguished by the work's sale to the public. The Court held, therefore, that copyright subsists in the work only to the extent provided by federal statute.[47] Finally, modern natural rights advocates rely upon copyright's free transferability to support their efforts to legitimize the copyright system by drawing parallels between copyright and tangible property.[48]

B. *The Continental Heritage: Property v. Personality*

In contrast to the utilitarian approach that dominates American copyright doctrine, Continental jurists have generally been re-

---

[43] *Millar*, 98 Eng. Rep. at 252 (L. Mansfield).

[44] Throughout the eighteenth century, publishers generally purchased all rights in a work for a lump sum. Finkelstein, *supra* note 39, at 1037. Licensing and royalty arrangements were not developed until later. The sale or license of rights in works of authorship is not the sole arrangement that would provide creators with enough financial security to produce original works. Creators could be supported by private or government grants, or, as very often is the case, receive a salary from an employer who owns the copyright. *See* Breyer, *supra* note 35, at 282-83 (discussing private and government grants); Brown, *supra* note 31, at 591 n.72 (noting that in the Netherlands the government pays a salary to recognized professional artists). One could also permit unrestricted use and copying of intellectual works, but require the payment of user fees set by regulation, similar to compulsory licensing systems in effect with regard to certain types of works. *See* Fisher, *supra* note 30, at 1725-26.

[45] Wheaton v. Peters, 33 U.S. (8 Pet.) 591, 657 (1834).

[46] *Id.*

[47] *Id.* at 661. In England, the argument for perpetual copyright was laid to rest by the House of Lords in its celebrated 1774 decision of Donaldson v. Becket, 1 Eng. Rep. 837 (1774). The court in *Donaldson* was sharply divided: seven of the eleven judges believed that the authors of a literary work and his assigns had an exclusive, perpetual right of printing and publishing the work at common law, but six judges voted that the right was preempted by the Statute of Anne. Lord Mansfield, a prominent supporter of the perpetual common law right, precluded himself from the proceedings. BIRRELL, *supra* note 29, at 124-28.

[48] *See, e.g.*, Gordon, *supra* note 21, at 1373-74.

luctant to see copyright as a sui generis, instrumentalist construct.[49] Instead, they have devoted substantial effort and imagination in the attempt to assimilate copyright within, or at least place it in relation to, the classical Roman law subdivision of rights: personality rights (rights of reputation, privacy, and other personal dignity interests), real rights (ownership, *usufruct*, easements) and personal rights (contract and tort claims).[50] In time, Continental copyright doctrine incorporated elements of all three categories, with a theoretical foundation consisting of a combination of natural rights doctrine and German idealism.

1. Continental Natural Rights Theory

The theory of natural law copyright was adopted by eighteenth century French authors as a tool for contesting the validity of royal printing privileges.[51] The theory achieved statutory recognition during the French Revolution, which swept away the royal printing privileges and replaced them with legislation based on the doctrine of intellectual property. The Revolutionary Laws of January 13-19, 1791, and July 19, 1793, codified inherent, exclusive rights of authors, dramatists, composers, and artists in their works.[52] The rights of such creators are viewed not as a statutory concession, but as a form of property that the legislature is obliged to recognize and protect.[53] The Law of July 19, 1793, explicitly conferred the

---

49 Even jurists who viewed copyright as a field apart from the classical rights generally categorized it as either a right that vests automatically upon the work's creation or a statutory privilege serving as a legitimate reward for social service, as opposed to an incentive for production. *See* Boudewijn Bouckaert, *What is Property?*, 13 HARV. J.L. & PUB. POL'Y 775, 792-93 (1990) (discussing the theories of Renouard, Roguin, and Picard); PIERRE RECHT, LE DROIT D'AUTEUR, UNE NOUVELLE FORME DE PROPRÍETÉ (1969) (discussing the intellectual property theory of Pouliett).

50 Bouckaert, *supra* note 49, at 793. *See also* RECHT, *supra* note 49 (discussing the competing theories of Continental jurists regarding the nature of author's rights and presenting his own conception of copyright as a new form of property).

51 Bouckaert, *supra* note 49, at 791. For an insightful and detailed account of the use of natural law theory by publishers and authors and the debate regarding the nature of authorship in revolutionary France, see Carla Hesse, *Enlightenment Epistemology and the Laws of Authorship in Revolutionary France*, 30 REPRESENTATIONS 109 (1990). As Hesse points out, French publishers claimed, like their English counterparts, that their rights derived from a perpetual natural right, rather than from a state privilege. French playwrights claimed a natural right in the work in an effort to wrest away control from theater owners, who held the sole royal privileges in dramatic works. *Id.* at 112, 122, 125-26.

52 *See* SAM RICKETSON, THE BERNE CONVENTION FOR THE PROTECTION OF LITERARY AND ARTISTIC WORKS 1886-1986, at 5-6 (1987).

53 In contrast to the copyright granted to authors by the Statute of Anne, the *droits d'auteur* arose automatically upon creation of a work, required no registration, deposit or other formalities, and extended for the life of the creator plus an additional five or ten years. (Even this was seen as a necessary, pragmatic compromise of the ideal of a perpetual property right.) *Id.* Limitations on the term of protection were justified by practical necessity. Lamartine, for example, distinguished the philosopher's recognition of a perpetual property right in an author's creation, akin to the natural right to the fruits of one's physi-

right to assign this property, and provided that assigns were to enjoy the same exclusive rights for the same period as the creator and his heirs.[54]

The alienability of the author's property rights was central to the natural rights component of *droits d'auteur.* Le Chapelier's report accompanying the 1793 revolutionary law referred to the author's work as " 'the most sacred and the most legitimate, the most unassailable and most personal of all of properties."[55] But this glowing pronouncement of authors' rights was tempered by other considerations. First, the Revolutionary legislators recognized the public interest in limiting the absolute character of the property right. Second, in the wake of the dissolution of royal privileges the legislators wished to provide publishers and theatrical companies with a legal basis for protecting their interests in intellectual works.[56] As in the United States, the limitation of the author's property right was justified by equating public dissemination with alienation. As Le Chapelier stated: "[W]hen an author has handed his work over to the public, [the author] has made [the public] a party to his property or, rather, he has transferred his property to it in full."[57] Publishers and theatrical companies found protection in the substitution of contract rights for royal privileges. By acquiring the author's property rights in a voluntary exchange, they obtained the legal authority to reproduce or perform the author's work and to prevent its infringement.[58]

The concept of ownership by natural right became the favored slogan of nineteenth-century Continental authors in their campaigns for legislative and international treaty recognition of economic rights in their work.[59] These efforts reached fruition in 1880 when the French Court of Cassation ruled that, except for the

---

cal labor, from the legislator's obligation to eschew absolute principals in favor of practical legislation reflective of the mores and customs of the time. E. LABOULAYE, ETUDES SUR LA PROPRIETE LITTERAIRE XX (1858), *quoted in* BIRRELL, *supra* note 29, at 19.

For a discussion of republican ideology in early French copyright law, see Hesse, *supra* note 51; Ginsburg, *supra* note 30.

54 RICKETSON, *supra* note 52, at 5-6.

55 André Kerever, *The French Revolution and Authors' Rights*, 141 R.I.D.A. 9 (1989); *see also* Radojkovic, *Copyright: A General Structural Survey*, 1 COPYRIGHT 57, 60 n.22 (1965).

56 *See* Kerever, *supra* note 55, at 9.

57 *Id.* (quoting Le Chapelier's Report Accompanying the Law of 19 July 1793) (emphasis omitted).

58 *Id.* at 10.

59 The 1858 Brussels Conference on Literary and Artistic Property and the 1878 Paris Conference of the International Literary Association (headed by Victor Hugo) both enacted resolutions calling for international recognition of authors' natural property rights in their works. *See* RICKETSON, *supra* note 52, at 42, 46. For a detailed chronological account of the use of traditional property theory to characterize and promote authors' rights in nineteenth-century Europe, see RECHT, *supra* note 49, 48-60.

limitation on its duration dictated by the public interest, literary and artistic property have the same characteristics as any other form of property, and must be treated in the same fashion.[60]

By 1880, however, the property analogy begun to encounter significant opposition among Continental jurists.[61] Some argued that the rights accorded to and claimed by authors did not comport with the essential characteristics of real rights.[62] For others, the concepts of property and intellectual property had come to connote a bourgeois exclusion of the general public from its common inheritance.[63] For still others, the property analogy did not adequately express the growing emphasis on individual personality and the personal connection between authors and their creations.[64] As a result of such opposition, Continental jurists turned increasingly to German idealism as the grounding point for copyright doctrine. They based their theory on the writings of Kant and Hegel, which posit a sharp distinction between inalienable person-

---

60 Judgment of Aug. 16, 1880 (Affaire Masson), Cass. civ. 3e, 1881 S. Jur. I 25, *quoted and discussed in* RECHT, *supra* note 49, at 50-51.

61 Although this marked the end of the effort to include copyright within the classical real-right construct, natural-law/property-right theory continues to influence Continental jurisprudence. The opening sentence of the French Act provides that "[t]he author of an intellectual work shall, by the mere fact of its creation, enjoy an exclusive incorporeal property right in the work, effective against all persons." FRENCH ACT, *supra* note 25, art. 1. Similarly, the German Constitutional Court has consistently held that protection of authors' rights is based on the guarantee of property afforded by the German Constitution. As a result, although the legislature has a degree of latitude in defining the scope of protection, it cannot derogate from the author's property rights in his work as recognized in the Constitution. Eugen Ulmer & Hans Hugo VanRauscher auf Weeg, *Germany (Federal Republic)*, *in* STEPHEN M. STEWART, INTERNATIONAL COPYRIGHT AND NEIGHBORING RIGHTS 417 (2d ed. 1989).

62 The limited duration and incorporeal subject matter of copyright were seen as the principle obstacles to its classification as property. *See* French government comment on the Law of 14 July 1866, *quoted in* RECHT, *supra* note 49, at 55-56 (explaining deletion of reference to property in title of authors' rights law by limited duration of authors' rights); E. POUILLET, TRAITE THEORIQUE ET PRATIQUE DE LA PROPRIETE LITTERAIRE ET ARTISTIQUE 28 (3d ed. 1908) (1879), *quoted in* RECHT, *supra* note 49, at 62-63 (maintaining that copyright is a separate form of property, different from traditional Roman concept because its subject matter is intangible). In 1887, the Court of Cassation reversed its position on the classification of copyright as property, and held that "authors' rights confer only a temporary exclusive privilege of commercial exploitation." Judgment of July 27, 1887 (Arrêt Ricordi), Cass. req., 1888 D.P. I 5, note Sarraute, *quoted and discussed in* RECHT, *supra* note 49, at 68 (translation is this author's).

The description of authors' rights as property continued in German courts through the early twentieth century and was codified in the German copyright laws of 1901 and 1907. RECHT, *supra* note 49, at 75.

63 RECHT, *supra* note 49, at 54-55. Proudhon, for example, rejected the notion of property in intellectual works on the grounds that ideas belong to the community and cannot be appropriated by the author. Thus, while the author may be entitled to a reward, he cannot be considered the owner of his mental products. Radojkovic, *supra* note 55, at 58-59.

64 *See* RECHT, *supra* note 49, at 56-57 (discussing the personalist theories of Bertauld and Morillot).

ality and alienable property.[65]

2. Copyright Doctrine in the Writings of Kant and Hegel

Kant characterized authors' rights as personality rather than property.[66] According to Kant, an author's words are a continuing expression of his inner self. They are an action, an exertion of the author's will, rather than an external thing.[67] An author's right in his work is thus fundamentally a personal right.[68] It is "not a right in an object, . . . but an innate right inherent in his own person."[69]

In essence, the author's personal right is the right to communicate one's thought, which Kant depicted as an aspect of autonomy and freedom, the "one sole original, inborn Right belonging to every man in virtue of his Humanity."[70] A literary work is a speech or discourse addressed to the public in a particular form.[71] It is a narration of the author's thought. The author alone may determine whether and how his words are to be disseminated. Any person who illicitly publishes and distributes a literary work infringes upon the author's freedom because he is speaking in the author's name without the author's consent.[72] The infringer is, in effect, forcing the author to speak against his will, in a forum and through a vehicle that is not of the author's choosing.[73]

The author's right of communication also implicates his contractual autonomy. Part and parcel of an individual's innate freedom is the right to not be be bound by others, except by choice.[74] A person may limit his active free will with respect to a given action or thing only by the autonomous exercise of his will in coming to

---

65 For an insightful analysis of the subject/object dichotomy in the work of Kant and Hegel, see Radin, *supra* note 1, at 1891-94.

66 For Kant, the only propertizable external objects of the will were external corporeal things, another's free will in performance of a particular act, and certain status relationships. IMMANUEL KANT, THE PHILOSOPHY OF LAW 64 (W. Hastie trans., photo reprint 1887) (1974). For an illuminating discussion of the development of early copyright theory in Germany during Kant's time, see MARTHA WOODMANSEE, THE AUTHOR, ART, AND THE MARKET: REREADING THE HISTORY OF AESTHETICS 35-55 (1994).

67 Kant differentiated between literary works, which he categorized as action ("opera"), or an exercise of the author's powers, and works of art, which he depicted as corporeal objects ("opus") that are beyond the ambit of copyright protection. *See infra* note 84.

68 IMMANUEL KANT, *Von der Unrechtm assigket des Buchernachdruckes, in* IMMANUEL KANTS WERKE 213, 221 (E. Cassirer ed., 1913) (1785).

69 "[I]st aber kein Recht in der Sache, . . . sondera ein angebornes Recht in seiner eignen Person." *Id.* at 221 n.1 (quote translated by author and Joël Dorkam).

70 KANT, *supra* note 66, at 56.

71 *Id.* at 129-31; KANT, *supra* note 68, at 221.

72 KANT, *supra* note 68, at 213-14; KANT, *supra* note 66, at 129-30.

73 *See* KANT, *supra* note 68, at 221 n.1 (an author may not be compelled to speak against his will).

74 KANT, *supra* note 66, at 56.

an agreement with another.[75]

The author's decision to create his work and have it published requires such an autonomous exercise of free will. Kant viewed the publication of a literary work as a tripartite transaction between the author, the publisher, and the public. The author creates the work and decides to communicate it to the public; the publisher disseminates the work on behalf of the author; and the public has certain rights to receive the work.[76] It is the author who must determine whether to conduct the transaction, and through which publisher his work is to be communicated. Viewed in this manner, the illicit publisher infringes upon the author's contractual autonomy, as well as upon his right of communication. By disseminating the author's work without the author's consent, the illicit publisher conducts a transaction as if on behalf of the author, but against the author's wishes.[77]

In Kant's view, however, the author does not have unlimited contractual freedom. While the author may grant to others the right to *use* his work, he may not transfer title in the work or assign his rights with respect to it.[78] Therefore, the publisher may disseminate a literary work only as the author's agent, in the author's name, and on the author's behalf.[79] The publisher's rights in the work derive solely from his agency commission, and not from any proprietary interest. In fact, the publisher's rights, even in an original manuscript that he has purported to have purchased from the author, do not extend beyond his use of the manuscript to further the transaction between the author and the public.[80]

The inalienability of the author's rights in his work follows from Kant's categorization of a literary work as part of the author's

---

75 KANT, *supra* note 68, at 219.

76 *Id.* at 213-16. Although the publication of a literary work is not a typical commercial transaction, it is founded upon contractual and quasi-contractual rights and duties. Thus, for example, an author may not grant publication rights to more than one publisher, since this would render superfluous the work of the first publisher. *Id.* at 215-16. At the same time, the publisher has certain obligations towards the public to disseminate the author's work. If the author dies without heirs prior to publication, the public may require that the publisher disseminate copies of the work in an adequate number and of an acceptable quality, or that he transfer the manuscript to another publisher who is able to do so. KANT, *supra* note 66, at 131.

77 KANT, *supra* note 68, at 215 n.1.

78 KANT, *supra* note 66, at 130.

79 *See id.* at 130-31; KANT, *supra* note 68, at 215-16. According to one commentator, Kant's desire to find a legal basis for protecting publishers was no less than his concern for authors. *See* 1 STIG STRÖMHOLM, LE DROIT MORAL DE L'AUTEUR 184 (1967). However, Kant believed that publisher's rights are, in essence, derived from those of the author, and do not amount to an independent proprietary interest. *See* KANT, *supra* note 66, at 124-25.

80 KANT, *supra* note 68, at 219-20.

person, as opposed to an external thing.[81] As a result of its identification with personality, a literary work is a component of the inalienable subject. It is not an object that may be acquired and exchanged by exercise of human will. Kant emphasized this distinction by contrasting books with money. For Kant, money expresses the transferability of external objects in its purest and most developed form. Money is "the greatest and most useable of all the Means of human intercommunication through Things, in the way of Purchase and Sale in commerce."[82] It "is a thing which can only be made use of, by being alienated or exchanged."[83] A book, on the other hand, is more than merely an external thing that can be bought and sold. It is the author's communication to the public, and thus is imbued with the personality of the author. It is the "means of carrying on the interchange of Thought," as opposed to commerce.[84]

In contrast to Kant, Hegel regarded intellectual works as external things, rather than extensions of personality. Although Hegel viewed mental ability as an inalienable part of the self, he maintained that the formulation of expression in an external medium could transform products of the mind into alienable property.[85] Mental products are externalized when they are expressed in a form that may be produced by other people.[86] For Hegel, both artistic and literary works met this criterion for propertization. A work of art is the portrayal of thought in an external medium that can be copied by another.[87] A literary work is an expression of thought in a series of separable abstract symbols that can be mechanically reproduced.[88] As in modern copyright law, the author does not necessarily alienate his right to reproduce his work

---

81 *Id.* at 220-21.

82 KANT, *supra* note 66, at 124.

83 *Id.* at 125.

84 *Id.* Curiously, Kant also differentiated between books and works of art, the latter of which he classified solely as objects. Immanuel Kant, *Was ist ein Buch?, in* DIE METAPHYSIK DIE SITTEN 405 (W. Weischedel ed., 1977), *quoted in translation in* Palmer, *Are Patents and Copyrights Morally Justified? The Philosophy of Property Rights and Ideal Objects,* 13 HARV. J.L. & PUB. POL'Y 817, 840 (1990).

85 GEORGE W. F. HEGEL, HEGEL'S PHILOSOPHY OF RIGHT §§ 43, 68 (T. Knot trans., 1952).

86 *Id.* § 68.

87 *Id.*

88 *Id.* Hegel also addressed the traditional idea-expression dichotomy in copyright doctrine, whereby the author's form of expression is protected, but the underlying idea is not. Hegel posited that ideas are not susceptible to protection because "the purpose of a product of mind is that people other than its author should understand it and make it the possession of their ideas . . . ." This, in turn, entitles the readers to express in their own way what they have learned, thereby converting their expression into a thing which they can alienate and regard as their own property. *Id.* at 55.

when he sells his manuscript or painting to another.[89] But since the right to reproduce is a part of the work's "external use," the author is free to part with the right "as a thing of value, or to attach no value to it all and surrender it together with the single exemplar of his work."[90]

3. The German Idealist Legacy

The writings of Kant and Hegel, as interpreted and applied by later theorists, have profoundly influenced the development of Continental copyright law. The Kantian conception of author's rights has found expression in the monist school of copyright theory, the most prominent proponents of which have been Otto von Gierke and Philipp Allfeld.[91] Monists hold that it is an author's fundamentally personal right[92] to determine when, in what form, and to what object his creative product is to be communicated to the public.[93] Intellectual works are part of the internal, personal sphere. Accordingly, an author's rights are rights of personality, rather than of property. They are akin to the dominion which one has over a part of oneself.[94]

Monists recognize that authors have an interest in economic exploitation of their works as well as a personal interest in the nature of their communication to the public. But monists see the economic interests as subsumed within the personal. Authors' rights may have patrimonial consequences or attributes, but there is no clear line of demarcation between these attributes and the fundamental core of personal interest prerogatives.[95] According to the monistic concept, the author's economic exploitation rights and personal rights are interrelated and mutually beneficial.[96] For example, the author's right to object to modifications of the work

---

89 *Id.* § 69.

90 *Id. But see* Justin Hughes, *The Philosophy of Intellectual Property*, 77 GEO. L.J. 287, 348-50 (1988). Hughes claims that Hegel posited that the complete alienation of an author's rights is an impermissible surrender of the self. Hughes's claim, however, is based upon a misreading of Hegel's explicit and much more limited statement that an author who transfers a copy of his work has simply "not necessarily alienated" the right to reproduce the work and "may reserve" that right to himself.

91 *See* STRÖMHOLM, *supra* note 79, at 329-31; FRANCIS J. KASE, COPYRIGHT THOUGHT IN CONTINENTAL EUROPE: ITS DEVELOPMENT, LEGAL THEORIES AND PHILOSOPHY 10-11, 16, 30-31 (1967). Gierke set forth his personalist theory of copyright in his two-volume work, DEUTSCHES PRIVATRECHT (1895). Allfeld expounded his views in KOMMENTAR ZU DEN GESETZEN (1902).

92 "Personal right" is referred to here in the sense of related to the self, and not to the classical Roman law meaning of the term.

93 *See* STRÖMHOLM, *supra* note 79, at 330; Radojkovic, *supra* note 55, at 61.

94 STRÖMHOLM, *supra* note 79, at 329.

95 *Id.* at 331.

96 *See* ADOLF DIETZ, COPYRIGHT LAW IN THE EUROPEAN COMMUNITY 67 (1978).

supports his personal interest in maintaining the integrity of his work, as well as his financial interest in preventing the work from being impaired by distortions.[97] At the same time, the successful commercial exploitation of the work serves the author's personal interests by disseminating his ideas and enhancing his reputation.[98]

The monists believe that authors' rights are unitary, personal, and inalienable.[99] Authors may grant licenses for the use and exploitation of their works, but they may not waive their rights or assign them to another.[100] Since the focus of the rights is the personality of the author and not his work, title to the rights must always remain with the author.

The monist theory of authors' rights was adopted by the German Act dealing with Copyright and Related Rights of September 9, 1965.[101] Under the German Act, copyright is a unitary right that protects the author with respect to his intellectual and personal relations to his work, as well as with respect to the exploitation of his work.[102] The German Act allows authors to grant licenses to use their works, but does not permit transfer of ownership, except by testamentary disposition.[103] The inalienability of copyright ownership is much more than a theoretical construct. Although an author may grant a global license of all exploitation rights in a work, upon termination of the license for any reason, all rights revert to the author.[104] Moreover, as discussed below, even during the term of the license, the author retains statutory rights that significantly restrict the licensee's right and ability to exploit the work.

In opposition to the Kantian-based monist theory of author's rights, Hegel's adherents developed a dualist theory, which assumes that the author's personal and economic interests are each protected by a legally and conceptually distinct set of rights.[105] Although the author has an indissoluble personal interest in the

---

97 *Id.*

98 *Id.*

99 STRÖMHOLM, *supra* note 79, at 331.

100 In examining the German Copyright Law of 1901, Allfeld concluded that the global alienation permitted by the law referred to alienation of use (der Ausübung nach) and not of title (der Substanz nach). *Id.*

101 *See* GERMAN ACT, *supra* note 22. The German Act has been amended in 1969, 1970, 1972, 1973, 1974 and 1985.

102 *See* GERMAN ACT, *supra* note 22, art. 11.

103 *Id.* arts. 29, 31. *See also* Dietz, *supra* note 25, at FRG-56.

104 Dietz, *supra* note 25, at FRG-48.

105 The author's personal interests are protected by the moral or personal rights of paternity, integrity, disclosure, and retraction. The author's pecuniary interests are protected by the rights to exploit the work commercially through reproduction or direct communication to the public.

way his work is presented to the world, he also enjoys the independent right to exploit his work commercially. The proponents of the dualist approach, the most prominent of which has been Josef Kohler,[106] follow Hegel's position that intellectual works are externalized products, which are separate and apart from the author's inner self.[107] Kohler posited that the author's pecuniary rights are essentially rights of property in "an incorporeal intangible legal commodity which stands outside man's personality."[108] But parallel to this classical "real right" are the author's personal prerogatives to have his work attributed to him and to determine when and in what form the work is to be presented to the public.[109] These prerogatives are anchored in the author's general rights of personality, which survive the market exploitation of the "immaterial good" produced by the author.

> [T]he writer can not only demand that no strange work be presented as his, but that his own work not be presented in a changed form. The author can make this demand even when he has given up his copyright. This demand is not so much an exercise of dominion over my own work, as it is of dominion over my being, over my personality which thus gives me the right to demand that no one shall share in my personality and have me say things which I have not said.[110]

The French Copyright Act of 1957[111] bears the imprint of dualist theory. The dualist nature of French *droits d'auteur* is expressed in Article 2 of the French Act, which accords authors an

---

106 KASE, *supra* note 91, at 12. Kohler characterized the author's personal rights as part of the general law protecting the individual's personality interests, and as such falling outside the law of intellectual property. *Id.* Other dualists see the author's economic and personal rights as parallel but distinct subdoctrines of the law regarding author's rights. *See* Strömholm, *supra* note 79, at 11-12.

107 *See supra* text accompanying notes 85-89. Kohler was influenced by Fichte and Schopenhauer as well as Hegel. KASE, *supra* note 91, at 39.

108 KASE, *supra* note 91, at 12 (quoting and translating JOSEF KOHLER, URHEBERRECHT AN SCHRIFTWERKEN UND VERLAGSRECHT 1 (1907)). Kohler held that an author has an exclusive, *sui generis* immaterial property right (*immaterial guter rechte*) in his work by virtue of his having created it, just as in primitive times the maker of a material object was automatically its owner. JOSEF KOHLER, DAS AUTORRECHT 98 (1880).

Intellectual productions may be subject to private ownership only temporarily, since "mental achievements become in time universal cultural possessions, and the formative material of human activity." JOSEF KOHLER, PHILOSOPHY OF LAW 122 (A. Albrecht trans., 1914).

109 JOSEF KOHLER, FORSCHUNGEN AUS DEM PATENTRECHT, MANNHEIM 114-16 (1888), *discussed and quoted in part in* RECHT, *supra* note 49, at 78-80. Kohler posited that the author's personal rights are "clamped together" but not "soldered to" the author's pecuniary rights. *Id.*

110 JOSEF KOHLER, URHEBERRECHT AN SCHRIFTWERKEN AND VERLAGSRECHT 15 (1907), *quoted and translated in* Damich, *supra* note 10, at 29.

111 *See* FRENCH ACT, *supra* note 25.

"exclusive incorporeal property right" in their works and enumerates two distinct subsets of that right: "attributes of an intellectual and moral nature," and attributes of "an economic nature."[112] The conceptual duality of the French *droits d'auteur* finds practical expression in the different treatment given to moral and economic rights in the French Act provisions governing alienability, transmission, and duration. The author's moral rights are "perpetual, inalienable and imprescriptible."[113] The author's exploitation rights, on the other hand, are assignable independently of the moral rights[114] and are of limited duration.[115]

The dual character of French *droits d'auteur* should not be overemphasized, however. French commentators speak of the interdependence of the moral and economic rights, and indeed, of the predominance of the former over the latter.[116] Moreover, authors' moral rights and other inalienable statutory rights impose significant restraints upon the transfer of economic rights, and provide for an indissoluble link between authors and their works. Thus, as one French commentator has concluded, although French law conceives of authors' creations as economically exploitable property, it does not permit the acquisition of full ownership in an intellectual work.[117]

III. The Moral Right And Its United States Parallels

Autonomy inalienabilities under Continental law arise principally from the idea that an author has a personal connection with his work that remains intact even if someone else has acquired the rights to exploit the work. This personal connection has been variously described as one of artistic reputation, emotional sensibility, and dominion of personality. To be certain, autonomy inalienabilities do serve to protect authors' standing in the community, subjective feelings of attachment to their work, and personal

---

112 Henri Desbois, Le Droit D'Auteur en France 275 (3d ed. 1978). The language of Article 2 seems to suggest that authors hold a single right with two sets of attributes. This could coincide with the monist view, depending upon the extent to which the attributes are viewed as interdependent and interrelated. Therefore, the dualist nature of French *droits d'auteur* would seem to be founded in the divergent treatment of moral and economic rights in French doctrine, rather than in the language of Article 2.

113 French Act, *supra* note 25, art. 6, para. 2.

114 *Id.* art. 30. Ironically, although transfers of ownership are fully permitted, French law does not recognize copyright licenses as such; authors grant "authorizations" that in fact amount to licenses of certain rights. Lucas & Plaisant, *supra* note 25, at FRA-59.

115 French Act, *supra* note 25, arts. 21-23. As a general rule, the exploitation rights continue for the life of the author, plus 50 years.

116 Desbois, *supra* note 112.

117 *See* Alphonse Tournier, *Peut-on Acquërir la Propriété d'une Oeuvre de l'Esprit selon la loi Francaise du 11 Mars 1957?*, 20 R.I.D.A. 3 (1958).

integrity. But the most important function of autonomy inalienabilities is the protection and promotion of author sovereignty and control over the process of creating and communicating intellectual works. In the aggregate, the restrictions on alienability serve to enhance the author's ability to determine whether, when, in what manner, by whom, and in whose name the work will be presented to the public.[118]

The doctrine of moral right represents the most significant restriction on alienability in Continental copyright law aside from Germany's flat-out prohibition of copyright assignments. In France and Germany, the doctrine of moral right includes four components: the rights of disclosure, withdrawal, attribution, and integrity. The right of disclosure gives to the author the exclusive right to determine whether to create the work, whether the work is completed, and whether and in what manner to disclose the work to the public.[119] The right of withdrawal permits the author to terminate the dissemination or exhibition of the work to the public, even after it has been disclosed.[120] The right of attribution enables the author to require that he be identified as the author of his work, or that the work be published either pseudonymously or anonymously.[121] The right of integrity allows the author to prevent uses or modifications of his work that would prejudice his reputation or other "intellectual interests" as an artist.[122]

As we shall see in this Part and the next, moral rights are not absolute. They are subject to limitations in scope and conditions of good faith exercise that are designed to give weight to competing interests of transferees, other users, and the public. Nevertheless, moral rights constitute a significant burden on a transferee's free use and exploitation of a work. As a general rule, these rights remain with the author even upon the transfer of pecuniary

---

118 Alongside the function of autonomy of expression, certain Continental copyright inalienabilities also serve to promote authors' material interests by guaranteeing authors a higher remuneration than they might otherwise obtain through unregulated negotiation. This interference with the alienability of copyright exploitation rights is part of a general move away from the traditional liberal model to contract freely. In the view of modern Continental theorists, as with many of their American counterparts, limitless freedom of contract is unwarranted where the parties have grossly unequal bargaining power. Eugen Ulmer, *Some Thoughts on the Law of Copyright Contracts*, 7 I.I.C. 202, 210-11 (1976). Continental law, when dealing with copyright contracts, uses the premise that the author is in a weaker economic and negotiating position than the transferee. It is also takes into account the special social value attached to literary and artistic works, and the need to provide economic maintenance for the creators of these works. *Id.* at 211-13.

119 *See infra* notes 129-55 and accompanying text.

120 *See infra* notes 156-64 and accompanying text.

121 *See infra* notes 165-88 and accompanying text.

122 *See infra* notes 189-226 and accompanying text.

rights.[123] Thus, a songwriter who has sold all worldwide exploitation rights in a song may still prevent the public performance of the song in a context or altered form that would damage the songwriter's reputation or vary significantly from the songwriter's artistic concept.[124] In addition, at least in theory, if the songwriter decides after a number of years that he no longer wishes to have the song communicated to the public, he may bring the dissemination of his song to an end.

United States law does not systematically recognize moral rights, although the Visual Artists Rights Act and a number of state acts accord limited moral rights protection to works of fine art. Recent years have seen an abundance of commentary concerning whether, despite the absence of explicit recognition, functional equivalents to moral rights can be found in United States federal and state law.[125] Many commentators contend that the combined legal effect of a patchwork of U.S. laws designed to protect a variety of economic, public, and personal interests results in colorable adherence to at least the moral rights requirements under Article 6*bis* of the Berne Convention.[126] Congress agreed with this conclusion

---

123 *See infra* notes 254-305 and accompanying text. *See also* Judgment of Dec. 12, 1988 (Delorme v. Catena-France), Cour d'appel, P.I.B.D. III, No. 454, 231 (assignment of copyright "for all purposes" did not confer the right to modify the work without the author's consent).

124 In the *Maske in Blau* decision, for example, the German Federal Court of Justice enjoined a stage production licensee from producing a version of an operetta that was said to distort the intent and mood of the original work. Judgment of Apr. 29, 1970, Bundesgerichtshofes [Supreme Court], 55 Entsheidungen des Bundesgerichtshofes in Zivilsacheh [BGHZ] 1.

125 *See, e.g.*, Amarnick, *supra* note 10; Damich, *supra* note 10; Kwall, *supra* note 10; Russell J. DaSilva, *Droit Moral and the Amoral Copyright: A Comparison of Artists' Rights in France and the United States*, 28 BULL. COPYRIGHT SOC'Y 1 (1980); Comment, *An Author's Artistic Reputation Under the Copyright Act of 1976*, 92 HARV. L. REV. 1490 (1979) [hereinafter *Reputation Comment*]; Susan L. Solomon, Comment, *Monty Python and the Lanham Act: In Search of the Moral Right*, 30 RUTGERS L. REV. 452 (1977); Comment, *Moral Rights for Artists Under the Lanham Act: Gilliam v. American Broad-casting Co.*, 18 WM. & MARY L. REV. 595 (1977); Joseph B. Valentine, Comment, *Copyright: Moral Right—A Proposal*, 43 FORDHAM L. REV. 793 (1975); Dominique Giocanti, *Moral Rights: Authors' Protection and Business Need*, 10 J. INT'L L. & ECON. 627 (1975); Comment, *Toward Artistic Integrity: Implementing Moral Right Through Extension of Existing American Legal Doctrines*, 60 GEO. L.J. 1539 (1972); James M. Treece, *American Law Analogues of the Authors' "Moral Right"*, 16 AM. J. COMP. L. 487 (1968); Comment, *The Moral Rights of the Author: A Comparative Study*, 71 DICK. L. REV. 93 (1966); William Strauss, *The Moral Right of the Author*, 4 AM. J. COMP. L. 506 (1955); Arthur L. Stevenson, Jr., *Moral Right and the Common Law: A Proposal*, 6 COPYRIGHT L. SYMP. (ASCAP) 89 (1953); Arthur S. Katz, *The Doctrine of Moral Right and American Copyright Law—A Proposal*, 24 S. CAL. L. REV. 375 (1951).

126 The relevant portions of Article 6bis read as follows:

> (1) Independently of the author's economic rights, and even after the transfer of the said rights, the author shall have the right to claim authorship of the work and to object to any distortion, mutilation or other modification of, or other derogatory action in relation to, the said work, which would be prejudicial to his honor or reputation.
>
> . . . .

in enacting the Berne Convention Implementation Act. The Act adopted the view that no expansion of U.S. law was necessary to meet the United States' obligations under Article 6*bis*.[127] But the Berne Convention's moral right requirements are considerably weaker than the provisions in effect in France, Germany, and other civil law countries.[128] As we shall see, the United States moral right analogues fall short of the more stringent French and German provisions, in terms of both their raw legal result and overall social effect. As such, Continental moral rights represent a considerably greater restriction on copyright alienability than do the U.S. analogues.

A. *The Right of Disclosure*

The right of disclosure is codified in both the French and German Acts.[129] Each provides that authors shall have the exclusive right to determine whether and how their work is disseminated.[130] The German Act goes beyond the French in one respect. In addition to the right to control the dissemination of the work itself, the German Act also gives the author the exclusive right to issue the first public summmary or description of a new and as yet unpublished work.[131] In other respects, however, the French provision appears to afford authors a greater measure of control than the German. As we will see, French doctrine and commentary strongly

---

> (3) The means of redress for safeguarding the rights granted by this Article shall be governed by the legislation of the country where protection is claimed.

Berne Convention, *supra* note 11, art. 6*bis*.

127 Berne Implementation Act provides that "[t]he obligations of the United States under the Berne Convention may be performed only pursuant to appropriate domestic law," and that "[t]he amendments made by this Act, together with the law as it exists on the date of the enactment of this Act, satisfy the obligations of the United States in adhering to the Berne Convention and no further rights or interests shall be recognized or created for that purpose." Pub. L. No. 100-568, § 2(2), (3), 102 Stat. 2853 (1988). The Act further provides that "[t]he provisions of the Berne Convention, the adherence of the United States thereto, and satisfaction of United States obligations thereunder, do not expand or reduce any right of an author of a work" with respect to the paternity or integrity right. *Id.* § 3(b).

128 The Berne Convention's moral right requirements are weaker in a number of ways. First, the Convention covers only the rights of attribution and integrity, and not the rights of disclosure and withdrawal. Second, the Berne integrity right arguably protects only against distortions that would damage an author's honor or reputaiton, and not against uses that simply would contradict the author's artistic concept. Third, the Convention arguably permits the waiver and transfer of the attribution and integrity rights independently from the author's pecuniary rights, whereas under French and German law the moral right is said to be inalienable.

129 French Act, *supra* note 25, art. 19; German Act, *supra* note 22, art. 12. The French right is generally translated as the right of divulgation, and the German right, the right of dissemination. "Right of disclosure" is used in this Article.

130 French Act, *supra* note 25, art. 19; German Act, *supra* note 22, art. 12.

131 German Act, *supra* note 22, art. 12(2).

suggest that the author's moral right of disclosure may override his contractual commitments to produce or allow public dissemination of his work. German doctrine is less clear on this point. Some commentators argue that the German disclosure right is essentially coterminous with the pecuniary right of publication; once an author has authorized publication, he is contractually bound to release his work.[132] Other German commentators insist that the disclosure right stands, in some fashion, independently from the publication right.[133] The analysis in this section will be drawn largely from French sources, with an understanding that its applicability to German law is somewhat speculative. In addition, the analysis will not extend to the disclosure right of authors of audiovisual works, since both the French and German Acts contain special provisions that sharply limit the right in the area of film production.[134]

The right of disclosure is founded upon two basic premises. First, an author's work cannot be said to exist as an independent thing that stands outside the author unless and until the author determines that it has been completed.[135] Until that time, the unfinished work is "as though it were retained in its creator's brain . . . a conversation between the author and himself."[136] As a result,

---

[132] Dietz, *supra* note 25, at FRG-84 to FRG-85. Recently, however, Dr. Dietz has noted that the disclosure right extends beyond the scope of the publication right in two respects. First, the disclosure right gives employed and commissioned authors the right to determine when their work is complete and ready to be handed over. Second, according to rules of private international law applicable to the German Act, foreign authors are automatically accorded the disclosure right (together with the attribution and integrity rights), but are accorded the publication right and other economic exploitation rights only when required by Germany's treaty obligations. Adolf Dietz, Legal Principles of Moral Rights in Civil Law Countries 7-8, Presented to the Association Litteraire et Artistique Internationale, Antwerp Congress on the Moral Right of the Author (Sept. 19-24, 1993).

[133] *See* Eric Marcus, *The Moral Right of the Artist in Germany*, 25 COPYRIGHT L. SYMP. (ASCAP) 93, 99 (1975) (noting that most German scholars do accept the moral right of disclosure as an independent right).

[134] The French provisions were added to the French Act by the controversial Law on Authors' Rights and on the Rights of Performers, Producers of Phonograms and Videograms and Audiovisual Communication Enterprises, July 3, 1985, No. 85-660, 1985 J.O. 1, *translated in* UNESCO, 2 COPYRIGHT LAWS AND TREATIES OF THE WORLD (1987) (hereinafter 1985 Amendments). Article 15 of the French Act now provides that if an author refuses or is unable to complete his contribution to an audiovisual work, he may not oppose the use of the part of his contribution already in existence for the purpose of completing the work. Article 19 of the French Act now provides that an author's disclosure right is subject to Article 63-1, which provides that the rights of authors of an audiovisual work, except for authors of its musical score, are deemed to have assigned to the producer their exploitation rights in the work, unless their contract stipulates otherwise. Article 89 of the German Act provides that authors of audiovisual works are deemed, in case of doubt, to have granted to the producer the exclusive right to exploit the work in every known manner.

[135] *See* Raymond Sarraute, *Current Theory on the Moral Right of Authors and Artists Under French Law*, 16 AM. J. COMP. L. 465, 467 (1968).

[136] *Id.* at 471.

a commissioned author's contractual obligation to transfer a work or the rights to exploit the work cannot take effect until the author determines that the work is complete and conforms to his original conception.[137] Thus, an author's good-faith inability to complete a work does not constitute a breach of a commission contract; the author's lack of inspiration is a normal risk contemplated by the parties.[138]

Second, even when a work has been completed, only the author may decide when and how the work will be publicly disclosed. At least under French law, the author enjoys this prerogative even when the work and all rights to exploit it are owned by a transferee.[139] As a result, an artist may prevent a transferee from reproducing and publicly exhibiting even a completed work that is in the transferee's possession. Likewise, an author may prohibit publication of a completed manuscript, even though he has assigned publication rights and delivered the manuscript to his publisher.[140]

The sole, although by no means insubstantial, caveat to the exercise of the right of disclosure, at least after the work has been completed, is the requirement that the author compensate the transferee for damages resulting from the author's breach of contract.[141] This requirement has led some commentators to suggest

---

137 This principle is well illustrated by the renowned case, Judgment of March 19, 1947 (L'Affaire Roualt), Cour d'appel, 1949 D.P. II 20 (Fr.), in which the painter, Roualt, agreed to transfer all of his work to Vollard, an art dealer. Vollard kept over 800 of Roualt's unfinished paintings locked in his gallery, where Roualt would come to apply finishing touches. Upon Vollard's death, his heirs claimed ownership of the paintings. Roualt maintained that the paintings were unfinished and therefore only he could decide when to effect their final delivery. The Paris Court of Appeal ruled in Roualt's favor:

> Whereas, one who negotiates with an artist for an uncompleted work which the author retains in his possession, reserving the right to finish it, contracts for future goods whose ownership can be only transferred by delivery without reservation after completion, and is not like the buyer who purchases an artistic production in any state which the painter intends definitively to part with even though it is in the form of a sketch; Therefore, until final delivery the painter remains master of his work, and may perfect it, modify it, or even leave it unfinished if he loses all hope of making it worthy of himself; This inalienable right, an attribute of the artist's moral right, persists notwithstanding any agreement to the contrary; and the breach of any such agreement exposes the author who changes his mind only to damages.

Discussed and quoted in English translation in Sarraute, *supra* note 135, at 469-70.

138 Sarraute, *supra* note 135, at 468; DESBOIS, *supra* note 112, at 476. In its ruling in the Roualt case, the Paris Court of Appeal suggested that an artist may be required to pay damages even if the artist's failure to deliver results from lack of inspiration. In that case, however, the court required only that the artist refund the advances he had received. Judgment of Mar. 19, 1947, 1949 D.P. II, at 20.

139 Damich, *supra* note 10, at 36; DaSilva, *supra* note 125, at 20.

140 Lucas & Plaisant, *supra* note 25, at FRA-95.

141 *See, e.g.,* Judgment of May 14, 1900 (Whistler v. Eden), Cass. civ., 1900 D.P. I 500 (Fr.) (holding that the artist, Whistler, was not required to deliver a completed portrait that had been commissioned by Eden, but that he had to compensate Eden for his breach of the commission contract). *But see* DESBOIS, *supra* note 112, at 476 (suggesting that in contrast

that the right of disclosure is merely a glorified version of the contract law proscription, found in common and civil law, against the imposition of specific performance in a personal service contract.[142] At first glance, this argument appears to have some merit. According to black-letter contract law, any person—not just an author—whose services have been retained may substitute money damages for promised performance.[143] Like the right of disclosure, this entitlement is inalienable, and any agreement purporting to forfeit it is invalid as a matter of law.[144]

The theoretical justification for the inalienable entitlement to substitute money damages for promised performance differs from that for the right of disclosure. The rule against compulsory performance of a personal service contract is based upon the two-fold rationale of administrative convenience and concern for personality interests. First, compulsory performance would require, in many instances, an inordinate amount of judicial supervision over an extended period of time. Courts would be called upon to undertake the difficult and time-consuming task of gauging whether the defendant is properly performing the services to the best of his ability.[145] Second, the specific performance of a contract requiring the promisor's ongoing personal cooperation with the other party

---

to the right of withdrawal, which the author may exercise only by compensating the transferee, the right of dissemination gives the author the absolute discretion to decide whether to publish the work, exercisable without an obligation to compensate the transferee). On the other hand, a court might order an author to deliver a completed work in accordance with a commission contract where the author seeks to exercise his right of disclosure in bad faith by attempting to obtain a higher price for the work from another party. Giocanti, *supra* note 125, at 634.

The French Act also makes an exception to the right of divulgation for cinematographic works, which combine the creative efforts of several persons. Article 15 provides that an author who refuses or is unable to complete his contribution to such a work may not oppose the use of the part of his contribution already in existence for the purpose of completing the work. FRENCH ACT, *supra* note 25, art. 15.

142 *See, e.g.*, STRÖMHOLM, *supra* note 79, at 23. Article 1142 of the French Civil Code limits the remedy for any contractual breach to an award of damages. André Françon & Jane Ginsburg, *Authors' Rights In France: The Moral Right of the Creator of a Commissioned Work to Compel the Commissioning Party to Complete the Work*, 9 COLUM.-VLA J.L. & ARTS 381 (1985).

143 SAMUEL WILLISTON, A TREATISE ON THE LAW OF CONTRACTS § 1423 (3d ed. 1972); RESTATEMENT (SECOND) OF THE LAW OF CONTRACTS § 367(1) (1981).

144 WILLISTON, *supra* note 143; RESTATEMENT (SECOND) OF THE LAW OF CONTRACTS, *supra* note 143.

145 WILLISTON, *supra* note 143; RESTATEMENT (SECOND) OF THE LAW OF CONTRACTS, *supra* note 143. *See also* Society of Survivors v. Huttenbach, 535 N.Y.S.2d 670, 675 (Sup. Ct. 1988) (society of Holocaust survivors and author not required to work together to complete and publish manuscript on the grounds that a court is unable to mandate cooperation between relevant parties).

Specific performance of plaintiff has an adequate legal remedy. WILLISTON, *supra* note 143, § 1423, at 786.

may threaten his autonomy, integrity, and self-respect.[146] A promisor who is compelled to perform may have to act in dissonance with newly-found but deeply-held convictions, desires, or goals. The inalienable entitlement of substituting money damages for performance enables the promisor to meet contractual obligations in a way that may be less intrusive upon his liberty and less denigrating to his person.[147]

The right of disclosure also touches upon personality interests, but these pertain specifically to the author's act of creation and subsequent continuing relationship with the thing created. Under French doctrine, and possibly under German law as well, a commissioned author enjoys a considerably greater measure of autonomy in deciding whether to comply with the contractual duty to create than does the promisor in a personal service contract in deciding whether to perform. By exercising the right of disclosure, the author who lacks the inspiration to create is apparently excused from the commission contract altogether. In contrast, a promisor who has agreed to provide other types of personal services must fulfill his obligations, if not by specific performance, then by payment of damages.

Recognizing the author's personal interest in controlling the dissemination of a work also yields a different result than protecting the autonomy and integrity of the promisor in a personal services contract. Under moral rights doctrine, even an author who has completed his work may avoid its delivery and public disclosure by compensating the transferee. But general contract doctrine would not entitle the author to substitute damages for performance. Having already performed the personal service of completing the work, the author would suffer no protectible injury to his autonomy and integrity by being compelled to deliver the product.[148] For this reason, when an author breaches his agreement to assign a copyright and deliver the manuscript in which the copyrighted work is embodied, U.S. courts may compel him to do so.[149]

In addition to the contract law doctrine of specific performance, some commentators point to the U.S. Copyright Act's first

---

146 *See* Anthony T. Kronman, *Paternalism and the Law of Contracts*, 92 YALE L.J. 763, 781-85 (1983).

147 *Id.*

148 Contracts for the sale of unique goods, such as a completed painting, are specifically enforceable since only a transfer of property, and not ongoing personal service under the direction of another, is required. *Id.* at 785.

149 *See* Hughes Tool Co. v. Fawcett Publications, Inc., 315 A.2d 577 (Del. 1974) (holding that the manuscript may be recovered at law by a claim for replevin or detinue, and the copyright assignment may be compelled at equity by mandatory injunction).

publication and public display rights as equivalents to the moral right of divulgation.[150] Section 106 of the U.S. Copyright Act accords copyright owners the exclusive right to distribute copies of a work to the public and to display the work publicly.[151] A U.S. author who holds the exclusive rights of publication and display may rely upon them to determine whether, and under what conditions, his work is disseminated. Like his Continental counterpart, he may require that his work be withheld from circulation even if he has transferred possession and title of a manuscript, canvas, or other physical object embodying the work.[152]

Although the U.S. Act's first publication right is essentially a pecuniary right, the Supreme Court has recognized that it also implicates the author's "personal interest in creative control."[153] Nevertheless, in contrast to the Continental moral right of disclosure, the first publication right is fully alienable by the author and any subsequent owner.[154] In fact, where the author created the work during the course of employment or transferred the first publica-

---

150 *See, e.g.*, Paul Goldstein, Copyright: Principles, Law And Practice 643-44 (1989). Prior to the 1976 Copyright Law revision, the right of authors to control first publication was grounded in common law copyright and the right to privacy. *See, e.g.*, Peay v. Curtis Publishing Co., 78 F. Supp. 305 (D.D.C. 1948) (unauthorized publication of plaintiff's photograph in a magazine constituted invasion of privacy). Accordingly, pre-revision commentators looked to these rights as the right of disclosure equivalent. *See, e.g.*, Treece, *supra* note 125, at 488-90; William Strauss, *The Moral Right of the Author, in* 2 Studies on Copyright 113, 136 (1963). The common law copyright and privacy right equivalents of the right of disclosure were preempted by the 1976 U.S. Copyright Act, and thus would no longer provide an independent basis for relief. *See* Goldstein, *supra*, at 646.

151 17 U.S.C. § 106 (1988).

152 Section 202 of the U.S. Copyright Act provides that the transfer of ownership of a material object such as a painting or manuscript does not in itself convey any rights in the copyrighted work embodied in the object. 17 U.S.C. § 202 (1988). On the other hand, the author could not rely on the Copyright Act to prevent any subsequent transfer of the painting or manuscript that amounts to publication. Under the Act, the transfer of ownership in a copy of a work brings into play the first sale doctrine exception to the right of first publication. 17 U.S.C. § 109(a) (1988). Section 109(a) provides that the transferee "is entitled, without the authority of the copyright owner, to sell 'or otherwise dispose . . . of that copy.' " *Id.* Since the term "[copy] includes the material object . . . in which the work is first fixed," 17 U.S.C. § 101 (1988), § 109(a) would require the author to rely upon the applicable state law right of privacy to prevent the exploitation of her previously unpublished work. The question of whether the sale of the original copy would constitute a waiver of the right of privacy would depend upon the particular factual circumstances surrounding the sale.

153 Harper & Row v. Nation Enterprises, 471 U.S. 539, 555 (1984).

154 17 U.S.C. § 201(d) (1988). This section provides that any of the exclusive rights comprised in a copyright may be transferred in whole or in part. The transfer of ownership in a copy of a work also effects a partial waiver of the first publication right under the first sale doctrine. *See supra* note 152; *see also* Society of Survivors v. Huttenbach, 535 N.Y.S.2d 670, 675 (Sup. Ct. 1988) (holding that publisher which had taken assignment of copyright could prevent author from publishing the work elsewhere, but also holding on the facts before it that publisher's publication of the work in the author's name without the author's consent would violate provisions of their contract, and would constitute passing off).

tion right prior to the work's creation, the author may not even be the right's first owner.[155] In that event, the right holder may freely disseminate the work, unhindered by any residual right of the author to prevent it.

B. *The Right of Withdrawal*

According to Continental doctrine, a work remains a continuing communication of the author's thought and expression after it is disseminated to the public. As a result, an author's autonomy interest in determining the conditions of this communication to the public extends beyond the initial divulgation and publication of the work. Moral rights doctrine protects this ongoing autonomy interest by according authors the right to withdraw a work from publication or to make modifications after the work is disseminated.

These rights are codified in Article 32 of the French Act.[156] Article 32 provides that even if the exploitation rights in a published work have been transferred and the work has been published, the author is entitled to withdraw or modify the work as long as he indemnifies the transferee in advance of the exercise of the right. The withdrawal right was long thought to be exercisable at the author's absolute discretion. The Court of Cassation has recently held, however, that an author may not exercise the right if his sole motivation for doing so is pecuniary.[157]

The corresponding provision in the German Act is somewhat more limited. In addition to indemnification, it requires, as a condition for the right's exercise, that the work no longer corresponds to the author's convictions and that the author's changed attitude is such that continued exploitation of the work cannot be expected of him.[158] Thus, in contrast to the French Act, which accords authors an absolute right, as long as his motive is not pecuniary, the German Act provides for court review of whether the author's changed attitude is such that continued exploitation of the work cannot be required. The German Act also contains no mention of the right of modification, although some commentators contend

---

155 In fact, under the Copyright Act, the "author" of a work-for-hire is the employer, and not the person who actually created the work. 17 U.S.C. § 201(b) (1988). The transfer of authors' interests in future works is discussed *infra* text accompanying notes 385-408.

156 Pursuant to the 1985 amendments to the French Act, the withdrawal right does not apply to computer software.

157 Judgment of May 14, 1991 (Chiavarino v. Ste SPC), Cass. civ., 151 R.I.D.A. 272 (1992).

158 GERMAN ACT, *supra* note 22, art. 42(1).

that this right is included in the right of withdrawal,[159] and the German Publishing Act of 1901 gives the author the waivable right to make changes in new editions "so far as they do not prejudice the lawful interests of the publisher."[160]

The right of withdrawal under both French and German laws is less expansive than might appear at first glance. In addition to the requirement of advance indemnification, both Acts give the transferee a right of first refusal on any subsequent publication of the work.[161] As a result of these restrictions, the right of withdrawal is infrequently exercised and has been the subject of few reported

---

159 As Strömholm points out, there is a fundamental flaw in this view that the right of withdrawal necessarily includes the right to alter the work. Unlike the right to terminate dissemination, the right of modification enables the author to compel performance of a publication contract with respect to a work that may be radically modified by the author. STRÖMHOLM, *supra* note 79, at 26. Other commentators maintain that the publisher cannot be forced to accept changes that would substantially alter the character of the work. *See, e.g.*, Aurelian Ionasco, *Le Droit de Repentir de l'Auteur*, 83 R.I.D.A. 33, 52 (1975); Giocanti, *supra* note 125, at 639; GÉRARD GAVIN, LE DROIT MORAL DE L'AUTEUR DANS LA JURISPRUDENCE ET LA LEGISLATION FRANCAISES 72 (1960).

160 An Act Concerning the Law of Publication 1901, art. 12, 1901 Reichsgesetzblatt [RGBl.] 217 (translated in UNESCO, 2 COPYRIGHT LAWS AND TREATIES OF THE WORLD (1987) [hereinafter German Publishing Act].

161 The French Act provides that the author must offer his exploitation rights to the transferee under the original conditions. FRENCH ACT, *supra* note 25, art. 32. The German Act permits the author to offer the licensee modified terms so long as they are reasonable. GERMAN ACT, *supra* note 22, art. 42(4). The rights of withdrawal and modification are also said to be inapplicable to the plastic arts. *See, e.g.*, DaSilva, *supra* note 125, at 25; Sarraute, *supra* note 135, at 477. Commentators reason that an artist who has transferred ownership of a painting or sculpture has no right to repossess his work. This view stems in part from a 1961 Paris Court of Appeals decision, which held that the painter, Vlaminck, who claimed that a painting sent to him for authentication was a forgery, had no right to erase his signature from the painting: "If the painter was correct in his estimate, he still had no right to alter another person's property. If, on the contrary, the painting was not a forgery, Vlaminck's moral right did not permit him to exercise a right of withdrawal after having sold the canvas." Judgment of Apr. 19, 1961, Cour d'appel Paris, 1961 Gazette du Palais [G.P.] 2.218 (Fr.).

The Paris court, and the commentators who have followed this reasoning, have missed the distinction between ownership rights in an article and copyright exploitation rights in a work embodied in the article. While the artist could not exercise the right of withdrawal in opposition to the transferees' ownership rights in the painting, he could preclude the transferee from publicly exhibiting and reproducing the painting. An author who cannot retrieve title to the original manuscript once it has been assigned may prevent his publisher from continued publication of the book.

The distinction between ownership rights and copyright was the basis for a recent decision of the German Federal Supreme Court on facts similar to the *Vlaminck* case. In the case the owner of two paintings signed with the name of deceased artist Emil Nolde sent the paintings to a foundation established by Nolde's widow and asked the foundation to certify their authenticity. The foundation claimed that the paintings were forgeries and refused to return them to their owner. The Court held that the foundation would have to return the paintings and refused to order that the paintings be marked to indicate that they were forgeries. However, in order to protect Nolde's paternity right not to be identified as author of a work that he did not create, the Court ordered that Nolde's name be removed from the painting. Judgment of June 8, 1989, Bundesgerichtshof, BGHZ 135, *reported in* 6 EUR. INTELL. PROP. REV. D-111 (1990).

decisions.[162] Nonetheless, the possibility that an author may exercise the right has been held to constitute a business risk that must be taken into account in any dealings between the author's transferee and other parties.[163] As such, the right represents a potentially significant restriction on alienability that has no parallel in U.S. law.[164]

C. *The Right of Attribution*

The right of attribution protects the author's interest in determining the authorship designation for his work. The right is said to be "based on the understanding that the 'natural link'"[165] between the author and his "intellectual child" is sacrosanct.[166] The attribution right consists of three subrights.[167] First, an author has the right to be identified as the author of his work, or to publish anonymously or pseudonymously.[168] Second, the author is entitled to prevent his work from being attributed to another.[169] Third, the author may prevent his name from appearing on works which he did not in fact create.[170]

---

162 Dietz, *supra* note 25, at FRG-55; DaSilva, *supra* note 125, at 24-25; Sarraute, *supra* note 135, at 477. In addition, Article 90 of the German Act provides that the withdrawal right does not apply to various exploitaiton rights involving cinematographic works. GERMAN ACT, *supra* note 22, art. 90.

163 Judgment of May 8, 1980 (Theatre du Gymnase Marie Bell v. Masmondet), Cass. soc., 107 R.I.D.A. 148 (Jan. 1981)(holding that where a playwright exercised his moral right to modify play by eliminating one of two characters that the defendant actress had been hired to play, the actress had no cause of action for terminating her employment contract with the play's producer).

164 Treece, *supra* note 125, at 500. In an applicable U.K. decision, the infant son of Charlie Chaplin had assigned away the copyright in his life story and later sought to enjoin publication. The court refused to intervene, holding that the copyright assignment constituted a present transfer of interest for value which may not be voided even by an infant author. Chaplin v. Leslie Frewin (Publishers), Ltd., 3 All E.R. 764, 772-73 (1965).

165 Dietz, *supra* note 25, at FRG-85.

166 *Id.*

167 The French and German Acts codify the attribution right in general terms, leaving the courts and commentators with the task of determining applications of the right. Article 6 of the French Act provides cryptically: "The author shall enjoy the right to respect for his name, his authorship, and his work." FRENCH ACT, *supra* note 25, art. 6. Article 13 of the German Act provides: "The author shall have the right of recognition of his authorship of the work. He can determine whether the work is to bear an author's designation and what designation is to be used." GERMAN ACT, *supra* note 22, art. 13.

168 Dietz, *supra* note 25, at FRG-85; Lucas & Plaisant, *supra* note 25, at FRA-96.

169 *See* DaSilva, *supra* note 125, at 26; Strauss, *supra* note 150, at 116.

170 DaSilva, *supra* note 125; Strauss, *supra* note 150. As several commentators have correctly noted, the right against false attribution is not properly included in the author's right of attribution, since it pertains to general reputational interests, rather than to the relationship between an author and his work. *See* Damich, *supra* note 10, at 13. I have nevertheless included the right against false attribution here, since it might serve as a supplement to the integrity right when used to prevent attribution of a distorted version of the author's work. *See* Stevens v. Nat'l Broadcasting Co., 148 U.S.P.Q. 755 (Cal. App. Dep't Super. Ct. 1966) (preliminary injunction issued to prevent the distortion of a film).

The scope of the attribution right is far-reaching. Even after contracting otherwise, an author may insist that his name (or a pseudonym) appear not only on the work itself, but also on all copies of the work and in references to the work in other material.[171] In collaborative works, such as films, each co-author is entitled to be identified as a creator of the work.[172] In collective works, such as newspapers, each author has the right to a byline for his article.[173]

According to one commentator, in comparison to Continental copyright law, U.S. law has traditionally shown "a callous disregard for the paternity rights of creative persons."[174] Except for the narrowly circumscribed attribution right under the Visual Artists Rights Act, U.S. copyright law accords authors no right to be identified with their works. An author who wishes to have his authorship recognized must generally extract from his transferee an enforceable promise to do so, although such a contractual requirement may conceivably be established by custom and usage applicable to a particular transaction.[175]

U.S. authors have successfully invoked a number of non-copyright theories to prevent both being falsely designated as authors of works that they did not create, and of having their works attributed to another. Principal among these theories have been state law defamation and privacy claims, and state and federal actions against deceptive trade practices.[176] In particular, a number of recent decisions have held that misattribution of authorship is actionable under Section 43(a) of the Lanham Act, which proscribes false designations of origin in the sale of goods and services.[177] An established author whose name has achieved significant public rec-

---

[171] Sarrautte, *supra* note 135; DaSilva, *supra* note 125, at 27. The extent to which the moral right of attribution may trump contractual obligations is more limited in Germany than in France. *See infra* text accompanying notes 267-72.

[172] Sarraute, *supra* note 135, at 478.

[173] Giocanti, *supra* note 125, at 636-37.

[174] Treece, *supra* note 125, at 494.

[175] *See, e.g.*, Vargas v. Esquire, Inc., 164 F.2d 522 (7th Cir. 1947) (artist who had transferred to Esquire magazine all of his rights in several of his drawings could not compel Esquire to attribute authorship to him without contractual obligation to do so); Melville B. Nimmer, *Implications of the Prospective Revisions of the Berne Convention and the United States Copyright Law*, 19 STAN. L. REV. 499, 520 (1967) (citing Poe v. Michael Todd Co., 151 F. Supp. 801 (S.D.N.Y. 1957)).

[176] *See Reputation Comment*, *supra* note 125, at 1490, 1496-99 (discussing applicability of state law prohibitions of defamation and deceptive trade practices); Jane Ginsburg & John Kernocham, *One Hundred and Two Years Later: The U.S. Joins the Berne Convention*, 141 R.I.D.A. 57, 145-49 (1989) (reviewing applications of trademark and Lanham Act, Section 43(a), to misattributions).

[177] *See, e.g.*, Lamothe v. Atlantic Recording Corp., 847 F.2d 1403 (9th Cir. 1988); Smith v. Montoro, 648 F.2d 602 (9th Cir. 1981) (involving substitution of film credit for actor); Dodd v. Fort Smith Special Sch. Dist. No. 100, 666 F. Supp. 1278 (W.D. Ark. 1987).

ognition in connection with his works may also register his name as a trademark in order to prevent misattributions of his works in circumstances likely to cause consumer confusion as to their source.[178]

These non-copyright theories are more limited in scope and applicability than their Continental attribution right counterparts. As of yet, no U.S. court has recognized an author claim, under any theory, against the simple failure to attribute authorship, as opposed to misattribution.[179] And even in the area of misattribution U.S. authors face material obstacles and limitations in asserting their claims. Defamation requires showing an injury to reputation, which may be difficult to prove.[180] Moreover, even a relatively unestablished author might be deemed a "limited purpose public figure," thus requiring a showing of actual malice.[181] The right of privacy has been successfully asserted to prevent the use of a person's name on a work that he did not create,[182] but it has been of little use in other attribution right areas.[183] Deceptive trade prac-

---

178 *See, e.g.*, *In re* Wood, 217 U.S.P.Q. 1345 (TTAB 1983) (in which the Trademarks Trial and Appeal Board upheld registration for an artist's name). A personal name may be registered as a trademark only upon proof that, through usage, it has acquired "distinctiveness" and "secondary meaning." In other words, the public must have come to recognize the name as a symbol that identifies and distinguishes the goods or services of only one seller. J. THOMAS MCCARTHY, MCCARTHY ON TRADEMARKS AND UNFAIR COMPETITION, § 13.02[1], at 13-3 to 13-5 (3d ed. 1992).

179 *Montoro*, 648 F.2d 602, and *Lamothe*, 847 F.2d 1403, are sometimes cited for the proposition that mere failure to give credit is a violation of Section 43(a) of the Lanham Act. But both cases involved misattribution, rather than simple non-attribution. In *Montoro* a film producer had removed the plaintiff's name from film credits and substituted another name. In *Lamothe* the name of one of several joint authors was deleted, which made it appear that the remaining authors were exclusively responsible for the work.

180 A defamation action would generally require a showing that the author has been exposed to contempt or public ridicule, thus injuring his professional standing. W. PAGE KEETON ET AL., PROSSER AND KEETON ON THE LAW OF TORTS § 117 (5th ed. 1984); Geisel v. Poynter Prods., Inc., 295 F. Supp. 331, 357 (S.D.N.Y. 1968). This could be a difficult showing even for a well-known author, and would effectively bar a defamation claim of a young author who has yet to build a professional reputation. Defamation actions also commonly require proof of special damages. *See* Harris v. Twentieth Century Fox Film Corp., 43 F. Supp. 119 (S.D.N.Y. 1942) (dismissing plaintiff's claim for libel resulting from defendant's crediting her with story research, rather than writing, for failure to plead special damages). Finally, even a plaintiff who succeeds on the merits will be unlikely to obtain injunctive relief. *See* Shostakovich v. Twentieth Century-Fox Film Corp., 80 N.Y.S.2d 575, 577-78 (Sup. Ct. 1948) (noting traditional rule, but stating that it would grant injunctive relief in a proper case).

181 *See, e.g.*, Wojnarowicz v. Am. Family Ass'n, 17 U.S.P.Q. 2d 1337, 1351 (S.D.N.Y. 1990) (artist's defamation claim denied because of failure to show that defendant who misrepresented fragments of artist's work as the complete work did so with knowledge or reckless disregard of the facts).

182 *See, e.g.*, Lord Byron v. Johnston, 35 Eng. Rep. 851 (1816) (enjoining circulation of a poem falsely attributed to Lord Byron); Eliot v. Jones, 120 N.Y.S. 989 (Sup. Ct. 1910), *aff'd mem.*, 125 N.Y.S. 1119 (1st Dep't 1910) (unauthorized use of the name of the editor of "Harvard Classics" in connection with rival publication).

183 *See, e.g.*, Ellis v. Hurst, 128 N.Y.S. 144 (Sup. Ct. 1910) (rejecting author's petition

tice statutes are designed to shield consumers from the false designation of goods and services, rather than to protect artistic reputation.[184] As a result, these statutes might not apply to misattributions of authorship that are unrelated to the marketing of a work to the public, such as in connection with the display of works of art in public places or references to a work in critical reviews or other nonpromotional materials.[185] Furthermore, none of these theories make actionable a publisher's refusal to market an author's work under the author's designated pseudonym, absent contractual agreement.[186]

Finally, the quasi-attribution rights enjoyed by U.S. authors are fully waivable. A ghostwriter who contracts to create a book under another's name forever relinquishes the right to prevent the false attribution of the work to another.[187] A screenwriter who agrees to contribute anonymously, cannot later insist on receiving authorship credit. Indeed, under the U.S. Copyright Act, when a work is created by an employee in the scope of his employment, the employer, and not the creator, is considered to be its author, unless the parties have otherwise agreed.[188] The employer has no obligation to attribute authorship to the work's "true author."

D. *Right of Integrity*

The right of integrity is generally seen as the central tenet of moral rights jurisprudence.[189] At a minimum, the right has a nega-

---

under state privacy statute to enjoin publisher from republishing the author's early pseudonymous works under the author's true name), *aff'd mem.*, 130 N.Y.S. 1110 (1911).

184 For a discussion of this distinction between deceptive trade practices and moral rights, see *Reputation Comment*, *supra* note 125, at 1499-1500.

185 Section 43(a) of the Lanham Act applies only to goods or services used "in commerce." 15 U.S.C. § 1125 (1988).

186 *See, e.g., Ellis,* 128 N.Y.S. at 144.

187 In theory the attribution of a book's authorship to a ghostwriter's client rather than to the ghostwriter constitutes impermissible reverse passing off under Section 43(a) of the Lanham Act. As such a ghostwriter's agreement to allow his work to be sold under another person's name might be unenforceable as a matter of public policy in order to protect consumers. On the other hand, however, even trademark owners maybe estopped from withdrawing their consent to another's use of their mark. The threat of consumer confusion from the continued use is only one factor in determining whether consent may be terminated. McCarthy, *supra* note 178, § 32.33[2], at 32-133 to 32-134. Accordingly, given that ghostwriting is a well-established practice and given the absence of any express protection for authorship attribution, it is highly unlikely that a U.S. court would countenance a ghostwriter's attempt to claim attribution in the face of a contrary contractual obligation.

188 17 U.S.C. § 201(b) (1988).

189 *See* DaSilva, *supra* note 125, at 31. In France, the right to integrity is codified principally in Article 6 of the French Act, which provides that "[t]he author shall enjoy . . . respect for his name, his authorship, and his work." French Act, *supra* note 25, art. 6. Article 14 of the German Act provides that "[t]he author shall have the right to prohibit any distortion or any other mutilation of his work which would prejudice his lawful intellectual or personal interests in the work." German Act, *supra* note 22, art. 14.

tive aspect. It entitles an author to prevent the public presentation of his work in a manner or context harmful to his reputation, or repugnant to the "feelings that he as an artist may cherish for the work he has created."[190] Some courts and commentators have also recognized an affirmative aspect of the integrity right, requiring public presentation of the author's work, and compelling its completion and preservation.[191] A purchaser of a work of art, or a publisher or producer, thus acquires the work or right to exploit a work subject to a duty to respect and possibly to promote the author's artistic conception.

The author's negative right is vividly illustrated in the oft-cited case of artist Bernard Buffet.[192] Buffet had painted designs on a refrigerator. The refrigerator's owner sought to dismantle it and sell each panel as a separate piece. Buffet claimed that the refrigerator was an indivisible artistic unit and sued to prevent its dismantling. The French Court of Cassation ruled that the owner could keep the dismantled panels at home, but that the public display or transfer of the artist's work in mutilated form would infringe the artist's personal rights in relation to the work.[193]

The negative right may also be asserted against an unfaithful presentation or an adaptation of the work that leaves the original version intact. Thus in *Bernard-Rousseau v. Galeries Lafayette*, a French department store was held to have violated painter Henri Rousseau's right of integrity by displaying reproductions of his work that differed in color and form from the original.[194] Similarly, a theater proprietor licensed to produce the operetta, Maske in Blau, was enjoined from deleting several parts of the original score and adding elements, including the theme from the American television detective series, Dragnet, which were unrelated to the original.[195] The German Federal Court of Justice found that the defendants' distortion of the work had violated the integrity right of the operetta composer and librettist.

The negative right might also apply to the performance or public display of a work in a context that is harmful to the author's reputation or contrary to his artistic conception. During the early

---

190 STRÖMHOLM, *supra* note 79, at 30 (quoting Swedish Copyright Law Commission Report, 1956 SOU No. 25, at 122).

191 *See* Damich, *supra* note 10, at 20-22.

192 Judgment of May 30, 1962 (Fersing v. Buffet), Cour de cassation, 1965 G.P. 126, *discussed in* Merryman, *supra* note 10.

193 *Id.*

194 Judgment of Mar. 13, 1973, Trib. gr. inst., 1974 J.C.P., No. 48, at 224, *discussed in* Damich, *supra* note 10, at 22.

195 55 BGHZ 1 (1970).

years of the Cold War, Twentieth Century-Fox released a film, entitled "The Iron Curtain," depicting Soviet espionage in Canada. As background music, the film included selections from the uncopyrighted works of Dmitri Shostakovich and three other Soviet composers. The composers sued to prevent the use of their music in the film, which, they claimed, cast upon them "a false imputation of being disloyal to their country."[196] Although a New York court rejected their claim,[197] they were successful in France.[198]

The author's positive right to compel public presentation of his work was dramatically demonstrated in the case of *Dubuffet v. Renault*.[199] The Renault corporation had commissioned artist Jean Dubuffet to design and prepare a model for a monumental sculpture that Renault was to construct at its plant. Renault approved Dubuffet's model and began to build the sculpture. As a result of cost overruns, however, Renault decided to abandon the project in the midst of construction. Dubuffet then brought suit to force completion on the basis of the moral rights of disclosure and integrity. In a ruling that was later confirmed by the Court of Cassation, the artist successfully obtained an order compelling Renault to complete the work and, implicitly, to preserve it as well.[200]

It is worth emphasizing that under French and German law the author's ongoing personal connection with his creation is said to extend beyond the protection of his reputational interests. The author is entitled to defend the work's integrity, as he views it, without any relation to how a given modification or use of the work might affect others' judgment of him, and regardless of whether the distorted work is attributed to him.[201] Critics may be of the

---

[196] Shostakovich v. Twentieth Century-Fox Film Corp., 80 N.Y.S.2d 575, 578 (Sup. Ct. 1948).

[197] Shostakovich v. Twentieth Century-Fox Film Corp., 87 N.Y.S. 2d 430 (1st Dep't 1949).

[198] Judgment of Jan. 13, 1953 (Soc. Le. Chant de Monde v. Soc. Fox Europe et Soc. Fox Americaine Twentieth Century), 1953 G.P. 191. Recently, the High Court of Berlin ruled that the publication of an author's poem, without the author's consent, in a lampoon of the former East German political organ, *Neues Deutschland*, violated the author's integrity right because, "in the eyes of the creator, the work had been placed in a context in which it did not belong." Adolf Dietz, *Copyright Law Developments in the Federal Republic of Germany (from 1989 to the beginning of 1993)*, 157 R.I.D.A. 128, 200-01 (October 1993) (summarizing Decision of 6 May 1988).

[199] Judgment of Mar. 23, 1977, Trib. gr. inst., 1977 R.I.D.A. 191 obs. Desbois (Fr.), *aff'd*, Judgment of June 2, 1978, 1980 G.P. 580 note Franck, *rev'd*, Judgment of Jan. 8, 1980, Cass. civ. 1re, 1980 J.C.P. II No. 1933 note Lindon.

[200] The *Dubuffet* decision was actually based on a fairly contrived reading of the sculptor's commission contract, rather than his moral rights. However, the court's interpretation of the contract and its unusual order of specific performance were heavily colored by Dubuffet's moral rights claim and lend considerable support to a positive right of integrity. *See* Françon & Ginsburg, *supra* note 142, at 391.

[201] *See* STRÖMHOLM, *supra* note 79, at 31. *See also* Judgment December 12, 1988 (De-

unanimous view that a given change in a work will only enhance the author's reputation, or that the public performance or display of a work in a certain context comports entirely with the author's persona and with the nature and quality of his other works. However, if the author sees his work and artistic endeavors in a different light, he has the right, with certain qualifications designed to prevent abuse, to enjoin such change or use.[202]

In the United States an ad hoc combination of defamation, contract and unfair competition law, together with certain provisions of the Copyright Act, provide a rough parallel to the right of integrity. The truncation or distortion of a work, or the work's presentation in an unfavorable context, might be actionable as a defamatory tort if it is attributed to the author and reflects adversely on the author's reputation.[203] A court might also enjoin the modification or use of a work that is contrary to an express or implied term of a contract.[204] In one such action, Otto Preminger sought to enjoin the licensing of his film, *Anatomy of a Murder*, for television broadcasting because of edited cuts for commercials.[205] Although the court rejected Preminger's claim, it recognized that a cause of action would have been stated if Preminger's contract with his distributor had expressly prohibited such cuts or if the cuts had been so extreme that they exceeded prevailing industry practice.[206]

The alteration of a work might also be prohibited on decep-

---

lorme v. Catena-France), Cours d'appel, P.I.B.D. III, No. 454, at 231, 10 EUROPEAN INT. PROP. REV. D-182 (1989) (upholding graphic designer's integrity right claim against modifications in company logo even though designer's name did not appear on logo and modifications consisted merely of changing the direction in which the logo was slanted).

202 Vexatious or abusive exercise of the author's moral rights is not permitted. *See* Lucas & Plaisant, *supra* note 25, at FRA-102. The author's objections to changes in or uses of his work must be shown to be real and substantial by some objective measure. In addition, authors who have authorized the adaptation of their work in another medium must accept changes that are necessitated by the transfer to another medium, so long as the essential spirit, character, and substance of the work is respected. For further discussion on this point see *infra* notes 295-305 and accompanying text.

203 *See, e.g.*, Edison v. Viva Int'l, Ltd., 421 N.Y.S.2d 203 (1979) (sustaining a libel action for publication of article in substantially different form and content); Granz v. Harris, 198 F.2d 585, 589 (2d Cir. 1952) (Frank, J., concurring). *But see* Shostakovich v. Twentieth Century-Fox Film Corp., 80 N.Y.S.2d 575 (Sup. Ct. 1948) (declining to enjoin alleged personal libel for distribution of author's musical compositions in a context that cast doubt on their loyalty to their country).

204 An author may clearly prohibit an assignee or licensee from making modifications to the author's work by express contractual provision.

205 Preminger v. Columbia Pictures Corp., 267 N.Y.S.2d 594 (Sup. Ct. 1966), *aff'd*, 269 N.Y.S.2d 913 (App. Div. 1966), *aff'd*, 219 N.E.2d 431 (N.Y. 1966).

Preminger concerns the claim of the film director, and not the author of the screenplay. As Nimmer has noted, however, the court's reasoning should be applicable to authors as well. NIMMER & NIMMER, *supra* note 12, § 8.21[C][1], at 8-258 n.53.

206 *Preminger*, 267 N.Y.S.2d at 603. *See also* Society of Survivors v. Huttenbach, 535 N.Y.S.2d 670, 674 (Sup. Ct. 1988) (indicating that if the contract is silent as to changes, the transferee may modify the work to the extent permitted by custom and usage in the trade).

tive trade practice theory. In *Gilliam v. American Broadcasting Co.*,[207] the Second Circuit ruled that ABC's broadcasting of unauthorized edited versions of previously televised skits of the English comedy group, Monty Python, violated Section 43(a) of the Lanham Act.[208] The court found that ABC's modifications were so substantial that in conjunction with the identification of the skits as the work of Monty Python, they created "a false impression of the product's origin."[209] The court suggested that it sought to protect the personal, as well as the proprietary, rights of authors.[210]

Despite the *Gilliam* court's reference to authors' personal interests, the Lanham Act provides significantly more limited protection for authors than do Continental moral rights. The Lanham Act's fundamental rationale is to prevent false advertising and consumer deception rather than to protect authors per se. As a result, only distortions that so change the character of a work that to attribute the work to its original authors would constitute a false designation of origin would be actionable under the Act. In *Gilliam* ABC had cut more than one quarter of the ninety-minute Monty Python program and had deleted material that was central to the group's repertoire. It is highly doubtful that a U.S. court would entertain a Section 43(a) claim against modifications, such as the colorization of a black-and-white film or the use of actresses to play male characters in a play, which leave the work essentially intact. Such modifications, however, have been enjoined by French courts as violative of the integrity right.[211] In addition, Section 43(a) proscribes only the false designation of *origin*, and not a work's multilation in and of itself. Accordingly, a mutilated film could lawfully be screened so long as it was clearly labeled as an

---

207 538 F.2d 14 (2d Cir. 1976).

208 *Id.* at 25. The court also rested its holding on grounds of breach of contract and copyright infringement.

209 *Id.* at 24. *See also* Rich v. RCA Corp., 390 F. Supp. 530, 531 (S.D.N.Y. 1975) (holding that the authorized publication of a previously written work and accompanied by a recent photograph of the author may violate Section 43(a) of the Lanham Act to the extent that the photograph suggests that the work is contemporary).

210 *Gilliam*, 538 F.2d at 24.

211 In a celebrated recent case the French Court of Cassation implicity recognized that the broadcasting in France of a colorized version of John Huston's film, *Asphalt Jungle*, violated the author's right of integrity. Judgment of May 28, 1991, Cas. civ. 1re, 149 R.I.D.A. 197 (1991). For an illuminating discussion of the *Asphalt Jungle* case, see Jane Ginsburg & Pierre Sirinelli, *Auteur, Création et Adaptation en Droit International Privé et en Droit Interne Français. Réflexions à Partir de l'Affaire Huston*, 150 R.I.D.A. 2 (1991). In another case, a French court found that a production of *Waiting for Godot* in which the lead roles were played by women, in contrast to Samuel Beckett's express instructions that the roles should be played by men, violated Beckett's moral right of integrity as asserted by his heirs. Lindon v. La Compagnie Brut de Beton, Trib. gr. inst. de Paris, 3e, 155 R.I.D.A. 225 (1993).

unauthorized edit, rather than the original author's work. In contrast, the integrity right has been held to apply even in the absence of authorship attribution.[212]

The U.S. Copyright Act within the rubric of various economic right also approximates certain features of the right of integrity.[213] The most important of these is the copyright owner's exclusive right to "prepare derivative works based upon the copyrighted work."[214] A derivative work may be a "translation, musical arrangement, dramatization, fictionalization, motion picture version, sound recording, art reproduction, abridgment, condensation, or any other form in which a work may be recast, transformed or adapted."[215] The term also includes "work consisting of editorial revisions, annotations, elaborations, or other modifications which, as a whole, represent an original work of authorship . . . ."[216] Accordingly, an author who holds the exclusive rights to make copies of, and to prepare derivative works based upon his work may prevent unauthorized distortions, truncations, modifications, and adaptions of the work. A slightly altered version of the author's work that remains "substantially similar" to the original work will be deemed to be an infringing copy.[217] A version in a different medium or that contains significant modifications, yet remains "based upon" the original work, will constitute an infringing deriva-

---

[212] Judgment of Dec. 12, 1988 (Delorme v. Catena-France), Cours d'appel, P.I.B.D. III, No. 454, at 231, 10 EUROPEAN INT. PROP. REV. D-182 (1989) (upholding graphic designer's integrity right claim against modifications in company logo even though defendant had not even known who had designed the logo).

[213] For a more detailed discussion of moral rights analogues in the U.S. Copyright Act, see Kwall, *supra* note 10.

[214] 17 U.S.C. § 106(2).

Another integrity right analogue is Section 115 of the Copyright Act. This section provides for a compulsory license for the making and distribution of phonorecords of a musical composition that has previously been recorded and distributed under the authority of the copyright owner. Section 115(a)(2) provides that the compulsory license includes the privilege of changing the musical arrangement of the work where necessary to conform arrangement to the style or manner of interpretation of performance, so long as no change is made in "the basic melody or fundamental character of the work." 17 U.S.C. § 115(a)(2) (1988). The House Report concerning § 115(a)(2) indicates that this qualification to the privilege of making musical arrangements was designed to prevent the original compositions from being "perverted, distorted or travestied." H.R. REP. No. 1476, 94th Cong., 2d Sess. (1976), *reprinted in* 1976 U.S.C.C.A.N. 5659, 5724.

Section 115(a)(2) evinces an awareness that copyright owners have an economic interest in preventing the preparation and dissemination of derivative works that distort the copyrighted work. This interest can generally be protected by imposing conditions to their grant of derivative work rights. Since this option is unavailable for copyright owners where a derivative work may be prepared without obtaining the owner's permission, as under the compulsory license provisions of § 115, Congress accorded a measure of protection for the interest under § 115(a)(2).

[215] 17 U.S.C. § 101.

[216] *Id.*

[217] *See* NIMMER & NIMMER, *supra* note 12, § 13.03, at 13-17 to 13-54.

tive work.[218] Thus, although Shostakovich could invoke U.S. copyright law to prevent the use of his work in an unfavorable context, Bernard Buffet might have successfully brought suit in the United States to enjoin the truncation of his refrigerator. In some circumstances, the public display or presentation of the original work in a new context might also constitute a transformation of the original amounting to a derivative work.[219]

The derivative right, therefore, is essentially coterminous with at least the negative aspect of the integrity right. Like their Continental counterparts, U.S. authors who hold the derivative right may prevent modifications to their work that run contrary to their artistic sensibilities, without any need to show consumer deception or harm to reputation. In fact, the derivative right may be freely exercised without the equitable, good-faith limitations that, as we shall see, have been imposed on the moral right.[220]

Under U.S. law, an author may grant to an assignee or licensee the right to make any and all changes in his work, even if such changes amount to a distortion or truncation. The author may also grant the right to present the work in any and all contexts, including those that may be contrary to the author's personal or artistic sensibilities. Both these grants can be made in gross and in advance of actual changes or presentation of the work. In the event of such a grant, the author may not thereafter complain of mutilations or repugnant uses of the work.[221] Indeed, once an au-

---

218 If the distortion is so extreme that the resulting work could not even be said to be "based on" the original work, then no cause of action will lie. *See* GOLDSTEIN, *supra* note 150, at 635. For an analysis drawing the line between the reproduction right to make the same or similar versions of a work and the right to make derivative works based upon the original work, see Paul Goldstein, *Derivative Rights and Derivative Works in Copyright*, 30 J. COPYRIGHT SOC'Y 209, 217 (1982-83).

219 *See* Mirage Editions, Inc., v. Albuquerque A.R.T. Co., 856 F.2d 1341, 1343 (9th Cir. 1988) (holding that removal of art print from a book and mounting it on a ceramic tile with a border constituted a recasting or transformation of the print amounting to an infringing derivative work).

220 *See infra* notes 279-89 and accompanying text. Of course, the derivative right is subject to fair use limitations under Section 107 of the Copyright Act.

221 Conceivably, an author's authorization to market a distorted version of a work under its original title or under the author's name would be unenforceable under the Lanham Act, Section 43(a), false advertising proscriptions. *See* MCCARTHY, *supra* note 178, § 18.11, at 18-53 to 18-55 (discussing assignment of literary titles). But this would not prevent the marketing of a distorted version that was accurately labeled as such. In addition, except in a particularly egregious case of consumer deception, the author would probably be estopped from terminating his prior consent to the grantee use. *See* MCCARTHY, *supra* 178, § 32.33[2], at 32-133 to 32-134. On the other hand, in those relatively few cases in which an author has registered a trademark in his name, he may not grant to another the right to market works under his name without some mechanism for author control over their quality. In fact, to the extent that an author's goodwill is personal to him, the personal name mark and the goodwill it represents may be incapable of being validly assigned to another person. *See* MCCARTHY, *supra* note 178, § 18.10 at 18-52 to 18-53.

thor has transferred his copyright, the exclusive right to make derivative works based upon the copyrighted work lies with the copyright owner, not with the author—and the same is true in work-for-hire cases, where the employer rather than employee-creator is deemed to be the first author for purposes of U.S. copyright law.[222]

A recent case involving Turner Entertainment's colorization of the black-and-white film, *Asphalt Jungle*, vividly illustrates the extent to which copyright alienability vitiates authors' control over their work in contrast to the Continental regime.[223] The heirs of John Huston, the film's director, objected to the colorization, which constituted a derivative work subject to the copyright owner's exclusive derivative right under U.S. copyright law. But Huston's heirs were barred from bringing an action under U.S. copyright law for two reasons. First, under U.S. work-for-hire rules a film's producer, rather than artistic director, is generally deemed to be the first author and copyright owner of the film. Second, Huston's film production contract contained a standard catch-all clause in which Huston assigned to the producer all rights that he may have had in the film.[224] However, when Turner granted to the French television channel La Cinq the right to broadcast the colorized film in France, Huston's heirs brought suit in that country to prevent the broadcast on the grounds that it would violate Huston's right of integrity. The French Court of Cassation refused to apply American law governing initial copyright ownership and contractual assignment. It ruled, under French domestic law, that Huston was the film's author and that his moral right of integrity had survived the blanket assignment of rights.[225] It held that Huston's heirs were entitled to challenge the broadcast of the colorized film and strongly suggested that the broadcast would in-

---

222 17 U.S.C. § 201(b). It has been suggested that to the extent authors who have relinquished the copyright retain a right, either as beneficial owners under section 501(b) of the U.S. Copyright Act, or as holders of a reversionary interest pursuant to the termination provisions, to prevent infringement or acts that might dilute the value of the copyright, such right might be used to prevent distortions. *See* Kwall, *supra* note 10, at 55. But even if such a right were recognized, it would not apply in cases of works-for-hire and could not be relied upon by authors who had granted a derivative work rights transferee unconditional authority to determine the form of the derivative work or who had otherwise waived the right to object to distortions.

223 Judgment of May 28, 1991, Cass. civ. 1re, 149 R.I.D.A. 197 (1991). For an illuminating discussion of the *Asphalt Jungle* case, see Ginsburg & Sirinelli, *supra* note 211.

224 Ginsburg & Sirinelli, *supra* note 211, at 4.

225 Even under French law, for film production contracts concluded after the effective date of the July 3, 1985 amendments to the French Act, the director's exploitation rights are presumptively transferred to the producer. But the director maintains certain moral rights despite the transfer.

fringe Huston's integrity right.[226]

E. *The Visual Artists Rights Act*

A review of United States analogues to moral rights would be incomplete without an examination of the Visual Artists Rights Act of 1990. The Visual Artists Rights Act represents the first, tentative step toward federal recognition of moral rights. The Act succeeds and largely preempts eleven state statutes that accord limited moral rights protection in the area of the visual arts.[227] The Act amends the U.S. Copyright Act to accord authors of certain original and limited edition works of visual art with narrowly circumscribed attribution and integrity rights. The Act's primary impetus is to bring "U.S. law into greater harmony with laws of other Berne countries,"[228] thus strengthening the United States' commitment

---

226 Ginsburg & Sirinelli, *supra* note 211, at 6, 24.

227 *See, e.g.*, CAL. CIV. CODE § 987 (West 1993); CONN. GEN. STAT. § 42-116t (West 1993); LA. REV. STAT. §§ 2151-2156 (West 1993); ME. REV. STAT. ANN. tit. 27, § 303 (West 1988); MASS. GEN. LAWS ANN. ch. 231, § 855 (West Supp. 1993); N.J. STAT. ANN. § 24:24A-4 (West 1993); N.Y. ARTS & CULT. AFF. § 11-14 (Consol. 1990); R.I. GEN. LAWS § 5-62-3 (1992).

Some of these statutes, including that of California, are designed to promote the public interest in preserving cultural and artistic creations, as well as to protect the artist's personal and economic interests. These statutes typically make actionable, by the artist or, in some instances, by a public official or body, the physical defacement, mutilation, alteration or destruction of works of fine art of "recognized quality." Other statutes, notably that of New York, serve essentially to protect the artist's reputational interests. These statutes prohibit the unauthorized public display, publication, or reproduction of a work of fine art in an altered, defaced, mutilated, or modified form when the work is identified or identifiable as being that of the artist, and when such act is likely to damage the artist's reputation. All of the statutes accord creators of works of fine art with a right of attribution. Typically, the artist is entitled "at all times" to claim authorship or, for "just and valid reason," to disclaim authorship.

Under the preemption provisions of section 301 of the Copyright Act, as amended by the Visual Artists Rights Act, the rights accorded under the state statutes are largely, although not entirely, preempted by the Visual Artists Rights Act. For preemption to occur, two criteria must be met. First, the applicable state statute provision must cover works falling within the subject matter covered by the Visual Artists Rights Act. Second, the rights sought to be vindicated under the state statute must be equivalent to the legal or equitable rights granted by the Act. Visual Artists House Report, *supra* note 16, at 21. Thus, to the extent that a state statute, such as that of New York (N.Y. ARTS & CULT. AFF. LAW § 14.53), makes actionable distortions of reproductions, as opposed to originals and limited edition copies, it would not be preempted by the Visual Artists Rights Act. *Id.* The protection of audiovisual works, as in the Massachusetts statute (MASS. ANN. LAWS ch. 231, at 85S) or of works of art in glass, as in California (CAL. CIV. CODE § 987(b)(2)) would similarly escape preemption. However, even these statutes might be preempted by the Coyright Act's derivative right to the extent that the distortions they seek to prevent constitute derivative works of the distorted originals, and so long as they do not require proof of a substantive element, such as harm to reputation, that falls outside the prima facie case for copyright right infringement.

228 *See Hearings on H.R. 2690 Before the Subcommittee on Courts, Intellectual Property, and the Administration of Justice of the House Committee on the Judiciary*, 101st Cong., 1st Sess. (1989) (statement of Ralph Oman, Register of Copyrights).

to the Berne Convention.[229] The Act is designed to protect "both the reputations of certain visual artists" and the integrity of "works of visual art that make up an important part of our cultural heritage."[230] In the true utilitarian tradition of U.S. copyright law, the House Report accompanying the Act states that the Act serves the public interest in encouraging artistic creation, in consonance with the Constitutional goal of promoting "the Progress of Science and useful Arts" by granting artists rights that are analogous to those protected by Article 6*bis*.[231]

The Visual Artists Rights Act's provisions extend to original drawings, prints, sculptures, and signed photographs that have been produced solely for exhibition,[232] and copies produced in limited editions of no more than 200 consecutively numbered copies bearing the artist's signature or, in the case of sculptures, another identifying mark.[233] Audiovisual works, applied art, books, newspapers, merchandising and promotional items, works made for hire, and various other works are explicitly excluded.[234]

Authors of qualifying works of visual art enjoy attribution rights consisting of both the right to require authorship attribution for the author's work and the right to prevent the misattribution of works that the author did not create.[235] However, the Act makes no general provision for anonymous or pseudonymous dissemination or display. An author is entitled to proscribe the use of his name only if the work has been distorted, mutilated or otherwise modified in such a way as to prejudice his honor or reputation.[236]

The author's integrity right is limited to preventing "intentional" distortions, mutilations and modifications that "would be prejudicial to his or her honor or reputation."[237] The House Report indicates that the harm to honor or reputation should be based on a finding of fact in each case as to the modification's adverse impact on the artist's professional reputation "as embodied in the work."[238] With respect to works of "recognized stature," the

---

229 136 CONG. REC. H13313 (daily ed. Oct. 27, 1990) (statement of Rep. Robert W. Kastenmeier).

230 *Id.*

231 Visual Artists House Report, *supra* note 16, at 5.

232 17 U.S.C. § 101 (1988 & Supp. II 1990).

233 *Id.*

234 *Id.*

235 17 U.S.C. § 106A(a)(2) (Supp. II 1990).

236 *Id.*

237 17 U.S.C. § 106A(a)(3)(A) (Supp. II 1990). The Act also makes actionable by the author the intentional or grossly negligent destruction of "a work of recognized stature." 17 U.S.C. § 106A(a)(3)(B).

238 Visual Artists House Report, *supra* note 16, at 15.

Report approaches the German and French position in noting that the modification of such works will generally be sufficient to establish harm to honor or reputation.[239] But, in contrast to Continental doctrine, the Act provides for no cause of action for distorting uses of the work, including reproductions, depictions, public presentations and portrayals that do not amount to a physical modification of the original or limited edition copy.[240]

The Visual Artists Rights Act provides that attribution and integrity rights are conferred only on the author, regardless of whether the author is the copyright owner.[241] The rights may not be transferred, but may be waived if the author expressly agrees in a written instrument signed by the author.[242] As indicated in the House Report, the Act "does not permit blanket waivers."[243] A waiver is effective only as to the works and uses of such works that are specifically identified in the written instrument,[244] and only as to the specific person to whom waiver is made.[245] Except as otherwise set forth in such a written instrument, neither the transfer of ownership of a copy of a qualifying work of visual art nor of any copyright interest therein constitutes a waiver of rights under the Act.[246]

The waiver provisions reflect an interim compromise, and may be revised in the future to strengthen author protection. The House Report recognizes that the assignment or transfer of the attribution or integrity rights would be contrary to their "personal nature."[247] It also notes that "[a]rguably, the best recognition of moral rights would countenance no waivers,"[248] both because the rights are personal to authors and because authors may routinely be required to bargain them away as a result of "a relatively weak economic position."[249] The Report concludes, however, that a no-waiver position "is probably too extreme for the U.S. system"[250] and that a narrow circumscription of waivers and the circumstances surrounding them would probably be sufficient to protect authors' in-

---

239 *Id.* at 16.
240 17 U.S.C. § 106A(c)(2), (3) (Supp. II 1990).
241 17 U.S.C. § 106A(b) (Supp. II 1990).
242 17 U.S.C. § 106A(e)(1) (Supp. II 1990).
243 Visual Artists House Report, *supra* note 16, at 19.
244 17 U.S.C. § 106A(e)(1).
245 Visual Artists House Report, *supra* note 16, at 18-19.
246 17 U.S.C. § 106A(e)(2) (Supp. II 1990).
247 Visual Artists House Report, *supra* note 16, at 18.
248 *Id.* (testimony of Professor Jane Ginsburg).
249 *Id.*
250 *Id.*

terests.[251] Nonetheless, the Act directs the Copyright Office to undertake a five-year review of the waiver provisions.[252] The purpose of the study is to determine whether any imbalance in bargaining power routinely compels artists to waive their rights, thus resulting in the evisceration of the Act's substantive provisions.[253]

IV. Alienability Of Moral Rights

As we have seen, alienability is one of the most significant areas in which the United States moral rights analogues appear to fall short of their Continental counterparts. Some United States analogues, including the U.S. Copyright Act's first publication and derivative works rights, are fully transferable and waivable. These rights are simply a part of the bundle of economic rights that the U.S. Copyright Act accords to a copyright owner, who may or may not be the author of the copyrighted work. Other United States moral rights analogues, including the causes of action for invasion of privacy, defamation, and the statutory fine arts paternity and integrity rights, are not transferable, but are waivable. The author's advance waiver of further control over the work will thus defeat a subsequent claim for defamation or invasion of privacy based on the publication of the work or a distorted version of the work. Although an author's rights under the Visual Artists Rights Act are not subject to blanket waiver, these rights may be irrevocably relinquished with respect to uses and users that are specified in a written instrument. Finally, with some limitations, rights derived from the deceptive trade practices analogues are effectively waived by an author who has agreed to give the transferee a free hand in modifications and description of origin.[254] These rights may also be transferred together with all of the assets of the author's business.

In contrast, German and French authors' rights doctrine is said to begin with the basic premise that an author's bond with his work is inseverable, thus making moral rights nonassignable and nonwaivable.[255] As one commentator has dramatically put it: the

---

251 *Id.* The Report also concurs with Professor Ginsburg's statement that a tight regulation of waiver might more effectively protect authors' interests than would an ideologically pure no-waiver law that might be rarely observed in practice. *Id.*

252 Pub. L. No. 101-650, § 608(a), 104 Stat. 5128 (1990).

253 Visual Artists House Report, *supra* note 16, at 22.

254 For a discussion of some possible limitations on author ability to effect a waiver of Lanham Act rights, see *supra* notes 187 and 221.

255 The French Act declares explicitly that the author's "right to respect for his name, his authorship, and his work [is] perpetual, inalienable and imprescriptible." French Act, *supra* note 25, art. 6. The German Act contains no such broad declaration, although commentators and courts take the inalienability principle as their starting point. *See, e.g.*, Dietz, *supra* note 25, at FRG-91 to FRG-92.2. The German Act, however, does explicitly provide

global renunciation of such rights would be tantamount to "intellectual suicide."[256] At the same time, the extent to which the inalienability principle is actually applied has troubled Continental commentators, as well as their American colleagues. As a leading German commentator notes: "It is relatively difficult to give a clear answer to the question whether, under German copyright law, an author has the power to transfer or waive his moral rights, since the answer is both yes and no at the same time."[257]

Much of the confusion regarding the extent to which moral rights are transferable and waivable stems from a lack of precision in defining the nature and scope of moral rights, and from the use of the terms transfer and waiver. Much of what some commentators have seen as a willingness to accept waivers or transfers can be described as the delimitation of the scope of moral rights, the conditions of their exercise, and the remedies available for their infringement. This tailoring of rights often serves to accommodate the interests of holders of contractual rights in authors' works. But it does not constitute the contractual relinquishment of moral rights by the author. A more careful use of definition and terminology cannot allay the real tension between absolutist sentiment espousing an inseverable bond between an author and his work, and the claims of exploitation right transferees, who, in a market economy, are necessary to bringing creative works to the public. But, as will be seen in this Section, a more careful use of definitions and terminology can help to differentiate between the inalienable core of moral rights protection and the partly alienable periphery.

---

that the right of revocation may not be waived in advance and that its exercise may not be precluded. GERMAN ACT, *supra* note 22, art. 42(2).

The Berne Convention requires that member states provide for rights of paternity and integrity that may be exercised by authors "[i]ndependently of the authors' economic rights, and even after the transfer of said rights." Berne Convention, art. 6*bis*. Most commentators maintain that this provision does not require the inalienability of paternity and integrity rights, but merely that said rights are not automatically transferred or waived by virtue of the transfer of the author's economic rights. *See, e.g*, Nimmer, *supra* note 175, at 523. *But see* Damich, Statement in Support of U.S. Adherence to the Berne Convention, Berne Hearings, *supra* note 12, at 553 (noting that the World Intellectual Property Organization Guide to the Berne Convention states that the provision "protects the author against himself" and concluding that the provision presumably means that an author cannot be held to agreements in which he has completely relinquished control over the integrity of his work).

256 DESBOIS, *supra* note 112, at 470. In this statement, Desbois refers to the global renunciation of moral rights, and not to their waiver in particular circumstances. Desbois's conclusion is that the term "inalienable" in article 6 of the French Act is inaccurate to the extent that it conveys the idea of an absolute or categorical prohibition on waiver.

257 Dietz, *supra* note 25, at FRG-91.

A. *Transfer*

To what extent are moral rights transferable? A complete transfer of moral rights would give the transferee the unrestricted power to dispose of such rights and to enforce them against other persons, including the author. For example, a transferee book publisher could authorize a third person to attribute authorship to himself and could, without taking the author's wishes into account, permit or prevent modifications to the book and to any derivative works based upon it; even modifications that will damage the reputation of or run contrary to the artistic conception of the author.[258]

Transfers like the one described above are not recognized in Continental law.[259] An author cannot convey to another a protectible personal interest in the author's work. Neither does a transferee of exploitation rights acquire any right that may be exercised independently of the author to enforce the author's personal interests. Thus, a book publisher that has obtained the publication rights to a novel does not, and cannot, acquire the moral right to determine when the work is to be disseminated. The author always may prevent publication or withdraw the work from circulation upon compensating the publisher for injury.[260] Similarly, a person in whose name a book is published pursuant to an agreement with a ghostwriter has no paternity right in his attributed authorship.[261] In fact, neither he nor the ghostwriter may prevent a third person from divulging the identity of the true author of the work.[262] Similarly, an exploitation rights transferee may only prevent third party modifications or uses of the work that infringe the transferee's exploitation rights.[263] Thus, the publisher of a novel who also holds

---

258 A transfer of moral rights could mean either that the transferee is entitled to assert the author's autonomy and reputational interests with respect to the work or that the transferee somehow acquires his own personal interests in relation to the work.

259 Eugen Ulmer, *Case Comments on Maske in Blau*, 2 I.I.C. 209, 218 (1971).

260 *See supra* notes 118-64 and accompanying text. Dietz characterizes the granting of the right to publish an unpublished work under conditions determined by the publisher as the author's authorization of the publisher to exercise the author's moral right of disclosure on the author's behalf. Dietz, *supra* note 25, at FRG-92. It would appear—and this is certainly the case if German law follows the French on this point—that this authorization is revocable. However, in a recent case concerning the right of the director of a feature film to determine when the film is ready for release, the Berlin Chamber Court declined to rule on the extent to which the right of disclosure might be transferable. Judgment of Oct. 25, 1985, Bundesgerichtshof, BGHZ 86, *discussed in* Adolf Dietz, *Letter from the Federal Republic of Germany: The Development of Copyright Between 1984 and the Beginning of 1989*, COPYRIGHT 77 (Feb. 1990) [hereinafter Dietz, Copyright 1990]. In any event, even under German Law, an author who could show that the work no longer corresponds with his convictions could effectively terminate such assignment.

261 *See* CLAUDE COLOMBET, PROPRIÉTÉ LITTÉRAIRE ET ARTISTIQUE 109 (6th ed. 1992).

262 F. FROMM & W. NORDEMANN, URHEBERRECHT 144 (5th ed. 1985).

263 In certain circumstances, the transferee may also prevent the author from modifying or using the work in a manner that would diminish the value of the exploitation rights that

the right to reproduce and produce adaptations of the novel may prevent the dissemination of a comic book version of the work only if the comic book is deemed to be either a reproduction of the novel or a type of adaptation to which the publisher holds the exclusive rights. The publisher may not prohibit dissemination of the comic book on the grounds that it is demeaning to the publisher or the author.

The single, partial caveat to the above is that, under German law, an author may authorize another to exercise and defend moral rights in the author's name; and an exploitation rights transferee acquires a similar derivate right to enforce the author's moral rights.[264] German law is uncertain whether the transferee may bring such an action in his own name or whether he must sue on behalf of the author.[265] In either event the author retains a superior and independent power of enforcement. Where the author and the transferee or authorized party disagree on whether to bring an enforcement action, the author's views prevail.[266]

B. *Waiver*

1. Disclosure and Withdrawal Rights

The rights of disclosure and withdrawal are not waivable.[267] This means that, regardless of what other rights an author has transferred or waived, theoretically, he may always prevent his work from being disseminated. In practice, however, authors will generally find it difficult to exercise these rights in the face of the exploitation right transferee's competing interests, since once the work has been completed, exercise is conditional upon compensating the transferee for damages.

---

the author has granted to the transferee. *See* STIG STRÖMHOLM, LA CONCURRENCE ENTRE L'AUTEUR D'UNE OEUVRE DE L'ESPRIT ET LE CONCESSIONAIRE D'UNE DROIT D'EXPLOITATION (1969).

264 *See* Deitz, *supra* note 25, at FRG-92; Ulmer, *supra* note 259, at 219.

265 In *Maske in Blau*, the German Federal Supreme Court explicitly declined to rule on the question of whether a transferee may sue in his own name for violation of the intellectual and personal interests of the author protected by the integrity right. The Court stated, somewhat quizzically, that the issue did not require a decision because the plaintiff transferee had withdrawn its claim for "immaterial damages" for infringement of the author's integrity right. Judgment of Apr. 29, 1970, 55 BGHZ 1. As pointed out by Professor Ulmer, however, under German Law a violation of moral rights may also give rise to injunctive relief and a claim for actual damages, and these remedies were sought by the plaintiff in *Maske in Blau.* Ulmer, *supra* note 259, at 218.

Professor Ulmer concludes that the plaintiff was merely acting with the author's authorization to defend the author's personal interests, and not suing to protect its own rights. *Id.* at 218-19. Fromm and Nordemann maintain, on the other hand, that the licensee may sue in his own name. FROMM & NORDEMANN, *supra* note 262, at 136.

266 Dietz, *supra* note 25, at FRG-92; FROMM & NORDEMANN, *supra* note 262, at 136.

267 Dietz, *supra* note 25, at FRG-55; Lucas & Plaisant, *supra* note 25, at FRA-95, FRA-102.

2. Attribution Right

It is sometimes suggested that the attribution right is waivable because it entitles an author to publish anonymously or pseudonymously rather than under his own name.[268] This position wholly misconceives the nature of the right and its exercise. The attribution right does not serve solely to allow authors to require that their works be identified as theirs; and even if it did, the failure of an author to so require in any given case does not constitute a waiver of the right but merely its non-exercise. Rather, the right gives authors control over what attribution is to be given to their works, whether it be the author's true name, another name, or no name at all.[269] Thus, if an author requires that his work be published anonymously or pseudonymously, this is an exercise of the attribution right, and not its waiver or non-exercise.

It follows that in considering whether the attribution right is waivable, the pertinent question, which has been described as "one of the most difficult in the entire realm of moral right,"[270] is whether an author may contractually bind himself to refrain from exercising his right to have the work published under his name or from publicly announcing that he is the true author of the work. French and German law diverge on this point. In France, agreements for anonymous publication or concealed collaboration are said to be unilaterally revocable by the author, who may disclose his authorship at any time.[271] In a recent case, the Paris Court of Appeals refused to recognize a ghostwriter's waiver of the attribution right, even though the contract was made in and governed by the laws of New York.[272] In Germany, an author's waiver of his

---

268 Dietz, *supra* note 25, at FRG-85 to FRG-86.

269 Lucas & Plaisant, *supra* note 25, at FRA-96; Dietz, *supra* note 25, at FRG-85. The attribution right provision of the German Act provides explicitly that the author may "determine whether the work is to bear an author's designation and what designation is to be used." GERMAN ACT, *supra* note 22, art. 13. The right of anonymous and pseudonymous publication under the French Act may be deduced from the references to such publication in various provisions of the Act, including those in Article 22 dealing with the period of copyright protection for anonymous and pseudonymous works.

270 Roeder, *supra* note 25, at 564.

271 *See* COLOMBET, *supra* note 261, at 109; Gautier, *L'Oeuvre Ecrite Par Autrui*, 139 R.I.D.A. 63, 81-83; Lucas & Plaisant, *supra* note 25, at FRA-107 (adding that an author who has consented to an anonymous or pseudonymous publication may not later claim damages for infringement of his paternity right); Schmidt, *L'Application Jurisprudentielle dela Loi du 11 Mars 1957*, 84 R.I.D.A. 91, 96 (1975). Prior to the enactment of the French Act in 1957, a body of opinion in France held that an author's waiver of the paternity right was binding unless contrary to the public interest in knowing the identity of the true author in a given instance. According to Desbois, this view ignores the fact that the traditional concept of droits d'auteur is to protect the pecuniary and moral rights of individuals, rather than the interests of society as a whole. DESBOIS, *supra* note 112, at 530.

272 Judgment of Feb. 1, 1989 (Michel de Grece), Cass civ. 1 re, 142 R.I.D.A. 301, *noted in* Lucas & Plaisant, *supra* note 25, at FRA-85. *See also* Judgment of May 5, 1993 (Villiers v.

right to recognition of authorship is deemed to be binding, except in certain unidentified "special circumstances where such an author can assert a legally protectible interest in becoming known as the creator of his work."[273]

3. Integrity Right

Uncertainty regarding the waivability of the right of integrity has centered upon the effect of the author's transfer of the exploitation right to adapt the work in another medium, such as for the production of a film, play, or opera based upon a novel. Both German and French law narrow the scope of the integrity right in such instances. The German Act provides that where an author has licensed the alteration or adaptation of his work, modifications in the work and its title to which the author cannot object in good faith are permissible.[274] Similarly, French judicial doctrine requires that an author who has authorized the adaptation of a work must accede to changes in the work that are necessitated by its transfer to another medium.[275]

Some Continental and United States commentators characterize these restrictions on an author's right to object to changes in the work as an implied waiver of the author's moral right of integrity.[276] They point to the restrictions as indicative of the limited scope and, indeed, illusory character of the principle of the inalienability of moral rights.[277] But the blanket characterization of the restrictions as an alienation of moral rights misconceives both the nature of the restrictions and the import of case law concerning author objections to modifications made by adaptation right's grantees.

Soton), Cass. civ., 158 R.I.D.A. 205 (1993) (holding that a contract clause by which an author purported to abdicate joint authorship credit could not constitute a definitive renunciation of her attribution right and was unenforceable where her co-author had acted in bad faith by taking sole authorship credit for the joint work).

[273] Dietz, *supra* note 25, at FRG-92. *See also* FROMM & NORDEMANN, *supra* note 262, at 144. Of course, even in Germany the waiver of the attribution right must be explicit, and does not arise from an assignment of exploitation rights. In fact, recent German decisions support the right of employees to receive authorship credit even if the employer holds the exploitation rights pursuant to a collective bargaining agreement and even if the employee has been lawfully dismissed prior to the work's completion. Dietz, *supra* note 198, at 198 (summarizing Judgment of Aug. 29, 1988, Landesarbeitsgerichte, 1989 Archiv für Presserecht 596 (collective bargaining agreement)); Judgment of July 5, 1991, Bundesgerichtshof, 1992 G.R.U.R. (co-editor who had helped give the work its particular shape did not lose attribution right as result of lawful dismissal).

[274] GERMAN ACT, *supra* note 22, art. 39(2).

[275] DaSilva, *supra* note 125, at 35.

[276] *See, e.g.*, DaSilva, *supra* note 125, at 16; Kwall, *supra* note 10, at 13; Paul Goldstein, *Adaptation Rights and Moral Rights in the United States and the Federal Republic of Germany*, 14 I.I.C. 43, 56 (1983); GAVIN, *supra* note 159, at 84.

[277] *Supra* note 276.

The extent to which the right of integrity can be alienated warrants a further examination of the contours of the right and of what is meant by its alienation. If the integrity right meant that the author may, at any time and under any circumstances, prevent another from modifying the author's work, then any rule that deviated from that seemingly unlimited mandate by permitting even minor modifications in the face of the author's objections would amount to a recognition of author forfeiture or waiver of the integrity right. But no abstractly-stated right is absolute. As Ronald Dworkin has noted, although rights tend to be formulated in expansive terms, they are in fact subject to various constraints, provisos, and competing interests.[278] Therefore, no matter how broadly the right of integrity may be expressed, it no more entitles the author to prevent all modifications than does the "right to free speech" give one license to libel or extort, or the "right to privacy" preclude all intrusions into one's personal affairs.[279]

In fact, the integrity right under French and German law is limited by the competing entitlements and interests of exploitation right transferees, editors, other authors and owners of material objects in which the author's work has been embodied.[280] In France the integrity right is generally expressed in absolute, maximalist terms that, if taken literally, would entitle the author to prevent any modifications.[281] But French courts have limited the right's application, first, by qualifying the meaning of "modification" and, second, by applying the doctrine prohibiting the bad faith exercise of rights. Courts have qualified the meaning of "modification" by limiting relief to alterations of the work's essential character, as determined by an objective standard, and not solely by the author's

---

278 Dworkin distinguishes between "abstract" and "concrete" rights. Abstract rights are statements of a "general political aim," such as the "right to free speech" or "equality," which do not indicate how that aim is to be weighed against other political claims in particular instances. Concrete rights are more precisely defined political aims that express with greater precision the weight they have against other political aims on particular occasions. RONALD DWORKIN, TAKING RIGHTS SERIOUSLY 93 (1977). By definition, however, a "right" must outweigh at least some social goals and must have a certain threshold weight against collective goals in general. *Id.* at 92.

279 For a detailed discussion of limitations to the right of privacy of public figures, see Robert Post, *The Social Foundations of Privacy: Community and Self in the Common Law Tort*, 77 CAL. L. REV. 957, 997-1008 (1989). For an analysis of the Supreme Court's seminal rulings regarding limitations to freedom of speech posed by the law of defamation and invasion of privacy see Melville B. Nimmer, *The Right to Speak from Times to Time: First Amendment Theory Applied to Libel and Misapplied to Privacy*, 56 CAL. L. REV. 935 (1968).

280 *See* DESBOIS, *supra* note 112, at 542-47; COLOMBET, *supra* note 261, at 112-15, 171-74.

281 *See, e.g.*, Lucas & Plaisant, *supra* note 25, at FRA-81. The reference to the integrity right in the French Act states cryptically that an "author shall enjoy the right to respect for . . . his work," without further delineating the meaning and scope of the right. FRENCH ACT, *supra* note 25, art. 6, para. 1.

sensibilities.[282] In one such case, Salvador Dali brought suit against a theater company, claiming that the addition of another artist's costumes and sets to those that Dali had designed for a ballet violated Dali's right of integrity.[283] Dali's claim was rejected on the grounds that the additions did not convey an inaccurate impression of the work.[284]

Under the doctrine of *abus de droit,* French courts will not countenance the author's bad faith or arbitrary exercise of the integrity right.[285] An author may not exercise the right "abusively to the detriment of third parties, nor unnecessarily impair interests he has granted to others in his works."[286] This rule enables courts to balance the interests of third parties, and to prevent manifestly vexatious claims.

The German formulation of the integrity right, as set forth in Article 14 of the German Act, suggests similar limitations to an absolutist conception of the right. Article 14 accords the author the right to prohibit "any distortion or other mutilation of his work

---

282 See Colombet, *supra* note 261, at 113. *Cf.* Desbois, *supra* note 112, at 541-44 (noting that an editor may correct undisputable factual errors and mistakes in spelling, punctuation and syntax so long as they are not deliberate expressions of the author's style). At least one commentator has questioned whether judges should be involved in determining what is the essential character of a work and whether particular modifications alter that character. Sarraute, *supra* note 135, at 482.

283 Judgment of Mar. 5, 1968, Cour de cassation, 1968 D.P. I 382 (Fr.); Judgment of May 11, 1965, Cour d'appel, 1967 D.S. Jur. 555 (Fr.), *discussed in* Colombet, *supra* note 261, at 113.

284 *Supra* note 283. The court might have had held differently if Dali's creation had been physically altered, rather than merely supplemented. *See* DaSilva, *supra* note 125, at 34.

285 Colombet, *supra* note 261, at 105-06; Lucas & Plaisant, *supra* note 25, at FRA-102. *But see* Judgment of June 5, 1984 (Maddalena v. Raffin), Cass. civ., 124 R.I.D.A. 150, 151 (1985) (stating, in contrast to the Court of Cassation's own rulings and practice on other occasions, that "the exercise of his moral right by the author of an original work is discretionary in nature and, therefore, it is beyond the competence of the court to assess whether the exercise is legitimate" (author's translation)).

For a general comparison of the French doctrine of *abus de droit* with U.S. equity doctrine, see Jacques Dufaux, *Equity and French Private Law, in* Equity in The World's Legal Systems: A Comparative Study (R.A. Newman ed., 1973). It is interesting to note that the concept of the moral right initially arose from judicial application of the same equitable principles set forth in article 1382 of the French Civil Code that gave birth to the doctrine of *abus de droit.* Damich, *supra* note 10, at 29.

286 Colombet, *supra* note 261, at 105-06; Lucas & Plaisant, *supra* note 25, at FRA-97. The author's obligation to act in good faith towards exploitation right transferees may, in certain circumstances, also limit the author's right to exercise other exploitation rights in the work or to exploit new, but similar, works where such acts would impair the transferee's ability to exercise his exploitation right. For an in-depth discussion of this issue, see generally Strömholm, *supra* note 79.

U.S. copyright law contains an interesting parallel to the French doctrine of *abus de droit* and German law requirements that authors must exercise good faith in exercising their integrity right. Several U.S. courts have intimated or held that the copyright owner's misuse of copyright, such as its use as an anti-competitive device, constitutes a valid equitable defense to a copyright infringement action. *See, e.g.,* Lasercomb America, Inc. v. Reynolds, 911 F.2d 970 (4th Cir. 1990).

which would prejudice his lawful intellectual or personal interests in the work."[287] The terms of the statute protect the author only against modifications that a court finds to be sufficiently substantial to warrant interference with the interests of the modifying party. In order to be actionable, a modification must be of sufficient proportion to amount to a "distortion or other mutilation" of the work, and must result in an objectively provable injury to the author's reputation or other interest accorded legal protection under the circumstances.[288] As a corollary to these constraints, the German Act contains specific requirements that the author exercise his integrity right in good faith. In essence, unless modification gives the author grounds for a good faith objection, a person who has the right to use the author's work, either as a grantee of an exploitation right, or under a compulsory license or right of fair use, may make modifications in the work and its title.[289] According to the German Federal Supreme Court, the determination of whether an author's objections are in "good faith" requires a case-by-case balancing of the author's interest in controlling his intellectual product against the user's interest in using or exploiting the work, or in creating a derivative work, by taking into account the nature of the author's work and the contemplated use.[290]

In addition to otherwise limiting the application of the integrity right, French and German law recognize that authors may give binding consent to specific changes in their work.[291] Therefore,

---

287 GERMAN ACT, *supra* note 22, art. 14.

288 *See* Dietz, *supra* note 25, at FRG-86.

289 Article 39(1) of the German Act provides that an exploitation rights licensee may not alter a work or its title unless the author has agreed to the alteration. Article 39(2), however, permits the licensee to make such "[m]odifications in the work and its title which the author cannot in good faith refuse . . . ." GERMAN ACT, *supra* note 22, art. 39(2). Article 62(1) provides that persons who are entitled, pursuant to Section VI of the German Act, to copy or disseminate a work without the author's consent, such as producers of works for personal use and organizers of a performance of a published work where spectators are admitted free of charge, may not alter the work or its title unless the author could not in good faith refuse to consent to such modification. Article 62(2) further provides that insofar as the purpose of the permitted use may require, the user may "make translations and such modifications to the work as amount merely to extracts or to transpositions into another key or pitch." *Id.* art. 62(2). Similarly, Article 62(3) provides that "[w]ith respect to artistic works and photographs, transpositions into a different scale and other modifications of the work shall be permissible to the extent required by the method of reproduction." *Id.* art. 62(3). Article 62(4) permits such modifications of literary works as are necessary for religious, school and instructional use, provided that the author has been given notice of the proposed modification and has not raised an objection within a month of such notice. *Id.* art. 62(4).

290 *See* Judgment of Apr. 24, 1970, 55 BGHZ 1 (holding that licensee's interpretation of a play that was designed to ridicule the work contained modifications to which the author could object in good faith and thus violated author's integrity right).

291 Article 56 of the French Act provides, for example, that a publisher may not modify the author's work "without the author's written consent," clearly indicating that modifica-

the right of integrity does not mean that all non-author modifications, or even mutilations, are prohibited. The right merely means that every modification—or at least every material modification—is subject to the author's consent.[292] An author's consent to a particular alteration of his work, however, does not necessarily constitute a waiver of his integrity right.[293] In essence, the integrity right gives the author continuing creative control over his work.[294] An author does not relinquish this control by agreeing to a particular modification in a particular context. The author would be surrendering creative control if he gave advance consent to whatever modifications the transferee wished to make. Such blanket consents are not enforceable under French or German law, precisely because they are seen as an impermissible waiver of the author's right of integrity.[295]

We have seen, therefore, that not every rule that permits non-author modifications necessitates an author waiver of the integrity right. We now return to the question of to what extent Continental

---

tions when permitted may not alter the work or its title unless the author could not in good faith refuse to consent to such modification. FRENCH ACT, *supra* note 25, art. 56. Article 39(1) of the German Act similarly provides that an exploitation rights licensee may not alter the work "[i]n the absence of any contrary agreement . . . ." GERMAN ACT, *supra* note 22, art. 39(1). The German Federal Supreme Court has stated in dicta that an author's consent to specific modifications, even substantial modifications that change a work's basic characteristics, will be upheld. Judgment of Apr. 24, 1970, 55 BGHZ 1.

292 *See* Dietz, *supra* note 25, at FRG-86.

293 This proposition has been supported by leading French commentators. *See, e.g.*, DESBOIS, *supra* note 112, at 539-46; COLOMBET, *supra* note 261, at 114-15. German commentators, on the other hand, tend to view an author's consent to modifications as a partial waiver of the integrity right. *See, e.g.*, Dietz, *supra* note 25, at FRG-87; Ulmer, *supra* note 259, at 218.

294 DESBOIS, *supra* note 112, at 542.

295 *Id.* at 539-41 (maintaining as well that a blanket consent to modifications in a publishing or production contract cannot be recognized under French law because it contradicts the fundamental purpose of such a contract, which is that the publisher or producer bring the work to the public with "servile fidelity to the author"); COLOMBET, *supra* note 261, at 114. *See also* Dietz *supra* note 25, at FRG-92 (stating that under German law the core of moral rights protection remains with the author despite contractual provisions purporting to effect a transfer of the author's right to alter his work or a waiver of this right to oppose alterations).

The author's consent to a particular modification may arguably be seen as a partial waiver of his integrity right only in one narrow sense. If the author truly maintained absolute creative control, then he would be free at any time to decide that he did not want his work modified after all and to require that the transferee refrain from making the modification or even re-modify the work to return it to its original state. Neither French nor German law would appear to permit the author freely to renege on his consent to a modification in this manner. *See* COLOMBET, *supra* note 261, at 115; Dietz, Copyright 1990, *supra* note 260, at 78 (writer may not waive the right to object to modifications in advance, but neither may he retrospectively object to changes that he had previously accepted). The author could effectively prevent dissemination of the modified work by invoking his right of withdrawal or correction. In this event, however, the author would be required to compensate the transferee for damages caused by the impairment of the transferee's exploitation right.

law restrictions on author control over adaptations in another medium may connote an implied waiver of the integrity right.

The author's grant of adaptation rights could treat the question of adapter freedom to modify the work in any of four basic ways. First, the transfer contract can provide that each part of the adapted work, including each and every variation from the original work, is subject to author approval.[296] In this case, Continental law imposes the good faith proviso to require that the author not unreasonably withhold consent to proposed modifications.[297] Second, the contract could explicitly state that the transferee may make whatever changes he wishes without consulting the author, and that the author waives any right to object to them.[298] Such provisions are either construed or reformed to limit adapter freedom. Adapter modifications are permitted only as long as the original work is interpreted in good faith and without distorting the work's essential character.[299] Third, the contract can explicitly authorize all changes and modifications that do not distort the spirit and character of the original. Such provisions are generally upheld.[300] Fourth, the contract can be silent with regard to the scope of adapter freedom, merely stating that the transferee may prepare

---

296 *See* Sarraute, *supra* note 135, at 482.

297 *Id. See also* Giocanti, *supra* note 125, at 642.

298 Such clauses are typical in the motion picture industry in the United States. *See, e.g.*, 2 A. LINDEY, LINDEY ON ENTERTAINMENT, PUBLISHING AND THE ARTS 806 (1990) (setting forth clause of standard contract for the grant of motion picture rights in a book that allows the grantee to make whatever modifications that "it in its sole discretion may deem advisable" and provides that the author waive his right to bring any action based on infringement of moral right or injury to professional reputation).

299 FROMM & NORDEMANN, *supra* note 262, at 259. In one early French case, a French court purported to uphold a blanket waiver clause, but nevertheless required the adapter to interpret the original work in good faith and without distorting its essential character. Judgment of July 23, 1933 (l'Affaire Bernstein), Trib. civ. seine, 1933 D.H. Jur., No. 5, at 33 (Fr.), *quoted in* DaSilva, *supra* note 125, at 35. In a more recent case, the Paris Tribunal de Grande Instance ruled that such a clause was null and void, given the inalienability of the author's integrity right and the clause's "negation of the dignity of the true author, [who was] reduced to the ridiculous status of commentator on the changes decided by the producer." Judgment of Feb. 24, 1970, Tr. gr. inst., 64 R.I.D.A. 180, 185. The court recognized that due allowance must be given to the producer's legitimate commercial and technical interests, but not to the point of recognizing a blanket waiver, designed to effect "the complete subjection of the artist" to the "discretion of a businessman," at the risk of "abasing the level of the work and degrading the taste of the audience."

An early U.S. case held that a writer's grant of motion picture rights authorizing the producer to "elaborate" on the story "however needed" did not entitle the producer to produce a film that bore no resemblance to the original work, but used its title and attributed authorship to the writer. Curwood v. Affiliated Distributors, 283 F. 219, 221 (S.D.N.Y. 1922). The court stated that the right to elaborate requires some "appropriate expression to the theme, thought, and main action of that which was originally written." *Id.* at 222. Today, U.S. motion picture producers commonly acquire the right to use the title of the original work even as the title of a motion picture that is not based on or suggested by the original work. *See* 2 LINDEY, *supra* note 298, at 803.

300 *See, e.g.*, Judgment of May 27, 1959, Trib. civ. seine, 24 R.I.D.A. 49.

a derivative work in a certain medium. In such instances, the author must accede to alterations that are dictated by the artistic, technical, and, to a more limited extent, commercial exigencies of the new medium.[301] At the same time, however, the adapter is required to transpose "with honesty, the spirit, character and substance of the work."[302] For example, in a film adaptation of a novel, the book's basic themes, plot, plan, episodes, and characters must be presented on the screen.[303]

The various standards for delineating the author's rights and transferees' obligations in these scenarios, as well as in instances in which no change of medium is contemplated, are sufficiently vague so as to elude definitive analysis. In fact, Continental commentators complain that the standards give courts overly broad discretion in considering claims involving violations of integrity rights.[304] Nevertheless, it would appear that the loss of creative control suffered by authors in transfer of medium cases is characterized more properly as a delimitation of the integrity right than a contractual waiver.[305] In the particular concrete circumstance in which an author has granted an exploitation right to another, the

---

[301] DaSilva, *supra* note 125, at 35; GAVIN, *supra* note 159, at 82.

[302] Schmidt, *supra* note 271, at 93.

[303] *Id.* at 95 (summarizing comments of Henri Desbois).

[304] *Id.* at 93-95.

[305] *See* Geller, *Introduction, in* 1 INTERNATIONAL COPYRIGHT LAW AND PRACTICE, *supra* note 25, at INT-197 (noting that judicial accommodation with competing rights avoids "the non sequitur of allowing inalienable rights to be contractually impaired"). In evaluating the waivability of the integrity right it is also instructive to review the difference between waiver, estoppel and the delimitation of an abstractly-stated right. A waiver is a voluntary and intentional relinquishment of a known right, privilege or claim. WILLISTON, *supra* note 143, § 678, at 239. But waiver is often used loosely to refer as well to estoppel in the sense of an involuntary abrogation of a right or bar from asserting a right because of something the right-holder has done or omitted to do. "Waiver is a troublesome term in the law" because of the many meanings and contexts with which it is used. *Id.* §§ 678-679, at 239-57. Estoppel has also been variously defined and applied. It generally relates to allegations of fact, but the term is also used, as in the text here, to mean the preclusion from asserting a right or taking inconsistent legal positions. For our purposes, the distinction between waiver and estoppel is important. Waiver is an expression of the intent of the affected party, whether expressly set forth or implied. *Id.* § 678, at 239-40. Estoppel is based upon public policy, fair dealing, good faith and justice. It is designed to prevent unfair injury to another. The delimitation of an abstractly-stated right is conceptually distinct from waiver and estoppel. Unlike waiver, it is derived from considerations of public policy and competing interests rather than intent. As opposed to estoppel, it requires no specific act or omission by the right holder, and need not carry with it a sense of protecting an innocent party from injustice. Nevertheless, the three concepts of waiver, estoppel and delimitation of rights often merge into one another. The intent to waive a right may be implied by words or conduct such that the right holder must, or another party may, reasonably expect that the right has been waived. The rightholder's subsequent attempt to assert the right might also be said to be estopped in order to prevent injustice to an innocent party who reasonably relied on the rightholder's words, acts or omissions. At the same time, the determination of what amounts to apparent intent to waive and what justifies reliance on the rightholder's words, acts or omissions depends to a large extent on customs of the trade, public policy and balancings of interests that define what the right holder and other par-

good faith proviso and accommodation of interests that are always at play in defining the scope of the integrity right require that the author permit the transferee to exercise the exploitation right in some reasonable fashion.[306] At the same time, like other rights that are seen as fundamental to the individual, the integrity right is accorded a certain threshold weight against competing interests. Accordingly, authors do not relinquish their right to prevent gross distortions even when they have purported to waive the integrity right. In short, the transfer of medium limitations reflect more a balancing of social goals, with the scales tipped towards the author, than a contractual impairment of the author's moral rights.

V. Additional Autonomy Inalienabilities

In complement to the doctrine of moral rights, Continental law contains a number of additional copyright alienability restrictions that serve the dual purpose of protecting authors' artistic control and promoting their material interests.[307] These include (i) the author's right to revoke a transfer if the transferee fails to meet statutory standards for exploiting the work, (ii) the requirement that copyright transfers be narrowly interpreted with respect to the rights assigned and technologies to be exploited, (iii) the prohibition against retransfer by the transferee without the author's consent, and (iv) restrictions on the transfer of future works.

A. *Assignee's Obligation to Exploit*

An unrestricted assignment of an asset or right gives the as-

---

ties may reasonably expect to be the consequences of their words and deeds under the circumstances.

306 Alternatively, the author's agreement to have his work transformed to another medium might be seen as an implied consent to those specific changes that are required for the transformation. An early U.S. case came to this result on the basis of a narrow interpretation of the contract clause requiring author approval of all alterations, eliminations and additions to be made in a play in converting it to a film. Manners v. Famous Players-Lasky Corp., 262 F. 811 (S.D.N.Y. 1919). The court held that a modification that is "faithfully consistent with the plan and sequence of the play" could not be said to constitute an alteration, elimination or addition within the meaning of the clause, and thus would not require author approval. 262 F. at 812. But, the author's implied consent to such modifications would not mean that he has waived the integrity right. The author's consent to particular changes in his work does not mean that he has surrendered creative control to the grantee. The requirement that an author may not later renege on his consent, at least without compensating the grantee, serves to avoid an injustice to the grantee, who may have incurred expenses and other burdens in reliance upon the author's consent. It is thus more correctly seen as an estoppel or delimitation of right, than a contractual waiver.

307 Other continental copyright alienability restrictions are related solely to exploitation contract payment terms. These include the author's right to proportionately participate in exploitation revenues (French Act, *supra* note 25, art. 35) and to bring a claim for equitable remuneration if exploitation revenues are grossly disproportionate to the contractually agreed upon income (German Act, *supra* note 22, art. 36).

signee the same freedom as previously enjoyed by the assignor to exploit the asset or right acquired, at the moment of choice, or to refrain completely from exploiting the asset. Under Continental copyright law, however, a transferee does not acquire the author's right to determine the conditions of exploitation or to refrain from exploitation. Rather, the transferee has a statutory obligation to exploit the assigned work in order to serve the author's personal interest in communicating his work.[308] The statutory obligation to exploit lends support to the positive aspect of the integrity right, which has been held, under certain circumstances, to entitle an author to compel the transferee to complete, preserve, and publicly display or disseminate the author's work.[309]

The obligation to exploit constitutes an integral part of copyright protection under French and German law. In France, the obligation is set out in several statutory provisions. Article 31 of the French Act provides that an assignee under an exploitation contract "shall undertake in such contract to endeavour to exploit the assigned right in conformity with professional usage."[310] Article 48 provides that an assignee's right to publish a work is subject to the "condition that he shall assure the publication and dissemination of the work."[311] Article 57 provides that a publisher "shall be required to ensure the sustained exploitation of the work without any interruption and its distribution through commercial channels according to the customs of the trade."[312] Article 57 has been the subject of much case law concerning the publication of musical works. French courts have consistently permitted authors to terminate contracts with publishers who publish sheet music, but fail to proceed with the recording and distribution of the work on records or cassettes.[313]

The assignee's obligation to exploit is viewed as the purpose of the assignment. French case law and commentary emphasize that the obligation is imposed to protect the author's personal and pe-

---

308 Ulmer & Von Rauscher auf Weeg, *supra* note 61, at 428. *See also supra* note 8 and accompanying text.

309 *See supra* notes 199-200 and accompanying text.

310 French Act, *supra* note 25, art. 31.

311 *Id.*, art. 48. On its face, Article 48 is phrased merely as a definition of a "publishing contract," rather than as a substantive provision. The Article is interpreted, however, to impose an obligation to see to it that the work is published and distributed. Henri Desbois, *L'obligation de publication et de diffusion des editeurs de musique*, 58 R.I.D.A. 163, 207, 231 (1968).

312 French Act, *supra* note 25, art. 57. Similarly, Article 63-5 provides that a producer of an audio visual work pursuant to a contract with the authors of the work "shall be required to exploit the audiovisual work in conformity with the practice of the profession." *Id.* art. 63-5.

313 Lucas & Plaisant, *supra* note 25, at FRA-76.

cuniary interests. "If the author deals with a publisher it is in order to communicate his work. A provision that would leave the [publisher] completely free not only to determine the time of publication, but also to decide whether or not it is desirable to publish the work at all, would be incompatible with the basic rationale for this relationship."[314] As a result, the author is entitled to terminate a publishing contract when the publisher breaches the obligation to publish and disseminate the work.[315]

Germany's Copyright Act does not impose an explicit obligation to exploit the licensed work, although some commentators maintain that such an obligation is nevertheless implied in all copyright contracts.[316] The German Act does, however, give the author the irrevocable right to terminate an exclusive license if the licensee fails to exercise his rights under the license, or does so inadequately, thereby causing serious injury to the author's interests.[317] The right of revocation may be exercised any time after two years from the grant or assignment of the license or the date of delivery of the work, if the delivery date is later.[318] The licensee must be given notice of the proposed revocation and an adequate period of time to exercise his rights under the license, unless such exercise is impossible or the extension would endanger the author's "primary interests."[319]

---

314 DESBOIS, *supra* note 112, at 171 (author's translation). The publisher's obligation to exploit and its basis in the author's moral rights were set forth in case law even prior to the enactment of the French Law in 1957. *See* Judgment of Dec. 8, 1925, Tribunal de commerce de la seine, 1926 G.P.I., *discussed in* Desbois, *supra* note 311, at 169-73 (1968).

315 FRENCH ACT, *supra* note 25, art. 63.

316 *See* Hans-Peter Hillig, *Contractual Freedom in German Copyright Law, in* COPYRIGHT CONTRACTS 121, 129 (H. Cohen Jehoram ed., 1977).

317 GERMAN ACT, *supra* note 22, art. 41(1). The revocation right does not apply to cinematographic works, except for licenses to adapt, transform, or otherwise use a pre-existing work for the production of a cinematographic work. GERMAN ACT, *supra* note 22, art. 90. Article 14 of the German Publishing Act provides that "[t]he publisher shall multiply and distribute the work in the appropriate and customary manner." German Publishing Act, *supra* note 160, art. 14. German courts also recognize the author's right to terminate an exploitation contract without notice if the licensee has acted so as to cause the author to lose confidence in him such that continuation of the contractual relationship is impossible. *See cases discussed in* Adolf Dietz, Letter from the Federal Republic of Germany: The Development of Copyright Between 1979 and the Beginning of 1984 (Second part), *in* COPYRIGHT 457, 462-63 (Dec. 1984) [hereinafter Dietz, Copyright 1984]. *See also* Judgment of Feb. 25, 1977, Bundesgerichtshof, BGHZ 237 (Schulze, J.), *discussed in* Adolf Dietz, Letter from the Federal Republic of Germany; Report on the Development of Copyright Between 1972 and 1979 (Second Part), 16 COPYRIGHT 129, 134 (Mar. 1980) [hereinafter Dietz, Copyright 1980].

318 GERMAN ACT, *supra* note 22, art. 41(2). In the case of a contribution to a newspaper, the period is three months, instead of two years. For contributions to periodicals the period ranges from six months to one year, depending upon the frequency of publication. *Id.* The author may agree to refrain from exercising the right of revocation for non-exercise for up to five years. *Id.* art. 41(4).

319 *Id.* art. 41(3).

The German Act requires that the author compensate the person affected by the revocation, but only to the extent that "fairness" requires.[320] The German Federal Court has declared invalid a contract clause permitting the author's right of revocation to be exercised only upon the reimbursement of fees already received. The Court held that the blanket requirement of full reimbursement conflicts with the statutory "fairness" limitation since in some circumstances fairness might require only partial reimbursement.[321]

Parallel to the author's right under the German Copyright Act to terminate an inadequately exploited license, the German Publishing Act of 1901 sharply limits the publisher's right unilaterally to terminate a publishing contract. Under the Publishing Act, a publisher may revoke a publishing contract only if the author's work is not delivered within the prescribed time or fails to meet the contract's specifications.[322] Publisher concerns about an author's marketability or even trustworthiness are insufficient grounds for revocation. Recent decisions in German regional courts have highlighted this restriction. The Regional Court of Passau held that a publisher could not terminate a publishing contract simply because the author's public image had significantly deteriorated following a sex change.[323] The Higher Regional Court of Munich held that a publisher could not unilaterally revoke its contract with a biographer who had been the subject of criticism that had cast serious doubt on the author's dependability and accuracy.[324]

United States law does not impose the same type of parallel obligation on the publisher to exploit the work, and does not provide the same type of parallel right to the author to terminate the publishing contract for breach of this obligation. United States authors have no statutory or common law right to have their works communicated to the public. As a result, exploitation right transferees have no obligation to disseminate authors' works except to the extent that the transfer of rights contract so requires. But this does not mean that authors' rights are in every instance contingent upon an express contractual provision requiring transferee exploitation. In a number of cases United States courts have held transferees to an implied duty to use reasonable efforts to exploit the work, even absent such a clause.

---

320 *Id.* art. 41(6).

321 Judgment of Feb. 18, 1982, Bundesgerichtshof, BGHZ 45, *discussed in* Dietz, Copyright 1984, *supra* note 317, at 458.

322 German Publishing Act, *supra* note 160, arts. 30 to 31.

323 *See* Dietz, *supra* note 198, at 234 (discussing Decision of 11 April 1991).

324 *Id.* (discussing Decision of 4 July 1991).

Book publishing has been a principal focus for judicial intervention in the United States. The typical book publishing contract requires the publisher to publish the book within twelve to eighteen months of receiving a complete and satisfactory manuscript, but leaves the publisher complete discretion as to the manner of publication, the number of copies printed, and the extent and means of promotion.[325] Nevertheless, courts have applied the covenant of fair dealing and good faith implied in every contract to impose upon the publisher a duty to exercise its discretion in good faith. A publisher must expend "reasonable efforts" to publish and promote a work.[326] In the seminal case of *Zilg v. Prentice Hall, Inc.*, the Second Circuit further defined this implied obligation. It ruled that the publisher must exert "a good faith effort to promote the book including a first printing and advertising budget adequate to give the book a reasonable chance of achieving market success in light of the subject matter and likely audience."[327]

This implied obligation to exploit appears to be considerably narrower than its Continental counterpart. As indicated above, Continental law recognizes the obligation to exploit as a corollary of the author's right to communicate the work to the public. Thus, the Continental obligation to exploit extends to all grantees and all means of exploitation (with certain limitations governing film production contracts under German law),[328] and may not be waived by contract.[329] In the United States, on the other hand, the rationale for judicial intervention is solely to protect the copyright owner's material interests, and not to enhance authors' ability to communicate their work. United States courts have recognized the grantee's implied duty to exploit only where, as in the typical book publishing contract, the author is to receive royalties measured by the

---

325 Melvin Simensky, *Redefining the Rights and Obligations of Publishers and Authors*, 5 Loy. Ent. L.J. 111, 122-23 (1985). *See also* E. Pearle & J. Williams, The Publishing Law Handbook § 2.07, at 2-22 (1992).

326 Zilg v. Prentice-Hall, Inc., 717 F.2d 671 (2d Cir. 1983), *cert. denied*, 466 U.S. 937 (1984); Contemporary Mission, Inc. v. Famous Music Corp., 557 F.2d 918, 923 (2d Cir. 1977).

327 *Zilg*, 717 F.2d at 680.

328 Article 90 of the German Act provides that the right of withdrawal by reason of non-exercise, as well as various other author rights, does not apply to exclusive licenses to reproduce, distribute, publicly present, or broadcast cinematographic works. The rights do apply to the exclusive licenses to make a cinematographic adaption of a non-cinematographic work, such as a book or play. German Act, *supra* note 22, art. 90. The French Act, on the other hand, explicitly extends the obligation to exploit to producers of audio-visual works. French Act, *supra* note 25, art. 63-5.

329 Under the German Act, the author's exercise of the right may be temporarily precluded by contract for up to five years, but may not otherwise be waived in advance. German Act, *supra* note 22, art. 41(4).

grantee's exploitation of the work.[330] Moreover, the grantee's implied duty arises regardless of whether or not the grantor is the author of the work or simply its copyright proprietor.[331]

In addition, the standard for fulfilling the obligation to exploit is generally more lax under United States law than under Continental law. *Zilg* requires that the publisher expend reasonable efforts to promote a book for its first printing. Once this initial obligation is fulfilled, the publisher is entitled to use good faith business judgment to decide whether further promotion is warranted, without being second-guessed by the court.[332]

Continental law imposes a more stringent obligation upon the publisher in two ways. First, at least in France the obligation to exploit appears to require greater publisher marketing efforts than the implied duty set out by United States courts. As one commentator notes, the French revocation provisions do not merely state that the publisher must reasonably promote. They require that the publisher see to it that the work is published and distributed.[333] Second, while the implied duty of the United States publisher does not extend past the first printing,[334] Continental law imposes upon publishers a continuing obligation to exploit the work.[335] It provides for author revocation if the publisher fails to publish and distribute the work for subsequent printings.[336]

The standard United States publishing contract contains a

---

330 *See* Nimmer & Nimmer, *supra* note 12, § 10.11[B], at 10-97 to 10-100. *Cf.* Moran v. London Records, Ltd., 827 F.2d 180, 183 (7th Cir. 1987) (noting that when a copyright owner assigns title in exchange for the right to receive royalties from the copyright's exploitation, a fiduciary relationship arises between the parties, entitling the assignor to sue for infringement as "beneficial owner" if the assignee fails to do so). For a typical book publishing contract royalty provision, see Lindey, *supra* note 297, at 128-31.

331 *See* Nimmer & Nimmer, *supra* note 12, § 10.11[B], at 10-97 to 10-100 (referring to "grantor" and not "author"). Under U.S. law, the source of the publisher's duty arises from the contract implied in law that a purchaser of property whose payment is based upon the earnings of the property transferred must make the property productive. Waterson, Berlin & Snyder Co. Fain v. Irving Trust Co., 48 F.2d 704, 709 (2d Cir. 1931).

332 *Zilg*, 717 F.2d at 680.

333 Desbois, *supra* note 310, at 231.

334 *Zilg*, 717 F.2d at 680.

335 *See* Lucas & Plaisant, *supra* note 25, at FRA-63.

336 In addition to French Act provisions requiring exploitation in the customary manner, Article 63 of the Act provides for author revocation if the publisher fails to reprint a work after the prior printing has been exhausted. A printing is considered exhausted if two purchase orders requesting the work are not filled within three months. French Act, *supra* note 25, art. 63. Similarly, Article 44 of the act provides that exclusive dramatic performance rights shall automatically terminate if the work has not been performed for two consecutive years. *Id.* art. 44. Like the French Act, the German Copyright Act's revocation for non-exercise provisions set no time limit on the grantee's exercise obligations. German Act, *supra* note 22, art. 41. In addition, under Article 17 of the German Publishing Act, absent a contractual provision to the contrary, the author may rescind a publishing contract upon the publisher's failure to issue a new edition within a time set by the author. *Id.* art. 17.

similar clause giving the author the right to terminate if the work remains out of print for more than six months after an author demands an additional printing.[337] However, a work is not deemed out of print as long as it is under contract or option for publication in the United States in any edition of the work, regardless of whether the work is actually being disseminated.[338]

Finally and most importantly, the obligation to exploit the work under United States law is derived from contract law, whereas the obligation under Continental law is an inherent part of the author's copyright. Therefore, in the United States the obligation attaches only to the author's immediate grantee. A remote assignee without notice of his assignor's obligations to the author or other copyright proprietor does not assume the obligation by the mere fact of the subassignment.[339] In addition, the publisher's obligation in the United States may be contractually impaired. The implied duty of good faith is based on typical contract clauses governing publisher discretion in the area of publication and promotion. Nothing would prevent the parties from expressly agreeing that the grantee is entitled to absolute discretion to refrain from any exploitation whatsoever, and that the author may not exploit the work in interference with the grantee's exclusive rights. In fact, this one-sided arrangement is typical of grants of motion picture rights in a book.[340] As long as the author receives consideration for foregoing the exploitation of his work, the clause will prevail over any implied duty to exploit.

B. *Narrow Scope of Copyright Transfers*

Continental copyright law restricts the alienability of copyright by narrowing the scope of copyright transfers. This is accomplished in two ways. First, contractual provisions defining the scope of the transfer are strictly interpreted against the transferee.[341] Second, certain copyright transfer provisions, no matter

---

337 *See* 2 LINDEY, *supra* note 298, at 136-37; PEARLE & WILLIAMS, *supra* note 325, § 2.15, at 2-44.

338 PEARLE & WILLIAMS, *supra* note 325, § 2.15, at 2-44.

339 Gay v. Robbins Music Corp., 38 N.Y.S.2d 337, 342 (N.Y. Sup. Ct. 1942), *cited in* NIMMER & NIMMER, *supra* note 12, § 10.11[B], at 10-97 n.11.

340 *See* 2 LINDEY, *supra* note 298, at 807.

341 The requirement of strict interpretation constitutes a restriction on alienability for two reasons. First, the requirement is more than simply a rule of narrow construction. It substantively reduces the scope of copyright transfers, by prohibiting the grant of rights with respect to means of exploitation that are unknown at the time of the making of the grant. Although such a grant is theoretically permitted if the author is given a participation in profits from such exploitation, it may be particularly difficult to arrive at an agreement as to profit participation given that the means of exploitation is unknown. Second, the requirement imposes a significant burden and obligation of foresight on parties that wish

how clearly and explicitly drafted, are deemed to be overbroad per se.

1. Strict Interpretation of Transfer Provisions

The requirement of strict interpretation of transfer provisions developed in case law and is now codified in both the French and German Copyright Acts.[342] The strict interpretation applies to both the exploitation right and the method or medium of exercising exploitation rights. Thus, an assignment of the right to reproduce a book will not be construed to imply the assignment of other exploitation rights, such as the right to distribute the book or recite it in public. Furthermore, the assignment of the right of public performance by wireless broadcast will not be construed to imply the assignment of the right of public performance through other media, such as cable transmission or stage dramatization.

Article 30 of the French Act provides that the transfer of either the right of performance or reproduction does not imply the transfer of the other right. The Article further provides that when a contract implies total transfer of one of these rights, the effect of the transfer is limited to the methods of exploitation explicitly set forth in the contract.[343] Article 31 requires that the transfer instrument specifically describe the transferred rights and their extent, purpose, place, and duration, thus further limiting judicial ability to give a liberal interpretation to copyright transfers.[344]

The French Act contains a number of narrow exceptions to the principle of strict interpretation. For example, under Article 45, a transfer of wireless broadcasting rights includes the transfer of the right to make simultaneous cable broadcasts to the same geographical area by the same entity that is authorized to make the wireless broadcasts.[345] In addition, Article 63(1) provides that film production contracts imply the assignment to the producer of the exclusive exploitation rights of various components of the film, un-

---

to effect global transfers. *See* Duncan Kennedy, *Distributive and Paternalist Motives in Contract and Tort Law, With Special Reference to Compulsory Terms and Unequal Bargaining Power*, 41 MD. L. REV. 563, 595-97 (1982) (noting that the non-disclaimability of a contract term is a relative concept, ranging from compulsory terms to requirements of a "clear statement" of waiver). Such parties must negotiate and include in the grant a specific enumeration of the transferred rights, which (at least in France) must encompass a description of the extent, purpose, place, and duration of each transferred right.

[342] André Françon, *Contractual Freedom in French Copyright*, *in* COPYRIGHT CONTRACTS 101, 108 (Herman Cohen Jehoram ed., 1977); Dietz, *supra* note 25, at FRG-50 to FRG-50.1.

[343] FRENCH ACT, *supra* note 25, art. 30. Articles 26, 27, and 28 of the French Act list the methods of exploitation for the rights of performance and reproduction. *Id.* arts. 26-28.

[344] *Id.* art. 31.

[345] *Id.* art. 45.

less otherwise stated in the contract.[346] Aside from these exceptions, the rule of narrow construction of copyright conveyances is strictly and uniformally applied in French statute and case law.[347]

German law, similarly requires strict interpretation of copyright transfers. Article 37 of the German Copyright Act provides that, in the case of doubt, the author retains certain adaptation, recording, and broadcast rights.[348] Article 37(1), for example, provides that where an author grants an exploitation license in his work, he is deemed to have reserved the publication and exploitation rights in any adaptation of the work, unless the contract unequivocally indicates otherwise.[349] On the other hand, Article 89(1) recognizes an implied assignment to film producers similar to Article 63(1) of the French Act.[350]

2. Voidance or Reformation of Overbroad Transfers

French and German law further limit the scope of copyright transfers by prohibiting gross transfers. Article 38 of the French Act forbids the transfer of the right to exploit a work in a manner unforeseen or unforeseeable at the time of transfer, unless it is explicitly set forth in the transfer instrument and the author is given a percentage of the exploitation profits.[351] In addition, Article 31 of the French Act provides that the transfer instrument must explicitly set forth each transferred right, together with the right's extent, purpose, place, and duration.[352] The Court of Cassation has recently confirmed that assignments purporting to transfer "all rights" violate the specificity requirements of Article 31 and are without any force and effect.[353]

The German Act contains parallel provisions. Article 31(4) provides that a transfer purporting to grant rights with respect to unknown means of exploitation is void.[354] Under this provision,

346 *Id.* art. 63(1).

347 Lucas & Plaisant, *supra* note 25, at FRA-55 (citing Judgment of Feb. 4, 1975, Cass civ. 1re, 1975 Bull. Civ. I, No. 47; Judgment of May 18, 1976, Cass civ. 1re, Bull Civ. I, No. 176.

348 German Act, *supra* note 22, art. 37.

349 *Id.* art. 37(1).

350 *Id.* art. 89(1). The implied assignment covers only technological applications known at the time of production. Judgment of Oct. 11, 1990, 22 I.I.C. 574 (1991) (holding that commercial distribution of a feature film on video cassette was an unknown use in 1968, and, therefore, not covered by the implied assignment to the producer).

351 French Act, *supra* note 25, art. 38. This provision allows the transfer of exploitation rights in unforeseeable ways if the two conditions set forth in it are met. The Article has been criticized by French commentators for failing to apply the doctrine of strict interpretation in a sufficiently stringent manner. Françon, *supra* note 342, at 109; Desbois, *supra* note 112, at 641-43.

352 French Act, *supra* note 25, art. 31.

353 Judgment of Oct. 9, 1991, Cass civ. 1re, 1991 J.C.P. II 429 (Fr.).

354 German Act, *supra* note 22, art. 31(4).

the author must retain the exclusive right to new means of exploitation that are developed after the grant is made. The German Federal Supreme Court has broadly interpreted this statute to favor authors. It has held that uses that are not yet commercially viable in Germany at the time of the grant constitute "unknown means of exploitation" within the meaning of the provision, even if the technical possibilities of use were already known.[355]

Article 31(5) of the German Act codifies the doctrine of transfer for a specified purpose (*Zweckubertrangugstheorie*). The Article provides that unless a grant of rights specifically enumerates the methods of exploitation, the scope of the grant is determined by the purpose for which it was made. The doctrine places the burden on the transferee to show that the unenumerated rights in question are within the purpose of the grant.[356] As one commentator stated: "The copyright, so to speak, tends to remain with the author as much as possible."[357]

The application of the doctrine of transfer for a specified purpose is illustrated by the Anneliese Rothenberger case.[358] In the case a television film producer acquired the exclusive right to use a manuscript "for all purposes, including radio broadcastings, television, joint antenna broadcasting, wire broadcasting and film uses, as well as for possible uses in these fields not yet known or not yet discovered."[359] After producing and televising a film based upon the manuscript, the producer sought to market video cassettes of the film for home viewing. The Federal Supreme Court held that despite the broad wording of the grant the audiovisual exploitation rights for nonpublic use had not been transferred to the producer.[360] Referring to the rule of narrow interpretation codified in Article 31(5), the Supreme Court ruled that the grant must be limited to its objective, as determined by the aim and purpose of the contract. The Court found that the sole purpose of the contract was for the production of a television program and, therefore, the reproduction and distribution of the work on video cassettes was precluded. In reaching this conclusion, the court emphasized that Article 31(5) serves to protect the author from the unfavorable

---

[355] Judgment of Oct. 11, 1990, 22 I.I.C. 574 (1991). The Court also held that the Article 31(4) restriction is applicable even where an employee has transferred exclusive exploitation rights to his employer.

[356] GERMAN ACT, *supra* note 22, art. 31(5).

[357] Ulmer, *supra* note 118, at 216.

[358] Judgment of Apr. 4, 1974, Bundesgerichtshof, 76 BGHZ 137.

[359] Ernest Pakuscher, *Recent Trends of the German Copyright Law*, 23 BULL. COPYRIGHT SOC'Y 65, 70 (1975).

[360] Dietz, Copyright 1980, *supra* note 317, at 129.

consequences of assigning several or all exploitation rights at once.[361]

3. United States Law

United States law contains no per se prohibition of global copyright transfers. It also contains no requirement that transferred rights be explicitly enumerated, and no limitation on grants with respect to unknown uses. Moreover, most American authorities eschew any notion that copyright grants are to be interpreted restrictively in order to protect the author. The traditional, majority view is simply that the scope of a copyright transfer is determined by general principles of contract interpretation.[362] In cases of ambiguity regarding the scope of a copyright transfer, United States courts adhering to this view determine the intent of the parties according to the language of the transfer instrument surrounding circumstances, and trade usage.[363] In the absence of any expression of intent, the principle that ambiguities are resolved against the drafter may work in favor of authors entering into standard publishing contracts and other contracts prepared by the transferee.[364] On the other hand, there appears to be a tendency, advocated by Nimmer, to construe copyright licenses liberally.[365] According to this approach, the license is not limited to expressly enumerated rights.[366] Rather, the licensee may pursue any use

---

361 *Id. See also* Pakuscher, *supra* note 359, at 70. The appellate court rejected the author's claim that Article 31(4) voided any purported transfer of the Super-8 film cassette rights. The court ruled that the distribution of film in this format did not constitute a new type of use. Judgment of Sept. 21, 1972, Oberlandesgericht, 72 OLGZ 6, *discussed in* Dietz, *Letter from the Federal Republic of Germany: The Development of Case Law Under the 1965 Copyright Act*, 10 COPYRIGHT 105 (1974). Recent lower court cases applying Article 31(5) have held that a grant for "all television and film purposes" did not include the right to screen video recordings of the television broadcasts at an international air show and that a grant of the right to broadcast a work of music on the radio did not include the right to broadcast the work for advertising purposes. Dietz, *supra* note 198, at 123 (discussing Higher Regional Court of Frankfurt, Decision of Dec. 22, 1988 (video recording) and Higher Regional Court of Hamburg, Decision of Mar. 1, 1990 (radio broadcast)).

362 NIMMER & NIMMER, *supra* note 12, § 10.08, at 10-71 n.1. The single exception to this statement is the presumed limitation of scope of the transfer of rights in a contribution to a collective work, such as the grant of magazine publication rights in an article. Section 201(c) of the United States Act provides: "In the absence of an express transfer of the copyright or of any rights under it, the owner of copyright in the collective work is presumed to have acquired only the privilege of reproducing and distributing the contribution as part of that particular collective work, any revision of that collective work, and any later collective work in the same series." 17 U.S.C. § 201(c) (1988).

363 NIMMER & NIMMER, *supra* note 12, § 10.10[B], at 10-85.

364 *See id.* § 10.08, at 10-71 to 10-72, and the cases cited therein. *See also* Rey v. Lafferty, 990 F.2d 1379 (1st Cir. 1993) (narrowly construing copyright grant where license agreement was drafted by licensee and the author-licensor was not represented by counsel).

365 NIMMER & NIMMER, *supra* note 12, § 10.10 [B], at 10-86.

366 *Id.*

which may reasonably be said to fall within the medium of exploitation described in the license.[367]

The rationale for this position, as expressed by Nimmer, is that where a transfer instrument includes any ambiguous term capable of an extended meaning, "it is surely more arbitrary and unjust to put the onus on the licensee by holding that he should have obtained a further clarification of a meaning which was already present than it is to hold that the licensor should have negated a meaning which the licensee might then or thereafter rely upon."[368] The burden is thus on the author to negate any possible interpretation that would expand the rights he intended to transfer, and not on the licensee to make certain that the transfer instrument explicitly includes the rights he intended to obtain.

The majority view leads to the opposite result than that reached in the Anneliese Rothenberger case. As pointed out by Nimmer, the approach of liberal construction would require that "a grant of the right to exhibit a motion picture by 'television' . . . includes any device by which the motion picture may be seen on television screens, including cable television and video cassette uses."[369] This was the result in *Platinum Record Co. v. Lucasfilm, Ltd.*,[370] which held that a grant executed in 1973 to exploit a motion picture "by any means or methods now or hereafter known" included the right to exploit by video cassettes and video discs, even though such methods of exploitation might not have been contemplated when the grant was made.[371]

In contrast to the majority view, the Ninth Circuit has recently taken the position that state law canons of contractual construction are subordinate to the federal copyright policy of protecting author rights.[372] As a result, a number of Ninth Circuit cases have enunciated the rule that copyright grants are assumed to prohibit

---

367 *Id.*

368 *Id.* at 10-87 (footnote omitted). *But see Rey*, 990 F.2d at 1388 (suggesting that narrow construction may be more appropriate where licensor lacks business acumen and has no reason to know of the potential new uses).

369 NIMMER & NIMMER, *supra* note 12, § 10.10[B], at 10-87.

370 566 F. Supp. 226 (D.N.J. 1983).

371 *Id.* at 227. *See also* Bartsch v. Metro-Goldwyn-Mayer, Inc., 391 F.2d 150 (2d Cir. 1968); Landon v. Twentieth Century-Fox Film Corp., 384 F. Supp. 450 (S.D.N.Y. 1974); Rooney v. Columbia Pictures Indust., 538 F. Supp. 211, 229 (S.D.N.Y. 1982) ("Where . . . a party has acquired a contractual right which may fairly be read as extending to media developed thereafter, the other party can hardly avoid the contract's application to such media by establishing that the precise nature of the advance was not anticipated.").

372 *See* S.O.S., Inc. v. Payday, Inc., 886 F.2d 1081, 1088 (9th Cir. 1989); Cohen v. Paramount Pictures Corp., 845 F.2d 851 (9th Cir. 1988); Apple Computer, Inc. v. Microsoft Corp., 759 F. Supp. 1444, 1451 (N.D. Cal. 1991).

any use not explicitly authorized.[373] In one such case, *Cohen v. Paramount Pictures Corp.*,[374] a grant of the right to reproduce and exhibit a motion picture by "means of television" was held not to include the right to distribute videocassettes of the film. In its ruling, the court cited the fact that videocassettes had not yet been invented when the license was executed and that language in the license reserving to the author all rights not granted be construed in accordance with the purpose underlying federal copyright law.[375]

C. *No Further Transfer Without the Author's Consent*

A fundamental tenet of ownership is the right to dispose of the object of ownership at one's will.[376] Accordingly, an assignee of an object or property right is generally free to reassign it to another without having to obtain the consent of the assignor. Continental copyright law, however, generally requires that a copyright transferee obtain the author's consent before transferring all or part of a copyright to a third party.

Article 62 of the French Act provides that a publisher may not transmit the benefits of a publishing contract to a third party, other than as part of a transfer of his business, without first obtaining the author's authorization. Even the assignment of "full title" of the copyright does not accord the publisher the right to reconvey to a third party without the author's consent.[377] If the publisher does transfer his business, the author is entitled to terminate the publishing contract if that is necessary to prevent serious injury to his material interests or moral rights. Similarly, Article 44 provides that a theatrical producer holding performance rights for a work may not transfer the rights without the author's formal, written consent.[378]

Under German law, a copyright may only be transfered by way of a license to use the right, and not by assignment of the right itself.[379] It is not surprising, therefore, that the transferee must obtain the author's consent before assigning the license or granting a

---

373 *Supra* note 371. *Cf.* Amarnick, *supra* note 10 (proposing that the scope of copyright transfers should be narrowly interpreted to protect the author's interest in maintaining the work's integrity).

374 845 F.2d 851 (9th Cir. 1988).

375 *Id.* at 854-55.

376 *See* Honore, *supra* note 1, at 118-19.

377 Judgment of June 17, 1993 (Defez v. Didier) Paris Cours d'appel, 158 R.I.D.A. 252 (1993).

378 The French Act does not contain a provision regarding audio-visual production contracts, suggesting that exploitation rights in audio-visual works may be freely reassigned.

379 GERMAN ACT, *supra* note 22, arts. 29, 31.

non-exclusive sublicense.[380] (However, the author may not in bad faith refuse to give such consent; and, no consent is required if the license is assigned as part of a sale of the licensee's business.)[381] As in France, the author cannot give a blanket consent to reassignment in advance.[382] The German Federal Supreme Court invalidated a clause in the standard copyright license contract of a broadcasting organization which purported to authorize the reassignment of the licensed rights without the consent of the author.[383]

United States copyright law imposes no restriction on subsequent copyright assignments, although, under general principles of law, a copyright licensee may not transfer his right to use a work without the consent of the licensor. A couple of cases have held that an owner of a copyright may rely upon a negative covenant to restrict the use of the work in the hands of a remote assignee.[384] But other cases have held that a remote assignee is not bound under a covenant restricting or forbidding transfers unless he had actual or constructive knowledge of the covenant.[385] In any event, it is unclear whether a covenant purporting to restrict further assignments without the author's consent would be enforceable.

D. *Future Works*

Publishers and other copyright grantees often seek to acquire rights in the author's subsequent works. From the grantee's perspective this represents a legitimate claim, given the grantee's efforts to build an audience for the author's prior work.[386] Continental law, however, seeks to protect the author's interest in his future production by restricting the transfer of future works. These restrictions serve to protect the author's material interests by preventing a young author's wholesale transfer of future rights at a time when he has little or no bargaining power.[387] In addition,

---

380 *Id.* arts. 34, 35. Consent is not required to grant a nonexclusive sublicense when the exclusive license is granted merely to safeguard the author's interests. An example of such a situation is a grant to an authors' collection society. *Id.* art. 35(1). In addition, the author's consent is not required for the assignment of an exclusive license or the grant of a non-exclusive license of various rights to exploit a cinematographic work. *Id.* art. 90.

381 *Id.* arts. 34(1), 34(3).

382 *Id.*

383 *See* Judgment of Feb. 18, 1981, Bundesgerichtshof, 82 BGHZ 81, *discussed in* Dietz, Copyright 1984, *supra* note 312, at 458.

384 *See* Capital Records v. Mercury Records Corp., 221 F.2d 657 (2d Cir. 1955) (stated with respect to common law copyright under New York law); *In re* Waterson, Berlin & Snyder Co., 48 F.2d 704 (2d Cir. 1931).

385 *See* NIMMER & NIMMER, *supra* note 12, § 10.12, at 10-101 and the cases cited therein.

386 *See* PEARLE & WILLIAMS, *supra* note 325, at 70.

387 Lucas & Plaisant, *supra* note 25, at FRA-55; Dietz, *supra* note 25, at FRG-59 to FRG-60.

Continental commentators point out that an author's long-term obligation to produce books for a particular publisher, or a painter's commitment to produce paintings for a particular dealer, runs counter to the creator's personal interest in determining when and how his work is communicated to the public.[388] Gierke argued that the global assignment of all future works, including works of a specific type, constitutes an illegal limitation on the development of the author's personality.[389] Allfeld held that global transfers are subject to voidance under Section 138 of the German Civil Code, which provides that any agreement contrary to good morals has no obligatory force. He posited that "undue restrictions on personal liberty" resulting from such transfers could amount to an injury to good morals within the meaning of the statute.[390] Strömholm maintains that an author's obligation concerning future production restricts his "right to create," a right rooted in moral rights and other doctrine.[391]

Article 33 of the French Act provides that transfer of all rights in future works is voidable by the author.[392] The rule applies whenever there is a conveyance of the entire copyright in two or more future works.[393] Some commentators maintain that the Article is also applicable to the conveyance of less than the entire copyright in future works.[394] An author may grant a preferential right to a publisher for the publication of his future works of a clearly specified kind.[395] However, the publisher's right must be limited to five new works of the specified kind, or to the works the author may produce within a term of five years from the date of signature of the publishing contract.[396] A clause conveying a preferential right to a publisher that does not contain one of those two limitations is voidable by the author.[397]

---

388 STRÖMHOLM, *supra* note 79, at 127.

389 *Id.* at 132.

390 *Id.* at 133.

391 *Id.* at 356.

392 The Article states that the "[t]otal transfer of future works is void." FRENCH ACT, *supra* note 25, art. 33. However, since only the author can invoke the statute, the total transfer is not void ab initio. Lucas & Plaisant, *supra* note 25, at FRA-55.

393 Lucas & Plaisant, *supra* note 25, at FRA-55.

394 Françon, *supra* note 342, at 106.

395 FRENCH ACT, *supra* note 25, art. 34. French courts have invalidated clauses granting a preferential right to "works of prose" on the grounds that the designation of the type of work is not sufficiently narrow and precise. André Françon, *Recent French Jurisprudence Concerning Publishers' Contracts, in* COPYRIGHT CONTRACTS 5, 9 (Herman Cohen Jehoram ed., 1977).

396 FRENCH ACT, *supra* note 25, art. 34.

397 Lucas & Plaisant, *supra* note 25, at FRA-57 (citing Judgment of July 8, 1972, 624 J.C.P. II, No. 17566, at 73); Françon, *supra* note 395, at 11 (citing Judgment of Jan. 31, 1970, Trib. gr. inst., 64 R.I.D.A. 176). In addition, when the publisher has successively refused two new

The German Act is somewhat less restrictive of the transfer of future works. A license of future works is permitted, but any license of unspecified future works may be terminated by either party after a period of five years from the date of the agreement.[398] Where the nature of the future works is not specified in detail, the license agreement must be in writing.[399] A transfer of future works for which the author received inadequate consideration may be voided by the author on general contract grounds.[400]

To understand their full import, the future works restrictions must be read in conjunction with the moral right of disclosure. The former voids contractual commitments for the transfer of future works that exceed the statutory limitations regarding duration and specificity. The latter gives the author a limited right to renege even upon contractual commitments that fall within the statutory limitations. Where the author fails to produce a commissioned work as a result of good faith lack of inspiration, he is simply excused from performance and absolved from liability. Where he produces but refuses to deliver the work or its copyright to the second party, he is still excused from specific performance, but must compensate the second party for injury and refrain from effecting a transfer to a third party without first offering the work to the second party. Ultimately, the author cannot be required to hand over his work to a publisher whose views, reputation, or manner of promotion he has come to find objectionable. At the same time, within the statutory restrictions designed to protect authors' personal and material interests, transferees may obtain some redress for the thwarting of legitimate contractual expectations.

The U.S. Copyright Act does not address the transfer of works that have yet to come into existence. As a result, courts in this country have looked to contract law to determine the enforceability of future works agreements. American case law in this area views such agreements as containing elements of both a sale of goods and a personal service contract. It reflects the view of copyright as property, tempered in part by a certain judicial reluctance

works of the specified kind, the author may terminate the publisher's preferential right to that kind of work as long as he refunds any advances he received from the publisher for such works. FRENCH ACT, *supra* note 25, art. 34.

398 GERMAN ACT, *supra* note 22, art. 40. The provision would also appear to apply where a publisher is given a preferential right to acquire the license for each work. STRÖMHOLM, *supra* note 79, at 125-27.

399 GERMAN ACT, *supra* note 22, art. 40.

400 Hillig, *supra* note 316, at 129. Section 138 of the Civil Code (Bürgerliches Gesetzbuch) provides for the voiding of contractual provisions which run counter to prevailing moral standards. *Id. See also* STRÖMHOLM, *supra* note 79, at 133-35.

to order specific performance of personal service commitments.[401]

At common law a vendor cannot transfer by present sale a thing that he does not own, even though he expects to acquire it. But, as noted by the Second Circuit in *T.B. Harms & Francis, Day & Hunter v. Stern*,[402] if a future work of authorship has been transferred, then like a vendor's sale of a future acquisition, the equitable title to the property attaches and vests in the grantee the moment the work comes into existence.[403] As a general rule, therefore, the grantee may require by specific performance the assignment of the author's interest in the work immediately upon its completion. At the same time, however, as further noted by the court in *T.B. Harms*, an author's agreement to give, in exchange for a present consideration, an exclusive right in all works that he might produce at any time in the future in exchange might be void as contrary to public policy.[404] This possible flaw would be cured if the author's obligation were sufficiently limited in time or by category or, conceivably, if the author were paid a royalty, rather than lump sum, so as not to erode his incentive to produce.[405]

U.S. courts have issued injunctions prohibiting authors who have undertaken to provide future works for a given party over a given period of time from providing those works to another person during that period.[406] However, such injunctions have issued only where the author's services are of a unique or extraordinary quality, such as where the author is particularly talented or well-known in relevant field.[407]

Finally, an author may be able to revoke a commitment to supply future works for an unlimited period. In some states a contract that is of indefinite duration may be terminable at will by either party. The Ninth Circuit, however, has recently held that California's terminable-at-will rule as applied to copyright licenses is preempted by the Copyright Act.[408] The court ruled that, absent a material breach on the part of the licensee, an author-licensor may terminate a copyright license only in accordance with Section 203

---

401 *See* NIMMER & NIMMER, *supra* note 12, § 10.03[A], at 10-36. *See also* Paige v. Banks, 80 U.S. (13 Wall.) 608 (1871) (holding that the right to publish an uncreated manuscript is a fully assignable property right). *But see* Associated Newspapers v. Phillips, 294 F. 845 (2d Cir. 1923) (holding that a journalist's agreement to furnish a newspaper with six articles per week is an employment contract, and not a contract for the sale of the articles).

402 229 F. 42 (2d Cir. 1915), *vacated on other grounds*, 231 F. 645 (2d Cir. 1916).

403 *Id.* at 48.

404 *Id.*

405 *Id.*

406 Associated Newspapers v. Phillips, 294 F. 845 (2d Cir. 1923).

407 *Id.* at 850; Kenner v. Simonds, 247 F. 822, 828 (S.D.N.Y. 1917).

408 Ramo v. Sipa Press, Inc., 987 F.2d 580 (9th Cir. 1993).

of the Act, which provides for author termination of a copyright grant at the close of 35 years following the grant.[409]

In sum, United States authors may be required, with certain limitations, to transfer their rights in their work or, alternatively, to refrain from realizing their rights altogether. Where these limitations are exceeded, author commitments to deliver as yet uncreated works are unenforceable.

VI. Conclusion

In contrast to the virulent personalist core of Continental autonomy inalienabilities, the United States analogues amount to a patchwork of legal doctrines designed to protect a variety of personal and economic interests, some pertaining to the author, some to whomever may be the copyright owner, and some to the public at large. It is not surprising, therefore, that Continental authors enjoy a measure of continuing control over whether, in what form, and through which agency their work is to be presented to the public that has no parallel in the United States. As opposed to their American colleagues, Continental authors may not be required to countenance, despite purported contractual obligations to the contrary, (1) the publication or continued dissemination of their work, (2) the public presentation of their work in a manner that significantly contradicts their artistic conception, regardless of its effect upon their reputation, (3) authorship attribution in a manner that does not accord with their wishes, (4) the failure of the exploitation right transferee to promote the work in accordance with statutory requirements, (5) the global transfer of all exploitation rights, (6) the exploitation right transferee's retransfer of the work, or (7) the unlimited transfer of future works, even if the author is to receive an additional payment for each work. In addition, in contrast to the majority view in the United States, the terms of Continental authors' exploitation rights grants are narrowly construed so as to maintain author control to the extent possible. To be sure, the exploitation rights of Continental authors are subject to a requirement of good faith and a certain accommodation to competing interests. However, even taking this into account the legal results from the application of United States analogues reach only a diminutive approximation of their Continental counterparts.

Moreover, the meaning of Continental autonomy inalienabilities cannot be measured solely by their legal result. The existence of a cohesive legal doctrine of author autonomy and personal con-

---

409 *Id.* at 585-86.

nectedness to one's original works promotes a very different conception of creative expression than does a proprietary copyright system. Legal rules help to determine the way we talk and think about ourselves, our possessions, attributes and community.[410] Thus, even if the United States analogues were to approximate similar legal results at this point in time, their overall social effect—and ultimate legal result—would vary substantially from that of Continental autonomy inalienabilities.

This conclusion does not necessarily mean that we should refrain from adopting autonomy inalienabilities in this country. The systematic implementation of such alienability restrictions would clearly entail a radical revision of our conception of creative expression. It would require that we view authors' works less as a market good and more as a constitutive part of personality.[411] At the same time, however, the Continental experience suggests that a significant decommodification of creative expression is possible even within the framework of a market society and need not prevent the widespread dissemination and commercial exploitation of authors' works.

---

410 *See* Cass Sunstein, *Legal Interference with Private Preferences*, 53 U. CHI. L. REV. 1129, 1146 (1986) ("It is hard to imagine a preference not shaped in part by legal arrangements.").

411 I have argued elsewhere that such a radical revision would better serve the interests of individual self-realization and diversity of expression than the current American proprietary copyright regime. *See* Neil Netanel, *Copyright Alienability Restrictions and the Enhancement of Author Autonomy: A Normative Evaluation*, 24 RUTGERS L.J. 347 (1993).

MORAL RIGHTS PROTECTION AND RESALE ROYALTIES FOR VISUAL ART IN THE UNITED STATES: DEVELOPMENT AND CURRENT STATUS

EDWARD J. DAMICH*

I. INTRODUCTION

The moral rights landscape in the United States is currently composed of federal moral rights legislation, state moral rights legislation, and other causes of action that have produced results similar to those codified in moral rights laws. The outstanding legal authority in this area, the Visual Artists Rights Act of 1990 ("VARA"),[1] amended the Copyright Act of 1976,[2] and for the first time expressly provided for national statutory moral rights protection for the visual arts. VARA grants the author of a work of visual art the right of attribution and the right of integrity.

Prior to 1980, lawyers representing visual artists were faced with making creative arguments based on causes of action that developed in response to more general problems, such as defamation, violations of the right of privacy, unfair competition, contract interpretation, and other provisions of the Copyright Act.[3] California was the first state to enact moral rights legislation, effective in 1980. Currently, only eleven states have express moral rights statutes.[4] In some cases these statutes and common law tort actions provide broader protection than VARA. Their availability, however, is qualified by the doctrine of preemption, which holds that federal statutes trump state statutes and common-law causes of ac-

---

* Copyright 1994, Edward J. Damich. Professor of Law, George Mason University School of Law; former Commissioner, Copyright Royalty Tribunal; J.S.D., L.L.M., Columbia University; J.D., Catholic University. This article was based on a paper presented by the author at the Bezalel Academy of Art and Design, Jerusalem, Israel.

1 Visual Artists Rights Act of 1990, Pub. L. No. 101-650, 104 Stat. 5128 (1991) (codified in scattered sections of 17 U.S.C.) [hereinafter VARA].

2 Copyright Act of 1976, Pub. L. No. 94-553 (1976).

3 In 1976, the United States Court of Appeals for the Second Circuit recognized a cause of action based on moral rights for the broadcasting of a truncated version of a Monty Python television program. The moral rights part of the decision was not followed by any other circuit. Gilliam v. American Broadcasting Co., 538 F.2d 14 (2d Cir. 1976).

4 CAL. CIV. CODE § 987 (West 1992); CONN. GEN. STAT. ANN. § 42-116s (West 1992); LA. REV. STAT. ANN. R.S. 51:2152 (West 1992); ME. REV. STAT. ANN. tit. 27, § 303 (West 1991); MASS. ANN. LAWS ch. 231, § 85S (Law Co-op 1992); NEV. REV. STAT. ANN. § 598.970 (Michie 1991); N.J. STAT. ANN. § 2A:24A-1 (West 1992); N.M. STAT. ANN. § 13-4B-2 (West 1992); N.Y. ARTS & CULT. AFF. § 14.01 (McKinney 1992); PA. STAT. ANN. tit. 73, § 2101 (Purdon Supp. 1991); R.I. GEN. LAWS § 5-62-2 (1987). *See also* R.I. GEN. LAWS § 42-75.2-3 (1993).

tion when there is conflict. In order to get an accurate picture of the strength and extent of moral rights protection, the complication and uncertainty inherent in the doctrine of preemption must be remembered. Courts have held that state statutory and common-law causes of action have been preempted by federal statutes when the state provides a right *in addition* to the federal right.[5] This reasoning is based on the proposition that in some cases, if Congress has *not* provided a right, it made a decision that no one should provide that right in the interests of national uniformity.[6]

The theoretical underpinning of moral rights is that the artist's work reflects and embodies his or her personality. However, the impetus for enactment of federal moral rights legislation did not come from the gradual acceptance of this theory. The concept that the artist should continue to control the destiny of his or her work even after it was sold conflicted with the traditional reverence for private property rights. That the artist should have a personal right based on the act of artistic creation itself seemed also to depart from the utilitarian basis for copyright protection found in the United States Constitution.[7] There were scholars, legislators, and members of the Copyright Bar who had accepted the personality theory, but the event that eventually led to VARA was the adherence of the United States to the Berne Convention on March 1, 1989. Article 6*bis* of the Berne Convention provides:

> (1) Independently of the author's economic rights, and even after the transfer of said rights, the author shall have the right to claim authorship of the work and to object to any distortion, mutilation or other modification of, or other derogatory action in relation to, the said work, which would be prejudicial to his honour or reputation.[8]

The legislation addressing the rights of article 6*bis* was not enacted until about two years after the passage of the Berne Convention Implementation Act.[9] Against all reason,[10] the United States

---

5 *See* Sears, Roebuck & Co. v. Stiffel Co., 376 U.S. 225 (1964). *See also* Compco Corp. v. Day-Brite Lighting, 376 U.S. 234 (1964) (companion case to *Sears*).

6 *Id.*

7 "The Congress shall have Power . . . To promote the Progress of Science and useful Arts, by securing for limited Times to Authors and Inventors the exclusive Right to their respective Writings and Discoveries." U.S. CONST. art. I, § 8, cl. 8.

8 *Guide to the Berne Convention, Art 6bis*, Pub. No. 615(E) (World Intellectual Property Organization) (1978) [hereinafter *Guide*].

9 Berne Convention Implementation Act of 1987, Pub. L. No. 100-568, 102 Stat. 2853 (codified in scattered sections of 17 U.S.C.).

10 *See generally Berne Convention Implementation Act of 1987: Hearings on H.R. 1623 Before the Subcomm. on Courts, Civil Liberties, and the Administration of Justice of the House Committee on the Judiciary*, 100th Cong., 1st and 2d Sess. 538 (1987) (statement of Edward J. Damich, Assoc. Prof. of Law, George Mason University School of Law).

delayed taking the position that the existing state statutes and other causes of action that produced moral rights-like results were sufficient to fulfill its obligations under article 6*bis* and therefore no federal moral rights statute was necessary.[11] As a result, the Berne Convention Implementation Act not only contained no moral rights provisions, but it also specifically denied the right to base a cause of action on the language of the Berne Convention, lest some hapless artist should attempt to obtain judicial relief based on article 6*bis* alone. Congress eventually enacted VARA, but it limited moral rights protection to the visual arts.

This article addresses the three features of the moral rights landscape in the United States: (1) the causes of action that yield moral rights-like results (coincidental causes of action), (2) the state moral rights statutes, and (3) VARA. This order was selected since it replicates the historical development of moral rights protection for visual art in the United States.

In this article, moral rights refers to the two general moral rights recognized by article 6*bis*: "the right of attribution" or "the right of paternity,"[12] and "the right of respect for the work" or the "right of respect"[13] and the various subrights included within them.

In addition, this article discusses the *droit de suite* or resale royalties; the right of the artist to obtain a payment from the resale of

---

[11] Dr. Arpad Bogsch, Director General of the World Intellectual Property Organization ("WIPO"), testified before the Senate Subcommittee on Patents, Copyrights and Trademarks in favor of this position. *See generally U.S. Adherence to the Berne Convention: Hearings Before the Subcomm. on Patents, Copyrights and Trademarks of the Senate Committee on the Judiciary*, 99th Cong., 1st and 2d Sess. 8 (1985) (statement of Dr. Arpad Bogsch, Director General, WIPO, Geneva, Switzerland).

[12] The right of attribution includes:

(1) the subright of proper attribution, that is, the subright against non-attribution of the author's work or attribution of the author's work to another;

(2) the subright against false attribution, that is, the subright against attributing to an author a work that she did not create or attributing a work to the author when it has been modified or distorted; and

(3) the subright of anonymity and pseudonymity, which includes the right to reject anonymity and pseudonymity. Note that the subright of proper attribution can be distinguished generally from the subright against false attribution because the former always involves the author's *work*, while the latter focuses primarily on the author's *name*.

[13] "Right of respect" refers to the right "to object to any distortion, mutilation or other modification of, or other derogatory action in relation to the work." *See Guide, supra* note 8, at 41.

This right includes:

(1) the subright against modification, that is, the subright to object to acts that physically affect the original of the work itself but do not utterly destroy it, such as painting an unpainted sculpture;

(2) the subright against unfaithful reproduction, that is, the subright to object to poor-quality reproductions or derivative works involving copies that pervert the work;

(3) the subright against destruction; and

(4) the subright against distortion, that is, the subright to object to any derogatory action that does not physically affect the original or involve reproduction.

his or her work. This right, which is optional under article 14*ter* of the Berne Convention, was included in an early version of VARA, and it has been the subject of a recent study by the United States Copyright Office.[14]

II. Coincidental Causes of Action

Until the California moral rights statute became effective in 1980, the only realistic hope for an artist to obtain moral rights protection for his or her work of visual art was through various common-law causes of action, Section 43(a) of the Lanham Act (the federal trademark and unfair competition statute), or some provisions of the Copyright Act.[15] These coincidental causes of action are still available to supplement other protection, but the common-law causes of action are subject to preemption.

Prior to 1976, courts routinely rejected causes of action based expressly on moral rights. For example, a muralist argued in the 1938 case *Crimi v. Rutgers Presbyterian Church*[16] that his moral rights were violated when a church had his mural painted over because it portrayed Christ with a bare chest.[17] The court unequivocally stated that "the claim of this plaintiff that an artist retains rights in his work after it has been unconditionally sold, where such rights are related to the protection of his artistic reputation, is not supported by the decisions of our courts."[18] Similarly, in 1947, when an artist complained that his moral rights were violated by a magazine's publication of his drawings without attribution, the court stated that "[t]he conception of 'moral rights' of authors so fully recognized and developed in the civil law countries has not yet received acceptance into the law of the United States."[19]

In 1976, the United States Court of Appeals for the Second Circuit in *Gilliam v. American Broadcasting Co.*[20] recognized a cause of action based simply on a violation of moral rights. However, the acceptance of a separate cause of action based on moral rights did not significantly improve, because no other court followed the lead of *Gilliam*.

---

14 *Droit de Suite: The Artist's Resale Royalty*, 1992 Reg. of Copyrights [hereinafter *Resale Royalty Report*].

15 *See generally* Edward J. Damich, *The Right of Personality: A Common-Law Basis for the Protection of the Moral Rights of Authors*, 23 Ga. L. Rev. 1, 35-75 (1988).

16 89 N.Y.S.2d 813 (N.Y. Sup. Ct. 1949).

17 *Id.* at 819.

18 *Id.*

19 Vargas v. Esquire, 164 F.2d 522, 526 (7th Cir. 1947), *cert. denied*, 335 U.S. 813 (1948) (quoting S. Ladas, The International Protection of Literary and Artistic Property 802 (1938)).

20 538 F.2d 14 (2d Cir. 1976).

The common-law causes of action that produce moral rights-like results in some instances involve defamation, the right of privacy, unfair competition, and contract interpretation.[21]

Except for contract interpretation, the common-law causes of action and Section 43(a) depend on deception, invasion of privacy, or injury to reputation.[22]

A. *Defamation*

The essence of the tort of defamation is injury to the reputation of the plaintiff by making a false statement to another. There is precedent for using the tort of defamation to protect the right of attribution, specifically, the subright against false attribution. In *D'Altomonte v. New York Herald Co.*,[23] the court held that the plaintiff's reputation was injured by the defendant's attribution to him of an article that he had never written. In *Edison v. Viva International*,[24] the court held that the plaintiff's reputation was injured when the defendant published a distorted version of the plaintiff's article and attributed it to him. In *Edison*, it was not the mere distortion of the plaintiff's work that gave rise to the cause of action but the injury to the plaintiff's reputation that resulted from the *attribution* of the distorted article to the plaintiff. Because of the nature of the tort of defamation, there must always be either explicit or implicit identification of the plaintiff as author of the work. Where the author's work is not attributed at all or where the author's work is attributed to another, there can be no injury to the author's reputation and, therefore, no defamation. Thus, the tort of defamation cannot be used to protect the subright of proper attribution or the subright of anonymity or pseudonymity nor can it protect the right of respect except indirectly.

Even in the case of the subright against false attribution, there can be no recovery if the author's reputation has not been injured. This is significantly different from the unqualified right of attribution found in the language of article 6*bis*.[25]

Finally, as a stand-in for the subright of false attribution, the tort of defamation has two other shortcomings: (1) courts are reluctant to grant injunctions against false attribution because of

---

21 In addition, there were various provisions in the Copyright Act of 1976 that provided some moral rights-like results, although the Act did not specifically recognize moral rights until the passage of VARA. *See* Damich, *supra* note 15, at 41-47.

22 *Id.* at 35-75.

23 139 N.Y.S. 200 (N.Y. Sup. Ct.), *aff'd*, 208 N.Y. 600 (1913).

24 421 N.Y.S.2d 203 (N.Y. Sup. Ct. 1979).

25 Note that arguably the requirement of prejudice to honor or reputation applies only to the right of respect. *See Guide*, *supra* note 8.

freedom of expression concerns, and (2) traditionally, the tort of defamation cannot be asserted posthumously.[26]

B. *Right of Privacy*

A cause of action based on the common-law right of privacy has been successfully used to vindicate the subright against false attribution and may possibly be used to vindicate the right of anonymity and pseudonymity. The *Restatement (Second) of Torts* lists four kinds of acts that give rise to a cause of action: (1) unreasonable intrusion upon the seclusion of another, (2) appropriation of the other's name or likeness, (3) unreasonable publicity given to the other's private life (or public disclosure of private facts), and (4) publicity that unreasonably places the other in a false light before the public.[27]

The subright against false attribution corresponds to publicity that places the other in a false light before the public or appropriation of the other's name or likeness.[28] Courts have recognized, such a right in various circumstances. In *Kerby v. Hal Roach Studios,*[29] the defendant attributed to the plaintiff and published a letter that the plaintiff did not write and that cast doubt on her moral character. Similarly, in *Stevens v. NBC*[30] the plaintiff obtained a preliminary injunction to prevent the distortion of the film, "A Place in the Sun," by the insertion of commercials during its television broadcast. In *Big Seven Music v. Lennon,*[31] the court, on the grounds of misappropriation, enjoined the release of a record album that was compiled from John Lennon's tapes without his permission and which Lennon claimed distorted his work. After analyzing these cases, it becomes clear that courts focus their attention on the improper association of the plaintiff's identity with the work and that the integrity of the work is protected coincidentally.

There is no definite precedent in United States law for protecting the rights to remain anonymous or pseudonymous by using the "public disclosure of private facts" prong of the Restatement's right of privacy despite similarity of concept,[32] although scholars

---

26 RESTATEMENT (SECOND) OF TORTS § 560 (1977).

27 *Id.* § 652A (1977).

28 *See* Damich, *supra* note 15, at 54.

29 127 P.2d 577 (Cal. Dist. Ct. App. 1942).

30 148 U.S.P.Q. (BNA) 755 (1966).

31 409 F. Supp. 122 (S.D.N.Y. 1976) (pertaining to an action brought by record company against ex-Beatle, John Lennon, for allegedly wrongfully preventing company's distribution of music produced by Lennon). The opinion is unclear whether the action was for invasion of privacy in addition to misappropriation or whether the misappropriation was the invasion of privacy.

32 *Id.*

often cite *Ellis v. Hurst*[33] for support. In *Ellis*, the plaintiff/author sued to prevent the publisher, who had the right to publish his book under a pseudonym, from publishing his book using his real name. However, a careful examination of *Ellis* reveals that it came before the same court twice, and that the second time the court found *against* the plaintiff.[34]

In sum, the right of privacy cases deal only with the right of attribution, not the right of respect.[35] Within the right of attribution, there is strong precedent protecting the subright against false attribution, where the attribution is to a work that has been tampered with. Authority is weaker for the subrights of anonymity and pseudonymity. The right of privacy cannot, however, be used to protect the subright of proper attribution if there is no attribution or if the author's work is attributed to another. In such cases, the artist's privacy has not been invaded since his or her identity is not used[36].

The right of privacy supplements the falsehood-dependent tort of defamation. For example, associating an anonymous author's real name with his or her work is not to make a false statement, and thus cannot be defamation, but it is an invasion of privacy. Even when a species of falsehood is involved, as in the case of "false light," the privacy cause of action does not focus on injury to the reputation but rather on loss of self-esteem.

C. *Unfair Competition*

The product identification aspect of the law of unfair competition yields moral rights-like results because it corresponds to the right of attribution. As in the tort of defamation and the right of privacy, the right of attribution can also indirectly enforce the right of respect. In general, the product identification aspect of unfair competition attacks all forms of "passing off,"[37] whether the defendant uses the name of the plaintiff to identify the defendant's product or whether the defendant uses his or her own name to identify the plaintiff's product ("reverse passing off").

Thus, unfair competition law has been used effectively to pro-

---

[33] 121 N.Y.S. 438 (N.Y. Sup. Ct. 1910) (granting temporary injunction to author to prevent publication under his real name of two stories which had previously been published under a pseudonym).

[34] 128 N.Y.S. 144 (N.Y. Sup. Ct. 1910), *aff'd*, 145 A.D. 918 (N.Y. 1911).

[35] However, the right of respect can be indirectly protected if the defendant insists on attributing to the author a modified or distorted version of his or her work.

[36] One could argue that authors of some works are easily identifiable and that there is implicit attribution as in the *Lennon* case.

[37] Charles R. McManis, Unfair Trade Practices in a Nutshell 200 (1993).

tect the subright against false attribution, when the author's name is used either in conjunction with a work he or she did not create or with one of the author's works that has been distorted. Moreover, unfair competition law can also be used to protect the subright of proper attribution when the author's work is attributed to someone else. In *Smith v. Montoro*,[38] the plaintiff recovered because his role in a film was attributed to someone else.[39] It is still unclear, however, whether unfair competition law protects an author when the work is not attributed at all.[40]

In *Gilliam v. ABC*,[41] a landmark case pointing out the weakness of the indirect protection of the right of respect that results from unfair competition law, the American Broadcasting Company ("ABC") televised truncated versions of "Monty Python" programs. When Monty Python sued for an injunction, the court stated that the plaintiffs had a cause of action grounded in the federal, statutory law of unfair competition based on Section 43(a) of the Lanham Act. Section 43(a) provided a cause of action for a "false description or representation . . . in connection with any goods or services."[42] But Judge Gurfein, in his concurrence, stated that with "an appropriate legend to indicate that the plaintiffs had not approved the editing of the ABC version . . . there is no conceivable violation of the Lanham Act."[43] Since unfair competition law, like

---

38 648 F.2d 602 (9th Cir. 1981) (concerning an actor's complaint that film distributors removed his name from credits and advertisements and substituted a different name and thereby stated a valid claim under the Lanham Act).

39 *Id.*

40 For example, Professor Nimmer cites *Smith v. Montoro* for this proposition despite the fact that the supportive language in the case is dictum because the case involved attribution of the author's work to another, not no attribution at all. M. NIMMER, COPYRIGHT § 8.21[E] nn.59.3-60.1 and accompanying text (1985); *see also* Roberta Rosenthal Kwall, *Copyright and the Moral Right: Is an American Marriage Possible?*, 38 VAND. L. REV. 1, 19 n.72 (1985).

41 538 F.2d 14 (2d Cir. 1976) (granting injunction to producers of television comedy programs to prevent broadcast of edited versions of their program).

42 15 U.S.C. § 1125(a)(1) (1988); This section provides:

> [a]ny person who, on or in connection with any goods or services, or any container for goods, uses in commerce any word, term, name, symbol, or device, or any combination thereof, or any false designation of origin, false or misleading description of fact, or false or misleading representation of fact, which—
>
> (A) is likely to cause confusion, or to cause mistake, or to deceive as to the affiliation, connection, or association of such person with another person, or as to the origin, sponsorship, or approval of his or her or another person's goods, services, or commercial activities by another person, or
>
> (B) in commercial advertising or promotion, misrepresents the nature, characteristics, qualities, or geographic origin of his or her or another person's goods, services, or commercial activities,
>
> shall be liable in a civil action by any person who believes that he or she is likely to be damaged by such act.

Pub. L. No. 100-667, 102 Stat. 3946 (1988).

43 538 F.2d at 27 (Gurfein, J., concurring).

defamation and the false light prong of the right of privacy, depends on deception, there is no cause of action if that deception is effectively removed. According to Judge Gurfein, a distorted version of Monty Python's programs could be attributed to Monty Python and broadcast, as long as there was a disclaimer. Under Judge Gurfein's reasoning, disclaimers can undermine the moral rights-like results of unfair competition law. Fortunately for the plaintiffs, the court held that under the circumstances, a disclaimer would not be effective.[44]

Another weakness of Section 43(a) of the Lanham Act is that the goods or services must be involved in interstate commerce.[45] If a work is purely local, however, the author can have recourse to state unfair competition law.

D. *Contract Interpretation*

On occasion, United States courts have construed contracts involving literary and artistic works to produce moral rights-like results. In *Clemens v. Press Publishing Co.*,[46] for example, Judge Seabury held in a concurring opinion that the plaintiff/author was entitled to attribution where the book publication contract was silent on the matter. The judge reasoned that the very nature of a publication contract of literary property implied that the work could not be published without attribution. He further explained that the publisher could not publish it in garbled form or attribute it to someone else.[47] Despite the logic behind this opinion, it was not followed by the court in *Vargas v. Esquire.*[48] The *Vargas* court flatly denied the right of attribution to an artist who sold the rights in his drawings and all the rights in his name. The court rejected

---

[44] Judge Lumbard, writing the majority opinion, noted that such a disclaimer would not "erase the indelible impression that is made by a television broadcast" and that a disclaimer at the beginning of the broadcast "would go unnoticed by viewers who tuned into the broadcast a few minutes after it began." *Id.* at 25 n.13.

[45] *See supra* note 42.

[46] 122 N.Y.S. 206, 208 (N.Y. App. 1910) (Seabury, J., concurring).

[47] Judge Seabury wrote:

> Even the matter of fact attitude of the law does not require us to consider the sale of rights to a literary production in the same way that we would consider the sale of a barrel of pork. Contracts are to be so construed as to give effect to the intention of the parties. . . . The rights of the parties are to be determined primarily by the contract which they make, and the interpretation of the contract is for the court. If the intent of the parties was that the defendant should purchase the rights to literary property and publish it, the author is entitled, not only to be paid for his work, but to have it published in the manner in which he wrote it. The purchaser cannot garble it, or put it out under another name than the author's; nor can he omit altogether the name of the author, unless his contract with the latter permits him so to do.

Id. at 207-08.

[48] 164 F.2d 522 (7th Cir. 1947).

the artist's contention that although the contract gave *Esquire* magazine the right to use his name and drawings, it did not give *Esquire* the right to publish his drawings without attribution.

Where the contract contains an express requirement to attribute the work, courts have used this kind of term to protect the integrity of the work. In *Granz v. Harris*,[49] the plaintiff/author of a master recording of a jazz concert entered into a contract with the defendant to make and distribute records of the concert. The contract provided for attribution, but it was silent regarding editing. The defendant produced and sold records of music from the concert which it had made from plaintiff's masters, but, although they were properly attributed, the records contained substantial deletions of music. The court held that the sale of the abbreviated records was a breach of contract. It reasoned that since the contract required the defendant to attribute the work to the plaintiff, there was an implied contractual duty not to make "the required legend a false representation."[50]

Courts have also protected the integrity of works without explicitly linking integrity to attribution. In *Preminger v. Columbia Pictures*,[51] the court construed the assignment of television rights to the movie "Anatomy of a Murder" to prohibit cutting and commercial interruptions that would amount to mutilation. Even in cases where the contract explicitly gives the right to edit, courts have held that a cause of action might lie for mutilation.[52]

E. *Copyright Act of 1976*

Aside from VARA, there are no provisions of the Copyright Act that expressly protect the right of attribution. The visual artist, however, can achieve some recognition of the right of respect by employing the right to prepare derivative works.[53] A derivative work is defined by the Copyright Act as "a work based upon one or more preexisting works . . . consisting of editorial revisions, annotations, elaborations, or other modifications."[54] If the artist has not transferred all of his or her copyright rights, he or she can argue that a physical change to the original is the unauthorized exercise of the right to prepare derivative works. But it may be asserted that the right to prepare derivative works is only exercised when the

49 198 F.2d 585 (2d Cir. 1952).
50 *Id.* at 588.
51 148 U.S.P.Q. (BNA) 398 (N.Y. Sup. Ct. 1966).
52 *See, e.g.*, Autry v. Republic Productions, 213 F.2d 667 (9th Cir. 1954).
53 17 U.S.C. §§ 101, 106(2) (1982).
54 *Id.* § 101.

change manifests additional creativity. Thus, the mere slashing of a canvas with a knife would not qualify nor would the utter destruction of the original.

If the artist licensed someone to make copies of his or her work, the artist could argue that a poor-quality reproduction was also an unauthorized exercise of the right to prepare derivative works. Again, however, the defendant could argue that a bad copy does not amount to a derivative work due to lack of any additional creativity.

F. *Summary*

Because defamation, privacy, and unfair competition all depend on the association of the artist with the work, they primarily yield results that imitate aspects of the right of attribution. Therefore, the right of respect is protected only insofar as it is linked with attribution. Violating the subright of false attribution—attributing to the artist a work that either she did not create or one that has been tampered with—the artist can look to the tort of defamation, the right of privacy, and unfair competition law. For violation of the subrights of anonymity or pseudonymity in its positive aspect—the right to remain anonymous or pseudonymous—the right of privacy, despite weak precedent, is most apt for this function. Unfair competition law provides protection against the attribution of the artist's work to another, but neither the common-law causes of action nor the Lanham Act provides protection when the artist's work is not attributed to anyone. Furthermore, when applying the tort of defamation, the artist must have sustained injury to his or her reputation, and in employing the Lanham Act, the artist's work must be in interstate commerce, and his or her remedy may be limited to a disclaimer.

Contract interpretation has produced results that imitate the right of attribution *and* the right of respect. There is weak precedent that an agreement to publish implies an agreement to attribute unless the agreement provides otherwise. There is also precedent that agreements to broadcast films imply that they cannot be edited to the point of distortion unless the agreement provides otherwise. It appears, however, that a United States court would enforce a contract that by its terms gave a party unlimited editing power.

Prior to VARA, and aside from the state statutes, only contract interpretation and the Copyright Act's right to prepare derivative works seemed to provide protection of the right of respect independent of the right of attribution. Neither the common law nor the Lanham Act provided a cause of action in cases where the perpetrator of the distortion removed the attribution. In addition, there is no clear precedent in these bodies of law for the aspect of the subright of proper attribution that allows the artist to require attribution. Even if there were such precedent, it seems anomalous to permit the artist to assert the subright of proper attribution so that his or her distorted painting is attributed to him or her in order to allow him or her to enforce the right of respect. Furthermore, even if the work were attributed, it is arguable that a disclaimer would remove the falsehood or deception which trigger most of these causes of action.

Although the coincidental causes of action do not provide comprehensive protection, they remain important features of the moral rights landscape. Insofar as they are not preempted, their application is not limited to particular kinds of works.

III. State Moral Rights Statutes

Due to the shortcomings of the common law, the Lanham Act, and the Copyright Act without VARA, some states enacted bona fide moral rights statutes. The eleven states with moral right statutes are: California, Connecticut, Louisiana, Maine, Massachusetts, Nevada, New Jersey, New Mexico, New York, Pennsylvania, and Rhode Island.[55] They can be divided into two groups: "California-type" statutes that provide rights more closely corresponding to article 6*bis* and "New York-type" statutes that condition the right of attribution on publication or public display and condition the right of respect on publication or public display and on attribution. Six states follow the New York pattern regarding the right of attribution, and six (sometimes different) states follow the New York pattern regarding the right of respect. There are only three states that are "California-type": California itself, Connecticut and Massachusetts. Thus, the linkage between falsehood and deception and moral rights that we saw in most of the common-law causes of action and the Lanham Act persisted in most of the state statutes. Moreover, five of the states that clearly have New York-type statutes also require some showing of prejudice to reputation for violations of the right of respect. The "California-type" statutes, by contrast, do not require prejudice to reputation; indeed, they go beyond article 6*bis* by not even requiring prejudice to honor.

None of the states protect all of the literary and artistic works that are contemplated by article 2 of the Berne Convention. In

[55] *See supra* note 4 and accompanying text.

general, they protect only works of visual or graphic art. Half of the states give moral rights protection only to works "of recognized quality" and only Massachusetts arguably protects motion pictures.

A. *Right of Attribution*

All of the states provide a right of attribution, but six state statutes apply the right only where there is some kind of public display or publication. The "California-type" statutes do not qualify the right of attribution in this way. For these states, the right of attribution includes the right "to claim authorship," and all but one also provide the right to disclaim authorship.[56] The right "to claim authorship" corresponds to the right to require proper attribution where the work is unattributed or where the artist's work is attributed to someone else. The right to disclaim authorship, however, provides the author with the right to—for example—affix a notice near an altered painting that he or she is not responsible for the change. Some statutes, however, define the right to disclaim to include the right to *prevent* attribution as well, thus providing the subright against false attribution. None of the state statutes explicitly provide the subright of anonymity, although it may be argued that this is implicit in the right to prevent attribution and the right to claim authorship. Only Massachusetts and New Mexico explicitly provide for pseudonymity, but, again, this right may be implicit in the right to prevent attribution and the right to claim authorship. Except for the publication/public display requirements of most of the states, the right of attribution provided by the state statutes includes most of the subrights of article 6*bis*.

B. *Right of Respect*

Virtually all the states couch the right of respect in terms of "alteration," "defacement," "mutilation," and "modification." Five states[57] are careful to add the modifier, "physical." Thus, all the states recognize the "subright against modification." Four states[58] also explicitly provide for a right against destruction, a right that is not explicitly provided for in article 6*bis*. Six states[59] seem to provide for the subright against unfaithful reproduction, but none of

---

56 Only Connecticut does not provide the right to disclaim authorship. *See supra* note 4.

57 These states are California, Connecticut, Massachusetts, New Mexico, and Pennsylvania. *See supra* note 4.

58 These states are California, Massachusetts, New Mexico, and Pennsylvania. *See supra* note 4.

59 These states are Louisiana, Maine, Nevada, New Jersey, New York, and Rhode Island. *See supra* note 4.

them go so far as the subright of distortion, that is, the right to object to derogatory action that does not physically affect the original or involve reproduction.

In sum, protection of the physical integrity of works of visual art is widespread among the moral rights states, protection of the quality of reproductions is fairly well represented, and some of the states provide a right against destruction. However, the publication/public display requirement, the attribution requirement, and the requirement of prejudice to reputation in most of the state statutes severely tarnishes the lustre of the right of respect.

C. *Duration and Waivability*

Five states[60] explicitly provide for a moral rights term of life plus fifty years, which corresponds to the economic rights in the Copyright Act and to article 6*bis*. Other states are silent, which implies either that they last in perpetuity or, because they are personal rights, they expire at death.

Six states[61] provide that moral rights are waivable in writing; five[62] have no waiver provision. Applying the presumption of alienability, moral rights in these states would be alienable and waivable, unless they were considered personal. If article 6*bis* is construed to forbid alienability and waivers, none of the states meet this standard.

D. *Summary*

The eleven state moral rights statutes were an advance over the coincidental causes of action at least for those artists connected with these states. First, the mere codification of moral rights would render them more certain than vague common-law causes of action for which, in an individual state, there might not be precedent. Second, the right of attribution in the state statutes is more comprehensive. In addition to the subright against false attribution, the state statutes recognize the subright of proper attribution and probably the subright of anonymity and pseudonymity. Third, five states[63] do not condition the exercise of the right of respect on attribution, although two[64] of these retain a requirement of publication or public display. However, prejudice to reputation and the

---

60 *See supra* note 57.

61 These states are California, Connecticut, Massachusetts, Nevada, New Mexico, and Pennsylvania. *See supra* note 4.

62 These states are Louisiana, Maine, New Jersey, New York, and Rhode Island. *See supra* note 4.

63 *See supra* note 57.

64 These states are New Mexico and Pennsylvania. *See supra* note 4.

availability of a disclaimer are also issues in the state statutes. The greatest drawback of the state statutes is the narrow subject matter that they protect—visual art (and in some states, "of recognized quality")—in contrast to the common-law causes of action, the Lanham Act, and the Copyright Act before VARA.

IV. Visual Artists Rights Act

The most obvious advantage of VARA over the state statutes is its national applicability. In addition, the right of respect is not linked to attribution, let alone to publication or public display. The subject matter of VARA is more limited than the state statutes, but it does not contain a quality test except for the subright against destruction. Perhaps its biggest drawback is that VARA does not provide for the subright against unfaithful reproduction.

A. *Right of Attribution*

VARA divides the right of attribution into three subrights: (1) the right to claim authorship; (2) the right to prevent the use of the author's name as author of a work that he or she did not create; and (3) the right to prevent the use of the author's name as author of a work "in the event of a distortion, mutilation, or other modification of the work which would be prejudicial to his or her honor or reputation . . . ."[65] The right to claim authorship corresponds to what I have called the subright of proper attribution.[66] The second and third rights correspond to the subright against false attribution. Although not explicitly mentioned, the legislative history states that the subrights of anonymity and pseudonymity are included.[67]

B. *Right of Respect*

The right of respect in VARA applies to any "intentional distortion, mutilation, or other modification" of the work which would be prejudicial to the author's honor or reputation.[68] This corresponds to my subright against modification. VARA also provides for the subright against destruction, but this subright applies only to works "of recognized stature," and it does not require preju-

---

65 17 U.S.C. § 106A(a).

66 For a discussion of the right of attribution, see *supra* note 12.

67 "Proposed Section 106A(a)(1) creates a right of attribution that extends not only to the right to be identified as the author of a work, or to prevent use of the author's name when he or she is improperly identified as the author of a work of visual art, but also to the right to publish anonymously or under a pseudonym." H.R. Rep. No. 514, 101st Cong., 2d. Sess. 14 (1990).

68 17 U.S.C. § 106A(a)(3)(A).

dice to honor or reputation.[69]

VARA does not recognize a subright against unfaithful reproduction, but it is arguable that it recognizes a subright against distortion, that is, a right to object to any derogatory action that does not physically affect the original or involve reproduction. This argument is based on the fact that the right of respect mentions "distortion," and there is an exception to the right of respect regarding "lighting and placement" of the work.[70] Neither lighting nor placement is a physical act done to the work itself; therefore it seems that there is a subright against distortion. Since reproductions, however, are not covered by VARA, and lighting and placement are excepted, the scope of protection is very narrow.

C. *Duration and Waiver*

Although in United States law the economic rights last for the life of the author plus fifty years,[71] the moral rights last only during the lifetime of the author.[72] This does not comply with the language of article 6*bis*. Under the provisions of VARA, artists may waive their moral rights in a signed writing that specifically identifies the works and uses, but moral rights may not be transferred.[73]

V. Comparison of VARA and State Moral Rights Statutes

The state statutes extend moral rights protection to more kinds of works than VARA. For example, although Massachusetts[74] limits protection to works "of recognized quality," it protects motion pictures, a category of works specifically excluded from VARA. Furthermore, despite the requirements of public divulgation and damage to reputation, several states protect reproductions.[75]

On balance, the scope of moral rights protection is broadened in state statutes, taken as a whole. For example, in almost all of the states the artist may disclaim authorship as long as she has a "just and valid reason,"[76] while under VARA the subright to prevent attribution may be exercised only if the work is not that of the artist or if the artist's right of respect has been violated.[77] More signifi-

---

69 *Id.* § 106A(a)(3)(B).
70 *Id.* § 106A(c)(2).
71 *Id.* § 302(a).
72 *Id.* § 106A(d).
73 *Id.* § 106A(e).
74 *See supra* note 4.
75 *See supra* note 57.
76 California, Louisiana, Maine, Massachusetts, New Jersey, New Mexico, New York, and Rhode Island provide that an author may disclaim for "just and valid reason(s)." *See supra* note 4.
77 *See* 17 U.S.C. § 106A.

cantly, several states recognize the subright against unfaithful reproduction.[78]

Clearly, the artist is better off with VARA if he or she lives in a state without a moral rights statute. However, depending on the work and the right asserted, the artist may be better off in one of the eleven states with moral rights statutes. But, will the artist be able to use the state moral rights statute or will he or she be precluded by the doctrine of preemption?

One of the prior versions of VARA stated that the state moral rights statutes would not be preempted "except to the extent that such . . . statutes would diminish or prevent"[79] the exercise of the federal moral rights. Instead, VARA contains a provision that closely tracks the preemption provision for the Copyright Act's Section 106 rights. There are, however, at least three arguments for an approach to preemption of moral rights that is more narrow than that for the Section 106 rights. First, the language of the VARA preemption provision is not as broad as the preemption provision for the section 106 rights.[80] Second, the VARA preemption provision provides a specific exception for rights "which extend beyond the life of the author."[81] Third, since Congress relied on the state statutes to demonstrate United States compliance with the moral rights provisions of the Berne Convention, it would be absurd for Congress to pass a federal moral rights statute that had the effect of weakening the moral rights protection available in the United States.

VARA and the state statutes combined do not produce the kind of moral rights protection envisioned by article 6*bis* of the Berne Convention. Hopefully, courts will not lessen the sum-total of moral rights protection in the United States by a draconian preemption analysis.

VI. United States Moral Rights Protection and Article 6bis

For the following reasons, United States law has a long way to go to comply with the language of article 6*bis*. First, article 6*bis* applies to all literary and artistic works. VARA applies only to a very narrow definition of visual art. The state statutes apply generally to works of visual and graphic art, but a little less than half require the work to be "of recognized quality." Only the common-

---

78 *See supra* note 57.
79 Transcript available from author.
80 For example, the VARA provision does not contain the phrase, "within the general scope of copyright." 17 U.S.C. § 301(a).
81 *Id.* § 301(f)(2)(C).

law causes of action and non-VARA provisions of the Copyright Act are not limited by kind of work. The common-law causes of action and the non-VARA provisions of the Copyright Act, however, do not provide the comprehensive protection of article 6*bis*, and the common-law causes of action depend on their acceptance in a particular jurisdiction.

Second, United States law, in general, does not provide the comprehensive protection of moral rights envisioned by article 6*bis*. Although VARA provides the same scope of protection of the right of attribution for visual art as article 6*bis* does, it falls short in the right of respect by not providing for the right against unfaithful reproduction. Only five states[82] recognize this right. It appears possible to achieve this kind of protection in the common law, however, through contract interpretation, as long as there is attribution.[83] The specific recognition of a right against destruction in VARA renders this right more secure in the United States than under article 6*bis*, which only arguably includes this right by implication as a "derogatory action."[84] Although the right against destruction applies only to works "of recognized stature,"[85] there is no need for a showing of prejudice to honor or reputation.

Third, the moral rights in VARA last only for the author's life.[86] As legislation passed *after* United States adherence, this does not conform to article 6*bis*, paragraph two.[87] Five states[88] comply better than VARA because their moral rights term equals the copyright term for economic rights. The remaining states that are silent and the common-law causes of action are susceptible to the argument that if these rights are purely personal, then they end with the artist's death.

Fourth, VARA's waiver provision goes beyond article 6*bis*, the official comments of which contemplate a much narrower scope for this practice.[89] Either explicitly or by presumption, all state statutes permit waiver. In general, common-law causes of action and the Lanham Act should be presumed waivable, although it may be argued that to waive defamation or false light is "anti-personal" and therefore unenforceable. The non-VARA provisions of the Copyright Act, of course, can be alienated.

---

82 *See supra* note 57.
83 Granz v. Harris, 198 F.2d 585 (2d Cir. 1952).
84 *See Guide, supra* note 8.
85 17 U.S.C. § 106A(a)(3)(B).
86 *Id.* § 106A(d).
87 *See Guide, supra* note 8.
88 *See supra* note 57.
89 *See Guide, supra* note 8, at 42.

The major failing of United States law *vis-a-vis* the language of article 6*bis* is its narrow subject matter coverage and its failure to provide clear causes of action for poor quality reproductions, as well as for perverse derivative works and adaptations.

VII. Resale Royalties

Article 14*ter* of the Berne Convention provides:

> (1) The author, or after his death the persons or institutions authorized by national legislation, shall, with respect to original works of art and original manuscripts of writers and composers, enjoy the inalienable right to an interest in any sale of the work subsequent to the first transfer by the author of the work.[90]

The theory behind resale royalties is that the author should share in the increase in value of his or her work. Although thirty-six countries recognize resale royalties, roughly half lack implementing legislation.[91] Aside from theory, resale royalties present problems in administration, such as determining the increase in value and collecting the royalty. Resale royalties have been successfully implemented in France, Germany, and Belgium; yet, in all three countries the resale royalty is levied on the total resale price rather than on the increase in value.[92] In Belgium and France, the royalty is levied effectively only on auction sales.[93] In Germany, resale royalties apply to auction sales and dealer sales, but on dealer sales the collecting society collects a flat percentage of gallery revenue paid partly to the qualifying artists and partly to an artists' social security fund.[94] Collecting societies appear to be essential to the smooth functioning of resale royalties, since only in those countries with efficient national authors' societies have resale royalties been successfully implemented.[95]

In the United States there is no federal resale royalties law, and only one state, California, has enacted resale royalties legislation. The California statute, passed in 1976, provides for a 5 percent royalty on the *total* resale price, if the resale price exceeds $1,000, *and* it equals or exceeds the prior purchase price paid by the seller.[96] Resale royalties are levied on resales of "fine art,"[97]

---

90 *Id.* at 90.

91 *See Resale Royalty Report, supra* note 14, at ii-iii.

92 *Id.*

93 French galleries, however, do make payments to an artist's social security. *See id.* at 125.

94 *See id.* at iv.

95 *Id.*

96 Cal. Civil Code § 986(a) (West Supp. 1992).

97 *Id.* at 68.

and they are payable to the artist or assignee, during the artist's lifetime or until twenty years after his or her death.

In a recently completed study of resale royalties pursuant to a provision of VARA[98], the Copyright Office concluded that it was "not persuaded that there are legitimate economic interests of visual artists that would be helped by a resale royalty."[99] The study notes that the market for contemporary art may well suffer, because the marginal initial purchaser will refrain from purchases due to an increased risk of loss from a smaller resale profit.[100] Most art depreciates in value. Successful artists share in the increased value of their works by commanding higher prices for new works. The study points out, however, that as with the Berne Convention, if the European Community includes resale royalties in its law harmonization process, the United States might very well feel obliged to follow suit.[101]

In anticipation, the Copyright Office study sets out a model resale royalties system for visual art in the United States.[102] The rate would be between three and five percent on the total gross sales price, and the royalty would be levied only on auction sales. There would be a presumption that the work has increased in value, but the reseller/purchaser would be able to rebut this presumption. The royalty would apply to visual art as defined in VARA and would last for the copyright term—the life of the author plus fifty years. The resale royalty would be inalienable, but the artist could assign his or her rights to a collecting society.

The United States has not taken the lead in the case of resale royalties in much the same way it lagged in adopting moral rights. Nevertheless, it will probably acquiesce in resale royalties in order to remain in step with the other developed countries

VIII. Conclusion

In order to bring United States law into real compliance with article 6*bis*, Congress must at least: (1) extend moral rights protection to all literary and artistic works, (2) recognize the right against unfaithful reproduction, (3) change the term of moral rights protection to the life of the author plus fifty years, and (4) eliminate the vestiges of formalities required for the exercise of the rights of

---

98 *See Resale Royalty Report, supra* note 14.

99 *Id.* at 143.

100 *Id.* at 72-73.

101 *Id.* at 148.

102 *Id.* at 151-55.

copyright. A bill called the Copyright Reform Act of 1993[103] is currently pending before Congress to accomplish (4) by repealing Sections 411 and 412 of the Copyright Act, but there is neither movement nor widespread sentiment in favor of (1)-(3).

Ironically, United States adherence to the Berne Convention and the passage of VARA may have made real compliance with article 6*bis* more difficult. Wasn't the United States permitted to join the Berne Union without *any* federal moral rights legislation? Didn't Dr. Arpad Bogsch, the General Director of WIPO, state that the United States was in substantial compliance with article 6*bis*? Hasn't the United States demonstrated its good faith by going beyond Dr. Bogsch by enacting VARA? Yet, as this article clearly demonstrates, literary and artistic work does not enjoy in the United States the protection envisioned by article 6*bis*.

Full compliance will depend on advocacy by author and authors' rights organizations, by academics and by principled legislators and government officials. After all, this coalition was able to pass VARA even after the incentive to join Berne had been removed. Full compliance may also be hastened by pressure from other countries. The United States rightly insists that Berne Union members fulfill their obligations regarding economic rights; other Berne Union countries should insist that the United States fulfill its obligations under article 6*bis*.

Passage of more comprehensive moral rights legislation can also be enhanced by meeting the objections of copyright users. Some foreign countries have been content with enacting very general moral rights statements, but there is no reason why United States legislation cannot be tailored to allay the fears of the publishing, movie, recording, and computer industries that implementing moral rights would be prohibitively expensive. Indeed, even countries with broad moral rights statements in their laws often qualify moral rights protection in practice.

Moral rights advocacy should not stop, but it should be tempered with pragmatism. Moral rights stonewalling should stop and be replaced by good faith negotiation.

---

103 S. 373/H.R. REP. No. 897, 103d Cong., 1st Sess. (1993). The identical bills sought to amend title 17 of the United States Code and were introduced on February 16. 1993.

ARCHITECT AS ARTIST: ARTISTS' RIGHTS AND HISTORIC PRESERVATION

Patty Gerstenblith*

I. Introduction

> For nearly three decades, it was one of the great rites of modern architecture: a walk through a eucalyptus grove to a serene courtyard overlooking the Pacific Ocean. But last week, half of that sequence . . . was gone. By itself, the grove had no particular value. But architecture is an art of procession, and the grove was . . . a symbolic wilderness through which one passed to reach the man-made order of the Salk's courtyard. To some, the grove represented the continent that ends at the Pacific. To others, it helped endow the courtyard with a spiritual presence rare among the austere forms of modern design.[1]

Many years ago, the famed architect, Louis Kahn, and the medical researcher, Dr. Jonas Salk, collaborated on the design and construction of the Salk Institute for Biological Sciences in La Jolla, California. A major addition to the Institute is now under construction and has led to considerable protest by members of Kahn's family and by an advisory committee of distinguished architects, including Philip Johnson, Frank Gehry, James Ingo Freed, Kevin Roche, Robert Venturi, and Richard Meier.[2] Even as bulldozers were digging trenches on the site, representatives of the Institute refused to meet with this advisory committee, which feels the new addition will destroy Kahn's vision and the spatial relationship among the original buildings.

The addition attempts to echo Kahn's style and will occupy a eucalyptus grove at the entrance to the laboratory complex.[3] Opponents of the plan believe the addition will "destroy Kahn's intention that visitors experience the institute as a sequence of landscaped spaces proceeding from the eucalyptus grove to an

---

* Associate Professor of Law, DePaul University College of Law; A.B., Bryn Mawr College; Ph.D., Harvard University; J.D., Northwestern University School of Law. This article is based on a paper first presented at the Bezalel Academy of Hebrew University, Jerusalem. I want to thank Judge Shoshana Berman and Dr. Siona Shimshi for their invitation to speak at the Bezalel Academy. I also want to acknowledge the support of the DePaul University College of Law and to thank Depak Sathy for his help in preparing this article.

1 Blair Kamin, *Cutting Criticism*, Chi. Trib., May 17, 1993, § 5, at 3.

2 *Id.*

3 Michael J. Crosbie, *Add and Subtract: The Controversial Building Addition at the Salk Institute is Examined*, 74 Progressive Architecture, Oct. 1993, at 48.

open courtyard framed by Kahn's two symmetrical laboratory buildings, with views of the Pacific Ocean beyond."[4] Supporters of the plan describe its opponents as "elitists who are insensitive to the institute's needs for expansion."[5]

This controversy exemplifies several of the legal issues arising more frequently in the United States and presents three major themes: 1) the rights of artists to preserve their work in its original form, with the artist, even after death, being represented by family members, former students, and colleagues; 2) the right of the public to preserve, from alteration or destruction, important elements of cultural property and heritage, including prominent examples of architecture and landmark buildings such as the Salk Institute; and 3) the rights of the owners and users of the cultural property to derive the most beneficial use from their property, with the assumption that progress, economic growth, and efficiency are thereby promoted.

In analyzing the legal issues implicated by these themes, it is necessary to examine two distinct societal developments which have had significant impact on the law of the United States: growth in the recognition of artists' rights in their work, and increased interest of the public in the preservation of the American cultural past.[6] The issue raised by these developments is, however, whether the past is best protected through recognition of architects' rights in their capacity as artists, or through recognition and expansion of the public's right to protect those examples of architecture which the public's representatives deem most worthy of such protection.

This article will first consider in Section II the position of the architect within the context of copyright law, and, second, the gradual recognition of the artist's moral rights within the framework of American copyright law. Section III then considers the effect on copyright law caused by the adoption of the Berne Convention, focussing on the inclusion of architectural works within the copyright system and the recognition of moral rights for artists. Section IV turns to the protection of architecture through

---

[4] Herbert Muschamp, *Altering a Kahn: Protest Widens*, N.Y. TIMES, May 6, 1993, at C17.

[5] *Id.* For a fuller discussion of the architectural significance of the building and the relationship between Kahn and Salk in creating the Institute, see Michael J. Crosbie, *Dissecting the Salk: Analysis of Louis Kahn's Salk Institute Complex*, 74 PROGRESSIVE ARCHITECTURE, Oct. 1993, at 40.

[6] Carol M. Rose, *Preservation and Community: New Directions in the Law of Historic Preservation*, 33 STAN. L. REV. 473, 479-94 (1981). Rose notes the evolution in motivations for historic preservation from nineteenth century patriotism, to early twentieth century interest in culture, art, and architecture, and finally to a modern concern for "the environmental and psychological effects of historic preservation." *Id.* at 479-80.

historical preservation and landmark statutes in the United States. Finally, in Section V, the article considers whether recognition of an architect's moral rights, or increased efforts for historic preservation through the landmark designation process, is the better mechanism for architectural preservation.

II. Background in the Rights of the Architect as Artist

Two major developments have recently taken place in American intellectual property law, the significance and application of which are, as yet, unclear. These developments occurred in response to the United States' adoption[7] of the Berne Convention for the Protection of Literary and Artistic Works[8] and ultimately resulted in the explicit recognition, through the federal Copyright Act, of artists' moral or personality rights in their works and of the place of architectural works within the copyright protection scheme. In order to understand these developments, however, it is first necessary to understand the conceptual underpinnings of American intellectual property law, particularly in the area of copyrights, as it existed until 1990. Following this introduction, a more detailed discussion of these more recent developments will be presented.

A. *Copyright Law*

In the Anglo-American legal system, the rights of the artist have primarily been protected through copyright laws. The United States Constitution provides: "The Congress shall have Power . . . (8) To promote the Progress of Science and useful Arts, by securing for limited Times to Authors and Inventors the exclusive Right to their respective Writings and Discoveries . . . ."[9] The primary motivation for the constitutionally provided protection for authors' and inventors' interest in their works is the benefit which the public will derive.[10] The public benefit is maximized by balancing the rights of original authors against the interests of subsequent au-

---

7 The Berne Convention Implementation Act of 1988, Pub. L. No. 100-568, 102 Stat. 2853 (1988).

8 Berne Convention for the Protection of Literary and Artistic Works, Sept. 9, 1886, revised in Paris on July 24, 1971, art. 6*bis*, 828 U.N.T.S. 221, 235.

9 U.S. Const. art. I, § 8, cl. 8.

10 Professor Jane C. Ginsburg disputes that the public benefit was originally intended as the exclusive purpose of the Constitution's copyright provision. Jane C. Ginsburg, *A Tale of Two Copyrights: Literary Property in Revolutionary France and America*, 64 Tul. L. Rev. 991, 998-1001 (1990). By examining late eighteenth century sources, she concludes that the utilitarian purpose of public benefit was equal in weight to the desire, inspired by Locke's notions of the origin of property rights, to protect authors' rights in their own creations and labor. However, she acknowledges that later Congressional enactments and statements of

thors.[11] This is accomplished by granting authors a time-limited monopoly in their creative works, so that others are then free to utilize the results of their creativity.[12]

The copyright laws are also viewed as providing protection exclusively for artists' pecuniary rights in their art works, rather than for artists' personal and personality rights inherent in the creative process.[13] Once the various economic rights embodied in the copyright laws are transferred, the artist is no longer viewed as having any continuing rights in the art work. The statutory scheme is intended to protect the copyright holder instead.[14] The notion of any continuing rights in the art work would conflict with the essential characteristics of property ownership recognized in the Anglo-American legal system.[15]

However, in recognition of the artist's limited bargaining power with the purchaser of the art work, the recent trend in American intellectual property law has been to provide increased protection for the artist. For example, the 1976 Copyright Act[16]

---

purpose emphasize primarily the public benefit aspect of copyright legislation. *Id.* at 999, 1001-02.

[11] For analysis of the balancing of the revenue and cost effects of the exclusive rights created by copyright protection, see William M. Landes & Richard A. Posner, *An Economic Analysis of Copyright Law*, 18 J. LEG. STUD. 325 (1989). *See also* Apple Computer, Inc. v. Microsoft Corp., 799 F. Supp. 1006, 1021 (N.D. Cal. 1992).

[12] For example, the Supreme Court has stated:

> the [Copyright] Act creates a balance between the artist's right to control the work during the term of the copyright protection and the public's need for access to creative works. The copyright term is limited so that the public will not be permanently deprived of the fruits of an artist's labors.

Stewart v. Abend, dba Authors Research Co., 495 U.S. 207, 228 (1990). *See also* Sony Corp. of America v. Universal City Studios, Inc., 464 U.S. 417, 429 (1984) (stating that the limited monopoly "is intended to motivate creative activity of authors and inventors by the provision of a special reward, and to allow the public access to the products of their genius after the limited period of exclusive control has expired."); Feist Publications, Inc. v. Rural Telephone Serv. Co., 499 U.S. 340, 349-50 (1991) (stating that "copyright assures authors the right to their original expression, but encourages others to build freely upon the ideas and information conveyed by a work."); Harper & Row, Publishers, Inc. v. Nation Enter., 471 U.S. 539, 545-46 (1985).

[13] Roberta R. Kwall, *Copyright and the Moral Right: Is An American Marriage Possible?*, 38 VAND. L. REV. 1, 2 (1985).

[14] MELVILLE B. NIMMER & DAVID NIMMER, NIMMER ON COPYRIGHT, § 8.21 (1991).

[15] *See, e.g.*, Colleen Battle, *Righting the "Tilted Scale": Expansion of Artists' Rights in the United States*, 34 CLEV. ST. L. REV. 445 (1986). Linda Lacey has recently questioned the fundamental differences in the rights accorded to the owners of personal and real property in contrast to the owners of intellectual property. Although she focusses, in particular, on the differences demonstrated in the fair use doctrine and the limited duration of copyright ownership, her analysis points to the need for a rethinking of the concepts of property ownership as applied to all aspects of intellectual property. Linda J. Lacey, *Of Bread and Roses and Copyrights*, 1989 DUKE L.J. 1532, 1544-67 (1989). She also notes, however, that the doctrine of moral rights may grant to the artist greater rights in his or her property than are given to the owners of other forms of personal property because moral rights continue in the particular object even after ownership has been transferred. *Id.* at 1548-53.

[16] 17 U.S.C. §§ 101-810 (1988).

modified the presumption that the copyright transferred with the physical object.[17] In addition, the 1976 Copyright Act, in combination with its various judicial interpretations, has tended to narrow the work-made-for-hire doctrine. This is significant because the copyright of a work-made-for-hire automatically belongs to the party who commissioned the work.[18] A narrowing of the doctrine results in more situations where the artist is considered the owner of the copyright.[19] While judicial interpretations of the 1976 Act are not uniform, and some of the lower federal courts have perhaps unduly restricted artists' rights, the sense that Congress intended the 1976 Act to expand upon artists' rights and to make it easier for the artist to protect them has generally influenced the course of judicial opinions.[20]

The position of the architect as artist, under the copyright laws, has been a very limited one. The Copyright Act is premised on the principle that its purpose is to protect items of aesthetic or artistic value.[21] It therefore excludes from protection any works

---

17 17 U.S.C. § 202. *See, e.g.*, Effects Assocs. Inc. v. Cohen, 908 F.2d 555, 557 (9th Cir. 1990) (holding that any ambiguity in contractual terms purporting to transfer copyright should be construed in favor of the author's retention of the copyright), *cert. denied*, 498 U.S. 1103 (1991). Cassway v. Chelsea Historic Properties I, L.P., 1993 U.S. Dist. LEXIS 5329, *10-11 (E.D. Pa. 1993) (holding that an agreement transferring ownership of architectural drawings is ambiguous and therefore does not transfer ownership of a copyright interest in the drawings). *See also* § 204(a) (requiring a signed writing to effect a transfer of copyright ownership); Eric M. Brooks, Comment, *"Tilted" Justice: Site-Specific Art and Moral Rights After U.S. Adherence to the Berne Convention*, 77 CAL. L. REV. 1431, 1444 (1989); Kwall, *supra* note 13, at 60.

18 17 U.S.C. § 201(b). *See also* Kwall, *supra* note 13, at 57-60.

19 Kwall, *supra* note 13, at 59-60. For example, the statute provides that a specially commissioned work does not automatically qualify as a "work-made-for-hire." 17 U.S.C. § 101(2).

20 In Community for Creative Non-Violence v. Reid, 490 U.S. 730 (1989), the Supreme Court rejected an expansive interpretation of the work-made-for-hire doctrine propounded, for example, by the Second Circuit in Aldon Accessories Ltd. v. Spiegel, Inc., 738 F.2d 548 (2d Cir.) (adopting the view that the "supervision and control standard" determines who is an employee for purposes of the work-made-for-hire doctrine), *cert. denied*, 469 U.S. 982 (1984). Only when the artist is considered an employee, rather than an independent contractor, or if the work falls into one of nine categories enumerated in the statute, will the work fall under the work-made-for-hire doctrine. Furthermore, the term "employee" should be determined by reference to the general common law of agency. *Reid*, 490 U.S. at 738-51. Factors to be examined in evaluating whether a hired party is an employee include the hiring party's right to control the manner and means of production, the skill required, the source of tools, location of the work, duration of the relationship, method of payment, the hired party's discretion over work conditions, tax treatment, and the provision of employee benefits. *Id.* at 751-52. The Supreme Court's test developed in *Reid* should result in fewer works of visual art being considered works-made-for-hire so that the artist will retain the copyright in more situations. *See also* Easter Seal Soc'y v. Playboy Enter., 815 F.2d 323, 327-34 (5th Cir. 1987), *cert. denied*, 485 U.S. 981 (1988).

21 In Mazer v. Stein, 347 U.S. 201, 218 (1954), the Supreme Court made it clear that while copyright protection extends to both the fine and applied arts, the copyright statute in fact protects only the artistic or aesthetic elements of useful articles and not their mechanical or utilitarian aspects. *Id.* Judge Walker stated the distinction more succinctly in considering the copyrightability of a computer program:

which are primarily utilitarian or functional in nature because it is thought that "progress and creativity are retarded by preventing useful objects from being available to others to use, adapt, or modify."[22] This is different from most European nations and other nations signatory to the Berne Convention which generally explicitly protect architectural works.

Under American copyright statutes and their judicial interpretations, now codified in the 1976 Act, a work which incorporates both utilitarian and aesthetic elements would be evaluated under the "separability test."[23] Thus, "if a pictorial, graphic, or sculptural work is of primarily utilitarian function, only its nonfunctional elements are eligible for copyright protection,"[24] and some elements of a work would be copyrightable while others would not. The elements of a work which are utilitarian in nature are considered more suitable for protection under the more stringent standards of the patent system than the copyright system.[25] However, the separability test has proven difficult to apply, particularly in the attempt to distinguish between industrial designs, on the one hand, and pictorial, graphic, and sculptural works, on the other.[26]

> The variations of expression found in purely creative compositions, as opposed to those found in utilitarian works, are not directed towards practical application. For example, a narration of Humpty Dumpty's demise, which would clearly be a creative composition, does not serve the same ends as, say, a recipe for scrambled eggs—which is a more process oriented text.

Computer Assocs Int'l, Inc. v. Altai, Inc., 982 F.2d 693, 704 (2d Cir. 1992). *See also* Eales v. Environmental Lifestyles, Inc., 958 F.2d 876, 879-80 (9th Cir. 1992) (holding that architectural plans do not fall under the "useful article" exception to the Copyright Act because they do not have a purely utilitarian function); Brooktree Corp. v. Advanced Micro Devices, Inc., 977 F.2d 1555, 1562 (Fed. Cir. 1992) (noting that, before enactment of the Semiconductor Chip Protection Act of 1984, Copyright Office had refused to register copyrights for patterns on printed circuit boards and semiconductor chips because the "pattern was deemed inseparable from the utilitarian function of the chip [and] no separate artistic aspects had been demonstrated.").

22 Raphael Winick, *Copyright Protection for Architecture after the Architectural Works Copyright Protection Act of 1990*, 41 DUKE L.J. 1598, 1602 (1992).

23 For early formulations of the tests by which to judge whether a work is aesthetic or utilitarian in nature, see Baker v. Selden, 101 U.S. 99, 104 (1879) (holding that a process or system is not eligible for copyright protection, although the explanation is); Mazer v. Stein, 347 U.S. 201, 213-18 (1954) (holding that copyright protection is available for applied art even though the art object may also be intended for use).

24 Winick, *supra* note 22, at 1602 n.24.

25 *Id.* at 1615 n.80, 1619-20.

26 The structural aspects of an architectural plan are also not copyrightable because of their purely functional nature. As such, they fall under the merger doctrine. *See infra* note 92. The status of copyright protection afforded architectural designs parallels, in some senses, the question of protection to be given to computer program designs. *See, e.g.*, Computer Associates International, Inc. v. Altai, Inc., 982 F.2d 693, 707-08 (2d Cir. 1992). *See also* Steven R. Englund, Note, *Idea, Process or Protected Expression? Determining the Scope of Copyright Protection of the Structure of Computer Programs*, 88 MICH. L. REV. 866, 875-79 (1990); Arthur R. Miller, *Copyright Protection for Computer Programs, Databases, and Computer-Generated Works: Is Anything New Since Contu?*, 106 HARV. L. REV. 977, 988 (1993).

Application of the utilitarian/aesthetic dichotomy to architecture leads to the result that the architect's technical plans and drawings are eligible for copyright protection.[27] However, the building, because it is a utilitarian work, is not, though some of the individual decorative elements, such as gargoyles and friezes, might be protected as sculptural works.[28] If one assumes that the architect is considered the author of the work (that is, not subject to the work-made-for-hire doctrine),[29] then the architect would own a copyright in the architectural plans and drawings but not in the three-dimensional building.[30] Thus, the allegation that a builder measured an existing building and reproduced a virtually identical one by copying the original would not result in a copyright violation.[31]

It is also important to note that the 1976 Copyright Act explicitly preempts state law from granting equivalent rights in types of art works protected by the federal act.[32] Thus, state common law and statutory protection do not exist if the subject matter is cov-

---

27 *See, e.g.*, Eales v. Environmental Lifestyles, Inc., 958 F.2d 876, 879-80 (9th Cir.) (explaining that architectural plans and drawings are eligible for copyright protection because their intrinsic function is to convey the information necessary to construct a building), *cert. denied,* 113 S. Ct. 605 (1992). Cases holding that architectural plans and drawings are eligible for copyright protection as "pictorial, graphic, or sculptural works" include Robert R. Jones Assoc. v. Nino Homes, 858 F.2d 274 (6th Cir. 1988); Imperial Homes Corp. v. Lamont, 458 F.2d 895 (5th Cir. 1972); Arthur Rutenberg Homes, Inc. v. Drew Homes, Inc., 829 F. Supp. 1314 (M.D. Fla. 1993); Demetriades v. Kaufmann, 680 F. Supp. 658 (S.D.N.Y. 1988). *Eales* further makes the point that architectural drawings are specifically not covered under the Architectural Works Copyright Protection Act of 1990. *Eales,* 958 F.2d at 880 n.2.

28 Winick, *supra* note 22, at 1610.

29 Because of the skill level required for their work, architects are often considered to be independent contractors; they are thus entitled to own the copyright in their works. *See, e.g.*, M.G.B. Homes, Inc. v. Ameron Homes, Inc., 903 F.2d 1486, 1492 (11th Cir. 1990) (finding drafting services to be highly skilled); Kunycia v. Melville Realty Co., 755 F. Supp. 566, 573-74 (S.D.N.Y. 1990) (finding an architect to be an independent contractor based on some of the factors enunciated in Community for Creative Non-Violence v. Reid, 490 U.S. 730 (1989)).

30 The 1976 Copyright Act specifically protects "pictorial, graphic, and sculptural works" including "technical drawings, diagrams, and models." 17 U.S.C. §§ 101, 102. The Senate Report states that "architect's plans and drawings would, of course, be protected by copyright." S. Rep. No. 1476, 94th Cong., 2d Sess. 55 (1976). *See also* Jacobs v. Westoaks Realtors, Inc., 205 Cal. Rptr. 620, 623 (1984).

31 M.G.B. Homes, Inc. v. Ameron Homes, Inc., 903 F.2d 1486 (11th Cir. 1990). *See also* Winick, *supra* note 22, at 1608-09 nn.51 & 53 and cases cited therein.

32 17 U.S.C. § 301 (1988). Section 301 provides:

> (a) . . . all legal or equitable rights that are equivalent to any of the exclusive rights within the general scope of copyright as specified by section 106 in works of authorship that are fixed in a tangible medium of expression and come within the subject matter of copyright as specified by sections 102 and 103 . . . are governed exclusively by this title. Thereafter, no person is entitled to any such right or equivalent right in any such work under the common law or statutes of any State.

Id. The judicial interpretation of this preemption provision, however, has not been very clear. *See* Brooks, *supra* note 17, at 1465-68; Edward J. Damich, *The New York Artists' Author-*

ered by the federal Copyright Act and the claimed right is equivalent to one granted by the federal Copyright Act.[33] The claimant may not then bring suit based on state law in state court but is limited to those protections offered by the federal act. This has particular relevance for the development of artists' moral rights because these rights first arose under state common law and statutory law and only recently became the subject of federal legislation.[34]

B. *The Development of Moral Rights in the United States*

In many of the European countries, the doctrine of an artist's "moral rights" developed at least as early as the period of the French Revolution.[35] While the French and German models of moral rights have their variances, both versions are distinctly different from the Anglo-American concept of copyright. The Anglo-American concept focusses on the economic rights which artists have in their work, rights which are subject to alienation, just like other economic rights. Moral rights, on the other hand, developed as a concept unique to the personality of the artist. As such they are inalienable and not waivable in many of the European models.[36]

---

ship Rights Act: A Comparative Critique, 84 COLUM. L. REV. 1733, 1737-39 (1984); Kwall, *supra* note 13, at 72-78.

[33] To avoid preemption, a cause of action based on state law must incorporate elements additional to those necessary to prove a violation based on federal copyright law and "must regulate conduct qualitatively different from the conduct governed by federal copyright law." Trandes Corp. v. Guy F. Atkinson Co., 996 F.2d 655, 659 (4th Cir.), *cert. denied*, 114 S. Ct. 443 (1993).

[34] For example, the federal Copyright Act, before enactment of the Visual Artists Rights Act, *see infra* notes 94-109 and accompanying text, was held not to preempt the New York State moral rights legislation in Wojnarowicz v. American Family Ass'n, 745 F. Supp. 130, 135-36 (S.D.N.Y. 1990). The court relied on the fact that the state legislature had a different purpose than the federal legislation in that the former aimed to protect the artist's reputation and required different elements of proof. The court concluded, however, that the New York statute may be preempted by VARA, which had been proposed but not yet enacted at the time of the decision. *Id.*

[35] For discussions of earlier forms of moral rights protection for authors, see Dan Rosen, *Artists' Moral Rights: A European Evolution, An American Revolution*, 2 CARDOZO ARTS & ENT. L.J. 165, 168-75 (1983); Harold C. Streibich, *The Moral Right of Ownership to Intellectual Property: Part I—From the Beginning to the Age of Printing*, 6 MEM. ST. U. L. REV. 1 (1975); *The Moral Right of Ownership to Intellectual Property: Part II—From the Age of Printing to the Future*, 7 MEM. ST. U. L. REV. 45 (1976) [hereinafter Streibich, *To the Future*]. Ginsburg, however, posits that the French legislative enactments at the time of the Revolution did not yet focus primarily on the authors' rights, rather than the public interest. Author-centrism developed later as a distinguishing feature of French intellectual property laws. Ginsburg, *supra* note 10, at 1005-14. For a summary of current French law protecting the artist's creative personality, see Edward J. Damich, *The Right of Personality: A Common-Law Basis for the Protection of the Moral Rights of Authors*, 23 GA. L. REV. 1, 6-35 (1988).

[36] For general discussions of the doctrine of moral rights and a comparison with the Anglo-American concept of copyright, see, e.g., Brooks, *supra* note 17, at 1434-39; Damich, *supra* note 35; Kwall, *supra* note 13, at 5-16; John Henry Merryman, *The Refrigerator of Ber-*

The copyright/moral rights distinction is founded on an underlying difference between positive law and natural law. The artist's moral rights are seen as inherent in the creative process. Therefore, they are part of the artist's natural rights and are only minimally subject to government intervention.[37] Copyright, however, is the product of positive law, a purely statutory creature, and thus it is entirely subject to government regulation and limitation.[38] Copyright is not so much a "right" as a governmentally-granted "privilege".[39] Because it is a "privilege," the legislature may impose any limitations or formalities on the right to copyright protection.[40]

The purposes of copyright and moral right are also fundamentally different. Copyright is motivated exclusively by the benefit which the public is to derive.[41] Moral rights, on the other hand, primarily vindicate the artist's individual rights, while the public derives secondary benefits from the recognition of the artist's rights.[42]

While specific moral rights granted in various nations differ, they generally are viewed as falling into the following categories: the right of attribution, the right of integrity, the right of disclosure, the droit de suite or resale royalty right, and the lesser recog-

---

nard Buffet, 27 HASTINGS L.J. 1023, 1025 (1976); Carl H. Settlemyer III, Note, *Between Thought and Possession: Artists' "Moral Rights" and Public Access to Creative Works*, 81 GEO. L.J. 2291, 2302-06 (1993).

37 Ginsburg, *supra* note 10, at 992-94.

38 The first modern copyright law was the Statute of Anne, enacted in 1710, which granted the exclusive right of publication of books to the author or his or her assigns for a period of 14 years from the date of publication. 8 Anne, ch. 19. *See* Streibich, *To the Future*, *supra* note 35, at 57; Ginsburg, *supra* note 10, at 998.

39 *See, e.g.*, Wheaton v. Peters, 33 U.S. 591 (1834).

40 Ginsburg, *supra* note 10, at 994. The Supreme Court has also implied that the legislature may expand upon those rights afforded by the Copyright Act, because such protection is a creature of statute. Mazer v. Stein, 347 U.S. 201, 214-15 (1954).

41 This purpose for the Statute of Anne was recognized by Lord Mansfield in Sayre v. Moore, 102 Eng. Rep. 139 (K.B. 1785). This sentiment was echoed by the United States Supreme Court in Mazer v. Stein, 347 U.S. 201 (1954), where the Court stated, "[t]he economic philosophy behind the clause empowering Congress to grant patents and copyrights is the conviction that encouragement of individual effort by personal gain is the best way to advance public welfare through the talents of authors and inventors . . . ." *Id.* at 219. Lacey provokes a need to re-evaluate what is meant by the "public interest" in the context of intellectual property, see *supra* note 15, at 1584-95, by distinguishing between a group of "autonomous individuals, each acting out of self-interest" and "an interdependent community with certain common interests that affect all its members." *Id.* at 1585. She suggests that intellectual property, at least in its definition of the fair use doctrine, needs to be premised on the latter definition of the "public interest." *Id.* at 1586-92.

42 Damich, *supra* note 32, at 1748-49 (noting that the purpose of protecting the droit moral, in French law, is the furtherance, not of the public interest, but of the artist's personal rights); Ginsburg, *supra* note 10, at 991-92. Ginsburg, however, also criticizes the view that the United States and the French systems of copyright protection are drastically different in practice. *Id.* at 994-95.

nized rights to withdraw a work from the public and to receive protection from excessive criticism.[43] The Berne Convention,[44] however, recognizes only the rights of attribution and integrity.[45]

In early American case law, there are examples of artists claiming some version of the European moral rights. Such claims were generally denied on the grounds that American law, especially federal copyright law, rejected recognition of the artist's moral rights in favor of the artist's exclusive pecuniary rights. The notion of an artist's continuing rights in a work after it has been conveyed conflicts directly with Anglo-American concepts of property law, according to which owners of an object are free to do with it as they wish. Such rights in the artist would present an inherent contradiction with American property law and would undermine and require a re-evaluation of essential characteristics in the nature of property ownership.

Most attempts by an artist to win explicit recognition of moral rights were rejected. One example of this is the 1938 decision, Crimi v. Rutgers Presbyterian Church.[46] In this case, the court held that the artist of a mural could not prevent its repainting once he conveyed it to the church which became its absolute owner.[47] In Shostakovich v. Twentieth Century-Fox Film Corp., the court rejected the plaintiffs' attempt to enjoin the use of their music and their names in a film with an anti-Russian bias, based on claims to the right to privacy, defamation, deliberate infliction of injury, and violation of the right of integrity.[48] Attempts to claim a right of attribution for literary authors and artists also have been rejected.[49] The well-known children's book author, Theodore Geisel (Dr. Seuss), failed to prevent a doll manufacturer from producing dolls and toys based on the illustrations in his books. In that case, in addition to rejecting claims based on moral rights, the court re-

---

[43] Brooks, *supra* note 17, at 1435; Kwall, *supra* note 13, at 5.

[44] Berne Convention art. 6*bis*.

[45] Brooks, *supra* note 17, at 1435; Edward J. Damich, *The Visual Artists Rights Act of 1990: Toward a Federal System of Moral Protection for Visual Art*, 39 CATH. U. L. REV. 945, 949-51 (1990).

[46] 89 N.Y.S.2d 813 (Sup. Ct. 1949); *see* Damich, *supra* note 32, at 1753.

[47] *Id.* at 818-19.

[48] 80 N.Y.S.2d 575, 578-79 (Sup. Ct. 1948), *aff'd*, 87 N.Y.S.2d 430 (App. Div. 1949). A French court, confronted with the same facts, held that the plaintiffs' moral rights were violated. Soc. Le Chant du Monde v. Soc. Fox Europe, Cours d'appel, Paris, D. Jur. 16, 80 (Jan. 13, 1953).

[49] Weinstein v. University of Illinois, 811 F.2d 1091 (7th Cir. 1987) (rejecting a claim to a right of attribution for a contributing author in a work published in an academic journal); Vargas v. Esquire, Inc, 164 F.2d 522, 526 (7th Cir. 1947), *cert. denied*, 335 U.S. 813 (1948) (rejecting a plaintiff's claim for a right of attribution for drawings published in Esquire Magazine); *see* Damich, *supra* note 32, at 1752-53.

jected claims based on copyright infringement and misrepresentation.[50]

Finally, in a controversy concerning his site-specific sculpture, "Tilted Arc", the sculptor Richard Serra failed to prevent the General Services Administration from removing the sculpture from Federal Plaza in lower Manhattan.[51] The sculpture, which consisted of an arc of steel 120 feet long, twelve feet tall, and several inches thick, had been commissioned by the federal government as part of its art-in-architecture program. This program requires that 1/2 of 1% of the cost of federal buildings be devoted to sculpture that will be placed in the building. Serra received the commission to execute a sculpture for the site, but soon after its completion, it became the subject of considerable controversy, and the GSA decided to remove it, barely four years after its installation.[52] Serra sued the government for allegedly violating his first amendment freedom of expression[53] and his right to due process.[54] He also claimed a moral right, based on state law.[55] His due process claim was rejected, at least in part, because he was not considered to have a protectable property interest in the sculpture once it was conveyed to the GSA.[56]

The case could also be viewed as presenting a conflict between the moral rights of Serra and the moral rights of the architects who designed the plaza and the buildings surrounding it. This perspective is bolstered by the fact that the architects had not been consulted when Serra's plans were accepted for the commission.[57]

> By his own admission, Serra set out to confront what the architects had done and to destroy the decorative character of their plaza. In the architects' view, Serra ignored the existing three-dimensional elements of the square and with his sculpture cut

---

50 Geisel v. Poynter Productions, Inc., 295 F. Supp. 331 (S.D.N.Y. 1968).

51 Serra v. United States Gen. Serv. Admin., 664 F. Supp. 798 (S.D.N.Y. 1987), *amended, 667 F. Supp. aff'd*, 847 F.2d 1045 (2d Cir. 1988). For detailed discussions of this case, see Balfe & Wyszomirski, *Public Art and Public Policy*, 15 J. ARTS MGMT. & L. 5 (1986); Brooks, *supra* note 17, at 1431-33; S. JORDAN, PUBLIC ART, PUBLIC CONTROVERSY: THE TILTED ARC ON TRIAL (1987).

52 *Serra*, 847 F. 2d at 1047.

53 *Id.* at 1048-51.

54 *Id.* at 1051-52.

55 664 F. Supp. at 802; 667 F. Supp. at 1051-52. The Court refused jurisdiction for the state-based claims because it had no federal jurisdiction for Serra's other claims.

56 847 F. 2nd at 1052. The court pointed out that Serra had no protectable property interest in the sculpture, once it had been conveyed to the GSA, pursuant to contract, and no protectable liberty or property interest which could be injured by relocation of the sculpture without an accompanying loss of employment.

57 1 JOHN HENRY MERRYMAN & ALBERT E. ELSEN, LAW, ETHICS, AND THE VISUAL ARTS 361 (2d ed. 1987).

across a handsome decorative stone pavement.[58]

Serra was successful only in preventing the re-installation of the sculpture in another location because a panel of art experts unanimously concluded that the sculpture was site-specific and therefore could not be displayed elsewhere without destroying its artistic integrity and intent.[59] The *Serra* controversy is but one example of such controversies concerning public art in the United States. These controversies have increased as federal, state, and local governments have enacted comparable art-in-architecture programs. In fact, controversies like that involving "Tilted Arc" have reportedly caused the repeal of such programs in some communities.[60]

In a few cases, however, courts have found other legal doctrines that could be used to grant protection to the artist's rights.[61] The best known of these cases is Gilliam v. American Broadcasting Co.[62] In *Gilliam*, the court rejected Monty Python Flying Circus' claim that ABC had violated its right of integrity, by significantly editing its programs. Nonetheless, the court held for the plaintiff by relying on principles of copyright, contract and, in particular, the misrepresentation and unfair competition provisions of the Lanham Act[63] because, after editing, the television programs could no longer be fairly considered the plaintiff's work. Thus, the court vindicated not the artists' right to control the future of their creations but rather the public's right to be properly informed of the nature of the work. Unless there is a statute which a court is willing to adapt to the artist's cause and some direct public benefit to be derived therefrom, any protection for an artist or author must

---

58 *Id.*

59 Douglas C. McGill, *Debating "Tilted Arc,"* N.Y. TIMES, Dec. 18, 1987, at C36.

60 Eric Scigliano, *Tacoma Repeals One-Percent Law*, ARTNEWS, March 1986, at 13-14, *reprinted in* 1 JOHN HENRY MERRYMAN & ALBERT E. ELSEN, LAW, ETHICS, AND THE VISUAL ARTS, 366-68 (2d ed. 1987). Others have questioned whether this controversy has deterred artists' freedom of self-expression in order to mute any public reaction or controversy. Michael Brenson, *The Messy Saga of "Tilted Arc" Is Far From Over*, N.Y. TIMES, Apr. 2, 1989, at B33.

61 Brooks, *supra* note 17, at 1449-61 (discussing use of the 1976 Copyright Act, the Lanham Act, and various common law actions based on contract, right of privacy, and right of publicity, to protect the artists' moral rights); Damich, *supra* note 35, at 41-75 (commenting on the 1976 Copyright Act, common-law copyright, the right of privacy, the right of publicity, unfair competition law, defamation, contract law, and waste, as doctrines which permit United States courts to recognize artists' right of personality in their work of art).

62 538 F.2d 14 (2d Cir. 1976).

63 Section 43(a) of the Lanham Act concerns the "use in connection with any goods or services . . . [of] any false description or representation, including words or other symbols tending falsely to describe or represent the same . . . ." 15 U.S.C. § 1125(a)(1988).

come from the contract rights specifically negotiated by the artist.[64] Therefore, protection for artists has depended almost entirely on their legal sophistication and economic bargaining power when entering into a contract for their work.[65]

While most American artists were meeting only limited success in their attempts to claim moral rights protection for their works, a few state legislatures chose to enact statutes to provide protection for a variety of moral rights.[66] These statutes vary in their purpose, the rights granted, the types of art works protected, and the remedies provided.

State moral rights legislation falls into two main categories depending on the primary justification chosen by the legislature. One such motivation is the public's interest in maintaining various categories of artistic works in their original condition. This approach may be viewed, at least in part, as a vehicle for accomplishing the goal of historic preservation. Such legislation is typified by the California statute, known as the California Art Preservation Act.[67] This Act grants rights of attribution and integrity for original paintings, sculptures, drawings, and works of art in glass, but only for those which are of recognized quality.[68] California is also the

---

64 The Ninth Circuit has also held that section 43(a) of the Lanham Act would apply to the claim of two songwriters who wished to assert the right of attribution for their musical compositions. Lamothe v. Atlantic Recording Corp., 847 F.2d 1403, 1405-08 (9th Cir. 1988).

65 Russ VerSteeg, *Federal Moral Rights for Visual Artists: Contract Theory and Analysis*, 67 WASH. L. REV. 827, 843-45 (1992) (discussing artists' bargaining position when entering into contracts).

66 As of 1991, eleven states had enacted such legislation. The eleven states were: California, CAL. CIV. CODE § 987 (West Supp. 1988); Connecticut, CONN. GEN. STAT. ANN. § 42-116 (West Supp. 1990); Louisiana, LA. REV. STAT. ANN. §§ 51:2151-51:2156 (West 1987); Maine, ME. REV. STAT. ANN. tit. 27, § 303 (West Supp. 1987-1988); Massachusetts, MASS. GEN. LAWS ANN. ch. 231, § 85S (West Supp. 1988); Nevada, NEV. REV. STAT. §§ 598.970-598.978 (1989); New Jersey, N.J. STAT. ANN. §§ 2A:24A-1—8 (West 1987); New Mexico, N.M. STAT. ANN. §§ 13-4b-1—3 (Michie 1992); New York, N.Y. ARTS & CULT. AFF. LAW §§ 14.51-14.59 (McKinney 1984); Pennsylvania, PA. STAT. ANN. tit. 73, §§ 2101-2110 (Supp. 1987); Rhode Island, R.I. GEN. LAWS §§ 5-62-2—6 (1987). *See* PAUL GOLDSTEIN, COPYRIGHT: PRINCIPLE, LAW AND PRACTICE 379 n.68 (Supp. 1992). For a general discussion of state moral rights statutes and the protections afforded, see Edward J. Damich, *State "Moral Rights" Statutes: An Analysis and Critique*, 13 COLUM.-VLA J.L. & ARTS 292 (1989).

67 CAL. CIV. CODE § 987 (West 1993). *See* Brooks, *supra* note 17, at 1462-63; Deborah Ann Chan, Note, *California Art Preservation Act: A Safe Hamlet for "Moral Rights" in the United States*, 14 U.C. DAVIS L. REV. 975 (1981); Karen Gantz, *Protecting Artists' Moral Rights: A Critique of the California Art Preservation Act as a Model for Statutory Reform*, 49 GEO. WASH. L. REV. 873 (1981); Peter H. Karlen, *Moral Rights in California*, 19 SAN DIEGO L. REV. 675 (1982); John G. Petrovich, *Artists' Statutory Droit Moral in California: A Critical Appraisal*, 15 LOY. L.A. L. REV. 29 (1981).

68 CAL. CIV. CODE § 987(b)(2) (West 1993). The Legislature's statement of intent actually cites as justifications both that "the physical alteration or destruction of fine art, which is an expression of the artist's personality, is detrimental to the artist's reputation" and that "there is also a public interest in preserving the integrity of cultural artistic creations." *Id.* § 987(a).

only state to recognize the author's droit de suite.[69] The other primary motivation for such legislation is to protect the artists' rights in their works. This group of statutes grants rights such as the right of attribution and the right of integrity, but only when a violation would injure the artist's reputation. This type of statute is typified by that of New York State.[70]

Thus, until 1990, artists who claimed any interests in their art work, other than copyright, were limited either to molding the claim into some other recognized legal doctrine, such as misrepresentation or breach of contract,[71] or to utilizing a state statute, if the artist was able to bring suit in a state with such a statute. The artist, however, was subject to the whims of the state with jurisdiction, the state's choice of protected art forms, and the state's choice of recognized moral rights.

III. United States Implementation of the Berne Convention

In the late 1980's, however, artists' rights began to change dramatically in the United States, prompted primarily by the United States' becoming a signatory to the Berne Convention. The decision of the United States to join the Berne Convention was motivated by other concerns—primarily the desire to achieve greater international protection for other forms of intellectual property,

---

69 Cal. Civ. Code § 986 (West 1993). The artist is entitled to receive 5% of the amount of the subsequent sale of any work of fine art which has a gross sales price greater than $1000. This right continues for twenty years after the death of the artist. *See* Ben W. Bloch et al., *An Economic Analysis of the California Art Royalty Statute*, 10 Conn. L. Rev. 689 (1978). This provision has survived constitutional and other challenges. Morseburg v. Balyon, 621 F.2d 977 (9th Cir.), *cert. denied*, 449 U.S. 983 (1980). VARA also directed the Register of Copyrights to study the feasibility of implementing a resale royalty requirement at the federal level. 17 U.S.C. § 106A (1992). *See infra* note 114.

70 The New York statute, known as the Artists' Authorship Rights Act, prohibits publication, without the artist's consent, of an art work "in an altered, defaced, mutilated or modified form if . . . damage to the artist's reputation is reasonably likely to result therefrom . . . ." N.Y. Arts & Cult. Aff. Law § 14.03 (McKinney Supp. 1990); *see* Brooks, *supra* note 17, at 1464-65; Damich, *supra* note 32, at 1741; Scott & Cohen, *An Introduction to the New York Artists' Authorship Rights Act*, 8 Colum.-VLA J.L. & Arts 369 (1984); Sarah Ann Smith, Note, *The New York Artists' Authorship Rights Act: Increased Protection and Enhanced Status for Visual Artists*, 70 Cornell L. Rev. 158 (1984). This provision was applied to enjoin the unauthorized publication of an artist's works that had been cropped and reproduced in a pamphlet decrying the NEA's support for such works. Wojnarowicz v. American Family Ass'n, 745 F. Supp. 130, 137-41 (S.D.N.Y. 1990).

71 For example, use of the Lanham Act to prevent distribution of a reproduction of plaintiffs' photographs, cropped in such a manner as to be misleading as to their content, was rejected because the pamphlets were not distributed for commercial purposes. *Wojnarowicz*, 745 F. Supp. at 141-42. The court also rejected plaintiff's claim based on defamation because the defendants did not act with actual malice under the standard of New York Times Co. v. Sullivan, 376 U.S. 254, 280 (1964), which requires that the defendant act "with knowledge that [the statement] was false or with reckless disregard of whether it was false or not." *Wojnarowicz*, 745 F. Supp. at 147-48.

particularly computer software.[72] However, it had the concomitant effect of requiring the United States to bring its intellectual property laws into conformity with other aspects of the Berne Convention. This meant both the recognition of artists' moral rights and the recognition of architecture as an art form with aesthetic value.

A. *The Architectural Works Copyright Protection Act (AWCPA)*

After the United States formally adopted the Berne Convention, debate raged both in Congress and throughout the intellectual property field as to whether any implementing legislation was required to bring the United States into compliance with Berne. Opponents to further legislation vehemently argued that the protections afforded artists' moral rights through the patchwork of common law legal doctrines and state and federal statutes already in existence constituted sufficient compliance with Berne. Others argued that modification of existing copyright laws would have detrimental effects.[73] However, because the Berne Convention explicitly grants copyright protection to buildings, as well as to technical architectural plans and drawings, it was difficult to argue that the United States was already in compliance with Berne with respect to architectural works.[74] The Paris text of the Berne Convention requires member nations to protect "works of . . . architecture; illustrations . . . plans, sketches and three-dimensional works relative to . . . architecture."[75] There was thus a direct contradiction between what Berne required and what the United States federal law granted.

In debating the creation of direct protection for architectural works, Congress was concerned with whether such protection would in fact diminish the creative process associated with the development of architectural forms. Many in the architectural field and academic commentators opposed the extension of such protection.[76] One commentator wrote

> An examination of the interrelationship between architecture, society, creativity, and the design process demonstrates that architectural creativity consists of the recombination of separate elements into forms that express both the new context of the

---

72 Settlemyer, *supra* note 36, at 2307 n.71.

73 *Id.* at 2306-11.

74 For a discussion of protections granted to architectural works in the Berne Convention and other nations, see Natalie Wargo, *Copyright Protection for Architecture and the Berne Convention,* 65 N.Y.U. L. REV. 403, 409-39 (1990).

75 Berne Convention art. 6*bis,* § 1.

76 *See, e.g.,* James Bucher, Comment, *Reinforcing the Foundation: The Case Against Copyright Protection for Works of Architecture,* 39 EMORY L.J. 1261, 1265-71 (1990).

> work and the originality of the architect. Legal norms that encourage incremental innovation and novel recombination of existing forms will foster such creativity, and benefit society.[77]

Because architecture is premised on the recombination of previously used forms and therefore reliant on copying, the extension of copyright protection could prevent creativity and the novel recombination of previously used forms into new structures. Arguments against the extension of copyright protection also focussed on the fact that architects, unlike other artists and authors, are considered fully compensated for their services in designing a unique item, i.e., the structure. Other types of authors usually rely on reproductions of their works before they achieve compensation commensurate with the value of their artistic efforts and creativity.[78] When Congress decided to amend the federal copyright statute, the motivation came not from a perceived need by the architectural community but rather from the recognition that the United States was clearly not in compliance with Berne on this issue.[79]

When the Architectural Works Copyright Protection Act[80] (hereinafter "AWCPA") was enacted, Congress established two requirements for architectural works to receive copyright protection. First, the work had to fall within the category of "architectural work," that was added to the list of protected "works of authorship."[81] Congress further defined this phrase as "the design of a building as embodied in any tangible medium of expression, including a building, architectural plans, or drawings. The work includes the overall form as well as the arrangement and composition of spaces and elements in the design, but does not include individual standard features."[82] While the use of the term "building" excludes many types of three-dimensional works worthy of copyright protection (such as bridges, walkways, and gardens), legislative history indicates that the word "building" should be interpreted broadly. As such, "buildings" include not only structures

---

[77] Winick, *supra* note 22, at 1604.

[78] *Id.* at 1606.

[79] *Id.* at 1611. Another commentator, however, noted that enactment of the AWCPA indicated Congress' recognition that "architecture is a form of artistic expression that performs a significant societal purpose, domestically and internationally." Marilyn Phelan, *A Synopsis of the Laws Protecting Our Cultural Heritage*, 28 New Eng. L. Rev. 63, 78 (1993).

[80] Pub. L. No. 101-650, 701, 703, 104 Stat. 5128, 5133 (1990) (codified at 17 U.S.C. § 101(5), 102(a)(8) (Supp. II 1990)).

[81] 17 U.S.C. § 102(a).

[82] Architectural Works Copyright Protection Act § 702(a), 17 U.S.C. § 101 (Supp. 1993). *See, e.g.*, The Value Group, Inc. v. Mendham Lake Estates, L.P., 800 F. Supp. 1228, 1231 (D.N.J. 1992) (extending copyright protection to both architectural plans and drawings and the works based on those plans and drawings).

inhabited by humans but also those used by humans, such as churches, pergolas, gazebos, and garden pavilions.[83] It has been suggested that as these terms are given clearer meaning through judicial interpretation, protection should not be extended either to structures that are primarily technical, engineering solutions (because these are not the product of aesthetic creativity) or to works such as gardens and parks which represent primarily spatial organizations rather than enclosed structures.[84]

Second, once a structure qualifies as a "building," its design must be considered both "original"[85] and "not wholly functional."[86] Thus, copyright protection may be granted to individual design elements, so long as they are not functionally required. Copyright protection may also be given to overall designs which meet a standard of originality, even if the separate elements would not qualify.[87]

---

83 Vanessa Scaglione, Note, *Building upon the Architectural Works Copyright Protection Act of 1990*, 61 FORDHAM L. REV. 193, 197-99 (1992).

84 Winick, *supra* note 22, at 1613. However, another commentator has argued in favor of a more expansive interpretation of "building," pointing out that the AWCPA does not explicitly require such a narrow reading. Scaglione, *supra* note 83, at 199-201.

85 For a recent discussion of the originality requirement, see Bellsouth Advertising & Publ. Co. v. Donnelley Information Publ., Inc., 999 F.2d 1436, 1439-40 (11th Cir. 1993) (applying the originality test to hold that the compilation of a telephone directory is not sufficiently original so as to be protectable).

86 If the possible ways of expressing an idea are limited or the form of expression is dictated by function and efficiency concerns, the idea and expression merge so as to render the expression unprotectable under the copyright laws. *See, e.g.*, Gates Rubber Co. v. Bando Chemical Indus., Inc., 9 F.3d 823, 838 (10th Cir. 1993) (discussing application of merger doctrine to computer program); *Bellsouth*, 999 F.2d at 1442-45 (applying the merger doctrine to deny copyright protection to a telephone directory compilation which could only be arranged in a limited number of ways or ways dictated only by function); Computer Associates International, Inc. v. Altai, Inc., 982 F.2d 693, 707-08 (2d Cir. 1992) (explaining that "expression" is not protected in those instances where there is only one or so few ways of expressing an idea that protection of the expression would be the equivalent to protection of the idea itself); Kregos v. Associated Press, 937 F.2d 700, 705 (2d Cir. 1991); CSM Investors, Inc. v. Everest Development Inc., 840 F. Supp. 1304 (D. Minn. 1994) (rejecting application of merger doctrine to architectural plans where the detailed specifications for construction were the same on the original and allegedly infringing plans).

87 Jane Ginsburg, *Copyright in the 101st Congress: Commentary on the Visual Artists Rights Act and the Architectural Works Copyright Protection Act of 1990*, 14 COLUM.-VLA J.L. & ARTS 477, 491 (1990). In True Value Group, Inc. v. Mendham Lake Estates, L.P., 800 F. Supp. 1228 (D.N.J. 1992), the court considered the degree of originality required under the low standard enunciated in Feist Publications, Inc. v. Rural Telephone Serv. Co., 499 U.S. 340, 345-48 (1991). The court acknowledged that copyright protection does not extend to individual standard features, 17 U.S.C. § 101, but maintained that so "long as an object embodies originality, copyright protection will not be displaced by the fact that the design was embodied in a 'useful article.'" The court further explained that a "useful" article is one with "an intrinsic utilitarian function that is not merely to portray the appearance of the article." The court used the example of a window as a useful article, and therefore not copyrightable, but the design on the window is not useful and is therefore eligible for copyright protection. *True Value Group*, 800 F. Supp. at 1232 & n.6. Finally, the court concluded that because the standard of originality is so low, copying was proven by the substantial similarity between the original and the infringing plans in their floor plan and

Four of the five exclusive rights granted under the Copyright Act have been extended to protectable architectural works. These are: the right to transform or adapt the work into another form ("the derivative works right"), the right to make copies, the right to distribute copies, and the right to display the work publicly.[88] One court has interpreted, albeit in dicta, the remedy which the AWCPA permits for copyright infringement of an architectural work. The District Court of New Jersey remarked that the AWCPA permits a court to enjoin the construction of an infringing building, rather than ordering impoundment of the infringing plans, which indirectly achieves the same result.[89]

The derivative works right, when applied to architectural works, was limited by a provision exempting from copyright protection two-dimensional representations of a building located in, or visible from, a public place.[90] This provision produces two anomalies. First, one is free to make two-dimensional, but not three-dimensional, reproductions of a protected architectural work. Second, because sculptures are now afforded greater protection than architectural works, a problem of classification has arisen. The House Report states that "monumental, nonfunctional works of architecture" should now be protected as architectural works and not as sculptural works.[91] The former category will thus be accorded a narrower version of the derivative works right and be denied any protections of the Visual Artists Rights Act.[92] This definitional distinction will therefore take on great significance, although it will arguably be difficult to determine.[93]

---

many of the details, such as placement, design, and size of the windows. *Id.* at 1233. *See also* CSM Investors, Inc. v. Everest Development Inc., 840 F. Supp. 1304 (D. Minn. 1994) (holding that a protected architectural "work" includes the form and design but not individual features).

88 Winick, *supra* note 22, at 1622.

89 *Compare* The Value Group, Inc. v. Mendham Lake Estates, L.P., 800 F. Supp. 1228, 1235 & n.8 (D.N.J. 1992) (enjoining the construction of an infringing building) *with* Demetriades v. Kaufmann, 690 F. Supp. 289, 295 (S.D.N.Y. 1988) (ordering the impoundment of infringing architectural plans).

90 AWCPA § 704(a), 17 U.S.C. § 120(a).

91 H.R. Rep. No. 735, 101st Cong., 2d Sess. at 20 & n.43 (1990) (commenting that architectural works should not be treated as pictorial, graphic, or sculptural works so as not to subject them to the separability test). On the other hand, architectural plans and drawings can now be protected as both "pictorial, graphic and sculptural works" and architectural works. CSM Investors, Inc. v. Everest Development Inc., 840 F. Supp. 1304 (D. Minn. 1994)

92 *See infra* notes 103-118 and accompanying text.

93 Ginsburg, *supra* note 87, at 494-95 & n.72; Scaglione, however, disagrees with Ginsburg's conclusion on this question, *supra* note 83, at 201-04. In Hart v. Sampley, 1992 U.S. Dist. LEXIS 1154 (D.D.C. 1992), the plaintiffs alleged a copyright infringement based on the allegation that defendants had reproduced and sold items depicting The Three Servicemen statue at the Vietnam Veterans' Memorial. One of the defendants' contentions rested on 17 U.S.C. § 120, in that, because the statue was in an "ordinarily visible and

The right to prevent alteration or destruction, in other words, the right of integrity, was specifically denied to architectural works. This was done so that a building owner could alter or destroy the building without seeking a transfer of the copyrights from the owner of the copyright or the architect.[94] This restriction was supported by the architectural community apparently out of fear that otherwise the architect would be routinely required to transfer the copyright.[95] The AWCPA's potential to preserve architectural works is thus nullified.[96]

B. *Federal Moral Rights Legislation (VARA)*

As was previously discussed in connection with the protection for architectural works, at the time of adoption of the Berne Convention, Congress debated whether any additional moral rights legislation was required to bring the United States into compliance with Berne. Some argued that other doctrines and statutes provided sufficient and equivalent protection to artists, as illustrated by the *Gilliam* decision.[97] Many others argued that this was not the type of protection required by the Berne Convention.[98]

The Berne Convention itself states, in Article 6*bis* that:

> (1) Independently of the author's economic rights, and even after the transfer of the said rights, the author shall have the right to claim authorship of the work and to object to any distortion, mutilation or other modification of, or other derogatory action in relation to, the said work, which would be prejudicial to his honour or reputation.[99]

---

public space," it did not receive copyright protection. Rather than considering the definitional aspects of this argument, the court merely rejected it because the statue was created in 1984, considerably before the applicable date of this provision. *Id.*

94 AWCPA § 704(a), 17 U.S.C. § 120(b).

95 Winick, *supra* note 22, at 1623-25. Winick also suggests, as will be discussed *infra* at notes 124-76 and accompanying text, that buildings of historic or architectural significance are better protected through local landmark and historic preservation laws, rather than through protection of individual architects' rights at the federal level. *Id.* The AWCPA also specifically states that it does not preempt such state and local laws. AWCPA § 705, 17 U.S.C. § 301(b)(2), (4). Another commentator has noted the curiousness of the position taken by architects who participated in the Congressional hearings. Ginsburg, *supra* note 87, at 494.

96 For a discussion of the duration of copyright protection for architectural works and the interrelationship with the work-made-for-hire doctrine, see Ginsburg, *supra* note 87, at 492-94.

97 *See supra* notes 67-71 and accompanying text.

98 *See, e.g.*, Brooks, *supra* note 17, at 1439-43, 1472-74; Edward J. Damich, *Moral Rights in the United States and Article 6bis of the Berne Convention: A Comment on the Preliminary Report of the Ad Hoc Working Group on U.S. Adherence to the Berne Convention*, 10 COLUM.-VLA J.L. & ARTS 143 (1986); Damich, *supra* note 35, at 3-4, 74-75; VerSteeg, *supra* note 65, at 830-33.

99 Berne Convention art. 6*bis*, § 1 (Paris Act 1971).

Thus, the Berne Convention recognizes two of the moral rights—the right to attribution (that is, the right to claim authorship) and the right to integrity (that is, the right to prevent the mutilation or destruction of the work).

Opposition to the adoption of the Berne Convention and to any modification of existing United States copyright law so as to recognize moral rights centered on a few main arguments. First, opponents argued that adoption of moral rights "would upset existing business practices" in the United States.[100] Second, the introduction of the European concept of moral rights would alter the natural evolution of American statutory and common law and would force or encourage American courts to look at judicial precedents and statutory interpretations of other nations.[101] The final primary argument was that artists' moral rights were already sufficiently protected by existing federal copyright laws, state moral rights legislation, a patchwork of other federal and state statutes, and common law causes of action.[102]

Despite these objections, Congress enacted the Visual Artists Rights Act (VARA) as an amendment to the 1976 Copyright Act.[103] VARA has limited relevance to the relationship between architecture and an artist's moral rights, because, as its title implies, it applies only to the visual arts.[104] A "work of visual art" is defined as

> a painting, drawing, print, or sculpture, existing in a single copy, in a limited edition of 200 copies or fewer . . . , or, in the case of a sculpture, [in 200 or fewer multiple casts]; or a still photographic image produced for exhibition purposes only, existing in a single copy . . . or in a limited edition of 200 copies or fewer . . . .[105]

Specifically excluded are "any poster, map, globe, chart, technical drawing, diagram, model, applied art, motion picture, or other audio visual work, book, magazine, newspaper, periodical, data base, electronic information service, electronic publication, or similar publication."[106] Also excluded are works made for hire and other

---

100 House Report on Berne Convention Implementation Act of 1988, H.R. Rep. No. 609, 100th Cong., 2d Sess., at 33-35 (1988). *See also generally* Settlemyer, *supra* note 36, at 2306-11.

101 H.R. Rep. No. 609, 100th Cong., 2d Sess., at 34-35.

102 *Id.* at 33-34.

103 Pub. L. No. 101-650, 603(a), 104 Stat. 5128 (1990) (codified at 17 U.S.C. § 106A (Supp. II 1990)). For a comparison of the moral rights provisions of VARA with those of the Berne Convention, see Damich, *supra* note 45, at 975-96.

104 VerSteeg, *supra* note 65, at 835-42.

105 Visual Artists Rights Act of 1990 § 602 (1)-(2), 17 U.S.C. § 101 (1)-(2).

106 VARA § 602 (2)(A)(i), 17 U.S.C. § 101 (2)(A)(i).

works not previously granted copyright protection under the existing federal statute.[107] The moral rights provisions thus deny an architect protection for both a completed architectural work and the architectural plans and drawings given the express exclusion of technical drawings and diagrams.

Only the rights of attribution and integrity are granted by VARA,[108] although the Copyright Office was directed to investigate the feasibility and practicality of adding the droit de suite at a future time.[109] The right of attribution includes the right to claim authorship of a work and the right to prevent the use of the artist's name as the author of a work not created by that artist. The right of integrity permits the artist to "prevent use of his or her name as the author . . . in the event of a distortion, mutilation, or other modification of the work which would be prejudicial to his or her honor or reputation."[110] The right of integrity also permits the artist

> (A) to prevent any intentional distortion, mutilation, or other modification of that work which would be prejudicial to his or her honor or reputation, and any intentional distortion, mutilation or modification of that work is a violation of that right, and (B) to prevent any destruction of a work of recognized stature, and any intentional or grossly negligent destruction of that work

---

107 VARA § 602(2)(B)-(C), 17 U.S.C. § 101(2)(B)-(C). The narrow scope of works protected by VARA will permit other forms of work to continue to be protected under the various state statutes and common law doctrines previously discussed, *supra* notes 61-71 and accompanying text. For example, VARA was held not to preempt state law protections for the right of attribution afforded to an artist when the art form involving puppetry was clearly not covered under VARA. The court read the statutory list as exhaustive rather than illustrative. Gegenhuber v. Hystopolis Prods, Inc., 1992 U.S. Dist. LEXIS 10156, at *9-12 (N.D. Ill. 1992).

108 Damich, *supra* note 45, at 958-66.

109 17 U.S.C. § 106A (1992). *See* Damich, *supra* note 45, at 973-74; Neil R. Siegel, *The Resale Royalty Provisions of the Visual Artists Rights Act: Their History and Theory*, 93 DICK L. REV. 1 (1988). Hearings on the possible enactment of a resale royalty right were held in San Francisco and New York in the spring of 1992. Andrea Maier, *If Art Is Resold, Should Artists Profit?*, N.Y. TIMES, Feb. 8, 1992, § 1, at 11; Daniel Grant, *Paying the Painter—Should Artists Get a Cut when Their Works are Resold?*, CHI. TRIB., Mar. 14, 1993, at C32. In December 1992, the Register of Copyrights presented its report prepared under the Congressional directive. This report recommended that the United States not establish a federal resale royalty right because the Copyright Office was "not persuaded that sufficient economic and copyright policy justification exists." It did, however, conclude that the federal copyright system could provide greater protection to visual artists by, for example, creating a broader public display right which would require that a fee be paid to the artist when a work is displayed in public. The Office also made various recommendations for a model federal system if Congress decided to enact a resale royalty right. This model includes a centralized collection agency and at least the initial application only to public auction sales. *Droit de Suite: The Artist's Resale Royalty*, Executive Summary, A Report of the Register of Copyrights xiii-xx (Dec. 1992). For a summary of United States law pertaining to the right of publication, a moral right not protected by VARA, see Settlemyer, *supra* note 36, at 2313-43.

110 VARA § 603(a)(2), 17 U.S.C. § 106A(a)(2).

is a violation of that right.[111]

Various types of modifications which result from the passage of time, conservation, and public presentation are excluded from being a destruction, distortion, or mutilation.

VARA thus attempts to vindicate both the author's personality interest in preserving the work of art when the artist's reputation is at stake and the public's interest in cultural property preservation, by requiring that the work be "of recognized stature" in order to receive such protection. VARA does not, however, define "recognized stature,"[112] and so this becomes a factual determination. This limitation has also been criticized for failing to follow the Berne Convention's extension of the right of integrity to all works of art which are otherwise protected by moral rights.[113]

For most works of art eligible to receive VARA protection, these rights will continue for the life of the artist.[114] This provision fails to provide as much protection for moral rights as for the economic rights provided under the Copyright Act.[115] One of the most controversial aspects of VARA is the provision pertaining to alienability. While the artist's moral rights are made non-transferable, they are waivable if the author expressly agrees in writing.[116] Many critics have suggested that this waiver provision converts moral rights into pecuniary rights, in direct contradiction to the Berne Convention. This provision will subject those artists with the least amount of bargaining power to routine pressure from dealers and collectors who want the artists to waive their rights.[117] Finally, VARA explicitly preempts equivalent state rights for works protected by VARA.[118]

There seems to be little direct linkage between the provisions of VARA and those of the AWCPA. Three points should, however,

---

111 VARA § 603(a)(3), 17 U.S.C. § 106A(a)(3).

112 VARA § 603(a), 17 U.S.C. § 106A(a)(3)(B). *See* VerSteeg, *supra* note 65, at 867-69.

113 Damich, *supra* note 45, at 953-55.

114 VARA § 603(a), 17 U.S.C. § 106A(d)(1).

115 *See* Damich, *supra* note 45, at 969-70 (noting that the Berne Convention in most instances requires moral rights to continue for as long as the economic rights in a work of art).

116 VARA § 603(a), 17 U.S.C. § 106A(e)(1)-(2).

117 Damich, *supra* note 45, at 966-68; VerSteeg, *supra* note 65, at 843-47 (noting, in particular, artists' generally weak bargaining position and their lack of knowledge concerning copyright and contract rights). Another commentator, however, suggested that at least some waivers should be permitted under federal moral rights legislation so as to accord with "the American tradition of balancing the interests of the artist with those of the purchaser and the public." Brooks, *supra* note 17, at 1479-81.

118 VARA § 605, 17 U.S.C. § 301 (f)(1)-(2). While this should not reduce the extent of protection granted, judicial interpretation of the preemption provision may have this effect depending on how narrowly the term "equivalent" is viewed. Damich, *supra* note 45, at 972-73.

be recalled. First, VARA's exclusion of technical plans and drawings from its definition of "visual art" seems to exclude architectural plans and drawings from any moral rights protection. Second, works of monumental sculpture may now be classified as architectural works, rather than as sculpture, and they therefore will not receive any protection under VARA. Third, the AWCPA's exclusion of the right of integrity for the architect or copyright owner gives the building owner the right to alter, destroy, or authorize the destruction of a building embodying an architectural work without the consent of the author or copyright owner of the architectural work.

Finally, one section of VARA deals specifically with the visual artist's rights when the art work is affixed to a building.[119] This section, however, limits the moral rights of the artist in order to protect the ownership rights of the property owner who later wishes to modify or destroy the building. If the artist agreed to the original installation, and if the art work is affixed in such a manner that it cannot be removed without significant damage, then the building owner may alter or destroy the building without the artist's consent. If the work can be removed without significant damage, then the building owner must attempt to notify the artist and give the artist ninety days in which to remove the work of art at the artist's expense.[120]

VARA's approach to this problem provides an interesting parallel and seems clearly to be an outgrowth of the decisions in both *Crimi* and *Serra.* Because the property owner has protectable or

---

119 VARA § 604, 17 U.S.C. § 113(d)(1)-(3). *See* Matthew A. Goodin, Comment, *The Visual Artists Rights Act of 1990: Further Defining the Rights and Duties of Artists and Real Property Owners*, 22 GOLDEN GATE U. L. REV. 567 (1992); VerSteeg, *supra* note 65, at 869-71. For discussion of the legislative history of this provision, see Keith A. Attlesey, Comment, *The Visual Artists Rights Act of 1990: The Art of Preserving Building Owners' Rights*, 22 GOLDEN GATE U. L. REV. 371, 382-84 (1992).

120 The California moral rights legislation has a similar provision, subjecting the artist's rights to those of the building owner. CAL. CIV. CODE § 987(h)(West 1993). VARA, however, appears to grant the artist greater protection than does the California statute. VARA protects the artist's right of integrity unless the artist waives the right in writing. The California statute, on the other hand, reverses the presumption, so that the artist's rights are protected only if reserved in a written instrument signed by the building owner. Attlesey, *supra* note 119, at 373-75 (arguing that VARA grants excessive protection to the artist's rights in this circumstance). In practice, it is likely that the artist will agree to waive rights protected by VARA because, without such a waiver, the building owner would probably refuse to install the art work. Perhaps the most significant difference in these approaches is that the California reservation of rights agreement must be recorded, so as to give notice to subsequent purchasers. However, the presence of the art work in the building gives inquiry notice to subsequent purchasers, even without a recorded instrument. Perhaps a weakness of VARA is its failure to deal with situations in which the art was attached to a building without the building owner's consent. *Id.* at 387-89. For an opposing view criticizing VARA as not granting sufficient protection to the artist, as opposed to the building owner, see Damich, *supra* note 45, at 955-58.

vested property rights in the building and in the land, while the artist has only contractual rights once the work of art itself has been conveyed, the property owner receives greater protection than does the artist.[121] Although VARA extends rights to the artist in the art work itself, even when the artist no longer owns the object, in a case of a conflict between the artist's rights and the rights of a real property owner, the latter will still receive greater protection.[122] Thus, the owner of the building and of real property is entitled to greater protection than the artist or the copyright owner, once again illustrating the relative values of different forms of "protectable" interests.

Professor Jane Ginsburg points out an ironic result of the dichotomy in treatment of removable and incorporated art works, when this distinction is applied to "site-specific" art such as Serra's "Tilted Arc." A site-specific work is generally removable without any resulting physical injury to the art work, but separation from its architectural or environmental context may arguably cause aesthetic destruction or mutilation of the work. The artist who asserts that the art object is site-specific and therefore cannot be moved because of the right of integrity may lose the right of integrity entirely because the art work may be classified as an incorporated art work.[123]

IV. Landmarking and Historic Preservation

It would be interesting to speculate on the linkage that might develop between VARA and AWCPA. Despite the expansion of both artists' rights and the rights of architects as artists, the combination of federal legislation would still fail to prevent the modifications of Louis Kahn's architectural masterpiece discussed at the beginning of this article. Even if the current legislation were to

---

[121] Battle, *supra* note 15, at 462-63 (noting that traditional concepts of property ownership endow the owner with freedom of alienability and terminate any rights of the seller in the property once it is sold).

[122] Under VARA, the artist's right of integrity is waivable by the artist. Thus, although VARA appears to protect this right after sale of the art work, in light of the artist's weaker bargaining position, it is likely that in many situations the artist will consent to such installation because otherwise the building owner will refuse to install the art work, 17 U.S.C. § 113 (d)(1)(A)-(B); *see also* VerSteeg, *supra* note 65, at 843-45 (noting artists' weaker bargaining position when entering into contracts). VARA places a further burden on the artist if the art work is one which could have been removed without injury. Then the building owner can remove it if the owner has attempted to notify the artist. 17 U.S.C. § 113(d)(2)(A)-(B) and § 113 (d)(3).

[123] Ginsburg, *supra* note 87, at 486-87. Contrary to Winick's view, Ginsburg suggests that at least the moral rights provisions of VARA could become an effective tool for accomplishing art preservation without creating conflict with the rights of copyright owners. *Id.* at 479.

apply to this building, the dilemma presented by the changes to the Salk Institute would fail to receive any protection for several reasons. First, the moral rights granted by VARA endure only for the lifetime of the author and cannot be asserted by family, friends, students, or colleagues of the author, even if they have a good basis for representing what the author might have wished. Second, in the case of architectural works, the right of integrity is explicitly denied to the author and copyright holder, even though such a right exists for the author of certain types of visual art works.[124] The reason for this lies in the sanctity accorded by Anglo-American law to property ownership and, in particular, real property ownership.

It is necessary therefore to consider the move in the United States toward protection of buildings and historical monuments, not through vindication of individual artists' rights, but through landmark preservation laws. In fact, historic preservation laws may encourage creativity in architectural design by providing incentives to building owners to use their buildings as a form of artistic expression.[125] These laws, which limit real property owners' use of their land, have withstood constitutional attack on the ground that they are a taking of property by the government without payment of just compensation, as required by the Fifth Amendment to the Constitution. This fact may demonstrate that such laws represent a more acceptable and productive method, at least within the existing framework of American property law, of protecting significant architectural works.

Just as in American intellectual property law, where the focus is on the benefit the public derives from the rights granted, in the area of historic preservation, the focus is on the rights the public may assert through the legislative and administrative branches of government. Throughout the United States, the federal government, all fifty states, and over 1000 city and local governments have enacted various forms of historic preservation legislation.[126] It is

---

124 Thus, although one commentator has suggested that enactment of the AWCPA demonstrates Congress' recognition of the importance of architecture as a form of cultural property, Phelan, *supra* note 79, at 78, this conclusion seems overly sanguine in light of the explicit rejection of a right of integrity for architects. Enactment of VARA, granting to authors the rights of integrity in any work of recognized stature, does serve a cultural property preservation purpose, Settlemyer, *supra* note 36, at 2311-12 & n.89, but does not further the more specific goal of architectural preservation.

125 Rose, *supra* note 6, at 501-02.

126 Examples of federal legislation include the National Trust for Historic Preservation Act, empowering the National Trust to receive donations of sites and buildings, 16 U.S.C. § 468-68d (1988); the National Historic Preservation Act of 1966, directing the maintenance of the National Register of historic districts, sites, buildings and structures, 16 U.S.C.

not possible to describe in detail these statutes and ordinances or the methods for landmarking which they establish. However, the New York City Landmarks Law,[127] under which over 1000 buildings and other structures have been declared landmarks, may serve as an illustration of this type of legislation.

The purpose of the ordinance is to protect, enhance, and perpetuate architectural features "of special character or special historical or aesthetic interest or value" that "represent or reflect elements of the city's cultural, social, economic, political and architectural history."[128] The Landmarks Law provides for an independent commission that has the power to designate landmark status on "any improvement, any part of which is thirty years old or older" which fits the stated purpose of the ordinance.[129] The Commission has authority to hold public hearings and then, at its own discretion, to declare a structure a landmark,[130] without the consent of the owner. Once a structure has been designated a landmark, the owner cannot "alter, reconstruct, demolish . . . [or] construct any improvement upon land embraced within such site or such parcel and located within such district."[131] In addition, all landmark owners must maintain and repair their structures at their own expense.[132]

The owner may receive an exemption from these restrictions for: safety reasons,[133] alterations that the Commission determines have no architectural effect,[134] alterations that the Commission determines to be architecturally appropriate,[135] and economic hardship so that the owner can earn a "reasonable return" on the property.[136] In the case of not-for-profit organizations, where reasonable return on investment is not an appropriate measure, the

---

§ 470a-w-b (1988 & Supp. III 1991); and the National Environmental Policy Act of 1969, requiring that environmental and cultural values be considered along with economic and technological issues in assessing the impact of federal projects, 42 U.S.C. § 4321-70a (1988 & Supp. III 1991). For a compilation of such legislation and other methods of historic preservation adopted by the state and federal governments, see James P. Beckwith, *Developments in the Law of Historic Preservation and a Reflection on Liberty*, 12 WAKE FOREST L. REV. 93 (1976), and Phelan, *supra* note 79, at 69-75. For a discussion of historic district designation and its potential role in building communities, see Rose, *supra* note 6, at 504-33.

127 N.Y. City Admin. Code §§ 25.301-25.321 (1992).

128 *Id.* § 25.301(b).

129 *Id.* §§ 25.303(a)(1), 25.302(n).

130 *Id.* § 25.303(a)(2)-(4).

131 *Id.* § 25.305(a)(1).

132 *Id.* § 25.311.

133 *Id.* § 25.312.

134 *Id.* § 25.306.

135 *Id.* § 25.307.

136 Reasonable return is defined as 6% net annual return on assessed value. *Id.* §§ 25-309, 25-302(v).

economic hardship or reasonable return on investment criterion is replaced with the test of whether the landmark designation interferes unreasonably with the organization's charitable purpose.[137]

This type of restriction must be distinguished from broader categories of land use regulation in which a town or city may be divided into various "zones" (hence the name zoning for this type of regulation), and particular uses, density, height, and methods of construction may be specified. In virtually every situation, the process of landmark or historic designation is in addition to, and sets a higher standard than, the more general zoning requirements for the particular area.

Two basic forms of challenges have been brought to landmarking designations in the United States. The first, and more general type of challenge, is that the regulation deprives the landowner of the use of the land, thus constituting a "taking" under the Fifth Amendment to the Constitution.[138] If a court determines that a particular regulation so deprives a landowner of the use of the property as to constitute a taking,[139] the government must then either pay the landowner "just compensation" or rescind the regulation.[140] This area of constitutional analysis has received considerable attention in recent years. Under the leadership of Justice Scalia, the Court seems to be breathing new life into the Takings Clause, as it applies to the area of "regulatory takings."[141]

A landowner can challenge governmental interference with economic rights that are premised on the ownership of the land involved. However, at least since the 1920's, restrictions on land

---

137 *See, e.g.*, Church of St. Paul and St. Andrew v. Barwick, 496 N.E.2d 183, 192 n.7 (N.Y. 1986).

138 The Takings Clause of the Fifth Amendment states, in part, "nor shall private property be taken for public use, without just compensation." U.S. CONST. amend. V. The Takings Clause has been made applicable to state governments through the Due Process Clause of the Fourteenth Amendment. Penn Central Transportation Co. v. City of New York, 438 U.S. 104, 122 (1978).

139 The Supreme Court recognized as early as its decision in Pennsylvania Coal Co. v. Mahon, 260 U.S. 393, 415 (1922), that the Takings Clause applied not only to physical deprivations of private property, but also to governmental regulations pursuant to the state's police power that were in some degree equivalent to a physical taking. How far a regulation had to go for it to be considered a taking is now the subject of considerable debate. *See, e.g.*, Lucas v. South Carolina Coastal Council, 112 S. Ct. 2886 (1992).

140 The Supreme Court determined that the owner of private property who was deprived of all use of the land by a governmental regulation was entitled to compensation for a "temporary" taking, even if the governmental authority subsequently rescinded the regulation. First English Evangelical Lutheran Church of Glendale v. County of Los Angeles, California, 482 U.S. 304 (1987).

141 *See, e.g.*, Nollan v. California Coastal Comm'n, 438 U.S. 825 (1987) (holding that a land-use regulation in the form of a development exaction for which the asserted state interest and the means of accomplishing that interest are not a close "fit" constitutes a taking); *Lucas*, 112 S. Ct. 2886 (holding that a land-use regulation which deprives the property owner of all economic value of the property constitutes a taking).

use for the promotion of public safety, health and welfare have been recognized as serving a legitimate governmental purpose.[142] Under both state constitutions and the federal constitution, this has been taken to include regulation for the preservation of aesthetic and historical values.[143]

In the landmark decision, Penn Central Transportation Co. v. New York City,[144] the United States Supreme Court conclusively decided that landmark preservation laws were, in fact, constitutional and presented no prima facie example of an unconstitutional exercise of governmental authority.[145] In that case, the owner of Grand Central Terminal was refused permission to construct a tower above the existing terminal because it had been designated a landmark.[146] In its decision, the Supreme Court also held that, so long as the owner could make reasonable use of the land (and, in fact, the landowner was allowed to continue the prior use of the land) and could realize a profit on his or her reasonable investment-backed expectations, the landmark designation did not constitute an unconstitutional taking of the property without compensation.[147]

More recent Supreme Court decisions have strengthened the effect of the Takings Clause, but it seems unlikely that these decisions will have any adverse impact on historic preservation laws.[148] In the Supreme Court's most recent decision concerning land use regulation, Lucas v. South Carolina Coastal Council,[149] Justice Scalia held that a regulation would constitute a taking when the landowner was deprived of *all* economic benefit in the regulated land.[150] Since most historic preservation laws only prevent the owner from altering the structure and permit the prior use to continue,[151] as in *Penn Central*,[152] most landmarking regulation would

---

142 *See, e.g.*, Village of Euclid, Ohio v. Ambler Realty Co., 272 U.S. 365 (1926).

143 *See, e.g.*, State of Missouri v. Berkeley, 458 S.W.2d 305 (Mo. 1970).

144 438 U.S. 104 (1978).

145 *Id.* at 128-35.

146 *Id.* at 116-18.

147 *Id.* at 137-38.

148 Since the Supreme Court's decision in *Penn Central*, *id.*, upholding the constitutionality of New York's landmark designation ordinance, the Supreme Court has apparently turned to the question of environmental regulation as a possible form of governmental taking, as is illustrated in the relatively recent decisions of Lucas v. South Carolina Coastal Council, 112 S. Ct. 2886 (1992); Nollan v. California Coastal Comm'n, 483 U.S. 825 (1987); First English Evangelical Lutheran Church of Glendale v. County of Los Angeles, 482 U.S. 304 (1987).

149 112 S. Ct. 2886 (1992).

150 *Id.* at 2893-95. This holding is partially qualified in that the government may abolish a harmful or noxious use which would be considered a nuisance under the state's common law definition of nuisance. *Id.* at 2896-2902.

151 For example, the New York City ordinance recognizes the owner's need to realize a

presumably pass constitutional muster. It is necessary to remember, however, that state constitutions can set a higher standard and so may preclude some forms of regulation that would be permissible under the Constitution.[153] Nonetheless, the basic constitutionality of landmark and historic preservation statutes has not been extensively challenged in recent years. The current areas of significant challenge are primarily in the field of environmental protection where greater restrictions are being placed on the uses to which landowners may put their land, such as occurred in *Lucas.*[154]

Landmark regulation has received more serious challenges when the landmarked building happens to be a church or some other type of structure with a religious use. Here, the landowner can raise not simply an economic claim but a religious claim, i.e., that the regulation denies the owner the first amendment right of religious free exercise.[155] When such a challenge is brought, the Supreme Court has traditionally given greater scrutiny in reviewing the constitutionality of the regulation. When the regulation imposes a substantial burden on the observation of a central religious practice, the regulation must be justified by a compelling governmental interest or purpose.[156]

In Employment Division v. Smith,[157] the Court, in an opinion written by Justice Scalia, held that there was no constitutionally compelled exemption to a generally applicable, otherwise valid statute or regulation.[158] Furthermore, the validity of such a regulation should be evaluated under the minimal standard of review, rather than the heightened scrutiny accorded to governmental actions which regulate fundamental rights.[159] Under this approach, buildings with religious uses would be subject to generally applica-

---

"reasonable" return from the building as a hardship factor and allows this need as the basis for an exemption from the ordinance.

152 438 U.S. 104 (1978).

153 *See, e.g.*, Society of Jesus v. Boston Landmarks Comm'n, 564 N.E.2d 571 (Mass. 1990) (holding that an ordinance prohibiting rearrangement of interior church architecture violated state's Declaration of Rights); First Covenant Church of Seattle v. City of Seattle, 787 P.2d 1352 (Wash. 1990) (holding that a landmark designation ordinance was unconstitutional as applied to buildings used for religious purposes under the state constitution, independent of its unconstitutionality under the Constitution).

154 112 S. Ct. 2886 (1992).

155 The First Amendment states, "Congress shall make no law respecting an Establishment of religion or prohibiting the free exercise thereof." U.S. CONST. amend. I.

156 *See, e.g.*, Sherbert v. Verner, 374 U.S. 398, 406-10 (1963); Thomas v. Review Bd of Indiana Employment Security Div., 450 U.S. 707, 718-19 (1981); Hobbie v. Unemployment Appeals Comm'n of Florida, 480 U.S. 136, 138-42 (1987); Hernandez v. Commissioner, 490 U.S. 680, 699 (1989).

157 494 U.S. 872 (1990).

158 *Id.* at 878-82.

159 *Id.* at 882-87.

ble, otherwise valid land use regulations, including landmark ordinances, even when the building owner attempts to raise the claim of a first amendment infringement. In Rectors, Wardens, and Members of Vestry of St. Bartholomew's Church v. City of New York,[160] this reasoning was used to validate the application of New York City's landmark ordinance which prevented a church from constructing an addition to be used as an office building.

On the other hand, the Massachusetts Supreme Court held that the Boston Landmark ordinance could not be applied to a church to prevent the church from altering its internal arrangement in accord with liturgical changes.[161] This decision, however, was based exclusively on Massachusetts' Declaration of Rights, rather than the federal Constitution's First Amendment, and therefore has little national significance.[162] The Washington State Supreme Court also held that a landmark ordinance violated both state and federal constitutions, when applied to religious structures, even though the ordinance provided an exemption for interior and external changes necessitated by liturgical changes.[163]

This area of takings clause jurisprudence may, however, change significantly with the recent enactment by Congress of the Religious Freedom Restoration Act. This Act restores the applica-

160 914 F.2d 348, 354 (2d Cir. 1990), *cert. denied*, 499 U.S. 901 (1991). For a discussion of this case and similar cases involving landmarking of religious buildings, see Thomas Pak, Note, *Free Exercise, Free Expression and Landmarks Preservation*, 91 COLUM. L. REV. 1813 (1991).

161 Society of Jesus v. Boston Landmarks Comm'n, 564 N.E.2d 571 (Mass. 1990).

162 564 N.E.2d at 572-73; *see also* Pak, *supra* note 160, at 1823 & n.68.

163 First Covenant Church of Seattle v. City of Seattle, 787 P.2d 1352 (Wash. 1990). At the time of the decision, the holding under the federal constitution seemed incorrect under Employment Division v. Smith, 494 U.S. 872, 878-87 (1990). This decision in *First Covenant Church* was vacated by the United States Supreme Court, 499 U.S. 901 (1991), but its holding based on the state constitution seems unassailable. However, upon reconsideration, the Washington Supreme Court reinstated its earlier holding and distinguished *Smith* on the grounds that the landmark designation ordinance was not a neutral regulation because it granted an exemption for architectural changes reflecting liturgical changes. First Covenant Church of Seattle v. City of Seattle, 840 P.2d 174, 180-81 (Wash. 1992). The ordinance was also not considered generally applicable because it contains a system of individualized exceptions which lend themselves to individualized governmental assessments of the conduct involved. *Id.* at 181. The Washington Supreme Court also distinguished this case from *Smith* on the grounds that the former involved a "hybrid" situation—that is, two constitutional rights, the freedom of speech as well as the free exercise of religion, were implicated. *Id.* at 181. The court then applied the *Sherbert v. Verner* compelling government interest test and concluded that the landmark ordinance could not apply to religious structures. *Id.* at 183. This reasoning may be significant because freedom of speech of the owner would apply to a large category of protected buildings and would thus significantly undermine the general applicability of historical preservation ordinances, beyond the religious context, throughout the nation. For a full discussion of the applicability of landmark preservation regulations to religious structures, see, e.g., Angela Carmella, *Houses of Worship and Religious Liberty: Constitutional Limits to Landmark Preservation and Architectural Review*, 36 VILL. L. REV. 401, 490-98 (1991); Pak, *supra* note 160, at 1840-43.

tion of the "compelling government interest" test to government regulation which substantially burdens the free exercise of religion,[164] as enunciated in Sherbert v. Verner[165] and Wisconsin v. Yoder.[166] It remains for future judicial decisions to interpret this Act, particularly in its application to historic preservation regulations.

V. Conclusion

The landmarking process is slow because it requires each building or historic district to be individually judged as to its value and significance. Nonetheless, there are now many (probably thousands) of designated buildings throughout the United States, so the process will likely continue.[167] It is interesting to note that the severe modification of the Salk Institute could have been pre-

---

164 107 Stat. § 1488 (1993). The Act, in part, reads:

> (a) In General.—Government shall not substantially burden a person's exercise of religion even if the burden results from a rule of general applicability, except as provided in subsection (b).
>
> (b) Exception.—Government may substantially burden a person's exercise of religion only if it demonstrates that application of the burden to the person—
>
> (1) is in furtherance of a compelling governmental interest; and
>
> (2) is the least restrictive means of furthering that compelling governmental interest.

Id. § 3. While these provisions would seem to substantiate decisions such as that of the Washington State Supreme Court, *supra* note 163, it remains for judicial opinions to interpret the statute's provisions concerning "substantial" burdens and, even more significantly, its apparent emphasis on the burdens placed on individuals' exercise of religion. While the First Amendment is perhaps unclear as to its focus on individuals, as opposed to institutions, some have argued that it is intended only to protect individual free exercise. *See, e.g.*, Ira Lupu, *Free Exercise Exemption and Religious Institutions: The Case of Employment Discrimination*, 67 B.U. L. Rev. 391, 419-31 (1987). *Contra* Mary Ann Glendon & Raul F. Yanes, *Structural Free Exercise*, 90 Mich. L. Rev. 477, 495-96 (1991). The Religious Freedom Restoration Act seems explicit in this regard. One could therefore posit that landmark ordinances burden institutions, that is most typically the corporate or associational owners of such buildings, and not individuals and that such ordinances are therefore not subject to the compelling government interest test.

Furthermore, even before the *Smith* decision, lower federal courts had held that buildings intended for religious uses were subject to land-use regulations in such decisions as Lakewood, Ohio Congregation of Jehovah's Witnesses, Inc. v. City of Lakewood, 699 F.2d 303 (6th Cir.), *cert. denied*, 464 U.S. 815 (1983) and Grosz v. City of Miami Beach, 721 F.2d 729 (11th Cir. 1983), *cert. denied*, 469 U.S. 827 (1984). Both of these decisions held that a community could deny an exemption for religious uses in an area where such uses were forbidden and there was no constitutionally-compelled exemption from such land-use regulations. *See* Scott D. Godshall, Note, *Land Use Regulation and the Free Exercise Clause*, 84 Colum. L. Rev. 1562 (1984). One could thus argue that even while the Supreme Court utilized a compelling government interest/strict scrutiny test for governmental burdens on the free exercise of religion, building uses were still subject to such generally applicable land-use regulations.

165 374 U.S. 398 (1963).

166 406 U.S. 205 (1972).

167 There are approximately 900 buildings which have been landmarked individually in New York City, but the number jumps to 18,000 if one includes historic districts. Pak, *supra* note 160, at 1814 n.10.

vented if that building had been given landmark status.[168] Even more noteworthy is the relative order of significance attached to the various interests represented by these types of conflicts.

The original purpose to the constitutional provision empowering Congress to legislate in the intellectual property field is premised primarily on the public benefit to be derived from granting authors and inventors rights in their creations.[169] Separately asserted rights, which are personal to the artist, must give way before the public interest. The corollary is that the artist's personal rights will also give way to the rights of the property owner (that is, the owner of the art object), with the public benefit to be derived from the vindication of such property rights simply assumed.[170] The dichotomy in the treatment of artists' rights applied to objects (that is, personal property) and the treatment of those rights when applied to land further illustrates the relative value given by the American legal system to various types of vested property interests.

Landmarking, on the other hand, because it serves only the public interest and is asserted only on behalf of the public (rather than individuals), is now granted priority over even the rights of the landowner.[171] For a society and a legal system, which purport to value the individual so highly, this subrogation of the individual's rights to those of the public represents an interesting paradox, a paradox well illustrated by the struggle of artists to achieve

---

168 Different state and federal legislation may require that a building be a certain age before it is eligible for landmark status. The Salk Institute may not have qualified for such status on that basis. The Federal Advisory Council on Historic Preservation has, however, requested information as to whether the Institute would fall under the National Historic Preservation Act. This Act requires council review of federal actions likely to affect historic properties. In the case of the Salk, the federal undertaking would be premised on the considerable funding being provided by the National Institutes of Health. Herbert Muschamp, *New Party Joins the Salk Addition Dispute,* N.Y. TIMES, June 17, 1993, at C14.

169 *But see* Lacey, *supra* note 15, at 1553-67 (questioning why the artist's rights in his or her property should be subjected to the public interest to a greater degree than the rights of owners of other types of private property).

170 Lacey critiques the relative hierarchy of rights accorded to different types of property ownership. However, she suggests that some moral rights, especially the rights of integrity, disclosure, and retraction, grant excessive rights to the artist, when they can be exercised for reasons other than the public's interest in cultural property preservation. In evaluating this interest, she suggests that the public should be defined as an interdependent community. Lacey, *supra* note 15, at 1593-95.

171 An alternative or additional mechanism to an aggressive landmarking program is to encourage the creation of easements or restrictive covenants donated by the property owner to the local government. The substance of such a restriction would be a negative promise by the landowner not to change or destroy the building without governmental permission. In exchange, the landowner would receive a tax deduction for the estimated value of the agreement to restrict the use of the property in this manner. Such a solution emphasizes private agreement, in that the landowner voluntarily agrees to restrict the use of the property, rather than having restrictions imposed on the landowner by the government. Such a system presumably would cause less friction between property owners and government because of its essentially voluntary nature.

recognition for their individual creative contributions to American society, and the even greater struggle to receive comparable recognition of architects, who, unfortunately, work in a medium with particular applications to the sanctity of real property rights.

In conclusion, public art, which should be taken to include both architecture and art placed in public places, requires an explicit balancing of the interests of the author, the present owner, and the public. This is not to deny that the premise underlying the grant of any protection to art works is in fact the benefit which the public will derive therefrom. This notion, however, conflicts directly with the other presumption of Anglo-American property law, that the public benefits the most from the free use and alienability of real property. In this area, therefore, we must recognize that while the application of moral rights to public art and architecture coincidentally helps to further the goals of protection and preservation, artists' rights are not intended primarily for that purpose. Furthermore, they are not the most effective tool for accomplishing these goals. The use of artists' moral rights for this purpose creates new problems and fails to resolve some old ones.

First, there is a major problem of enforcement. In some nations, the moral right does not last beyond the life of the author; so, once the author dies, there is no one to protect the art work. Even if the right outlives the author, there is a question as to who should have standing to enforce it. What qualifies the artist's heirs to assert it, and, even if they are "qualified," will they have the incentive or desire to do so?[172]

Second, even if enforcement may be left to the artist's heirs, are the author and the heirs the most appropriate judges of what the art work's future should be? While authors should have continuing moral rights to their works, particularly the rights of integrity and attribution, there may well come a point when the public should be able to decide what is to be protected and how, especially for those works to be displayed in public and to be maintained by the public or by the owner.[173] This suggestion would fit

---

[172] In some nations, such as Brazil, Italy and Portugal, after the creator's death, the creator's moral rights are exercised by a governmental authority rather than by the creator's heirs or legatees, as in France. *See* Kwall, *supra* note 13, at 16 n.65. This type of mechanism should better serve society's interest in preserving its cultural property. *See also* Lacey, *supra* note 15, at 1594 (positing that moral rights should not outlast the author because "at that point, the bond between the artist and her work is broken or at least weakened, and the interest of the community in experiencing the work becomes paramount").

[173] The right of attribution seems distinguishable from the right of integrity, the former deserving perpetual protection or at least protection significantly beyond the lifetime of

the goal of balancing the interests implicit in the case law, even if not explicit in the statutory law.

The alternative, to the extension of the right of integrity beyond the life of the author, is to rely on an aggressive landmarking process to represent the public's interest in the preservation of public art and architecture. As landmarking exists in the United States today, the process is not perfect; buildings have been lost to destruction before they have been landmarked, and landmark commissions may give permission for alterations to which others may object. Nonetheless, it is a process which in recent years has been the subject of relatively little controversy, from either landowners or the artistic and architectural communities.

The proposed model would incorporate a system similar to that currently used by the United States for architecture. However, the concept of landmark should be extended to individual art works in the public and the private domain. Many other nations, in order to protect their ancient past, have declared blanket national ownership of all objects and archaeological sites that are more than a certain age.[174] On the other hand, in the United States, with relatively few exceptions for cultural property found on publicly-owned land, virtually no cultural property of this sort is protected.[175]

Blanket national protection for all public art may not be the solution. Nevertheless, individual works of art, as well as buildings, can be granted landmark status that would require the owner,

---

the artist. There may at times arise a problem of proper attribution, but, so long as this can be accurately determined, there is no reason not to require it.

174 For example, in Israel, all objects considered "antiquities," although not all owned by the national government, are subject to strict restrictions on ownership, trade, and especially export. In Israel, any antiquity found or discovered after February 10, 1978 and the surrounding area necessary for the object's preservation are the property of the State. Antiquities include any object which is the product of human activity dating from before the year 1700, any zoological or botanical remains dating before the year 1300, and more recently produced objects which the Minister of Education and Culture declares to have historical importance. 885 SEFER HAHUKIM 776 §§ 1 and 2(a) (Feb. 10, 1978). *See* Shoshana Berman, *Antiquities in Israel in a Maze of Controversy*, 19 CASE W. RES. J. INT'L L. 343, 344, 351 (1987). *See also* LYNDEL PROTT & PATRICK O'KEEFE, LAW AND THE CULTURAL HERITAGE. I: DISCOVERY AND EXCAVATION (1984); III: MOVEMENT (1989).

175 Several states have in recent years enacted special legislation prohibiting the possession, sale, transfer, and public display of human remains and associated grave goods. *See, e.g.*, CAL. PUB. RES. CODE ANN. §§ 5097.98 and 5097.99 (West & Supp. 1992); IDAHO CODE § 27-501(2)(a)-(c) (1989). Several states have also enacted legislation protecting unmarked burial sites, often even when found on private land, and requiring that human remains and associated grave goods be returned either to descendants or to related ethnic, kin, or tribal groups, when such groups are identifiable, or sometimes reburied, when such descendants or related groups are not identifiable. *See, e.g.*, CAL. PUB. RES. CODE § 5097.98; FLA. STAT. § 872.05 (West 1991); IND. CODE §§ 14-3-3.4—16 (Burns 1990); KAN. STAT. ANN. §§ 74-2742—2748 (1992); MD. CODE ANN. § 5-627(a)-(b) (1991); MO. REV. STAT. §§ 194.400-194.410 (1992).

whether public or private, to maintain and protect the art work. In the case of an object, it should not need to be as old as the thirty years required by New York landmark law.[176] Thirty years is too long for personal property. Artists should be given the opportunity to seek landmark status during their lifetime, allowing them to vindicate the moral right of integrity. For the same reason, a shorter time could also be required for architectural works. However, the decision to require preservation would not be a unilateral one by the artist. Rather, only a decision by a body responsible to the public, and including representatives of the artistic community, could impose on the owner the duty to preserve and maintain the art work.

While expansion of the artist's or architect's moral right is desirable in the short run, in the long term, this does not seem to take sufficient account of the public interest. However, an aggressive plan of landmarking of both architectural works and individual art objects would represent the appropriate and necessary balancing of interests between the artist, the owner, and the public, if the goal of preservation of artistic monuments is to be accomplished.

---

176 N.Y. City Admin. Code § 25-302(n) (defining "landmark" as "any improvement, any part of which is thirty years old or older.").

CAMPBELL v. ACUFF-ROSE: JUSTICE SOUTER'S RESCUE OF FAIR USE*

PIERRE N. LEVAL**

I. *2 LIVE CREW*

Last month, as you know, the Supreme Court delivered its opinion in *Campbell v. Acuff-Rose*, involving the 2 Live Crew's rap parody of "Oh, Pretty Woman."[1] It will come as no surprise that the opinion brought me enormous joy. I will not try to disguise that my vanity was enormously gratified by Justice Souter's very generous citation of my article on fair use standards.[2] Another part of my joy, however, came from a different source. This was the sense that the fair use doctrine had been lost adrift for a turbulent decade and now, at last, through Justice Souter's magnificent opinion had found its way.

I believe the doctrine got lost as a result of overreaction to the Supreme Court's opinion in *Sony* in 1984.[3] I have never disagreed with the bottom line of *Sony*.[4] I do not think an actionable copyright infringement has occurred when Mom and Pop record Masterpiece Theatre while they are out to dinner so they can watch it after they come home. (I am not at all sure that this result required reference to fair use.) In any event, the Supreme Court opinion included propositions that, unintendedly, cast fair use adrift. Previously, the most significant force driving a fair use finding had been the notion that *fair uses are "productive."*[5] Because time-shifting was difficult to square with the notion of "productivity," the Supreme Court announced that productivity was not an

---

* This was originally delivered at the Benjamin N. Cardozo School of Law as the keynote speech at "Copyright in the Twenty-First Century," a symposium held on April 12, 1994, sponsored by the *Cardozo Arts and Entertainment Law Journal*.

** The author is a judge of the United States Court of Appeals for the Second Circuit.

1 114 S. Ct. 1164 (1994).

2 Pierre N. Leval, *Toward a Fair Use Standard*, 103 HARV. L. REV. 1105 (1990).

3 Sony Corp. of Am. v. Universal City Studios, Inc., 464 U.S. 417 (1984).

4 The Court in *Sony* held that private home videotaping of a copyrighted television program to be used solely to permit a one-time *private* non-commercial home viewing at a time more convenient than the hour of broadcast, would not infringe the copyright because it would constitute a fair use. *Id.* at 442.

5 *See, e.g., Sony*, 464 U.S. at 478-82 (Blackmun, J., dissenting); Universal City Studios, Inc. v. Sony Corp. of Am., 659 F.2d 963, 970 (9th Cir. 1981); Pacific & Southern Co. v. Duncan, 572 F. Supp. 1186 (N.D. Ga. 1983), *aff'd in part and rev'd in part*, 744 F.2d 1490 (11th Cir. 1984), *cert. denied*, 471 U.S. 1004 (1985); WILLIAM F. PATRY, THE FAIR USE PRIVILEGE IN COPYRIGHT LAW at xi, 3, 17, 205 (BNA Books 1985); WILLIAM F. PATRY, LATMAN'S THE COPYRIGHT LAW 240 (BNA Books 1986).

essential requirement of fair use.[6] Justice Stevens' opinion does not suggest he intended to *overturn* the entire history of fair use thinking. Nor does the *Sony* opinion purport to define the heart of fair use. All this opinion said was that while "[t]he distinction between 'productive' and unproductive uses may be helpful, . . . it cannot be wholly determinative."[7] Unfortunately, the world of copyright lawyers, scholars, and judges overreacted. The Supreme Court's holding was generally taken to mean that productivity was no longer a useful or important standard. The notion of productivity abruptly disappeared from fair use discussions. Having been deprived of its most important compass bearing, the doctrine then drifted aimlessly without a governing standard for ten years.

Having lost their guiding standard, courts began to grope for other guides that might help explain an individual ruling. The first groping came in *Sony* itself. Searching for a rationale for its decision, the Supreme Court stressed how harmless Mom and Pop's *noncommercial* time shift was.[8] To emphasize a helpful contrast, the Court set up a straw man, a dictum that was in no way essential to the reasoning of the case: "[E]very commercial use of copyrighted material is presumptively unfair."[9] And practically every Supreme Court opinion since that time has ritualistically repeated that phrase.[10] Until the Sixth Circuit's decision in *2 Live Crew,* this slogan did not do much harm. Courts that dealt frequently with copyright issues soon realized that virtually all uses are commercial.[11] Newspapers, criticism, commentary, history—it's all published for money. When the courts found something that they thought *for other reasons* was an infringement, they would chime: "Commercial uses are presumptively unfair." On the other hand, when they believed a fair use was involved, courts would simply

---

6 *Sony,* 464 U.S. at 455 n.40.

7 *Id.* at 455.

8 *Id.* at 481 (Blackmun, J., dissenting).

9 *Id.* at 451.

10 *See, e.g.,* Harper & Row Publishers, Inc. v. Nation Enters., 471 U.S. 539, 562 (1985); Stewart v. Abend, 459 U.S. 207, 237 (1990).

11 *See, e.g., Harper & Row,* 471 U.S. at 592 (Brennan, J., dissenting). The Court recognized this issue in *Acuff-Rose* stating "[i]f, indeed, commerciality carried presumptive force against a finding of fairness, the presumption would swallow nearly all of the illustrative uses listed in the preamble paragraph of § 107, including news reporting, comment, criticism, teaching, scholarship, and research, since these articles 'are generally conducted for profit in this country.' " *Acuff-Rose,* 114 S. Ct. at 1174 (quoting the dissent in *Harper & Row*); *see also* American Geophysical Union v. Texaco, Inc., No. 92-9341, 1994 U.S. App. LEXIS 30437, at *25 (2d Cir. Oct. 28, 1994) ("Since many, if not most, secondary users seek at least some measure of commercial gain from their use, unduly emphasizing the commercial motivation of a copier will lead to an overly restrictive view of fair use.").

omit any mention of the "commercial" thing. This "rule" was thus given occasional lip service, but no real force.

The Sixth Circuit, however, took the Supreme Court's utterances seriously.[12] It detected the presence of commercial motivation in the 2 Live Crew rap. That was presumptively unfair. The case became very easy to decide. If the presumptive unfairness of commercial uses was really a rule, virtually all cases would be easily decided as commercial motivation is virtually ubiquitous in publishing. Fair use would become a faint memory.

In cases subsequent to *Sony* the courts groped for more "rules" that might help explain this now directionless doctrine. We were told things like:

> (1) "[T]he unpublished nature of a work is a key, though not necessarily determinative, factor tending to negate a defense of fair use."[13]
> (2) Factual works are more prone to fair use than fiction.[14]
> (3) The fourth factor [effect on the market] is by far the most important.[15]
> (4) One wins the first factor [purpose and character of the use] simply by producing a work in the area of criticism, comment, news reporting, or scholarship.[16]

Then we were told that because it is so easy to win the first factor, winning the first factor doesn't mean anything.[17]

None of these utterances offered any meaningful help in understanding the doctrine of fair use. Some were extremely harmful. Collectively they instilled fear in the publishing world. Publishers, who must lay out the money, became extremely wary of the unpredictable shark-infested waters. The cost was great. The public, which is the intended beneficiary of the copyright law,[18] lost the publication of a number of illuminating historical works.[19]

---

[12] Acuff-Rose Music, Inc. v. Campbell, 972 F.2d 1429 (6th Cir. 1992).

[13] *Harper & Row*, 471 U.S. at 554 (internal quotes and citations omitted).

[14] *Id.* at 563.

[15] *Id.* at 566.

[16] Salinger v. Random House, Inc., 811 F.2d 90, 96 (2d Cir.), *reh'g denied*, 818 F.2d 252 (2d Cir.), *cert. denied*, 484 U.S. 890 (1987); New Era Publications Int'l, ApS v. Henry Holt & Co., 873 F.2d 576, 583 (2d Cir. 1989).

[17] *Salinger*, 811 F.2d at 97; *New Era*, 873 F.2d at 583.

[18] L. RAY PATTERSON & STANLEY W. LINDBERG, THE NATURE OF COPYRIGHT: A LAW OF USERS' RIGHTS 70 (1991); Jessica Litman, *The Public Domain*, 39 EMORY L.J. 965, 978 (1990).

[19] In *Salinger*, 811 F.2d 90, the novelist J.D. Salinger was successful in suppressing the use of his personal letters in a biography written by Ian Hamilton. "Hamilton would be forced to rewrite his book twice. Initially called 'J.D. Salinger: A Writing Life,' the book would eventually be recast as the saga of writing a biography of an author who does not want the story of his life written." Katherine Stephen, *A Biographer's Quest for J.D. Salinger*, L.A. TIMES, Aug. 5, 1988, at 1, 22; *see also* Amy Gamerman, *Unfair Use: Copyright Decision*

Other works that *were* published were less valuable and interesting than they might otherwise have been because of the suppression of interesting material that might lose in a fair use tussle in which no one understood the rules.[20]

I suggest to you that *2 Live Crew* fixed the rudder and restored the compass bearing. It has dispelled all those unhelpful slogans from the fair use discussions—particularly the pernicious "commercial use" presumption. And what are the new bearings? The most important thing *2 Live Crew* teaches about fair use is that it is a doctrine of the copyright law that seeks to advance the goal of copyright. That familiar goal is to bring intellectual enrichment to the public by giving authors a *limited* control over their writings to provide them with financial incentive to create. The control is *limited* because of the recognition that a stranglehold would be counterproductive.

The law of fair use focuses on one aspect of where those limits should be drawn. As one of the eighteenth-century lords put it, "[o]ne must not manacle science."[21] Every advance in knowledge or art builds on previous advances. An author's exclusive control must not be so stringent as to prevent those who come after from using the prior work for further advancement. The *2 Live Crew* opinion refocuses the fair use doctrine on the central purpose of copyright.

The opinion teaches us further that every fair use factor is to be understood as a subset of that overall goal. They are not separate factors. Each is part of a multifaceted assessment of the question: Where should the author's exclusivity *stop* in order to best serve these familiar overall objectives of the copyright law?

The opinion stresses this dynamic interrelationship. Of cardinal importance is the close interdependence of the first and fourth factors. The fourth factor looks at the harm which the secondary work may do to the copyright market of the original *by offering itself as a substitute* (for either the original or its derivatives). The first factor looks primarily at whether the use made of the original seeks to *transform* the taken material into a new purpose or message, distinct from purposes of the original. It follows logically that the

---

Cramps Writers' Style, WALL ST. J., Apr. 10, 1990, at A16; *see* David A. Kaplan, *The End of History?*, NEWSWEEK, Dec. 25, 1989, at 80 ("To avoid their books being shelved judicially, book publishers are censoring themselves.").

20 *See, e.g.*, Gamerman, *Unfair Use*, WALL ST. J., Apr. 10, 1990 (discussing the "emasculation" of Bruce Perry's biography of Malcolm X). After the *Salinger* and *Nation* decisions, Mr. Perry excised Malcolm X's previously unpublished letters from his forthcoming biography.

21 Cary v. Kearsley, 170 Eng. Rep. 679, 680 (K.B. 1802) (Lord Ellenborough).

more the appropriator is using the material for new *transformed* purposes, the less likely it is that appropriative use will be a substitute for the original, and therefore the less impact it is likely to have on the protected market opportunities of the original.

The opinion thus restores the lost emphasis on "productive use," but now in the context of a far more sophisticated discussion, related in every detail to the basic objectives of copyright doctrine.

The *2 Live Crew* opinion does not ensure perfect answers to all future disputes. I have heard it criticized from the protectionist wing of the copyright bar as interfering excessively with the *absolute right* of an author to exercise total control over the use of the author's creations. With all respect, I don't think the copyright law provides such an absolute right. I have heard criticism also from the appropriation art lobby for insufficient protection of the right to appropriate.[22] In my view, some of these statements have been so extreme in the proposition that *any change* rebuts infringement that they threaten to swallow much of the copyright law, leaving authors and artists defenseless. If minor changes will circumvent the protection of copyright law, what will protect the ability of authors, composers, and artists to earn a living through their creations?

One thing is certain: under the *2 Live Crew* standards, as under any standard, the courts will produce decisions that will not satisfy one hundred percent of the copyright community; no standards could. But I submit that *2 Live Crew* has restored valid compass bearings to the fair use doctrine by relating it in each of its component inquiries to the overarching central purpose of copyright.

II. Appropriation

This rethinking of fair use as an essential tool in achieving the public-enriching goal of copyright also illuminates the analysis of *remedies* when the fair use defense fails. This subject has particular bearing on the hotly debated issues of appropriation art. I suggest that all of us who deal with copyright—lawyers, judges, authors, appropriators—have gone much too far in attaching opprobrium to a judgment of infringement. Courts are quick to decorate a finding of infringement with dramatic invective like "piracy" and "stealing." The world of authors, appropriators, and the consum-

---

[22] Appropriation art ranges from Andy Warhol's use of Campbell's trademarked soup cans, to Sherrie Levine's virtual reproductions of Walker Evan's photographs; *see generally* John Carlin, *Culture Vultures: Artistic Appropriation and Intellectual Property Law*, 13 COLUM.-VLA J.L. & ARTS 103 (1988).

ing public is quick to draw the inference that a judgment of infringement maligns the worth of an appropriating work. These attitudes go hand-in-hand with the hair-trigger inclination of courts to accompany findings of infringement with injunctive relief—to wipe the infringing work from the face of the earth.

In my view there is no necessary logic to these associations. A finding of infringement does not necessarily contradict high utility and original authorship in the infringing work. While many infringing works represent scandalous larceny whose existence is unjustified, in other cases a valuable work narrowly fails the fair use test. True, compensation is owed for use of material from an original. But in such instances courts inflict unjustifiable harm *on the public* by coupling a finding of infringement with the grant of an injunction. A finding of infringement can thus mean nothing more than an entitlement to compensation.

Artists, no matter how great, must pay for what they use in making their works. They pay for paint, for canvas, for steel, for clay, for a model's time. Why should they not also pay a reasonable fee for the use of another artist's work as part of a new work? A finding of such an obligation to pay need not imply a derogatory judgment of the new appropriative work.

We have tended to think of appropriative works as falling into two categories: (i) those that infringe, and (ii) those that pass the fair use test and therefore do not infringe. I would suggest that we should revise that thinking and divide appropriative works into *three* zones:

> (i) At one extremity are the works properly described as acts of piracy, those that deserve to be enjoined.
> (ii) At the other end is the band that satisfies the fair use test and achieves immunity from *any* judicial remedy because there is no infringement.
> (iii) In the center is a numerically small but important band encompassing works which, although they fail the fair use test, have originality and independent value, and represent a sufficiently small threat to the economic entitlements of the author of the original, so that the public-enriching objectives of the copyright law are better served by withholding injunctive relief. Such infringements should be compensated only by damages.[23]

[23] *See* Universal City Studios v. Sony Corp. of Am., 659 F.2d 963, 976 (9th Cir. 1981), *rev'd on other grounds*, 464 U.S. 417 (1984) (awarding damages over an injunction); Honorable James L. Oakes, *Copyrights and Copyremedies: Unfair Use and Injunctions*, 18 HOFSTRA L. REV. 983 (1990); Paul Goldstein, *Copyright and the First Amendment*, 70 COLUM. L. REV. 983, 1030 (1970) ("[A]n award of damages should be preferred to the injunction relief remedy.") [Judge Leval's position is evidenced in several of his cases; *see* Salinger v. Random

> And the damages should be in a carefully measured amount, an amount designed to provide reasonable compensation to the initial author for the use of her material and to compensate for any modest loss of market opportunity.

As I read it, the Supreme Court in *2 Live Crew* has directed the adoption of such an approach. In footnote 10, which may become one of the most-often cited parts of this opinion, the Supreme Court said, "Because the fair use inquiry often requires close questions of judgment as to the extent of permissible borrowing in cases involving parodies (or other critical works), courts may also wish to bear in mind that the goals of the copyright law, 'to stimulate the creation and publication of edifying matter are not always best served by . . . automatically granting injunctive relief.' "[24] The footnote goes on to point out that § 502(a) provides only that a court "may" grant injunctions.[25]

In debatable cases of the fair use defense, where *transformative* objectives offer some justification, albeit insufficient to pass fair use, and the harm to the original author's commercial interests is not excessive, courts should remember that there is no automatic right to an injunction.

When I have talked about this notion in the past, I have been asked if I am advocating a system of compulsory license. That is not the description I would choose, for it implies the *withdrawal* of a remedy *provided* by the copyright law. A preferable view is that the copyright statute confers *limited* rights and remedies, which exist, furthermore, to serve the public good. Against some appropriations, there is no remedy at all because they are protected by fair use. Against some, a remedy lies for *reasonable compensation*. In some cases, the remedy of statutory damages authorizes damages in large amounts.[26] And, finally, in some cases, the axe! But courts should distinguish carefully among these different categories and should not grant the discretionary remedy of injunction except in appropriate cases.

House, 650 F. Supp. 413, 426 (S.D.N.Y. 1986), *rev'd*, 811 F.2d 90 (2d Cir. 1987) (injunction issued); New Era Publications v. Henry Holt & Co., 695 F. Supp. 1493, 1525-28 (S.D.N.Y. 1988), *aff'd*, 873 F.2d 576 (2d Cir. 1989) (majority rejected Judge Leval's reasoning but nevertheless declined to issue an injunction on the basis of the doctrine of laches). At the Second Circuit Chief Judge Oakes concurred with the majority opinion but split on this issue. *Henry Holt*, 873 F.2d at 595. Judge Oakes agreed with Leval that "enjoining publication of a book is not to be done lightly." *Id.* at 596. *Eds.*].

[24] *Acuff-Rose*, 114 S. Ct. at 1171 n.10 (internal quotes and citation omitted).

[25] *Id.*

[26] The Copyright Act permits a court to award statutory damages up to $100,000 for a wilful infringement. 17 U.S.C. § 504(c)(2) (1988). Court costs and attorney's fees may also be awarded to the prevailing party. 17 U.S.C. § 505 (1988).

I believe the adoption of such an approach will better serve the goals of copyright in dealing with the difficult problems of appropriation. Useful appropriators who do not pass the fair use test unquestionably owe compensation, but the public may be entitled to the survival of their works.

In *2 Live Crew* the Supreme Court has reoriented the doctrine of fair use to serve the central goal of copyright—to promote the growth and dissemination of knowledge. This same reorientation promises also to enlighten our understanding of copyright's remedies.

Join me in a toast to fair use which, like Odysseus, suffered ten storm-tossed years, lost and wandering, but has now refixed its compass on its goal.

THE EXCLUSIVE RIGHT TO READ

Jessica Litman*

> *For what the king fundamentally insisted upon was that his authority should be respected. He tolerated no disobedience. He was an absolute monarch. But, because he was a very good man, he made his orders reasonable.*
>
> — The Little Prince[1]

The hottest of hot topics in the copyright community these days is the information superhighway, officially dubbed the National Information Infrastructure.[2] Copyright specialists are attending conferences, writing articles and speeches, convening advisory councils, holding public hearings, and caucusing over the Internet about how the information superhighway will, indeed must, be paved with copyright asphalt.[3] Some view the coming of the information superhighway as an opportunity to redesign intellectual property policy before stakeholders acquire vested interests;[4] others see an occasion to consolidate the advantages they currently enjoy under the copyright law or to close copyright "loopholes" that they feel have inadvertently sprung up in their way.[5]

---

* Professor of Law, Wayne State University. I would like to thank Marci Hamilton and Pamela Samuelson for helpful comments on earlier drafts, and, as always, Jonathan Weinberg, who read many drafts and had insightful comments on each of them. I am also grateful to Mary Jensen and the Coalition for Networked Information for moderating CNI's provocative copyright mailing list.

1 Antoine de Saint-Exupery, The Little Prince 42 (1943).

2 *See* Request for Comments on Intellectual Property Issues Involved in the National Information Infrastructure Initiative, 58 Fed. Reg. 53,917 (1993).

3 *See, e.g.*, United States Patent & Trademark Office, United States Department of Commerce, *National Information Infrastructure Task Force Working Group on Intellectual Property, Public Hearing on Intellectual Property Issues Involved in the National Information Infrastructure Initiative* (Nov. 18, 1993) [hereinafter *NII Hearing*]. A transcript of the November 18, 1993 Hearing, along with other relevant documents, is available in a compilation of material related to the work of the Working Group, which is collected on the University of South Dakota gopher server, sunbird.usd.edu., in the Academics Divisions directory, School of Law subdirectory, under the heading NII Working Group on Intellectual Property. URL: gopher: //sunbird.usd.edu:70/11/Academic%20Divisions/School%20of%20Law/NII%20Working%20Group%20on%20Intellectual%20Property.

4 *See, e.g.*, Software 2000: A View of the Future 2-16 to 2-20 (Brian Randell et al. eds., 1994); David Lange, *At Play in the Fields of the Word: Copyright and the Construction of Authorship in the Post-Literate Millennium*, 55 Law & Contemp. Probs. 139 (1992); John P. Barlow, *The Economy of Ideas: A framework for rethinking patents and copyrights in the Digital Age (Everything you know about intellectual property is wrong)*, Wired, Mar. 1994, at 84.

5 *See, e.g.*, *NII Hearing*, *supra* note 3, at 107-21 (testimony of Hilary B. Rosen, Recording Industry Association of America); *id.* at 193-201 (testimony of Ronald J. Palenski, Information Technology Association of America); *id.* at 211-20 (testimony of Thomas M. Lemberg, Business Software Alliance and Alliance to Promote Software Innovation).

The federal government's Information Infrastructure Task Force[6] has, with much fanfare,[7] issued a Draft Report containing its preliminary analysis of copyright issues affecting and affected by the Information Infrastructure, and its suggestions for copyright revision.[8] The Draft Report recommends what it characterizes as minor clarifications of well-settled principles, and modest alterations to better secure copyright owners' control over works they produce.[9] The minor changes it recommends, however, would amount to a radical recalibration of the intellectual property balance.

The Report takes the position that current law secures to the copyright owner control over virtually any reproduction,[10] but finds the state of current law regarding transmission to be less than clear.[11] It therefore recommends amending the law in several respects. First, the distribution right should be amended to "reflect that copies of works can be distributed to the public by transmission, and such transmissions fall within the exclusive distribution right of the copyright owner."[12] Second, the Draft Report recommends expanding the current definition of "transmit" in section 101, to encompass transmissions of reproductions as well as transmissions of performances or displays,[13] and to add a test distinguishing between transmissions of reproductions and transmissions of performances and displays based on "the primary

---

6 President Clinton appointed the Information Infrastructure Task Force last year, and asked Commerce Secretary Ronald Brown to serve as its chair. The IITF is charged with coming up with "comprehensive telecommunications and information policies aimed at articulating and implementing the Administration's vision for the NII." *NII Hearing, supra* note 3, at 8 (opening remarks of Bruce A. Lehman, Chairman, Assistant Secretary of Commerce and Commissioner for Patents and Trademarks). The IITF set up a Working Group on Intellectual Property Rights, chaired by Patent Commissioner Bruce A. Lehman, to assess the intellectual property implications of the NII. *See* 58 Fed. Reg. 53,917, *supra* note 2. The Working Group held a public hearing and solicited written comments on intellectual property issues before formulating its recommendations. *See id.*; *NII Hearing, supra* note 3.

7 *See* Heather Bruce, *Study Urges Copyright Update for Digital Age*, BOSTON GLOBE, July 8, 1994, at 61; Jeff Leeds, *Cyberspace Copyright Proposal Draws Praise*, L.A. TIMES, July 8, 1994, at D1; Theresa Riordan, *Writing Copyright Law for an Information Age*, N.Y. TIMES, July 7, 1994, at D1; Sandra Sugawara, *What's Out of Line, When On Line? White House Report Says Copying of Computer Service Files May be Illegal*, WASH. POST, July 7, 1994, at D9.

8 INFORMATION INFRASTRUCTURE TASK FORCE, INTELLECTUAL PROPERTY AND THE NATIONAL INFORMATION INFRASTRUCTURE: A PRELIMINARY DRAFT OF THE REPORT OF THE WORKING GROUP ON INTELLECTUAL PROPERTY RIGHTS (July 1994) [hereinafter IITF GREEN PAPER]. An electronic copy of the Green Paper is available on the University of South Dakota gopher server, sunbird.usd.edu., see *supra* note 3.

9 *See* IITF GREEN PAPER, *supra* note 8, at 120-34.

10 *See id.* at 35-37.

11 *See id.* at 42-43, 121.

12 *Id.* at 121.

13 *Id.* at 122.

purpose and effect of the transmission."[14] Third, the Draft Report suggests an amendment making it clear that transmission of a work into the United States violates the copyright owner's exclusive importation rights.[15] Fourth, the Report suggests that the first sale doctrine, which allows the owner of a lawfully made copy to sell, loan, rent or otherwise dispose of the possession of that copy, be repealed insofar as it might apply to transmissions.[16] Finally, the Draft Report offers miscellaneous suggestions to forestall the emergence of other perceived threats to the copyright owners' bundle of rights.[17]

By vesting copyright owners with control of any reproduction or transmission of their works, and then defining reproduction and transmission to include any appearance, even a fleeting one, of a protected work in any computer, and any transfer of that work to, from, or through any other computer,[18] the Draft Report's recommendations would enhance the exclusive rights in the copyright bundle so far as to give the copyright owner the exclusive right to

---

14 *Id.* My initial reaction to this proposal was to wonder why the Report's drafters believed such a test to be necessary. If, as the Report asserts, any transmission would involve an actionable reproduction, I could not immediately see why a test would be needed to resolve whether the right it would violate in addition to the reproduction right would be the display right, the performance right, or the distribution right. Because copyright is divisible, however, the different rights in the copyright bundle can be, and often are, owned or controlled by different entities. If the copyrighted work is a popular song, for example, the reproduction and distribution rights are typically owned by a music publisher and licensed through the Harry Fox Agency to record companies, while the performance right is licensed through a performing rights society like ASCAP. The proposal to treat a transmission as an invasion of the distribution right rather than the performance right, therefore, drew intense opposition from ASCAP and enthusiastic support from the record companies and music publishers during the September 1994, public hearings on the Green Paper. The "primary purpose and effect" test drew nearly unanimous protest.

15 *Id.* at 123.

16 *Id.* at 124-25 & n.353. The Report promises that its ongoing work includes examining all of the statutory exceptions to the copyright owner's distribution right to ascertain whether they, too, should be rescinded in the context of distribution by transmission. *Id.* at 125. The statutory exceptions it mentions are ones that are incidental to a statutory reproduction privilege. Section 108(d) permits libraries to make photocopies of protected works in specific circumstances for the purpose of interlibrary loan and to distribute those photocopies to the users requesting them. Section 112(c) allows a non-profit organization to make a single copy of a performance of religious music and distribute it at no charge, so long as the copy is never publicly performed except pursuant to a license and is destroyed within a year. Section 115, the mechanical compulsory license, permits the making of cover versions of previously recorded music, and the distribution of those recordings to the public, on payment of a statutory royalty. Repealing the incidental distribution privileges would, of course, make the reproduction privileges pretty useless: what good does it do a library to be entitled to make a copy for purposes of interlibrary loan if the copy cannot be passed on to the person requesting it?

17 *See supra* note 16 and *infra* notes 21, 49.

18 *See* IITF Green Paper, *supra* note 8, at 36-39, 54-55, 120-23. The Draft Report does appear to recognize that a work might, as a theoretical matter, reside in a computer's random access memory for too brief an interval to invade the copyright owner's rights, *see id.* at 37, but does not offer any examples of an appearance that would be sufficiently fleeting to qualify.

control reading, viewing or listening to any work in digitized form. The Draft Report comes down firmly on the side of increased rights for copyright owners and it endorses the goal of enhanced copyright protection without acknowledging any countervailing concerns.[19] Because it is an advocacy document, it at times misrepresents the state of current law.[20] It gives voice to only one side of complicated policy debates.[21] In some cases, the Report identifies

---

19 During the November 18, 1993 Hearing, copyright-affected industries presented their wish lists to the Working Group. *See NII Hearing, supra* note 3. Although the majority of the twenty-eight witnesses at that Hearing represented copyright-owner interests, there were a few witnesses who did not. Robert Oakley, Professor of Law and Director of the Law Library at Georgetown University, and an ACCORD Commissioner, testified on behalf of thirteen library and educational organizations; John Masten testified on behalf of the New York Public Library; Gary J. Shapiro testified on behalf of the Electronic Industries Association and the Home Recording Rights Coalition; Professors Henry Perritt and Frank W. Connolly appeared in their individual capacities. The Draft Report, however, takes the side of copyright owner interests in every dispute. Indeed, it reads as if it were Santa Claus' response to the wish lists presented by current stakeholders.

20 Two examples are the Report's assertion that it is settled law that loading a protected work into a computer's random access memory is an actionable reproduction, IITF GREEN PAPER, *supra* note 8, at 36, see *infra* notes 54-64 and accompanying text, and its crabbed reading of Supreme Court cases on fair use under 17 U.S.C. § 107. IITF GREEN PAPER, *supra* note 8, at 45-52.

21 One example is the Draft Report's endorsement of a broad prohibition of devices and services that defeat technological copy-protection or other means of blocking access or reproduction.

> The Working Group finds that prohibition of devices, products, components and services that defeat technological methods of preventing unauthorized use is in the public interest. Consumers of copyrighted works pay for the acts of infringers. The price of copyrighted works for legitimate users is higher due to infringement losses suffered by copyright owners. The public will also have access to more works via the NII if copyright owners can more effectively protect their works from infringement.
>
> Therefore, the Working Group recommends that the Copyright Act be amended to prohibit the importation, manufacture and distribution of devices, as well as the provision of services, that defeat anti-copying systems.

IITF GREEN PAPER, *supra* note 8, at 126. Devices that overcome technological copy-protection methods can have legitimate uses. *See, e.g.*, Vault Corp. v. Quaid Software, Ltd., 847 F.2d 255 (5th Cir. 1988); OFFICE OF TECHNOLOGY ASSESSMENT, U.S. CONGRESS, COPYRIGHT & HOME COPYING: TECHNOLOGY CHALLENGES THE LAW 52-61 (1989) [hereinafter OTA, COPYRIGHT & HOME COPYING]. Copy protection devices can, after all, block access in situations when the copyright statute would privilege it. In addition, relying on technological copy protection can be self-defeating:

> I would argue that initial efforts to protect digital copyright by copy protection contributed to the current condition in which most otherwise ethical computer users seem morally untroubled by their possession of pirated software.
>
> Instead of cultivating among the newly computerized a sense of respect for the work of their fellows, early reliance on copy protection led to the subliminal notion that cracking into a software package somehow "earned" one the right to use it. Limited not by conscience but by technical skill, many soon felt free to do whatever they could get away with.

Barlow, *supra* note 4, at 129. For these reasons, and others, requests to reinforce technological copy-protection tools with legal prohibitions have generated opposition from a variety of camps. Prior suggestions to outlaw such devices have therefore been narrowly drawn. *See generally Audio Home Recording Act of 1991: Hearing Before the Subcomm. on Intellectual Property of the House Comm. on the Judiciary*, H.R. 3204, 102d Cong., 2d Sess. (1992). Congress enacted one such prohibition in the Audio Home Recording Act of 1992 (codi-

a particular alternative as more desirable *because* it gives copyright owners rights subject to fewer exceptions.[22] The Report's drafters apparently did not perceive objectivity or balance to be their job.

Nor is anyone else clamoring to volunteer. The general public's interest in copyright legislation is diffuse; a grass-roots revolt of copyright users seems unlikely. Interest groups with copyright on their agendas have a long history of dropping their opposition to copyright amendments of general application in return for narrow provisions addressing their specific concerns.[23] Congress, for its part, has, since the turn of the century, been delegating the policy choices involved in copyright matters to the industries affected by copyright.[24] But, before we succumb to calls for further enhance-

---

fied at 17 U.S.C. §§ 1001-1010). The audio recording device prohibition was sufficiently controversial that, after the introduction of legislation in 1987, four years of negotiations among record companies, hardware manufacturers, songwriters, music publishers, and performing rights societies were required to reach agreement on the form and specifications of a limited prohibition. *See* H.R. REP. 873, 102d Cong., 2d Sess., pt. 1, at 14-18 (1992); Gary S. Lutzker, Note, *DAT's All Folks:* Cahn v. Sony *and the Audio Home Recording Act of 1991—Merrie Melodies or Looney Tunes*, 11 CARDOZO ARTS & ENT. L.J. 145 (1992). During the legislative process, the prohibition was narrowed and narrowed again to ensure that it would not be construed to apply to devices other than home audio recording devices. As enacted, it was balanced by a provision preventing the imposition of copyright liability for noncommercial copying of audio recordings, or for manufacturing, importing or selling audio recorders. *See* 17 U.S.C. § 1008 (Supp. V 1988). The Communications Act has a provision relating to the manufacture or distribution of descrambling equipment. *See* 47 U.S.C. § 605 (1988). It, too, is narrow in scope, and carefully distinguishes between legal and illegal uses. Broadly phrased prohibitions can interfere with legitimate behavior, and can hamstring technology in unanticipated ways. In presenting its finding that such devices should be prohibited across the board, the Working Group's Draft Report does not mention any countervailing concerns.

22 Thus the Draft Report notes: "One of the important aspects of defining a transaction as a 'reproduction' rather than something else is that the potentially relevant exceptions to the reproduction right are substantially fewer in number than those that apply to certain other rights . . . ." IITF GREEN PAPER, *supra* note 8, at 36 n.107. A few pages later, the Report discusses the exclusive distribution right, and notes that it is limited by the first sale doctrine codified in 17 U.S.C. § 109. *Id.* at 38. In considering how to characterize the dissemination of a work by means of the NII, the Report concludes that "the reproduction right, rather than the distribution right, may be both more logically applicable and more legally appropriate (by virtue of its more limited exceptions)." *Id.* at 39. The Report nonetheless proposes to amend the first sale doctrine to prohibit owners of copies of protected works from transmitting their copies. *Id.* at 124-25. *See supra* note 16 and accompanying text.

23 *See generally* Jessica Litman, *Copyright Legislation and Technological Change*, 68 OR. L. REV. 275 (1989). Thus, to pick a single example, the American Library Association and the American Association of Law Libraries initially opposed the partial repeal of the first sale doctrine as it applied to sound recordings and computer programs. Both associations switched their positions when the proponents of the bill agreed to exempt non-profit libraries from the legislation. *See id.* at 351-52.

24 *See generally* Litman, *supra* note 23; 1 HOWARD B. ABRAMS, THE LAW OF COPYRIGHT § 1.03[A] (release #3 1994); Abe A. Goldman, *The History of U.S.A. Copyright Law Revision from 1901 to 1954* (1955), *reprinted in* SUBCOMM. ON PATENTS, COPYRIGHTS AND TRADEMARKS OF THE SENATE COMM. ON THE JUDICIARY, 86TH CONG., 1ST SESS. COPYRIGHT LAW REVISION STUDIES (Comm. Print. 1960); Jessica Litman, *Copyright, Compromise and Legislative History*, 72 CORNELL L. REV. 857 (1987); Thomas P. Olson, *The Iron Law of Consensus: Congressional Responses to Proposed Copyright Reforms Since the 1909 Act*, 36 J. COPYRIGHT SOC'Y 109 (1989).

ment of the rights in the copyright bundle, we need to reexamine the intellectual property bargain from the vantage point of the public, on whose behalf, after all, the copyright deal is said to be struck in the first place.[25] Does the shape of the law as it currently stands make sense? Do the changes that are being proposed cause it to make more sense, or less sense?

I.

At the turn of the century, U.S. copyright law was technical, inconsistent, and difficult to understand,[26] but it didn't apply to very many people or very many things.[27] If one were an author or publisher of books, maps, charts, paintings, sculpture, photographs or sheet music, a playwright or producer of plays, or a printer, the copyright law bore on one's business. Booksellers, piano-roll and phonograph record publishers, motion picture producers, musicians, scholars, members of Congress, and ordinary consumers could go about their business without ever encountering a copyright problem.[28]

Ninety years later, the U.S. copyright law is even more technical, inconsistent and difficult to understand; more importantly, it touches everyone and everything. In the intervening years, copyright has reached out to embrace much of the paraphernalia of modern society.[29] The current copyright statute weighs in at 142 pages. Technology, heedless of law, has developed modes that insert multiple acts of reproduction and transmission—potentially actionable events under the copyright statute—into commonplace daily transactions.[30] Most of us can no longer spend even an hour

---

25 *See* Sony Corp. of Am. v. Universal City Studios, Inc., 464 U.S. 417, 429 (1984).

26 *See* L. Ray Patterson & Stanley W. Lindberg, The Nature of Copyright: A Law of Users' Rights 74-77 (1991); Library of Congress, Report of the Librarian of Congress for the Fiscal Year Ending June 30, 1903, H.R. Doc. No. 10, 58th Cong., 2d Sess. 68-69 (1903).

27 *See* Office of Technology Assessment, U.S. Congress, Intellectual Property Rights in an Age of Electronics and Information 190-93 (1986) [hereinafter OTA, Intellectual Property Rights].

28 *See* Patterson & Lindberg, *supra* note 26, at 71-72; Litman, *supra* note 23, at 284-98.

29 Copyright now extends to works as diverse as computer programs, buildings, stuffed animals, doodles, electronic mail, picture postcards, snapshots and shopping lists. Everything you see on television, hear on the radio, read in the newspaper, or see posted as signage or scrawled on the wall of the subway or bus on the way to work is protected by copyright; as is everything you write, or draw, or tape. *See* Jessica Litman, *The Public Domain*, 39 Emory L.J. 965 (1990).

30 Consider the fax machine. One could send a document to its recipient by courier or U.S. mail, but it now can travel more quickly by facsimile. The original document will remain with the sender while it is both reproduced and transmitted to its recipient. Faxing documents has become sufficiently common that there are pay-facsimile booths in many metropolitan airports, and at least one major airline has plans to install facsimile devices in passenger seat-backs.

without colliding with the copyright law. Reading one's mail or picking up one's telephone messages these days requires many of us to commit acts that the government's Information Infrastructure Task Force now tells us ought to be viewed as unauthorized reproductions or transmissions.

What we know about the general public's impression of the shape of copyright law suggests that the public believes that the copyright statute confers on authors the exclusive right to profit commercially from their copyrighted works, but does not reach private or non-commercial conduct.[31] The law in this country has never been that simple; the copyright statute has never expressly privileged private or non-commercial use.[32] Until recently, however, the public's impression was not a bad approximation of the scope of copyright rights likely, in practice, to be enforced. If copyright owners insisted, as sometimes they did, that copyright gave them broad rights to control their works in any manner and in all forms,[33] the practical costs of enforcing those rights against individual consumers dissuaded them from testing their claims in court.[34] So long as nobody proposed to sue the nation's teenagers for copying music onto audio cassette tapes, or copying computer games onto floppy disks, what did it matter that some folks argued that if

---

31 *See, e.g.*, OTA, INTELLECTUAL PROPERTY RIGHTS, *supra* note 27, at 121-23, 208-09; OTA, COPYRIGHT & HOME COPYING, *supra* note 21, at 163-65; Pamela Samuelson, *Modifying Copyrighted Software: Adjusting Copyright Doctrine to Accommodate a Technology*, 28 JURIMETRICS 179, 198-99 (1988).

32 *See, e.g.*, Pamela Samuelson, *Fair Use for Computer Programs and Other Copyrightable Works in Digital Form: The Implications of* Sony, Galoob *and* Sega, 1 J. INTELLECTUAL PROP. L. 49, 67-73 (1993). *But see* PATTERSON & LINDBERG, *supra* note 26, at 177-96 (arguing that copyright is or should be so limited).

33 *See, e.g.*, Daly v. Palmer, 6 F. Cas. 1132 (C.C.S.D.N.Y. 1868); Baker v. Selden, 101 U.S. 99 (1879); Bobbs-Merrill Co. v. Straus, 210 U.S. 339 (1908); Jewelers' Circular Publishing Co. v. Keystone Publishing Co., 281 F. 83 (2d Cir.), *cert. denied*, 259 U.S. 581 (1922); Aldrich v. Remington Rand, Inc., 52 F. Supp. 732 (N.D. Tex. 1942); Twentieth Century Music v. Aiken, 422 U.S. 151 (1975); West Publishing Co. v. Mead Data Central, 799 F.2d 1219 (8th Cir. 1986); Educational Testing Servs. v. Katzman, 793 F.2d 533 (3d Cir. 1986); Worlds of Wonder, Inc. v. Vector Intercontinental, Inc., 653 F. Supp. 135 (N.D. Ohio 1986); Acuff-Rose Music, Inc. v. Campbell, 972 F.2d 1429 (6th Cir. 1992), *rev'd*, 114 S. Ct. 1164 (1994); Sega Enters. v. Accolade, Inc., 977 F.2d 1510 (9th Cir. 1992); Lotus Dev. Corp. v. Borland, Int'l, Inc., 799 F. Supp. 203 (D. Mass. 1993).

34 *See, e.g.*, *Audio Home Recording Act of 1991: Hearing on H.R. 3204 before the Subcomm. on Intellectual Property and Judicial Administration of the House Comm. on the Judiciary*, 102d Cong., 2d Sess. (1993). In a small number of recent cases, copyright owners joined allegedly representative individuals as nominal parties defendant to lawsuits challenging the sale of goods or services said to facilitate infringement, but neither sought nor received relief against them. *See, e.g.*, Universal City Studios, Inc. v. Sony Corp. of Am., 480 F. Supp. 429 (C.D. Cal. 1979), *aff'd in part, rev'd in part*, 659 F.2d 963 (9th Cir. 1981), *rev'd*, 464 U.S. 417 (1984); Edwin McDowell, *Ideas and Trends: College "Copy Mills" Grind Quickly, So Publishers Sue*, N.Y. TIMES, Dec. 19, 1982, § 4, at 18; Samuelson, *supra* note 32. *But cf.* Demetriades v. Kaufmann, 690 F. Supp. 289 (S.D.N.Y. 1988) (individual home buyers sued for hiring builder to construct look-alike house).

they chose to sue they could win?[35]

Nonetheless, by asserting that what members of the public think of as ordinary use of copyrighted works was, in fact, flagrant piracy, and that, as such, it undermined the national economy,[36] copyright owners may well have won a rhetorical battle the rest of the country never realized was being fought. As industries lobby, scholars analyze, and bureaucrats convene in too many meetings to consider the shape of the new-and-improved national information infrastructure, few people have seriously challenged copyright owners' claims to control all access to and use of the material they say they own.[37] Arguments for universal access are, so far, cast in terms of good citizenship rather than entitlement.[38] Even those who favor liberal subsidy of public access to the information highway seem to accept the contention that if copyright owners cannot maintain control of their asserted property, the wellspring of

---

[35] *See, e.g., Home Video Recording: Hearing on Providing Information on the Issue of Home Video Recording Before the Senate Comm. on the Judiciary*, 99th Cong., 2d Sess. 22-27 (1987) (memorandum from Jon Baumgarten, Proskauer Rose Goetz & Mendelsohn).

[36] *See, e.g., Copyright Reform Act of 1993: Hearing on S. 373 Before the Subcomm. on Patents, Copyrights and Trademarks of the Senate Comm. on the Judiciary*, 103d Cong., 1st Sess. (Oct. 19, 1993) (prepared statement of Enid Green Waldholtz, Software Publisher's Association); *Copyright Amendments Act of 1991: Hearings on H.R. 2372 Before the Subcomm. on Intellectual Property and Judicial Administration of the House Comm. on the Judiciary*, 102d Cong., 1st Sess. 99-100 (1991) (statement of James M. Burger, Apple Computer, Inc.); *Fair Use and Unpublished Works: Joint Hearing on S. 2370 and H.R. 4263 Before the Subcomm. on Patents, Trademarks and Copyrights of the Senate Comm. on the Judiciary and the Subcomm. on Courts, Intellectual Property, and the Administration of Justice of the House Comm. on the Judiciary*, 101st Cong., 2d Sess. 278 (1990) (written statement of the Electronic Industries Association); *Home Recording of Copyrighted Works: Hearings on H.R. 4783, H.R. 4794, H.R. 4808, H.R. 5250, H.R. 5488, and H.R. 5705 Before the Subcomm. on Courts, Civil Liberties, and the Administration of Justice of the House Comm. on the Judiciary*, 97th Cong., 2d Sess. 4-5 (1982) (statement of Jack Valenti, Motion Picture Association of America).

[37] Professor L. Ray Patterson has recently published an articulate expression of the minority view.

> The author receives the reward for making his or her original work of authorship accessible to all. Contrary to the common notion, the reward is not for the act of creation, but for distribution to provide public access: public learning comes not from the creation of a work, but from reading and studying it, a truism that copyright owners have apparently managed to hide from courts for many years.

L. Ray Patterson, *Copyright and "The Exclusive Right" of Authors*, 1 J. INTELLECTUAL PROP. L. 1, 37 (1993).

[38] In one of the Draft Report's rare nods to the possible conflicting claims of copyright owners and the public, we find the following discussion:

> The Copyright Act exists for the benefit of the public. To fulfill its constitutional purpose, the law should strive to make the information contained in protected works of authorship freely available to the public. "Freely available," of course, does not necessarily mean "available free." The Working Group does not believe that authors should be required to donate access time to their works on-line, but some reasonable approach must be adopted to ensure that the economically disadvantaged in this country are not further disadvantaged or disenfranchised by the information revolution.

IITF GREEN PAPER, *supra* note 8, at 133.

American creativity will dry up, our trade deficit will turn into a mushroom cloud, and our balance of payments will drop off and fall into the sea.[39] Meanwhile, because the assumptions underlying copyright owners' claims to expansive control over the works they create and disseminate crept into our discourse without much examination at a time when the price of acknowledging them was only nominal, we have so far allowed important policy choices to be made without debate.

II.

Imagine that you have been retained as the public's copyright lawyer. One morning, your client, the public, walks into your office to consult you about a deal that it has been offered. It seems that all of the industries with substantial economic stakes in copyright have gotten together and written up a proposal. Here it is: the current copyright statute. It's 142 pages long, and, frankly, it's a little hard to decipher. Your client stayed up all night to read it, and can't seem to make head or tail of it. In any event, your client drops this 142 page tome on your desk.

> *Client:* "So, whaddya think? Should I sign it? Is it a good deal?"
> *You (temporizing):* "It depends," you say. "What sort of a bargain do you want?"
> *Client:* "Look; I'm not out to get something for nothing. I understand that authors won't write stuff if they can't get paid. I want them to make new works and I'm willing to pay them to do so. I want to encourage authors to write as many new works as they can. As for me, I want to be able to read, see, hear or download any work in captivity, and pay appropriate royalties for doing so.[40] Will this proposal let me do that?"

Would you recommend that your client sign on the dotted line?

I would not. The text we're considering wasn't really written with your client's interests in mind. Most of it was drafted by the representatives of copyright-intensive businesses and institutions, who were chiefly concerned about their interaction with other copyright-intensive businesses and institutions.[41] For that reason, there's lots of verbiage speaking to the behavior of a public televi-

---

39 *See* IITF GREEN PAPER, *supra* note 8, at 6.

40 I have appropriated the turns of phrase from Dani Zweig. I have never met Dr. Zweig, but we have corresponded electronically.

41 *See* 1 ABRAMS, *supra* note 24, § 1.03[A][2][b]; 1 NICHOLAS HENRY, COPYRIGHT, CONGRESS AND TECHNOLOGY: THE PUBLIC RECORD xi-xxii (1978); Litman, *supra* note 23, at 311-54; Olson, *supra* note 24.

sion station or a cable system operator with respect to the programming it might transmit,[42] but very few words addressing the behavior of a consumer with respect to the programming she might watch or record. You can find a fair amount of language relevant to the actions of a publisher bringing out an author's new novel, and the film producer that seeks to adapt the story for the screen,[43] but not so much about the actions of the police officer who buys and reads the book, rents and sees the film, and wishes the producer had not cast Tom Cruise in the leading role.[44] The law has a specific provision for retail stores who play the radio for their customers, but no language that seems to contemplate fraternities who play loud music for their neighbors.[45] Thus, the statute fails to discuss your client's ability or obligation to pay appropriate royalties in return for access, and there is no provision securing your client's opportunity to read, see, hear, or download copyrighted works.

One can draw different conclusions from the paucity of language speaking to the behavior of individuals who are consuming rather than exploiting copyrighted material. One conclusion that is commonly voiced is that the statute really doesn't address the legal obligations of individuals acting in their private capacities.[46] An equally plausible interpretation, favored by copyright owners and copyright lawyers, is that the statute forbids private individuals, acting without permission, to invade the copyright owner's broad rights unless their behavior falls within an express statutory exception.[47] In the words of the Draft Report: "Users are not granted

---

42 *See* 17 U.S.C. §§ 111, 118 (1988).

43 *See, e.g.*, 17 U.S.C. §§ 106, 201, 203 (1988).

44 *See Anne Rice Jabs Stake Into Cruise*, USA TODAY, May 23, 1994, at D2. In theory, the police officer who succumbs to temptation and imagines the film as it might have looked if Daniel Day Lewis had been cast in Tom Cruise's role may be violating the copyright owners' exclusive rights under 17 U.S.C. § 106(2) to prepare derivative works, since a violation of the derivative work right requires no tangible embodiment whatsoever. *See* H.R. REP. 1476, 94th Cong., 2d Sess. 62 (1976).

45 Public performances of copyrighted works are copyright infringement unless privileged by §§ 107-119. Section 110(5) permits:

> communication of a transmission embodying a performance or display of a work by the public reception of the transmission on a single receiving apparatus of a kind commonly used in private homes, unless—
>
> (A) a direct charge is made to see or hear the transmission; or
>
> (B) the transmission thus received is further transmitted to the public;

17 U.S.C. § 110(5) (1988). The subsection expressly privileges the use of home-style televisions or radios (but not records, tapes or disks) in small commercial establishments. *See, e.g.*, ROBERT A. GORMAN AND JANE C. GINSBURG, COPYRIGHT FOR THE NINETIES 46 (4th ed. 1993). No comparable provision exists for use of a boom-box in public, or the playing of automotive stereo equipment in a car with its windows rolled down.

46 *See, e.g.*, OTA, INTELLECTUAL PROPERTY RIGHTS, *supra* note 27, at 190-93; OTA, COPYRIGHT & HOME COPYING, *supra* note 21, at 5-6; *see also supra* note 45.

47 *See, e.g.*, Litman, *Copyright, Compromise, and Legislative History supra*, note 24, at 883-84.

any affirmative 'rights' under the Copyright Act; rather, copyright owners' rights are limited by certain exemptions from user liability."[48] There are not very many specific exceptions addressed to individuals' private actions, which means that individuals are routinely prohibited from doing the sorts of things that businesses have statutory exemptions for unless they first secure the copyright owner's permission.[49]

Either way, though, it doesn't seem as if the agreement reflected in the 142 pages is yet in your client's interest as your client has expressed it. Perhaps the changes suggested by the Draft Report will help.

III.

The IITF Draft Report presents its task as the proposal of modest adjustments to repair the unintended damage that the passage of time and the growth of technology have had on the copyright law:

> It is difficult for intellectual property laws to keep pace with technology. When technological advances cause ambiguity in the law, courts rely on the law's purposes to resolve that ambiguity. However, when technology gets too far ahead of the law, and it becomes difficult and awkward to apply the old principles, it is time for reevaluation and change. "Even though the 1976 Copyright Act was carefully drafted to be flexible enough to be applied to future innovations, technology has a habit of outstripping even the most flexible statutes."
>
> The coat is getting a little tight. There is no need for a new one, but the old one needs a few alterations.[50]

The Draft Report recapitulates oft-voiced complaints about the damage to the integrity of the rights in the copyright bundle caused by the unanticipated fallout from digital technology.[51] The ease of digital copying is frequently said to pose a profound threat to copyright at its core.[52] The same technological miracles that

48 IITF GREEN PAPER, *supra* note 8, at 44-45 n.130.

49 Individuals can, of course, seek to rely on the fair use privilege codified in 17 U.S.C. § 107. *See* Samuelson, *supra* note 32, at 67-73; OTA, COPYRIGHT & HOME COPYING, *supra* note 21, at 68-70. The Draft Report suggests that, in the context of the NII, the fair use privilege should not be generously construed. *See* IITF GREEN PAPER, *supra* note 8, at 45-53, 133-34.

50 IITF GREEN PAPER, *supra* note 8, at 120 (footnotes omitted) (quoting H.R. REP. 735, 101st Cong., 2d Sess. 7 (1990)); *see also id.* at 9-10.

51 *See id.* at 8, 71-72, 120-21.

52 *See, e.g., U.S. Adherence to the Berne Convention: Hearings before the Subcomm. on Patents, Copyrights and Trademarks of the Senate Comm. on the Judiciary*, 99th Cong., 1st & 2d Sess. 47 (1987) (prepared statement of Barbara Ringer, former Register of Copyrights); *NII Hear-*

pose the threat, however, have served up some unanticipated windfalls for the copyright owner.[53] The most crucial example is the evolution of the reproduction right into something more encompassing than envisioned in any copyright revision until now. United States copyright law has always given copyright owners some form of exclusive reproduction right.[54] It has never before now given them an exclusive *reading* right, and it is hard to make a plausible argument that Congress would have enacted a law giving copyright owners control of reading. A handful of recent interpretations of the statute, however, insist that one reproduces a work every time one reads it into a computer's random access memory.[55] For all works encoded in digital form, any act of reading or viewing the work would require the use of a computer, and would, under this interpretation, involve an actionable reproduction. One might therefore expect an analysis proposing modest alterations of the law (to fix unintended ambiguities) to suggest clarifying this point: amending the law to provide explicitly that an individual's ordinary reading, viewing, or listening to an authorized copy of a work does not invade the copyright owner's rights. Instead, debates on the intellectual property underpinnings of the proposed National Information Infrastructure have proceeded on the assumption that copyright does, and should, assure such rights to the copyright

---

ing, supra note 3, at 211-20 (testimony of Thomas M. Lemberg, Business Software Alliance and Alliance to Promote Software Innovation); Eric Fleischmann, *The Impact of Digital Technology on Copyright Law,* J. PAT. & TRADEMARK OFFICE SOC'Y, Jan. 1988, at 5; William H. O'Dowd, Note: *The Need for a Public Performance Right in Sound Recordings,* 31 HARV. J. ON LEGIS. 249 (1993); *see also* Barlow, *supra* note 4.

Current stakeholders are not responding to the perceived threat by recommending fundamental changes to the copyright law, with which they appear to be well satisfied; rather, they want to make sure that tomorrow's players will have to play by today's rules. *See NII Hearing, supra* note 3, at 14-23 (testimony of Steven J. Metalitz, Information Industry Council); *id.* at 31-40 (testimony of Stephen L. Haynes, West Publishing Company); *id.* at 40-50 (testimony of Lisa Freeman, Association of American University Presses); *id.* at 99-107 (testimony of Fritz Attaway, Motion Picture Association of America); *id.* at 130-41 (testimony of Benjamin F.P. Ivins, National Association of Broadcasters).

53 *See* Jerome H. Reichman, *Electronic Information Tools—The Outer Edge of World Intellectual Property Law,* 17 U. DAYTON L. REV. 797 (1992).

54 *See* Act of May 31, 1790, ch. 15, § 1, 1 Stat. 124; Act of Apr. 29, 1802, ch. 36, § 2, 2 Stat. 171; Act of Feb. 3, 1831, ch. 16, § 1, 4 Stat. 436; Act of July 8, 1870, ch. 230, § 86, 16 Stat. 198, 212; Rev. Stat. § 4952; Copyright Act of Mar. 4, 1909, § 1(a), 35 Stat. 1075; 17 U.S.C. § 106(1); *see generally* L. RAY PATTERSON & STANLEY W. LINDBERG, *supra* note 26; LIBRARY OF CONGRESS, COPYRIGHT ENACTMENTS: LAWS PASSED IN THE UNITED STATES RELATING TO COPYRIGHT (1963).

55 *See* MAI Sys. Corp. v. Peak Computer, Inc., 991 F.2d 511 (9th Cir. 1993); Triad Sys. Corp. v. Southeastern Express Co., 31 U.S.P.Q. 2d (BNA) 1239 (N.D. Cal. Mar. 18, 1994); Advanced Computer Servs. v. MAI Sys. Corp., 845 F. Supp. 356 (E.D. Va. 1994); *see also* NATIONAL COMMISSION ON NEW TECHNOLOGICAL USES OF COPYRIGHTED WORKS, FINAL REPORT 39 (1978) ("The protection afforded by section 106 of the new law seemingly would prohibit the unauthorized storage of a work within a computer memory, which would be merely one form of reproduction . . . .").

owner.[56] The Draft Report adopts this view; it claims that "[i]t has long been clear that under U.S. law the placement of a work into a computer's memory amounts to a reproduction of that work"[57] and suggests that the expansiveness of the reproduction right should be exploited to ensure copyright owners' enhanced control of protected works.[58]

In fact, the Draft Report's characterization of current law is dubious, and the Report does not cite authority to support it. There is support available: the Report could have mentioned three recent cases,[59] a stray remark in the CONTU Report,[60] and brief

---

56 *See NII Hearing*, *supra* note 3, at 130 (testimony of Benjamin F.P. Ivins, National Association of Broadcasters); *id.* at 14 (testimony of Steven J. Metalitz, Information Industry Association); *id.* at 201 (testimony of Mark Traphagen, Software Publishers Association).

57 IITF Green Paper, *supra* note 8, at 36. It is apparent from the Draft Report's examples of infringing reproductions, see *supra* note 21, that by "placement . . . into a computer's memory" the Report means reading a work into random access memory, or RAM. A work's appearance in RAM is, by its nature, temporary; the work will disappear from RAM when the computer is turned off.

58 The Draft Report puts it this way:

> This fundamental right—to reproduce copyrighted works in copies and phonorecords—appears likely to be implicated in innumerable NII transactions. Indeed, because of the nature of computer-to-computer communications, it appears to be a right that will be implicated in most NII transactions. For example, when a computer user simply "browses" a document resident on another computer, the image on the user's screen exists—under contemporary technology—only by virtue of the copy that has been reproduced *in the user's computer memory*. It has long been clear under U.S. law that the placement of a work into a computer's memory amounts to a reproduction of that work (because the work may be, in the law's terms, "perceived, reproduced, or . . . communicated . . . with the aid of a machine or device").
>
> In each of the instances set out below, one or more copies is made, and, necessarily, in the absence of a proof of fair use or other relevant defense, there is an infringement of the reproduction right:
>
> • When a work is placed into a computer, whether on a disk, diskette, ROM, or other storage device or in RAM for more than a very brief period, a copy is made.
>
> • When a printed work is "scanned" into a digital file, a copy—the digital file itself—is made.
>
> • When other works—including photographs, motion pictures, or sound recordings—are digitized, copies are made.
>
> • Whenever a digitized file is "uploaded" from a user's computer to a bulletin board system or other server, a copy is made.
>
> • Whenever a digitized file is "downloaded" from a BBS or other server, a copy is made.
>
> • When a file is transferred from one computer network user to another, multiple copies are made.
>
> • Under current technology, when a user's computer is being used as a "dumb" terminal to "look at" a file resident on another computer (such as a BBS or Internet host), a copy of the portion viewed is made in the user's computer. (Without such copying into the RAM or buffer of the user's computer, no screen display would be possible.) As long as the amount viewed is more than *de minimis*, it is an infringement unless authorized or specifically exempt.

IITF Green Paper, *supra* note 8, at 35-37 (emphasis in original) (footnotes omitted).

59 MAI Sys. Corp., 991 F.2d 511; Triad Sys. Corp., 31 U.S.P.Q. 2d (BNA) 1239; Advanced Computer Servs., 845 F. Supp. 356.

60 *See* National Commission on New Technological Uses of Copyrighted Works,

discussions in a couple of recent law review articles.[61] This is some support, but it is hard to argue that the proposition "has long been clear under U.S. law." The CONTU reference is ambiguous; the other sources are recent. Authority on the other side of the question includes the statutory language,[62] and the following passage from the House Report accompanying the 1976 Act:

> Reproduction under clause (1) of section 106 is to be distinguished from "display" under clause (5). For a work to be "reproduced," its fixation in tangible form must be "sufficiently permanent or stable to permit it to be perceived, reproduced, or otherwise communicated for a period of more than transitory duration." Thus, the showing of images on a screen or tube would not be a violation of clause (1), although it might come within the scope of clause (5).[63]

I would argue that the better view of the law is that the act of reading a work into a computer's random access memory is too transitory to create a reproduction within the meaning of section 106(1).[64]

FINAL REPORT 39 (1978) ("The protection afforded by section 106 of the new law seemingly would prohibit the unauthorized storage of a work within a computer memory, which would be merely one form of reproduction . . . .").

61 *See, e.g.,* Jane C. Ginsburg, *Copyright Without Walls?: Speculations on Literary Property in the Library of the Future,* 42 REPRESENTATIONS 53, 56, 70 n.17 (1993).

62 The relevant language states:

> "Copies" are material objects, other than phonorecords, in which a work is fixed by any method now known or later developed . . . .
>
> A work is "fixed" in a tangible medium of expression when its embodiment in a copy or phonorecord, by or under the authority of the author, is sufficiently permanent or stable to permit it to be perceived, reproduced, or otherwise communicated for a period of more than transitory duration. . . .
>
> "Phonorecords" are material objects in which sounds . . . are fixed by any method now known or later developed. . . .

17 U.S.C. § 101 (1988).

"[T]he owner of copyright under this title has the exclusive rights to do and to authorize any of the following:

(1) to reproduce the copyrighted work in copies or phonorecords . . . ." 17 U.S.C. § 106(1)(1988).

63 H.R. REP. No. 1476, *supra* note 44, at 62. *See also* Pamela Samuelson, *Legally Speaking: The NII Intellectual Property Report,* Communications of the ACM, Dec. 1994, at —.

> Proponents of the view that RAM copies infringe copyrights argue that as long as the machine is on—and it can be on indefinitely—a copy of the copyrighted work stored there can be perceived or reproduced, thereby satisfying the "more than transitory duration" standard. (By this logic, holding a mirror up to a book would be infringement because the book's image could be perceived there for more than a transitory duration, i.e., however long one has the patience to hold the mirror.)

Id.

64 Indeed, the Draft Report itself seems a little confused about this; compare IITF GREEN PAPER, *supra* note 8, at 14 ("A transmission is not a fixation. While a transmission may result in a fixation, a work is not fixed by virtue of the transmission alone.") with *id.* at 36 ("[W]hen a computer user simply 'browses' a document resident on another's computer, the image on the user's screen exists—under contemporary technology—only by

In any event, even if the Draft Report's characterization of current law were not skewed, its endorsement of what it presents as well-settled law deserves examination. If a bargain between the public and the authors and producers of copyrighted works were negotiated (at arms length) and drafted up today, it might include a reproduction right, but it surely wouldn't include a "reading" right. It might include a performance right but not a "listening" right; it might have a display right, but it wouldn't have a "viewing" right. From the public's vantage point, the fact that copyright owners are now in a position to claim exclusive "reading," "listening," and "viewing" rights is an accident of drafting: when Congress awarded authors an exclusive reproduction right, it did not mean what it may mean today.

The Draft Report's proposed resolution of the ambiguities introduced into the law by the passage of time and the invention of new media is not, from the public's point of view, an improvement. If you were the public's copyright lawyer, you would, in my view, be hard pressed to assure your client that the Draft Report's proposals for modest alterations were in fact a good deal.

IV.

The Draft Report argues that its proposed enhancement of copyright owner's rights is without question in the public interest, for it is a necessary first step in the creation of the information superhighway. This is the central justification for further enhancing the rights in the copyright bundle: without strong copyright protection, there will be no national information infrastructure. The public might believe that what it wants is unfettered access to copyrighted works in return for reasonable royalty payments to authors, but, if we let the public set the freight charges, we risk underproduction of freight. If authors and publishers cannot reliably control their works, they will decline to make them available at all. The Draft Report puts it this way:

> [T]he potential of the NII will not be realized if the information and entertainment products protectible by intellectual property laws are not protected effectively when disseminated via the NII. Owners of intellectual property rights will not be willing to put their interests at risk if appropriate systems—both in the U.S. and internationally—are not in place to permit them to set and enforce the terms and conditions under which their works are

virtue of the copy that has been reproduced *in the user's computer memory*." (emphasis in original)).

> made available in the NII environment. Likewise, the public will not use the services available on the NII and generate the market necessary for its success unless access to a wide variety of works is provided under equitable and reasonable terms and conditions, and the integrity of those works is assured. All the computers, telephones, fax machines, scanners, cameras, keyboards, televisions, monitors, printers, switches, routers, wires, cables, networks and satellites in the world will not create a successful NII, if there is not *content*. What will drive the NII is the content moving through it.[65]

If the public wishes an NII, the argument goes, it must offer strong copyright protection as a bribe to those whom it hopes to persuade to create enough stuff to make an NII worthwhile. Relying on a hope that if the public only builds the infrastructure, the information to travel it will come is said to be naive; of course the owners of protectible works will refuse to permit those works to be exploited unless their ownership rights are secure.

It appears to follow from that analysis that my thought experiment is ill-considered. We should not pursue the public's hypothetical interest in paying reasonable fees in return for unfettered access to copyrighted works because the deal cannot be struck on those terms. If the public stops promising authors "a reward in the form of control,"[66] we will soon run short of new copyrighted works to read, see, hear or download. Representatives of copyright owners have made this argument repeatedly in the context of the NII.[67] They couldn't be bluffing about that, could they?

A.

Imagine for a moment that some upstart revolutionary proposed that we eliminate all intellectual property protection for fashion design. No longer could a designer secure federal copyright protection for the cut of a dress or the sleeve of a blouse. Unscrupulous mass-marketers could run off thousands of knock-off

---

65 IITF GREEN PAPER, *supra* note 8, at 6-7 (emphasis in original).

66 Goldstein v. California, 412 U.S. 546, 555 (1973).

67 *See, e.g., NII Hearing, supra* note 3 (testimony of Steven Metalitz, Information Industry Association):

> If we aren't able to protect copyright in the new information environment, then the information that will be available, the useful information, the supply of that will be drastically be curtailed. [sic] Or just as troubling, it will be limited to the information that the government chooses to create or some other powerful institution chooses to create.

It's worth noting that the Internet, which the Draft Report uses as its model for the NII, see IITF GREEN PAPER, *supra* note 8, at 2 n.2, is experiencing no dearth of material. *See infra* text accompanying notes 83-84.

copies of any designer's evening ensemble, and flood the marketplace with cheap imitations of haute couture. In the short run, perhaps, clothing prices would come down as legitimate designers tried to meet the prices of their free-riding competitors. In the long run, though, as we know all too well, the diminution in the incentives for designing new fashions would take its toll. Designers would still wish to design, at least initially, but clothing manufacturers with no exclusive rights to rely on would be reluctant to make the investment involved in manufacturing those designs and distributing them to the public. The dynamic American fashion industry would wither, and its most talented designers would forsake clothing design for some more remunerative calling like litigation. And all of us would be forced either to wear last year's garments year in and year out, or to import our clothing from abroad.

Or, perhaps, imagine that Congress suddenly repealed federal intellectual property protection for food creations.[68] Recipes would become common property. Downscale restaurants could freely recreate the signature chocolate desserts of their upscale sisters. Uncle Ben's® would market Minute® Risotto (*microwavable!*); the Ladies' Home Journal® would reprint recipes it had stolen from Gourmet® Magazine. Great chefs would be unable to find book publishers willing to buy their cookbooks. Then, expensive gourmet restaurants would reduce their prices to meet the prices of the competition; soon they would either close or fire their chefs to cut costs; promising young cooks would either move to Europe or get a day job (perhaps the law) and cook only on weekends. Ultimately, we would all be stuck eating Uncle Ben's Minute Risotto® (*eleven yummy flavors!!*) for every meal.

But, I'm boring you, you tell me; you've heard all of this before. It's the same argument motion picture producers make about why we need to extend the duration of copyright protection another 20 years;[69] the same argument software publishers make about what will happen if we permit other software publishers to decompile and reverse-engineer their software products;[70] the

---

68 *See generally* Malla A. Pollack, Note, *Intellectual Property Protection for the Creative Chef, or How to Copyright a Cake: A Modest Proposal*, 12 CARDOZO L. REV. 1477 (1991).

69 *See Copyright Office: Hearing Held on Possible Extension of Copyright Term*, 46 PAT., TRADEMARK & COPYRIGHT J. (BNA) 466 (Sept. 30, 1993).

70 *See, e.g., Copyright Amendments Act of 1991: Hearings on H.R. 2372 Before the Subcommittee on Intellectual Property and Judicial Administration of the House Committee on the Judiciary*, 102d Cong., 1st Sess. 115 (1993)(testimony of William Neukom, Software Publishers Association); ANTHONY LAWRENCE CLAPES, SOFTWARS: THE LEGAL BATTLES FOR CONTROL OF THE GLOBAL SOFTWARE INDUSTRY 6-9 (1993); Arthur R. Miller, *Copyright Protection for Computer Programs, Databases, and Computer-Generated Works: Is Anything New Since CONTU?*, 106 HARV. L. REV. 97, 1013-32 (1993); *see generally* Charles R. McManis, *Intellectual Property Protection*

same argument database proprietors make about the huge social cost of a failure to protect their rights in their data.[71] Perhaps the most important reason why we have intellectual property protection is our conclusion that incentives are required to spur the creation and dissemination of a sufficient number and variety of intellectual creations like films, software, databases, fashions and food.

Of course, we don't give copyright protection to fashions or food.[72] We never have.

B.

The model suggesting that production and dissemination of valuable, protectible works is directly related to the degree of available intellectual property protection is much too simplistic.[73] In fact, history teaches us a more equivocal lesson. Whenever we have discovered or enacted a copyright exception, an industry has grown up within its shelter. Player piano rolls became ubiquitous after courts ruled that they did not infringe the copyright in the underlying musical composition;[74] phonograph records superseded both piano rolls and sheet music with the aid of the compulsory license for mechanical reproductions;[75] the jukebox industry arose to take advantage of the copyright exemption accorded to "the reproduction or rendition of a musical composition by or upon coin-operated machines."[76] Composers continued to write music, and found ways to exploit these new media for their works.

The videotape rental business swept the nation shielded from copyright liability by the first sale doctrine.[77] The motion picture

---

and Reverse Engineering of Computer Programs in the United States and the European Community, 8 HIGH TECH. L.J. 25 (1993).

71 *Cf.* Jane C. Ginsburg, *No "Sweat"? Copyright and Other Protection of Works of Information after* Feist v. Rural Telephone, 92 COLUM. L. REV. 338, 353 (1992) ("Absent protection for the effort and expense of compiling information, one may fear the substantial diminution of incentives to invest in compiling information.").

72 *See, e.g.*, Pollack, *supra* note 68; Malla A. Pollack, *A Rose Is a Rose Is a Rose, But Is a Costume a Dress? An Alternative Solution in* Whimsicality, Inc. v. Rubie's Costume Co., 41 J. COPYRIGHT SOC'Y 1 (1993).

73 *See* Stephen Breyer, *The Uneasy Case for Copyright: A Study of Copyright in Books, Photocopies, and Computer Programs*, 84 HARV. L. REV. 281, 291-323 (1970); William W. Fisher III, *Reconstructing the Fair Use Doctrine*, 101 HARV. L. REV. 1659, 1700-39 (1988); *see also* Barlow, *supra* note 4, at 127.

74 *See* Kennedy v. McTammany, 33 F. 584 (C.C.D. Mass. 1888); White-Smith Music Publishing Co. v. Apollo Co., 209 U.S. 1 (1908).

75 Copyright Act of 1909, Pub. L. No. § 1(e), 35 Stat. 1075; *see* U.S. LIBRARY OF CONGRESS, SECOND SUPPLEMENTARY REPORT OF THE REGISTER OF COPYRIGHTS ON THE GENERAL REVISION OF THE U.S. COPYRIGHT LAW: 1975 REVISION BILL, Ch. IX (1975).

76 Copyright Act of 1909, *supra* note 75; *see* U.S. LIBRARY OF CONGRESS, *supra* note 75, at ch. X.

77 *See* 17 U.S.C. § 109 (1988).

industry predicted that if Congress failed to rush in to correct the problems posed by the invention and marketing of the videocassette recorder, American television would slowly be destroyed, and American motion picture production would sustain grave injury.[78] Howard Wayne Oliver, Executive Secretary of AFTRA (American Federation of Television and Radio Artists) told the House Subcommittee:

> Unless we do something to ensure that the creators of the material are not exploited by the electronics revolution, that same revolution which will make it possible for almost every household to have an audio and video recorder will surely undermine, cripple, and eventually wash away the very industries on which it feeds and which provide employment for thousands of our citizens.[79]

Notwithstanding all of the gloom and doom, however, both the motion picture and television industries discovered that the videocassette recorder generated new markets for prerecorded versions of their material.

Cable television began spreading across America with the aid of a copyright exemption;[80] it eclipsed broadcast television while sheltered by the cable compulsory license.[81] Yet, there is no dearth of television programming,[82] and the popular media image of the new information superhighway includes 500 television channels to accommodate it all.[83]

Even an erroneous assumption of copyright immunity can stimulate a nascent industry. The commercial photocopy shop prospered in part because of the university coursepack business made possible by a supposed fair use privilege.[84] Commercial and

---

78 *See Video and Audio Home Taping: Hearing on S. 31 and S. 175 Before the Subcomm. on Patents, Trademarks and Copyrights of the Senate Comm. on the Judiciary*, 98th Cong., 1st Sess. 276-306 (1983) (testimony of Jack Valenti, Motion Picture Association of America); *id.* at 307-09 (testimony of Kay Peters, Screen Actors Guild); *Home Recording of Copyrighted Works: Hearings on H.R. 4783, H.R. 4794, H.R. 4808, H.R. 5250, H.R. 5488, and H.R. 5705 Before the Subcommittee on Courts, Civil Liberties and the Administration of Justice of the House Comm. on the Judiciary*, 97th Cong., 2d Sess. 4-16 (1982) (testimony of Jack Valenti, Motion Picture Association of America).

79 *Home Recording of Copyrighted Works, supra* note 78, at 142.

80 *See* Teleprompter Corp. v. Columbia Broadcasting Sys. Inc., 415 U.S. 394 (1974); Fortnightly Corp. v. United Artists Television, 392 U.S. 390 (1968).

81 *See* 17 U.S.C. § 111; Litman, *supra* note 23, at 342-46.

82 *See, e.g., NII Hearing, supra* note 3, at 130-41 (testimony of Richard Ducey and Benjamin F.P. Ivins, National Association of Broadcasters).

83 *See, e.g.*, Paul Farhi, *TCI's Malone Quietly Assembling an Empire*, WASH. POST, Oct. 14, 1993, at A1; Benjamin J. Stein, *More Channels, More Laziness*, WASH. POST, Nov. 2, 1993, at A19.

84 *See* Basic Books, Inc. v. Kinko's Graphics Corp., 758 F. Supp. 1522 (S.D.N.Y. 1991); Princeton Univ. Press v. Michigan Document Serv., 855 F. Supp. 905 (E.D. Mich. 1994).

non-commercial subscriptions to services providing access to the Internet are increasing geometrically,[85] and much of the activity on the net takes place on the mistaken assumption that any material on the Internet is free from copyright unless expressly declared to be otherwise. Nonetheless, there are scores of electronic magazines and news services developed specifically for electronic distribution, and many commercial publishers are currently releasing their works over the Internet despite the absence of effective coercive means of protection.[86]

Of course, copyright owners would prefer to maximize their own control over the works they produce. Of course, if we ask them to come up with an optimal copyright law, they will draft one that meets that specification. If the general public had a lawyer to sit at the copyright negotiating table on its behalf, however, the law that emerged from the negotiating process might be a different one.

V.

Neither the authors of the Draft Report nor the current stakeholders whose views the Report appears to endorse are oblivious of public opinion. They realize that some of their proposals would be controversial, indeed, even unpopular to some segments of the public, if the public were paying attention. The Draft Report suggests that one solution to this problem is education.[87] The Report acknowledges that the task might not be easy.[88]

We know quite a bit about the problems that inhere in educating the public about copyright law, because copyright owners have

---

The popularity of the course-pack services provided by commercial photocopy shops eventually enabled publishers to establish a lucrative course-pack photocopy licensing business. *See id.*

85 *See* SOFTWARE 2000, *supra* note 4, at 2-5 to 2-15; Philip Elmer-Dewitt, *Technology: Battle for the Soul of the Internet*, TIME, July 25, 1994, at 50; Peter H. Lewis, *A Boom for On-Line Services*, N.Y. TIMES, July 12, 1994, at D1; Peter H. Lewis, *Business Technology; Even in Cyberspace, Overcrowding*, N.Y. TIMES, Feb. 2, 1994, at D1.

86 An "Electronic Newsstand" at enews.com, URL: gopher://gopher.enews.com:70/11/magazines/alphabetic, offers free samples from magazines including BUSINESS WEEK, the ECONOMIST, the NEW REPUBLIC and the NEW YORKER to encourage the purchase of subscriptions. Tor Books, URL: gopher://gopher.panix.com:70/11/TBON, and Del Rey Books, URL: gopher://gopher.panix.com:70/11/DRB, offer free excerpts from forthcoming novels on the Panix Gopher Server. Associated Press, UPI and Reuters are available on Compuserve, and TIME magazine maintains a presence on America Online. Meanwhile, both West Publishing Company and Mead Data Corporation conduct extensive (and expensive) online information services notwithstanding the rudimentary state of available protections for the material they have at their disposal.

87 IITF GREEN PAPER, *supra* note 8, at 117-19.

88 *Id.* The major difficulties highlighted in the Draft Report are practical, rather than substantive concerns. My own view is that the substantive problems far outweigh the logistical questions. *See infra* text accompanying notes 89-106.

been expending huge sums of energy, time, and money with that goal in mind. The music performing rights societies have been trying to educate a recalcitrant public for the past eighty years, and the effort has hardly made a dent in the psyches of their customers or the people who patronize them.[89] Restaurateurs would not think of selling their patrons stolen food, or sitting them in stolen chairs, but they think nothing of selling them stolen music; many of those who buy performing rights licenses from ASCAP, BMI and SESAC say that they do so only because they are afraid of the copyright police.[90]

The performing rights situation is straightforward: if you run an establishment open to the public, you need to buy a license to perform music unless your performances fit into one of the exceptions; and licenses are sold relatively cheaply.[91] But, compliance is grudging at best.[92] People perceive the law to be grossly unfair,[93] partly because enforcement is incomplete and uneven; there's no guarantee that the business down the street is licensed, and who wants to be a chump?[94] Then there are all of the exceptions in section 110, which don't make any sense.[95] How come a bar with one 27" television doesn't need a license, while another bar with

---

89 *See generally Music Licensing Practices of Performing Rights Societies: Oversight Hearing Before the Subcomm. on Intellectual Property and Judicial Administration of the House Comm. on the Judiciary*, 103d Cong., 2d Sess. (Feb. 23-24, 1994) [hereinafter *Music Licensing Hearing*]; Ralph Oman, *Source Licensing: The Latest Skirmish in an Old Battle*, 11 COLUM.-VLA J.L. & ARTS 251 (1987).

90 *See Music Licensing Hearings*, *supra* note 89, at — (testimony of Guy Gregg, Owner, The Publick House Restaurant).

91 *See id.* at — (testimony of Morton Gould, American Society of Composers, Authors and Publishers); *id.* at — (statement of Marvin L. Berenson, Broadcast Music, Inc.); *id.* at — (statement of Representative Craig Thomas).

92 The music performing rights situation is exemplary; I choose it because of the longstanding campaigns waged by ASCAP, BMI and SESAC to educate the public. Organizations like the Software Publishers Association have been in business for far fewer years, with no more success. On compliance with the copyright law as it concerns software, John Perry Barlow recently wrote:

> The laws regarding unlicensed reproduction of commercial software are clear and stern . . . and rarely observed. Software piracy laws are so practically unenforceable and breaking them has become so socially acceptable that only a thin minority appears compelled, either by fear or by conscience, to obey them. When I give speeches on this subject, I always ask how many people in the audience can honestly claim to have no unauthorized software on their hard disk. I've never seen more than 10 percent of the hands go up.
>
> Whenever there is such profound divergence between law and social practice, it is not society that adapts. Against the swift tide of custom, the software publishers' current practice of hanging a few visible scapegoats is so obviously capricious as to only further diminish respect for the law.

Barlow, *supra* note 4, at 88.

93 *See Music Licensing Hearings*, *supra* note 89, at — (statement of Joe Johnson, National Licensed Beverage Association).

94 *See id.* at — (statement of John Deion, Owner, Last Call Saloon).

95 *See id.* at — (statement of Mike Leonard, National Licensed Beverage Association).

two 13" televisions does? Copyright lawyers might understand that the reason for this is that the words in section 110(5) say "*single* receiving apparatus of a kind commonly used in private homes,"[96] but there is nothing intuitively appealing about the distinction. Some prospective licensees fail to buy licenses because they believe the law could not possibly have been intended to apply to their situation; others find its complex provisions arbitrary and incomprehensible, and, therefore, unfair. And, every single year, despite the fact that the liability of unlicensed commercial establishments is well settled, people choose to *litigate* rather than pay up. And, of course, they lose. Their lawyers could have told them they would lose at the beginning, but they go through the painful and expensive litigation process anyway.

The moral of the story: some things are easier to teach than others. The current copyright statute has proved to be remarkably education-resistant. One part of the problem is that many people persist in believing that laws make sense. If someone claims that a law provides such and such, but such and such seems to make no sense, then perhaps that isn't really the law, or wasn't intended to be the way the law worked, or was the law at one time but not today, or is one of those laws, like the sodomy law, that it is okay to ignore. Our current copyright statute has more than merely a provision or two or three or ten that don't make a lot of sense; it's chock-full of them.[97] That is a direct result of the process we use to come up with our copyright laws. Whatever the strengths of the negotiated legislation approach to an area as complex as copyright, the statutes that result from the process are long, complex, and counterintuitive.[98]

The dynamics inherent in the negotiation process discourage brevity and intuitive appeal. Lawyers representing affected interests respond to the issues raised by new technology by ratifying all of the "accidents" that favor their clients and repudiating the "accidents" that work to their disadvantage. You know the drill: One does this by claiming that the first sort of accident is no accident at all, but part of Congress's grand design; while the second sort of accident is a completely unintended, unexpected "loophole." That is precisely the approach taken by the Draft Report, which treats the apparent expansiveness of the reproduction right as a design feature of the copyright law,[99] but presents the apparent leaks in

96 17 U.S.C. § 110(5) (1988) (emphasis added); *see supra* note 45.
97 *See* Jessica Litman, *Copyright as Myth*, 53 U. PITT. L. REV. 235 (1991).
98 *See* Litman, *supra* note 23.
99 *See* IITF GREEN PAPER, *supra* note 8, at 35-37.

the transmission right as accidental ambiguities that Congress should plug.[100] If interested parties disagree on which accidents are which, there is a predictable negotiated solution. Negotiating stakeholders have always resolved differences through specificity and detail.[101] By the time we're done the new statute is even worse than the old one. Thus, the recent Audio Home Recording Act,[102] even in its streamlined "DART Lite" version,[103] is one of the longest and least comprehensible copyright enactments of all time. And while it is easy to claim that the interplay among all of the interests affected by copyright provides a proxy for the public interest, the statutes that interplay produces demonstrate that it isn't so.[104]

Our current copyright law is a descendent of the copyright laws in force at the turn of the century and before, which were designed to bring order to the interaction among affected industries. Because affected industries, and their lawyers, were invited to draft those rules themselves, the law became so technical, detailed, and counterintuitive that those industries now need to bring their copyright lawyers along to tell them how to play. If the law is intended to affect only the behavior of players with substantial economic stakes in copyright-affected matters, there is not much wrong with that degree of complexity. As soon, however, as the law is claimed to control the ordinary behavior of ordinary members of the public going about their ordinary daily business, then that species of law will no longer serve.

If we want ordinary people to look at unlicensed music, unlicensed software, and unlicensed digital reading material the same way they see stolen personal property, and to treat them accordingly, then we need to teach them the rules that govern intellectual property when we teach them the rules that govern other personal property, which is to say, in elementary school. That proposition should not be controversial; the Draft Report suggests that very thing.[105] The problem, though, is that our current copyright statute could not be taught in elementary school, because elementary school students couldn't understand it. Indeed, their teachers couldn't understand it. Copyright lawyers don't understand it.[106]

---

100 *See id.* at 120-23.

101 *See* Litman, *supra* note 23.

102 Audio Home Recording Act of 1992, Pub. L. No. 102-563, 106 Stat. 4237, *codified at* 17 U.S.C. §§ 1001-1010; *see Audio Home Recording Act Hearings*, *supra* note 21; H.R. Rep. No. 873, *supra* note 21.

103 *See* H.R. Rep. 873, *supra* note 21.

104 *See supra* notes 24-45 and accompanying text.

105 IITF Green Paper, *supra* note 8, at 117-19.

106 I make this statement with no intention of being hyperbolic. Anyone with access to the Internet can join a number of online virtual communities in which copyright law is

If we are going to teach the copyright law to school children, then we need the law to be sensible, intuitive, and short enough that school children can hold its essential provisions in their heads. What we have now is not even close. We need, in other words, to abandon entirely the idea that we can make members of the public conduct their daily affairs under rules thought up by and for major players in copyright-affected industries. If the public is to play by copyright rules, then those rules must be designed with the public's interests in mind.

VI.

Imagine once again that the public has retained you as its copyright lawyer. Acting in your new role, you review the current statute, and the government's proposals for adjusting it, and you chat with your client about where to go from here:

> *You:* "Look. I think the copyright concept is a good one, but I'm not happy with the details. There are a bunch of places where I think the language is unfortunate, and not in your long term best interest. Let me take it home and see if I can draft up a counterproposal that'll meet your needs, here."
> *Client:* "Gee. That's great; that's what I hoped you'd say. But lookit. This time, when you're writing it up, could you make it real short? I don't read so fast, and this is real important to me. I want to understand what it says."

So, you have yourself a drafting project. Your job is to construct a copyright law that affords members of the public the opportunity to read, see, hear, and otherwise experience, download, buy, borrow and keep copies of all, or at least most, of the works that are

---

discussed by groups including experts and interested laypeople. One story I like to tell involves a debate that went on for a couple of months on a wonderful copyright mailing list that has more than 1000 subscribers, some of whom are prominent experts in the field. The debate was over whether one could dedicate one's electronic postings to the public domain, and, if so, how might that be accomplished, and could one, having done that, attach any conditions to the further distribution of the contents of those posts? Participants were not sure that it was possible to dedicate works to the public domain anymore, after the Berne Implementation Act, Pub. L. No. 100-568, 102 Stat. 2853 (1988); they were not sure how, if it were possible, one could accomplish it; they could not agree on what words to use. None of these folks are copyright naifs; both the original inquirer and most of the posters offering views on this particular issue had substantial copyright backgrounds. But, if 1000 sophisticated people with enormous copyright expertise among them cannot over a two month period resolve this simple a question, then the law has gotten way too complicated for any purpose; it surely cannot be taught to school children.

Someone asked me the other day why, if music stores could play music without a performing rights license, videotape stores couldn't play videotapes without a performing license, and why, if television stores were not allowed to play all of their television sets without a license, they did it all the time? Can you think of an answer to those questions that would sell in junior high school? I can't.

out there, while according ample compensation to the authors and publishers of copyrighted works, and encouraging them to produce and disseminate as many copyrighted works as they are able to. The law should be about three pages long, should strike more folks than not as more fair than not, and should be sufficiently intuitive to appeal to school children. Let's say that you take about an hour, and come up with some language that meets spec.[107] Your client approves it. You take it over to Congress. Or maybe you take it over to the Patent and Trademark Office at the U.S. Commerce Department, home of the Information Infrastructure Task Force's Working Group on Intellectual Property Rights. Or, maybe, you sign on to the Internet and post it for all to read. You have only one final problem: Congress isn't going to enact it.

The only way that copyright laws get passed in this country is for all of the lawyers who represent the current stakeholders to get together and hash out all of the details among themselves.[108] In the past, this process has produced laws that are unworkable from the vantage point of people who were not among the negotiating parties,[109] and it won't generate any better results this time. The public needs to sit at the negotiating table and insist that any solution must seriously address its interests, as well as theirs.

What the public needs is a copyright lawyer of its own to represent it in the revision or replacement of the copyright law we now have, and the proposals for amending it that the National Information Infrastructure is inspiring. If you were unable to take the assignment yourself, where would you send your prospective client to find someone who would act as the copyright lawyer for the general public? Where would you send your prospective client to find someone who could do it well?

That is supposed to be Congress's job, of course. Congress *is* the public's copyright lawyer. The problem is that Congress is also the public's bankruptcy lawyer, and our trade lawyer, and our outer-space lawyer. Congress seems to lack the interest, expertise, and institutional memory to represent the public on this particular project; indeed, what Congress has done more often than not is delegate the job of coming up with legislation to interested private

---

107 My own view is that a number of different approaches would each yield a copyright law more hospitable to the public's interests than the one we have now. My three page proposal would differ from yours, but perhaps no more so than would any lawyer's draft of a short agreement on a more conventional topic. I am much less confident that anything I write will persuade readers to attempt the exercise than I am with my suggestion that an hour's concentrated thought would generate interesting and probably useful language.

108 *See supra* note 24.

109 *See* Litman, *supra* note 23.

parties, which is how the statute got so long and convoluted in the first place.

But, Congress *has* a copyright lawyer of its own. That is the Copyright Office's job. The Copyright Office *does* have both the expertise and institutional memory; it has functioned as Congress's copyright lawyer and copyright expert for almost a century. The Office has, of course, some history of being "captured" by industry for most of the usual reasons (limited budgets, revolving doors, and the growing perception that copyright owners were in fact the Office's real constituency), but the public badly needs a copyright lawyer. The Copyright Office is in the very best position to perform that function. Besides, the Draft Report issued by the Working Group headquartered in the Patent and Trademark Office indicates that the Patent Office has already managed to assume much of the job of serving the interests of industry. This may be an unusually good moment for the Copyright Office to think very hard about redefining its role.

The Copyright Office's enormous expertise could enable it not only to persuade all of us (that is, both stakeholders and individual members of the public) that the public's interests *are* compatible rather than adverse to the interests of copyright owners, but also to make it so. What it would require, though, is a different sort of legislative proposal than the ones we have gotten used to seeing over the years. The Copyright Office has focused much of its recent attention on the threats that technology might unbalance the copyright bargain to the detriment of copyright owners, and has failed to attend to the danger that the bargain might unbalance to the detriment of the public. All it would take would be for the Office to view the public as its copyright client. And somebody certainly should.

WILL THE COPYRIGHT OFFICE BE OBSOLETE IN THE TWENTY-FIRST CENTURY?

PAMELA SAMUELSON*

When contemplating possible futures for copyright law in the twenty-first century, we should not forget to consider what future the U.S. Copyright Office may have. During the century now drawing to a close, the Office has played an important role in the formation of copyright policy in the United States and in its administration.[1] When a governmental institution has existed for as long as the U.S. Copyright Office, one tends to take for granted that the institution will continue for the indefinite future and will play the same role in the future that it has played in the past. Abolition of a government agency is, after all, an exceedingly rare event in U.S. history. In view of this, the Copyright Office would seem to have a secure future.

And yet, I perceive a number of circumstances that might cause the Copyright Office to become obsolete in the coming century. This article will discuss these circumstances—some of which are offered with tongue only partly in cheek—and will make some more general observations about possible futures for copyright law in the twenty-first century. The future of the law of copyright and of the Office responsible for its administration are, as one might expect, closely intertwined.

Here, then, are some circumstances which might render the U.S. Copyright Office obsolete.

I. REPEAL OF THE REGISTRATION AND DEPOSIT REQUIREMENTS

First, if the U.S. Congress repeals the registration and deposit provisions of the current copyright statute, there may be little or nothing for the Copyright Office to do. In this event, Congress might decide to abolish the Office entirely. Under the current stat-

---

* Professor of Law, University of Pittsburgh Law School. I offer my thanks to Marci Hamilton for having organized the symposium at which I had the opportunity to give the talk on which this article is based.

1 From 1790 to 1870, registration of claims to copyright was the responsibility of clerks of the federal district courts for the district in which the author resided. The Library of Congress took over this responsibility in 1870. Congress appropriated money for a Copyright Department of the Library of Congress (which became the U.S. Copyright Office) in 1897. The Copyright Act of 1976 contains many provisions setting forth the responsibilities and registration procedures of the Office. 1 PAUL GOLDSTEIN, COPYRIGHT PRINCIPLES, LAW & PRACTICE § 3.19 (1989); *see* 17 U.S.C. §§ 408-409, 701-710 (1988).

ute, registration of a claim of copyright is not required as a precondition for protection of a work.[2] However, registration is a precondition, at least for U.S. authors, for enforcing one's copyright interests; that is, to initiate a lawsuit for copyright infringement, U.S. authors must have obtained a certificate of registration from the Copyright Office.[3] In the process of registering copyright claims with the Office, authors can also satisfy the requirement that they deposit copies of their works, thereby enhancing the collection of the Library of Congress.[4]

Those who deplore the registration and deposit requirements of U.S. copyright law as vestiges of a formality-ridden past support repeal of the requirements.[5] Congress has been considering legislation that would effect a repeal as part of a copyright law reform package.[6]

Those who support the repeal of the registration and deposit requirements do not openly advocate abolition of the Copyright Office. Indeed, some anticipate that authors would continue to register their works with the Office on a voluntary basis.[7] A blue-ribbon panel established by the Librarian of Congress to consider possible repeal of these requirements made a number of suggestions for changes to current registration requirements that a majority of the panel thought would enhance registration on a voluntary basis.[8]

As well-meaning as these proposals are, it is difficult to believe that voluntary registration would be widely used if the registration and deposit requirements were repealed and a sister proposal permitting plaintiffs to be awarded attorney's fees and statutory damages without prompt registration of copyright claims were

---

2 17 U.S.C. § 408(a)(1988).

3 17 U.S.C. § 411(a) (Supp V 1988). Authors who reside in Berne member nations other than the U.S. may bring infringement suits without registering their claims of copyright.

4 Section 407 sets forth the deposit requirement. 17 U.S.C. § 407 (1988). Section 408 concerns deposits of copies of copyrighted works as part of the copyright registration process. 17 U.S.C. § 408 (1988).

5 For a helpful discussion of the history of formalities in U.S. copyright law and their subsidence as a precondition of U.S. adherence to the Berne Convention, see, e.g., Jane C. Ginsburg & John M. Kernochan, *One Hundred and Two Years Later: The U.S. Joins the Berne Convention*, 13 COLUM.-VLA J. LAW & ARTS 1 (1988). For an argument that U.S. copyright law still has too many formalities, see Shira Perlmutter, *Freeing Copyright from Formalities*, 13 CARDOZO ARTS & ENT. L.J. (forthcoming 1995).

6 *See* H.R. 897, 103d Cong., 1st Sess. (1993); *see also* S. 373, 103d Cong., 1st Sess. (1993).

7 *See, e.g.*, Perlmutter, *supra* note 5.

8 *See* ROBERT WEDGEWORTH & BARBARA RINGER, ADVISORY COMMITTEE ON COPYRIGHT REGISTRATION AND DEPOSIT, THE LIBRARY OF CONGRESS, REPORT OF THE CO-CHAIRS (Sept. 1993) [hereinafter ACCORD].

implemented.[9] If these changes go into effect, registration may no longer offer any significant benefit to copyright owners.[10] If registration dropped off precipitously in the aftermath of adoption of such legislation,[11] it would be difficult to justify the continued existence of the Copyright Office.

II. Automated Registration

Even if the registration and deposit requirements are not repealed, a Copyright Office staffed by humans will not really be needed if computerized registration and deposit procedures become the norm.[12] To automate registration and deposit functions, all that would seem to be required is a server connected to the Internet. An electronic version of the work could then be sent, along with an electronic form provided by the server. The server would automatically scan the new work and compare it with documents in the system; assuming that no close or exact match was identified, the server could issue an electronic certificate of registration which would then be e-mailed to the registrant. Much the same procedure might be used for recording transfers of copyright interests.[13]

Because people have more confidence in the ability of human

---

9 *See* 17 U.S.C. § 412 (1988) (conditioning the award of attorney's fees and statutory damages on registration within three months of publication). The same bill that would do away with the current requirement that a work be registered before an infringement action can be brought would repeal § 412 as well as § 11. *See* Letter from Robert Oakley, ACCORD Committee Member, to James Billington, Librarian of Congress (Sept. 27, 1993) (dissenting from the ACCORD Report and expressing concern that the repeal of §§ 411 and 412 would cause a drop in registrations) [hereinafter ACCORD Dissent] (on file with the *Cardozo Arts & Entertainment Law Journal*).

10 Lawyers may regard the fact that a registration certificate is prima facie evidence of the validity of an author's claim of copyright as a meaningful inducement to registration. *See* 17 U.S.C. § 410(c) (1988). Authors, however, are unlikely to be attuned to the fine points of evidence law.

11 There are a number of reasons why Congress may decide not to repeal the current registration and deposit requirements. *See* ACCORD Dissent, *supra* note 9. Interestingly, many publishers do not support these changes. The Copyright Reform Act of 1993: Hearings on S. 373 Before the Subcomm. on Patents, Copyrights and Trademarks of the Senate Comm. on the Judiciary, 103d Cong., 1st Sess. (1993) (statement of the Association of American University Presses and the Association of American Publishers). One of the important functions of the current registration process is to limit the number of frivolous copyright claims for blank forms, useful articles and the like with which the U.S. courts would otherwise have to deal. Thus, repeal of the registration and deposit requirements would probably lead to an increase in copyright litigation. Jon Baumgarten and Peter Jaszi, Working Paper #4a, *in* ACCORD, *supra* note 8, app. at 85, 88.

12 *See, e.g.*, Robert E. Kahn, *Deposit, Registration, and Recordation in an Electronic Copyright Management System*, 1 IMA Intell. Prop. Project Procs. 111 (1994).

13 The Copyright Office currently maintains records on transfers of copyright in addition to records on initial registration of copyright claims. *See* 17 U.S.C. § 205 (1988). Kahn's model for an electronic copyright management system would also provide this function. Kahn, *supra* note 12.

examiners than in automated examiners to identify truly "original" work, perhaps the current presumption of validity of a copyright claim that arises from prompt registration would have to be changed.[14] However, the loss of this presumption seems a modest price to pay for the elimination of an unnecessary federal agency.

III. Improved Technological Protection of Intellectual Property Rights in a Digital Networked Environment

Much promising research has focused on the development of technological strategies for protecting intellectual products in digital form. Some of this research was presented at a recent conference jointly sponsored by the Coalition for Networked Information, the Interactive Multimedia Association, the Science, Technology, and Public Policy Program of Harvard University's John F. Kennedy School of Government, and the Massachusetts Institute of Technology's Program on Digital Open High-Resolution Systems.[15]

Some of the presentations at the Conference focused on techniques for encrypting the contents of digitized works.[16] Distributing encrypted works in a digital networked environment would not threaten the economic interests of copyright owners because in order to consume or enjoy copyrighted works, a potential consumer would have to obtain a decryption "key." A user would have to pay a specified fee to obtain the key, or would have to otherwise be eligible to receive it. One presentation featured a model for an Internet billing server that could carry out transactions for obtaining decrypted versions of digitized works on the Internet.[17]

None of these proposals is foolproof.[18] After all, once one person has possession of a decrypted copy, it may be difficult to stop that person from redistributing it over the network. Additionally, distribution of copyrighted works in encrypted form may be

---

14 *See* 17 U.S.C. § 410(c).

15 *See Proceedings on Technological Strategies for Protecting Intellectual Property in the Networked Multimedia Environment,* 1 IMA Intell. Prop. Project Procs. 1 (1994).

16 *See, e.g.,* Benoit Macq & Jean-Jacques Quisquater, *Digital Images Multiresolution Encryption,* 1 IMA Intell. Prop. Project Procs. 179 (1994).

17 *See* Marvin A. Sirbu, *Internet Billing Service Design and Prototype Implementation,* 1 IMA Intell. Prop. Project Procs. 67 (1994).

18 Another promising technological strategy for protecting intellectual property in digital networked environments would be to distribute works with a program that could "rat" on abusive consumers. That is, such documents might be programmed to send a message to the owner of the copyright to inform the owner that too many copies had been made or that some digital manipulation of the contents had occurred. This, however, would not be foolproof either since users might construct programs to deactivate the ratting program.

viewed by some technically proficient "hackers" as a challenging problem in need of a solution, and may encourage efforts to defeat encryption.[19] Workshop participants seemed to regard technological strategies for protecting digitized intellectual property in networked environments as having decided advantages over the alternative of sending the most highly-prized intellectual products of the day out on the Net in unencrypted form, in the hopes that all of those who consume will send back sufficient revenues to justify further investments in the creation of more highly prized works.[20]

Those who look to technological means to protect intellectual property should, however, recognize the past failure of one effort to use technological means to protect digitized intellectual property, namely, copy-protected mass-marketed software.[21] The main reason for the failure of copy protection schemes was that consumers did not favor them.[22] Software consumers felt that they should be able to make backup copies of their programs. They could not do this with copy-protected software.[23] Companies marketing only copy-protected software found themselves losing out in the marketplace to those firms willing to risk distribution of unprotected programs. Eventually, software developers adapted to market demands by abandoning sales of copy-protected software altogether.

Also contributing to the downfall of copy protection systems was the reality that it had become a sport for programmers to write programs to undo copy protection.[24] Even more upsetting than this, markets began to develop for anti-copy-protection programs. However, the first litigation seeking to outlaw the sale of anti-copy-

---

19 As John P. Barlow recently observed, "a social overreliance on protection by barricades [such as encryption] rather than conscience will eventually wither the latter by turning intrusion and theft into a sport, rather than a crime." John P. Barlow, *The Economy of Ideas*, WIRED, Mar. 1994, at 84, 129.

20 This concern also underlies the recent Green Paper. INFORMATION INFRASTRUCTURE TASK FORCE, INTELLECTUAL PROPERTY AND THE NATIONAL INFORMATION INFRASTRUCTURE: A PRELIMINARY DRAFT OF THE REPORT OF THE WORKING GROUP ON INTELLECTUAL PROPERTY RIGHTS (July 1994) [hereinafter IITF GREEN PAPER].

21 Copy protection for software products was accomplished by placing an additional program besides the application the consumer sought to acquire on the disk. This prevented copying of the software.

22 *See* Barlow, *supra* note 19, at 129.

23 It is considered sound practice in the computing community for users to make backup copies of programs because computer failures, among other things, can cause a particular copy of a program to be destroyed. *See* Mary M. Meisner, *Archival Backup Copying of Software: How Broad a Right?*, 14 RUTGERS COMPUTER & TECH. L.J. 391 (1988). The legitimacy of backup copying is also recognized in the copyright statute. *See* 17 U.S.C. § 117 (1988).

24 As John P. Barlow has noted, "early reliance on copy protection led to the subliminal notion that cracking into a software package somehow 'earned' one the right to use it." Barlow, *supra* note 19, at 129.

protection programs proved unsuccessful.[25] The National Information Infrastructure Task Force's Working Group on Intellectual Property Rights ("the Working Group") advocates making any attempt to bypass technological means for protecting digitized intellectual products illegal.[26] This would legislatively reverse the results of the early litigation. The Working Group hopes that doing so will open the way for highly effective protection of digital intellectual property distributed in networked environments.

If the technology to protect intellectual property becomes very effective and if attempts to defeat it are made illegal, it would seem that not only the Copyright Office, but copyright law itself, might become obsolete. Why would one need copyright protection, let alone need to register a claim of copyright with a Copyright Office, if it becomes virtually impossible to copy a work because of the technological protection attached to it? Perhaps there would be a symbolic purpose for maintaining copyright law as a kind of "deus ex machina" justifying the assertion of intellectual property rights in the first place, but the Copyright Office itself would surely not be needed in a technologically secure environment.

IV. Header Contracts

Some believe that contractual strategies will supplement, or possibly even supplant, technological strategies for protecting intellectual property rights in digital networked environments.[27] Contracts are already the primary means for protecting many commercially valuable digitized information services in the market today.[28] But some envision an even broader future for contractual means of protecting intellectual products in digital form through use of "header contracts" for obtaining rights to use digital information.[29]

An example will help illustrate the potential utility of header contracts. Imagine that you are a person in need of information of a particular sort. You know that the information must be out there

25 *See* Vault Corp. v. Quaid Software, Ltd., 847 F.2d 255 (5th Cir. 1988) (defendant's RAMKEY program was designed to "unlock" plaintiff's PROLOK program; because defendant's program did not reproduce expression from the plaintiff's program, it was noninfringing).

26 IITF Green Paper, *supra* note 20, at 126-30.

27 *See, e.g.*, Henry J. Perritt, *Permission Headers and Contract Law*, 1 IMA Intell. Prop. Project Procs. 27 (1994).

28 *See, e.g.*, Pamela Samuelson & Robert J. Glushko, *Intellectual Property Rights for Digital Library and Hypertext Publishing Systems*, 6 Harv. J.L. & Tech. 237, 242-43 (1993).

29 For a discussion of one prototype system of this sort, see Luella Upthegrove & Tom Roberts, *Intellectual Property Header Descriptors: A Dynamic Approach*, 1 IMA Intell. Prop. Project Procs. 63 (1994).

on the Net somewhere, but you don't know exactly where, and you don't know under what conditions it will be made available to you. To assist you in your search, you call upon a "knowbot," an intelligent search program that has been trained to be attentive to your particular preferences.[30] You send the "knowbot" out into cyberspace to search for the information you need. When it has located sources that contain the information, the "knowbot" sends you messages about each source. The header for each source informs you of the conditions under which the information will be made available to you. After you choose the source from which you wish to order the information, you reply to the source's header. By replying, you will have ordered the information and will have bound yourself to the terms described in the header.

Header contracts appear to offer important protection to digital works, whether the contracts are employed separately or are used in conjunction with technological protection.[31] One wonders what there would be for copyright law or the Copyright Office to do if individual contracts bound all who used intellectual property distributed in digital networked environments.[32] The need for copyright law itself would become questionable if one could bind every user to limitations on access to every information product available in the market.

V. A Hostile Takeover by the Patent & Trademark Office

A more immediate threat to the viability of the Copyright Office as an institution than technological and contractual strategies for protecting intellectual property distributed in digital networked environments is the prospect of a "hostile takeover" by the Patent and Trademark Office. The Patent and Trademark Office could conceivably assume all of the Copyright Office's functions.

Bruce Lehman, the current Commissioner of Patents and Trademarks and an Assistant Secretary of Commerce, would seem

---

30 For a discussion of "knowbots," see Robert E. Kahn & Vinton G. Cerf, *An Open Architecture for a Digital Library System and a Plan for its Development*, The Digital Library Project, Volume 1: The World of Knowbots (DRAFT) 60-62 Corporation for National Research Initiatives (1988). *See also* Perritt, *supra* note 27.

31 Header contracts are much more likely than shrinkwrap licenses to be regarded as imposing meaningful contractual limitations on the ability of copyright owners to limit consumer uses of copyrighted works. *See, e.g.*, Brian Kahin, *The Strategic Environment for Protecting Multimedia*, 1 IMA Intell. Prop. Project Procs. 1, 6-7 (1994); *see also* Perritt, *supra* note 27.

32 Those wishing to take action against persons who receive digital data from someone who contracted with an information provider, even though the second recipients had not themselves contracted with the information provider, might rely on implied contract or unjust enrichment theory.

to be the ideal person to accomplish the "takeover." Commissioner Lehman is a lawyer whose experience in copyright is even more extensive than his experience in trademark or patent law.[33] During the long interregnum in which the Register of Copyright position was open,[34] Commissioner Lehman attended to a number of important copyright policy matters. He is currently chair of the Working Group on Intellectual Property Rights for the National Information Infrastructure Task Force.[35] This group recently issued a "Green Paper" which aims to modify copyright law so that it will better respond to the evolving needs of intellectual property rights owners who want to distribute their works in digital networked environments.[36] He was also active in the Clinton Administration's efforts to persuade Japan not to adopt a provision that would have permitted decompilation of computer programs as a means to access, for example, the information needed to construct programs that could interoperate with a particular program.[37]

Lehman may perceive the desirability of continuing to streamline the structure of the U.S. government in relation to its intellectual property policy. Some reorganization was achieved before Lehman became Commissioner. At one time the Patent Office and the Trademark Office were two separate departments within the Department of Commerce. They were consolidated in 1975.[38] From the standpoint of organizational efficiency, there would seem to be no reason to continue to maintain an administratively separate Copyright Office when it could so easily be folded into the Patent and Trademark Office.

The Copyright Office is, after all, a very odd duck, as government agencies go. It is not part of a "real" federal agency; rather, it is a subdivision of the Library of Congress and hence a part of the legislative branch of the U.S. government.[39] It would be simple

---

33 Some opposition to Lehman's candidacy for the position of Commissioner of Patents & Trademarks arose because Lehman's background in copyright is stronger than his background in patent or trademark law. *See, e.g.*, Teresa Riordan, *Profile: Even In a 'Big Tent,' Little Insults, Little Compromises*, N.Y. TIMES, May 29, 1994, § 3, at 5.

34 Ralph Oman resigned as Register of Copyrights in August 1993; Mary Beth Peters was named as his successor in August 1994.

35 IITF GREEN PAPER, *supra* note 20, at 1. This project is in furtherance of a Congressional initiative to ensure that intellectual property rights are protected in digital networked environments. *See* 15 U.S.C. § 5512(c)(1988).

36 IITF GREEN PAPER, *supra* note 20, at 5-10.

37 *See, e.g.*, T.R. Reid & Peter Behr, *A Software Fight's Blurred Battle Lines*, WASH. POST, Jan. 11, 1994, at D1.

38 Pub. L. No. 93-596, § 3, 88 Stat. 1949 (1975).

39 *See* GOLDSTEIN, *supra* note 1.

and sensible to sever this odd appendage of the legislative branch and join it with the Patent and Trademark Office.

Rather than cluttering up the name of the Office with a reference to yet another area of intellectual property law, the Office should be renamed the Office of Intellectual Property Policy (OIPP). And while the urge to reorganize remains strong, not only copyright and semiconductor chip protection laws,[40] which are currently administered by the Copyright Office, but also the Plant Variety Protection Act,[41] and any subsequently enacted U.S. intellectual property law (e.g. an industrial design law should Congress ever enact one) should be placed under the jurisdiction of OIPP. Different subdivisions of OIPP could oversee each area of law, headed by an official responsible to the Commissioner of OIPP.

Additionally, the Office of the Commissioner of OIPP should include a bureau of competition policy, a bureau of legislative policy, and a bureau of international relations. In this way, the policy initiatives for the various intellectual property laws could be more smoothly developed and could be coordinated in a manner that would enhance the overall performance of the Office and the industries whose interests it regulates.

This reorganization of U.S. intellectual property law administration would leave no room for the Copyright Office as we know it. As an institution, it would cease to exist. Even if some functions or personnel were carried over to a reconstituted Office within the Commerce Department, the Office might well be unrecognizable to traditionalists. No longer would the head of the Office be known as "Register." In the newly-created OIPP, the head of each subdivision might be known by a standardized term such as "Chief of [name of subdivision]." No longer would such an official report to the Librarian of Congress (i.e., to someone who necessarily cares about learning and the dissemination of knowledge), but rather, to a Commerce Department official (i.e., to someone whose job it is to facilitate the success of American businesses).

It is with some regret that I express the view that the administrative reorganization set forth here is inevitable, whether Commissioner Lehman brings it about or not. The regret arises because I believe that learning and the dissemination of knowledge are essential purposes of copyright law. These purposes have, on occasion, served as important constraints on the extent to which

40 17 U.S.C. §§ 901-914 (1988).
41 7 U.S.C. §§ 2401-2404 (1988).

copyright owners can exercise control over the use of copyrighted works.[42] These purposes are in danger of being undervalued or forgotten entirely if the Copyright Office is transplanted from the Library of Congress to the department responsible for promoting commerce in American products, whether they are widgets or informational works.

VI. Another Alternative: Takeover by the F.B.I.

Now that it appears that virtually every copyright infringement is a misdemeanor,[43] and that a great many are felonies,[44] an alternative administrative home for the U.S. Copyright Office might be the Federal Bureau of Investigation.[45] To judge by their recent promotional campaign against "software piracy," it would probably be easy to persuade members of the Software Publishers Association ("SPA") to volunteer to serve as agents of the FBI if they were authorized to arrest all those who had made unauthorized copies of computer programs.[46] The SPA already maintains a hotline that disgruntled employees, alienated teenagers, former girlfriends and boyfriends, and other "informants" can use to report the unauthorized copying of software.[47] Deputizing SPA "auditors" as federal agents could only enhance enforcement efforts in this area. This would also relieve "regular" FBI agents of an otherwise burdensome additional task and allow them to focus on bank robberies and kidnappings.

Of course, the SPA would probably not want to enforce any copyrights except those for software, but it might be willing to train

42 *See, e.g.*, Sony Corp. of Am. v. Universal City Studios, Inc., 464 U.S. 417, 450-51 (1984)("[A] use that has no demonstrable effect upon the potential market for, or the value of, the copyrighted work need not be prohibited in order to protect the author's incentive to create. The prohibition of such noncommercial uses would merely inhibit access to ideas without any countervailing benefit.").

43 Under Title 17 of the United States Code, § 506(a), anyone who infringes a copyright willfully and for commercial advantage or private financial gain has engaged in criminal copyright infringement. 17 U.S.C. § 506(a). This crime is punishable by up to a year in prison, unless the criteria for felony punishment are met. *See* 18 U.S.C. § 2319(b)(3)(1988). Those who take a broad view of this provision would likely argue that anyone who knowingly makes an unauthorized copy of a copyrighted work has violated the provision. The private financial gain element could be met, under this view, on the theory that the defendant benefited by possessing a copy of the work without having to pay the customary price.

44 *See* 18 U.S.C. § 2319(b)(1)-(2)(1988).

45 *See, e.g.*, Jessica Litman, *The Exclusive Right to Read*, 13 Cardozo Arts & Ent. L.J. 29 (1994) (discussing copyright police).

46 The SPA was one of the strongest proponents of the felony provisions for copyright infringement. *See* discussion *supra* note 43. One SPA-sponsored billboard features a picture of a pair of handcuffs above which appears the slogan: "This is the hardware you can get for free if you make unauthorized copies of software."

47 *See* Kahin, *supra* note 31, at 5.

members of the American Society of Composers, Authors, and Publishers (ASCAP); Broadcast Music, Inc. (BMI), and the Copyright Clearance Center (CCC) in copyright enforcement techniques it has mastered in enforcing software copyrights.[48] ASCAP, BMI, and CCC could then supplement the SPA's enforcement efforts so that copyright infringement crimes would not go unpunished.

Publishers have long thought of unauthorized reproduction of copyrighted work as a species of theft,[49] no matter what excuse a defendant might make based on the doctrine adherents refer to as "fair use."[50] Now that intellectual property is coming to be recognized as one of the principal sources of America's economic strength, perhaps infringement will finally be seen as the theft that publishers always thought it to be. What better way could there be to get tough on this rampant crime than to make the U.S. Copyright Office part of the FBI?

Another benefit of making the Copyright Office part of the FBI is that doing so could provide the agency with a new tool for enforcement. In many cases, imaginative prosecutors could add criminal copyright infringement charges to ordinary criminal indictments. For example, someone who breaks into a bank computing system and alters banking records in order to steal money could be charged with criminal copyright infringement, on the grounds that he or she had made an unauthorized derivative work of the banking records willfully and for the sake of private financial gain. The culprit could also be charged with criminal infringement for the unauthorized copying of copyrighted bank records and of the software used to access the records beyond the use-copying privilege set forth in section 117 of the United States Code, title 17.[51] One who engages in espionage against defense contractors to obtain information vital to the national security could conceivably be prosecuted for criminal copyright infringement as well. Espionage typically involves photocopying or photographing documents which copyright law protects automatically from the moment of

---

48 These entities already have enforcement staff and active copyright enforcement programs, but they have principally focused on civil enforcement efforts.

49 *See Sony Corp. of Am.*, 464 U.S. at 450 n.33 (1984) (discussing a proferred analogy between private use copying of copyrighted works and the theft of jewelry for private use only; ultimately rejecting the analogy because one who copies a copyrighted work does not deprive the lawful owner of its rightful possession of the work).

50 The fair use doctrine is found in the copyright statute at 17 U.S.C. § 107 (1988).

51 *See* 17 U.S.C. §§ 106, 506(a)(1988). Only lawful owners of copies of copyrighted software are eligible for the § 117 privilege to make copies of programs in a computer in order to be able to use those programs. 17 U.S.C. § 117.

the first fixation of each document in tangible form.[52] These copies would infringe the exclusive rights of copyright and would be criminal if the copies were made willfully and for private gain.[53] However, until Congress amends the copyright statute to eliminate the rule that works of the U.S. government cannot be copyrighted,[54] the usefulness of criminal copyright infringement charges to punish and deter espionage against the government would be impaired.[55]

While many other examples could be given of the potential benefit of using criminal copyright infringement penalties to punish crimes that have not traditionally been conceived of in copyright terms, let me end with one example that may not seem as far-fetched as those given above. It seems quite likely that those who attempt to decrypt digitized works that have been distributed over a network in encrypted form will eventually be prosecuted for criminal copyright infringement if civil penalties do not prove an effective deterrent.[56] The Green Paper recently published by the NII Working Group on Intellectual Property Rights seems to contemplate this.[57]

To understand how very different a view of copyright this kind of criminal enforcement would bring about, one need only describe the "crime" somewhat differently. Someone who decrypts an encrypted work does so in order to "read" the content of a publicly-distributed, and perhaps even mass-marketed, copyrighted work. Thomas Jefferson would, I think, weep at the thought that the law of copyright, which has historically promoted the dissemination of

---

52 17 U.S.C. § 302(a)(1988) (copyright protection subsists from creation).

53 *See* 17 U.S.C. § 506 (1988); 18 U.S.C. § 2319 (1988).

54 17 U.S.C. § 105 (1988).

55 I mention this "limitation" of copyright law, as presently written, as a way of illustrating that if one reconceives the purpose of copyright law, certain provisions that are quite consistent with the historical purpose of copyright (e.g., promoting the dissemination of knowledge) may be perceived differently.

56 The Ninth Circuit Court of Appeals recently upheld the legality of decompilation of object code forms of computer programs when necessary to get such information as how to construct a compatible program. *See* Sega Enter. v. Accolade, Inc., 977 F.2d 1510 (9th Cir. 1992). Decompilation involves intermediate copying of a copyrighted work in order to understand its contents, which makes it similar to the intermediate copying that would be necessary to decrypt an encrypted copy of a copyrighted work. Given that the court in *Sega* emphasized that the defendant had to have a legitimate purpose in engaging in decompilation, such as seeking to develop a compatible noninfringing program, and that the information being sought was not available except by decompilation, *id.* at 1514, it is doubtful that a decrypter who was simply trying to get a copy of a copyrighted work for less than the customary price would be able to raise a successful *Sega* defense.

57 IITF GREEN PAPER, *supra* note 20, at 125-30. The Working Group points out that if efforts to bypass technological protection constituted copyright infringement, the criminal copyright provisions could be used to punish those who sell decryption or bypass technologies. *See* 17 U.S.C. § 506 (1988); 18 U.S.C. § 2319 (1988) (concerning the criminal copyright provisions).

knowledge, was instead becoming a law which served primarily to prevent information from being disseminated to anyone who has not tithed to the publisher.[58]

VII. Conclusion

The twenty-first century will surely witness many profound changes in legal and social institutions. Among them will be changes in the law of copyright and in the institutional arrangements by which works of authorship are created, readied for market, distributed, and consumed.[59] Inevitably, these changes will affect the Copyright Office. In fact, they may result in its demise. But even assuming that the Office continues to exist, its role in copyright administration is likely to change. Some of the ministerial activities that the Office currently conducts may, in fact, be automated; staff would then be freed-up to engage in more demanding tasks. If one conceives of the Copyright Office's registration data as a valuable repository of useful information, as the Office currently does,[60] the value of constructing a computer database in which this information could be enhanced with additional data provided by copyright owners becomes apparent; it would facilitate low-cost licensing of copyrighted work.[61] This would provide a valuable public service, and would take advantage of opportunities that new technologies provide to redefine and expand the role of the Copyright Office in a socially beneficial way. If the Copyright Office becomes a kind of clearance center for information about the licensing of copyrighted works, the Office will

---

[58] Jefferson, after all, was a believer in the dissemination of knowledge, as is clear from his oft-quoted statement:

> If nature has made any one thing less susceptible than all others of exclusive property, it is the action of the thinking power called an idea, which an individual may exclusively possess as long as he keeps it to himself; but the moment it is divulged, it forces itself into the possession of every one, and the receiver cannot dispossess himself of it . . . . He who receives an idea from me, receives instruction himself without lessening mine; as he who lights his taper at mine, receives light without darkening me. That ideas should freely spread from one to another over the globe, for the moral and mutual instruction of man, and improvement of his condition, seems to have been peculiarly and benevolently designed by nature . . . .

Graham v. John Deere Co., 383 U.S. 1, 8 (1966) (quoting VI Writings of Thomas Jefferson at 180-81 (Washington ed. 1854)).

[59] In previous essays, I have argued that the nature of the digital medium will contribute to these changes. *See* Pamela Samuelson, *Digital Media and the Changing Face of Intellectual Property Law*, 16 Rutgers Computer and Tech. L.J. 323 (1990); Pamela Samuelson, *Some New Kinds of Authorship Made Possible by Computers & Some Intellectual Property Questions They Raise*, 53 U. Pitt. L. Rev. 685 (1992).

[60] *See* Eric Schwartz, *The Role of the Copyright Office in the Age of Information*, 13 Cardozo Arts & Ent. L.J. 69 (1994).

[61] *Id. See also* Kahn & Cerf, *supra* note 30.

be acting in a manner consistent with the historical purpose of copyright law—facilitating the dissemination of knowledge. Because I believe that this purpose should have as much importance in the future as it has had in the past, I applaud the Office's efforts to redefine its role in a manner that will keep the historical function of copyright law vital. This is one strategy that promises to keep the Office alive in the twenty-first century. I wish it well in its efforts.

CHARTING THE COLLAPSE OF THE PATENT-COPYRIGHT DICHOTOMY: PREMISES FOR A RESTRUCTURED INTERNATIONAL INTELLECTUAL PROPERTY SYSTEM

J.H. Reichman*

Introduction

Governments adopt intellectual property laws in the belief that a privileged, monopolistic domain operating on the margins of the free-market economy promotes long-term cultural and technological progress better than a regime of unbridled competition.[1]

---

* B.A. 1955, University of Chicago; J.D. 1979, Yale Law School; Professor of Law, Vanderbilt University, Nashville, TN, U.S.A. © J.H. Reichman, 1995.

The author gratefully acknowledges the thoughtful advice and suggestions that Professors Wendy Gordon, Marci Hamilton, Pamela Samuelson, and Paul Geller have kindly provided.

[1] Intellectual property laws typically provide qualified creators with temporary grants

Ordinary tangible goods that acquire value by satisfying known human needs in more or less standardized ways cannot escape the price-setting function of the competitive market. In contrast, intellectual goods acquire value by deviating from standard solutions to known human needs in ways that yield more efficient outcomes or that capture the public's fancy. Because intellectual goods define relevant market segments in terms of the novelty or the originality they purvey, their creators invent their own markets by stimulating demand for goods that did not previously exist.[2]

By the end of the twentieth century, the role of intellectual property rights in stimulating post-industrial economic development had become so vital that it figured on the agenda for the Uruguay Round of multilateral trade negotiations.[3] The Final Act embodying the results of that Round incorporates an Agreement on Trade-Related Aspects of Intellectual Property Rights ("TRIPS" Agreement) into the Marrakesh Agreement Establishing the World Trade Organization ("WTO").[4] The universal minimum standards

---

of exclusive property rights that derogate from the norms of free competition in order to overcome the "public goods" problem inherent in the commercial exploitation of intangible creations. *See, e.g.*, ROBERT P. BENKO, PROTECTING INTELLECTUAL PROPERTY RIGHTS—ISSUES AND CONTROVERSIES 17-19, 21 (1987) [hereinafter BENKO] (stressing that "knowledge goods . . . create problems of market failure, externalities, and appropriability" and citing the relevant literature); WILLIAM KINGSTON, INNOVATION, CREATIVITY AND LAW 79-106 (1990); *see also* Wendy J. Gordon, *Fair Use as Market Failure: A Structural and Economic Analysis of the* Betamax *Case and its Predecessors*, 82 COLUM. L. REV. 1600, 1610-32 (1982) (stressing role of intellectual property rights in market formation) [hereinafter Gordon, *Fair Use*]. The "public good" characteristic of information and intangible creations generally stems from their indivisibility; no single person's consumption diminishes its availability to others. *See, e.g.*, BENKO, *supra*, at 21; Steven N. S. Cheung, *Property Rights and Invention, in* 8 RESEARCH IN LAW AND ECONOMICS—THE ECONOMICS OF PATENTS AND COPYRIGHTS 5-18 (1986) [hereinafter ECONOMICS OF PATENTS AND COPYRIGHTS] (contrasting views of Arrow with those of Bentham, Taussig, Pigou, and Plant, among others); *see also* Stanley M. Besen & Leo J. Raskind, *An Introduction to the Law and Economics of Intellectual Property*, 5 J. ECON. PERSP. 3, 5 [hereinafter Besen & Raskind] (stating that the "objective of intellectual property protection is to create incentives that maximize the difference between the value of the . . . property . . . created and used and the social cost of its creation, including the cost of administering the system"); Edmund W. Kitch, *Patents: Monopolies or Property Rights?, in* ECONOMICS OF PATENTS AND COPYRIGHTS, *supra*, at 31 [hereinafter Kitch].

2 *See, e.g.*, BENKO, *supra* note 1, at 22-23 (literary, artistic, and scientific works largely "define a society and create new products and markets"); Paul Roubier, *Unité et synthèse des droits de propriété industrielle, in* ETUDES SUR LA PROPRIÉTÉ LITTERAIRE ARTISTIQUE: MELANGE MARCEL PLAISANT 161, 162-66 (1960) (stressing that "industrial competition ends—despite everything—in a process of constant renewal"); *see also* Michael Lehmann, *Property and Intellectual Property—Property Rights as Restrictions on Competition in Furtherance of Competition*, 20 INT'L REV. INDUS. PROP. & COPYRIGHT L. (IIC) 1 (1989).

3 *See* Ministerial Declaration of Punta del Este of September 20, 1986, General Agreement on Tariffs and Trade Doc., MIN. DEC. No. 86-1572 (Sept. 20, 1986), *reprinted in* LAW AND PRACTICE UNDER THE GATT, III.A.3 (K. Simmonds & B. Hill eds. 1989); *see generally* J.H. Reichman, *Intellectual Property in International Trade: Opportunities and Risks of a GATT Connection*, 22 VAND. J. TRANSNAT'L L. 747, 751-68 (1989) [hereinafter Reichman, *GATT Connection*] (contrasting theses of major protagonists in multilateral trade negotiations).

4 *See* Final Act Embodying the Results of the Uruguay Round of Multilateral Trade Negotiations, Marrakesh Agreement Establishing the World Trade Organization, *signed at*

of protection set out in the TRIPS Agreement tend to detach intellectual property rights from their historical roots in territorial law and to align them more closely with general norms of public and private international law applicable to older, more tangible forms of property.[5]

In so doing, however, the drafters of the TRIPS Agreement undertook no new economic or legal analysis to justify or validate the elevation of pre-existing intellectual property rights to the status of universal norms.[6] On the contrary, they deliberately built upon the Paris Convention for the Protection of Industrial Property (1883) and the Berne Convention for the Protection of Literary and Artistic Works (1886),[7] as progressively developed[8] and

---

Marrakesh (Morocco), April 15, 1994 [hereinafter WTO Agreement], Annex 1C, Agreement on Trade-Related Aspects of Intellectual Property Rights [hereinafter TRIPS Agreement], *reprinted in* THE RESULTS OF THE URUGUAY ROUND OF MULTILATERAL TRADE NEGOTIATIONS—THE LEGAL TEXTS 1-19, 365-403 (GATT Secretariat, ed. 1994).

5 *See generally* J.H. Reichman, *Universal Minimum Standards of Intellectual Property Protection Under the TRIPS Component of the WTO Agreement,* 29 INT'L LAW. 345 (1995) [hereinafter Reichman, *Universal Minimum Standards*]; J.H. Reichman, *The TRIPS Component of the GATT's Uruguay Round: Competitive Prospects for Intellectual Property Owners in an Integrated World Market,* 4 FORDHAM INTELL. PROP., MEDIA & ENTERT. L.J. 171, 173-78, 191-202, 224-42 (1993) [hereinafter Reichman, *TRIPS Component*]; *see also* Paul Edward Geller, *Intellectual Property in the Global Marketplace: Impact of TRIPS Dispute Settlements?,* 29 INT'L LAW 99, 101-03 (1995) [hereinafter Geller, *Dispute Settlements*]; J.H. Reichman, *Beyond the Historical Lines of Demarcation: Competition Law, Intellectual Property Rights, and International Trade After the GATT's Uruguay Round,* 20 BROOKLYN J. INT'L L. 75 (1993) [hereinafter Reichman, *Competition, Intellectual Property and Trade*]. The industrialized countries' demand for improved international protection of intellectual goods within the framework of a GATT agreement can be construed as a collective declaration that pre-existing rules of public international law that disfavored intangible forms of property must change in order to keep pace with changed economic conditions. *See* Reichman, *GATT Connection, supra* note 3, at 810-11. However, harmonization at the international level requires states to abandon deeply entrenched local practices, and consensus remains hard to achieve even among countries that are otherwise similarly situated. *See, e.g.,* HAROLD C. WEGNER, PATENT HARMONIZATION—BY TREATY OR DOMESTIC REFORM 23-26, 44-77 (1993) [hereinafter WEGNER] (discussing bases of United States resistance to proposed patent harmonization treaty).

6 For the grudging acceptance of orthodox legal and economic justifications of intellectual property rights, and the continuing resistance to these justifications in certain quarters, see *infra* notes 46-52 and accompanying text.

7 Paris Convention for the Protection of Industrial Property, March 20, 1883, *as last revised* at Stockholm, July 14, 1967, 21 U.S.T. 1583, T.I.A.S. No. 6923, 828 U.N.T.S. 305 [hereinafter Paris Convention]; Berne Convention for the Protection of Literary and Artistic Works, Sept. 9, 1886, *as last revised* at Paris, July 24, 1971, 828 U.N.T.S. 22 [hereinafter Berne Convention]. The TRIPS Agreement requires all WTO member countries to comply with articles 1 through 21 of the Berne Convention (1971) and the Appendix thereto, but not with Article 6*bis* on moral rights. *See* TRIPS Agreement, *supra* note 4, art. 9. It also mandates compliance with articles 1 - 12 and 19 of the Paris Convention. *See* TRIPS Agreement, *supra* note 4, art. 2(1).

8 The Paris and Berne Conventions, *supra* note 7, were revised at periodic intervals up to 1967 and 1971, respectively. *See, e.g.,* G.H.C. BODENHAUSEN, GUIDE TO THE APPLICATION OF THE PARIS CONVENTION FOR THE PROTECTION OF INDUSTRIAL PROPERTY AS REVISED AT STOCKHOLM IN 1967, 9-11 (1968) [hereinafter BODENHAUSEN]; WORLD INTELLECTUAL PROPERTY ORGANIZATION (W.I.P.O.), GUIDE TO THE BERNE CONVENTION FOR THE PROTECTION OF LITERARY AND ARTISTIC WORKS (PARIS ACT 1971) at 6 (1978) [hereinafter GUIDE TO THE BERNE CONVENTION]. For the gradual formation of consensually recognized international

supplemented by other international agreements.[9] These "Great Conventions," as they are known, established a worldwide constitutional framework that directly or indirectly configures the various domestic systems on which it rests.[10] Their nineteenth-century conceptual underpinnings remain central to the operations of the international intellectual property system as further broadened and strengthened by the TRIPS Agreement.

This Article is one in a series of studies[11] that questions the

---

minimum standards of protection, see, e.g., STEPHEN P. LADAS, PATENTS, TRADEMARKS AND RELATED RIGHTS: NATIONAL AND INTERNATIONAL PROTECTION 59-94, 1884, 1887-88, 1904-05 (1975) [hereinafter LADAS, INDUSTRIAL PROPERTY]; David Ladd, *To Cope With the World Upheaval in Copyright*, 19 COPYRIGHT (W.I.P.O.) 289, 290 (Oct. 1983) (stressing that, in the past, "domestic law-making served as a precursor of gradual elaboration of the Berne Convention"). The failure of later efforts to revise the Paris Convention gave rise to multilateral trade negotiations to resolve the impasse.

9 The single most important treaty supplementing both the Paris and Berne Conventions is now the TRIPS Agreement, *supra* note 4. Examples of other important treaties that supplement the protection of industrial property under the Paris Convention include the Patent Cooperation Treaty, June 19, 1970, 28 U.S.T. 7645, *with regulations at* 28 U.S.T. 7813; Convention on the Grant of European Patents, October 5, 1973, 1160 U.N.T.S. 231 [European Patent Convention]; The Treaty on Intellectual Property in Respect of Integrated Circuits, *opened for signature at* Washington, May 26, 1989 [IPIC Treaty]; The Madrid Agreement Concerning the International Registration of Marks, April 14, 1891, *as last revised* July 14, 1967, Stockholm, U.N.T.S. 11852; Budapest Treaty on the International Recognition of the Deposit of Microorganisms for the Purposes of Patent Procedure, April 28, 1977, 32 U.S.T. 1241, 17 I.L.M. 285 *with regulations at* 32 U.S.T. 1252; International Convention for the Protection of New Varieties of Plants, December 2, 1961, 33 U.S.T. 2703, 815 U.N.T.S. 89 [UPOV], *as last revised* March 19, 1991; Hague Agreement Concerning the International Registration of Industrial Designs and Models, June 2, 1934, 205 L.N.T.S. 179, *as amended* at the Hague, Nov. 28, 1960 [Hague Agreement]. The TRIPS Agreement mandates compliance with main provisions of the IPIC treaty covering integrated circuit designs. *See* TRIPS Agreement, *supra* note 4, art. 35.

On the copyright side of the ledger, the Universal Copyright Convention, Sept. 6, 1952, 6 U.S.T. 2731, 216 U.N.T.S. 133, *as last revised* July 24, 1971, 25 U.S.T. 1341 [hereinafter U.C.C.], constructed a bridge between Berne and non-Berne countries that has diminished in importance since the United States adhered to Berne in 1989. *See, e.g.*, STEPHEN M. STEWART WITH HAMISH SANDISON, INTERNATIONAL COPYRIGHT AND NEIGHBORING RIGHTS 146-49 (2d ed. 1989) [hereinafter STEWART]. Of growing importance, in contrast, are the treaties regulating so-called rights allied to or neighboring on copyright law. *See, e.g.*, International Convention for the Protection of Performers, Producers of Phonograms and Broadcasting Organizations, *done* at Rome, Italy, Oct. 26, 1961, 496 U.N.T.S. 43 [hereinafter Rome Convention]; Convention for the Protection of Producers of Phonograms Against Unauthorized Duplication of Their Phonograms, *done* at Geneva, Switzerland, Oct. 29, 1971, 25 U.S.T. 309, 866 U.N.T.S. 67; *see generally* WORLD INTELLECTUAL PROPERTY ORGANIZATION (W.I.P.O.), GUIDE TO THE ROME CONVENTION AND TO THE PHONOGRAMS CONVENTION 7-13 (1981) [hereinafter GUIDE TO THE ROME CONVENTION]. The U.S. does not adhere to the Rome Convention.

10 *See, e.g.*, 1 LADAS, INDUSTRIAL PROPERTY, *supra* note 8, at 14-15; SAM RICKETSON, THE BERNE CONVENTION FOR THE PROTECTION OF LITERARY AND ARTISTIC WORKS: 1886-1986, at 39-41, 917-21 (1987) [hereinafter RICKETSON].

11 *See, e.g.*, J.H. Reichman, *Legal Hybrids Between the Patent and Copyright Paradigms*, 94 COLUM. L. REV. 2432 (1994) [hereinafter *Legal Hybrids*]; Pamela Samuelson, Randall Davis, Mitchell D. Kapor, & J.H. Reichman, *A Manifesto Concerning the Legal Protection of Computer Programs*, 94 COLUM. L. REV. 2308 (1994) [hereinafter Samuelson et. al, *Manifesto*]; *see also* Jerome H. Reichman, *Electronic Information Tools—The Outer Edge of World Intellectual Property Law*, 24 I.I.C. 446 (1993) [hereinafter Reichman, *Electronic Information Tools*]; J.H. Reichman, *Computer Programs as Applied Scientific Know-How: Implications of Copyright Protec-*

capability of this inherited institutional framework to meet the needs of creators, innovators and investors operating under the changed conditions of an Information Age.[12] It re-examines certain negative economic premises underlying the patent and copyright paradigms and explains how these premises are tacitly implemented in a compartmentalized, bipolar framework that supports the international intellectual property system as historically conceived. The Article then suggests that a proliferation of hybrid legal regimes falling outside this classical framework routinely violates its cardinal economic premises and disrupts the historical balance between free competition and legal incentives to create. Once these hybrid or deviant regimes are taken into account, the real structure of the international intellectual property system as it empirically operates at the end of the twentieth century differs radically from the bipolar structure embodied in the Great Conventions at the end of the nineteenth century.

The Article concludes with the thought that efforts to balance the public and private interests at stake in devising legal incentives for twenty-first-century innovation are likely to produce cycles of under- and overprotection until the economic implications of existing hybrid legal regimes are better understood. Another study, entitled *Legal Hybrids Between the Patent and Copyright Paradigms,*[13] has recently begun this task. Meanwhile, the discrepancies between the nineteenth-century historical construct and the twentieth-century empirical realities charted in this Article suggest that the TRIPS Agreement could yield fewer beneficial results than anticipated and, in some areas, could even compound the social disutilities stemming from an obsolete and increasingly dysfunctional institutional framework.[14] The Article ends by reaffirming the need for a new intellectual property paradigm[15] specifically devised for the conditions that induce legislators everywhere to enact hybrid regimes that deviate from the legal and economic logic of the international intellectual property system as historically conceived.

---

tion for Commercialized University Research, 42 VAND. L. REV. 639, 648-67 (1989) [hereinafter Reichman, *Programs as Know-How*].

12 *See, e.g.,* STEPHEN SAXBY, THE AGE OF INFORMATION 11-40 (1990); ANNE WELLS BRANSCOMB, WHO OWNS INFORMATION? 174-86 (1994); EJAN MACKAAY, ECONOMICS OF INFORMATION AND LAW 107-72 (1982).

13 *See supra* note 11.

14 *See also* Reichman, *Competition, Intellectual Property Rights and Trade, supra* note 5, at 113-19.

15 *See generally Legal Hybrids, supra* note 11, at 2504-2557.

I. Bipolar Structure of the International Intellectual Property System

The term "intellectual property" was not coined until the late nineteenth century. Only when Josef Kohler and Edmond Picard perceived that copyright, patent, and trademark laws had more in common with each other than with the older forms of property known to Roman law was it recognized that a new class of rights in intangible creations had arisen.[16] Their use of the term "intellectual property" thus coincided with the drive for international regulation of both artistic and industrial property, a movement destined to produce a fully articulated and universally recognized legal discourse in little more than a century.[17]

A. *Nature and Limits of the Dominant Intellectual Property Paradigms*

Taken together, the Paris and Berne Conventions purport to subdivide the international intellectual property system into two hermetically sealed compartments separated by a common line of demarcation. Literary and artistic property rights occupy one of these compartments; so-called industrial property rights occupy the other.[18]

1. The Patent and Copyright Subsystems

The origins of the bipolar structure can be traced to cornerstone provisions of the Great Conventions extant since their inception and to corresponding state practices recognized by most

---

16 *See* 1 Stephen P. Ladas, The International Protection of Literary and Artistic Property 9-10 (1938) [hereinafter Ladas, Artistic Property]; *see also* Pierre Recht, Le Droit d'Auteur: Une Nouvelle Forme De Propriété 229-33 (1969); Paul Edward Geller, *International Copyright Law: An Introduction*, *in* 1 International Copyright Law and Practice § 1[3] [a] (P.E. Geller rev. ed., 1994) ("Copyright might well be said to be . . . a bundle of rights in search of a doctrine") [hereinafter International Copyright Law and Practice].

17 *See, e.g.*, 1 Ladas, Industrial Property, *supra* note 8, at 3 (stating that international protection of industrial property rights "could not possibly begin before the last century" and emphasizing that maturation of industrial property law often coincided with its international protection). *See generally* Arpad Bogsch, *The First Hundred Years of the Paris Convention for the Protection of Industrial Property*, 19 Indus. Prop. 191 (1983); Arpad Bogsch, *The First Hundred Years of the Berne Convention for the Protection of Literary and Artistic Works*, 22 Copyright (W.I.P.O.) 291 (1986).

18 *See, e.g.*, 1 Ladas, Industrial Property, *supra* note 8, at 1 (stating that "the division of intellectual property into literary or artistic and industrial property is very generally admitted"). Industrial property rights in this context embrace both legal monopolies to stimulate individual creations, such as patents, utility models, and design rights, and the very different regimes concerned with trademarks, trade names, appellations of origin and unfair competition in general. The assimilation of these diverse rights under a single rubric termed "industrial property" within a comprehensive, foundational treaty was largely a matter of convenience and historical accident. *See, e.g.*, 1 *id.* at 2-3, 2 *id.* at 967-70 (stressing the comparatively recent origins of most intellectual property rights).

developed intellectual property systems. On the one hand, Article 1 of the Berne Convention established "a Union for the protection of the rights of authors in their literary and artistic works."[19] Such works, categorized at length in Article 2(1), should receive automatic and mandatory protection in the domestic copyright laws of the member states.[20] To avoid censorship and to liberate authors from overt and covert forms of patronage,[21] these laws entitle almost all independently created works falling within the designated subject matter categories to a generous but relatively soft form of protection against copying only that lasts a long period of time.[22]

On the other hand, Articles 1(1) and 1(2) of the Paris Convention established "a Union for the protection of industrial property"[23] and identified certain legal institutions as the "object" of industrial property protection, namely, "patents, utility models, industrial designs, trademarks, service marks, trade names, indications of source . . . and the repression of unfair competition."[24] While some international minimum standards and the rule of national treatment apply to all these institutions,[25] the Paris Convention entrusted the protection of industrial creations primarily to "the various kinds of industrial patents recognized by the laws of

---

19 *See* Berne Convention, *supra* note 7, Preamble, art. 1; GUIDE TO THE BERNE CONVENTION, *supra* note 8, at 5-11.

20 *See* Berne convention, *supra* note 7, arts. 2(1), 2(6). Article 2(1), which derives from article 4 of the 1886 text, states that the "expression 'literary and artistic works' shall include every production in the literary, scientific and artistic domain, whatever may be the mode or form of its expression," and then provides a detailed list of mandatory subject matters. *Id.*; *cf.* 17 U.S.C. § 102(a) (1988) (providing copyright protection for "original works of authorship" and listing eligible subject-matter categories).

21 *See* 1 LADAS, ARTISTIC PROPERTY, *supra* note 16, at 10-11; RICKETSON, *supra* note 10, at 3-8.

22 *See* Berne Convention, *supra* note 7, arts. 2(1), 2(6), 5(2), 7(1) (requiring minimum term of life plus fifty years). Although the Berne Convention imposes no international minimum standard of eligibility, the domestic copyright laws are remarkably similar in the following respects: only originality or subjective novelty is required, not objective novelty; only the form or expression is protected, not ideas; and proof of independent creation constitutes a valid defense to an action for infringement. *See, e.g.*, GUIDE TO THE BERNE CONVENTION, *supra* note 8, at 12, 17; ALAIN STROWEL, DROIT D'AUTEUR ET COPYRIGHT—DIVERGENCES ET CONVERGENCES 391-401, 468-81, 623-33, 644-51 (1993); 1 PAUL GOLDSTEIN, PRINCIPLES, LAW AND PRACTICE §§ 1.2 - 1.10 (1989 and Supp. 1994) [hereinafter GOLDSTEIN]. *But see* IVAN CHERPILLOD, L'OBJET DU DROIT D'AUTEUR 59-109, 183-85 (1985) (rejecting idea-expression distinction in both theory and practice). State practice generally recognizes the principle that forbids discrimination on the basis of artistic merit. *See, e.g.*, GUIDE TO THE BERNE CONVENTION, *supra* note 8, at 12-13; Bleistein v. Donaldson Lithographing Co., 188 U.S. 239, 251 (1903).

23 *See* Paris Convention, *supra* note 7, art. 1(1).

24 *Id.* art. 1(2) (stating that the "protection of *industrial property* has as its *object* patents, utility models; [etc.]") (emphasis added).

25 *See id.* art. 2(1) (rule of national treatment "as regards the protection of industrial property"); 1 LADAS, INDUSTRIAL PROPERTY, *supra* note 8, 271-76 ("unionist treatment"); BODENHAUSEN, *supra* note 8, at 13-16.

the countries of the Union."[26] The patent paradigm and variants thereof classically confer a tougher form of protection on strict formal and substantive conditions for a relatively short period of time.[27]

2. The Historical Line of Demarcation

Because the domestic patent and copyright regimes afford fundamentally different types of protection, the line of demarcation between the Paris and Berne Conventions becomes of paramount importance. A line that appears unclear or poorly defended will tempt entrepreneurs to circumvent the strict prerequisites of patent law, with its basic requirements of novelty, utility, and nonobviousness, in order to shelter industrial creations within the more receptive and generous embrace of copyright law, which applies without regard to artistic merit.[28] An unclear line of demarcation also leads to the risk that the same subject matter will attract different proprietary regimes. This, in turn, renders classical intellectual property theory incoherent and breeds endless contradictions.[29]

A body of historical evidence pertaining to industrial design makes it logical to characterize this line of demarcation in terms of a discredited dichotomy between "art" and "utility."[30] However, the international conventions did not expressly sanction this inter-

---

26 Paris Convention, *supra* note 7, art. 1(4) (not defining patents and recognizing, among others, "patents of importation, patents of improvement, patents and certificates of addition, etc.")

27 *See, e.g.*, JAY DRATLER, JR., INTELLECTUAL PROPERTY LAW: COMMERCIAL, CREATIVE AND INDUSTRIAL PROPERTY § 103[1] (1992) [hereinafter DRATLER] ("Patents provide the strongest protection of any form of intellectual property"). The domestic patent laws normally apply stringent requirements of objective novelty and nonobviousness (or an "inventive step"), which limit the patent paradigm to exceptional or non-routine advances in the art. *See, e.g.*, 35 U.S.C. §§ 102, 103, 271(a), (b) (1994); DRATLER, *supra* (stating that the patent law's "right to exclude is well-nigh absolute"). A weakness of the Paris Convention is that it imposes no international minimum standards concerning the subject matter of patentability, substantive prerequisites, or duration. However, the TRIPS Agreement, *supra* note 4, arts. 27-34, now mandates the extension of patentability to virtually all fields of technology recognized in developed patent systems, prolongs patent protection to a uniform term of twenty years from the date of filing (formerly seventeen years from issuance in U.S. law, 35 U.S.C. § 154 (1994)), and lays down detailed obligations concerning the exclusive rights to be granted. *See generally* Reichman, *Universal Minimum Standards*, *supra* note 5, pt. II.A; Reichman, *Competition, Intellectual Property and Trade*, *supra* note 5, at 98-105.

28 *See* 35 U.S.C. §§ 102, 103 (1994); Baker v. Selden, 101 U.S. 99 (1879); *supra* note 22 (principle of nondiscrimination as to merit).

29 *See, e.g.*, J.H. Reichman, *Overlapping Proprietary Rights in University-Generated Research Products: The Case of Computer Programs*, 17 COLUM.-VLA J.L. & ARTS 51, 60-109 (1992) [hereinafter Reichman, *Overlapping Proprietary Rights*]; Marie-Angèle Pérot-Morel, *La double protection des dessins et modèles*, *in* LE DROIT D'AUTEUR AUJOURDHUI 117-20 (Isabelle de Lamberterie ed., 1991) (case of commercial designs).

30 *See, e.g.*, FRANÇOIS PERRET, L'AUTONOMIE DU REGIME DE PROTECTION DES DESSINS ET MODÈLES 26-29 (1974); *see also* Mazer v. Stein, 347 U.S. 201 (1954).

pretation or others, equally intractable,[31] that appeal to philosophical or even political biases. Rather, the Great Conventions took a more empirical approach, adopted for mundane economic purposes, that turned on the definition of "industrial property" in Article 1(3) of the Paris Convention.[32]

This definition deliberately left nothing to the discretion of the member states. It dictated that "industrial property shall be understood in the broadest sense and shall apply not only to industry and commerce proper, but likewise to agricultural and extractive industries and to all manufactured or natural *products*, for example, wines, grain, tobacco leaf, fruit, cattle, minerals, mineral waters, beer, flowers, and flour."[33] In effect, this provision casts "industrial property" in terms of every conceivable product available for sale on the general products market in order "to avoid excluding . . . activities or products which would otherwise run the risk of not being assimilated to those of industry proper."[34] Its sole major exclusion is for those literary and artistic works subject to domestic copyright laws that were later covered by Article 2(1) of the Berne Convention and by Article I of the Universal Copyright Convention (U.C.C.).[35]

Apart from the rule of national treatment, states members of the Paris Union are seldom required to take any particular action with regard to any of the product categories listed in this broad definition of industrial property.[36] The industrial property defined in Article 1(3) thus constitutes the true subject matter of protection under the Paris Convention, as distinct from the legal regimes, such as the domestic patent and trademark laws, through which its protection may or may not be perfected.[37] At the same time, the

---

31 *See generally* J.H. Reichman, *Design Protection in Domestic and Foreign Copyright Law: From the Berne Revision of 1948 to the Copyright Act of 1976*, 1983 DUKE L.J. 1143, 1153-70 [hereinafter Reichman, *Design Protection*] (citing authorities).

32 Paris Convention, *supra* note 7, art. 1(3).

33 *Id.*, art. 1(3) (definition of industrial property) (emphasis added).

34 BODENHAUSEN, *supra* note 8, at 25.

35 *See* Berne Convention, *supra* note 7, art. 2(1), U.C.C., *supra* note 9, art. I (obliging member states "to provide for the adequate and effective protection of the rights of authors and other copyright proprietors in literary, scientific and artistic works").

36 Paris Convention, *supra* note 7, art. 2(1) (mandating national treatment); BODENHAUSEN, *supra* note 8 at 25; 1 LADAS, INDUSTRIAL PROPERTY, *supra* note 8, at 265; *see also supra* note 27.

37 *See, e.g.*, BODENHAUSEN, *supra* note 8, at 24, 25. To the extent that these states choose to protect intangible industrial property rights in any of the products within article 1(3) of the Paris Convention, and do so by means of the legal institutions set out in article 1(2), then they must recognize the minimum international standards that apply to these legal institutions in addition to the rule of national treatment. *See* Paris Convention, *supra* note 7, arts. 1(2), 2(1); 1 LADAS, INDUSTRIAL PROPERTY, *supra* note 8, at 263-65, 271-76; BODENHAUSEN, *supra* note 8, at 13-16. If, however, states members choose to protect "industrial property"—as objectively defined in article 1(3)—outside the confines of these

definition of industrial property functionally determines the jurisdictional reach of the Paris Convention in relation to the international copyright conventions. In effect, this line of demarcation appears to turn not strictly on the "art versus utility" criterion, but rather on the distinction between "products" of industrial and commercial activity "in the broadest sense"[38] that are sold on the general products market, and literary and artistic "productions"[39] that are not.

In principle, the patent and copyright subsystems thus meet each other face to face across this common frontier.[40] The clarity of this juncture is enhanced by noting that domestic and international industrial property laws normally exclude technical writings as such from eligibility as patentable subject matter.[41] Conversely, technical and utilitarian writings normally fall within the jurisdiction of national and international copyright laws, at least to the extent of their expression and not their ideas.[42]

That this line of demarcation has become less air tight and unequivocal over time than the nineteenth-century draftsmen had intended cannot be denied. The old puzzle of industrial art (*i.e.*,

---

legal institutions or by means of new legal institutions not known to the founding fathers, then only the rule of national treatment but not the minimum standards would continue to apply. In either case, subject only to the cardinal principle of national treatment set out in article 2(1), the states members remained largely free to determine both the nature and level of protection to be afforded any product category, in keeping with their own economic self-interest vis-a-vis other states participating in a competitive world market. *See* Paris Convention, *supra* note 7, art. 2(1); Reichman, *GATT Connection, supra* note 3, at 847-48, 851-53. The TRIPS Agreement, *supra* note 4, greatly limits this freedom. *See supra* note 27.

38 Paris Convention, *supra* note 7, art. 1(3) (definition of industrial property).

39 For the technical distinction between literary and artistic productions in general and the "works" that are objects of international copyright protection, see Berne Convention, *supra* note 7, art. 2(1).

40 *See also infra* notes 98-100 and accompanying text, and Figure 1.

41 *See, e.g.*, PETER D. ROSENBERG, PATENT LAW FUNDAMENTALS § 6.02[3] (2d ed. 1994) (stating that "printed matter by itself is nonstatutory subject matter," although printed matter "in combination with physical means . . . may engender a new functional relationship") (emphasis deleted). In U.S. law, the technical rationale is that an arrangement of words conveys novelty of concepts rather than of physical structure. *Id.* For echoes of the international demarcation line in the U.S. Constitution, see U.S. CONST., art. I, § 8, cl. 8 (distinguishing "Authors and Writings" from "Inventors and Discoveries"); *see also* DRATLER, *supra* note 27, § 1.01[3] (noting constitutional authority for treating inventions and works of authorship as "distinct fields of subject matter" and stating that, at the time of the Industrial Revolution "printed matter was the only commercially significant subject of copyright law and the fields of industrial technology and publishing were quite distinct").

42 *See supra* note 20 (quoting Berne Convention, *supra* note 7, art. 2(1)); 17 U.S.C. § 101 (definitions of pictorial, graphic and sculptural works and of literary works), §§ 102(a), (b), 113(a) (1988); Baker v. Selden, 101 U.S. 99 (1879); 2 GOLDSTEIN, *supra* note 22, §§ 8.4 (factual works), 8.5 (functional works). For parallel practices in foreign copyright law, see Reichman, *Electronic Information Tools, supra* note 11, at 449-51; *see also* Jane C. Ginsberg, *Creation and Commercial Value: Copyright Protection of Works of Information*, 90 COLUM. L. REV. 1865, 1881-1900 (1990) (distinguishing between low- and high-authorship works and criticizing personality-based theories of copyright protection).

commercial designs) and the new puzzle of industrial literature (*i.e.*, computer programs), for example, conjure up endless ambiguities.[43] For present purposes, nonetheless, it suffices to establish, *first, that "industrial property" and "literary and artistic works" entirely occupied the classical intellectual property universe at the international level;*[44] *and second, that the predominant legal subsystems operating within that universe of discourse were historically separated by a line of demarcation cast in terms of the general products market.* As will be seen from the next section, this bipolar structure rested upon a shrewd economic calculus.

B. *Negative Economic Premises Underlying the Dominant Legal Paradigms*

The liberal economic system of the nineteenth century formally recognized only two fundamental exceptions to the general norms of competition, one for patentable inventions that took a major step beyond the pre-existing prior art, and another for literary and artistic works subject to the very different and far more generous modalities of the copyright paradigm.[45] Since then, economists have become increasingly convinced that the exceptions to the rules of competition that patent and copyright laws carve out for inventors and authors at any given level of innovation actually stimulate competition in the long run by eliciting the production of scarce intangible goods and by elevating routine technical skills to ever higher levels.[46] Succinctly stated, this body of law

---

43 *See, e.g.*, Reichman, *Design Protection, supra* note 31, at 1153-1170; Samuelson et. al, *Manifesto, supra* note 11, at 2347-56.

44 After the Second World War, additional international conventions recognizing rights related to copyright or "Neighboring Rights Conventions" were adopted, with a view to strengthening the protection of performances, sound recordings, and broadcasts. *See supra* note 9; Herman Cohen Jehoram, *The Nature of Neighboring Rights of Performing Artists, Phonogram Producers and Broadcasting Organizations,* 15 COLUM.-VLA J.L. & ARTS 75 (1990).

45 Article 2 of the Paris Convention, as redacted in 1883, also recognized industrial designs for purposes of national treatment, without mandating their protection. *See* Convention of Paris for the Protection of Industrial Property, Mar. 20, 1883, art. 2, *reprinted in* WORLD INTELLECTUAL PROPERTY ORGANIZATION [W.I.P.O.], 1 MANUAL OF INDUSTRIAL PROPERTY CONVENTIONS, item A-1 (1978). The protection of designs was mandated in 1958. *See* Paris Convention, *supra* note 7, art. 5*quinquies.* Utility models are also recognized for purposes of national treatment and priority. *See id.* arts. 1(2), 2(1), 4A(1).

46 *See, e.g.*, F.M. SCHERER, INNOVATION AND GROWTH 127 (1984) ("What is needed for a rapid state of technological advance is the proper blend of competition and monopoly."); Lehmann, *supra* note 2, at 11-15; *see also* Michael Lehmann, *The Theory of Property Rights and the Protection of Intellectual and Industrial Property,* 16 I.I.C. 525 (1985) [hereinafter Lehmann (1985)]; William M. Landes & Richard A. Posner, *An Economic Analysis of Copyright Law,* 18 J. LEGAL STUD. 325 (1989); Edmund W. Kitch, *The Nature and Function of The Patent System,* 20 J. L. & ECON. 265 (1977) [hereinafter Kitch, *Patent System*]. Consumers and users are thought to benefit from these exceptions, despite the diminished price competition, by gaining the opportunity to choose new products or processes over previously available products and processes that are perceived as inferior.

grants creators a bundle of exclusive property rights devised to overcome the "public good" problem arising from the intangible, indivisible and inexhaustible nature of intellectual creations, which allows them to be copied by second comers who have not shared in the costs and risks of the creative endeavor.[47]

The literature also attributes a number of important ancillary functions to the temporary monopolies emanating from these regimes. Patents, for example, stimulate disclosure of major discoveries that might otherwise remain under trade secret law.[48] In addition, both patents and copyrights provide a winner-take-all reward in case of commercial success, which helps to overcome the risk aversion inherent in prospecting for path-breaking discoveries or for artistic works that enrich the culture or that capture the pub-

---

[47] *See supra* note 1. Intellectual goods in general are "scarce" before the acts of creation and divulgation, when risk aversion is high and the success of the innovative enterprise uncertain. The scarcity of any particular intellectual good tends to vanish with creation and disclosure, absent the fictitious "portable fences" of intellectual property law, backed by the power of the state. These fences neutralize essential attributes of property that possession would ordinarily confer and restrict the possessors' rights to use the achievements embodied in the artifacts even within the confines of their private estates. *See, e.g.*, MACKAAY, *supra* note 12, at 115-17; Wendy J. Gordon, *An Inquiry Into the Merits of Copyright: The Challenges of Consistency, Consent, and Encouragement Theory*, 41 STAN. L. REV. 1343, 1378-84 (1989) [hereinafter Gordon, *Inquiry*] ("Because the nature of intellectual property and tangible property boundaries differ, the natures of 'trespass' and 'infringement' differ. Yet the boundaries function alike in identifying what constitutes 'property.' "). To the extent that neither originators nor the entrepreneurs who exploit their output can erect fences around creations that are both intangible and inexhaustible, second comers who obtain material embodiments of these creations from the stream of commerce may appropriate future profits without having shared in the costs and risks of the creative endeavor. *See, e.g.*, BENKO, *supra* note 1, at 17, 21-24; Lehmann (1985), *supra* note 46, at 534 (stressing vulnerability of technical knowledge and information); Hans Ullrich, *The Importance of Industrial Property and Other Legal Measures in the Promotion of Technological Innovation*, 28 INDUS. PROP. 102, 103-04 (1989). In effect, exclusive intellectual property rights substitute relatively long statutory periods of artificial lead time for the uncertain period of natural lead time that competition in intellectual achievements otherwise tends to produce. *Cf. Legal Hybrids*, *supra* note 11, at 2438-42. *But see* BENKO, *supra* note 1, at 19 (critics of intellectual property system believe innovators gain sufficient natural lead time over competitors who must master technological know-how). Exclusive intellectual property rights also mandate a contractual relation between creator and exploiter that prevents competitors from using the creator's contribution in specified ways without paying for the privilege. *See, e.g.*, Roubier, *supra* note 2, at 164 (stressing that the exclusive right to reproduce, which constitutes an essential element of intellectual property, gives intellectual creations the quality of "goods" in both the legal and economic sense of the term). This, in turn, allows the market for intellectual creations to develop and organize itself with a relative degree of efficiency, in keeping with the efficiencies generally thought to derive from the recognition of property rights in material objects. *See, e.g.*, Ejan MacKaay, *Economic Incentives in Markets for Information and Innovation*, 13 HARV. J.L. & PUB. POL'Y 867, 885-906 (1990) [hereinafter MacKaay, *Economic Incentives*]; Lehmann, *supra* note 2, at 11-15; Wendy J. Gordon, *Asymmetric Market Failure and Prisoner's Dilemma in Intellectual Property*, 17 U. DAYTON L. REV. 853, 854-59 (1992) (discussing conditions for market failure).

[48] *See, e.g.*, Jack Hirshleifer, *The Private and Social Value of Information and the Reward to Inventive Activity*, 61 AM. ECON. REV. 561, 569-73 (1971); Rebecca S. Eisenberg, *Proprietary Rights and the Norms of Science in Biotechnology Research*, 97 YALE L.J. 177, 190-91 (1987).

lic's fancy.[49] Exclusive property rights facilitate a reasonably efficient allocation of resources to the tasks of transferring major scientific breakthroughs to industry,[50] or of organizing the costly public dissemination of artistic works whose commercial value cannot be determined in advance.

Whether, and under what conditions, such a system actually delivers a relatively efficient market for intellectual goods remains controversial,[51] and little would be served either by rehashing the abundant literature this enduring controversy still elicits or by reviewing in detail the positive modalities by which states implement the mature patent and copyright paradigms.[52] Of primary concern here, instead, are certain *negative economic premises* that appear to underlie the dominant legal paradigms but that have attracted less attention from scholars and publicists. To understand why the classical intellectual property system has begun to break down, one must first grasp the nature and role of these negative premises. One must then test the accuracy of the behavioral assumptions on which they rest against the realities of legislative and judicial action in the second half of the twentieth century, a task that has been carried out in another study.[53]

For example, the positive modalities of patent law are known to provide inventors in developed countries with an absolute right of exclusion for a relatively short period of time if they satisfy the strict substantive prerequisites of novelty, utility, and above all, nonobviousness.[54] Yet, one also finds at least four negative eco-

---

49 *See* Kitch, *Patent System*, *supra* note 46, at 266-75.

50 *Id.* at 276-80.

51 *See, e.g.*, George L. Priest, *What Economists Can Tell Lawyers About Intellectual Property: Comment on Cheung*, 8 RES. IN L. AND ECON. 19, 21 (John Palmer ed., 1986) (stating that there is no consensus about the effect on social welfare of intellectual property systems); *see also* Tom G. Palmer, *Are Patents and Copyrights Morally Justified? The Philosophy of Property Rights and Ideal Objects*, 13 HARV. J.L. & PUB. POL'Y 817 (1990); David Vaver, *Some Agnostic Observations on Intellectual Property*, 6 INTELL. PROP. J. 125 (1990); Stephen Breyer, *The Uneasy Case for Copyright: A Study of Copyright in Books, Photocopies, and Computer Programs*, 84 HARV. L. REV. 281 (1970); Roger E. Meiners & Robert J. Staaf, *Patents, Copyrights, and Trademarks: Property or Monopoly?*, 13 HARV. J.L. & PUB. POL'Y 911, 912-13 (1990). For a major statement of the negative view, tempered by a certain realism, see STAFF OF SENATE SUBCOMM. ON PATENTS, TRADEMARKS AND COPYRIGHTS, SENATE COMM. OF THE JUDICIARY, 85TH CONG., 2D SESS., AN ECONOMIC REVIEW OF THE PATENT SYSTEM 80 (Comm. Print 1958) (FRITZ MACHLUP) (finding that "[i]f we did not have a patent system it would be irresponsible . . . to recommend instituting one"). In effect, most of these scholars continue to fight the Great Patents Controversy of the nineteenth century, see Fritz Machlup & Edith Penrose, *The Patent Controversy in the Nineteenth Century*, 10 J. ECON. HIST. 1, 3-9, 11-29 (1950), whereas mainline economic opinion focuses attention on issues concerning scope of protection and licensing.

52 *See supra* notes 20-22, 27, 46-50 and accompanying text.

53 *See infra* text accompanying notes 109-180; *see also Legal Hybrids*, *supra* note 11, at 2453-2504.

54 *See* 35 U.S.C. § 101-103, 271 (1994); WEGNER, *supra* note 5, at 77-134; *supra* note 27.

nomic premises implicit in the structural arrangements given these modalities:

1) Unpatented innovations remain subject to price competition and may be imitated if disclosed;[55]
2) Undisclosed, unpatented innovations may be reverse-engineered but not stolen;[56]
3) Patented inventions are not infringed by nonequivalent innovation;[57]
4) Unfair competition law should not repress imitation of unpatented products in the absence of confusion or deception.[58]

Similarly, the positive modalities of copyright law (or of "authors' rights" laws as they are known in most non-English-speaking countries)[59] provide virtually all authors and artists who independently create their own works with relatively soft protection against copying only that lasts a very long period of time.[60] By the same token, one also finds at least four negative economic premises implicit in the structural arrangements given these modalities:

1) Noncopyrightable productions or components thereof remain subject to price competition and may be imitated if disclosed.[61]
2) Nonprotectable ideas underlying clusters of independent creation may be used but may not be stolen [built-in reverse-

---

55 *See, e.g.*, Bonito Boats, Inc. v. Thunder Craft Boats Inc., 489 U.S. 141, 151, 156-60 (1989) ("free exploitation of ideas will be the rule, to which the protection of a federal patent is the exception"); Compco Corp. v. Day-Brite Lighting, Inc., 376 U.S. 234, 237 (1964); Sears Roebuck & Co. v. Stiffel Co., 376 U.S. 225 (1994).

56 *See* Uniform Trade Secrets Act § 1(2), 1(4), 14 U.L.A. 438 (1985) [hereinafter U.T.S.A.] (adopted by a majority of states); Kewanee Oil Co. v. Bicron Corp., 416 U.S. 470, 476, 490 (1974).

57 Under the doctrine of equivalents, second comers will not avoid infringement by making trivial variations if their product or process "performs substantially the same function [as the patented invention] in substantially the same way to obtain the same result." Graver Tank & Mfg. Co., Inc. v. Linde Air Products Co., 339 U.S. 605, 608 (1950); *see also* Robert P. Merges & Richard R. Nelson, *On the Complex Economics of Patent Scope*, 90 COLUM. L. REV. 839, 853-68 (1990) (stressing complex economics applicable to the determination of equivalents in specific cases); Martin J. Adelman & Gary J. Francione, *The Doctrine of Equivalents in Patent Law: Questions That* Pennawalt *Did Not Answer*, 137 U. PA. L. REV. 673 (1989).

58 *See Bonito Boats*, 489 U.S. at 159 (The "protection" guaranteed a particular design under the law of unfair competition is thus limited to the context where consumer confusion is likely to result.).

59 *See, e.g.*, STROWEL, *supra* note 22, at 17-27; *see also* Paul Edward Geller, *Toward an Overriding Norm in Copyright: Sign Wealth*, 159 REVUE INTERNATIONALE DU DROIT D'AUTEUR. [R.I.D.A] 2, 13-30 (1994) [hereinafter Geller, *Sign Wealth*] (discussing historical differences between "copyright" and "authors' rights" traditions).

60 *See, e.g.*, 17 U.S.C. §§ 101, 102, 103, 106, 304, 501 (1988); *supra* note 22.

61 *See, e.g.*, 17 U.S.C. § 301 (1988), *supra* note 55.

engineering].[62]

3) Cultural policies are not applicable to the general products market.[63]
4) Unfair competition laws should not limit users' rights in the absence of confusion or deception.[64]

1. Patents for Inventions

Taken together, these negative premises serve to remind both partisans and critics of the patent system that its strict substantive prerequisites—when faithfully applied—implicitly ensure that the great bulk of nonpatentable innovation remains subject to price competition on the general products market. The competitors' rights freely to imitate any unpatented products once distributed to the public thus constitute a normative premise of the free-market economy, one that presumably benefits consumers by gearing prices to production efficiencies and to incremental technical progress.[65]

Historically, the right to imitate subpatentable products and the ability to do so did not go hand in hand. Had it been otherwise, unpatented tangible products would have remained as vulnerable to instant duplication as so many intangible intellectual creations are by their very nature. The ensuing lack of appropriability would have diminished incentives to invest in ordinary product development. Today, it is sometimes hard to recall just how difficult it was to reverse-engineer ordinary industrial products by proper means in the late nineteenth and early twentieth centuries.[66] The legal duty to do so gave innovators a period of

---

62 *See, e.g.*, 17 U.S.C. §§ 102(b), 106, 107 (1988); Baker v. Selden, 101 U.S. 99 (1879); Feist Publications, Inc. v. Rural Tel. Serv. Co., 111 S.Ct. 1282 (1991); *supra* notes 55-56.

63 *See, e.g.*, Baker v. Selden, 101 U.S. 99 (1879); J.H. Reichman, *Goldstein on Copyright Law: A Realist's Approach to a Technological Age*, 43 STAN. L. REV. 943, 947-48 (1991) [hereinafter Reichman, *Realist's Approach*].

64 *See supra* notes 55 and 61.

65 *See, e.g.*, *Bonito Boats*, 489 U.S. at 141; Sears Roebuck & Co. v. Stiffel Co., 376 U.S. 225 (1964); Compco Corp. v. Day-Brite Lighting, Inc., 376 U.S. 234 (1964); *Kewanee Oil Co.*, 416 U.S. at 482-87. *See also* Paul Goldstein, *The Competitive Mandate: From* Sears *to* Lear, 59 CALIF. L. REV. 873 (1971).

66 Despite certain "property-like" qualities, "liability for the appropriation of a trade secret rests on a breach of confidence or other wrongful conduct in acquiring, using, or disclosing secret information." RESTATEMENT (THIRD) OF UNFAIR COMPETITION LAW, cmt. a, at 23-24 (1995); *see also id.* § 40 ("Appropriation of Trade Secrets"); U.T.S.A., *supra* note 56, § 1(2); John C. Stedman, *Trade Secrets*, 23 OHIO ST. L.J. 4, 8 (1962) (trade secrets not protected when the information is independently discovered or when obtained by analysis or inspection of publicly distributed products). Assuming that undisclosed but sufficiently definite infórmation fits within the operative definition of a trade secret, *see* U.T.S.A., § 1(4), and reasonable precautions are taken to preserve its secrecy, trade secret law confers no exclusive rights to make, use, sell, or reproduce it in the manner of patents or of other statutory intellectual property rights. *See, e.g.*, U.T.S.A., § 1(4); *Bonito Boats*, 489 U.S.

natural lead time in which to secure a foothold in the market and to recuperate their costs of research and development.[67]

By the same token, a competitor's right to shorten the routine innovator's natural lead time by lawful forms of reverse-engineering stimulates investment in research and development looking to future innovation and technical improvements.[68] For this and other reasons, the United States Supreme Court has endowed the competitor's right to reverse-engineer unpatented, noncopyrightable innovation with constitutional underpinnings.[69]

Even with regard to patented inventions meeting the threshold test of nonobviousness, moreover, competitors remain free to work around the matter claimed in the patents and to make use of pre-existing, substitute products and processes whose market-driven costs limit the patentees' own pricing opportunities.[70] How courts apply the doctrine of equivalents in particular cases thus largely determines the negative economic impact of the patent system on day-to-day investment and licensing decisions.[71]

Corollary principles of unfair competition law then allow second comers who take steps to avoid confusing consumers to imitate

---

at 160; *Kewanee Oil Co.*, 416 U.S. at 476, 490; 2 ROGER M. MILGRIM, MILGRIM ON TRADE SECRETS § 7.08 (1994) [hereinafter MILGRIM]. *See also* Rockwell Graphic Sys., Inc. v. Dev Indus. Inc., 925 F.2d 174, 179 (7th Cir. 1991) (suggesting that a theory that gave the trade secret holder a property right valid against the world would be preempted by the federal patent statute); Stedman, *supra*, at 21-24 (characterizing trade secrets as "a strange form of 'property' that disappears when the information becomes public or others independently make the same discovery").

67 *See* Machlup & Penrose, *supra* note 51, at 18 (explaining the view that, in the "exploitation of industrial inventions . . . the head start of the first user should as a rule suffice to enable him to earn enough to cover a reward for the inventor"); Ralph S. Brown, *Design Protection: An Overview*, 34 U.C.L.A. L. REV. 1341, 1388 (1987) ("[T]he originator will have had a head start. That is often the only advantage our system grants . . . and it is often enough."); *see also* Richard C. Levin, Alvin K. Klevorick, Richard R. Nelson & Sidney G. Winter, *Appropriating the Returns from Industrial Research and Development*, *in* 3 BROOKINGS PAPERS ON ECONOMIC ACTIVITY 783, 784 (1987) [hereinafter Levin et al.] (finding that, even with patents, gaining lead time and exploiting learning curve advantages are primary methods of appropriating returns from investment).

68 "The possibility of subsequent independent discovery is the prime risk. . . . [i]mplicit in reliance upon trade secret protection." 1 MILGRIM, *supra* note 66, § 5.04[1]. However, trade secret laws require would be competitors who do not enter licensing contracts to extract an innovator's undisclosed information by proper methods of reverse engineering. *See, e.g.*, U.T.S.A., *supra* note 56, § 1(2). For these purposes, permissible reverse engineering occurs when a second comer starts with the innovator's known product and works backward to derive the process that aided in its development or manufacture. *See Kewanee Oil Co.*, 416 U.S. at 476. The duty to reverse engineer by proper means favors investments in improvements and new applications of the innovation in question. *See, e.g.*, Levin et al., *supra* note 67, at 805-07; David D. Friedman, William M. Landes & Richard Posner, *Some Economics of Trade Secret Law*, J. ECON. PERSP. (Winter 1991), at 61, 67, 69.

69 *See Bonito Boats*, 489 U.S. at 159-64.

70 *See, e.g.*, 35 U.S.C. §§ 112, 271(a) (1994); *supra* note 57 and accompanying text.

71 *See, e.g.*, 4 DONALD S. CHISUM, PATENTS § 18.04[2] (1993) (broader range of equivalents in pioneer patents); Merges & Nelson, *supra* note 57, at 868-80 (favoring strict construction of claims and ample room for improvers under doctrine of equivalents).

unpatented products generally, including those which they have reverse-engineered by proper means.[72] In practice, some courts in all countries, including the United States, periodically deviate from this norm, especially in times of economic downturn.[73] As important new technologies fall into the penumbra between the patent and copyright paradigms, moreover, a growing reliance on misappropriation theories has culminated abroad in statutory anticopying laws outside the framework of classical intellectual property systems.[74] These measures testify to the pressures exerted on the patent and copyright paradigms under modern conditions,[75] even

---

72 *See, e.g.*, Paris Convention, *supra* note 7, art. 10*bis* (which was the prototype for Lanham Act, § 43(a) (codified at 15 U.S.C. § 1125(a) (1994)); RESTATEMENT (THIRD) OF UNFAIR COMPETITION LAW § 1 (1995) (recognizing entrepreneur's freedom to compete without liability except for acts or practices pertaining to "deceptive marketing," "infringement of trademarks or other indicia of identification," and "appropriation of intangible trade values" or similar acts or practices); 3 LADAS, INDUSTRIAL PROPERTY, *supra* note 8, at 1675-78 (stressing "public interest in competition and advertising and avoiding dishonesty"). Laws protecting trademarks, trade names, trade dress, service marks, and geographical appellations of origin are specialized applications of general unfair competition norms that enable consumers to identify products and their sources. *See, e.g.*, Besen & Raskind, *supra* note 1, at 20-21; William Landes & Richard Posner, *Trademark Law: An Economic Perspective*, 30 J.L. & ECON. 265, 269-70, 275 (1987) (stressing that trademarks reduce search costs to consumers and stimulate manufacturers to "maintain a consistent quality over time and across consumers"). The extent to which unfair competition law should extend beyond these roots in the "passing off" doctrine to protect innovation and information not otherwise covered by intellectual property laws remains controversial, despite growing recourse to a "misappropriation" rationale for this purpose in both domestic and foreign law. *See, e.g.*, Wendy J. Gordon, *On Owning Information: Intellectual Property and the Restitutionary Impulse*, 78 VA. L. REV. 149 (1992) [hereinafter Gordon, *Restitutionary Impulse*]; Dennis S. Karjala, *Misappropriation as a Third Intellectual Property Paradigm*, 94 COLUM. L.REV. 2594, 2604-08 (1994). *But see* Leo J. Raskind, *The Misappropriation Doctrine as a Competitive Norm of Intellectual Property Law*, 75 U. MINN. L. REV. 875 (1991).

73 *See generally* ERIC GOLAZ, L'IMITATION SERVILE DES PRODUITS ET DE LEUR PRÉSENTATION 103-21 (1992) (comparing French, German, Belgian and Swiss laws); 3 LADAS, INDUSTRIAL PROPERTY, *supra* note 8, 1675-1717. For periodic deviations by the United States Supreme Court, see International News Serv. v. Associated Press, 248 U.S. 215 (1918); Goldstein v. California, 412 U.S. 546 (1973). Courts eager to repress what they view as "piracy" tend to equate imitation with confusion as a matter of law. By such means, the United States federal appellate courts have created a judge-made design law out of the traditional protection of trade dress under section 43(a) of the Lanham Act. *See generally* J.H. Reichman, *Design Protection and the New Technologies: The United States Experience in a Transnational Perspective*, 19 U. BALT. L. REV. 6, 98-123 (1989/1990) [hereinafter Reichman, *Designs and New Technologies*]; *see also* J.H. Reichman, *Past and Current Trends in the Evolution of Design Protection Law—A Comment*, 4 FORDHAM INTELL. PROP. MEDIA & ENT. L.J. 387, 392-97 (1993) [hereinafter Reichman, *Evolution of Design Protection*).

74 *See Legal Hybrids*, *supra* note 11, at 2474-76 (discussing Swiss Unfair Competition Law of 1986 and Japanese Unfair Competition Law of 1993); *see also* JEAN-PAUL TRIAILLE, UNFAIR AND PARASITIC COMPETITION (Centre de Recherches Informatique et Droit, F.N.D.P. (1990)) (reviewing the protection of information under the unfair competition laws of seven countries); Friedrich-Karl Beier, *The Law of Unfair Competition in the European Community—Its Development and Present Status*, 16 I.I.C. 139 (1985).

75 *See, e.g.*, Ulrich Loewenheim, *Legal Protection for Computer Programs in West Germany*, 4 HIGH TECH. L.J. 187 (1989) (protection of computer programs in German unfair competition law prior to E.C. Directive on copyright protection for software); Dick van Engelen, *The Misappropriation Doctrine in the Netherlands*, 22 I.I.C. 11 (1991) (discussing role of unfair competition when legislatures cannot keep pace with new technological developments); *see*

as they enable unfair competition law to perform its historic role of identifying marginal cases in need of legislative relief.[76] Nevertheless, the legal mythology of all market economies requires courts formally to acknowledge the competitor's right to imitate pre-existing products, and Supreme Courts everywhere are prone to vindicate this principle at intervals, often in periods of economic growth.[77]

2. Literary and Artistic Works

Taken together, the negative economic premises identified above further remind both partisans and critics of intellectual property law that the mature copyright paradigm is predicated on the very absence of the natural lead time that trade secret law attempts to defend. Because authors normally embody their intangible creations in tangible mediums of expression, the distribution of these material supports to the public at large negates any further possibility of concealing the product of creative know-how in the manner of trade secrets.[78] Because every artistic work thus bears its author's intellectual creation on its face, would-be competitors need only obtain some tangible embodiment of that expression to duplicate it without incurring the investment of time, money, or skill inherent in the process of reverse-engineering unpatented in-

---

also Jean-Marc Mousseron, La protection du savoir-faire [know-how], paper presented to the conference on Exporter Notre Technologie—Protection et Transfert Internationaux des Innovations, 10-14 (University of Ottawa, Canada, Faculty of Law, Nov. 1993) (proposing new unfair competition norm against parasitic copying); Gordon, *Restitutionary Impulse*, *supra* note 72.

76 *See, e.g.*, 3 LADAS, INDUSTRIAL PROPERTY, *supra* note 8, at 1675 (unfair competition law "forms the background and constitutes the general principle of which the law protecting the various branches of industrial property are only special aspects or particular applications"); *see also* Douglas G. Baird, *Common Law Intellectual Property and the Legacy of* International News Service v. Associated Press, 50 U. CHI. L. REV. 411 (1983); *Developments in the Law—Competitive Torts*, 77 HARV. L. REV. 888, 932-941 (1963/1964).

77 *See, e.g.*, *Bonito Boats*, 489 U.S. 141; Besen & Raskind, *supra* note 1, at 24-25; *see also* GOLAZ, *supra* note 73, at 103-21; PETER J. KAUFMANN, PASSING OFF AND MISAPPROPRIATION—AN ECONOMIC AND LEGAL ANALYSIS OF THE LAW OF UNFAIR COMPETITION IN THE UNITED STATES AND CONTINENTAL EUROPE 7-30 (1986).

78 *Cf.* Justin Hughes, *The Philosophy of Intellectual Property*, 77 GEO. L. J. 287, 315 (1988); F.D. Prager, *The Early Growth and Influence of Intellectual Property*, 34 J. PAT. OFF. SOC'Y 106, 108-09 (1952). Even in the depths of the anti-patent movement during the nineteenth century, see *supra* note 51, it was widely believed that natural lead time was "too short in the book-publishing business, where cheaper pirated editions can be put on the market almost without delay, making it impossible for the first publisher to earn enough to pay the author." Machlup & Penrose, *supra* note 51, at 18 (citing authority). The legitimacy of copyright law thus escaped challenge at a time when patent laws were being rolled back. Ironically, when the protectionist movement in the late twentieth century succeeded in greatly strengthening United States patent law, see, e.g., Martin Adelman, *The New World of Patents Created by the Court of Appeals for the Federal Circuit*, 20 U. MICH. J.L. REF. 979, 979-82 (1982), the copyright law came under serious abolitionist fire. *See, e.g.*, Breyer, *supra* note 51; Palmer, *supra* note 51.

dustrial innovation. Third parties who rapidly duplicate a successful literary or artistic work may reduce the author's natural lead time to zero, or even minus zero if they possess sufficient market power, simply by selling the same artistic production at a price below the average cost to publish or disseminate the original work.[79] The copyright system thus deals with intellectual goods not protectable as trade secrets that require no reverse-engineering to appropriate.

The system responds by providing long periods of artificial lead time in the form of exclusive property rights to all independent creators without regard to merit and without requiring originators to preselect those works thought to be worth the costs of formal registration or administrative examination.[80] Wary of unreliable value judgements about art and unable to predict which of even the most successful author's future works will capture or recapture the public's fancy, the copyright laws embrace all literary and artistic works simply by virtue of their being creations and leave the assessment of both merit and pecuniary worth entirely to the market.[81]

Unlike patent law, however, copyright law never prevents third parties from independently creating works of authorship similar to those already on the market.[82] Nor does copyright law invest authors with any generally recognized right to control the end use of

---

[79] *See, e.g.*, Benko, *supra* note 1, at 21; Dratler, *supra* note 27, § 1.01[1]; Ralph S. Brown, *Eligibility for Copyright Protection: A Search for Principled Standards*, 70 Minn. L. Rev. 579, 596 (1985) [hereinafter Brown, *Eligibility*]; *see also* Yves Gaubiac, *Les Nouveaux Moyens Techniques de Reproduction et le Droit d'Auteur*, 123 R.I.D.A. 22, 26 (1986).

[80] *See, e.g.*, Ricketson, *supra* note 10, at 231-232; Guide to the Berne Convention, *supra* note 8, at 17; Adolph Dietz, Copyright Law in the European Community: A Comparative Investigation of National Copyright Legislation 32, 30-31 (1978). *See also* 1 Ladas, Artistic Property, *supra* note 16, at 269-75; Dratler, *supra* note 27, § 102[1] (stressing that "patents are the only form of intellectual property whose coverage depends upon the precise legal description of the protected subject matter in a government grant").

[81] *See, e.g.*, Feist Publications, Inc. v. Rural Tel. Serv. Co., 111 S. Ct. 1282 (1991); Bleistein v. Donaldson Lithographing Co., 188 U.S. 239 (1903); *supra* notes 19-22 and accompanying text. In practice, the exclusive rights of copyright law provide a pecuniary reward only to those authors and artists who successfully explore the public's taste. *Cf.* Kitch, *Patent System, supra* note 46 (stressing role of prospecting function in patent system). By thus securing a winner-take-all return for those relatively few creators able to capture the public's fancy, the copyright incentives help to overcome high risk aversion otherwise apt to discourage investment in the dissemination of cultural goods. *See, e.g.*, David Ladd, *The Harm of the Concept of Harm in Copyright*, 30 J. Copyright Soc'y 421, 431 (1983) (stressing the negative influence of broad fair use exceptions on risk-taking in authorship and publishing); *see also* Mackaay, *supra* note 12, at 115-17. The exclusive rights also permit creators to defray the costs of past failures by preventing second comers from prematurely siphoning off the fruits of any lucky strike that happens to result.

[82] *See, e.g.*, Guide to the Berne Convention, *supra* note 8, at 17-18; Ricketson, *supra* note 10, at 231-32; 1 Goldstein, *supra* note 22, § 1.2.2.3; *see also* Dratler, *supra* note 27, § 1.03[1] (independent creation is no defence to an action for patent infringement).

protected works as such.[83] On the contrary, by encouraging third parties to make free and abundant use of nonprotectable matter underlying the protected expression, *copyright laws foster a built-in process of "reverse-engineering" that enables many independently created and copyrightable works to cluster around common themes or ideas.*[84]

If the exclusive rights bestowed on authors thus stimulate the production and dissemination of literary and artistic works under free-market conditions,[85] the overall objective is "to promote the progress of science" and not just the drive for economic efficiency in general.[86] To this end, domestic copyright laws foster certain cultural policies that are sometimes inconsistent with the efficient allocation of resources on the market for literary and artistic productions as such. For example, incentive theory[87] will not adequately account for the long period of protection, which enables living authors and their immediate heirs to partake of revenues generated many years after the creation of their works, nor for such paternalistic measures as the right to terminate transfers under the United States Copyright Act of 1976, nor the moral rights that permeate foreign copyright laws.[88] True, the incentive

---

83 *See, e.g.*, Brown, *Eligibility, supra* note 79, at 588-89. Professor Brown states: "The right to control the use of a work, although granted to inventors, has never been part of copyright except as performance may be considered 'use.' Indeed, the absence of a 'use right' helps justify the relatively casual approach to granting copyright as opposed to the more searching tests for patentability." *Id. See generally* FREDERIC POLLAUD-DULIAN, LE DROIT DE DESTINATION 279-399 (1989) (noting subtle variations from one national system to another). *But see* F. GOTZEN, HET BESTIMMINGSRECHT VAN DE AUTEUR (1975) (favoring generalized right to control end use).

84 *See, e.g.*, Baker v. Selden, 101 U.S. 99 (1879); Jessica Litman, *The Public Domain*, 39 EMORY L.J. 965, 1015, 1023 (1990); Brown, *Eligibility, supra* note 79, at 590, 601-05.

85 *See, e.g.*, 1 GOLDSTEIN, *supra* note 22, § 1.2.

86 U.S. CONST. art. I, § 8, cl. 1; L. RAY PATTERSON & STANLEY W. LINDBERG, THE NATURE OF COPYRIGHT—A LAW OF USER'S RIGHTS 49 (1991); *see also* Gordon, *Inquiry, supra* note 47, at 1468 (rejecting economic efficiency as overall goal though recognizing need to avoid market failure; and affirming that "[c]reativity is too important to human life, economically, psychologically, and culturally, to have its legal treatment subordinated to the legal policies regulating the tangible domain").

87 The incentive theory of copyright law, which prevails in the English-speaking countries, emphasizes the need to stimulate optimum production of literary and artistic works and to overcome the problem of appropriability. *See, e.g.*, Landes & Posner, *Copyrights, supra* note 46; Gordon, *Fair Use, supra* note 1, at 1610-32; *see generally* Alain Strowel, *L'analyse économique du droit d'auteur—Une revue critique des arguments invoqués*, *in* THE SOCIO-ECONOMIC ROLE OF INTELLECTUAL PROPERTY RIGHTS 105-34 (M. Van Hoecke ed. 1991) (skeptically reviewing the literature as a whole). This approach contrasts with natural rights and personality-based theories that traditionally prevailed in the rest of the world. *See, e.g.*, STROWEL, *supra* note 22, at 81-129; Alfred C. Yen, *Restoring the Natural Law: Copyright as Labor and Possession*, 51 OHIO ST. L. J. 517 (1990); *see also* Wendy J. Gordon, *A Property Right in Self-Expression: Equality and Individualism in the Natural Law of Intellectual Property*, 102 YALE L.J. 1533 (1993).

88 *See, e.g.*, Th. Limpberg, *Duration of Copyright Protection*, 103 R.I.D.A. 53, 68-69, 75-77 (1980); Zecharia Chafee, Jr., *Reflections on the Law of Copyright*, 45 COLUM. L. REV., 503, 507-08 (1945); 17 U.S.C. §§ 203, 304(c) (1988) (termination of transfers); *see also* Reichman, *Realist's Approach, supra* note 63, at 947-48. On moral rights, which prevent those who have

theory of copyright law, which predominates in the United Kingdom and the United States,[89] serves to limit actual inefficiencies by emphasizing the public interest in free competition.[90] However, it underestimates the extent to which all industrialized countries, to varying degrees, have deliberately subordinated efficiency to cultural policy goals in the specialized market for literary and artistic works.[91]

Phrased differently, any efficiencies that copyright law produces in the market for literary and artistic works are an integral part of the larger cultural policy this body of law seeks to implement. By the same token, the most fundamental of all the negative economic premises underlying the mature copyright paradigm is that the peculiar mix of cultural and economic policies it implements on the market for artistic works *should not disrupt competition in the general products market as regulated by the mature patent paradigm.*[92] For this reason, legislators deny copyright protection to "any idea, procedure, process, system, method of operation, concept, principle, or discovery, regardless of the form in which it is described, explained, illustrated, or embodied" in original works of authorship.[93] This premise also explains why courts traditionally afford factual and functional works only "thin" protection against literal reproduction;[94] why legislators and courts will not allow the exclusive reproduction rights of copyright law indirectly to prevent

---

paid to commercialize an author's work from doing so in a manner that could prejudice the author's honor or reputation, see, e.g., Berne Convention, *supra* note 7, art. 6*bis*; W.R. CORNISH, INTELLECTUAL PROPERTY: PATENTS, COPYRIGHTS, TRADE MARKS AND ALLIED RIGHTS 309 (2d ed. 1989); Edward J. Damich, *The Right of Personality: A Common Law Basis for the Protection of the Moral Rights of Authors*, 23 GA. L. REV. 1, 8-25 (1988); *see generally* STIG STRÖMHOLM, LE DROIT MORAL DE L'AUTEUR (1967).

89 *See generally* STROWEL, *supra* note 22, at 81-173 (noting convergence between copyright and authors' rights systems).

90 *See, e.g.*, 1 GOLDSTEIN, *supra* note 22, § 1.2; *see also* Landes & Posner, *Copyrights*, *supra* note 46, at 361 (discussing whether limiting term of protection avoids monopoly profits and tracing costs).

91 The coherence of these cultural policies may have diminished with the growing attack on the classical view that emphasizes protection of the author's personality as manifested in works of authorship. *See, e.g.*, Paul Edward Geller, *Must Copyright Be Forever Caught Between Marketplace and Authorship Norms?*, *in* OF AUTHORS AND ORIGINS: ESSAYS ON COPYRIGHT 178-81 (Brad Sherman & Alain Strowel eds. 1994) [hereinafter Geller, *Authorship Norms*]; Robert H. Rotstein, *Beyond Metaphor: Copyright Infringement and the Fiction of the Work*, 68 CHI.-KENT. L. REV. 725, 727-28 (1993); Marci A. Hamilton, *Art Speech* (1994-95) (unpublished manuscript, on file with the *Cardozo Arts & Entertainment Law Journal*). *See also* György Boytha, *The Justification of the Protection of Authors' Rights as Reflected in Their Historical Development*, 151 R.I.D.A. 53 (1992).

92 *See* Baker v. Selden, 101 U.S. 99 (1879); *supra* notes 55 and 63.

93 17 U.S.C. § 102(b); *see generally* Pamela Samuelson, *Computer Programs, User Interfaces and Section 102(b) of the Copyright Act of 1976: A Critique of* Lotus v. Paperback, 55 LAW & CONTEM. PROBS. 311, 322-23, 325-31 (1992).

94 *See, e.g.*, Feist Publications v. Rural Tel. Serv. Co., 111 S. Ct. 1282, 1289 (1991); *see generally* 2 GOLDSTEIN, *supra* note 22, §§ 8.4, 8.5.

the use of unprotectable utilitarian matter by third parties;[95] and why legislators try to dissuade courts from opening unfair competition law to matter denied protection in copyright law.[96]

C. *Apparent Locus of the Deviant Regimes*

The foregoing observations attempted to describe how the world's intellectual property system carves up its universe of discourse and to identify some of the behavioral assumptions that were implicitly made concerning the standard objects of protection. In considering the extent to which late twentieth-century intellectual property law still conforms to these nineteenth-century foundations, it is helpful to visualize the constitutional framework of the Great Conventions as operating within two broad spheres or spectra of protected activity that are geared, respectively, to "industrial" and "artistic" property.[97]

1. A Thickness Syndrome Under the Classical Models

The subdivision between traditional forms of industrial and artistic property underlying the Great Conventions is represented graphically in Figure 1, entitled "Pressure on the Dominant Paradigms: Selected Legal Hybrids." Figure 1 portrays the two traditional spheres as meeting at the line of demarcation identified earlier in this Article, namely, at the general products market, which the patent paradigm nominally governs.[98] The broad ends of the two spectra represent the locus of classical objects of intellectual property protection, namely, patents for inventive but conventionally engineered applications of science to industry,[99] on the

---

95 *See, e.g.*, 17 U.S.C. §§ 101, 113(b) (compelling this result when a three-dimensional utilitarian article is portrayed in a two-dimensional copyrighted work, such as a dress design or a boiler design, and a competitor reverse engineers the same design by copying the three-dimensional dress or boiler); Baker v. Selden, 101 U.S. at 103 (compelling the same result with regard to literary works); Sega Enters. Ltd. v. Accolade, Inc., 977 F. 2d 1510 (9th Cir. 1992); *see generally* Reichman, *Programs as Know-How*, *supra* note 11, at 693, 693 n.288 (rehabilitating the pristine function of *Baker v. Selden*, which prevents the reproduction rights from indirectly protecting ineligible functional matter); 1 GOLDSTEIN, *supra* note 22, § 5.2.1.4 (Supp. 1994) (reaching same result on the basis of codified fair-use criterion).

96 *See supra* notes 55 and 61.

97 *See supra* text accompanying notes 18-27.

98 *See supra* text accompanying notes 38-42.

99 The phrase "inventive but conventionally engineered applications of science to industry" is meant to embrace the traditional subject matters of patentability, but not necessarily such borderline cases as computer programs, industrial designs, plant varieties, and certain products of biogenetic engineering, especially living microorganisms, whose collocation within the modern patent system remains controversial. *See, e.g.*, ROBERT P. MERGES, PATENT LAW AND POLICY—CASES AND MATERIALS 35-147, 1001-1005 (1992) (distinguishing computer software, algorithms, business methods, living subject matter, and medical devices as borderline cases and industrial designs as a special case).

one hand and works of art and literature in the traditional and ordinary sense, on the other.[100]

FIGURE 1: PRESSURE ON THE DOMINANT PARADIGMS: SELECTED LEGAL HYBRIDS

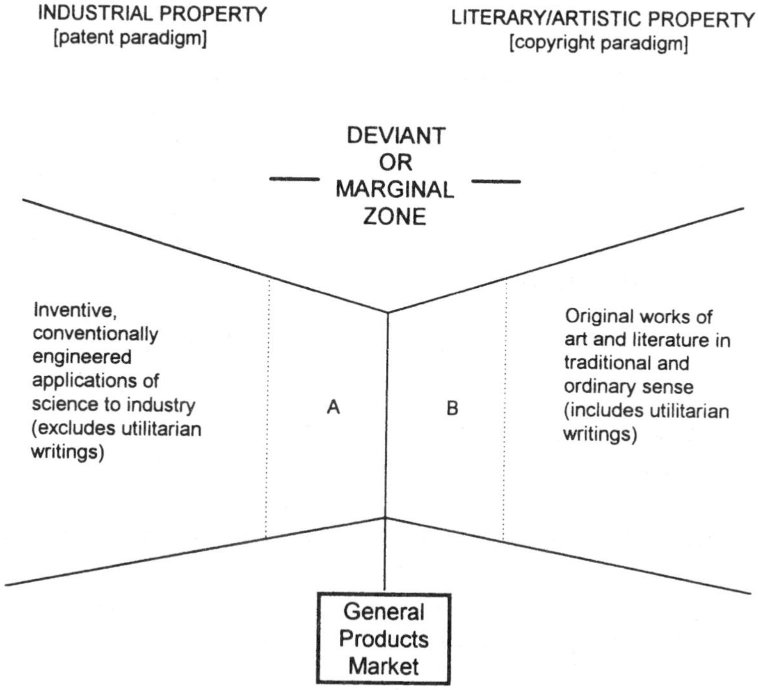

That the spectra appear broader at their outer ends signifies that even the standard objects of protection—if otherwise qualified—do not uniformly obtain the maximum scope of protection available under the dominant legal paradigms. Questions always arise concerning the extent to which any given subject matter category (or any particular patent or copyright falling within given subject matter categories) will obtain protection against other than literal or nearly exact copying. The international intellectual property system provides virtually no minimum standards to constrain

[100] *See, e.g.*, Bailie v. Fisher [Register of Copyrights], 258 F. 2d 425, 426 (D.C. Cir. 1958) (per curiam) (citing Rosenthal v. Stein, 205 F. 2d 633, 635 (9th Cir. 1953)); Reichman, *Design Protection*, *supra* note 31, at 1174-82.

domestic judicial decisions in this regard.[101] Yet, how courts answer these questions determines the true level of protection available from any given domestic system and greatly affects the overall calculus of social costs and benefits flowing from these systems.[102]

Studies suggest, for example, that courts and administrators provide pioneer inventions with a broader or "thicker" range of equivalents than patents in an already crowded field and that, at the limit, so-called blocking patents covering a broad set of claims may dominate a "subservient" patent that relies on narrower claims to some improved feature of the same invention.[103] Likewise in copyright law, certain disfavored subject matters, such as factual and functional works, routinely received relatively "thin" protection compared with more expressive literary and artistic works.[104] Patent courts, overtly or covertly, often engage in similar discriminations.[105]

---

101 This remains true even under the TRIPS Agreement, *supra* note 4, which otherwise elevates the standards of protection generally. The TRIPS Agreement, however, does introduce periodic trade policy review mechanisms as well as binding dispute-resolution mechanisms that could lead to quasi-common-law adjudications at the international level. Arguably, states could challenge or contest the scope of protection practices of other states in these forums. *See, e.g.*, Geller, *Dispute Settlements, supra* note 5, at 107-14; Reichman, *TRIPS Component, supra* note 5, at 256-63; *see also* Reichman, *Competition, Intellectual Property and Trade, supra* note 5, at 108-09 (predicting future round of multilateral trade talks to establish international guidelines governing misuse of intellectual property rights).

102 *Cf.* Merges & Nelson, *supra* note 57, at 908-16 (concluding that rapid technological achievement is encouraged by narrower patents); Geller, *Sign Wealth, supra* note 59, at 85-89 (broad derivative rights may limit access to public domain); Paul Goldstein, *Derivative Rights and Derivative Works in Copyright*, 30 J. COPYRIGHT SOC'Y 209 (1983) (protection of derivative works encourages investment in creative expression).

103 *See, e.g.*, Westinghouse v. Boyden Power Brake Co., 170 U.S. 537, 561-62 (1898); 5 CHISUM, *supra* note 71, § 20.03[3]; Merges & Nelson, *supra* note 57, at 854 (who find that courts relate the range of equivalents to the degree of advance over the prior art, and in the case of a pioneer patent, "will stretch to find infringement even by a product whose characteristics lie considerably outside the boundaries of the literal claims.") Inventions falling between patentable improvements and pioneer inventions receive "an intermediate range of equivalents." *Id.* at 854 n.68 (citing authorities). "Two patents are said to block each other when one patentee has a broad patent on an invention and another has a narrower patent on some improved feature of that invention. The broad patent is said to 'dominate' the narrower one." *Id.* at 860. In such cases, apportioned royalties or cross licensing appears to be the logical result. *See, e.g.*, 5 CHISUM, *supra* note 71, § 20.03 [3].

104 *See, e.g.,,* Feist Publications v. Rural Tel. Serv. Co. 111 S. Ct. 1282 (1991) (thin protection of factual works in copyright law); Baker v. Selden, 101 U.S. at 102-04; Atari, Inc. v. North Am. Phillips Consumer Elecs. Corp., 672 F.2d 607, 614-16 (7th Cir. 1982) (Posner, C.J.) (discussing a similar spectrum in copyright law, which is thicker for traditional artistic works than for borderline creations); *see generally* Reichman, *Realist's Approach, supra* note 63, at 966-76.

105 In the United States, for example, courts hostile to design patents seldom recognized any range of equivalents and traditionally afforded relief against servile imitation only. *See, e.g.*, Mathew Nimetz, *Design Protection*, 15 COPYRIGHT L. SYMP. (ASCAP) 79, 101 (1967) (showing hostility of U.S. federal courts to design patents); Reichman, *Designs and New Technologies, supra* note 73, at 25, 42-43, 51-53 (showing Federal Circuit's willingness to recognize some range of equivalents in recent years). Most countries eventually removed design protection from patent law, in part to square outcomes with legal doctrine.

As a general proposition, the spectra represented in Figure 1 reflect this "thickness syndrome" by indicating a broader scope of protection for some subject-matter categories and a narrower scope of protection for others. Whether a stronger case can be made for creators or for second comers when determining either the range of equivalents in patent law or the breadth of the exclusive rights to prepare derivative works in copyright law varies with the different theories of protection that appeal to different decision makers. Economic analysis provides no clear resolution of these differences.[106]

Experience does nonetheless suggest that a particularly thin scope of protection will turn out to be a characteristic feature of all the intellectual property regimes whose objects of protection deviate from true "inventions" or from the "works of art or literature in the ordinary and historical sense" that fall within the standard patent and copyright subsystems. Industrial designs, for example, seldom obtain more than protection against slavish imitation even when subjected to full or modified patent regimes.[107] Other deviant regimes are explored at length in this investigator's previous studies, especially his *Legal Hybrids* monograph.[108] For present purposes, these rough empirical observations concerning the tensions surrounding scope of protection issues under the dominant intellectual property paradigms—encapsulated here in the notion of a "thickness syndrome"—provide a clue to ascertaining the probable locus of deviant protective phenomena within the larger universe of discourse that the international patent and copyright systems formally stake out.

2. The Deviant Regimes

If, under standard operating assumptions, the patent and copyright subsystems meet face to face at a common line of demarcation, as shown in Figure 1, the existence of a "thickness syn-

---

106 *Compare, e.g.*, Kitch, *Patent System, supra* note 46 (suggesting that under prospecting theory of patent law the granting of a broader scope to an initial inventor may induce more effective development and future invention) *with* Merges & Nelson, *supra* note 57, at 843-44, 854 (concluding that without "extensively reducing the pioneer's incentives, the law should attempt at the margin to favor a competitive environment for improvements, rather than an environment dominated by the pioneer firm"); *see also* Peter Jaszi, *Toward a Theory of Copyright: The Metamorphosis of Authorship*, 1991 Duke L.J. 455, 477-85, 501-02 (criticizing myth of personal creation and resulting doctrinal excesses); Geller, *Authorship Norms, supra* note 91, at 178-81 (contending that personality-based copyright theories tend unduly to broaden the scope of protection for literary works).

107 *See, e.g., Legal Hybrids, supra* note 11, at 2463-65 (supporting the proposition in the text and discussing its implications for a unified field approach).

108 *See generally Legal Hybrids, supra* note 11, at 2455-63, 2465-2500.

drome" operating within the dominant paradigms makes it plausible to expect deviant or marginal intellectual property models to occupy a position at or near the narrow ends of the spectra shown in Figure 1. There, for one reason or another, the scope of protection was posited as likely to attain its weakest levels. To facilitate further analysis, Marginal Zones A and B have been added to Figure 1, in keeping with these premises. Figure 1 thus provisionally incorporates selected deviant intellectual property models into the open spectra of industrial and artistic property, in harmony with the "thickness syndrome" identified above.

For example, in Marginal Zone A (on the industrial property side of the dividing line), one finds such deviant protective regimes as utility model laws,[109] registered design laws,[110] plant variety protection laws,[111] and unregistered design protection laws (like that

---

109 The pristine purpose of early utility model laws was to protect functional improvements in the design of hand tools and other everyday implements that were achieved by means of novel, three-dimensional forms or shapes. Such improvements typically lacked the level of nonobviousness required for patent protection. *See, e.g., id.* at 2455-59 (citing German, Italian and Japanese authorities); *see also* Reichman, *Electronic Information Tools*, supra note 11, at 451-55 ("Tool Design in Comparative Industrial Property Law"). Over time, utility model laws tend to degenerate into longer and stronger petty patent regimes that provide patent-like protection of small inventions generally, for a relatively short period of time. In this form, they become less strictly tied to three-dimensional, functional shapes of tools and everyday implements. *See, e.g., Legal Hybrids, supra* note 11, at 2457-59 (noting reform of German utility model law in 1990, which abolished the requirement of a three-dimensional configuration and made electronic circuit designs eligible for the first time). Nevertheless, the European Union seems destined to adopt a community-wide directive mandating the protection of utility models. *See, e.g., Proposal of the Max Planck Institute for a European Utility Model*, 25 I.I.C. 700 (1994); Michael Kern, *Towards a European Utility Model Law*, 25 I.I.C. 627 (1994).

110 Registered design protection laws normally protect two-dimensional designs or three-dimensional models that enhance the appearance of industrial products by means of their forms or of a particular combination of lines, colors or other features that appeal to the eye. Generally speaking, such laws require registration and deposit, but not necessarily a full examination of the prior art, in addition to objective novelty and some degree of qualitative innovation not rising to the level of nonobviousness. Most design laws exclude functionally determined designs, and they typically provide patent-like protection for a term of ten or fifteen years. *See, e.g., Legal Hybrids, supra* note 11, at 2461-63; *see also* Reichman, *Designs and New Technologies, supra* note 73, at 8-10, 20-26 (noting that most European countries and Japan have sui generis, registered design laws, but not the United States, which applies patent law to industrial designs). The European Union appears likely to adopt a new, registered design law, with Community-wide application. *See* Commission of the European Communities, Proposal for a European Parliament and Council Regulation on the Community Design, COM (93)342 final at 463 (Dec. 3, 1993) [hereinafter Proposed EC Design Directive].

111 Plant variety protection laws as initially adopted provided plant breeders with copyright-like protection for novel varieties of certain plants (e.g., sexually reproduced plants in the U.S.) that demonstrate sufficient stability, uniformity and distinctiveness over time. *See, e.g.,* Plant Variety Protection Act (PVPA), Pub. L. No. 91-577, 84 Stat. 1542 (1970) (amended 1980) (current version at 7 U.S.C. §§ 2321-2583 (1988)); *see generally Legal Hybrids, supra* note 11, at 2465-67. Countries adopting similar laws usually adhered to the International Convention for the Protection of New Varieties of Plants (UPOV), *supra* note 9. In 1991, the member countries amended UPOV and moved toward more patent-like protection. In 1994, the United States amended the PVPA to conform to the 1991 revision

the United Kingdom enacted in 1988).[112] Also included in this zone are recent unfair competition laws that, to varying degrees, restrain third parties from copying unpatented, noncopyrightable innovation without any corresponding investment of their own.[113] Logically included in this zone, but not analyzed in this investigator's previous studies, are several other hybrid regimes, both existing and proposed, such as sui generis regimes protecting typeface designs;[114] regimes that issue inventors' certificates or that reward individual rationalization proposals (largely a heritage of the centrally planned economies);[115] and, arguably, proposed amendments to the United States patent law that would lower the standards of eligibility for certain discoveries in biogenetic

---

of the UPOV treaty. *See* PVPA Amendments of 1994, Pub. L. No. 103-349, 108 Stat. 3136 (1994); *see generally Legal Hybrids, supra* note 11, at 2467-72.

112 Dissatisfaction with patent-like protection of industrial designs under registered design laws led the United Kingdom to provide copyright-like protection of unregistered designs, whether functionally determined or aesthetic in nature, for a fifteen-year period. *See* Copyright, Designs and Patent Act, ch. 48, §§ 213-264 (1988) (U.K.); Christine Fellner, *The New United Kingdom Industrial Design Law,* 19 U. BALT. L.REV. 369, 388-89 (1989/90). The Proposed EC Design Directive, *supra* note 110, also provides for a much less radical regime of unregistered protection, which applies only to appearance designs and would last, without formalities, for three years from the date on which a given design was first made publicly available. *See* Proposed EC Design Directive, *supra* note 110, arts. 1(2), 7(a), 12; *see also* Bernard Posner, The Proposal for a EU Design, paper presented to the International Conference on the Legal Protection of Industrial Designs (Tokyo and Kyoto, Japan, Nov. 8-12, 1994).

The most radical form of unregistered design protection for appearance designs, as distinct from functionally determined designs, is currently provided by the United States federal appellate courts' broad reading of Lanham Act § 43(a). These courts treat product configurations as unregistered "appearance trade dress," protectable under Lanham Act § 43(a) for an indefinite period of time. *See, e.g.,* Reichman, *Designs and New Technologies,* supra note 73, at 98-123 (citing authorities); *see further* Reichman, *Evolution of Design Protection, supra* note 73, at 392-97 (appearance trade dress from *Bonito Boats v. Thunder Craft Boats,* 489 U.S. 141 (1989) to *Two Pesos v. Taco Cabana,* 112 S. Ct. 2753 (1992)); J.H. Reichman, *Design Protection and the Legislative Agenda,* 55 LAW & CONTEMP. PROBS. 281, 284-90 (1992) [hereinafter Reichman, *Designs and Legislative Agenda*].

113 *See, e.g., Legal Hybrids, supra* note 11, at 2472-76 (discussing Swiss unfair competition law of 1986 and Japanese unfair competition law of 1993). The Swiss law focuses on protecting investment in unpatented technologies in general, and carries no specified time limit for the innovator's reasonable return on his or her investment. The less open-ended Japanese law simply forbids slavish duplication of new industrial product configurations for a three-year period from the time the relevant products become available to the public. *See* Federal Law on Unfair Competition 1986 [Switzerland], art. 5(c) (effective March 1, 1988), *reprinted in* 5 INDUS. PROP. LAW. & TREATIES (Supp., Sept. 1988); The Unfair Competition Act [Japan], Law No. 47/1993, § 2(3) (May 19, 1993).

114 *See* Vienna Agreement for the Protection of Type Faces and Their International Deposit and Protocol Concerning the Term of Protection, June 12, 1973, Records of the Vienna Diplomatic Conference on the Protection of Typefaces 1973, at 10 (W.I.P.O. 1980); *see also* Phillip W. Snyder, *Typeface Design After the Desktop Revolution: A New Case for Legal Protection,* 16 COLUM.-VLA J.L. & ARTS 97 (1991).

115 *See, e.g.,* Stojan Pretnar, *Inventor's Certificates, Rationalization Proposals and Discoveries, in* 14 INTERNATIONAL ENCYCLOPEDIA OF COMPARATIVE LAW: COPYRIGHT AND INDUSTRIAL PROPERTY, ch. 6 (Eugene Ulmer ed. 1983).

engineering.[116]

Similarly, in Marginal Zone B (on the artistic property side of the dividing line), one finds such deviant regimes as sui generis laws protecting computer programs (now largely superseded);[117] laws protecting integrated circuit designs on copyright-like principles;[118] and miscellaneous sui generis laws protecting such items as data bases and catalogues,[119] applied art,[120] and engineering projects.[121] Also included in this zone is the European Union's ex-

---

116 *See, e.g.*, H.R. 587, 104th Cong., 1st Sess. (1995) (proposing to overrule *In re Durden*, 763 F.2d 1406, 1410 (Fed. Cir. 1985), by mandating that a novel input or output could make a process as a whole nonobvious).

117 France protected computer programs under a sui generis law, built on modified copyright principles, that was attached to the Copyright Law of 1985. *See Legal Hybrids*, *supra* note 11, at 2481-83 (citing authorities). Although it formally recognized computer programs as copyrightable works, the French law explicitly excepted computer programs from many principles of copyright law and otherwise established a sui generis regime. However, the European Community's Directive on the Legal Protection of Computer Programs, Council Directive 91/250, 1991 O.J. (L 122) 42 [hereinafter EC Directive on Computer Programs], will override inconsistent provisions of the 1985 French law in the interest of harmonizing copyright law in the E.U. *See, e.g.*, André Lucas, *The Council Directive of 14 May 1991 Concerning the Legal Protection of Computer Programs and Its Implications in French Law*, 14 EUR. INTELL. PROP. REV. 28, 31 (1992).

118 *See, e.g.*, Semiconductor Chip Protection Act of 1984 (SCPA), Pub. L. No. 98-620, 98 Stat. 3347 (1984) (codified as amended at 17 U.S.C. § 901 *et seq.* (1988)) [hereinafter SCPA] (providing copyright-like protection for one class of functional designs, viz., "mask works" or integrated circuit designs); IPIC Treaty, *supra* note 9 (internationalizing this approach); *Legal Hybrids*, *supra* note 11, at 2478-80.

119 In the Nordic countries, sui generis laws protecting non-copyrightable compilations against slavish imitation have existed for several decades. *See, e.g.*, Gunnar Karnell, *The Nordic Catalogue Rule*, *in* PROTECTING WORKS OF FACT 67-72 (E.J. Dommering & P.B. Hugenholtz eds., 1991). More recently, the Commission of the European Communities has proposed an innovative Directive on the Legal Protection of Databases, loosely modeled on the Nordic Catalogue rule, that protects electronic information tools outside of the domestic copyright laws. *See* Proposal for a Council Directive on the Legal Protection of Databases, COM(92)24 final at SYN 393 (1992) [hereinafter First EC Directive on Databases]; Amended Proposal for a Council Directive on the Legal Protection of Databases, COM(93)464 final at SYN 393 (1993) [hereinafter Amended EC Directive on Databases]; *see also Legal Hybrids*, *supra* note 11, at 2493-98 (analyzing and criticizing these proposals).

120 See Berne Convention, *supra* note 7, arts 2(7), 7(4) (allowing lesser degree of copyright protection for works of applied art). The inclusion of designs in both Marginal Zones A & B of Figure 1 results from the fact that works of applied art overlap industrial designs as such in most domestic intellectual property systems, while the criteria for distinguishing one from the other produce uncertain results. *See, e.g.*, Reichman, *Designs and New Technologies*, *supra* note 73, at 8-17 (citing authorities); Reichman, *Design Protection*, *supra* note 31, at 1153-59, 1182-86, 1213-23. Nevertheless, apart from the U.S. (and one or two other countries), which still protects industrial designs under the full patent paradigm, and France, which still protects them under the full copyright paradigm, *see infra* note 124 and accompanying text, most developed countries during the second half of the twentieth century resorted to registered, sui generis design laws built on modified patent principles.

121 While many countries, including the United States, treat technical drawings, blueprints and engineering projects differently from other copyrightable works, see, *e.g.*, 17 U.S.C. § 113(b); Reichman, *Electronics Information Tools*, *supra* note 11, at 448-51, one country—Italy—protects noncopyrightable engineering projects under a neighboring rights law built on liability principles. *See* Italian Copyright Law, Law No. 633 of April 22, 1941, *as amended through* July 29, 1989, art. 99; EDUARDO PIOLA CASELLI, CODICE DEL DIRITTO DI AUTORE 510-511 (1943); PAOLO GRECO & PAOLO VERCELLONE, I DIRITTI SULLE OPERE

perimental adaptation of copyright law to computer programs,[122] as well as certain aberrational experiments in the domestic copyright laws, such as full copyright protection of functional designs in the United Kingdom (now superseded);[123] full copyright protection of mostly non-functional appearance designs in France;[124] and modified forms of copyright protection for certain borderline functional works, such as measures concerning technical drawings and engineering projects in Germany and the United States.[125] Logically included in Marginal Zone B but not highlighted in this or earlier studies are the more traditional rights, related to or "neighboring" on copyright law, which protect performers, broadcasting organizations, and the producers of sound recordings,[126] and which turn out to be less deviant than appears on the surface.[127]

DELL' INGEGNO 395-96 (1974); *see also* Antonio Cataudella, *Rilettura delle norme a tutela degli autori di progetti di ingegneria*, 1988 RIVISTA DEL DIRITTO COMMERCIALI E DEL DIRITTO GENERALE DELLE OBLIGAZIONE 1. "Article 99 . . . allows authors of engineering projects or other analogous productions who contribute novel (but not nonobvious) solutions to technical problems to obtain a reasonable royalty from third parties who commercially exploit their technical contributions without authorization. This right to 'equitable compensation' lasts twenty years from the date of registration, and appropriate notice must appear on copies of the plans." *Legal Hybrids*, *supra* note 11, at 2477.

122 *See* EC Directive on Computer Programs, *supra* note 117. "[T]he European Community, bowing to pressure from the United States, produced the Council Directive on Computer Programs, which adopts a copyright approach while subtly incorporating important tailor-made exceptions and limitations." *Legal Hybrids*, *supra* note 11, at 2484-85; *see further id.* at 2485-88.

123 "Between 1968 and 1988, British courts . . . protected a 'host of wholly functional, nonregisterable articles designed without regard to appearance' on a par with true literary and artistic works merely 'because they started life as engineering drawings because copying could be indirect as well' as direct, and because it could be done by reproducing a two-dimensional work (the plaintiff's drawing) in three-dimensional form.' Items protected . . . included screws, bolts, washers, clerical collars, paper-mache bedpans, pulley wheels, and plastic knock-down drawers." *Legal Hybrids*, *supra* note 11, at 2489 (quoting Fellner, *supra* note 112, at 373).

124 The French "unity of art doctrine allows any appearance design to obtain cumulative protection as 'works of art' in copyright law regardless of its status under the design protection law in force. By combining a boundless definition of 'art' with exaggerated deference to the principle of nondiscrimination, French courts have conferred full copyright protection on purely functional designs of all kinds . . . ." *Legal Hybrids*, *supra* note 11, at 2489 (citing authorities).

125 *See supra* note 121 and accompanying text.

126 *See* Rome Convention, *supra* note 9 (creating international framework for coordinating domestic laws that protect performers' renditions, broadcasts, and producers of sound recordings); *see also* Stephen M. Stewart & Hamish Sandison, *Neighboring Rights*, *in* INTERNATIONAL COPYRIGHT AND NEIGHBORING RIGHTS, *supra* note 9, at 185-220; Cohen Jehoram, *supra* note 44, at 76-84.

127 "Despite occasional dependence on new technologies, these neighboring rights laws neither stimulate technological innovation nor systematically violate cardinal economic premises underlying the patent and copyright paradigms. On the contrary, they establish the outer limits of artistic property law without blurring or undermining the classical line of demarcation separating artistic from industrial property laws." *Legal Hybrids*, *supra* note 11, at 2500.

Figure 1 thus visually represents a working hypothesis about a putative marginal zone taking root somewhere between the patent and copyright paradigms that is further verified in the *Legal Hybrids* study. The collocation of deviant phenomena in this zone also attempts to portray the relative distance separating deviant objects of protection from the prototypical objects of patent and copyright protection, and it emphasizes the relative proximity of deviant cases to the historical line of demarcation running between industrial and artistic property law. While the reader is advised that the empirical survey of deviant models undertaken in the *Legal Hybrids* study ultimately required a rectification of this working hypothesis and its graphic representation,[128] a glance at the contents of Marginal Zones A and B in Figure 1 suffices to support what all experienced practitioners intuitively know: namely, that the real universe of world intellectual property law is inhabited by constellations of deviant protective modalities that violate its key operating assumptions, especially the negative economic premises set out above.[129]

Some of these misfits or mutants are truly new and readily identifiable with today's important new technologies. Others, however, are almost as old as the world's intellectual property system itself. Whether the latest deviants represent a novel response to new empirical phenomena or merely variants of responses to earlier phenomena that had long challenged the systemic integrity of the classical foundation is investigated in the *Legal Hybrids* article. Some of the preliminary conclusions drawn from that investigation are set out below, and any attempt to reconceptualize the field as a whole[130] must take them into account.

II. Empirical Limits of the Classical Bipolar Structure

The survey of deviant regimes carried out in the *Legal Hybrids* study confirms that the classical "vision that subdivided world intellectual property law into discrete and mutually exclusive compartments for industrial and artistic property has irretrievably broken down."[131] To the extent that the patent and copyright models underlying the Great Conventions represent a coherent theory about the way intellectual creations behave in the world at large, that theory has been discredited by its inability to account for, or ade-

128 *See infra* text accompanying notes 151-55.

129 *See supra* text accompanying notes 45-96.

130 *See further Legal Hybrids, supra* note 11, at 2500-2557.

131 *Id.* at 2500; *see generally id.* at 2453-2504.

quately deal with, the behavior of so many commercially valuable intellectual creations that actually inhabit that universe.[132]

The real objects of protection that increasingly elude the classical scheme often constitute the cutting edge of technological innovation at the end of the twentieth century; they account for an ever growing share of the gross domestic products in both developed and developing countries.[133] Yet, one cannot reconcile the hybrid legal regimes summoned to protect these creations with the economic justifications of the classical intellectual property system. On the contrary, the proponents of these regimes invariably make a virtue out of a vice by justifying the need for new intellectual property rights in terms of the shortcomings or limits of the dominant legal paradigms.

In these and other respects, the hybrid legal regimes proliferating within today's international intellectual property system resemble the Ptolemaic epicycles with which the earth-centered theory of the universe was continually adjusted in a bygone day.[134] These adjustments enable observers only to account for past deviations from existing norms without being able to predict the behavior of the relevant legal constellations in the future.

A. *Real Locus of the Deviant Regimes*

To escape these after-the-fact rationalizations, a helpful first step is to reconsider the theoretical foundations of the classical framework in order to obtain a more precise understanding of how—and where—it empirically accommodates the deviant regimes. As portrayed in Figure 1, regimes protecting industrial property were separated in principle from regimes protecting literary and artistic works by a line of demarcation set out in article 1(3) of the Paris Convention.[135] That line of demarcation relegated the legal protection of "products" to industrial property laws while implicitly confining literary and artistic productions, as nonproducts, to a specialized market governed by different regulatory principles that were far more generous to creators.[136]

---

132 *Id.*; *cf. also* Hermann Kronz, *Patent Protection for Innovations: A Model* (pt. 1), 7 E.I.P.R. 178, 180 (1983) (stressing irrelevance of patent system to real problem of transforming "technical knowledge into products and investment under much more difficult market entry conditions").

133 *Cf.* Reichman, *TRIPS Component*, *supra* note 5, at 263-66; *see also* Reichman, *GATT Connection*, *supra* note 3, at 754-66.

134 *See* THOMAS KUHN, THE STRUCTURE OF SCIENTIFIC REVOLUTIONS 69-70 (1970).

135 *See supra* text accompanying notes 28-44, 65-96.

136 *Compare* Paris Convention, *supra* note 7, art. 1(3) ("all manufactured or natural products") *with* Berne Convention, *supra* note 7, art. 2(1) ("every production in the literary, scientific and artistic domain"). *See also* P. Bernt Hugenholz, *Convergence and Divergence in*

1. A Permeable Line of Demarcation

The evidence suggests, instead, that *the marginal cases on either side of that line seem to flow into one another without encountering any meaningful resistance from it.* A typeface design converted into a computer program will claim entry into copyright law,[137] as will the digitized design of a dress nominally excluded from the same copyright law on other grounds.[138] Electronic circuit designs traditionally excluded from utility model laws may at different times qualify for protection as an unregistered design, as a computer program, as a technical drawing, as an integrated circuit design, and as a patentable invention, not to mention trade secret protection of the pertinent know-how.[139] That the marginal cases on either side of the dividing line appear to flow into one another also tallies with complaints that the nonobvious standard has been falling lower and lower,[140] or that patent law increasingly protects mathematical formulas and mental steps,[141] or that artistic property law sometimes affords patent-like protection, say, of computer programs.[142]

Given such a permeable line of demarcation and the growing tendency of the two compartments to overlap in practice,[143] legal issues of ownership and scope of protection in any particular case may vary with accidental or trivial aspects of the innovation in question. A university professor may own copyrightable components of a computer program he or she has created, but not the patentable components, because the applicable laws impose different owner-

---

Intellectual Property Law: The Case of the Software Directive, in INFORMATION LAW TOWARDS THE 21ST CENTURY 319, 320 (W.F. Korthals Altes et al. eds. 1992) ("In the old days, cumulative protection by copyright and patent law would have been unthinkable.").

137 *See, e.g.*, Snyder, *supra* note 114, at 113-15 (discussing Copyright Office decision to register computer programs that generate specific typeface design for copyright protection); *see also* Eltra Corp. v. Ringer, 579 F.2d 294, 298 (4th Cir. 1978) (long-standing judicial denial of copyrightability to type-face design had been "acquiesced in by Congress").

138 *Cf. supra* notes 120-25 and accompanying text (contradictory treatment of industrial art and literature).

139 *See Legal Hybrids, supra* note 11, at 2455-65, 2477-88; *see also* Reichman, *Overlapping Propriety Rights, supra* note 29, at 65. In 1990, the German utility model law was revised to admit electronic circuit designs. *See, e.g.*, Roland Leisegang, *German Utility Models After the 1990 Reform Act*, 20 A.I.P.L.A. Q.J. 1,2 (1992).

140 *See, e.g.*, Samuelson et. al, *Manifesto, supra* note 11, at 2345-47, 2361-64. The heads of both the Italian and Belgian patent offices have voiced such complaints to this author at recent conferences.

141 *See, e.g.*, *In re* Alappat, 33 F.3d 1526, 1542-45 (Fed. Cir. 1994) (Rich, J.); *id.* at 1545, 1562-68 (Archer, C.J., dissenting); *see also* Pamela Samuelson, Benson *Revisited: The Case Against Patent Protection for Algorithms and Other Computer Program-Related Inventions*, 39 EMORY L.J. 1025, 1059-1132 (1990); Hugenholz, *supra* note 136, at 319.

142 *See, e.g.*, Whelan Assocs., Inc. v. Jaslow Dental Laboratories, Inc., 797 F.2d 1222 (3rd Cir. 1986), *cert. denied*, 107 S. Ct. 877 (1987).

143 *Cf.* Frederich-Karl Beier, *The Future of Intellectual Property in Europe*, 22 I.I.C. 157, 161 (1991) (stating that the "areas of industrial property law . . . and copyright law . . . , formerly so neatly segregated, show a noticeable tendency to overlap and grow together").

ship criteria and biases.[144] Unpatented, noncopyrightable applications of know-how that may constitute the commercially most valuable components of the same program will respond to the very different ownership criteria and protective apparatus of trade secret law.[145] The cumulative legal product seems a caricature of the international intellectual property system as conceived at the end of the nineteenth century.

When the hybrid legal regimes are examined one by one, moreover, the evidence confirms *that their objects of protection actually resemble each other more than they resemble either works of art or industrial inventions, the prototypical subject matters of the dominant paradigms.* It is useful to reconsider some of their common characteristics in this light. Few, if any, of the subject matters governed by hybrid legal regimes actually partake of art in the historical and ordinary sense.[146] In addition, none of the hybrid regimes require the strict evaluation of merit characteristic of a mature patent system,[147] while all of them tend to allow the market, directly or indirectly, to validate the eligibility of their respective subject matters or to influence the scope of protection. To the extent that even the validity of traditional utility patents in the United States increasingly depends on secondary factors, such as commercial success and copying, the patent law itself is opening towards market-determined legal outcomes.[148] Finally, most of the deviant subject matters also lead a dualist existence that enables them to compete either as disembodied graphic or verbal representations of copyrightable works or as functional components of material supports that are distributed on the products market.[149]

That the objects of the deviant regimes actually resemble each other more than they resemble works of art or industrial inventions

---

144 *See generally*, Reichman, *Overlapping Proprietary Rights*, *supra* note 29, at 66-88.

145 *See generally id.* at 88-109; Rochelle Cooper Dreyfuss, *The Creative Employee and the Copyright Act of 1976*, 54 U. CHI. L. REV. 590, 597-600 (1987); *see also* BRANSCOMB, *supra* note 12, at 138-58.

146 *See generally Legal Hybrids*, *supra* note 11, at 2455-98 (discussing utility models, industrial designs, plant varieties, technical drawings and engineering projects, semiconductor chip designs, computer programs, and electronic data bases). Exceptions might include works of applied art and certain directories or other compilations that do constitute original and creative works of authorship. *See, e.g.*, *id.* at 2460, 2460 n.122, 2491.

147 *See supra* note 54 and accompanying text.

148 *See, e.g.*, Panduit Corp. v. Dennison Mfg. Co., 774 F.2d 1082, 1099-1100 (Fed. Cir. 1985); Alco Standard Corp. v. Tennessee Valley Authority, 808 F.2d 1490 (Fed. Cir. 1986); Hybridtech, Inc. v. Monoclonal Antibodies, Inc., 802 F.2d 1367 (Fed. Cir. 1986), *cert. denied*, 480 U.S. 947 (1987). *See also* Robert P. Merges, *Commercial Success and Patent Standards: Economic Perspectives on Innovation*, 76 CAL. L. REV. 803 (1988) (criticizing this trend).

149 *See Legal Hybrids*, *supra* note 11, at 2460-64 (case of industrial designs), 2477-78 (case of technical drawings, blueprints and engineering projects), 2480-88, 2493-98 (case of electronic information tools).

is of capital importance in arriving at a systematic clarification of the marginal cases in general. It should be remembered that Kohler and Picard coined the term "intellectual property" because they thought patents, copyrights, and trade marks had more in common with each other than with the categories of tangible property inherited from antiquity.[150] *That the creations governed by hybrid legal regimes resemble each other more than they resemble the true objects of classical copyright and patent systems likewise suggests that one is witnessing the formation of a new intellectual property paradigm that has much to reveal about the economics of competition in a post-industrial marketplace.*

2. Overlapping Jurisdictional Spheres

These findings mandate a rectification of the working hypothesis adopted at the outset of this Article. There it was posited that deviant intellectual property regimes were likely to group themselves at the "thin" edges of their respective jurisdictional spheres, as illustrated in zones A and B of Figure 1.[151] What the survey evidence actually reveals is that the patent and copyright paradigms have thrust deeper and deeper into each other's domains in order to provide some makeshift or emergency form of protection for marginal subject matters that resemble each other more than they resemble "inventions" or "works of art."[152] This finding is represented in Figure 2, entitled "Overlapping Jurisdictional Spheres."

One may note parenthetically that nothing emerged from the survey of legal hybrids that undermines the continuing validity of the master paradigms with respect to true inventions or works of art in the ordinary and historical sense. To the extent that current literature continues to challenge or defend the workings of these paradigms with respect to their traditional objects of protection, neither side can take much comfort from the data reported here.[153] *Serious problems arise in the penumbra or intermediate zone emerging between the patent and copyright paradigms.* Analysis of this zone has been handicapped, however, by the difficulties of map-

150 *See supra* notes 16-17 and accompanying text.

151 *See supra* text accompanying notes 97-130.

152 Contrary to the classical tenets of the international intellectual property system, in other words, the jurisdictional spheres governing inventions and artistic works overlap each other notwithstanding the historical premises of the Great Conventions, which posited two distinct legal compartments meeting at a common line of demarcation. *See supra* text accompanying notes 29-44.

153 *See supra* notes 1-2, 51-52 and accompanying text. *See also* Robert P. Merges, *Of Property Rules, Coase, and Intellectual Property*, 94 COLUM. L. REV. 2655-74 (1994) (critiquing liability rules without evaluating the adverse economic effects of exclusive property rights on small-scale incremental innovation falling in the penumbra between the patent and copyright paradigms).

FIGURE 2: OVERLAPPING JURISDICTIONAL SPHERES

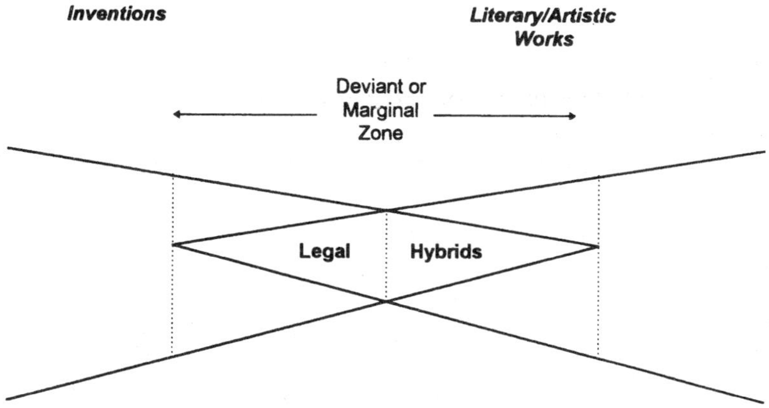

ping its overall dimensions or even of pinpointing its locus within an international intellectual property system still premised on the nonexistence of any operative space between the constituent subsystems of a bipolar structure.

The results of this author's empirical survey of the legal hybrids resolve this paradox by showing that the dominant paradigms actually overlap instead of meeting face to face.[154] As Figure 2 indicates, *the supposedly nonexistent space between the two distinct compartments actually lies within the intersecting regions of the dominant paradigms themselves, on either side of the classical line of demarcation.* The deviant or marginal zone of copyright law thus extends into the industrial property spectrum and mingles almost imperceptibly with its natural constituents; the deviant or marginal zone of industrial property law likewise extends into the sphere of artistic property and mingles almost imperceptibly with its regular constituents. The inability of the classical line of demarcation to impede these developments suggests that the line itself has become increasingly meaningless under modern conditions. The true outlines of the intermediate zone as a whole become visible, indeed, only when the observer ignores that line altogether and focuses attention on the similarities of its overlapping constituent parts rather than on the dissimilarities of "art" and "inventions."

---

154 *See Legal Hybrids, supra* note 11, at 2453-2504.

To portray how the legal regimes that constitute the intellectual property universe really behave at the end of the twentieth century, therefore, one needs to expunge the classical line of demarcation between the dominant paradigms from within the deviant zone and then to remove that zone from the jurisdiction of the dominant subsystems so that it appears as an entity in its own right. These adjustments conform to the evidence showing that, within the marginal zone, the formal line of demarcation constitutes a permeable non-barrier. They also express the fact that, within the marginal zone, all the constituent members affect the products market in one way or another as will be seen below, and that few, if any, partake of art in the historical and ordinary sense. These adjustments are illustrated in Figure 3, entitled "Real Locus of the Deviant Zone."

The proximity of the deviant zone to the dominant paradigms still conveys a false sense of homogeneity, however, which wrongly suggests that some facile relation between this zone and its bigger and more established neighbors lies readily at hand. In reality, *the classical distinction between patents and copyrights breaks down altogether within the marginal or intermediate zone.* There one finds an amalga-

FIGURE 3: REAL LOCUS OF THE DEVIANT ZONE

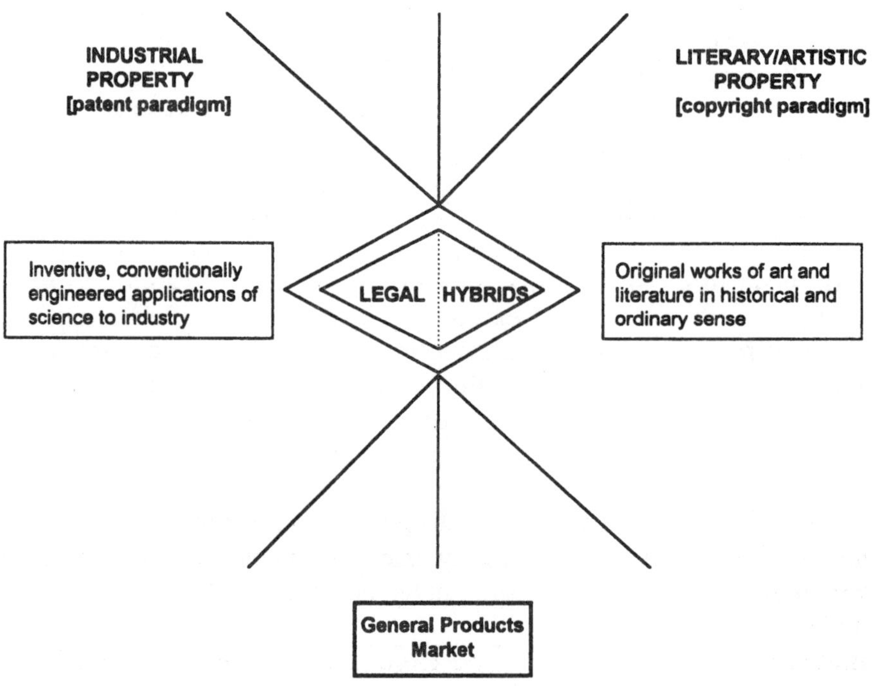

mation of protective devices drawn from both of the dominant models and meted out in a heterogeneous and sometimes almost haphazard fashion that varies with the artificial legal pigeonholes any given creation happens to fit.

To emphasize the interrelatedness of all the hybrid solutions, one should, therefore, portray the marginal zone as an autonomous entity independent of its evolutionary locus at the juncture of the dominant intellectual property subsystems. One can then logically detach this entity from its historical matrix and situate it at a certain distance from its overarching progenitors, in order to suggest its potentially autonomous character. These adjustments are accomplished in Figure 4, entitled "The Legal Hybrids as a Potentially Autonomous Entity."

FIGURE 4: THE LEGAL HYBRIDS AS A POTENTIALLY AUTONOMOUS ENTITY

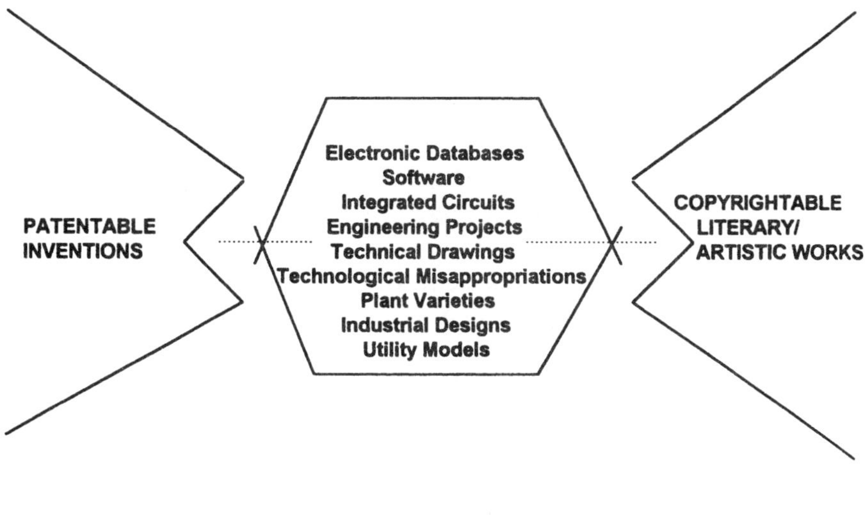

Viewed this way, the survey evidence confirms that, in the space where the patent and copyright systems overlap, legal hybrids multiply and thrive notwithstanding the contradictions they breed. This common domain, largely hidden from view by the paradigmatic blinders of ordinary legal thought, operates with a different legal and economic logic that increasingly distorts and destabilizes the workings of the master paradigms themselves. Identifying the common denominator that underlies these regimes, and devising a unified response to the challenge it poses, then become primary objects of inquiry.

B. *The Competitive Ethos Under Attack*

All of the marginal cases examined in the *Legal Hybrids* survey violate the negative economic premises of their respective master paradigms.[155] These deviations reveal the extent to which the economic justifications of the dominant intellectual property paradigms no longer meet the needs of those engaged in advanced technological innovation. At the same time, their cumulative anticompetitive effects cast doubt on the wisdom of the ad hoc legislative initiatives that continue to breed new intellectual property rights.

1. Overriding the Negative Economic Premises

On the patents side of the ledger, *all of the hybrid legal institutions protect innovation that normally fails the nonobviousness test of eligibility*. To the extent that economists justify industrial property protection in terms of the technical superiority it engenders,[156] that claim breaks down empirically as one enters the marginal zone. In this zone, one detects a palpable diminution in the strictness of the threshold prerequisites as one moves downwards from the "thick" to the "thin" end of the industrial property spectrum,[157] as shown in Figure 1.

For example, plant varieties, most commercial designs and, increasingly, even utility models need only show some form of "novelty" to qualify under their respective hybrid regimes.[158] Noncommonplace industrial designs that are independently created may qualify for protection under the United Kingdom's unregistered design right of 1988 even if they are functionally determined.[159] This unregistered design right, like the laws protecting

155 *See supra* text accompanying notes 45-96.

156 *See supra* notes 45-54 and accompanying text.

157 *See supra* text accompanying notes 98-107.

158 *See Legal Hybrids, supra* note 11, at 2502, 2502 n. 392 (citing authorities). *See also supra* note 139 and accompanying text (noting codification of lower standard in German utility model law.) All of these subject matters tended to obtain no appreciable range of equivalents when initially protected. However, the UPOV Agreement, as amended in 1991, *see supra* note 111, extends the range of equivalents afforded eligible plant varieties without elevating the standard of eligibility. *See Legal Hybrids, supra* note 11, at 2469-70. This would potentially make the latest UPOV model one of the most extreme deviants.

159 *See supra* note 112; Fellner, *supra* note 112, at 377-78.

integrated circuit designs and even Switzerland's technology misappropriation law, abandon even the pretense of a qualitative standard of achievement.[160] Yet, a statutory indifference to the level of achievement, wherever it materializes, approximates the copyright standard applicable to literary and artistic works.[161]

On the artistic property side of the ledger, meanwhile, *most of the hybrid institutions restrain competition with respect to nonartistic goods that are distributed on the general products market.* This violates the cardinal negative premise limiting application of the copyright paradigm to cultural goods.[162] Such distortions typically occur when creations falling within the marginal zone are susceptible of a "dualist" form of existence. When put forward as disembodied, two-dimensional representations of functional or factual matter, such as source codes of computer programs or as the drawing of an industrial object, they mimic the form of literary or artistic productions. The principle forbidding discrimination on the basis of merit then nudges them into copyright law.[163] When the same matter is subsequently embodied in three-dimensional products, the manufacturer extends copyright protection to market segments on which industrial, rather than cultural exploitation occurs.

The survey of legal hybrids revealed, in short, that the worldwide intellectual property system now routinely dispenses its legal monopolies to *less than nonobvious innovation that competes on the general products market.* Regardless of whether the hybrid legal regimes that increasingly occupy the forefront of attention protect cutting-edge technologies or more traditional forms of innovation, they defy the economic and social justifications for the classical intellectual property systems that were put forward at the end of the nineteenth century.[164]

2. Cumulative Restraints on Trade

The anti-competitive effects likely to ensue from this creeping generalization of the "two-market conundrum"[165] are potentially

160 *See Legal Hybrids, supra* note 11, at 2464-65, 2472-76, 2478-80, 2490.

161 *See supra* notes 79-84 and accompanying text.

162 *See supra* text accompanying notes 85-96.

163 *See supra* notes 80-81, 149 and accompanying text.

164 *See supra* text accompanying notes 45-52.

165 *See supra* text accompanying notes 162-63. The "two-market conundrum" is historically associated with industrial designs. Producers whose product designs gain entry into copyright law *qua* artistic creations may use the exclusive reproduction rights to control commercial exploitation of the underlying material supports *qua* industrial products on the general products market. *See, e.g.*, Reichman, *Designs and New Technologies, supra* note 73, at 130-32.

more far-reaching than those that the older marginal cases might have engendered fifty to a hundred years ago. In the nineteenth century, for example, industrial design was truly marginal in the economic sense, because industrial objects reproduced in series still competed on the basis of technical yields, not style;[166] moreover, electronic information processing had yet to be invented. Today, instead, industrial design drives the products market[167] and computer programs constitute a primary engine of economic development.[168] Yet, because virtually every product bears a functionally integrated configuration that could fall within, say, an unregistered design law[169] or increasingly, within a utility model law,[170] and because every computer program is potentially copyrightable,[171] *the cumulative effect of the marginal cases is to suspend the operation of the normal rules of competition at the very core of the post-industrial economy.*

Taken one by one, the protection provided by each of the hybrid legal regimes seeks to overcome the free-rider problem that threatens to inhibit investment in a particular type of innovation.[172] Taken together, these regimes introduce a strong protectionist bias into domestic economies driven by constant innovation that

> contradicts even the liberalizing thrust of multilateral trade negotiations seeking greater competition in an integrated world market. The risk is that liberalization . . . will largely affect traditional products of the industrial revolution, while producers of non-traditional, high-tech products and processes increasingly take ad hoc protectionist barriers for granted on both the domestic and international markets.[173]

---

166 *See, e.g.*, F. PERRET, *supra* note 30, at 13 (citing authorities). The marginal character of design protection laws in the nineteenth century was expressed in the phrase, "the poor relations in the family group of industrial property," that commentators often used. *See, e.g.*, 2 LADAS, INDUSTRIAL PROPERTY, *supra* note 8, at 828.

167 *See, e.g.*, D. O. UGHANWA & M. J. BAKER, THE ROLE OF DESIGN IN INTERNATIONAL COMPETITIVENESS 346 (1989) (stating that "the review of the literature and our empirical findings reveal that most of the important factors stimulating international competitiveness are design-driven"); *see also* F. PERRET, *supra* note 30, at 13-17.

168 *See generally* SAXBY, *supra* note 12, at 147-258.

169 *See, e.g.*, *Legal Hybrids*, *supra* note 11, at 2490; *see also* Reichman, *Evolution of Design Protection*, *supra* note 73, at 397-400.

170 *See, e.g.*, *Proposal of the Max Planck Institute for a European Utility Model Law*, 25 I.I.C. 700 (1994); Kern, *supra* note 109.

171 *See supra* notes 117 & 122 and accompanying text; TRIPS Agreement, *supra* note 4, art. 10(1); *see further* J.H. Reichman, *The Know-How Gap in TRIPS: Why Software Fared Badly, and What Are the Solutions*, 17 COMM/ENT __ (forthcoming 1995).

172 *See supra* notes 107-127 and accompanying text; *Legal Hybrids*, *supra* note 11, at 2442-44, 2511-17.

173 *See generally* Reichman, *Competition, Intellectual Property, and Trade*, *supra* note 5, at 94-98. The TRIPS Agreement, *supra* note 4, requires careful evaluation in this light. As re-

The protectionist tide rising with respect to nontraditional objects of legal protection could thus offset competitive gains expected to flow from the harmonization of laws pertaining to more traditional objects of protection whose relative share of total investment in research and development seems likely to decline over time.

These transnational legislative trends have virtually eclipsed the cautious and skeptical view of intellectual property rights that prevailed in the nineteenth and early twentieth centuries. In that period, compelling economic and social justifications were required for any legal monopoly that derogated from the basic norm of free competition. Even the paradigmatic intellectual property regimes recognized in the Paris and Berne Conventions accordingly evolved with strict limitations and exceptions that balance the public interest in competition against specific incentives to create.[174] "In contrast, the hybrid legal regimes appear to have been crafted without comparable inhibitions."[175] They represent an improvised set of responses to sectoral protectionist demands that lack any coherent theoretical foundations and that rest upon altogether different economic premises.

The competitive mandate of nineteenth-century economic law is thus giving way to an assortment of hybrid legal regimes under which virtually every product of important new technologies will come freighted with some improvised grant of exclusive property rights. As the protectionist momentum building up in the sphere of nontraditional innovation continues unabated, moreover, the paradigmatic foundations of the international intellectual property system are further destabilized by the tendency of patent, copyright and trademark laws to mutate under the pressure of events. Both tendencies lack any unifying principle or standards to guide courts and administrators, and history shows that both are likely to breed recurring cyclical states of chronic under- and over-protection.[176]

---

gards new technologies, in particular, this Agreement either leaves major gaps in the overall fabric of international intellectual property protection or consecrates reliance on the sector-by-sector hybrid regimes. *See generally* Reichman, *Universal Minimum Standards, supra* note 5, pt. II. C.

174 *See supra* text and accompanying notes 45-51.

175 *Legal Hybrids, supra* note 11, at 2503. For remorse and renewed dedication to free-market principles, *see* Robert W. Kastenmeier & Michael J. Remington, *The Semiconductor Chip Protection Act of 1984: A Swamp or Firm Ground?*, 70 MINN. L. REV. 417, 438-42 (1985). However, Chairman Kastenmeier was not re-elected and these tenets have seldom influenced subsequent legislative deliberations.

176 *See Legal Hybrids, supra* note 11, at 2503-04. Factors pulling for over- or underprotection already exist on both sides of the classical line of demarcation. On the copyright side of Figure 1, for example, a broad derivative work right sometimes overprotects by favoring overlapping claims to incremental innovation while restricting access to ideas, methods and processes by indirect means and for a very long duration. *See, e.g.*, Reichman, *Electronic*

It may be doubted that nineteenth-century notions of unrestricted competition adequately meet the needs of a post-industrial economy in which the most valuable commercial products often consist of costly, intangible bundles of information that third parties can duplicate without defraying the costs of their own research and development.[177] This theme colors the unified approach proposed in this author's *Legal Hybrids* study,[178] although it is worth noting here that the United States Supreme Court apparently relied on the nineteenth-century view in major recent decisions touching the free-rider problem.[179] Yet, what the empirical survey of legal hybrids showed, if nothing else, was that application of the nineteenth-century competitive model, as adjusted by its classical patent and copyright systems, had become increasingly chimerical in practice. *That model has been overwhelmed by the rise and rapid expansion of a countervailing group of deviant models that apply different and seldom explored economic principles.*

The bigger picture that emerges from the empirical survey of legal hybrids does not, therefore, concern just the evolution of intellectual property rights. It concerns the changing nature of competition in the so-called information society, changes that all the attention bestowed on the classical patent and copyright systems in recent years may paradoxically have obscured. In effect, the hybrid legal regimes "turn the nineteenth-century outlook upside down by presupposing a universe of commercial intercourse in which legal protection becomes a necessary and constant component of eco-

---

Information Tools, supra note 11, at 456-61 ("The Derivative Work at Odds with Information Technologies"). Yet, underprotection can result from the inability of copyright-like models to protect the internal dynamic features of technological innovation, in which idea and expression merge, and also from the lack of any exclusive right to control end use. *See* Samuelson et. al, *Manifesto, supra* note 11, at 2356-65. Similarly, on the industrial property side of Figure 1, "overprotection results from the progressive monopolization of ever smaller aggregates of inventive activity, which elevate social costs in return for no clearly equilibrated social benefits. Yet, the nonobviousness standard and its variants can also induce states of chronic underprotection by excluding the bulk of the incremental innovations that underlie today's most promising technologies." *Legal Hybrids, supra* note 11, at 2504 n.401.

The oscillations of industrial designs between recurring states of over- or underprotection during a two-hundred year period of regulatory activity were charted in this author's earlier studies. *See id.* at 2460-64 (citing authorities). In this and other respects, design protection laws appear to have been a precursor of the many legal hybrids that world intellectual property law would strive to accommodate in the last half of the twentieth century.

177 *See, e.g.*, Gordon, *Restitutionary Impulse, supra* note 72, at 277-78; Rochelle C. Dreyfuss, *Information Products: A Challenge to Intellectual Property Theory*, 20 N.Y.U. J. INT'L. L. & POL. 897, 908-12 (1988); William Kingston, *The Thesis Chapters, in* DIRECT PROTECTION OF INNOVATION 21-33 (William Kingston, ed. 1987). *See also* Karjala, *supra* note 72, at 2596-2601.

178 *See Legal Hybrids, supra* note 11, at 2504-58.

179 *See, e.g.*, Bonito Boats, Inc. v. Thunder Craft Boats, Inc., 489 U.S. 141 (1989); Feist Publications, 111 S. Ct. at 1289-91.

nomic life."[180] If, as the old cliché declares, the classical patent and copyright systems were once islands of protection in a sea of competition, the legal hybrids—taken together—conjure up the vision of a sea of protection in which intrepid entrepreneurs encounter remote islands of free competition.

3. Need for a New Intellectual Property Paradigm

Governments seeking to maintain high levels of investment in technological innovation face an increasingly difficult task as the twentieth century draws to a close. They must preserve or restore the bases for healthy competition at a time when information is increasingly becoming the medium from which the most socially valuable artifacts are likely to be constructed.[181] This task will require the elaboration of a new intellectual property paradigm that looks "beyond art and inventions."[182] Such a paradigm must deal directly with the pervasive threat of market failure facing investors in unpatentable, noncopyrightable innovation under present-day conditions, without multiplying ill-conceived, socially harmful regimes of exclusive property rights.[183]

This topic is addressed at length in *Legal Hybrids Between the Patent and Copyright Paradigms*,[184] a monograph that recently appeared in a symposium issue of the Columbia Law Review.[185] A companion article in that symposium, co-authored by Pamela Samuelson, Randall Davis, Mitchell D. Kapor and this author, presents concrete proposals for a new intellectual property regime to protect unpatentable, noncopyrightable components of computer programs.[186] Such a regime, built on modified liability principles that break with the exclusive property rights tradition,[187] would implement the unified field approach this author believes should gradually replace all existing hybrid regimes in a restructured

---

180 *Legal Hybrids*, *supra* note 11, at 2504.

181 *See* Samuelson et al., *Manifesto*, *supra* note 11, at 2320-24 ("Program text is, . . . like steel and plastic, a medium in which other works can be created").

182 *See supra* text accompanying notes 18-44; *see generally Legal Hybrids*, *supra* note 11, at 2504-06.

183 *See id.*, at 2442-44, 2506-19. *See also* Reichman, *Programs as Know-How*, *supra* note 11, at 648-67 ("New Directions in Legal Protection of Industrial Know-How").

184 *See supra* note 11.

185 *See generally* Symposium: Toward a Third Intellectual Property Paradigm, 94 Colum. L. Rev. 2307-2677 (1994).

186 *See* Samuelson et al., *Manifesto*, *supra* note 11, at 2413-29. Samuelson is professor of law at the University of Pittsburgh; Davis is a Professor of Computer Science and Associate Director of the Artificial Intelligence Laboratory, Massachusetts Institute of Technology; Kapor founded Lotus Development Corporation, designed Lotus 1-2-3, and is Chairman of the Board of the Electronic Frontier Foundation.

187 *See id.* at 2413-29.

intellectual property system.[188]

Taken together, these studies demonstrate that the failure of the patent and copyright models to deal adequately with the most important new technologies, including computer programs, biogenetic engineering, and industrial designs, does not stem from inherent conceptual defects in those models. Rather, the real problems arise from a breakdown of classical trade secret law under modern conditions. In effect, the nineteenth-century view of competition takes it for granted that some measure of natural lead time will result from the duty of second comers to reverse-engineer unpatented, noncopyrightable innovation by proper means.[189] In other words, competition with respect to the products of incremental innovation—as distinct from patentable inventions and copyrightable literary or artistic works—presupposes that trade secret laws (or equivalent laws of confidential information) typically supply enough lead time to overcome the problem of appropriability inherent in public goods.[190]

On analysis, trade secret law can most usefully be conceived as a set of default liability rules regulating relations between members of any given technical community. These rules provide innovators with natural lead time and they require second comers to contribute, directly or indirectly, to the technical community's overall costs of research and development.[191] Although trade secret laws always suffered from the risk of irrational and capricious results at the margins, where secrecy either did not exist at all or proved impervious to reverse-engineering, the total competitive picture entails an "historical dependence of intellectual property systems on a substratum of liability rules."[192]

These ancillary liability rules break down under modern conditions, however, because information becomes a primary medium of construction for the most innovative products and also because

---

188 *See Legal Hybrids, supra* note 11, at 2519-57.

189 *See id.* at 2438-42, 2520-25. "On the margins of the pure market economy . . ., trade secret laws (and related laws protecting confidential information) . . . provide a loosely constructed set of liability rules that . . . mediate between the potential for overprotection inherent in statutory grants of exclusive property rights and the potential for underprotection inherent in the competitor's unfettered ability to appropriate the fruits of investment in unpatented incremental innovation. The temporary or "disappearing" quantum of natural lead time they provide solves the free-rider problem . . . without resort to arbitrarily imposed barriers to entry characteristic of all regimes built around exclusive property rights." *Id.* at 2439-40 (citing authorities).

190 *Id.*, at 2506-11; *supra* notes 1, 65-69 and accompanying text. For empirical evidence, *see, e.g.*, Levin et. al., *supra* note 67, at 784. *See also* Friedman, Landes & Posner, *supra* note 68, at 67-69; Stedman, *supra* note 66, at 8-9.

191 *See Legal Hybrids, supra* note 11, at 2434-36, 2521-25.

192 *See id.* at 2434-36 (citing authorities).

the design components of new technologies—which transcend the old product-process distinction of patent law—are routinely embodied in the end products that are distributed in the open market. As a result, "incremental innovation bearing know-how on its face" tends to obtain zero lead time from classical trade secret law in most design-rich or design-dependent applications of advanced technical know-how to industry.[193] The resulting threat of market failure leads to the proliferation of hybrid legal regimes, usually built on modified patent and copyright principles, that have cropped up here and abroad. Collectively evaluated, their cumulative restraints on competition appear worse, in the sense of overprotection, than the chronic state of underprotection they seek to redress.[194]

The solution to the real problems facing twenty-first century innovation is not mindlessly to multiply exclusive property rights for each new technology that heaves into sight. Rather, the task is to develop a substitute liability regime that rationalizes the economic functions of classical trade secret law under the very different conditions of an Information Age: it requires, so to speak, the formulation of a "portable trade secret" regime whose economic benefits do not depend on the often socially irrelevant condition of actual secrecy.[195] To this end, the "default liability regime for applied know-how" outlined in the *Legal Hybrids* article[196] is devised specifically for unpatentable, noncopyrightable innovations that fall into the penumbra between the international patent and copyright systems. It provides innovators with short periods of artificial lead time in which to recoup their investment, and it also endows competitors with a menu of standardized, automatic licenses that encourage them to make incremental improvements while contributing to the originator's costs of research and development.[197] This minimalist, pro-competitive approach overcomes market failure and the attendant free-rider problem without multiplying exclusive property rights or creating other barriers to entry.

These and other studies thus confirm that today's most commercially valuable applications of scientific and technical know-

---

193 *See* Samuelson et al., *Manifesto, supra* note 11, at 2320-24; *Legal Hybrids, supra* note 11, at 2442-44, 2506-19. *See also* Dreyfuss, *supra* note 177, at 898-905; Wendy J. Gordon, *Assertive Modesty: An Economics of Intangibles*, 94 COLUM. L. REV. 2579, 2585-90 (1995); Richard R. Nelson, *Intellectual Property Protection for Cumulative Systems Technology*, 94 COLUM. L. REV. 2674, 2676-77 (1994).

194 *See Legal Hybrids, supra* note 11, at 2511-19.

195 *See id.* at 2519-21.

196 *See id.* at 2504-06, 2529-57.

197 *See id.* at 2529-57; *see also* Samuelson et al., *Manifesto, supra* note 11, at 2426-29.

how to industry often fall through the cracks of the classical bipolar structure enshrined in existing international conventions, including the TRIPS Agreement.[198] Policymakers charged with the task of restructuring the world's intellectual property system have yet to grasp the true nature of the problems that limit the flow of investment to incremental innovation under present-day conditions. As a result, the bases for healthy competition in an integrated world market risk being constantly undermined by a chronic shortage of natural lead time and by a welter of anticompetitive trade restraints that Ptolemaic tinkering with an obsolete historical construct tends to engender. Sooner or later, unless legislators combat these twin evils in the interests of a more rational and constructive approach that seeks to place both innovators and borrowers in a win-win position over time,[199] an increasingly discredited intellectual property system risks collapsing of its own protectionist weight.

---

198 *See supra* text accompanying notes 6-10, 18-44.

199 *See Legal Hybrids, supra* note 11, at 2535 ("Default liability rules that improve on existing trade secret laws should . . . promote the interest of the relevant technological community as a whole and the larger public interest with which they must be reconciled . . . Determining the interest of the technical community initially requires a recognition that most of its members do not pertain immutably to either the category of innovators or that of borrowers; they shift back and forth between these categories at different phases in the evolution of particular types of innovation").

THE PRECARIOUS BALANCE: MORAL RIGHTS, PARODY, AND FAIR USE

GERI J. YONOVER*

* ©1996, Geri J. Yonover. Professor of Law, Valparaiso University School of Law. B.A., University of Chicago, 1964; J.D., Chicago-Kent College of Law, 1983. I appreciate the very helpful comments of Jack Hiller, Dave Myers, and Curt Cichowski on an earlier version of this article, which appears at 29 VAL. U. L. REV. 935 (1995). I am grateful to Peter Yelkovac and Lynda Sloane, Class of 1994, for their excellent research assistance and to Terry Bloede for her enthusiastic secretarial support. Thanks are also due to the School of Law and Valparaiso University for the sabbatical leave that provided the time to think deeply about art and law.

Parody is 'the tribute that mediocrity pays to genius.'[1]
Parodies and caricatures are the most penetrating of criticisms.[2]

Art is both evolutionary and revolutionary. Art mutates according to the conscious, or even unconscious, sensibilities of the artist. That which has come before is fodder for artistic creation and is linked inextricably to the present. Art is history; at the same time it derives from history and affects history. In a real sense, the cave paintings of Lascaux and those recently discovered in Chauvet are our artistic ancestors. Lascaux's wooly mammoths relate to Picasso's bulls as the archaic smile on the faces of Hellenic sculpture informs the enigmatic smile of the *Mona Lisa.* "What's past, is prologue."[3] But art, like history, is not static. Changes come slowly or in sudden spurts. Sometimes artistic vision breaks out of the mold and gives us a new way to look at the world. Still other artists refer explicitly to earlier works. They appropriate them and, by adding humor, sarcasm, or comment, send a parodic message to the viewer about what these earlier works now mean to contemporary society.

Society needs the "parent" and the "child": the first artist and the parodist. Because art progresses on the shoulders of prior art, we want to protect the creator of the referent and the referencer. However, the tension between the first artist and the second artist will never disappear. Our goal should be to balance their economic and personal interests very, very carefully so as not to diminish the sum of art which enriches our lives.

When Congress enacted the Visual Artists Rights Act of 1990[4] ("VARA") as a measure subsequent to the United States joining the Berne Convention,[5] it represented the first explicit federal recogni-

---

1 Robert Bernstein, *Parody and Fair Use in Copyright Law,* 31 Copyright L. Symp. (ASCAP) 1, 12 (1984) (quoting Oscar Wilde).

2 *Id.* (quoting Aldous Huxley).

3 William Shakespeare, The Tempest act 2, sc. 1.

4 Visual Artists Rights Act of 1990, Pub. L. No. 101-650, tit. VI, 104 Stat. 5128 (1990) (codified in scattered sections of 17 U.S.C.).

5 Berne Convention Implementation Act of 1988, Pub. L. No. 100-568, 102 Stat. 2853 (1988) (codified at 17 U.S.C. §§ 401, 408, 411-412 (1994)). Article 6*bis* of the Berne Convention for the Protection of Literary and Artistic Works (Paris Text, 1971) provides:

> (1) Independently of the author's economic rights, and even after the transfer of said rights, the author shall have the right to claim authorship of the work and to object to any distortion, mutilation or other modification of, or other derogatory action in relation to, the said work, which would be prejudicial to his honor or reputation.
>
> (2) The rights granted to the author in accordance with the preceding para-

tion of the continental European notion of protecting an artist's moral rights,[6] specifically the rights of attribution and integrity.[7]

---

graph shall, after his death, be maintained, at least until the expiry of the economic rights, and shall be exercisable by the persons or institutions authorized by the legislation of the country where protection is claimed. However, those countries whose legislation, at the moment of their ratification of or accession to this Act, does not provide for the protection after the death of the author of all the rights set out in the preceding paragraph may provide that some of these rights may, after his death, cease to be maintained.

(3) The means of redress for safeguarding the rights granted by this Article shall be governed by the legislation of the country where protection is claimed.

Berne Convention for the Protection of Literary and Artistic Works, Sept. 9, 1886, *as last revised* at Paris, July 24, 1971, 828 U.N.T.S. 221 [hereinafter Berne Convention], art. 6[bis], *translated in* UNITED NATIONS EDUCATIONAL, SCIENTIFIC AND CULTURAL ORGANIZATION, 1 COPYRIGHT LAWS AND TREATIES OF THE WORLD, at Berne Copyright Union—Paris Act, 1971: Item H-1, at 3-4 (Supp. 1971) [hereinafter COPYRIGHT LAWS AND TREATIES OF THE WORLD].

As of 1985, seventy-six nations adhered to the Berne Convention, which was signed initially in 1896 and is the oldest multilateral treaty providing for copyright protection. Roberta R. Kwall, *Copyright and the Moral Right: Is an American Marriage Possible?*, 38 VAND. L. REV. 1, 10 & n.38 (1985). In order to join the Berne Convention, which required member nations to afford moral rights protection, *see* art. 6[bis](1), the United States had to represent that moral rights were already given some protection by various methods, including the Copyright Act of 1976, Pub. L. No. 94-553, 90 Stat. 2541 (1976) (codified as amended at 17 U.S.C. §§ 101-810, 18 U.S.C. § 2319 (1994)), which, until VARA, did not afford explicit protection for moral rights. *See* S. REP. NO. 352, 100th Cong., 2d Sess. 9-10 (1988), *reprinted in* 1988 U.S.C.C.A.N. 3706, 3714-15; *see also* FINAL REPORT OF THE AD HOC WORKING GROUP ON U.S. ADHERENCE TO THE BERNE CONVENTION 35-45, *reproduced in* 10 COLUM.-VLA J.L. & ARTS 513, 547-557 (1986).

[6] Several authors have examined the nature and extent of moral rights. *See, e.g.*, Robert A. Jacobs, *Work-For-Hire and the Moral Right Dilemma in the European Community: A U.S. Perspective*, 16 B.C. INT'L & COMP. L. REV. 29 (1993); John M. Kernochan, *Moral Rights in U.S. Theatrical Productions: A Possible Paradigm*, 17 COLUM.-VLA J.L. & ARTS 385 (1993); Brett Sirota, Note, *The Visual Artists Rights Act: Federal Versus State Moral Rights*, 21 HOFSTRA L. REV. 461 (1992); Moana Weir, *Making Sense of Copyright Law Relating to Parody: A Moral Rights Perspective*, 18 MONASH U. L. REV. 194 (1992); Patrick G. Zabatta, Note, *Moral Rights and Musical Works: Are Composers Getting Berned?*, 43 SYRACUSE L. REV. 1095 (1992); Joseph Zuber, *The Visual Artists Rights Act of 1990—What it Does, and What it Preempts*, 23 PAC. L.J. 445 (1992); Otto W. Konrad, *A Federal Recognition of Performance Art of Author Moral Rights*, 48 WASH. & LEE L. REV. 1579 (1991); Edward J. Damich, *The Visual Artists Rights Act of 1990: Toward a Federal System of Moral Rights Protection for Visual Art*, 39 CATH. U. L. REV. 945 (1990); Eric M. Brooks, Comment, *"Tilted" Justice: Site-Specific Art and Moral Rights After U.S. Adherence to the Berne Convention*, 77 CAL. L. REV. 1431 (1989); Lawrence A. Beyer, *Intentionalism, Art, and the Suppression of Innovation: Film Colorization and the Philosophy of Moral Rights*, 82 NW. U. L. REV. 1011 (1988); Kwall, *supra* note 5; Sydney A. Diamond, *Legal Protection for the "Moral Rights" of Authors and Other Creators*, 68 TRADEMARK REP. 244 (1978); John H. Merryman, *The Refrigerator of Bernard Buffet*, 27 HASTINGS L.J. 1023 (1976); Raymond Sarraute, *Current Theory on the Moral Right of Authors and Artists Under French Law*, 16 AM. J. COMP. L. 465 (1968); William Strauss, *The Moral Right of the Author*, 4 AM. J. COMP. L. 506 (1955); Martin A. Roeder, *The Doctrine of Moral Right: A Study in the Law of Artists, Authors, and Creators*, 53 HARV. L. REV. 554 (1940).

[7] 17 U.S.C. § 106A (1994) provides in relevant part:

(a) Rights of Attribution and Integrity. Subject to section 107 and independent of the exclusive rights provided in section 106, the author of a work of visual art—

(1) shall have the right—

(A) to claim authorship of that work, and

(B) to prevent the use of his or her name as the author of any work of visual art which he or she did not create;

(2) shall have the right to prevent the use of his or her name as the author

To date, there has been little litigation brought under VARA—none involving parody.[8] Thus, in assessing the proper balance between the protection of an artist's moral rights, the fairness of an alleged infringer's use of the artist's work in parodying that work, and society's interest in providing incentives to create more art, this article is, in one sense, writing on a clean slate. But prior case law focusing on parody and fair use,[9] especially the recent

---

> of the work of visual art in the event of a distortion, mutilation, or other modification of the work which would be prejudicial to his or her honor or reputation; and
>
> (3) subject to the limitations set forth in section 113(d), shall have the right—
>
> > (A) to prevent any intentional distortion, mutilation, or other modification of that work which would be prejudicial to his or her honor or reputation, and any intentional distortion, mutilation, or modification of that work is a violation of that right, and
> >
> > (B) to prevent any destruction of a work of recognized stature, and any intentional or grossly negligent destruction of that work is a violation of that right.

8 Since the effective date of VARA, June 1, 1991, there have been few reported cases brought under the statute. *See, e.g.*, Pavia v. 1120 Avenue of the Americas Assocs., 901 F. Supp. 620 (S.D.N.Y. 1995) (holding that VARA does not protect an artist whose work was altered before VARA's effective date). In Carter v. Helmsley-Spear, Inc., 852 F. Supp. 228 (S.D.N.Y. 1994), three sculptors sought to prevent building owners from dismantling a large sculptural installation from a lobby of a former Macy's warehouse in Queens, New York. In August 1994, Judge Edelstein granted plaintiffs an injunction that permits them to visit the unfinished work and restricts defendants from removing the sculpture. The ruling was based on plaintiff's claim that defendant's attempted removal would "deface, modify, or mutilate" the work in violation of § 106A(a)(2) and (a)(3). *Carter*, 852 F. Supp. at 232. Recently, the Second Circuit reversed, holding the sculpture to be a work made for hire and therefore not protected under VARA. Carter v. Helmsley-Spear, Inc., 71 F.3d 77 (2d Cir. 1995).

The issues raised in *Carter* are not new. In 1980, the New York branch of The Bank of Tokyo cut up a large sculpture by the noted artist and architect, Isamo Noguchi, and removed it from the bank's Wall Street office without notifying Noguchi. *See* George Glueck, *Bank Cuts Up a Noguchi Sculpture and Stores It*, N.Y. TIMES, Apr. 19, 1980, at A1. This occurred more than a decade before VARA and more than five years before a New York moral rights statute became effective. Thus, Noguchi, unlike the *Carter* sculptors, had no remedy. *See* Edward J. Damich, *The New York Artists' Authorship Rights Act: A Comparative Critique*, 84 COLUM. L. REV. 1733 (1984). However, the New York statute, N.Y. ARTS & CULT. AFF. LAW § 14.03 (McKinney Supp. 1996), does not protect the artist against destruction of the work. *See* Zuber, *supra* note 6, at 465; *cf.* Crimi v. Rutgers Presbyterian Church, 89 N.Y.S.2d 813 (N.Y. Sup. Ct. 1949) (holding that an artist had no remedy when defendant obliterated a church fresco painted by him). *Crimi* was decided well before the enactment of the New York statute.

In a Canadian case brought on similar facts, a sculptor succeded in preventing the Toronto Eaton Centre from tying Christmas ribbons around the necks of the sixty geese making up his sculpture. Snow v. The Eaton Centre Ltd., 70 C.P.R.2d 105 (Ont. High Ct. 1982). The plaintiff claimed that the ribbons around the geese's necks were similar to dangling earrings on the *Venus de Milo*. *Id.* Canadian copyright law has an express provision for protection of the right to integrity. *See* R.S.C. ch. C-30, §§ 14.1-14.2, 28.1-28.2 (4th Supp. 1989) (Can.). Authors of paintings, sculptures, and engravings do not have to show prejudice to honor or reputation, as do other authors. Rather, the distortion, modification, or mutilation of these works are presumed to cause the requisite harm. *Id.* § 28.2(2). *See generally* LESLEY E. HARRIS, CANADIAN COPYRIGHT LAW (1992).

9 *See infra* notes 133-41, 143-44, 146-48, and accompanying text.

Supreme Court decision in *Campbell v. Acuff-Rose Music, Inc.*,[10] as well as a significant body of literature that addresses the parody and fair use issue in a non-moral rights context,[11] does inform the discussion herein, which is based on the following hypothetical facts.

Assume that sometime after June 1, 1991,[12] a modern Leonardo da Vinci executed a portrait of Mona Lisa[13] and made a limited edition of 100 lithographs. He numbered them consecutively, 1/100, 2/100, and so on, and signed each one.[14] Leonardo com-

---

10 114 S. Ct. 1164 (1994).

11 *See, e.g.*, William F. Patry & Shira Perlmutter, *Fair Use Misconstrued: Profit, Presumptions, and Parody*, 11 CARDOZO ARTS & ENT. L.J. 667 (1993); Brian R. Landy, Comment, *The Two Strands of the Fair Use Web: A Theory for Resolving the Dilemma of Music Parody*, 54 OHIO ST. L.J. 227 (1993); E. Kenley Ames, Note, *Beyond* Rogers v. Koons: *A Fair Use Standard for Appropriation*, 93 COLUM. L. REV. 1473 (1993); Richard Posner, *When is Parody Fair Use?*, 21 J. LEGIS. STUD. 67 (1992); Alfred C. Yen, *When Authors Won't Sell: Parody, Fair Use, and Efficiency in Copyright Law*, 62 U. COLO. L. REV. 79 (1991); Steven R. Gordon & Charles J. Sanders, *Strangers in Parodies—Weird Al and the Law of Musical Satire*, 1 FORDHAM ENT. MEDIA & INTELL. PROP. L.F. 11 (1990); Michael A. Chagares, *Parody or Piracy: The Protective Scope of the Fair Use Defense to Copyright Infringement Actions Regarding Parodies*, 12 COLUM.-VLA J.L. & ARTS 229 (1988); Harriette K. Dorsen, *Satiric Appropriation and the Law of Libel, Trademark, and Copyright: Remedies Without Wrongs*, 65 B.U. L. REV. 923 (1985); Charles C. Goetsch, *Parody as Free Speech—The Replacement of the Fair Use Doctrine by First Amendment Protection*, 3 W. NEW ENG. L. REV. 39 (1980); Sheldon N. Light, *Parody, Burlesque, and the Economic Rationale for Copyright*, 11 CONN. L. REV. 615 (1979). For an excellent treatise on the subject, see WILLIAM F. PATRY, THE FAIR USE PRIVILEGE IN COPYRIGHT LAW (1985).

12 Under VARA, to receive federal protection against interference with the right of integrity, a work must be destroyed, distorted, mutilated, or modified after June 1, 1991, the effective date of VARA. VARA § 610(a), 104 Stat. 5132; *see Pavia*, 901 F. Supp. 620.

13 Leonardo's portrait has been described as enigmatic and mysterious. It is at once a rendition of a particular individual, probably the wife of a Florentine merchant named Giocondo, and an expression of the High Renaissance ideal of woman. The woman's features, her half-smile, and the "sfumato" (hazy) background have intrigued viewers for more than four hundred years, inspiring songwriters (like Nat King Cole, who wrote "Mona Lisa") and other artists, including Marcel Duchamp. The *Mona Lisa* is "the most reproduced . . . image in all art." CAROL STRICKLAND & JOHN BOSWELL, THE ANNOTATED MONA LISA 34 (1992). To some, the portrait "embodies a quality of maternal tenderness which was to Leonardo the essence of womanhood." HORST W. JANSON, HISTORY OF ART 421 (2d ed. 1977). It has been suggested by computer artist Lillian Schwartz that the *Mona Lisa* is actually a self-portrait of Leonardo. *See* Louis Montana, *Commercial Applications of Realist Art: Lillian Schwartz*, 54 AM. ARTIST 60-65 (1990). If this is so, then maybe Duchamp's moustache reveals Leonardo's "secret."

It is conceivable that Leonardo may have used parody in the *Mona Lisa*. Her intriguing smile evokes the "Archaic smile" of Greek figures of the fifth and sixth centuries B.C. *See* JANSON, *supra*, at 421.

14 Our modern Leonardo's work is protected by VARA because it qualifies as a "work of visual art" as defined in 17 U.S.C. § 101:

> (1) a painting, drawing, print, or sculpture, existing in a single copy, in a limited edition of 200 copies or fewer that are signed and consecutively numbered by the author, or, in the case of a sculpture, in multiple cast, carved, or fabricated sculptures of 200 or fewer that are consecutively numbered by the author and bear the signature or other identifying mark of the author; or
>
> (2) a still photographic image produced for exhibition purposes only, existing in a single copy that is signed by the author, or in a limited edition of 200 copies or fewer that are signed and consecutively numbered by the author.

plied with all provisions of the relevant copyright statute.[15] Assume also that in July 1991, a contemporary Marcel Duchamp[16] bought one of these lithographs and added a moustache to the face of Mona Lisa, not unlike what Duchamp actually did in 1919. Duchamp then exhibits this picture at a local art gallery, whereupon Leonardo files a complaint in federal district court, alleging, *inter alia,*[17] a violation of VARA.[18] Duchamp answers the complaint in typical fashion: (1) he did not infringe, and (2) even if he did, his use is a fair one,[19] based on parody, which immunizes his al-

---

15 Leonardo's "modern" *Mona Lisa* is protected by copyright, as it qualifies as an "original work . . . of authorship fixed in [a] tangible medium of expression." 17 U.S.C. § 102(a). As a pictorial work created after March 1, 1989, affixation of copyright notice, registration of the work in the copyright office, and recordation as a precondition to suit are discretionary, not mandatory. *See* Berne Convention Implementation Act, *supra* note 5.

16 Duchamp was one of the founders of the post-World War I self-titled "Dada" artistic movement. Dada allegedly was a random word choice, considered an infantile "all-purpose" word. Dada, in part, stood for anti-art and was a reaction to the senseless destruction caused by the War. Duchamp is probably most remembered for his 1912 *Nude Descending a Staircase, No. 2,* a cubist portrait of a woman's continuous motion as she walks down a flight of stairs. *See* JANSON, *supra* note 13, at 660 & fig. 820. The *Nude* was the most talked about hit of the famous 1913 Armory show in New York, which showed 1,600 modern works. *See* MARCEL JEAN, THE HISTORY OF SURREALIST PAINTING 31 (1960). The Armory Show, exhibiting works of such artists as Duchamp, Matisse, and Picasso, has been called the "most significant art show in American History," because "it burst the bubble of American provincialism." The *New York Times* called the show "pathological." Public officials demanded the closing of the Armory show "to safeguard public morals." STRICKLAND & BOSWELL, *supra* note 13, at 150.

For insight into Duchamp's creative mind, combining both wit and scientific precision, see MARCEL DUCHAMP, THE BRIDE STRIPPED BARE BY HER BACHELORS EVEN (George H. Hamilton trans., 1960). In fact, Duchamp's mathematical precision is not unlike that with which Leonardo planned his paintings. *Mona Lisa* is drawn in the shape of a truncated cone, one example of Leonardo's thinking that "every branch of knowledge dovetails with every other." LIANA BORTOLON, THE LIFE, TIMES AND ART OF LEONARDO 72 (1965).

17 The claims might include copyright infringement under 17 U.S.C. § 106(1), (2); unfair competition claim under section 43(a) of the Lanham Act, 15 U.S.C. § 1125 (1994); and assorted state claims such as unfair competition, defamation, and misrepresentation.

18 17 U.S.C. § 106A (violation of rights of attribution and integrity). Federal question jurisdiction is based on 28 U.S.C. §§ 1331, 1338 (1994).

19 The moral rights given to visual artists are tempered explicitly by VARA, 17 U.S.C. § 106A. Section 107 delineates fair use:

> Notwithstanding the provisions of sections 106 and 106A, the fair use of a copyrighted work, including such use by reproduction in copies or phonorecords or by any other means specified by that section, for purposes such as criticism, comment, news reporting, teaching (including multiple copies for classroom use), scholarship, or research, is not an infringement of copyright. In determining whether the use made of a work in any particular case is a fair use the factors to be considered shall include—
> (1) the purpose and character of the use, including whether such use is of a commercial nature or is for nonprofit educational purposes;
> (2) the nature of the copyrighted work;
> (3) the amount and substantiality of the portion used in relation to the copyrighted work as a whole; and
> (4) the effect of the use upon the potential market for or value of the copyrighted work.
> The fact that a work is unpublished shall not itself bar a finding of fair use if such finding is made upon consideration of all the above factors.

leged infringement. The case of *Leonardo v. Duchamp* may well be one of first impression and illustrates the inherent conflict between moral rights on the one hand and parody on the other, with fair use as the arbiter.

The imaginary juxtaposition of these two artists is not without some logic.[20] Leonardo's renown persists through the centuries not only because of his few but incredibly beautiful paintings, such as *The Last Supper*, the *Mona Lisa*, and *The Virgin of the Rocks*, but because of his encompassing vision of the artist as inventor, scientist, physicist, and architect, which led to innumerable detailed drawings of flying machines, embryos in the womb, human anatomy, and a host of other subjects. His approach to these drawings was scientific and analytical. Leonardo believed that artists should "know not only the rules of perspective but also all laws of nature . . . ."[21] In short, Leonardo tried to bridge the gap between art and craft, between painting and science. Similarly, Duchamp, in his "Ready-Mades," for example, a very slightly embellished bicycle, urinal, or bottlerack, and in his precise, scientific drawings, which are "a sort of mathematics of signs and significations,"[22] attempted, like Leonardo, to bridge the gap between art and science. Thus, in one sense, *L.H.O.O.Q.*[23] (the mustachioed *Mona Lisa*) represents a conscious or subconscious attempt to link Duchamp with Leonardo—art as science, art as both homage and critique, art as parody.

This article will discuss the appropriate resolution of the moral rights issues raised in *Leonardo v. Duchamp*. The discussion in part I focuses on the current state of moral rights protection.[24] Part II focuses on parody[25] and fair use.[26] Part III proposes that fair use, based on a parody that infringes upon an artist's moral

---

17 U.S.C. § 107.

20 The artificial placing of two or more chronologically and/or geographically separate individuals who interact in the same place and time is a frequent literary device. *See, e.g.*, E.L. DOCTOROW, RAGTIME (1974) (book involving Henry Ford, Emma Goldman, Harry Houdini, J.P. Morgan, Theodore Dreiser, Sigmund Freud, and Emiliano Zapata); TOM STOPPARD, TRAVESTIES (1974) (play involving Lenin; James Joyce; and Tristan Tzara, a noted and early Dadaist (*Travesties* is itself a parody of OSCAR WILDE, THE IMPORTANCE OF BEING EARNEST (1895)); STEVE MARTIN, PICASSO AT THE LAPIN AGILE (1993) (play in which Picasso and Einstein meet at the noted Parisian bistro).

21 JANSON, *supra* note 13, at 421.

22 JEAN, *supra* note 16, at 36. In Venice, the 1993 Biennale presented a Duchamp retrospective at the Palazzo Grassi, which contained several of his readymades, paintings, and drawings. The germ of this article was formed when I viewed this exhibit.

23 This acronym has several meanings; *see infra* text accompanying notes 125-26.

24 *See infra* notes 32-120 and accompanying text.

25 *See infra* notes 121-33 and accompanying text.

26 *See infra* notes 134-73 and accompanying text.

right of integrity,[27] should be given a wide berth.[28] Put another way, under fair use an artist's moral right of integrity should in most circumstances yield to the right of the parodist. Part III also explores other means of resolving the tension between parody and moral rights, including a per se rule of non-liability, based either on copyright law or First Amendment considerations,[29] a limitation of remedies where the use is determined to be unfair,[30] and the availability of a compulsory license for the parodist.[31] The article concludes that these alternatives will not be as effective as an interpretation of fair use that presumes a parodist's use is fair when section 106A rights of integrity are at stake.

I. Moral Rights

Until the enactment of VARA,[32] the focus of the 1976 Copyright Act was on protecting the pecuniary rights of copyright owners.[33] However, the European concept of moral rights differs significantly from the English and American copyright models[34] and fits, as a newcomer to our shores, very uneasily into our copyright scheme. Unlike United States copyright law's emphasis on economic rights, the concept of moral rights is based upon the notion that an artist expresses her individualism, her personality, in her art—that, in effect, we cannot "separate the dancer from the dance."[35] Moral rights encompass personality rights[36] that inure to

---

27 17 U.S.C. § 106A(a)(3)(A).

28 *See infra* notes 213-45 and accompanying text.

29 *See infra* notes 201-12 and accompanying text.

30 *See infra* notes 195-201 and accompanying text.

31 *See infra* notes 178-94 and accompanying text.

32 17 U.S.C. § 106A.

33 A copyright owner could be the author, an employer, or one who commissions a certain type of work under the provisions of 17 U.S.C. § 101(1) or (2), or someone who now owns the copyright due to transfer of ownership under the provisions of 17 U.S.C. §§ 201-205.

34 United States copyright law was modeled after the Statute of Anne, 8 Anne, ch. 19 (1709). These laws protected the economic, rather than the personal, rights of authors. The pecuniary protection afforded copyright owners by the 1976 Act is the ability to prevent and be compensated for wrongful use of the particular work. Such unpermitted use of the protected work constitutes infringement. Infringement occurs when an unauthorized party violates one or more of the exclusive bundle of rights afforded by section 106, such as the right to reproduce, to make derivative works, to distribute, to display, or to perform. To prove infringement, the copyright owner must prove a valid copyright in the work and copying by defendant.

35 William B. Yeats, *Among School Children, in* The Tower 8 (1928).

36 S. Ladas, The International Protection of Literary and Artistic Property 272 (1938). The author uses the German word "urheberpersonlichkeitsrecht," translated as "right of the author's personality." It is noteworthy that most countries that provide moral rights protection do not recognize a fair use defense. *See* Anne Moebes, *Negotiating International Copyright Protection: The United States and European Positions*, 14 Loy. L.A. Int'l & Comp. L.J. 301, 320 (1992).

the artist as creator, protect the artistic integrity of the artist's creation, and require the recognition of the artist as author/creator.[37]

A. *The European Experience*

In any one country, the bundle of personal moral rights may also include, in addition to the right of integrity, the right of disclosure (the exclusive ability to decide when or if the work should be disseminated publicly), the right of withdrawal (the exclusive ability after publication of the work to recall all existing copies of the work), and the right to prevent excessive criticism where its only purpose is to abuse the author.[38] As of 1981, there were approximately three dozen countries in Asia, Africa, Europe, and South America that recognized one or more of the personal, moral rights of artists.[39] These countries were and are predominantly civil rather than common law jurisdictions. It is in these countries, perhaps especially in France,[40] Italy,[41] and Germany,[42] that the eight-

---

[37] Sarraute, *supra* note 6, at 478. The latter right is known as the "right of paternity." *Id.*

[38] Kwall, *supra* note 5, at 5-8. Another right that is both personal and explicitly pecuniary is the "droit de suite," or resale royalty provisions, which require the owner of a work of art, should it be resold, to pay a percentage of the resale price to the artist, even if the artist is no longer the copyright owner. The "droit de suite" is a French concept dating from 1920. *See generally* Elliot C. Alderman, *Resale Royalties in the United States for Fine Visual Artists: An Alien Concept*, 40 J. COPYRIGHT SOC'Y 265 (1993); John H. Merryman, *The Wrath of Robert Rauschenberg*, 40 J. COPYRIGHT SOC'Y 241 (1993); Shira Perlmutter, *Resale Royalties for Artists: An Analysis of the Register of Copyrights' Report*, 40 J. COPYRIGHT SOC'Y 284 (1993); Carol Sky, *Report of the Register of Copyrights Concerning "Droit de Suite," the Artist's Resale Royalty: A Response*, 40 J. COPYRIGHT SOC'Y 315 (1993). The authors split 2/2 on the advisability of "droit de suite" in this country: Merryman and Alderman against; Perlmutter and Sky believing it worth exploring. A constitutional challenge to California's Resale Royalty Act, CAL. CIV. CODE § 986 (West Supp. 1995), was rejected. *See* Morseburg v. Balyon, 201 U.S.P.Q. (BNA) 518 (C.D. Cal. 1978).

[39] Kwall, *supra* note 5, at 97-100.

[40] Law No. 57-298 on Literary and Artistic Property, Mar. 11, 1957, *as amended* up to July 3, 1985, arts. 6, 19, 32 (Fr.) (the inalienable right of paternity, the right of disclosure, and right of withdrawal when the artist agrees to indemnify the owner of the work), *translated in* 1 COPYRIGHT LAWS AND TREATIES OF THE WORLD, *supra* note 5, at France: Item 1, at 1, 3, 5 (Supp. 1984-86). France is thought to be the foremost exponent of an artist's personal rights, Russell J. Da Silva, *Droit Moral and the Amoral Copyright*, 28 BULL. COPYRIGHT SOC'Y 1, 2 (1980), followed by Germany and Italy. *See* Sydney A. Diamond, *Legal Protection for the "Moral Rights" of Authors and Other Creators*, 68 TRADEMARK REP. 244, 247 (1978).

A leading scholar on civil law systems notes:

> The moral right of the artist in French law is entirely judicial in origin. This is in itself remarkable, since one of the most treasured tenets of the conventional wisdom about the civil law is that law is made by legislators and executives, not by judges. The development of the moral right of the artist is merely another example of the extent to which this tattered brocard is inapplicable to France.

JOHN H. MERRYMAN ET AL., THE CIVIL LAW TRADITION: EUROPE, LATIN AMERICA AND EAST ASIA (1994); *see* JOHN H. MERRYMAN & ALBERT E. ELSEN, LAW, ETHICS AND THE VISUAL ARTS 144 (2d ed. 1987); Jack A. Hiller, *The Law-Creative Role of Appellate Courts in The Third World*, *in* ESSAYS ON THIRD WORLD PERSPECTIVES IN JURISPRUDENCE 226-27 & nn.270-77 (M.L. Marisinghe & William E. Conklin eds., 1994).

The statutory data given in this note and notes 41-42 *infra* is gleaned from the World

eenth century romantic notions of authorship took hold—art as an expression of the unique personality of an author who captures and records the very essence of culture.[43] Once artists are regarded in this manner, it is practically inevitable that legal doctrine would appear to protect the personal, if not also the pecuniary, rights of artists.

Several French cases, brought on the basis of a moral rights violation, illustrate how powerful a tool the concept of moral rights is in the hands of the artist. Perhaps the paradigmatic moral rights case is the one involving the painter Bernard Buffet and his refrigerator.[44] Buffet had painted a refrigerator's six sides and regarded the finished piece as one painting, thus signing only one of the panels. After auctioning the refrigerator, Buffet became aware of another auction that offered one of the six painted panels. He sued to prevent this sale, as he regarded the six-panelled work as an indivisible artistic whole. The Paris Court of Appeals agreed, and the Cour de cassation affirmed that this violated Buffet's right

---

Intellectual Property Organization Copyright Law Survey, as reported in Kwall, *supra* note 5, at 98-100.

41 Law No. 633 of Apr. 22, 1941 for Protection of Copyright and Other Rights Connected with the Exercise Thereof, *as amended* up to July 29, 1981, arts. 20, 142 (Italy) (rights of paternity, integrity, and withdrawal subject to indemnity), *translated in* 2 COPYRIGHT LAWS AND TREATIES OF THE WORLD, *supra* note 5, at Italy: Item 1, at 3-4 (Supp. 1981-83), 22-23 (Supp. 1979-80). In an illustrative Italian case, De Chirico v. Ente Autonomo "La Biennale" di Venezia, [1951] Diritto de Autori 220, [1951] Temi 568, [1952] 50 Rivista Diritto Commerciale [Riv. Div. Comm.] II. 128 (Tribunal di Venezia) (note by Fioretta), the trial court ruled in favor of artist Giorgio de Chirico's claim that a proposed exhibition of a number of the artist's works in the Biennale misrepresented him by including too many early works and not including enough later works. *See* Merryman, *supra* note 6, at 1032-33 & nn.29-33.

42 Act dealing with Copyright and Related Rights, Sept. 9, 1965, *as amended* up to June 24, 1985, arts. 12-14, 42, 46(4) (F.R.G.) (rights of disclosure, paternity, integrity, to revoke a license, with indemnity, if work no longer reflects artist's views), *translated in* 2 COPYRIGHT LAWS AND TREATIES OF THE WORLD, *supra* note 5, at Germany: Item 1, at 2a, 7-8 (Supp. 1984-1986).

The *Rocky Island with Sirens*, 79 RGZ 397 (BGH 1912), case is typical. By commission, plaintiff painted a mural in the stairway of defendant's home. The homeowner objected to the naked sirens and had them painted with clothing. The court said that the homeowner violated the artist's right against unauthorized changes. *See* Strauss, *supra* note 6, at 510 n.22. The statutory data given in this note and notes 72-73 *infra* is gleaned from the World Intellectual Property Organization Copyright Law Survey, as reported in Kwall, *supra* note 5, at 98-100.

Moral rights are on the march. There is sentiment within the European Community that moral rights should be strengthened, especially in connection with the film industry. *See EC Moral Rights Measures Proposed*, 5 J. PROPRIETARY RTS. 34 (1993). In May 1991, the former U.S.S.R. Supreme Soviet passed a law granting authors and their heirs the right of integrity, among others. *See* Eric J. Schwartz, *Recent Developments in the Copyright Regimes of the Soviet Union and Eastern Europe*, 38 J. COPYRIGHT SOC'Y 123 (1991).

43 *See generally* Peter Jaszi, *On the Author Effect: Contemporary Copyright and Collective Creativity*, 10 CARDOZO ARTS & ENT. L.J. 293 (1992); Christopher Aide, *A More Comprehensive Soul: Romantic Conceptions of Authorship and the Copyright Doctrine of Moral Right*, 48 U. TORONTO FAC. L. REV. 211 (1990).

44 *See generally* Merryman, *supra* note 6.

of integrity and ordered that there be no separate sale of one panel.[45]

Three other French decisions confirm the commitment of France to moral rights by recognizing the special bond that exists between creator and creation. A late nineteenth-century case involved Whistler's mother's son, James McNeill Whistler. Lord Eden had commissioned a portrait of his wife, which Whistler painted. Whistler then altered and refused to deliver the portrait to Lord and Lady Eden. When Lord Eden sued Whistler, the court held that Eden should receive restitution and damages for Whistler's breach of contract, but that Whistler would be required neither to restore nor to deliver the commissioned portrait.[46] Half a century later, the Russian composer Dimitry Shostakovich met with similar success in French courts. Twentieth Century Fox had distributed a movie, "The Iron Curtain," with a decidedly anti-Soviet theme. (The halcyon days of World War II "friendship" between the United States and the Soviet Union had quickly palled). The picture depicted Soviet espionage in Canada and contained approximately forty-five minutes of music, credited to all individual composers, including Shostakovich. Shostakovich sought to enjoin the use of his name and music in the picture and in any advertising or publicity matter relating to the film, claiming that his moral right as a composer was violated because the use of his music indicated his "approval," "endorsement," and "participation" in an anti-Soviet theme, thereby "false[ly] imput[ing] disloyal[ty]" to his country.[47] The French court ruled in favor of Shostakovich, ordered the film seized, and declared that Shostakovich sustained "moral damage."[48]

In a more recent moral rights case brought in France, the court in 1991 again ruled in favor of an artist's personal rights. In *Huston v. Societé de l'Exploitation de la Cinquieme Châine*,[49] the estate

---

45 Buffet v. Fersing, [1962] Recueil Dalloz [D. Jur.] 570 (Cour d'appel, Paris). *See generally* Merryman, *supra* note 6.

46 Eden v. Whistler, [1898] Recueil Dalloz [D.P. II] 465 (Cour d'appel, Paris), *aff'd*, 1900 Cass. civ. 1re 489 (Cour de cassation). *See* Merryman, *supra* note 6, at 1024, 1028; Saurraute, *supra* note 6, at 467-68.

47 These facts are taken from the identical case brought in New York, but the composer was not successful in the New York case. *See* Shostakovich v. Twentieth Century-Fox Film Corp., 80 N.Y.S.2d 575 (N.Y. Sup. Ct. 1948).

48 Soc. Le Chant du Monde v. Soc. Fox Europe, [1953] Recueil Dalloz [D. Jur.] 16, 80 (Cour d'appel, Paris); *see* Strauss, *supra* note 6, at 534-35 n.56. Strauss, then Attorney Advisor at the Copyright Office, worries about the result in the French Shostakovich case: "To arm a composer with the right to suppress the use of his music in a film because he disproves of the political view expressed in the film, would come close to censorship and would have little, if anything, to do with the protection of his personality." *Id.* at 534.

49 1991 Cass. civ. 1re, 149 R.I.D.A. 197 (Cour de cassation). For a thorough history of

of director John Huston sued to enjoin a French television broadcast of a colorized version[50] of Huston's black and white film, *Asphalt Jungle.* Although in the United States colorized films are subject only to the most minimal constraints,[51] the French trial court enjoined the broadcast of Huston's film. On appeal, the Cour d'appel reversed. It noted that although French law permits such relief, American law would not recognize Huston's (who was not the copyright owner) moral rights. The Cour d'appel did, however, require the television station to state Huston's objections and to remind the audience that they could tune their television sets to blot out the color. The next appeal, to the Cour de cassation, was successful. This court reversed the intermediate appellate court and stated that moral rights inure to the benefit of an author, even a foreign one.[52]

---

this case, see Paul E. Geller, *French High Court Remands Huston Colorization Case,* 39 J. COPYRIGHT SOC'Y 252 (1992).

50 Technology permits a computer to scan a black and white film for shades of gray, and then an appropriate color is applied. *See* James T. Duggan & Neil V. Pennella, *The Case for Copyrights in "Colorized" Versions of Public Domain Feature Films,* 34 J. COPYRIGHT SOC'Y 333 (1987). Provided the colorized version indicates authorship, then the colorized film could be granted copyright registration as a derivative work. *See* 37 C.F.R. § 202.3 (1995). "Colorization" is a registered trademark of Colorization, Inc. *See Official Gazette of the United States Patent and Trademark Office,* Nov. 3, 1987, at TM 3.

Colorization, which has been compared to "painting a mustache on the *Mona Lisa,*" *see* Jennifer T. Olson, Note, *Rights in Fine Art Photography: Through a Lens Darkly,* 70 TEX. L. REV. 1489, 1514 & nn.150-51 (1992), is a subject of tremendous controversy in this country. Woody Allen and other filmmakers have testified frequently in Congress that colorization interferes with their right of integrity. *Legal Issues that Arise when Color is Added to Films Originally Produced, Sold and Distributed in Black and White: Hearings Before the Senate Subcomm. on Technology and the Law of the Senate Comm. on the Judiciary,* 100th Cong., 1st Sess. 62 (1987). However, congressional response has been relatively meager. The National Film Preservation Acts of 1988 and 1992 are a very small sop to Woody Allen and others like him. *See infra* note 51.

The colorization debate is a lively one. *See, e.g.,* Craig A. Wagner, Note, *Motion Picture Colorization, Authenticity, and the Elusive Moral Right,* 64 N.Y.U. L. REV. 628 (1989); Beyer, *supra* note 6; Daniel McK. Sessa, Note, *Moral Rights Protections in the Colorization of Black and White Motion Pictures: A Black and White Issue,* 16 HOFSTRA L. REV. 503 (1988); Alberta L. Cook, *Colorization; Actors and Directors: Color Them Mad as Hell,* NAT'L L.J., July 27, 1987, at 10, 11; Roger L. Mayer et al., *Colorization: The Arguments For,* 17 J. ARTS MGMT. & L. No. 3, at 64 (1987); Woody Allen et al., *Colorization: The Arguments Against,* 17 J. ARTS MGMT. & L. No. 3, at 79 (1987).

51 *See, e.g.,* National Film Preservation Act of 1992, Pub. L. No. 102-307, tit. II, 106 Stat. 267 (1992) (codified at 2 U.S.C. §§ 179-179k (1994)), creating a panel to include up to twenty-five movies per year in a national registry of classic films. *See generally* David A. Honicky, *Film Labelling as a Cure for Colorization [and other Alterations]: A Band-Aid for a Hatchet Job,* 12 CARDOZO ARTS & ENT. L.J. 409 (1994); Warren H. Husband, *Resurrecting Hollywood's Golden Age: Balancing the Rights of Film Owners, Artistic Authors and Consumers,* 13 COLUM.-VLA J.L. & ARTS 327 (1993). The authors agree that currently there is inadequate protection for authors of altered films. One solution was proposed in the Film Disclosure Act of 1993, H.R. 1731, 103d Cong., 1st Sess. (1993), which would have amended the Lanham Act by adding 15 U.S.C. § 1125(c), under which networks or distributors which would have had to comport with certain requirements should they have wished to show a materially altered film.

52 *See* Jeffrey L. Graubart, *U.S. Moral Rights: Fact or Fiction?,* N.Y.L.J., Aug. 7, 1992, at 5.

The Whistler,[53] Shostakovich,[54] Buffet,[55] and Huston[56] cases (none involving parody) illustrate the extensive moral rights protections afforded artists under French law and are typical of the moral rights approach in those countries that have a much longer history of "droit moral" than the United States. The following sections discuss why moral rights may have bloomed so late in our country. The state of moral rights protection that existed in this country prior and subsequent to VARA is then described.

B. *Moral Rights in the United States*

There are several answers to the question of why the moral rights doctrine took so long to gain a foothold in this country. One theory is that United States copyright law is very much the child of Anglo-Saxon jurisprudence with its emphasis on economic property rights.[57] The American notion of copyright as protective of economic property rights, rather than personal rights, was borne directly from its earlier English counterpart.[58]

Aside from the genealogical explanation for tardy moral rights acceptance in this country, the history and geography of art may also be a factor.[59] In terms of the history of western art, the art capital of the western civilized world over the course of centuries has moved westward—from the classical period in Athens, the neoclassical in Rome, the medieval and gothic art in various continental European cities, the high Renaissance in Florence, and the late nineteenth-century impressionism in Paris. It is only in the twentieth century that New York has become a major art center.[60] This is not to suggest that prior to 1913 America had not seen its share of important visual artists; James Whistler,[61] Thomas Eakins, Mary Cassatt, and Winslow Homer were but a few. But it is only quite recently that American visual artists have achieved international recognition, and that the American public has paid the kind of attention and homage to art previously found in the art centers of Europe. In the last sixty years, such American artists as Robert

---

53 *See supra* note 46 and accompanying text.

54 *See supra* note 47 and accompanying text.

55 *See supra* note 45 and accompanying text.

56 *See supra* note 49 and accompanying text.

57 *See supra* note 34.

58 *See* Kwall, *supra* note 5, at 17 n.67.

59 *See* Merryman, *supra* note 6, at 1042.

60 This may find its roots in the Armory Show of 1913, which brought together approximately 1,600 seminal works of art. Critics called it "the most significant art show in American history." STRICKLAND & BOSWELL, *supra* note 13, at 150.

61 For a discussion of the French moral rights case involving Whistler, see *supra* note 46 and accompanying text.

Rauschenberg,[62] Jim Dine, Jasper Johns,[63] Robert Indiana, Roy Lichtenstein, Andy Warhol, Larry Rivers, Georgia O'Keefe, Edward Hopper, and Alexander Calder have established our country as a significant art center, and major art movements such as the "Ash Can School" and "Pop Art" developed and flourished within our borders.[64] Some commentators believe the relative youth of our country and its art may explain why moral rights protection in this country lagged so far behind the international art communities.[65] The artist as hero, icon, celebrity, and media event is a recent phenomenon in this country. It has been suggested, for example, that Chicagoans will not burn down the city over a painting—"Paris maybe, but Americans have never taken culture that seriously."[66]

The delayed birth of moral rights in this country may also be due to the strong values we attach to free expression, as embodied in the First Amendment.[67] In civil law countries, such as France, Germany, and Italy, moral rights have received their greatest reception. These countries have no explicit speech protection analo-

---

62 Rauschenberg parodied *Mona Lisa*. *See infra* note 123 and accompanying text.

63 Johns also parodied *Mona Lisa*. *See infra* note 123 and accompanying text.

64 *See* JANSON, *supra* note 13, at 675. George Bellows represents the Ash Can School's emphasis on realistic, gritty scenes. STRICKLAND & BOSWELL, *supra* note 13, at 154-55. Roy Lichtenstein and Andy Warhol ("the Pope of Pop") were Pop Artists who depersonalized art and used consumer items as "art." *Id.* at 174-75. As such, they may represent the artistic progeny of Duchamp.

65 *See* Merryman, *supra* note 6, at 1042; Roeder, *supra* note 6, at 557. Even internationally, the notion of art as reflection of an artist's personality did not achieve recognition until the age of positivism and Freud. *See* Albert Elsen, *Why Do We Care About Art?*, 27 HASTINGS L.J. 951, 954 (1976). Elsen, an art historian, explains:

> [T]he concept of self-expression is historically recent in art, originating in the last century, when pioneering modernists such as the Impressionists took it upon themselves to work from personal experience in individually acquired styles rather than by interpreting the experience of others in academically approved modes. With the development of abstract art early in this century, artists looked for art's sources in the self. They radically changed the conditions of art in order to capture the unique qualities of their private vision, and this change resulted in the creation of the very vocabulary and grammar of their art. Painters such as Kandinsky could look upon their art as creations and as intimate extensions of themselves. Picasso saw his art as a diary. . . . By extension, the modern artist's work, grounded in the self, becomes a tangible manifestation of his personality. In view of their country's early leadership in modern art, it is not surprising that by the mid-19th century French jurists began to recognize and protect this intimate relationship between the artist and the work of art.

Id. at 954-55.

66 Nelson v. Streeter, 16 F.3d 145, 150 (7th Cir. 1994) (Posner, J.). In May 1988, three Chicago aldermen removed a painting of Harold Washington in women's frilly white lingerie from the School of the Art Institute. The student painter filed a civil rights suit that was settled for $95,000. *See* Matt O'Connor, *Suit Ended on Picture of Washington*, CHI. TRIB., Sept. 21, 1994, § 2, at 1.

67 The First Amendment provides: "Congress shall make no law respecting an establishment of religion, or prohibiting the free exercise thereof; or abridging the freedom of speech, or of the press, or the right of the people peaceably to assemble, and to petition the Government for a redress of grievances." U.S. CONST. amend. I.

gous to our 200-year experience with an amendment that tops the hierarchy of rights enumerated in the Bill of Rights. Because the moral right of integrity directly affects expression, such as a parody that may injure an artist's honor or reputation, First Amendment concerns may lurk behind our slow acceptance of moral rights. While traditional copyright law also affects expression, relying on fair use to effect the proper balance, it does not protect "honor and reputation" per se, but rather the pecuniary rights of artists. In contrast, "honor and reputation" issues have up until now been subsumed in defamation law with its concomitant constitutional constraints.[68]

1. Moral Rights in the United States before VARA

Prior to our adherence to Berne[69] and subsequent enactment of explicit but limited federal moral rights protection for certain visual arts under section 106A,[70] there were differing views about the extent of quasi-moral rights protection under copyright or other federal or state doctrines. While many commentators have thought that the personal rights of artists were insufficiently protected prior to VARA,[71] at least one observer found that as of 1986 United States law did offer several meaningful equivalents to moral rights protection.[72] However, most of the controversies that arose between artists and defendants resulted in judicial decisions that strain to apply doctrine ill-fitting to the moral right issues raised in those cases.

a. State Law and Moral Rights

In one of the earliest cases directly raising a moral rights claim, *Shostakovich v. Twentieth Century-Fox Film Corp.*,[73] the New

---

68 *See* New York Times Co. v. Sullivan, 376 U.S. 254 (1964); *cf.* Hustler Magazine v. Falwell, 485 U.S. 46 (1988) (holding that the reckless disregard standard is also required for intentional infliction of emotional distress claims brought by public figures). *See generally* Laura Cohen, *Beyond* Silberman v. Georges*: Shielding the Artist from Claims of Libel,* 17 COLUM. HUM. RTS. L. REV. 235 (1986); Leslie K. Trieger, *Protecting Satire Against Libel Claims: A New Reading of the First Amendment's Opinion Privilege,* 98 YALE L.J. 1215 (1989).

69 Berne Convention, *supra* note 5.

70 17 U.S.C. § 106A.

71 *See* Kwall, *supra* note 5, at 18 & n.68.

72 *See* FINAL REPORT OF THE AD HOC WORKING GROUP ON U.S. ADHERENCE TO THE BERNE CONVENTION, *supra* note 5, at 547-57; *see also* Sam Ricketson, *U.S. Accession to Berne: An Outsider's Appreciation (Part 2),* 8 INTELL. PROP. J. 87, 103-04 (1993) (quoting letter from Dr. Arpad Bogsch, Director General, World Intellectual Property Organization, to Irwin Karp, Esq., June 16, 1987).

73 80 N.Y.S.2d 575; *see supra* note 47 and accompanying text for a more extended discussion of the case. Other cases denying the validity of moral rights claims include Vargas v. Esquire, Inc., 164 F.2d 522 (7th Cir. 1947) (holding that the defendant need not attribute authorship), *cert. denied,* 335 U.S. 813 (1948); Crimi v. Rutgers Presbyterian Church,

York court rejected Shostakovich's argument that use of his music in an anti-Soviet movie violated his moral rights such that it falsely imputed to him disloyalty to his country. The court reasoned:

> There is no charge of distortion of the compositions nor any claim that they have not been faithfully reproduced. Conceivably, under the doctrine of Moral Right the court could in a proper case, prevent the use of a composition or work, in the public domain, in such a manner as would be violative of the author's rights. The application of the doctrine presents much difficulty however. With reference to that which is in the public domain there arises a conflict between the moral right and the well established rights of others to use such works. So, too, there arises the question of the norm by which the use of such work is to be tested to determine whether or not the author's moral right as an author has been violated. Is the standard to be good taste, artistic worth, political beliefs, moral concepts or what is it to be? In the present state of our law the very existence of the right is not clear, the relative position of the rights thereunder with reference to the rights of others is not defined nor has the nature of the proper remedy been determined.[74]

Still other plaintiffs have sought to cast their moral rights claim in other legal clothes such as contract, but not necessarily with any more success.[75] Other state doctrines relied upon by plaintiffs seeking to vindicate their moral rights include invasion of privacy,[76] defamation,[77] and unfair competition.[78] However, the lack of a uniform approach and the unpredictability of results in these moral rights cases make state law protection problematic. Further, lurking behind any of these state law claims is the possibility of pre-emption under one or more federal laws, especially the Copyright Act.[79]

---

89 N.Y.S.2d 813 (N.Y. Sup. Ct. 1949) (finding that the defendant could obliterate the plaintiff's fresco).

74 *Shostakovich*, 80 N.Y.S.2d at 578-79 (citation omitted).

75 *See, e.g.*, Edison v. Viva Int'l, Ltd., 421 N.Y.S.2d 203, 205 (N.Y. App. Div. 1979) (plaintiff's moral rights claim was subsumed in his contract right to seek remedy for mutilation of his article and must be dismissed). *But see* Zim v. Western Pub. Co., 573 F.2d 1318 (5th Cir. 1978) (publication of revised version of plaintiff's book violated agreement between author and publisher); Granz v. Harris, 198 F.2d 585, 588 (2d Cir. 1952) (defendant breached contract by selling abbreviated records made from plaintiff's master discs; contract required appropriate attribution of authorship); Packard v. Fox Film Corp., 202 N.Y.S. 164 (N.Y. App. Div. 1923) (stating that false attribution and unauthorized use of author's name constitutes breach of contract).

76 *Zim*, 573 F.2d at 1326; *Geisel*, 295 F. Supp. at 340 n.5.

77 *Edison*, 421 N.Y.S.2d at 207.

78 *Granz*, 198 F.2d at 588; Jaeger v. American Int'l Pictures, Inc., 330 F. Supp. 274, 278 (S.D.N.Y. 1971); *Geisel*, 295 F. Supp. at 354 n.15.

79 17 U.S.C. § 301(a) provides:

In the last decade or so, perhaps as a response to this murky state of moral rights protection, a number of states enacted artist and author rights statutes. The House Report on VARA noted that as of 1990 eleven states had such statutes:[80] California,[81] Connecticut,[82] Illinois,[83] Louisiana,[84] Maine,[85] Massachusetts,[86] New

---

> On and after January 1, 1978, all legal or equitable rights that are equivalent to any of the exclusive rights within the general scope of copyright as specified by section 106 in works of authorship that are fixed in a tangible medium of expression . . ., whether created before or after that date and whether published or unpublished, are governed exclusively by this title. Thereafter, no person is entitled to any such right or equivalent right in any such work under the common law or statutes of any State.

Even without the specific preemption language of § 301, state law moral rights claims could be preempted if (1) Congress has occupied the field in such manner as to foreclose state law, *see* Hines v. Davidowitz, 312 U.S. 52, 67 (1941), or (2) state law conflicts with the objectives of a federal statute. *See* Pacific Gas & Elec. Co. v. State Energy Resources Conservation & Div. Comm'n, 461 U.S. 190, 203-04 (1983).

Intellectual property plaintiffs usually are well aware of the preemption problem, but nevertheless may try to bring claims in state courts for a variety of reasons. *See generally* Ted D. Lee & Ann Livingston, *The Road Less Traveled: State Court Resolution of Patent, Trademark, or Copyright Disputes*, 19 ST. MARY'S L.J. 703 (1988). Plaintiffs may prefer state courts because of different jury pools, decreased litigation costs, greater familiarity with state court, less crowded dockets, and other reasons. *Id.*

The Supreme Court has considered the intellectual property/preemption issue in several cases. *See* Bonito Boats, Inc. v. Thunder Craft Boats, Inc., 489 U.S. 141 (1989) (stating that a state plug molding statute was preempted by the Patent Act); Kewanee Oil Co. v. Bicron Corp., 416 U.S. 470 (1974) (holding that a state trade secret law was not preempted by the Patent Act); Goldstein v. California, 412 U.S. 546 (1973) (holding that a state antipiracy statute protecting sound records (then not protected under federal copyright law) was not preempted); Sears Roebuck & Co. v. Stiffel Co., 376 U.S. 225 (1964); and Compco Corp. v. Day-Brite Lighting, Inc., 376 U.S. 234 (1964) (holding that a state unfair competition law was preempted by the Patent and Copyright Acts). For a discussion of preemption under § 301 of the 1976 Act see Paul Goldstein, *Preempted State Doctrines, Involuntary Transfers and Compulsory Licenses: Testing the Limits of Copyright*, 24 UCLA L. REV. 1107 (1977). For a discussion of preemption under the 1909 Act, see MELVILLE B. NIMMER, 1 NIMMER ON COPYRIGHT § 1.01 (1988).

80 H.R. REP. NO. 514, 101st Cong., 2d Sess. 9 (1990), *reprinted in* 1990 U.S.C.C.A.N. 6915, 6919. Three other states protect artists' rights. Nevada, NEV. REV. STAT. ANN. § 597.720-.760 (Michie 1994); South Dakota, S.D. CODIFIED LAWS ANN. § 1-22-16 (1992); and Utah, UTAH CODE ANN. § 9-6-409 (1996). Nevada law grants the rights of attribution and integrity, NEV. REV. STAT. ANN. §§ 597.730, .740. South Dakota grants the rights of attribution and integrity to an artist whose work has been acquired by the state. S.D. CODIFIED LAWS ANN. § 1-22-16(1) to -16(3). Utah grants to artists who create art work commissioned by its Arts Development Program the right of attribution and integrity. UTAH CODE ANN. § 9-6-409(2), (5).

81 CAL. CIV. CODE § 987 (West Supp. 1995). The California Art Preservation Act is intended to prevent a person who acquires "fine art" from physically altering or destroying that art. The statute prohibits "any physical defacement, mutilation, alteration, or destruction of a work of fine art" by anyone other than the artist herself who owns and possesses the work. *Id.* § 987(c)(1). The same prohibitions apply to a person who mutilates, alters, or destroys a work of fine art through gross negligence. *Id.* § 987(c)(2).

For a general discussion of the Act, see G.L. Francione, *The California Art Preservation Act and Federal Preemption by the 1976 Copyright Act—Equivalence and Actual Conflict*, 18 CAL. W. L. REV. 189 (1982); John Petrovich, *Artists' Statutory "Droit Moral" in California: A Critical Appraisal*, 15 LOY. L.A. L. REV. 29 (1981).

82 CONN. GEN. STAT. ANN. §§ 42-116s to -116t (West 1992 & Supp. 1996) protects artists from intentional physical defacement or alteration of their fine art by another person.

83 ILL. ANN. STAT. ch. 815, paras. 320/1-320/8 (Smith-Hurd 1993). The Illinois statute

Jersey,[87] New Mexico,[88] New York,[89] Pennsylvania,[90] and Rhode Island.[91] The protections these statutes afford the moral rights of

---

does not address explicitly an artist's moral right to ensure the unaltered maintenance of a piece of art. However, the statute does hold an art dealer liable for the "loss of or damage to" a work of fine art while in the dealer's possession. *Id.* para. 320/2 § 2(5). The statute also prohibits an art dealer who accepts fine art on consignment from using or displaying the art or a photograph of the art unless notice is given to persons who use or view the art that the product is the artist's creation. *Id.* para. 320/5 § 5(d).

84 LA. REV. STAT. ANN. §§ 51:2151-2156 (West 1987) prohibits a person other than the artist or person acting with the artist's consent from displaying, making accessible to the public, or publishing a work of fine art that has been altered, defaced, modified, or mutilated.

85 ME. REV. STAT. ANN. tit. 27, § 303 (West 1988) provides that no person other than an artist or person authorized by an artist may *knowingly display* in a place accessible to the public *or publish* fine art or a reproduction of fine art that is in an "altered, defaced, mutilated or modified form" if: (1) the work is represented as the work of the artist or could reasonably be regarded as his work, and (2) the artist's reputation is reasonably likely to be damaged as a result of displaying, reproducing, or publishing the art. *Id.* § 303(3) (emphasis added). In addition, if conservation work on a piece of fine art is grossly negligent, the statute will apply. *Id.* § 303(4).

86 MASS. GEN. LAWS ANN. ch. 231, § 85S (West Supp. 1996). The law's purpose is to prevent the "physical alteration or destruction of fine art" in order to prevent harm to the artist's reputation. Further, the public has an interest in "preserving the integrity of cultural and artistic creations." *Id.* § 85S(a). This statute prohibits anyone other than the artist who owns and possesses the art, or a person authorized by the artist, from intentionally defacing, mutilating, altering, or destroying fine art. Intent includes gross negligence, as well as deliberate action. *Id.* § 85S(c). For a general overview of the Massachusetts Act, see Vance R. Koven, *Observations on the Massachusetts Art Preservation Act*, 71 MASS. L. REV. 101 (1986).

87 N.J. STAT. ANN. §§ 2A:24A-1 to -8 (West 1987). The "Artists' Rights Act" recognizes that the physical nature of fine art "is of enduring and crucial importance to the artist and the artist's reputation," and that the alteration, defacement, mutilation, or modification of fine art could affect this. Consequently, the statute recognizes that destruction of the integrity of the art causes a loss to the artist and his reputation.

88 N.M. STAT. ANN. §§ 13-4B-1 to -3 (Michie 1978). The "Fine Art in Public Buildings" Act protects an artist's right of integrity, *id.* § 13-4B-3(A), and attribution, *id.* § 13-4B-3(B), provided the work is "fine art . . . of recognized quality." *Id.* § 13-4B-2(B).

89 N.Y. ARTS & CULT. AFF. LAW § 14.03. The statute prohibits anyone other than the artist or a person duly authorized by the artist from knowingly displaying in a place accessible to the public or from publishing "a work of fine art or limited edition multiple of not more than three hundred copies by that artist or a reproduction thereof in an altered, defaced, mutilated or modified form." *Id.* § 14.03(1). This prohibition will apply if the work is claimed, or could reasonably be regarded, as being the artist's work and if the artist's reputation is reasonably likely to be damaged by the injurious act. *Id.*

Artists have tried to avail themselves of the Act's protections with not much success. *See, e.g.*, Monta v. Omni Publications Int'l, Ltd., 741 F. Supp. 1107, 1114-15 (S.D.N.Y. 1990) (defendant's placement of plaintiff's sculpture with an anti-nuclear message in a pro-nuclear text is not a mutilation or alteration under the Act); Tracy v. Skate Key, Inc., 697 F. Supp. 748, 751 (S.D.N.Y. 1988) (plaintiff's claim under the New York Act is preempted by the Copyright Act as it "tracks the rights protected by the Copyright Act").

For a general discussion of the New York Act, see Damich, *supra* note 8; Sarah A. Smith, Note, *The New York Artists' Authorship Rights Act: Increased Protection and Enhanced Status for Visual Artists*, 70 CORNELL L. REV. 158 (1984).

90 PA. STAT. ANN. tit. 73, §§ 2101-2110 (1993). The "Fine Arts Preservation Act" prohibits a person other than an artist who owns and possesses a work he created from committing or authorizing, in an intentional manner, "any physical defacement, mutilation, alteration or destruction" of fine art. *Id.* § 2104(a). The statute applies only to fine art that is displayed in Pennsylvania in a place that the public can access. *Id.* § 2110(a).

91 R.I. GEN. LAWS §§ 5-62-2 to -6 (1995) prohibit anyone other than the artist or person

artists vary greatly. New York is probably most protective of an artist's personal rights, while California seems to stress the preservation of art with no provision for affronts to an artist's reputation. The laws of Connecticut, Massachusetts, Pennsylvania, and Rhode Island are of the California model, while Louisiana, Maine, and New Jersey focus, like New York, on the artist's reputation. These varying laws have been described by an artists' rights attorney as a "patchwork of rules which by itself vitiates somewhat the single, unified system of copyright . . . ."[92] However, Congress said that certain statutes, like those discussed above, were sufficient safeguards of the rights of paternity and integrity such that Article 6*bis* of Berne[93] could be satisfied:

> This existing U.S. law includes various provisions of the Copyright Act and the Lanham Act, *various state statutes*, and common law principles such as libel, defamation, misrepresentation, and unfair competition, which have been applied by the courts to redress authors' invocation of the right to claim authorship or the right to object to distortion.[94]

b. Pre-VARA Protection of Moral Rights under Federal Law

Prior to VARA, federal copyright law offered only minimal and indirect protection of the personal rights of artists. Professor Kwall noted the possibility that sections 115(a)(2), 106(2), 203, 304, and 501(b) of the Copyright Act might be read to protect an artist's moral rights, but to date this has not been the case.[95]

However, another federal statute, the Lanham Act, specifically its unfair competition provision,[96] furnished the basis for the high-water mark of federal moral rights protection pre-VARA. In *Gilliam v. American Broadcasting Companies, Inc.*,[97] the Monty Python com-

---

authorized by the artist from knowingly and publicly displaying fine art, or from publishing a reproduction of fine art, in an "altered, defaced, mutilated or modified form," if the work is represented as that of the artist or if the work would reasonably be considered as being that of the artist. *Id.* § 5-62-3.

92 H.R. Rep. No. 514, *supra* note 80, at 9, *reprinted in* 1990 U.S.C.C.A.N. at 6919 (testimony of John Koegel, Esq.).

93 Berne Convention, *supra* note 5.

94 S. Rep. No. 352, *supra* note 5, at 9-10, *reprinted in* 1988 U.S.C.C.A.N. at 3714-15 (emphasis added). *See* H.R. Rep. No. 609, 100th Cong., 2d Sess. 32-40 (1988).

95 Kwall, *supra* note 5, at 38-56.

96 15 U.S.C. § 1125(a) provides in part:

> Any person who, on or in connection with any goods or services . . . uses a false designation of origin . . . or any false or misleading representation . . . and [causes] such goods or services to enter commerce . . . shall be liable to a civil action by any person . . . who believes that he is or is likely to be damaged by the use of any such false description or representation.

97 538 F.2d 14 (2d Cir. 1976).

edy group sued to enjoin ABC from broadcasting two ninety-minute specials of Monty Python programs. Without Monty Python's permission, ABC had cut twenty-four minutes out of each of the ninety-minute programs. ABC had edited the material to make time for commercial advertising and to eliminate "offensive or obscene matter."[98] Python argued, and both the trial and appellate courts agreed, that broadcasting the Monty Python shows in the truncated ABC version violated the integrity of Python's work and could make Python subject to criticism—the focus of section 1125(a)'s protection.[99]

Section 1125(a) of the Lanham Act, as interpreted creatively by *Gilliam* and other courts,[100] indicates the lengths to which some courts will go to protect an artist's moral rights even in the absence of explicit federal law. Unlike the patchwork of state moral rights, section 1125(a) could provide national uniformity. However, most commentators and a few courts believe the fit between the Lanham Act and *droit moral* is an extremely tenuous one.[101]

2. Moral Rights under VARA

Despite state moral rights statutes,[102] various state law doctrines,[103] and strained reliance on Lanham Act provisions,[104] it was not until June 1, 1991, the effective date of VARA,[105] that copyright law explicitly protected the moral rights of attribution and integrity. Thus, VARA creates the potential for a nationwide, uniform scheme, albeit limited, of moral rights safeguards. Whether Congress enacted VARA to comport with Berne moral rights requirements,[106] or as a supremely political compromise between the arguments tendered by folks in both camps of the colorization de-

---

98 *Id.* at 18. ABC deleted such words as "hell" and "damn." *Id.* at 23.

99 *Id.* at 24.

100 *See, e.g.*, Waits v. Frito-Lay, Inc., 978 F.2d 1093, 1110 (9th Cir. 1992) (stating that the Lanham Act provides a remedy to plaintiff in a "sound-alike" suit because of "an economic interest akin to that of a trademark holder in controlling the commercial exploitation of his or her identity"), *cert. denied*, 113 S. Ct. 1047 (1993); Smith v. Montoro, 648 F.2d 602 (9th Cir. 1981) (holding that the substitution of plaintiff's name constitutes "reverse passing off" actionable under § 1125).

101 *See, e.g.*, Halicki v. United Artists, 812 F.2d 1213 (9th Cir. 1987); *Gilliam*, 538 F.2d at 26-27 (Gurfein, J., concurring); Kwall, *supra* note 5, at 24 & n.89. *But see* Diana E. Pinover, *The Rights of Authors, Artists and Performers under Section 43(a) of the Lanham Act*, 83 TRADEMARK REP. 38 (1993).

102 *See supra* notes 80-91 and accompanying text.

103 *See supra* notes 74-78 and accompanying text.

104 *See supra* notes 96-99 and accompanying text.

105 17 U.S.C. § 106A.

106 Recall that Congress had, perhaps disengenuously, stated that moral rights in this country were sufficient to admit the U.S. into Berne. *See supra* note 94. Adherence to Berne was desired to curb international piracy and to make the United States an effective participant in international copyright. *See* Carl H. Settlemyer III, *Between Thought and Pos-*

bate,[107] is not made clear by VARA's dubious legislative history.[108]

To highlight the coverage now afforded by VARA and the unresolved copyright issues created by the addition of these moral rights to what previously was a pecuniary-based protection scheme, let us now return to our imaginary case of *Leonardo v. Duchamp.* The issue is whether VARA offers any redress when Duchamp purchases a single copy of Leonardo's *Mona Lisa* edition of 100 and draws a moustache upon those famous smiling lips. Initially, Leonardo will need to show that the *Mona Lisa* edition is a "work of visual art" protected by VARA. Since the *Mona Lisa* lithographs are a limited edition of under 200 copies, and are signed and numbered by Leonardo, he could satisfy the definitional requirements of section 101(1).[109] However, not only must the protected work be a work of visual art, but the offending work must also be a work of visual art.[110] Duchamp's *L.H.O.O.Q.* is such a work. Because the hypothetical assumes that Leonardo created the *Mona Lisa* after June 1, 1991 and that he is still alive today, the rights afforded by section 106A are in full force and are independent of any of the exclusive rights provided in section 106A.[111]

Leonardo's main claim under VARA is that Duchamp, in adding a moustache to one of Leonardo's lithographs, intentionally distorted, mutilated, or modified the work in a way "prejudicial to his . . . honor or reputation."[112] In short, Duchamp violated Leonardo's right of integrity.[113] In order to succeed on his integrity claim, Leonardo will not have much difficulty showing that Duchamp intentionally distorted, mutilated, or modified his *Mona Lisa.* Duchamp clearly knew what he was doing and intended at least to "modify" the work to accomplish the desired result—"a

---

session: Artists' "Moral Rights" and Public Access to Creative Works, 81 GEO. L.J. 2291, 2307 n.71 (1993).

107 *See supra* note 50. The narrow range of works protected by VARA was not unintentional. *See* 17 U.S.C. § 101. *Compare* 136 CONG. REC. H3113 (daily ed. June 5, 1990) (Rep. Kastenmeier stated: "We will continue to consider whether claims arising in the film context meet the same standards as visual artists' claims did.") *with id.* at H3115 (Rep. Fish stated: "[T]his legislation should not be viewed as a precedent for the extension of so-called moral rights into other areas.").

108 *See* George C. Smith, *Let the Buyer of Art Beware; Artists' Moral Rights Trump Owners' Property Rights under the Visual Artists Rights Act,* RECORDER, Jan. 10, 1991, at 4. Smith believes VARA was passed only because it was linked to critical judgeships legislation. *Id.*

109 17 U.S.C. § 101(1). Note that if we had not massaged the facts, Leonardo's portrait might be considered as owned by Signore Giocando as a work for hire, *id.*, and thus not a "work of visual art" protected by VARA. 17 U.S.C. § 101(2)(B); *see Carter,* 71 F.3d 77.

110 *See* 17 U.S.C. § 106A(c)(3).

111 *See id.* § 106A(a).

112 *Id.* § 106A(a)(3)(A).

113 *See id.* § 106A(a)(1)(A).

risqué joke on the Giocanda!"[114]

A more sticky issue arises as to whether Duchamp's parodic modification "would be prejudicial to [Leonardo's] honor or reputation."[115] The fuzziness of the term "prejudicial . . . to honor or reputation" is not made appreciably clearer by VARA's legislative history. The House Report on VARA tells us to focus on "the artistic or professional honor or reputation of the individual as embodied in the work that is protected. . . . [W]hile no per se rule exists, modification of a work of recognized stature will generally establish harm to honor or reputation."[116] But the House Report emphasizes that the standard of harm "is not analogous to that of a defamation case, where the general character of the plaintiff is at issue."[117] Based on this amorphous standard—harm to artistic honor or reputation—it is not very clear what Leonardo would have to show, although Judge Edelstein's recent decision in *Carter v. Helmsley-Spear, Inc.*[118] gives some guidance.

Assuming that Leonardo can show the requisite harm, the only barrier to recovery under the panoply of remedies of the Copyright Act[119] would be the fair use doctrine.[120] As a parodist, Duchamp would attempt to raise this defense. The following sections will discuss the nature of parody and fair use (part II) and the proper resolution of Leonardo's claim against Duchamp (part III).

II. Parody and Fair Use

A. *Parody in the Visual Arts*

The visual arts have seen more than their fair share of parody.

---

114 Marcel Duchamp, Marcel Duchamp 289 n.131 (Anne D'Harnocourt & Kynaston McShine eds., 1973).

115 17 U.S.C. § 106A(a)(3)(A).

116 H.R. Rep. No. 514, *supra* note 80, at 15-16, *reprinted in* 1990 U.S.C.C.A.N. at 6925-26.

117 *Id.* at 15, *reprinted in* 1990 U.S.C.A.A.N. at 6925.

118 861 F. Supp. 303 (S.D.N.Y. 1994), *rev'd*, 71 F.3d 77 (2d Cir. 1995). The district court focused upon "good name, public esteem, or reputation in the artistic community" and relied on expert testimony. *Carter*, 861 F. Supp. at 323.

119 These include injunctions, impoundment, damages, and profits or statutory damages, costs, and reasonable attorney's fees. *See* 17 U.S.C. §§ 501-505. Section 501 makes explicit that these remedies are available to authors whose section 106A(a) rights are violated. *See id.* § 501(a). Note that even if Leonardo's actual damages are slight or difficult to quantify, he may elect, alternatively, to seek statutory damages under section 504(c). Recently doubled under section 10 of the Berne Convention Implementation Act of 1988, *supra* note 5, 102 Stat. 2860, the statutory damages generally range from a $500 minimum to a $20,000 maximum. However, the ceiling increases to $100,000 for willful infringements, and the floor decreases to $200 for innocent infringements. On the *Duchamp* facts hypothesized here, Duchamp would probably be found to have infringed willfully. Willfulness could be shown by reckless disregard of Leonardo's copyright; *see* Lauratex Textile Corp. v. Allton Knitting Mills, 519 F. Supp. 730 (S.D.N.Y. 1981), or by Duchamp's infringement; *see* Broadcast Music, Inc. v. Xanthas, Inc., 855 F.2d 233, 236 (5th Cir. 1988).

120 17 U.S.C. § 107; *see infra* notes 137-72 and accompanying text.

The 1919 Duchamp parody of Leonardo's 1506 *Mona Lisa*, which is illustrative of the moral rights/parody dilemma, is one example of "appropriation art."[121] Others range from the ridiculous, which includes *Mad* magazine's *Sports Titillated*, a parody of the swimsuit issue of *Sports Illustrated*; to the sublime, such as Titian's *Venus* (1538), parodied by Manet's *Olympia* (1893), in turn parodied by Mel Ramos in 1974; and the putatively sublime, such as Andy Warhol's 1963 parody of the *Mona Lisa*, entitled *Thirty Are Better Than One*; the 1970 film *M*A*S*H*, containing a parody of Leonardo's *The Last Supper* (ca. 1497); and Larry Rivers's 1970 parody of Manet's *Olympia*, entitled *I Like Olympia in Blackface*. Warhol's parody, which reproduces identical images of the *Mona Lisa* in rows six across and five down, was intended to critique "a consumer society that loves quantity more than quality and [which] can use a popular icon of highbrow art as a mass-produced product."[122] Several other prominent twentieth-century artists also have parodied the *Mona Lisa*: Charles Addams (*Monster Rally 89* (1950)) (a cartoon of Mona Lisa sitting in a movie audience); Robert Rauschenberg (*Mona Lisa* (1958)); Jasper Johns (*Figure 7* (1969)); Tom Wesselman (*Great American Nude #35* (1962)); Philippe Halsman (*Mona Dali; What Dali sees when he looks at Mona Lisa* (1954)); Marisol (*Mona Lisa* (1961-62)); Robert Arneson (*George [Washington] and Mona in the Baths of Coloma* (1976)); Shusaku Arakawa (*Portrait of Mona Lisa* (1971)); and Peter Max (*Mona Lisa* (1991)).[123] More recently, the Museums of Stonybrook, New York, mounted an intriguing exhibit: "Parodies of the American Masters: Rediscovering the Society of American Fakirs, 1891-1914." The Fakirs were a group of art students who painted outrageous parodies, neither kind nor gentle, based on subject matter and titles of such well-known artists as George Bellows, Winslow Homer, and John Singer Sargent. All these paradigmatic parodies[124] (some of which

---

[121] Appropriationism in art refers to the incorporation into new art works of existing images; collage, montage, and Duchamp's "ready-mades" involve appropriation. *See* Heather J. Meeker, Comment, *The Ineluctable Modality of the Visible: Fair Use and Fine Arts in the Post-Modern Era*, 10 U. MIAMI ENT. & SPORTS L. REV. 195, 213-16 (1993).

[122] LINDA HUTCHEON, A THEORY OF PARODY 47 (1985). *Thirty Are Better Than One* is reproduced in the appendix. As for American art, Grant Woods's *American Gothic* must be one of the top ten targets for parody.

[123] JEAN LIPMAN & RICHARD MARSHALL, ART ABOUT ART 28, 58-62 (1978). A recently formed art group, the "Guerrilla Girls," produced a poster of Mona Lisa with a fig leaf covering her mouth to protest censorship and sexism. STRICKLAND & BOSWELL, *supra* note 13, at 194. As of 1952, there were more than five dozen versions of the *Mona Lisa*, *id.* at 34, one of which is reproduced in the appendix.

[124] Parody has been a recognized art form for thousands of years. *See* LIPMAN & MARSHALL, *supra* note 123; Leon R. Yankwich, *Parody and Burlesque in the Law of Copyright*, 33 CAN. B. REV. 1130, 1133 (1955). It should be noted that copyright is not the only branch of

are reproduced in the appendix), based on almost universal familiarity with the *Mona Lisa* and other works, send a message to the viewer about artistic creation and the nature of art itself as revolution.

Thus, Duchamp's parody is well-grounded in a long and solid parodic tradition. While the hypothetical case of *Leonardo v. Duchamp* is based on a chronological glitch with a moral rights twist, the "invasion" is much the same as in Duchamp's actual 1919 parody, which is an exact reproduction of the *Mona Lisa* with several zingers. First, Duchamp painted a large black moustache and small goatee—graffiti—on what is undoubtedly one of the most celebrated, if not one of the most beautiful and serene female faces in western art. Second, Duchamp changed the title of the work to the initials *L.H.O.O.Q.*, which serve as a French acronym for "elle a chaud au cul," which translates into something along the lines of "She has a hot ass"[125] or, more daintily, "She has hot pants."[126] *L.H.O.O.Q.* can be pronounced phonetically in English as the single word "look," referring perhaps to the enigmatic countenance of *La Giocanda.* These visual and aural puns are what gives

intellectual property that involves problems of parody. Trademark parodies are fairly common, and infringement is judged by a "likelihood of confusion" test. *See* 15 U.S.C. § 1114(1) (1994). Representative trademark cases alleging infringement by parody include Anheuser-Busch, Inc. v. Balducci Publications, 28 F.3d 769 (8th Cir. 1994) ("Michelob Oily" parody in defendant's humor magazine *Snicker*), *cert. denied,* 115 S. Ct. 903 (1995); Anheuser-Busch, Inc. v. L&L Wings, Inc., 962 F.2d 316 (4th Cir.) ("King of Beaches" parody of Bud slogan on T-shirt), *cert. denied,* 113 S. Ct. 206 (1992); Cliffs Notes, Inc. v. Bantam Doubleday Dell Pub. Group, Inc., 886 F.2d 490 (2d Cir. 1989) (printing "Satire" prominently on "Spy Notes" parody of Cliffs Notes unlikely to cause confusion); Jordache Enter., Inc. v. Hoggwyld, Ltd., 828 F.2d 1482 (10th Cir. 1987) ("Lardashe" parody of Jordache jeans); Shieffelin & Co. v. Jack Co. of Boca, Inc., 850 F. Supp. 232 (S.D.N.Y. 1994) ("Dom Popignon," a popcorn product mark, infringes upon "Dom Perignon" champagne trademark); Nike, Inc. v. "Just Did It" Enters., 799 F. Supp. 894 (N.D. Ill. 1992) (parody of Nike's "Just Do It" slogan); General Elec. Co. v. Alumpa Coal Co., 205 U.S.P.Q. (BNA) 1036 (D. Mass 1979) ("Genital Electric" parody). *See generally* Tammi A. Gauthier, Note, *Fun & Profit: When Commercial Parodies Constitute Copyright or Trademark Infringement,* 21 PEPP. L. REV. 165 (1993); Peter W. Smith, Note, *Trademarks, Parody, and Consumer Confusion: A Workable Lanham Act Infringement Standard,* 12 CARDOZO L. REV. 1525 (1991); Tyrone Tasker, *Parody or Satire as a Defense to Trademark Infringement,* 77 TRADEMARK REP. 216 (1987).

Should a parodist seek trademark protection for her mark, the Lanham Act poses several hurdles. 15 U.S.C. § 1052(d) (1994) provides that no mark can be registered if it is likely to cause confusion, mistake, or deception with a previously registered mark. Further, unlike copyright law, which has no explicit content-based restriction for protection (and courts have rejected reading such a restriction into the copyright act, *see, e.g.,* Mitchell Bros. Film Group v. Cinema Adult Theater, 604 F.2d 852 (5th Cir. 1979), *cert. denied,* 445 U.S. 917 (1980)), the Lanham Act rejects protection for immoral, deceptive, or scandalous marks. *See* 15 U.S.C. § 1052(a).

125 *See* HORST W. JANSON, HISTORY OF ART 693 (3d ed. 1986).

126 *See* LAWRENCE D. STEEFEL, JR., THE POSITION OF DUCHAMP'S "GLASS" IN THE DEVELOPMENT OF HIS ART 368 n.40 (1977). Such punning is hardly surprising from an artist who made a self-portrait entitled *With My Tongue in My Cheek* (1959).

Duchamp's parody its kick to its viewers and its sting to Leonardo's moral rights as an artist.

B. *Parody and Fair Use*

Parody, by its very nature, smacks of irreverence. Whether it involves a send-up of a work protected by traditional copyright law,[127] or one protected additionally by the new moral rights provisions of state[128] or federal law,[129] a parody is almost always quasi-revolutionary[130] in concept, and rarely is it a loving, respectful, or deferential use of the underlying work. One example of this is, of course, Duchamp's hirsute and bawdy version of Leonardo's *Mona Lisa.* Given the essential, even if subtle, naughtiness of most parodies, it is highly unlikely that any author or author's estate[131] will voluntarily permit the parodist to use the underlying work. This may be especially true when the moral right of integrity, the protection of "honor or reputation,"[132] is at stake. If parody is intended to criticize or mock an author's work, then almost inevitably an artist's "honor or reputation" is on the line.

In parody, imitation is most often *not* the sincerest form of flattery, as numerous examples will illustrate.[133] As the Ninth Circuit noted in *Fisher v. Dees,* "[t]he parody defense to copyright infringement exists precisely to make possible a use that generally cannot be bought."[134] It cannot be bought because the original artist fears not only a deleterious economic effect on her work (a hit on the pocketbook, which is protected by traditional copyright law), but also the negative effect on her artistic sensibilities, reputation, and honor (a hit on the psyche, the subject of moral rights protection). Indeed, the authors of a leading copyright casebook note that a licensed parody is oxymoronic.[135] To obtain permis-

---

127 17 U.S.C. § 106.

128 *See supra* notes 79-91 and accompanying text.

129 17 U.S.C. § 106A.

130 Parody as revolution is as recent as Chinese political discontent. People wore "dissatisfaction T-shirts," which turned political party propaganda into parody. *See* ORVILLE SCHELL, MANDATE OF HEAVEN 273-74 (1994).

131 The Copyright Act of 1976 affords protection against infringement for the author's life plus fifty years. 17 U.S.C. § 302(a) (for works created after Jan. 1, 1978). Federal moral rights expire with the author's death. 17 U.S.C. § 106A(d).

132 *Id.* § 106A(a)(3)(A).

133 *See, e.g., Acuff-Rose,* 114 S. Ct. 1164; Walt Disney Prods. v. Air Pirates, 581 F.2d 751 (9th Cir. 1978), *cert. denied sub nom.* O'Neill v. Walt Disney Prods., 439 U.S. 1132 (1979).

134 Fisher v. Dees, 794 F.2d 432, 437 (9th Cir. 1986) (citations omitted); *see also* Wendy J. Gordon, *Fair Use as Market Failure: A Structural and Economic Analysis of the Betamax Case and its Predecessors,* 82 COLUM. L. REV. 1600 (1982).

135 ALAN LATMAN ET AL., COPYRIGHT FOR THE NINETIES 600 n.5 (4th ed. 1993); *cf. Acuff-Rose,* 114 S. Ct. at 1178 (stating that it is "unlike[ly] that creators of imaginative works will license critical review or lampoons of their own productions"); Richard H. Posner, *When Is*

sion from an artist who may assert personal, moral rights would seem to be virtually impossible. Further, we may well wonder how parody could function effectively as commentary and critique if the authority to satirize, criticize, ridicule, or jibe is given. Permission connotes approval—few parodists wish that blessing, and few artists whose moral rights of integrity are at risk would wish that curse.

The chilling effect of this is self-evident. To escape liability for infringement based on an unauthorized use of the underlying work, there are only two avenues open to parodists: silence (not to use the protected work), or reliance on the fair use defense. When an artist's moral rights of honor and reputation are at stake, the parodist may well decide to self-censor, fearing that the current formulation of the fair use doctrine might not sufficiently immunize her. Silence will not, of course, add to society's storehouse of "useful arts" contemplated by the constitutional grant of limited copyright monopoly.[136]

1. Case Law Prior to 1994: Lower Court Decisions

Almost four decades of copyright cases charging parodists with infringement[137] have not resulted in any consistent, predictable,

Parody Fair Use?, 21 J. LEGAL STUD. 67, 69 (1992) ("The credibility of book reviews . . . would be undermined if a reviewer needed the author's permission to quote from the book."); Vincent Blasi, *Toward a Theory of Prior Restraint: The Central Linkage*, 66 MINN. L. REV. 11, 67 (1981) ("[T]he granting of a license . . . constitutes an official seal of approval, the modern day equivalent of an imprimatur."). The front cover of Ronald Richard Roberts's (pseudonym) *The Ditches of Edison County* (1993) has stamped upon it "unauthorized . . . a parody." It would be hard to imagine that Robert James Waller, the author of *The Bridges of Madison County*, would permit this second author to ridicule his book so barbedly.

136 U.S. CONST. art. I, § 8, cl. 8 provides that copyright protection be for "limited Times."

137 Representative parody/fair use cases since the 1950s include, in chronological order: Loew's, Inc. v. Columbia Broadcasting Sys., Inc., 131 F. Supp. 165 (S.D. Cal. 1955), *aff'd sub nom.* Benny v. Loew's, Inc., 239 F.2d 532 (9th Cir. 1956) (holding that the Jack Benny "Autolight" parody was not fair use), *aff'd by an equally divided Court*, 356 U.S. 43 (1958); Columbia Pictures Corp. v. National Broadcasting Corp., 137 F. Supp. 348 (S.D. Cal. 1955) (holding that the parody "From Here to Obscurity" was fair use); Berlin v. E.C. Publications, Inc., 329 F.2d 541 (2d Cir.) (holding that *Mad* magazine's satirical lyrics sung to twenty-five of Irving Berlin's songs was fair use), *cert. denied*, 379 U.S. 822 (1964); *Air Pirates*, 581 F.2d 751 (holding that bawdy counter-culture depiction of Disney cartoon characters was not fair use); MGM, Inc. v. Showcase Atlanta Coop Prods., 479 F. Supp. 351 (N.D. Ga. 1979) (holding that reenactment of *Gone with the Wind* as a comedy was not fair use); Elsmere Music, Inc. v. National Broadcasting Corp., 482 F. Supp. 741 (S.D.N.Y.) (holding that "I Love Sodom," an eighteen second Saturday Night Live skit, was fair use), *aff'd*, 623 F.2d 252 (2d Cir. 1980) (per curiam); MCA, Inc. v. Wilson, 677 F.2d 180 (2d Cir. 1981) (holding that the parody song "Cunnilingus Champion of Company C" was not fair use); Pillsbury Co. v. Milky Way Prods., 215 U.S.P.Q. (BNA) 124 (N.D. Ga. 1981) (holding that depiction of Pillsbury characters engaging in sexual intercourse and fellatio, and reproduction of the Pillsbury baking song, was not fair use); Warner Bros., Inc. v. American Broadcasting Cos., 720 F.2d 231 (2d Cir. 1983) (holding that the television show "The Greatest American Hero" did not infringe upon the plaintiff's "Superman" character); *Fisher*, 794 F.2d 432 (holding that the parody song "When Sonny Sniffs Glue" was fair use); Original Appalachian Artworks, Inc. v. Topps Chewing Gum, Inc., 642 F. Supp. 1031 (N.D. Ga.

and coherent application of the fair use doctrine, at least until the Supreme Court's attempt in *Campbell v. Acuff-Rose Music, Inc.*[138] Neither the relative outrageousness of the parody nor the cleverness of the newly titled song seem to be a reliable predictor of whether the use will be deemed a fair one.[139] Additionally, courts have expressed divergent views about fair use, depending upon the focus of the infringing parody. The Sixth Circuit held in *Acuff-Rose* that a "fair" parody cannot be a general social commentary, but must target plaintiff's specific protected work.[140] In contrast, the Second Circuit in *Elsmere* squarely rejected the notion that the challenged parody must poke fun at the original work, rather than using that work as a means to facilitate a more general critique of society.[141]

Still other courts have articulated what has come to be known as the "conjure up test." Recognizing that the very nature of parody requires the audience to make the connection between the original work and the parodying work, some courts concede that a parodist must necessarily use "a substantial enough portion of [the original and fairly well-known work[142]] to evoke recognition," to make both a successful and fair parody.[143] These courts acknowledge, as they should, that the artistic genre itself requires significant use of the protected work. The "joinder of reference and ridicule" is thus the essence of parody.[144]

However, the line between a fair "conjuring up" and an imper-

---

1986) (holding that "Garbage Pail Kids" was not fair use); New Line Cinema Corp. v. Bertelsmann Music Group, Inc., 693 F. Supp. 1517 (S.D.N.Y. 1988) (holding that alleged parody of "Freddy Krueger," a character from the movie *A Nightmare on Elm Street*, was not fair use); Tin Pan Apple, Inc. v. Miller Brewing Co., 737 F. Supp. 826 (S.D.N.Y. 1990) (holding that a beer company's use of a sound-alike and look-alike rap group in a commercial parody not a viable fair use defense); Eveready Battery Co. v. Adolph Coors Co., 765 F. Supp. 440 (N.D. Ill. 1991) (holding that a defendant's use of a plaintiff's mechanical rabbit beating on a drum was presumed to be fair use); Rogers v. Koons, 960 F.2d 301 (2d Cir.) (holding that a derivative sculpture based on a photo of a man and a woman holding seven puppies was not fair use), *cert. denied*, 113 S. Ct. 365 (1992); Acuff-Rose Music, Inc. v. Campbell, 972 F.2d 1429 (6th Cir. 1992) (holding that "Oh Hairy Woman" parody by the Rap group 2 Live Crew was not fair use), *rev'd*, 114 S. Ct. 1164 (reasoning that a commercial parody is not presumptively unfair).

It is not surprising that most of the parody cases emanate from the Ninth and Second Circuits, in which Hollywood and New York are respectively located.

138 114 S. Ct. 1164.

139 *Compare Fisher*, 794 F.2d 432 (holding that "When Sonny Sniffs Glue" is a fair use parody of "When Sunny Gets Blue") *with MCA*, 677 F.2d 180 (holding that "Cunnilingus Champion of Company C" is not a fair use of "The Boogie Woogie Bugle Boy of Company B").

140 *Acuff-Rose*, 972 F.2d at 1436 n.8.

141 *Elsmere Music*, 623 F.2d at 253 n.1.

142 Recognition gives parody its punch.

143 *See Fisher*, 794 F.2d at 435 n.2.

144 *Acuff-Rose*, 114 S. Ct. at 1173.

missible pirated taking is often quite difficult to draw. This lack of a bright-line test is hardly surprising, as the classic definition of parody is "counter song," a song beside another.[145] Thus, for the parodying work to succeed at all it must be sung, painted, written, sculpted, in short, *expressed* in such a way as to be evocative of the underlying work. In other words, to parody, the second artist must always take from the first artist. On the other hand, if the second work amounts to a substantial taking, that is, something considerably more than evoking or conjuring up the original work, the parody/fair use defense generally fails.[146]

As the above discussion indicates, when the Supreme Court decided *Acuff-Rose*,[147] it was writing on its own clean slate,[148] but on a national slate made very rough and murky by inconsistent, confusing, and uneasily reconcilable lower court opinions of the last four decades. The following discussion will present a brief overview of the Supreme Court's *Acuff-Rose* decision, which should facilitate later analysis of the clash between moral rights and parody, as tempered by fair use.

2. Parody and Fair Use in the Supreme Court: *Campbell v. Acuff-Rose Music, Inc.*

Although the judicially crafted doctrine of fair use has been available to defendants at least since 1841[149] and was codified in the 1976 Copyright Act without any substantial change,[150] the Supreme Court did not address fair use until 1984 in *Sony*[151] and again a year later in *Harper & Row*.[152] Neither *Sony* nor *Harper & Row* involved parody. In *Acuff-Rose*, the Supreme Court expanded

---

145 WEBSTER'S NEW WORLD DICTIONARY OF THE AMERICAN LANGUAGE 1064 (1957 ed.). It derives from the Greek, "paroidia," "para" meaning beside, and "oide" meaning song. *Id.*

146 The *Fisher* court describes the delicate balance. *See Fisher*, 794 F.2d at 439 (citing *Walt Disney Prods.*, 581 F.2d 751).

147 114 S. Ct. 1164.

148 The Supreme Court had granted certiorari in Columbia Broadcasting Sys. v. Loews Inc., 353 U.S. 946 (1957), but, due to Justice Douglas's recusal, was equally divided and did not issue a written opinion. 356 U.S. 43 (1958).

149 Folsom v. Marsh, 9 F. Cas. 342 (C.C.D. Mass. 1841) (No. 4,901). Justice Story described the defense as an "intricate and embarrassing [question] . . . [where it was not] easy to arrive at any satisfactory conclusion, or to lay down any general principles applicable to all cases." *Id.* at 344. But he then proceeded to do so: "[W]e must . . . look to the nature and objects of the selections made, the quantity and value of the materials used, and the degree in which the use may prejudice the sale, or diminish the profits, or supersede the objects, of the original work." *Id.* at 348.

150 Congress intended, by statutory enactment, " 'to restate the present judicial doctrine of fair use, not to change, narrow, or enlarge it in any way.' " *Acuff-Rose*, 114 S. Ct. at 1170 (quoting H.R. REP. NO. 1476, 94th Cong., 2d Sess. 66 (1976), *reprinted in* 1976 U.S.C.C.A.N. 5659, 5679-80; S. REP. NO. 473, 94th Cong., 2d Sess. 62 (1975)).

151 Sony Corp. v. Universal City Studios, Inc., 464 U.S. 417, 451 (1984).

152 Harper & Row Publishers, Inc. v. Nation Enters., 471 U.S. 539 (1985). The Supreme

upon its earlier analyses of fair use and considered the special problems posed by the intersection of parody and fair use. In concluding unanimously[153] that 2 Live Crew's use of Ray Orbison's ballad, "Oh, Pretty Woman," might be fair, the Court alternatively relied upon and distinguished *Sony* and *Harper & Row.*

Sony contained language that significantly impacted the Sixth Circuit's two-to-one decision in *Acuff-Rose,* which found 2 Live Crew's alleged parody to be an unfair use.[154] The *Sony* majority stated that use for "a commercial or profit-making purpose . . . [is] presumptively . . . unfair," while the contrary presumption, that non-commercial use is presumptively fair, would and did benefit Sony.[155] This latter presumption seemed to convince the *Sony* Court of the fairness of the use even though the activity at issue, taping, was merely reproductive.[156]

The presumption of unfairness attached to commercial use was reiterated the very next year by the majority in *Harper & Row,*[157] even in the context of news reporting that exemplifies a transformative and productive work subject to fair use.[158] In *Harper & Row,* defendant *The Nation* magazine had "scooped" parts of former President Ford's memoirs, which were to appear, by agreement, in *Time* magazine. The Court, stressing strongly the right of first publication and the fact that *The Nation* took the heart of Ford's memoirs about Ford's pardon of Nixon, concluded *The Nation's* infringement was not excused as a fair use.[159]

Neither *Harper & Row* nor *Sony* involved parody, albeit a commercial parody. Taken together, however, it would appear that prior to *Acuff-Rose* the Supreme Court meant what it said—if an alleged infringer uses the copyrighted work for commercial purposes the use is presumptively unfair, even if it results in a transformative, productive, or creative work like the news reporting in

---

Court also discussed fair use in Stewart v. Abend, 495 U.S. 207, 236-38 (1990), but the treatment was relatively brief and unremarkable for purposes of this article.

153 Justice Kennedy concurred to stress that while he agreed substantially with the Court's fair use analysis, he believed it could still be possible for the district court on remand to find that 2 Live Crew's song was not fair use. *Acuff-Rose,* 114 S. Ct. at 1182 (Kennedy, J., concurring).

154 *Acuff-Rose,* 972 F.2d 1429, *rev'd,* 114 S. Ct. 1164.

155 *Sony,* 464 U.S. at 499.

156 Justice Blackmun, on the other hand, stressed the notion that fair use should generally not apply when the use is reproductive, rather than productive, although he would not suggest "that every productive use is a fair use." *Sony,* 464 U.S. at 479 (Blackmun, J., dissenting).

157 *Harper & Row,* 471 U.S. at 562 ("[E]very commercial use of copyrighted material is presumptively an unfair exploitation of the monopoly privilege that belongs to the owner of the copyright." (quoting *Sony,* 464 U.S. at 451)).

158 *See* 17 U.S.C. § 107.

159 *Harper & Row,* 471 U.S. at 569.

Harper & Row. Since fair use is an affirmative defense,[160] a commercial-use defendant would thus be hard-pressed to overcome that presumption. *Acuff-Rose* reined in the presumption, at least with regard to parody. Justice Souter, writing for the Court, said that despite its language *Sony* "called for no hard evidentiary presumption."[161] Thus, when the Sixth Circuit elevated this one sentence to a "per se rule," it was both "counter to *Sony* itself [and] . . . to the common-law tradition of fair use adjudication."[162] The commercial nature of the use is but one factor to be added onto the scales with the other non-exclusive section 107 inquiries.[163]

What triggered the Court's apparent softening of what seemed to be inexplicably clear language in *Sony,* which was reiterated in *Harper & Row?* First, Justice Souter noted the transformative nature of 2 Live Crew's song: as a transformative work, the song furthered copyright's goal "to promote science and the arts."[164] Second, Justice Souter appreciated "parody's need for the recognizable sight or sound"[165]—the "conjure up" test.[166] Finally, in assessing the effect of 2 Live Crew's use upon the potential market for the copyrighted song, Justice Souter emphasized that in the case of parody, even a commercial one, it is likely that the second work "will not affect the market for the original in a way cognizable"[167] by the fair use doctrine. This is so because there is "no protectable derivative market for criticism."[168] Since it is not likely that creators will authorize the slings and arrows of criticism, the "potential licensing market" for such is simply not present.

Acuff-Rose, although it is based on "traditional" copyright infringement (property rights), teaches several lessons which are important in resolving the hypothetical *Leonardo v. Duchamp* case based on a moral rights violation. First, *Acuff-Rose* indicates that there are no fixed presumptions with regard to the commercial character of use, at least in the parody situation. Rather, the for-profit character of the use is to be regarded as one ingredient in the fair use recipe. Second, transformative uses, as are both Duchamp's and 2 Live Crew's, serve copyright's goal and "the

---

160 The affirmative nature of the defense has been stressed since Justice Story's decision in *Folsom,* 9 F. Cas. 342. *See* PATRY, *supra* note 11, at 22, 477-78.

161 *Acuff-Rose,* 114 S. Ct. at 1174.

162 *Id.*

163 *Id.*

164 *Id.* at 1171.

165 *Id.* at 1176.

166 *Id.*; *see Elsmere Music,* 623 F.2d at 253 n.1; *Fisher,* 794 F.2d at 438-39.

167 114 S. Ct. at 1177; *cf.* 17 U.S.C. § 107(4).

168 *Acuff-Rose,* 114 S. Ct. at 1178 ("People ask . . . for criticism, but they only want praise." (quoting SOMERSET MAUGHAM, OF HUMAN BONDAGE 241 (1992)).

more transformative the new work, the less will be the significance of other factors, like commercialism, that may weigh against a finding of fair use."[169] Third, the Court gave its seal of approval to the "conjure up" test, articulated heretofore by a few lower courts,[170] which recognizes the special needs of parody as an art form: Mimesis is the sine qua non of parody. Moreover, the nature of parody as criticism requires a sensitive inquiry into the potential market effect.[171] It is one thing to reduce the potential market by disparagement and criticism. This is *not* the negative market effect contemplated by section 107. It is quite another to reduce demand by the substitution effect of the parodying work. In short, defendant can destroy plaintiff's market, but cannot replace it. This would violate section 107(4) and thus would not likely be fair use.

Finally, we are left then with no bright-line test in traditional copyright infringement cases. Each case must be analyzed on its own, and all section 107 factors are to be considered together.[172] In thus eschewing any hard and fast application of the fair use doctrine, the Court sacrificed, of course, a certain degree of predictability and uniformity. But this sacrifice, presumably at the altar of copyright's purpose to foster creativity,[173] may complicate the application of the fair use defense raised in conjunction with a moral rights claim.

Nevertheless, even though *Acuff-Rose* dealt with traditional property rights-based copyright infringement, its lessons for us in the moral rights context have great import, even though I reject an *Acuff-Rose* type solution to the very different problem of a moral rights violation based on parody.

III. Resolving the Moral Rights/Parody Dilemma Through Fair Use

In *Acuff-Rose*, a non-moral rights case, the Supreme Court specifically and even-handedly rejected two proffered and contrary presumptions. The first proposal, from defendant 2 Live Crew, was

---

169 *Id.* at 1171.

170 *See supra* note 166 and accompanying text.

171 *Acuff-Rose*, 114 S. Ct. at 1177.

172 *See id.* at 1169 (citing Pierre Leval, *Toward a Fair Use Standard*, 103 Harv. L. Rev. 1105, 1110-11 (1990)); Patry & Perlmutter, *supra* note 11, at 685-87.

173 *Id.* at 1170 (citing *Stewart*, 495 U.S. at 236). This emphasis on "creativity" is also found in Feist Publications, Inc. v. Rural Tel. Serv. Co., 499 U.S. 340 (1991). In *Feist*, Justice O'Connor, writing for the Court, mentioned originality and authorship numerous times in assessing the copyrightability of telephone white pages. *Id.* at 345-64. Professor Goldstein has noted that Justice O'Connor refers to originality thirteen times. *See* Paul Goldstein, Copyright § 2.2.1 n.11 (Supp. 1993).

to treat parody as presumptively fair use.[174] The second, put forth by Acuff-Rose and adopted by the Sixth Circuit,[175] was to view commercial use as presumptively unfair use, even in the context of parody. While neither presumption succeeded in *Acuff-Rose*, in the moral rights setting involving parody, a parodist's use should be presumed fair. On the one hand section 106A(a) makes explicit that the right of integrity is subject to section 107's fair use defense.[176] On the other hand, Congress has expressed ambivalence about the viability of the fair use defense in the moral rights arena.[177] Given this somewhat schizophrenic situation with respect to fair use in the moral rights context, it might be wise to consider solutions, other than giving a presumption of fair use to the moral rights/parodist defendant, which might balance effectively the rights of the artist and parodist.

A. *Compulsory License*

The relationship between artist and critic can be described as one of worthy adversaries, supportive and empathetic friendship, symbiosis at its finest, or the art world equivalent of a dysfunctional family—a "can't live with 'em/can't live without 'em" conundrum. Although artists may "ask . . . for criticism," even if implicitly so by putting their creations out for public consumption, "they only want praise."[178] Parody is critical and it is rarely kind, gentle, affectionate, or sought for by the artist. In fact, I suspect that if all the art, theater, dance, and book critics, as well as parodists, would vanish from this world, artists worldwide would be dry-eyed. Thus, when moral rights, "honor or reputation," are at risk this monopoly might be used to prevent or chill the critic/parodist.

The concern that artists could use their copyright (including and especially moral rights) to censor parody might be alleviated by establishing a "Parody Licensing Clearance Center" which would be authorized by Congress to provide a license on a percentage of revenue basis to anyone who chooses to parody the pro-

174 *See Acuff-Rose*, 114 S. Ct. at 1168.

175 *Acuff-Rose*, 972 F.2d at 1435, 1437. The Sixth Circuit "ostensibly [and erroneously] culled" this presumption from *Sony*. *Acuff-Rose*, 114 S. Ct. at 1173-74 (citing *Sony*, 464 U.S. at 451).

176 17 U.S.C. § 106A(a).

177 H.R. REP. NO. 514, *supra* note 80, at 22, *reprinted in* 1990 U.S.C.C.A.N. at 6932. The stark contrast between explicit statutory language and legislative history may be explained by VARA's somewhat hasty passage in Congress. *See* Smith, *supra* note 108 and text accompanying note 108.

178 SOMERSET MAUGHAM, OF HUMAN BONDAGE 241 (1992), *quoted in Acuff-Rose*, 114 S. Ct. at 1178.

tected work.[179] Compulsory licenses function as "permission to use intellectual property, compelled by the government to accomplish some political or social objective;"[180] for example, to encourage more art. Presumably, in the moral rights context, a compulsory license would afford some monetary incentive to Leonardo without endangering Duchamp any more than by requiring him to pay a royalty.

Compulsory license is rare in copyright law, but no stranger. At one time or another, the 1976 Copyright Act listed six areas covered by compulsory license: cable television transmissions;[181] making and distributing phonorecords;[182] jukebox recording or performing of musical compositions;[183] non-commercial, for example, public broadcasting;[184] satellite retransmissions;[185] and importation and manufacture of digital audio recording devices.[186] At one time the Register of Copyrights suggested that the political compromise between the "protected interests of creators" and the "pressures . . . of newly emergent user industries" might result in more, rather than less use of compulsory license.[187] In one sense, this is true. In reviewing the then-new 1976 Act, Professor Paul Goldstein listed the four areas subject to compulsory license: cable transmissions; phonorecords; jukeboxes; and public broadcasting.[188] Since 1977, two new areas were added: satellite retransmissions and digital audio recording devices.[189] On the other hand, Congress recently has endorsed private, voluntary licensing negotiations and arbitration with reference to government fiat as a last resort.[190]

---

179 *See* Edmund W. Kitch & Harvey S. Perlman, Legal Regulation of The Competitive Process 212-13 (4th rev. ed. 1993). The authors' suggestion did not address the § 106A(a) parody problem, but it works equally well or equally ineffectively in the moral rights context.

180 J.T. McCarthy, McCarthy's Desk Encyclopedia of Intellectual Property 51-52 (1991).

181 17 U.S.C. § 111(c), (d).

182 *Id.* § 115.

183 *Id.* § 116. Currently, § 116 problems are handled either by a negotiated license, which may include arbitration, *id.* § 116A(b), (c), or by compulsory license under 17 U.S.C. § 116.

184 *Id.* § 118 (determining the royalty fee either by negotiated license or compulsory license; *see id.* § 118(b)(2)).

185 *Id.* § 119(b). After Dec. 31, 1992, the royalty fee is determined by voluntary negotiation or compulsory arbitration. *Id.* § 119(c)(1).

186 *Id.* §§ 1003-1004 (1994).

187 Barbara Ringer, *Copyright and the Future of Authorship*, 101 Libr. J. 229, 231 (1976).

188 Goldstein, *supra* note 79, at 1127-35.

189 *See supra* notes 185-86; *see also* Michael L. Baroni, *A Pirate's Palette: The Dilemmas of Digital Sound Sampling and a Proposed Compulsory License Solution*, 11 U. Miami Ent. & Sports L. Rev. 65 (1993).

190 *See* 17 U.S.C. §§ 801-803.

Compulsory license for parody seems problematic even in the economic rights context, but seems particularly inappropriate to the moral right of integrity. Compulsory license works best, or at least seems most necessary, when new technology presents issues of copyright infringement not even dreamed of when the 1909 or 1976 copyright laws were enacted. Thus, such uses as satellite transmissions and digital recording devices seem amenable to compulsory license—parody affecting moral rights does not. The 1976 Act compulsory license scheme for making and distributing phonorecords illustrates this point. A compulsory license is *not available* to someone who changes the protected work.[191] Similarly, a compulsory license would not be available to a parodist who infringes upon an artist's moral right of integrity by some fundamental change—which parody always makes—to the protected work. It is not a question of accommodating emerging technology by political compromise.[192] The compulsory license scheme ill-fits the balancing of interests between an artist's moral rights and a parodist's right to "conjure up" and fundamentally change that work to achieve the desired parodic effect.

Two further difficulties arise in connection with a compulsory license scheme. The first relates to the essence of the right of integrity. Designed to protect an artist's honor and reputation, the right would be threatened into extinction if the author is forced to "approve" the parodist's use by compulsory license. The second difficulty relates to the nature of parody which thrives, perhaps, on its iconoclastic and unpermitted status. Compulsory license, though freeing the parodist from liability, takes away from the zing that is the essence of parody: the "civil disobedience"[193] of art. A compulsory license affects negatively the transgressive quality of

---

[191] 17 U.S.C. § 115(a)(2) provides:

> A compulsory license includes the privilege of making a musical arrangement of the work to the extent necessary to conform it to the style or manner of interpretation of the performance involved, *but the arrangement shall not change the basic melody or fundamental character of the work, and shall not be subject to protection as a derivative work . . . except with the express consent of the copyright owner.*

Id. (emphasis added).

[192] *See* Goldstein, *supra* note 79, at 1128 n.83.

[193] John Carlin, Remarks at A.A.L.S. Annual Meeting, Intellectual Property Law Section (Orlando, Fla., Jan. 7, 1994) [hereinafter A.A.L.S. Meeting]. Dr. Carlin is an art historian, former Professor of Art History, sometime curator at the Whitney Museum of American Art, and Director of the Red Hot Organization, New York. In speaking about the history of the appropriation art movement in the visual arts, Dr. Carlin called Duchamp the "King of appropriation." *Id.* In balancing the interests implicated in appropriation art, Carlin proposes, *inter alia*, a model, voluntary license agreement. *See* John Carlin, *Culture Vultures: Artistic Appropriation and Intellectual Property Law*, 13 COLUM.-VLA J.L. & ARTS 103, 139-41 (1988).

parody.[194] How can you "up the establishment" if the establishment says "right on?"

B. *Limitation of Remedies*

While the first solution, compulsory license, affects the "liability" phase, this second alternative focuses on the "damage" phase; we assume that a parodist has been found liable to the original artist through infringement and a failed fair use defense. As described earlier, the Copyright Act affords to copyright owners, including those who assert moral rights violations, a full range of remedies including injunctions, damages, and profits.[195] One way to accommodate the interests of parodists and first artists is to tinker with the remedy phase.

One model that would preserve an artist's honor and reputation while alleviating the hit on the parodist's purse would permit an injunction, but no money damages or profits. But this would ill-serve our copyright goal to encourage more art. Injunctions are silencers. Permanent injunctions involving works of a derivative nature, such as parody, are frequently blanket. That is, a court will enjoin dissemination of the whole parody, even if it consists of both infringing and non-infringing material, since such are often inextricably intertwined.[196] Thus, parodies would not be seen or heard. Further, it is questionable whether an injunction truly protects artistic honor. Injunctions might issue too late to ameliorate the "dissing"[197] effect of the parody, and pre-publication injunctions are generally disfavored as prior censorship.[198]

A second possibility is to eschew entirely injunctive relief, and award damages and profits to the artist whose right of integrity is sullied. This would seem to work well when it is difficult to separate the infringing from the non-infringing parts of the parodist's work. Where "the proportion [used of plaintiff's work] is so insignificant compared with the injury from stopping [defendant's] use

---

194 *Cf.* A.A.L.S. Meeting, *supra* note 193 (remarks of Prof. Peter Jaszi).

195 17 U.S.C. §§ 502, 504; *see supra* note 119.

196 *See* PAUL GOLDSTEIN, COPYRIGHT, PATENT, TRADEMARK AND RELATED STATE DOCTRINES 725 n.7 (3d rev. ed. 1993).

197 "Diss" has become an idiomatic expression for disrespect or disparagement. Although it is pure slang, it seems to have been coined by rap musicians as a short and concise verb, "to diss," to express a noun, such as disrespect. *See* Lee Bey, *Kickin' The Ballistics and Resurrecting Old Verbs; New Dictionary Preserves Lively Language of Blacks*, CHI. SUN-TIMES, Aug. 28, 1994, Show Section, at 14; Larry Fiquette, *Do Your Own Thing, Reporters*, ST. LOUIS POST-DISPATCH, June 12, 1994, at 2A.

198 *See* Pierre N. Leval, *Toward a Fair Use Standard*, 103 HARV. L. REV. 1105, 1130-35 & n.112 (1990). Note that Judge Leval believes that our copyright law seems "incompatible" with moral rights. *Id.* at 1128.

. . . an injunction would be unconscionable," and plaintiff should recover only money damages.[199] Similarly, in *Acuff-Rose*, the Court urged sensitive inquiry into whether injunctive relief should be awarded "when parodists are found to have gone beyond the bounds of fair use."[200]

It is not clear, however, that the legal remedy of monetary damages, as opposed to the equitable remedy of injunctive relief, will well serve the interests of artist, parodist, and public, at least under the present formulation of the fair use doctrine. Under the existing formulation of fair use, where the parodist has the burden of proof, the second artist may be disinclined to parody, especially when the parody will trample on the first artist's "honor and reputation." Thus, the silencing problem inherent in the injunctive remedy model may still be unsolved in the damages only model. In addition, the damages only model does not give artists asserting moral rights what they really want[201]—freedom from criticism which injures their honor or reputation.

C. *Per Se Rule of Non-Liability*

A per se rule of non-liability is an effective shield for Duchamp, but eviscerates entirely Leonardo's section 106A rights. A right without a remedy is, of course, no right at all. So if Congress enacted a new section 106B, which makes explicit that the remedies afforded by sections 501-505 are not available in actions involving moral rights, it would render section 106A a nullity and, arguably, jeopardize our status as an adherent to Berne.

D. *Moral Rights, Copyright, and the First Amendment*

One author has argued that in the context of moral rights, a First Amendment[202] defense to liability should be established, as moral and First Amendment rights inevitably conflict.[203] Several

199 Dun v. Lumbermen's Credit Ass'n, 209 U.S. 20, 23-24 (1908). Seventy-six years later, Justice Blackmun recognized the need for a sensitive tailoring of remedies to accommodate "traditional copyright principles." *Sony*, 464 U.S. at 500 (Blackmun, J., dissenting); *see* A.A.L.S. Meeting, *supra* note 193 (remarks of Prof. Marci Hamilton, "Possible Property Models for Art Appropriation").

200 *Acuff-Rose*, 114 S. Ct. at 1171 n.10 (citations omitted).

201 Professor Gordon refers to the "[a]nti-[d]issemination motives" of plaintiffs in parody suits, which have little to do with the economic value of plaintiff's copyright. Gordon, *supra* note 134, at 1632.

202 U.S. Const. amend. I.

203 *See* Kathryn A. Kelly, *Moral Rights and the First Amendment: Putting Honor Before Free Speech?*, 11 U. Miami Ent. & Sports L. Rev. 211 (1994). The proposed test would vary with the speech at issue, for example, "[v]iolations of . . . integrity would be analyzed under *Central Hudson* . . . ." *Id.* at 249 (citing Central Hudson Gas & Elec. Corp. v. Pub. Serv. Comm'n of N.Y., 447 U.S. 557 (1980)); *see also* Beyer, *supra* note 6, at 1070-71.

other authors have recognized the delicate relationship between copyright monopoly and First Amendment freedom of speech.[204] Professor Denicola argues for a limited First Amendment privilege to allow potential users access to protected expression when traditional copyright law does not so permit.[205] Professor Goldstein proposes constitutional tests when copyright protections encroach upon "overtly constitutional areas."[206] A student author opines that "[i]f the *Mona Lisa* were copyrighted and da Vinci sued for infringement, Duchamp's First Amendment defense should clearly prevail."[207]

Courts, however, have been fairly uniform in rejecting First Amendment defenses in copyright cases. In *Air Pirates* (the bawdy, promiscuous Mickey Mouse parody), defendants urged that the "First Amendment should bar liability for their parody because otherwise protected criticism would be discouraged."[208] The Ninth Circuit recognized the possible tension between copyright and First Amendment, but held that the First Amendment argument failed because defendants "could have expressed their theme without copying Disney's protected expression . . . ."[209] Similarly, in *Dallas Cowboys Cheerleaders* (poster of partially nude cheerleaders), the court noted: "The judgment of the constitution is that free expression is enriched by protecting the creations of authors from exploitation by others, and the Copyright Act is the congressional implementation of that judgment. . . . The first amendment is not a license to trammel on legally recognized rights in intellectual property."[210] In 1985, the Supreme Court forestalled further development of any separate First Amendment defense in copyright cases. In *Harper & Row* (*The Nation* magazine's news scoop of

---

204 *See, e.g.*, David A. Householder, *The Progress of Knowledge: A Reexamination of the Fundamental Principles of Copyright Law*, 14 Loy. L.A. Ent. L.J. 1, 38-42 (1993); Floyd Abrams, *First Amendment and Copyright*, 35 J. Copyright Soc'y 1 (1987); Patricia Krieg, Note, *Copyright, Free Speech, and the Visual Arts*, 93 Yale L.J. 1565, 1584 (1984); Robert C. Denicola, *Copyright and Free Speech: Constitutional Limitations on the Protection of Expression*, 67 Cal. L. Rev. 283 (1979); Paul Goldstein, *Copyright and The First Amendment*, 70 Colum. L. Rev. 983 (1970); Melville B. Nimmer, *Does Copyright Abridge the First Amendment Guarantees of Free Speech and Press?*, 17 UCLA L. Rev. 1180 (1970).

205 Denicola, *supra* note 204, at 316.

206 Goldstein, *supra* note 204, at 1057.

207 Krieg, *supra* note 204, at 1584.

208 *Walt Disney Prods.*, 581 F.2d at 758.

209 *Id.* at 758-59 (citing Sid & Marty Krofft Television Prods., Inc. v. McDonald's Corp., 562 F.2d 1157, 1170 (9th Cir. 1977); Zacchini v. Scripps-Howard Broadcasting Co., 433 U.S. 562, 577 & n.13 (1977)).

210 Dallas Cowboys Cheerleaders, Inc. v. Scoreboard Posters, Inc., 600 F.2d 1184, 1187-88 (5th Cir. 1979) (citations omitted). *But see* Triangle Publications, Inc. v. Knight-Ridder Newspapers, Inc., 445 F. Supp. 875 (S.D. Fla. 1978), *aff'd on other grounds*, 626 F.2d 1171, 1178 (5th Cir. 1980). In *Triangle*, the district court held defendant's use not to be fair, but privileged nonetheless under the commercial speech prong of the First Amendment.

Time's publication of parts of President Ford's memoirs), the Court found no inherent conflict between the Copyright Act and the First Amendment.[211] Rather, the Court noted:

> In view of the First Amendment protections already embodied in the Copyright Act's distinction between copyrightable expression and uncopyrightable facts and ideas, and the latitude for scholarship and comment traditionally afforded by fair use, we see no warrant for expanding the doctrine of fair use to create what amounts to a public figure exception to copyright . . . .[212]

Having shown that neither compulsory license, remedy tinkering, per se non-liability, nor a separate First Amendment privilege will resolve appropriately the hypothetical *Leonardo v. Duchamp* case, we are left then with fair use—the final barrier to liability both in section 106 and section 106A cases.

E. *Presumptive Fair Use for Parodists Who Violate an Artist's Right of Integrity*

An analysis of the four fair use factors shows that even in cases involving commercial parodies and section 106A(a)(3)(A), Duchamp should be afforded presumptive fair use. In one sense, this conclusion is made possible because *Acuff-Rose* eschewed a presumption of unfairness when the use is commercial,[213] thus levelling the playing field. What I am suggesting then is to tilt this ground. Even though the Court did not treat parody as presumptive fair use in a property-based, traditional copyright suit, this should not foreclose shifting the burden from defendant/parodist in a moral rights case. Previously, fair use has been viewed as an affirmative defense that a defendant, parodist or not, had to plead and prove.[214] Instead, in moral rights cases based on infringement of the right of integrity, the first artist should bear the burden of pleading and proving that a review of the four section 107 factors shows that the parodist's use was unfair. This tinkering with the fair use doctrine to accomplish the desired effect is not foreclosed by section 107. Section 107 represents not the "creation of new law," but rather, "a direction to the courts to continue to develop the common law."[215] Faced with a bundle of new and odd-fitting[216]

---

[211] *Harper & Row*, 471 U.S. at 560.
[212] *Id.*
[213] *Acuff-Rose*, 114 S. Ct. at 1174.
[214] *Id.* at 1177.
[215] Patry & Perlmutter, *supra* note 11, at 674; *see Stewart*, 495 U.S. at 236. The process began with Justice Story in *Folsom*, 9 F. Cas. at 342.

rights, such as the personal right of integrity, courts should be free to tailor the fair use doctrine to the particular case.

1. The Purpose and Character of the Use

Parody, as criticism or comment, is one of the favored purposes specified in section 107. Though parody is not afforded a per se non-infringement status, such productive, transformative material is often treated as fair use, even when it is for-profit.[217] As is often the case, a parody "adds something new, with a further purpose or different character, altering . . . with new expression, meaning, or message" the host work; thus, it furthers "the goal of copyright to promote science and the arts."[218] Because parody relies on recognition of the host work, it necessarily "copies" at least enough of that work to conjure it up for the viewing or listening public. Thus, a parody that comments upon, targets, or criticizes the original work, as *L.H.O.O.Q.* surely does, is the special focus of section 107.

Additionally, it is no longer crucial that Duchamp exhibited *L.H.O.O.Q.* at a local art gallery and sold the painting to an enamored viewer. The presumption of unfairness attached to commercial use, arguably arising from the *Harper & Row*[219] and *Sony*[220] cases, exists no more.[221]

2. The Nature of the Copyrighted Work

Nor is it critical that Duchamp has copied Leonardo's creative expression (rather than a fact-based work). *Acuff-Rose* teaches that "[t]his fact . . . is not much help . . . in separating the fair use sheep from the infringing goats in a parody case, since most parodies almost invariably copy publicly known, expressive works."[222] So, although Leonardo's *Mona Lisa* "falls within the core of . . . copyright's protective purposes,"[223] the *L.H.O.O.Q.*s of this world must conjure up that creative expression. To afford any weight to Leonardo on this score is, for all practical purposes, to destroy parody as a genre.

---

216 *See supra* notes 157-59 & 167 and accompanying text.

217 *See, e.g., Acuff-Rose*, 114 S. Ct. 1164 (holding that 2 Live Crew's parody may be fair use); *Fisher*, 794 F.2d at 432; *Eveready Battery Co.*, 765 F. Supp. at 440; *Elsmere Music*, 482 F. Supp. at 741.

218 *Acuff-Rose*, 114 S. Ct. at 1171.

219 *Harper & Row*, 471 U.S. at 539.

220 *Sony*, 464 U.S. at 417.

221 *Acuff-Rose*, 114 S. Ct. at 1174.

222 *Id.* at 1175.

223 *Id.*

3. The Amount and Substantiality of Defendant's Use

Under the proposed scheme, Leonardo would have the burden here, as with the other section 107 factors, to show that both the quantity and quality[224] of Duchamp's use exceeds the boundaries of fairness. This determination is to be made with a view "to the copyrighted work as a whole."[225] Because "the extent of permissible copying varies with the purpose and character of the use,"[226] Duchamp's parody necessarily must evoke the *Mona Lisa* to succeed at all as parody. The problem here, of course, is that unlike 2 Live Crew's less than total use of Roy Orbison's song,[227] Duchamp has taken one hundred percent of Leonardo's work, merely adding some hair to lip and chin and changing the title. Leonardo would have to show then that this use went far beyond the necessity to conjure up his *Mona Lisa.* The conjure up test recognizes that Duchamp must use the "most distinctive or memorable features, which the parodist can be sure the audience will know,"[228] but it might be argued that Duchamp went beyond the pale. On the other hand, the iconographic stature and nature of the *Mona Lisa* as portrait suggests that to parody it at all requires almost an entire appropriation. In fact, virtually all the other artists who have parodied the *Mona Lisa* have used it almost in its entirety.[229] Very few visual artists have been able to conjure up a host work merely by outlining it: for example, Larry Rivers, *Outline of History* (1976) and Shusaku Arakawa, *Next to the Last* (1971) (both reproduced in appendix). Thus, parody of a visual art, which is the only type of work protected under section 106A, may necessitate a more total appropriation than a parody of a non-section 106A work, such as a song or a play. Less than verbatim copying of "I Love New York" or "Oh Pretty Woman" may still result in parody, while visual art parodies may require very substantial, near verbatim, copying.[230]

---

224 *Cf. Harper & Row,* 471 U.S. at 564-66, 568.

225 17 U.S.C. § 107(3).

226 *Acuff-Rose,* 114 S. Ct at 1175.

227 *Id.* at 1176-77.

228 *Id.* at 1176; *cf. Cliffs Notes,* 886 F.2d at 494 ("The keystone of parody is imitation.").

229 *See supra* note 123 and accompanying text.

230 Justice Kennedy suggests this conclusion in *Acuff-Rose,* 114 S. Ct. at 1181 (Kennedy, J., concurring). *Cf.* MELVILLE B. NIMMER, 3 NIMMER ON COPYRIGHT § 13.05D, at 13-211 to 225 (1994) ("[T]here may be certain very limited situations wherein copying of even the entire work for a different functional purpose may be regarded as fair use."). Although Nimmer's text refers to use in judicial proceedings, incidental reproduction, and reverse engineering of computer software, it does cite Haberman v. Hustler Magazine, 626 F. Supp. 201 (D. Mass. 1986), where the court held that full reproduction of a fine art postcard was necessary for the purpose of comment.

4. The Effect of Duchamp's Use upon the Potential Market for or Value of the *Mona Lisa*

Although "[t]his last factor is undoubtedly the single most important element of fair use,"[231] the impairment of the marketability of the underlying work is affected differently when the use is parody, rather than another form of use. As both *Fisher* and *Acuff-Rose* note, the economic effect of parody contemplated is not its likelihood of destroying or lessening the market for the original, which any parody as critique may do, but whether the parody has a substitutive effect on the host work.[232] "[P]arody may quite legitimately aim at garroting the original, destroying it commercially as well as artistically," but that is not the harm encompassed by copyright law.[233]

In some ways it is difficult to apply this fourth fair use factor to a right of integrity claim. Section 107(4) focuses upon hits on Leonardo's pocket, not upon attacks on his artistic sensibilities of honor and reputation. Yet, Congress notes that expert testimony can show whether the use in fact affects the honor or reputation of the artist.[234] Presumably this testimony will proffer evidence as to whether damage to reputation is indicated by actual or potential deleterious market effects on the *Mona Lisa.* However, the Supreme Court cautions that when "the second use is transformative [as in parody], market substitution is at least less certain and market harm may not be so readily inferred."[235] Further, Leonardo's market for other permitted derivative parodying works is very limited. There is little or "no derivative market for critical works."[236] As noted earlier, artists are unlikely to authorize criticism or to license disparagement.[237]

To shift the burden of pleading and proof on this factor from Duchamp to Leonardo in a right of integrity case does not seem unfair. This is for several reasons. First, section 106A(a)(3)(A)'s

---

231 *Harper & Row,* 471 U.S. at 566 (citations omitted).

232 *See Fisher,* 794 F.2d at 438; *Acuff-Rose,* 114 S. Ct. at 1177-79; *id.* at 1181 (Kennedy, J., concurring).

233 *Acuff-Rose,* 114 S. Ct. at 1178 (citing BENJAMIN KAPLAN, AN UNHURRIED VIEW OF COPYRIGHT 69 (1967)).

234 H.R. REP. NO. 514, *supra* note 80, at 16, *reprinted in* 1990 U.S.C.C.A.N. at 6926.

235 *Acuff-Rose,* 114 S. Ct. at 1177; *cf.* H.R. REP. NO. 2237, 89th Cong., 2d Sess. 64 (1966); H.R. REP. NO. 83, 90th Cong., 1st Sess. 35 (1967) ("[W]ith *certain exceptions* (*use in parodies* or as evidence in court proceedings . . . .) a use which supplants any part of the normal market for a copyrighted work would ordinarily be considered an infringement." (emphasis added)); Patry & Perlmutter, *supra* note 11, at 693 (stating that, in most parody cases, the effect on plaintiff's potential market "will tend to favor fair use," since there is little chance the parody will supplant the market for the original).

236 *Acuff-Rose,* 114 S. Ct. at 1178.

237 *See supra* notes 133-34 and accompanying text; *cf.* Strauss, *supra* note 6, at 534.

concept of prejudice to honor or reputation is relatively amorphous. It tracks the language of article 6*bis* of Berne, but in our country honor and reputation issues have arisen mostly in conjunction with defamation law, with outermost limits constrained by the First Amendment.[238] In copyright law, fair use itself is thought to represent the compromise, the "breathing space" between copyright monopoly and First Amendment free expression interests,[239] but the reputational interests in right of integrity cases are not so unlike those in defamation cases where plaintiff does bear the burden of proof.[240]

The second reason that supports the shift of the burden from Duchamp to Leonardo to demonstrate negative market effects relates to access to such proof. "Such proof is peculiarly in the hands of the copyright owner, and consequently he should have the burden of proof."[241] Presumably, Leonardo knows whether prejudice to his honor or reputation has occurred and already has to show reputation damage in conjunction with his section 106A suit. Thus, we would not be imposing a new and difficult burden.

5. The Effect of Burden Shifting

In the easiest copyright (economic rights) cases, for example, where defendant's use is productive (parody), but not for profit, it might make little difference who carries the burden of pleading and proving the four fair use factors. But in harder moral rights cases where the parody that strikes at the artist's right of integrity is a commercial use, or even not-for-profit, the potential censoring effect[242] of section 106A(a)(3)(A) is mitigated by shifting proof of the fair use factors from Duchamp to Leonardo. In "hard" moral

---

238 *New York Times*, 376 U.S. 254. Negative opinions, such as most parodies that ridicule original authors or artists, are constitutionally protected. *See* Hustler Magazine v. Falwell, 485 U.S. 46 (1988).

239 *Acuff-Rose*, 114 S. Ct. at 1171; *see supra* notes 203-07 and accompanying text.

240 In defamation cases, plaintiff must proffer evidence "from which harm to reputation could reasonably be inferred or direct evidence of harm to reputation." W. PAGE KEETON ET AL., PROSSER AND KEETON ON THE LAW OF TORTS § 113, at 797 (5th ed. 1984).

241 *Cf.* HOUSE COMM. ON THE JUDICIARY, 89TH CONG., 1ST SESS., COPYRIGHT LAW REVISION PART 5: 1964 REVISION BILL WITH DISCUSSIONS AND COMMENTS 98-100 (Comm. Print 1965) (remarks of Harry N. Rosenfield, counsel for the Ad Hoc Committee of Educational Organizations on Copyright Law Revision). Although Rosenfield's comments were made in the context of nonprofit educational uses, I would argue that it is equally applicable in right of integrity/parody cases.

242 *Cf.* Yen, *supra* note 11, at 107 ("[A]uthors [may] value their copyright rights for nonmonetary reasons . . . [and] authors will consistently refuse to sell others the rights to use their works because money will not be an adequate substitute for any interests harmed by the contemplated use."). Granting authors an "aesthetic veto" has resulted in numerous European decisions in which expression has been prevented. *See* Robert A. Gorman, *Federal Moral Rights Legislation: The Need for Caution*, 14 NOVA L. REV. 422, 424-27 & nn.3-15 (1990).

rights cases, doubts should be resolved in favor of the parodist;[243] we should have more art rather than less. This solution balances appropriately the three interests served by current copyright law—protection of an artist's personal and proprietary (economic) rights, protection of the parodist's right to create transformative works, and protection of the public's interest in fostering the kind of creativity that promotes science and the arts.[244] That this tinkering with what had been viewed as the affirmative nature of the fair use defense is necessary is due to the attempt to fit a square peg into a round hole—natural, personal, moral rights into an economic rights-based copyright scheme.[245]

CONCLUSION

More art than law.[246]

"Whatever else art is good for, its chief effectiveness lies in propagating more art . . . of all the things art has an impact on, art is the most susceptible and responsive. All art is infested by other art."[247] This is hardly surprising given the nature of the artistic muse. Robert Motherwell, a noted American artist of this century, explained the import of prior art: "Every intelligent painter carries the whole culture of modern painting in his head. It is his real subject, of which everything he paints is both an homage and a

243 In a non-moral rights claim, doubts would be resolved in favor of the first artist. *See Acuff-Rose*, 114 S. Ct. at 1181 (Kennedy, J., concurring).

244 *Cf.* Fogerty v. Fantasy, Inc., 114 S. Ct. 1023, 1030 (1994) ("[C]opyright law ultimately serves the purpose of enriching the general public through access to creative works . . . ."); *Acuff Rose*, 114 S. Ct. at 1171 (stating that transformative works are "at the heart of the fair use doctrine's guarantee of breathing space within the confines of copyright"); *Harper & Row*, 471 U.S. at 546 (stating that copyright "rewards the individual author in order to benefit the public"); *Sony*, 464 U.S. at 429 (holding that copyright "makes reward to the owner a secondary consideration") (quoting United States v. Paramount Pictures, Inc., 334 U.S. 131, 158 (1948)). That these goals remain the core of copyright is evidenced by § 801's balancing of maximizing the availability of creative works to the public and giving the copyright owner a fair return and the user a fair income. 17 U.S.C. § 801(b)(1)(A), (B).

245 *Cf.* Leval, *supra* note 198, at 1128 ("Our copyright law has developed over hundreds of years for a very different purpose and with rules and inconsequences that are incompatible with the *droit moral.*"). Judge Leval authored two important copyright/fair use decisions that did not survive appellate review: New Era Publications Int'l v. Henry Holt & Co., 695 F. Supp. 1493 (S.D.N.Y. 1988), *aff'd on other grounds*, 873 F.2d 576 (2d Cir. 1989); Salinger v. Random House, Inc., 650 F. Supp. 413 (S.D.N.Y. 1986), *rev'd*, 811 F.2d 90 (2d Cir.), *cert. denied*, 484 U.S. 890 (1987). His fair use article was frequently cited by the Supreme Court in *Acuff-Rose.*

246 The charge given to me by Prof. Sherri Burr, Chairwoman of the A.A.L.S. Art Law program on parody in New Orleans, Jan. 5, 1995. As one of the panelists, I spoke very briefly, but showed four dozen art parody slides, some of which are reproduced with permission in the appendix.

247 LIPMAN & MARSHALL, *supra* note 123, at 9.

critique."[248] Contrary to the advice given by Polonius to his son Laertes, "[n]either a borrower nor a lender be,"[249] many artists have their feet (or paintbrushes, pens, sculpting tools, and pianos, among other things) in both camps. They use ideas, plots, themes, often parodying earlier works, while still other artists feed on this art. In this sense, much art is symbiotic. That legal doctrine which can protect both "host" artist and "parasite" artist, or at least balances carefully the interests of both, best serves the artistic and cultural needs of society and "promote[s] the Progress of Science and [the] useful Arts . . . ."[250] But the balance is a delicate one. Too much protection for the "host" artist can stifle creation of new, transformative works. Too much protection for the second artist might cause our original artist to lose the incentive to create.

Because art begets art, society needs to furnish incentives for artists to create. Copyright is one vehicle by which to accomplish this. But the monopolistic property and moral rights given to authors under sections 106 and 106A of the Copyright Act, even though moderated by fair use, are often in inherent conflict with the ability to create freely and without fear of lawsuits. Courts have, however, endeavored to resolve the conflict by employing, often successfully, the fair use doctrine on a case-by-case basis in traditional, "property" rights cases. Whether there can be similar successful use of the doctrine as an affirmative defense on such an ad hoc basis in the context of moral rights, that is, Leonardo's freedom from an "intentional distortion, mutilation, or . . . modification of [his] . . . work which would be prejudicial to his . . . honor or reputation,"[251] is much more problematic. This is so for several reasons. First, a moral rights violation is fuzzier than a property rights violation. Second, it must be conceded that artists rarely seek out criticism and most endure it grudgingly. This, in turn, raises a third difficulty: artists could use section 106A to chill or prevent art. Since monopoly is the heart of copyright, artists may use the new grant of moral rights to censor. Because of these concerns, this article proposed that when moral rights under section 106A are asserted against a parodist, such as Duchamp in the hypothetical case, a court should presume that the parodist's use is a fair one, even if it is a commercial use. This presumption recognizes the need to protect both da Vinci and Duchamp, but gives

248 *Id.* at 7.

249 William Shakespeare, Hamlet act 1, sc. 3.

250 U.S. Const. art. I, § 8, cl. 8.

251 17 U.S.C. § 106A(a)(3)(A).

Duchamp, as parodist, the benefit of a fair use presumption in section 106A/right of integrity cases.

APPENDIX

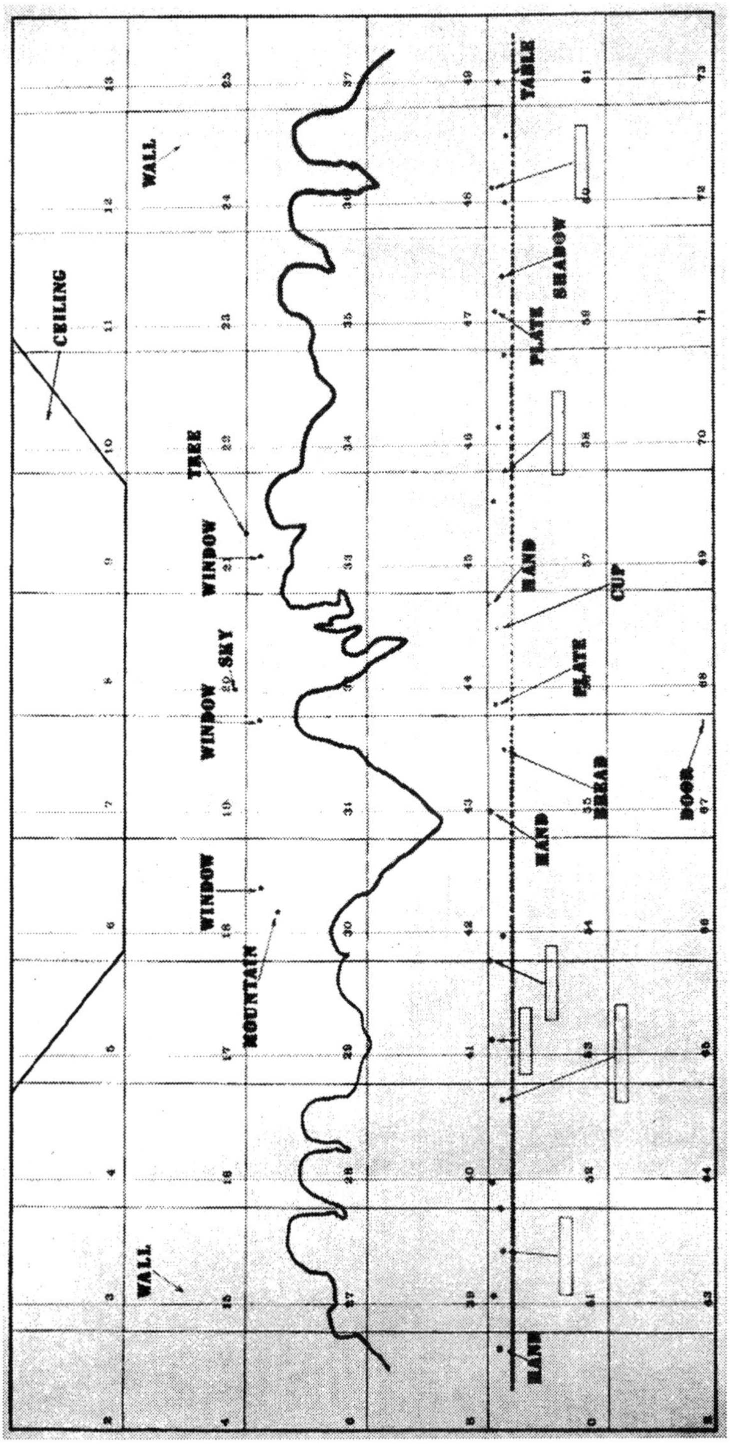

SHUSAKU ARAKAWA. *Next to the Last.* 1967-71. Serigraph, printed in color, composition: $27^{1}/_{4} \times 42^{5}/_{16}$" (69.2 × 107.4 cm). The Museum of Modern Art, New York. Reiss-Cohen Fund. Photograph © 1996 The Museum of Modern Art, New York.

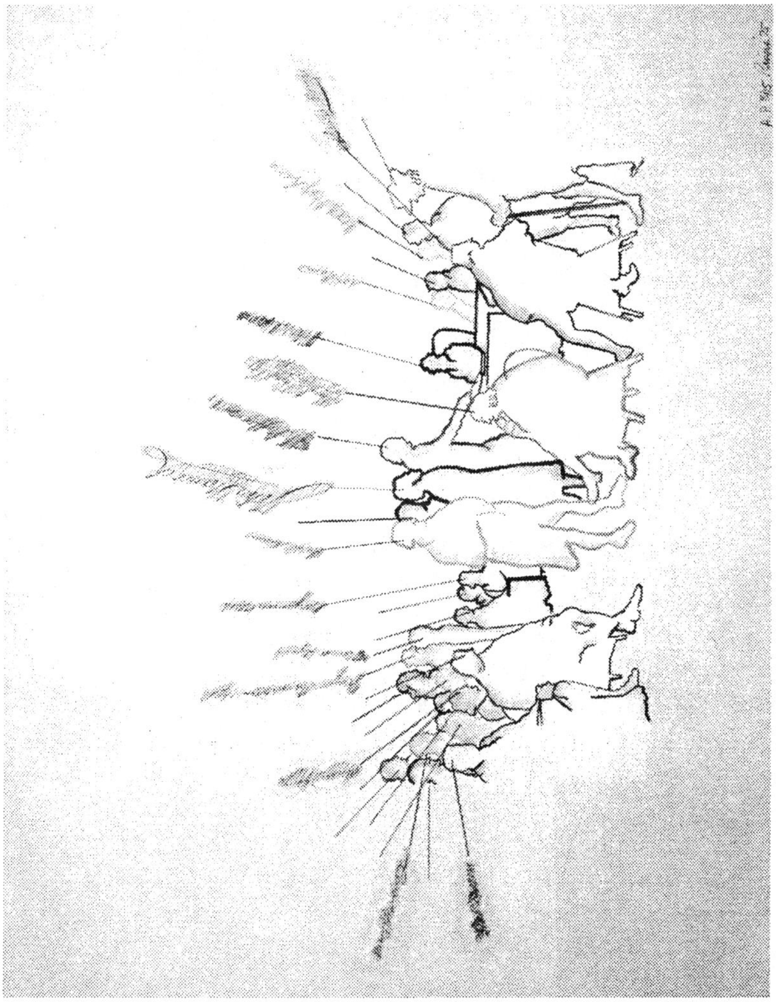

Larry Rivers, *Outline of History*, 1976. © 1996 Larry Rivers/Licensed by VAGA, New York, NY.

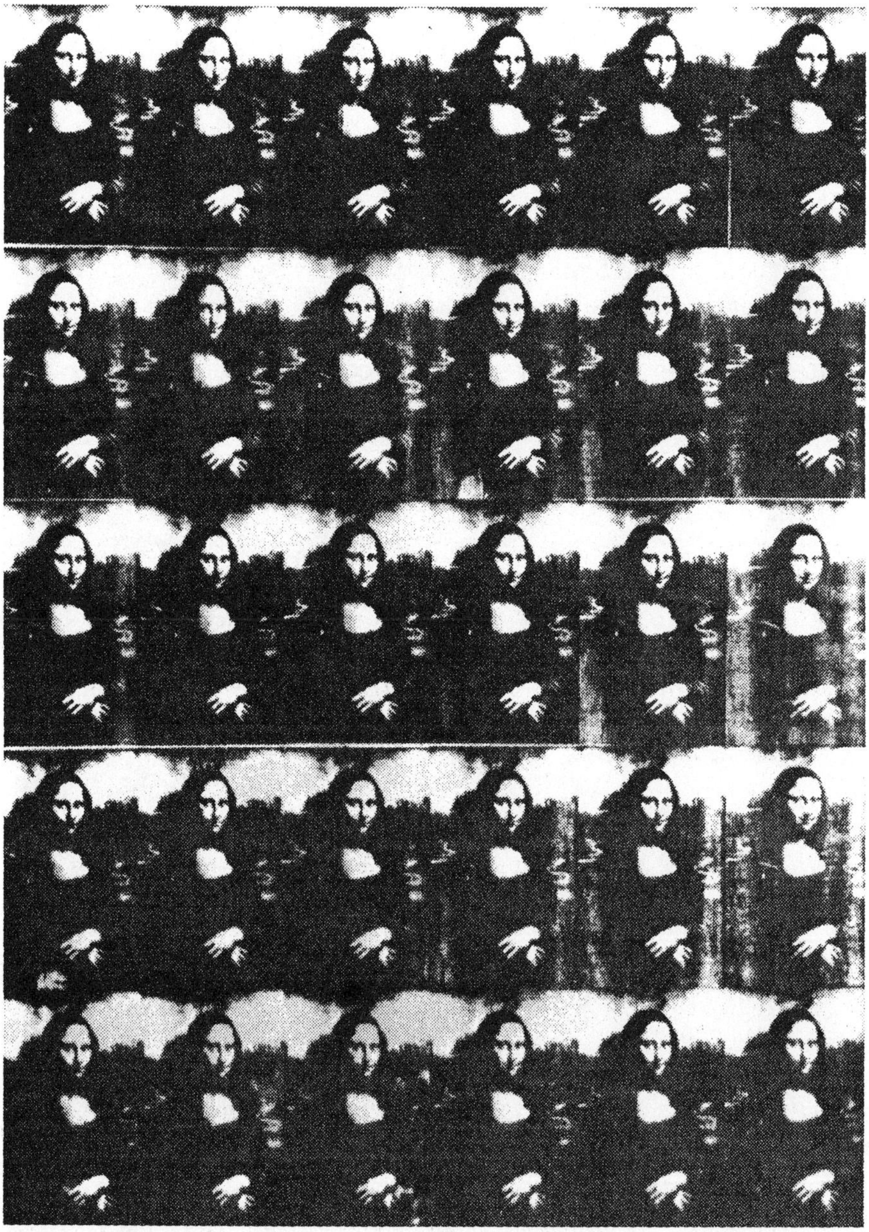

ANDY WARHOL, *Thirty Are Better Than One*, 1963. Synthetic polymer paint and silkscreen ink on canvas, 9'2" × 7'10½". Reproduced by permission of The Andy Warhol Foundation, Inc.

COPYRIGHT AND THE LEGISLATIVE PROCESS: A PERSONAL PERSPECTIVE

WILLIAM F. PATRY*

I'd like to begin in an unorthodox way, by reciting a few excerpts from a March 12 *Washington Post* article on the House of Representatives majority whip Tom DeLay, Republican of Texas.[1] On March 31, 1995, the *New York Times* published a somewhat similar article on the Senate Judiciary Committee,[2] but it lacks the candor that makes the *Washington Post* piece so useful.

The *Washington Post* article is entitled *Rep. DeLay Makes Companies Full Partners in the [GOP] Movement*,[3] and was obviously written with his cooperation. It details his efforts, in conjunction with business lobbyists, to pass a moratorium on new federal regulations. Although the bill passed the House,[4] the Senate substantially revised it before passing it on March 29, 1995.[5] The Senate is being viewed with increasing fondness by House Democrats, and perhaps by some moderate Republicans. This is quite a switch. A few years ago, when the Democrats controlled both the House and the Senate, a Democratic congressman remarked about House Republicans, "they may be the opposition, but the Senate is the enemy." This is no longer the case.

Here is the first quote:

> [A]lthough several provisions of the "Contract with America" adopted by Republican House candidates last fall take specific aim at rolling back federal regulations, the moratorium was not part of that. In fact, as outlined . . . *in* DeLay's office by Gordon Gooch, an oversized, folksy lobbyist for energy and petrochemi-

* Associate Professor of Law, Benjamin N. Cardozo School of Law, Yeshiva University, New York. Formerly counsel, Subcommittee on Intellectual Property & Judicial Administration, Committee on the Judiciary, U.S. House of Representatives; Policy Planning Advisor to the Register of Copyrights, U.S. Copyright Office.

This article was adapted from a speech given on Apr. 3, 1995, at the Benjamin N. Cardozo School of Law, Yeshiva University, and sponsored by the *Cardozo Arts & Entertainment Law Journal* and the Cardozo Intellectual Property Law Program. The author wishes to thank Dean Frank J. Macchiarola and Professor Marci Hamilton, for the honor of being selected as the Tenzer Distinguished Lecturer for 1995.

1 Michael Weisskopf & David Maraniss, *Forging an Alliance for Deregulation; Rep. DeLay Makes Companies Full Partners in the Movement*, WASH. POST, Mar. 12, 1995, at A1 (This article was part of a series entitled *Inside The Revolution: Business and the House Republicans*).

2 Stephen Engelberg, *Business Leaves the Lobby And Sits at Congress's Table*, N.Y. TIMES, Mar. 31, 1995, at A1.

3 Weisskopf & Maraniss, *supra* note 1, at A1.

4 H.R. 450, 104th Cong., 1st Sess. § 3(a) (1995).

5 S. 219, 104th Cong., 1st Sess. § 3(a) (1995).

> cal interests who served as the congressman's initial legislative ghost writer, the first draft of the bill called for a limited, 100-day moratorium on rule-making while the House pushed through the more comprehensive anti-regulatory plank in the Contract. But his fellow lobbyists in the inner circle argued that was too timid, according to participants in the meeting. Over the next few days, several drafts were exchanged by the corporate agents. Each new version sharpened and expanded the moratorium bill, often with the interests of clients in mind—one provision favoring California motor fleets, another protecting industrial consumers of natural gas, and a third keeping alive Union Carbide Corp.'s hopes for altering a labor department requirement. As the measure progressed, the roles of legislator and lobbyist blurred. DeLay and his assistants guided industry supporters in an ad hoc group whose name, Project Relief, sounded more like a Third World humanitarian aid effort than a corporate alliance with a half-million-dollar communications budget. On key amendments, the coalition provided the draftsman. And once the bill and the debate moved to the House floor, lobbyists hovered nearby, tapping out talking points on a laptop computer for delivery to Republican floor leaders . . . . Turning to business lobbyists to draft legislation makes sense, according to DeLay, because "they have the expertise."[6]

The word "expertise" is a misnomer in this case. The lobbyists were not information providers, explaining the meaning of technically difficult regulations. Instead, their "expertise" was in drafting a bill that took care of their clients. Mr. Gooch, the over-sized lobbyist, is quoted in the article as saying: "I'm not claiming to be a Boy Scout . . . . No question I thought what I was doing was in the best interests of my clients."[7] Students of the legislative process will recognize this as an excellent example of public choice theory.[8]

The *Washington Post* article also puts forth a reason other than "expertise" that may have caused Mr. DeLay to turn to business lobbyists. When he decided to run for the leadership position of majority whip (at a time when the Democrats were still in the majority), Mr. DeLay, who has been in the House for ten years, knew that a very effective way to get support for his bid was to raise money for fellow Republicans running for the first time—not his

---

6 Weisskopf & Maraniss, *supra* note 1, at A1.

7 *Id.*

8 For a review of public choice theory, see generally DANIEL A. FARBER & PHILIP P. FRICKEY, LAW AND PUBLIC CHOICE: A CRITICAL INTRODUCTION (1991).

own money, of course, but that of the lobbyists. A short quote from the same *Washington Post* article:

> [T]he large number of open congressional seats and collection of strong Republican challengers offered [DeLay] an unusual opportunity. He turned to his network of business friends and lobbyists. "I sometimes overly prevailed on" these allies, DeLay said. In the 1994 elections, he was the second-leading fund-raiser for House Republican candidates, behind only [Newt] Gingrich [Speaker of the House]. In adding up contributions he had solicited for others, DeLay said, he lost count at about $2 million.[9]

That the lobbyists know how the system works is revealed in the final passage I'll quote:

> "[w]e'd rustle up checks for the guy and make sure Tom [DeLay] got the credit," said . . . [a] beer lobbyist. "So when new members voted for majority whip, they'd say, I wouldn't be here if it wasn't for Tom DeLay."[10]

Is the Tom DeLay story relevant to copyright legislation? Do liberal copyright lawyers and lobbyists engage in the same type of activity hoping to have the same impact as conservative business lobbyists?

Yes, you bet they do. Copyright interest groups hold fund raisers for members of Congress, write campaign songs, invite members of Congress (and their staff) to private movie screenings or sold-out concerts, and draft legislation they expect Congress to pass without any changes. In the 104th Congress, they are drafting the committee reports and haggling among themselves about what needs to be in the report. In my experience, some copyright lawyers and lobbyists actually resent members of Congress and staff interfering with what they view as *their* legislation and *their* committee report. With the 104th Congress we have, I believe, reached a point where legislative history *must* be ignored because not even the hands of congressional staff have touched committee reports.

The House Intellectual Property Subcommittee under the chairmanship of my then-boss, Representative William Hughes,[11] was once described to me by a lobbyist as a "Ford operation"— "we've got a better idea." I think this characterization reveals resentment that Mr. Hughes, or any member of the subcommittee, would have *any* idea of his own, or else disgust that Mr. Hughes

---

9 Weisskopf & Maraniss, *supra* note 1.
10 Weisskopf & Maraniss, *supra* note 1.
11 Rep. William Hughes (D-N.J.) served in Congress between 1975 and 1995.

mistook his role as a member of Congress as actually involving making policy. Undoubtedly to those who agree with the Ford characterization, one of Mr. Hughes's sins was the introduction of the Copyright Reform Act of 1993[12] without, as one copyright lawyer put it in an article in the *New York Law Journal*, getting sage advice from the "gray beards" of the copyright bar.[13] It was indeed a shocking display of congressional independence: just the kind of independence copyright lawyers would applaud if the legislation involved civil rights or crime.

But Mr. Hughes's greatest sin may have been the opposite type of independence: rejecting an industry draft. While Mr. Hughes welcomed suggestions for legislation and criticism of his own initiatives, he strongly believed that Congress, not industry, should draft legislation. On May 11, 1994, the music industry gave Mr. Hughes an unsolicited "industry consensus" draft bill *to replace* a bill Mr. Hughes had drafted and introduced to extend digital performance rights to sound recordings.[14] Congressman Hughes rejected the draft on policy grounds, although he tried to incorporate some of its features in a revised version of his bill.[15]

In March 1995, at a hearing before the Senate Judiciary Committee on new digital performance rights legislation, a number of witnesses repeated, mantra-like, the position that Congress should enact the May 11, 1994 industry draft.[16] The message at the hearing was "we drafted it, the best thing for you to do is to enact it down to the commas." The Committee did just that on June 29, 1995, favorably reporting a revised bill drafted entirely by the industry.[17] You can guess who drafted the committee report. On July 27, my old House Subcommittee on Intellectual Property & Judicial Administration marked-up the Senate version, with one member of the subcommittee saluting the chairman for insisting that the parties work things out for themselves. How times have changed.

You might ask, especially if you are a lawyer representing the industry, isn't that what matters?

No, that isn't all that matters. It isn't even close to being the

---

[12] H.R. 897, 103d Cong., 1st Sess. (1993).

[13] Alan J. Hartnick, *Gray Beards & The Copyright Reform Act of 1993*, N.Y.L.J., May 21, 1993, at 5.

[14] *See Senators Endorse Limited Digital Music Performance Bill*, AUDIO WEEK, Mar. 13, 1995, at 10.

[15] H.R. 2576, 103d Cong., 1st Sess. (1993).

[16] *The Performance Rights in Sound Recordings Act of 1995: Hearing on S. 227 Before the Senate Comm. on the Judiciary*, 104th Cong., 1st Sess. (1995).

[17] SENATE COMM. ON THE JUDICIARY, DIGITAL PERFORMANCE RIGHTS IN SOUND RECORDINGS ACT OF 1995, S. REP. NO. 128, 104th Cong., 1st Sess. (1995).

most important consideration. The most important consideration is whether a proposal, anyone's proposal, represents good policy; a decision—along with the drafting—that should only be made by Congress.

Don't get me wrong. Industry must be involved in the legislative process. Legislation regulates industry and those who are regulated must have the opportunity to fully present their views on how or if such regulation should occur. Industry understands far better than Congress the "real world" of how its businesses work.

This does not mean, however, that Congress should let industry regulate itself by writing legislation or determining its content. Enacting turn-key industry bills is not legislating. It is letting those who had a seat at the private sector table divvy up the spoils among themselves. And, as philosopher Isaiah Berlin said, "when the wolves get their liberty, the lambs lose their lives."[18]

The lambs in the copyright system are usually individual authors, although even corporations can get carved up if they are not at the table. For example, the Digital Performance Rights Act[19] will currently affect only one company, DMEX. Yet, to the best of my knowledge, the industry never invited DMEX to participate in its meetings, even though DMEX is the only party that will be required to pay royalties under the bill. Those who will receive the royalties and those who piggishly insisted on exemptions were all well represented.

My greatest concern, though, is with how well the Copyright Act[20] currently protects and will in the future protect the interests of individual authors. I am not talking only about technological innovations, the information superhighway, work-made-for-hire abuses, or a trend toward corporate authorship. Instead, the concern is with classic copyright, traditional cases where a work, such as a musical composition or a novel, is created by an individual who subsequently enters into a contract with a publisher to exploit that work. The current bills in the House and Senate to extend the term of protection, Senate Bill 483 and House Bill 989, illustrate the point because there is still an opportunity to influence the outcome of these bills.[21]

First, though, a review of some of the important forces helping

---

18 Isaiah Berlin, Four Essays on Liberty (1969).

19 Act of Nov. 1, 1995, Pub. L. No. 104-39, 109 Stat. 336 (1995).

20 Copyright Act of 1976, 90 Stat. 2541 (1976) (codified as amended at 17 U.S.C. §§ 101-803 (1994), 18 U.S.C. § 2319 (1994)).

21 Copyright Term Extension Act of 1995, S. 483, 104th Cong., 1st Sess. (1995); H.R. 989, 104th Cong., 1st Sess. (1995).

to shape any copyright legislation, including the current term extension bills before both houses of Congress.

I. Copyright Legislation is Discretionary

Unlike appropriations bills, copyright bills are almost always discretionary: if a bill does not pass one Congress, it can be taken up by the next Congress. This fact typically leads to a relatively long gestation period for copyright legislation, which may, in individual cases, be a good thing. But the discretionary nature of copyright legislation also leads to an unfortunate unwillingness to take up controversial issues.

II. Congress Lacks Copyright Expertise

A. *Congressmen as Generalists*

Members of Congress are generalists; they are not and cannot be specialists in copyright. Utah Republican Senator Orrin Hatch, for example, as chairman of the Judiciary Committee and an important national figure, has been involved in tremendously important issues, including: the Balanced Budget Amendment,[22] crime legislation, term limits, the line-item veto, welfare reform, tort reform, judicial nominations, and foreign policy, along with constituent matters, and Republican party issues. On many of the bills, he was or will be the floor manager. Some may recall that the Senate spent over thirty days debating the Balanced Budget Amendment, compared with just two days in the House.[23] As the floor manager, Senator Hatch had to spend most of those thirty days on the floor. Not surprisingly, he hit the roof when it didn't pass.[24]

B. *Congressional Staff Cuts*

Senator Hatch genuinely wants to make good copyright policy, but he simply has too little time to devote to copyright issues. If he does not have an expert staff, who will understand the issues and thereby help him make the policy? Senator Hatch's staff is spread thin due to a one-third committee staff cut imposed this Congress,[25] a reduction that came on top of the often forgotten but still substantial cuts imposed during the last Congress.

This point is directly related to the *Washington Post* article on

---

22 H.R.J. Res. 1, 104th Cong., 1st Sess. (1995).

23 *Id.*

24 *See* Karen Hosler, *Democrats Sack Balanced Budget Amendment*, Baltimore Sun, Mar. 3, 1995, at 1A.

25 H.R.J. Res. 6, 104th Cong., 1st Sess. § 101(a) (1995).

majority whip DeLay.[26] While the one-third reduction in committee staffs for this Congress was depicted by Republicans as a symbol of their willingness to reduce the size of government, the reduction was also designed to impact seriously on Democrats' ability to oppose Republican initiatives. The number of Republican committee staff substantially *increased* (as did their pay), while there were no cuts at all in members' personal staff, which outnumbered committee staff even before the one-third cuts. My former committee, the House Judiciary Committee, is an example. In the last Congress, the 103d, there were approximately seventy-five staff, fifty Democrats and twenty-five Republicans. This Congress, the 104th, staff was cut one-third, to approximately fifty, of which thirty-four are Republicans and sixteen are Democrats. Thus, the Republican staff increased from twenty-five to thirty-four, while the Democrats' decreased from fifty to sixteen.

C. *A Legislative Power Shift to the Private Sector*

Less obvious to those outside the Washington, D.C. beltway, the committee staff reductions shifted power away from Congress to the private sector. With fewer committee staff and more legislation to be accomplished in a very short, arbitrarily imposed time-limit—100 days in the case of the Contract For America—someone has to do the work. With a Republican Congress and a Democratic Administration, the Republican majority party in Congress is certainly not going to rely on the Clinton Administration for drafting assistance. As the DeLay story and the Digital Performance Rights legislation shows, it is the private sector who will do the drafting.

III. Why Copyright Legislation is Unique

Almost alone among the issues faced by the judiciary committees, copyright legislation is not about politics as is crime or abortion legislation. Copyright legislation is economic legislation. It is, in other words, about money and not principles. As a result, those with the most money are the best organized and represented, and therefore, have the greatest opportunity to succeed. The interests of individual authors, who are rarely well-organized, get trampled in the process. It is a vicious circle: members of Congress, even those who might be sympathetic to the plight of individual authors, only hear from industry groups and thus, in the absence of input

26 Weisskopf & Maraniss, *supra* note 1, at A1.

from individual authors, come to the understandable conclusion that individual authors don't object to the proposal.

IV. Copyright Debate Occurs Outside the View of the Public

A. *The House of Representatives*

Unlike important social and political issues, where the critical debates and votes take place at the floor level for all to watch on C-SPAN, the "real" action on copyright bills takes place at a very low level: in the House of Representatives, at the subcommittee level. Copyright bills are usually rubber-stamped by the full House Judiciary Committee, and pass on the floor on the suspension calendar, under which no amendments are permitted. The low level of deliberation in the House results in decisions being made by a very small group of people.

B. *The Senate*

On the Senate side, there is no copyright subcommittee, and at the floor level, copyright legislation is considered under unanimous consent agreements, which causes one of two undesirable results.

Under the first option, the legislation is "dumbed down": made so innocuous or limited that one may well ask whether it is worth the trouble. The Digital Performance Rights Act for sound recordings is an excellent example of a *really* dumbed down bill.[27] It has been so dumbed down that even in the form in which it was introduced, it would have failed to accomplish important United States objectives, such as obtaining reciprocal foreign royalties and letting the United States participate in a proposed new multilateral treaty for sound recordings.[28] Notwithstanding its anemic condition on introduction, the process of running the legislative gauntlet of every piggish private sector roadblock drained it of all life and logic.

Second, if a bill isn't dumbed down, perhaps because a senator irrationally decides to take a principled stand, he or she will be confronted with what might be called the "Darth Vader" or the "dark side" principle: any single senator can effectively block any copyright bill from reaching the floor by merely placing a hold on

---

[27] S. 227, 104th Cong., 1st Sess. (1995).

[28] *See, e.g., Committee of Experts on a Possible Instrument for the Protection of the Rights of Performers and Producers of Phonograms*, First Sess. (June 28 - July 2, 1993), World Intellectual Property Organization Doc. No. /NR/CE/I/2.

it. Since copyright legislation does not command enough importance to be called up on the Senate floor in regular order for debate and a majority vote, it has to be brought up by unanimous consent, and I mean unanimous. *Any* one senator can object to the bill's even being considered by placing a "hold" on it.

Amazingly, at least for those outside the Senate, holds are secret. You may remember recent efforts at congressional reform. One proposal was to require senators placing holds to come to the floor and do so in public. The proposal was so offensive to a majority of the Senate that it never stood a chance of passage.

Even more amazingly, sponsors of bills can't find out which senator has placed the hold. Holds do not even have to be related to an objection to the content of the bill. Frequently, holds act as a form of log-rolling: "I'll lift my hold if you'll agree to add an unrelated piece of legislation."

In 1993, for example, the House passed a bill to abolish the Copyright Royalty Tribunal ("CRT").[29] A companion bill was sponsored by Senators DeConcini and Hatch.[30] When the bill was "hotwired," that is, pre-cleared for unanimous consent consideration, the Republican cloakroom[31] indicated that there was a Republican hold on the bill. Senator Hatch's staff tried to find out who put the hold on, to no avail. Senator Hatch himself then went to the cloakroom, also to no avail. The cloakroom did agree to tell the hold-placing senator that Senator Hatch wanted to talk to him. Days went by with no word, and this was at the end of the session, when hours can mean the difference between a bill passing or not.

Finally, Senator Alan Simpson, Republican of Wyoming, called Senator Hatch and said he had placed the hold. When asked why, Senator Simpson stated that he was sending a message to Congressman Hughes about Hughes's failure to move a House bill on film labelling. How a Democratic House member was supposed to get such a message from a secret hold put on an unrelated bill by a Republican senator mad about the failure to move a *House* bill—Simpson had his own bill in the Senate—was a mystery, but Mr. Hughes called Simpson, stroked him, and got the hold removed.

In the meantime, though, a second hold had been placed, this

---

29 Copyright Royalty Tribunal Act of 1993, Pub. L. No. 103-198, 107 Stat. 2304 (1993).

30 S. 1346, 103d Cong., 1st Sess. (1993).

31 Both the House of Representatives and the Senate have cloakrooms for the Democrats and the Republicans. The cloakrooms monitor floor activity and inform their party's members about any on-going floor debate. Members retire from the floor to take calls and argue out important votes outside the view of reporters and C-SPAN. *See* Benjamin Sheffner, *How to Follow the Floor Show—Know These Rules: No Cheering, No Electronic Gadgets. And What's a One-Minute, Anyway?*, ROLL CALL, Apr. 17, 1995.

time by Senator Ted Stevens, a Republican from Alaska. Senator Stevens wanted to tack on to the CRT legislation an amendment to benefit Alaska longshoremen. Since the House bill was not co-sponsored by a Republican, *I* had to convince House Republicans to agree to a Senate Republican amendment to benefit the Alaskan fishing industry. The bill was finally passed, but not before a third hold had been placed by Kansas Republican Senator Robert Dole at the request of religious broadcasters.

Sometimes, though, you cannot work things out because you do not have anything to trade. In these circumstances, the unanimous consent requirement gives enormous, destructive power to defeat the majority's will, including bills that passed the House without a negative vote, and which would overwhelmingly pass the Senate if they could make it to a vote. It is one thing for Republican Senator Mark Hatfield of Oregon to be the single vote that brought down the Balanced Budget Amendment,[32] but at least the amendment was put to a vote. It is quite another for one senator to be able to prevent a bill from *ever* being voted on. However, this is the sad truth about the way the system currently works for copyright legislation.

V. The Effects on Current Copyright Legislation

Let's tie all this together to legislation currently pending to extend the term of copyright protection, House Bill 989 and Senate Bill 483.[33] These bills are sometimes referred to as the "life plus seventy" bills, because one section would extend the current copyright term for works by individuals created on or after January 1, 1978[34] from the life of the author plus fifty years to the life of the author plus seventy years.[35] Advocates of the bills are using the European Union's term directive as the bill's rallying flag. The European Union, as of July 1, 1995, went from a term of "life plus fifty" to "life plus seventy" years, but foreign works will be granted this extra twenty years of copyright protection only on a reciprocal basis.[36] Thus, according to some, United States copyright owners will be deprived of protection and money in Europe unless the United States also goes to a "life plus seventy" year term. Of course, as with

---

32 141 Cong. Rec. S3314 (daily ed. Mar. 2, 1995) (vote on the Balanced Budget Amendment).

33 S. 483; H.R. 989.

34 Jan. 1, 1978 is the effective date of the Copyright Act of 1976.

35 S. 483; H.R. 989.

36 Eur. Ecn. Council (Oct. 29, 1993). Council Directive 93/98, harmonizing the Term of Protection of Copyright and Certain Related Rights, 1993 J.O. (L 290) art. 1, 7.

most European Union efforts, members have been slow to actually implement this directive.

But the bill really isn't motivated by the "life plus seventy" term, or even getting European royalties. Instead, the bill is actually concerned with "old act works"—specifically, musical compositions published in the 1920s and 30s. Many of you probably saw the February 23, 1995 article in the *New York Times* describing AMSONG, a group of the children of famous composers and lyricists.[37] The article focused less on European and more on domestic royalties (which are bound to be more substantial than foreign royalties), and on preventing uses that we ordinarily consider violations of moral rights. For example, Frank Loesser's daughter talks about having made it her task to police her father's artistic legacy for authenticity.[38]

My purpose is not to debate the merits of how long copyright should last, or whether the children of famous composers should have moral rights. At the same time, the Constitution mandates that copyright must cease at some point.[39] The arguments of some of these heirs that the term of copyright must be extended because the music is still generating royalties is not very persuasive. The parade has to stop some time, and fifty years after your father died doesn't seem terribly stingy.

What should be talked about is how the bill fails to help individual authors or their children nearly as much as it could. The *New York Times* article on the AMSONG group makes much of the fact that a few composers outlived some of their copyrights under the 1909 Act and that some of the composers' children may also outlive that same term.[40] The 1909 Act, of course, had a term of protection measured from the date of publication rather than by the life of the author.[41]

If Congress really wants to solve the problem of authors outliving their copyrights or being unable to provide for their children as long as the children would like, the best solution is to go to a term of life of the author plus fifty or seventy years for *old act works.* Old act works that were unpublished works on January 1, 1978, the effective date of the 1976 Act, were granted a minimum term of life

---

37 Ralph Blumenthal, *A Rights Movement with Song at Its Heart*, N.Y. TIMES, Feb. 23, 1995, at C13.

38 *Id.*

39 U.S. CONST. art. I, § 8, cl. 8 ("To promote the Progress of Science and useful Arts, by securing *for limited Times* to Authors and Inventors the exclusive Right to their respective Writings and Discoveries." (emphasis added)).

40 Act of Mar. 4, 1909, ch. 320, 35 Stat. 1075 (1909).

41 Act of Mar. 4, 1909, ch. 320, § 23, 35 Stat. at 1080.

plus fifty years.[42] So this is hardly a new solution.

Congress did consider giving published old act works a life plus fifty term in the 1976 Act, but declined to do so, persuaded by the argument that this would be unfair to transferees who had purchased both the original and renewal terms from authors, and who would, therefore, be deprived of the full benefit of their bargain. As a result, for old act works the 1976 Act continued the old act's structure of an initial term of twenty-eight years from publication plus an additional twenty-eight year renewal term.[43] At the same time, Congress added nineteen years to the renewal term, for a total of seventy-five years.[44]

Who got these extra nineteen years? In a constitutional system that gives Congress the power to grant copyright only to authors, one would think the authors. There could be no argument that giving the nineteen years to authors would deprive transferees of the full benefit of their bargain, since they had bargained only for fifty-six years, and the nineteen years were tacked on after those fifty-six years had expired. But *no*, the extra nineteen years did not go to authors where the author had transferred his or her rights. The extra nineteen years were instead granted to the transferee, even though the transferee had not bargained for it at the making of the contract.[45]

It is true that in section 304, Congress gave authors the right to terminate the transfer for the extra nineteen years.[46] But what Congress gave with one hand, it virtually took away with the other, since it unfairly placed the burden on the individual author to terminate the transfer.[47] To make matters worse, only a five-year window was provided for authors to terminate.[48] This can hardly be described as a "pro-author" copyright law. The ineffectiveness of the termination of transfer provisions is amply borne out by the Copyright Office records, which reveal that only about 0.72% of the works renewed have been the subject of a recorded termination notice.[49]

This year, in House Bill 989 and Senate Bill 483, an additional twenty years is proposed to be tacked on to the renewal term, for a

---

42 17 U.S.C. § 304.

43 Act of Mar. 4, 1909, ch. 320, §§ 23, 24, 35 Stat. at 1080; 17 U.S.C. § 304(a).

44 17 U.S.C. § 304.

45 *Id.*

46 *Id.* § 304(a).

47 *Id.* § 304(c).

48 *Id.* § 304(c)(3)-(c)(4).

49 These statistics have been provided to the author in his former capacity as Policy Planning Advisor to the Register of Copyrights, U.S. Copyright Office.

total of ninety-five years for old act works.[50] If Congress decides to grant this twenty years, who is going to get it? Do the additional twenty years vest automatically in the author? No they do not, notwithstanding the excellent precedent in the GATT legislation, which vested, as of January 1, 1995, and restored copyright in the author.[51] Congress rejected an industry draft that the GATT rights vest in transferees. I had hoped that the GATT retroactive provision might lead to a greater willingness to recognize the author as the principal beneficiary of copyright, but I was obviously wrong.

VI. No New Termination Right

Do House Bill 989 or Senate Bill 483 provide a termination right for the new extra twenty years? Will authors fare at least as poorly as they did under the 1976 Act? No, some of them will fare worse. There is no special termination of transfer right for the new twenty years. Instead, the bills will apply the existing termination right in section 304. Or will they? Because the time limits for termination have not been amended, for works first published between 1920 and 1933 (coincidentally important years for the AMSONG group), the five-year window for termination has already passed. These authors or their children, even if they want to, cannot terminate. And with each successive year, authors or their children will lose the ability to terminate for another year's works: in 1996, authors and their children will no longer be able to terminate for works first published in 1934.

Who will the copyright in the extra twenty years go to then? It will go to the transferee, without any opportunity for the author or children to get it back. Does this tell you anything about who is the real principal beneficiary of the bill? The answer is *not* authors or their children.

Music publishers, of course, will have to pay the composer according to the terms of the contract, so it is not as if they are trying to get the twenty years free and clear except, importantly, in cases where a lump sum payment was made for the copyright. But composers and their children do not have to and should not settle for such a raw deal. Indeed, far and away the best public policy is vesting all rights in the twenty-year extension in authors and making publishers renegotiate the contract. Under no circumstances, however, should a publisher be granted the twenty-year term without the author being able to terminate. There is no reason to deprive

50 S. 483; H.R. 989.

51 Uruguay Round Agreements Act of 1994, 108 Stat. 4809 (1994).

authors or their heirs of the opportunity to renegotiate a contract that may have been written as long ago as 1920 in order to get the benefit of today's market value. After all, music publishers are going to charge users today's market value. Why the author or the author's heirs should have to settle for decades old market value is a mystery.

I would also throw the reversal of *Mills Music v. Snyder* into the mix,[52] since that decision deprived composers and other authors of much of the benefit of the paltry termination right.

I do not mean to suggest that publishers or other middlemen are doing anything unethical or wrong. They are just protecting their interests, which are not the same as the interests of authors or the larger public good. But this gets me back to my main theme: that industry-drafted bills, like the "life plus seventy" bills, do not look out for the public interest.

In the *Washington Post* on Sunday, April 2, 1995, there was an article about the fight over the Balanced Budget Amendment.[53] The article contained a short interview with former Senator James Abourezk,[54] who quit in disgust after one term in the 1970s. Abourezk is described as not having enjoyed his time in the Senate, but as appreciating the education in our system of government that he received: " 'I learned about my government,' he sa[id] . . . smiling impishly. 'I learned that very little gets done in the public interest. When it does, it's usually by accident.' "[55]

The content of the "life plus seventy" bills is not an accident. Your mission, as today's law students and tomorrow's intellectual property attorneys and legislators, is to make more "accidents" happen to better serve the public interest than the current copyright legislative process does.

52 469 U.S. 153 (1985). In *Mills*, a frequently criticized decision, the Supreme Court held that an author's termination of an assignee's copyright license did not terminate the assignee's rights to share in royalties derived from any sub-licensed derivative works.

53 *The World's Greatest Talkative Body*, WASH. POST, Apr. 2, 1995 (magazine), at W30.

54 James George Abourezk was elected as a Democrat from South Dakota to the Ninety-Second Congress, serving for one term between 1972 and 1974. In 1973, Abourezk was elected to the Senate and served a single term, from 1974 to 1980.

55 *The World's Greatest Talkative Body*, *supra* note 53, at W31.

CYBERLAW AND SOCIAL CHANGE: A DEMOCRATIC APPROACH TO COPYRIGHT LAW IN CYBERSPACE

NIVA ELKIN-KOREN*

* Faculty Member, University of Haifa School of Law. LL.B 1989, Tel-Aviv University; LL.M 1991, Harvard Law School; J.S.D 1995, Stanford Law School. I am grateful to John Barton, Yochai Benkler, Jody Freeman, Paul Goldstein, Guy Mundluk, Neil Netanel and Margaret Radin, for their insightful comments on earlier drafts of this paper. I also wish to thank Tal Noy and Ariel Olsewer for their valuable research assistance. The author alone is responsible for errors and misunderstandings set forth in this paper.

Introduction

As cyberspace becomes central to the creation and exchange of information, the debate over the future of copyright law in cyberspace is getting heated. For a long time, scholars were pointing at the need to revise copyright law to accommodate the new digitized environment.[1] The nature and extent of copyright reform remained controversial, however. Some believe that copyright law is flexible enough for managing rights in information technologies despite the increasing disparity between the rapid development of new technologies and the lumbering pace of copyright revisions.[2] Others, however, believe that copyright law was tailored to address the special needs of the print technology; needs that are no longer valid in a digitized environment.[3]

What began as a controversy over the appropriatness of copyright law to accommodate the technological changes, became a political battle over the distribution of the potential gains that cyberspace offers.[4] The challenges of digital technology go significantly beyond mere conceptual controversies and beyond disagreement on how to divide potential gains. The challenges of digital technology are, first and foremost, challenges to society. The debate over the future of copyright, therefore, should focus on political questions. Introducing political questions to the debate at this formative stage of the information superhighway is crucial for the future of cyberspace. The infrastructure may be designed and regulated in a way that would be irreversible or difficult to change. This moment presents us with an opportunity to shape cyberspace in a way that is consistent, and supportive of democracy. Introducing democratic theory to the debate would provide an adequate basis for a critical evaluation of the legal rules formulated by the

---

1 *See* Paul Goldstein, Copyright Highway: From Gutenberg to the Celestial Jukebox 197-236 (1994); Pamela Samuelson, *Digital Media and the Changing Face of Intellectual Property Law*, 16 Rutgers Computer & Tech. L.J. 323 (1990) [hereinafter Samuelson, *Digital Media*]; Ann Wells Branscomb, Who Owns Information? From Privacy to Public Access (1994).

2 *See, e.g.*, Information Infrastructure Task Force, Intellectual Property and the National Information Infrastructure: The Report of the Working Group on Intellectual Property Rights (Sept. 1995) [hereinafter IITF White Paper]; Arthur R. Miller, *Copyright Protection For Computer Programs, Databases, and Computer-Generated Works: Is Anything New Since CONTU*, 106 Harv. L. Rev. 977 (1993) [hereinafter Miller, *Copyright Protection Since CONTU*].

3 *See, e.g.*, Pamela Samuelson et al., *A Manifesto Concerning the Legal Protection of Computer Programs*, 94 Colum. L. Rev. 2308 (1994) [hereinafter Samuelson et al., *Manifesto*]; M. Ethan Katsh, The Electronic Media and the Transformation of Law 172-81 (1989); John P. Barlow, *The Economy of Ideas, A Framework for Patents and Copyrights in the Digital Age*, Wired, Mar. 1994, at 85 (arguing that copyright law was developed to convey forms and methods of expression entirely different from digitized medium).

4 Pamela Samuelson, *The Copyright Grab*, Wired, Jan. 1996, at 134.

legislature, and for the considerations and legal arguments made in courts.

This Article argues that the future of copyright law in cyberspace is crucial for democracy. It suggests that laws regulating the flow of information in cyberspace should be based on democratic principles. It argues that copyright law should be modified to serve the promise of decentralization and to facilitate participation in the production of knowledge. This argument relies on three claims. The first involves democratic theory; the second involves technology and social change; and the third deals with the relationship between technological development and the law.

Part I hypothesizes that the future of copyright law in cyberspace is crucial for democracy. Cyberspace and democracy often intermingle in political speeches, visionary accounts, and even in scholarly works. Yet, neither the nature of cyberspace, nor the definition of democracy are definite. Consequently, the meaning of "Cyber-Democracy" is very loose. For some, cyberspace promises a more democratic environment that is capable of facilitating direct access to decision makers. Thus, sending e-mail to the White House,[5] or acquiring access to bills introduced in Congress,[6] symbolizes the promise of a whole new way of governance. Others believe that cyberspace may democratize society by electronically generating the old New England Town Hall Meetings that allow the public at large to deliberate.[7] Both views assume that technological applications improve the functioning of existing institutions of mass democracies.

Although this Article shares the hope that cyberspace will facilitate democracy, it argues that the transformative power of cyberspace lies in its capability to decentralize the production and dissemination of knowledge. The vision of democracy that cyber-

---

5 The attempt to make government deliberations more accessible to the public underlies the creation of an electronic bulletin board that would allow citizens to communicate their concerns and opinions to the White House and to their representatives. *See* BRANSCOMB, *supra* note 1, at 162-63.

6 House Speaker Newt Gingrich, in testimony before the Ways and Means Committee on January 6, 1995, announced a new on-line service named after Thomas Jefferson, operated by the Library of Congress. This system makes available information ranging from the complete text of every bill introduced in Congress since 1992 to every word uttered in House and Senate floor speeches. *See Cybercitizens On-line*, SEATTLE TIMES, Jan. 9, 1995, at B4. Gingrich announced his vision that a revolution could take place, if more citizens would be able to surf the Internet and "get information beyond the cynicism of the elite." Edmund L. Andrews, *The 104th Congress: The Internet, Mr. Smith Goes to Cyberspace*, N.Y. TIMES, Jan. 6, 1995, at A22. This Article suggests that it is necessary for democracy to do more than merely provide electronic access to government deliberations.

7 For example, H. Ross Perot put forth this position in his 1992 presidential campaign. *See* BRANSCOMB, *supra* note 1, at 172.

space may promote is one that is based on participation and decentralization of power. This vision incorporates the insight of deliberative theorists who perceive "will formation processes" as essential for democracy. It therefore emphasizes active dialogic participation, rather than the sporadic passive procedural participation (voting) as key for democratizing decision-making processes. Part I introduces the participatory approach to democracy and discusses the significance of participation and decentralization of social dialogue for democracy.

Part II demonstrates how digital networks may decentralize meaning-making processes. Cyberspace is a medium in which meaning-making processes, identity formation, will formation, preferences, ideas, and ideologies are increasingly being created and manifested. Digital networking, it is argued, may transform the way we create and exchange information, form our preferences, and define our identities. It shifts power among social agents in the context of social and political discourses and meaning-making processes. The special characteristics of digital media may support a particular construction of power relations. By empowering individuals, decentralizing power relations, inducing collaboration, and enhancing accessibility of information, digitization may facilitate a more decentralized and non-hierarchical social dialogue. It has the potential of making social dialogue more dialogic. It may also, however, support a centralized, closely monitored, and exclusionary structure of social dialogue.

Part III demonstrates the role of law in shaping the social outcome of cyberspace. Law in general, and intellectual property law in particular, may play a major role in shaping technological implementation. The significance of copyright law for structuring technological uses and directing technological development is two-fold. First, copyright law shapes the structure of the market in which any given technology develops, by defining the scope of property rights and the circumstances under which they are granted. Second, copyright law, as any other social institution, reflects and communicates an ideology. It, therefore, serves to shape the technological choices that society members perceive as feasible.

I. Democracy as Participation in Social Dialogue

Digital networks may transform the way we create, exchange, and access information.[8] They may also transform the way we in-

[8] *See infra* part II.B and note 100 and accompanying text.

teract in private and in public.[9] Furthermore, digital networks may transform our ideas about private and public, and make it difficult to apply our traditional concepts of public interaction. Why would those changes in the way we interact with one another, with old traditions, with culture and subcultures, be significant for democracy? What is the significance of social dialogue for democracy?

A. *The Public Sphere and Democratic Theory*

The institutional structure of existing democracies in western societies reflects a liberal model of democracy. Society under this liberal model is perceived as a market-structured network of interactions among private persons.[10] These autonomous individuals enter the political arena with preexisting interests and preferences, and struggle within the system to maximize the satisfaction of those interests.[11]

The assumption that preferences, interests, and values are apolitical and prior to the political process, defines the role of politics under this model. For liberalism, "politics" is a mediating process among predetermined private interests.[12] Collective goals are determined through the competition between conflicting interests and preferences. The political process does not aim at reaching a "common good," but instead, seeks to arrive at a formula that would satisfy as many private interests as possible.[13]

The prevailing method for aggregating the sum of private preexisting interests is voting. The political process, therefore, focuses

---

9 *Id.*

10 The discussion of the Liberal Model is based on the works of Ronald Dworkin. Ronald Dworkin, *What is Equality? Part I: Equality of Welfare*, 10 PHIL. & PUB. AFF. 185 (1981); Ronald Dworkin, *What is Equality? Part II: Equality of Resources*, 10 PHIL. & PUB. AFF. 283 (1981); Ronald Dworkin, *What is Equality? Part III: The Place of Liberty*, 73 IOWA L. REV. 1 (1987); JOHN RAWLS, POLITICAL LIBERALISM: NOZICK, ANARCHY, STATE AND UTOPIA (1974). For an analysis of the assumptions of the liberal model, see Jurgen Habermas, *Three Normative Models of Democracy*, 1 CONSTELLATIONS 1 (1994); see also Nancy Fraser, *Rethinking the Public Sphere: A Contribution to the Critique of Actually Existing Democracy*, *in* HABERMAS AND THE PUBLIC SPHERE 130 (Craig Calhoun ed. 1993).

11 Fraser, *supra* note 10, at 130. For a critical discussion of the liberal approach, see Stephen M. Feldman, *The Persistence of Power and the Struggle for Dialogic Standards in Postmodern Constitutional Jurisprudence: Michelman, Habermas, and Civic Republicanism*, 81 GEO. L.J. 2243-44 (1993).

12 *Id.*

13 *See* Fraser, *supra* note 10, at 140.

> [T]he liberal-individualist model stresses the view of politics as the aggregation of self-interested, individual preferences. Deliberation in the strict sense drops out altogether. Instead, political discourse consists in registering individual preferences and in bargaining, looking for formulas, that satisfy as many private interests as possible. It is assumed that there is no such thing as the common good over and above the sum of all the various individual goods, and so private interests are the legitimate stuff of political discourse.

Id.

on voting. The political process is premised on a market structure and aims at facilitating free and equal competition among interests. The political outcome reflects the aggregated sum of preexisting interests reached under the conditions of free and equal competition. Consequently, the liberal model of democracy requires that the political process be based on neutrality and equally weighted voting rights.[14]

While the political process should guarantee the neutral and equal aggregation of private interests into a socially operative agenda, democratic institutions aim at programming the government in the interest of society.[15] The assumption is that the institutions of democracy (elections, parliamentary bodies, government) would reflect the aggregation of those interests in an operative way.[16] The majority rule is restricted by a separation of powers, bill of rights, and judicial review, to guarantee a democratic (just) result.[17] Democracy is thus understood as a mechanism for mediating preexisting private interests into a political will that defines the mandate of government.

One of the most influential attacks on the liberal model is the critique of deliberative theorists.[18] From their perspective, the liberal model fails to adequately address the relationship between the political process and will formation processes.[19] By excluding will

14 JOHN HART ELY, DEMOCRACY AND DISTRUST, A THEORY OF JUDICIAL REVIEW (1980); *see* Morton Horwitz, *The Constitution of Change: Legal Fundamentality Without Fundamentalism*, 107 HARV. L. REV. 30 (1993) (describing the correlation between the introduction of the "one person one vote" principle into American constitutional law and the rise of the concept of democracy in Supreme Court opinions).

15 Government is thus perceived as the mechanism which specializes in administratively employing political power for collective goals.

16 Habermas, *Three Normative Models of Democracy*, *supra* note 10, at 3 ("[Political rights] give citizens the opportunity to assert their private interests in such a way that by means of elections, the composition of parliamentary bodies, and the formation of a government, these interests are finally aggregated into a political will that makes an impact on the administration.").

17 *See* ELY, *supra* note 14.

18 For the purposes of this analysis "deliberative democracy" is understood as any model of democracy that looks at political participation in a broad sense. Namely, any view that rejects the narrow perception of politics under the liberal model and includes not only participation in strictly political institutions (for example voting), but also taking part in any discursive will formation processes in social and cultural spheres.

19 Even though deliberative approaches to democracy are distinct from one another in many respects, those distinctions are irrelevant for the current analysis. Mapping democratic theory by distinguishing between liberal and deliberative approaches allows me to discuss both the civic republican view of democracy (often referred to as "participatory democracy") and the discursive model of democracy (Habermas, Benhabib, Baynes) under the label of "deliberative approaches."

For a further discussion of this distinction, see Seyla Benhabib, *Models of Public Space: Hannah Arendt, the Liberal Tradition, and Jurgen Habermas*, *in* HABERMAS AND THE PUBLIC SPHERE 73 (Craig Calhoun ed., 1993) [hereinafter Benhabib, *Models of Public Space*] (distinguishing between the notion of participatory democracy in critical theory and this notion

formation processes, which are crucial for political outcomes, the liberal model fails to articulate the democratic process.

This critique of deliberative theorists is based on several factors.[20] First, critics claim that the liberal model of democracy is based on dubious assumptions about will formation processes. By assuming that individuals' preferences, interests, and identities are given *prior* to the political process, the liberal model fails to recognize that they are in fact constituted by it. The liberal model fails to conceptualize that preferences, interests, and identities are affected and shaped *throughout* political process. Thus, the liberal model does not provide an accurate description of the complexity of modern democracies.

The assumption of exogenous preferences also causes the liberal model to disregard the problem of power. Preferences, interests, and identities are vulnerable to manipulation by power. If they are not pre-political, but are shaped instead by the political process, then it is necessary to guarantee that will formation processes are also democratic. Therefore, equal weight cannot be achieved simply by securing equal rights to citizens (one person one vote).

The model of deliberative democracy seeks to address these deficiencies of the liberal model by shifting the focus of democratic theory. The deliberative democracy model shifts from a narrow view of politics as democratic institutions, to a broader view of politics as discursive will formation processes.[21] Under the deliberative model, political will is not fixed, but instead discursive and constituted through dialogue. This claim is buttressed on several grounds. First, the act of deliberation may itself affect individuals'

---

under the civic republican vision); see also Habermas, *Three Normative Models of Democracy*, *supra* note 10 (distinguishing discursive democracy from the republican view of Michelman). For Michelman's dialogic view of politics, see Frank Michelman, *Law's Republic*, 97 YALE L.J. 1493 (1988); Frank Michelman, *Conceptions of Democracy in American Constitutional Argument: The Case of Pornography Regulation*, 56 TENN. L. REV. 291 (1989) [hereinafter Michelman, *The Case of Pornography Regulation*]; Frank Michelman, *Conceptions of Democracy in American Constitutional Argument: Voting Rights*, 41 FLA. L. REV. 443 (1989) [hereinafter Michelman, *Voting Rights*]; Frank Michelman, *Personal But Not Split: Radin Versus Rorty*, 63 S. CAL. L. REV. 1783 (1990) [hereinafter Michelman, *Personal But Not Split*].

20 The deliberative model also criticizes liberalism for excluding questions of values from politics. The argument is that the liberal model seeks to guarantee neutral politics by excluding assertions of any concept of the good. *See* BRUCE ACKERMAN, SOCIAL JUSTICE IN THE LIBERAL STATE 11 (1980). This model was criticized by deliberative theorists for failing to be neutral. This is because the nature of an issue as an issue of justice or of the good life is not an inherent characteristic of it. Defining the nature of an issue requires the process of an unconstrained public dialogue. *See* Benhabib, *Models of Public Space*, *supra* note 19, at 82. The perception of the political process under the model of deliberative democracy is different from the liberal model in that politics is conceived of as a contest over questions of values and not simply questions of preferences. *See* Habermas, *Three Models of Democracy*, *supra* note 10. This debate is, however, beyond the scope of the current discussion.

21 *See* Benhabib, *Models of Public Space*, *supra* note 19, at 86.

preferences and opinions. Political deliberation is reflexive in the sense that it requires individuals to be aware of the perspective of all involved, in order to gain the support of their co-deliberators.[22] Furthermore, it is only through political deliberation that individuals are confronted with new information about their preferences and the various ethical and political perspectives of others.[23] The liberal assumption that people in a complex society are able to grasp the consequences and relative merits of each of their potential choices in advance is unrealistic.[24]

From this perspective politics is understood as an ongoing transformative dialogue among citizens.[25] In such a dialogue, citizens confront one another, challenging their "linguistically encoded self-understandings, sensibilities, and ways of knowing."[26] Politics, therefore, does not have the structure of a market in which citizens merely negotiate and bargain for a collective agenda that would satisfy as many private interests as possible.[27] Politics is instead about deliberation. The exchange of views becomes the es-

---

22 Seyla Benhabib, *Deliberative Rationality and Models of Democratic Legitimacy*, 1 CONSTELLATIONS 1, 16 (1994) [hereinafter Benhabib, *Deliberative Rationality*].

> When presenting their point of view and position to others, individuals must support them by articulating good reason in a public context to their co-deliberator. The process of articulating good reasons in public forces the individual to think of what would count as a good reason for all others involved. One is thus forced to think from the standpoint of all involved for whose agreement one is "wooing."

Id. This argument assumes that political deliberation is strategic in that it aims at persuading rather than understanding. It may therefore be inconsistent with the Habermasian model of communicative action. For Habermas, action may take two forms—strategic action, namely purposive-rational action, and communicative action, action aimed at reaching an understanding. Political deliberation should aim at mutual understanding or "communicatively achieved consensus." *See* Habermas, *Three Normative Models of Democracy*, *supra* note 10, at 2.

23 Bernard Manin, *On Legitimacy and Deliberation*, 15 POL. THEORY 338, 338-68 (Elly Stein & Jayne Mansbrige trans., 1987) (Deliberative processes are processes that impart information. It is only through deliberation that individuals become aware of the various ethical and political perspectives of others, and of the relevant information necessary to a decision that would affect all.).

24 Benhabib rejects the assumption, influenced by economic methodology, that individuals have an "ordered set of coherent preferences." This assumption, she argues, is fictional and irrelevant in a complex political world. The idea that individuals have a coherent set of preferences assumes that they can be aware in advance of "the consequences and relative merits" of each of their potential choices. In fact such awareness can only be produced through the deliberative process itself. Benhabib, *Models of Public Space*, *supra* note 19, at 16.

25 Habermas, *Three Normative Models of Democracy*, *supra* note 10, at 1.

> Politics is conceived as the reflective form of substantial ethical life, namely as the medium in which the members of somehow solidary communities become aware of their dependence on one another and acting with full deliberation as citizens, further shape and develop existing relations of reciprocal recognition into an association of free and equal consociates under law.

Id.

26 Michelman, *Personal But Not Split*, *supra* note 19, at 1786.

27 *See* Fraser, *supra* note 10, at 140.

sence of politics. Politics under the deliberative model should have the structure of a public dialogue, namely, public communication oriented towards mutual understanding.

The model of deliberative democracy thus makes both a sociological claim and a normative claim. As a sociological model it claims that preferences are formed through dialogue. Political preferences are shaped reflexively, through confrontation with opposing points of view and access to relevant information.[28] Consequently, politics is about will formation. This suggests that politics encompasses both an opportunity and a vulnerability. Ideally, the political process would allow citizens to transform themselves through dialogue,[29] but it is also the sphere in which community members would be most vulnerable to manipulation and the use of power. These opportunities and vulnerabilities require that participation in social dialogue should be shielded from manipulation by power.

However, the model of deliberative democracy also makes a normative claim that seeks to legitimize the use of coercive power by the state.[30] Imposing political decisions on all would be legitimate under the deliberative model only if "all" (that is, "all" who are affected by a decision) are allowed to participate in the deliberation.[31] To be sure, the deliberative model is not an argument for the replacement of existing democratic political institutions (such as voting) with alternative processes in civil society. Instead it suggests that processes in civil society are significant for democracy and may supplement formal political institutions. The deliberative model makes civil society only a supplement to democratic institutions and recognizes the significance of formal political institutions for the operation of mass democracies. Will formation processes alone, though significant for the democratic process, are incapable of fulfilling the needs of modern societies.[32] Even though social

---

28 Benhabib, *Deliberative Rationality*, *supra* note 22, at 32.

29 Michelman, *Voting Rights*, *supra* note 19, at 485 ("[P]olitics is a field in which persons reciprocally exercise their capacities for changing and becoming by and through communicative relations.").

30 See Manin, *supra* note 23, at 352 ("It is the process by which everyone's will is formed that confers its legitimacy on the outcome, rather than the sum of already formed wills.").

31 Democracy therefore requires an inclusive will formation process "in which free and equal citizens reach an understanding on which goals and norms lie in the equal interests of all." Habermas, *Three Normative Models of Democracy*, *supra* note 10, at 3.

32 Indeed, under the Habermasian model of system and lifeworld, "social dialogue" should not be subject to the functional requirements that are fundamental to the "system." The two different institutional orders necessary for a functioning social order are institutions that are largely integrated through consensually accepted norms (society as lifeworld), and institutions that are largely defined by their capacity to respond to the functional requirements imposed by the environment (society as a system). *See* KENNETH

dialogue may not replace the institutions of the administrative state, it complements these institutions by generating mass loyalty[33] and legitimacy.[34]

B. *Social Dialogue and Deliberative Democracy*

Both aspects of the deliberative model—the sociological (phenomenological) claim and the normative standard—make social dialogue significant for democracy. Under the deliberative model, the importance of social dialogue for democracy may be understood in several ways. The deliberative model may be seen as a claim that extends the reach of democratic theory to cover will formation processes. There are other ways, however, to understand the interface between processes in civil society and institutional politics. For example, one may perceive them as two separate spheres which are mutually dependent. From this perspective, processes in civil society are significant for democracy since they have an indirect influence on the outcome of institutional politics. A third way to understand social dialogue under the deliberative model is to view social dialogue as a potential source of legitimacy for institutional democracy.

The following discussion will critically examine these three claims about social dialogue. I will first discuss the second and third claims, and present a critique of these claims, informed by the insight of postmodern theorists. Then, I will return to the first claim, and suggest a reading of the deliberative model that may coexist with the postmodern critique.

1. Indirect Influence

The claim that social dialogue in civil society has an indirect influence upon institutional politics deserves further explanation. Habermas describes this course of influence: "[i]nformal public opinion-formation generates 'influence'; influence is transformed

---

BAYNES, THE NORMATIVE GROUNDS OF SOCIAL CRITICISM, KANT, RAWLS AND HABERMAS 179 (1992) (arguing that the political system has to produce mechanisms for accountable decision making and to guarantee an adequate concern for the "common good of the republic as a whole").

33 Money, administrative power, and solidarity are perceived by Habermas as the three resources from which modern societies meet their needs for integration. While society as a system (that state and the market) relies on money and administrative power, it fails to generate solidarity. Solidarity is formed through overlapping practical discourses in civil society. *See* Habermas, *Three Normative Models of Democracy*, *supra* note 10, at 14-15.

34 Baynes's discussion of the Habermasian approach suggests an illuminating metaphor: "Thus, rather than calling for the dismantling of the formal political system, Habermas has instead spoken of the need for secondary associations of the public sphere to surround and 'besiege' it, without however conquering it." BAYNES, *supra* note 32, at 179.

into 'communicative power' through the channels of political elections; and communicative power is again transformed into 'administrative power' through legislation."[35]

It follows that democratic principles should apply to discursive will formation to guarantee that formal political institutions accurately reflect *the will of the citizens.* Undemocratic processes in the public sphere may distort the outcome of the political system in that the political system would fail to produce political norms that are consistent with the public good. Under this view, will formation processes in civil society should conform with democratic principles in order to guarantee that the outcome of political institutions is undistorted.

This argument is based on two assumptions. The first of these assumptions presumes that it is possible to distinguish between a sphere of meaning (the "lifeworld") and a sphere of action (the "system"), and to purify the sphere of meaning from the prevalence of power. The perception of civil society as a distinct sphere of meaning is founded on Habermas's distinction between the "system" and the "lifeworld." The system/lifeworld dichotomy distinguishes between two different institutional orders in modern societies. Civil society (society as a lifeworld) in this sense is distinct from both the (public) administrative state and the (private) economy in the broad sense of these terms. Civil society is different from "political society of parties, political organizations, and political publics (in particular, parliaments)."[36] It is thus a sphere of human action that is distinct from the state. This sphere is not, however, private. It is distinct from "economic society composed of organizations of production and distribution, usually firms, cooperatives, partnerships, and so on."[37]

Civil society consists of institutions that are largely integrated through consensually accepted norms, while the economic and administrative states consist of institutions that are largely defined by their capacity to respond to the functional requirements imposed by the environment.[38] While civil society is situated in the sphere

---

35 Habermas, *Three Normative Models of Democracy*, *supra* note 10, at 13.

36 JEAN L. COHEN & ANDREW ARATO, CIVIL SOCIETY AND POLITICAL THEORY (1994). Cohen and Arato understand civil society as "a sphere of social interaction between economy and state, composed above all of the intimate sphere (especially the family), the sphere of associations (especially voluntary associations), social movements, and forms of public communication."

37 *Id.* Both the lifeworld and the system consist of private and public subcategories. While the system consist of the (private) economy and the (public) administrative state, the informal institutions of the lifeworld consist of the (private) family and the public sphere. *See* BAYNES, *supra* note 32, at 174, 177-78.

38 *Id.*

of meaning (society as lifeworld), the state and the economy are located in the sphere of action (the system).

Habermas's lifeworld/system distinction requires that social dialogue in civil society be sufficiently shielded from the "colonization" effects of the capitalist market and the administrative state.[39] Without this shield, the public sphere would merely reproduce the effects of money and power in the market and in the administrative state.[40]

Postmodern theorists reject this attempt to define a sphere of human actions that is separable from power. The system/lifeworld distinction, it is argued, functions as a kind of dualism which enables communication to be separated from power. "Ultimately, the distinction is based upon two theoretical fictions, namely, that an action system can occur independently of the normative building of consensus, and that a communicatively integrated action sphere, the lifeworld, can occur independently of domination by relations of power."[41] Power, however, resides not merely in readily-identifiable institutions (the state or the market), but in the play of opposing forces and actions.[42] For postmodern theorists, institutions always represent the dominant narrative which is internalized by all.[43] Foucault, for instance, describes how bureaucracy uses resources and knowledge to control and manipulate individual behavior. Its social agents internalize power and thereby become regimented, isolated, and self policing. Consequently, social dialogue cannot occur independently of domination by relations of power.[44]

---

39 The idea of "colonization" of the lifeworld under the Habermasian model requires further explanation. The system/lifeworld distinction is grounded in Habermas's theory of language which distinguishes between communicative actions and strategic actions, and maintains the primacy of the former over the latter. The colonization of the lifeworld is "the taking over of communicative imperatives by strategic imperatives." *See* DAVID M. RASMUSSEN, READING HABERMAS 35 (1990). In other words, the colonization of the lifeworld is the spill-over of attempts to meet the requirements of system maintenance into the domain of the lifeworld. *See* BAYNES, *supra* note 32, at 174.

40 BAYNES, *supra* note 32, at 178.

> Measures need to be implemented to insure that public opinion is not simply a commodity manufactured by advertising agencies for the capitalist economy, nor something that can be readily manipulated by campaign managers whose primary allegiance is to the party elite.

Id.

41 *See* RASMUSSEN, *supra* note 39, at 51 (discussing the critique of Axel Honneth).

42 *See* MICHAEL GARDINER, THE DIALOGICS OF CRITIQUE, M.M. BAKHTIN AND THE THEORY OF IDEOLOGY 156 (1992).

43 *See* FOUCAULT, POWER/KNOWLEDGE: SELECTED INTERVIEWS AND WRITINGS 1972-77 (C. Gordon ed., 1980); *see also* GARDINER, *supra* note 42, at 152-58.

44 Foucault's power/knowledge matrix is based on a relational concept of power in which power resides not in readily-identifiable institutions (the state or the market), but in the play of opposing forces and actions. Power resides everywhere, that is, everything exists within a matrix of power/knowledge. *See* GARDINER, *supra* note 42, at 156.

The second assumption underlying the claims regarding indirect influence presumes that it is merely the diffusion of power from the system (the market and administrative state) into the public sphere that distorts social dialogue. A public sphere which is adequately shielded from the colonizing effect of the system would be based on consensus and rational reasoning.[45] Democratic processes should, therefore, prevent dominant social groups from manipulating these will formation processes so that these processes exclusively reflect their interests and preferences.

While it is likely that a political system that excludes some segments of the population will be biased, in that it may generate public values that strongly represent the interests of the dominant social groups, it does not necessarily follow that a political system that is inclusive would accurately reflect the will of the people. In fact, critical theorists attack the very possibility of reaching a consensus over the "common good."[46] What is a "common good" may only be determined by participants in the deliberative process, and would be affected by the power relations among the participants. A consensus reached under conditions of systematic social inequality is tainted by the effects of dominance and subordination.[47]

The critique of the system/lifeworld distinction should not, however, completely undermine the significance of this distinction as an analytic tool. Identifying a separate realm of human interactions that is distinct from the economy and the state may be significant even if those spheres overlap and are not entirely distinguishable in reality. First, the system/lifeworld distinction acknowledges the existence of another realm of human action and interaction which is relevant to the operation of modern democracies. This conceptual framework recognizes that the modern state cannot be fully understood either in terms of the market, or in terms of the relationship between the market and the administrative state. It therefore facilitates a discussion of actions that are independent of both the market and the state.

Furthermore, the system/lifeworld distinction focuses atten-

---

45 For Habermas the lifeworld has primacy over the system in that it allows reason and rationalization to occur uncorrupted by relations of domination. *See* RASMUSSEN, *supra* note 39, at 51. Therefore the colonization of the lifeworld by the system distorts the ability to reach a rational result. Consequently, if the "system" colonizes the public sphere then no rational outcome may be reached, and the outcome would be inconsistent with the public good.

46 Fraser, *supra* note 10, at 131 ("[W]hen social arrangements operate to the systemic profit of some groups of people and to the systemic detriment of others, there are prima facie reasons for thinking that the postulation of a common good shared by exploiters and exploited may well be a mystification.").

47 *Id.*

tion on the way power may flow between the spheres. From this perspective, the democratic project should be extended from merely securing the freedom of citizens from state intervention, to an attempt to shield participation in the public sphere from the effect of power accumulated in the market. The critique of critical theorists suggests, however, that it is necessary to adapt a more sophisticated analysis of power which looks beyond the effect of power that is inflicted by institutions. This would be particularly important for the analysis set forth in this paper, which focuses on the way technology may affect power relations in the public sphere.

2. Legitimacy

The deliberative model further claims that democratic practices in civil society would provide the democratic process with legitimacy. This potential of civil society to generate legitimacy makes it the primary locus for strengthening democracy and supplementing democratic institutions under the deliberative model. The legitimacy of formal democratic institutions stems from the presumption that all have equal power to effect the democratic result (one person one vote).[48] Consequently, if the participation in the political process of any communal member is coerced, dominated, excluded, or otherwise distorted by power, the outcome of the political process would lose its sense of legitimacy.[49]

Legitimacy under the deliberative model is decentered.[50] It requires that all those affected by general social norms have a say in the adoption of those norms. The set of prescriptive conditions that social dialogue needs to satisfy in order to generate legitimacy

---

48 Civic Republicans challenge the liberal model of democracy, for denying the effect of economic power and disparities of power, on the ability to equally participate in the public sphere. Economic power subverts democracy in two ways. First, economic power is translated into power in the public sphere in ways that undermine equality and participation. That was the rationale behind attempts to limit expenditures and contribution in campaigns. *See, e.g.*, Citizens Against Rent Control v. City of Berkeley, 545 U.S. 290 (1981). Another way by which economic power subverts the equal opportunities for effective participation is psychological. Experiences of dependency in the private spheres of work and consumption preclude personal and political autonomy. For instance, the need of those who lack property to submit to the direction of those who have it in order to earn their living. *See* William H. Simon, *Social-Republican Property*, 38 UCLA L. REV. 1335 (1991).

49 Feldman, *supra* note 11, at 2245.

50 Under the liberal view, legitimate power is power used by the state and restricted by negative rights of citizens vis-a-vis the state and other citizens. These rights seek to guarantee freedom of external compulsion (governmental intervention). Legitimacy is based on the aggregation of will as reflected in election results. Under the deliberative model, power is decentered and arises from the power of autonomous individuals acting together.

Legitimacy under the liberal model is external to the political process. Legitimacy under the deliberative model stems from a decentered public sphere in which will-formation processes occur.

varies among theorists of deliberative democracy.[51] For Habermas, social dialogue would reflect consensus rather than coercion only if it satisfies the condition of an "ideal speech situation."[52] For Michelman, legitimacy depends on the idea that dialogue must be open to all within the community and be undistorted by the distribution and orientation of power.[53] The assumption accepted by all these theorists of deliberative democracy, however, is that it is the ability of all to equally participate in a meaningful way in generating social norms of action that makes these norms legitimate.

It is this attempt to legitimize the use of power by the state that postmodern theorists criticize. For these theorists, the idea that there is a set of prescriptive procedural conditions such that one's undergoing a dialogic modulation of one's understandings would not be considered coercive[54] is naive.[55] It overlooks the hegemonic ideological power embedded in institutions and culture. If citizens indeed internalize the dominant narrative in a way that prevents them from even recognizing that the so-called consensus does not adequately include them,[56] then even though it may seem that they have granted their consent, their consent is nonetheless coerced.[57]

---

51 Legitimacy under the liberal model also is grounded in the notion of social dialogue. Yet, Habermasian dialogue, unlike liberal dialogue, is not subject to criteria of neutrality, but instead is evaluated by the model of "practical discourse."

52 Legitimacy stems from the exercise of social dialogue that conforms with the model of "practical discourse." These procedural constraints of the "ideal speech situation" seek to guarantee that all those affected by general social norms would have a say in their adoption. Social dialogue would reflect consensus only if it meets the following conditions: 1) each participant must have an equal chance to initiate and to continue communication; 2) each must have an equal chance to make assertions, recommendations, explanations, and to challenge justifications; 3) all must have equal chances as actors to express their wishes, feelings, and intentions; and 4) the speakers must act as if in contexts of action there is an equal distribution of chances. *See* JURGEN HABERMAS, THEORY OF COMMUNICATIVE ACTION (Vol. 1, 1984; Vol. 2, 1987) [hereinafter HABERMAS, THEORY OF COMMUNICATIVE ACTION]; *see also* SEYLA BENHABIB, CRITIQUE, NORM, AND UTOPIA, A STUDY OF THE FOUNDATION OF CRITICAL THEORY 284 (1986) [hereinafter BENHABIB, CRITIQUE OF CRITICAL THEORY]. While the first three requirements may be expressed in terms of access and power, the fourth requirement looks at the type of arguments that may be legitimately made in such discourse.

53 In *Law's Republic*, Michelman focuses on the legitimacy of American Constitutionalism, and asks what conditions are presupposed by the Constitution. *See* Michelman, *Law's Republic*, *supra* note 19.

54 *See* HABERMAS, THEORY OF COMMUNICATIVE ACTION, *supra* note 52; *see also* Michelman, *Law's Republic*, *supra* note 19, at 1526-27.

55 *See* Dana R. Villa, *Postmodernism and the Public Sphere*, 86 AM. POL. SCI. REV. 712, 715 (1992) (the severe limitations of the public realm theory in coming to grips with the nature of modern power are most apparent in its naive reliance upon conditions of symmetry, non-hierarchy, and reciprocity as adequate guarantees of a "coercion-free" space).

56 Fraser, *supra* note 10, at 130. Indeed the Foucauldian idea is that subjects internalize the dominant power since it constitutes them. There is no external existence of the subject outside the matrix of power/knowledge relations, since subjects are being constituted by it. For a critical view of this Foucauldian approach, see GARDINER, *supra* note 42, at 158.

57 Villa, *supra* note 55, at 715 ("The criterion of consensus is too blunt an instrument . . . since it leaves unexamined the self-surveillance of the civically virtuous citizen (who has

This Article does not seek to legitimize the use of power by the state. The critical view suggests that our ability to legitimize the use of power by the state is limited. The insight of critical theory (Foucauldian) is significant in that it broadens the notion of power beyond the explicit effect of coercive institutions or the simple reproduction of economic relations, to cover all levels of the social system.[58] It channels the analysis of power to look at the way the hegemonic ideologies are generated and internalized. Yet, this view in itself cannot provide a basis for public policy. It does not suggest how power can be resisted. Foucauldianism assumes that people are not self-directed autonomous agents, but instead are constituted by the matrix of power/knowledge relations. This assumption makes it difficult to conceive of how those agents could possibly engage in alternative forms of action.[59] It further fails to show how social institutions may be modified to decentralize the effect of power. If power resides at every conceivable level of social relations, then transcending one power system would only result in constituting a new one.[60]

Incorporating the insights of critical theory into the model of deliberative democracy formulates questions about power within a normative framework. This framework establishes a norm against which to evaluate the use of power, and therefore facilitates a discussion over the extent to which a particular use of power is consistent with democracy. The deliberative model establishes the link between democracy and will formation processes in civil society. The insights of postmodern theorists allow the deliberative model a mechanism through which to address the complexity of power relations. The deliberative model, modified by critical insight, may become the basis of social policy.

3. Extending the Reach of Democratic Principles

A third reading of the deliberative model suggests another way of understanding the significance of social dialogue within this model. The claim that political will formation is inseparable from the political process requires that will formation processes be governed by democratic principles. Recognizing that norms of action

internalized the hegemonic conception of the public good) or communicatively rational agent (who has internalized the hegemonic conception of what constitutes 'the better argument.' ")).

58 Foucault shares with Bakhtin the non-reductionist perception of society. Society is perceived not as a fixed structure but as a constellation or dispersed fields of opposed forces and strategies. *See* GARDINER, *supra* note 42, at 158-61.

59 *Id.*

60 *Id.* at 162.

are defined and affected by on-going meaning-making processes makes the public sphere an arena in which the democratic process takes place. In other words, when democracy is defined not merely by formal political institutions, but as a process of "discursive will formation," *participation is no longer confined to a narrowly defined political realm, but is instead perceived as an activity that can be realized in the social and cultural spheres* as well.[61]

Furthermore, if political will formation is not prior to, but rather part of the political process, it ought to be governed by democratic principles. To achieve democracy, it is necessary that all those who are affected by norms of action be able to participate in their creation. Social dialogue should be democratic since it is inseparable from politics.

There are two consequences for the concept of participation in democracy. First, it is necessary to guarantee participation at all levels of social dialogue in which political will is being formed. If norms of action are determined not merely by formal political procedures, but also through informal discourse in the public sphere, it is necessary to guarantee the ability of all affected to participate in such debate. Informal discourse in an overlapping and decentralized network of civil associations should be encouraged.[62]

Second, it is necessary to guarantee the *ability*, and not merely the *right*, to participate. In other words, to achieve democracy, it is not enough to focus merely on negative rights (neutrality and equality of representation procedures), but also to secure a positive right—an actual possibility of participation.

The ability to equally participate in the deliberative process depends on power. When power accumulates in the economic market, or by state administrators, and is used in the public sphere, it tends to distort equal participation and merely reproduce the effects of money and power in the market and the administrative state. "Measures need to be implemented to insure that public opinion is not simply a commodity manufactured by advertising agencies for the capitalist economy, nor something that can be readily manipulated by campaign managers whose primary allegiance is to the party elite."[63]

The ability to equally participate in social dialogue also de-

---

61 Benhabib, *Models of Public Space*, *supra* note 19, at 87 ("This conception of participation, which emphasizes the determination of norms of action through the practical debate of all affected by them, has the distinct advantage over the republican or civic virtue conception that it articulates a vision of the political true to the realities of complex modern societies.").

62 BAYNES, *supra* note 32, at 179.

63 *Id.* at 178.

pends on disparities of power among participants. One's ability to participate in the political process in a meaningful way depends on her position relative to other participants in this process.[64] In other words, participation depends on how much power one has over other people and institutions, and on the power she is subjected to. The political process should therefore guarantee that disparities of power do not distort the way people form their preferences. The challenge for democracy is to identify the impact of disparities of power on the ability to participate, and to minimize that effect. Finally, the ability to participate depends on the accessibility of social dialogue, accessibility of information, and control over resources.

The following discussion will, therefore, focus on the ability to participate in social dialogue in a meaningful way. Before discussing the technological context and the way it affects social dialogue, an introduction to the concept of social dialogue is required.

C. *Social Dialogue as a Meaning-Making Process*

The discussion of social dialogue is distinct from the normative approach to political theory. Normative political theory asks what conditions should be satisfied by a political dialogue to legitimize the norms of action that it generates. I propose that social dialogue should be considered in the broad sense of the term. While normative political theory looks at the conditions under which public debate on public issues would generate authoritative bases for political action,[65] discursive will formation processes are not limited to political discourses. Neither are they aimed at agreement over norms of action. Instead, discursive will formation processes include any social interaction by which social agents engage in meaning-making processes. This understanding of social dialogue includes everything from arts and sciences, to writing and reading a book, interpreting old texts, exchanging ideas about

---

64 The concept of power I use here is positional in the sense that it examines disparity of power between agents in any given context, and accepts the idea that agents may enjoy different levels of power in different contexts. Power is understood as the capacity to impose one's will on others and to resist the same imposed by others. *See* Note, *Distributive Liberty: A Relational Model of Freedom, Coercion, and Property Law*, 107 HARV. L. REV. 859, 864 (1994).

65 *See* Craig Calhoun, *Introduction*, *in* HABERMAS AND THE PUBLIC SPHERE (Craig Calhoun ed., 1993). Calhoun posits that democratic theory looks at the social conditions under which the rational-critical debate about public issues determines decisions. For instance, the normative approach would look at the type of arguments that would be legitimate in a social dialogue—should values and interests be excluded from social dialogue, or are they necessary to constitute the legitimacy of social dialogue?

family values, searching information on a database, and creating and consuming artifacts.

Political opinions depend on ideas and understandings about the world, values, and concepts of good. Such belief systems, as any other signifying practice, are generated in particular social contexts through dialogue.[66] Identities are also formed through dialogical interaction with others (family, community, associations), tradition, and shared cultural symbols. We form our views about what is socially appropriate, what is socially desirable, and what future we wish for ourselves based on interaction. Preferences are affected by information about what is available to us and to others. Priorities are affected by our information on the potential consequences of a certain course of action. The type of information we are able to access determines the available options. Therefore, our ability to access information (such as surveys, movies, and historical texts), and to communicate and interact with others, is crucial for the broad understanding of will formation processes.[67]

Social dialogue is understood here as a meaning-making process. This approach perceives all possible forms of human interaction and cultural artifacts as modes of symbolic communication; that is, as semiotic practices which display certain textual or quasi-textual properties that are read and responded to dialogically.[68] Texts, broadly understood as any expression or self-reflection of individuals through symbolic communication, contain no absolute fixed meaning.[69] Consequently, they are necessarily mediated by dialogic relations.[70]

Various social agents are engaged in an on-going process of constructing the meaning of symbols. Through this process, social agents give meaning to the objective world and define their own identity. The process of creating and communicating information

---

66 Bakhtin's perception of ideology as a signifying practice (a symbolic medium through which all social relations are necessarily constituted) makes it inherently dialogic (just like language). Gardiner notes that "[w]hen colonized (or 'monologized') by dominant cultural forms and institutional arrangements, particular ideological discourses can play a crucial role in the maintenance of asymmetrical power relations." GARDINER, *supra* note 42, at 7.

67 In Bakhtin's words, the "world of the text . . . is a world which can play a vital role vis-a-vis our self-awareness and our moral and political choices in the here and now." *Id.* at 136.

68 *Id.* at 106.

69 *Id.* at 137.

70 Bakhtin distinguishes between dialogic relations, which are subject-subject relations between living persons, and natural relations, which unlike dialogic relations can be understood in terms of causality and quantity. *Id.* at 105.

is a process of creating meaning.[71] The public sphere is thus perceived as an on-going process of meaning-making through communicative activities.[72] This sphere is both constituted by and constitutes the individuals engaged in it.[73] The politics of meaning-making aims at fixing and transforming meanings.[74] It reflects disparities of power among social agents depending on their ability to control access to sources of signification and dissemination.[75]

This perception of social dialogue rejects the idea that political deliberation occurs only in specific institutions, such as courts or parliaments, and perceives it as a network of social interactions that take place at endless levels and arenas. Social dialogue, as an on-going meaning-making process, takes place in overlapping networks.[76] It may occur simultaneously in a wide range of institutions, from informal movements and associations through the public mass media, to the more formal institutions of parliamentary debate and legal argumentation.[77] The underlying assump-

---

[71] Margaret Chon, *Postmodern "Progress": Reconsidering the Copyright and Patent Power*, 43 DePaul L. Rev. 97, 122-24 (1993).

[72] Bakhtin, for instance, perceives fictional text as having a capacity to shape the contours of mass consciousness, and therefore as significant for the organization and the subversion of ideological hegemony.

[73] This concept of dialogism is based on Mikhail Bakhtin. *See* Gardiner, *supra* note 42; *see also* T. Todorov, Mikhail Bakhtin: The Dialogical Principle ix (1984).

[74] Rosemary J. Coombe, *Objects of Property and Subject of Politics: Intellectual Property Laws and Democratic Dialogue*, 69 Tex. L. Rev. 1853, 1860-61 (1991).

[75] *See* Gardiner, *supra* note 42, at 7; Coombe, *supra* note 74, at 1860-61. Coombe argues that intellectual property laws suppress dialogic practices by "preventing us from using the most powerful, prevalent, and accessible cultural forms to express identity, community, and difference." *Id.* at 1855. I wouldn't go that far. I believe that some level of property rights in works is necessary to secure freedom. Yet, the scope of rights should be adjusted to accommodate free dialogue. For further discussion of this issue, see *infra* part III.

[76] Social dialogue under the deliberative model is understood as a network of overlapping discourses in which discursive will-formation occurs. The idea of an overlapping network is confusing. The public sphere is fragmented and decentralized, and does not treat the entire citizenry, at any single moment, as equal participants, as they are treated by institutions of the formal political system (such as elections). Participation is nevertheless realized through a network of ongoing overlapping discourse. "Although the idea of a practical discourse in which the entire citizenry participate as free and equal persons is not directly realized within any one of these forums, the entire network of institutions should be designed in such a way that this idea is appropriately mirrored in them." Baynes, *supra* note 32, at 180. Furthermore,

> [i]t is in this sense, too, that Habermas has spoken of a "proceduralization" of the Rousseauean conception of popular sovereignty in which the notion of a localized sovereign body is replaced with that of an anonymous network of communication processes comprised of autonomous associations, independent mass media, and other institutions of the public sphere. On this model, the "moment" of deliberation, so to speak, does not reside primarily with the judiciary (Sunstein) nor with the body of elected representatives (Madison), but is dispersed throughout a vast communicative network.

Id.

[77] *See* Baynes, *supra* note 32, at 180. Political dialogue should occur in many forums. Civil society is thus conceived as "a pluralist public sphere in which citizens define the

tion of part II is that these social interactions affect the way identities, interests, and values are being formed. Rather then focusing merely on the chance of actors to express themselves in a political dialogue, social dialogue looks at how their objectives, values, and views are constituted. From this perspective, social dialogue does not aim at reaching any binding decision.

The following discussion looks at actual social conditions in which discourse occurs and attempts to track the impact of power on the way meaning is generated. Social dialogue is perceived as a historical phenomenon that is affected by social, political, and technological changes.[78] This discussion is restricted to the way technological changes affect social dialogue, and the way the law may intervene to determine the direction of those effects.

II. Social Dialogue in Cyberspace

We have seen that an inclusive social dialogue is essential for democracy. Social dialogue in a democracy should promote participation of all members affected and should minimize the effects of coercion and power. This part looks at social dialogue and its implementation in digital networks. The question is whether the media, which facilitates dialogue, affects its nature and structure. I would argue that interactions on digital media, when compared with other forms of communication, may affect the disposition of social dialogue.

Since on-line services are facilitating an increasing portion of

---

terms and conditions of their common life and in which debate and argument about collective norms, social policies, and political decisions take place." *Id.* at 178; *see* Michelman, *Law's Republic*, *supra* note 19, at 1531 (identifying many "arenas of potentially transformative dialogue").

[78] The Habermasian model of the public sphere is historical. In *The Structural Transformation of the Public Sphere*, Habermas describes an autonomous sphere that emerged in modernity. *See* Jurgen Habermas, The Structural Transformation of the Public Sphere (Thomas Burger trans., 1989) (1962). The emergence of the public sphere in the eighteenth century is described as part of the changes in sociocultural institutions. The bourgeois public sphere of the eighteenth century emerged in the form of private clubs, coffee houses, learned societies and literary associations, publishing houses, journals, and newspapers. Therefore, even though the Habermasian concept of the public sphere is analytic, and relates to a sphere (realm of human activities), rather than a place, and to a type of activities (reasoning private persons) rather than a specific institution, it relates to a quality of social institutions that may be affected by technological and social changes. The Habermasian model is particularly appealing in the context of the information superhighway not only because it is perceived as a historical phenomena, but also because of the focus on communication acts. Furthermore, Habermas's perception of overlapping discourses in civil society is reflected in the reality (and the metaphor) of the Internet. For the use of Habermasian ideas to develop a social theory of media see John B. Thompson, *Social Theory and the Media*, *in* Communication Theory Today 24 (David Crowley & David Mitchell eds., 1994).

our social interactions,[79] digital networks are displacing our cultural attention, and may transform the way we understand information and information exchanges.[80]

This discussion demonstrates how digitization may affect the capability of individuals to participate in social dialogue. First, I will explore several characteristics of digital media, such as flexibility and interactivity, which may decentralize the meaning-making process, and enhance the ability of individuals to effectively participate in social dialogue. Second, I will illustrate how digitization opens social dialogue for participation by enhancing accessibility to different means of creation and communication. Cyberspace may facilitate active, rather than passive participation in the deliberative process and enhance the ability of individuals to access relevant information that may be crucial for will formation processes.

A. *Decentralizing Control Over Meaning*

Digitization has the potential to redistribute meaning-making power by shifting that power over meaning from authors, and other producers of information, to users. This is due to several characteristics of digital media. One such characteristic is the flexibility of digital representation, which allows meaning to be created by various social agents at various times. Another aspect of digital media that supports decentralization is interactivity, which enables users to act upon works. Consequently, the meaning of works may reflect not only the author's meaning, but also mutual influences of authors and users.

1. Fixity and Flexibility

Perhaps the most significant characteristic of digital media is that it stores information in electronic codes rather than in a physical form.[81] This flexible form of representation is easy to manipulate and modify. The costs of manipulation in a digitized form are

---

79 The visionaries of cyberspace anticipate that digital networks will replace all other methods of communication. For the current analysis however, it is not necessary to assume that digital networks would entirely replace all methods of communication. Even if digital networks merely offer an alternative for existing communication methods, they would still have the potential for transforming social dialogue. This is because introducing an alternative to the current structures of communication entrusts participants with an option, and thus subverts the hegemony of prevailing structures.

80 *See* Michael Benedikt, Cyberspace: Some Proposals, in Cyberspace—First Steps 124 (1991) ("[J]ust as printing did not replace but displaced writing, and writing did not replace but displaced storytelling, and just as movies did not replace theater nor television movies . . . cyberspace will not replace either objective reality or dreaming and thinking in their historical modes.").

81 George P. Landow, Hypertext, The Convergence of Contemporary Critical Theory and Technology 18 (1992).

relatively low, partly since manipulation may occur on the same media that carries the original message. Revisions of text in a physical medium, by contrast, often require the use of a new media, which, in turn, increases the cost of creating new versions.[82] Digital representation is nonetheless fixed, in the sense that it may be communicated to many receivers over time and distance in the form in which it was recorded. While the significance of writing and printing technologies is considered to be the ability to create and disseminate static fixed records,[83] the significance of digital representation is that it combines fixity and flexibility.

It is unnecessary to predetermine any aspect of a digitized work because it is easy and inexpensive to revise it, even after the creation of the work has been completed.[84] Physical media, by contrast, are static and require a choice regarding the final version of the work prior to its completion.[85] Consequently, digitized works tend to be indefinite and subject to change. David Bolter remarks that

> [t]his restlessness is inherent in a technology that records information by collecting for fractions of a second evanescent electrons at tiny junctions of silicon and metal. All information, all data, in the computer world is a kind of controlled movement, and so the natural inclination of computer writing is to change.[86]

The flexibility of digitized media shifts power among social agents. Consider, for instance, the shift from retrieval methods based on physical media, such as card catalogs, printed indexes, tables of contents, pagination, or bibliographies, to computerized databases. Physical retrieval methods are based on a fixed, linear representation and tend to concentrate meaning-making power in

---

82 Consider for instance the routine activity of revising a printed text. Whereas such revisions used to require mechanical deletion (for example, covering with a whitener), or printing the text all over again, the same revisions on a wordprocessor may be performed in a matter of seconds.

83 The invention of writing allowed the creation of fixed records—of data and ideas—to be shared by people in different places and at different times. The invention of the print by Gutenberg allowed the dissemination of such records in multiple copies. *See* ELIZABETH EISENSTEIN, AGENT OF CHANGE 229 (1976); LANDOW, *supra* note 81, at 18; ITHIEL DE SOLA POOL, TECHNOLOGIES OF FREEDOM: ON FREE SPEECH IN AN ELECTRONIC AGE (1983).

84 One may change a work altogether by adjusting the size of a design, or altering the colors of a image or a digitized drawing.

85 For instance, once a painting has been drawn on canvas, the colors and size may not be modified.

86 DAVID BOLTER, WRITING SPACE: THE COMPUTER IN THE HISTORY OF LITERACY 31 (1990) ("Electronic text is the first text in which the elements of meaning, of structure, and of visual display are fundamentally unstable. Unlike the printing press or the medieval codex, the computer does not require that any aspect of writing be determined in advance for the whole life of a text.").

the hands of the few who construct them. Meaning is constructed through the selection and the organization of information. The way a piece of information is defined and categorized determines the path that will locate it, and enable people to access it.[87] Any information structure reflects specific assumptions by the compiler regarding the meaning of that information. For instance, the decision to classify a group that uses violence to achieve political goals as either a "terrorist group" or a "liberation organization" depends on one's political perspective.[88] The meaning defined by the classifier is imposed by controlling access to information. Unless the user's set of assumptions matches the set of assumptions used by the compiler, the user would fail to retrieve any relevant information. Retrieving information by following a constructed path requires accepting, or at the very least acknowledging, the underlying assumptions of the classifier.[89] Thus, physical retrieval methods serve to perpetuate meanings assumed by the compiler.[90]

Another source of control exercised by compilers of information in physical media is the power to determine which chunks of reality are to be categorized, and those which do not merit a special category. In this sense, compilers have the power of language creators. This power may significantly affect our perception of the world.[91] It follows that those who control the means of arranging

---

87 The rigidity of previous methods of information retrieval troubled one of the pioneers of hypertext—Vannevar Bush, who as early as 1946 wrote: "[Information] can be in only one place, unless duplicates are used; one has to have rules as to which path will locate it, and the rules are cumbersome. Having found one item, moreover, one has to emerge from the system and re-enter on a new path." VANNEVAR BUSH, ENDLESS HORIZONS 31 (1946).

88 The construction of information is not reflected merely through classification, but also through the network of links that creates the path which leads to the information.

89 "Some level of recognition" is used here to cover a whole range of different levels of recognizing the underlying assumptions in order to access information. This goes from internalizing or adapting the meanings assumed by the compiler, studying those meanings in a critical way, or completely rejecting them. Even if one does not fully accept the meaning attached to information through the way it is organized, the fact that the compiler's assumptions are being repetitively used, as the only path to the information, gives that specific meaning a dominant role.

90 It is arguable that to some extent, in order to create an effective system of classification, a classifier must be responsive to existing common understandings and perceptions, and must reflect those in her classification. To that extent existing meanings are perpetuated.

91 This may also be demonstrated in the context of legal research. Defining a problem as one of private or public law, as one of tort or contract law, may invoke different interests and considerations. Structuring the law by defining legal categories was part of an effort of late-nineteenth-century legal scholars to depoliticize legal thought. *See* MORTON HORWITZ, THE TRANSFORMATION OF AMERICAN LAW 1870-1960, THE CRISIS OF LEGAL ORTHODOXY 10 (1992). The content of legal categories, and the organizational structure of the law, had always been debated. Legal categories served not only functional but also political purposes. *Id.* at 10-27. The impact of on-line legal research, which increasingly dominates American legal education, on legal categories is yet to be seen. When students and practi-

and tagging information possess the power to impose specific meanings. The more control one has over information resources, the more one is able to impose her meanings and force users to conform to those meanings.

Digitization of information retrieval methods decentralizes control over meaning in several ways. First, representation of information is flexible and neutral, and may be classified in endless ways. Whereas physical retrieval methods rely on rigid mechanisms, such as reference to text by page numbers, or reference to books by call numbers, digitized representation is not linked to any specific classification and organization. Consequently, it allows reference to information in various ways. The fact that digitized classifications may be constantly modified reduces the dependency on preexisting classifications and allows constant change of meanings.

Second, whereas manual research methods follow a single path defined by rigid categories,[92] computerized research allows the use of endless categories, or several categories simultaneously. It is, therefore, less dependent on familiarity and compliance with preexisting concepts. One may employ, for instance, a keyword search that would provide direct access to all the documents which contain a certain combination of words, even though such combination was never previously contemplated. Consequently, several meanings may be affixed to any single piece of information.[93] It thereby reduces the dependency of users on preexisting classifications and assumptions regarding the meaning of symbols, liberates researchers from conforming with prevailing methods of classification, and facilitates the creation of new meanings.[94]

Nevertheless, digitized data also reflects the programmer's set of assumptions.[95] Access to digitized information depends on retrieval programs that may limit the accessibility of information.

---

tioners are able to access cases directly, and no longer dependent on legal classification in books and manuals, the structure of the law may transform.

92 "When data of any sort are placed in storage, they are filed alphabetically or numerically, and information is found (when it is) by tracing it down from subclass to subclass. It can be in only one place, unless duplicates are used; one has to have rules as to which path will locate it, and the rules are cumbersome. Having found one item, however, one has to emerge from the system and re-enter on a new path." BUSH, *supra* note 87, at 31.

93 Compare, for instance, research using the West manual key system with research on LEXIS. Using the key system one has to conform to the existing categories, including different areas of law and existing legal doctrines. Classification of a case as one of private law or constitutional law may be crucial for the legal outcome. In a digitized environment one may look up a case by using words that assume (or eventually establish) a different meaning.

94 Computerized legal research, for instance, may change the classic classification of legal fields such as contract law and criminal law. This may allow the creation of new fields of knowledge which combine previously distinct disciplines.

95 *See* Muriel Zimmermann, *Reconstruction of a Profession: New Roles for Writers In the Com-*

The syntax used by a computer program does structure and define the information retrieved. However, retrieval programs may vary in the rigidity of their search strategies, and many would allow users to choose various search parameters. Furthermore, the flexible form of representation, and the ability to separate the recording of information and the retrieval mechanisms, allow access by different research programs simultaneously.[96] Many computer programs run on the same database, and thus allow different social agents to apply their meaning to that information. This may reduce the hegemony enjoyed by information compilers and may allow diversity in research strategies.[97]

Another feature of flexible representation is non-linearity. Digital information allows one to access a bit of information directly, without following any given sequence and without having to read any other information. One may use the automated "search" command of a word processor, for instance, to go directly to the desired paragraph. Books, by contrast, are linear and are commonly read from beginning to end.[98] Non-linearity transfers meaning-making power from authors to readers. If a user is able to enter the text at any point, she may disregard what the author considered to be the meaning of the text, and may use the fragmented material as she wishes.[99]

The overall effect of the flexible nature of digital representation tends to decentralize control over meaning-making processes,[100] and invites more individuals to participate.

---

puter Industry, *in* THE SOCIETY OF TEXT, HYPERTEXT, HYPERMEDIA, AND THE SOCIAL CONSTRUCTION OF INFORMATION 244 (Edward Barrett ed., 1989).

96 Physical retrieval methods, by contrast, require the classification of the information itself, such as by attaching a call number to books and physically placing them together in the library, or by organizing text in pages, and referring in an index to specific page numbers.

97 From the perspective of copyright law, one question is whether users can adapt works to reflect their own meanings. I argue that new conditions created in the digitized environment suggest that the law should not prohibit this type of application.

98 LANDOW, *supra* note 81, at 21 ("Whereas analogue recording of sound and visual information requires serial, linear processing, digital technology removes the need for sequence by permitting one to go directly to a particular bit of information.").

99 From the perspective of copyright law this aspect of digital technology raises some interesting questions regarding the rights of a database owner to prevent the use of computer applications over its database. The question is whether, considering opportunities for participation in the digital era, copyright law should permit activities such as this. This question is discussed in part III, *infra*.

100 *See* MICHAEL HEIM, ELECTRIC LANGUAGE: A PHILOSOPHICAL STUDY OF WORD PROCESSING 220 (1987).

> Fragments, reused material, the trails and intricate pathways of "hypertext", as Ted Nelson terms it, all these advance the disintegration of the centering voice of contemplative thought. The arbitrariness and availability of database searching decreases the felt sense of an authorial control over what is written.

Id.

2. Interactivity

Digitized systems tend to be more interactive than works in traditional forms. This is due to the fact that manipulation of digitized works is relatively easy and inexpensive, and therefore allows input of users to be integrated into works. Non-digital media, such as printed text, film or sound recording, carry only a single form of the work at any given time.[101]

The level of a user's involvement in the creation of the final work may vary. Some interactive systems allow users to select one way of reading (or experiencing) a work from among several options. Interactive films, for instance, allow the audience to choose the development of the plot. Other interactive systems allow one to incorporate one's own input into the work. Interactive TV, for instance, allows viewers to choose what they see and to manipulate it. Viewers can grab and manipulate photographs or sound samples, recolor a cartoon, or play an interactive film. Other interactive works are compilations of various materials, either crude (such as sound samples or colors) or highly processed (such as blocks of text). The user is invited to interact with the media and reflect her personal preferences by integrating several elements into a single presentation.

Interactivity decentralizes meaning-making power by shifting meaning-making power from authors to users. Compare, for instance, writing text on paper and writing with hypertext.[102] Hypertext is "text composed of blocks of words (or images) linked electronically by multiple paths, chains or trails in an open-ended, perpetually unfinished textuality described by the terms link, node, network, web and path."[103] In other words, those are blocks of text linked electronically that permit multiple readings. While authors

---

101 Ithiel de Sola Pool, Technologies Without Boundaries, On Telecommunications in a Global Age 50 (1990).

102 The significance of the hypertext example is twofold. First, interactive electronic linkage is not unique to hypertext. It is a feature shared by any electronic text. When text written on a wordprocessor is connected to the network, it functions in a hypertext environment, namely, it may be linked to other texts, converged with them, in whole or in pieces, and be placed in the "same psychic framework." *See* Heim, *supra* note 100, at 160-61. Thus hypertext provides an appropriate context for studying the interactive linkage, as well as a context from which generalization may be drawn. Additionally, from the perspective of copyright law, it is interesting to examine the changes in writing (in the narrow sense of drafting text). The reason is that the print technology was central for adapting copyright laws, and it is therefore still central to fundamental concepts of copyright.

103 Landow, *supra* note 81, at 3. The term "hypertext" was first defined in the 1960s by Theodore H. Nelson as "nonsequential writing—text that branches and allows choices to the reader, best read at an interactive screen. As popularly conceived, this is a series of text chunks connected by links which offer the reader different pathways." Theodor H. Nelson, Literary Machines 0/2 (1981) (emphasis omitted).

of printed text would organize their ideas in advance and put them into specific words and order, authors of hypertext do not control the organization of themes in the text. Instead, writing involves creating fragments of information or text which are then selected and organized by users in each reading of the text.[104] The openendness of text that allows readers to contribute their input is sometimes referred to as "un-authored," "authorless,"[105] or a "book that's sort of written as you read it, by your finger when you touch the screen."[106]

The Hypertext example illustrates the effect of interactivity on decentralizing meaning-making power. Authoring by the reader may take three forms: first, by creating meaningful text by linking specific blocks of text; second, by annotating text written by others; and third, by creating links between separate documents.[107] Each of these "reader created meanings" deserves further elaboration.

Authoring by linking occurs when the reader determines how to move through different texts. Thus, even though the reader may not change the text produced by another writer, she is constructing a meaningful text while reading it.

Annotating text permits readers to add their comments and make revisions in the text.[108] Such annotations are no longer external to the text, but may converge with it, and may be shared among readers.[109] This makes text more vulnerable, and reduces the power of writers to govern meaning.

Creating links between separate documents makes each text vulnerable to changes and convergence with others.[110] Here, readers may alter and change a text to create a new text, and a new

---

104 Or, fragments of information or text are selected and organized by users in each and every running of the program. *See* Edward Barrett, Text, Context, and Hypertext: Writing with and for the Computer (1988).

105 *See* Zimmermann, *supra* note 95, at 245. Zimmermann forecasts that in the next generation of computer documentation, using database methodologies, there will be no unique authors. Writers will contribute fragmented texts into a database in which it will be maintained and reused.

106 *See* Stewart Brand, The Media Lab: Inventing the Future at M.I.T. 141 (1987).

107 *See* Landow, *supra* note 81, at 71.

108 Landow perceives this to be a crucial liberating and empowering quality of hypertext: "[a]s long as any reader has the power to enter the system and leave his or her mark, neither the tyranny of the center nor that of the majority can impose itself." *Id.* at 178.

109 Compare, for instance, annotating a book one owns in the privacy of one's house with annotating text on a hypertext system where the new version of that text may be instantly read and further revised by other users.

110 *See* Landow, *supra* note 81, at 71-72. From a philosophical perspective, "[h]ypertext . . . narrow[s] the phenomenological distance that separates individual documents from one another in the worlds of print and manuscript." *Id.* at 71.

meaning. As a result, authors may no longer control the meaning of their text.

It is arguable that the ability to change texts and place them in different contexts also exists in physical media. Critical theorists have long attributed meaning-making functions to readers of printed text.[111] Yet, digitization translates this abstract idea about the meaning of art into a concrete framework of activities. Whereas unilateral communication, such as broadcasting or the printing press, imposes an authoritative uniform meaning on its audience,[112] digital technology allows meaning to be created through dialogue. A plurality of meanings may be constructed by a variety of individual users who interact with the text.

By making readers more active, hypertext systems combine writing and reading, and transfer meaning-making power from authors to readers.[113] Meaning thus becomes multicentered.[114]

3. Participation and Empowerment

a. Expanding the Circle of Creators

For readers, interactivity is empowering. It transforms readers from relatively passive receivers of a message, into potential participants in the creation process.[115] Thus, interactive systems such as Hypertext empowers readers with creative powers and expands the number of people who may participate in the creation process.

Interactivity transforms the hierarchical nature of one-way communication. In a non-digitized environment, a message is put together by the originator (that is, a book publisher or a broadcaster) and is disseminated to passive receivers. Receivers may dispute the message and respond in a separate message of their own. For example, one may write "letters to the editor" in response to a disputed article, or respond instantly to a program on a television

---

111 *See* RONALD BARTHES, S/Z (1974).

112 *See* COLIN CHERRY, THE AGE OF ACCESS: INFORMATION TECHNOLOGY AND SOCIAL REVOLUTION 64 (1985).

> [Broadcasting] . . . is essentially a unilateral system, sending out . . . its educational material, etc. from an authoritative center to the multitude, who cannot effectively respond as *individuals*; broadcasting has enormous responsibilities for this very reason, that it essentially extends and enhances the power of authority.

Id.

113 LANDOW, *supra* note 81, at 71.

114 Interactivity may break the monopolistic stranglehold of the mass media. This monopoly is maintained by separating consumers from producers, and turning viewers to passive receivers. Interactivity allows the audience to participate in choice and makes receivers potential transmitters. *See* Peter Jukes, *The Work of Art*, STATESMAN AND SOC'Y, July 1992, at 40.

115 *Id.*

talk show. Such responses may not, however, become part of the original message. Interactivity allows a convergence of the message with the adjustments made by the receiver/user. Thus, the ability to change the original message is empowering for individuals. It opens up actual ways for individuals to resist a message, redefine it, or create a mutual message. In this sense interactivity facilitates dialogue and participation.

Interactivity mitigates the need for professional training in order to participate in social dialogue. It allows amateurs to participate in creating works. Use of computers as artistic tools replaces some of the labor involved in the creation process and may expand the range of participants in creative activities. Computer music, for instance, allows people to compose music regardless of their proficiency in playing musical instruments.[116] Sound may be generated digitally or may be processed from pre-existing recordings of instruments through sampling. Interactive music composition lets users compose their own music out of pre-constructed parts, re-mix or re-arrange a composition, control the tempo and mood of the composition, or play as one of the band's members.[117] Other interactive systems introduce users to the process of writing music,[118] or offer an interactive experience which combines music art and games. Interactive systems break the link between instrument-playing techniques and sound creation, and change the roles and the significance of the traditional participants in the creation process. If technical skills are no longer necessary, then more people may be able to express themselves through computer assisted creation.[119]

Interactivity may transform the very meaning of authorship. Authors may focus increasingly on facilitating creativity of others, rather than devoting themselves to the generation of fixed and completed works. From a political perspective, the overall effect of interactivity is to empower individuals to take an active role when experiencing works of others. It creates opportunities for more individuals to express themselves and may democratize social

116 *No World Order*, is a system by Todd Rundgren, which runs on CD-I and Macintosh systems, and contains a database of more than 1500 musical segments and phrases from which users may create their own composition. *See* Fred Davis, *I Want My (Desktop) MTV!*, WIRED, July 1993, at 86.

117 *Id.* at 85.

118 See for instance Peter Gabriel's *Explora* CD-ROM, which is an interactive tour of the process of creating music. Gabriel's aspiration is to empower his audience. "I hope this technology will empower people who have a sense that they have as much right and ability for self-expression as anyone who goes under the officially approved category [of artist]." *Id.* at 84.

119 *See* RAYMOND KURZWEIL, THE AGE OF INTELLIGENT MACHINES 368 (1990).

relations.[120]

b. Cut and Paste

Another aspect of digitization with the potential to expand the circle of creators is the capability of cut and paste. Creators in digital environments are gradually more occupied with processing signals, making decisions about selection and organization, and using computerized commands. Authorship in digital media involves processing fragmented works as building blocks. It takes the form of creating a meaningful text by selecting specific blocks of text, linking them and revising them. Reconstructing blocks of text redefines boundaries and provides a new meaning.

Consider, for instance, "Digital Sampling." Once an analog sound wave is converted into a digital code it may be reused, manipulated or combined with other digitized or recorded sounds using digital data processors.[121] Recording engineers can mix snippets of music from various sources. As in music, designers can incorporate actual shapes and textures, capture them on video or photograph, and then convert them to a digitized form. Such images may then be manipulated or combined with other pictures and images to create new computer-collages. The same cut and paste process is applicable for texts which incorporate preexisting texts. The challenge for the artist, however, remains the same—to create a meaningful text. The musician, for instance, must still choose the right timbres and melodies to express her musical ideas.[122]

The fact that cut and paste techniques occupy a large chunk of the creation process is significant for several reasons. If the essence of creation becomes the processing of signals and preexisting texts, then those become the building blocks of the creation process.

---

120 *See* Brenda Laural, *Immersive Technology*, WIRED, Dec. 1993, at 107 ("In the world of immersion, authorship is no longer the transmission of experience, but rather the construction of utterly personal experiences."). For further discussion of the effect of digitization on transforming the notion of authorship, see Niva Elkin-Koren, *Copyright Law and Social Dialogue on the Information Superhighway: The Case Against Copyright Liability of Bulletin Board Operators*, 13 CARDOZO ARTS & ENT. L.J. 345, 390-99 (1995).

121 *See* Judith Greenberg Finell, *How a Musicologist Views Digital Sampling Issues*, N.Y.L.J., May 22, 1992, at 5.

122 *See* KURZWEIL, *supra* note 119, at 355. The shift in the focus of the creation process to manipulation of signals is demonstrated not only by the use of the "cut" and "paste" commands, but also by new techniques used in computerized images. Drawings may be created by defining rules and providing information to a program. *See* Randall Davis, *Intellectual Property and Software: The Assumptions are Broken*, *in* WORLD INTELLECTUAL PROPERTY ORGANIZATION, WORLDWIDE SYMPOSIUM ON THE INTELLECTUAL PROPERTY ASPECTS OF ARTIFICIAL INTELLIGENCE (1991).

Identifying which are the building blocks of the creation process is significant for property rights. Building blocks are the resources of writers for further creation. Allowing one to exercise control over building blocks, and depriving everyone else of this resource, may inappropriately restrict creation.[123] The distinction between ideas and expressions draws the line between what is a resource for further creation and is, therefore, excluded from the reach of property right, and what is to be considered the final product of a creation process (expression) and is, therefore, an appropriate object of property rights. It is arguable, therefore, that the rules that allow property rights to reside in expressions may require adjustment.

c. Customizing the Creation Process[124]

Digitization allows works to be made according to individual needs or personal specifications. Two aspects of digital technology facilitate this transition: the availability of two-way communication, and the ease of manipulating digitized works.[125] The existence of a two-way channel between producers and users allows information about individual preferences and interests to be communicated and gathered more efficiently.[126] Consequently, users are increasingly involved in determining what they wish to watch, read, or otherwise consume.[127] The manipulability of digitized media al-

---

123 *See supra* notes 86 & 100 and accompanying text.

124 "Customization" is relevant both for the creation and the dissemination of works. The difficulty of classifying customization as either an aspect of creation or as an aspect of dissemination, reflects the difficulty of applying our concepts to digital environment. In a digital world the two activities—creation and dissemination—converge. Dissemination is concerned with communicating works to potential recipients. Yet, if works are customized then distribution no longer involves duplicating an identical work, but instead, distributing individualized works. Customization also means that works are being created while distributed, and not before—as used to be the case.

125 The shift to customized products also occurs in manufacturing. Manufacturing shifts from mass production to the manufacturing of tailored-based products. *See* ITHIEL DE SOLA POOL, *supra* note 101, at 12, 251. Computerization allows flexibility in the production process, and the ability to constantly gather information regarding the consumer's changing needs. Computer aided design allows much more flexibility in the design process by enabling rapid changes, and by allowing designers to try a large number of models. Computerized systems that control the manufacturing process allow the adjustment of the assembly lines to respond to consumers' individualized demands. Consequently, assembly lines are able to produce based on individual orders rather than on speculations over future demand. This saves storage costs and makes production more efficient. On the other hand, it increases transaction costs of gathering information regarding the interests and desires of potential consumers. For the effect of computer technology on the production process see SHOSHANA ZUBOFF, IN THE AGE OF THE SMART MACHINE: THE FUTURE OF WORK AND POWER (1988).

126 ITHIEL DE SOLA POOL, *supra* note 101, at 10.

127 For example *First!* is a customized newspaper published by Individual, Inc. of Cambridge, Massachusetts. Individuals' software automatically generates a daily individualized newspaper filtered and compiled from the daily newspapers and news services, according

lows producers to attune to individuals' preferences.[128] Users may add their input and shape a digitized work to meet their individual preferences in a cost effective way. The passiveness of consuming mass products is replaced by constructing individualized experiences.[129] Consequently, works increasingly exist in multiple individualized versions.[130] Producing artistic works used to involve the creation of a single prototype ("the work"), and the subsequent duplication[131] of the work in copies.[132] Walter Benjamin perceived the trend towards reproduction of works of art as having a liberating effect on society. Benjamin saw the democratic potential of mass production in eroding the possessive fetishism of the art object, allowing works of art to become more accessible. Digitization may shift the focus of production from duplicating multiple *reproductions* of a work, to creating *personalized* or *customized* works. The process of creation may thus shift from mass duplication of a single prototype to the creation of tailored-made works.[133] This may further advance the democratizing trends observed by Benjamin. While mass duplication of works provided individuals with an unlimited access to works of art, digitization provides them with the power to act upon works. By allowing customization, digitization enables individuals to incorporate their personal expression into the cultural products they consume.

Customization and interactivity modify the market in which the process of creation takes place. Mass consumption is gradually being replaced by customized consumption. The value of works rests in the works' ability to adjust to the specific preferences of

---

to the subscriber's profile. The customized newspaper is delivered to subscribers by fax or by e-mail. *See* Kathleen K. Wiegner, *All the News that Fits*, FORBES, Apr. 30, 1990, at 174-75.

128 Digitized newspapers, for instance, allow users to define their interests, and compile for each customer an individualized newspaper which consists of only the news that falls within the scope of the client's interest. Pool discusses the transformation of the mass media—"[I]nstead of identical messages being disseminated to millions of people, electronic technology permits the adaptation of electronic messages to the specialized or unique needs of individuals." ITHIEL DE SOLA POOL, *supra* note 101, at 8.

129 As described by one writer, "on our own again, after the long mediation of top-down authored experience, of broadcast culture and mass produced objects of desire." Brenda Laurel, *Immersive Technology*, WIRED, Dec. 1993, at 107.

130 ITHIEL DE SOLA POOL, *supra* note 101, at 10.

131 Duplication may take the form of a limited edition such as in the case of lithographs, or the form of mass reproduction such as printed books.

132 *See* Walter Benjamin, *The Work of Art in the Age of Mechanical Reproduction*, *in* ILLUMINATIONS (Hannah Arendt ed., Schocken Books 1969) (1936).

133 Pool discusses an example of computer-controlled composition that allowed newspapers to appear in local and specialized editions which contained different ideas and features. *See* ITHIEL DE SOLA POOL, *supra* note 101, at 12. For further discussion of the potential social impact of customization and the way it may be inhibited by copyright law, see *infra* notes 263-77 and accompanying text.

users.[134] Consequently, the creation process is gradually aiming at creating works that may be customized; in other words, works that may be individualized according to the choices and preferences of the users.[135]

The ability to customize works permits more individuals to incorporate their input into cultural products. Even where there is minimal ability to customize works, it may still empower individuals by providing them with choices. The individual's ability to choose one's cultural experiences allows individual expression through the consumption of commodities that are adapted to meet one's own agenda.[136] This, in turn, promotes diversity and individuality by voicing individuals' choices. The ability of individuals to choose their cultural experiences is crucial for participation, since it is the very process of choosing and adapting a work to one's own meaning which defines social dialogue. In other words, participation requires individuals to recognize themselves and their aspirations in the range of representations offered within the central communication sectors, and to contribute to the development of these sectors.[137] To the extent that users contribute their input into objects they consume, the power and significance of the dominant source of meaning and standards declines.[138]

Some argue that customization may weaken the sense of social experience. If people are exposed to more individualized messages, the significance of a common social experience declines. This has become a matter of concern for several scholars who point at the danger it poses for society's consolidation. The concern is

134 A customized record may allow the music to be tailored to the listener's circumstances. Individuals may be able to program their CD-I to respond to their changing needs—for instance compiling music for a dance party.

135 From an economic perspective the availability of customized works means that we may no longer talk about a single demand for copies of a single work, but about various demands for particular individualized goods. We may still, however, talk about a single demand for a work that is flexible enough to be adjusted to meet individualized needs.

136 Consider, for instance, the ability of users to customize digitized stories and change the names and gender of the characters. This may be crucial for one's ability to relate to the arts and to popular culture, as demonstrated by the controversy over banning controversial books in libraries and schools. When a book is controversial, such as *Heather Has Two Mommies* and *Daddy's Roommate* (featuring illustrations of gay couples) it can either be banned or approved by public libraries and schools. *See* Michael Granberry, *Besieged by Book Banners*, L.A. TIMES, May 10, 1993, at A1. If, however, children and parents are able to change the characters and the plot, they are more likely to find the story consistent with their family perception. The controversy over what books should be included on the New York City public schools' list of suggested bibliography for teachers, further demonstrates the significance of decentralizing dissemination of information.

137 *See* Graham Murdock, *Poverty and Political Inequality*, *in* CITIZENSHIP IN THE AGE OF PRIVATIZED COMMUNICATION: THE INFORMATION GAP 180 (Marsha Siefert et al. eds., 1989).

138 It has been argued that digital technology encompasses more choices than one can or wishes to handle. Note also that some people may resent choice, or may wish to have less choice. *See* Davis, *supra* note 116.

that in the absence of a common cultural experience, social dialogue will weaken.[139] This critique assumes that it is necessary in social dialogue for all members of the community to have a shared set of concerns. It overlooks the possibility of establishing a dispersed social dialogue in a vast of overlapping discourses.

B. *Expanding Access to Social Dialogue*

The transformative power of digital dissemination methods[140] may be clarified when contrasted with previous distribution technologies, namely, the printing press and electronic communication.[141] The printing press, which began with Gutenberg's metal typeface system over 550 years ago, allows delivery of a permanent version of a work in multiple copies over distance. It was heavily based on the idea that once a work was created, many copies could be reproduced on paper and distributed to the public. Digital technology differs from the printing press by shifting the focus of dissemination from the distribution of copies to access.

Electronic communication, which emerged during the twentieth century, expanded the distribution potential of print. It introduced the capacity of massive diffusion of information, using electric currents by radio and television broadcasting.[142] Digital communication combines electronic communication with digital technology. It departs from electronic communication by introducing two new features. First, it allows all forms of electronic communication to be transmitted through a single channel. Second, it permits the logical manipulation of the message.[143] Conse-

---

139 *See* Ithiel de Sola Pool, *supra* note 101.

140 Computer networks connect computer work stations through cables that carry digital signals. Networks differ from one another in their distribution structures. Computer conferences allow contributions of participants to be communicated to other participants. Systems differ from one another in their restrictions on participants—some are open to all, and some are exclusive to selective subscribers; they may involve various degrees of editing of the content; and they may be centralized, distributing all materials to and from a single center, or wide-spread, allowing redistributing materials among subscribers. For the most part they allow direct communication among computer users, and remote access to files and data bases.

141 Information may be distributed digitally on a physical medium that records it, such as a diskette or a CD-ROM. This method of distribution resembles distribution in a non-digitized environment. It differs, however, from traditional distribution methods in the sense that it allows all types of text to be represented on the same media. Written texts, sounds and images are homogenized into a single digitized form, allowing the creation and distribution of mixtures of formats that used to be represented by different symbols and on different types of media.

142 Electronic communication began in the twentieth century, although its roots can be traced back to the late eighteenth century with the invention of the telegraph by Samuel Morse in 1844. *See* Ithiel de Sola Pool, *supra* note 101, at 8-9.

143 A message in a digitized form may be manipulated and transformed while being transmitted. This elasticity of representation reverses the effect of the mass media revolu-

quently, the processes of creation and distribution are merged into a single process.

1. Dissemination by Access

Several services on the digital networks, such as e-mail and file transfer, allow users to distribute copies of works to single or multiple recipients.[144] Yet, although transferring files or sending messages by e-mail resembles distribution of copies, the two distribution methods differ substantially. Digitization undermines the very notion of a "copy." A "copy" reflects a distinction between a medium, such as a book or a record, and content, such as text or music. Whereas printed text is embodied on paper or another object, digitized text may be delivered through the network without any physical medium. Digitized copies of a work are electronic versions of the primary version that resides in the computer's memory.[145] The dematerialization of the medium allows the distribution of information in its abstract. Publishing is gradually becoming a matter of providing users with access to information in an abstract form, rather than distributing physical copies.[146]

The shift from physical distribution of copies to furnishing access has several implications for power relations. First, it decreases the significance of distance as a barrier to communication.[147] Whereas distribution costs in print (such as the costs of shipping or

---

tion. Instead of disseminating an identical messages to millions of people, digital dissemination allows the adaptation of messages to meet individuals' needs.

144 Copies of files may be transmitted to any user of a network and also to people who are subscribers of other networks, and in some cases even to people who are only connected to a fax machine. *See, e.g.*, COMPUSERVE USERS MANUAL, QUICK START GUIDE 35 (1994).

145 Landow calls this feature "Virtual Text." *See* LANDOW, *supra* note 81, at 19:

> Since electronic text processing is a matter of manipulating computer-manipulated codes, all texts that the reader-writer encounters on the screen are virtual texts . . . all texts the reader and the writer encounter on a computer screen exist as versions created specifically for them while an electronic primary version resides in the computer's memory. One therefore works on an electronic copy until the versions converge when one commands the computer to "save" one's own version of the text by placing it in memory. At this point the text on screen and in the computer's memory briefly coincide, but the reader always encounters a virtual image of the stored text and not the original version itself; in fact, in descriptions of electronic word processing, such terms and such distinctions do not make much sense.

146 *See id.* at 23. For instance, digital networks provide remote access to large databases on mainframe computers. Information may be available to users by downloading from a bulletin board or a database. Another way of dissemination by access is by making files available on the network for the use of the general public. Anonymous FTP (File Transfer Protocol) is the posing of files for remote retrieval by the public, in a publicly accessible directory. Anyone is able to log in anonymously and retrieve the files in the public access directory.

147 ITHIEL DE SOLA POOL, *supra* note 101, at 8.

coordinating distribution) increase with distance, digital networks allow the transmission of information over distance at a very low cost. In fact, communication costs do not depend on the distance a message is going.[148] The distribution cost is primarily the costs of preparing the work for distribution and the cost of occupying the network, measured by the network's prices for connection time or volume. This may allow individuals to publish their works to multiple users in a wide range of places.

Digital communication may also effect the organization of human activity. The ability to communicate internationally may effect national boundaries by opening up communication channels across national borders. For instance, newsgroups on USENET facilitate discussion groups of general interest that range from recreational activities, arts, and social issues, to discussions of political questions.[149] The ability to exchange views and develop affiliations with other people beyond one's geographical place may change the relationship between individuals and their local communities.[150] Electronic communities may supplement affiliation on the basis of geographical boundaries (residency or workplace), with other affiliations that are based on mutual interest and deliberation, such as affiliations with professional groups, special interest groups, or groups deliberating on political issues.[151] From a political and legal perspective, the question is whether on-line communities should be recognized as independent jurisdictions and what their status should be vis-a vis traditional jurisdictions such as states and local governments.

---

[148] Digital communication has an advantage over analog communication. Digital signals depend on an on-off pattern, which is less affected by long distance transmission. Analog signals, by contrast, weaken in long distance transmission, and it is difficult to recognize their its exact frequency or amplitude. *Id.* at 21-22.

[149] *See* Ed Krol, The Whole Internet User's Guide 153 (1994).

[150] It is arguable that this characteristic is definitive of any communication method. Digital networks, it is argued, are not any different from previous modes of communication (such as television or the telephone). Digital networks allow, however, more information, of all types, to be exchanged at a lower cost. Consequently, they are likely to take over a large portion of our everyday interactions. It may replace (and enhance) communication via telephone, television and newspapers. On-line interactions may therefore become more influential over individual's ideas and identities, and crucial to an individual's sense of belonging. Therefore, the quantitative difference between digital networks and other methods of communication may become a qualitative one.

[151] Pool is discussing the impact of electronic communication on the boundaries of nations. He argues that once the distance a message is going does not alter the costs of communication, there is no reason to restrict communication to the national boundaries. Therefore he predicts that cities and nations will be transformed. *See* Ithiel de Sola Pool, *supra* note 101, at 13. Digital communication may also effect national boundaries indirectly by changing industry and production and consequently transforming the structure of national markets. For the legal implications, see David R. Johnson & David G. Post, *Law and Borders: The Rise of Law in Cyberspace*, 48 Stan L. Rev. (forthcoming 1996).

An international network that is gradually becoming a major medium of interaction also challenges the law as an institution that operates on a territorial basis. The authority of laws is usually restricted to the territorial boundaries of the sovereign. But on-line communications take place beyond these boundaries. Consequently, international arrangements would have to receive an increased emphasis. In addition, past problems dealt with domestically would have to be addressed on a multinational level.[152] The issues raised by electronic communities are not limited to questions of enforcement. The erosion of geographic boundaries in electronic communities may complicate the use of legal rules that rely on the notion of a community.[153]

Network communication allows a variety of participants to directly communicate and disseminate each others ideas.[154] Direct

---

152 For instance, cyberspace makes it very difficult, if not impossible, for governments to prevent citizens from accessing information. Laws of the sovereign are only enforceable within its jurisdiction, while cyberspace functions across national borders. Consequently, legislation of a European country that restrict access to specific information would not apply to an American citizen who wishes to post that information on her web home page, which is accessible to all. But see the controversial Communications Decency Act, passed as part of the Telecommunications Act of 1996, tit. V, §§ 501-512, Pub. L. No. 104-104, 110 Stat. 56 (1996) (to be codified at 47 U.S.C. § 223(a)-(h)) that seeks to regulate transmission of offensive materials on the Internet. Furthermore, the ability of individual users to transfer information from one state to another, without crossing any borders, may complicate the enforcement of intellectual property rights. In the absence of any of the previous bottlenecks (customs, detectable distribution mechanisms) infringements would be very difficult to detect and prevent. This would cause greater reliance on international treaties and collaborative efforts to harmonize and enforce intellectual property rights. For further discussion of the complexity of cyberspace in the context of international law, see John D. Faucher, *Let the Chips Fall Where They May: Choice of Law in Computer Bulletin Board Defamation Cases*, 26 U.C. DAVIS L. REV. 1045 (1993).

153 For instance, the standard for determining whether materials describing or depicting sexual conduct are obscene, requires that the average person, applying a contemporary community standard, would find that the work, taken as a whole, appeals to the prurient interest. *See* Miller v. California, 413 U.S. 15 (1973). In United States v. Thomas, 74 F.3d 701 (6th Cir. 1996), a California couple ran a sexually explicit BBS in San Francisco, which was accessible to users from anywhere in the United States. The couple was charged and convicted in Memphis, Tennessee, after investigators downloaded selected image files to a computer in Tennessee. What community standard should be applied to a BBS that disseminates sexually explicit materials to its subscribers? At least three community standards are applicable: one is the standard of the prosecuting community; a second is the standard of the defendant's community; and a third is the standard of the community of users, in which the materials are actually distributed. The standard of the prosecuting community, in which the offense took place, makes sense in the print environment, that involves distribution in public. What reason is there, however, to impose the prosecutor's standard on a BBS operator who disseminates materials directly to users, without serving the community as a whole? The court of appeals concluded that a new definition of "community" should not be adopted for the purpose of BBS in regard to prosecutions related to obscene materials. For an excellent analysis of these questions, see Y. BENKLER, RULES OF THE ROAD FOR THE INFORMATION SUPERHIGHWAY: ELECTRONIC MAIL AND THE LAW (forthcoming 1996).

154 From the perspective of access, network communication may allow employees to access information about their employer that was not accessible to employees at their level in the institution itself.

communication between users opens channels of communication between participants in the social dialogue. It thereby transforms hierarchical structures of communication between originators of message and facilitators of dissemination: writers and publishers, performers and broadcasters. It may also weaken the power enjoyed by central generators of information to restrict the flow of information.

Network communication also eliminates visual clues regarding the participants' status, gender, race, national origin, or disabilities.[155] It allows direct communication with the network subscribers regardless of, among other things, their position, education, economic status. One may log-in to a list or a bulletin board and communicate their messages to others. The absence of visual clues levels differences between users and reduces disparities of power. It may open new channels of communication that bypass the inhibiting effects of institutions. This allows participants of all levels to input their contributions and establish an on-line dialogue in which all contributions are equally judged according to their content.[156]

Dissemination by access, however, may also enhance the power of information providers to monitor and restrict access to information. A carrier who runs the network may control and supervise the content being transferred.[157] Furthermore, if the essence of "publishing" becomes gaining access to the network, text which is excluded from the network may be marginalized. Networking makes text easy to access, locate and connect to other resources. As a result, digitized distribution is gradually becoming the dominant distribution method. Text which would not be available on the network is likely to be avoided.[158] The power to control access to the network becomes enormous[159] and this power will depend on the users' alternatives. The more users are able to

---

155 *See* Trotter Hardy, *Electronic Conferences: The Report of an Experiment*, 6 HARV. J.L. & TECH. 213, 222 (1993) ("You cannot see what the other participants are wearing, cannot hear their accents, cannot distinguish them by race, age, national origin, or disability.").

156 It may also provide a channel for expressing complaints, or criticizing one's superiors anonymously. It may thereby create a forum in which management and employees, or government officials and citizens may communicate.

157 For the use of power to terminate access, consider the controversy between Prodigy's management and the network's users over censorship policies employed by the network. *See Sex Talk Prompts Prodigy to Shutter Bulletin Board*, CHI. TRIB., Feb. 1, 1993, at B2.

158 For instance, a law review article published in a law review that does not appear on LEXIS or Westlaw is unlikely to gain large audience. With on-line searches on LEXIS and Westlaw becoming the primary methods of legal research, the chances of finding out about an article that was published only in a hard copy are slim.

159 *See* LANDOW, supra note 81, at 188 ("[G]aining access to a network permits a text to exist *as a text* in this new information world.").

switch between on-line providers and gain access to the network in multiple ways, the weaker the power of on-line providers to control access.

2. Self-Publishing and Redistribution

The print world allowed only the wealthy, who could afford the costs of publishing a book, or those who had established themselves in the market, to become published authors. The digital environment, by contrast, makes it possible for an increasing number of people to become self-published authors. Personal computers and laser printers provide writers with personal publishing capabilities, without the specialization and capital necessary for mechanical print.[160] They allow most of the editorial and formatting activities to be performed with high quality by the authors themselves.

Digitization also allows users to easily retransmit materials. Users may use scanners to digitize photos or texts that are published in a traditional form. A digitized copy that was delivered through the network may be downloaded by the user and retransmitted. Retransmission through digitized versions is both easy and inexpensive. Everything digitized may be reproduced in seconds and at low cost. Self-publishing is also available through network communication. While only a couple of years ago it was predicted that "continuing improvements in desktop publishing and laser printing will produce a late efflorescence of the text as a physical object,"[161] it now seems that network publishing will soon replace desktop publishing.

Cyberspace integrates the generation and distribution of information. Digital networks provide direct communication between authors and potential readers.[162] An author may transmit her text directly from the work-station on which it was created without any additional processing, aside from technical adjustments of the format. In most cases those technical adjustments are made on the same computer which generated the document. Consequently,

---

160 *See* HEIM, *supra* note 100, at 219.

161 *See* LANDOW, *supra* note 81, at 23.

162 This already was anticipated by scholars in the early 1980s. *See, e.g.*, Brian Aveney, *Post Industrial Publishing*, ELECTRONIC PUBLISHING AND BOOKSELLING, Jan. 1984, at 1.

> Distribution will become largely obsolete as a separate function in publishing with the eventual disappearance of the edition-printed products of industrial model publishing. Distribution will become a computer-controlled process of downloading text or video signals to the user's personal computer memory or directly to a printer or viewer. In a reversal of current realities distribution will occur before manufacturing in the on-demand environment.

Id.

everyone with access to a computer network may become a publisher. Network distribution creates a continuum that goes from personal writing on one hand, to publication on the other, with many degrees of connectivity and access permissions in between.[163]

The significance of self-publishing is in facilitating the distribution of works in print. The printed word conveys authority and tends to be taken more seriously.[164] Written statements provide authors with more control over their works. The print provides exact duplications of works (rather than a paraphrase). Even though readers may not adapt any specific position expressed in a printed text, its permanent nature affects the discourse by formulating the questions at stake, and determining the language being used. Accordingly, the ability of an increasing number of people to express their thoughts and feelings in print is important for social and political participation.

It is arguable that since more text becomes available in print, the authority of printed text will decrease. The ability to self-publish, it is argued, would undermine the quality of texts being published.[165] Under this theory, the authority of the printed text stems from the contribution and reputation of editors. So, even though more people may be able to get their word out in print, the printed word will lose its authoritative power.

I find this elitist argument difficult to accept. First, it assumes that the individuals who in the past had exclusive access to means of publication are worthy of being heard, while others are not.[166] It also assumes that there are social agents (editors, publishers)

---

163 Heim points at the dangers of making what he calls "the psychic framework" public. *See* HEIM, *supra* note 100, at 160-64. He also recognizes, however, the potential of connectivity for collaborative interaction and a new kind of community. For a further discussion of digital dissemination and the private/public distinction in the context of copyright law, see Elkin-Koren, *supra* note 120, at 390-99.

164 *See* ITHIEL DE SOLA POOL, *supra* note 101, at 245 (noting that under the Judeo-Christian tradition, the written word is deemed scared, regarded more seriously, and considered more definitive than oral statement).

165 *See* HEIM, *supra* note 100, at 219.

> [C]omputer-mediated communication creates a psychic framework in which more text will become easily available but the text will be probably less intelligent, less carefully formulated, less thoughtful text. Computers may boost productivity, according to this criticism, only to have a greater production of written stupidity, even decreasing the likelihood of finding worthwhile material.

Id.

166 Another version of this argument is that "deliberation should be exercised by professionals (novelists, poets, ethnographers, journalists, and docudramatists), who can best express the pain and humiliation of other, unfamiliar sorts of people." RICHARD RORTY, CONTINGENCY, IRONY, AND SOLIDARITY xvi, 94 (1989). Rorty assumes that the oppressed groups cannot directly express themselves, and require others to adequately speak for them. *Id.*

that are able to determine which text is suitable for reaching the public. These assumptions are inconsistent with any concept of democracy and social dialogue. The fact that means of publication were opened only to a selective group of people in itself created disparities of power.[167] Some were able to communicate their ideas in an authoritative way, while others lacked the access and its attendant power. Making "publishing" more accessible may indeed transform the meaning of the printed word, and may weaken its authoritative power. Yet, it may also eliminate disparities of power. The hierarchical nature of dissemination will be transformed, and an increasing number of people will be able to participate in any social dialogue.

3. Intermediaries and Direct Communication

Another aspect of the shift to network distribution is the weakening role of intermediaries, such as publishers, broadcasters and distributors, in the distribution process.[168] Intermediaries currently play a central role in distributing non-digitized works because of the capital necessary to distribute works via physical media. These costs have an economy of scale, and are therefore lower if publishing is centrally executed. Intermediaries who specialize in distribution to the public are therefore necessary for disseminating information in a cost-effective way. Distribution by intermediaries centralizes social dialogue. It permits intermediaries to select the works and the messages to be published, when, and with what level of marketing support.

Distribution by intermediaries further centralizes social dialogue by making decisions about what to produce and disseminate

---

167 *See* J. David Bolter, Writing Space: The Computer in the History of Literacy 148-49 (1990). Bolter argues that the printing press created an inequality of power that was not present in previous writing practices.

> Because printing a book is a costly and laborious task, few readers have the opportunity to become published authors. An author is a person whose words are faithfully copied and sent around the literary world, whereas readers are merely the audience for those words. The distinction meant less in the age of manuscript, when "publication" was less of an event and when the reader's own notes and glosses had the same status as the text itself. Any reader could decide to cross over and become an author: one simply sat down and wrote a treatise or put one's notes in a form for others to read. Once the treatise was written, there was no difference between it and the works of other "published" writers, except that the more famous works existed in more copies.

Id.

Bolter's argument overlooks the fact that prior to Gutenberg's invention, only a limited number of individuals were able to read and write. Overall, the introduction of the printing press made writing and reading more popular and thereby initiated a major social transformation. *See* Eisenstein, *supra* note 83.

168 *See* Elkin-Koren, *supra* note 120, at 401-07.

tightly connected with economic considerations. Recovering investments by charging for copies of a work, collecting fees for its use, or selling commercials, create economic dependency. The need to guarantee success in the market increasingly dictates the content of works. Intermediaries thus tend to disseminate works that are likely to gain public approval.[169]

Network distribution may transform the information flow. The current centralized information flow of "one to many" may be replaced by a distribution pattern of "many to many." Network distribution allows direct communication among users and therefore weakens the role of intermediaries in the production and dissemination of information. It decentralizes the production of information by breaking the financial barriers to publication. By making means of expression more accessible, digitization transforms the hierarchical relations between authors and publishers.[170] By reducing dependency on commercial sponsorship, network distribution may increase diversity of information that is made available to the public.[171]

Network distribution also undermines the editorial role of publishers. Direct communication enables authors to become publishers. Consequently, authors are free from having to negotiate the content of a work before publishing.[172] Publishers and broadcasters in the non-digital environment currently play a dual role: selecting or screening information, and making it available to the public. Publishers of professional journals, for instance, provide editorial services such as selection and review, that are linked to their reputation. Potential readers would regularly read a publication of their choice, and would receive the editor's selection. From

---

169 Publishers prefer products that may increase their potential markets. Advertisers encourage producers to create and disseminate content that would increase the media's potential reach. *See* EDWIN C. BAKER, ADVERTISING AND A DEMOCRATIC PRESS 62-66 (1994). For further discussion, see *infra* notes 200-07 and accompanying text.

170 Even if network distribution ends up being merely a supplementary method of distribution, rather than fully replacing print, it may still have a liberating effect on the flow of information. The availability of videodiscs or CD-ROMs, for instance, opened up dissemination channels for photographers as an alternative to major magazines and books.

171 Furthermore, the fact that more raw, unfiltered sources of information would reach people, is an advantage not only from the perspective of democracy and participation. Kapor argues that "noise is just the price we pay for signal. In fact, without junk, there is less of a chance for real quality to emerge. Let the marketplace of ideas rule." *See* Mitchell Kapor, *Where Is the Digital Highway Really Heading? The Case for a Jeffersonian Information Policy*, WIRED, Jul./Aug. 1993, at 53, 94.

172 *See* HEIM, *supra* note 100, at 219.

> The individual with a laser printer can create virtually typeset manuscripts, with the user controlling more of the final product. Self-publishing in this sense is more direct: no editor intervenes; the author has hands on the final look and wording of documents without having to answer to copy editors.

Id.

the author's perspective, the publisher's reputation would determine the chances of reaching a large audience.

In cyberspace, however, intermediaries are no longer necessary for providing access to information.[173] First, digital dissemination disintegrates journals, books, or other publications as stand alone, independent products. Once on-line, articles become part of a pile of text.[174] Also, there is no longer any compelling reason for publishing a single copy of a journal.[175] A journal may be transformed into a series of articles delivered to the subscribers upon completion.[176] Second, due to the nonlinear nature of digital representation, users are able to directly access specific articles or excerpts that interest them. Users have direct and immediate access to the entire database and may make their selection by using technical devices.[177] Consequently, the authority of the publisher and the significance of its reputation decline. The development of powerful browsers that facilitate access to information in a nonstructured way, further weakens the role of intermediaries.[178] Other technological efforts are made in the direction of developing electronic agents, which would allow users to define a general interest or a specific question, and execute searches on their behalf.[179]

---

173 When publishers are not only selectors but also providers, one cannot access the information unless one purchases the book, journal, or a particular channel on cable television. In digital networks, one may use a screening agent to gather the information, or access it directly using retrieval programs.

174 Take the context of legal publications as an example. In a print world it was likely that an article published in the *Harvard Law Review* would reach a larger audience than an article that was published in a nameless publication. *Harvard Law Review*'s reputation increased the likelihood that libraries would carry it, students and scholars would browse through it, and authors would refer to it.

175 Journals serve the economic necessities created by print technology in that they organize several articles to be distributed together and thereby reduce the distribution cost. The economic circumstances of cyberspace render the continued value of journals unclear.

176 *See* Jacques Leslie, *Good-bye, Gutenberg, Pixelating Peer Review is Revolutionizing Scholarly Journals*, WIRED, Oct. 1994, at 68-71.

177 In a world of computer legal research services (LEXIS and Westlaw), it has become crucial to be on-line. The hard copy of a publication becomes less significant.

178 Internet browsers are becoming more user-friendly and allow users to easily access on-line information. One example is the World Wide Web ("WWW"), which is a hypertext based system for finding and accessing Internet resources. The WWW defines a standard for data which allows users to turn almost any document (text, image, sound, video) into hypertext. The WWW is supported by several browsers that allow users to move between documents. *See* KROL, *supra* note 149, at 515. Mosaic, for instance, is a computer program with a graphical user-friendly interface, that retrieves and interprets documents on the WWW and allows users to navigate through on-line information. Gary Wolf, *The (Second Phase of the) Revolution Has Begun*, WIRED, Oct. 1994, at 116.

179 For example, a program allowing individualized news research already exists. *See* Wiegner, *supra* note 127. The idea of electronic agents also begins to be implemented in the context of commercial on-line transactions. *See* David Kline, *I Want Marc Porat and His Agents of Change*, WIRED, Jan. 1995, at 108.

Digital networks introduce, however, a new type of intermediaries, namely, the network itself. Every network has its own policy on the type of services that are permitted. Distribution of some materials may be restricted.[180] The question is whether author-network relationships are different from author-publisher relationships. It seems that publishers would be more involved in the content of a work, while network operators would merely transmit the information. In the past, communication companies merely carried signals and did not generate information.[181] Yet, digitization is modifying the role of the carriers. Digitization allows carriers to effect the content they deliver and blurs the distinctions between carriers and publishers. To the extent the networks function like publishers, they enjoy more power over users than publishers in a non-digitized world.

4. Accessibility of Information

Accessibility of information introduces another context in which digitization effects participation in social dialogue.[182] At the most obvious level, participation requires community access to information necessary to establish views about political issues, and the means to pursue rights effectively. Accordingly, it is necessary that communities have access to diverse information and debates[183] which are in the public interest. At another level, the accessible information affects self-perception and views about the world, defines the horizon of expectations and determines the per-

---

180 For instance, Bitnet's policies were revised in November 1990 to permit fee-based services in support of academic research. *See generally* KROL, *supra* note 149, at 35-47, 495-96.

181 The distinction between information carriers and information generators is significant in determining the appropriate level of government control over the operation of communication companies. Under the traditional paradigm of government intervention in communication activities, the more involved networks get in the content they transmit, the less they are allowed to maintain a monopoly and restrict First Amendment rights. Yet, as producers of content communication, companies are less regulated and the government has limited power to monitor their operation and restrict their First Amendment rights.

182 The market approach to communication and information products addresses people primarily through their identity as consumers, both from the information products they consume and from the products promoted in the expanded advertising system that finances some communicative services. This marginalizes or displaces other identities, particularly the identity of citizen. *See* Graham Murdock & Peter Golding, *Information Poverty and Political Inequality: Citizenship in the Age of Privatized Communication, in* THE INFORMATION GAP: HOW COMPUTERS AND OTHER NEW COMMUNICATION TECHNOLOGIES AFFECT THE SOCIAL DISTRIBUTION OF POWER 180 (Marsha Siefert et al. eds., 1990).

183 Lasch argues that democracy depends on public debate and not on information, and therefore concludes that the press should provide access to political debates, and should not pretend to report facts objectively. *See* Christopher Lasch, *Journalism, Publicity and the Lost Art of Argument*, GANNETT CTR. J., Spring 1990, at 1.

ceived choices.[184] Accessibility of information also affects the relative power of participants in social dialogue. The ability of people to access information translates into power.

Accessibility may be measured by the number of people for which information becomes accessible, the type of information that becomes accessible—in terms of volume and content, and the quality of access.[185] Digitization has the potential to enhance access in all three respects. More access to information expands opportunities for participation in social and political life.[186]

Distribution in a digitized form makes information more accessible by allowing more information to be distributed to more

---

184 One's information about what is available (such as job opportunities or medical care) would determine what she perceives to be her options. For instance, pregnant women whose physicians fail to provide them with information about abortions may not consider abortion as an option. At another level, internalizing information that is available determines what individuals perceive as their choices. Consider, for instance, access to information about the law. The law may be perceived as a mechanism for regulating behavior by communicating to people information about what is expected, what is forbidden, and what are the consequences of taking a certain course of action. *See* Marc Galanter, *The Legal Malaise; Or, Justice Observed*, 19 LAW & SOC'Y REV. 537, 545 (1985). Galanter argues that the law should be perceived as information transfer, rather then the exercise of force.

> For example, when we speak of deterrence, we are talking about the effect of information about what the law is and how it is administered. Similarly, when we describe "bargaining in the shadow of the law," we refer to regulation accomplished by the flow of information rather than directly by authoritative decision. Again, "legal socialization" is accomplished by the transmission of information. In a vast number of instances the application of law is, so to speak, self administered—people regulate their conduct (and judge the conduct of others) on the basis of their knowledge about legal standards, possibilities and constraints.

Id.

185 Quality of access looks at the way people are able to approach information: Are they able to choose what information they wish to see? Are they able to affect the information to which they are exposed? The special characteristics of digital media that affect quality of access were demonstrated in the previous discussion of interactivity and customization.

186 Accessibility of information was recently recognized by Congress as a goal to be achieved under the National Information Infrastructure Act of 1993. Congress found that high-performance computing and high-speed networks have become powerful tools for, among other things, the "mak[ing] a wide array of information available for a variety of applications." NATIONAL INFORMATION INFRASTRUCTURE ACT OF 1993, H.R. DOC. NO. 1757, 103d Cong., 1st Sess. § 2(1) (1993). The finding focused on the potential empowerment of underprivileged groups such as people with disabilities. Thus, the status refers to the ability of networks "to expand opportunities for participation for Americans who have disabilities and to improve equality of opportunity, full participation, independent living, and economic self-sufficiency for Americans with disabilities." *Id.* § 2(4). This reference to disabled people is typical of the language often used to introduce new technologies. It is interesting that those applications become the focus of the discussion of new technologies. One plausible explanation may be an attempt to shift attention from other social implications that may be more controversial (for example, class issues). *See* High-Performance Computing Act, Pub. L. No. 102-194, 105 Stat. 1594 (1991), which discusses the relationship between technology and accessibility and participation. Both laws also emphasize the need to develop means of protection for copyright in the digital environment. The question discussed in this Article is whether the digitized environment requires some changes in the property schemes—not merely an adjustment of the administration of rights but an adjustment of the rights themselves.

people at less costs. One reason is that digitized reproduction is less expensive then mechanical reproduction.[187] Furthermore, digitized reproduction does not cause any decrease in quality.[188] Copies are identical to the original, and there is no generational loss.[189]

Network distribution reduces the cost of disseminating information because digitized information is communicated in its abstract. From an economic perspective, information, whether digitized or not, is considered a public good.[190] Its use by one person does not diminish its usefulness to another. A book, for instance, once written, can never be used up. It may be read and reproduced over and over again without ever exhausting it or depriving anyone else of its use. Since additional use does not reduce the utility to other users,[191] the marginal cost of any additional use is zero. Consequently, transferring information carries a very low marginal cost.[192] Scarcity, however, does apply to the tangible in-

---

187 In text, for instance, it would be less expensive to copy one thousand pages onto a disk than to print or reproduce it on paper. There is also no need for special equipment. The same computer that was used to generate the text may be used in its reproduction.

188 Digital audio tapes ("DAT"), for instance, allow consumers to make copies of an audio CD-ROM, preserving its original characteristics. Stephen E. Arnold, *Storage Technology: A Review of Options and Their Implications for Electronic Publishing*, ON-LINE INC., July 1991, at 39.

189 Data is represented in unit pulses rather than continuous variation of some characteristics of the flow. Data transmitted digitally will therefore be identical to both the sender and the receiver, even though it may have been manipulated during the digital transmission or in the process of receiving it (saving it, for instance, in the computer's memory). This characteristic provides optimal conditions for delivering and processing digital signals under changing circumstances.

190 A public good has two distinguishing characteristics. One is non-excludability, namely, the difficulty of excluding non-payers. Given a good for which the marginal cost of exclusion is greater than the marginal cost of provision, it is inefficient to expend resources to exclude non-purchasers. The second characteristic is non-rivalrous competition, namely, that any use of the good does not reduce the supply of the good available to others. One person's consumption of a good does not diminish another person's consumption of the same good. Non-excludability facilitates "free-riding," and consequently makes it difficult to recapture the investment on the creation of the good. This reduces the supply of information below the optimal level or inhibits the extent to which it is shared. *See* William M. Landes & Richard A. Posner, *An Economic Analysis of Copyright Law*, 18 J. LEGAL STUD. 325 (1989).

191 Moreover, the use of information by additional users may increase the utility to others due to the existence of network externalities. Network externalities exist in markets of products for which the utility or satisfaction that a consumer derives from the product increases with the increase in the number of other consumers of the product. For instance, increased use of operating systems for computers facilitates the interchangeability of data and programs among the machines of different manufacturers and allows the user to combine equipment of different suppliers. It may also lower the search costs of finding a compatible application program that runs on their operating system and reduces the costs from adapting and learning a new system. *See* Peter S. Menell, *An Analysis of the Scope of Copyright Protection for Application Programs*, 41 STAN. L. REV. 1045 (1989); *see also* Brock, *Competition, Standard and Self-Regulation in the Computer Industry*, *in* REGULATING THE PRODUCT: QUALITY AND VARIETY 75 (R. Caves & M. Roberts eds., 1975).

192 This is also true for maintaining and upgrading information. Updating software, for

corporation of information. If one holds a book, for instance, she may deprive everyone else of reading that copy of the book.[193] Since digitized information is represented abstractly, it is no longer governed by scarcity. Consequently, providing access to digitized information is less costly than doing so for printed information.[194] Furthermore, when a message is communicated through the network, "the 'sender' doesn't lose the message—he retains it, either in memory, or even as a duplicated copy. The two people then both have it—shared."[195] This may open up an opportunity for a more cooperative environment in which information can be shared, and may make intellectual products more accessible to users.[196] Another feature of network distribution that reduces dissemination costs is narrowcast, namely, selective, rather than broad, transmission of works. This allows publishers to disseminate works only to interested subscribers, rather than spending resources on covering the whole market.[197]

Reducing distribution costs affects access to information in several ways. Obviously, it allows more volume to be disseminated at the same cost.[198] This allows more information to be accessible without decreasing the level of compensation for authors. When

---

instance, used to involve distributing diskettes. Now, however, users may update their software on the Internet by logging onto a server and following simple instructions. Maintenance may be done automatically by a server that informs all users of a bug and installs a repair program. Avoiding the high cost of distributing diskettes permits more frequent updates at a lower price.

193 Tangible goods are scarce and only may be used by a single social agent at a time. If one is working land, for instance, she deprives everyone else from doing so at the same time. This loss to others represents the social cost of her working the land.

194 Note that furnishing access still carries some cost of transmission through the network.

195 *See* CHERRY, *supra* note 112, at 43. For that reason Cherry argues that messages can never be exchanged but only shared. Yet, this feature of digital communication is perceived as the main threat to intellectual property laws. *See infra* notes 240-41 and accompanying text.

196 Digital technology is often described as technology that promotes collaboration. It transforms authorship from an individualistic undertaking into a process of sharing and interacting with others. *See* PAMELA MCCORDUCK, THE UNIVERSAL MACHINE: CONFESSION OF A TECHNOLOGICAL OPTIMIST 65 (1985) ("One salient fact of computing, and one of the most important world-wide effects of computing might be computing's introduction of a new ethos of cooperation.").

197 Although narrowcasting may reduce the costs of disseminating information, it also reduces the potential market of any given work. Broadcasting exposes all consumers to all works, and thus allows consumers to expand and modify their interests. Narrowcasting, by contrast, requires users to define their interests in advance and be exposed to specific types of materials. This creates a new intellectual environment.

198 The question of who is going to benefit from this cost reduction is a distributive question and is affected by social and legal arrangements. It is possible that publishers will grab the surplus by charging the same for works disseminated over the network, depriving users of the cost savings. The surplus may be used to reduce prices for works and consequently for distributing information to more people. However, the surplus may be used to provide the same circle of users with more information.

communication is inexpensive, information may be accessible to a larger number of users at distant places.[199] Furthermore, digital networks may allow equal access to information regardless of one's area of residence.

But the reduction in distribution costs is also significant to access in a less obvious way. It may contribute to the diversity of content being produced and communicated. As noted earlier, the large financial investment involved in distribution mechanisms affects decisions about which works are distributed. Consequently, publishers and broadcasters tend to disseminate information that they believe adheres to the public taste.

The expenses involved in creating and distributing works are often paid by advertisers. Advertisers play a central role in creation and distribution of works through the mass media. The market structure of advertising by the media is fairly simple. Advertisers seek to capture maximum consumer attention to their products and are therefore willing to pay the costs of creating and distributing works which could captivate consumers' attention.[200] The mass media is therefore often described as an industry that sells audiences to advertisers.

Advertising affects social dialogue via the media both directly, through advertisements, and indirectly, by shaping the content created and distributed by the mass media. Advertisements constitute a large portion of the content that is delivered by the media,[201] and this content creates a symbolic structure that not only affects our consumption habits, but also shapes our sense of values[202] and concept of the world. In addition, advertising affects the content created and disseminated by the mass media in a way that is more relevant to the current discussion. It encourages producers to create and disseminate content that would induce a buying mood among readers and viewers,[203] increase the media's potential reach

---

199 *See* ITHIEL DE SOLA POOL, *supra* note 101, at 260 (asserting the democratic power of network communication).

200 While radio and television sponsorship by advertisers constitutes the main income of the networks, the economics of newspapers is slightly different. Here, consumers are also charged a price for the newspaper, though lower than the actual cost of producing it. *See* BAKER, *supra* note 169, at 62-66.

201 Baker cites studies that show that advertisements constitute about sixty-five percent of newspaper space and twenty-two percent of television time. *Id.* at 45.

202 *Id.*

203 *Id.* at 62-66. Baker describes the way advertisers encourage the creation of light, noncontroversial, and simple content that they believe makes the audience responsive to their commercial messages. He concludes that:

> [t]o the extent that the media respond to advertisers' concern with program packaging, they are guided by neither what the viewers want nor what media professional think the public needs. Instead, advertisers pay the media to pro-

by reducing partisanship, and select content that is particularly targeted towards higher-income audiences.[204] The effect of the advertising industry on the media may be the most cynical way in which power accumulated in the market is being used in the public sphere. What is often described as a "free market of ideas" is in fact vulnerable to manipulation by corporations which use their financial power to affect social dialogue. It is often argued that advertising increases access to information by reducing the price of information to users (such as by subsidizing the price of newspapers) or diminishing it altogether (such as in the case of radio and television). Advertisers are thus said to have a democratizing effect on social dialogue by making information available for larger portions of the population. However, advertising is often aimed at the wealthier segments of the population, and may therefore further marginalize the poor.[205]

Cyberspace transforms the role of advertisers in the dissemination of information. Commercial sponsorship may no longer be necessary in network distribution, where subscribers may be charged directly and individually for their specific uses. The reduced costs would allow more individuals to avoid subsidy by advertisers.[206] Reduction in distribution costs may also free dissemination from commercial sponsorship and consequently may increase diversity and promote individualism.[207]

However, digitization may also inhibit access to information and may cause disparities in accessibility of information to individuals that do not exist in print. To some extent, what seems to be a reduction of the distribution cost is only a reallocation of that cost by transferring it from publishers to end-users. The availability of digitized information to users depends on access to equipment.

> vide content the advertisers believes will leave the audience emotionally and intellectually most vulnerable to commercial messages.

Id. at 63.

204 *Id.* at 44.

205 *Id.* at 66.

206 Yet, the reason for advertising sponsorship is not only the failure to collect fees, but also an attempt to lower the price paid for the information. Newspapers, for instance, are subsidized by advertisements, and thus advertisers and consumers share the costs of publishing. Nevertheless, it has been suggested that advertising in its current form may no longer exist in the digital world, since interactive television will allow individuals to filter out commercials. Consequently, it is argued, advertisers will have to pay viewers to watch their advertisements. This also shifts power between advertisers and viewers. For a discussion of the future of advertising in the digital era, see Michael Schrage, *Is Advertising Dead?*, WIRED, Feb. 1994, at 71.

207 It has been argued that such diversity may facilitate the growth of specialized intellectual subcultures, and thereby may divide society and endanger the sense of social cohesion. This notion of social cohesion is based on common themes of interests and attention. *See* ITHIEL DE SOLA POOL, *supra* note 101, at 261.

Digitized access to information requires some use of a computer, a modem, a telephone or a data line, special software, storage capacity, processing power, graphics capabilities, and so on. The costs of publication through the network therefore shift to the end-users in that they must pay for communication equipment. Ownership, or other opportunity to use even basic end-user equipment, such as a telephone, a computer, or a VCR, is extremely limited among lower income groups.[208] Consequently, many people that were unprivileged by the current system would not be able to improve their opportunities via digital technology.

Furthermore, the dependency on end-users' equipment creates disparities between individuals. Initial purchasing power not only allows access to information, but also determines the type of services available on the network to users. If, for instance, a computer program is placed in a FTP for remote retrieval, the ability of a user to download the file would depend on the storage capacity and processing capabilities of her computer. Furthermore, end-users' equipment may create a large disparity between users' abilities to utilize the network. For instance, a user working on an on-line service with a 28,000 bps modem is likely to be able to download more information for less money than a user who is working with a 14,400 modem.[209] The effectiveness and efficiency of end-users' equipment would, in turn, increase relative to its cost.

Consequently, it is arguable that digital distribution may increase socioeconomic inequalities in society. Murdock discusses the relationship between market based communication technologies and inequality. He argues that "[w]henever access to the communications and information resources required for full citizenship depends upon purchasing power (as expressed directly through customer payments or indirectly through the unequal distribution of advertising subsidies to production), substantial inequalities are generated that undermine the nominal universality of citizenship."[210]

The fact that access to information increasingly depends on end-users' equipment inhibits accessibility of information in a digitized world in a way that print technology does not. However, end-users' equipment continually becomes cheaper and more available. There has been a dramatic change in the availability of this digital

---

208 *See* Murdock, *supra* note 137, at 190.

209 This depends on the pricing method used by the network, which may vary from charging for on-line time, volume, services, or any combination of those factors.

210 Murdock, *supra* note 137, at 184. On the relationship between citizenship and disparities of power among citizens, see *supra* note 64 and accompanying text.

technology in the past several years.[211] Besides, even the simplest equipment performs the basic functions of reproduction and redistribution of information. Furthermore, the quality of access changes—digital access allows users to actively participate in choosing and formulating the information they receive. It therefore seems that the overall effect of digitization is to enhance access to information, and it is the responsibility of the law to outweigh the inhibiting affects it may have on accessibility.

Networking may provide publishers with more control over the usage of disseminated works. When one acquires a book, for instance, one is entitled to use the information it contains as she pleases, subject, of course, to some general restrictions, such as copyrights. On the other hand, on-line access to information may be restricted at any point. Whereas acquiring a book is a one time purchase that provides the purchaser with a perpetual license to use,[212] accessing information on-line requires an on-going relationship between users and publishers. This may strengthen the power that publishers exercise over users.[213] While, in the print world, the expiration of a contractual relationship would effect the supply of future information, it would have left the information already supplied intact. Terminating a contractual relationship with an on-line provider may deny users any access to information altogether.[214]

The weakening power of users is also apparent in the changing nature of libraries. Libraries are public depositories of information that provide the public with relatively free access to that

---

211 This is due to several reasons. First, the dramatic change in price and performance made computers more affordable. Second, computers are physically more accessible since they became more mobile and connected through communication lines. *See* John Sculley, *Computer Communications and Content*, CCI, 1992, at 15.

212 The purchaser acquires property rights in the copy of the work. These rights are protected notwithstanding the copyright in the book itself. Thus, under the first sale doctrine, copyright owners may not prevent any disposition of a book sold to a consumer. For further discussion see *infra* notes 246-48 and accompanying text.

213 Such on-going relationships between publishers and users may undermine the justification for copyright protection, since such relationships will allow authors to establish contractual relationships with users and rely on technological means of exclusion monitoring of use. *See supra* notes 168-73 and accompanying text.

214 An example of the new power balance introduced in the context of dissemination by digital access, is the previously discussed conflict between Prodigy and its subscribers. Dissemination by digital access allows providers of on-line information to monitor and restrict access and exclude certain types of users or certain types of uses of information. Prodigy, for instance, decided to cut off service for users who used the network to protest the company's pricing policy. Whereas Prodigy was able to deprive users of any access to the network due to usage it did not approve, an owner of a book in the print world was never under the threat of having to surrender her copy due to her behavior. Dissemination by digital access thus alters the balance of power between users and publishers. For a discussion of the Prodigy case, see *Sex Talk Prompts Prodigy to Shutter Bulletin Board*, *supra* note 157, at B2.

information. Such access is, however, limited, and subject to various restrictions. Libraries are gradually being converted to electronic form, first by changing their card catalogs to electronic inventories accessible from remote terminals,[215] and ultimately by storing full texts in electronic form.[216] This will make libraries equivalent to databases and will make information accessible instantly at any time and from anywhere over the networks. Electronic libraries may no longer provide free access to information they own, but instead provide gateways to information owned by others. The flip side of this is that in many cases libraries would not own the physical medium that carries the information, as they did in the past, and therefore would be more dependent on information suppliers. While current policies secure the right of people to access information through institutions such as libraries, the ability to monitor and restrict access through the network may require the administration of those institutions in a fresh way.

III. Copyright in Cyberspace and the Future of Social Dialogue

Parts I and II of this Article discussed in great detail the potential of digital technology in general, and of digital networks in particular, for participatory democracy. While cyberspace enables individuals to access, manipulate and distribute information, and thereby to participate in political deliberation, it also enhances capabilities of restricting and monitoring access to information. Thus cyberspace may either centralize or decentralize social dialogue. The following discussion demonstrates how copyright law may affect the way social dialogue will be constructed in cyberspace.

Copyright law has an inherent centralizing effect. It allows the commodification of information, and thereby facilitates a market in which control over the use of information could be accumulated.[217] Copyright law restricts access to information and reduces

---

215 This transformation created multimedia libraries: most materials are stored in print form or other format, but cataloging and other library systems are now electronic.

216 Project Mercury at Carnegie Mellon University, for instance, is aimed at building a pilot electronic library. It is one of the efforts that will transform research libraries from print to electronic entities. *See* Lauren H. Seiler, *The Concept of Book in the Age of the Digital Electronic Medium*, Lib. Software Rev., Jan. 1992, at 19.

217 *See* Chon, *supra* note 71, at 129; Kapor, *supra* note 171, at 53; *see also* Ben H. Bagdikian, The Media Monopoly ix-xix (1992) (few private corporations control most of the U.S. media); Final Report of the National Commission on New Technological Uses of Copyrighted Works 36 (1979) (Hersey, Comm'r., dissenting) ("The country has lately seen an alarming trend toward the concentration of economic power in all the communications industries.").

the use of information by allowing copyright owners to resort to the power of the state to enforce their exclusive rights. Yet, the purpose of such a temporary restriction is to allow access of more individuals to more information.[218]

Employing copyright principles in cyberspace, without any adaptation to the change of circumstances, may increase the social cost involved. First, it may jeopardize the new opportunities introduced by cyberspace for decentralizing social dialogue. Second, when combined with new technological means of controlling and monitoring use, it may enhance the power of copyright owners in an unprecedented way.

Cyberspace is arguably different from previous technologies that were traditionally covered by copyright law in many respects. It is different in the way information is represented (digits). It is also different in speed, in the resources its consumes, and in its capabilities. The issue of *relevant difference* is complicated. The argument that two things are different or alike is relative to a governing principle of relevancy. It is one thing to show that digital technology differs from other technologies in terms of the way the information is represented, in the speed of processing information, and in the shape and costs of processors. It is quite another thing to determine which of these differences is relevant for the assignment of rights in digitized products. A report that was released in the U.S. by the Information Infrastructure Task Force (the IITF Report) focussed only on the differences that are relevant to the interests of the stakeholders under current copyright law.[219] Instead, this Article suggests that one should focus on the differences that are *relevant* to the promotion of the constitutional goals of copyright law. The relevant changes created by digital technology are those that affect the balance of power between copyright owners and users. To understand the implications of digital technology one must understand how digital technology changes that balance of power, and how that change affects the function of copyright law in the pursuit of knowledge and learning.

Cyberspace does not merely bring about a quantitative change, by making reproduction easier, less costly, and by expediting information delivery. As the discussion in part II demon-

---

218 *See* Niva Elkin-Koren, *The Challenges of Technological Change to Copyright Law*, 17 SCI. COMM. 186, 194 (1995). This stems from the constitutional purpose of copyright law "to promote the progress of science and the useful arts." U.S. CONST. art. I, § 8, cl. 8. Alternatively, one may argue that progress would be best served by providing more information to a limited number of people who can best promote it. *See* RORTY, *supra* note 166, at xvi.

219 IITF WHITE PAPER, *supra* note 2, at 5.

strated,[220] cyberspace has the potential of decentralizing the structure of creation and dissemination of information, which may radically affect social structures.[221] This potential may be crucial for democracy.

The following discussion examines copyright law from the perspective of social dialogue. It demonstrates how copyright principles may be used in cyberspace to expand the rights and privileges of parties who currently benefit from the copyright regime. It challenges the justification for granting these broad rights in cyberspace. This discussion further highlights the social cost involved in applying copyright law in cyberspace, and suggests that this cost should be considered when defining the scope of copyright law in cyberspace.

A. *From Reproduction to Use*

Section 106(1) of the 1976 Copyright Act provides owners with an exclusive right to "reproduce the copyrighted work in copies or phonorecords." The right to reproduce was understood by the IITF Report to cover any placement of a work into a computer's memory, since the work may be "perceived, reproduced, or communicated . . . with the aid of a machine or device."[222] This was also the court's approach in several cases which held that digital copies that were merely "fixed" in RAM constituted infringing copies.[223] These controversial rulings were criticized, however, for be-

---

220 *See supra* notes 79-216 and accompanying text.

221 For example, Pool points at five aspects of electronic communication that are likely to change society: overcoming the barrier of distance in communication, convergence of speech text and pictures in a single form of representation, the growing share of information handling in all of human activities, the convergence of computing and communicating, and the reversal of the media revolution. *See* ITHIEL DE SOLA POOL, *supra* note 101, at 8.

222 IITF WHITE PAPER, *supra* note 2, at 25-26 (citing 17 U.S.C. § 101 (1994)).

223 MAI Sys. Corp. v. Peak Computer, Inc., 991 F.2d 511, 519 (9th Cir. 1993), *cert. denied*, 114 S. Ct. 671 (1994). This decision has been recently sustained by the Court of Appeals for the Seventh Circuit, in a way, however, that restricts its application. NLFC, Inc. v. Devcom Mid-America, Inc., 45 F.3d 231 (7th Cir. 1995), involved a suit against a computer service company that directly accessed and serviced its customers' computers via leased or dedicated phone lines and dumb terminals. The court believed the service company's assertions that it did not download the software onto its own computers in order to perform work, and found no support for the inference that a printed copy of the source code was produced by the service company's computer. The court found no violations of the Copyright Act, holding that the service company did not illegally copy software in the process of servicing that software. The court's analysis ignored reproduction on the RAM. Once the court found that no copy was downloaded onto the defendant's computer, it concluded that there was no copying.

> Devcom did not, during its course of business with either lab, download the software onto its computers in order to work on it. Instead, Devcom directly accessed the laboratory computers, via leased or dedicated phone lines and the use of dumb terminals. . . . Devcom accessed the memory or hard drive of one

ing inconsistent with the language of the statute and the legislative history, which indicates a Congressional intention to limit the scope of the reproduction right to sufficiently permanent or stable copies.[224]

This broad interpretation of the right to reproduce prohibits any unauthorized digitization of a work by scanning it into a digitized file, and any uploading or downloading of works from or onto a server. It further prohibits creating any incidental copy in the course of using a file. Every digital transmission involves a reproduction, since copies are made during the transmission and when the transmission arrives at its destination. Furthermore, potential infringement of the reproduction rights occurs whenever someone browses a document on-line,[225] or loads a work into a computer's RAM. Indeed, the IITF Report concluded that the reproduction right "appears to be a right that will be implicated in most NII transactions."[226]

The exclusive right to reproduce—as interpreted by the IITF Report and by courts—provides copyright owners with a broad monopoly compared with their rights in non-digitized works. Works in a digitized form must be reproduced in one way or another to allow any access to them. Digitized works are represented ab-

---

> of the laboratory computers directly through a dedicated phone line, and that the source codes were printed directly from that source. There is no support here for the inference that this information originated from one of Devcom's computers.

Id. at 12-13. Thus, even though the court explicitly cited *MAI*, the fact that it did not distinguish between reproduction on the RAM and reproduction on a hard drive, and the fact that it did not consider copying on the RAM to be infringement, departs from the *MAI* decision and restricts the meaning of reproduction to the creation of a permanent copy.

224 *See* H.R. Rep. No. 1476, 94th Cong., 2d Sess. 62 (1976).

> "Reproduction" under clause (1) of section 106 is to be distinguished from "display" under clause (5). For a work to be "reproduced", its fixation in tangible form must be "sufficiently permanent or stable to permit it to be perceived, reproduced, or otherwise communicated for a period of more than transitory duration." Thus, the showing of images on a screen or tube would not be a violation of clause (1), although it might come within the scope of clause (5).

Id.; *see* Samuelson, *Digital Media*, *supra* note 1, at 323 (arguing that the same logic that underlies the view that RAM copies infringe copyrights, would find infringement in holding a mirror up to a book, because the book's image could be perceived there for more than a transitory duration); Jessica Litman, *The Exclusive Right to Read*, 13 Cardozo Arts & Ent. L.J. 29, 42-43 (1994).

225 IITF White Paper, *supra* note 2, at 64 ("[W]hen a computer user simply 'browses' a document resident on another computer, the image on the user's screen exists—under contemporary technology—only by virtue of the copy that has been reproduced in the user's computer memory."). The court in Religious Technology Ctr. v. Netcom On-line Communication Servs., 907 F. Supp. 1361, 1378 (N.D. Cal. 1995) concluded that "[a]bsent a commercial or profit-depriving use, digital browsing is probably a fair use . . . ." The court emphasized that browsing will not have much market effect. *Id.*

226 IITF White Paper, *supra* note 2, at 64. As a result, the Report concluded that there is no reason to change the definition of the exclusive right to reproduce. *Id.*

stractly in ones and zeros, and require the use of a processor to access them. Such processing always involves the creation of a copy. Consequently, every access to digitized works falls under the copyright monopoly.

In the print world, the notion of copying was used to distinguish between legitimate and infringing uses. The use of this same concept—copying—in a digitized environment would be too inclusive.[227] Copyright owners were never able to prevent *the use* of their works.[228] Under the current copyright regime, owners are granted only limited rights over the use of their works. These rights are strictly defined by section 106, and do not undertake to grant owners control over all conceivable uses of their works. The rights are subject to further restrictions under sections 107 to 118 of the 1976 Copyright Act.[229] There is a wide range of permissible uses of works that is not at all regulated by copyright law.[230] Those uses that are not explicitly subject to owners' control under copyright law remain in the public domain.

Consider browsing through a document on the computer, for instance. Every act of reading a text on-line, examining it, flipping through it, or even glancing at its titles, involves its reproduction by the machine that displays it. Consequently, all acts like reading e-mail, surfing the Internet, or following links of Hypertext files[231] may constitute copyright infringement. A law that perceives all

---

227 *See* Litman, *supra* note 224, at 43 (arguing that the Report's characterization of current law allows copyright owners to claim exclusive "reading," "listening," and "viewing" rights).

228 The bundle of rights granted to copyright owners under section 106 does not allow owners to control the use of their copyrighted works. In fact, this is one of the main differences between copyright law and patent law. *See* Ralph S. Brown, *Eligibility for Copyright Protection: A Search for Principled Standards*, 70 MINN. L. REV. 579, 588-89 (1985).

> The right to control the use of a work, although granted to inventors, has never been part of copyright except as performance may be considered "use." Indeed, the absence of a "use right" helps justify the relatively casual approach to granting copyright as opposed to the more searching tests for patentability.

Id. (footnotes omitted).

229 17 U.S.C. §§ 107-118 (1994). It does not follow, however, that all unauthorized uses of a work are prohibited unless they fall under the exceptions.

230 For a description of copyright law as a regime that is regulated, rather than defined in terms of property, see L. RAY PATTERSON & STANLEY W. LINDBERG, THE NATURE OF COPYRIGHT, A LAW OF USERS' RIGHTS 193 (1991).

231 Does a link between documents on the World Wide Web constitute copyright infringement under the broad interpretation of the Working Group? The World Wide Web is a hypertext based system that allows access to Internet resources in the form of Hypertext documents. KROL, *supra* note 149, at 515. "Hypertext documents are documents that contain links to other documents; selecting a link automatically displays the second document." *Id.* at 508. It is arguable that a link is very similar to a bibliography entry. It refers users of one document to other documents that may be relevant. It also provides the location of further information. A locator, however, is codified digitally and operates automatically when a user clicks on the screen. This connects the user to the host Web site, which responds by sending a copy of the linked document to the user's screen.

such incidental reproductions as falling within the scope of the copyright monopoly, makes browsing illegal.[232]

Browsing, however, is crucial for any notion of progress. Any creation of knowledge depends on exposure to new information. We refine our ideas about the world through interaction with others' ideas, feelings, beliefs and discoveries. A law that allows owners to charge money for any such interaction is detrimental to any vision of learning and growth.

If copyright owners are able to charge for all browsing, fewer people will be able to gain even limited access to information. While, under the current regime users are able to freely browse through books in the bookstore or through different sections of a newspaper, a regime that makes browsing an infringement would restrict such behavior.

Furthermore, making browsing a copyright infringement inherently limits opportunities for progress and change by restricting random access to information. Random access to information is essential for individuals' ability to shape their interests, preferences, and positions. If browsing involved a fee, users would be required to choose in advance whether they wish to engage in such a transaction. They must be able to determine *a priori* what kind of information they are interested in. But how would people know what they are interested in before they even know what is available? How can their expectations be shaped in the absence of random observation of what is available to them? The need to choose in advance one's areas of interest may narrow individuals' experience of the world and of themselves. It may also limit the ability of people to change.[233]

Perceiving browsing as part of the copyright monopoly is also significant for social dialogue. A right to control browsing relo-

---

Under the IITF White Paper, selecting a linked document would appear to create an infringing copy. IITF WHITE PAPER, *supra* note 2, at 64.

232 *See* Litman, *supra* note 224.

233 For instance, when we read a newspaper, we carefully read the sections we are the most interested in (book review, front page, business section), and we flip through the others. This is the underlying assumption of the whole industry of advertisements in newspapers. *See* BAKER, *supra* note 169, at 64. Once in a while browsing will lead to a news item which we couldn't expect we would be interested in reading. This new information may challenge our previous views. A monopoly over browsing limits those opportunities.

This same problem exists with screening agents that are selecting information that fits one's interests and needs. Consider for instance, a system that creates individualized newspapers according to one's profile. Such systems also require defining one's interests in advance. Yet, intelligent agents may include a component of random selection, which would provide the user with several arbitrarily chosen items. Such random selection would be limited, however, in a regime that perceives browsing as covered within the rights of copyright owners.

cates a privilege enjoyed by the public, within the scope of the private monopoly of copyright owners. It therefore enhances the ability of owners to exclude access to cultural forms. It may therefore limit access to information on the basis of economic power.

Browsing is part of our everyday behavior. For example, we flip through books at the bookstore, read books in the library, glance at a photograph or a drawing in a store or a museum. If cyberspace is to become the main channel for distributing information, all this information will become available on-line. In the absence of any alternative to current practices of browsing, we would be deprived of a large portion of our current capacity to access information at low cost.

It thus becomes apparent that even though digital technology may make works more accessible, broad copyright in a digital environment may limit access to works in an unprecedented way. The expansive use of the notion of "copying" in a digitized environment would fail to take advantage of the full potential of the technology.

If the right to reproduce is to be used in the digitized context, it should preserve the fundamental trade off between granting the public perpetual use of the work in exchange for a monopoly over the initial distribution of a work. Accordingly, the reproduction right should be confined to its original meaning in a pre-digitized world, namely the right to control the preparation of fixed copies which allow repeated, unrestricted use of the work. It should explicitly exclude any behaviors which do not aim at the preparation of such copies, such as browsing or linking documents.

The significance of the incomprehensible nature of digitized representation—that it is codified in a machine readable form and must be re-presented in a human readable form in order to become accessible to users—has been most directly discussed in the context of fair use. It has been argued, for example, that it is necessary to copy a computer program in order to study it.[234] Disassembly, namely, the process that transforms the object code into a comprehensible form, is required in order to read a program, study and analyze it, to understand the ideas and functions it contains. In *Sega v. Accolade*, the court held that disassembling of copyrighted object code is a fair use of the copyrighted work if such

---

234 This argument was raised in the *Sega* case, regarding the copying of the Sega Genesis software by Accolade. In an *amicus curiae* brief filed in Court of Appeals for the Ninth Circuit in support of Accolade's position, the *amici* argued that, contrary to other works protected by copyright, object code is incomprehensible. Sega Enters. Ltd. v. Accolade, Inc., 977 F.2d 1510 (9th Cir. 1992).

disassembly provides the only means of access to those elements of the code that are not protected by copyright.[235] This suggests that in cyberspace, where the right to reproduce may cover any access to works, the scope of this right should be limited.

B. *Distribution, Transmission and Access*

Section 106(3) of the 1976 Copyright Act provides copyright owners with the exclusive right to "distribute copies . . . of the copyrighted work to the public by sale or other transfer of ownership, or by rental, lease, or lending."[236] Several courts have concluded that on-line dissemination constitutes public distribution.[237] The IITF Report argued that on-line dissemination differs from previous methods of distribution because it involves "proliferation of copies." The dissemination of works does not involve the distribution of copies, but the creation of new copies, and therefore falls under the exclusive right to reproduce.[238] The Working Group noted that even though no material objects are involved, the transmission of a copy of the work from one location to several others results in the distribution of additional copies of the work. Therefore, the Report recommended expanding the meaning of "distribution" to cover dissemination by transmission.[239]

On-line dissemination of works changes the balance between copyright owners and users. The expansion of copyright monopoly, to cover not only distribution of copies, but also on-line dissemination, poses a threat to copyright policies.[240] Transmission and distribution are essentially different.[241] "Distribution" requires dis-

---

235 *Id.*

236 17 U.S.C. § 106(3) (1994).

237 *See, e.g.*, Playboy Enters., Inc. v. Frena, 839 F. Supp. 1552 (M.D. Fla. 1993) (a bulletin board operator was found liable for infringing the plaintiff's exclusive rights to publicly distribute Playboy's copyrighted photographs).

238 Every agent in the dissemination chain may both disseminate the work and retain her own copy. IITF WHITE PAPER, *supra* note 2, at 213.

239 Under copyright law owners retain the exclusive right to "distribute copies . . . of the copyrighted work to the public by sale or other transfer of ownership, or by rental, lease, or lending." The Report recommended to add "or by transmission" after "lending" in the statute. *See* IITF WHITE PAPER, *supra* note 2, at 213, 217, & 219.

240 *See* PATTERSON & LINDBERG, *supra* note 230, at 99-100. Even though Patterson & Lindberg discuss television broadcasts, the concerns they raise also are applicable to cyberspace. The underlying assumption of the public performance clause is that performance is equivalent to publication, and thereby supposedly satisfies the promotion of learning condition required by copyright. Patterson & Lindberg argue that the protection of a live broadcast on television (under what they call "electronic copyright") reflects three fictions: the corporate copyright fiction which perceives the employer as an author, the fiction of fixation which perceives a broadcast as being fixed even if it is being transmitted, and the fiction that performance is equivalent to publication. *Id.*

241 The IITF White Paper argued that digital dissemination differs from previous methods of distribution in that it involves "proliferation of copies." The dissemination of works

semination of copies to the public for profit. Consequently, it guarantees public access to the work. The existence of a copy of the work, that is not controlled by the copyright laws, guarantees that the work will eventually fall into the public domain.

The economic structure of on-line dissemination is, however, entirely different. It requires only the communication of a work over the network to obtain both copyright protection and a profit. A work that is disseminated on-line does not become available to the general public for subsequent use. Copyright owners maintain control over any further access to their works.[242] Publishers may restrict access to information and control *uses* that are not protected under copyright law. Consequently, users become more dependent on publishers for access. While copies allow repetitive use of the copyrighted work, on-line dissemination does not guarantee such access.[243]

Copyright law traditionally served to protect copyright interests when the publisher lost the physical control over the copies. Mass distribution of works required a substitute for contractual or physical restraints over the use. The context of cyberspace is en-

---

does not involve the distribution of copies, but the creation of new copies. Every agent in the dissemination chain may both disseminate the work and retain her own copy. Therefore, the Working Group concluded, "under the current law, the reproduction right, rather than the distribution right, may be both more logically applicable and more legally appropriate (by virtue of its more limited exceptions). IITF WHITE PAPER, *supra* note 2, at 216. The IITF White Paper further noted that the reproduction right would be more appropriate for the NII since it is subject to less exceptions. Justifying the preference of the reproduction right over the distribution right, by the fact that it is subject to more limited exceptions, is peculiar. The Working Group was entrusted with the task of recommending the amendments necessary in copyright law to meet the new circumstances created by the NII. Therefore, the Report should have critically examined which exceptions of the reproduction rights and distribution rights would be appropriate in the context of the NII, instead of treating the current right and limitations as a package deal.

242 *Id.* at 216; *see* Jerome H. Reichman, *Electronic Information Tools—The Outer Edge of World Intellectual Property Law*, 17 DAYTON L. REV. 797, 823 (1992).

> For example, to the extent that publishers supply on-line information to a network of licensed subscribers from computerized and constantly updated data bases kept on their own premises, they avoid the kind of dissemination in hard copies that made intellectual creations vulnerable to third-party appropriation in the past.

Id.

243 The lack of physical medium alters the balance of power between users and publishers. On-line services may exercise continuous control over the use of works. When one acquires a book for instance, one gains unrestricted access to the information it contains. On the other hand, access to information on an on-line service may be restricted or cut off all together at any time. Its use may also be continuously restricted by the on-line provider. While acquiring a book is a one time purchase that provides the buyer with property rights over the book, accessing information on-line requires an ongoing relationship between users and providers of on-line services. In the absence of rights analogous to the power exercised by users of tangible copies, users' freedom to access and use information becomes more vulnerable. This creates a sweeping right at the hands of the copyright owner in a digitized environment that she has never had in the past.

tirely different. On-line dissemination allows publishers to control the use of disseminated information even in cases of mass distribution. The use of works may be subject to contractual restraints,[244] supplemented by technical means of monitoring and enforcing license restrictions. On-line dissemination increases the feasibility of monitoring and restricting the use of copyrighted works. Networking allows more control over the type of use (browsing, downloading, annotating) the number of uses, and the identity of users. It allows applying different price policies to different users and charging different prices for different uses. This gives the copyright owner an absolute power over the licensing of her work. This ability of copyright owners to monitor and control the use of their works on-line, weakens the case for copyright protection in cyberspace.

Furthermore, distribution rights under copyright law seek to guarantee the ability of copyright owners to commodify their works in the market by selling copies or exclusive licenses.[245] The exclusive right to distribute is granted to copyright owners against competitors in the market. A right to control on-line dissemination expands the power of owners to control not only uses by competitors but also any transmission by individual users.

The overall impact of on-line dissemination is to deny users any unrestricted perpetual right to use the information. Access to works increasingly depends on a relationship with the copyright owner. Copyright law should serve to supplement the otherwise limited ability of copyright owners to protect their interests in the market place. Yet, if on-line dissemination turns out to enhance the power of copyright owners to control the use of their works, the role of copyright law should be reconsidered.

Network distribution shifts the essence of dissemination from

---

244 Reichman, *supra* note 242, at 823. Yet, the status of on-line contracts and the circumstances that would constitute an on-line agreement are unclear.

245 *Id.* at 820-21.

> In effect, copyright law established a surrogate form of ownership by instituting a system of portable fences, valid against the world and backed by the power of the state, that accompany an author's creation on its journey from mind to mind. Even though third parties legitimately exercise dominion over artifacts that embody original intellectual creations, these fictitious portable fences neutralize essential attributes of property that possession would ordinarily confer. The exclusive right to reproduce thus mandates a consensual relation between creator and would-be exploiters that prevents the latter from using the former's contribution in specified ways without paying for the privilege. This right constitutes the essential element of intellectual property law, and it gives intellectual creations the quality of "goods" in both the legal and economic sense of the term.

Id.

distribution of copies to *access* and *use.* This weakens the dependency of users on a tangible copy, but increases their need for information in a form that is constantly updated, manipulated, and combined with other sources. The common characteristics of a sale transaction may not be applicable to network distribution. Therefore, it is necessary to develop a new typology to describe the legal relationships that are established in network distribution. It is also necessary to come up with an alternative mechanism that would allow users to do the same things they are able to do in a non-digitized environment. Purchasers of books, for instance, are entitled to share their book with a friend or a colleague, and also to dispose of it. The first sale doctrine restricts the power of distributors to control secondary markets for their works. Under section 109(a) of the 1976 Copyright Act,[246] the exclusive right to distribute copies to the public is limited to the right to make an initial distribution of a particular copy. The first sale doctrine allows the owner of a copy to dispose of her possession of that copy at her will. The freedom of individuals to share information with others, and the power of secondary players in the marketplace to redistribute and disseminate already distributed works, stimulates dissemination of information.[247] Furthermore, alternative channels of distribution have the effect of decentralizing dissemination. Since the first sale doctrine applies to distribution of physical copies, it remains unclear whether the doctrine applies to on-line transmission. The IITF Report recommended explicitly to exclude transmission from the reach of the first sale doctrine.[248] Abolishing the first sale doctrine would further enhance owners' power to control secondary markets of their works and would further centralize the dissemination of information, rather than supporting the decentralizing opportunities created by digital networks.

C. *Derivative Rights*

The 1976 Copyright Act provides copyright holders with an exclusive right to prepare, and authorize others to prepare, a derivative work.[249] A derivative work is defined by the 1976 Copyright Act as "a work based upon one or more preexisting works . . . ."[250]

---

246 17 U.S.C § 109(a) (1994).

247 *See* PAUL GOLDSTEIN, COPYRIGHT: PRINCIPLES, LAW AND PRACTICE § 5.6.1 (1994) ("The intent behind section 109(a) was to provide that, once the copyright owner parts with ownership of a copy or phonorecord, everyone in the succeeding chain of title—owners and nonowners alike—will enjoy the privilege.").

248 IITF WHITE PAPER, *supra* note 2, at 91.

249 17 U.S.C. § 106(2) (1994).

250 17 U.S.C § 101.

This right allows copyright owners to exploit additional markets beyond the original market for the work.[251] It thus enlarges the prospective market for the copyrighted work, and increases incentives to invest in the development of works.[252] This guarantees proper levels of investment in creating works and also encourages early publication of works. The concern is that without an exclusive right to create derivative works, authors will withhold publication of the original works until they are ready to exploit other potential markets, without losing their head start.[253] Derivative rights also enable owners to divide their property interest and enhance to value of their bundle of rights.[254]

The question is to what extent copyright owners of digitized works should be able to control the preparation of enhancements and modifications of their works. The ability to manipulate works in cyberspace is substantially different from the manipulability of non-digitized works. The potential for manipulation is different in quality in that it allows transforming the entire work. The ability to manipulate works in a digitized form makes it substantially easier to create transformative uses of works. This difference introduces a new set of interests to be considered.

The primary difference between annotating printed text and annotating a downloaded file is that text in a digitized form is flexi-

---

> A "derivative work" is a work based upon one or more preexisting works, such as a translation, musical arrangement, dramatization . . . abridgment, condensation, or any other form in which a work may be recast, transformed, or adapted. A work consisting of editorial revisions, annotations, elaborations, or other modifications which, as a whole, represent an original work of authorship, is a "derivative work."

Id.

251 *See* Reichman, *supra* note 242, at 813 ("This right enables an author to recoup revenues generated from different uses of his or her work on each of the market segments where its expressive features are commercially exploited either in original or adapted form."). Thus, an author enjoys the exclusive right to make a movie based on her novel and Disney has the exclusive right to make posters, T-shirts, and toys in the image of its movie characters. The idea that the interest of copyright owners includes a legitimate expectation of future markets is also significant to fair use analysis. The fourth fair use factor is "the effect of the use upon the potential market for or value of the copyrighted work." 17 U.S.C. § 107(4) (1994). In Campbell v. Acuff-Rose Music, Inc., 114 S. Ct. 1164 (1994), the Supreme Court held that the fourth factor of the fair use analysis requires the courts to consider not only the harm to the market of the original work, but also the potential market for derivative works. Any substantial harm to the market for derivative works "would weigh against a finding of fair use, because the licensing of derivatives is an important economic incentive to the creation of originals." *Id.* at 114 (footnotes omitted).

252 GOLDSTEIN, *supra* note 247, at 571 ("Derivative rights enable prospective copyright owners to proportion their investment to the returns they hope to receive not only from the market in which their work will first be published, but from other, derivative, markets as well.").

253 For economic analysis of the adaptation right, see Landes & Posner, *supra* note 190, at 354-55.

254 *See* GOLDSTEIN, *supra* note 252, at 575.

ble and manipulable and allows users to integrate their comments into the original work itself. This aspect of digitization was down played by the Working Group. Physical modes of representation stand alone.[255] Therefore, annotating printed text creates a distinct work, consisting of the original work and the comments as separate features. Annotating text in a digitized form transforms the text itself.[256] The disappearance of the physical boundaries between original and derivative components, and the ease of manipulation are significant both for users and for authors.

From the perspective of authors, the physical boundaries help define and protect the integrity of the work. When the original work is fixed in a certain form, and may be preserved in the form in which it was created by the author, it is feasible to sustain its completeness, original meanings and qualities. It is also easier to protect a work from being distorted. The existence of a fixed format of the work provides a baseline to which all modifications may be compared, and thus makes detection of distortions easier.[257] The physical boundaries also communicate a clear signal to users as to the scope of the work. In the absence of a clear division between works of different sources, they may all become part of a single web.[258] Finally, the flexible nature of digital representation makes it easy and inexpensive to modify the original work.

Although derivative rights under United States copyright law protect an economic interest of copyright owners in potential related markets, it has been suggested that they may also serve to protect the integrity of copyrighted works.[259] The monopoly over derivative works may allow authors to prevent any distortion, misrepresentation, misuse, or transformation of her work without proper authority.[260] In many cases, however, copyright owners are

---

255 If one is writing comments on a book, she creates a separate text that accompanies the printed text. If she wishes to print her comments and physically incorporate them into the original, she must retype the entire book. In a digitized text, one may simply add her comments with or without marking them, and may also directly modify the original text.

256 *See* Bolter, *supra* note 167, at 29.

257 Consider, for instance, handwritten comments on a book, or changes of color on a painting or a photograph.

258 Consider, for instance, the experience of following pointers to web sites or reading responses to messages posted on a bulletin board.

259 Thus, derivative rights allowed the United States to join the Berne convention without having to explicitly add moral rights to the bundle of rights provided to authors, and consequently, without having to compromise the "utilitarian ethos" that underlies its copyright law. *See* Goldstein, *supra* note 252, §§ 5.2.3, 7.1.2, 7.3.2; Reichman, *supra* note 242, at 813; Neil Netanel, *Alienability Restrictions and the Enhancement of Author Autonomy in United States and Continental Copyright Law*, 12 Cardozo Arts & Ent. L.J. 1, 42-43 (1994).

260 *See* Netanel, *supra* note 259, at 43 ("The derivative right, therefore, is essentially coterminous with at least the negative aspect of the integrity right. Like their Continental counterparts, U.S. authors who hold the derivative right may prevent modifications to their

not the authors of the original works; this is the case when copyright is transferred to others, such as movie producers or book publishers. This is also the case when the work is considered a work-made-for-hire, in which the employer is classified as the first author of the work.[261] The vast majority of copyrighted materials that are on the market are not owned by the actual author. Corporate copyright weakens the case for protecting the integrity of the work, or other moral rights, under derivative rights.

From the user's perspective, the ability to interact, change and modify works is empowering. It is this vulnerability of digitized works to modification and manipulation that makes them so valuable for social dialogue. It allows users to participate in creating the meaning of cultural artifacts. Users may incorporate their input into works of others, customize it to serve their preferences and reflect their choices, or create new meaning by linking texts to one another, or integrating fragments of text together.[262] No special equipment training or skills are necessary for changing a downloaded file. Usually the same equipment that allows access to a work would allow its manipulation.[263]

Cyberspace allows individual users to add their input and shape digitized works to meet their individual preferences in a cost-effective way. Users may be increasingly involved in determining what they watch, read, or otherwise consume. The technological ability to customize allows users to recognize their personal expressions in the works they consume.[264] The passivity of consuming mass products may thus be replaced with actively constructing indi-

---

work that run contrary to their artistic sensibilities, without any need to show consumer deception or harm to reputation."). Another legal arrangement that allows copyright owners to protect the integrity of a work is section 115(a)(2) of the Copyright Act. Under section 115, a musical composition that was previously licensed by the copyright owner to be recorded and distributed is subject to a compulsory license for further recordings. Under section 115(a)(2) licensees are free to make changes in the musical arrangement of the work where necessary to conform with the style or manner of interpretation or performance, so long as no change is made in the basic melody or fundamental character of the work. 17 U.S.C. § 115(a)(2) (1994). The House Report notes that this qualification intended to prevent the original compositions from being perverted, distorted or travestied. *See* H.R. Rep. No. 1476, 94th Cong., 2d Sess. (1976).

261 17 U.S.C § 201(b) (1994); Netanel, *supra* note 259, at 43-44.

262 For further discussion of the potential of digitization for decentralizing meaning-making process, see part II.A & note 100.

263 The shift of emphasis to personal use shakes the fundamental scheme of copyright law. The ultimate goal of granting copyright protection is to allow authors to share their works in public, and at the same time protect their economic interests in the market.

264 The ability of users to customize digitized stories, for instance, may be crucial to their sense of affiliation with a community, and to their ability to relate to the culture they consume. The controversy over what books should be included on the New York City public schools' suggested bibliography for teachers further demonstrates the significance of decentralizing dissemination of information. *See supra* note 136.

vidualized experiences. This may facilitate the constitutional purpose underlying copyright law of promoting progress. Moreover, if works may exist in multiple individualized versions, then diversity of works and expressions would be enhanced. The opportunities for more individuals to add their input and take part in creating cultural artifacts serves the primary goal of copyright law—promoting progress.

If annotating a downloaded file infringes the adaptation rights, copyright owners will be entitled to restrict, or entirely prohibit any such use of their works. Alternatively, copyright owners may license such use for a fee. The overall effect of granting owners the right to control any annotation of their works is to reduce such activity.[265] In other words, while digital technology opens up opportunities for grass roots participation in the creation of cultural forms, granting broad derivative rights inhibits that potential. While manipulability of digitized works creates an opportunity for decentralizing meaning-making processes, an opportunity that is significant both from the perspective of copyright principles and of democratic theory, it also threatens the boundaries of the work's integrity.[266] The interest in the integrity of works is limited to human authors, however, and does not present itself as clearly in the case of corporate copyright.

What should be the appropriate scope of derivative rights in a digitized context? To what extent should copyright holders in cyberspace be able to control the preparation of enhancements and modifications of their works? Should copyright law facilitate a regime in which users are encouraged to adapt works to reflect their own meanings?

Very broad derivative rights may unduly impede opportunities for participation in meaning-making processes. It would severely limit the ability of users to customize works, interact and respond to them, or use them as building blocks of their own creation. Broad derivative rights may serve to block the potential for decentralizing meaning. In other words, the technological advantages of cyberspace may be outlawed. Thus copyright law may be used to

---

265 This is either because copyright owners would not license it or because users would not value it enough to pay the fee set by the owner. Copyright owners would have an incentive to set the price for licensing derivative works higher in order to maintain their monopoly. In any event, any charges for derivative use would decrease the level of such use, and would allow a more limited group of users, who can afford paying for the derivative rights, to make derivative uses of works.

266 In the context of industrial property, the competing interests are slightly different: very broad derivative work rights can unduly impede competition in the general products marketplace. On the other hand, lack of appropriate means to control derivative uses of a technical innovation may cause under-investment in creation or delay publication.

create and maintain power over meaning-making processes. It may be used to preserve the centralized structure of social dialogue.

How should we resolve the tension between the threat to integrity and the potential for empowering users? How should we resolve the tension between the threat to the owner's market posed by individual users and the social benefit generated by such use? Copyright policy should promote public access to means of distribution not only as passive recipients but also as originators.[267] In *Campbell v. Acuff-Rose Music, Inc.*,[268] the Supreme Court found the transformative use of works to be the single most important factor under fair use analysis.[269] This was because "the goal of copyright, to promote science and the arts, is generally furthered by the creation of transformative works."[270]

Broad derivative rights may also jeopardize the efficient use of works in digital form by limiting the ability of individuals to customize copyrighted works.[271] This would impair one of the most significant contributions of digitization to social dialogue: the ability of users to integrate their contribution to works and to adapt them to their own meaning.

Digitized works are distinct from conventional works in that they allow access, use and manipulation by various functional applications. Broad derivative rights may allow the copyright owners to control the distribution of functional applications such as computer programs that create new options of selection, change the speed or color of works, or allow the work to be combined with other sources of information.[272]

Copyright reform should focus on encouraging and not impeding the creation of transformative works. The enhanced op-

---

267 *See* Sega Enters. Ltd. v. Accolade, Inc., 977 F.2d 1510 (9th Cir. 1992). The court held that "the immediate effect of our copyright law is to secure a fair return for an 'author's' creative labor. But the ultimate aim is, by this incentive, to stimulate artistic creativity for the general public good." *Id.* at 1527 (quoting *Sony*, 464 U.S. at 432).

268 114 S. Ct. 1164. The Court discussed the extent to which a commercial derivative work (parody) should be exempted under fair use doctrine.

269 *Id.* The Court noted that "[t]he more transformative the new work, the less will be the significance of other factors, like commercialism, that may weigh against a finding of fair use." *Id.* at 1166.

270 *Id.* at 1171. Transformative works, the Court held, "lie at the heart of the fair use doctrine's guarantee of breathing space within the confines of copyright." *Id.*

271 For further discussion see *supra* notes 124-39 and accompanying text.

272 What rights do copyright holders have against competitors that are marketing compatible devices? Does an enhancing product constitute a derivative work, and does the output created through the use of such products amount to a derivative work? This second question may be of great importance. Even if the compatible device does not, by itself, infringe the exclusive right to adapt, the distributor of such a device may still be liable for copyright infringement. For instance, if an output of a program that runs on a multimedia system is considered to be a derivative work, then an unauthorized publisher of such a program may be liable for contributory infringement.

portunities for modifying, customizing, or otherwise manipulating digitized works may promote this purpose of copyright law. A broad derivative right may, however, impede this potential. It is therefore necessary to reexamine the appropriateness of the adaptation right to the digitized context.

It is arguable that the appropriate balance between the owner's monopoly over derivative uses of her work and users' freedom to manipulate, should be resolved under the fair use doctrine. The scheme of providing a broad right to control derivative use, subject to fair use exemption, puts users at a disadvantage. Under fair use, users' rights are less stable. Rights would depend on judicial determination. Users would have to act under the threat that their acts would be found infringing. The prospects of potential litigation may have an inhibiting effect on users. Users are more likely to be risk averse than copyright owners, and therefore less likely to engage in acts that may be found infringing, subjecting liability to pay compensations.[273]

Copyright reform should incorporate these principles into the statute. The exclusive right to create derivative works should explicitly exclude transformative uses. Explicitly providing that transformative use is not infringing would communicate a clear message to owners and users. It may encourage transformative uses in cyberspace and allow the technology to serve the purpose of copyright law.

D. *Fair Use*

Fair use doctrine had been one of the most important means of promoting public access to works under copyright law. Fair use reflects a fundamental principle of copyright law, namely, that rights of copyright owners are limited.[274] When a use is considered "fair," the user is exempted from copyright liability. The following discussion looks at two aspects of cyberspace that are relevant to fair use doctrine. One is the on-going controversy over whether personal use should be considered fair use. A second issue relevant to fair use analysis in cyberspace is the effect of the availability of licensing arrangements and monitoring measures.

1. Is Personal Use a Fair Use?

One of the most controversial issues in fair use is whether per-

---

[273] Furthermore, fair use is a defense, and therefore imposes the burden of proof on defendants, namely, potential users.

[274] *See* Reichman, *supra* note 242, at 821.

sonal use should be considered fair use. Personal use is "the private use of a work for one's own learning, enjoyment, or sharing with a colleague or friend—without any motive for profit."[275] The advocates of the personal use exemption maintain that widespread use of information by individuals is the ultimate purpose of copyright law, and that the law should only protect copyright owners against commercial competitors in the market place.[276] Opponents claim, however, that even private noncommercial copying provides users with the benefit of a copy for which they haven't paid, and therefore reduces the expected return of copyright owners.[277]

This controversy takes on new meaning in a digitized context. Part II demonstrated how users become major players in the dissemination of information over digital networks. This change in the role of users from passive consumers to potentially active participants upsets the balance previously drawn between the public right of access and the need to secure the economic interests of copyright owners.

On the one hand, cyberspace makes personal use of copyrighted works for noncommercial purposes feasible for more people. Increasing direct access of individuals to works is one of the most significant advantages of digital technology. Traditionally, the process of communicating a message to an audience required economic resources. The large investment involved in publishing a book or producing a record, imposed a centralized mechanism of selection and allowed only the few who could afford the necessary investment or who had established themselves in the market, to become published.[278] Networking, by contrast, allows individual

---

275 PATTERSON & LINDBERG, *supra* note 230, at 11-12.

276 In *Sony*, for instance, the Supreme Court presumed that private noncommercial copying is fair use. *Sony*, 464 U.S. at 455. ("Copying for commercial gain has a much weaker claim to fair use than copying for personal enrichment."); *see* Williams & Wilkins Co. v. United States, 487 F.2d 1345 (Ct. Cl. 1973), *aff'd per curiam*, 420 U.S. 376 (1975) (holding that personal individual photocopying is non-infringing). The status of photocopying for personal use is less clear under Basic Books, Inc. v. Kinko's Graphics Corp., 785 F. Supp. 1522 (S.D.N.Y. 1991). Personal use is protected under some European laws—section VI of the German Act entitles users to copy or disseminate a work without the author's consent. *See* Netanel, *supra* note 259, at 43.

277 Justice Blackmun's dissent in *Sony* noted: "[t]he making of even a single videotape recording at home falls within this definition; the VTR user produces a material object from which the copyrighted work later can be perceived. Unless Congress intended a special exemption for the making of a single copy for personal use, I must conclude that VTR recording is contrary to the exclusive rights granted by section 106(1)." *Sony*, 464 U.S. at 464 (Blackmun, J., dissenting). And further, "[n]either the statute nor its legislative history suggests any intent to create a general exemption for a single copy made for personal or private use." *Id.*

278 *See supra* notes 169-81 and accompanying text on intermediaries and direct communication.

users to directly communicate their works to others and liberates authors from dependency on intermediators. It makes it possible for an increasing number of people to become self-published authors. Information may thus increasingly be originated by individual users, and continuously updated, revised and reused by other users. Users are able to share information in high quality with a large number of people. Thus, cyberspace enhances the opportunities of a wide range of users to effectively participate in exchanging information. The promotion of learning in society no longer depends solely on appropriate incentives for publishers, but also on direct exchanges among users.

On the other hand, personal use by individuals may threaten the commercial interests of copyright owners in an unprecedented way. The ability of individual users to cause a substantial commercial harm to copyright owners by sporadic non-commercial uses is typical of a digitized context.[279] No special equipment training or skills are necessary for downloading a file, changing it or redistributing it. Usually the same equipment that allows access to a work would permit its redistribution. Individual users are not competing with the copyright owner in the market place, and in many cases they would not receive any financial advantage from disseminating works over cyberspace. Yet, they may still effect this market. There is an accumulative effect of a large number of users, each using the work individually for personal purposes and displacing the market of the copyrighted work.

The ability of individual users to cause harm to copyright owners by personal use is a fundamental feature of cyberspace. Consequently, in a digitized context users are increasingly becoming the target of copyright owners. In this sense, cyberspace diverts substantially from traditional copyright environments. Even though copyright owners have always insisted that the scope of copyright covers private or non-commercial use, these rights are rarely enforced.[280] Digital networks, however, establish direct communication among users and distributors, and creates greater capabilities for monitoring the use of works. Therefore, the likelihood of ac-

---

[279] For instance, the ability of individual users to threaten the market for CD's by producing perfect copies of recorded music by using DAT (Digital Audio Tape) led to the enactment of the Audio Home Recording Act of 1992, Pub. L. No. 102-563, § 1, 106 Stat. 4248; *see* MELVILLE B. NIMMER, NIMMER ON COPYRIGHT §§ 8B.01[A], 8B.6-7.

[280] *See* Litman, *supra* note 224, at 35 ("If copyright owners insisted, as sometimes they did, that copyright gave them broad rights to control their works in any manner and in all forms, the practical costs of enforcing those rights against individual consumers dissuaded them from testing their claims in court."); *see also Audio Home Recording Act of 1991: Hearing on H.R. 3204 before the Subcomm. on Intellectual Property and Judicial Administration of the House Comm. on the Judiciary*, 102d Cong., 2d Sess. (1993).

tual infringement suits against private users increases.[281] Furthermore, achieving consensus over the claim of copyright owners to control private uses may effect their rights, even in the absence of enforcement efforts. This is because many users may wish to avoid potential liability for copyright infringment, even if the odds of being sued are low. Such expensive definition of owners' rights becomes the underlying assumption of the current debate over the future of copyright in cyberspace.[282]

The change of circumstances in cyberspace also means, however, that granting owners a right to control personal use would involve different considerations. The shift to personal use shakes the fundamental scheme of copyright law. The ultimate goal of granting copyright protection is to allow authors to share works in public, and at the same time to protect their economic interests in the market. Striking a balance between users' rights of personal use, and owners' economic interests involves the following issues.

First, enhancing the ability of individual users to access, use, and transform preexisting works is the ultimate purpose of copyright law.[283] Users are playing an active role in both disseminating and retrieving information.[284] The power of copyright owners to

---

281 The reason is that for copyright owners to have an incentive to sue for copyright infringements by private users, they must perceive their expected damages (namely, the actual harm multiplied by the odds of winning in litigation) as higher then the cost of detecting infringement and bringing a suit to court. Since in a non-digitized environment detecting infringements by private users was extraordinarily expensive, the likelihood of suit was very low. In cyberspace, however, with direct communication between users and distributors, and the greater capabilities of technical control, the likelihood of actual suits by private users for copyright infringements would increase.

282 *See* Patterson & Lindberg, *supra* note 230, at 7-11 (arguing that the ultimate reason for the misconception of copyright law is due to copyright owner's effort to promote an industry-oriented view of copyright, and warning that "[i]f such fallacies go unchallenged long enough, they are likely to become a substitute for the truth"); *see also* Litman, *supra* note 224, at 36 ("[B]y asserting that what members of the public think of as ordinary use of copyrighted works was, in fact, flagrant piracy, and that, as such, it undermined the national economy, copyright owners may well have won a rhetorical battle the rest of the country never realized was being fought.").

283 *Sony*, 464 U.S. at 431-32.

> The limited scope of the copyright holder's statutory monopoly, like the limited copyright duration required by the Constitution, reflects a balance of competing claims upon the public interest: Creative work is to be encouraged and rewarded, but private motivation must ultimately serve the cause of promoting broad public availability of literature, music, and the other arts. The immediate effect of our copyright law is to secure a fair return for an "author's" creative labor. But the ultimate aim is, by this incentive, to stimulate artistic creativity for the general public good. "The sole interest of the United States and the primary object in conferring the monopoly," this Court has said, "lie in the general benefits derived by the public from the labors of authors."

Id. (citations omitted).

284 The potentially interactive nature of the use of digitized works may also support finding of fair use. Thus, in *Acuff-Rose*, 114 S. Ct. 1164, the Supreme Court held that the central purpose of fair use analysis is to allow transformative uses of works, namely, a use

control and limit personal use would increase the social costs involved in applying copyright law to cyberspace. The potential public benefit in facilitating personal use and decentralization should be weighed against the prospective loss of private gain.[285]

Second, copyright law has always reflected a trade-off between the cost of restricting the availability of the work against the benefits of providing incentives to create the work in the first place. Finding the correct balance between access and incentives is the central issue in any copyright case.[286] The legal powers granted under copyright law seek to guarantee incentives to create. They allow copyright owners to prevent competitors from distributing their works at a lower price, thus decreasing the incentives to create.[287] Copyright law is thus equipped to balance the rights of copyright owners against competitors in the market place.[288] A monopoly over personal use levies a tax on *every* use, not just uses for commercial gains. It may further reduce competition and consequently the use of copyrighted works.[289]

---

which supplants the original, adds something new, or alters the first with new expression, meaning, or message.

> Although such transformative use is not absolutely necessary for a finding of fair use, . . . the goal of copyright, to promote science and the arts, is generally furthered by the creation of transformative works. Such works thus lie at the heart of the fair use doctrine's guarantee of breathing space within the confines of copyright, . . . and the more transformative the new work, the less will be the significance of other factors, like commercialism, that may weigh against a finding of fair use.

Id. at 1171.

285 *See* GOLDSTEIN, *supra* note 248, at 821 (arguing that fair use doctrine would exempt certain unauthorized uses because the resulting public benefit is thought to outweigh the loss of private gain).

286 S.J. Liebowitz, *Copyright Law, Photocopying, and Price Discrimination*, 8 RESEARCH IN L. & ECON. 181, 184 (1986); *see* Landes & Posner, *supra* note 190, at 326.

287 The underlying assumption of the copyright model is that to guarantee an optimal level of investment in the creation of new works, it is necessary to allow creators to reap that investment. Publishers need to cover cost of development plus cost of distribution. Competitors, however, may copy the work and only pay the cost of distribution. Consequently, competitors are able to charge a lower price for works, and impair the ability of publishers to reap the rewards of their initial investment. If copies made by the creator are priced close to marginal cost, others may be discouraged from making copies. However, creator's total revenues may not be sufficient to cover the cost of creating the work. If the creator cannot reap the marginal value of his efforts, he will undersupply the works. Copyright law seeks to correct this market failure by granting owners with the legal power to prevent such exploitation of their works. *See* Landes & Posner, *supra* note 190, at 326.

288 PATTERSON & LINDBERG, *supra* note 230, at 192 ("The only protection that copyright owners need is protection against the piracy of their works by competitors in the marketplace.").

289 *Id.* Patterson & Lindberg argue that protection against consumers rather than against competitors, means securing profits from monopoly rather than a market.

> The greater the protection they can obtain, of course, the less their competition - and the higher the price they can charge. The less their protection, the more competitive their prices must be. The ultimate goal of such copyright owners, it appears, is to transmute copyright from a device to protect the work for a market (a limited monopoly) into a device for guaranteeing a profit (an

Furthermore, the right of the public to access copyrighted works is partly secured under the 1976 Copyright Act by special privileges of libraries under section 108.[290] The transition from distribution of copies to dissemination by access suggests that libraries would either cease to exist, or transform their role and function. Libraries may no longer facilitate users' access to physical copies of works. In an entirely networked environment it is no longer necessary to administer large warehouses of books, which involve large expenses of space and maintenance and lack the advantages of on-line information such as connectivity with other information, manipulability and accessibility.[291] Libraries would be transformed from depositories of books into access providers. The weakening role of libraries requires, however, expanding the privileges of individual users to use copyrighted works. This is because the public interest in providing free access to information may no longer be satisfied through the privileges of libraries.

Fair use analysis, however, should also allow consideration of personal use that has the effect of a "competitive use." The Supreme Court in *Sony* had recognized this potential harming effect of personal use:

> A challenge to a noncommercial use of a copyrighted work requires proof either that the particular use is harmful, or that *if it should become widespread, it would adversely affect the potential market for the copyrighted work.*[292]

Applying this standard in cyberspace, however, involves a high cost. The enhanced opportunities of personal use are of great value both for the constitutional purpose of promoting learning, and from the democratic perspective of decentralizing meaning-making processes and facilitating effective participation. Any restric-

---

> absolute monopoly). In other words, they want copyright to protect the work not only against the competitor but also against the customer.

Id. at 192.

290 17 U.S.C. § 108.

291 *See* Lauren H. Seiler, *The Concept of Book In the Age of the Digital Electronic Medium*, 11 LIB. SOFTWARE REV. 19 (1992) (predicting that libraries will not remain as warehouses for stored information, but will be transformed into on-line databases.); *see also* RICHARD LANHAM, THE ELECTRONIC WORD, DEMOCRACY, TECHNOLOGY AND THE ARTS 134 (1993).

> The library world feels depayse today, and rightly so. Both of its physical entities, the buildings and the books they contain, can no longer form the basis for planing. And the curatorial function has metamorphosed, to borrow a phrase from an archivist acquaintance, "from curatorial to interpretive." Librarian of electronic information find their job now a radically rhetorical one—they must consciously construct human attention-structures rather than assemble a collection of books according to commonly accepted rules.

Id.

292 *Sony*, 464 U.S. at 451.

tion on personal use would repress, rather than promote, the opportunities for individuals' participation in exchanging information.

It may be useful, instead, to distinguish between the accumulative effect of reproduction by individual users for personal use, and personal use that mimics the effect of a competitor. Thus, a use that merely reduces the market for the original work, denying the owner compensation for a particular use, may still be considered fair use. On the other hand, a use that assumes the role of a competitor should be excluded from fair use. That includes any act that satisfies a large demand for a copyrighted work by directly competing with the copyright owner, such as mass distribution of copies of the work.

2. The Ability to Control and License the Use

In most transactions that involve tangible goods, the owner is able to physically exclude others from utilizing the good without a license.[293] Excluding non-payers from the use of intangibles had always been a problem.[294] Copyright law seeks to substitute the physical ability to exclude non-payers with the legal right to use the power of the state to exclude certain exploitations of copyrighted works.[295] The more excludable a work is, however, the less justification there is for copyright protection.[296]

The shift from distribution of copies to electronic dissemination might give distributors more control over the use of their works. Distribution by access allows copyright owners to rely on technological means to monitor the use[297] and charge different

---

293 Thus, a landlord may either fence her parcel, or hire guards to protect the property against trespasses. Property interest in tangible goods and intangibles had always been distinguished on the ground that intangibles are non-excludable, and therefore require the intervention of the state to allow their distribution. The reality of rights in tangibles, however, challenges this distinction. Property laws and the police may play a role in excluding trespasses by defining the boundaries of rights one exercises over one's property and deterring unauthorized use of property. It is therefore inaccurate, and even misleading, to argue that property rights in tangibles rely entirely on the ability to physically exclude non-payers.

294 *See* Landes & Posner, *supra* note 190, at 327.

295 Reichman, *supra* note 242, at 820-21.

296 Landes & Posner, *supra* note 190, at 326.

297 Reichman, *supra* note 242, at 823.

> Because subscribers entering any given data base must log in and out, the proprietors' physical control over the data may enable them to charge for each and every use of electronically processed information, even though the copyright law itself grants no exclusive right to control either end use in general or the use of disparate facts in particular. Even when dissemination occurs in hard copy form, such as a CD[-]ROM, digital technology facilitates the control of end use by enabling intermediate providers, such as libraries, to monitor actual

prices for different uses and/or users.[298] Thus, it gives copyright owners the power to prevent *any* unauthorized use and not just uses that are protected under copyright law.[299] Consequently, copyright owners may exercise more control over the use of their works.

Furthermore, dissemination in cyberspace substantially enhances the capabilities of licensing. Networking establishes direct communication between publishers and users. It provides the means for negotiating and entering licensing agreements for different uses of works. Since on-line providers control the physical access to their works, they may make access contingent upon accepting the terms of their license.[300] How should the feasibility of licensing effect the fair use analysis?

The market approach to fair use maintains that a use should be considered fair if, among other things, the user could not have

---

> usage and by permitting originators to charge, directly or indirectly, for all uses.

Id.

298 For instance, copyright owners could distribute encrypted works that could only be read by paying users.

299 Reichman, *supra* note 242, at 823-24.

300 America On-line, for instance, subjects any use of its services to the following license:

> (a) Proprietary Rights. All content is copyrighted as a collective work under the U.S. Copyright laws, and AOL Inc. owns a copyright in the selection, coordination, arrangement and enhancement of such content. Members may not modify, publish, transmit, participate in the transfer or sale, create derivative works, or in any way exploit any of the content, in whole or in part. If no specific restrictions are displayed, members may make copies of portions of content, including copyrighted material, trademarks, or other proprietary materials, provided that the copies are made only for member's personal use.

America On-Line Terms of Service. The validity of such license restrictions may be challenged under both contract law and copyright law.. From a contractual perspective, it is necessary to determine whether a contract was formed, namely whether there was adequate acceptance, whether the formalities of forming a contract were satisfied and, and also whether the license's provisions are enforceable under the unconscionability doctrine. From a copyright perspective it is then necessary to examine whether the license provisions are consistent with copyright doctrines, and whether the laws that hold them valid are preempted by copyright law. Courts may also refuse to enforce license provisions that restrict the user's rights under copyright law by declaring them contrary to public policy. Thus, it was held that there is no obligation to pay royalties pursuant to a copyright license after the expiration of the underlying copyright. April Prods. v. G. Schirmer, Inc., 126 N.E.2d 283 (N.Y. 1955). Technological means also provide the means for monitoring and enforcing contractual provisions. The overall effect of dissemination on the NII is to enhance the capability of copyright owners to collect compensations for the use of their works. *See* Reichman, *supra* note 242, at 824-25.

> Indeed, by facilitating implementation of the pay-per-use principle on a scale hitherto unthinkable, computerization tends to reduce the need for the blanket licenses and collection agencies that other copyright industries employ. In effect, the electronic information publisher becomes increasingly capable of serving as his own collection society, subject to no consent decrees, no membership controls, and no external regulation other than the threat of litigation for abuse of copyright.

Id.

purchased the use through the market.[301] An uncompensated use is justifiable, under this approach, when it is impossible to reach consensual bargain.[302] For instance, high transaction costs would traditionally create such a market failure. If the costs of receiving a license are higher than the anticipated profits from the transaction, users will be reluctant to make such use, even though it may be socially desirable.[303]

Yet, considering the ability to license as the basis of fair use analysis creates a circular argument.[304] This way of posing the question of fair use assumes the answer. Rather than defining what *should* be the scope of copyright monopoly, and therefore what uses are to be considered beyond its reach, the license standard assumes that every use which copyright owners would offer to license should be covered by copyright.[305]

This issue was the focus of the court in *American Geophysical Union v. Texaco, Inc.*[306] The court examined the applicability of the fair use doctrine to photocopying done by a researcher in a commercial corporation for personal archival purposes.[307] The court

---

301 *See* GOLDSTEIN, *supra* note 247, at 821 (describing the Private Benefit Approach).

302 The underlying assumption of this principle is that in the absence of any market barriers, the parties would achieve the most efficient allocation of resources. *See* Wendy Gordon, *Fair Use as Market Failure: A Structural and Economic Analysis of the Betamax Case and its Predecessors*, 82 COLUM. L. REV. 1600 (1982). This argument, however, takes property rights of the copyright owner as its baseline, and defines exceptions for this absolute right under market conditions which create inefficiencies. Alternatively, one may identify the situations in which property rights are justifiable in the first place. From this perspective, the inability to contract serves to justify copyright law, and the ability to contract may undermine the justification for copyright protection altogether.

303 *Id.* at 1628-29.

304 *See Williams & Wilkins*, 487 F.2d at 1357.

> It is wrong to measure the detriment to plaintiff by loss of presumed royalty income—a standard which necessarily assumed that plaintiff had a right to issue licenses. That would be true, of course, only if it were first decided that the defendant's practices did not constitute "fair use". In determining whether the company has been sufficiently hurt to cause these practices to become "unfair," one cannot assume at the start the merit of the plaintiff's position.

Id.

305 This view was reflected in the dissenting opinion in American Geophysical Union v. Texaco, Inc., 37 F.3d 881, 904 (2d. Cir. 1994).

> There is a circularity to the problem: the market will not crystallize unless courts reject the fair use argument that Texaco presents; but, under the statutory test, we cannot declare a use to be an infringement unless (assuming other factors also weigh in favor of the secondary user) there is a market to be harmed.

Id.

306 *Id.* at 881.

307 The availability of licenses for the allegedly infringing use is considered under the fourth statutory fair use factor, namely, "the effect of the use upon the potential market for or value of the copyrighted work." 17 U.S.C. § 107(4). In analyzing this fourth factor, which the Supreme Court and commentators recognize as "the single most important element of fair use," courts would assess, among other things, the availability of license. *See Harper & Row*, 471 U.S. at 566.

held that the impact on potential licensing revenues should be considered in assessing the fourth factor, namely, "the effect upon the potential market for or value of the copyrighted work."[308] The court recognized, however, that not every effect on potential licensing revenues should enter the fair use analysis. It is only licensing of "traditional, reasonable, or likely to be developed markets" that is appropriate for consideration under the fourth factor.[309]

The court's reasoning, however, fails to distinguish between the right of copyright owners to *license their copyright* and their power *to license the use of the work.* Copyright law provides owners with control over the *use of the copyright,* namely, the uses that fall within the scope of their exclusive rights. It does not empower owners to control *any use of their works.*[310] The copyright interest that is protected is a limited one. It lasts only a limited period and is restricted under the statutory provisions of sections 107-120.[311] Fair use itself is defined as a limitation on the copyright owner's exclusive rights.[312] As the Supreme Court in *Acuff-Rose* had recently stated, fair use doctrine is a necessary exception to authors' monopoly privileges needed in order to fulfill copyright's purpose to promote the arts and sciences.[313] Therefore, the question of what would be considered a use that the copyright owner may be license, depends on the extent to which the use is necessary under considerations of public policy.[314] It does not depend on the

---

308 *American Geophysical Union,* 37 F.3d at 897 ("It is indisputable that, as a general matter, a copyright holder is entitled to demand a royalty for licensing others to use its copyrighted work . . . and that the impact on potential licensing revenues is a proper subject for consideration in assessing the fourth factor."); *see Acuff-Rose,* 114 S. Ct. at 1178; *Harper & Row,* 471 U.S. at 568-69.

309 *American Geophysical Union,* 37 F.3d at 898. This standard allowed the court to distinguish *Williams & Wilkins* from the circumstances at hand. The Second Circuit quoted the District Court: "To the extent the copying practice was 'reasonable' in 1973 [when *Williams & Wilkins* was decided], it has ceased to be 'reasonable' as the reasons that justified it before [photocopying licensing] have ceased to exist." *Id.* at 892 (quoting 802 F. Supp. at 25).

310 For a discussion of this distinction, see PATTERSON & LINDBERG, *supra* note 230, at 181-86. Publishers however, seek to expand their power by "acting on a belief that any use of the work is the use of the copyright and vice versa." *Id.* Patterson & Lindberg demonstrate their argument by analyzing the provisions of common copyright licenses and copyright notices, including the license of the Copyright Clearance Center ("CCC"). The CCC license purports to license any use of published works notwithstanding the provisions of section 107 ("Fair Use"), or section 108 ("Limitations on Exclusive Rights: Reproduction by Libraries and Archives"), which specifically exclude certain uses from the monopoly of the copyright owner. *Id.* at 183-84.

311 17 U.S.C. §§ 107-120.

312 17 U.S.C. § 107 ("Limitation on exclusive rights: Fair Use").

313 *See Acuff-Rose,* 114 S. Ct. at 1169 ("From the infancy of copyright protection, some opportunity for fair use of copyrighted materials has been thought necessary to fulfill copyright's very purpose, 'to promote the Progress of Science and useful Arts . . . .' " (quoting U.S. CONST. art. I, § 8, cl. 8)).

314 For a discussion of the public benefit approach to fair use *see generally* GOLDSTEIN,

owner's willingness to license a certain use.[315]

The interpretation of fair use doctrine should be consistent with the constitutional provisions.[316] The feasibility of licensing arrangements should only be an affirmative criterion. In other words, when it is impossible to license a certain use, or prohibitively expensive to do so due to high transaction costs, the fourth factor would support the finding of fair use. Yet, the fact that a license is available does not weigh the fourth factor against fair use. This is supported by the cases cited by the Supreme Court in *Acuff-Rose*. In all of those cases, the availability of a license was considered only as a negative standard, namely, as a factor that limits the right of the copyright holder and supports the finding of fair use.[317]

The availability of licenses becomes even more critical in the context of digital networks. In digital dissemination all uses become potentially infringing. The availability of contractual arrangements between distributors and users introduces a threat to "the public's ability to foster certain socially beneficial uses of that same information at acceptable costs."[318] An approach that limits fair use doctrine to incidents where a license is unavailable expands the control enjoyed by publishers over uses of their works. In such a case copyright law would serve to supplement an already expanded power of copyright owners to control the use of their works. This is complemented by the physical ability to monitor the

---

supra note 247 (public benefit approach to fair use will excuse uses if the social benefit of the use outweighs the loss to the copyright owner).

315 The defendant in *American Geophysical Union*, made a similar argument. Texaco argued that considering the impact on potential licensing revenues assumes that publishers are entitled to demand and receive licensing royalties and fees for photocopying. The question of whether publishers are entitled to demand fees for permission to make photocopies, however, is the very question that the fair use analysis is supposed to answer. *See* 37 F.3d at 897.

316 464 U.S. at 432 ("When technological change has rendered its literal terms ambiguous, the Copyright Act must be construed in light of this basic purpose.") (citations omitted).

317 In other words, the absence of a market or an ability to license favored the finding of fair use. None of the cases cited by the court supported the conclusion that the availability of licenses negates the finding of fair use. In *Acuff-Rose*, the Supreme Court found support for the finding of fair use in the "unlikelihood that creators of imaginative works will license critical reviews or lampoons of their works." 114 S. Ct. at 1178. The Court cited other courts that found the fourth factor to support the finding of fair use when the allegedly infringing use effects only "a potential market or value that the copyright holder has not typically sought to, or reasonably been able to, obtain or capture." *American Geophysical Union*, 37 F.3d at 898 (quoting *Twin Peaks*, 996 F.2d at 1377 and noting that fourth factor will favor secondary user when use "filled a market niche that the [copyright owner] simply had no interest in occupying"); Pacific and S. Co. v. Duncan, 744 F.2d 1490, 1496 (11th Cir. 1984), *cert. denied*, 471 U.S. 1004 (1985) (noting that the fourth factor may not favor copyright owner when the secondary user "profits from an activity that the owner could not possibly take advantage of").

318 Reichman, *supra* note 242, at 824.

use of the work and would lead to an abolishment of fair use defense.

From the perspective of social dialogue and political participation, the inability of users to use and act upon copyrighted works, along with their absolute dependency on licensing by the copyright owner is dangerous. "For if the copyright owner has the power to grant a license to use the work, the copyright owner would then also have the power to deny the license completely."[319] It is widely recognized that some uses, such as parodies, would usually not be licensed by copyright owners.[320] Less attention, however, was granted to the power of copyright owners to refuse to license certain uses in order to maintain their economic and or political power.[321] The ability of copyright owners to license a use and thus to establish an additional market and prospective profits, does not call for copyright protection of that power. It is conceivable that in some cases the law should not allow copyright owners to exercise both their monopoly under copyright law and under licenses.

The content of the fair use doctrine would define the future of the public domain; namely, the works and uses that are free for all to use. The public domain is no less essential to copyright than the rights of copyright owners. Enriching the public domain is the ultimate purpose of copyright law. Cyberspace poses a direct threat to the public domain that is no less valid than the threats it poses to current interests of copyright owners. These considerations should enter the fair use calculus in specific cases of infringement in cyberspace.

CONCLUSION

In the introduction to his book *Copyright Highway*, Paul Goldstein redefines the challenges presented to copyright law by digital networks:

---

319 PATTERSON & LINDBERG, *supra* note 230, at 185-86. Patterson & Lindberg describe this as "a matter of censorship in both instances, although for profit motives rather than political reason." *Id.*

320 *See* GOLDSTEIN, *supra* note 247, at 238. Goldstein suggests that "there are two types of uses that copyright owners will usually be reluctant to license: crude parodies or advertisements quoting from the copyrighted work." *Id.* In those cases, he argues, the use should be protected as fair under the fourth factor; the copyright owners should seek relief under other regimes (such as reputational torts, passing off and misrepresentation).

321 This concern links considerations of property and democracy, allocation of resources and free speech. Copyright owners may use their power to restrict licenses in order to maintains their monopoly power. The centralized structure of the information flow which draws a clear line between producers and paying consumers is beneficial for copyright owners, and they are most likely to maintain it. What incentive would a copyright owner have to license users to create their own customized version of a movie?

> This book does not ask, as would some legal specialists, whether copyright will survive the new technologies. That question is about as bootless as asking whether politics will survive democracy. The real question is what steps it will take to ensure that the promised new era of information and entertainment survives copyright.[322]

This Article suggested that the promise of cyberspace lies first and foremost in its potential for decentralizing and democratizing social dialogue. Cyberspace has the potential of transforming the production and dissemination of knowledge. It has the potential of transforming our social and cultural structures.

This paper demonstrated how copyright law, when combined with new technological means of controlling and monitoring use, may enhance the power of copyright owners to restrict access to information in an unprecedented way. The overall effect of enforcing copyright law in cyberspace is to limit the public domain. The combination of physical control over the use of information, on the one hand, with property rights, on the other hand, may give copyright owners absolute control over the use of their works. Owners get both the physical control over any access to their works, and legal control provided by copyright law.

The important advantage of cyberspace is its potential for enhancing wide participation of individuals in social dialogue. Participation, from a democratic perspective, has a value in and of itself. Expensive copyright suppresses such participation by allowing copyright owners to limit the use of information. At a minimum, expensive copyrights allow owners to repress competition with their works and thus secure their economic interests at a price of restricting diversity of information and cultural forms. At the extreme, expensive copyright may also be used to suppress the use of information for purposes that are inconsistent with the long term political and economic goals of copyright owners.

"Universal Service" became one of the prevalent slogans of the public debate over the future of cyberspace. The public debate over universal access had so far focussed on issues such as who controls the wires and to what extent access to cyberspace should be regulated. But universal access is also about the ability to access content in cyberspace, and to take part in its creation. If copyright law does not evolve to take those considerations into account, the benefits of cyberspace will be denied to the public and distributed among a limited group of stakeholders.

---

322 GOLDSTEIN, *supra* note 1, at 36.

COPYRIGHT WITHOUT BORDERS? CHOICE OF FORUM AND CHOICE OF LAW FOR COPYRIGHT INFRINGEMENT IN CYBERSPACE

JANE C. GINSBURG*

I. INTRODUCTION

I stress the question mark in the title of this paper. Here is the problem: claims of copyright infringement are arising out of the communication of works over digital networks such as the Internet. These networks are indifferent to national borders. But copyright owners today pursue infringement claims before courts and under legal rules whose competencies are territorial. How does one reconcile the ubiquity of the infringement with the boundaries of adjudication?

To illustrate the problem, let me begin with a true story. Former French President François Mittérand died in January 1996. Within a few days of his death, his former personal physician published a memoir, titled *Le Grand Secret* (*The Big Secret*). The doctor disclosed that the cancer that ultimately killed Mittérand had already metastasized when Mittérand first assumed the presidency. Indeed, the doctor claimed, toward the end of his second seven-year term, Mittérand was no longer able to exercise the functions of his office. The book's publication drew Mittérand's family's ire; the family invoked the late President's post-mortem right of privacy under French law to obtain a court order against the book's dissemination. Within days of its publication, the book was withdrawn from circulation.

Before every copy disappeared from bookstore shelves, however, the entrepreneur of a "cyberspace cafe" in a provincial French city acquired a copy, scanned all 190 pages, and posted the image files to an Internet site. Patrons of his cafe could log onto the site, as could remote users elsewhere in France who enjoyed Internet access. The event proved to be the best publicity the In-

---

* Morton L. Janklow Professor of Literary and Artistic Property Law, Columbia University School of Law. This Article expands on the Herbert Tenzer Distinguished Lecture in Intellectual Property Law, given at the Benjamin N. Cardozo School of Law, October 15, 1996.

Many thanks for substantive suggestions to Professor Jessica Litman, Professor Henry Monaghan, and to the participants in the Columbia Law School faculty symposium, and for research assistance to Deirdre von Dornum, Columbia Law School 1997.

ternet could have received in France. More than 30,000 people simultaneously tried to access the site, provoking a "crash" of telephone service in eastern France. Faced with threats from Mittérand's family, the entrepreneur declared that if pursued, he would simply delete the material from the French server, and send his files to a website in the United States.[1]

So far, this story lacks a role for the copyright owner. In real life, the author and the publisher were caught in the middle. The entrepreneur's actions clearly violated their rights under French copyright law, notwithstanding his self-serving declarations that his acts fell within a juridical void. The author's and publisher's difficulty was not with the copyright law, it was with the politics of the situation. They, after all, were contesting the withdrawal of the book. While the entrepreneur had treated the copyright cavalierly, he had also eluded the censorship that the late President's family had so far succeeded in imposing.

But suppose that the entrepreneur had uploaded his files to a U.S. website, and that the French copyright owners had sought to prevent dissemination of the work in the United States? Or that the entrepreneur uploaded the files to a United Kingdom website, and the copyright owners sought to prevent the dissemination from the United Kingdom? (*Le Grand Secret* was in fact found on websites in the United States, Canada, and the United Kingdom.) Whom would the copyright owner pursue? In what forum (fora)? And what law(s) would apply?

The implications of this scenario contest a central commonplace of international copyright law. Traditionally copyright protection has been territorial. That is, national law will apply to acts of infringement committed in a particular country, regardless of the national origin of the work infringed. The principal multilateral copyright conventions aim to promote international exchange of works of authorship by mandating the nondiscrimination rule of "national treatment." While promoting the permeability of national boundaries by copyrighted works, this rule also preserves national sovereignty by confining any country's copyright regime to local borders. But the concept of territoriality becomes elusive when the alleged infringements are accomplished by means of digital communications originating offshore. Traditional international copyright rules seem to presume that international

---

[1] *See* Michel Alberganti & Hervé Morin, *Internet contourne la censure du livre du docteur Gubler*, LE MONDE, Jan. 25, 1996; Paul-André Tavoillot, *Le droit de l'Internet existe personne ne l'a rencontré*, LA TRIBUNE, Jan. 25, 1996, at 6; David Dufresne, *Besançon, site sismique*, LE CAHIER MULTIMEDIA DE LIBÉRATION, Jan. 26, 1996, at I-II.

infringements will occur sequentially and slowly; but digital networks make possible multinational infringements that are simultaneous and pervasive. As a result, it may be time to rethink this basic rule of international copyright.

The disjunction between territorial treatment of copyright claims and the ubiquity of cyberspace has led some commentators to urge abandonment of landlocked notions of judicial and legislative competence. Since digital communications resist grounding in particular fora, or governance by individual national laws, these writers contend it would be best to devise a cyberian legal system that would supply cyber-specific substantive copyright law, and/or virtual dispute settlers whose competence—and whose determinations—would transcend national borders.[2]

My analysis will be more earthbound. This is not to belittle the important ongoing efforts to achieve international harmony of substantive copyright rules.[3] Nor is it in any way to disparage the virtual magistrate concept, under which parties (especially copyright holders and on-line service providers) would remit their disputes to on-line arbitrators.[4] Rather, as a practical matter, I doubt that either of these approaches will immediately displace national disparities in copyright rules or adjudication in national courts. As a result, I will consider how courts may apply existing principles of judicial and legislative competence to resolve as fully as possible in a single forum a claim of multinational copyright infringement occurring through cyberspace. To keep an admittedly complex inquiry relatively simple, I will limit the focus of the analysis to U.S. legal concepts of judicial and legislative competence. I acknowledge, however, that U.S. concepts may sometimes differ significantly from those applied in other common law or civil law countries.[5]

II. Choice of Forum

Recall our story of the posting of *Le Grand Secret* to websites in

---

[2] *See, e.g.*, David R. Johnson & David Post, *Law and Borders—The Rise of Law in Cyberspace*, 48 Stan. L. Rev. 1367 (1996); Henry H. Perritt, Jr., *Jurisdiction in Cyberspace*, 41 Vill. L. Rev. 1 (1996); *see also* Paul Edward Geller, *New Dynamics in International Copyright*, 16 Colum.-VLA J.L. & Arts 461 (1992).

[3] *See, e.g.*, WIPO Copyright Treaty, Dec. 20, 1996. A "special agreement" to "introduce new international rules and clarify the interpretation of certain existing rules in order to provide adequate solutions to the questions raised by new economic, social, cultural and technological developments." *Id.* preamble.

[4] *See, e.g.*, Johnson & Post, *supra* note 2 (advocating a separate legal system for cyberspace, developed and regulated by users and service providers).

[5] *See* W.R. Cornish, *Intellectual Property Infringement and Private International Law: Challenging the Common Law Approach*, 4 GRUR Int'l 285 (1996).

the United States and the United Kingdom. The copyright owner's goal in pursuing an infringement action is to bring as many parties and claims as possible before a single forum. Can the French publishers obtain personal jurisdiction in a U.S. court over the French national that originated the communication? Over the operator of the U.S. website? Over the operator of the U.K. site? Over the commercial on-line service (if any) that carries the website? (The question whether, on the merits, the website operator or on-line service would be liable for direct or secondary copyright infringement is a different matter. For present purposes, we are concerned with whether that entity can be haled before a U.S. court.)

A. *Jurisdiction Based on Defendant's Domicile or the Place or Origin of the Harm*

To address this question, it may be helpful to recall some general principles of judicial competence in the United States. First, although jurisdiction over the subject matter of copyright claims is exclusively federal,[6] federal courts look initially to the law of the forum state to supply the rules of jurisdiction over the parties.[7] As a general matter, a defendant may be sued at its domicile or principal place of business, regardless of whether or not the claim arose there.[8] Thus, for example, were the French publishers to initiate their copyright action against CompuServe in Ohio, or against America Online ("AOL") in Virginia, the Ohio or Virginia federal court would have jurisdiction over those parties. Moreover, because the court would be asserting general jurisdiction over those parties, it would have power to hear not only claims arising out of the U.S. distribution of the copyrighted work, but also claims arising out of the distribution of the work in other countries. (What law applies to extra-U.S. distribution is a matter I will take up in a later section of this Article.) But what about the website operators

---

6 28 U.S.C. § 1338 (1994).

7 *See* FED. R. CIV. P. 4. Although it has yet to do so, Congress could enact national rules of judicial competence. However, when the claim arises under federal law, and minimum contacts with any one state are lacking, a federal court will have jurisdiction over a defendant whose aggregate contacts with the United States meet constitutional standards for assertion of personal jurisdiction. *See id.* 4(k)(2), discussed *infra* text accompanying notes 22-24.

8 *See* 4 CHARLES ALAN WRIGHT & ARTHUR R. MILLER, FEDERAL PRACTICE AND PROCEDURE §§ 1065-67 (2d ed. 1987). This basis of judicial competence is generally recognized outside of the United States as well. *See also* Judicial Enforcement of Judgments in Civil and Commercial Matters, sec. 2, art. 5.2, 1978 O.J. 1978 (L 304) 77; RUDOLF B. SCHLESINGER, COMPARATIVE LAW: CASES, TEXTS, MATERIALS 383 (1988); European Communities Convention on Jurisdiction and Enforcement of Judgments in Civil and Commercial Matters, Sept. 27, 1968, 8 I.L.M. 229, arts. 2, 5.3 [hereinafter Brussels Convention] (judicial competence within the European Union).

(if those entities are different from an on-line service and are not residents of Ohio or Virginia) and the French national?

A second basis of judicial competence focuses on the place of the harm. The place of harm can be understood as either the place of generation of the harm or the locations of its impact. Under the former characterization, the non-resident defendants could be subject to suit at the point of origin of the communication.[9] This raises the problem of localizing the origin of the communication. Under one view, the communication of *Le Grand Secret* originated in Besançon, France, whence the cybercafe entrepreneur sent it to the U.S. and U.K. websites. Economically, however, this point of origin seems rather fortuitous: the communication does not become accessible (and thus economically threatening) until it has been received at the website. The alleged harm is caused by the public availability of the work for access and downloading from the website, not from the home or cafe computer of the French national (who, in any event, deleted it from his server).[10] From the perspective of the members of the public seeking to obtain *Le Grand Secret*, the website is the distribution center for the work.[11] Thus, jurisdiction in a U.S. court over the website operator and over the foreign national who deliberately sent the work to that site would be proper at the U.S. location of the server. The territorial scope of the claim would cover not only distributions of the work to U.S. users, but distributions to foreign users who access and download from the U.S. website. (Again, choice of law is another matter.)

B. *Long-Arm Jurisdiction*

This brings us to the final basis of judicial competence: the forum as the place of impact of the harm. In our hypothetical, the party over whom the copyright owner would be asserting this basis of personal jurisdiction in a U.S. court would be the U.K. website

---

9 The prevailing view in the United States and abroad is that plaintiff can sue in tort either where the harm originated or where it impacted. *See, e.g.*, Wright & Miller, *supra* note 8, § 1069; Schlesinger, *supra* note 8, at 391; Dominique Holleaux, Jacques Foyer, Géraud de Geouffre de La Pradelle, Droit international privé §§ 713-26 (1987); Brussels Convention, *supra* note 8, art. 5.3; Case 68/93, Shevill v. Presse Alliance, SA, 1995 E.C.R. 289 (Mar. 7), ¶ 20.

10 *Cf.* Summers v. The Washington Times, 21 Med. L. Rep. 2127 (D.D.C. 1993), *quoted in* Givens v. Quinn, 877 F. Supp. 485, 491 (W.D. Mo. 1994) (in libel action, "publication" held to occur not when newspaper's source sent allegedly defamatory statements to the newspaper, but when alleged defamation became "available to the general public").

11 *Cf.* CompuServe, Inc. v. Patterson, 89 F.3d 1257 (6th Cir. 1996) (personal jurisdiction in Ohio over non-resident declaratory judgment defendant justified because, *inter alia*, defendant regularly sent software to CompuServe for distribution over its shareware network).

operator. Here, unlike the case of the U.S. website operator, there is no U.S. "distribution center." But there could be receipt in the United States, assuming U.S. users contacted the U.K. site, rather than the U.S. site, in order to obtain the work. In any event, once a work is on the web, it is available all over the world, whatever the physical location of the server. Is this availability of material sufficient to justify exercise of personal jurisdiction over the non-U.S. site operator?

1. Jurisdiction over the parties

The answer depends first on constitutional limitations on judicial competence. The constitutional limits are generous: it suffices for assertion of specific jurisdiction that defendant have "certain minimum contacts with [the forum] such that the maintenance of the suit does not offend 'traditional notions of fair play and substantial justice.'"[12] There will be "minimum contacts" with the forum if there is "some act by which the defendant purposefully avails itself of the privilege of conducting activities within the forum State, thus invoking the benefits and protections of its laws."[13]

For constitutional purposes, then, the question would be whether making copyrighted works available to users in the forum for viewing and downloading is tantamount to purposefully availing oneself of the privilege of conducting activities in the forum. If we were talking about traditional distribution of infringing hard copies or traditional broadcasting to the forum, the answer, I believe, would clearly be "yes."[14] For distributions through cyberspace that do not specifically target the forum, the defendant's relationship to the forum may be similar to that of a foreign defendant who merely injects a product into the "stream of commerce." That act alone may not suffice.[15] On the other hand, even if the defendant has not specifically targeted the forum, the defendant knows that "[b]y simply setting up, and posting informa-

---

[12] International Shoe Co. v. Washington, 326 U.S. 310, 316 (1945).

[13] Hanson v. Denckla, 357 U.S. 235, 253 (1958).

[14] *See generally* Martin Schwimmer, *World Wide Web—Nationwide Jurisdiction?*, 65 COPYRIGHT WORLD 15, 16-17 (1996) (discussing mail-order catalog cases).

[15] *See, e.g.*, Worldwide Volkswagen Corp. v. Woodson, 444 U.S. 286 (1980); Asahi Metal Indus. v. Superior Ct., 480 U.S. 102 (1987). In international stream of commerce cases, courts must

> consider the procedural and substantive interests of other nations whose interests are affected by the assertion of jurisdiction . . . . In every case, however, those interests . . . will be best served by a careful inquiry into the reasonableness of the assertion of jurisdiction in the particular case, and an unwillingness to find the serious burdens on an alien defendant outweighed by minimal interests on the part of the plaintiff or the forum State.

Asahi Metal Indus., 480 U.S. at 115-16.

tion at [ ] a website in the form of an advertisement or solicitation, one has done everything necessary to reach the global [I]nternet audience,"[16] and thus has "purposefully availed" oneself of the benefits of each forum from which one hopes to attract customers.

A recent trademark infringement case in the Southern District of New York affords an example of the "mere injection" approach to Internet postings. The case involved a Missouri website that advertised a local jazz club called the Blue Note. The website was accessible in New York, where the better-known plaintiff Blue Note jazz club is located. The judge held that "[c]reating a site, like placing a product into the stream of commerce, may be felt nationwide—or even worldwide—but, without more, is not an act purposefully directed toward the forum state."[17] In that case, the court stressed that Internet users could not purchase tickets to shows at the Missouri Blue Note through the website. To buy tickets or see a show, New Yorkers would have to travel to Missouri (although they could order tickets from New York via the defendant's 800 number). Thus, the court concluded, the website advertised to New Yorkers (and to anyone else with Internet access), but did not initiate a transaction via the web with these users.

By contrast, in another recent Internet-related trademark infringement case, a federal district court in Connecticut held that the minimum contacts standard was met when an out of state software producer's website was accessible to Connecticut residents, and invited them to call an 800 number to place orders.[18] The Connecticut court did not inquire whether any 800 number transactions had taken place, or even if Connecticut residents with Internet access had in fact logged onto defendant's site. The potential for access to and transactions from the forum apparently sufficed.

In the same vein, while a Missouri court faced with another Internet trademark infringement controversy took evidence on the number of "hits" the defendant's site had received from Missouri, the court's disposition rested more on the potential of the Internet as a marketing tool to the forum, than on the quantifiable in-state

---

16 Maritz, Inc. v. Cybergold, Inc., 947 F. Supp. 1328, 1332 (E.D. Mo. 1996).

17 Bensusan Restaurant Corp. v. King, 937 F. Supp. 295, 301 (S.D.N.Y. 1996).

18 *See* Inset Sys., Inc. v. Instruction Set, Inc., 937 F. Supp. 161 (D. Conn. 1996). *But see* Richard S. Zembek, Comment, *Jurisdiction and the Internet: Fundamental Fairness in the Networked World of Cyberspace*, 6 ALB. L.J. SCI. & TECH. 339, 367-75 (1996) (drawing analogies to cases involving interstate advertising and 1-800 numbers, which held that neither the advertisement, nor the toll-free number, standing alone, sufficed to satisfy the minimum contacts standard); *see also* Dan L. Burk, *Federalism in Cyberspace*, 28 CONN. L. REV. 1095, 1111 n.70 (1996) (criticizing *Inset* on the ground that it could lead to assertion of personal jurisdiction over remote users who access websites located in other states).

impact of the website. The court stressed that "the nature and quality of contacts provided by the maintenance of a website on the [I]nternet are clearly of a different nature and quality than other means of contact with a forum such as the mass mailing of solicitations into a forum."[19] Or, as another district court recently concluded, a commercial website operator "should not be permitted to take advantage of modern technology through an Internet Web page and [CompuServe] forum and simultaneously escape traditional notions of jurisdiction."[20]

Another federal district court has assessed and attempted to rationalize these decisions by distinguishing "passive Website[s]" such as the Missouri Blue Note's from interactive sites either "involving the knowing and repeated transmission of computer files over the Internet," or at least permitting a user to "exchange information with the host computer."[21] Applying this analysis to our hypothetical, the out of state website that offers *Le Grand Secret* is "interactive": it does not simply inform users that they can buy the book elsewhere (or through other media); it enables them to acquire it directly from the site.

If interactivity is the key to minimum contacts, must in-state residents have in fact interacted with the website, or does the potential for in-state viewing and storage suffice? Courts that have found the minimum contacts standard satisfied by the in-state accessibility of an out-of-state webpage appear to emphasize potential access by in-state computer users, rather than actual in-state access measured by the number of "hits" to the website. Where in-state users have viewed or downloaded *Le Grand Secret* from the foreign site, it should be clear that the out of state website operator has initiated infringing transactions within the forum. Where the site is accessible in-state but no evidence is submitted as to actual hits, the "potential access" view of minimum contacts would hold that, by inviting residents to view or acquire infringing copies directly from the website, the out-of-state operator avails itself of the benefits of conducting activities within the state.

On the other hand, were the evaluation of minimum contacts limited to actual hits, it is conceivable that no single state would

---

19 *Maritz*, 947 F. Supp. at 1333; *accord* Minnesota v. Granite Gate Resorts (Minn. 2d Dist. 1996) (visited Feb. 17, 1997) <www.leepfrog.com/E-law/Cases/Minn_v_Granite_Gate.html> (offshore on-line gambling service based in Belize held to have established minimum contacts with Minnesota because its webpage solicitation was "a direct marketing campaign to the State of Minnesota").

20 EDIAS Software Int'l v. BASIS Int'l Ltd., 947 F. Supp. 413, 420 (D. Ariz. 1996).

21 Zippo Mfg. Co. v. Zippo Dot Com, 1997 U.S. Dist. LEXIS 1701 *12-13 (W.D. Pa. 1997).

have sufficient contacts with the offshore website operator. But this need not mean that no U.S. court will be competent to hear a copyright infringement claim against the foreign defendant. Because the claim arises under federal copyright law, Federal Rule of Civil Procedure 4(k)(2) affords a special basis of personal jurisdiction in exactly this kind of situation. The Rule provides:

> If the exercise of jurisdiction is consistent with the Constitution and laws of the United States, serving a summons or filing a waiver of service is also effective, with respect to claims arising under federal law, to establish personal jurisdiction over the person of any defendant who is not subject to the jurisdiction of the courts of general jurisdiction of any state.[22]

Thus, so long as there are a sufficient number of *nationwide* hits to satisfy minimum contacts standards, a federal district court will have personal jurisdiction over the foreign website operator. In applying Rule 4(k)(2) to foreign (non-U.S.) corporations, federal courts have held that "personal jurisdiction may be asserted by courts where a foreign corporation, through an act performed elsewhere, causes an effect in the United States."[23] Similarly,

> where American residents have been intentionally solicited or targeted by the allegedly tortious conduct and there are sufficient contacts overall with the United States, a court may find that the exercise of personal jurisdiction would not offend the minimum contacts requirement of due process even where the conduct that proximately causes the injury occurs outside this country's borders.[24]

A U.S. federal court could determine that the invitation from the operator of U.K. website to U.S. users to download *Le Grand Secret* is an act causing an effect (creation of infringing copies) in the United States.

Rule 4(k)(2) only applies, however, in the event that all state courts would lack judicial competence. In many, if not most, instances it is likely that a state's doctrine on personal jurisdiction would reach the foreign website operator, particularly if the state's

---

22 FED. R. CIV. P. 4(k)(2).

23 Eskofot A/S v. E.I. Du Pont De Nemours & Co., 872 F. Supp. 81, 87 (S.D.N.Y. 1995) (antitrust claim by Danish corporation against U.K. corporation alleging anticompetitive acts in Europe that barred plaintiff's entry into U.S. market); *accord* United States v. Int'l Bhd. of Teamsters, 945 F. Supp. 609 (S.D.N.Y. 1996) (RICO claim against Canadian corporation).

24 Aerogroup Int'l Inc. v. Marlboro Footworks, Ltd., No. 96 CIV. 2717 (DLC), 1996 U.S. Dist. LEXIS 19051, *41 (S.D.N.Y. Dec. 24, 1996) (applying Rule 4(k)(2) in a trademark infringement action and finding insufficient nation-wide contacts).

long-arm statute is coextensive with constitutional standards. But in some states constitutional norms may not supply the only limits on the court's competence; the long-arm statute in force in the state in which the federal court sits may decline to exercise the state's power over foreign defendants to the full extent allowed by the federal Constitution.[25] Take, for example, the New York long-arm statute. Section 302 of New York Civil Practice Law and Rules offers two relevant bases for asserting personal jurisdiction over the U.K. defendant. One is based on "commit[ting] a tortious act within the state," when the claim arises from that act.[26] Another basis is more circumscribed. It recognizes jurisdiction based on tortious acts committed outside the state that cause injury within the state, but also requires that defendant reasonably should have expected its acts to have in-state consequences, and that the defendant "derive[d] substantial revenue from interstate or international commerce."[27]

When in-state users access and download allegedly infringing copies from the foreign website, has a tort been committed in the state, thus triggering the first basis for personal jurisdiction? Or does the tort (unauthorized copying or distribution) originate out-of-state, with only an impact (the copies) occurring in-state, thus triggering the potentially more restrictive second basis for judicial competence?

The prevailing view (at least in the United States and the European Union) on communication of works over digital networks holds that copies are made when the work is received, even temporarily, in the memory of a computer.[28] As a result, when the in-

---

25 *Compare* R.I. GEN. LAWS § 9-5-33 (1956), CAL. CIV. CODE § 410.10 (West 1973), N.J. STAT. ANN. § 4:4-4 (West 1996), TEX. REV. CIV. STAT. ANN. art. 2031b (West 1996), *and* TENN. CODE ANN. § 20-2-214 (1994) (state long-arms going to full extent permitted by constitution) *with* MD. CODE ANN., CTS. & JUD. PROC. §§ 6-102 to -103 (1995), FLA. STAT. ANN. § 48.193(1)(g) (West 1997), *and* GA. CODE ANN. § 9-10-91 (1996) (state long-arms of more limited reach).

26 N.Y. C.P.L.R. § 302(a)(2) (McKinney 1996).

27 *Id.* § 302(a)(3)(ii).

28 Electronic distribution entails the making of "copies" within the meaning of the 1976 Copyright Act, 17 U.S.C. § 101 (1994), at least as amended in 1980, when Congress adopted the recommendations of the Commission on New Technological Uses ("CONTU"). Under the CONTU approach, a "copy" is made when a computer program (or by extension, any work expressed digitally) is received into the computer's temporary memory. *See* FINAL REPORT OF THE NATIONAL COMMISSION ON NEW TECHNOLOGICAL USES OF COPYRIGHTED WORKS (1978), *cited in* ROBERT A. GORMAN & JANE C. GINSBURG, COPYRIGHT FOR THE NINETIES 692 & n.164 (4th ed. 1993). This approach is the premise for section 117 of the U.S. Copyright Act, and has been followed in the European Union. *See* Council Directive 91/250, art. 4(a), 1991 O.J. (L 122) 42. American courts have also applied this principle. *See, e.g.*, MAI Sys. Corp. v. Peak Computer, Inc., 991 F.2d 511, 517 (9th Cir. 1993); Advanced Computer Servs. v. MAI Sys. Corp., 845 F. Supp. 356, 362 (E.D. Va. 1994) (unauthorized loading of a program into computer's temporary memory held to create an

state receiver accesses or downloads *Le Grand Secret* at her home computer, she has created an unauthorized copy; a tortious act has thus been committed in the state. But by whom? The offshore website operator has not engaged in-state copying, it has simply made it possible for in-state actors to copy. Under this reasoning, the operator could be seen as a contributory infringer.[29]

But one might also characterize the offshore defendant's activities as directly effecting a distribution in the state. In a recent Southern District of New York decision, Judge Scheindlin held that an Italian defendant who operated an Italian website from which U.S. users could access and download images from *Playmen* magazine—in violation of the trademark rights of *Playboy* magazine—was not only distributing the images, but was engaging in distribution within the United States. This distribution violated a 1980 order enjoining the defendant from distributing *Playmen* (then extant only in print format) in the U.S. The foreign website operator had contended that it was "merely posting pictorial images on a computer server in Italy [where distribution of *Playmen* was lawful],[30] rather than distributing those images to anyone within the United States."[31] In effect, argued the defendant, U.S. users are taking a virtual voyage to Italy, acquiring *Playmen* there, and returning to the United States with their copies. The court rejected this argument, stressing "[t]hat the local user 'pulls' these images from [defendant's] computer in Italy, as opposed to [defendant]

---

infringing copy); Telerate Sys. Inc. v. Caro, 689 F. Supp. 221, 231 (S.D.N.Y. 1988) (unauthorized remote access to database: receipt of data in unauthorized user's computer held to create a copy). Thus, to receive an electronic distribution is to make a copy, even if no further, more permanent, copy follows. *See generally* INFORMATION INFRASTRUCTURE TASK FORCE, INTELLECTUAL PROPERTY AND THE NATIONAL INFORMATION INFRASTRUCTURE: THE REPORT OF THE WORKING GROUP ON INTELLECTUAL PROPERTY RIGHTS 64 & n.66 (1995).

However, several commentators have questioned or even strongly criticized the proposition that receipt in a computer's random access memory entails making a "copy." *See, e.g.*, David Post, *New Wine, Old Bottles: The Evanescent Copy*, AM. LAW., May, 1995, at 103 (questioning); Jessica Litman, *The Exclusive Right to Read*, 13 CARDOZO ARTS & ENT. L.J. 29, 40 & n.43 (1994) (criticizing); Pamela Samuelson, *Legally Speaking: The NII Intellectual Property Report*, COMM. ACM, Dec. 1994, at 21, 22 (criticizing). *But cf.* Ira L. Brandriss, *Writing in Frost on a Window Pane: E-mail and Chatting on RAM and Copyright Fixation*, 43 J. COPYRIGHT SOC'Y 237 (1996) (distinguishing infringing copying—which may be accomplished by transitory perceptible access—from fixation in creating a work of authorship, which should require a more stable format).

29 *See, e.g.*, Fonovisa, Inc. v. Cherry Auction, Inc., 76 F.3d 259 (9th Cir. 1996); Gershwin Publ'g Corp. v. Columbia Artists Management, Inc., 443 F.2d 1159 (2d Cir. 1971); Polygram Int'l Publ'g, Inc. v. Nevada/TIG, Inc., 855 F. Supp. 1314 (D. Mass. 1994).

30 *See* Playboy Enters., Inc. v. Chuckleberry Publ'g, Inc., 486 F. Supp. 414, 423 & nn. 11-12 (S.D.N.Y. 1980) (noting that PEI "succeeded in preventing dilution of the mark by Playmen everywhere but Italy, where a standard inconsistent with our law was applied to deny Playboy any protection").

31 Playboy Enters. v. Chuckleberry Publ'g, Inc., 939 F. Supp. 1032, 1039 (S.D.N.Y. 1996) (granting motion for a finding of contempt).

'sending' them to this country, is irrelevant. By inviting United States users to download these images, [defendant] is causing and contributing to their distribution in the United States."[32]

By contrast, in an earlier ruling on the motion for a finding of contempt, the court had found that a distribution in the United States had occurred when U.S. users, upon viewing the *Playmen* teaser screens ("Playmen Lite"), requested a password to view more ("Playmen Pro"). In this opinion, Judge Scheindlin was less clear as to whether simply viewing the "Playmen Lite" images in the United States (without the additional e-mail or fax transaction to obtain the password to "Playmen Pro") constituted a distribution in the United States.[33] There was a distribution, but its localization at first seemed uncertain.

In the *Le Grand Secret* hypothetical, the difference between distributing in the United States and distributing in some unspecified location correlates to the two long-arm bases cited earlier: tortious act committed in the state and tortious act committed out of state, with impact in state (and additional conditions). If the U.K. website operator were making *Le Grand Secret* available to U.S. users without requiring additional transactions (such as the purchase of a password), under the reasoning of Judge Scheindlin's second opinion in *Playboy Enters.* there would still be a U.S. distribution because U.S. users would be receiving copies on their screens that they could also printout or download to permanent memory. Under her first opinion in *Playboy Enters.*, by contrast, the place of distribution being uncertain, perhaps the only basis of personal jurisdiction (in a federal court sitting in a state with a long-arm statute like New York's) would be the latter one. In that case, the copyright owner would need to show that the U.K. website operator should have foreseen U.S. downloads, and that the U.K. defendant derived substantial revenue from interstate or international commerce.

With respect to the defendant's source of revenue, one might expect that the copyright owner would not attempt to secure jurisdiction in the U.S. courts over the U.K. website operator if the operator lacked assets in the United States against which a judgment could be enforced. But that may be too swift an assumption. Suppose that the plaintiff was seeking an injunction to block access by U.S. users to the U.K. website.[34] (Plaintiff could, of course, go

[32] *Id.* at 1044 (denying motion for reconsideration).

[33] *See id.* at 1039.

[34] U.S. courts may enter injunctions "sufficiently broad to include actions taken outside

against the U.K. actor in the United Kingdom, but it would prefer to get as much coverage as possible in a single action.[35]) In that case, the "substantial revenue" limitation could bar asserting the claim against the offshore actor.

As for foreseeability, it should be clear that once a document is posted on a website, it is foreseeable that it can be accessed anywhere in the world (assuming that the operator has not specifically limited access).

2. Scope of the claim

Assuming that the contacts between the offshore website operator and the U.S. forum are not too tenuous to justify assertion of personal jurisdiction over our hypothetical U.K. operator, the next question is: what is the territorial scope of the claim? If the claim is based on the intra-U.S. impact of an infringement originating outside the United States, then the non-resident alleged infringer would normally be obliged to defend against only those acts that can be localized in the United States.[36] The plaintiff would not be able to bootstrap extraterritorial acts, such as the distribution of copies in the United Kingdom or elsewhere in the world, to its U.S. claim. Otherwise, as a practical matter, there would be no difference between the "specific" jurisdiction exercised against a non-resident defendant under a long-arm statute and the "general" jurisdiction to which a resident defendant would be subject.

Now, that makes some sense if one is thinking only in terms of the normally appropriate power of the court to hale a foreign defendant before it. If one is thinking of the plaintiff who is facing a worldwide infringement, this reasoning means that the plaintiff may have to litigate its infringement claims around the world, in each country of receipt/access. Of course, plaintiff could go to the source country of the infringement, or the domicile of the in-

---

the United States which have a significant impact on U.S. commerce." Nintendo of America, Inc. v. Aeropower Co., 34 F.3d 246, 249 (4th Cir. 1994).

[35] Moreover, under U.K. jurisdictional approaches, the plaintiff may not be able to try in a U.K. court those aspects of the claim that involve infringements taking place outside the United Kingdom. *See* Cornish, *supra* note 5, at 286 , 287 n.7.

[36] *Accord Shevill*, 1995 E.C.R. 289, ¶ 33. In a libel action, Brussels Convention, *supra* note 8, art. 5.3, authorizes a victim to

> bring an action for damages against the publisher either before the courts of the contracting state of the place where the publisher of the defamatory publication is established, which have jurisdiction to award damages for all the harm caused by the defamation, or before the courts of each contracting state in which the publication was distributed and where the victim claims to have suffered injury to his reputation, which have jurisdiction to rule solely in respect of the harm caused in the state of the court seised.

Id.

fringer, but this alternative presents at least two problems. First, as illustrated by the entrepreneurial copier of *Le Grand Secret* who uploaded the book to sites in the United States, the United Kingdom, and Canada, there may be more than one source country. Second, even assuming a single source, a rule that limits trial of the entire action to the source country or to defendant's domicile may well spawn opportunistic relocation of servers and corporate domiciles to the copyright equivalent of the Cayman Islands.

Is there an alternative to litigating either everywhere, or, as a practical matter, nowhere? Libel and defamation law may supply a helpful analogy. The "single publication rule" responds to a similar problem. When a defamatory statement has been published, broadcast, or transmitted to many jurisdictions, one could imagine that receipt of the libel in each jurisdiction constitutes a distinct tort,[37] thus obliging the plaintiff to sue in many fora, and putting defendant at risk of inconsistent outcomes. Instead, the "single publication rule" (judge-made in some states, legislated in others) deems an "aggregate communication," such as an edition of a newspaper or a radio broadcast, a "single publication"; while plaintiff may still select among potentially competent fora, she may only choose one.[38] Moreover, "recovery in any action shall include all damages for any such tort suffered by the plaintiff in all jurisdictions."[39] The purpose of the rule is "avoiding multiplicity of suits, as well as harassment of defendants and possible hardship upon the plaintiff himself."[40] In effect, the single publication rule makes compulsory the joinder of claims that the plaintiff could have brought against the defendant in other fora.

Does the territorial scope of the damages claim asserted under the single publication rule transcend U.S. borders? While I am not aware of any U.S. defamation decisions awarding damages for extraterritorial publications,[41] the *Restatement (Second) of Torts* is clear that a plaintiff may so recover:

> In [plaintiff's] single action he may recover damages for the publication to all persons whom the communication has reached or may be expected to reach . . . . This is true even though the publication has crossed state lines and has been read, heard or seen in every state and in foreign countries; and

---

37 *See* Keeton v. Hustler Magazine, 465 U.S. 770, 777 (1984) ("The tort of libel is generally held to occur wherever the offending material is circulated.").

38 *See* Restatement (Second) of Torts § 577A (1977).

39 Unif. Single Publication Act § 1, 14 U.L.A. 377 (1990).

40 Restatement, *supra* note 38, § 577A, cmt. d.

41 *Cf.* Watt v. Longsdon, 1 K.B. 130 (1930) (calculating damages to include distribution of English publication in Morocco).

> all damages sustained in all jurisdictions may be recovered in the one action.[42]

Were courts to adapt the single publication rule to copyright infringement in cyberspace, a U.S. court with personal jurisdiction over our hypothetical U.K. website operator would be able to award damages not only for U.S. downloads, but for all downloads, wherever localized (assuming it were possible to calculate or estimate their extent).[43] The rule thus could usefully simplify the plaintiff's claim, as well as the defendant's exposure to subsequent litigation. The rule's actual effectiveness would depend on whether the U.K. defendant has sufficient U.S. assets to satisfy the judgment, or if not, whether a U.K. court would recognize such a judgment.[44]

Now, if a single publication rule for international copyright infringement claims is such a good idea, why haven't U.S. courts already adopted it? After all, multinational infringements are not new with cyberspace, although cyberspace certainly aggravates the problem. One reason may be that, with respect to multinational infringements that did not involve distribution or public performance of works in the United States, there may have been no basis for personal jurisdiction over a foreign infringer. In cyberspace, by contrast, even far away infringements can come to the United States, and thus potentially subject the offshore defendant to the jurisdiction of our courts. A more significant reason may be that, in the United States, copyright is exclusive federal subject matter. Courts and litigants did not *need* a single publication rule for copyright, because one copyright action already covered the whole na-

---

42 RESTATEMENT, *supra* note 38, § 577A, cmt. e; *see id.* illus. 8:

> A publishes in a magazine of national circulation an article in which he states that B beats his wife. The magazine is read by a million readers in all states of the United States and in foreign countries. B brings an action against A for a defamation. In this action B may recover damages based on the communication to all of these readers.

43 There may be some question as to whether there has been a "single publication" when the work is "distributed" not by communication to users who receive the copies or the performance at the same time, but rather by means of the users themselves, whose access to the work will be intermittent and disjoined in time. Nonetheless, since each user is presumably receiving the same communication from the same website, the "single" quality of the publication should persist. *See id.* § 577A, cmt. d.

44 It is not clear whether a U.K. court would recognize the judgment. The single publication rule appears inconsistent with the European Court of Justice's determination in *Shevill*, 1995 E.C.R. 289. *See supra* note 36.

Outside the European Union, a British Columbian court, in a libel action where the libel was published in British Columbia, Alberta, and Saskatchewan, awarded damages for harm caused by the publication in all three jurisdictions; this was permissible because the libel was wrongful under the law of all the jurisdictions and there were no significant differences in the libel laws of the jurisdictions. *See* Hubert v. DeCamillis [1963] 41 D.L.R. (2d) 495. Thus, it seems that other jurisdictions could apply the single publication rule.

tional territory.[45] On the other hand, even U.S.-originated infringements can impact abroad, notably in Canada. As to these claims, however, litigants in the past appear to have concentrated on whether U.S. copyright law could apply to extraterritorial acts or impacts, not on whether plaintiff could be compelled to add the foreign claim to the U.S. action. As a U.S. court has emphasized, "[t]he single publication rule is not a choice-of-law rule. Instead, the single publication rule determines how many causes of action a plaintiff might have . . . ."[46] And with this distinction between the single publication rule and choice of law, it is now appropriate to turn to the latter issue.

III. Choice of Law

First, if my proposal to adopt a single publication rule for multinational infringements in cyberspace were adopted, would the choice of law analysis be simplified as well? Not necessarily. While in single publication rule cases the forum applies its own law to determine the applicable statute of limitations,[47] it is unclear what law applies to the substance of the defamation claim. Indeed, it is not even clear if the forum should apply one law,[48] or as many laws as there are jurisdictions to which the libel was communicated.[49] Ultimately, the appropriateness of the forum applying its own law (and only its own law) may depend on the facts of the alleged infringement.

A. *The U.S. Forum is Defendant's Domicile—or is the Point of Origin of the Infringement*

Let us return to the comparatively straightforward situation in which the allegedly infringing communication originates from a U.S. website. Clearly, U.S. copyright law would apply to all U.S. access of the work, and the court should be able to enjoin the oper-

45 *Cf.* Ettore v. Philco Television Broad. Corp., 229 F.2d 481 (3d Cir. 1956) (adjudicating right of publicity claims by Pennsylvania resident arising out of unauthorized television broadcast received in Pennsylvania, Delaware, New Jersey, and New York; right of publicity claims, albeit a form of intellectual property, are state rather than federal claims).

46 *Givens,* 877 F. Supp. at 488.

47 *See* Sun Oil v. Wortman, 486 U.S. 717 (1988). This is true even if the forum ends up applying another state's statute of limitations; it would have done so under its own "borrowing statute," which directs the forum to look to the statute of limitations in force in the state of first publication. *See Givens,* 877 F. Supp. at 487.

48 *See* David S. Welkowitz, *Preemption, Extraterritoriality, and the Problem of State Antidilution Laws,* 67 Tul. L. Rev. 1, 21 (1992) ("There is scant precedent as to what law should apply, although the logic of the single publication rule and judicial economy considerations suggest that a single state law should apply to the entire transaction.").

49 *See Ettore,* 229 F.2d at 481 (distributive application of the law of each state where unauthorized broadcast of prizefight was received).

ation of the U.S. site altogether. But what law applies to copies made outside the United States, when offshore users logged onto the U.S. site? Still U.S. law, or the laws of the countries of end use? Our ever-present desire to keep things simple would counsel application of U.S. law, even to infringements that culminate offshore. The case law, however, is conflicted. There appears to be a split between the Ninth Circuit and other courts, most notably the Second Circuit.

In a series of decisions dating back to 1939, the Second Circuit has upheld the application of U.S. law to distribution of copies abroad, when the foreign copies were further reproductions of an initial infringing reproduction committed in the United States.[50] Other courts have also applied this master copy approach to the extraterritorial extension of U.S. copyright law.[51] The Second Circuit has, however, distinguished the master copy cases when plaintiff sought recovery for offshore live *performances* of copyrighted works. When an unauthorized performance takes place abroad, the material connection to the United States provided by an initial unauthorized reproduction is considered lacking.[52]

The Ninth Circuit appears more reluctant to apply U.S. copyright law to extraterritorial acts. In a recent decision concerning videocassette rights to the Beatles' film *Yellow Submarine*, the court declined to apply U.S. law to a claim that the U.S. defendant had "authorized" offshore actors to make and distribute videocassettes of the film, in violation of plaintiff's alleged rights.[53] None of the allegedly infringing videocassettes were manufactured or sold in the United States.

Although the U.S. Copyright Act confers on authors the exclu-

---

50 *See, e.g.*, Sheldon v. Metro-Goldwyn Pictures, Corp., 106 F.2d 45 (2d Cir. 1939), *aff'd*, 309 U.S. 390 (1940) (distribution in Canada of motion picture held to infringe plaintiff's play); Update Art Inc. v. Modiin Publ'g Ltd., 843 F.2d 67 (2d Cir. 1988) (publication in Israel of photograph of poster; initial copy of photograph allegedly made in United States and sent to Israel for further copying and distribution); Famous Music Corp. v. Seeco Records, Inc., 201 F. Supp. 560 (S.D.N.Y. 1961) (pirate records sold in Europe allegedly made from illicit U.S. master tape); *see also* Fun-Damental Too, Ltd. v. Gemmy Indus. Corp., No. 96 CIV. 1103 (MBM), 1996 U.S. Dist. LEXIS 18653, at *19 (S.D.N.Y. Dec. 16, 1996) (dismissing copyright infringement claim because plaintiff "failed to allege an infringement within the United States that led to extraterritorial infringement").

51 *See* P & D Int'l v. Halsey Publ'g Co., 672 F. Supp. 1429 (S.D. Fla. 1987) (unauthorized exhibition on cruise ship of film print made without authorization in Miami).

52 *See* Robert Stigwood Group Ltd. v. O'Reilly, 530 F.2d 1096, 1100 (2d Cir. 1976) (distinguishing *Sheldon*, 106 F.2d 45, on the ground that case involved a U.S. reproduction further reproduced in Canada, while case at bar concerned live performances in Canada); Gasté v. Kaiserman, 683 F. Supp. 63, 65 (S.D.N.Y.), *aff'd*, 863 F.2d 1061 (2d Cir. 1988) (no recovery for infringing performances abroad, unless plaintiff can show that these performances "resulted from the reproduction of recordings originally made in the United States").

53 Subafilms, Ltd. v. MGM-Pathe Communications Co., 24 F.3d 1088 (9th Cir. 1994).

sive rights "to do and to authorize" certain acts, including reproduction, distribution, and public performance,[54] the Ninth Circuit held that "authorization" alone is insufficient to justify the application of U.S. law.[55] Invoking the national treatment principle of the Berne Convention,[56] the Ninth Circuit stressed that copyright is territorial, and that courts should therefore apply the law of the countries where the infringing distribution takes place.[57]

Subafilms was not necessarily inconsistent with the Second Circuit decisions, since no infringing master copy was alleged to have been made in California, and the Second Circuit cases did not involve "mere authorization." A later Ninth Circuit decision, however, seems more in tension. In a controversy concerning the diversion of the Showtime cable signal to Canadian viewers, the Ninth Circuit held that it made no difference whether the U.S. defendant had authorized Canadians to appropriate the signal, or had instead itself broadcast the signal from the United States to Canada. "In either case, the potential infringement was only completed in Canada once the signal was received and viewed."[58]

The Ninth Circuit's approach has provoked criticism from commentators[59] and, to date, one district court, in Tennessee.[60] For that court, the Ninth Circuit's analysis was artificial and out of touch. "[P]iracy has changed since the Barbary days," the *Curb* court emphasized.[61]

> Today, the raider need not grab the bounty with his own hands; he need only transmit his go-ahead by wire or telefax to start the presses in a distant land. *Subafilms* ignores this economic reality .... Under [the Ninth Circuit's] view, a phone call to Nebraska [from the United States] results in liability; the same phone call to France results in riches. In a global marketplace, it is literally a distinction without a difference.[62]

---

54 17 U.S.C. § 106 (1994).

55 *Subafilms*, 24 F.3d 1088.

56 Berne Convention for the Protection of Literary and Artistic Works, *as last amended* Oct. 2, 1979, 828 U.N.T.S. 221 [hereinafter Berne Convention].

57 "Extraterritorial application of American law would be contrary to the spirit of the Berne Convention, and might offend other member nations by effectively displacing their law in circumstances in which previously it was assumed to govern." *Subafilms*, 24 F.3d at 1097.

58 Allarcom Pay TV Ltd. v. General Instrument Corp., 69 F.3d 381, 387 (9th Cir. 1995).

59 *See, e.g.*, Michael W. Ballance, *Third-Party Innocence: Domestic Authorization of Foreign Copyright Infringement and Subafilms, Ltd. v. MGM-Pathé Communications Co.*, 20 N.C.J. INT'L L. & COM. REG. 435 (1995); Jason S. Hartley, *Subafilms, Ltd. v. MGM-Pathé Communications Co.: The Ninth Circuit Allows Direct Copyright Infringers to Escape Liability*, 4 TUL. J. INT'L & COMP. L. 345 (1996).

60 Curb v. MCA Records, Inc., 898 F. Supp. 586 (M.D. Tenn. 1995).

61 *Id.* at 595.

62 *Id.* The court may have overstated its proposition, given that the same act that vio-

What is the relationship of this debate to our hypothetical U.S. website? When foreign users log onto the U.S. site and download copies to their computers outside the United States, these acts could be characterized as further reproductions made from the illicit master copy on the U.S. website, and thus within the scope of U.S. law, as the Second Circuit has articulated the law's reach. Alternatively, applying the Ninth Circuit's approach, one might view the website as an invitation ("authorization") to all Internet users to access the document and produce copies. U.S. downloads would be governed by U.S. law (that would be true were the server located in the United Kingdom as well), but foreign downloads, since they "culminate" off shore, would be subject to the law of the place of receipt.

One begins to appreciate the Tennessee court's frustration with insistence on the dual conditions of territoriality and materiality. Perhaps courts should be less materialistic about identifying infringement, and recognize that intellectual acts of planning unauthorized acts of copying, public performance, or distribution can be localized here in the United States.[63] In the networked world of dematerialized copies, the U.S. originator of an infringing communication can attempt to elude the application of her own law by ensuring that copies are initially "sent" from a server outside the United States to destinations outside the United States. This illustrates the problem with confining legislative competence over the alleged infringement to the place where copies are made.[64] It may make more sense to identify the place where the plan to engage in unauthorized dissemination was devised, and then to consider the application of that place's law. I would argue that if it is possible to localize in the United States the point from which the unauthorized communication becomes available to the public (wherever that public be located), then U.S. law should apply to all unauthorized copies, wherever communicated. Similarly, where the United States is the nerve center for foreign distributions, the domestic

---

lates U.S. law might well violate French copyright law, so riches might not ultimately result there, either. On the other hand, the defendant could achieve a substantial practical advantage if a U.S. court, persuaded that U.S. law does not apply, and that the laws of the countries where the physical copying occurred did apply, then dismissed the claim on *forum non conveniens* grounds, remitting the plaintiff to suing in each of the countries where copying occurred. *See* discussion *infra*, section III.B.

63 *Cf.* Brown & Williamson Tobacco Corp. v. Philip Morris, Inc., 101 A.D.2d 753 (N.Y. Sup. Ct. 1984) (retaining jurisdiction to apply New York unfair competition law to New York headquartered defendant who allegedly conceived and directed from New York a scheme to infringe plaintiff's trademark rights in many foreign countries).

64 *See* Burk, *supra* note 18, at 1111-15 (discussing the difficulty of discerning physical locations of Internet users).

acts of planning and intellectually implementing the offshore acts should suffice to justify the application of U.S. law to the foreign communications.

Is this recommendation consistent with the conflicts rule of the Berne Convention, which directs application of the law of the country "where protection is claimed" to govern infringement claims?[65] One can read that text to require distributive application of the laws of all of the countries in which infringing copies appear.[66] Or one could contend that the "country where protection is claimed" is the forum country when that is the country from which the infringement originated, and which is best placed to accord an effective international remedy.[67]

Similarly, if the basis of judicial competence is the U.S. domicile of the defendant, rather than the U.S. point of origin of the communication, I would argue that U.S. law should still apply to the entirety of the infringing acts. Indeed, to some extent, the "point of origin" approach and the defendant's domicile may converge: the defendant's domicile is likely to be the same as the place from which defendant planned a series of unauthorized acts, many of them culminating abroad.[68] Moreover, the law of headquarters (especially when that is the place from which defendant devised and executed its program of international infringement) has a close relationship to all the alleged illicit acts; that law will produce the same result, whatever the destination of the pirated copies. In addition, under U.S. conflict of laws principles, the forum has a strong interest in regulating the activities of its domiciliaries.[69]

This analysis has focused on application by a U.S. court of its own law when that law is the law of the point of origin of the allegedly infringing digital communication, or of defendant's domicile. The "domicile" and "origin of the communication" points of attachment are not fully generalizable: to make these the choice of law rules in all cases would again spur manipulation of these criteria in order to localize them in the "Cayman Islands of copyright."

---

65 Berne Convention, *supra* note 56, art. 5.2.

66 *See, e.g.*, Pierre-Yves Gautier, *Du droit applicable dans le <<village planétaire>>, au titre de l'usage immatériel des œuvres*, D.S. Jur. 131 (1996).

67 *Cf.* Paul Edward Geller, *Conflict of Laws in Cyberspace: Rethinking International Copyright in a Digitally Networked World*, 20 COLUM.-VLA J.L. & ARTS 571, 597 (1996) (making a similar argument, in the context of infringements for which a point of origin cannot easily be identified); Michel Vivant, *Cybermonde: Droit et droits des réseaux*, JCP [1996] I [3969], para. 6.

68 *Cf. Shevill*, 1995 E.C.R. 289, ¶ 24 (reconciling judicial competence under Brussels Convention, *supra* note 8, art. 2—defendant's habitual residence—and art. 5.3—point of origin of a multinational tort—on the ground that these will often be the same).

69 *See, e.g.*, Gulf Oil Corp. v. Gilbert, 330 U.S. 501, 508-09 (1947).

Thus, any generalization of these criteria would require that a court ascertain whether the law designated by these points of attachment meets minimum standards of copyright protection, such as those set forth in the Berne Convention and the Agreement on Trade Related aspects of Intellectual Property ("TRIPS").[70]

B. *The Infringement Originated Outside the U.S. Forum, and Defendant Is a Non-Domiciliary*

Finally, let us return to the U.K. website operator, who is before the U.S. courts on a long-arm basis. The single publication rule (if adapted to international copyright cases) would subject the foreign defendant to suit in the United States for non-U.S. distributions as well, but we have yet to resolve which law(s) apply to those distributions. While the simplest solution would be to apply U.S. copyright law to all downloads, the relationship of the U.S. to foreign downloads from a foreign website seems too attenuated (assuming the operator is also non-U.S.) to justify such extensive application of U.S. law. Rather, the court should either apply the law of the place of the server or of the defendant's domicile. However, if these places are copyright havens, then the court should revert to the traditional territorial approach and apply the law of each country of receipt. Copyright is a "transitory cause of action": so long as the court has personal jurisdiction over the foreign defendant, it can apply a foreign copyright law.[71]

Moreover, the court *should* apply foreign law, especially when the claim presents many points of attachment with the forum, and no other forum is likely to be able to adjudicate the entirety of the action. U.S. courts too often dismiss on grounds of *forum non conveniens* when called upon to apply foreign law.[72] For example, in a

---

[70] *See generally* Agreement on Trade-Related Aspects of Intellectual Property Rights, Including Trade in Counterfeit Goods, Apr. 15, 1994, Marrakesh Agreement Establishing the World Trade Organization, Annex 1C, LEGAL INSTRUMENT—RESULTS OF THE URUGUAY ROUND vol. 31, 33 I.L.M. 81 (1994); *cf.* Comment 10 to proposed section 2B-106 of the Uniform Commercial Code (draft 1996) (protective rule if the foreign law otherwise applicable confers too low a level of protection) (visited Feb. 18, 1997) <www.law.uh.edu/ucc2b/>.

[71] *See, e.g.*, London Film Prods. Ltd. v. Intercontinental Communications, Inc., 580 F. Supp. 47 (S.D.N.Y. 1984); III PAUL GOLDSTEIN, COPYRIGHT: PRINCIPLES, LAW & PRACTICE § 16.2 (2d ed. 1996).

[72] *See* Timberlane Lumber Co. v. Bank of Am. Nat'l Trust & Sav. Ass'n, 549 F.2d 597, 616 (9th Cir. 1976) (dismissing antitrust claim on *forum non conveniens* grounds because, *inter alia*, Honduran law applied); *see also Gulf Oil Corp.*, 330 U.S. at 509 (stating that it is appropriate to try a diversity case "in a forum that is at home with the state law that must govern the case, rather than having a court in some other forum untangle problems in conflict of laws, and in law foreign to itself."). *But see London Film Prods.*, 580 F. Supp. at 49 (retaining exercise of federal diversity jurisdiction over foreign law claim by U.K. plaintiff against U.S. defendant alleged to have licensed plaintiff's films for exhibition in South

recent decision involving worldwide videocassette rights to Stravinsky's *Rite of Spring*, recorded on the soundtrack to Disney's *Fantasia*, the Southern District of New York dismissed the action, remitting the plaintiff music publisher to trying its copyright infringement claims in each of the eighteen foreign countries where videocassettes of *Fantasia* were distributed.[73] Because the U.S. copyright in the work had never been secured, there was no U.S. copyright claim. There were nonetheless substantial U.S. contacts to the litigation: defendant was a U.S. corporation; the contract in which Stravinsky granted rights to record *Rite of Spring* onto the film soundtrack was signed in New York and governed by New York law. The court justified its *forum non conveniens* dismissal on the grounds that the substantive copyright issues would best be tried in the countries whose domestic copyright laws would be called into play.

This is a weak basis for dismissal when the United States probably was the only forum in which all eighteen copyright claims could have been adjudicated. Nor would the copyright issues necessarily have been better resolved in eighteen different proceedings. The substantive issue in the case was whether a 1939 contract authorizing recording of the music onto the film's soundtrack for exhibition of the film in theaters should be interpreted to authorize reproduction and public distribution of videocassettes of the film. The Southern District of New York could have heard proof on the resolution of the old license/new media issue under the laws of the eighteen countries at issue. While other countries may resolve that issue differently, the issue under foreign law is no more elusive than it is under U.S. law.

Assuming that the court should apply foreign copyright law to the non-U.S. based claims, must the plaintiff plead and prove the laws of all 100 or more other countries where the work could have been received, and for which the plaintiff seeks damages? Perhaps resorting to a presumption that foreign copyright law resembles U.S. copyright law would help. U.S. courts have occasionally applied such a presumption, leaving it to the defendant to demonstrate that, in certain jurisdictions, the law is different.[74] The

America, without plaintiff's authorization, and in violation of plaintiff's rights in the South American countries at issue).

[73] Boosey & Hawkes Music Publishers, Ltd. v. Walt Disney Co., 934 F. Supp. 119 (S.D.N.Y. 1996).

[74] *See, e.g.*, Louknitsky v. Louknitsky, 266 P.2d 910 (1954); Leary v. Gledhill, 84 A.2d 725 (1951). *But cf.* Phillips Petroleum Co. v. Shutts, 472 U.S. 797 (1985) (declining to apply Kansas law when that law conflicted with that of other jurisdictions, and Kansas had little connection to either the class action plaintiffs or the suit's subject matter); Castano v. American Tobacco Co., 84 F.3d 734, 740-44 (5th Cir. 1996) (decertifying multistate class

presumption may be particularly appropriate in the copyright area, where over 100 countries are members of the Berne Convention, a multilateral treaty that imposes substantive minimum standards of copyright protection.[75]

IV. Conclusion

To conclude, let us return to the site—physical as well as digital—at which our story began. Back in eastern France, our cybercafe entrepreneur was enjoying considerable notoriety as a result of his Internet exploits. All the major papers carried the story of his scanning and uploading *Le Grand Secret.* But his fifteen minutes of fame ultimately did him in. The authorities did pursue him, although not for copyright infringement, nor for post-mortem privacy violations. Rather, the national press coverage awakened local officials in another part of France to a trail that had run cold: our entrepreneur went to jail for "family abandonment" and failure to pay child support.[76]

---

action because the district court failed adequately to analyze possible variations in state law).

[75] *Cf. In re* "Agent Orange" Prod. Liab. Litig., 580 F. Supp. 690, 708-13 (1984) (not necessary to apply presumption regarding the content of foreign law, since the court instead determined that the states whose laws were at issue would all apply a "national consensus" law to the mass tort claim at issue). *But see In re* Rhone-Poulenc Rorer, Inc., 51 F.3d 1293, 1300-02 (7th Cir. 1995) (district court exceeded discretion in proposing to apply an amalgamated common law standard to determine negligence in a 50-state class action suit).

[76] *See Besançon: Pascal Barbaud écroué*, Le Figaro, Jan. 27, 1996, at p. B9, col. 8.

AN INTRODUCTION TO THE LAW AND ECONOMICS OF THE V-CHIP*

MATTHEW L. SPITZER**

* Prepared for the Duke Conference on Violence in the Media.

** California Institute of Technology, Division of Social Sciences and University of Southern California Law School. I thank the participants at the Duke Conference on Media Violence and Public Policy, in an Olin Workshop at Cornell University, participants at the legal theory workshop at the University of Southern California, participants at the Law and Economics Workshop at the University of Chicago, Erwin Chemerinsky, Larry Simon, Jean Spitzer, and Eric Talley. Research assistance was provided by James Mixon, Alec Harrell, Young Dae Moon, Janene Bassett, and Brian Hickey. Errors remain my own. I can be reached at mspitzer@law.usc.edu.

INTRODUCTION

The Telecommunications Act of 1996[1] requires that all television sets sold in the United States contain a special computer chip—popularly called a "V-chip"—that will allow the viewer to program his or her television. This V-chip will allow the viewer to program the television to reject any show that has been rated too sexual, violent, or offensive in some other way. Television shows' ratings will be electronically encoded in the signal that is transmitted to the set, so the viewer will be able to program the television to reject entire classes of shows, rather than be required to make individual decisions about every program.

A television ratings system now appears to be in place.[2] Television programs will be rated in a hierarchy: "TV-G" (for all ages), "TV-PG" (parental guidance suggested), "TV-14" (may be inappropriate for children under 14), and "TV-M" (for adults).[3] Once large numbers of people purchase sets (or add-on boxes[4]) with the V-chip, we will likely alter our television viewing habits substantially. In reaction, the nature of the television market may change,

---

1 Pub. L. No. 104-104, 110 Stat. 56 (1996).

2 *See* Jane Hall & Brian Lowry, *Industry Unveils Its Ratings System for TV Programs*, L.A. TIMES, Dec. 20, 1996, at A1. All studios and broadcast networks, except for NBC, have agreed to the industry plan. Jane Hall, *Ratings Plan Set to Go to the FCC*, L.A. TIMES, July 26, 1997, at F1. As I explain below, this system may or may not survive administrative review.

3 *Id.* There are also other ratings: "TV-Y" (suitable for youngsters), "TV-Y7" (appropriate for children 7 and over), "S" (sex), "L" (language), "V" (violence), and "D" (suggestive dialogue). It is not clear if a program rated TV-Y7 will pass through a V-chip set for TV-PG. It is also unclear if a program rated "S", "L", "V", or "D" will pass through a V-chip set for TV-PG, TV-14, or even TV-M.

4 Add-on boxes will likely retail for around $40. *See V-Chip Technology Waits for Washington*, BROADCASTING & CABLE, Dec. 30, 1996, at 8 (reporting that Soundview Technology will sell a "V Chip Converter" for around $ 40).

and the fare available to children and adults may, in turn, transform.

Reactions to the V-chip have varied from ecstatic[5] to indifferent[6] to outraged.[7] Legal analysis of the V-chip has been uneven.[8] Some of those who like the idea of the V-chip have trouble paying even the most cursory attention to the question of possible constitutional problems,[9] while one commentator who is outraged sees obvious constitutional violations.[10]

---

5 *See Why the Markey Chip Won't Hurt You,* BROADCASTING & CABLE, Aug. 14, 1995, at 10 (interview with Rep. Edward J. Markey (D-Mass.)); Reed E. Hundt, *The Public's Airwaves: What Does the Public Interest Require of Television Broadcasters?,* 45 DUKE L.J. 1089, 1126 (1996). For a more sophisticated and satisfying defense of the V-chip on policy grounds, see James T. Hamilton, *Private Interests in "Public Interest" Programming: An Economic Assessment of Broadcaster Incentives,* 45 DUKE L.J. 1177 (1996). *See also* Mark M. MacCarthy, *Broadcast Self-Regulation: The NAB Codes, Family Viewing Hour, and Television Violence,* 13 CARDOZO ARTS & ENT. L.J. 667 (1995) (explaining why "self regulation" does not work); Kevin W. Saunders, *Media Self-Regulation of Depictions of Violence: A Last Opportunity,* 47 OKLA. L. REV. 445 (1994) (explaining why "self regulation" does not work).

6 *See* Ronald J. Krotoszynski, Jr., *Into the Woods: Broadcasters, Bureaucrats, and Children's Television Programming,* 45 DUKE L.J. 1193, 1194 (1996); David B. Kopel, *Massaging the Medium: Analyzing and Responding to Media Violence Without Harming the First Amendment,* 4 KAN. J.L. & PUB. POL'Y 17 (1995).

7 *See* Ted Hearn, *Lawmaker Fields Calls V-Chip Unconstitutional,* MULTICHANNEL NEWS, Nov. 27, 1995, at 152; Robert Corn-Revere, *What, Me Worry? (or, Why Mainstream Advertisers Should Pay Attention to the New Censorship),* 24 CATO INSTITUTE BRIEFING PAPER, Aug. 3, 1995 [hereinafter Corn-Revere, *What, Me Worry?*]; Robert Corn-Revere, *Television Violence and the Limits of Voluntarism,* 12 YALE J. ON REG. 187 (1995) [hereinafter Corn-Revere, *Television Violence and the Limits of Voluntarism*]; *see also* Rep. Tom Coburn, *V-Chipping Away at Parental Responsibility Is Not the Solution to TV's Morality Crisis,* ROLL CALL, Oct. 23, 1995 (opposing version of V-chip that would have governmental body do ratings, but supporting one that had parents making decisions). Bob Dole, Senator Paul Simon (D-Ill.), and Representative Jack Fields (R-Tex.) all opposed the V-chip before passage, though they stopped short of outrage. *See* Christopher Stern, *Industry Battles Ratings, V-Chip,* BROADCASTING & CABLE, June 26, 1995, at 16.

8 There have been some very good pieces discussing, in general, the constitutionality of regulating violence on television. *See* Thomas G. Krattenmaker & L.A. Powe, Jr., *Televised Violence: First Amendment Principles and Social Science Theory,* 64 VA. L. REV. 1123 (1978); Harry T. Edwards & Mitchell N. Berman, *Regulating Violence on Television,* 89 NW. U.L. REV. 1487 (1995); James Albert, *Constitutional Regulation of Televised Violence,* 64 VA. L. REV. 1299 (1978); Dennis L. DeLeon & Robert L. Naon, Note, *The Regulation of Televised Violence,* 26 STAN. L. REV. 1291 (1974); Ian Matheson Ballard, Jr., Note, *See No Evil, Hear No Evil: Television Violence and the First Amendment,* 81 VA. L. REV. 175 (1995). For a first-rate analysis of the constitutional problems involved in regulating indecent political speech, see Lili Levi, *The FCC, Indecency, and Anti-Abortion Political Advertising,* 3 VILL. SPORTS & ENT. L.J. 85 (1996).

9 *See* Hundt, *supra* note 5; Krotoszynski, Jr., *supra* note 6; David V. Scott, Comment, *The V-Chip Debate: Blocking Television Sex, Violence, and the First Amendment,* 16 LOY. L.A. ENT. L.J. 741 (1996).

10 *See* Corn-Revere, *Television Violence and the Limits of Voluntarism, supra* note 7. Although clearly not outraged by the V-chip, Edwards & Bermon analyze the V-chip in a way suggesting that it has constitutional problems. Edwards & Berman, *supra* note 8, at 1513-15. They state that "[t]he regulation will raise problems only if the government ordains the program characteristics upon which a lockout mechanism could operate, thereby disadvantaging speech by content or subject matter." *Id.* As we will see *infra* notes 15-17 and accompanying text, the Telecommunications Act of 1996 seems to have done just that.

No one has yet provided a thorough analysis of the likely effects of the V-chip on the video market.[11] Will adding a V-chip decrease, increase, or leave unchanged the amount of sex and violence on television? What information would we need in order to answer this question? A full economic treatment of the V-chip would answer at least some of these questions. And many of the answers are crucial to evaluating the constitutionality of the V-chip. However, to date no one has attempted to provide a full, systematic economic analysis. This paper fills that void.[12]

This article provides the first economic analysis of the V-chip and the market for television shows. It also provides an introduction to some of the constitutional issues surrounding the V-chip.[13] Now that the broadcast and cable industries have announced their rating system, enough can be discerned to allow us to sketch out the major issues under the First Amendment. Before we can proceed to the constitutional law and economics of the V-chip, however, we need to explain the statutory background.

Section 551 of the Telecommunications Act of 1996 creates an administrative system for rating and regulating violence and sex on television.[14] Section 551(e) gives the industry's "distributors of video programming" one year from the date of passage of the Act to:

---

[11] Legal analyses of the V-chip are starting to appear. *See* Scott, *supra* note 9; J.M. Balkin, *Media Filters, the V-Chip, and the Foundations of Broadcast Regulation*, 45 DUKE L.J. 1131 (1996).

[12] This paper will not discuss the question of why governmental coercion is needed, rather than relying on the voluntary actions of industry members. The answer may be that there is a coordination game, where no single set of actors wants to proceed unless they are reasonably certain that the rest of the industry will proceed with a rating system. The producers will not bother to rate programs and embed the ratings in the programs, for example, unless the producers are certain that the set manufacturers will install chips that can read and filter on the basis of the ratings.

A completely voluntary system for Internet sites is currently being developed by the Recreational Software Advisory Council. This voluntary system, which relies on the "Platform for Internet Content Selection" ("PICS" codes) system for embedding codes into Internet sites, relies on voluntary ratings of sites by the operators. *See* Hiawatha Bray, *Rated P for Preemptive: System to Shield Kids from Adult Web Material Also Seeks to Keep Censors Off Net*, BOSTON GLOBE (July 25, 1996) <http://www.rsac.org/press/960725.html>\; *see also* Whit Andrews, *Site-Rating System Slow to Catch On*, WEBWEEK (July 8, 1996) <http://www.webweek.com/96July8/comm/rating.html>; RSAC, *USWeb Affiliate Network to Use RSAC Internet Rating System* (July 16, 1996) <http://www.rsac.org/press/960716.html>.

[13] In Hundt, *supra* note 5, at 1126 (implicitly assuming away the constitutional issue), the chairman of the Federal Communications Commission ("FCC") concludes that there is no constitutional issue worth discussion relating to the V-chip. *Accord* Krotoszynski, Jr., *supra* note 6, at 1194. As my discussion below shows, they are almost certainly wrong.

[14] Throughout this draft "television" should be understood to include broadcast and cable television, unless the context makes it clear that this is not the case. In addition, I will often use "violence" as a shorthand for violent, sexually explicit, or laced with strong language.

> "(A) establish[ ] voluntary rules for rating video programming that contains sexual, violent, or other indecent material about which parents should be informed before it is displayed to children, . . . ; and
>
> (B) agree[ ] voluntarily to broadcast signals that contain ratings of such programming."[15]

I will refer to this year-long period as "Stage One." The "voluntary" rating system implemented during Stage One must be "acceptable to the [Federal Communications] Commission [("FCC")]."[16] The FCC is to determine whether an acceptable voluntary rating system has been adopted by the distributors of video programming by consulting with "appropriate public interest groups and interested individuals."[17] At this time we are waiting for the FCC's decision to approve, or not approve, the industry's rating system.

If, at the end of a year, the distributors of video programming have failed to adopt an acceptable rating system, the administrative system enters "Stage Two." During Stage Two the FCC is authorized to create a special advisory committee. The advisory committee is to mirror the polity and the industry,[18] and must submit a report to the FCC recommending a ratings system.[19] Based on the report and recommendations of the advisory committee, the administrative system enters "Stage Three." In Stage Three, the FCC must prescribe two different types of regulations. First, the FCC must promulgate "guidelines and recommended procedures" for rating video programming containing "sexual, violent, or other indecent material about which parents should be informed."[20] These regulations will not require anyone to rate programming. Instead, the regulations are only a recommended system for anyone who might choose to rate programs. Second, with respect to any video programming that has been rated, the FCC must promulgate rules "requiring distributors of such video programming to transmit" the rating in a way that would allow the V-chip to block the rated programming. These regulations will require distributors of video programming to transmit the ratings.

---

15 Telecommunications Act of 1996, § 551(e), Pub. L. No. 104-104, 110 Stat. 56, 142 (amending 47 U.S.C. § 303).

16 *Id.*

17 *Id.*

18 The FCC must "ensure that such committee is composed of parents, television broadcasters, television programming producers, cable operators, appropriate public interest groups, and other interested individuals from the private sector and is fairly balanced in terms of political affiliation, the points of view represented." *Id.* § 551(b)(2)(A).

19 The advisory committee's report must be submitted within one year of the appointment of the committee's "initial members." *Id.*

20 *Id.*

To summarize the V-chip administrative system in Stage Three, the FCC's recommendations for rating video programming *will not be* binding, while the FCC's rules for transmitting any such ratings *will be* binding. The V-chip administrative system in Stage Three says to the industry "you need not rate, but if you do, you *must* transmit the rating." The conference report accompanying the Act directly supports this interpretation.

The rules prescribed for transmitting a rating are requirements. In contrast, the guidelines and recommended procedures for a rating system are not rules and do not include requirements. They are intended to provide the industry with a carefully considered and practical system for rating programs if the industry does not develop such a system itself. However, nothing in subsection (b)(1) of section 551 authorizes, and "the conferees do not intend, that the Commission require the adoption of the recommended rating system nor that any particular program be rated."[21]

Regardless of what happens with rating television programs, all new television sets with screens at least thirteen inches in diagonal must have a V-chip installed.[22] Nothing in the Act seems to cover the tuner section in a VCR.

In sum, then, the Act's plan looks something like the following:

	Stage One	Stage Two (max one year)	Stage Three
Ratings:	Voluntary	Advisory Committee Report	FCC "Guidelines"
Transmission:	Voluntary	Nothing	FCC Rules Require
Chip:	Must Be Installed	Must Be Installed	Must Be Installed

Does such a plan violate the First Amendment to the Constitution? To answer this question I will analyze the question under alternative assumptions. First, I will assume that the ratings system is done in Stage One and resembles the one already proposed by the industry. Second, I will assume that Stage One fails and that the FCC must promulgate recommendations and rules in Stage Three.

In part I of this article I will first outline the "state action" doctrine—the rules that govern when "private behavior" will be treated as if it were behavior of the state and hence subject to the require-

21 H.R. CONF. REP. NO. 104-458, § 551—Parental Choice in Television Programming, Conference Agreement (1996).

22 Actually, the TV must "be equipped with a feature designed to enable viewers to block display of all programs with a common rating." Telecommunications Act of 1996 § 551(c).

ments of the First Amendment. I will then apply the state action rules to the V-chip ratings system adopted in Stage One. Part I concludes that the industry's decision to adopt a V-chip ratings system in Stage One will be treated as state action and hence will be subject to scrutiny under the First Amendment. The form of the system, however, may well be regarded as private behavior. In part II, I conduct a similar analysis, but focus on a V-chip ratings system adopted in Stage Three. I conclude that the V-chip rating system will be subject to the First Amendment if the system is adopted in Stage Three. Part III of this article concludes that the Court will likely find the V-chip system constitutional under substantive First Amendment analysis. The reasons for my conclusion will differ depending on the precise nature of the First Amendment claim. A producer claiming that the entire V-chip system produces a chilling effect will fail, at this point, to demonstrate the chill.[23] A producer complaining about his individual rating will fail, possibly because of special state action problems, and possibly because of the justifications for the ratings system.

I. The State Action Requirement in Stage One: "Voluntary" Ratings

Under this alternative (Stage One) I will analyze the system already adopted by the broadcast and cable industry, including the studios. Television programs will be rated in a hierarchy: "TV-G" (for all ages), "TV-PG" (parental guidance suggested), "TV-14" (may be inappropriate for children under 14), and "TV-M" (for adults).[24] Considerations of violence, sex, and language will be collapsed into one variable, coded for age-appropriateness. All of the major broadcast and cable networks will encode a program's ratings and transmit them with the program to the viewer. If, for example, the viewer sets a V-chip for TV-PG, then no program with a rating of TV-14 or TV-M will appear on that viewer's set.

Let us assume that someone, either a program producer or a viewer's group, objects to the V-chip plan as a violation of the First Amendment. Further, assume that such a person or group has standing to bring the objection before a federal court.[25] The first,

---

23 This assumes that the producer bears the burden of proof. *See infra* discussion at note 115 and accompanying text.

24 *See* Hall & Lowry, *supra* note 2. There are also other ratings: "TV-Y" (suitable for youngsters), "TV-Y7" (appropriate for children 7 and over), "S" (sex), "L" (language), "V" (violence), and "D" (suggestive dialogue). Jane Hall, *Ratings Plan Set to Go to the FCC*, L.A. Times, July 26, 1997, at F1. It is not clear if a program rated TV-Y7 will pass through a V-chip set for TV-PG.

25 The Supreme Court has held that a film distributor had standing to object to the

and most important defense that such a litigant will face is termed the "state action" requirement.

The First Amendment begins "Congress shall make no law." As a consequence, the First Amendment restricts only the actions of the government, and does not restrain private behavior.[26] When a private party restrains another private party's speech, the First Amendment provides no impediment to the practice. In fact, under certain circumstances, such as when an editor of a newspaper chooses not to print certain content, the First Amendment protects the private party's right to "restrict" the speech of another private party.[27] The need to find government action before the First Amendment controls the case is called the "state action" requirement.

As applied to this situation, the government and (presumably) the distributors of video programming will claim that the ratings and the transmission of the ratings within the shows result only from private, not government, action.[28] After all, they will say, the ratings are being done by program producers, studios, or video distributors, all of whom are private actors. The decision to rate a television program for violence and sex, like a newspaper editor's decision to print an article, is not constrained by the First Amendment and cannot be challenged on that constitutional basis in court. As a consequence, they will argue, we need not even discuss First Amendment doctrine or policy. The case ends before it begins.

How should we evaluate this claim by the government? To provide a sophisticated and nuanced evaluation, we must first learn a little bit of doctrinal and theoretical background about the state action doctrine, and then apply this to the V-chip rating facts.

U.S. government's labeling his film "political propaganda" because of the potential harm to the distributor's reputation. *See* Meese v. Keene, 481 U.S. 465, 472-77 (1987). Such a theory might apply to give standing to the program producer who may suffer damage to his or her reputation from having his product labeled "violent" or "sexual."

[26] *See* San Francisco Arts & Athletics, Inc. v. United States Olympic Comm., 483 U.S. 522 (1987); Lebron v. National R.R. Passenger Corp., 115 S. Ct. 961 (1995).

[27] *See* Miami Herald Publ'g Co. v. Tornillo, 418 U.S. 241 (1974).

[28] *See* Don West & Christopher Stern, *Jack of All Trades: The Man in the Middle on the V-Chip*, BROADCASTING & CABLE, Mar. 18, 1996, at 26, 29 (Jack Valenti, who is spearheading the industry's effort to rate programming, says "I'm just saying to you, what we're doing is voluntary. The law does not command us to do it."). This is logically consistent with Valenti's earlier pronouncement about controlling violence on television. Three years earlier Valenti wrote that what "should chill the blood of every citizen is the heavy hand of government slowly, steadily, remorselessly intruding into the outer perimeter of the First Amendment." Jack Valenti, *Whose Children are They, Anyway?*, L.A. TIMES, Oct. 4, 1993, at B7.

A. *Background on the State Action Doctrine*

The state action doctrine applies to more than just the First Amendment. Most of the Constitution's protections for individual rights apply only to the state.[29] Constitutional guarantees of freedom from racial discrimination,[30] the right to be represented by counsel at a criminal trial,[31] freedom from unlawful search and seizure,[32] and the right to a fair procedure before important rights are taken away,[33] only apply to state action. If private individuals discriminate on racial grounds, interfere with the right to counsel, unlawfully search or seize evidence, or refuse to give someone a fair procedure, the Constitution is not violated. The aggrieved parties must look to some other source of law, such as the 1964 Civil Rights Act,[34] for protection.

The state action doctrine attempts to draw the line between private action—which is unconstrained by most constitutional guarantees—and state action—which must comply with the requirements of the Constitution.[35] Most of the Supreme Court's cases finding state action involved racial discrimination.[36] Because the V-chip raises no racial discrimination issue I will concentrate on precedents without this factor.

1. Cases Without Racial Discrimination Issues

In the absence of a racial discrimination issue, the Supreme Court is most willing to find state action when either of two different theories applies. First, if a private party performs a function that has traditionally and exclusively been a government function, then the Court is more likely to find state action.[37] Second, if the

---

29 *See* ERWIN CHEMERINSKY, CONSTITUTIONAL LAW: PRINCIPLES AND POLICIES § 6.4 (1997) (forthcoming).

30 *See* Virginia v. Rives, 100 U.S. 313 (1879); The Civil Rights Cases, 109 U.S. 3 (1883); *see also* C. VANN WOODWARD, REUNION AND REACTION: THE COMPROMISE OF 1877 AND THE END OF RECONSTRUCTION (1966).

31 *See* Polk County v. Dodson, 454 U.S. 312 (1981).

32 *See* Soldal v. Cook County, Ill., 113 S. Ct. 538 (1992).

33 *See* Jackson v. Metro. Edison Co., 419 U.S. 345 (1974); Memphis Light, Gas & Water Div. v. Craft, 436 U.S. 1 (1978); Flagg Bros., Inc. v. Brooks, 436 U.S. 149 (1978).

34 42 U.S.C. §§ 2000 to 2000bb-4 (1994 & Supp. 1997).

35 *See* Charles L. Black, Jr., *Foreword: "State Action," Equal Protection, and California's Proposition 14*, 81 HARV. L. REV. 69, 95 (1967); Edmondson v. Leesville Concrete Co., 500 U.S. 614, 632 (1991) ("cases deciding when private action might be deemed that of the state have not been a model of consistency").

36 *E.g.,* Reitman v. Mulkey, 387 U.S. 369 (1967) (finding state action in an amendment to the California Constitution guaranteeing private landlords the right to refuse to rent property for any reason, including racial prejudice); Shelly v. Kramer, 334 U.S. 1 (1948) (finding state action in judicial enforcement of racially restrictive land covenants).

37 Most of the cases finding a government function basis for state action involved racial discrimination. This continues the general theme noted in the sections above. For example, Texas attempted to delegate the business of elections to a private political party, which

government has become entangled in private conduct by providing strong incentives or encouragement for private individuals to behave in some way, then the private parties' behavior may be deemed "state action." Because the V-chip raises only the government entanglement issue, I will not discuss the government function theory.

The government entanglement "theory" asks whether the government has so involved itself, either by providing incentives, encouragement, or resources, with private behavior, that the actions of a private party must be deemed that of the state.[38]

The Court is often unwilling to find state action in cases involving no racial discrimination, although sometimes the Court does so.[39] Most important for purposes of this paper, the Court appears to have established that granting a license to a private party does not turn the private party's actions into state actions.[40]

---

excluded blacks from participating. *See* Nixon v. Herndon, 273 U.S. 536 (1927); Nixon v. Condon, 286 U.S. 73 (1932); Smith v. Allwright, 321 U.S. 649 (1944), *rev'g* Grovey v. Townsend, 295 U.S. 45 (1935); Terry v. Adams, 345 U.S. 461 (1953). Similarly, where a city tried to avoid desegregating a public park by turning control of the park over to a private entity that would refuse to allow blacks into the park, the Supreme Court balked and found state action. *See* Evans v. Newton, 382 U.S. 296 (1966). A few cases do not involve racial discrimination. *E.g.*, Marsh v. Alabama, 326 U.S. 501 (1946) (company town); Rendell-Baker v. Kohn, 457 U.S. 830 (1982) (running a school); National Collegiate Athletic Assoc. v. Tarkanian, 488 U.S. 179 (1988) (regulating collegiate athletics).

38 As with the government function theory, described in the paragraph above, the archetypal cases finding state action tend to be at least two decades old, and frequently involve racial discrimination. The most famous case in this area is *Shelley*, 334 U.S. 1, in which the Supreme Court held that a court enforcing a racially restrictive covenant in a land sale constituted state action. Prior to the decision in *Shelley* many residential properties were burdened by promises not to sell the properties to black people. These promises, which were made as part of previous sales of residential property between private parties, were supposed to "run with the land" and be enforceable against any subsequent purchaser. Hence, if a private owner of land burdened by a racially restrictive covenant attempted to sell the land to a black purchaser, a neighbor could sue the seller and have the attempted sale voided. The Supreme Court ruled that the court's enforcement of these covenants would constitute state action, and hence be unconstitutional. Cases involving the racially-restrictive use of preemptory challenges have also found state action. *See* Batson v. Kentucky, 476 U.S. 79 (1986); *Edmonson*, 500 U.S. 614; Georgia v. McCollum, 505 U.S. 42, 50 (1992). Subsequent cases involving racial discrimination and which seem to raise the state action question have frequently found the Court ducking the issue. *See* Bell v. Maryland, 378 U.S. 226 (1964) (Justices Douglas and Black debating the issue, while the rest of the Court ducked the issue); Lombard v. Louisiana, 373 U.S. 267 (1963) (overturning trespass convictions of civil rights protestors, but ducking the *Shelley* issue); Peterson v. Greenville, 373 U.S. 244 (1963).

39 *Compare, e.g.*, *Flagg Bros. Inc.*, 436 U.S. 149 (refusing to find state action in a private creditor's use of a self-help repossession statute, despite the sheriff's involvement for storage of goods at a warehouse), *with* Lugar v. Edmondson Oil Co., 457 U.S. 922 (1982) (finding state action when creditor obtained a writ of prejudgment attachment from a court).

40 *See* Moose Lodge Number 107 v. Irvis, 407 U.S. 163 (1972) (refusing to find that a liquor license turned the Moose Lodge's actions into state action, despite the Lodge's explicit racial discrimination); CBS v. Democratic Nat'l Comm., 412 U.S. 94 (1973) (Three justices refused to find that a broadcasting license turned a broadcaster's refusal to accept

Likewise, state subsidies to private actors do not to trigger state action.[41] For example, in *Rendell-Baker v. Kohn*,[42] a school that received over ninety percent of its income from the state fired a teacher because she had been critical of the school's administration. The Supreme Court refused to find state action, stating that the firing was not "compelled or even influenced by any state regulation."[43] In *Blum v. Yaretsky*,[44] government Medicaid funding rules essentially required the transfer of hospital patients to less well-equipped care facilities under certain circumstances. Despite the fact that Medicaid provided over ninety percent of the funds for the patients, the decision to transfer remained, according to the Court, a private one.

2. Broadcasting and Cable Cases

Several cases evaluate the government's attempt to reduce the amount of violent programming,[45] sexually explicit programming,[46] or drug-oriented rock and roll.[47] These cases raise the issue of whether the broadcasters' or cable operators' refusal to carry particular material constitutes state action. The most recent and important case is *Denver Area Educational Telecommunications Consortium v. FCC*.[48]

Cable television operators control the content on almost all of the channels on the cable system. On a few channels—termed "access" channels—the cable operator may not control the content. Leased access channels are those that have been set aside, pursuant

---

paid political advertisements into state action. Note that *no issue* in this case garnered five votes.); *Jackson*, 419 U.S. 345 (refusing to find that state-granted monopoly turned electric company into state actor).

41 When racial discrimination is present, the Court tends to find state action. *See, e.g.*, Norwood v. Harrison, 413 U.S. 455 (1973) (free textbooks given to all schools, including racially segregated schools, constituted state action); Gilmore v. City of Montgomery, Ala., 417 U.S. 556 (1974) (giving exclusive use of city-owned recreational facilities to segregated private schools created state action).

42 457 U.S. 830.

43 *Id.* at 841.

44 697 F.2d 302 (1982).

45 *See* Writers Guild of America, West v. FCC, 423 F. Supp. 1064 (C.D. Cal. 1976), *vacated and remanded on jurisdictional grounds sub nom.* Writers Guild of America, West v. ABC, 609 F.2d 355 (9th Cir. 1979).

46 *See Denver Area Educ. Telecomms. Consortium*, 116 S. Ct. 2374. Several cases considering whether a state public utility commission's grant of permission to a franchised monopoly telephone company to refuse to carry dial-a-porn turned the telephone company's subsequent refusal into state action have also refused to equate permission with state coercion. *See, e.g.*, Carlin Comms., Inc. v. Mountain States Tel. & Tel. Co., 827 F.2d 1291 (9th Cir. 1987); Carlin Comm., Inc. v. Southern Bell Tel. & Tel. Co., 802 F.2d 1352 (11th Cir. 1986); *see also* Dial Info. Servs. Corp. v. Thornburgh, 938 F.2d 1535 (2d Cir. 1991); Information Providers' Coalition v. FCC, 928 F.2d 866 (9th Cir. 1991).

47 *See* Yale Broad. Co. v. FCC, 478 F.2d 594 (D.C. Cir. 1973).

48 *Denver Area Educ. Telecomms. Consortium*, 116 S. Ct. 2374.

to requirements in the Cable Act of 1984, for lease by commercial entities not affiliated with the cable operator. Public, educational, and governmental ("PEG") access channels are those that are set aside, pursuant to contract with the local municipality, for use by members of the public, educational institutions, or governmental bodies. In the 1992 Cable Act[49] Congress changed the rules for leased access and PEG access channels on cable television systems. Under section 10(a) of the 1992 Cable Act, a cable operator gained authority to refuse to carry indecent programming on leased access channels.[50] If a cable operator decided to carry indecent programming on leased access, it had to put the indecent programming on a single channel, block the channel from cable subscribers, and only unblock the channel in response to a written request from a particular subscriber.[51] Section 10(c) of the 1992 Cable Act required the FCC to allow cable operators to prohibit "any programming which contains obscene material, sexually explicit conduct, or material soliciting or promoting unlawful conduct."[52] Section 10(d) removes the cable operators' previously granted immunity from criminal liability for carrying obscenity on access channels.

The Supreme Court issued three opinions in *Denver Area.* Justice Breyer, writing for Justices Stevens, O'Connor, and Souter,

---

49 Cable Television Consumer Protection and Competition Act of 1992, Pub. L. No. 102-385, 106 Stat. 1460 (1992) (codified at 47 U.S.C. § 531 (1994)).

50 *Id.* § 10. Children's Protection From Indecent Programming on Leased Access Channels

> (a) Authority to Enforce.—Section 612(h) of the Communications Act of 1934 (47 U.S.C. 532(h)) is amended—. . .
>
> (2) by adding at the end thereof the following: "This subsection shall permit a cable operator to enforce prospectively a written and published policy of prohibiting programming that the cable operator reasonably believes describes or depicts sexual or excretory activities or organs in a patently offensive manner as measured by contemporary community standards."

Id.

51 *Id.* § 10.

> (b) Commission Regulations—Section 612 of the Communications Act of 1934 (47 U.S.C. 532) is amended by inserting the following new subsection:
>
> (j)(1) Within 120 days following the date of the enactment of this subsection, the Commission shall promulgate regulations designed to limit the access of children to indecent programming, as defined by Commission regulations, and which cable operators have not voluntarily prohibited under subsection (h) [§ 10(a)] by—
>
> > (A) requiring cable operators to place on a single channel all indecent programs, as identified by program providers, intended for carriage on channels designated for commercial use under this section;
> >
> > (B) requiring cable operators to block such single channel unless the subscriber requests access to such channel in writing; and
> >
> > (C) requiring programmers to inform cable operators if the program would be indecent as defined by Commission regulations.

Id.

52 *Id.* § 10(c).

seemed to find state action in sections 10(a) and 10(c). The conclusion is only slightly uncertain because Justice Breyer first stated the issue rather clearly and then, without explicitly answering the state action question, proceeded to a lengthy discussion of the substantive First Amendment claims.[53] The substantive discussion would have been quite irrelevant unless Justice Breyer had implicitly found that a cable operator's decision to refuse to carry indecency would have been state action.

Justice Kennedy, writing with Justice Ginsburg, explicitly found state action as to both sections 10(a) and 10(c).

> The plurality at least recognizes this as state action . . . avoiding the mistake made by the Court of Appeals . . . . State action lies in the enactment of a statute altering legal relations between persons, including the selective withdrawal from one group of legal protections against private acts, regardless of whether the private acts are attributable to the State.[54]

Justice Thomas, writing for Chief Justice Rehnquist and Justice Scalia, did not confront the state action issue. Instead, he asked to what extent the First Amendment protects cable operators, programmers, and viewers from state action. Justice Thomas argued that all of the speech rights start with the cable operator, and that access channels represent a (constitutionally questionable) infringement of cable operators' rights. Creating the access channels does not, consequently, create any First Amendment interests in programmers or viewers. Hence, they cannot object to the regulations. Only cable operators may object.[55]

B. *Application of State Action to V-Chip Ratings in Stage One*

> [T]he drafting of both the present ratings and brawnier new system was as voluntary as facing a firing squad. Both came in response to withering pressure from TV reformers and especially, the federal government, with some vote-driven, opportunistic members of Congress joining true believers in embracing an issue they felt would resonate like a thunderbolt—not only with much of the public but with the media. The industry's

[53] Justice Breyer wrote, "[w]e recognize that the First Amendment, the terms of which apply to governmental action, ordinarily does not itself throw into constitutional doubt the decisions of private citizens to permit, or to restrict, speech . . . ." *Denver Area Educ. Telecomms. Consortium*, 116 S. Ct. at 2383. He then outlined the petitioners' arguments for finding state action under these circumstances and proceeded directly to the substantive arguments. *Id.* at 2383-84.

[54] *Id.* at 2404-05.

[55] *Id.* at 2409-12.

choice: with or without the blindfold?[56]

To apply the state action doctrine to the V-chip we must make a distinction. The plaintiff producer's claim might be that the existence of any ratings system, in and of itself, chills speech and stifles the marketplace of ideas. If this is the claim, then the issue is whether there is state action in bringing the ratings system into existence. The plaintiff producer's claim might, however, be more specific. The producer might object to a ratings system that is both age-based and content-based, rather than just age-based.[57] In that case, the producer would object to the *form* of the rating system adopted by the industry. Last, the producer might object to the rating that was given to one of his shows. The producer's show might have been given a TV-M, but the producer thinks that the show deserves only a TV-G. In this case, the question will be whether there is state action in the assignment of a particular rating to a show. The three different types of producer claims may get different answers to the question of state action.

There are several possible arguments as to why the "voluntary" ratings and transmission scheme is actually government action. All of these arguments refer to the "excessive entanglement" branch of the state action doctrine.

1. Political Economy and the "Free" Digital Channel for Broadcasters

One change facing broadcasting in the near future is that broadcasters will have to give up the six megahertz of spectrum that they are now using for analog broadcasting. New digital broadcasting channels, also most likely six megahertz, will be allocated for digital broadcast transmissions. These new licenses will give the broadcasters the flexibility to deliver one high definition picture with six channel sound, or to deliver several lower quality signals.

Existing broadcasters want the federal government to give each of them a six megahertz "digital" license (for free) and allow the broadcasters to keep the existing analog licenses for as long a period as possible before surrendering the analog licenses to the FCC.[58] Many in the House and Senate, including former Senator

56 Howard Rosenberg, *Holdout by NBC to Provide Real Test*, L.A. TIMES, July 30, 1997, at F1.

57 A content-based ratings system gives information about the amount of sexual, violent, or other types of content in the program. *See infra* note 86 and accompanying text.

58 *See* Edmund L. Andrews, *On Their Way to Being Digital, Broadcasters Feel They Are Still Entitled to Cost-Free Airwaves*, N.Y. TIMES, Jan. 22, 1996, at D7; *Prepared Statement of Kevin*

Dole, have suggested auctioning off the new digital licenses to the highest bidders.[59] The public treasury, rather than existing broadcasters, would reap the benefits from the new spectrum. Such a prospect has terrified existing broadcasters, and has compelled them to give Congress whatever is wanted. What is wanted, in short, is a "voluntary" rating system.[60]

This trade of "free" spectrum for good behavior in restraining broadcast violence has occasionally reached the level of explicit public musings by FCC officials or Congressmen.[61] These public musings almost always take the form of a veiled threat. The broadcasters' good behavior is described as a "quid pro quo" or part of a "social compact" for free spectrum.[62] The argument is that the carrot of a "free" digital channel, combined with the stick of surrendering the analog channel, has overwhelmed the broadcasters' free will regarding ratings. As a consequence, the "voluntary" ratings system is actually government action.

The description is absolutely correct as a matter of political economy, and it might also serve to establish state action, *at least as to the industry's agreeing to create and implement a ratings system.* Note that none of these carrots or sticks have been offered in exchange for rating any particular show in any way. Hence, the political economy argument will not help an individual producer who is objecting to the way in which his program was rated to establish state action in the individual exercise of discretion. Rather, the political

---

O'Brien, Vice President and General Manager KTVU-TV, Channel 2, San Francisco, CA and Chairman of the Board (The Association of Local Television Stations) Before The House Commerce Committee, FED. INFO. SYS. CORP., FED. NEWS SERV., Mar. 21, 1996; *Fields Chides Broadcasters on Tax Ads,* DIVERSIFIED PUB. GROUP, MULTICHANNEL NEWS, Mar. 25, 1996; *Domenici Tunes Out TV Auction Plan,* U.P.I., WASH. NEWS, Mar. 14, 1996. This is close to the deal that the FCC had worked out before the passage of the Telecommunications Act of 1996. 142 CONG. REC. S.1528 (1996).

59 *See* Mike Milla & Paul Farhi, *Dole Statement Snags Phone, Cable TV Bill; Senator Fights Free Digital Broadcast Licenses,* WASH. POST, Jan. 11, 1996, at D8; Mike Milla & Paul Farhi, *Dole's Warning To Broadcasters; He'd End Free Licenses,* INT'L HERALD TRIB., Jan. 12, 1996; 142 CONG. REC. H.1145, H.1150 (1996); 142 CONG. REC. S.684 (1996); 141 CONG. REC. S.14471, S.14513 (1995); 141 CONG. REC. S.7881, S.7898 (1996).

60 Newspaper accounts frequently link the two issues. *See* Mike Milla & Paul Farhi, *Dole Statement Snags Phone, Cable TV Bill; Senator Fights Free Digital Broadcast Licenses,* WASH. POST, Jan. 11, 1996, at D8; *see also* Andrews, *supra* note 58, at D7; Edmund L. Andrews, *Digital TV, Dollars and Dissent; The Political Battle Grows Over the Use of New Broadcast Technology,* N.Y. TIMES, Mar. 18, 1996, at D1; Mike Milla & Paul Farhi, *Dole's Warning To Broadcasters; He'd End Free Licenses,* INT'L HERALD TRIB., Jan. 12, 1996; Brian Lowry, *The Ratings: Inside and Out,* L.A. TIMES, July 12, 1997, at F1.

61 *See* Corn-Revere, *Television Violence and the Limits of Voluntarism, supra* note 7, at 199-200 (discussing the comments of former FCC Chairman Alfred Sikes, Congressman Ed Markey, and current FCC Chairman Reed Hundt). On the political economy, and its connection to spectrum auctions, see Thomas Hazlett, *Assigning Property Rights to Radio Spectrum Users: Why Did FCC License Auctions Take 67 Years?,* WORKING PAPER, July 11, 1995.

62 *See* Corn-Revere, *Television Violence and the Limits of Voluntarism, supra* note 7, 199-200.

pressure has been directed at getting a ratings system. Hence, this may help establish state action for a plaintiff whose theory objects to the existence of the ratings process.

There has been at least one case holding that official threats and links between broadcast violence and licenses constitutes state action.[63] On the other hand, there has been no explicit statutory or administrative link between the two issues. It remains perfectly possible for the broadcasters to gain the free channel without instituting a ratings system. Hence, the Supreme Court may be more likely to view the digital channel as political background, but not legal entanglement or coercion.

2. Requiring the Chip in the Set

The next argument focuses on the undisputed state action of requiring that the V-chip be installed in the set. This is more, goes the argument, than just requiring an "on/off" switch be installed in television sets. The only purpose of a V-chip is to facilitate a ratings and screening system. By regulating one part of the ratings and screening system, the government has so injected itself into the process as to constitute excessive encouragement in the entire enterprise. Requiring the chip may also put the government's imprimatur on whatever system evolves.

This argument, standing by itself, is weak. A Court that is loathe to find government action where Medicare rules virtually coerce the transfer of an elderly patient is also unlikely to find government action, based solely on requiring the chip, when program producers decide to implement a ratings scheme. However, in combination with other factors, this argument may gain importance. After all, the producers' and networks' decision to implement a ratings scheme can only come after mandatory installation of V-chips in the sets.[64] Hence, we have clear state action in the first step in implementing a ratings system. What is more, this argument would seem to work equally well for a plaintiff objecting to either an individual instance of rating a program, or for one objecting to the entire ratings system. However, to complete the state action argument we must rely on other considerations, such as the political economy argument discussed immediately above, or the other concerns to which we turn in the sections below.

---

63 *See Writers Guild of America, West*, 423 F. Supp. 1064. *But see CBS*, 412 U.S. 94 (a plurality refusing to find state action in the bare licensing of television broadcasters).

64 I am presuming that absent regulation the V-chip would not have been installed.

3. Governmental "Approval"

The government might have become so involved in the process that its approval and encouragement for ratings have stepped over the line into impermissible entanglement. I believe that this argument has considerable power with regard to the industry's decision to adopt a ratings system. Recent events have extended this argument's force to the *type* of ratings system adopted.

The federal government has pressured the industry to adopt a ratings system. Consider the meeting between President Bill Clinton and leaders of the broadcast and cable industry[65] at the White House. President Clinton called the industry leaders to the White House, asked for a commitment to implement a "voluntary" ratings system, and got it on the spot. In addition, President Clinton, while trying to verbally distance himself from the process, has indicated that he intends to stay involved:

> Q (LOS ANGELES TIMES): What kind of a role do you foresee for yourself, for the White House, in monitoring the implementation of this system and making sure it's done right?
>
> A (PRESIDENT CLINTON): Well, the first thing I think is that the government should not be involved in the process by which the system is developed and then implemented. Just like we're not involved in the movie ratings. I don't believe we should be involved.
>
> I think the industry, if you look at the movie ratings or even if you look at the advisories that we see now on television before certain programs, I think its clear that once the industry decides to do this and hold itself publicly accountable, that there's a very high probability that a good job will be done on this.
>
> What I think I can do is to, first of all, receive the results of their efforts since they sort of kicked it off here. If they'd like to come back, I invited them to come back and make a report to

---

65 The list of 30 included Ted Turner (TBS), Rupert Murdoch (Fox), Barry Diller (Silver King), Michael Ovitz (Disney), Frank Mancuso (MGM), Kay Koplovitz (USA Network), Alan Levine (Sony), Bob Wright (NBC), Michael Jordan (Westinghouse), Richard Masur (Actor's Guild), Eddie Fritts (NAB), Peter Lund (CBS), Jack Valenti (MPAA), Judith McHale (Discovery), Ray Rodriguez (Univision), Gene Reynolds (Director's Guild), Brian Roberts (Comcast), Ron Meyer (MCA), Bob Iger (Cap Cities/ABC), Lucy Salhany (United Paramount), Rich Frank (C-3), Ervin Duggan (PBS), Haim Saban (Saban Entertainment), Brad Radnitz (President, Writers Guild of America, West), Terry Semel (Chairman/co-CEO, Warner Bros., Warner Music Group), Robert A. Daly (Chairman/co-CEO, Warner Bros., Warner Music Group), Jeffrey Katzenberg (Founder, Dreamworks SKG), Jonathan L. Dolgen (Chairman, Viacom), Robert L. Johnson (President/CEO, Black Entertainment Television), and Decker Anstrom (President NCTA). *See The Elegant Surrender: Industry Capitulates on V-Chip Without Firing a Shot*, BROADCASTING & CABLE, Mar. 4, 1996; John M. Broder & Jane Hall, *President Hears TV Executives Commit to Ratings System*, L.A. TIMES, Mar. 1, 1996, at A1.

> me and to bring in the members of Congress, and I'm trying to keep this in a very nonpolitical way.
>
> So one of the things we might be able to do is to highlight the work once its done, to emphasize it, and then to make sure that we do everything we can to explain to people how the V-chip works and how they should access it as they buy new televisions. And for those who do not have the V-chip—and for several years there will be millions of Americans who won't have it—to encourage them still to become familiar with the rating system and to use it at home anyway.
>
> "Q (LOS ANGELES TIMES): Is there a place for jawboning or exhortation about overall quality in programming?
>
> A (PRESIDENT CLINTON): Well, I think that's the next follow-up."[66]

In addition, one could also consider governmental involvement left over from implementation of the Television Violence Act.[67] When the networks were slow to implement a standard, Senator Paul Simon told the industry that if it failed to reduce violence within the following sixty days, congressional action would follow.[68]

In a recent televised meeting between Senator Joseph Lieberman (D-Conn.) and Representative Edward Markey (D-Mass.) and Hollywood producers Steven Bochco (*NYPD Blue*), John Wells (*ER*), Marta Kaufman (*Friends*), and others, the discussion of the V-chip boiled over into threats. Producer Lionel Chetwynd attacked the politicians by saying "'It's all a charade. They've made Hollywood a target of opposition in a political season. . . . Never before in the history of the republic has the coercive power of the state been enlisted to control or in any way limit the [First] Amendment.'"[69] In response, Senator Lieberman said "'I find these comments to be dispiriting. . . . Folks, if you keep on down this road in a state of denial, there's a group of folks behind me and [Representative] Markey that don't have the same concern for the [First] Amendment that we do.'"[70]

As to the *type* of ratings system actually adopted, two factors push toward finding state action. First, consider the requirement

---

66 *Q&A with President Clinton*, L.A. TIMES, Mar. 2, 1996, at F1.

67 Television Program Improvement Act of 1990, 47 U.S.C. § 303 (1995).

68 *See* Jason Moody, STATES NEWS SERV., Aug. 1, 1989, *available in* LEXIS, News Library, Wires File.

69 Greg Braxton, *Confusion, Anger Mark Discussion About V-Chip*, L.A. TIMES, Oct. 4, 1996, at F1.

70 *Id.* at F25. Jack Valenti, who is in charge of putting together the rating system, retorted "'I'm not worried about those people in back of you, because we will be in federal court in a nanosecond' if there is any attempt by lawmakers to impose censorship." *Id.*

that the FCC find the voluntary ratings system acceptable, or else the process proceeds to Stage Two.[71] This appears to border on the government adopting the private system as its own, indicating that there is state action. Second, government pressure has helped shape the ratings system. When the industry first attempted to adopt a pure age-based system, (TV-Y, TG-G, etc.), the choice seemed to be private. Prior to the industry's preliminary choice of the age-based ratings system, interest groups and politicians pressured the industry to adopt a content-based system. A content-based system would give the information about the level of sex, violence, and strong language in a program, and permit the viewer to filter based on those factors. Academics,[72] interest groups,[73] and congressmen[74] argued that the public wanted and needed a content-based system. The pressure was strong enough that Vice Presi-

---

71 The FCC must also approve the technology that will be used in the V-chip itself. This gives another added measure of control. *See V-Chip Technology Waits for Washington, supra* note 4.

72 Prof. Joel Federman, Co-director of the Center for Communication and Social Policy at the University of California at Santa Barbara, argued:

> The industry has pledged that its ratings will be useful to parents, helping them to block unwanted shows using the much-heralded V-chip. But a recent national survey of parents sponsored by the PTA and conducted by University of Wisconsin researchers found that 80% of parents would prefer a system that identifies programs by content rather than the age group for which the programming is appropriate. Parents surveyed said the HBO rating system, which specifies the type and level of sex, violence and language, is significantly more helpful to them and more objective than the MPAA ratings.

Joel Federman, *Let's Pave a High Road for TV Ratings System*, L.A. TIMES, Dec. 9, 1996, at F3.

73
> But the aggressive strategy chosen by MPAA Chairman Jack Valenti and other entertainment executives could set the stage for a political showdown with a spectrum of critics, from the conservative Traditional Values Coalition to the liberal Center for Media Education, which want information made public in advance about the level of sex, violence and bad language on individual shows.

Jube Shiver, Jr., *TV Industry to Use Ratings Before Regulatory Review*, L.A. TIMES, Dec. 19, 1996, at A1.

74
> [S]ome children's television advocates and members of Congress . . . strongly favor a content-based TV rating system that would give parents more specific—information about the sex, violence or foul language found in every entertainment program.
>
> "Parents have reviewed Hollywood's age-based system and given it two thumbs down," said Rep. Edward J. Markey (D-Mass.). "Now is the time for their voices to be heard."
>
> Markey, one of several members of Congress who have spoken out against the industry's design, said he has requested a meeting with the president to try to change his mind.
>
> "We should not spend 10 months trying out a system that child psychologists, pediatricians, religious leaders and educators agree is seriously flawed," Markey said.
>
> Earlier this week the battle between the two sides reached a boiling point. Sen. Joseph I. Lieberman (D-Conn.) threatened to introduce legislation requiring a content-based system. But Valenti, the chief architect of the industry's proposal, countered that he would file a [First] Amendment lawsuit to keep the government from intervening, which would likely stall the introduction of the system.

dent Al Gore met with representatives from several interest groups that wanted President Clinton to intervene in the process.[75] The industry, however, coalesced around an age-based ratings system[76] and then at first refused to give in to pressure.

Relentless political from Senator John McCain (R-Ariz.), Representative Ed Markey (D-Mass.), and Vice President Al Gore ensued. After key industry executives were given "assurances from key members of Congress of a moratorium of several years on legislation to modify the system still further,"[77] the industry (except for NBC) caved in and agreed to add "V", "S", "L", and "D". This whole scenario—industry resistance, intense political pressure, and capitulation, suggests state action in the type of ratings system. Through Jack Valenti, the Chairman of the industry ratings committee, the industry has been moderately pugnacious:

> Referring to Rep. Edward J. Markey (D-Mass.), who joined [Senator] Lieberman in strongly criticizing the TV industry's system Thursday, Valenti said, "Ed Markey wants the government to be Big Brother . . . and have us do what he wants to do. If Congressman Markey leads the troops on the White House floor to pass any legislation that we believe torments the 1st Amendment, we'll see him in court."
>
> Valenti also dismissed suggestions from industry critics that the Federal Communications Commission, which must give its approval to the ratings system, could reject the industry's plan and impose one of its own.
>
> "If the FCC says that what we present is unsuitable, we're under no obligation to use any other design," he said. "We will not use any other TV ratings guidelines except the ones that we are going to announce next week."[78]

The combination of these factors provide a reasonably strong argument for finding state action, at least as to the creation of the

---

Elizabeth Shogren, *Clinton Supports Industry on TV Ratings Proposal*, L.A. TIMES, Dec. 14, 1996, at A1.

75 The Vice President apparently told them to take their fight to the FCC.

> "The Vice President assured us that the White House neither endorses nor condemns the TV ratings system, said Kathryn Montgomery, president of the Center for Media Education, a Washington communications advocacy group. But, she said, "there will be an open process at the FCC for debate and comment on this issue."

Shiver, Jr., *supra* note 73.

76 A ratings "committee member acknowledged that an alternative to the MPAA-based system was never seriously considered."

"'This was the only system the whole TV industry would agree to,' the committee member said." Hall & Lowry, *supra* note 2.

77 Jane Hall, *TV Industry Reportedly Oks New Ratings*, L.A. TIMES, July 10, 1997, at A1.

78 Jane Hall, *TV Ratings Architect Vows to Fight Federal Intervention*, L.A. TIMES, Dec. 13, 1996, at D1.

ratings system. The involvement of President Clinton, the required approval of the ratings system by the FCC, and threats by Lieberman and Markey provide a reasonably strong case that the intensity of government involvement has passed the point where the ratings can be thought of as private, voluntary behavior. Telling the President "No" after you have been summoned to the White House, particularly if you are a firm in a partially regulated industry, requires great courage. Continuing to resist when members of Congress are issuing veiled threats and the FCC must approve your ratings system is, in short, too much to expect. In sum, the total level of involvement by the government is so great that the industry's behavior should be viewed, in part, as government behavior.[79]

Similar factors suggest state action in the *type* of ratings system that has been chosen. The industry's initial resistance to pressure and choice of a purely age-based system, followed by intense political pressure and the industry's agreement to content-based ratings, indicates state action. When one adds the need for subsequent FCC approval, the facts suggest that the industry's age-based system should be viewed as state action, and not as a private, independent choice.[80]

4. Ratings vs. Transmission of Ratings

To the extent that the Court is willing to consider the transmission of ratings apart from the ratings system, it is more likely that the voluntary transmission of ratings will be regarded as state action. This conclusion follows from the *requirement* in Stage Three that any ratings *must* be transmitted. If program distributors refuse to "voluntarily" transmit the ratings in Stage One, they will be

---

79 The response, I suppose, is to focus on the lack of explicit coercion. President Clinton was only making a request, not giving an order. The background legislation does not require ratings. And Lieberman and Markey were only pointing out that *other* Members of Congress would not be as friendly as they are. Hence, the decision to rate programs remains private.

This response fails. It does not address the level of government involvement. The Clinton administration and Congress have been deeply and forcefully involved in the V-chip issue. The administration's extremely active involvement in shaping the content of children's television on closely related issues, such as educational television, underscores how seriously broadcasters must regard the administration's pressure. The White House recently brokered a deal for the FCC to require three hours per week of educational programming for children. Again, meetings were held at the White House. *See* Sheryl Stolberg & Jane Hall, *Educational Children's TV Shows to Air*, L.A. TIMES, July 30, 1996, at A12. The industry's adoption of a V-chip ratings system should, in short, likely be regarded as state action.

80 Congress has also pressured broadcasters to reinstate the "family hour"—child-friendly programming during the first hour of prime time. In May "100 members of Congress signed an open letter to the presidents of six broadcast networks, asking them to bring back the family hour . . . as a 'voluntary covenant with the viewing public.'" Aaron Barnhart, *Networks to Dance Again with 'Family Hour,'* KAN. CITY STAR, July 20, 1997, at J1.

forced to transmit in Stage Three. Hence, the form of the regulation is "volunteer to do X now, or in a year we will force you to do X." As a consequence, there is no real private choice.

There are at least two possible responses. The first response is that the decision to transmit the ratings during Stage One is still voluntary. The law does not impose any penalty for failing to transmit the rating during Stage One. Once we reach Stage Three transmission will be required by the law, and then there will be state action. The second response is that under the Act the distributor will only be required to transmit ratings in Stage Three if the program producers have adopted a ratings system. If not, there will be nothing to transmit. Hence, the actual form of the regulation is "volunteer to do X now, or in a year we might force you to do X." This is not sufficient encouragement or coercion to constitute state action.

C. *Putting All of the Stage One State Action Arguments Together*

When one combines the effect of the various arguments—requiring the chip in the set, requiring the transmission of ratings in Stage Three, the carrot of 6 megahertz of "free spectrum," pressure from President Clinton, threats from congressmen, and the requirement of FCC approval of a "voluntary" system—it is hard to conclude that the system is voluntary. In the absence of these factors, no V-chip rating system would likely be created, and virtually all of these pressures have been brought to bear for the purpose of pushing the industry to adopt a ratings system. In other words, I suggest that the Court should find state action present in the creation of a Stage One V-chip rating system.[81] State action extends to the type of ratings system—mixes age-based and content-based—finally adopted.

This does not imply that the court should (or would) find state action in the decision to impose any particular rating on a particular program. Government actors have not (to my knowledge) been trying to get any particular show rated in a particular way. *Blum v. Yaretsky*[82] would seem to be the natural comparison. In *Blum*, the government clearly created the reimbursement system that created the entirely foreseeable consequence of transferring patients to facilities with fewer capabilities. However, no particular decision to transfer was made by the government, and the Court

---

[81] *Accord* Corn-Revere, *What, Me Worry?*, *supra* note 7; Corn-Revere, *Television Violence and the Limits of Voluntarism*, *supra* note 7.
[82] 697 F.2d 302.

declined to find state action in a particular transfer. Here, the government may be free to argue that although the rating system was produced by state action, the operation of the rating system as to individual cases is still private action. The V-chip ratings system could apply any rating to any particular show without government involvement.

II. State Action in Stage Three: The FCC's "Suggested" Rating System

The existence of state action in Stage Three, or not, will depend in part on the continued behavior of President Clinton and other powerful politicians.[83] Let us assume that the "voluntary" system from Stage One fails, political involvement decreases, the FCC forms an advisory committee, and then the committee submits a report within one year. Next, assume that the FCC issues two different types of directives. With respect to ratings, the FCC promulgates "guidelines and recommended procedures." With respect to transmission, the FCC requires that the ratings be transmitted when the ratings have been implemented. Under these assumptions, what are the arguments for state action (different from the arguments elucidated above)?[84]

A. *Requiring Transmission*

If a ratings plan has been adopted by the studios and networks,[85] then the transmission of those ratings would be required. This would almost certainly qualify as sufficient compulsion to turn the networks' actions (regarding transmission) into state action.

---

83 *See supra* notes 74 & 80.

84 Note that my assumption about decreasing involvement by politicians suggests that the general entanglement theory will be much weaker here.

85 This is probably the only circumstance under which a complaining program producer or viewer could get standing in Stage Three. On the requirement of injury in standing, see Director, OWCP v. Perini, 459 U.S. 297 (1983) (holding that the presence of an injured employee as respondent allowed the petitioner, the Director of the Office of Worker's Compensation Program, to have standing to argue the merits of the case because the respondent's presence assured that the court would be reviewing a case with an actual injury redressable by the court); Sierra Club v. Morton, 405 U.S. 727 (1972) (holding that the "injury in fact" test for standing to sue under the Administrative Procedure Act requires more than injury to a cognizable interest and requires that the party seeking review be himself among the injured); Enos v. Marsh, 769 F.2d 1363 (1985) (holding that plaintiff lacked standing to bring a claim for relief under the Administrative Procedure Act since plaintiff had presented no fact showing that actual injury would occur if the Army Corp. of Engineers were to use a lower discount rate in cost-benefit computations for a harbor project); Zoslaw v. MCA Distrib. Corp., 594 F. Supp. 1022 (1984) (finding that former operators of a retail record store could have standing to complain of another record retailer's alleged favorable treatment from record distributors who violated price discrimination provisions of the Robinson-Patman Act only if the two record retailers were competitors in the same market).

Note that this will probably suffice to establish "state action" for different sorts of complaints. A producer complaining of the "chill" from the entire ratings system will be able to show that *all* of the ratings under the system must be transmitted. And a producer complaining about the rating his show was given by a review board may show that the law requires that *the producer's* show's rating be transmitted.

B. *The FCC's "Suggested" Rating System*

Perhaps the act of constituting an advisory committee, taking its report, and promulgating "guidelines and recommended procedures" so involves the government that private action becomes public. This involves the government in the ratings system far more than just finding the "voluntary" system in Stage One "acceptable." (Clearly that did not happen here, for if it had we would not have gotten to Stage Three.) When combined with the admitted requirements of installing V-chips and transmitting ratings, the entire system might constitute government action.

I will spend little time evaluating this argument because the courts will likely find state action in the requirement of transmission, and the substantive First Amendment analysis of requiring transmission will also require an analysis of the rating system. To see this, just try to answer the question "why require transmission"? without referring to the arguments for and against the substance of the ratings that are being transmitted. I contend that this cannot be done. For example, assume that the FCC's suggested system rated *only* stories involving explicit descriptions of intercourse as appropriate for all ages, and attached ratings to shows based on this idea. Programs with explicit descriptions of intercourse would be rated "family fare," while programs lacking such material would be given "adults only" ratings. Such ratings, once attached to a program, would have to be transmitted. A producer or broadcaster objecting to the requirement of transmitting ratings, based on the First Amendment's general unfriendliness to forced speech,[86] would likely prevail. The government's attempt to justify requiring transmission would likely fail, because the underlying ratings system is useless. The government could neither claim that the transmission was needed to protect children, nor that rational parents would use the transmitted ratings to choose shows (because shows

---

86 *See* Hurley v. Irish-American Gay, Lesbian, & Bisexual Group, 115 S. Ct. 2338 (1995); Riley v. National Fed'n of the Blind, 487 U.S. 781 (1988); Wooley v. Maynard, 430 U.S. 705, 714 (1977).

including explicit descriptions of intercourse always go through the filter). In just this way, any attempt to evaluate under the First Amendment the requirement of transmitting ratings will end up focusing on the substance of the V-chip ratings system.[87]

III. The Substantive First Amendment Claim Against the V-Chip

Assuming that a litigant can get past the state action requirement, he must still convince a court that the V-chip ratings system violates the substantive requirements of the First Amendment. Proving that the V-chip rating constituted state action, but losing the claim that the First Amendment was violated, would provide the litigant no relief.

Any court evaluating such a First Amendment claim would need to cover many issues to fully treat the case. I will attempt no such thorough treatment in this section.[88] Instead, I will discuss only a subset of the issues. I will divide the analysis, once again, according to whether the suit challenges a system devised in Stage One or Stage Three.

A. *Substantive First Amendment Analysis in Stage One*

1. The Nature of the Infringement of Speech

To analyze the substantive First Amendment claim, we must first spell out the nature of the infringement claim. This claim will differ, at least in Stage One, based on the nature of the producer's complaint. If the producer is attacking the entire V-chip ratings system, he will likely claim that the system, in general, chills speech. This could be a claim about any ratings system, or, more likely, a claim about the type of ratings system actually adopted. In either case, the producer will claim that the existence of the system causes producers, networks, and others to alter their speech in ways to satisfy the system.[89] The mix of speech produced by the market

[87] This argument would likely be available to both a plaintiff objecting to the entire V-chip ratings system, and to one who is objecting to the rating attached to a particular show. The ratings must be transmitted in general, and as to any particular show that has been rated. Hence, at both levels, there is state action.

[88] For example, I will not discuss the "forced speech" issue.

[89] The closest analogy would be the "vagueness" and "overbreadth" cases in First Amendment law. The cases on vagueness require that speech regulation be precise, so as to give those subject to the regulations notice of exactly what is prohibited. The Court desires to reign in governmental prosecutorial discretion, Kolender v. Lawson, 461 U.S. 352 (1983), and to avoid "chilling" speech by those who are uncertain as to the reach of the regulations, Houston v. Hill, 482 U.S. 451 (1987); Smith v. Goguen, 415 U.S. 566 (1974); Baggett v. Bullitt, 377 U.S. 360 (1964); NAACP v. Button, 371 U.S. 415 (1963). In overbreadth cases, the Court invalidates speech regulations that reach substantial amounts

will, in turn, change. Disfavored speech will be produced less.[90]

An alternative theory of infringement will likely be advanced by a producer who is complaining about the rating his particular program receives. Such a producer will claim that the rating for his program burdens his individual speech, much like a tax or a license would burden his speech. When his programs have ratings that will cause more V-chips to reject the program, his speech is limited.[91]

2. Chilling Effect

I will discuss the chill argument first and then return to the license argument. To evaluate the chill argument we will need some way to analyze the likely effect of the V-chip on the market. *Broadcasting & Cable Magazine* seems to think that the effects have already arrived:

> Hollywood's broadcast network producers and programers say they are stoically bracing themselves for the future under a new television ratings system they contend will place a premium on blandness rather than creativity.
>
> Although most are taking a wait-and-see attitude, some have stepped up production or orders for family-friendly shows since the passage last February of legislation mandating a V-chip device that will allow parents to block certain programing, and

---

of protected speech, in addition to unprotected speech, and allows those challenging the regulations to assert that the protected speech of third parties will be "chilled" by the regulations. *See* Secretary of State v. J.H. Munson Co., 467 U.S. 947 (1984); Schad v. Mt. Ephraim, 452 U.S. 61 (1981); Broadrick v. Oklahoma, 413 U.S. 601 (1973).

The Court has often used the (sometimes presumed) change in the mix of speech in the marketplace produced by a change in incentives from government regulations as a basis for invalidating various restrictions on speech. *See* United States v. National Treasury Employees Union, 115 S. Ct. 1003 (1995) (declaring unconstitutional a federal law preventing government employees from being paid for off-the-job speeches and writings so as to avoid chill to these expressive activities); Simon & Schuster v. Members of the N.Y. State Crime Victims Bd., 502 U.S. 105 (1991) (striking down state law preventing criminal from profiting from sale of story so as to avoid chill to criminals' speech); *Miami Herald*, 418 U.S. 241 (Court struck down a "right of reply" statute in newspapers, in part on the basis that the statute would chill newspapers' editorializing); New York Times v. Sullivan, 376 U.S. 254 (1964) (limiting reach of state defamation laws to reduce potential chill to criticisms of public officials). For similar concerns about the "fairness doctrine," *see* 1985 Fairness Doctrine Report and Order, 102 FCC 2d 145 (1985).

90 Clearly some government officials, including President Clinton and Representative Edward Markey (D-Mass.) are hoping for a chilling effect. *See infra* note 93.

91 The second theory, of course, suffers from the state action problems reviewed above. There are two additional problems, both resembling state action, that may plague this cause of action. First, producers rate their own shows, at least in the first instance. Hence, a producer unhappy with his rating could rerate himself. The recently-announced system will include a 19-member appeals board to resolve ratings disputes, so it is possible that self-help may not be available. Hall, *supra* note 78. In addition, viewers must choose to set the V-chip filter before any shows are removed from the set. These actions may serve to cut the link between any government action and individual producer injury.

> Hollywood's subsequent agreement to develop a companion ratings system.
>
> At least one prominent producer thinks that the atmosphere already is restricting creative freedom . . . .[92]

Broadcasting & Cable Magazine may or may not be right about the V-chip. As I will show below, the market effects of the V-chip will depend on crucial details, which one cannot reasonably expect government officials[93] or perhaps even from members of the industry to reveal. Hence, whoever has the burden of proof in showing a chill will likely fail.

The nature and source of the appropriate burden of proof in this issue lies beyond the scope of this article. However, I must point out that the Supreme Court, starting with *Ginsberg v. New York*[94] and going to the present,[95] has utilized a very light burden of proof for the connection between children's exposure to indecent material and ill effects from the exposure. The Court has been willing to presume bad effects, or accept rather thin evidence to satisfy the burden. Such an attitude could produce an analogous result in the case of the V-chip, leading the Court to require a large burden of proof to show a chill from regulations designed to shelter children from "inappropriate" material.

a. Basic Method of Analyzing Television Competition

I will analyze the market behavior of TV broadcasters and cablecasters by utilizing spatial models. These models were originally used to describe competitive behavior of business firms,[96] but were later adapted to describe competition between candidates in elections.[97] In these models I assume a one dimensional continuum. For analytical purposes I will presume a content-based rating

92 David Topenkin, *It's All in the Family TV*, BROADCASTING & CABLE MAG., June 3, 1996, at 24; *see* Howard Rosenberg, *Dick Wolf: Rating TV's New Order*, L.A. TIMES, Jan. 3, 1997, at F1 (quoting veteran producer as fearing chill of "the 10 o'clock drama").

93 Clearly some government officials are hoping for a chilling effect. "V-chip proponent Rep. Edward J. Markey (D-Mass.) has said that if even a small percentage of parents take advantage of the technology, ratings would decline for objectionable programming, thus reducing levels of violence." Brian Lowry, *So, They Fixed TV . . .*, L.A. TIMES, Dec. 29, 1996, at 3. "President Clinton has said that if enough viewers respond to these initiatives, 'It will change programming, hopefully for the better.'" *Id.*

94 390 U.S. 629 (1968).

95 *See Denver Area Educ. Telecomms. Consortium*, 116 S. Ct. 2374, discussed *infra* notes 158-63 and accompanying text; Community for Creative Non-Violence v. Reid, 490 U.S. 730 (1989).

96 *See* H. Hotelling, *Stability in Competition*, 39 ECON. J. 41 (1929); B. Curtis Eaton & Richard G. Lipsey, *The Principle of Minimum Differentiation Reconsidered: Some New Developments in the Theory of Spatial Competition*, 42 REV. ECON. STUD. 27 (1975).

97 *See* Gary W. Cox, *Multicandidate Spatial Competition*, *in* ADVANCES IN THE SPATIAL THEORY OF VOTING (James Enelow & Melvin Hinich eds., Cambridge Univ. Press 1990).

system. I will consider the unit on the real line, with the most violent shows at "0" and the least violent shows at "1." Note that this does not correspond directly to the age-based portion of the system adopted by the industry. However, it corresponds directly to the "V", "S", "L", and "D" portions of the system.

I assume that viewers have single-peaked preferences over the types of shows, and for most of the analysis I will assume that viewers' ideal program types are distributed evenly (for example, there is a rectangular distribution).[98] Viewers choose to watch the show that is closest to their ideal type.[99] Broadcasters and cablecasters choose the type of program that they air to garner the maximum number of viewers.[100] (There are no moral considerations constraining the broadcasters and cablecasters in this model.) I also presume that none of the other proposed methods of dealing with the violence on television issue are being implemented simultaneously. These would include removing advertisers' ability to sponsor individual programs,[101] taxing advertising-derived revenues and giving the proceeds to broadcasters on the basis of how many viewers they garner,[102] strengthening craft unions to allow them to negotiate over content,[103] or giving control of the broadcasting business to those who have a "personal stake" in quality.[104]

To get a feel for the operation of the model, consider a market with two broadcasters. I will use a 0 conjectural variation, in which the broadcasters choose their type of programming under the assumption that the other broadcaster will remain constant. Under these assumptions, what will the broadcasters do? They will both choose to locate in the center of the violence spectrum, showing programs that are one half as violent as the maximum possible.

---

98 This means that there are the same number of viewers whose ideal point lies between 0 and 0.1 as there are viewers whose ideal point lies in any other interval of length 0.1, such as 0.4 to 0.5 or 0.75 to 0.85. We will denote an interval "a" to "b" by [a,b].

99 Modern literature sometimes relaxes this assumption, claiming instead only that a consumer's choice is a probabilistic function of the relative distances. *See* SIMON P. ANDERSON ET AL., DISCRETE CHOICE THEORY OF PRODUCT DIFFERENTIATION 284, 300 (MIT Press 1992).

100 This model does not take into account the mixed nature of funding in the broadcast and cable business. Broadcast is entirely advertiser-supported, while expanded basic channels are supported by a mix of advertiser and viewer payments, and premium cable channels are almost entirely supported by viewer payments. I know of no model of spatial competition that incorporates different methods of payment for the competitors. For my purposes, however, assuming audience maximization is quite acceptable. All of these forms of payment respond positively to increases in audience size.

101 *See* Stephen J. Kim, *"Viewer Discretion is Advised:" A Structural Approach to the Issue of Television Violence,* 142 U. PA. L. REV. 1383, 1434 (1994).

102 *See* C. EDWIN BAKER, ADVERTISING AND A DEMOCRATIC PRESS 85-91 (1994).

103 *See* Kim, *supra* note 101, at 1437.

104 *See* C. Edwin Baker, *Mergerphobia,* NATION, Nov. 8, 1993, at 520.

FIGURE 1

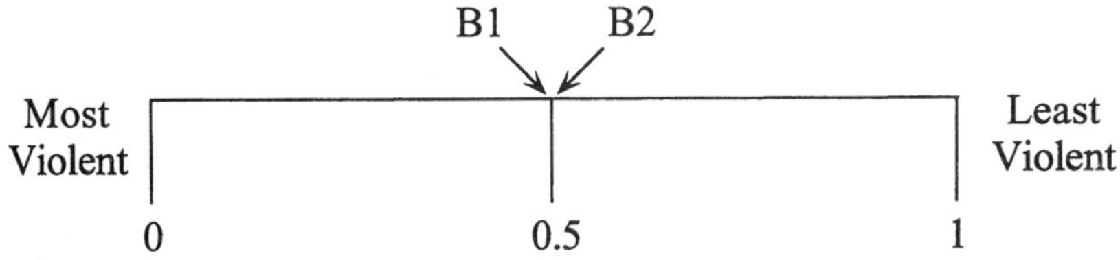

Both broadcasters locate at .5.

Under these circumstances, each broadcaster gets fifty percent of the total audience. The broadcasters are in equilibrium because neither broadcaster has an incentive to relocate. To see this, ask what would happen if one of the broadcasters, say B_1, were to decide to provide more violent fare, and locate at 0.4.

FIGURE 2

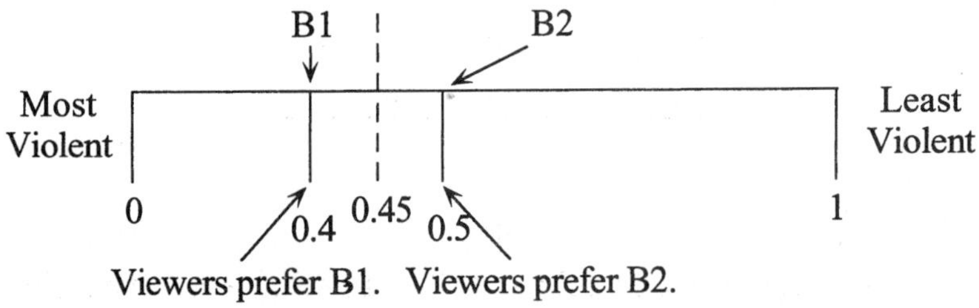

Then B_1 would garner all of the viewers between 0 and 0.4, and also the viewers between 0.4 and 0.45. (B_2 would get all the rest.) As a consequence, B_1 would have forty-five percent of the total audience, which is not as good as the fifty percent that B_1 had when located at 0.5. Hence, B_1 would not make such a move. Similarly, B_1 would not make a move to the right and program less violent fare. The same reasoning applies to B_2 as long as B_1 is at 0.5. In sum, neither broadcaster will change position.

Such models will not always have equilibria. To see this, consider what happens with three broadcasters.[105] What would happen if all three broadcasters were to locate at 0.5? Under this arrangement each broadcaster would have 1/3 of the total audience. It would then immediately pay one of the broadcasters, say B_1, to move epsilon to the right (or left). Once B_1 had done so, it would have approximately fifty percent of the audience, and B_2 and B_3 would have twenty-five percent each.

105 Assuming that firm strategies or consumer choices are probabilistic can restore some equilibria. *See* ANDERSON, *supra* note 99, at 284, 300.

FIGURE 3

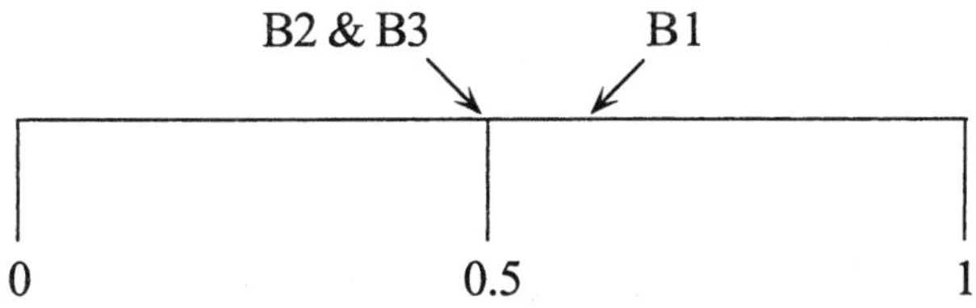

B1 gets all viewers between B1 and 1.

But once this happens it would pay either B_2 or B_3 to leapfrog over the other to the left (or, if B_1 had gone left, then to the right). If, say, B_2 were to do so, and locate epsilon to the left of 0.5, then B_1 and B_2 would each get approximately fifty percent of the viewers and B_3 would get virtually nothing.

FIGURE 4

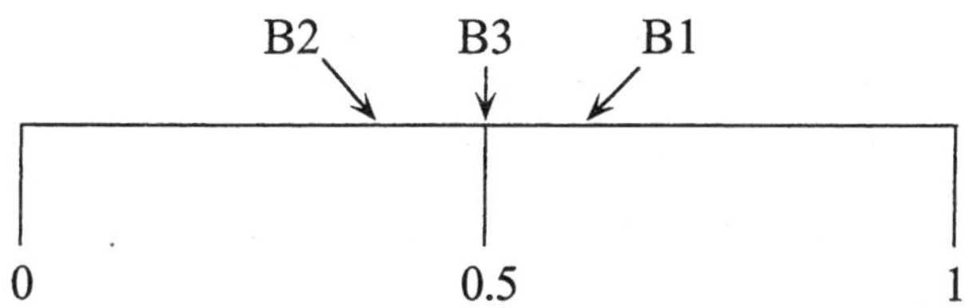

B3 is trapped beneath B1 and B2, garnering few viewers.

Now B_3 has an incentive to leapfrog over either B_1 or B_2 and garner the viewers on one side or the other. Assume that B_3 leapfrogs over B_1. Then B_1 will find itself trapped.

FIGURE 5

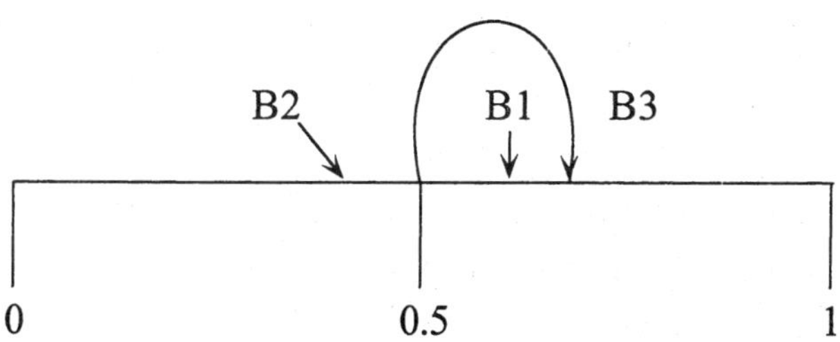

B3 leapfrogs B1, trapping B1.

Now B_1 will have an incentive to leapfrog over B_2 or B_3. This leapfrogging will continue until the broadcasters are so far from the center that it suddenly pays one of them to return to the center.

FIGURE 6

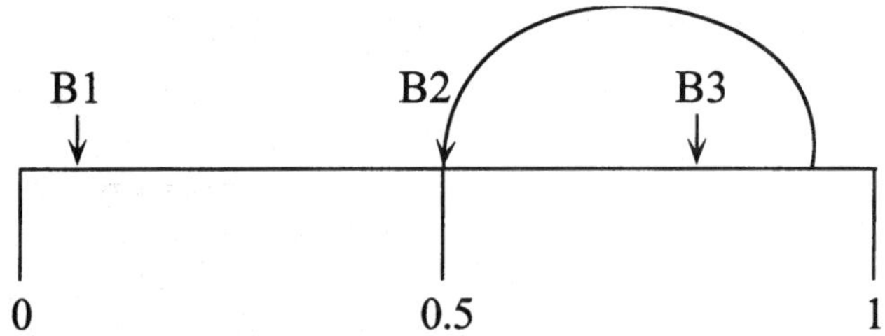

B2 jumps back to the middle.

However, once one of the broadcasters has returned to the center each of the other two broadcasters will have an incentive to move in close and crowd the broadcaster in the center, garnering virtually all of the viewers on either side. Once this happens the leapfrogging starts all over again. In fact, under these circumstances, there is no stable arrangement of broadcasters; the leapfrogging, return, crowding, and leapfrogging behavior will continue forever.

As a brief side note, such a prediction might explain the appearance of rapid turnover and churning in broadcast television. The networks, particularly when there were only three, were constantly programming and counterprogramming. This behavior might represent a market without an equilibrium.

In contrast to the market with three broadcasters, with four or more broadcasters there are stable arrangements. However, with four or more broadcasters, not all the programming will be clustered in the middle. Consider the case of four broadcasters. Two broadcasters will pair off at 0.25 and two more will pair off at 0.75. Each broadcaster will garner twenty-five percent of available viewers. This equilibrium is unique.

FIGURE 7

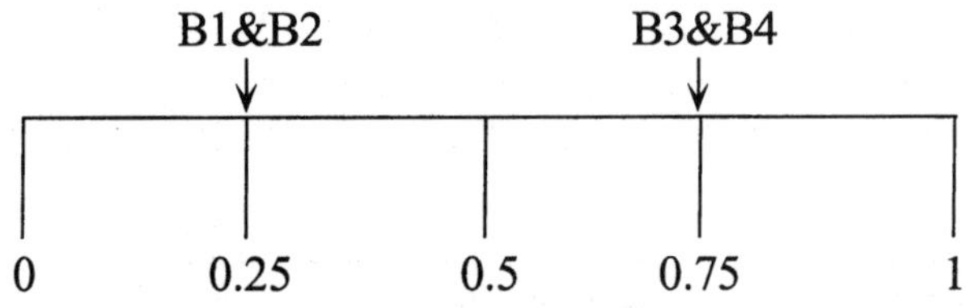

With four broadcasters we get two pair.

With six or more firms in a market the equilibria are no longer unique. However, every equilibrium is characterized by the following conditions:

(1) Peripheral broadcasters—those closest to either 0 or

1—are paired.[106] Thus, every equilibrium with six or more firms must look like the figure immediately below.

FIGURE 8

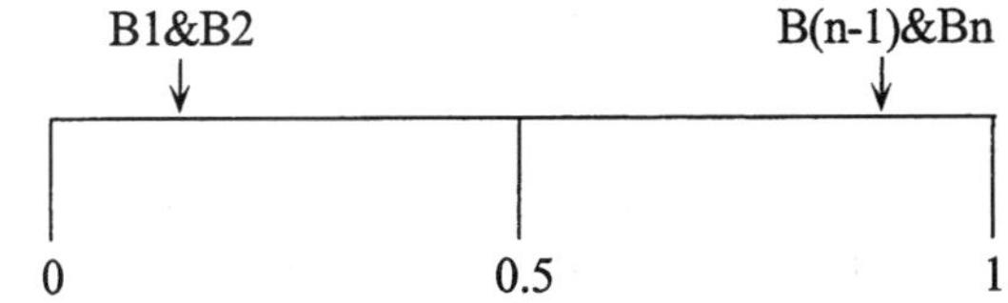

With six or more firms, the peripheral firms are paired.

(2) No broadcaster can have an audience smaller than the audience of the peripheral firms.[107]

(3) No broadcaster can have an audience more than twice as large as any other broadcaster's audience.[108]

b. Putting the V-Chip into the Market

Now, how will adding the V-chip change the offerings in broadcasting markets? The answer is "it depends." The V-chip will change the broadcasting market in different ways depending on the number of broadcasters in the market, the rating system's decision about which programs to consider violent, and the way in which the viewers will use the technology.

To get a feeling for how the V-chip can change the market, I will analyze a market with two broadcasters. I will use a very simple assumption about how the government (or industry) rates television programs: the ratings administrator rates a program as violent or nonviolent. This, in essence, means that the ratings administration picks a standard, v, at some place on the violence continuum, and rates all programs to the left of that standard "violent" and all programs to the right of that standard "nonviolent."[109]

---

106 *See* Eaton & Lipsey, *supra* note 96, at 29.

107 *Id.* at 31.

108 *Id.*

109 The V-chip may actually utilize several grades of violence. Thus, an administrator might rate programs on a scale of v_1 to v_{10}, where v_1 is most violent and v_{10} is least violent. A viewer might choose some standard, say v_6, and then the V-chip would block all programs with ratings from v_1 through v_6, but allow programs rated from $v_7$7 through v_{10} to appear on the television set. In appendix 6, *infra*, I take a few preliminary steps at analyzing a video market where the V-chip ratings system has many settings.

FIGURE 9

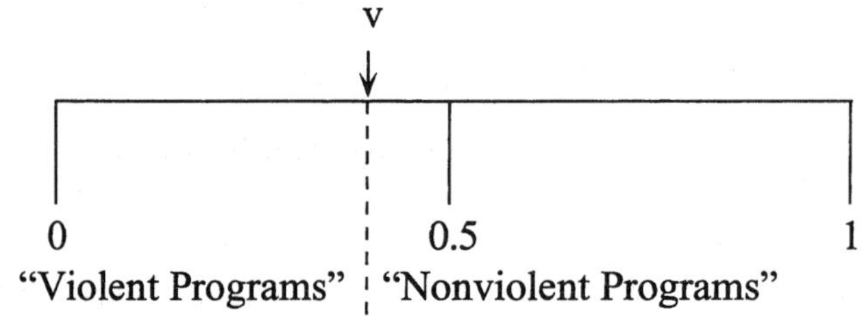

How will viewers respond to the V-chip? Who will choose to use the V-chip and block out all those programs that are rated more violent than the standard? I will use two alternative assumptions about who uses the V-chip. Recall that viewers are characterized by having an ideal type of program on the violence continuum, and that I have assumed that these ideal types are distributed evenly over [0, 1].

i. Assumption A1 Regarding V-Chip Use

My first assumption about the distribution of those who choose to use the V-chip is that they are distributed across the violence spectrum in the same way that viewers in general are distributed across the violence spectrum. Hence, if *x*% of viewers whose ideal point is 0.6 use the V-chip, then *x*% of viewers with any other ideal point use the V-chip.

Discussion: This assumption is somewhat counterintuitive. After all, one would think that those who have ideal points to the *left* of *v*, the government standard, would not use the V-chip. After all, using the V-chip removes the user's favorite type of program. The response to this reasoning runs something like the following: those who use the V-chip are not doing so for themselves. Instead, the V-chip helps parents remove violent programs from the household, regardless of whether the parent would like to see violent programs. As long as we are counting only the adults as viewers, then this assumption may well be correct. What of the children?[110] Perhaps parents whose children who love violent programming use the V-chip more frequently than parents with children who do not

110 *See* James T. Hamilton, Does Viewer Discretion Prompt Advertiser Discretion? The Impact of Violence Warnings on the Television Advertising Market (June 29, 1996) (draft presented at Duke Conference on Media Violence and Public Policy), indicates that the advertising rates for violent programs do not change with respect to changes in the number of children in the audience. If Professor Hamilton's results are correct, then we would need to know at what point on the violence continuum (i.e., 0.6?, 0.8?) children start to "count" to complete the analysis. This complication is beyond the scope of this paper.

like violence. In this case the assumption would be inaccurate, but inaccurate in a way that is opposite to our original concern. Perhaps the phenomenon of parents removing children who love violence from the audience counterbalances the phenomenon of adults without children refusing to use the V-chip if v is to the right of the adult's favorite program type. There is one additional consideration. If any security procedure that is good enough to keep children from removing the V-chip filter will also be complex enough to keep most adults from turning it on and off, then parents must also screen themselves out of violent, sexual, and other programming, along with their kids. If parents who like violent shows but do not want their children to see violence are just as likely to activate the V-chip as parents who dislike violent shows, then *Assumption A1* will be satisfied, and adults and children will be removed from part of the audience in uniform fashion.

ii. Assumption A2 Regarding V-Chip Use

Those who use the V-chip are located only to the right of v, the government rating standard. But those to the right of v who choose to use the V-chip are distributed in the same way as viewers are generally distributed over this range.

Discussion: This assumption posits that parents cannot easily turn the V-chip on and off, and are willing to exercise control over their children's viewing right up to the point that doing so would remove the adult's favorite program from the set. At that point the parent gives up and stops using the V-chip.

Of course, I could utilize an almost infinite number of variations on these assumptions about the characteristics of those who will use the V-chip.[111] Each variation might produce some change in the results of the analysis. To get a feeling for the style of the analysis and the form of the results (both in economics and in the First Amendment) we will proceed with the two assumptions listed above.

iii. Two Broadcasters, Rectangular Viewer Distribution, Assumption A1 Regarding V-Chip Use

The results of this model will depend on whether v is greater than or less than 0.5. If v is less than 0.5, then both broadcasters will locate at 0.5, and the equilibrium will be unchanged from the case in which there is no V-chip.

---

111 A full treatment would endogenize the behavior of viewers in a game, but that is beyond the scope of this article.

If v is greater than 0.5, then there are two different equilibria. First, define p to be the percentage of the viewers who use the V-chip.

Case i: $2(1-p)v < 1$. In this case both broadcasters locate at v and earn $1/2$ of the available viewers.[112]

FIGURE 10

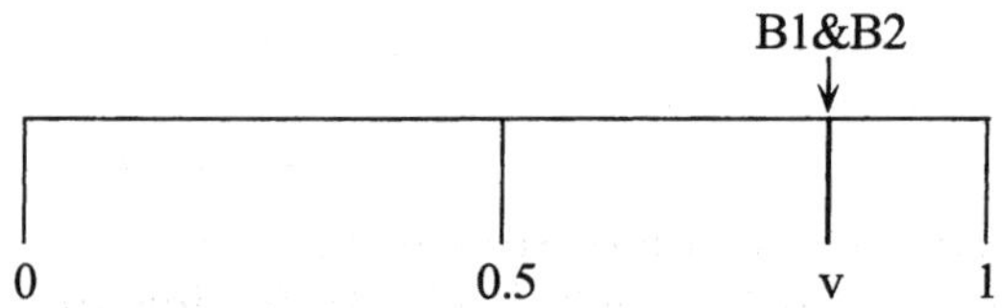

Both broadcasters remain at v.

Case ii: $2(1-p)v > 1$. There are two subcases. If $v < p+0.5$ then there is no equilibrium. If $v > p+0.5$, then there is an equilibrium with both broadcasters locating at 0.5.[113]

SUMMARY

Parameter Conditions	$v < 0.5$	$v > 0.5$ and $2(1-p)v < 1$	$v > 0.5$ and $2(1-p)>1$ and $v < p+0.5$	$v > 0.5$ and $2(1-p)>1$ and $v > p+0.5$
Equilibrium Outcome	Pair at 0.5	Pair at v	No Equilibrium	Pair at 0.5

Thus, we see that the V-chip and government rating of television programs can make the market more complex. Under certain circumstances, the equilibrium was completely destroyed. Where the equilibrium exists, it is either unchanged from the case with no V-chip—both broadcasters locate at 0.5—or changed such that both broadcasters locate at v. The next part of the analysis, immediately below, will reveal a very different story.

iv. Two Broadcasters, Rectangular Viewer Distribution, Assumption A2 Regarding V-Chip Use

Recall that assumption A2 posits that only viewers whose ideal point lies to the right of v will use the V-chip. The results in this general case depend on whether v is to the right or left of 0.5.

If v is to the left of 0.5, then the equilibrium exists and is identical to the case without the V-chip. Both broadcasters locate at 0.5.

---

112 *See infra* appendix 1.

113 *See id.*

FIGURE 11

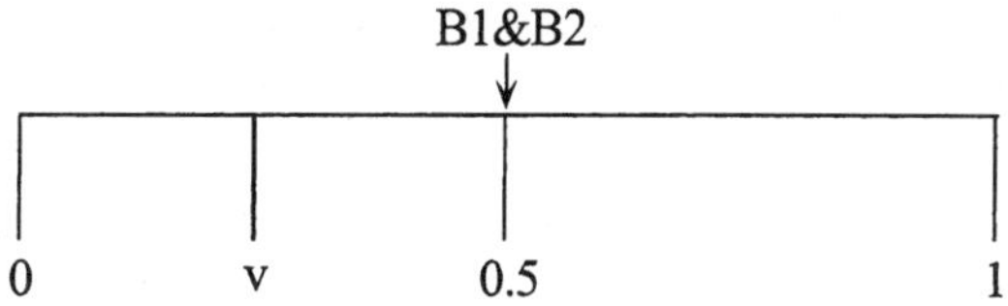

If v is to the right of 0.5, then we cannot get an equilibrium pair at v. We can get an equilibrium at $e = (^1/_2)\ [v+(1-p)(1-v)]$ if and only if $e > (1+p;)(1-v)$.[114] Where such an equilibrium exists, if p is small and v is large, the programming could be *more* violent than it would without the V-chip. In other words, e may be less than 0.5. This slightly counterintuitive result makes sense only because of the behavior of viewers.[115]

c. Preliminary Implications From Two-Broadcaster Markets

Analyzing markets with only two broadcasters gives a dizzying array of results. Depending upon the assumptions regarding the percentage of people who choose to use the V-chip, the way they use it (assumptions A1 or A2), and the placement of the violence standard, the equilibrium may be destroyed. Where the equilibrium exists it may be less violent, equally violent, or more violent than that found in the market without the V-chip. Predicting which of these outcomes is likely to obtain requires a fairly good knowledge of the parameters in the model.

What, if anything, is the likely legal import of this? It depends on where the Court places the burden of proof to show a chill of violent speech. If there is a heavy burden on the plaintiff, and showing the possibility of a chill is not enough, then the plaintiff will likely lose. There is no evidence that anyone involved in the V-chip ratings process, including program producers, politicians, or (eventually) judges, has a good idea of the parameters in the model. I certainly have no good idea about them. Unless the plaintiff can get a good source of data, the plaintiff will lose. On the other hand, if the Court essentially places the burden on the defendant to show no chilling effect, the defendant will lose. Certainly a chill of violent speech is possible, and ruling it out would

114 *See infra* appendix 9.

115 This resembles the sentiments of Brian Lowry of the *L.A. Times*.

> In the realm of unintended consequences, there have been indications at least with the MPAA's movie rating codes, on which the new TV system is based, that a "G" rating can be off-putting to adults without children. Since advertising is sold primarily off how many young adults tune in, ratings for wholesome family shows could thus theoretically be hurt by the system.

Lowry, *supra* note 93.

require data on the parameters in the model. Hence, at this stage, I would suggest that he who bears the burden loses. Of course, subsequent events could change all of this. If, after we have gained substantial experience with the behavior of viewers using the V-chip, governmental actors again tinker with the process, then this theory of First Amendment violation could gain substantial strength.

d. Larger Markets

Perhaps there is something special about the two-broadcaster market that produced the results. Perhaps there is some overwhelming pattern from three- or four-broadcaster markets that would lead us to conclude something different. We will examine some three- and four-broadcaster markets and find that no great pattern emerges.

i. Three Broadcasters, Rectangular Viewer Distribution, Assumption A1 on V-Chip Use:

Recall that there was no equilibrium in the absence of a V-chip. Are there any equilibria with the V-chip? Only in very limited circumstances, which are described below.

Certainly there can be no equilibrium with three broadcasters clustered on the interior of either range *(0, v)* or *(v, 1)*, for the same reason that there is no equilibrium with three broadcasters and no V-chip; the "trapped" broadcaster will leapfrog to the outside of one of the other broadcasters.

Can there be an equilibrium with a cluster of only two? There are only three likely possibilities:

(a)

FIGURE 101

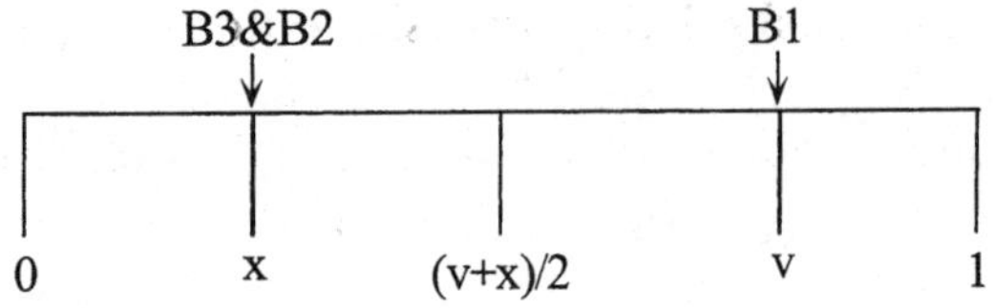

(b)

FIGURE 102

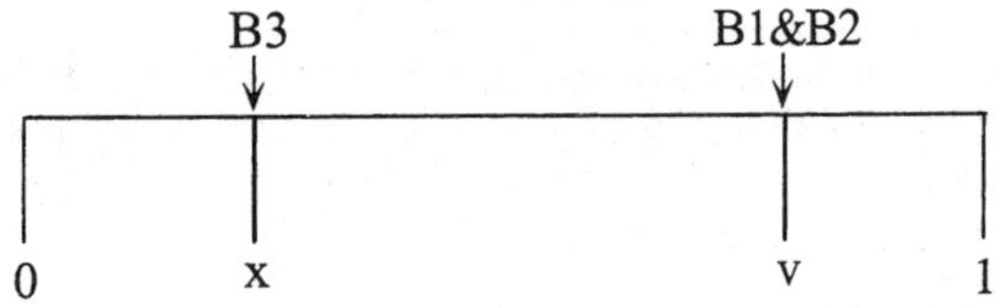

(c) FIGURE 103

There are no equilibria possible in Figure 101.[116] In addition, there can be no equilibrium in Figure 102. This results from B_3's incentive to slide over and crowd B_1 and B_2 on the left side. Under some circumstances, however, there may be an equilibrium in Figure 103. If the relationship between *p*, the percentage of the population that uses the V-chip, and *v*, the location of the violence standard, satisfies two conditions, then equilibrium can exist.

> (i) $1-v < 1/3$. This condition keeps B_1 (or B_2 or B_3) from moving slightly to the right and crowding the other two broadcasters.
>
> (ii) $(1-p)v < 1/3$. This condition keeps each broadcaster from moving slightly to the left and crowding the other two.

Putting these two conditions together greatly restricts the range of equilibria. Condition (i) implies that $v > 2/3$. And putting this into condition (ii) suggests that $p > 1/2$. What would a sample equilibrium be? If $v = 5/6$ and $p = 0.7$, then all three broadcasters would remain at *v* and Figure 103 would be in equilibrium. However, there is no guarantee that there is any pair (v,p) that satisfies conditions (i) and (ii), and also the functional relationship between *v* and *p* that is defined by viewers' behavior. In other words, if the government sets the violence standard at greater than 2/3, less than fifty percent of viewers may choose to use the V-chip.

Notice that if an equilibrium exists in Figure 103, the equilibrium will tend to be pushed very far to the right, and that the equilibrium will have crushed the diversity of offerings found where there was no V-chip or no equilibrium at all. An alternative way of characterizing the result is that the V-chip has allowed viewers effectively to control violent programming.

ii. Three Broadcasters, Rectangular Viewer Distribution, Assumption A2 Regarding V-Chip Use

Under these circumstances, there are no equilibria with three broadcasters clustered together.[117] Also, there can be no equilibrium

116 *See infra* appendix 3.
117 *See infra* appendix 4.

rium in Figure 102. B_3 has an incentive to slide over and crowd B_1. The only remaining possibility is for an equilibrium looking like Figure 101, and this fails as well.[118]

In sum, in three-broadcaster markets, the V-chip can create an equilibrium only in a limited range of circumstances. The viewers must use the V-chip in accord with assumption A1 rather than A2, and viewers must be willing to use the V-chip at a rather high rate, even when the violence rating standard is extremely strict.

iii. Four Broadcasters, Rectangular Viewer Distribution, Assumption A1 Regarding V-Chip Use

Recall that without a V-chip the equilibrium had two pairs of broadcasters, one pair located at 0.25 and the other at 0.75. How does the V-chip change things?

If $v < 0.25$, the equilibrium is unchanged. What happens if $0.25 < v$? There are two different sorts of possible equilibria. The first, depicted in Figure 12, has a pair of broadcasters located at v, and another pair located to the right of v.

FIGURE 12

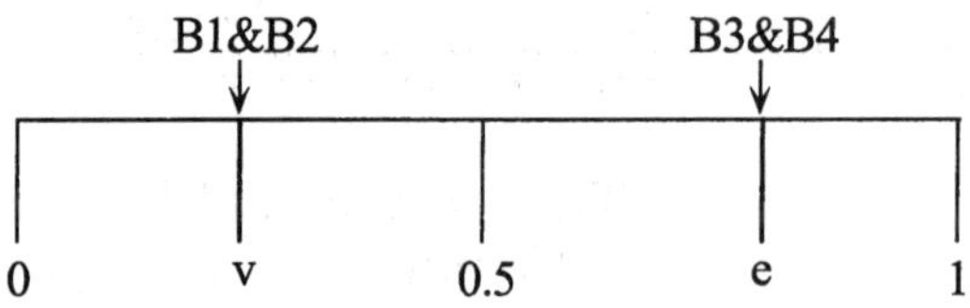

To be in equilibrium, certain relationships must be maintained. First, $(1-p)v \leq 1-e$. Further, $2(1-e) = e-v$. This implies that $2+ = 3e$. For example, $v = 1/3$, $e = 7/9$, $p \leq 1/3$ is an equilibrium. As the violence standard v is made more strict (by moving farther to the right), e must move farther to the right, and p, the percentage of people using the V-chip, must rise. Thus, consider the equilibrium if v is set at 2/3. Then $e = 8/9$ and $p = 5/6$. That is a startlingly high percentage of people using the V-chip, particularly when the standard is strict. Hence, I suspect that as v becomes more strict, this equilibrium becomes less likely.

There is, however, one other possibility, and that is depicted in Figure 13. In order for this to be an equilibrium, two conditions must be satisfied. First, $3e = v$. Second, $1-v = e(1-p)$. Such equilibria can exist only when $3/4 < v < 1$.[119] For example, $v = 9/10$, $e = 3/$

118 *See id.*

119 Substitute $v/3$ for e into $1\text{-}v = e(1\text{-}p)$, and get $(3\text{-}3v)/v = (1\text{-}p)$. If $p = 0$, $v = 3/4$, while if $p = 1$, $v = 1$.

10, and $p = 2/3$ is an equilibrium. Again, I regard such an equilibrium as unlikely.

FIGURE 13

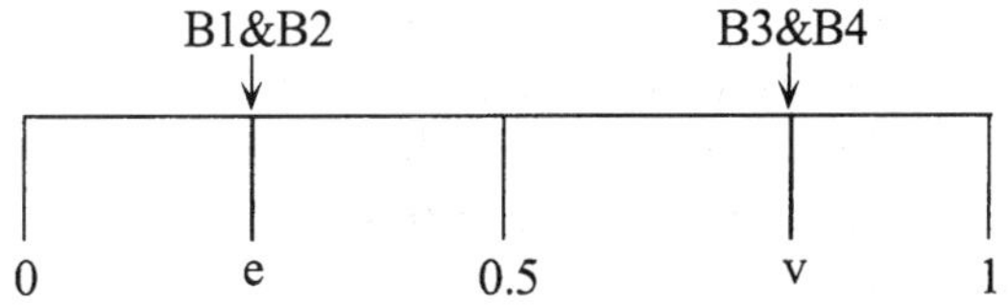

iv. Four Broadcasters, Rectangular Viewer Distribution, Assumption A2 Regarding V-Chip Use

The results in this model depend, again, on what v is. If $0 < v < 0.25$ or if $0.25 < v < 0.75$, then the equilibrium is identical to the case without a V-chip. Two broadcasters pair at 0.25, and the other two pair at 0.75. When $0 < v < 0.25$ the reasoning is identical to the case with no V-chip. When $0.25 < v < 0.75$, the reasoning, but not the results, differ.[120] When $0.75 < v < 1$, there is no equilibrium.[121]

In sum, in four-broadcaster markets equilibria may not exist. If equilibria do exist they may be unchanged from the situation without a V-chip, or they may look quite different. Again, the particular outcome depends on the parameters in the model.

e. Implications From Two-, Three- and Four-Broadcaster Markets

There is no clear pattern of effects from the V-chip. The parameters of the models are crucial to determine whether an equilibrium exists and what its nature is. Again, there is no evidence at this juncture that anyone has any useful knowledge of these parameters. Consequently, he who bears the burden under a "chill" theory of a First Amendment violation can gain no comfort here. As I noted earlier, subsequent actions by government officials could change these conclusions.

f. Variations and Extensions

i. Stigma and Ratings

Some broadcasters have claimed that there will be a stigma associated with broadcasting shows that have been rated violent (or sexual or laced with strong language).[122] This stigma, it is claimed,

---

120 *See infra* appendix 5.
121 *See infra* appendix 8.
122 *See* Christopher Stern, *The V-Chip First Amendment Infringement v. Empowerment Tool*,

will cause broadcasters to eschew programming material likely to be so rated. As a consequence, it will be difficult to find such material on television.

There are at least two ways to interpret such a claim. The first regards broadcasters as engaged in something akin to consumption. In contrast to the assumption in the models above, broadcasters get utility from being "good citizens," as well as from making money. The stigma from being rated reduces the consumption utility from broadcasting at a point toward 0 on the violence continuum. The equilibrium, if any, might well be shifted to the right.

The crucial question in evaluating such a claim about stigma (as affecting consumption) is whether it is generally true of broadcasters.[123] Finding *some* broadcasters who care about such matters will not tell us whether or not the equilibria will shift. If a few broadcasters care, but others do not, then we would expect the overall equilibrium to be unchanged, but only those who feel no stigma to be producing and programming the stronger fare. We already know that some producers, such as Hugh Hefner or Al Goldstein, seem to feel little remorse at producing and programming sexual material. It may be fairly easy to find a supply of those who care little about being rated.

A second interpretation of the stigma argument is that advertisers will not want to be labeled as supportive of violent (or sexual or otherwise negatively controversial) programming.[124] Again, it is the rating, rather than the programming, that plays the crucial role in the argument. As a consequence, advertisers and programmers will pay less for those viewers whose preferences lie on the left hand side of the violence continuum, at least when such viewers are attracted by violent fare. This process will push equilibria toward the nonviolent end of the spectrum.

To evaluate such a claim, one must decide whether or not the price of advertising on shows rated violent will decline. For such a

---

BROADCASTING & CABLE, Feb. 12, 1996; *Violence Code Could Be Economic Scarlet Letter; Code for Violence on Television Programs Could Reduce Advertising Revenues*, BROADCASTING & CABLE, June 21, 1993; *Clinton Puts V-Chip on Fast Track; Momentum Grows for Mandatory Violence-Blocking Technology for TV*, BROADCASTING & CABLE, July 17, 1995, at 6.

Hamilton, *supra* note 110, has shown that advisories of strong content before motion pictures shown on television reduce advertising revenues. "Broadcasters run more network promotions and fewer general product ads on theatrical films with warnings, consistent with the theory that warnings cause advertiser pullouts that lower prices." *Id.* at 4. If these results were to carry over into the V-chip framework, the stigma argument would gain great force.

123 Note that the stigma comes not from broadcasting violent material, but from being *labeled* as a broadcaster of violence.

124 *See* Hamilton, *supra* note 110 (presenting theory and data supporting the stigma argument).

thing to happen, one must find more than two or three advertisers whose demand for time is reduced by the stigma. For the stigma to reduce the market price for advertising on shows rated violent, the *marginal* advertisers' demand must be reduced by stigma. Marginal advertisers are those who value ad time on violent programs at no more than the prevailing market rate. If price goes up, they shift to other advertising media—nonviolent television programming, newspapers, radio, magazines, billboards, and others. What is more, it will not do to find a few marginal advertisers who are currently advertising on shows that would be rated violent and conclude that the price of ad time would fall from V-chip ratings. There may be other marginal advertisers who are currently indifferent between buying ad time on violent programs and buying it elsewhere. If enough of these marginal advertisers are not affected by the stigma, then they will take the place of those marginal advertisers who are affected by the stigma and who therefore switch away from advertising on programs rated violent when V-chip ratings start. Because ad prices will not change in such circumstances, no change in programming should occur. Instead, one will only see a reshuffling of advertisements on shows.

There is no way to know, at this point, if either of the stigma arguments is correct. If they are right on the facts, then changes in equilibrium television output may well follow.

ii. Violence Unleashed[125]

"Tom Wildmon, vice president of the Tupelo, Miss.—based American Family Assn., objects to any ratings, claiming they merely give the networks 'more license to do whatever they want to, under the guise of "Hey, we warned you."' "[126] The amount of sex and violence in the marketplace might go up, rather than down, because of the V-chip ratings. Some broadcasters will feel free to program more violent fare than in the past because the broadcasters can deflect criticism with the V-chip. If a potential viewer objects to the violence, the broadcaster can say "use the V-chip to filter us out."

Such an argument can be interpreted in at least three ways. First, such an argument may refer to a broadcaster's need to deal with the reduction in profits stemming from unpopular, controversial programming. If sexual or violent programming angers

---

125 Geoff Miller, Professor of Law, New York University Law School first suggested this argument to me.

126 Brian Lowry, *The Ratings: Inside and Out*, L.A. TIMES, July 12, 1997, at F1.

enough potential viewers, the broadcaster may be made to suffer lost profits. Viewers may threaten to organize boycotts of advertisers' products, or opinion leaders may indicate that there is substantial social stigma from watching particular programs. Advertisers, in turn, may shy away from certain shows. If enough advertisers (particularly those on the margin) behave in this way, broadcasters' revenues may be hurt. The V-chip, however, may give broadcasters a way to defuse such situations without watering down sexual or violent programming. If saying "just filter us out" suffices to reduce outrage to mere grumbling, the broadcasters may face smaller (or no) problems from programming sex and violence when the V-chip is in the market. Consequently, the V-chip will increase the profitability of sex and violence. As a consequence, concludes this argument, equilibria shift to the left.

This version of the argument makes logical sense. However, pending some empirical evidence on the truth of the various assumptions in the argument, there is no way to know whether the argument correctly applies to the V-chip.

Second, this argument may be similar to the consumption version of the stigma argument reviewed above, but opposite in direction. Broadcasters, who get utility from broadcasting above and beyond that realized from maximizing profits, will get more utility from broadcasting violent fare once a V-chip rating system is in place. The increase in utility will derive from the ability to say "just filter us out" when outraged consumers object to the programming. The increased utility may shift equilibria to the left.

To evaluate such an argument, one needs to know essentially the same facts as those needed to evaluate the stigma argument. First, one needs to know if the underlying assertions about broadcaster motivations were true. Second, these assertions would have to be true of the broadcasters who had been presenting violent fare. If those who would suffer from the stigma from showing violence had been showing nonviolent fare, then instituting the V-chip would produce no change in the mix in the market. This is because those who had been showing violence suffered no stigma from showing violence, and consequently they could not be released from any stigma by instituting the V-chip ratings system.

Third, such an argument might be about the removal of an implicit regulatory constraint against showing highly violent fare. Indeed, at least as to programs showing indecency, instituting the V-chip ratings system *might* undercut the rationale for time zoning indecency on broadcast television.[127] In a forceful piece entitled *Media Filters, the V-Chip, and the Foundations of Broadcast Regulation,* J. M. Balkin argues that the V-chip will ultimately require reworking (and reducing) the restraints on televised broadcast indecency.[128] If the Court were now to rule that governmental regulations requiring time-zoning indecent television broadcasts were unconstitutional because the V-chip ratings provided a much less intrusive alternative, then we might expect some indecent content during hours when children might be expected to be in the audience.[129] Such programming would undoubtedly be rated for sexual content. As to violent but nonsexual programming, it is not clear that there has been any regulatory constraint. Hence, the V-chip ratings system probably cannot remove any constraint regarding violence.

iii. Allowing More Values of *V* or "Picky" Viewers

What happens if there can be more than one value of *v*? In my model above, consumers had only the choice of turning the V-chip on or off, and *v* was set equal to one value. What if the consumer has a choice of several settings? Do the results change greatly?

I am afraid I cannot yet answer this question fully. I have investigated the effect of giving the consumer an infinite number of values from which to select. In such a system, the consumer could select any number between 0 and 1, such as 0.3257 or 0.86156, for *v*, and then the consumer would have infinitely fine control over which shows came into the house. Appendix 6 contains a proof that if the consumer has an *infinite* number of values from which to select, all equilibria may be destroyed.

In my model, viewers always watched whatever show was closest to their ideal points. What happens if viewers are "picky" and turn off the set if no alternative is close enough to their ideal points? The answer depends on how picky the viewers are.[130] In some cir-

---

127 Part of the rationale used in *FCC v. Pacifica Foundation*, 438 U.S. 726 (1978), to uphold time-shifting of indecent programming was to enable parents to control the broadcast diet of children. Of course, as to broadcast television, the V-chip now seems to provide a less intrusive alternative. The Court also hinted at the purpose of protecting children, with the state as a surrogate parent. *See* M. SPITZER, SEVEN DIRTY WORDS AND SIX OTHER STORIES 129-30 (1986).

128 Balkin, *supra* note 11; *see* Note, *Constitutional Law—Freedom of Speech*, 109 HARV. L. REV. 864, 867-68 (1996) (making the same point).

129 *See infra* appendix 7. Even this prediction is not as clear cut as it might seem. Such a regulatory constraint can destroy equilibria in some markets.

130 This is similar to the problem of voters who refuse to vote unless there is a candidate that is close enough to the voter's ideal. *See* Melvin J. Hinich & Peter C. Ordeshook, *Plural-*

cumstances, new equilibria can be created that have more diversity than in markets without picky consumers. For example, consider a two-broadcaster market. Recall that the equilibrium without the V-chip was for both broadcasters to locate at 0.5. If consumers will watch if and only if there is an offering within 0.25 of their ideal points, then a new equilibrium will be obtained. One broadcaster will locate at 0.25, while the other will locate at 0.75.

I have not yet worked out the implications of a V-chip in such a market. Perhaps further research awaits.

iv. Entry and Number of Stations

How does potential entry, particularly in cable television, affect the ability of the V-chip to change equilibria in the broadcasting market?[131] The formal answer is "I don't know." My guess is that entry makes sustaining any equilibrium in which large segments of the violence continuum are unserved quite unlikely. Large, unserved areas of the consumers' tastes would provide profitable opportunities and invite entry.

The big question is the expense of entry. In broadcasting, where one needs a license, entry is quite difficult. In cable, where no license is needed to start a new cable network,[132] entry is possible, but requires capital. The cheaper entry becomes, the more offerings we can expect in equilibrium. And as the number of outlets grows, we can generally expect a more diverse set of offerings in equilibrium.[133]

v. Unrated Programs

How will the existence and treatment of unrated programs change the analysis? I witnessed a demonstration of a beta-system by Tim Collings, inventor of the V-chip, at the Duke Conference on Violence in the Media. In the demonstrated system, the viewer had the option of allowing through or blocking all unrated program material. If the final system has this feature, then the decisions of viewers on treating unrated material might change the

---

ity Maximization vs. Vote Maximization: A Spatial Analysis with Variable Participation, 64 AM. POL. SCI. REV. 772 (1970) (Assumption 7); Melvin J. Hinich & Peter C. Ordeshook, *Abstentions and Equilibrium in the Electoral Process*, 8 PUB. CHOICE 81 (1969); Melvin J. Hinich et al., *Nonvoting and the Existence of Equilibrium Under Majority Rule*, 4 J. ECON. THEORY 144 (1972); Richard D. McKelvey, *Policy Related Voting and Electoral Equilibrium*, 43 ECONOMETRICA 814 (1975).

131 This is similar to the question of candidate entry in political science. *See* Thomas R. Palfrey, *Spatial Equilibrium with Entry*, 51 REV. ECON. STUD. 139 (1984).

132 This is not to be confused with the franchise, which is usually needed to build a cable system in a community.

133 *See* BRUCE OWEN & STEVEN WILDMAN, VIDEO ECONOMICS 142-44 (1992).

equilibrium. If *all* viewers choose to block unrated material, then the models described above work perfectly—all producers will choose to rate their programs, for that will be the only way that anyone will be able to receive the programs. On the other hand, if enough viewers choose to allow unrated programming through, some producers may choose not to rate their programs. Depending upon which viewers choose to allow through unrated programs, the equilibrium might be changed. Computing these changes awaits further research.

vi. Summary of Variations and Extensions

I do not know all of the answers to the questions posed in this section. The answers I do know, however, do not all point in one direction. Depending upon which variation one examines, the V-chip might produce effects in one direction or another. Hence, I would conclude that there is nothing here that would give any aid or comfort to a plaintiff trying to prove a chill-based cause of action against the V-chip ratings system.

g. Summary of Various "Chill" Arguments

Assuming the plaintiff had the burden of proof to show the chill, his cause of action would fail because of an inability to demonstrate an infringement of speech by the V-chip. This leads us to consider the alternative theory of infringement that might be propounded by a complaining producer—the V-chip operates like a tax on his expression, reducing its range of delivery.

3. The License Theory of Infringement[134]

A complaining producer's argument would be straightfor-

[134] There is an additional theory that the producer could propound that is beyond the scope of this article. The producer could claim that the V-chip ratings system, which requires the producer to rate the show, represents compelled speech, and as such violates the producer's right not to speak. There are a number of cases that uphold, in general, the right not to speak. *See* West Virginia State Bd. of Educ. v. Barnette, 319 U.S. 624 (1943) (invalidating a state requirement that children salute the U.S. flag); *Wooley*, 430 U.S. 705 (holding that individuals have constitutional rights to obscure the motto "Live Free or Die" on a license plate); McIntyre v. Ohio Elections Comm'n, 115 S. Ct. 1511 (1995) (invalidating requirement that campaign literature identify the author). The two cases that are most similar to the V-chip rating system are *Lamont v. Postmaster General*, 381 U.S. 301 (1965) (invalidating the federal statute requiring U.S. Post Office to identify "communist political propaganda" and requiring that those wanting such material request the delivery in writing) and *Meese*, 481 U.S. 465 (upholding the requirement that motion picture exhibitors place the words "political propaganda" at the start of foreign films that had been identified as propaganda by the U.S. government).

ward.[135] The V-chip ratings system prevents him from distributing his product to everyone who might otherwise be able to receive it. The program's rating will cause it to be filtered out of the sets in many homes. In this way, the V-chip ratings system is standing between the producer and otherwise able (and willing?) recipients.

First Amendment "licensing" cases represent the closest analogy to the producer's claims. The licensing cases consider various circumstances in which the government, through an administrative apparatus, makes governmental permission a prerequisite to communication. Representative cases have struck down schemes requiring permission from a City Manager to distribute literature,[136] requiring a permit to use a sound amplification system on a motor vehicle,[137] or requiring a permit—to be issued at the unfettered discretion of the mayor—for placing a newspaper vending machine on public property.[138] Although some licensing cases have been upheld,[139] the Court remains very skeptical of licensing schemes.[140]

Many of the licensing cases considered attempts by state and local governments to create permit systems for motion pictures. The federal courts tend to treat governmental regulations that license motion pictures very harshly. These regulations, which restrict the ability of motion picture theaters to show sexual or violent fare to children and teenagers, were routinely struck down.[141] The film ordinances and the V-chip ratings system bear a certain similarity because these film ordinances were undoubtedly passed, in part, for the purpose of protecting children, and because the film licensing ordinances attempted to filter children out of the audience.

---

135 Here we must presume that the producer prevailed on his somewhat shaky state action argument in the section before.

136 *See* Lovell v. City of Griffin, 303 U.S. 444 (1938).

137 *See* Saia v. New York, 334 U.S. 558 (1948).

138 *See* City of Lakewood v. Plain Dealer Publ'g Co., 486 U.S. 750 (1988).

139 *See, e.g.*, Kovacs v. Cooper, 336 U.S. 77 (1949); Cox v. New Hampshire, 312 U.S. 569 (1941).

140 *See* Forsyth County v. Nationalist Movement, 505 U.S. 123 (1992). This should be understood as part of the Court's general hostility toward any regulation that gets classed as a "prior restraint" of speech. *See* CHEMERINSKY, supra note 29, § 11.2.3.

141 *See* Interstate Circuit, Inc. v. Dallas, 390 U.S. 676, 678-81 (1968); Holmby Prods., Inc. v. Vaughn, 350 U.S. 870 (1955); Commercial Pictures Corp. v. Regents, 346 U.S. 863 (1954); Superior Films, Inc. v. Department of Ed., 346 U.S. 587 (1954); Kingsley Int'l Pictures Corp. v. Regents, 360 U.S. 684 (1953); Gelling v. Texas, 343 U.S. 960 (1952); Joseph Burstyn, Inc. v. Wilson, 343 U.S. 495 (1952); Paramount Film Distrib. Corp. v. Chicago, 172 F. Supp. 69 (N.D. Ill. 1959).

State court cases include Police Comm'r v. Siegel Enters., Inc., 162 A.2d 727 (court year); People v. Kahan, 206 N.E.2d 333 (1965); People v. Bookcase, Inc., 201 N.E.2d 14 (1964); Hallmark Productions, Inc. v. Carroll, 121 A.2d 584 (1956).

The Court should find that the V-chip ratings scheme differs from the film licensing scheme in two important ways. First, the film licensing schemes were designed to prevent children (and sometimes adults)[142] from seeing harmful material, regardless of the views of the families involved. In contrast, the V-chip will allow families to make decisions for themselves. This both greatly reduces the burden on distributing the rated material, and also allows more precise filtering of material to children according to parents' wishes.[143] Second, a motion picture ratings system could allow children to see movies if accompanied by a parent or guardian, much as the private Motion Picture Association of America ("MPAA") rating system does with "R" rated movies.[144] This imposes substantial costs on any parent wishing to let his or her child see the rated motion picture. In contrast, the V-chip ratings scheme will impose very low costs on any such parent.

My guess—that these two reasons will serve to distinguish the film licensing cases—rests in part on the federal courts' attitude toward "time zoning" indecent broadcast material.[145] Indecency, which has much more to do with sex and language than with violence, can be regulated so as to keep it away from children. Broadcast indecency may therefore be restricted to certain portions of the day.[146] As Judge Harry Edwards and Mitchell Berman have forcefully pointed out, this represents a burden to those parents who wish to expose their children to indecent broadcasts.[147] And despite this burden, such restrictions on broadcast indecency have been upheld. Where better filtering can be implemented, such as with indecency over the telephone (also known as "dial-a-porn"),

---

142 Criminal prosecution, rather than licensing, has been used to keep material away from consenting adults. *E.g.*, New York v. Mature Enters., 343 N.Y.S.2d 911 (1973) (finding the film *Deep Throat* obscene).

143 One way of looking at the choices of private parties to utilize the V-chip is that they might "cut the causal chain" between governmental action and the infringement. The producers might respond that the definition of the categories, and the decision to use an age-based system, establishes enough rigidity in the system that the viewer's choice to use the V-chip rating system does not let the government off the First Amendment state action hook.

144 *See Interstate Circuit, Inc.*, 390 U.S. at 678-81.

145 On the regulation of broadcast indecency, see THOMAS G. KRATTENMAKER & LUCAS A. POWE, JR., REGULATING BROADCAST PROGRAMMING 103-41 (1994); Lili Levi, *The Hard Case of Broadcast Indecency*, 20 N.Y.U. REV. L. & SOC. CHANGE 49 (1992).

146 *See* Sable Comms., Inc. v. FCC, 492 U.S. 115 (1989); *Pacifica Found.*, 438 U.S. 726; Action for Children's Television v. FCC (ACT III), 58 F.3d 654 (D.C. Cir. 1995) (en banc), *cert. denied sub nom.* Pacifica Found. v. FCC, 116 S. Ct. 701 (1996); Action for Children's Television v. FCC (ACT II), 932 F.2d 1504 (D.C. Cir. 1991), *cert. denied sub nom.* Children's Legal Found. v. Action for Children's Television, 503 U.S. 913 (1992); Action for Children's Television v. FCC (ACT I), 852 F.2d 1332 (D.C. Cir. 1988).

147 Edwards & Berman, *supra* note 8.

the government must implement better filters.[148] Once children, but not adults, are screened out, the regulation of telephonic indecency passes constitutional muster.

The V-chip ratings system compares very favorably to the indecency regulations that have been upheld. The V-chip ratings are not nearly as intrusive as the time zoning regulations for broadcast indecency.[149] Under the V-chip ratings system, very violent, sexual, or profanity-laced programming may be broadcast or cablecast at any hour of the day. It will be up to adults (parents for their children and other adults for themselves) to filter out the content. The V-chip ratings also compare favorably to the filtering approaches (for example, requiring a credit card) adopted for dial-a-porn. The cost and potential risk from setting a V-chip is clearly lower than that involved in giving out a credit card number over the telephone.[150]

The grounds on which the V-chip ratings scheme can be distinguished from the motion picture licensing precedents—parental autonomy and low cost—match closely the ways in which the V-chip is less burdensome than the indecency regulations that have been approved. As a consequence I expect the Court to distinguish, as a general matter, the motion picture precedents when ruling on the constitutionality of the V-chip.

4. Sufficient Justification for the Infringement?

Assuming the Court concludes the V-chip ratings system, and perhaps its application, constitutes state action, and that the system infringes upon speech in some judicially cognizable fashion, the Court must still confront the questions of whether the infringements are sufficiently justified. Particularly, the Court must decide whether the government has a good enough reason for infringing this sort of speech, and whether the V-chip ratings system is sufficiently closely connected to the government's good reasons.

---

148 *See Sable Comms., Inc.*, 492 U.S. 115; Balkin, *supra* note 11.

149 I am presuming that the two sorts of regulations are substitutes, not complements. *See* Balkin, *supra* note 11 (arguing that they must be substitutes).

150 Kim, *supra* note 101, analyzes part of the First Amendment issue correctly. He perceives that the Court's view of ratings as content-based regulation will lead to strict scrutiny, which will demand that regulations be narrowly tailored to a compelling state interest. Then, unfortunately, Kim gives the reader only the following sentence, "Given the ongoing controversy over the precise effects of media violence and the problem of definition, the government would face a tough battle in demonstrating both its compelling interest and the required fit between means and ends." *Id.* at 1406. Kim later acknowledges that the D.C. Circuit did find that enabling parents to control children's television viewing represented a compelling state interest, but fails to follow up with a serious analysis of whether ratings and the V-chip would be narrowly tailored. *Id.* at 1408-09.

a. Finding the Standard of Review

In theory, a court must first choose a standard of review with which to evaluate a regulation of speech. Usually the choice of a standard is crucial, for the more demanding the standard, the less likely the regulation will pass muster. However, as I will explain in detail below, I believe that the choice of a standard in this case will not be particularly important. *The V-Chip regulations are likely to pass the most demanding level of scrutiny, and hence will also pass less demanding levels of review.*

The two standards of review that will contend for the court's choice are "strict" scrutiny and "intermediate" scrutiny. Strict scrutiny generally requires that the regulation of speech be designed to serve a "compelling state interest," and that the regulation must be "carefully tailored to achieve" the compelling interest.[151] This formulation, which is supposed to express skepticism about the validity of the regulations at issue, is to be applied to regulations that are "content-based."[152] Such regulations, which reward or punish speakers based, in part, on the content of speech, are presumptively invalid.[153] "Intermediate" scrutiny, in contrast, demands only an "important" governmental interest to justify the regulation. In addition, the regulation of speech must directly implement the important governmental interest, but need not be as narrowly tailored to the task as those that are tested under "strict" scrutiny.[154] "Intermediate" scrutiny is often used to test content-neutral regulations[155] or content-based regulations in the field of broadcasting,[156] as well as regulations that have incidental effects on speech.[157]

In *Denver Area Educational Telecommunications Consortium v. FCC*,[158] the Supreme Court split five to four on whether the federal

---

151 *See* R.A.V. v. City of St. Paul, 505 U.S. 377 (1992); *Sable Comms.*, 492 U.S. at 126; Consolidated Edison Co. v. Public Serv. Comm'n, 447 U.S. 530, 540 (1980). This standard is also used in many other areas of constitutional analysis. *See, e.g.*, Adarand Constructors v. Pena, 115 S. Ct. 2097 (1995); Sugarman v. Dougall, 413 U.S. 634 (1973); Sherbert v. Verner, 374 U.S. 398 (1963).

152 *See R.A.V.*, 505 U.S. at 382.

153 *Id.*; Texas v. Johnson, 491 U.S. 397, 412 (1992). Another implication of this statement is that the government has the burden of proof in such cases. *See* CHEMERINSKY, supra note 29, § 6.5.

154 *See* Turner Broad. Sys. v. FCC, 114 S. Ct. 2445 (1994); Bellsouth Corp. v. U.S., 868 F. Supp. 1335, 1342 n.10 (N.D. Ala. 1994).

155 *See* the discussion in *Turner*, 114 S. Ct. at 2459. Sometimes a regulation that is facially "content-based" is regarded as content-neutral if the *motivation* for the regulation is unrelated to suppressing or encouraging particular types of content. *See* Renton v. Playtime Theaters, 475 U.S. 41 (1986).

156 *See* FCC v. League of Women Voters of Cal., 468 U.S. 364 (1984).

157 *See* United States v. O'Brien, 391 U.S. 367 (1968).

158 116 S. Ct. 2374.

courts should apply traditional formulations of the First Amendment doctrine in the field of telecommunications. Justice Breyer, writing for himself and three other justices, claimed not. The field of telecommunications is changing too rapidly, said Justice Breyer, to allow the Court to use one of the traditional verbal formulations for testing federal regulations under the First Amendment:

> [N]o definitive choice among competing analogies (broadcast, common carrier, bookstore) allows us to declare a rigid single standard, good for now and for all future media and purposes. That is not to say that we reject all the more specific formulations of the standard—they appropriately cover the vast majority of cases involving Government regulation of speech. Rather, aware as we are of the changes taking place in the law, the technology, and the industrial structure, related to telecommunications, we believe it unwise and unnecessary definitively to pick one analogy or one specific set of words now. . . .
>
> Rather than decide these issues, we can decide this case more narrowly, by closely scrutinizing [section] 10(a) to assure that it properly addresses an extremely important problem, without imposing, in light of the relevant interests, an unnecessarily great restriction on speech.[159]

Note that Justice Breyer appears to be substituting a new formulation—"properly address[ing] an extremely important problem, without imposing, in light of the relevant interests, an unnecessarily great restriction on speech"—for the old standards. However, because Justice Breyer took such pains to deny that he was picking a standard, I will assume that Justice Breyer's plurality opinion chose no doctrinal structure that can be applied directly to the next case.[160]

---

159 *Id.* at 2385. In his concurrence Justice Souter echoed Justice Breyer's sentiments about technological uncertainty counseling against picking a First Amendment doctrine for testing the regulations at issue:

> All of the relevant characteristics of cable are presently in a state of technological and regulatory flux. . . . As cable and telephone companies begin their competition for control over the single wire that will carry both their services, we can hardly settle rules for review of regulation on the assumption that cable will remain a separable and useful category of First Amendment scrutiny. And as broadcast, cable, and the cyber-technology of the Internet and the World Wide Web approach the day of using a common receiver, we can hardly assume that standards for judging the regulation of one of them will not have immense, but now unknown and unknowable, effects on the others.

Id. at 2402 (footnote omitted).

160 This aspect of Justice Breyer's opinion has received some harsh treatment. *See* Paul M. Barrett, *Cable Ruling May Portend Internet Curbs*, WALL ST. J., July 1, 1996, at B1 (quoting Laurence Tribe as saying Breyer's opinion is a "sugar-coated poison pill for the First Amendment"); James C. Goodale, *Caught in Breyer's Patch*, 216 N.Y.L.J. 1 (1996) (describing Breyer's opinion as "the nadir of the Court's First Amendment jurisprudence").

In contrast, Justice Kennedy, joined by Justice Ginsburg, applied traditional First Amendment doctrine. "When confronted with a threat to free speech in the context of an emerging technology, we ought to have the discipline to analyze the case by reference to existing elaborations of constant First Amendment principles."[161] Justice Kennedy rejected the plurality's reliance upon technological and economic change to delay developing standards. "The plurality seems distracted by the many changes in technology and competition in the cable industry. The laws challenged here, however, do not retool the structure of the cable industry . . . ."[162] Justice Kennedy applied strict scrutiny and found all aspects of the statute unconstitutional.

Justice Thomas, writing for the Chief Justice and Justice Scalia, also embraced traditional First Amendment standards and rejected the plurality's reliance upon technological and economic change to justify any other course of action.[163]

b. Finding a Good Reason

Regardless of whether the Court chooses one of the traditional standards, "strict" or "intermediate" scrutiny, or pursues Justice Breyer's formulation—looking for extremely important problems and regulations that do not unnecessarily restrict speech—the government will likely claim that the V-chip ratings system helps parents control children's diet of violent, sexually explicit, or profanity-laced programming. Will such a purpose—empowering parental control of children's television viewing—be regarded as *compelling*? If so, then the purpose will suffice for "strict" scrutiny and also for "intermediate" scrutiny and (probably) for Justice Breyer's "approach" as well.

I think that the recent trends in judicial reasoning on closely analogous subjects will push the Court to regard empowering parents as a compelling justification. The Court of Appeals for the Eighth Circuit held that protecting the "physical and psychological well-being of minors" from violence in video tapes represented a

---

161 *Denver Area Educ. Telecomms. Consortium*, 116 S. Ct. at 2404.

162 *Id.* at 2406.

163 Justice Thomas wrote:

> Curiously, the plurality relies on "changes taking place in the law, the technology, and the industrial structure, relating to telecommunications," to justify its avoidance of traditional First Amendment standards. If anything, as the plurality recognizes those recent developments . . . suggest that local cable operators have little or no monopoly power . . . thus effectively negating the primary justifications for treating cable operators differently from other First Amendment speakers.

Id. at 2422 n.3 (citations omitted).

compelling state interest.[164] And the Court of Appeals for the District of Columbia Circuit has already ruled that "helping parents supervise their children" is a compelling governmental interest.[165] In addition, the Supreme Court has in the past been solicitous of protecting children and empowering parents, at least in the somewhat analogous area of indecent telecommunications.[166] Justice Thomas recently characterized the law in the following language: "Our precedents establish that government may support parental authority to direct the moral upbringing of their children by imposing a blocking requirement as a default position."[167] The trend, in short, is for the Court to approve governmental allocation of control of offensive television programming to parents. Given the political tenor of our times, I would bet that the Supreme Court will continue down this line[168] and find that empowering parents to control children's viewing provides a compelling government interest. *A fortiori*, empowering parents would also be an important governmental interest, and therefore satisfy intermediate scrutiny.

c. Finding a Close Connection Between the V-Chip and Empowering Parents

Is the V-chip ratings system, approved in Stage One, sufficiently "narrowly tailored" to pass "strict" scrutiny? If so, then the

---

164 Video Software Dealers Assoc. v. Webster, 968 F.2d 684 (8th Cir. 1992). The Eighth Circuit struck down the Missouri law aimed at protecting children because the law was vague and not narrowly tailored. The purpose, however, was conceded to be compelling. *Accord* Davis-Kidd Booksellers, Inc. v. McWherter, 866 S.W.2d 520 (Tenn. 1993). For a list of the various interests the state has invoked to justify protecting children from broadcast indecency, see Edythe Wise, *A Historical Perspective on the Protection of Children From Broadcast Indecency*, 3 VILL. SPORTS & ENT. L.J. 15, 19 (1996).

165 Action for Children's Television v. FCC, 11 F.3d 170, 177 (D.C. Cir. 1993).

166 *See Sable Comms., Inc.*, 492 U.S. 115; *Pacifica Found.*, 438 U.S. 726. In addition, the Supreme Court seems to have coalesced around protecting children from "sexually explicit" material as a compelling state interest. *See Denver Area Educ. Telecomms. Consortium*, 116 S. Ct. at 2390 (Breyer, J.); *id.* at 2416 ("Congress does have . . . a compelling interest in protecting children from indecent speech.") (Kennedy, J.); *id.* at 2429 ("The parties agree that Congress has a 'compelling interest in protecting the physical and psychological well-being of minors' and that its interest 'extends to shielding minors from the influence of [indecent speech] that is not obscene by adult standards.'") (Thomas, J.). Note that this is only slightly different from empowering parents.

167 *Denver Area Educ. Telecomms. Consortium*, 116 S. Ct. at 2429 (while discussing indecency regulation). The Supreme Court also analogized cable to broadcast, finding that cable has a "uniquely pervasive presence" and that patently offensive material can "'confront the citizen' in the 'privacy of the home.'" *Id.* at 2386. Justice Breyer used this characterization to justify the constitutionality of extending indecency regulation to cable television.

168 *See* James A. Stimson et al., *Dynamic Representation*, 89 AM. POL. SCI. REV. 543 (1995); Charles H. Franklin & Liane C. Kosaki, *Republican Schoolmaster: The U.S. Supreme Court, Public Opinion, and Abortion*, 83 AM. POL. SCI. REV. 752 (1989).

V-chip ratings system will also pass the "directness" requirement of "intermediate" scrutiny.

The answer to the narrow tailoring inquiry will depend, in part, on the details of implementing the V-chip. The harder the V-chip is for adults to work, and the easier it is for children to circumvent, the less well-tailored is the ratings system. If we assume that the V-chip will be easy for adults and difficult for children, then the Court should regard the ratings system as narrowly tailored. The Court should find that the V-chip places little burden on adults' choice of shows, but effectively empowers parents.[169] Those adults without children in the house can just turn the V-chip off, thereby allowing the set to receive everything. Those adults with children in the house can set the V-chip to screen out the unwanted material for children.

Are there less intrusive alternatives to the V-chip that accomplish the same purpose? There are two obvious alternatives to the V-chip ratings system's approach. First, parents could closely monitor their children's viewing. This might require sitting and watching the shows, or at least frequently monitoring what is on the set. Second, the V-chip could allow only blocking by day, time, and channel, thereby forcing parents to make an independent judgment about the worth of individual shows.[170] The Court should find the two alternatives to the V-chip ratings system to be too costly and time-consuming for parents, or not sufficiently effective to invalidate the V-chip ratings system.

Requiring parents to closely monitor their children's viewing sounds ideal on the surface. However, many parents cannot afford to spend large amounts of time sitting with their children and monitoring what is on the set.[171] Even when the parent is home, he or she must often perform other tasks to keep the household

---

169 Note that when the purpose is to empower parents, the question of whether the criteria for age-rating the programming are appropriate becomes an inquiry into the types of programming that most parents would like to control.

170 Justice Breyer mentioned the "lockbox" as an example of a less intrusive alternative to segregating and blocking indecent material in *Denver Area Educ. Telecomms. Consortium*, 116 S. Ct. at 2393-94. As a result, the segregate and block requirement of section 10(b) is unconstitutional. The lockbox, however, would likely provide no reason for striking down the V-chip; the V-chip is *easier* to use than the lockbox, whereas the section 10(b) was harder for parents to use than the lockbox.

Justice Breyer mentioned the V-chip in favorable terms in the same case, *id.* at 2392, describing the V-chip as a reason to strike down the more intrusive alternative of requiring cable operators to segregate and block all indecent programming on access channels. Although, as Justice Breyer noted, the constitutionality of the V-chip was not at issue in *Denver Area*, his use of the V-chip indicates a favorable predisposition toward the new technology of program filtering.

171 In the lower income strata there is often no parent present to do the monitoring.

running. Once a child has learned to use the channel control, turning the set to a child-friendly show and leaving the room is quite risky. One leaves the child with *Sesame Street*, and may return to find the child watching MTV.

The second alternative, requiring the parent to program the set by date, time and channel, is likely to be ineffective. First, it would be quite costly. Any household that gets, for example, fifty channels of cable television, will have to monitor and decide about *(50)(24)=1200* hours of television *every day*. This is likely to be a time-consuming task, even with the repetition in show lineup on some channels. Further, the programming task may well be beyond the competence of many parents. As a consequence, few parents will actually do the programming. Together, these arguments suggest that the first two alternatives to the V-chip ratings system are much more costly and thus less likely to be effective. Hence, the government should not be required to use one of the first two alternatives.[172]

5. First Amendment Process and the V-Chip

If the Supreme Court finds the V-chip ratings system to be enough like film licensing to apply the precedents, it may well conclude that some form of First Amendment due process guarantees apply to the system.[173] The form that the guarantees take will depend on whether the Court follows the film licensing cases directly, or engages in a more free-form sort of balancing suggested by *Matthews v. Eldridge.*[174]

---

172 One caveat should be mentioned here. If, in operation, the V-chip effectively chases all violence, sex, and strong language off of the air, so that adults are reduced to watching only material that is "fit for children," then in operation the V-chip might well offend principles of First Amendment law found in *Butler v. Michigan*, 352 U.S. 380 (1957).

If the Court were to conceive of the purpose of the V-chip to be reducing the amount of sexual and violent material on the air, rather than helping parents to control their children's diet, and if reducing (but not eliminating) such material were held to be a valid purpose, then the economic analysis of the V-chip presented in notes 92-133 and accompanying text, *supra*, would bear directly on the question of narrow tailoring. In order for the V-chip to be lawful it would have to implement, to some degree, the purposes of the law. Depending on the placement and weight of the burden of proof to show narrow tailoring (or "directly implementing" under middle tier scrutiny), the indeterminacy of the analysis might help establish, or fail to rebut a presumption of, narrow tailoring.

I will not discuss in the text the possible justification of overriding parents' judgments about what material is appropriate for children, mainly because the V-chip rating system allows parents to let all material into the home if they wish. Hence, the V-chip rating system seems to be very poorly tailored toward the purpose of reversing paternal judgment.

173 Note that such a claim of process would likely be brought by a producer who is unhappy with the way in which his product was rated. As I noted below, such a claim would face severe problems with the state action requirement. *See supra* note 57 and accompanying text.

174 424 U.S. 319 (1976).

a. *Freedman v. Maryland*

The film precedents define the process rights of producers who are unhappy with the ratings of their motion pictures. Assume for the moment that the Court applies these precedents to the V-chip ratings system. Because the V-chip ratings system has a process for reversing producer ratings, perhaps where someone deems them to be "unreasonable," the appeals process issue may be central.[175]

In *Freedman v. Maryland*,[176] the Court considered the criminal conviction of a motion picture exhibitor who refused to submit his film to the Maryland State Board of Censors for prior approval. The Court first held that a state had the authority to require films to be submitted to a state review board. However, the Maryland statute violated the First Amendment because the procedures for reviewing an adverse censorial finding were too slow and costly to the film exhibitor. In particular, the *Freedman* Court ruled that (1) the film censor must bear the burden of proof; (2) any restraint on speech prior to a judicial determination must be limited to preserving the status quo and must be for as short a period of time as is possible for a reasonable judicial process; and (3) a final judicial determination on the censor's ruling *must* be guaranteed to issue promptly.[177] Failure to provide such procedural safeguards would amount to giving unlimited discretion to an administrative official to disallow speech—something that the Court has consistently ruled unconstitutional.[178] The Court was particularly sensitive to the economic needs of film distributors for quick procedures, so as not to interfere with their incentives to distribute the film.[179]

---

175 The industry's rating system includes a review board. "Valenti . . . disclosed that a 19-member board will be established to resolve disputes over the ratings. But the appeals board will consist entirely of people who work in television, rather than including any parents from the outside, as the MPAA uses with its movie ratings." Jane Hall, *TV Architect Vows to Fight Federal Intervention*, L.A. TIMES, Dec. 13, 1996, at D1.

It may be relatively easy to get one person to declare another's rating to be unreasonable. When a large sample of the public was asked to rate current television shows using the MPAA rating system (G, PG, PG-13, R, NC-17), the sample produced large differences of opinion as to how certain shows should be rated. *See* Michael Schneider, *How "Bad" Does the Public Think TV Is? Media Executives Have a Committee To Devise a Content Ratings System for Television*, ELECTRONIC MEDIA 3, July 29, 1996, *available in* 1996 WL 7535273.

176 380 U.S. 51 (1965).

177 *Id.* at 58-60; *see* United States v. One Carton Positive Motion Picture Film Entitled "491", 367 F.2d 889 (2d Cir. 1966) (applying *Freedman*). *See generally* Annotation: Constitutionality of Regulation of Obscene Motion Pictures—Federal Cases, 22 L. Ed. 2d 949 (1970).

178 *Freedman*, 380 U.S. at 56. For a more recent example of the general principle, see Freeman v. Burson, 504 U.S. 191 (1992).

179 Particularly in the case of motion pictures, it may take very little to deter exhibition in a given locality. The exhibitor's stake in any one picture may be insufficient to warrant a protracted and onerous course of litigation. The distributor,

As applied to any V-chip ratings system that contains a process for reversing an "unreasonable" initial rating that a program producer assigns to his or her own product, the *Freedman* procedural requirements might require a lot.[180] The rationale—that the economics of the medium will give the rater unfettered discretion unless review is very quick and inexpensive—would seem to apply directly. A program producer who is unhappy with an "adults only" type of V-chip rating, such as "TV-M," will need a quick and inexpensive process to help him position his product and make whatever changes, if any, are needed to attain the desired V-chip rating. As a consequence, I would expect the Court to hold that (1) the burden of proof must be on the V-chip rater who is reversing a program producer's rating of his own show; (2) prompt[181] judicial resolution of the ratings dispute be guaranteed; and (possibly) (3) the producer's own rating will apply until the process is

---

> on the other hand, may be equally unwilling to accept the burdens and delays of litigation in a particular area when, without such difficulties, he can freely exhibit his film in most of the rest of the country.

Freedman, 380 U.S. at 59.

The Court has, in general, followed the procedural requirements outlined in *Freedman*. *See* FW/PBS, Inc. v. City of Dallas, 493 U.S. 215, 226-230 (1990) (requiring a licensing scheme for sexually explicit businesses to act administratively and provide judicial review within a short period of time, but declining to put the burden of proof on city inspectors); Southeastern Promotions, Ltd. v. Conrad, 420 U.S. 546, 559-62 (1975) (striking down a city's refusal to allow the musical *Hair* to be staged in a municipal theater because the city's decision making failed to follow the *Freedman* procedures); *see also Riley*, 487 U.S. 781; Heller v. New York, 413 U.S. 483, 489-90 (1973) (approving, under *Freedman*, a judge's viewing of a film before issuing a warrant for seizure of the film under obscenity statutes); Paris Adult Theater I v. Slaton, 413 U.S. 49, 55 (1973) (commenting favorably upon civil injunction scheme for obscene materials). A recent film case, *Meese*, 481 U.S. 465, approved a U.S. government film labeling scheme, but did not address the issue of procedures. For an angry response to *Meese*, see Scott Lewis Landsbaum, Note, *How to Censor Films Without Really Trying: The Beirut Agreement and the Foreign Agents Registration Act*, 62 S. CAL. L. REV. 685 (1989).

180 One could argue that the *Freedman* procedural requirements should not apply to a V-chip ratings system. The *Freedman* requirements were designed for dealing with administrative suppression of a motion picture, at least as to people under 21. Because the administrative treatment of motion pictures was so harsh, the corresponding procedural protections needed to be great. In contrast, one might argue, a V-chip rating will not suppress a television program to the same degree that motion picture regulation suppressed movies, and the procedural protections can correspondingly be more lax. The rebuttal, I suppose, would focus on the *greater* speed with which most television product must be brought to market. Because television shows are often created in a very short period of time, and much closer to the time of airing than motion pictures, the need for speedy and effective review of ratings might be greater in television than in motion pictures. For the purposes of this article, I will assume that the rebuttal will carry the day and that the *Freedman* procedural requirements will apply.

181 Prompt means less than eight weeks of administrative process for movies. *See* Teitel Film Corp. v. Cusack, 390 U.S. 139 (1968). Because the lead time for television episodes is much less than for movies, I would expect that the process would have to be faster for V-chip determinations.

complete.[182] Of course, it might be difficult for the "voluntary" system to guarantee speedy judicial review without some further legislative action by Congress. The Telecommunications Act of 1996 gave disappointed producers no right to jump to the front of the line in court. Perhaps applying for temporary restraining orders and preliminary injunctions would suffice, but I doubt it. The substantive requirements for these procedures includes demonstrating likelihood of success on the merits. This may represent too much of a burden. If so, then processes currently available to disappointed producers would fail the *Freedman* requirements. In the absence of further congressional action that improves review procedures in court, the Stage One system might be put to a stark choice: either allow "unreasonable" ratings by program producers to stand unchallenged, or else risk the entire ratings systems foundering on *Freedman*'s requirement of a speedy process.

Any Stage One V-chip system that satisfies the *Freedman* requirements is likely to be quite expensive. The V-chip system will have to rate huge numbers of hours of programs. Consider the following quote by Jack Valenti.

> Let me put it to you in stark terms. A single cable system today, with 70 channels on the average, operating 24 hours a day, will produce 611,520 hours of programing a year. That amounts to 2,000 hours a day. Now, if you cut that in half and say half of it is going to be non-rateable—news, sports—you get down to a thousand hours a day. That's the equivalent of rating 500 motion pictures a day. The movie ratings system rates two movies a day, sometimes three. So you have three movies a day versus 500.[183]

If there are disputes regarding only three percent of the episodes rated, that will amount to fifteen movies' worth of time per day that must be rerated by some administrative process and then put onto a fast judicial track. What is more, these fifteen movies of time per day might well turn into twenty or twenty-five separate cases, because many television programs are only thirty minutes long. Further, the V-chip rating system must be prepared to deal with peak load problems; some weeks will have thirty movies' worth of time per day that must be re-rated, while other weeks will have none. The system must be able to deal with the periods of peak demand for re-rating without slowing up. This means that the sys-

182 This might represent preserving the status quo and would certainly give the V-chip ratings system incentives for speedy process.

183 West & Stern, *supra* note 28, at 26 (comments of Jack Valenti).

tem will have to maintain excess capacity most of the time, and along with it a substantial expense. In practical terms it means that the V-chip ratings system will have to hire many re-raters and lawyers (for the subsequent judicial process).

There may be some ways of reducing these costs. First, once a show has been rated for exhibition in one market, that rating could be used for exhibiting the same show in other markets. An old episode of *The Mary Tyler Moore* show that is rated as "appropriate for children" over a cable system in Charleston, SC, should also be rated "appropriate for children" over a local broadcast in Ithaca, NY. Second, one could try rating series programming by sampling several episodes of the series and then presumptively using the rating derived from the sample for the entire series.[184] Producers would be responsible for notifying the raters of any surprises in particular episodes. Third, distribution contracts could specify arbitration of any disputes. Such clauses might raise antitrust or First Amendment process concerns, but if such concerns were overcome, the monetary savings could be substantial.

b. *Mathews v. Eldridge*

Is there any possible response on the part of the government to the process requirements outlined above? Yes. The government might be able to persuade the Court to apply the modern balancing approach to procedural due process, rather than the "First Amendment" process approach from film cases, to the V-chip ratings system. In *Mathews v. Eldridge*,[185] the Court defined a balancing test for deciding which procedures are required under the Fourteenth Amendment.

> First, the private interest that will be affected by the official action, second, the risk of an erroneous deprivation of such interest through the procedures used, and the probable value, if any, of additional or substitute procedural safeguards; and finally, the Government's interest, including the function involved and the fiscal and administrative burdens that the additional or substitute procedural requirement would entail.[186]

In the 1980s and 1990s, the Court has been somewhat deferential

---

184 "A panel of network and studio representatives led by Motion Picture Association of America President Jack Valenti has been meeting since March to hammer out [V-chip] standards. . . . Shows probably will be rated on a seasonal basis unless there are indications of significant variance by episode." Topenkin, *supra* note 92, at 28.

185 424 U.S. 319 (1976).

186 *Id.* at 335.

to the government's choice of procedures under this test.[187] As applied to the V-chip ratings system there would seem to be significant interests on both sides of the balance. The producer's First Amendment rights are at stake, and the economics of the business makes a speedy determination of the proper rating very valuable to the producer. However, the great expense involved will count as a reason to reduce the procedural protections under *Mathews v. Eldridge*. I have no idea how the Court would or should do the balancing. But I am certain that this approach will give the government a better chance of victory than will the film licensing cases.

6. Summary of Stage One and the First Amendment

In Stage One, the Court should probably find the V-chip ratings system to be constitutional. The Court should regard empowering parents to control their children's television viewing as a compelling state interest, and then find the V-chip narrowly tailored to that purpose. Hence, a First Amendment claim based on the type of V-chip ratings system should fail. Further, the Court may require the V-chip ratings system to satisfy the procedural requirements of *Freedman v. Maryland*, and doing so may require further congressional action.

B. *Substantive First Amendment Analysis in Stage Three*

I will have very little to say in this section, mainly because I think the substantive First Amendment analysis is quite similar to that described above. One point needs elaboration, however. Recall that in Stage Three we established state action, in part, by the requirement that if a show is rated then the broadcasters *must* transmit the rating. Hence, as to the transmission, there is clear state compulsion.

To evaluate the constitutionality of compelling transmission, one must evaluate the ratings system. To see this, ask what the state interest in compelling transmission might be. As I point out above,[188] the government will have to show that parents will want to use the ratings to control their children's viewing to justify forcing broadcasters and cable systems to transmit the ratings. This leads us directly back into the analysis of justifications from Stage One of the V-chip ratings system.

---

187 *See* CHEMERINSKY, *supra* note 29, § 7.4.3.

188 *See supra* notes 92-133 and accompanying text.

Conclusion

In Stage One, the industry's decision to adopt a ratings system likely should be regarded as state action. In addition, the Court should also view the particular age-based mixed with content-based system that the industry was pressured to adopt as state action. In contrast, the rating assigned to any particular show should be regarded as private action. In Stage Three the state action calculus may change. The Act's requirement that ratings be transmitted probably establishes state action across the board.

The V-chip ratings system may well be constitutional under the First Amendment. The litigant bearing the burden of proof of showing or negating a chill from the ratings system should probably lose at this point. Also, the government may be able to justify the V-chip ratings system, even under strict scrutiny, as supporting parental authority to control their children's diet of television. All of these conclusions are tentative. Further government actions and industry reactions could change any of the conclusions.

APPENDIX 1

In this appendix we will derive the results for two broadcasters competing with a rectangular viewer distribution and assumption A1 regarding V-chip use.

> *case i:* $2(1-p)v < 1$. In this case both broadcasters locate at v and earn $1/2$ of the available viewers. *Discussion:* Will either broadcaster move from v? Consider an extremely small move to the left of v. If B_1 were to do that, B_1 would earn all of the viewers between v and 1 who did *not* use the V-chip, which is $(1-p)v$, and B_2 would get the rest, $(1-v)$. Because $(1-p)v < 1/2$, it would not pay B_1 to make such a move. Any other move would garner B_1 even fewer viewers, so we know that B_1 will choose to remain at v, paired with B_2.
>
> *case ii:* $2(1-p)v > 1$. There are two subcases. If $v < p+0.5$ then there is no equilibrium. If $v > p+0.5$, then there is an equilibrium with both broadcasters locating at 0.5.

Discussion: If $2(1-p)v > 1$, then there can be no equilibrium with both broadcasters at v. If they were both located there, each would get fifty percent of the available viewers. Then one, say B_1, would move slightly to the left, and garner $(1-p)v$, which by assumption is greater than $1/2$. B_2 will then get $(1-v)$, which is less than $1/2$. Then B_2 will move to either pair with B_1 and earn $(1-p)/2$, or leapfrog B_1 and earn slightly less than $(1-p)v$. Because $v > 0.5$, it clearly pays to leapfrog. But then the same will be true of B_1 when deciding whether or not to leapfrog B_2. This leapfrogging will continue all the way to 0.5, where it will stop, and 0.5 will be paired at local equilibrium. This means that neither will have any incentive to move a small distance away from 0.5 as long as it thinks the other broadcaster will remain at 0.5. At this point, will either broadcaster have an incentive to "jump" over to v? By doing so, B_1 (or B_2) could garner $1-(0.5+v)/2$, while B_2 would get $(1-p)(0.5+v)/2$. B_1 will make this jump if and only if $1-(0.5+v)/2 > (1-p)(0.5+v)/2$. This reduces to $v < p+0.5$. However, if $v < p+0.5$ and B_1 jumps to v, then B_2 will slide over and crowd B_1. Leapfrogging will ensue, and no equilibrium can exist.

APPENDIX 2

This appendix contains a demonstration of the results in the case with two broadcasters, rectangular distribution, and assumption A2 regarding V-chip use.

If v is to the left of 0.5, then the equilibrium exists and is identical to the case without the V-chip. Both broadcasters locate at 0.5.

FIGURE 11

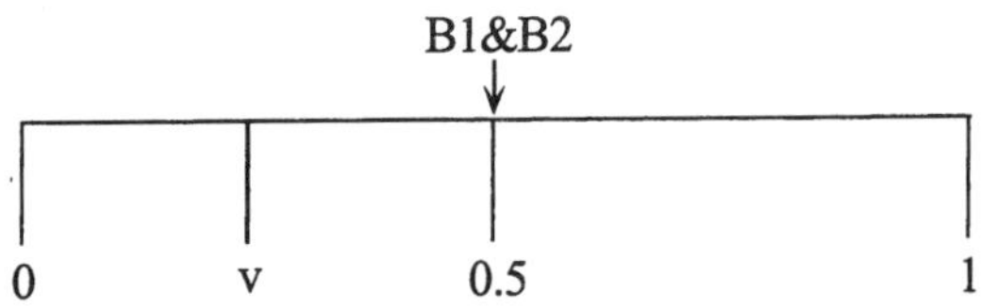

If v is to the right of 0.5, then we cannot get an equilibrium pair at v. We can get an equilibrium at $e = (1/2)[v+(1-p)(1-v)]$ if $e > (1-p)(1-v)$. *Discussion:* Assume that we start with a pair of broadcasters at v. Both broadcasters will be getting fifty percent of the available viewers. If B_1 moves slightly to the left, he gets (almost) v viewers. (Remember that those viewers whose ideal points are to the left of v do not use the V-chip with assumption A2.) This is better for B_1, as $v > 1/2$. Now, B_2 will leapfrog over B_1 and this will continue until they reach $e = (v-e)+(1-p)(1-v)$, which is where the right hand payoff just equals the left hand payoff. This simplifies to $e = (1/2)[v+(1-p)(1-v)]$. Will either broadcaster have the incentive to jump to v? If B_1 were to do so, it would garner $(v-(e-v)/2)+(1-v)$ viewers. For a jump to be appealing to B_1, that quantity must be greater than $(1/2)(v+(1-p)(1-v))$. This simplifies to $e < (1-p)(1-v)$. Under these circumstances, B_1 will jump to v, and then B_2 will slide over and crowd B_1, and leapfrogging will ensue. Under A2, the percentage of viewers who use the V-chip is not a function of v. Hence, the government can ensure that an equilibrium will exist by making v large enough. This entails rating more programs violent.

Now, we can deduce that e is less than $1/2$. To see this, note that e is exactly equal to $1/2$ when $p = 0$. When p is greater than zero, $(1-p)$ is less than one, so the expression in the brackets falls to less than one. One half times something less than one (but greater than zero) is less than $1/2$. Hence, $e < 1/2$. This means that the equilibrium, where it exists, will be *more* violent than the equilibrium without the V-chip. This slightly counterintuitive result makes sense only because of the behavior of viewers. Because the viewers on the right end of the violence spectrum are the only ones to use the V-chip, the broadcasters care less about the preferences of those who like non-violent programs.

Appendix 3

This appendix contains a demonstration that given three broadcasters, rectangular viewer distribution, and assumption A1 on V-chip use, there is no equilibrium in the configuration represented by Figure 101. In Figure 101, B_2 and B_3 each get $(1/2)((1-p)(v+x)/2$, and B_1 gets $1-(v+x)/2$. In order for Figure 101 to be an equilibrium, six conditions would need to be satisfied:

1. $(1-p)/3 < 1-(v+x)/2$. This condition prevents B_1 from moving left and duplicating x, the position of B_2 and B_3.

2R. $(1-p)(1-x) < 1-(v+x)/2$. This condition prevents B_1 from moving left and crowding B_2 and B_3 on the right hand side.

2L. $(1-p)x < 1-(v+x)/2$. This condition prevents B_1 from moving right and crowding B_2 and B_3 on the left hand side.

3L. $(1-p)(1-(v+x)/2) < (1-p)(v+x)/4$. This condition prevents B_2 (or B_3) from sliding over and crowding B_1 on the left hand side.

3R. $(1-v) < (1-p)(v+x)/4$. This condition prevents B_2 (or B_3) from sliding over and crowding B_1 on the right hand side.

4. $(1/2)(1-(v+x)/2) < (1-p)(v+x)/4$. This condition prevents B_2 (or B_3) from moving over and duplicating B_1.

These conditions are mutually inconsistent. First, subtract equation 2L from 2R to obtain

$$(1-p)(1-x)-(1-p)x < 0.$$

This simplifies to: $x > 1/2$.

Now, subtract equation 1 from equation 2R and obtain:

$$(1-p)/3-(1-p)(1-x) < 0.$$

This simplifies to: $x < 2/3$.

Now, subtract equation 4 from equation 3L and obtain:

$$(1/2-p)(1-(v+x)/2) < 0.$$

Because $v+x < 2$, we know $(1-(v+x)/2) > 0$, which means $(1/2-p) < 0$, or

$$p > 1/2.$$

Now, subtract equation 3R from equation 4 and obtain:

$$(1/2)(1-(v+x)/2)-(1-v) < 0.$$

This simplifies to $v > (2+x)/3$. Since $x > 1/2$ (our first result, above), we know

$$v > 5/6.$$

But now equation 2R is impossible.

APPENDIX 4

Three broadcasters, rectangular viewer distribution, assumption (A2) on V-Chip use: To see that there are no equilibria, first consider whether the three broadcasters can cluster on v, much as in Figure 103. Under this circumstance, each broadcaster has an incentive to move to the "long" side (the left) and crowd the other two. Leap-frogging ensues.

Can there be an equilibrium at $e \neq v$, similar to the case with two broadcasters? No. To see this, realize that when all three broadcasters are clustered at e, where $v > 0.5$ and $e < v$, each broadcaster earns $1/3[(1-p)(1-v)+v]$. For e to be an equilibrium, two conditions must be satisfied:

> (i) $e < 1/3[(1-p)(1-v)+v]$. This condition removes the incentive for the broadcasters to move left slightly and crowd the other two.
>
> (ii) $(v-e)+(1-p)(1-v) < 1/3[(1-p)(1-v)+v]$. This condition removes the incentive for the broadcasters to move right slightly and crowd the other two.

Now, add (I) and (ii) together to obtain:

$$v+(1-p)(1-v) < 2/3[(1-p)(1-v)+v].$$

This reduces to $v+(1-p)(1-v) < 0$. Since $v > 0$ and $p > 0$, this is impossible. Hence, there is no clustered equilibrium.

There also cannot be any equilibrium in the configuration in Figure 101. For that to be an equilibrium, at least the following two conditions must be satisfied:

> (i) $x < (1/2)(v+x)/2$. This condition removes the incentive for B_2 or B_3 to move to the left slightly and crowd the other.
>
> (ii) $x < 1-(v+x)/2$. This condition removes the incentive for B_1 to slide over and crowd B_2 and B_3 on the left.

The only way for these two conditions to hold simultaneously is for $x < 0$, which is impossible. Hence, there is no equilibrium.

APPENDIX 5

What if $0.25 < v < 0.75$? Then the situation looks as it does in Figure 14.

FIGURE 14

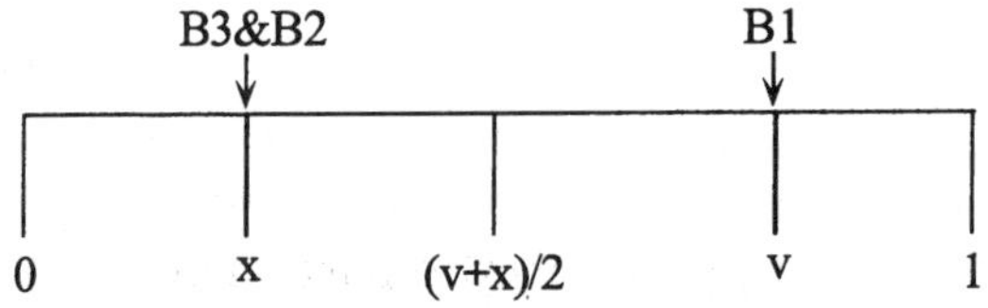

I have divided the range into four parts, d_1, d_2, d_3 and d_4. The only possible equilibria would have two broadcasters paired on either end, and we have labeled the two positions e_1 and e_2. Now, the number of viewers garnered by B_1 and B_2 in the first two ranges (and split equally between them) are:

d_1: e_1

d_2: $(v-e_1)+(1-p)((e_1+e_2)/2-v)$.

The number of viewers garnered by B_3 and B_4 (and split equally between them) in the final two zones are:

d_3: $(e_2-1/2(e_1+e_2))+p(^1/_2(e_1+e_2)$[189]

d_4: $1-e_2$.

In order for this to be an equilibrium, three conditions must be satisfied.

(1) $e_1 = (1-p)[^1/_2(e_1+e_2)-v]$. This removes the incentive for either B_1 or B_2 to move slightly to the right or left and crowd the other one.

(2) $e_2-1/2(e_1+e_2)+p(^1/_2(e_1+e_2)-v) = 1-e_2$. This removes the incentive for either B_3 or B_4 to move slightly to the left or right and crowd the other.

(3) $v-e_1+(1-p)[^1/_2(e_1+e_2)-v]=e_2-1/2(e_1+e_2)+p(^1/_2(e_1+e_2)-v)$. This removes the incentive for either B_1 or B_2 to move to the right and crowd B_3 and B_3 on the left hand side.

But (3) is true $\Leftrightarrow$ either $p=0$ or $^1/_2(e_1+e_2) = v$. Assume that $p > 0$. Then from conditions (1) and (2) we have $^1/_2(e_1+e_2) = v = 0.5$. This, in turn, implies $e_1 = 0.25$, and $e_2 = 0.75$.

---

189 The second term in this expression represents all those viewers between v and $^1/_2(e_1+_2)$ who used the V-chip and turned to the offering at e_2, the only available viewing for them.

Appendix 6

What happens if we greatly increase the number of settings of *v*? The answer to this question, just as the answer to the question about what happens with only one setting of *v*, is "it depends." To get a feeling for a possible change, this appendix sets forth a framework of analysis of what may happen if the *v* rating is continuous over the range [0,1]. In other words, if a show could be rated at any point on this range, and a consumer could set *v* at any point, how would the system work? For example, a show might be rated 0.361, and a consumer might set *v* at 0.45. In this case, the V-chip would filter out the show. Or, a show might be rated 0.572, and then pass through the V-chip set at 0.45.

How would the market be affected by such a system? Let us assume, again, that viewer ideal points are uniformly distributed on [0,1], that viewers watch the closest program available, that broadcasters are profit maximizers, etc. We must still make some assumption about how viewers will choose to set *v*. Let us make a particularly simple assumption that makes the analysis tractable. Viewers choose *v* at slightly less than their ideal points. This says, in essence, that the parents are willing to let their kids watch anything, as long as it is not more violent than the kids' ideal type of programming. Alternatively, if kids and parents ideal points are identical, then the parents are willing to let the kids watch anything as long as it is not more violent than the parents' ideal type of programming.

If there are two broadcasters, there is no equilibrium. To see this, first note that there can be no equilibrium where the two broadcasters are paired. Assume that B_1 and B_2 are located at the same point, sharing equally in the available viewers. Then each of the broadcasters has an incentive to move slightly to the left and garner almost all of the viewers that the two broadcasters were sharing. (Note that moving right slightly would be counterproductive, for no one to the right of a broadcaster can get the signal.) If B_1 were to do so, then B_2 would have an incentive to leapfrog over B_1. Leapfrogging would ensue until one broadcaster would return to 1. At that point the other would slide over to slightly less than 1 and garner almost all of the viewers. Leapfrogging ensues.

Similarly, no arrangement where the two broadcasters are any significant space apart can be an equilibrium. The broadcaster on the left would slide over and crowd the broadcaster that was further to the right, and garner almost all of the viewers. Leapfrogging ensues.

If there are more than two broadcasters, there is no equilibrium. To see this, consider any market with *n* broadcasters that is claimed to be in equilibrium. Consider the two broadcasters who are located closest to 1. They cannot be located at the same point, for one would move slightly to the left. Leapfrogging would ensue. They cannot be located any appreciable distance apart, for then the broadcaster closest to 1 would be vulnerable to crowding (on the left) by the broadcaster that is the next closest to 1. Leapfrogging ensues.

Appendix 7

An alternative model of regulation might posit that under the pre-V-chip regulatory regime there was, in essence, a constraint against showing really violent matter on *broadcast* television. This could be modeled as a barrier, say at 0.6, preventing any programming between 0 and 0.5. Then the broadcasters, restricted to [.6,1], would regard demand as a mass point at 0.5, equal in magnitude to all of the viewers located (uniformly) on [.6,1]. Under these circumstances, what would an equilibrium look like without a V-chip? With two broadcasters, both locate at 0.6. With four broadcasters, there is no equilibrium.

Appendix 8

There are only two genuine possible equilibria when $v > 0.75$, and both fail. First, we could have the same arrangement—two broadcasters at 0.25 and two at 0.75—as we had when $v < 0.75$. The difficulty is that the two broadcasters at 0.75 would each garner less than twenty-five percent of the available viewers, while the broadcasters at 0.25 would each get twenty-five percent of the viewers. The reason for this is that the two broadcasters will be broadcasting "violent" programming, and the viewers to the right of v who have activated the V-chip will not get the broadcasters' programs. In contrast, the broadcasters at 0.25 will be dealing with a universe of viewers (those in [0, 0.5]) who have *not* activated the V-chip. As a consequence, each of the broadcasters at 0.75 will have an incentive to slide over and crowd the two broadcasters at 0.25, taking twenty-five percent of the audience either on the right or left of 0.25.

The other possible equilibrium is that depicted in Figure 13. In order for this to be an equilibrium, each of the four broadcasters must earn twenty-five percent of the audience. Now B_1 and B_2 each get $\frac{1}{2}((e+v)/2)$, while B_2 and B_4 each get $\frac{1}{2}(1-(e+v)/2)$. Equating these two, we derive $e+v = 1$. Since $v > 0.75$ we know $e < 0.25$. But this cannot be an equilibrium, for $v-e > \frac{1}{2}$. If , say, B_3 were to slide over and crowd B_1 and B_2 on the interior, B_3 would get $\frac{1}{2}(v-e)$, which we know is greater than 1/4. Hence, B_3 will not remain at v.

APPENDIX 9

In such an equilibrium three conditions must be satisfied:

1. $(^1/_2)(v+(1-p)(1-v)) \geq e$. This prevents either broadcaster from having an incentive to move ε to the left.

2. $(^1/_2)(v+(1-p)(1-v)) \geq (v-e)+(1-p)(1-v)$. This prevents either broadcaster from having an incentive to move ε to the right.

3. $(^1/_2)(v+(1-p)(1-v)) \geq (1-v)+(^1/_2)(v-e)$. This prevents either broadcaster from having an incentive to move to v.

By rearranging (2) we can get $(-v/2)+e \geq (^1/_2)(1-p)(1-v)$, or $e \geq (^1/_2)(v+(1-p)(1-v))$. Putting this together with (1), we have $(^1/_2)(v+(1-p)(1-v)) = e$.

Next, rearrange (3) to get $e > (1-v)(1-p)$.

THE PERSONALITY INTEREST OF ARTISTS AND INVENTORS IN INTELLECTUAL PROPERTY*

JUSTIN HUGHES**

I. INTRODUCTION

Like all social institutions, property rights are justified by the benefits they bring to individuals in society. The dominant understanding of this justification for all types of property has been an economic formula: property rights are the most efficient means to produce social wealth. Judges and commentators considering intellectual property have historically remained true to this formula; copyrights and patents are viewed as an *ex ante* incentive structure to produce the most social wealth at the least cost.

The same general justification—benefits brought to individuals in society—has given rise to discussions of the non-economic benefits of intellectual property. Property rights, it was observed, are a means to protect the personality interest or "personhood" of individuals; this seemed especially true with intellectual property rights that are draped over creations of the human mind. Along these lines, personhood proponents could understandably be found in the vanguard of "moral rights" for authors, "reverse shop rights" for inventors, and "rights of publicity" for everyone.

While personhood theory challenged economics' prior monopoly on explanations of property, the "pro-property" personhood theory was itself met with a deconstructionist reply specific to intellectual property: that creators' rights to control intellectual property should be limited to permit non-owners to manipulate the communicative messages, shape their own messages, and, thereby, increase the personhood benefits that intellectual creations bring to those non-owners. This argument is akin to the consumer benefit side of economic analysis. It repeats the established formula with only slightly different formulation: the creator's personality interest in her work must be balanced against the

* In addition to those mentioned in footnote 12, this article has benefitted from the helpful comments of George Fisher, Owen Jones, Lance Liebman and George Shepherd. The author is counsel in the International and Legislative Office of the U.S. Patent and Trademark Office ("PTO"), Department of Commerce. This article was written substantially prior to the author joining the Department of Commerce; the views expressed are neither those of the Department nor the PTO.

** B.A., Oberlin, 1982; J.D., Harvard, 1986; Henry Luce Scholar, 1988; Mellon Fellow in the Humanities, 1989.

personality interest of consumers—who will be further creators—using her work in their own acts of creation/expression. Along these lines it is argued that authors need greater liberty to quote existing texts, minority groups need greater liberty to manipulate existing cultural symbols (like celebrity images), and performing artists need more liberty to interpret theatrical works.

The interesting arguments in this area have obscured a deeper problem: we do not have a good grip on what constitutes the "personality" or "personhood" interests that may be present in a particular piece of intellectual property. We know that we can think about the "personhood interest" being held by one person, a few people (as in joint works), or, in the deconstructionist critique, in the multitude who are users, consumers, or the audience. We know that the personality interest may lead us into a highly subjective world, in which some proclaimed personality interests may strike us as illegitimate or unhealthy.[1]

Beyond this, there has not been much mapping of the possible constitutive elements of the "personhood" interest in intellectual property. This article explores some of the interests which might live under the personhood tent. Drawing on a variety of problems, this article describes three identifiably separate personhood interests in an intellectual property *res*:[2] (1) creativity; (2) intentionality; and (3) identification as the source of the *res*. Without claiming that these three strands of personhood are exhaustive, I will explore areas of the law where these interests seem to influence and other areas where they do not, but perhaps should, hold weight.

Part I describes the background for the search for "personhood" interests in property and then explores how much "creativity"—a fundamental notion in our copyright law—is a core personhood interest, that blurs the notions of originality and personal expression. But this does not mean that creativity occupies the same conceptual space as the idea of the *individual* "author"—an apparent assumption of some recent commentators. In fact, the notion of creativity comfortably co-exists with the idea of collaborative or co-created works. This article's discussion of creativity concludes by suggesting that the linkage of creativity to personal

---

1 Margaret J. Radin, *Property and Personhood*, 34 Stan. L. Rev. 957, 968-70 (1982); Justin Hughes, *The Philosophy of Intellectual Property*, 77 Geo. L.J. 287, 335 (1988).

2 Res is everything that may form an object of rights and includes an object, subject-matter, or status. Black's Law Dictionary 1304 (6th ed. 1990) (quoting *In re* Riggles Will, 205 N.Y.S.2d 19, 21, 22 (N.Y. App. Div. 1960).

expression creates a generally unrecognized dilemma—one the legal system might solve by what I will call a "moral shop right."

At the same time, one of the basic propositions of this article is that the notion of creativity, despite this complexity, does not explain all the personhood interests in an intellectual property *res* that may be worthy of protection. Indeed, too much attention on "creativity" has pushed other personhood interests into the background. The result is *ad hoc* reasoning by courts, catch-all phrases in statutes,[3] or efforts to shoehorn or redefine those interests into paradigms called, sometimes derisively, the "Romantic genius" and the "inventor-hero."[4] A personhood theory of intellectual property needs to provide for the inventor-hero's creativity. However, it can also provide for the inventor who identifies with his improved widget only in the same way that his neighbor takes pride in a recently purchased sports car. This article proposes that we might improve on such phrases with two additional concepts for personhood interests: "intentionality" and "sourcehood." Part II discusses "intentionality," a significant personality interest, and arguably more important than creativity. Part II's discussion shows how the concept of intentionality can help us understand copyright's "made-for-hire" doctrine as well as the personhood interest of inventors, photo-journalists, and "inadvertent" creators—problems that have always seemed ill at ease with a creativity-based property justification.

Finally, Part III considers whether merely being the source of a *res* creates legitimate personhood interests that justify protection of some sort. For example, I propose that personhood interests can arise from simply being the human source of an intellectual property *res*. Examples might be true "eureka" discoveries or profoundly accidental intellectual products. That personhood interests may arise in such settings is not surprising, particularly to the extent that we believe, as David Gauthier suggests, that "each person identifies with those capacities, physical and mental, to which he had direct access, and we see that this identification affords each person a normative sense of self . . . ."[5] An individual's per-

[3] For example, one country's law grants copyrights to anthologies only if "they are distinguishable by their originality, or their coordination *or by any other personal effort justifying protection.*" Egyptian Copyright Law, Part I, Article 4(3), Law No. 354, June 24, 1954, as amended by Law No. 34, 6/17/75, art. 4 (emphasis added).

[4] For descriptions of the inventor-hero and use of this phrase, *see* ANNE L. MACDONALD, FEMININE INGENUITY: WOMEN AND INVENTION IN AMERICA (1994); Steven Cherensky, *A Penny for Their Thoughts: Employee-Inventors, Preinvention, Assignment Agreements, Property, and Personhood,* 81 CAL. L. REV. 595 (1993).

[5] DAVID GAUTHIER, MORALS BY AGREEMENT 210 (1986).

sonal identification with all of her physical and mental capacities could give rise to personal identification with the intellectual products of those capacities—without any reference to what we would call "creativity."[6] If an individual has a "sense of self" from her capacities, we should explore if and when the use of those capacities for intellectual production should lead to protectable personhood interests.[7] This "sourcehood" helps explain the personhood interests of inventors and suggests that in 1990 plaintiff Moore may have had a better case for rights over cells generated from his spleen than the California Supreme Court was willing to recognize in *Moore v. University of California*.[8]

This discussion of creativity, intentionality, and sourcehood is a descriptive framework for better understanding the sentiments of creators and the educated classes from which they largely come and for whom they (partially) create. The question remains whether we *should* protect such interests. It may be wrong for people to (1) identify with their capacities; and then, (2) identify with the intellectual products of those capacities. Taking a cue from Rawls, we might believe that an individual does not have any particular entitlement to her talents,[9] jeopardizing any justification based on personality interests. Or we may question whether (2) is a legitimate move. To transpose Robert Nozick's classic query, why should we think putting our personality out into the world gives us rights to the things we create? Why should we not assume that

---

6 Actually, we should imagine an intermediary step. If a person identifies with his or her own mental capacities, this may cause that person to identify, first, with the *process* of using those capacities and, second, with the *products* of those processes. It is conceivable that someone would identify with the *process* without identifying (as strongly) with the *product*.

7 Are personhood justifications compatible with the Copyright and Patent Clauses of the Constitution? The wording of Article I, Section 8, Clause 8 ("to promote the progress of science and the useful arts") expresses an instrumental view of intellectual property law, a goal of "stimulat[ing] original investigation whether in literature, science, or art, for the betterment of the people that they might be instructed and improved with respect to those subjects." Ansehl v. Puritan Pharm. Co., 61 F.2d 131, 133-34 (8th Cir. 1932). But this incentive structure may just as easily encompass, for example, moral rights as economic rights. Acknowledgment as an author or an inventor may be a critical incentive for lots of people.

8 793 P.2d 479 (Cal. 1990).

9 Assume that individuals identify with (1) their capacities; and, thereby (2) the processes of using those capacities; and, thereby, (3) the intellectual products of these processes. We might conclude, as John Rawls suggests, that step (1) is wrong, that the individual does not have any particular entitlement to identify with the talents with which she is endowed. Professor Rawls considers even the ability to expend effort to be determined by factors outside a person's control and hence a morally impermissible criterion for distribution. *See* JOHN RAWLS, A THEORY OF JUSTICE 104 (1971) ("The assertion that a man deserves the superior character that enables him to make the effort to cultivate his abilities is equally problematic; for his character depends in large part upon fortunate family and social circumstances for which he can claim no credit."); *id.* at 312.

when we mix our personality with the world, we lose part of our personality instead of gaining part of the world?[10] At another level, the discussion that follows is a mix of both descriptive and normative accounts of our legal system. For example, the proposal that intentionality helps explain the work-for-hire doctrine is: (1) a proposal that (descriptively) the concept is already at work in the thinking of courts and parties; and (2) a proposal that (normatively) we should bring the concept into the light of day to help make our conscious framework better fit our case law. This transiting between experience and logic, "being and meaning," is a regular process of legal thinking.[11] Perhaps the transiting is so regular that we too often forget when we are trying to describe how the world is and when we are prescribing how the world should be.

Throughout this article, the discussion has benefited from the thoughts and impressions of a variety of creators. While not at all the kind of empirical work that is needed in legal scholarship on property,[12] the ideas of these people have helped shape the expressions in this article.[13]

II. Personhood Interests from Creativity, Originality, and Personal Expression

In her classic analysis of "personhood" in property, Margaret Jane Radin drew upon familiar material objects—a wedding ring, a portrait, a family home. When Radin describes how these objects become "bound up with personhood,"[14] we intuitively understand

10 Robert Nozick, Anarchy, State and Utopia 174-75 (1974) (questioning why Locke thought "mixing" one's labor with the world gave that person property rights, instead of causing the person to lose the value of their labor).

11 As Professor Leff wrote, the law's life is "an attempt to create and maintain a coherent species of 'logic' that would not too ridiculously fail to reflect, or even refract, experience. It has been, in short, an attempt to construct a legal system that accommodates the equally exigent demands of being and meaning, and to do so in a universe in which what a thing does is only one of the things that it means, everything that it means is something else that it does." Arthur Allen Leff, *Law and*, 87 Yale L.J. 989 (1978).

12 George Priest's observation about patent scholarship is generally true of all intellectual property scholarship, *i.e.*, that "the ratio of empirical demonstration to assumption in this literature must be very close to zero." George Priest, *What Economists can Tell Lawyers about Intellectual Property*, 8 Res. L. & Econ. 19 (1986). Priest concludes that there is, at present, an "inability of economists to resolve the question of whether activity stimulated by the patent system or other forms of protection of intellectual property enhances or diminishes social welfare . . ." *id.* at 21, and that without empirical research "economic analysis" in this area is akin to "applied moral philosophy." *Id.* at 22.

13 I am grateful for discussions with a variety of creators, ranging from a four-time Emmy-winning screenwriter to the "first scientists in the world to express a human protein in bacteria" ((Stephen Hall, *Invisible Frontiers*): actors Shelley Hack, William Sadler; visual artist Brigitte Palmerl; inventors Arthur Riggs, Keiichi Itakura; writers Mark Saltzman, April Smith; cinematographer Arnold Glassman; and researcher Rob Lempert).

14 Radin, *supra* note 1, at 959.

what she means. The individual probably had no role in the material object's design or creation; most of us neither designed nor constructed the houses, furniture, and clothes we live with. Nonetheless, we come to identify with these objects and they come to be imbued with our "personhood."

With a wedding ring, an individual's personality seems to *move into* an existing object. Years ago, a husband and wife could have chosen a completely different set of rings but now the rings have great sentimental significance. In fact, our "personhood" may often be wrapped up in external objects we consider imperfect, inconvenient, or even ugly. The table inherited from Aunt May has an honored place in the home not because it is pretty, but because it is imbued with family history.[15] The same kind of identification can happen with intellectual property: a poem learned while young can become particularly important to the individual, a piece of music first heard on an important occasion can become imbued with personal meaning.

Professor Radin gave us examples of situations where "commodification," treating a physical *res* as fungible property, disrupts a personhood interest. For instance, a tenant may lose an apartment for market reasons—like increasing rent or a decision to redevelop the property—even though that tenant has greater personal identification with the apartment than the landlord. However, commodification of intellectual property does not engender the same disruptive separation of person from (personhood embodying) *res*. Intellectual creations are "public goods" in the economic sense.[16] They are "non-excludable"[17] in that once one has had some access to the intellectual property *res*, one can-

---

15 Another possibility in the case of existing objects is that the personality does not "move into" the object so much as the object "moves into" the personality. Consider some of Milan Kundera's thoughts on personal development:

> There are two methods of cultivating the uniqueness of the self: the method of *addition* and the method of *subtraction*. [One character] subtracts from herself everything that is exterior and borrowed . . . [another character], she keeps adding to it more and more attributes and she attempts to identify herself with them . . . . Th[is] method of addition is quite charming if it involves adding to the self such things as a cat, a dog, roast pork, love of the sea or of cold showers. But the matter becomes less idyllic if a person decides to add love for communism, for the homeland, for Mussolini, for Catholicism or atheism, for fascism or antifascism.

MILAN KUNDERA, IMMORTALITY 100-01 (Peter Kussi trans., 1991).

16 A "public good" is a good for which "it is possible at no cost for additional persons to enjoy the same unit." Harold Demsetz, *The Private Production of Public Goods*, 13 J.L. & ECON. 293, 295 (1970). Put another way, the public good is subject to "non-rivalrous consumption." Stephen L. Carter, *Owning What Doesn't Exist*, 13 HARV. J. L. & PUB. POL'Y 99, 102 (1990). The sweep of a lighthouse beam is a public good that can be enjoyed by any and all ships along the coast; a clock atop city hall offers a public good— accurate information on the time—to all who pass nearby. The subjects of intellectual property are the prototyp-

not be completely separated from it. If a person were deprived of all his music and books, he would have a great sense of personal loss, but yet would still know Satie's "Gymnopedies" by heart, would still remember much of Faulkner, and could still go to the library to read or listen to these favorites.[18]

Of course, commodification of intellectual property may, as with commodification of physical property, systemically prevent *prospective* personhood interests from *developing*. When Mr. Potter's ownership of all the buildings in town prevents Emily & Geoff from buying an affordable house in Pottersville, prospective personhood interests are frustrated. Similarly, when the high royalties demanded by authors keeps Curt from buying books (and curtails the library's acquisitions), Curt's prospective personhood interests are frustrated. He cannot identify with a book to which he is denied access.

So far this has been a discussion of personhood interests commonly linked to sentimental attachment or opportunity for personal growth. Intellectual property also brings to mind an intuitively different set of personhood interests. When we first encounter a *res* of intellectual property, instead of noting that an individual's personality has moved *into* an existing object, we may note that an individual's personality caused the object to come into existence. The object comes into the world already an embodiment or reflection of some particular individual.[19] So Delacroix called paintings "a bridge linking the painter's mind with that of the viewer," Solzhenitsyn said that literature "transmits incontrovertible condensed experience," and Thomas Jefferson called in-

ical public good; indeed, the lighthouse and the city hall clock are not far from intellectual property since the commonly shared public good is *information*.

17 Carter, *supra* note 16, at 102.

18 A distinction should be clear here: the difference between the intellectual property *res* and the particular, physical manifestation of that *res*. The copy of *Lady Chatterly's Lover* on my shelf belonged to my grandmother; it is that *copy*, not the novel, which has personal significance for me. Personhood interests in a physical object, whether a book or a wedding ring, were the subject of Radin's initial inquiries. While the intellectual property *res* is distinct from the object, it is also true that access to a poem, symphony, or fictional story is made much easier by owning physical objects. On that account, it might be noted, for example, that the bankruptcy laws of most states allow a bankrupt person to retain their home (often the greatest repository of personhood interests) and a dollar amount of personal effects; within that amount, the individual can choose the optimal personhood-preserving mix of family heirlooms, library, etc.

19 Many physical objects also come into the world imbued with someone's personality, like a hand-built cabin or a hand-made Christmas wreath. But if we continue this line of thinking, the distinction between material property and intellectual property starts to blur because the material objects that most obviously come into the world imbued with personhood interests are also more likely to be objects of intellectual property laws, i.e., paintings or art pottery.

ventions "the fugitive fermentation of an individual brain."[20] Armed with this belief about the nexus between the individual person and the intellectual product, we believe that rights to these intellectual products are desirable because "they strengthen our sense of individuality."[21]

But what does this have to do with our individuality? What is at stake? For example, "creativity" is a characteristic we cultivate in our children, linking it intimately with their development as autonomous individuals. We look at nearly indistinguishable finger paintings, praise them as original, make posters of them, and imagine that one of these children will be a new Pollock. Throughout our culture, we link, if not blur, our notions of creativity, originality, and personal expression. This linkage occurs whether we are turning our attention to kindergarten finger-painting or Carnegie Hall performances; whether our critical faculty is focused on intensely original work—like Picasso's *Les Desmoiselles d'Avignon* when it was first viewed[22]—or on works whose subtle variations are appreciated only by a few. In some situations, a work's origin may cry out to the whole world. It does not take much familiarity with modern painting to recognize most of Picasso's work as Picasso or most of Miro's work as Miro. However, the identification of some specific work with some specific individual occurs with subtler expression, similar to a particular defensive play in a chess tournament, a solution to a computer programming problem, the juxtaposition of a certain painting with another at an exhibition, a particular style of lighting scenes in a film,[23] or even the layout of sand traps and

---

[20] Letter from Thomas Jefferson to Isaac McPherson, *in* THE WRITINGS OF THOMAS JEFFERSON 333 (Saul K. Padover ed., 1967). *See also*, WILLIAM KINGSTON, INNOVATION, CREATIVITY, AND LAW 89 (1990) ("Legal protection of disembodied information thenceforward reflected the view that the work of writers and inventors is an extension of their personalities, and consequently in some sense, 'theirs.'"); JOHN H. MERRYMAN & ALBERT E. ELSEN, LAW, ETHICS, AND THE VISUAL ARTS 145 (2d ed. 1987) ("The primary justification for the protection of moral rights is the idea that the work of art is the extension of the artist's personality, an expression of his most innermost being. To mistreat the work of art is to mistreat the artist . . . to impair his personality.").

[21] Lynn S. Paine, *Trade Secrets and the Justification of Intellectual Property: A Comment on Hettinger*, 20 PHILA. & PUB. AFF. 247, 252 (1991).

[22] Discussing this painting one commentator said, "[t]he consequences of one individual act of perception were and remain incalculable . . . . This individual act of perception is recorded in a painting by Picasso, now called *Les Demoiselles d'Avignon.*" HERBERT READ, A CONCISE HISTORY OF MODERN PAINTING 67 (1974). The painting was "recognized instantly" as a "summit of achievement." PIERRE DAIX, PICASSO LIFE AND ART 65-78 (Olivia Emmett trans., Harper Collins 1993).

[23] In discussing the development of a few leading cinematographers from the Hollywood studio system of the 1930s, John Bailey said: "[C]oming out of that [studio system were] some really stellar people . . . who had such strength and such individual voice that they kind of transcended whatever studio they happened to be working for. Today you can look back and very easily recognize their films from the look irrespective of the director." VISIONS OF LIGHT (Arnold Glassman, director, 1994).

greens on a golf course.[24] A few years ago, a foreign affairs article appeared in a scholarly journal attributed to "Z". The speculation about the author included numerous people claiming it read like Ambassador Jean J. Kirkpatrick or Zbigniew Braezinski.[25] In these latter, subtle cases, we may search for some new terminology like "critical judgment" or "intellectual insight." However, it is hard to deny that some sense of personal style is what lurks behind the terminology and, in turn, that this notion of "style" is some alloy of creativity and personal expression.[26]

So it should be no surprise that the three ideas—creativity, originality, and personal expression—are so thoroughly alloyed in American case law that there may be no principled way to disentangle them, despite efforts by some courts and commentators to keep originality and creativity conceptually asunder. In the 1991 *Feist* decision,[27] the U.S. Supreme Court made it clear that "originality" as used in copyright law should be defined, in part, by means of creativity:

> Original, as the term is used in copyright, means only that the work was independently created by the author (as opposed to copied from other works) and that it possesses at least some minimal degree of creativity. To be sure, the requisite level of creativity is extremely low, even a slight amount will suffice.[28]

This "linkage" of creative-original-personal expression produces a complex or "multivalent" concept of creativity. One question is whether this linkage is inevitable or merely the result of historical accident; if the law developed at a time when these notions were culturally linked, although the cultural linkage might break down

---

24 For example, the Southern California courses designed by George C. Thomas (including the Riviera Country Club) show his particular style of fairway and green architecture. Steve Springer, *The L.A. Open Not The Retiring Kind: George Clifford Thomas Jr. Thought He Was Through Designing Golf Courses Before the L.A. Athletic Club Persuaded Him to Build Riviera in Santa Monica Canyon*, L.A. TIMES, Feb. 22, 1993, at 3.

25 Z, *To the Stalin Mausoleum*, 119 DAEDALUS, Winter 1990, at 295. *See also* David Warsh, *Was It Daedalus or Icarus? Mystery Essay May Prove to be a Jape Gone Awry; The "Z" Affair*, BOSTON GLOBE, Feb. 18, 1990, at A25; *The Mysterious Mr.-or Ms.- Z*, TIME, Jan. 15, 1990, at 33 (speculating on author's identity because of stilted prose).

26 This remains true whether one adopts a "modern" or "post-modern" view of personality. For an interesting discussion of this problem with photographic images, *see* Jeffrey Malkan, *Stolen Photographs: Personality, Publicity, and Privacy*, 75 TEX. L. REV. 779 (1997). Malkan observes that "style" is a matter of what's "on the inside" and quotes Cocteau's observation that "[d]ecorative style has never existed. . . . Style is the soul . . . ." *Id.* at 833.

27 Feist Publications, Inc. v. Rural Tel. Serv. Co., 499 U.S. 340 (1991).

28 *Id.* at 345. In the statutory grant that "[c]opyright protection subsists . . . in original works of authorship," 17 U.S.C. § 102(a) (1988 & Supp. IV 1992), "original" is interpreted as having "originality" or meeting the "requirement of originality . . . ." *See* Key Publications v. Chinatown Today Publications, 945 F.2d 509, 512 (1991).

over time, the conceptual linkage in jurisprudence might continue.

This is the spirit of the deconstructionist's observations about the single "author" and the immutable "text." The deconstructionists reason that the solitary author-genius is a creation of Romanticism that became embedded in American jurisprudence in the nineteenth century. Now, the argument continues, in a world of high technology and collaborative creative work, this construct needs to be replaced. There is much that is interesting, but also much that is dissatisfying about these deconstructionist observations. Assuming the "author" reflects the creative process of another time, the deconstructionists give us little real evidence of how our creative process is different. The evidence the deconstructionists do marshal is as much evidence of a benign, complex notion of creativity as it is evidence that the "author" lurks beneath intellectual property decisions. Instead of being a historical accident, there is good reason to think that the linkage between creativity, originality, and personal expression is both historically rooted and, at a deeper level, inevitable. That linkage, in turn, raises the issue of what I will tentatively call the "moral shop right."

A. *The Romantic Author-Genius and the Place of Creativity*

In recent years, critical legal studies imported the deconstructionist attack against "authors" and "texts" from French literary criticism. This wave of law review articles[29] has explored how copyright law developed with, and came to rely on the Romantic notion of creative authorship, "an extreme assertion of the self and the value of the individual experience . . . together with the infinite

---

[29] *See, e.g.*, Jessica Litman, *The Public Domain*, 39 EMORY L.J. 965, 1007 (1990); Peter Jaszi, *Toward a Theory of Copyright: The Metamorphoses of Authorship*, 41 DUKE L.J. 455 (1991) [hereinafter Jaszi, *Theory of Copyright*]; Martha Woodmansee, *On The Author Effect: Recovering Collectivity*, 10 CARDOZO ARTS & ENT. L.J. 279 (1992); James Boyle, *A Theory of Law and Information: Copyright, Spleens, Blackmail and Insider Trading*, 80 CAL. L. REV. 1413 (1992); Peter Jaszi, *On the Author Effect: Contemporary Copyright and Collective Creativity*, 10 CARDOZO ARTS & ENT. L. J. 293 (1992) [hereinafter Jaszi, *Author Effect*]; Andrea A. Lunsford & Lisa Ede, *Collaborative Authorship and the Teaching of Writing*, 10 CARDOZO ARTS & ENT. L.J. 681 (1992); Keith Aoki, *Adrift in the Intertext: Authorship and Audience "Recording Rights,"* 68 CHI.-KENT L. REV. 805 (1993) [hereinafter Aoki, *Adrift*]; Keith Aoki, *Foreword: Innovation and the Information Environment: Interrogating the Entrepreneur*, 75 OR. L. REV. 1 (1996) [hereinafter Aoki, *Foreword*]; Keith Aoki, *Property and Sovereignty: Notes Toward a Cultural Geography of Authorship*, 48 STAN. L. REV. 1293 (1996) [hereinafter Aoki, *Sovereignty*]; Margaret Chon, *Symposium: Innovation and the Information Environment: New Wine Bursting From Old Bottles: Collaborative Internet Art, Joint Works, and Entrepreneurship*, 75 OR. L. REV. 257, 265 (1996) ("The binary structure of copyright law, dependent as it is on a strict division between author and reader, or original artist and copyist, is being corroded by networked digital information.").

and the transcendental."[30] The "author" is seen as a historically contingent social construct that arose to capture the creative process in the nineteenth century and did not exist before that time.[31] In general, the deconstructionists view "the persistent judicial reliance on author-reasoning as a method of resolving ambiguity and suppressing the complexity of the world."[32] In a tempered, wide-ranging presentation, Professor James Boyle has even argued that the author construct gets used in economic analyses of legal controls on information.[33]

For the deconstructionists, the problem is that the author construct is unsuitable to an increasingly complex world of group, corporate, and collaborative creativity.[34] Sometimes, the deconstructionists present the "death of authorship" as a *fait accompli*, in both literary theory and writers' practices; it only remains for jurists to sign off on the death certificate. Other times, sometimes breathlessly in the same article, the deconstructionist sees a resurgence of the individualistic Romantic author construct with destructive consequences for less typical sources of intellectual production. There is valuable work in this deconstructionist jurisprudence, but there are questions about both its picture of how the world is and its vision of how the world should be.[35]

---

[30] Jaszi, *Theory of Copyright, supra* note 29, at 455 (quoting THE OXFORD COMPANION TO ENGLISH LITERATURE 842 (M. Drabble ed., 5th ed., 1985)).

[31] Boyle, *supra* note 29, at 1526 ("[T]he idea of [the] author[ship] is socially constructed and historically contingent."). Woodmansee, for example, quotes a 1753 German text to show us that "[t]he scholar and the writer" were held on a par with "the papermaker, the type founder, the typesetter and the printer, the proofreader, the publisher, the book-binder." Woodmansee, *supra* note 29, at 280. But, the book she draws this inference from is an "economic dictionary" and all these professionals are held on a par as to their respective *economic* effect on "this branch of manufacture." *Id.* This does not address the social place of "the scholar and the writer." This would be the same as taking, as evidence of their similar social station today, a statement like "book publishing is an *X* billion dollar business, providing jobs for authors, editors, graphics technicians, book store clerks, and lumberjacks." Would such a statement make you believe that we treat authors and lumberjacks on a par?

[32] Aoki, *Adrift, supra* note 29, at 816.

[33] "The values of romantic authorship seem to seep—consciously or unconsciously—into economic analysis. And because in most conflicts the paradigm of authorship tends to fit one side better than the other, this romantic grounding provides economic analysis with at least the illusion of certainty. Authors tend to win." Boyle, *supra* note 29, at 1527. Professor Boyle has expanded this argument in JAMES BOYLE, SHAMANS, SOFTWARE, AND SPLEENS: LAW AND THE CONSTRUCTION OF THE INFORMATION SOCIETY (1996).

[34] *See, e.g.*, Aoki, *Foreword, supra* note 29; Boyle, *supra* note 29; Jaszi, *Author Effect, supra* note 29; Jaszi, *Theory of Copyright, supra* note 29; and Woodmansee, *supra* note 29. The focus on the author "drive[s us] to confer property rights in information on those who come closest to the image of the romantic author . . . . This is a bad thing for reasons of both efficiency and justice." Aoki, *Foreword, supra* note 29, at 6.

[35] Some deconstructionists also see the development of the "work" as a construct used to disempower authors. But the increasingly broad property protection engendered by the "work" construct is a mixed, often valuable, gift for authors. In early copyright cases, any concept of "work" was limited to the exact physical embodiment of the author's copy.

It is hard to disagree with this proposition. Even if one believes in the possibility of private language, most ideas remain social constructs. If the point is that the individual author "construct" is out of synch with the times—for which we need a more collectivist paradigm of creative output—then three observations are in order.

First, the case for this new descriptive account of the world has not been made (and it will be difficult to make). It is difficult to measure how much more collective and collaborative the creative process has become compared to the past. The evidence mustered seems about as convincing as Bertolt Brecht having himself photographed in the 1930s "writing poetry in the midst of a crowd of workers to emphasize that the days of romantic political individualism were dead and poetry was now a collective proletarian activity."[36] On this point, the evidence assembled focuses on writing—particularly books, lectures, stories—without reference to closely related arts and activities.[37] For example, plays—collaborative efforts of playwrights, actors, set designers, and musicians[38]—have been a continuously vibrant part of both western and Japanese cultures for centuries. Renaissance frescoes were often collaborative works among similarly stationed individuals—as was the Brancacci Chapel in Florence by the painters Masaccio and Masolino.[39] There are also old literary traditions, western and eastern, of col-

This resulted in authors losing value at the hands of less creative market players. *See, e.g.*, Stowe v. Thomas, 23 F. Cas. 201 (E.D. Pa. 1853) (holding that copyright of *Uncle Tom's Cabin* is not infringed by non-English translation); White-Smith Music Publ'g v. Apollo Co., 209 U.S. 1 (1908) (copyright in printed sheet not infringed by the making of player piano roll for such music). *See also* Edward Samuels, *The Idea-Expression Dichotomy in Copyright Law*, 56 TENN. L. REV. 321, 334-47 (1989).

36 PAUL JOHNSON, INTELLECTUALS 178 (1988). The authors often overstate the situation. For example, Professor Margaret Chon in a thoughtful discussion of "chain art" and other collaborative projects on the Internet, recently commented that "[w]hether the work is an e-mail conversation or a serialized document, the individual-based notion of 'work' does not describe what is actually occurring in this new medium." Chon, *supra* note 29, at 271. But an "e-mail conversation" is not fundamentally different from a regular correspondence—a genre of historic publication that has flourished in the world of the "author" and "work."

37 This is even true of many articles focusing on the Internet. *See, e.g.*, Rebecca Tushnet, *Legal Fictions: Copyright, Fan Fiction and a New Common Law*, 17 LOY. L.A. ENT. L.J. 651 (1997). However, there is also a growing literature about "collaborative" images on the Net. *See, e.g.*, Chon, *supra* note 29; Raphael Winick, *Intellectual Property, Defamation and the Digital Alteration of Images*, 21 COLUM.-VLA J.L. & ARTS 143 (1997).

38 For example, songwriting, in all its subgenres, had often been a collaborative venture, including the works of Elton John and Brian Tauper, David Bowie and Brian Eno, Tim Rice and Andrew Lloyd Webber, and Jay Livingston and Ray Evans (winners of three Academy Awards and authors of compositions like *Mona Lisa*, *Que Sera Sera*, and *Silver Bells*). *See* Rachel Fischer, *Piano Men*, L.A. TIMES, Aug. 18, 1996 (Westside Weekly Supp.), at 1; *See e.g.*, Patricia T. Perkens, *"Hey! What's the Score?" Copyright in the Orchestration of Broadway Musicals*, 16 COLUM.-VLA J.L. & ARTS 475 (1992).

39 *See* PERRI LEE ROBERTS, MASOLINO DA PANICALE 53-83 (Oxford Univ. Press 1994).

laborative writing, like the Japanese renga.[40]

Consider the role of the "studio." At the close of this century, leading architects like I.M. Pei and Antoine Predock have studios staffed with junior partners and assistants who do much of the work on the building commissions given to the named architect.[41] Arguably the most striking feature of Louis Kahn's greatest work—the Salk Institute in San Diego—was not originally Kahn's idea.[42] The deconstructionists are correct to note that even when learned critics focus on the works coming out of such studios, the analysis is intensely individualistic, e.g., "what was Predock trying to achieve?" or "what did Kahn mean?" But this does not mean an old way of thinking is being imposed on a new way of producing intellectual works. Scores of understudies in the studios of Michelangelo and Leonardo worked on the masters' projects. The point is not that the "old" way was individualistic *or* collective; the point is that the "new" way has not been shown to be *more* collective.

Second, even if this descriptive account of present-day intellectual production is correct, this new nature of the process might not "diffuse and diminish emotions of original discovery and exclusive ownership."[43] It is possible, for example, that even as the process of intellectual production becomes more collaborative, personal *feelings* become more individualized and atomized.[44] A general, increasing individualism in western society has been noted by many

---

[40] In Japanese literature, there is the "renga," a traditional form of poetry in which several poets author one poem together. The poets "write successively stanzas of three and of two lines, without rhyme, but with a fixed syllabic measure." OCTAVIO PAZ & CHARLES TOMLINSON, AIRBORN/HIJOS DEL AIRE 5 (1981). Inspired by the renga, Octavio Paz and Charles Tomlinson later took to writing sonnets together by correspondence. *Id.* at 5-7.

[41] In the 1980s and 1990s, Predock, for example, employed between 15 and 40 people in his architecture studio. *See* David Dillon, *Antoine Predock: American Visionary*, ARCHITECTURE, Mar. 1, 1995, at 55.

[42] When Louis Kahn asked Luis Barragin how he would landscape the area between the two buildings at the Salk Institute, "the Mexican architect walked over to one building, touched its concrete, and corrected Kahn's question at its premise. The space should not be a garden at all, Barragin concluded . . . but a plaza paved in stone cut by a channel of water. . . . The rest is architectural history: a square surfaced in travertine with a rivulet channeled straight down the middle to the Pacific." Joseph Giovannini, *The Salk Addition*, ARCHITECTURE, Mar. 1, 1996, at 75.

[43] BENJAMIN KAPLAN, AN UNHURRIED VIEW OF COPYRIGHT 117 (1967) (Kaplan expressed this hope in this seminal work).

[44] As Professor Chon has observed:

> [E]ven in intensely collaborative environments, individual feelings of ownership (or perhaps possessiveness) emerge . . . . Whatever the futureoligists predict, the Internet has not yet erased the vestiges of earlier historical views of authorship and works - views reinforced by cultural practices that persist despite successive waves of different kinds of "mechanical reproduction," appropriation art, post-structuralist theory and critical thinking in the law.

Chon, *supra* note 29, at 274 (noting that students participating in a "chain art" project on the Internet were often upset when someone changed the joint image in a way they were unhappy with).

authors.[45] Architects and filmmakers, working in a *historically* collaborative, studio-oriented milieu appear as or more intensely individualistic as novelists who work alone.[46] Scientists and engineers working in research teams have, as courts have noted, a tendency to remember their own work on the team in a magnified form.[47] Academics and entertainers both effusively thank their "collaborators" (in footnotes and award acceptance speeches, respectively) without sharing the billing or too much of the spotlight. There was just a touch of irony when two of the leading proponents of the "collective process" wrote back-to-back articles in one journal. Each article was entitled *Author Effect* and each author thanked the other author in the first footnote. But the articles were not co-written; each retained *individual* authorship of *one* article.[48] Apparently, their own works have not become *that* "polyvocal." Of the people who write about the contemporary collaborative writing

---

45 *See, e.g.*, JEAN BETHKE ELSHTAIN, DEMOCRACY ON TRIAL 15-57, 129 (1993) (arguing that the civic notion of "rights" has been replaced by rights as the entitlements of individuals freed from "any and all ties of reciprocal obligations and mutual interdependence"); CHRISTOPHER LASCH, THE REVOLT OF THE ELITES: AND THE BETRAYAL OF DEMOCRACY (1995) (noting that elite classes have abandoned their civic role for individual mobility and choice). But this same observation about the civic-minded liberty of the ancients versus the modern liberty of the individual to develop his capacities without hindrance even from his community was made by Benjamin Constant in the late eighteenth and nineteenth centuries. *See* BENJAMIN CONSTANT, POLITICAL WRITINGS 309-28 (Biancamaria Fontana trans., 1988); Biancamaria Fontana, *Introduction* to Political Writings, *id*, at 18-28.

46 For example, Louis Kahn proudly recounted the following tale from his childhood:

> One day as a small boy I was copying the portrait of Napoleon. His left eye was giving me trouble. Already I had erased the drawing of it several times. My father leaned over and lovingly corrected my work. I threw the paper and pencil across the room saying, "Now it is your drawing, not mine." Two cannot make a single drawing. I am sure the most skillful imitation can be detected by the originator.

LOUIS KAHN, THE NOTEBOOKS AND DRAWINGS OF LOUIS KAHN, (Foreword) (1974). And it is hard to fathom Walt Disney's motives when it came to attribution in Disney films. The classic Walt Disney movies from the "golden age" of animation—Snow White, Fantasia, Jungle Book, Bambi—were created by the "Nine Old Men" of Disney, including Frank Thomas and Ollie Johnston, but Walt Disney—whose singular name is identified with that treasure trove—"would not allow any animator to take sole credit for a character in a film." Scott Collins, *Frank, Ollie Ride Again*, L.A. TIMES, Oct. 19, 1995, at F1.

47 For example, one court recounted the following:

> At trial, however, Green testified that the anvil groove was his basic idea, and that he was the prime mover in getting it done. At the time of the development of the [patented invention], the engineers at Van Dyck worked in groups, the members of which regularly met, interacted, and exchanged ideas. The three patentees regularly interacted in this setting in an effort to solve the problem of proper staple firing and formation. Given this scenario, and after reviewing the testimony of Green, it is clear that although Green felt the idea for the anvil groove was "his," it really was the product of the work of all three.

United States Surgical Corp. v. Hospital Prod. Int'l Party Ltd., 701 F. Supp. 314, 340 (D. Conn. 1988). As another court commented, there is the "temptation for honest witnesses, who have worked years with a patentee to implement his ideas, to forget whose ideas they were." Acme Highway Prod. Corp. v. D.S. Brown, 431 F.2d 1074, 1083 (6th Cir. 1970).

48 *See* Woodmansee, *supra* note 29; Jaszi, *Author Effect*, *supra* note 29, at 293.

process, Andrea Lumsford and Lisa Ede seem to be rare exceptions who put their pens—and their empirical research—where their theories are.[49] Their work has not yet gone far enough to prove increasing feelings of a non-individualistic, collaborative process.[50] And what would we do if we concluded that intellectual production had become more collaborative, while that identification with intellectual products remained intensely individualistic?

Third and finally, if both the creative process and sentiments arising from intellectual production are more collaborative, we still do not have much idea of how and how much a system of legal rights should protect all contributors to a given work. There are good arguments that the basic system should remain the same.[51] A scheme for attribution rights would probably not be difficult to sort out. Artists seem generally amenable to such attribution. Our popular culture already thrives on recognizably collective, albeit extremely hierarchical creativity. It is "Bruce Springsteen and the E Street Band," "Prince and the New Power Generation," or "Huey Lewis and the News." Still, one wonders how far such a scheme must go. In her 1990 album *Attainable Love*, folksinger Christine Lavin went so far as to thank one person for "the E chord" in a song and another colleague for suggesting *one* word for the lyrics of a different track.[52]

---

49 Lunsford & Ede, *supra* note 29; Lisa Ede & Andrea A. Lunsford, *Why . . . Write Together?*, 1 RHETORIC REV. 150 (1983).

50 An exception to this—so rare as to prove the individualism of artists in collaborative enterprises—was Julie Andrews' 1996 refusal to be nominated for a Tony Award for her role in the Broadway production of *Victor/Victoria*. After the 318th standing ovation—which followed the 318th performance of the show—Andrews announced her decision to decline the nomination saying, "I have searched my conscience and my heart and find that I cannot accept this nomination and prefer to stand instead with the egregiously overlooked . . . members of the *Victor/Victoria* family." Andrews specifically named 12 people to whom she attributed the success of the show, including the lighting and costume designers. *See* Joseph Steuer, *Andrews' Bomb: "No" to Tony Nom*, HOLLYWOOD REP., May 9, 1996, at 1.

51 For example, Andre Lucas, of the University of Nantes, has observed:

> I do not think that interactivity . . . fundamentally changes the facts of the matter. True, in making the "consumer" play a more active role, it takes away from the "aura" surrounding the act of creation. Nonetheless, the fact remains that, no matter what people say, there is indeed an "imaginer" and this suffices to restore the traditional basis. This does not mean that the new technologies do not complicate matters. For example, it may be difficult to separate the contributions of the computer programmer and the artist, or that of the provider of the basic scenario and that of the "adopter." However, this is basically a classic problem.

Jean-Loup Tournier, *Author's Rights and New Modes of Exploitation*, 16 COLUM.-VLA J.L. & ARTS 441, 458 (1992).

52 CHRISTINE LAVIN, ATTAINABLE LOVE (1990) (Liner notes read "All songs written by Christine Lavin except *Sensitive New Age Guys* co-written with John Gorka; the E chord in *Kind of Love* suggested by Bill Kollar; the word 'luminescent' in *Venus* contributed by Noah Adams.")

Beyond attribution, what rights belong to whom? One option would be to extend the present system, effectively giving each contributor rights to prevent any particular use (license, novelization, broadcast, etc.). This would produce a "veto" system which would surely diminish society's access to jointly written works. In such a system, pressures would be strong to create a background hierarchy of contributors so that not every contributor could prevent release of the work. Such a system could produce elaborate differentiation rights for different contributors.[53]

While questions remain about what is happening in the production of intellectual works and how law *could* address such changes, the reality is that the single author idea remains powerful in our legal system. As Professor Keith Aoki has noted, it is ironic that while some scholars have been marshaling European literary criticism against "authors," other scholars and lawmakers have been importing European notions of "moral rights"—legal privileges which elevate the importance of the individual who produces intellectual works.[54] Declaring the end of the romantic "author" and thoughtfully calling for programs to reshape the law without this nuisance concept seems just a little out of touch. We must first consider a dozen legislatures who have already passed moral rights laws for visual artists, and Congress which has grudgingly embraced the moral rights requirements of the Berne Convention.[55] If these laws are any indicia, then it may be, as James Boyle believes, that "the romantic vision of authorship is more important today than it was to Fichte and Krause, Pope and Macaulay."[56]

Other things, however, could be at work. First, the rise of the

---

53 The European Community's "Directive 92/100/EEC of 19 November 1992 on Rental Right and Lending Rights . . ." distinguishes between producers, directors, and actors with possible inclusion of script writers and authors of underlying works as "co-authors" of films but enjoying different rights. *See* Said Mosteshar, *Surprises in Store: Future Mandatory Rental Rights*, 22 INT'L BUS. L. 37 (1994).

54 Aoki, *Adrift*, *supra* note 29, at 816-21. As Aoki has more recently noted on intellectual property laws in the brave new world of the Net, "[c]opyright law does not seem to be on the verge of consignment to the dustbin of history anytime in the near future, prophesies of eminent cyberpundits aside." Aoki, *Sovereignty*, *supra* note 29, at 1308.

55 In 1990, Congress enacted the Visual Artists' Rights Act, 17 U.S.C. § 106A (1988 & Supp. IV 1992), which provides limited attribution and integrity rights for artists who create graphic, sculptural, or photographic works, either in original or limited editions. In addition, several states have moral rights of varying strength for visual artists. *See* California Art Preservation Act, CAL. CIV. CODE §§ 980-89 (West Supp. 1993); CONN. GEN. STAT. ANN. §§ 42-116s to 42-116t (West 1992); Artists' Authorship Rights Act, LA. REV. STAT. ANN. §§ 51:2151 to 51:2156 (West 1987); ME. REV. STAT. ANN. tit. 27, § 303 (West 1988); Fine Arts Preservation Act, PA. STAT. ANN. tit. 73, §§ 2102-2110 (West Supp. 1992); R.I. GEN. LAWS §§ 5-62-2 to -6 (1987).

56 Boyle, *supra* note 29. Rights are "but one example of how the Romantic conception of 'authorship' is displaying a literally unprecedented measure of ideological autonomy in legal context." Jaszi, *Author Effect*, *supra* note 29, at 299.

"author" in eighteenth and nineteenth century cultural norms and its migration about that time into jurisprudence does not tell us that the word "author" in present-day court opinions has either the same content or the same influence it may once have had. We cannot condemn a social construct purely on its pedigree without reference to its present uses.[57] If the history of ideas teaches us anything, it is that ideas are not stable. The question is not whether the concept is historically contingent, but *how* contingent it is. The concept of a "republic" is also historically contingent, but that does not mean it lacks utility or applicability.[58] No doubt "romantic author" is a more historically contingent construct than "author"—just as "federal republic" would be a more historically contingent construct than "republic." If the point is to show us that "author" in American jurisprudence always carries "romantic author" imbedded in it, then there is a great deal yet to prove.

Second, while the phenomenon being studied may be a word whose meaning has migrated, the student of the phenomenon must make sure her concepts are clear, limited, and do not migrate. Sometimes, it appears that in order to find "author-reasoning" in a variety of places, the deconstructionists often morph their concept of author. They began with a "romantic author" and move through "romantic author-geniuses,"[59] to "master mind,"[60] and then, a romanticized, Faustian vision of "entrepreneurship."[61]

Studying a historically evolved concept may call for such leeway,[62] but the result may be that symptoms of "author-reasoning" can be found everywhere. If one began searching for iridium in geological samples, then started subtracting or adding electrons

57 If we did, we would, for example, have to attack the notion of "diversity" in college admissions. It appears that "diversity" became an issue at Harvard College in the early nineteenth century as a call for greater geographic diversity—thereby giving Harvard officials a fig leaf to admit more "WASPs" from the Midwest and fewer first generation immigrant Jews from the East coast. *See* Alan M. Dershowitz & Laura Hanft, *Affirmative Action and the Harvard College Diversity-Discretion Model: Paradigm or Pretext?*, 1 CARDOZO L. REV. 379, 386-400 (1979).

58 *See generally* PAUL A. RAHE, REPUBLICS ANCIENT AND MODERN: CLASSICAL REPUBLICANISM AND THE AMERICAN REVOLUTION (1992); CLAUDE NICOLET, L'IDÉA RÉPUBICAINE EN FRANCE (1982); Philippe Raynaud, *Destin de l'idéologie républicaine*, ESPRIT (Dec., 1983); LE SIÉCLE DE L'AVÉNEMENT RÉPUBLICAIN (Francois Furet & Mona Ozouf eds., 1993).

59 Aoki, *Adrift*, *supra* note 29, at 820.

60 Jaszi, *Theory of Copyright*, *supra* note 29, at 487.

61 Boyle, *supra* note 29, at 1508 (linking romantic images of innovative entrepreneur to romantic images of authors).

62 This terminological "drift" also makes for more comfortable reading; ironically, it follows in the tradition of intellectual property case law which has been attacked for the same kind of imprecision. For example, in the 1884 *Burrow-Giles Lithographic Co. v. Sarony* case, Justice Miller used almost a score of different phrases to describe what was protectable by copyright, ranging from "original intellectual conceptions" to "originality of thought" to "intellectual production." 111 U.S. 53, 58-61 (1884).

and protons as to what molecules would count as iridium, it would not take long to find "iridium" all around us. Because concepts in the social sciences lack the precision of atomic element descriptions, we must be cautious that "drift" in our concepts does not cause us to overexpand, and thereby undercut, our observations.

After exploring the notion of creativity, the discussion below will sketch out how the deconstructionists' observations about "author reasoning" can just as well be diagnosed as the law's sometimes uncritical reliance on the notion of "creativity."

B. *The Multivalent Notion of Creativity*

From the deconstructionist perspective, copyright law "is grounded on an uncritical belief in the existence of a distinct and privileged category of activity"[63] called authorship. However fascinating the historical account of romantic author-genius' arrival into Anglo American law may be, our courts, like our art professors and theater critics, are more concerned with creativity than authorship.

Yet understanding "creativity" is no easy task. To psychologists and psychiatrists, "[t]he more one studies the subject of creativity, the more complex and bewildering it seems."[64] Freud himself reluctantly concluded that "before the problem of the creative artist, analysis must, alas, lay down its arms."[65] And to many artists "the most important element" of their works remains completely "inexplicable."[66] We do not even know what kind of relationship it has with other constructs of human activity, such as labor.[67] This is

---

63 Jaszi, *Theory of Copyright*, *supra* note 29, at 466.

64 As Leon Berman elaborates:

> Attempts to define the creative process have focused on . . . regression in the service of the ego; and such diverse affects as awe, wonderment, loneliness, inspiration, and ecstasy. Significant life experiences have been considered as well as innate endowments. Traumatogenic theories of creativity have implicated childhood abuse, loss, illness, and congenital deformity.
>
> In the midst of all this attention, the character of the poor artist has been idealized, diagnosed, and defamed. He has been associated with the infant, the child, and the adolescent; the dreamer, the prophet, and the rebel; the neurotic, the impostor, the sociopath, the pervert, the criminal, and the psychotic.

Leon Berman, *An Artist Destroys His Work: Comments on Creativity and Destructiveness*, *in* CREATIVITY AND MADNESS: PSYCHOLOGICAL STUDIES IN ART AND ARTISTS 59 (Panter et al. eds., 1995). Berman adds, "it must be concluded that we know a great deal more about madness than we do about creativity." *Id.* at 61.

65 SIGMUND FREUD, DOSTOYEVSKI AND PATRICIDE 177 (Standard ed., 1928).

66 "I have never known one great painter—not one!—who hasn't told me in some way or other that the most important element in his best works, as in the masterpieces of other painters, was inexplicable—no matter whether that implied mystery or clarity." ANDRE MALRAUX, PICASSO'S MASK 235 (June Guicharnaud trans., 1976).

67 There is a very ambiguous relationship between creative work as "work" and as pleasure. For example, watching the young Renoir paint, the critic Charles Gleyre asked him,

serious baggage for someone arguing that creativity better explains judicial reasoning than the "romantic author." To meet that burden, the discussion that follows explores the popular notion of creativity and how its constituent elements provide a personality justification for intellectual property rights. Although creativity bears some aspects of "a distinct and privileged category of activity," it has over the decades actually required dilution of the romantic notion of creative *genius* and, in its place, put increasing emphasis on *originality* and *personal expression.*

1. The Melding of Originality and Creativity

In *Feist* a unanimous Supreme Court defined originality by reference to creativity.[68] But it is important to remember the path to this conclusion. The Copyright Act limits property rights to "original works of authorship."[69] The adjective "original" has led courts to create a threshold issue in copyright disputes of whether a work shows "originality." The Supreme Court packed the notion of creativity into the notion of originality in the context of using "originality" as a requirement for copyright protection. This is decidedly different from a social scientist's effort to unpack the notion of creativity; the Court was considering a judicial construct versus a social scientist exploring a social convention. Still, *Feist* is a starting point because the Court concludes that everything juridically *original* is also juridically *creative.* That logically entails the proposition that decided *Feist*: if something is not juridically *creative,* it cannot be juridically *original.* ("*If j-original, then j-creative.*")[70]

This equation (*if j-original, then j-creative*) was in reaction to a long line of case law that had supported the view that the requirement of originality was "little more than a prohibition of actual copying."[71] This juridical notion of originality, like the popular no-

"No doubt, it is to amuse yourself that you are dabbing in paint?" To which Renoir is supposed to have replied, "Why, of course, and if it did not amuse me, I beg you to believe that I would not do it." OTTO FRIEDRICH, OLYMPIA: PARIS IN THE AGE OF MANET 242 (1992). Aristotle was probably the first to observe that the "sciences which do not aim at giving pleasure or at the necessities of life were discovered, . . . first in the places where men first began to have leisure. This is why mathematical arts were founded in Egypt; for there the priestly caste was allowed to be at leisure." ARISTOTLE, 1 METAPHYSICS, 690-91 (Random House ed. 1941). Thus started the quandary of how an experience of leisure could be a process of labor. *See* Hughes, *supra* note 1, at 302-05.

68 Feist Publications, Inc. v. Rural Tel. Serv. Co., 499 U.S. 340 (1991).

69 17 U.S.C. § 102(a) (1988 & Supp. IV 1992).

70 "Juridically original" (*j-original*) and "juridically creative" (*j-creative*) should be distinguished as legal concepts from general social conventions. For those familiar with symbolic logic, let's summarize the *Feist* decision as saying: *if j-original, then j-creative,* which is logically equivalent to *if not j-creative, then not j-original* (*~j-creative→~j-original*).

71 Alfred Bell & Co., v. Catalda Fine Arts, Inc., 191 F.2d 99, 103 (2d Cir. 1951). This is a view unquestioned by scholars writing prior to *Feist. See, e.g.,* Litman, *supra* note 29, at 999

tion of originality, owes its currency to the idea of something's "origin": if a song owes its origin to Leslie, it must be *original* to Leslie. This measure of "originality" dates back to Justice Story's early nineteenth century opinions[72] and gave us a fairly bright line test: if the work was the independent creation of someone, it was "original" to that person.[73] (As described earlier, this minimalist sense of "original"—owing its origin to someone—is what we will explore below as the notion of "sourcehood." If the song owes its origin to Leslie, Leslie is the source of the song; if the cell line owes it origin to a skin sample taken from Tim's wrist, then Tim is the source of the cell line).

This pedigree of "originality" leads to a problem: originality meant that something could be juridically "original" in the sense that it was not copied, but the thing still might not be considered creative in the popular sense. Because American law makes originality the gate keeper of copyright protection, the *Feist* Court backed away from this narrow sense of "original." Instead, the Court embraced a formula tying originality with creativity. The Second Circuit and Professor Nimmer were among those who had already explicitly linked originality to creativity[74] while many copyright decisions had already required "creativity" for copyright protection—meaning that it was either embedded in the notion of "originality" or it stood as a separate requirement.[75]

The program in *Feist* adopts the formula "*if j-original, then j-creative*" because this provides the more important rule, "*if not j-creative, then not j-original.*" Embedding creativity in originality certainly makes the originality test more complicated than it would be as a mere test of sourcehood.[76] But beyond that where are we led?

("Copyright's threshold requirement of originality . . . requires neither newness nor creativity, but merely creation without copying."); Robert C. Denicola, *Copyright in Collections of Facts: A Theory for the Protection of Nonfiction Literary Works*, 81 COLUM. L. REV. 516, 520-21 (1981).

[72] Gray v. Russell, 10 F.Cas. 1035 (D. Mass. 1839) (Story, J); Emerson v. Davies, 8 F.Cas. (D. Mass. 1845) (Story, J.).

[73] *See* Russ VerSteeg, *Rethinking Originality*, 34 WM. & MARY L. REV. 801, 806 (1993) (calling this "Type I originality"); Dale P. Olson, *Copyright Originality*, 48 MO. L. REV. 29, 36 (1983).

[74] L. Batlin & Son, Inc. v. Snyder, 536 F.2d 486, 490 (2d Cir. 1976) (en banc); 1 MELVILLE B. NIMMER, THE LAW OF COPYRIGHT § 10.2 (1975). Prior to the *Feist* decision, Professor Litman also suggested that the "symbolic power" of originality was rooted in the "romantic model of authorship." Litman, *supra* note 29, at 1007. While not subscribing to the scholarship of the "romantic author" construct, I take Litman to have recognized that the legal notion of "originality" always required creativity.

[75] The ambiguous place of the creativity requirement goes back at least to Justice Miller's formulation in *Trade-Mark Cases* that copyright protection applies to works "only such as are original, and are founded in the creative powers of the mind." *In re* Trade-Mark Cases, 100 U.S. 82, 94 (1879).

[76] Prompting one commentator to, perhaps inadvertently, enter the deconstructionist's

What counts as creative in the juridical sense? What counts as creative in the popular sense? In *Feist,* the court tells us only that creativity is *not* variations that are "mechanical," "entirely typical," or "garden variety." Intellectual products that result from choices about composition that are obvious, inevitable, or "age old practice(s)" do not count as minimally creative.

There is nothing objectionable in any of these pronouncements or the fact that the Court would not say more. Supreme Court opinions are understandably restrained by fear that legions of lawyers will try to shoehorn a wide range of future human activity into choice phrases from opinions. But if judicial creativity is the same as the popular notion of creativity, we have a problem because the popular notion of creativity turns back to and depends on the popular notion of originality.

As Russ VerSteeg has pointed out, "creativity" traces its etymological roots to the Latin verb *creo,* meaning "to beget" or "to give birth to."[77] The Latin root also means "to make" or "to produce" and is related to the verb *cresco* meaning "to grow up" or "to spring forth."[78] In short, the words' roots do nothing to help distinguish "creating" from "originating," or being the source of something.

A better starting point is that the idea of *being the source of* something, of *originating* something, and of *creating* something all rely on the idea of transforming existing materials into something that is identifiably different. Imagine that Patty purchases ten pounds of red clay from Adam, who dug the clay from a hillside on his farm. Patty uses five pounds of the clay to make a vase; she gives this vase to Kevin. She also gives the five remaining pounds of clay to Kevin (perhaps with a note about the pleasures of the potter's wheel). It is non-controversial that if someone asked you, knowing all this, "what is the origin of the vase?" you would probably say "Patty" and that the same reply would hold true if you substituted "source," i.e. "what is the source of the vase?" If you rephrased the question into "who created the vase?" you would again get "Patty" as the answer.

Now consider if someone asked about the clay, i.e., "what is the origin of the clay?" or "what is the source of the clay?" This is more difficult. If you understood this question to be "how did the clay get here?" you might answer "Patty," but it seems more likely that you would treat this as a question about the clay's provenance,

---

fray by recently suggesting that creativity be cordoned off in a separate requirement of "authorship" or a "work." *See* VerSteeg, *supra* note 73, at 813-14.

77 *Id.* at 826 (quoting OXFORD LATIN DICTIONARY 456 (P.G.W. Glare ed., 1982)).

78 CASSELL'S LATIN DICTIONARY 142 (Marchant et al. eds., 1948).

i.e. "where did it come from?" In that case, if someone asked you "what is the origin of the clay?" you would probably say "Adam" or "Adam's farm." Again, the same answer would come if "source" was substituted for "origin." The probable answer would be "Adam" or "Adam's farm."

But what if someone asked who *created* the clay? The question might evoke "God," "Nature," or some explanation that Adam dug it up, but didn't "create" it. I believe that this question gets a different answer because Adam does not seem to have transformed the materials available to him when he dug them up. But this still does not evince a great difference between the popular ideas of "creating" and "originating." In fact, we could arrange a hierarchy of questions which, to increasing degrees, evoke the question of when an object first appears in the world (or first appears in the world in the form it now has):

> "What is the provenance of *X*?"
> "Where/who did *X* come from?"
> "What is the source of *X*?"
> "What is the origin of *X*?"
> "Who/what created *X*?"

Substitute Patty's vase or Adam's clay for *X* in this series of questions—the questions initially can be met with an intermediary answer ("the delivery truck," "the back seat of Patty's car," etc.). However, as you go down the list, what is increasingly demanded is an answer about when *X* first appears in the world identifiable as *X*. This would hold true if you ran through this list replacing *X* with a commercial jetliner, an antique chest, or a manuscript, anonymous because the title page has been torn off. Point to a commercial jet at an airport and ask where did it come from; its last stop—Boston, Cincinnati, Denver—will be a fine answer. But point to the same aircraft and ask who created it; nothing but "Boeing" will do as an answer. The moment when something first appeared in the world in its present form is synonymous with the moment when other things were transformed to the new thing.

The point of the hierarchy of questions is that it shows that both creativity and originality are rooted in the transformative process.[79] But there are many details that need attention. First, there

---

[79] The view that transformation or novelty is fundamental to creativity is also put forward in ROBERT WEISBERG, CREATIVITY: BEYOND THE MYTH OF GENIUS 4-5, 247-48 (1993), a book that came to my attention after this article was written. Weisberg provides a thoughtful survey of psychological efforts to explore creativity, particularly how it differs from regular thinking—an issue that this discussion does not address.

is the issue of whether the transformative process of "creating" or "originating" focuses on the materials actually at the disposal of the person *or* the total world of materials or elements possibly available. Notions, especially populist notions, of both creativity and originality are context-specific; they measure transformation by what the person actually had available. For example, discussing "creativity," Robert Nozick writes,

> Whether or not there really is anything new under the sun, a creative act produces something new or novel in comparison to what the creator had encountered and known previously. If unbeknownst to the creator someone else had produced something similar or identical . . . still the creator's act would have been an act of creation. All that matters is that the effects of this earlier discovery have not seeped through and become known to the new discoverer in a way that makes his act less novel. Calling an act "creative" characterizes it only in relation to the materials it actually arose from, the earlier experiences and knowledge of the creator, not in relation to everything that has preceded it in the history of the universe.[80]

On this approach, if Ted, the chess novice, hits upon the Evans gambit in a chess game today, as his opponent, I may call his moves "creative" or "original" even though his moves are exactly how Captain W. D. Evans executed the game in the 1820s.

But others would apply a more demanding measure. In considering Rembrandt and the master forger, Mihaly Csikszentmihaly reasons that only "Rembrandt's work is creative because he introduced some variations in the domain of painting at a certain point in history, when those variations were novel . . . . The very same variations a few years later were no longer creative, because then they simply reproduced existing forms."[81] Csikszentmihaly's definition of creative differs from Nozick's not in the test—which remains a test of identifiable difference—but in the reference set used for the test. Whereas Nozick refers to what the *creator* had encountered and known previously, Csikszentmihaly compares to all that has come before.

Whether the benchmark is an identifiable difference from what the creator had encountered or from *all* of what was known previously, the popular measure for the "original" or the "creative" still seems to be whether the thing seems identifiably different to

---

80 Robert Nozick, The Examined Life 35 (1989).

81 Mihaly Csikszentmihaly, *Society, Culture, and Person: A Systems View of Creativity, in* Nature of Creativity (Robert J. Sternberg ed., 1988).

us, not the creator. This is a problem we sometimes encounter with children: the child piles up sand in her sand box and asks us to look at what she has "made." We feign interest, but it does not look like anything has been "made" at all. No transformation is apparent to us; nothing in the sand box looks much different than the pre-existing conditions.

The law rarely needs to worry about the sensitivities of infants, but the problem returns in the case of faithful reproductions and derivative works. The master copier example makes clear that the question of "transformation" from pre-existing materials is a question of mental or intellectual materials, not physical materials. Consider a case where the master copier reproduced *Pineapple Bud*, not on a canvas but in a different medium—a holographic image of *Pineapple Bud*, a tile mural of *Pineapple Bud*, etc. Professor Nimmer reasonably took the position that "mere reproduction of a work of art in a different medium should not constitute the required originality"; Nimmer reasoned that "no one can claim to have independently evolved any particular medium."[82] But while the result seems right, the reasoning is suspect. The real reason must be because expression of the *same* image in a known medium, while an identifiably different object, is not an identifiably different image.

That reproduction in another medium does not constitute transformation was emphasized by the Second Circuit in the 1995 *American Geophysical Union v. Texaco Inc.* case.[83] In *American Geophysical*, publishers of scientific journals brought suit against Texaco for Texaco's extensive copying of scholarly articles for researchers in its laboratories. The battle was engaged over the question of whether Texaco's copying constituted a fair use and, on that basis, both the trial court and the appellate court looked at a sample of Texaco's activities against the four factor test set out in 17 U.S.C. §107(1)-(4). As to the first factor of whether the copying was a "transformative (or productive)"[84] use of the original, Texaco argued that its use of the articles was "transformative" because: "photocopying the article separated it from a bulky journal, made it more amenable to markings, and provided a document that could be readily replaced if damaged in a laboratory, all of which 'transformed' the original article into a form that better served [the sci-

82 1 Melville B. Nimmer & David Nimmer, Nimmer On Copyright § 2.08(c)(2) (1995).
83 60 F.3d 913 (2d Cir. 1994).
84 A question recognized as central to analysis under the first factor. *See* Campbell v. Acuff-Rose Music, Inc., 510 U.S. 569, 579 (1994) ("[T]he goal of copyright, to promote science and the arts, is generally furthered by the creation of transformative works.").

entist's] research needs."[85]

Both the district court and the Second Circuit soundly rejected this argument on the grounds that "Texaco's photocopying merely transforms the material object embodying the intangible article that is copyrighted work."[86] Texaco's activities were found to fall on the side of "untransformed duplication," which made no "contribution of new intellectual value"; instead, being "little or nothing more than the value that inheres in the original."[87] On that basis, the first factor weighed against a finding of fair use.

The *American Geophysical* opinion equates "transformative" as producing new "value," but then implicitly recognizes that "new" value can always be found. So some distinction is necessary between value that "inheres" in the work and "new" value. In an intellectual culture steeped in law and economics, we can understand a court trying to objectify its analysis in terms of "value." But beyond this conceptual dressing, it is clear that the distinction between inherent value and new value really *relies* on a judgment about transformation and not vice versa. New value depends on transformation and transformation depends on identifiable differences from what has come before.

Does transformation—and thus a judgment of originality or creativity—depend on anything more than *identifiable* difference? Does it depend on *significant* differences or *important* differences or *extensive* differences? Some quantum of difference—either quantitative or qualitative? One author broadly identified creativity as: "(1) originality—new or unusual elements must be involved, and (2) adaptation to reality—outcomes must be meaningful to others rather than random or idiosyncratic."[88] Here the popular notion of creativity is being defined in terms of originality, which is not at all surprising given our discussion. "New or unusual elements" adds little to this. What is more interesting is the "non-random" requirement.

There are a few ways we could understand this. One prospect is that if "non-randomness" is a requirement for something to be creative, it is because random organization of existing elements are not identifiably different from what occurs (has occurred or could occur) in the background world.[89] The child's arrangement of

---

85 *American Geophysical*, 60 F.3d at 920.

86 *Id.* at 923.

87 *Id.*

88 Ruth Richards et al., *Assessing Everyday Creativity: Characteristics of the Lifetime Creativity Scales and Validation with Three Large Samples*, 54 J. PERSONALITY & SOC. PSYCHOL. 476 (1988); *see generally*, FRANK X. BARRON, CREATIVE PERSON AND CREATIVE PROCESS (1969).

89 There is no question that the showing of some random choice defeats creativity in

blocks does not seem "creative" if it looks no more than random. Another prospect is that what is "non-random" is non-random because it is meaningful. Both these interpretations can be read from Aristotle's discussion of the concept of art. "Art" for Aristotle was that which owed its origin to a person and did *not* have its existence in the background world:

> [A]rt is identical with a state of capacity to make, involving a true course of reasoning. All art is considered with coming into being, i.e., with contriving and considering how something may come into being which is capable of either being or not being, and *whose origin is in the maker and not in the thing made; for art is concerned neither with things that are or come into being by necessity nor with things that do so in accordance with nature (since these have their origin in themselves).*[90]

In other words, creativity/originality requires a transformation not arising from the background order, whether that order is considered random or deterministic. But whatever the ontology, the candidate to whom we always turn to explain the transformation separate from the background world is the person—personal *expression*, personal *intention, reflections* of the person.

2. The Connection between Creativity and the Personal

It is said that Diego Rivera's affair with his wife's sister, Christina, was discovered because of the way he painted Christina's image into a mural at the Mexican National Palace—in an "ecstasy pose,"[91] while the extraordinary paintings of his wife, Frida Kahlo, reflected her own experiences—spinal injuries from a car accident,

---

the eyes of some judges. Toro v. R&R Prods., 787 F.2d 1208, 1213 (10th Cir. 1986). As the court said in *Mitel, Inc. v. Iqtel, Inc.*, 124 F.3d 1366 (10th Cir. 1997):

> Mitel's arbitrary selection of a combination of three or four numbers required de minimis creative effort, Mitel's own witness testified to the arbitrariness of the command codes . . . . [A] Mitel marketer who selected some of the "registers" and "descriptions" testified that he selected the numbers arbitrarily, without any attempt to place his mark on them. . . . We agree with the district court that the random and arbitrary use of numbers in the public domain does not evince enough originality to distinguish authorship.

Id. at 1373-74.

90 Aristotle, Nicomachean Ethics, Book VI, Ch. 4 (Terence Irwin trans., 1985) (emphasis added). Aristotle distinguished art as concerned with the "variable" versus scientific knowledge which is concerned with the "invariable" and the universal. But both art and science are "states by virtue of which the soul possesses truth by way of affirmation or denial." *Id.* at Book III. But Aristotle later has a more difficult time identifying the "truth" of art than of scientific knowledge. He says, "wisdom in the arts we ascribe to their most finished exponents, e.g. to Phidias as a sculptor . . . and here we mean nothing by wisdom except excellence in art." *Id.* at Book VII.

91 Joan F. DiGiovanni and Ronald R. Lee, *The Art and Suffering of Frida Kahlo, in* Creativity and Madness, *supra* note 64, at 81, 85.

a miscarriage, and struggles with Catholicism.[92] Edward Munch's first major work, *The Sick Child*, recalls the death of his sister Sophie from tuberculosis. It was a scene he would repaint six times in his life.[93] Julian Green acknowledges that several of his characters "inherited" his own fascination "for long, adventurous walks" through the streets of Paris[94] while Eudora Welty sees the emphasis in her stories on weather, schoolteachers, and parades all stemming from childhood memories.[95] Ibsen was even more direct in transforming personal experiences into literature. He was known to abruptly start inviting individuals to dinner parties, then just as unceremoniously drop them from his social list, once he had enough of their manners, speech, and attitudes to create a character.[96] Even animators draw upon their experiences with humans to draw memorable characters and creatures.[97] We could fill an encyclopedia with such examples of "art" based on the artist's experiences.[98] As Bono, lead singer of "U2" remarked, "musicians, painters, whatever, they have no choice but to describe where they live."[99]

From such examples, we know that there is a connection between creativity and personal experience. The connection could be one of practicality and prudence, the most successful creators staying close to what they know. Kahlo herself explained that many of her paintings were self-portraits "[b]ecause I am the subject I know best."[100] In giving advice to a young writer, Jane Austen suggested "[L]et [your characters] go to Ireland, but as you know nothing of the Manners there, you had better not go with them. You will be in danger of giving false representations . . . ."[101] But it

---

92 *Id.* at 88-95. *See also* HAYDEN HERRERA, FRIDA: A BIOGRAPHY OF FRIDA KAHLO (1983).

93 Lawrence Warick & Elaine Warick, *Edvard Munch: A Study of Loss, Grief and Creativity*, *in* CREATIVITY AND MADNESS, *supra* note 64, at 177-78 (discussing repeated paintings of his mother and paintings of three characters when he was involved with a married woman).

94 JULIAN GREEN, PARIS 129 (1991).

95 EUDORA WELTY, ONE WRITER'S BEGINNING 4-37 (1984). Miss Welty also describes how her college experience reading Yeats in the library stacks while it was snowing outside became a scene in a story she wrote, *id.* at 81, and how the poem *The Song of Wandering Aegus* runs through the stories in her collection, *The Golden Apples. Id.*

96 JOHNSON, *supra* note 36, at 102 (describing the character Kaja Folsi in *The Master Builder* as "an act of human larceny."). Johnson also details how Ibsen developed characters from his father, *id.* at 84, Emilie Bardach, an Austrian girl with whom he corresponded, *id.* at 101-02, and his friend Bjornson, *id.* at 95-96.

97 Betsy Sharkey, *The Heart and Soul of a New Animator*, N.Y. TIMES, May 19, 1996, at B1 (describing how animator Andreas Deja relies on his own personal experiences "to make a character real").

98 For an example of art discussing how art is derived from experience, *see* YASUNARI KAWABATA, BEAUTY AND SADNESS 31-33 (First Vintage Int'l ed., 1996) (One of the main characters, Oki, is a novelist whose greatest work was a fictionalized account of his true life affair with a 16 year old, Otoko.). *See generally*, Weisberg, *supra* note 79 at 233.

99 Jon Pareles, *Searching for a Sound to Bridge the Decades*, N.Y. TIMES, Feb. 9, 1997, at B34.

100 Warick & Warick, *supra* note 93, at 178.

101 Letter from Jane Austen to Anna (Aug. 10, 1814). Jane Austen also displayed her

appears to be something more than creativity conveniently married to personal memories. Many of us—perhaps most of us—move uncritically from a belief that intellectual works *reflect* personal *experiences* to a belief that intellectual works are personal *expressions.* This is worth exploring. It is important to consider how personal expression may be something different from repeating or reproducing personal experiences.

a. Weak and Strong Views of Creativity-as-Reflection

Faithfully reconstructing a situation from one's personal past—memory regurgitation—would be an act of personal reflection. It would reflect personal experiences as though the person was a passive, if imperfect, mirror of extra-person reality. But let's consider two distinct strands of the view that intellectual works reflect the personal experiences of those that produce them.

First, it is certainly easy to believe that an intellectual work is a *personal reflection* of the individual—a reflection of their infancy, their childhood, their recent experiences, or what they had for lunch today. As Welty writes, "any writer is in part all of his characters. How otherwise would they be known to him, occur to him, become what they are?"[102] Liam Hudson and Bernadine Jacot believe, for example, that the broad choice of what field academics and professionals enter is a reflection of parent/child relations in infancy.[103] At a more refined level, Hudson and Jacot believe that the research projects undertaken by many eminent social scientists reflect neither random choices nor strategic career opportunities nor influential teachers, but "the mind helping make the raw edges of personal experience smooth."[104] Their examples include both

---

lack of personal experience when writing to Clarke, the Prince Regent's librarian, about a novel featuring a clergyman much like the Reverend Clarke:

> I am quite honoured by your thinking me capable of drawing such a clergyman . . . . But I assure you I am not. The comic part I might be equal to, but not the good, the enthusiastic, the literary. Such a man's conversations must at times be on subjects of science and philosophy, of which I know nothing; or at least be occasionally abundant in quotations and allusions which a woman who, like me, knows only her mother tongue, and has read very little in that, would be totally without the power of giving.

Letter from Jane Austen to James Stanier Clarke (Dec. 11, 1815), *in* JANE AUSTEN'S LETTERS 442 (R.W. Chapman ed., 2d ed. 1979).

102 WELTY, *supra* note 95, at 101.

103 LIAN HUDSON & BERNADINE JACOT, THE WAY MEN THINK 81-82 (1991). Hudson and Jacot believe that the "science and technology, far from requiring an extension or distortion of imaginative processes that are properly personal, provide the 'male' imagination with venues within which it can be deployed in its most fluent and spontaneous form." They also believe that male artists turn their imagination away from this "natural home" by refocusing on the "female body from which it initially took flight." *Id.* at 172.

104 *Id.* at 15.

Sigmund Freud and Alfred Kinsey pushed to their respective works in sexuality—the former highly normative, the latter dispassionately descriptive—by their own homosexual experiences.[105]

In these last cases, personal experiences *reflect* in intellectual works because they are deep causes in the course of events that produce the works. But the "reflection" theory has a much more explicit side. The possibility is that personal reflection, personal expression, and creativity should all collapse on one another, i.e., that "creativity" is only a fancy covering for observation—the direct reproduction of things we have experienced.[106] The Athenian Greeks were the first to conclude that art was an act of reproduction or imitation,[107] a view that was reflected in Aristotle's reference to fine arts as "imitative arts" and "modes of imitation." In this spirit, Emily Dickinson described the eminent painter as "[o]ne who could repeat the Summer day" and "reproduce the Sun."[108] Dickens modeled a character in *Bleak House,* Harold Skimpole, so precisely after Leigh Hunt that Dickens noted to a friend that his fictional character was "[T]he most exact portrait that was ever painted in words . . . . It is an absolute reproduction of the real man."[109] Kundera tells us that "Hemingway's work is but a coded form of Hemingway's life."[110] Perhaps even sometimes an individual's personality is most manifest in a *res* as a negative inference: I recognize that the emotions or the vision in the intellectual work come from some human experience, but I know that it could *not* come from my experience.[111]

---

105 *Id.* at 2-12. *See also* Weisberg, *supra* note 79 at 233.

106 As in the New Englander who thought Thoreau got his ideas from conversations with one of Emerson's relatives: "He did set them [Bulkey Emerson's views] down, but he didn't give Bulkey the credit. . . . I think Thoreau was nothing more than an early new journalist. He was an excellent reporter, but he was nonobjective and he was very bad about his sources." JOHN MANSON MITCHELL, CEREMONIAL TIME 141 (1984). In considering "creativity" as an act of our experiences, we should not underestimate how much the process of building memories may itself be at least individual physiology, if not individual personality. Neurological researchers are only beginning to establish the exact chemistry involved in real-time selection and sorting data for short term memory and long-term memory. David Brown, *Substance Resembling a Marijuana Component Helps Brain Sort, Store Information,* WASH. POST, Aug. 21, 1997, at A15.

107 JOHN DEWEY, ART AS EXPERIENCE 7 (1932).

108 EMILY DICKINSON, Poem 307, *in* THE COMPLETE POEMS OF EMILY DICKINSON 145 (Thomas H. Johnson ed., 1960).

109 ANN BLAINEY, IMMORTAL BOY: A PORTRAIT OF LEIGH HUNT 189 (1985).

110 KUNDERA, *supra* note 15, at 336. In Eudora Welty's words, "[m]y imagination takes its strength and guides its direction from what I see and hear and learn and feel and remember of my living world." WELTY, *supra* note 95, at 76. Or as one reviewer wrote of Edmund White's novel *The Farewell Symphony,* "Edmund White is writing his autobiography the old-fashioned way: He's disguising it as fiction." David Streitfeld, *Who's Who,* WASH. POST, Oct. 12, 1997, at 15 (book review).

111 In describing the emotional power of a fictional singer, Peter Hoeg writes:

I still have [his] record. It's still an unforgettable recording. I've sometimes

Indeed, the label "impressionism" came from a very imitative, passive interpretation of what the impressionist painters were doing. Jules Antoine Castagnary characterized them as "impressionists in the sense that they render not the landscape, but the sensation produced by the landscape."[112] Other critics considered the impressionist as direct, immediate representation of *light*, rather than *objects* seen "indirectly" by the play of light they produce.[113]

But while the "weak" view of creativity-as-reflection is beyond cavil, the "strong" reflection view does not make sense. Indeed, in ancient Greece, there was already a sense that pure representation was not a complete explanation[114] and, as Dewey observed, "imitation" to the Greeks may not have meant a "literal copying of objects" as much as an effort to reproduce "the emotions and ideas that [were] associated with the chief institutions of social life." Thus Aristotle viewed music as the *most* imitative of all the arts, not because it captured "the twittering of birds [and] the gurgling of brooks [but because it] reproduces by means of sounds the affections, the emotional impressions, that are produced by martial, sad, triumphant, sexually orgasmic, objects and scenes."[115]

The initial explanation of impressionist painting gave way to a difficult effort among critics to reconcile the notions that the "impression" (and the resulting painting) was both "an 'accurate' view of nature and an individualized or an 'original' sensation belonging to a particular artist."[116] In the aesthetic theory of many late nineteenth century French thinkers, the "impression" of nature born on a tableau carried the unique temperament of the artist.[117] Posner terms this vision of artistic production "the older idea of creativity as imitation with enrichment."[118] Given the enormous

---

> thought that the body, our very physical existence, puts a limit of how much pain a mind can bear. And that [he], on that record, reaches that limit. So that afterward the rest of us can listen and make that journey without going there ourselves.

PETER HOEG, SMILLA'S SENSE OF SNOW 215 (1993).

[112] Jules Antoine Castagnary, *L'Exposition du Boulevard des Capucines: Les Impressionnistes*, LE SIÈCLE, 29 April 1874, *reprinted in* Hélène Aclhémar, *L'Exposition de 1874 chez Nadar*, CENTENAIRE DE L'IMPRESSIONNISME 265 (Paris 1974).

[113] *See* John Rewald, The History of Impressionism 330-38 (1961).

[114] As S.H. Butcher says, "[t]he idea of imitation is connected in our minds with a literal or servile copying; and the word as transmitted from Plato to Aristotle, was already tinged by some such disparaging associations." S.H. BUTCHER, ARISTOTLE'S THEORY OF POETRY AND FINE ART 121 (1951).

[115] DEWEY, *supra* note 107, at 252.

[116] RICHARD SHIFF, CEZANNE AND THE END OF IMPRESSIONISM 18 (1984).

[117] *Id.* at 27-38 (discussing views of Eugène Veron, Eugène Delacroix, and Émile Zola).

[118] RICHARD POSNER, LAW AND LITERATURE: A MISUNDERSTOOD RELATIONSHIP 348-49 (1988) (discussing T.S. Eliot).

break between classic painting on the one hand and Manet and the impressionists on the other, what may be surprising to us is that critics of the time did not put more emphasis on the "temperament" of the new wave of artists. What was the "enrichment" added by the artist? The next section addresses that hanging question with what we might call the "robust" view of creativity-as-expression.

b. Simple and Robust Views of Creativity-as-Expression

Today, as Barthes notes, "it is impossible to write without labeling oneself,"[119] but this was not always true. The connection between intellectual works and personal expression has not been universal across time. As Andre Malraux observed: "our civilization [has not] relinquished *expression.* That an artist wants to express something—even himself, especially at a time when individualism reigns supreme—goes without saying . . . [but f]or four or five thousand years works of art—whether expressions of the artist or of the sacred—were, like contemplation, anonymous."[120] We may never know for sure what gave rise to the current social convention that artists unanonymously *express* themselves. One possibility is that the Industrial Revolution freed (or removed) the artist from the role of *artisan,* a producer of objects used in daily life. John Dewey believed that this isolation of the artist from the regular flow of social services and the productive activities of daily life gave rise to the individualist impulse in modern times.[121]

However, once it becomes a social convention that creative works are expressions, this social norm could easily become self-sustaining. Creators may decide to express themselves because, regardless of what they really want to do, audiences will take their creations as personal statements. Some artists might conclude, on the strength of social convention, that committing themselves to "express" some message in their works is the way to be creative.

---

119 ROLAND BARTHES, WRITING DEGREE ZERO 1 (Annette Lavers and Colin Smith trans., 1968).

120 MALRAUX, *supra* note 66, at 221. Barthes describes pre-classical literature as a time when "[m]en are still engaged in the task of getting to know nature, and not yet in that of giving expression to man's existence." BARTHES, *supra* note 119, at 55.

121
> Because of changes in industrial conditions, the artist has been pushed to one side from the main streams of active interests. . . . He is less integrated than formerly in the normal flow of social services. A particular esthetic "individualism" results. Artists find it incumbent upon themselves to betake themselves to their work as an isolated means of "self-expression." In order not to cater to the trend of economic forces they often feel obliged to exaggerate their separateness to the point of eccentricity. Consequently artistic products take on to a still greater degree the air of something independent and esoteric.

DEWEY, *supra* note 107, at 9-10.

The notion that an artistic work makes some clear statement from the artist could be called the simple view of creativity-as-expression.

At the same time, many creators, such as Picasso, Borges, Stravinsky, and Graham Greene, strived against this view of creativity, often saying that they are not making personal expressions in their works.[122] The simple view of creativity-as-expression also seems ill fitting with the repeated observation that artists fail when they are too directly or self-consciously expressive. Octavio Paz, Parra Nicanor, and Milan Kundera have all criticized efforts of their colleagues to write poetry with political messages.[123] John Dewey—to whose theories we will return—put part of the case against direct expression this way: "indifference to response of the immediate audience is a necessary trait of all artists who have something new to say."[124]

But this places before us two questions. First, if many of our greatest artists do not believe that their works are personal expressions, what general proposition can we put forward that creativity involves expression? Second, whatever creativity is, we know that it relies on—uses as fuel—the personal experiences of the creator. Something *more* than those experiences must be produced for us to say that the individual has been *creative.* That is why creativity and originality are so intertwined. But what about the "more"—how and in what sense is it expression of the individual? Let us con-

---

122 *See* JORGE L. BORGES, Borges and I, in LABYRINTHS 246 (James E. Irvy trans., 1964), *quoted in* Hughes, *supra* note 1, at 366 n.241. Picasso repeatedly expressed the feeling to Andre Malraux that he was compelled to paint, indeed taken over by painting. He told Malraux that "[p]ainting makes me do just what it wants me to." MALRAUX, *supra* note 66, at 17, 188. "I can talk about Van Gogh maybe," he told Malraux, "But not about painting. [Painting] makes me do what it wants me to: to press on, to press on further and further, to press on even further than that . . . ." *Id.* at 118. Later in life, Malraux, himself an accomplished writer, agreed with Picasso's distance from his work: "I was of the same mind as Picasso when it came to his exhibitions: all that's about a guy who has the same name as mine." *Id.* at 145. More radically, Igor Stravinsky believed that "music [wa]s . . . powerless to *express* anything at all, whether a feeling, an attitude of mind, a psychological mood." IGOR STRAVINKSY, AN AUTOBIOGRAPHY 83, 256, 274-76 (1936). Even Che Guevara, editing the diaries of a trip he took around South America in his mid-twenties, wrote, "[t]he person who wrote these notes died the day he stepped back on Argentine soil. The person who is reorganizing them and polishing them, me, is no longer me, at least I'm not the me I was." ERNESTO CHE GUEVARA, THE MOTORCYCLE DIARIES 12 (Ann Wright trans., 1995). Critical acclaim for Beck's song *Loser* was similarly misguided: "[e]veryone assumed I was the song," Beck told one reporter, "It was a bad case of mistaken identity." Robert Hilburn, *The Freewheelin' Beck*, L.A. TIMES, Feb. 26, 1997, at F1.

123 Octavio Paz commented on his inability to write poetry about too political, too propagandistic subjects. *See* SELDEN RODMAN, TONGUES OF FALLEN ANGELS 158 (1974). Parra Nicanor, in discussing Pablo Neruda, also commented on the "metaphysical impossibility" of writing a "political poem." *Id.* at 83.

124 DEWEY, *supra* note 107, at 104. Dewey also attacked Samuel Johnson's "[p]hilistine's sturdy preference for reproduction of the familiar" with true art. *Id.* at 79.

sider some possible refinements of our notion of creativity that may provide some insight into these questions.

The non-mechanical and non-necessary. One of Robert Nozick's suggestions is that "for a product to be creative it must not only differ from what came before but also stand in no specific obvious relationship to its predecessors."[125] Professor Nozick initially proposes that when a new object is derivable from predecessors by "mechanical application of a clear rule" it stands in a kind of "specific obvious relationship" to that predecessor and it is not creative. This harkens back to Aristotle's observation that the artistic is not determined by nature. Things at T_2 which owe their origin to "necessity" or to "nature," are things which arise from mechanical application of rules to the background situation at T_1. If you know there are so many seeds in a particular type of soil, with particular amounts of water, and sun at T_1, then you can be pretty certain that at T_2 you will have plants which are the "mechanical" result of biological rules. If you are looking through a kaleidoscope at T_1, you know how a kaleidoscope works, and you turn the kaleidoscope, then the new pattern at T_2 is the result of the mechanical, albeit elaborate, application of rules about how kaleidoscopes work and the initial pattern of glass in your kaleidoscope.

This advances us some.[126] The discussion of creativity and originality had concluded that both require a transformative process so something identifiably new is produced—something that did not exist before. To this we can add Nozick's suggestion that no matter how transformed the new result is—no matter how many turns of the kaleidoscope—it will not be creative unless it does *not* come from the application of mechanical rules.

In the discussion of creativity and originality, we also held out the possibility that the new result needed to be non-random in order to be "original." I suggested that a random result would be a result of the background situation—the sand in the sandbox having whatever shape the winds and local fauna last gave it. A non-random result would be a result apparently *not* from the background situation—and this again would fit with Aristotle identifying "nature" or "necessity" as places that art does not come from.

---

125 NOZICK, *supra* note 80, at 36.

126 Many psychological descriptive accounts of creativity could still reduce creativity to a "mechanical" activity—at least for a sufficiently large mind. For example, if creativity is the combination of "remotely associated" ideas—a view put forward by Keith Simonton—then one only needs to mechanically combine more and more remote ideas to get something creative; if it involves "lateral thinking"—the view of Edward deBono—then one needs only keep recombining patterns laterally to get something creative. *See* WEISBERG, *supra* note 79, at 56-67.

The point is that the background situation can be treated as deterministic or random (or with elements of both—as with the kaleidoscope example). Something will be considered "creative" only when it appears to come from neither a purely mechanical process, nor a purely random one. We identify this process that navigates between determinism and randomness—this process that produces the "non-mechanical new"—as something that goes on inside the individual person.[127] But this still may not provide any strong evidence that the process is "expressive" of those individual persons.

Self-restoration. Another possibility is that creativity is, as Graham Greene said, "a form of therapy."[128] This could explain why so many artists describe their work as critical to their psychological well-being—"a physical and spiritual necessity," as Sam Francis said.[129] Nozick has also recognized that:

> The creative work and product come to stands, sometimes unconsciously, for herself or for a missing piece or part, or for a defective one, or for part of a better self. The work is a surrogate for the creator, analog of her, a little voodoo doll to tinker with and transform and remake in something analogous to the way she herself, or a part, needs to be transformed, remade, or healed. . . . Important and needed work on the self is modeled in the process of artistic creation and symbolized there.[130]

But viewing creativity as a therapeutic process, a surrogate reworking of part of the self, does not mean that the work is an "expression" in the sense of an act of communication. Perhaps we could solve this problem by saying that the process of producing intellectual works should be likened to therapy in which one *expresses* problems to a therapist. An artist's work may be her statement to an unknown audience and, like the confessional, there may be some candor-inducing comfort in at least the veneer of audience anonymity. What is said may be frank or opaque, just as one may

---

127 For an example of how a creator can fail to navigate these two extremes, see *Mitel, Inc. v. Iqtel, Inc.*, 124 F.3d 1366 (10th Cir. 1997), in which, on the one hand the plaintiff's command codes were found to be unprotected because they were the result of "random" and "arbitrary" number selection, *id.* at 1373-74, while, on the other hand, the plaintiff's command "values" were found to be "unprotectable . . . because they were dictated by external functionality and compatibility requirements . . . ." *Id.* at 1376.

128 "Art is a form of therapy. Sometimes I wonder how all those who do not write, compose, or paint can escape the madness, the melancholia, the panic-fear inherent in the human situation." CREATIVITY AND MADNESS, supra note 64, at 137 (quoting Graham Greene).

129 In addition to describing his painting as "a physical and spiritual necessity" Francis said "[w]hen I'm disturbed, upset in my life, it all comes up to the surface boiling." Sam Francis Exhibition, Jeu de Paume Museum, Paris (Jan. 1996).

130 NOZICK, supra note 80, at 39.

tell a therapist things directly or obliquely, candidly or metaphorically.

Creativity as generalization. Another aspect of creativity that finds favor in some descriptive accounts is the idea that creativity involves generalization from personal experiences, i.e., creativity as the successful quest for universal truths. Edmund Wilson lavished praise on Edna St. Vincent Millay in just these terms:

> In giving supreme expression to profoundly personal experiences, she was able to identify herself with more general human experiences and stand forth as a spokesman for the human spirit, announcing its predicaments, its vicissitudes, but as a master of human expression, by the splendour of expression itself, putting herself beyond common embarrassments, common oppressions, and panics.[131]

In less majestic terms Garrison Keillor has noted that "experience" only becomes literature when it moves beyond what actually happened to the author, "when it no longer matters to the reader whether the story is true or not."[132]

But describing creativity this way seems to exacerbate our search for personal expression in creativity. The uncovering of universal themes in personal experiences sounds a bit like a spirit—alien, foreign, different—descending on the person: the Muse seizing them and their experiences for the purpose of a universal statement, not a personal statement. Producers of intellectual property—both artists and inventors—often speak this way. However, if their comments were accurate descriptions of these cases, it is possible that the only personality justification to link the intellectual work to the individual would be, what I will call below, a "sourcehood" interest. The more *deux ex machina* arrival of some universal insight, the less that process of intellectual creation seems to be a form of personal expression.

Synthesis of the Old and the New. Each of these options—self-restoration, generalization, and non-mechanical newness—offers insights on creativity, but does not much advance our understanding of how the creative process could be fundamentally an expressive process. We are left with only a few options. One option is to

---

131 Edmund Wilson, The Portable Edmund Wilson 72 (1983).

132 Garrison Keillor, *The Poetry Judge*, Atlantic Monthly, Feb. 1996, at 93. In comparing Shakespeare's characters to those of the French dramatist Pierre Corneille, one author commented that "Shakespeare's Romans are Romans, while Corneille's characters are Normans," noting that "Corneille was unable to detach his own personality from the characters he created. He endowed them with his own attitudes. Shakespeare had the genius of dissociating the characters he was describing from his own personality." Leon R. Yankwich, *Originality in the Law of Intellectual Property*, 11 F.R.D. 457, 473 (1952).

admit that we are using "personal expression" as a bridge concept between an act of purely reflecting personal experiences and the production of the non-mechanical new. To the extent that an object appears to be anything more than a direct reflection of personal history, we label the "more" as personal expression and, therefore, creativity.

This still leaves creativity as an unknown, unknowable phenomena. It is a black box—or more properly, a set of black boxes, one inside each of us. Ignorant of their provenance and with no knowledge of their content, we tend to assume that all these black boxes have the same innards. This assumption is strengthened by the common vocabulary used by creators to speak about the process; a songwriter says her experiences "go through her imaginary brain" and "come out in an imaginary place";[133] a painter says his works come from a "state of hallucination"; and a fiction writer attributes her work to "all sorts of vision, dream, illusion, hallucination, obsession, and memory."[134] But the similarity of these descriptions may speak more to the poverty of our language than the actual sameness of the phenomena. When we say some creation is a "personal expression," what we mean is that we have located this sort of unknown phenomenon in one particular person—their little black box. "Expression," then, is just the *externalization* of something from the black box: the processes going on in a black hole *expressed* in effects on the surrounding space and time.

One of the century's most influential and rich accounts of the artistic process was John Dewey's William James lectures subsequently published as *Art as Experience*.[135] Although Dewey was dealing mainly with artistic production, he believed that much about artistic and inventive production was the same. Dewey's lectures explore the various ways in which creativity is the interaction of old personal experiences and the new environment. Some of his com-

---

[133] [My characters] are made from the clay of people I know, but they go through my imaginary brain, they come out in an imaginary place. I never write about people really that I know. I can't do it. I can't write about myself. When I try to write about myself and something that really happened, I'm a really poor writer. I write like a twelve year old's diary. So I make it into a pretend palace where I can work it out.

Videotape: Conversation on Creativity at Santa Monica College (Rickie Lee Jones 1995) (on file with the Public Relations Office, Santa Monica College).

[134] "[All] sorts of vision, dream, illusion, hallucination, obsession, and that most wonderful interior vision which is memory, have all gone to make up my stories . . . ." WELTY, *supra* note 95, at 89.

[135] DEWEY, *supra* note 107.

ments could be taken as sympathetic of the self-restorative[136] or generalization views of creativity.[137] Others of his comments seem to endorse the view that creativity is a nexus of old and new experiences if only because, as Hudson and Jacot argue, our old experiences shape our personal interests which control our creative efforts:

> Because interest is the dynamic force in the selection and assemblage of materials, products of minds are marked by individuality, just as products of mechanism are marked by uniformity. No amount of technical skill and craftsmanship can take the place of vital interest; "inspiration" without it is fleeting and futile. A trivial and badly ordered mind accomplishes things like unto itself in art as elsewhere, because it lacks the push and the centralizing energy of interest.[138]

Thus, each of our respective creative agendas bears, through our interests, the imprint of our respective personal experiences. This can apply to both arts and sciences, but Dewey has a stronger view of creativity as synthesis in which both perception and imagination are the synthesis of old experiences stored in memory and new circumstances being experienced by the individual:

> [an] experience becomes conscious, a matter of perception, only when meanings enter it that are derived from prior experiences. Imagination is the only gateway through which these meanings can find their way into a present interaction; or rather . . . the conscious adjustment of the new and the old *is* imagination.[139]

Note that Dewey's view seems to be that consciousness itself, not just imagination, requires this synthesis: "experience is rendered conscious by means of that fusion of old meanings and new situations that transfigures both (a transformation that defines imagination)," he writes.[140] What makes for consciousness also seems to make for expression:

---

136 For example:

> From the first manifestation by a child of an impulse to draw up to the creations of a Rembrandt, the self is created in the creation of objects, a creation that demands active adaptation to external materials, including a modification of the self so as to utilize and thereby overcome external necessities by incorporating them in an individual vision and expression.

Id. at 282.

137 "The act is expressive only as there is in it a union of something stored from past experiences, *something therefore generalized*, with present conditions." *Id.* at 71.

138 *Id.* at 266.

139 *Id.* at 272.

140 *Id.* at 275.

> The junction of the new and the old is not a mere composition of forces, but is a recreation in which the present impulsion gets form and solidity while the old, the "stored," material is literally revived, given new life and soul through having to meet the new situation. It is this double change that converts an activity into an act of expression. Things in the environment that would otherwise be mere smooth channels or else blind obstructions become means, media. At the same time, things retained from the past experience that would grow stale from routine or inert from lack of use, become coefficients in new adventures and put on a rainment of fresh meaning. Here are all the elements needed to define expression.[141]

Perhaps because he identifies creativity with consciousness, Dewey is able to dismiss the "eureka" theory—some ideas *seem* to hit us like lightning bolts only because the synthesis occurs below the "threshold of consciousness."[142] Dewey, it seems, would not need the sourcehood justification discussed below. His view is that both the subjects our minds engage and what we do with those subjects are the results of personal experience being reworked in the present tense. Because each of us is a unique experiential time line, whatever we produce constitutes personal expression.

This allows us to return to an interesting question about the relationship between creativity and the "non-mechanical." Robert Nozick has suggested that even if our neuro-scientists came to have a very mechanical, biochemical explanation of how a Beethoven or a Chopin generated musical ideas, we still might view it as a "creative" process: "[f]or when it is a person's brain that generates ideas, however 'mechanical' the explanation of how it does so turns out to be, we see those ideas as expressive and revelatory of something about the person."[143] Let us merge this thought with Dewey's view and the kaleidoscope metaphor used above. As kaleidoscopes share the same kind, color, and roughly the same size and shape of glass bits, we share many of the same kind and roughly the same details of human experiences. Each of us is a unique order of experiences and each new creation, like the results of a turn of the kaleidoscope, might somehow be predictable

---

141 *Id.* at 60-61.

142 Suddenness of emergence belongs to appearance of material above the threshold of consciousness, not to its generation. Could we trace any such manifestation to its roots and follow it through its history, we should find at the beginning an emotion comparatively gross and undefined. We should find that it assumed definite shape only as it worked itself through a series of changes in imagined material.

Id. at 75.

143 Nozick, *supra* note 80, at 38.

and mechanical while staying beautiful and unique.[144]

C. *The Explanatory Power of the Author Construct Versus the Notion of Creativity*

The deconstructionist might say that the alloy of personal expression into creativity only reinforces the power of the "romantic author." But instead of seeing personal expression as manifesting the "romantic author," it is better to see the melding of personal expression into "creativity" as an egalitarian society's effort to move the "romantic author" off center stage.

Intellectual property protection in the western countries has now been extended widely, to what some might view as "the meanest levels of creative activity,"[145] and others as the subtlest forms of creative activity consistent with a workable system of copyright enforcement. It has been pointed out that this movement to a lower common denominator of creativity served the needs of capitalists investing in idea industries.[146] But it is also true that extending legal protection to the meanest levels of creative activity has been in keeping with the rise of liberalism and a society of autonomous, equal citizens. However much we love fingerpainting, we know that not all of our children will grow up to be artistic geniuses. A highly stratified society might accept that certain rights would pertain only to "romantic geniuses," a kind of "idea-ed gentry." But that is not our society. The author of a bland script about a love triangle has just as much right that it not be stolen by a major studio as does the author of a radically innovative who-done-it. That our democratic and egalitarian traditions have affected our conception of intellectual progress was not lost on Luigi Barzini, one of the twentieth century's most lucid observers. As Barzini wrote,

---

144 Despite that beauty, would it still be creative and personally expressive, if we could predict the results of that kaleidoscope turn? Nozick seems to believe so:

> Although we—on the outside—may have some mechanical explanation for how the creator generates her ideas, is it still "expression" if the generation of ideas feels—on the inside—like a mechanical process. Is it possible that Beethoven will feel the music is self-expressive or self-relevatory only if it does not feel mechanical? A mechanical process would be, after all, antithetical to a transformative process, a process of growth."

Id.

145 Jaszi, *Theory of Copyright*, *supra* note 29, at 483. Professor Peter Jaszi is one of those authors who both sees the "author" construct as powerful, while recognizing its modern dilution.

146 The deconstructionists interested in expurgating the "author" from the case law do not mention the large number of cases where the "author" already seems absent, but copyright is acknowledged. *See, e.g.*, Ansehl v. Puritan Pharm. Co., 61 F.2d 131 (8th Cir. 1932) (holding arrangement and elements in advertisement of cosmetics are to be protected without attributing advertisement to one author).

> Time, Americans thought . . . was a gentleman, did not cheat, and would eventually take care of everything; somewhere surely there always is a still unknown young man (or a team of them) making revolutionary inventions, discovering new miracle drugs, formulating a new scientific law, devising a machine, working out the answers. He did not always have to be a genius, like Leonardo da Vinci. More often he was just "one of us."
>
> Incidentally, this seems to be another constant trait. For some reason, Americans like to think that Great Men are like everybody else . . . . Deep emotions or high thoughts often are expressed in the form of weak jokes. The press always reports these quotations eagerly, to confirm the myth that "all men are more or less the same" and that practically anybody could write the Faulkner opus, discover the structure of DNA, or write a great symphony, if only he had the proper equipment and took the time.[147]

The sentiment Barzini observed about our culture has been picked up in our legal system. Copyright and patent law have large chunks of case law showing the rejection of "genius" as the foundation for intellectual property protection. In the realm of copyright, the case law on advertising has emphasized, over and over, that "creative genius"[148] is not necessary for copyright protection and that expressive elements are protectable even if they are "characterized as an advertising gimmick or 'Madison Avenue' kitsch."[149] In patent law there has been—as Barzini would have guessed—the express repudiation of the "spark of genius" requirement. All of this should make us doubtful of the "author" construct.

Yet to the deconstructionist, the individual "romantic author" is both the explanation for and the problem with recent decisions by American courts. Aoki argues, for example, that by applying a creativity test which denied copyright protection to the producers of the white pages, the *Feist* Court, "discounted the collaborative and collective nature of fact-gathering reflected in the assembly and composition of a white pages directory in favor of a particular vision of clearly individuated authorship and originality."[150] Jaszi

---

147 Luigi Barzini, Memories of Mistresses: Reflections from a Life 136-37 (1986) (an essay on Americans called *Loners in the World*).

148 Jacobs v. Robitaille, 406 F. Supp. 1145, 1149 (D.N.H. 1976).

149 Chuck Blore & Don Richman, Inc. v. 20/20 Adver., Inc., 674 F. Supp. 671, 677 n.5 (D. Minn. 1987).

150 Aoki, *Adrift, supra* note 29, at 812. Aoki also sees the *Feist* result implicitly reasoning that "because only clearly individuated authors can possess sufficient creative originality to justify copyright protection, the absence of such an authorial subject foreclosed copyright protection for the white pages." *Id.*

similarly sees the Second Circuit's *Rogers v. Koons*[151] decision as embodying copyright's continued preference for the single, creative individual author over alternative, collaborative efforts to produce art. In *Rogers*, photographer Art Rogers brought suit against sculptor Jeff Koons for literal copying of one of Koons' postcards, *Puppies*, into a three dimensional sculpture, *String of Puppies*. Koons' artistic approach was to produce sculptural collages in which he would juxtapose existing cultural images against one another. Having chosen the images, arrangement, and materials, Koons would employ artisans in workshops to do the actual fabrication and crafting of the three dimensional sculpture. In *Rogers*, the Second Circuit found that the Koons' artwork infringed Rogers' pre-existing copyright in his photographs. Jaszi views the *Rogers* case as showing the court's preference for the solo artist versus the collaborative fabrication of art by artisans in a workshop.[152]

These interpretations of *Feist* and *Rogers* unnecessarily conflate the notions of "creativity" and "individuated authorship." In *Feist*, two *organizations* (collaborative efforts at production) squared off against each another with no creativity to be seen. The Court said the plaintiff lost because there was no creativity in its work. Not only did the case lack a creative "individuated author," but it also lacked a creative collaborative group. *Feist's* emphasis on creativity means that the 150 Harvard students who set out each summer to write *Let's Go: Europe* know that their compendium of facts will have a degree of copyright protection that the *Feist* phone books do not.[153]

The *Rogers* case is more interesting because the individual artist—photographer Rogers—does triumph over the sculpture resulting from collaborative work under artist Koons' direction. But it is just as easy to see the *Rogers* court as being *solicitous* of collaborative efforts instead of being biased towards the individual artist. Part of Jeff Koons' negative ethos with the court may have been his failure to give artistic credit to the artisans who fabricated his sculptures. The court's dissatisfaction with Koons' hands-off attitude to-

---

151 960 F.2d 301 (2d Cir. 1992).

152 Jaszi, *Author Effect, supra* note 29, at 308.

153 Jaszi may point out, in contrast to *Feist*, the Second Circuit's subsequent decision in *Key Publications v. Chinatown Today Publishing Enterprises*, 945 F.2d 509 (2d Cir. 1991), in which copyright was recognized for a Chinese-American Yellow Pages for New York City when the Court attributed the yellow pages to Key's president, Lynn Wang, and repeatedly referred to her personal role in assembling the yellow pages. *Id.* at 513-14. But again *Feist* and *Key* can also be distinguished on the different amounts of creativity discussed by the respective opinions. And the *Key* court, while acknowledging copyright, was not so solicitous of Ms. Wang, the single author, since there was a finding that the defendant's phone book had not infringed the creative elements of Ms. Wang's phone book.

ward "his" art[154] may have been dissatisfaction with Koons' failure to give artistic credit to the collaborative group.[155]

Indeed, the evidence mustered by the deconstructionists to show the importance of "author-reasoning" can just as well be interpreted as courts searching for means to make workable a copyright system that has stretched the "creativity" tent far beyond the "romantic author." A good example of this is the separate copyrightability requirement for joint authors. In the 1991 *Childress v. Taylor*[156] case, the Second Circuit squarely confronted this problem. One issue in the case was whether, as some courts and the Register of Copyright had reasoned, each author in a joint work would have to make a *separately* copyrightable *contribution* to the work. What was refreshing about Judge Newman's opinion is that it correctly recognized that this requirement makes no sense, either as an element of the instrumental purpose of the Copyright Clause or the meaning of "author."[157] Nonetheless, Judge Newman's opinion embraced the separate copyrightability requirement on the policy grounds that it may "serve to prevent some spurious claims by those who might otherwise try to share the fruits of a sole author."[158] While one may disagree with this outcome, it is understandable as the result of a court explicitly trying to protect the legitimate claims of both sole authors and co-authors.[159]

The same issue—practical enforcement considerations—has arisen in cases considering when an arrangement of a song is a separate "derivative" work from the underlying song. While these courts have not stated the issues with the candor of the *Childress* panel, the reasoning of these derivative song cases is so unusual—and sounds so much more like patent than copyright doctrine—that it is apparent some special considerations must be at work.

In the 1994 case *Woods v. Bourne Co.*,[160] a New York district

---

154 "[Koons] gave the artisans one of Rogers' notecards and told them to copy it." *Rogers*, 960 F.2d at 305.

155 Another irony resulting from interpreting *Rogers* as a case about the classic artist as opposed to a new form of artistic endeavor is that Rogers was a photographer, one of the last kinds of artist to be accepted by the courts (and the artistic community) as "art" while Koons was a sculptor or, at least, a "producer" of sculptures—one of the classic art forms.

156 945 F.2d 500 (2d Cir. 1991).

157
> If the focus is solely on the objective of copyright law to encourage the production of creative works, it is difficult to see why the contributions of all joint authors need be copyrightable . . . . The "author" of an uncopyrightable idea is nonetheless its author even though, for entirely valid reasons, the law denies him a copyright . . . .

Id. at 506.

158 *Id.* at 507.

159 *Id.* at 504.

160 841 F. Supp. 118 (S.D.N.Y. 1994), *rev'd in part*, 60 F.3d 978 (2d Cir. 1995).

court faced a copyright renewal situation bringing claims of derivative works to a head. In *Woods*, the heirs of the composer of *When the Red, Red Robin Comes Bob-Bob-Bobbin Along* were found to have the copyright to the song during its renewal period. But the song's original publisher, Bourne, contended that *every* version of the song it had published was a "derivative work" for which Bourne still had the copyright. Bourne reasoned that the composer had given Bourne only a "lead sheet" with nothing more than the melodic line, so that all the "musical arrangements" Bourne had published were separately copyrighted derivative works. Bourne relied on 17 U.S.C. §101 which states that derivative works include musical arrangements.

The court found it incredible that Bourne claimed that the first published piano and voice version was a "derivative work," if only because the composer "played the song for [the publisher] when he brought it into the firm."[161] But even assuming the publisher's people added something to the melodic line, the court held that this was not enough: "[i]n order to qualify as a musically 'derivative work,' there must be present more than mere cocktail pianist variations of the piece that are standard fare in the music trade by any competent musician."[162] The *Woods* court relied on earlier cases similarly finding that a derivative work could not arise from "the addition of certain inconsequential melodic and harmonic embellishments such as are frequently improvised by any competent musician,"[163] and that: "[i]n music it may be said that anything which a fairly good musician can make, the same old tune being preserved, could not be the subject of copyright."[164] This language would be disconcerting to almost any other class of beneficiaries of copyright law. If we substituted "screenwriter" or "painter" in place of "musician," we would have opinions denying copyrights to works that are the "standard fare in the trade by any competent screenwriter," or "anything a fairly good painter c[ould] make." These phrases sound much more like the patent law standard for novelty than the post-*Bleistein* standard for copyright protection.[165]

---

161 *Id.* at 121.

162 *Id.*

163 McIntyre v. Double-A Music Corp., 166 F. Supp. 681 (D. Cal. 1958).

164 Cooper v. James, M.D., 213 F. 871, 872 (N.D. Ga. 1914).

165 In fact, the full quotation from the *Cooper v. James* case—a pre-*Bleistein* case—directly connected patents and copyrights in music: "[i]n patents, we say that any improvement which a good mechanic could make is not the subject of a patent, so in music it may be said that anything which a fairly good musician can make, the same old tune being preserved, could not be the subject of a copyright." *Id.* at 872. But as the *Alfred Bell* court noted, "[A] multitude of books rest safely under copyright which show only ordinary skill

A deconstructionist who read these cases might see them as an ugly resurgence of the "romantic author" such that "artists who work from personal experience, in proximity to the natural raw materials of the creative process, are given a legal preference over those who merely rework prior art."[166] But the opposite is just as likely: the fact that this patentesque doctrine has existed for most of the century, when the concept of author was steadily becoming more egalitarian, suggests that the force giving discipline to the doctrine is not the "romantic author" at all.

Even if the "author" does not explain these cases, it still might explain the case law better than creativity. What is the difference between these two interpretations—one seeing the courts driven by the "author," and one seeing the courts moved by "creativity"? That may turn, in part, on our unspoken accounts of what goes on in a judge's mind. The deconstructionists' image might be a judge writing a copyright opinion while above his head there is a balloon-cloud with Shakespeare scrivening with a quill pen. Perhaps there is no such vivid image for the judge moved by "creativity." Yet a sentiment may serve instead. The judge whose opinions are driven by creativity calls up her own experiences. Indeed, the bench is filled with people, who in their younger days (if not now) dabbled in writing poetry, essays, and short stories, did some high school or college acting, or worked as a research assistant to a biology, philosophy, or law professor. Perhaps the judge mulling about creativity conjures up and relies upon feelings of that *process.*

Is this feeling of *process* any different than the judge seeing himself as an *author*? I believe it is. First, the decision-makers' creative experiences may come from collaborative efforts, particularly those in which he was a junior partner (research assistant, assistant editor of a student publication, acting, or lighting director for a play). This means that the judge's understanding of the creative process need not be encased in the "prerogatives of the autonomous individual"[167] which the deconstructionists perceive to be at the heart of the "author" construct. Second, most of us who dabbled in high school poetry and college drama do not have any preconceptions of our own "genius" in these fields. Let us assume the same is true with judges: if they are influenced by their own understanding of the creative process, it need not be encased in

and diligence in their preparation . . . ." Alfred Bell & Co. v. Catalda Fine Arts, Inc., 191 F.2d 99, 103 (2d Cir. 1951) (quoting Henderson v. Tompkins, C.C., 60 F. 758, 764 (1st Cir. 1894)).

166 Jaszi, *Theory of Copyright, supra* note 29, at 495.

167 *Id.* at 502.

the vision of "genius" which again seems central to the deconstructionists' author construct.

In the end, the truth is probably some amalgam of these visions. In an excellent discussion, Boyle sees the author construct as sharing the stage with "originality": "[t]ogether, the *figure* of the romantic author, the *theme* of originality, and the *conceptual distinction* between idea and expression seem to offer one of the most convincing mediations of the tensions described earlier [in access to forms of information]."[168] Similarly, Professor Jessica Litman has written about the nurturing of "authorship" and the "enterprise of authorship" instead of reifying a process into the "author."[169] Focusing on the activity of "authoring" and insisting that it be viewed as a process of "translation and recombination"[170] moves the discourse about the "author" closer to a discourse about creativity. In the end, the reified figure of the "romantic author" is not much needed. If we had to choose between them, we would be better off—for both a descriptive account of the case law and a normative prescription for the legal system—to view courts as relying on a notion of the process of creativity.

D. *The Moral Shop Right*

One of the rare, but disconcerting aspects of our intellectual property law is that occasionally a creator can suffer some legal consequences because her recent creation is found to impinge upon the propertied region of one of her prior creations. These legal consequences could be either the inability to assert some intellectual property right[171] or, more commonly, having her own freedom limited by property rights now held by someone else.

Perhaps the most important example of this problem is the 1914 case of *Gross, et al. v. Seligman,*[172] in which the Second Circuit found that a photographer's new work had infringed a prior photograph he had taken. Seligman had taken a photograph of a young woman which he entitled *Grace of Youth.* He transferred his rights in that image to another party. Then, two years later, Selig-

---

168 Boyle, *supra* note 29, at 1510.

169 Litman, *supra* note 29, at 969, 991.

170 *Id.* at 966.

171 In the realm of patent, it is possible that a creator could suffer adverse consequences while holding all rights to both the prior and more recent creation. Imagine that Dr. Dale sues Hoth Corporation for infringing his 1992 patent; Hoth Corporation defends on the grounds that Dale's 1992 patent is preempted by a 1988 patent that Dr. Dale also holds. The 1992 patent may be found invalid for that reason. Although Dr. Dale may succeed in asserting the 1988 patent against Hoth Corporation, it may turn out that only claims in the 1992 patent—now invalid—could be asserted against Hoth.

172 212 F.930 (2d Cir. 1914).

man employed the same model and produced a new photograph. He was sued by the holder of the copyright on the *Grace of Youth* photograph. The court found that "the many close identities of pose, light, and shade, etc. indicate very strongly that the first picture was used to produce the second."[173] In finding infringement, the *Gross* court concluded: "[t]he one thing, viz., the exercise of artistic talent, which made the first photographic picture a subject of copyright, has been used not to produce another picture, but to duplicate the original."[174]

This choice of language is interesting. Note that the court did not say that there was *no* exercise of artistic talent, but that artistic talent had been exercised for the purpose of copying. This is the sort of comment one might apply to a talented forger copying a Manet: artistic talent given over to being a human Xerox machine. The *artist*, a person who creates forms, had lowered himself to an *artisan*, a person who copies forms.[175]

While the *Seligman* case remains an oddity, the situation could arise again. In the *Koons* cases (which we have considered and will consider again) Second Circuit courts held that artist Jeff Koons could not use copyrighted images in his sculptures. In one of those cases, *United Features Syndicate, Inc. v. Koons*,[176] the copyright in the "Odie" character from the *Garfield* cartoon was owned by United Features Syndicate ("UFS"). In finding that Koons infringed the "Odie" image, the court inadvertently pointed to a *Seligman*-like problem:

> [T]he Court notes that the existence of even three of these sculptures would prejudice UFS's ability to exploit this potential market. For example, the creator of the "Garfield" comic strip, James Davis, is an accomplished artist and may, at some point, decide to create artistic sculptures of characters for commercial sale. . . . Moreover to the extent that UFS would sell the rights to produce such sculptures to another artist, the market for such sculptures has been reduced by the unauthorized use of the "Odie" character.[177]

Reading this passage, one must ask, what if James Davis wanted to do sculptures of the *Garfield* characters and UFS objected (perhaps, because it had already sold the right to do such sculptures to

---

173 *Id.* at 931.

174 *Id.*

175 *See, e.g.*, MALRAUX, *supra* note 66, at 193 (asking whether particular pieces of African art are done by artists—intentionally changing the form—or artisans, copying the forms).

176 817 F. Supp. 370 (S.D.N.Y. 1993).

177 *Id.* at 382.

"another artist")? What if, later in life, Davis becomes cynical of the world and he can find no better way to express "the cynical and empty nature of society" than by using his own characters in devastating sculptures? If UFS tried to stop him, whose side would the law take?

The *Gross* opinion is probably wrong on a factual analysis: it appears that Seligman's new photograph was visibly different from *Grace of Youth.* The Court recognized differences in the backgrounds of the photographs, the props, and the emotions visible on the model's face[178]—elements of the composition clearly under Seligman's control.[179]

But the *Gross* decision is more troubling for its analytic framework. If Seligman had been copying a Manet, perhaps the *Gross* analysis would be right. In copying a Manet, Seligman would have been engaging in an activity apparently devoid of his own personality; he would be an "artisan" instead of an artist. But that is the critical difference. Even if Seligman's second photograph were absolutely indistinguishable from his prior *Grace of Youth,* he could have been trying to *recapture* and *reconvey* his own personal expression; just as James Davis might want to re-express himself through his own idiom—the *Garfield* characters.

Consider some variations on this and the *Gross* situation. Imagine that Seligman had sold the rights to *Grace of Youth,* but then had decided to do a coffee table book of photographs of young women from different walks of life in the same graceful pose. Would these new photographs infringe the *Grace of Youth* copyright? This problem about a collection of photos leads us to the question of an artist's personal "style" and a curious, but little noted problem in the relationship of creativity, originality, and personal expression. There is no question that we place great value on creators having individual "styles," what is, for an author, a "marked writing characteristically the expression of a person's 'mind' or 'psyche.'" Faulkner and Hemingway wrote in such distinctive styles that there are now contests to mimic them. For visual

---

178 From some reports, it appears that the two photographs were not that similar. The *Grace of Youth* was a model in the nude. Two years later, the same model was used for *Cherry Ripe,* probably "in the identical pose" except that "the model wore a smile and held a cherry stem between her teeth . . . while in the first she was posed with her face in repose." Silvers v. Russell, 113 F. Supp. 119, 123-24 (S.D. Cal. 1953).

179 The Court also commented that "the young woman was two years older when the later photograph was taken, and some slight changes in the contours of her figure were discoverable." *Gross,* 212 F. at 931. In context, it sounds like the court does not consider this a meaningful change since the photographer had no control over the model's aging; on the other hand, Seligman did choose this same model while aware of her aging.

or auditory arts, there are those qualities, some gross, some subtle, that make a work identifiably Manet or Monet, Mozart or Mahler.

But that is the rub. If Miro's newest painting manifests so much "creativity," why is it so identifiably similar to his old paintings? If each Mozart concerto is so creative, how can a person who has heard several Mozart concerti recognize a concerto he has never heard before as Mozart? The very existence of a Miro or Mozart "style" speaks of collective sameness to a group of works.[180] It is sometimes asked jokingly whether Vivaldi wrote 400 concerti or the same concerto 400 times. Surely this means that subsequent works by the same author were not as creative as they could have been. This point has not been lost on artists and critics. "A painter's worst enemy is style," Picasso once said. He attacked artists conscious of their personal style who "make themselves a little cake mold; then they make cakes."[181] His friend Malraux was more blunt: "Continuity of style is hell," he said.[182] Roland Barthes traces one route of a writer's development in which style eradicates personal expression premised on freedom:

> [M]echanical habits are developed in the very place where freedom existed, a network of set forms hem in more and more the pristine freshness of discourse, a mode of writing appears afresh in lieu of an indefinite language. The writer taking his place as a "classic," becomes the slavish imitator of his original creation, society demotes his writing to a mere manner, and returns him a prisoner of his own formal myths.[183]

Along with Picasso and Barthes, we could go so far as to say that there may be a negative correlation between (1) the degree to which we can identify a work as manifesting a particular person's identity; and (2) creativity in its purest, most extreme sense of bringing something into existence which is different from anything that has existed before. If we can confidently say that *Escalier de la Nuit* is *clearly* the work of Miro, then that judgment is possible only because *Escalier de la Nuit* looks like other works by Miro. It is less "original" compared to these works than to all art by people other

---

180 *See, e.g.*, LEON PLANTINGA, ROMANTIC MUSIC 362-89 (1984) (characterizing the individual styles of several Russian composers).

181 After all, you can only work against something. Even if it's yourself. That's very important. Most painters make themselves a little cake mold; then they make cakes. Always the same cakes. And they're very pleased with themselves. A painter should never do what people expect of him. A painter's worst enemy is style.

MALRAUX, *supra* note 66, at 140.

182 *Id.* at 18.

183 BARTHES, *supra* note 118, at 78.

than Miro.[184]

To think of it another way, would *Escalier de la Nuit* be *more* innovative if no other works of Miro existed? This is a peculiar question, so peculiar that no answer is obvious. If only *one* Miro work existed in all the world, it would not have the *economic* value that it does as part of the oeuvre of Miro. It might be ignored, or kept as a trinket by someone who thought it sad that there was no chance to see what else this artist might have produced. But would it be perceived as equally or *more* creative? An affirmative answer is suggested by cases where an artist changes style radically. Dali's *The Great Masturbator*[185] and Mondrian's *Still Life with Ginger Jar* paintings[186] were great breaks with their works up to that time; if they had stopped at that point we would have still considered these final works very creative. On the other hand, we might get a negative answer from the case of Stravinsky. It seems that appreciation of Stravinsky's music suffered because he drew from such a wide range of idioms from the whole history of music. One critic wrote that his "incredible diversity of stylistic procedures . . . amount[ed] to an absence of style," but more importantly it appears that this lack of an identifiable style pervading his music fueled detractors to accuse him of "a lack of originality, a failure of invention."[187]

When a work of art is judged "creative," it is usually judged so against two benchmarks to which we apply different standards: (1) the rest of the world except for other works from the same source; and (2) other works from the same source. It is not that Miro's other works don't count to judge *Escalier de la Nuit*; they just count differently. If nothing else, the difference expected between same-source works is smaller. When a painter has an exhibition of new works, the audience judges the individual works against one an-

---

184 The only possibility—a kind of maximum creativity possibility—was attributed to Picasso's works by Malraux: "Those particular works resembled one another by the very fact of their not bearing any resemblance to the others." MALRAUX, *supra* note 66, at 32. Could this be possible? For a bunch of one artist's works to "resemble" one another simply by being equally distant from works that had existed before, while each of those artist's works was similarly distant from the artist's other works? *See also* Weisberg, supra *note* 79 at 202-208 (discussing how even a powerfully new Picasso painting like *Guernica* had clear antecedents in his prior work, including a lithograph called *Minotauromachy*).

185 MEREDITH ETHERINGTON-SMITH, THE PERSISTENCE OF MEMORY: A BIOGRAPHY OF DALI 14-15 (1992).

186 Mondrian's move to Paris and his two paintings *Still Life with Ginger Jar I* (1911-12) and *Still Life with Ginger Jar II* (1912) marked his embracing of cubism—which would evolve over time into what is popularly known now as the "Mondrian" style. *Still Life with Ginger Jar II* is, to the untrained eye, more purely cubist, but both paintings are regarded as a break with his work up until that time. Indeed, the artist may have sensed a new period in his life, as these are the first paintings signed "Mondrian" instead of "Mondriaan." *See generally* JOHN MILNER, MONDRIAN 90-92 (1992).

187 MILAN KUNDERA, TESTAMENTS BETRAYED 76 (1995).

other ("I prefer this one in the corner") and the new collections against prior works ("I prefer his use of color now to what he was doing in the 1980s.") Works may be condemned for being too similar to the artist's prior achievements, particularly in a field like architecture where the specific needs of a particular commission offer strong reasons to vary from prior work.[188] We enjoy making such judgments. There is no question that we enjoy "placing" a work, not just among all novels or buildings or symphonies, but among those of the particular creator.[189]

Of course, few souls are as inventive as a Picasso or a Stravinsky.[190] Most of us, if we create at all, find a few idioms, a few "signatures" in which we are both comfortable and successful. Thus, Richard Meier's architecture is distinguishable by its use of white enamel panels and similar materials; I.M. Pei's work by its emphasis on triangular forms and particular combinations of concrete, glass, and tubular steel. In her characteristic modesty, Eudora Welty commented: "I had been writing a number of stories, more or less one after the other, before it belatedly dawned on me that some of the characters in one story were, and had been all the time, the same characters who had already appeared in another story."[191] Academics, it is often said, hit upon a few ideas and themes in their early career which they spend subsequent decades spinning out and elaborating.

Conscious of these limitations, many artists take up intentional self-reference. Self-reference may take many forms. New works of art may consciously and obviously refer to prior works. David

---

188 Lawrence J. Vale, Power, Architecture, and National Identity 244-47 (1992) (criticizing Louis Kahn's Parliament Building in Bangladesh as "curiously similar" to his Exeter Library design, particularly considering the different needs at the two sites).

189 This understanding, however, might not be focused on the *creativity* of the latest piece; it might be focused on understanding the artist or the artist's intent. As Dewey writes,

> [T]he discrimination of a critic has to be assisted by a knowledge of the development of an artist, as that is manifested in the succession of his works. Only rarely can an artist be criticized by a single specimen of his activity. The inability is not merely because Homer sometimes nods, but because understanding of the logic of the development of an artist is necessary to discrimination of his intent in any single work.

Dewey, *supra* note 107, at 312.

190 Unless one takes a strong version of the "post-modern" view of personality, i.e., "[i]f we bargain away one personality there is nothing to stop us from generating a new one." Malkan, *supra* note 26, at 783.

191 Welty, *supra* note 95, at 98. Welty's comment is a real-life example of the humorous plot in Vargas Llosa's *Aunt Julia and the Scriptwriter* in which the radio soap opera scriptwriter is writing several plotlines simultaneously, but the hero is suspiciously similar in all of them and, over time (and to the desperation of an enraptured radio audience), characters literally start to bleed from one soap opera into other soap operas. Mario Vargas Llosa, La Tía Julia y el Escribidor (5th ed. 1983).

Bowie's *Ashes to Ashes* explicitly makes use of the "Major Tom" character created in his 1972 *Space Oddity*. When a middle-aged John Travolta hesitatingly danced the jitterbug in the 1994 film *Pulp Fiction*, it could not help but be a playful reference to his more youthful role in *Saturday Night Fever*. An artist's performance of her established repertoire may intentionally poke fun or criticize a former "self" either explicitly[192] or with accentuated mannerisms.[193]

The point of all this is that artistic style could be sharply curtailed if an infringing copy was one "which comes so near the original as to give every person seeing it the idea created by the original."[194] It is precisely the fact that works by the same artist "come near" one another which creates the familial sameness of an artist's "style." This suggests that we might want the law to use a double standard, by which the creator of a copyrighted work is permitted to use much more of the "look and feel" of the copyrighted work than other non-owners.

Let us call this idea a "moral shop right" because (1) it has a similarity to the "moral rights" granted artists under continental legal systems; and (2) it is akin to the "shop right" which permits an employer to use an invention invented on his premises even though the employee has title to the invention and has all other rights to assign, license, or otherwise exploit the invention. At the onset, be clear that the use of "rights" talk does not mean I am advocating the establishment of a new "right" in the strong Constitutional or civil rights sense. What is suggested here is an equitable doctrine to fortify the position of intellectual producers; this doctrine—if it was ultimately found desirable—could be developed by legislative history, by courts explicitly, or by courts implicitly. The reasons for this "moral shop right" are twofold. First, it would protect personhood interests of the individual creator. Second, it

192 For example, in her 1987 concerts at Carnegie Hall, Liza Minelli sang the 1966 Kander and Ebb classic *Cabaret*, which she originally sang for the film of the same name. In the original version, a vivacious Sally Bowles refers to her prostitute-roommate dying of "too much pills and liquor." In response to the neighbors coming to "snicker," Sally Bowles sings "she was the happiest corpse I had ever seen . . . . and as for me, I made my mind up back in Chelsea, and when I go, I'm going like Elsie." JOHN KANDER & FRED EBB, Cabaret, on Cabaret (1972). In the Carnegie Hall recordings of a soberer late 1980's, Minelli changes the words to "And as for me, I made my mind up back in Chelsea, and when I go, I'm *not* going like Elsie." JOHN KANDER & FRED EBB, Cabaret, on Liza Minnelli at Carnegie Hall (Telarc Digital 1987).

193 Stephen Holden, *Self-Parody as a Part of the Pop Singer's Art*, N.Y. TIMES, Oct. 22, 1989, at B32 (In a positive review of a Bob Dylan concert, Holden wrote "[h]ow could a star, who is now 48, carry off the role of the hippest, most arrogant adolescent ever born, I wondered? It had to be partly at least a self-parody. Not even Christopher Guest's savage Dylan caricatures . . . were as exaggerated as the mannerisms Mr. Dylan flaunted at the [concert].").

194 West v. Francis, 106 Eng. Rep. 1361 (K.B. 1822).

probably would serve the public's interests. Assuming most producers of intellectual works are not as innovative and ground-breaking as Picasso, a moral right would ensure that these people could "exhaust" their own idiom.

It is worth noting that this idea may already be implicit in the reasoning of a few cases. For example, in the 1954 case *Warner Bros. Pictures, Inc. v. Columbia Broadcasting System, Inc.*,[195] Warner Brothers, as the owner of the rights to Dashiell Hammett's *Maltese Falcon*, tried to stop Hammett's use of "Sam Spade" and other characters from *Maltese Falcon* in subsequent radio broadcasts called *The Adventures of Sam Spade.* The Ninth Circuit's opinion was blurry on several issues, but we are concerned more with the spirit of the case than the precise reasoning.

The court looked at the contract between Hammett and Warner, noting that it transferred rights to the *Maltese Falcon* story and that title, but was silent on any transfer of rights to the characters. Interpreting the contracts against Warner Brothers, who prepared them and was "a large, experienced movie picture producer,"[196] the court concluded that "since the use of characters and character names are nowhere specifically mentioned in the agreements . . . the character rights with the names cannot be held to be within the grants . . . [and] the contract, properly construed, does not deprive Hammett of their use."[197]

All of this reasoning is compatible with the premise that Hammett's characters were copyrightable, but when the court considered this issue, it seemed to conclude that Congress did not intend to include characters as protectable work under the Copyright Clause. The *Warner Bros.* opinion is most famous for its now discredited conclusion on protection of characters. But the court did not say that characters were uncopyrightable because of something about characters; rather the court tried to glean congressional intent, reasoning that since "[t]he practice of writers to compose sequels to stories is old," congressional silence on the question of character protection was incompatible with Congress intending "that the sale of the right to publish a copyrighted story would foreclose the author's use of its characters in subsequent works."[198] Thus, both general principles of contract interpretation and the background copyright law favored Hammett retaining the right to use his characters. This reasoning was not about the inherent un-

195 216 F.2d 945 (9th Cir. 1954).
196 *Id.* at 949.
197 *Id.*
198 *Id.* at 950.

copyrightability of characters—which would have allowed use of Sam Spade, but rather it was about the practices of creators. The court was also clear in its motives: "[t]he characters of an author's imagination and the art of his descriptive talent, like a painter's or like a person with his penmanship, are always limited and always fall into limited patterns."[199] The court even went so far as to quote Oliver Wendell Holmes on how much intelligent people repeat themselves.[200]

In other words, the driving force of the *Warner Bros.* case was not that "Sam Spade" could not be copyrighted. Indeed, the Court made it clear that Warner Brothers had a protectable interest in the character Sam Spade.[201] In a parallel declaratory action brought in New York (but later dismissed in favor of the California case), the Second Circuit similarly thought that "[t]o use Sam Spade is to use a valuable part of the Maltese Falcon."[202] Despite these protectable interests, Warner Brothers could not stop Hammett from using characters of his own creation. In other words, the driving force in this case is something akin to a moral shop right.

The moral shop right can be thought of in several ways: (1) as analogous to the "shop right" under patent law; (2) as a kind of special fair use doctrine; and (3) as a complement to common views on non-competition clauses in employment contracts. For example, the "shop right" is an equitable doctrine developed by the common law to give the employer a non-exclusive license to any invention an employee makes on the employer's premises. This provision of the common law is largely forgotten now that most employment contracts deal with intellectual property ownership, but the doctrine was intended to recognize the employer's contribution to the employee's work. By the same token, this "moral shop right" might, in a sense, give the creator a very limited, non-exclusive reverse license.

The moral shop right could also be thought of as a kind of special fair use doctrine for creators. Consider the *Harper &*

---

199 *Id.* at 949.

200 The court found that ruling that an author transferred the rights to the characters in a work when he transferred the work would be contrary to the copyright law's purpose in "encourag[ing] the production of the arts." *Id.*

201 In considering the unfair competition claim Warner brought, the court said, "[i]t is patent that the characters of the *Maltese Falcon* could not fairly be used in such a manner as to cause the Falcon to be materially lessened in it's commercial worth. . . ." *Id.* at 951. Such a comment was possible because Hammett's new stories were seen as enriching or, at least, not detracting from the "Falcon." But what if Hammett was the one cheapening the characters?

202 Hammett v. Warner Bros. Pictures, Inc., 176 F.2d 145, 147 (2d Cir. 1949).

Row[203] case. Imagine that the contract between President Ford and Harper & Row had transferred copyright to Harper & Row, but did not impose any contractual duties on President Ford in terms of book promotion or publicity. Now, consider if President Ford had done some interviews with news magazines near the book's debut in which he reported—pretty much verbatim—the same language that the *New Republic* excerpted from his book. Let's also assume this made Harper & Row a little unhappy. Would we find that the author infringed the copyright of the book as readily as we would find that the *New Republic* infringed? The answer may be no for several reasons, i.e., Ford's interviews could increase sales of the book. But one of those possible reasons may be that we willingly give creators more leeway to reuse elements of their creations than we give non-creators to *use* elements of those creations.[204]

Finally, one could think of the "moral shop right" as an extension of common law on non-competition clauses. The case-law in most jurisdictions subjects covenants not-to-compete to a reasonableness test. Frequently, part of that reasonableness test is whether the covenant still permits the restricted individual to earn a living: restrictive covenants "which tend to prevent an employee from pursuing a similar vocation after termination of employment are disfavored by the law,"[205] because, there are "powerful considerations of public policy which militate against sanctioning the loss of a man's livelihood."[206] In refusing to uphold a non-competition clause that covered the entirety of the United States and Canada, the Indiana Supreme Court in 1955 noted: "our courts will zealously guard every individual against even his own commitments which would limit or thwart *the greatest constructive employment and enjoyment of his faculties from this moment forward* unless the manner of his living would contravene public policy . . . ."[207] In this spirit, the idea of a "moral shop right" is to safeguard the full constructive employment of an individual's intellectual abilities, to ensure that a person who

203 Harper & Row Publishers, Inc. v. Nation Enters., 471 U.S. 539, 589 (1985).

204 Admittedly, even if President Ford were virtually repeating verbatim passages from his book, we might treat this as drawing from his memories, not his copyrighted *memoirs*.

205 Columbia Ribbon v. A-1-A Corp., 369 N.E.2d 4, 6 (N.Y. 1977) (refusing to uphold broad non-competition clause against departing employee).

206 Purchasing Assoc., Inc. v. Weitz, 196 N.E.2d 245, 247 (N.Y. 1963); see also Arthur Young & Co. v. Black, 466 N.Y.S.2d 10, 12 (N.Y. App. Div. 1983) (court refused to enforce non-competition agreement against departing accounting firm partner to the extent that it would strip him of clients he brought to the firm, because "[t]o deny defendant the right to service those clients who had been developed over many years by his father and himself is to inflict on him a grievous personal injury.").

207 Donahue v. Permacel Tape Corp., 127 N.E.2d 235, 240 (Ind. 1955) (emphasis added).

is talented, but not as innovative as a Picasso, could fully enjoy their creative faculties.

About any potential new right, we should ask whether reasonable limits to the right are possible. In the case of the "moral shop right," the issue would be just how *close* the artist may come to his previous, now-alienated work. Would it pertain only to "style," or would it extend to more specific copyrighted items, such as individual fictional characters? Would it extend to *whole* works, such as an entire symphony, or only to elements of transferred works? Consider three situations. In the first, a composer writes the score for a musical with a dozen songs, an overture, and incidental music; a librettist pens the "book" for the musical. In the second, a computer programmer writes a program for a video game involving thousands of subroutines and images. In the third, a chef and a photographer collaborate on a recipe book with a few dozen recipes and photos of both the dishes and luscious settings for dinner.

In all these cases, let's assume that the individuals conveyed copyright to a third party, but continue to work in that field. Assume that the contracts by which copyright was conveyed expressly include rights to put the whole work in a different medium, i.e., the stage musical may be adapted for the screen, the video program may be adapted to CD-ROM, and perhaps, the cookbook may be turned into a video. These transfers are not at issue. But I believe that the intuitive pull of a "moral shop right" increases dramatically when we focus on elements, parts, or themes of each work. Should the composer be free to use sections of the melodic line of the musical score for a symphony?[208] Should the programmer be free to use subroutines she wrote in another program? May the chef include several slight variants of the recipes from the book in his new collection? In these situations, we could imagine cases where we might want to give the creator more leeway to recycle, reuse, and reform the materials found in the transferred work. Recall Eudora Welty's comments about how much her work involves similar characters and how much artists like Kahlo and Munch repainted similar themes.

The problem of drawing these boundaries remains. Gene Roddenberry, the creator of *Star Trek*, transferred the rights of *Star Trek* to Paramount. What if he became dissatisfied with how the studio exploited the franchise? What if Stan Lee, creator of nu-

[208] As when Grieg wrote incidental music for Brecht's 1876 *Peer Gynt* and later orchestrated that music as the *Peer Gynt Suite #1, opus 46* (1888) and the *Peer Gynt Suite #2, opus 55* (1891).

merous comic book characters, was disturbed with the plot of *Spiderman* comics or cartoons? First, the extra leeway of the "moral shop right" should only come into play for the creator's continuing expression of herself, and not to "correct" the course of the work that has been alienated. Such "correction" is the province of standard moral rights and involves us in thorny questions of an artist's relationship to his existing works. The "moral shop right" concerns the artist's subsequent expression—how much subsequent expression may "play off" or appear to derive from certain existing works. Admittedly, this distinction—in a sense between proactive and creative behavior by the creator—would be very hard to police. Is Roddenberry feeling the need to write a new intergalactic, starship-driven science fiction series because he can only express himself through this kind of vehicle or does he feel the need to express himself because of what he thinks Paramount has done with *Star Trek*? Would we prevent Stan Lee from doing a *Spiderman* book, but allow him to create a troubled, but responsible young man superhero, *The Arachnid*? The questions remain vexing.

Those vexing questions lead us to the odd relationship between a "moral shop right" and other moral rights. A "moral shop right" might diminish the importance we attach to other moral rights. If an artist has the right to continue in a particular style and produce fraternal works, then the artist's need to prevent destruction or mutilation of a pre-existing work may not be as great. (In fact, we could quell some controversy over artists' rights by granting a "special moral shop right": where the owner of a *res* destroys or irreparably and substantially damages a work, the artist might be given the "moral shop right" to *recreate* the work.)

Free marketeers may resist any thought of a "moral shop right" on the grounds that, like all moral rights, it abridges free economic activity. Although patents abridge free economic activity, few people propose abolishing patents. We could however, try to get by without them, relying on a trade secrets system providing economic rents for innovation recovered only in the period until competitors learn to duplicate one's technology. The difference is that moral rights—like child labor laws—*bar*, not shape, certain economic activity. Like child labor laws, they say a certain type of transfer may tend to happen because of economic disparity and that it should not happen.[209] At first blush, a "moral shop right"

---

209 We should also note that moral rights come to American jurisprudence from a less "rights oriented" legal culture. Just as, as a practical matter, rights in America are often sculpted around the exigencies of society, moral rights can be "trumped" by public policy. *See, e.g.*, Foujita v. SARL Art Conception Realisation, Fleet Street Reports 523 (1988)

does not have the same corrosive effect on chattel property rights that makes other moral rights so unnerving to studio executives, art gallery owners, and conservative jurists. Stephen Carter, for example, has called moral rights an "elitist and despotic doctrine," because it deprives property owners of the "right to do with their possessions as they wish."[210] (Never mind that on economic indicators, it is usually the property owner—the art collector, the studio mogul—who is more "elite" than the creator who would have the moral rights.) Carter objects to an artist having the power to stop the owner of a painting from putting a moustache on it; he objects to the idea that a film director could stop a studio from colorizing that film.

These criticisms might not stick to a "moral shop right." A "moral shop right" need not interrupt the relationship between object and owner, it would not give the artist any power to frustrate the owner's whims and predilections. What it would do is alter the potential value of the owned object; the photographer's retention of the right to do a photo in the same style may diminish the value of the *res* owned by the holder of the photograph's copyright. But the linkage between the value of a piece of art and the subsequent activities of its creator already exists. Just an artist staying alive affects an object's value. In fact, this linkage between value and lineage occurs in all kinds of areas. A computer's value is certainly linked to whether or not it is part of a successful line of computers; a house may be more marketable if the builder enjoys a continuing reputation in the area for quality home construction; a piece of art deco pottery will have its value determined by the kiln having a successful (but preferably limited) lifetime. In keeping with these examples, the effect of a "moral shop right" would be both indirect and uncertain. In fact, the artist's right to continue in a particular style might increase the value of earlier works in that style. (But so too might the artist's timely intervention to prevent a moustache from being painted onto the portrait.)

Situations in which Libby's paintings are purchased to hang in one's living room and Libby continues painting similar scenes are not particularly worrisome. But transfers of copyright are often motivated by the intent of the transferee to invest a substantial amount of money—substantially more than available to the trans-

---

(Court of Appeals, Versailles, 1987) (exercise of moral right by widow of artist Leonard Foujita to prevent publication of book on Foujita and his works was unreasonable and an abuse of moral rights considering quality of proposed book, artist's publicity policy during his lifetime, and lack of materials on his work published in French).

210 Carter, *supra* note 16, at 100-01.

feror—to exploit the work. This investment usually entails the creation of new, derivative works in other media. If the creator of "Batman" or "Jessica Fletcher" or "Winnie the Pooh" had the inalienable right to reuse these characters, the investment in downstream derivative works would be much more precarious.

One suggestion is to take a cue from patent law's "shop right" doctrine. Under the "shop right" doctrine, when an employee invents something in his employer's shop, the employer has a right to use the patented invention in his own "shop," but does not have the right to further license the invention—that right is held by the inventor. So too, the individual who produces an intellectual work and then transfers that work could retain a "moral shop right" to use elements of the work in her own creations without having the right to license those protected elements to others for *their* creation of derivative works. In other words, a novelist who wrote a novel with several characters and contracted away the development rights to that first novel could have the "moral shop right" to use a character from the first novel in a new novel, but not to license that character (as it appears in the new novel) for use in a feature film based on the new novel.

A "moral shop right" might be needed for patent law as well, since an inventor can sign away even her own right to use the invention. As one commentator has rightly noted, "[a]n inventor's individuation is threatened when an employer can preclude an inventor from continuing to work with her creation even after she leaves the employment relationship. Some degree of inventive continuity is required to make possible, and protect, the constituting of individuating personhood in inventive work."[211] This is an interesting problem. Patent law already has a safeguard in a patent equivalent of "fair use" doctrine: there is no patent infringement where the patented process is used purely for research. Just as patent law has drawn limits on what counts as "research" for the inventor's use of her alienated invention, copyright law could develop limits to a "moral shop right" to ensure that, while artists and writers are not stymied from self-expression, those who invest in derivative works based on artistic creations are guaranteed just returns from those investments.

III. Personhood Interests from Intentionality[212]

Modern western philosophy has devoted considerable energy

[211] Cherensky, *supra* note 4, at 648.

[212] "Intentionality" is used here as a counterpart to "creativity" and as a constituent of

to the idea of "intention" and what it means to *intend* something, particularly in areas like just war theory and medical ethics. While we all seem to have a rough idea of what an "intention" is, philosophers have grappled with different ways to characterize the process of forming and having intentions. It is generally agreed, for example, that intentions are "parasitic" on beliefs, i.e., I cannot *intend* to jog tomorrow morning when the sun rises unless I *believe* that the sun will rise and that I will be physically able, at that time, to jog. Intentions seem related to, but different from, predictions, i.e., I cannot *intend* to jog tomorrow morning unless I am willing to *predict* that I will jog in the morning;[213] as Wilfrid Sellars suggested, *intending* is more than, but includes, thinking that something will be the case.[214]

Philosophers have tried different formulations of the relationship between intention and other concepts for mental states ranging from describing an intention as a "decision" or a "resolution" of a question about actions[215] to proposing that "desire" be understood as an "intentional" state of mind.[216] One of the most important writers in this area, G.E.M. Anscombe, sought to distinguish "intention" or "purpose" from "motives" or "causes"; she saw "[a] man's intention [as] *what* he aims at or chooses," in contrast to a "motive," which more amorphously determines his intention.[217] Anscombe suggested that this difference between "intention" and "motive" in philosophers' parlance reflects a difference in popular usage—that a motive, i.e., doing it out of love or pity, is expressive of the "spirit" in which some action is undertaken, while an inten-

---

"personality." In other words, "intentionality" is used in the sense in which Bentham introduced the word to distinguish between acts that are intended and those that are unintended. "Intentionality" is not used in the Husserlian sense. *See* EDMUND HUSSERL, IDEEN ZU EINER REINEN PHENOMEMOLOGIE UND PHANOMENOLOGISCHEN PHILOSOPHIE (1913), *translated in* IDEAS: GENERAL INTRODUCTION TO PURE PHENOMENOLOGY (William R. Boyce Gibson trans., 1931).

213 HECTOR-NESI CASTANEDA, THINKING AND DOING 41-42 (1975).

214 Wilfrid Sellars, *Thought and Action*, *in* FREEDOM AND DETERMINISM 126 (Keith Lehrer ed., 1966); *see also* Hector-Nesi Castaneda, *Some Reflections on Wilfrid Sellars' Theory of Intentions*, *in* ACTION, KNOWLEDGE AND REALITY: CRITICAL STUDIES IN HONOR OF WILFRID SELLARS 30 (1975).

215 CASTANEDA, *supra* note 213, at 170 (In discussing the grammatical similarity of "intending" to go to a place and "deciding" to go to that same place, Castaneda offers a "theoretical thesis" that "the very same thought content that is a decision, or resolution, is also an intention. Whether an intention is a decision or not, then, depends solely on whether a psychological process of deciding or deliberating has the intention as its ending element.").

216 Charles Taylor, *Action as Expression*, *in* INTENTION AND INTENTIONALITY: ESSAYS IN HONOUR OF G.E.M. ANSCOMBE 85 (C. Diamond & J. Teichman eds., 1979).

217 G.E.M. Anscombe, *Intention*, 57 PROCEEDINGS ARISTOTELIAN SOC'Y 321-32 (1956-57), *reprinted in* 2 THE COLLECTED PHILOSOPHICAL PAPERS OF G.E.M. ANSCOMBE, METAPHYSICS AND THE PHILOSOPHY OF MIND 77 (1981).

tion is descriptive of the end being sought.[218]

Anscombe's dichotomy agrees with the emphasis other writers have put on the focus—both temporal and conceptual—of an intention. Sellars proposed that an intention is a volition—a thought, to the effect that one shall do some action *now*,[219] while Castaneda has suggested that "[a]n intention is a possible first-person answer to the question 'Shall I do that?' or the question 'What shall I do?,' understanding that answers of the sort like 'I don't know' cannot be included."[220] Castaneda has suggested that it may also be helpful to think of an intention as a first person analog of ordering, entreating, or advising someone to do something.[221]

A common theme in philosophical discussions of intentions is a sense of their "nowness"—that an intention is a desire or decision being put into action. Aristotle's passing remarks on the problem seem to suggest that he viewed the mental state of intending as focused on the means to achieve a given goal.[222] Modern writers strike a similar chord. Castaneda writes: "[i]ntending to do something is to be already in the process of doing it, even if merely by having undergone a re-arrangement of the causal powers within oneself in the direction of the action one intends to do,"[223] while Charles Taylor has suggested that any "awareness of [an] intention incorporates, and may be nothing more than, our awareness of what we are doing intentionally."[224]

While an intentional state usually includes awareness of both goal and means to that goal (the actions we will or *are* undertaking), there may not be a full understanding of the goal—Wittgenstein, for example, noticed that when a chess novice "intends" to play a game of chess, it is unlikely that "intention" includes an understanding of all the rules of chess. The same problem can (and perhaps should) trouble public policy experts. When the Federal Reserve Board lowers interest rates, they no doubt "intend" to increase borrowing. They probably also intend to increase new

---

218 *Id.* at 78-79.

219 WILFRID SELLARS, SCIENCE AND METAPHYSICS 177 (1967). *See also* Sellars, *supra* note 214, at 109.

220 CASTANEDA, *supra* note 213, at 41.

221 *Id.* at 172 ("We could use the word 'intention' and 'decision' to refer to first-person contents of acts of deciding or intending conceived as analogous to ordering, entreating, advising, requesting, and commanding.").

222 "We deliberate not about ends, but about means. For a doctor does not deliberate about whether he shall heal, nor an orator whether he shall persuade . . . they assume the end and consider how and by what means it is to be obtained." ARISTOTLE, supra note 90, at Book III, ch. 3.

223 CASTANEDA, *supra* note 213, at 41.

224 Taylor, *supra* note 216, at 87.

home construction—an element of the economy well known to be sensitive to interest rate changes. But, for example, was it their "intent" to cause the 1993 national lumber shortage that resulted from a rapid increase in housing starts?

To the degree that an intention is separate from the "spirit" of an action, this might help us distinguish intention from the creative impetus behind a project. While Taylor may be correct that desire is an intentional state, the important difference for our purposes between a "desire" and an "intention" is that the latter is *operational*; you can "desire" some end without doing anything to achieve that end, but "intending" something connotes making a plan and putting it into action. An intention includes an awareness of a personal goal, awareness of a means to achieve that goal, and a commitment to pursue that means with personal actions.

There is no question that artistic works that seem imbued with creativity also seem imbued with the artist's intention or purpose. In his seminal work on theory of art, Dewey remarked that: "[n]o matter how imaginative the material for a work of art, it issues from the state of reverie to become the matter of a work of art only when it is ordered and organized, and this effect is produced only when *purpose* controls selection and development of material."[225]

In our common discourse about art, exploration of the artist's expression quickly moves into exploration of his intentions, i.e., "what was he trying to express?" easily becomes "what was his intention?" To John Dewey, purpose was as keenly connected to one's personality as creativity:

> Purpose implicates in the most organic way an individual self. It is the purpose he entertains and acts upon that an individual most completely exhibits and realizes his most intimate selfhood. Control of material by a "self" is control by more than just "mind": it is control by the personality that has mind incorporated within it.[226]

For Dewey intent was a requirement of art; Dewey likened a bird building a nest and a beaver building a dam to the work of artisans transforming materials, but recognized that "[w]e may hesitate to apply the word 'art' since we doubt the presence of directive intent."[227]

One question, however, is whether only certain types of intent

---

225 DEWEY, *supra* note 107, at 276.

226 *Id.* at 277.

227 *Id.* at 24; *see also* Daniel Dennett, *The Interpretation of Text, People, and other Artifacts*, 50 PHIL. & PHENOMENOLOGICAL RES. 177-94 (1990) (reasoning that people view other minds as having an "intentional stance" and artifacts as having a parallel "design stance.")

are associated with intellectual products. While Dewey recognized that artisans transformed materials, Malraux, like many, distinguished artisans from *artists* on the grounds that the former copy, while only the latter *intend* to produce previously non-existent images and forms. While the artisan might reproduce images, taking wood blocks and recreating a known mask or idol shape, "what is important is that [the artist] altered the previous work intentionally."[228] We may conclude that just any *intent* is not enough for a personhood interest in intellectual products; perhaps the individual must *intend* to produce some form or shape that does not yet exist.

A. *Intentionality as the Personhood Interest in Research and Exploration Programs*

Earlier, I noted that Jefferson called inventions the "fermentation of an individual brain";[229] in his turn, Lincoln praised the incentive structure of the patent system as adding fuel to "the fire of genius."[230] But once we are beyond the flowery language, there is something deeply dissatisfying about trying to shoehorn scientific invention into the same "personhood" justification as painting and composing music. We have only a couple of options to resolve this apparent discontinuity. In the first, all our talk of creativity and personal expression simply misunderstands the artistic process. Instead, artistic creativity and scientific discovery are actually as W.V.O. Quine puts it, "all of a piece."[231] If the photographer feels only that he "captures" a vista that already exists, and if the sculptor thinks that "he chips away bits to expose a shape that was inside the stone all along,"[232] then they are explorers cut of the same cloth as the great "discoverers" of the fifteenth and sixteenth centuries. The Muses carry away the artist just as the trade winds carried away explorers. This notion of creativity-as-discovery also finds comfort in a Platonic metaphysics. As Quine writes, "[i]f the fantasy of the *UNIVERSAL LIBRARY* were realized, literary creativity would likewise reduce to discovery: the author's book would await him on the shelf."[233]

From what has been discussed above, I do not subscribe to this

---

228 MALRAUX, *supra* note 66, at 194.

229 *See supra* note 21.

230 Abraham Lincoln, Lecture on Discoveries and Inventions (Feb. 11, 1859), *in* THE POLITICAL THOUGHT OF ABRAHAM LINCOLN 112, 121 (Richard N. Current ed., 1967).

231 W.V. QUINE, QUIDDITIES 39 (1987).

232 *Id.* at 38.

233 *Id.* at 39.

creativity-as-discovery paradigm. We treat art and science (convincingly) differently. When Mary Cassatt exhibited some paintings or Walt Whitman wrote a poem, they might be questioned about the "meaning" of their work. When Dennis Gabor discovered the principles of holography or when Barbara McClintock hypothesized that genes move from one chromosomal site to another, the questions about what he or she "meant" by this discovery were probably few. On those occasions when a Gabor or McClintock is asked about the "meaning" of their new discoveries, the question is actually about the future effects of the discovery: "What does this mean to society?" is actually "What is the likely impact on society?" Admittedly, this also happens to the artist: questions about the "meaning" of their new works can be questions about the future effect, i.e., "Mr. Bernstein, what does *West Side Story* mean for the future of American musical theater?" But usually the "meaning" question directed at the artist is about symbolism, embedded messages, and communication. The poem, dance, or film is thought to have an internal meaning that does not involve its prospective effect on other facts or events. This internal meaning is assumed not to exist with scientific discovery.[234]

But if the inventor's personhood interest seems further removed from personal expression, there still seems to be a strong personhood interest of some sort. It is this that we should try to explain. One explanation is that the inventor's insight is the direct product of that unknowable "raw creativity" discussed above; this would jibe with the frequent accounts of inventors who say that they may have been working on a problem for some time, and then the breakthrough idea just occurred to them on a particular day, at a particular place, without explanation. We will turn to this possibility in the next section's discussion of "sourcehood."

Another possibility is that the personhood interest we perceive derives from intentionality. For while the breakthrough idea may

---

234 Scientific advances have at least one other kind of "meaning"—how the discovery leads to other conclusions and revisions about the world. These are often inferences about history, not projections about the future. Edwin Powell Hubble's discovery in the 1920s that the Andromeda nebula contains short period variable stars led to the conclusion that the Andromeda nebula is a separate galaxy from the Milky Way. Back on Earth, the reconceptualization in the 1970s of the Burgess Shale fossil record by Harry Whittington, Derek Briggs, and Simon Conway Morris led to new conclusions about evolution. Hubble's discovery of short-period variable stars *meant* star clusters distinct from the Milky Way existed. The reconstruction of the Burgess Shale *meant* evolution followed a previously unaccepted course of diversification and decimation. *See* STEPHEN J. GOULD, WONDERFUL LIFE: THE BURGESS SHALE AND THE NATURE OF HISTORY (1989). Instead of an effect on future events, this "meaning" is an effect on the probability of the truth of other historic events. This "external" meaning is still very different from the "internal" meaning of poetry, music, dance, and visual arts.

be a bolt from the blue that strikes randomly, its effects may not be random. Of the people taking fireside naps in Ghent on a night in 1865, perhaps only one, Friedrich Auguste Kekulé, had been pondering the possible structure of the benzene molecule.[235] When Kekulé dreamt of the circular snake biting its own tail, he awoke, and immediately decided to test the hypothesis that the molecule had a ring shape—a hypothesis that proved true. It does not matter much whether you view Kekulé's dream as a freak occurrence or his unconscious brain continuing to explore possible options to his problem. In either case, the breakthrough was the result of Kekulé's intent to pursue a particular research program, itself a manifestation of a more general intent to reach a goal—understanding benzene.

This is clearly so if the self-consuming snake was the work of a mind continuing to explore possible theories in the subconscious language of metaphor. But it is also true if the dream was a total random occurrence—if *X* number of people over *Y* days will have *Z* dreams of self-consuming snakes. If such a random event happens to a physicist contemplating space/time, it might inspire him to try some new hypothesis about wormholes. Most of us who enjoy dozing in the morning never have "Eureka-like" solutions to problems of chemistry or genetic engineering. At a minimum, that is because most of us do not put ourselves on a path to solve problems of chemistry or genetic engineering. The intentional dedication to a particular research program empowers one to take advantage of particular random occurrences. As Louis Pasteur said, "chance favors only those minds which are prepared."[236]

There is also the intentionality aspect, that one must not only be empowered to take advantage of random occurrences, but one must take advantage of them: as Kekulé himself said, "[l]et us learn to dream, gentlemen, but let us also beware of publishing our dreams until they have been examined by the wakened mind."[237] Even if Kekulé's dream was a "Eureka act," it required

---

235 *See* William H. Brock, The Norton History of Chemistry 265 (1992). Later in life, Kekulé, one of the great figures of nineteenth century chemistry, also said that one of his earlier advances, the conception of the carbon chain, came to him while he was drowsing one summer afternoon in 1854 on the upper deck of a London omnibus. *Id.* at 252. Dreams continue to be known as major inspiration to inventors. In 1997, Bertram V. Burke received patent #5,621,640 on a change-depositing system inspired by a dream he had about coins rolling off his dresser, down the hall, and out to a neighborhood drain. *See* Teresa Riordan, *Patents: Funneling Change to Useful Pursuits*, N.Y. Times, June 9, 1997, at D2. Mr. Burke, ironically, is a psychoanalyst.

236 Louis Pasteur, A Treasury of the World's Great Speeches 473 (Houston Peterson ed., 1954).

237 Brock, *supra* note 235, at 265. Brock adds:

confirming laboratory work. Interestingly, John Dewey made roughly the same observation about painting:

> Even if we were to suppose that the image first presented itself in a dream, it would still be true that its material had to be organized in terms of objective material and operations that moved consistently and without a break to consummation in the public that is a public object in a common world.[238]

When it comes to science, unlike art, there is a greater sense of inevitability. But this need not disrupt the intentionality interest.

For example, even if Kekulé thought, as it appears that he may have, that the discovery of the structure of benzene was inevitable given not just his own research program, but the research program of his colleagues,[239] nonetheless, from Kekulé's perspective, his personality interest might arise from being the source of the directed labor. This is similar to the runner who is intent on crossing the finish line first even though several other athletes are running in the same direction. The scientists who made an important discovery from the hypothalamus gland characterized their work in much the same terms of highly directed labor: "[n]obody before had to process millions of hypothalami. . . . The key factor is not the money, it's the will . . . the brutal force of putting in 60 hours a week for a year." They likened the experience to "fighting Hitler . . . you have cut him down."[240]

It is worthwhile to consider the parallel between inventors of the twentieth century and explorers in the Age of Discovery. On the whole, we probably do not consider particular voyages or land discoveries to be "creative" acts. Perhaps Columbus' initial insistence on sailing west to reach the East was a creative idea. But once it was known that land could be reached by sailing west, were the voyages of Cabot, Balboa, Ponce de Leon, and Cartier *creative*

> While historians of science are happy to concede that the well-springs of scientific innovation are often to be found outside the culture of science, and there is no particularly strong reason to doubt Kekulé's account of the hypothetico-deductive method in action, others have argued to the contrary that Kekulé invented the story to ensure his priority over other possible hexagon claimants. Whatever the truth of the matter, the consequences of any subconscious creation of the ring concept had to be honed and perfected at the laboratory bench.

Id.

238 DEWEY, *supra* note 107, at 277.

239 "Kekulé was undoubtably right to note deprecatingly that the hexagon was bound to have occurred to anyone who tinkered long enough with the structure theory. 'What else,' he asked, could a chemist 'have done with the two valences' left over on benzene other than form a ring with them?" BROCK, *supra* note 235, at 265.

240 BRUNO LATOUR & STEVE WOOLGAR, LABORATORY LIFE: THE CONSTRUCTION OF SCIENTIFIC FACTS 118 (1986).

acts? These missions were imbued with intention and purpose, but they do not seem to manifest creativity. Once the gross generalities of the geography were known, the French and English explorations of the Great Lakes or the Portuguese penetration along the African coast seem like research programs, not creative acts.

The inventor, like an explorer, usually deals with an area where some general facts are known but much is uncertain. The inventor and the explorer work with general hypotheses. Other individuals are exploring the same area. There is often a sense of competition as to who will pick the research approach that will succeed—as with the explorer's sense of who has the best intuitive guess on trade winds and where the elusive goal—the northwest passage, the fountain of youth—might be found. Just as scientific researchers are not asked what they "mean" by a discovery, explorers were not asked what they "meant" by new cartographic discoveries. Whether we refer to the discovery of tau neutrinos by CERN researchers or the discovery of Hudson Bay, any discussion of meaning is a discussion of the likely effects on future developments (or inferences about the past). The similarities between the process of geographic exploration and scientific invention were not lost on our juridical ancestors. In fact, in the early days of American patent law, inventors were sometimes referred to as "discoverers."[241]

The parallels between the two processes may not be complete. Robert Nozick, for example, draws a distinction between exploration and experimentation.[242] He suggests that exploration, while a directed activity, "does not have the structure of a well designed experiment . . . fixed observation along well-defined alternatives."[243] Certainly the voyages of a Christopher Columbus (or a Jean-Luc Picard) seem less controlled than the experiments of a modern medical lab, but this may be an issue of comparative scale or our own technological moment. At other times, scientific experiments may have been less structured and well-defined. Benjamin Franklin's holding a kite during a thunderstorm seemed to open him up to some not so "well-defined alternatives." The same could be said of Madame Curie's more technologically advanced experiments—those experiments killed her by unexpected "alternatives" as surely as Magellan's fatal and (we guess) unexpected encounter

---

[241] *See, e.g.*, Alfred Bell & Co. v. Catalda Fine Arts, Inc., 191 F.2d 99, 101 n.7 (2d Cir. 1951).

[242] To be accurate, Nozick was discussing "intellectual explorations," not the great geographic explorations of the late fifteenth to the early nineteenth centuries.

[243] Nozick, *supra* note 80, at 44.

with Filipino natives in 1521.[244]

Programs of discovery—scientific or geographic—may have varying degrees of clarity about the expected goal. Or they may have clarity about the desired goal with varying degrees of certainty about the probabilities of other outcomes. When scientists designed and deployed NASA's Cosmic Background Explorer ("COBE") satellite they knew precisely what they were looking for: fluctuations in background microwave radiation levels that would support the hypothesis that uneven distribution of matter in the early ages of the universe led to the formation of galaxies. Variations were detected, although perhaps smaller than anticipated.[245] So too with geographic programs of exploration, Lewis and Clark sought a better commercial route to the Pacific, hoping to find that the Missouri was navigable much further than then known and that only a short portage would connect it to the headwaters of the Columbia. The climate and topography they found was far less hospitable to commercial transportation than they had hoped.[246] The *result* of the research program may be unanticipated in the sense that there are details in the result that were not expected when the individual settled on the particular goal and particular program. This fits with the philosophical problem of what is included in an intention; Wittgenstein's novice chess player may have had no idea that the intention to play a game of chess included the intention to castle or to take a pawn *en passant*, or to permit her opponent to exploit these lesser known details of the game.

This might appear to push us towards the position that the person's intentionality is intention in the *process* which led to creation of the *res*, not intention in the *res* itself. But we can (and do) still speak about the inventor's intentions *vis-à-vis* the final product. Patent infringement actions have, for example, aspects akin to literary interpretation symposia. When a product or process is scrutinized for alleged infringement of a patent, it is *not* compared to the actual real world product or process of the patentee. Instead, the alleged infringing product or process is compared to the *claims* the inventor made in the patent.

---

244 Professor Nozick does not elaborate on the concept of "experimentation" or his exploration/experimentation dichotomy. He considers "exploration" to be a process of accumulating "directed observations" in which "you explore in a place or direction you think is likely to be fruitful, and you allow things to roll in upon you, prepared to notice within general categories and to pursue interesting facts or possibilities." *Id.*

245 John D. Barrow et al., The Lefthand of Creation: The Origin and Evolution of the Expanding Universe 75-79 (1983).

246 Stephen E. Ambrose, Undaunted Courage: Meriwether Lewis, Thomas Jefferson, and the Opening of the American West (1996); Meriwether Lewis, The Lewis and Clark Expedition (1814 ed., J.P. Lippencott Co., 1961).

The inquiry into the "scope" of the patent claims becomes a search for the intent of the inventor reminiscent to the search for a writer's intentions in his novel.[247] But while literary criticism can tolerate the subconscious or subliminal meaning of an author, the inventor needs to have some awareness that he intended this or that in the wording of the patent claims. And just as an author's personal correspondence contemporaneous with a novel can show the motives and factors shaping the fiction, a scientist's correspondence and notes can show what was the conscious goal of her invention.[248]

B. *Intentionality and the Research Program of Journalists*

Intentionality may also provide an improved perspective on what is happening in some film and videotaping cases. In *Time, Inc. v. Bernard Geis Assocs.*, a copyright was recognized for an amateur photographer's raw footage of the Kennedy assassination on the grounds that selection of the type of camera, film, lens, time, and position of camera were all sufficiently "original" to merit protection.[249] More recently, in *Los Angeles News Service v. Tullo*, the Ninth Circuit held that raw videotape of a train accident by Los Angeles News Service ("LANS") was similarly protected because of the creator's decisions about "the newsworthiness of the events and how to best tell the stories . . . the selection of camera lenses, angles and exposures; the choices of the heights and directions from which to tape and what portion of the events to film and for how long."[250] Indeed, in finding the LANS videotapes had sufficient originality to warrant protection, Judge Browing went so far as to quote one of LANS' camera people "describ[ing] herself as 'an artist. I use a paint brush. I use the camera to tell a story.'"[251]

Whatever gloss witnesses and jurists give to these cases, it is a stretch to pour the making of the Zapruder film and the LANS videotapes into the mold of creative acts. My suggestion here is that we would do better to recognize the personhood interest in these works as arising from intentionality, not creativity. Like the explorer or the scientist, the journalist goes to work with a program to capture "bolts from the blue." Someone like Mr. Zapruder is at

---

[247] *See generally* Tandon Corp. v. United States Int'l Trade Comm'n, 831 F.2d 1017, 1023-24 (5th Cir. 1987).

[248] Autogiro Co. of Am. v. United States, 384 F.2d 391, 397 (Ct. Cl. 1967).

[249] 293 F. Supp. 130, 142-43 (S.D.N.Y. 1968).

[250] 973 F.2d 791 (9th Cir. 1992).

[251] *Id.* at 794. (It is unclear whether she meant she uses a paint brush at home—to show she was an artist generally—or whether she meant the camera was her paintbrush.).

the right place at a tragically correct time, but it is rarely by complete coincidence. The photo-journalist's plan is like the explorer's plan: we could characterize the photo-journalist's goal as being to "record the afternoon air show and whatever happens,"[252] just as we could characterize the explorer's intention as being to "map the northern coast and whatever is found there."

As a personhood interest, intentionality may still point to a different result between, on the one hand, the LANS videotapes and the videotape of the Rodney King beating—the latter taken by a citizen from his balcony who had been awoken by the din of police brutality, and perhaps deserving less or no copyright protection. On the other hand, amateur videographer George Holliday had the general intention to capture things on video—he had just bought a video camera—and a specific intention that night to make as complete and as clear a record of what he was seeing.[253]

C. *Intentionality, the Work-For-Hire Doctrine, and the Common Law of Employer-Owned Inventions*

Intentionality also may give us some insights into copyright's "work for hire"[254] doctrine. The "work for hire" regime runs counter to most copyright law by permitting creators to transfer their copyright *before* creation of the *res.* Under the 1909 Copyright Act, a work was a "work for hire" if an "employer" hired another to make the work, absent an agreement to the contrary.[255] The 1909 law did not define an "employer". Under the case law, "employer" was limited to the traditional employer/employee relationship until the mid-1960s when the Second and Ninth Circuits expanded "employers" to include those who hire independent contractors

---

[252] As Kundera writes:

> A burning plane had crashed into a crowd of onlookers. The photographs were large, each one a full page. They showed terrified people fleeing in all directions, charred clothing, burned skin, flames rising from bodies. Agnes could not help staring at the pictures, and she thought of the wild joy of the photographer who had been bored watching the banal spectacle and suddenly saw that luck was falling his way from the sky in the shape of a burning airplane.

Kundera, *supra* note 15, at 30.

[253] *See* Beth Shuster, *Man Who Taped King Beating Defends LAPD,* L.A. TIMES, Mar. 10, 1996, at B1 ("Holliday, who had given the video camera to his first wife for Valentine's Day, had been playing with it earlier in the evening, trying to figure out the focusing mechanism, among others things.").

[254] Following Justice Marshall's acute sense of English, this section "use[s] the phrase 'work for hire' interchangeably with the more cumbersome statutory phrase 'work made for hire,'" found in 17 U.S.C. § 101 (1988 & Supp. IV 1992). Community for Creative Non-Violence v. Reid, 490 U.S. 730, 737 n.3 (1989).

[255] Section 62 of the 1909 Copyright Act was 17 U.S.C. § 26 (1976) which provided that "the word 'author' shall include an employer in the case of works made for hire." Tobani v. Carl Fischer, Inc., 98 F.2d 57, 59-60 (2d Cir. 1938).

where the work was made at the "instance and expense" of the hiring party.[256] Over the next decade, courts, particularly the Second Circuit, filled out the "instance and expense" test finding different occasions when a hiring party was an "employer" and, therefore, the produced work was a "work-for-hire." Tests included whether the hiring party was "the motivating factor in producing the work"[257] and whether the hiring party had the right "to direct and supervise the manner in which the writer perform[ed] his work."[258]

The 1976 Copyright Act offered the prospect of sweeping this framework away by statutorily elaborating specific conditions for works-for-hire. According to the 1976 Copyright Act, a "work for hire" is:

> (1) a work prepared by an employee within the scope of his or her employment; or
>
> (2) a work specially ordered or commissioned for use as a contribution to a collective work . . . if the parties expressly agree in a written instrument signed by them that the work shall be considered a work made for hire.[259]

The statute specifically recognizes only nine types of works which can be subject to the subsection (2) "ordered or commissioned" provision.

It might be tempting to think that both the 1909 and 1976 work-for-hire doctrines are statutory recognition of the power of capital. The only test in 1909 and the first test set out in the present statute is whether or not the creator(s) are employee(s) of the entity claiming copyright; the second test under the 1976 law might also favor capital—artists and writers doing work on order or commission are rarely successful enough to be in a position to turn down projects because those financing the project propose a written contract which transfers copyright.

What has happened since the 1976 Copyright Act became law is more interesting. Because § 101(2) requires a "written instrument" acknowledging that a work was "made for hire," court cases under this provision confront judges with little more than interpretations of ambiguous contractual provisions.[260] Instead, § 101(1)'s

---

256 Lin-Brook Builders Hardware v. Gertler, 352 F.2d 298, 300 (9th Cir. 1965); Brattleboro Publ'g Co. v. Winmill Publ'g Corp., 369 F.2d 565, 567-68 (2d Cir. 1966).

257 Seigel v. National Periodical Publications, 508 F.2d 909, 914 (2d Cir. 1974).

258 Picture Music, Inc. v. Bourne, Inc., 457 F.2d 1213, 1216 (2d Cir. 1972); Scherr v. Universal Match Corp., 417 F.2d 497, 500 (2d Cir. 1969).

259 17 U.S.C. § 101 (1988 & Supp. IV 1992).

260 An interesting problem is raised by the fact that § 101(2) enumerates nine types of works potentially subject to a copyright-transferring "made for hire" contract: what if the

"employee within the scope of . . . employment" provision has remained the battleground for work-for- hire disputes—so much so that 1909 law and 1976 law cases look much the same.[261]

After the 1976 Copyright Act introduced the § 101(1) and (2) dichotomy between "employment" works and "commissioned" works there was a split among the courts concerning "employment." Forced into a renewed analysis of "employment," the Second Circuit required *actual* control over the work's creation to be exercised by the hiring party.[262] This was a higher requirement than the *right to control* doctrine which the Second Circuit had earlier championed, and which continued to hold sway in some courts.[263] About the same time, the Ninth Circuit interpreted § 101(1) "employment" most narrowly, requiring it to be formal, salaried employment.[264]

In *Community for Creative Non-Violence v. Reid*,[265] the Supreme Court resolved these differences in favor of, de facto, the old *right to control* standard. In *Reid*, the Community for Creative Non-Violence ("CCNV") had commissioned Reid, a Baltimore sculptor, to prepare the figures for a sculpture depicting the plight of the homeless in Washington, D.C., through the metaphor of the modern nativity scene. CCNV prepared the base of the sculpture, which was an integral part of the work. CCNV also worked with Reid in providing him with human models for the sculpture, rejected some of Reid's proposals for elements of the sculpture, and may have reviewed sketches to approve stages of the work's development. Not falling within a § 101(2) "commission" category, the ownership dispute that eventually broke out took the form of whether Reid was an "employee" of CCNV. The Supreme Court

parties executed a clear "made for hire" contract covering a type of work not set out in § 101(2)? For example, the Supreme Court has recognized both that "sculpture does not fit within any of the nine categories" and that "no written agreement between the parties established [the sculpture] as a work for hire." Community for Creative Non-Violence v. Reid, 490 U.S. 730, 738 (1989). But what if the written agreement had made clear it was a work for hire, although it was not one of the enumerated nine categories?

261 *See* Philadelphia Orchestra Ass'n v. Walt Disney Co., 821 F. Supp. 341 (E.D. Pa. 1993) (soundtrack to "Fantasia" was work-for-hire owned by Disney because Orchestra members had signed agreements acknowledging that they had been "employed" by Disney); Respect Inc. v. Committee on Status of Women, 815 F. Supp. 1112, 1117-18 (N.D. Ill. 1993) (workbook was not work-for-hire because writer was not an employee of the Committee); Playboy Enters., Inc. v. Dumas, 831 F. Supp. 295 (S.D.N.Y. 1993), *rev'd in part*, 53 F.3d 549 (2d Cir. 1995) (copyright in Patrick Nagel's artwork belonged to Nagel's widow because Nagel was not a *Playboy* employee); Forward v. Thorogood, 985 F.2d 604 (1st Cir. 1993) (Thorogood's music recordings not work for hire).

262 Aldon Accessories Ltd. v. Spiegel, Inc., 738 F.2d 548 (2d Cir. 1984).

263 *See, e.g*, Peregrine v. Lauren Corp., 601 F. Supp. 828, 829 (Colo. 1985).

264 Dumas v. Gommerman, 865 F.2d 1093 (9th Cir. 1989).

265 490 U.S. 730 (1989).

adopted the Fifth Circuit's view that "the term 'employee' within § 101(1) carries its common-law agency meaning."[266] However, the Court then found that in order to have a uniform nationwide law, it would be necessary to use "the general common law of agency, rather than the law of any particular State."[267]

The Court then held that "[i]n determining whether a hired party is an employee under the general common law of agency, [one] consider[s] the hiring party's right to control the manner and means by which the product is accomplished."[268] That test, in turn, would be settled by considering a variety of factors drawn from the *Restatement of Agency*, "[n]o one of these factors being determinative."[269] These factors include the location of the work, ownership of the "instrumentalities and tools," the right to assign additional projects, provision of employee benefits, and the hired party's role in hiring assistants. In short, the *Reid* opinion set the stage for gestalt consideration of the relationship between hiring and hired; almost nothing is ruled out.

Because of all the *possible* factors bearing on an agency question, issues of raw economic power can have a weakened role.[270] Jaszi has noted that work-for-hire cases under § 101(1) typically de-emphasize the capital investment of the employer and emphasize the employer's creative contribution. To Jaszi, "[i]ronically, the employer's claims are rationalized in terms of the Romantic conception of 'authorship' with its concomitant values of 'originality' and 'inspiration.'"[271] Jaszi is correct on the de-emphasis on capital. For example, if economic underwriting was the pure measure of a § 101(1) work-for-hire, then the First Circuit's *Forward v. Thorogood*[272] case should have come out differently. Forward arranged and paid for the recording sessions of various songs by George Thorogood and the Destroyers at a time when Thorogood had no means to do so himself. On a *but-for* economic test, one might conclude that these recordings would not have happened without Forward. But a First Circuit panel held that this was not enough because Forward provided no direction and exercised no control over the recordings as a project: "[f]orward was a fan and

266 *Id.* at 739 (citing Easter Seal Soc'y for Crippled Children, et al. v. Playboy Enters., 815 F.2d 323 (5th Cir. 1987)).
267 *Id.* at 740.
268 *Id.* at 750-51.
269 *Id.* at 752.
270 *See, e.g.*, Hi-Tech Video Prods. v. Capital Cities/ABC, Inc., 58 F.3d 1093 (6th Cir. 1995) (although company exercised actual control over video's production, other factors established that hired parties were not employees for purposes of § 101(1)).
271 Jaszi, *Theory of Copyright*, *supra* note 29, at 486-88.
272 985 F.2d 604 (1st Cir. 1993).

friend who financed this effort, not the Archbishop of Salzburg commissioning works by Mozart."[273] The reference to the Archbishop of Salzburg, a great patron of the arts, is telling.

Although we are exploring the §101(1) criteria for when someone is an employee and *not* the § 101(2) question of a commissioned work, the characteristics of a work being "commissioned" suddenly can become central to the analysis. In *Philadelphia Orchestra*, the *Fantasia* soundtrack was found to be a work-for-hire owned by Disney in part because Disney had selected the music, provided the instruments and recording facilities, and controlled the recording process.[274] Harkening back to the Medicis reviewing Leonardo's handiwork, the court noted, approvingly, "Walt Disney himself attended the recording."[275]

Of course, "commission" language can be put in purely economic terms: discussion of whether an entity has "commissioned" a work frequently appears hand-in-hand with discussion of whether the entity undertook *all* the *financial risk* that the project would have no value. For example, in the *Fantasia* case, Disney undertook all the risk that the Philadelphia Orchestra's recordings would be worthless, while in *Playboy Enterprises v. Dumas* the trial court reasoned that the artwork of Patrick Nagel was not work-for-hire because, in part, "Nagel was the one who bore the risk because there was no commitment on the part of Playboy to purchase the works . . . ."[276] Looking to the allocation of financial risk makes sense in work-for-hire cases because that allocation reasonably reflects people's expectations. When a person knows his work has been specially *ordered* by someone, he usually does not expect to own it. When a patron commissions a work by an artist, the artist does not expect that tableau to be sitting around her studio years after it is done. The statutory test just reflects our usual expectations in a wider array of special orders; whether it is a tailored suit, a specially ordered automobile, or the advance purchase of a farmer's hay crop.

---

273 *Id.* at 606.

274 Philadelphia Orchestra Ass'n v. Walt Disney Co., 821 F. Supp. 341, 348 (E.D. Pa. 1993); *see also* Playboy Enters., Inc. v. Dumas, 831 F. Supp 295 (S.D.N.Y. 1993), *rev'd in part*, 53 F.3d 549 (2d Cir. 1995) (*Playboy* held not to be the owner of art works because it did not specially order or commission them).

275 *Philadelphia Orchestra*, 821 F. Supp. at 348.

276 *Playboy Enters.*, 831 F. Supp. at 299 ("In producing these [art]works, Nagel used his own equipment, tools, and materials; he worked in his own studio, on days and at times of his own choosing . . . ."). This finding was later reversed by the Circuit Court. *See also* Brattleboro Publ'g Co. v. Winmill Publ'g Corp., 369 F.2d 565, 567 (2d Cir. 1966) (establishing a presumption that a *res* is a work made for hire when the *res* is "produced at the instance and expense of the employer").

Despite this economic explanation for the notion of "commission" percolating into questions about employment, I would offer another possibility. There is much to suggest that the "commission" test reflects intentionality and if "employment" is sometimes measured by tests that sound like commissioning, this is partly because intentionality, and hence personhood, interests are at work. When a patron commissions a specific work, it is intended to fulfill a pre-established need. This need may be very general—as in a particular size tableau to fill an unusually shaped wall—or it may be very specific. The classic commission was specific at least as to theme: a statute or portrait to depict a particular individual with known physical features in a particular fashion (serious, formal, intelligent, at home, at battle, at leisure). A commission typically includes the power to reject a work. All this put tremendous control over the artistic program in the hands of the "patron." This extensive control over the artistic expression continues in modern life where, for corporations, commissioned art can have an important public relations impact. On this reasoning the "commission" test is not a financial measure, but a measure of whether the patron's intentions imbue and control the artistic endeavor. The case law reflects this in two ways.

First, courts frequently conclude that a work-for-hire is made when the "motivating factor in producing the work was the [patron] who induced the creation . . . ."[277] In *Playboy Enterprises,* the Second Circuit affirmed that a necessary condition for a § 101(1) work-for-hire is that it was made at the "instance" of the entity claiming ownership.[278] The *Thorogood* case discussed above provides an even better example of the "motivating factor" test. George Thorogood and the Destroyers were inspired to make music—in fact, to make the particular songs they were practicing and intent on recording—with or without Forward. The Thorogood artistic program was already settled when Forward provided the financing. Another way to think of this is that while Forward's money might have been the *but for* cause of the recordings being made, Forward was not a *sufficient* cause of the artistic program. Similarly, in a recent case in Illinois, *Respect v. Committee on Women,*[279] the court found that Mast, the author of sexual educational books on abstinence, was the author of the books in question, not

---

[277] Siegel v. National Periodical Publications, 508 F.2d 909, 914 (2d Cir. 1974); *Philadelphia Orchestra,* 821 F. Supp at 348; Picture Music, Inc. v. Bourne, Inc., 457 F.2d 1213 (2d Cir. 1972).

[278] *Playboy Enters.,* 53 F.3d at 553-56.

[279] 815 F. Supp. 1112 (N.D. Ill. 1993).

the Committee that funded her. The court's description makes it clear that Mast's "program" was already in place before the Committee funded her and that the Committee did not greatly affect that program;

> Well before Committee came onto the scene, Mast was an experienced teacher who was at the forefront of abstinence education. When she entered into discussions with Committee she continued to act as an entrepreneur. . . . Though Committee did have a limited kind of input to the books - for example, by suggesting revisions . . . [i]t was Mast and not Committee who was responsible for the books' content and flavor.[280]

Contrast these examples with the *Philadelphia Orchestra* case. In that case, it is clear that the Disney Studios were intent on making an animated vehicle for Mickey Mouse and, later, intent on including that project as part of an animated feature film set to classical music. From what we know about the facts, it appears that Disney would have made the project with or without the Philadelphia Orchestra.[281] It is Disney who had put a "program" in place and filled it with the Orchestra. The archetype of a commission is one where a specific development—such as the painting of the Sistine Chapel ceiling—is going to happen whether or not this particular artist is chosen. One screenwriter, who had just completed her first novel, when asked about the difference between working as a studio screenwriter and writing a novel, felt that the insignificance of a screenwriter comes from the fact that the script is going to get written with or without you. In this sense, the patron is a *sufficient* cause for some development to happen.[282]

Second, in these types of work-for-hire cases, courts inquire as to how much control the patron had over the artistic program. As

---

280 *Id.* at 1118. Note, however, that the case has language suggesting that the Department of Health and Human Services ("HHS"), which funded the Committee, actually had greater theoretical control on the work: "HHS conditioned its grant in part on the submission, for suggestion and pre-approved, of drafts and final versions of all printed materials developed with grant funds." *Id.* at 1115. But HHS did not claim to hold copyright in these books.

281 In fact, the recording of *The Sorcerer's Apprentice* used in *Fantasia* was *not* done by the Philadelphia Orchestra, but by an orchestra that Disney assembled and Leopold Stokowski conducted. *Philadelphia Orchestra*, 821 F. Supp. at 343. In an earlier contract dealing with the project, Disney had contracted for Stokowski to "select and employ a complete symphony orchestra," *id.* at 348, underscoring that the project would have gone forward with or without the Philadelphia Orchestra.

282 This may also parallel the modern distinction between a "commission" on the one hand and a "grant" or "fellowship" on the other. A grant or fellowship is given to a person to allow them to pursue a research agenda or artistic endeavor of *their own* selection versus one selected by the granting authority. The granting authority may provide the money to make the research or art possible, but if some other granting authority had provided the money, the researcher or artist would have pursued the same course.

the Supreme Court has said, the party who commissions a work "by definition has a right to specify the characteristics of the product desired . . . ."[283] In the *Thorogood* case, "the trial judge noted that Forward did request that certain songs be played [for the demo tape]" but "the band then played those songs in precisely the same manner that it always played them."[284] To the court, this was evidence that Forward made no artistic contribution to the tapes. But it is also evidence that Forward exercised no control; without his presence, the songs would have been exactly what they were. In *Picture Music v. Bourne Inc.*,[285] the court held the *res* was a work-for-hire where a motion picture producer had control over the original song, engaged the creator to adapt the song, and remained free to accept, reject, or modify the work. The Second Circuit remains firm that a work must be (1) at the patron's expense; (2) at the patron's instance; and (3) the patron must have had "the right to control and supervise."[286]

As much as the patron intervenes—or can intervene—in the process of intellectual production, the artist may feel that *less* of their personalities are involved in the creation. One visual artist I interviewed works mainly in her studio, but had recently completed a mural on commission. Without hesitation she characterized the two experiences as "completely different" and said that although her patron had given her great "creative leeway," she could not put her "heart and soul" into the work. Perhaps the relationship between the artist's creativity and patron's intentionality is or is often close to a zero sum game.[287] In many cases, we will never

---

283 Community for Creative Non-Violence v. Reid, 490 U.S. 730, 741 (1989). In *Reid*, the Supreme Court also set indicia for judging when someone is an employee (versus an independent contractor). *Id.* at 751-52. Interestingly, those indicia do not focus on *control* of the project.

284 Forward v. Thorogood, 985 F.2d 604, 607 (1st Cir. 1993).

285 457 F.2d 1213 (2d Cir. 1972).

286 Playboy Enters., Inc. v. Dumas, 53 F.3d 549, 555 (2d Cir. 1995). *See* ALAN LATMAN, ET AL., COPYRIGHT FOR THE NINETIES 309 (3rd ed., 1989); *Philadelphia Orchestra*, 821 F. Supp. at 348 ("[T]he test for actual control by the commissioning party slackened in the sixties to become a mere right to control (even if not exercised) standard."). Ironically, while the "employer" test under § 101(1) seems to have all the elements of a classic commission relationship—expense, instance, and right of artistic control—the Second Circuit has opined that under the § 101(2) test for a commissioned work, "the hiring party need not possess or exercise artistic control over the product." *Playboy Enters.*, 53 F.3d at 561. It's not clear whether this was a rejection of the *actual* control test—which would accord with *Aldon Accessories*—or a rejection of the *right* of control—which would make the § 101(2) standard less demanding than the § 101(1) standard.

287 This is suggested by at least one court's reasoning that "[the hiring party's] control of the video production thus weighs in favor of finding an employer-employee relationship, but not significantly, in light of the skill required of the assistants, as well as the assistant's artistic contributions to the product." Hi-Tech Video Prods. v. Capital Cities/ABC, Inc., 58 F.3d 1093, 1097 (6th Cir. 1995); *see also* Marco v. Accent Publ'g, 969 F.2d 1547, 1552 (3d Cir. 1992).

know the score in that game because "the interplay of ideas within such designer/client partnerships cannot usually be clearly charted or differentiated."[288] The degree to which the commission imposes a "pre-existent matrix" on the art is the degree from which it detracts from the artist's originality.[289] On the other hand, it would be depressing indeed to think that Michelangelo's work, the Sistine Chapel, does not embody the "heart and soul" of the artist. A large chunk of civilization's masterpieces were commissions. How can we reconcile this fact with a theory that trades off artist's creativity and patron's intentionality? Two possibilities come to mind.

First, why are the patron's demands not viewed by the artists as simple obstacles in the creative program, no more diminishing the artist's creativity than flaws in the block of marble from which Michelangelo sculpted the *David*, or the practical constraint on a director that his film should run under two hours? One answer is that the artist knows that the constraint of the patron is the result of another person's *will*. Unlike the flaws in the stone, the available pigments of painting, or the impersonal facts of audience attention span that rule all performing arts, the patron's intention is the product of a human mind. It may be that a great artist overcomes this difference, coming to view his patron's intentions as no more than troublesome random constraints.[290] Louis Kahn, for example, seemed obsessed with buildings as they appear as ruins, writing that ruins "reveal . . . the spirit" of a building because the building is then "freed from use"—a rhapsodized prose that seems to put the client's intentions, the occupants of the building, and the needs for which it was built all on a par as constraints.[291]

But there is another explanation for soulful commissioned

---

288 VALE, *supra* note 188, at 7 (discussing efforts to trace the different "meanings" or "intentions" of architects and politicians in national capital building projects).

289 For example, Milan Kundera credits Beethoven with being the first to change the structure of the compositions, so that the framework of each piece was "radically individual." He sees Beethoven as the first to understand that the "composition (the architectural organization of a work) should not be seen as some pre-existent matrix, loaned to an author for him to fill out with his invention; the composition should itself be an invention, an invention that engages all the author's originality." KUNDERA, supra note 187, at 172.

290 But the opposite is possible; it is easy to imagine the stereotypical prima donna anthropomorphizing every constraint as people conspiring against her art. This might happen when economic constraints demand that a commissioned work be changed. Are economic considerations akin to physical flaws in the marble to be sculpted or do they manifest weakness of will on the part of the patron (who may be, for example, unwilling to move monies from the welfare budget to the arts)? *See, e.g.*, Adele Freedman, *A Mall, Not a City Hall*, ARCHITECTURE, Jan. 1, 1995, at 43. (Architect Moshe Safdie threatened to sue the City of Ottawa when the city removed plans for a 56-foot high tower from Safdie's design for the new Ottawa City Hall to cut costs.)

291 ALEXANDRA TYNG, KAHN'S PHILOSOPHY OF ARCHITECTURE 166 (1984) (quoting letter from Kahn to Harriet Pattison).

works—one which respects the idea of a zero sum game between artist creativity and patron intentionality. Commissioned work and "artist-originated" work are just extreme characterizations. In the world of commissioned works, the amount of control (intention) exercised by the patron depends greatly on the stature of the artist. As screenwriter Mark Saltzman put it:

> [W]hen Spielberg did a movie in the 1980's, he was technically working for Universal but no one questioned that he got to do whatever he wanted. A recent USC grad might sign the same directing contract and there will be 20 Universal executives looking through the lens on each shot.[292]

The artist of sufficient stature may turn the tables on his patron, demanding resources or leeway beyond anything the patron intended.[293]

The choice of the word "patron" in this discussion was done partly with this point in mind. If we consider the classic "patron," he was not the sort of foil that would easily become—to a deconstructionist—a "construct" explaining the work-for-hire cases. A patron invested in an artist's career, giving the artist freer and freer rein as confidence in the artist's creative powers grew.

The recent *Playboy Enterprises* opinion shows the courts wrestling with a truer "patron" situation—facts somewhere between the *Philadelphia Orchestra* and the *Thorogood* situations. In *Playboy Enterprises,* Patrick Nagel began producing artwork for *Playboy* in 1974 and continued to provide monthly contributions until 1984.[294] The relationship between magazine and artist had the hallmarks of an increasingly relaxed patron/artist relationship: "Nagel accepted some specific assignments, at least until 1976. However, as time went on, he was given greater freedom to submit the paintings he wanted, which apparently matched what Playboy was interested in publishing."[295]

The court received evidence about specific assignments Nagel received, such as illustrations for a story on Lillian Hellman and an article on sex with aliens.[296] But these works were not at issue. What was at issue were five artworks done after August 1978 which *Playboy* had reproduced and marketed as the *Playboy Collection by Patrick Nagel.* These works came from a time when an independent

---

292 Interview with Mark Saltzman in Los Angeles, Cal. (Feb. 2, 1998).

293 Safdie prevailed in having a tower gridwork erected, giving his overall design the originally intended shape. *See* Freedman, *supra* note 290.

294 *Playboy Enter.,* 53 F.3d at 552.

295 Playboy Enters., Inc. v. Dumas, 831 F. Supp. 295, 300 (S.D.N.Y. 1993).

296 *Id.* at 310.

market for Nagel's works was already developing[297] and the parties had settled into a loose, but consistent relationship:

> Sometime after January 1977, but before August 1978, Nagel and Playboy fell into a course of conduct whereby Nagel would produce a few works for Playboy expecting them to be published; Playboy, in turn, expected to publish a few of Nagel's works . . . . Neither party appears to have tested the boundaries of the other.[298]

This fact pattern falls into a grey zone between the various measures we have been discussing. Although both parties knew that "there were subjects which would not have been accepted by Playboy . . . apparently no Nagel work was ever rejected outright."[299] Hugh Hefner himself provided some key evidence, but unlike Disney's presence at the recording session, Hefner went on record saying that *Playboy* gave up trying to direct Nagel's art.[300] The freedom given to Nagel, the apparent right Nagel would have to use any art *Playboy* would reject, the fact that Nagel was developing similar art independently—all suggest that the correct result was reached as to the "intentionality" at issue in the case.

It is useful to compare the statutory work-for-hire doctrine in copyright law with the common law's allocation of patent rights between employers and employee-inventors in the absence of a written assignment agreement. The common law doctrine of an employer's right to an employee's inventions bears the same mark of concern for "intentionality." The common law recognizes three distinct kinds of employees who could be inventors:

(1) employees who do not have inventive activities as part of their job description. Examples of this first category would be someone hired to be the accountant for a jet engine company or the receptionist for a biotechnology research lab.

(2) persons in "general" inventive employment, i.e. research, design or development. An example of this second category might be a technician hired to join the biotech lab.

(3) persons employed for the specific purpose of creating employer-specified inventions. An example of this third cate-

---

297 *Id.* at 313.

298 *Id.* at 310-11.

299 *Id.* at 310.

300 "At first we asked [Nagel] to illustrate a particular [subject] . . . but soon it was clear that trying to funnel such a large talent so narrowly was like telling Irwin Shaw or Ray Bradbury what to write about." Playboy Enters., Inc. v. Dumas, 53 F.3d 549, 562 (2d Cir. 1995).

> gory might be an engineer hired to solve a particular problem of airflow in a type of jet engine.

Of course, it's easy to imagine borderline situations between these categories.[301]

The common law draws a distinction among these categories as to the rights enjoyed by the employer. In general, all inventions are the property of employee-inventors who fall in (1) and (2). However, in cases where the employee used the employer's "time, facilities, and materials to attain a concrete result," equity entitles the employer to a non-exclusive "shop right" to practice the invention.[302]

The one exception to ownership by the employee-inventor is category (3): the employer has title to an invention when the employee-inventor made an *employer-specified* invention,[303] i.e., the inventor was employed to invent the super-widget and actually invented the super-widget. Fitting with our discussion of intentionality, in this tripartite classification of the common law, the employer-specified invention program is most analogous to the classic artistic commission. Both impose specific demands on the creator; in both cases, the patron is imbuing the creative process with her own intention.[304] There is a program already set upon—to make the engine run cooler or to fill the blank wall with a seascape. This kind of inventive work is employer-driven (or patron-driven) versus inventor-driven (or artist-driven). Thus, in the *Dubilier* case, the Supreme Court found that the patents belonged to Dunmore and

301 For example, what if the lab technician is hired to do general work in the lab, but receives written project assignments which transfer her from "team" to "team," each with a particular, explicitly stated inventive goal. Would she then fall in category (1) or (2)? Because preinvention assignment agreements are so prevalent in research organizations, this sort of question may not reach the courts.

302 United States v. Dubilier Condeser Corp., 289 U.S. 178 (1933), *amended by* 289 U.S. 706 (1933); Cherensky, *supra* note 4, at 616-27. In *Dubilier*, the Supreme Court found that the common law gave the inventor title to the invention even when the employee was working in a research lab because employment "to design or to construct or to devise methods of manufacture is not the same thing as employment to invent." *Dubilier*, 289 U.S. at 178. Justice Stone provided a reasonable, common-sense dissent from this result, finding that the distinction between employment to work in a research lab and employment to invent was too fine a distinction: "They were not, of course, engaged to invent, in the sense in which a carpenter is employed to build a chest, but they were employed to conduct scientific investigations in a laboratory devoted principally to applied rather than pure science, with full knowledge and expectation of all concerned that their investigations might normally lead, as they did, to inventions." *Id.* at 211.

303 *Dublilier*, 289 U.S. at 188; Cherensky, *supra* note 4, at 616-27.

304 To be fair, as in the case of artistic commissions, we could explain the common law of invention ownership by reference to expectations. If an inventor was paid to invent the super-widget, he should reasonably expect that any resulting super-widget will belong to the person who paid him. As the Court said in *Dubilier*, "[a] term of the [employment] agreement necessarily is that what he is paid to produce belongs to his paymaster." 289 U.S. at 187.

Lowell, the employees, because they were self-motivated in their inventive work: "Dunmore was wrestling, in his own mind, impelled thereto solely by his own scientific curiosity, with the subject of substituting house lighting alternating current for direct battery current in radio apparatus . . . . [The project] was independent of their work and voluntarily assumed."[305]

Steven Cherensky advocates a form of "corporate inventorship" that would allow corporate entities to be listed as the "inventor" of patented innovations just as corporations can be the "authors" of copyrighted works under the work-for-hire doctrine. It is interesting to note *when* Cherensky would consider "corporate inventorship" appropriate. After considering and rejecting different possible standards for when "corporate inventorship" should be invoked, Cherensky settles on a test rich in intentionality: "[a] better definition of corporate inventions would . . . [be] limit[ing] a corporate invention to *an anticipated result of corporate direction* that was conceived and reduced to practice using significant corporate resources."[306] This formula certainly has parallels to elements of the work-for-hire doctrine; Cherensky believes an invention is the "corporation's" when "corporate direction" determined the inventive quest—the same intent and purpose which can place a copyrighted intellectual work in the hands of someone who did not actually produce the work.

D. *Intentionality and the Artisan's Unforeseen Results*

Recognizing personhood interest through the intentionality in a plan of action also gives us a different perspective on another vexing doctrine of copyright law, the problem of mistakes. Pioneer animators Frank Thomas and Ollie Johnston of the Disney studios "recall stumbling upon many of their best discoveries almost by accident"[307] and Alfred Stieglitz's grand-niece is convinced that many of the great photographers' works turned out differently than he intended, but that he explained away these unintended effects.[308] Copyright law protects variations that are unplanned or inadvertent. As Jerome Frank said in an often quoted passage of *Alfred Bell*: "[a] copyist's bad eyesight or defective musculature or a shock

---

[305] *Id.* at 184-85.

[306] Cherensky, *supra* note 4, at 656-57 (emphasis added).

[307] Scott Collins, *supra* note 46, at F1.

[308] Hunter Drohojowska-Philp, *Stieglitz in Sharp Focus*, L.A. TIMES, Oct. 19, 1995, at F1 (Stieglitz's niece, Sue Davidson Lowe, believed that the making of any of Stieglitz's cloud photographs was a "pasttime" and "once it was in print, it was frozen. He was not good at saying he'd made a mistake, so his instinct was to embellish it.").

caused by a clap of thunder, may yield sufficiently distinguishable variations. Having hit upon such a variation, the 'author' may adopt it as his and copyright it."[309]

Some commentators have interpreted Frank as "declar[ing] that 'intent' was not an element of originality" and that "an author's lack of intent cannot negate originality."[310] Judge Frank, however, seemed less certain. Indeed, in an earlier opinion he noted that lack of intention might prevent copyrightability, commenting, "[i]f one made an unintentional error in copying which he perceived to add distinctiveness to the product, he might perhaps obtain a valid copyright on his copy, although the question would then arise whether originality is precluded by lack of intention."[311]

It would be an understatement to say that protection of inadvertent originality is a nettlesome problem for the personal expression paradigm. If the artist did not *intend* to badly distort the woman's nose, how can such distortion be his *personal expression*? If the variation was the reaction to "shock caused by a clap of thunder," we do not even have the fig-leaf of explanation offered by the artist's unconscious. As Nozick has commented, "[i]t won't count as creative if it simply happens by accident."[312]

At one time, this may have been a pretty limited problem, but twentieth century painting, musical composition, playwrighting, and filmaking have broadened the issue. For the issue is no longer the quirky result of "defective eyesight" or a muscular twitch—at least these could be explained by reference to the artist's body. Now, there are artists for whom a major "technique" is capturing random occurrences or the spontaneous reaction of others—an entire artistic approach that seems to rob us of our comfortable notion that the artist "means" something or "expresses" something.

We have already explored the problems embedded in the notion of personal expression, but we should note that one commentator has suggested that the "transformative" process of creativity is actually closer to the inadvertent mistake than we would like to admit. Litman has noted that the "imperfect eyesight [and] flawed execution" of Judge Frank's opinions "can serve as a metaphor for authorship in general."[313] Recognizing how our minds record experiences, Litman insightfully (and admiringly) characterizes au-

---

309 Alfred Bell & Co. v. Catalda Fine Arts, Inc., 191 F.2d 99, 105 (2d Cir. 1951).

310 VerSteeg, *supra* note 73, at 845.

311 Chamberlin v. Uris Sales Corp., 150 F.2d 512, 513 (2d Cir. 1945).

312 NOZICK, supra note 80, at 35.

313 Litman, *supra* note 29, at 1010.

thorship as a "combination of absorption, astigmatism, and amnesia." This is an interesting thought—that "creativity" is the result of an inability to process the world of experience with the accuracy we now demand of our high technology. (In placing our creativity in our shortcomings, Litman is not too far from a more familiar view that creativity springs from the individual's psychological inability to cope with the world.) Litman's suggestion gives us the problem of inadvertent mistake or Jackson Pollack splashes writ large: it robs us wholesale of the idea of "meaning" and "expression."

Intentionality offers us a prospective answer. The artist intended to splatter certain paints on the canvas; the playwright or director intended to assemble actors of a particular sort and give them general directions of a particular sort. But what are the limits of this explanation—does it apply to so many circumstances that it applies to none? Consider an example the *Alfred Bell* court drew from Plutarch: "[a] painter, enraged because he could not depict the foam that filled a horse's mouth from champing at the bit, threw a sponge at his painting; the sponge splashed against the wall—and achieved the desired result."[314] I think this is beyond the extreme of inclusion in an "intentional program." Unlike Pollock spilling paint across a canvas, Plutarch's painter seems to be stepping outside his "intentional program" to vent his anger. Throwing the sponge was not part of a plan to achieve a desired result; in fact, at the moment he threw the sponge, the artist may have expected that, if anything, the impact of the sponge would move him away from the desired result by damaging part of the painting.

Along the same lines, we might conclude that a genetic mutation would be so far beyond the pale of intention (or creativity) that these could not justify personality interests in valuable cell-lines—a topic considered in a few lines.

IV. Personhood Interests in Being the Source of the *Res*; The Desire for Social Place

Aside from creativity and intentionality, there may be a simpler, starker personality interest: identification as the source of the *res.* The idea of "sourcehood" takes two forms. The first is the purely private self-identification with the *res.* This is a private belief that one is the source of the *res.* A ghost-writer or the author of an anonymous *Economist* story can have a private sense of pride in her

---

314 *Alfred Bell*, 191 F.2d at 105 n.23.

work.[315] Contrast this with the desire for the attention of others, recognition, or *social place*; a person who wants others to identify her and might try to achieve this recognition by "marking" things as her own.[316] There are those so desperate for social recognition that they identify things as their own when they have no other connection to the things they have "marked" other than that they mark them. Perhaps some cases of graffiti fall into this sort of behavior.[317]

Self-identification and the desire for recognition from others are conceptually distinct. One can imagine creative people who identify with their work and do *not* want social recognition. In fact, a well-known reason to avoid social recognition is to maintain greater creative freedom.[318] But these two notions—self-identification as the source of a *res* and desire for social recognition through the *res*—are rarely disentangled. More often, they are combined on an assumption that the person seeks social identification for those things with which she already self-identifies. I call this a "sourcehood" interest and suggest that this simple interest, in being identified as the source of some intellectual work, may be a personality justification. Even for one commentator who finds intellectual property rights generally problematic, there remains a belief that "[a]n author's or inventor's sense of worth and dignity requires public acknowledgment by those who use the writing or discovery. . . ."[319] Indeed, the personhood interest in intellectual property is most often protected with a guarantee of social recognition: the right of attribution. This protection takes the form of social mores as much as laws. For example, there is the convention in the scientific community that newly discovered species or geographic features may be christened by their discoverers. Among academics, at least, the social opprobrium of plagiarism is distinct from the legal liability of copyright infringement.

Although attribution rights protect sourcehood interests, in America those rights are much more inchoate than in continental

---

315 The ghostwriter is used only as an example of private pride; obviously the writer may have a creativity interest, not just the raw sourcehood interest being described here.

316 *See generally* Hegel's Philosophy of Right ¶ ¶ 54-58 (T.M. Knox trans., 1967).

317 *See* Victor Pelevin, *Assertive,* N.Y. TIMES SUN. MAG., June 9. 1997, 65 ("The American Teen-ager . . . in tracing his esoteric, indecipherable signature, is an image-maker adding his own logo to the cluttered symbols around him. When he traces a mysterious zigzag on . . . a bridge, he is already beginning to carve out his niche in life.").

318 Jane Austen sensibly expressed this concern: "I am gratified by her having pleasure in what I wrote—but I wish the knowledge of my being exposed to her discerning criticism, may not hurt my style, by inducing too great a solicitude." Letter from Jane Austin, *in* JANE AUSTEN'S LETTERS (Jan. 24, 1809).

319 Edwin C. Hettinger, *Justifying Intellectual Property,* 18 PHIL. & PUB. AFF. 31, 45 (1989).

legal systems. The default assumption of our copyright system is that a source of an intellectual property *res* does not have a right of attribution.[320] American patent law works better to protect this personality interest than does copyright law, requiring that the named inventor(s) on a patent application—and any patent issued—be natural persons who actually invented the invention.[321] Compare this with copyright law which permits someone who did not create the copyrighted work (an employer) to be treated as the "author" of that work.[322]

If the right of attribution has only a toehold in our mores and laws, even more problematic is the extension of any other rights (i.e. to control the intellectual property *res*) on the slender reed that someone self-identifies with that *res*. This section explores (1) some of the situations in which self-identification might arise from "sourcehood"; (2) the descriptive question of how intellectual property law has responded to such situations; and (3) the normative question of whether intellectual property law should respond to such interests.

We are concerned here with situations in which a person is the source of some valuable intellectual property but something about the situation seems to deny us the instruments explored above—creativity or intentionality. One could be the "Eureka" situation, a useful thought that just pops into a person's head or a totally unintended, undirected discovery: Scott's golf ball flies off course, lands at the entrance of an undiscovered cave, and with one step inside he finds the fossils of a previously unknown species. A sourcehood interest could also arise through labor or effort, even though that effort has not led to anything apparently creative. A common example of this sort might be cases of painstaking repro-

---

320 *See, e.g.*, Cleary v. News Corp., 30 F.3d 1255, 1259-60 (9th Cir. 1994); Vargas v. Esquire, Inc., 164 F.2d 522, 524-27 (7th Cir. 1947) (holding that an artist could not claim a right of attribution against a magazine where the artist granted the magazine all rights to his drawings in exchange for monthly compensation); Nelson v. Radio Corp. of Am., 148 F. Supp. 1 (S.D. Fla. 1957) (denying a singer a right of attribution in the context of a master/servant relationship between recording company and singer and absent agreement to provide label credit).

321 *See* 35 U.S.C. §115 (1988) (requiring that the "applicant shall make oath that he believes himself to be the original and first inventor of the [invention] for which he solicits a patent"); 6 DONALD S. CHISUM, PATENTS: A TREATISE ON THE LAW OF PATENTABILITY, VALIDITY, AND INFRINGEMENT § 22.01 (1992). Steven Cherensky is one of those to recognize, "[t]his non-transferable, non-assignable, market-inalienable inventorship identification is a form of protection of a personhood interest—the association of the person with her invention." Cherensky, *supra* note 4, at 653.

322 17 U.S.C. §§ 101, 201(b) (1988 & Supp. III 1991). *See also* The Semiconductor Chip Protection Act of 1984, which provides that "authorship" of a new chip mask design may belong to the entity financing the design. 17 U.S.C. §§ 901(6), 902 (1988 & Supp. IV 1992).

duction; we must consider whether intentionality still provides an explanation of the personality interest in these situations. A sourcehood interest could also come from being the passive source of valuable genetic information; this is the *Moore v. University of California*[323] problem. In all these situations, however, the legal system does not grant protection—and therefore does not seem to recognize a personhood interest—unless other elements are present. This point has been noted frequently by deconstructionists espousing the "romantic genius" role in our legal system. But, again, the juxtaposition does not have to be unprotected "sources" from protected "geniuses"; the undervaluing of "sources" may be rooted in the idea of human agency (of the sort described in the above discussions of creativity and intentionality) as the ingredient that removes something from the Lockean commons.[324]

A. *The "Eureka" Problem*

The "Eureka" situation happens when a new and important thought just springs into the head of a person or someone stumbles upon a completely unintended discovery, i.e., a hiker who finds an extraordinary fossil. The "Eureka" situation could prove vexing in extreme cases. Imagine Allen wakes up one morning with a complex mathematical formula pounding in his head. He writes it down simply to lessen the pounding in his head, finding his work is impaired by this formula's presence in his head, and, finally asks a physicist friend what the formula might mean. Instead of telling him that he is uncontrollably recalling a formula from a "physics for poets" college course, the physicist tells Allen "he" has quite possibly solved a problem about warping space with gravity fields. At first, Allen says "Not me." Yet as the formula gains notoriety, so does he. Indeed, after a time he comes to enjoy attending physics symposia and, imitating Chauncy in *Being There*, speaking in poetic metaphors about astrophysics. His sole claim to the formula is that it afflicted his consciousness; if it was "in the air," he was the person it happened to alight upon.

As fanciful as this tale is, there are many cases where the individual knows he is the "source" of an idea, but he feels disconnected from it—it has no relation to his person or personality. Richard Evans, source of the 1994 book *The Christmas Box* repeatedly said in interviews that he did not feel like the author of that

323 793 P.2d 479 (Cal. 1990).

324 *See* Holmes v. Hurst, 174 U.S. 82, 86 (1899); Jefferys v. Boosey, 10 Eng. Rep. 681, 702 (H.L. 1854) (describing words as "elements of matter").

story as much as the "messenger" who simply told it. Picasso was known to say he could not control his paintings.[325] Miro said his paintings were "always born in a state of hallucination induced by shock, objective or subjective, for which I am not personally responsible."[326]

This sentiment is at least as common in the sciences and philosophy as it is in the arts. Nietzsche loudly opposed the Cartesian formula "I think," noting that "a thought comes when 'it' wants to and not when 'I' want it to . . . [and that a philosopher's thoughts come] from outside, from above or below, like events or thunderbolts heading for him."[327] In the sciences, Eureka-esque stories occur again and again. Kepler was drawing at the board in a mathematics class he was teaching one day when he was struck with an idea so forceful, that he believed he had stumbled onto the secret of creation: it was the basis to justify a heliocentric solar system that would eventually topple Ptolemaic astronomy. "The delight I took in my discovery," he exclaimed, "I shall never be able to describe in words."[328] Arthur Koestler once said, "[t]he more original a discovery, the more obvious it seems afterwards." And the more obvious something seems, the less it may seem like one person's mind.

In all these cases, the "Eureka" feeling and the sense of internal disassociation with the work may not be shared by external observers.[329] External observers may see creativity or intentionality at

---

325 When he looked at some of his early works, he commented to Malraux, "It's not me who chooses now." MALRAUX, *supra* note 66, at 79.

326 Attributed to Miro at the exhibit Miro: Spirit of the Orient, Hong Kong Museum of Art, (Sept. 1995 to Oct. 1995). *See supra* note 122.

327 The role of the "I" of thinking has been a subject of much Western philosophy. Although Leibniz sought, in the seventeenth century, to distance himself from Cartesianism, he expressed a view akin to Nietzsche's, but arguably compatible with Dewey's: that although we do not "form" our ideas, the ideas "form themselves through us, not in consequence of our will, but in accordance with our nature and that of things." GOTTFRIED W. LEIBNIZ, THEODICY: ESSAYS ON THE GOODNESS OF GOD, THE FREEDOM OF MAN, AND THE ORIGIN OF EVIL § 403, at 364 (E.M. Huggard trans., 1985).

328 ARTHUR KOESTLER, THE SLEEPWALKERS: A HISTORY OF MAN'S CHANGING VISION OF THE UNIVERSE 247 (1959); *see also* HUDSON & JACOT, *supra* note 103, at 111

> [I]t is perfectly normal for a scientist to be seized with an idea that seems to him unchallengeable, a bolt from the blue so dramatic as to arrive as a revelation; and normal too, for a life's work to be built around such dazzling insight. It is also commonplace for such insights to be false.

Id.

329 Among those doubtful of such claims is Steven Pinker.

> Unfortunately, creative people are at their most creative when writing their autobiographies. Historians have scrutinized their diaries, notebooks, manuscripts, and correspondence looking for signs of the temperamental seer periodically struck by bolts from the unconscious. Alas, they have found that the creative genius is more Salieri than Amadeus.

STEVEN PINKER, HOW THE MIND WORKS 361 (1997). Similarly, Weisberg discusses, but does

work. If one embraces the broad explication of potential intentionality interests in the videotape and inadvertent artist discussions above, there may be little room for pure sourcehood. If Columbus' intention was to reach the Far East, then he got nowhere; if his intention was to reach land by sailing west, then his intention program was largely achieved. With almost any scientific or research program, a personhood interest could be rooted in the purposeful direction of the individual's mental life; even if the scientists claims it came to him "out of the blue," we may see it as the result of years of education, or some other personal factor. The same applies to exploratory artistic programs. The Eureka idea comes to the artist or inventor because he has been setting traps to catch it.

But the point is that for the most extreme Eureka situations—such as Allen the reluctant physicist—Radin's original explication of personhood interests is still good. While much of this article has focused on the *personal* which becomes an *expression*, in the sourcehood situation there may be *expressions* which become the *personal*. In the story above, Allen comes to identify with the physics formula that came to him. The legal system has not handled cases like this, but if it did, we might feel that some protectable interest should be recognized. This becomes clearer in a case that did come to the courts: the dispute between John Moore and the University of California over rights to genetic information from his cells.

B. *Being the Source of Bodily Information*

When viewed in the historic sweep of Anglo-American political thought, one of the most strangely reasoned opinions of the late twentieth century may be the majority opinion in *Moore v. Regents of University of California.*[330] Doctors at UCLA Medical Center had removed Moore's spleen in the course of cancer treatment, and then used Moore's cells to create a patented cell-line. In *Moore,* the California Supreme Court held that the doctors may have breached their fiduciary duty to Moore, but that Moore had no property interest in his own body's cells.

The *Moore* majority was not concerned with the moral dimension of extending property rights over living tissue—an issue apparently settled in America but still hotly debated in Europe.[331] The

---

not believe this "messenger" view of creativity. *See* Weisberg, *supra* note 79 at 215, 231 (analyzing such claims by William Blake, Dostoyevski, and others).

330 793 P.2d 479 (Cal. 1990.

331 See Andrew Kimbrell, *Life for Sale,* UTNE READER, July/Aug. 1995, at 24 (discussing

Moore court did not question the propriety of the patents issued to the physicians who had cultured Moore's spleen cells. Instead, the majority opinion, authored by Justice Panelli, called Moore's own claim to have a property interest in the biological materials derived from his own body "novel" and "problematical at best."[332] Justice Panelli's opinion on why a person's biological material is not his own property gives one the distinct impression that John Locke was not on the judge's shelf. It is Locke's 300-year-old claim that people own their own arms and legs—very much biological material—which provides the first step in a labor theory of property which has influenced American law since the Founding Fathers.[333] This is not to say that Locke's initial premise cannot be questioned,[334] but if that was Panelli's intent, he might have done more than label Moore's claim "novel" and "problematic." One irony of the *Moore* case is that the conventions of the scientific community did a better job of recognizing Moore's contribution than the legal system did: as issued, the patent covers the "Mo cell line."

The *Moore* majority opinion has been criticized by many writers for different reasons. James Boyle has accurately critiqued the *Moore* opinion for its inexplicable discussion of uniqueness as a requisite for a property right in human cells.[335] The *Moore* court focused on the genetic code for production of lymphokines, finding that this tiny part of Moore's gene code could not be different from anyone else's.[336] The proper focus of analysis, however, was not the gene code, but the cells (or whatever aspect of the cells—possibly including code) that were responsible for Moore's higher than normal level of lymphokines production. Even if the court had done a tighter factual analysis, there would be no justification for the court's uniqueness requirement on Moore's property claim. Uniqueness is a requirement only of patent law; it is not required for most other property regimes and certainly not for rights to one's own labor—one's own bodily toil.

European Parliament's rejection of patenting scheme for life forms); Chester Bisbee, *Defeat of European Draft Directive Clouds Animal Patenting Issue,* GENETIC ENGINEERING NEWS, Apr. 15, 1995, at 1.

332 *Moore,* 793 P.2d at 493.

333 JOHN LOCKE, TWO TREATISES OF GOVERNMENT (Peter Laslett rev. ed., Cambridge Univ. Press 1963).

334 As Moritz Schlick, one of the Vienna Positivists noted: "[t]he grammar of the word 'owner' is similar to that of the word 'my': it makes sense only where it is logically possible for a thing to change its owner, *i.e.*, where the relation between the owner and the owned object is empirical, not logical." Moritz Schlick, *Meaning and Justification,* 45 PHIL. REV. 339, 366 (1936). If a particular gene code could not change its "owner," perhaps it has no "owner" at all.

335 Boyle, *supra* note 29, at 1516-18.

336 *Moore,* 793 P.2d at 490.

To Boyle, *Moore* is also another case in which "sources" of new intellectual property are undervalued while the manipulators who use source material are aggrandized by the "author" construct,[337] a point reinforced by dissenting Justice Mosk's comment that "no one can question Moore's crucial contribution to the invention."[338] The *Moore* court emphasized the patented work of the UCLA researchers in producing a *cell line* from Moore's cells, opining that "adaptation and growth of human tissues and cells in culture is difficult—often considered an art" and that the patent granted to the cell line applied to the results of this "inventive effort . . . not the *discovery of naturally occurring* raw materials."[339] Again, this part of the opinion's reasoning is not relevant to Moore's claim of body-snatching. Simply put, the patent rights of the UCLA researchers do not bear directly on property rights to the *source material*; Charles Allen's process for extracting alumina from bauxite did not confer on him ownership of the bauxite he used to produce the first batch of alumina. The amount of art Rodin put into the *Kiss* would not alter property rights to the original bronze or marble; Rodin might own the copyrightable image of the *Kiss* and still be liable for stealing marble. The issue that should have been directly confronted is whether Moore had a property right to his cells—does Locke's theory of self-ownership extend to the cellular level or does "ownership" simply make no sense when applied to body parts? The majority opinion fails to get to the root questions of cell ownership.

The *Moore* case does not, however, offer us a platform to explore some other fundamental issues. While we might be pre-disposed to recognize that Moore had a property right in his biological cells, would we have said the same thing if the issue was only his property right to the genetic *information* in whatever gene in his code prompts zealous lymphokine production? Imagine that instead of taking his cells—removing physical material—in surgery, in the course of treating Moore, the UCLA physicians had been able to scan and "read" the sequence of amino acids in his DNA and had discovered which portion of it was responsible for heightened lymphokine production. In one sense, this would be like a news reporter who had permission to be in your study opening a drawer, reading and memorizing a portion of your unpublished

337 Boyle believes that in the *Moore* opinion "the issue is once again being restated, whether consciously or unconsciously, in terms of the ideology of authorship." Boyle, *supra* note 29, at 1516.

338 *Moore*, 793 P.2d at 511.

339 *Id.* at 492 (emphasis added).

manuscript, and using verbatim quotations from it in his own articles. In both cases, although there was permission given, there is still invasion of privacy. In both cases, there is no physical taking, just a taking of information and expression.[340] The great difference, however, is that people have no conscious personal experience, creativity, or intentionality embedded in their genetic codes. Does a personhood interest in this information arise nonetheless because you are the source of the information? The *Moore* court drifted toward a negative answer without fully appreciating the depths of the waters they skirted.

In truth, Moore's experience was not far from that of Bela Lugosi's heirs at the hands of the same court a few years earlier—another troubling page in any account of "sourcehood" recognition. In *Lugosi v. Universal Pictures*,[341] a majority of the California Supreme Court held that Lugosi's heirs could not prevent Universal Studios from licensing an image of "Dracula" that clearly included Lugosi's likeness. Lugosi had granted Universal a right to use his likeness in promoting specific *Dracula* films, but Universal had discovered, as Disney had with Mickey Mouse, that the "Dracula" character—particularly Lugosi's rendition of it—was a valuable property separate from any films in which it appeared. Universal widely licensed the Lugosi-Dracula character for merchandise unconnected to any re-release or promotion of the films. Lugosi's heirs argued that Lugosi's grant to Universal did not extend to such uses.

The majority found that Lugosi's right to control his name and likeness was personal, and, therefore, nondescendible. This left Universal free to exploit the Lugosi-Dracula image after Lugosi's death. The majority concluded that "neither society's interests in the free dissemination of ideas nor the artist's rights to the fruits of his own labor would be served" by recognizing the right to descend to Lugosi's heirs.[342] The court also justified their nondescendibility ruling by "the difficulty in judicially selecting an ap-

---

340 Ironically, in biochemistry, "expression" is used to refer to duplication of an amino acid code.

341 603 P.2d 425 (Cal. 1979). The connection between genetic information and persona has not gone unnoticed. *See* Stephen Ashley Mortinger, Comment, *Spleen for Sale;* Moore v. Regents of University of California *and the Right to Sell Parts of Your Body,* 51 OHIO ST. L.J. 499, 514 (1990) (holding that "a cause of action for appropriation of the commercial value of a person's genetic structure [is not] far removed from the Court's current recognition of the right of a person to claim appropriation of his unique likeness or persona.") *But see* Thomas P. Dillon, *Source Compensation for Tissues and Cells Used in Biotechnical Research: Why A Source Should not Share in the Profits,* 64 NOTRE DAME L. REV. 628 (1989) (not recognizing any personality interests).

342 *Lugosi,* 603 P.2d at 431.

propriate durational limitation" if heirs were allowed to inherit a property right in a likeness.[343] Justice Mosk provided a concurrence which touched on different issues, but was principally driven by his belief that "[m]erely playing a role" creates no property interest in that dramatic role.

The *Lugosi* case is not easily analyzed as a "source" versus "romantic author" battle. In *Lugosi*, the original author plays no part because the character created by the author, Bram Stoker, had already entered the public domain. On one hand, the case centered on a popular *artiste's* battle against an anonymous collaborative institution. On the other hand, that artist, Lugosi, was clearly using someone else's material. The only hint of Mr. Lugosi being an underappreciated "source" may have been Justice Mosk saying that Lugosi "was a talented actor [b]ut . . . he was not a playwright, an innovator, a creator or an entrepreneur."[344]

Still, the prevailing arguments in *Lugosi* bear scrutiny. The court's reasoning that the "artist's right to the fruits of his labor" would not be served by descendible rights certainly seems at odds with Congress' conclusion that laboring artists are well served by permitting copyrights to descend to heirs. Justice Mosk similarly seemed to misstep when he reasoned that Lugosi's "performance gave him no more claim on Dracula than that of countless actors of Hamlet who have portrayed the Dane in a unique manner."[345] That comment misses the point. The issue was not whether Lugosi's heirs had rights over the *Dracula role*, but whether Lugosi's heirs had rights over the Lugosi-Dracula *image*: as Justice Bird pointed out, when Universal granted licenses, it "specifically authorized the use of Lugosi's likeness from his portrayal of Count Dracula."[346] Universal did this even though other actors had played the *Dracula* role in other Universal films.

Justice Bird provided the sole dissent[347] and the only recognition that the right of publicity could have justifications separate from privacy and similar to that of other intellectual property. She was correct that this was a case about an image; at our present level of technology, we can understand that image as a compendium of information. It could be digital information used to create the image on a computer; it could also be genetic information which largely (although not completely) constituted Lugosi's physiog-

---

343 *Id.* at 431 n.8.
344 *Id.* at 432.
345 *Id.* at 432.
346 *Id.* at 435 (Bird, J., dissenting).
347 *Id.* at 434.

nomy coupled with some information on make-up. It might be said that this oversimplifies the case because the Lugosi-Dracula image was rooted in an intentional, dramatic performance. But the simplification is justified by the widespread use of the image separate from the films and the fact that many consumers of the image—particularly young people—have no experience with Lugosi's dramatic performance as Dracula. This is what arguably makes any personhood justification for protecting the Lugosi-Dracula image so different from protection for the images of Madonna, Prince, Humphrey Bogart or a Hollywood starlet. In those cases the individual's image and overall persona is a product imbued with intention and purpose. But the rise of the image of Lugosi-Dracula, an image sold to teenagers who do not know who Bela Lugosi was, seems comparatively accidental. Separated from Lugosi's dramatic performances, Lugosi's vampirial likeness becomes a possible sourcehood example, one in which we might want to recognize a personhood interest even where no creativity or intentionality is at play.

This is not to say that the wrong result was reached in *Lugosi*. Both the *Moore* and *Lugosi* cases share a strong concern about policy considerations, particularly the duration of property rights and their impact on future users. The *Lugosi* court felt that the practical question of the proper duration of a descendible right of publicity weighed against recognizing such a right.[348] Justice Bird proposed solving this problem by adopting a copyright standard of a certain number of years after the image owner's death. Justice Bird's proposal has much to recommend it—to a legislature, if not to a court. One of the most laudable aspects of intellectual property rights is that they are of limited duration; once those rights expire, the protected art or technology becomes part of the public domain—a true "common" of information, images, and expressions available to anyone for free. It would be inconsistent to create perpetual property rights for being the source of some biologically-based information—whether a cell line or a famous face—while we put a sunset on rights arising more from the life of the mind. I believe

348 As discussed above, the *Lugosi* court's conclusion that a descendible right of publicity would not serve the society's interests seems at odds with Congress's conclusion in this respect about other intellectual property rights—but if an "image" developed without international efforts—if it was the result of accident and the person's only claim to it was the result of accident and the person's only claim to it was one of "sourcehood," then it would make some sense to say that the same inventive structure does not exist. In 1988, California enacted a descendibility statute for rights of publicity. *See* CAL CIV. CODE § 990 (West 1998).

that those states that have rights of publicity in perpetuity err on this count.

Duration issues also vexed the *Moore* court which repeatedly expressed concern for future researchers who might have to trace title to cell-lines. This problem may have been overblown. If property rights had been recognized, the medical system would have undoubtedly responded with written waivers by which a patient surrendered property rights in their cells in exchange—we hope—not just for surgery, but for some interest in any patent that would result from research in her cells.

C. *The Problem of Labor*

Beyond examples like the *Moore* case, a final area of case law *may* offer some insights into the sourcehood justification of personality interests. Intellectual property law is rich in cases holding that *mere* labor or effort does not lead to intellectual property protection. Justice Brennan cautioned against seeing protectable interests arising from labor in the 1985 case brought against the *Nation* for printing excerpts of former President Ford's memoirs:

> Limiting the inquiry to the propriety of a subsequent author's use of the copyright owner's literary form is not easy in the case of a work of history. Protection against only substantial appropriation of literary form does not ensure historians a return commensurate with the full value of their labors. The literary form contained in works like "A Time to Heal" reflects only a part of the labor that goes into the book. It is the labor of collecting, sifting, organizing, and reflecting that predominates in the creation of works of history such as this one. The value this labor produces lies primarily in the information and ideas revealed, and not in the particular collection of words through which the information and ideas are expressed. Copyright thus does not protect that which is often of most value in a work of history, and courts must resist the tendency to reject the fair use defense on the basis of their feeling that an author of history has been deprived of the full value of his or her labor. A subsequent author's taking of information and ideas is in no sense pirating because copyright law simply does not create any property interest in information and ideas.[349]

The "tendency" against which Brennan warns might be couched as the "labor" problem — whether protectable (personality) interests

---

349 Harper & Row Publishers, Inc. v. Nation Enters., 471 U.S. 539, 589 (1985).

can arise from seemingly non-creative labor that produces valuable works.

The "collecting, sifting, and organizing" that constitutes such a large part of some works is a kind of activity which does not seem to be creative. Yet many of us believe that such researchers are justified in feeling deep personality interests in their own work. Unlike the *Moore* case, the research labor situation may involve intentionality; clearly, the "collecting, sifting, and organizing" is a goal-directed, conscious activity. But the intentionality—the will behind the research—may belong to someone else. If the purpose, approach, and design of the research is completely determined by an employer *and* the research activity is not judged creative, does the researcher have any personhood interest in the results just from being the source of the labor?

Patent law does not do anything to positively embrace this possible "sourcehood" interest, but it does leave open the possibility for such recognition. Following the 1984 amendments to the patent law, 35 U.S.C. § 166 provides that: "Inventors may apply for a patent jointly even though (1) they did not physically work together or at the same time; (2) each did not make the same type or amount of contribution; or (3) each did not make a contribution to the subject matter of every claim of the patent." The 1984 amendments codified case law recognizing that there may be a hierarchy of contributions by these different individuals. In *Monsanto Co. v. Kamp*,[350] the court held that a joint invention must be the result of "collaboration of the inventive endeavors of two or more persons working toward the same end . . ." but recognized that the nature of the contributions to the collaboration could vary:

> Each needs to perform but a part of the task if an invention emerges from all of the steps taken together. . . . One may take a step at one time, the other an approach at different times. One may do more of the experimental work while the other makes suggestions from time to time. The fact that each of the inventors plays a different role and that the contribution of one may not be as great as that of another does not detract from the fact that the invention is joint if each makes some original contribution, though partial, to the final solution of the problem.[351]

The *Monsanto* opinion recognized that the level of contribution to the invention by different individuals may be quite disparate,

350 269 F. Supp. 818, 824 (D.D.C. 1967).
351 *Id.* at 824.

although it continued to call on "original" contribution from each. More recently, in *Lert v. A.C. Nielsen Co.*,[352] the court refused to grant summary judgment to a defendant attacking a patent with an invalidity charge based on misjoinder of inventors. The evidence most favorable to the plaintiffs/patent holders showed relatively minor contributions by the second and third named inventors. The third named inventor, John Cornelius, had worked on the prototype and "conceived and designed the method of detecting network logos as cue signals,"[353] while the second inventor—primary inventor John Lert's brother—appears to have only worked on the prototype with John and "noted problems with some of John's ideas and caused John to think through those problems and arrive at solutions."[354] Nonetheless, this was viewed as an arguably sufficient contribution. Cases like the *Lert* case suggest that non-creative labor under someone else's direction may receive attribution and other intellectual property rights under patent law. If patent law tolerates the naming of such members of research teams as inventors, then the decision whether such non-creative labor is rewarded falls to the mores of that particular scientific community, that particular institution, and even that particular laboratory.

Another area of arguably non-creative, non-intentional labor is painstaking reproduction. When such painstaking reproduction takes nature as its subject, there was no problem distinguishing the *res* from its underlying inspiration—no matter how realistic, a painting is distinguishable from the meadow or fruit bowl it portrays. But when these skills of painstaking reproduction are focused on an object which is already the subject of intellectual property rights, problems arise. How can we grant property rights to painting *X*, a painstaking reproduction of painting *Y*, without compromising the intellectual property rights to *Y*? If an artist creates art by painstakingly reproducing something—a known artistic image like Mickey Mouse or Manet's Olympe—she will be denied copyright protection on the grounds that there is no meaningful variation from the prior art.

This was the result in *Gracen v. Bradford Exchange*, in which an artist who had faithfully recreated Dorothy from *The Wizard of Oz* on collector's plates was unable to prevent her image from being pirated.[355] Bradford had sponsored a contest to create a collector's plate image of Dorothy; the arguably schizophrenic contest instruc-

352 33 U.S.P.Q.2d (B.N.A.) 1026, 1029 (N.D. Ill. 1994).
353 *Id.*
354 *Id.*
355 698 F.2d 300 (7th Cir. 1983).

tions stated that Bradford sought the artist's "interpretation" of Dorothy but that this interpretation of "Judy/Dorothy must be very recognizable as everybody's Judy/Dorothy."[356] Gracen had initially won the contest, but when Grace and Bradford could not agree on the price for Gracen's work, Bradford hired another artist to copy Gracen's work. Gracen sued, claiming that the second artist had, at Bradford's direction, pirated her copyrighted image of Dorothy. Gracen lost on summary judgment—later affirmed by Judge Posner—on the basis that Gracen's image had insufficient variation from the Dorothy images in the film. In John Shepherd Wiley's words, "[t]he prize for faithful accuracy doomed Gracen's copyright suit .... The court condemned Grace for achieving precisely her creative goal."[357] Wiley argues that Gracen should have had some copyright recognized and that, in general, copyright should be rewarded where the artist has painstakingly reproduced something.

It is instructive that faithful reproduction like Gracen's work are often shoehorned into the "creativity" model. Bradford had originally praised Gracen's painting of the *Wizard of Oz,* saying that it "was the one painting that conveyed the essence of Judy's character in the film . . . ."[358] The idea of "conveying" or "capturing" the "essence" of something is very much in the romantic spirit. The difference between a northern European Renaissance painter and Gracen is that the romantic painter was usually capturing the "essence" of some aspect of nature or human activity,[359] whereas Gracen was capturing the essence of prior, protected art.

It is possible that the practical problem of sorting out rights between the original and derivative work compels the *Gracen* conclusion. It is also possible that Gracen's case was not compelling because we feel there is little or no personality interest in her work, that the use of the word "creative" is just misplaced. No one would ask Gracen what her Dorothy "meant" because it was an image so undistinguishable from the Dorothy of the movies that no one would have thought it to be a different creation.

As long as high fidelity copying could only be done by humans—and a very few, dedicated humans—it was easy to believe that some very subtle but nonetheless unique work went into "cap-

---

356 *Id.* at 301 (emphasis omitted).

357 John S. Wiley, Jr., *Copyright at the School of Patent,* 58 U. CHI. L. REV. 119, 136-37 (1991).

358 *Gracen,* 698 F.2d at 301 (emphasis omitted).

359 E.H. GOMBRICH, THE STORY OF ART 167-82 (14th ed., 1984) (discussing highly representational art of that period).

turing" the "essence" of the image. In describing the modern advent of the "author" construct, Boyle thinks that "the most cursory historical study reveals that '[m]edieval church writers actively disapproved of the elements of originality and creativity;'"[360] and he quotes Ernst Goldschmidt's conclusions that medieval theologians

> [V]alued extant old books more highly than any recent lucubrations and they put the work of the scribe and the copyist above that of the author. The real task of the scholars [was] . . . a discovery of great old books, their multiplication and the placing of copies where they would be accessible to future generations of readers.[361]

The point about the value of the "author" is well taken.[362] But Goldschmidt's conclusion about the relative position of scribes and authors speaks to something more than the lower station occupied by authors in pre-modern times; his comment must be read against the technological level of medieval times. Prior to the printing press, the accurate scribe or copying provided a very valuable, uniquely human skill.

To a medieval pair of eyes, the scribe's work seemed far less "mechanical" than it does to us. To return to one of Nozick's ideas—the juxtaposition of the creative and the mechanical—if scribe copying seemed less mechanical back then, it probably seemed more "creative" back then. What is the proper analogy? Perhaps in medieval times, the scribe's skills appeared like the airline pilot's skills appear to us: we know what the pilot does, we know that pilots do the same thing again and again, but we also think that each time they land a plane they employ skill, finesse, and intuitive judgments unavailable to most of us and not yet reduced to mechanical algorithms. Scribes were, in the medieval context, understandably special.[363]

---

360 Boyle, *supra* note 29, at 1463.

361 Ernst P. Goldschmidt, Medieval Texts and their First Appearance in Print 112 (Biblo-Moser eds., 1969).

362 Of course, "medieval church writers" probably "actively disapproved" of elements of democracy, liberty, and most human rights. To many, the fact that medieval church writers disapprove of something more or less recommends it.

363 Prior to mechanical copying, copyists were also more important because of the power that they wielded. This is a point made by A.C. Milner in the context of Malay rulers of the sixteenth to eighteenth centuries controlling access to copies of historical accounts of each dynasty:

> as a mid-nineteenth century traveler noted in Kedah, for instance, a [written tale] might be "quoted over and over again" even by opposing factions "to support their jarring interests and theories." In such circumstances, the *author or copyist* was a man of consequence; he might further the claims of one party or another by the way he portrayed events. It has been noted that rulers jealously guarded texts, allowing them to be heard but not copied.

Technology foiled this equation. It is no accident that realism in painting ebbed as photography flowed. It has become harder to see "personality" in painstaking reproductions of images or sounds. What personal meaning can be conveyed in doing what a machine can do? And as our machines have become more clever and adept, the problem has become more severe.

Reproduction remains, however, a means by which we can see the sourcehood interest in very non-creative labor and where the legal system does not permit rights to flow from that interest. Gracen had an understandable attachment to her work—something Judge Posner may have implicitly recognized in permitting her to continue to use her Dorothy image in her own portfolio. At the margins, we might find that the fair use doctrine, for example, gives some breathing space to sourcehood interests in reproductions—but not much.

V. CONCLUSION

Patents owe their origin to Renaissance Venice, and copyright protection of a sort dates back to ancient Rome, but it is in the United States where intellectual property law has found its most fertile ground for development. To some cultures, America may seem obsessed with intellectual property protection.[364]

For some, this is a recent obsession related to our competitive position in a world economy—disadvantaged in areas like manual labor costs but still with great advantages in knowledge, information, and technology.[365] At a deeper level, our society emphasizes the rights of the individual to act alone or in groups of her choice and this emphasis increases the importance of a network of rights to make private actions easier, more secure, and more successful. Regardless of our international economic position, extensive intellectual property rights may be a natural outgrowth of a culture with

A.C. MILNER, KERAJAAN: MALAY POLITICAL CULTURE ON THE EVE OF COLONIAL RULE 65 (Univ. of Ariz., 1982).

364 If one considers the American government's view on the intellectual property protection offered by our trading partners, one gets the clear impression that no one takes intellectual property rights as seriously as the United States. In mid-1994, for example, the U.S. Trade Representative's Office had placed the following countries on various "watch" lists for their shortcomings in protecting our intellectual property: Argentina, Australia, Brazil, Canada, Chile, China, Colombia, Cyprus, Egypt, El Salvador, the European Union (including Belgium, France, Germany, Greece, Holland, Italy, Portugal, Spain, and the U.K.), Guatemala, Honduras, India, Indonesia, Israel, Japan, Korea, Pakistan, Panama, Paraguay, Peru, the Philippines, Poland, Russia, Saudi Arabia, Singapore, Taiwan, Thailand, Turkey, the United Arab Emirates, and Venezuela. *See* 195 COPYRIGHT LAW REPORTS at 1 (June 20, 1994). Who among our trading partners was not named?

365 Paula Dwyer, et al., *The Battle Raging Over 'Intellectual Property,'* BUS. WK., May 22, 1989, at 80.

such emphasis on "private" activities. Then there is the pleasant, if silly, thought that perhaps Americans emphasize extensive intellectual property rights because we are "the most idea-based civilization in history."[366]

Property rights are traditionally justified in terms of economic efficiency, but in the realm of intellectual property such justifications, however persuasive, do not have a strong empirical basis. "Personhood" interests can also be used to justify property rights or, in some cases, rules bending or mitigating the effect of property rights. Behind the shield of property rights, personhood flourishes in our homes, automobiles, clothes, gardens, and the things we collect—be it art, baseball cards, books, toys, music, pottery, model ships, or sport trophies. In the world of artistic and scientific creations, personhood interests take a different turn. It often seems that an individual's personality is already "expressed" in an intellectual property *res*. Courts have recognized the "personal expression," "creativity," "genius," and "intellectual labor" of intellectual property—all intimating that protection of the creator's personhood interests is at issue.

But beyond saying that someone's personality is expressed in an intellectual work, is there anything more we can say about the personhood interests? This article has argued that creativity or personal "expression," personal "intention," and "sourcehood" are three candidate conditions for personhood interests, with varying degrees of protection possible for each. Along the way, creativity has been presented as a complex notion that serves as an equally good explanatory device for recent copyright cases which deconstructionist scholars have criticized as relying unduly on the "romantic author" construct. I have proposed that the concept of intentionality may explain personality interests in research programs and photojournalism. This sort of personality interest may help explain occasions when we grant property protection as well as occasions when courts deny rights, but we feel a tug of regret that we cannot grant those rights.

Law's on-going exploration of the concepts it uses is no different than that in any other structured system of thinking. Such thinking is, as Susan Sontag put it, "an insatiable project, endlessly producing and consuming 'systems,' metaphor-haunted classifications of an ultimately opaque reality."[367] The concepts of "originality" and "creativity" are explicit elements of law's classificatory

---

366 Newt Gingrich, To Renew America 30 (1995).

367 Susan Sontag, *Introduction to* Barthes, *supra* note 118, at xx.

scheme; "personhood," "romantic author," and "intentionality" are all explanatory devices by which we try to shore up, tear down, or induce mutation in the classificatory system. One of Sontag's comments on art criticism is largely applicable to legal scholarship:

> Someday perhaps a demystification of the myth of "art" (as an absolute activity) will be possible and will take place, but it seems far from that moment now. At this stage, only new myths can subdue—even for the brief time to permit contemplation—the old myths which move convulsively about us.[368]

This article has explored a set of myths that are sturdy and highly serviceable to make the intellectual property system respond to the opaque, but nonetheless very real personhood interests of creators.

In the end, the process of intellectual exploration—whether it is modern painting, Darwin's voyages, or a video journalist looking for a new angle on a Latin American election—may be much the same. Whether we call it a profession or a preoccupation, when we return to the same activity again and again, what we learn in the exploratory process transforms us. In this spiral of activity we explore, digest, create, transform ourselves, and explore again.

368 *Id.* at xxi.

FUTURE DIRECTIONS IN INTERNATIONAL COPYRIGHT

SHIRA PERLMUTTER*

I. INTRODUCTION

Originally this talk was to be entitled, "The Future of International Copyright." Because that title sounded overly portentous, and seemed to demand a dramatic black or white conclusion (with the subtitle "obsolescence or apotheosis?"), I abandoned it in favor of one suggesting the more modest goal of identifying some paths where copyright is likely to meander in the coming years.

The future is becoming more and more difficult to fix clearly in our sights, as technologies of creation, dissemination, and use of copyrighted works evolve at an exponentially increasing pace. When the Copyright Office recently commissioned a study of the directions of new technology from Professor I. Trotter Hardy,[1] we envisioned a long-term view. After extensive discussions with Professor Hardy, we narrowed it down to a bare five years in the future—the furthest he believed it was possible to project. We have learned to speak not of the long term, but of the relatively longer term.

Despite this unavoidable myopia, it seems both possible and worthwhile to take a step back from the maelstrom of current issues, in all their intensity and urgency, to gain some perspective on where we are today on the international stage, and where we are going. My talk will be divided into three parts, roughly comparable to today, tomorrow, and the day after. First, an overview of international copyright today; second, a description of the issues just around the corner; and finally, some modest predictions—an assessment of where the focus of attention and activity is likely to turn in the longer run.

II. INTERNATIONAL COPYRIGHT TODAY

Let me start by setting the framework. What is international copyright law? It is a basic axiom that copyrights are territorial—in

* Associate Register of Copyrights for Policy and International Affairs, U.S. Copyright Office. This article is based on a lecture given at the Benjamin N. Cardozo School of Law, March 27, 1997.

1 Professor of Law, Marshall-Wythe School of Law, College of William and Mary, Williamsburg, Virginia. The study is titled: *Project Looking Forward: Sketching the Future of Copyright in a Newtworked World.*

other words, that they are granted, delineated, and enforced in any given country by the operation of that country's laws. As a result, the concept of international copyright must begin with the basic foundation of the national copyright laws. Links are forged between those laws by international relationships, including formal treaties, regional commitments, and the ongoing give and take of trade interactions.

The foundation of national laws, along with their various links, makes up the international legal structure. The other key component, built on top of the legal foundation, is the private side: how works are actually exploited on an international scale. While such exploitation includes both commercial and noncommercial uses, I will refer to it generally as the "market." The market establishes its own structure that allows works to be licensed and sold around the world—a structure that evolves rapidly in response to changing economic, social, and technological conditions. Just as in the domestic arena, the relationship between the global market and international law is a symbiotic one, with each being shaped by changes in the other.

A. *National Laws*

One distinct trend in the foundation of national laws is a broadening in global coverage. Most nations today do protect copyrights—including developing countries and former socialist economies. And the ranks of those that do not are rapidly dwindling, as more and more countries become convinced of the benefits that copyright can bring and choose to join the international community.

In addition to becoming broader, the foundation is becoming more uniform. There is considerably less divergence among national laws today than in the past. While one can still see distinctive individual approaches to various issues, a tremendous amount of harmonization has taken place on the core concepts of copyright. In particular, the subject matter of copyright, its duration, and the basic rights granted are relatively consistent from one country to another. The reasons for this harmonization may be complex, but the result is plain. More variety exists in delineating the precise scope of rights through exceptions and limitations, although certain general categories are common.

Coexisting with the core areas of agreement are various recurring points of contention. They include issues of new subject matter, parallel importation, national treatment, retroactive protection, and enforcement. As to new subject matter, issues about coverage of computer programs and original databases have been essentially resolved in the past few years in the course of treaty negotiations; the current iteration involves non-original databases and multimedia works. The issue of whether copyright owners should be able to control parallel imports—i.e., the importation into one country of copies sold lawfully in another—is one that deeply divides the world today.

Similar controversy attends the question of national treatment: whether foreign authors should be given the same rights as domestic authors, or only those rights that the foreign country gives to authors under its own system. There are divergent perspectives on national treatment, including whether it should be the generally applicable approach to intellectual property, or whether countries should be free to condition on reciprocity the grant of new rights to foreigners, in order to pressure other countries to implement the new rights. This has become particularly contentious in the area of levy systems for private copying, where countries establish pools of money for distribution to copyright owners to compensate them for private copying, and may not allow participation by nationals of countries that do not provide similar schemes, despite the fact that their works represent a significant proportion of all works copied in that country.

Retroactivity is the label used to describe the principle of a law protecting not just subsequently-created works, but works already in existence at the time the law is enacted. The use of this term is unfortunate, since it sounds like something extraordinary and perhaps even dangerous—like radioactivity. It is also a misnomer, since it refers to *prospective* protection for pre-existing works, and will not impose liability for past acts. The principle is of particular importance in the international context, because when a country joins a copyright treaty, it takes on obligations to protect works from other countries that are party to the treaty. At that point, of course, many valuable works already exist in those other countries, and those countries therefore have a strong interest in ensuring that the works are protected abroad for the remainder of the copyright term. The terms and conditions upon which such retroactive protection is provided vary from country to country, and have been the subject of dispute.

Additional harmonization has also been accomplished on a regional level. The major initiatives to date have taken place within the common market of the European Union ("E.U."). The E.U. has engaged in a process of harmonizing the copyright laws of the member states in areas that affect their common market, by issuing several directives requiring them to implement detailed provisions relating to specific rights or subject matter. While there have been some difficulties with adequate and timely implementation, the eventual result will be greater homogeneity within the E.U., beyond the level of harmonization that has been achieved elsewhere. As other countries line up for membership in the E.U., they are increasingly implementing existing directives in preparation. At the same time, by conditioning rights for non-Europeans on reciprocity, these directives apply real economic pressure on other countries to harmonize their systems to the same extent.

B. *Copyright Treaties*

One major set of links among national systems is supplied by international treaties on the subject of copyright and neighboring rights. Chief among these treaties is the Berne Convention for the Protection of Literary and Artistic Works ("Berne Convention").[2] Dating back to 1886, the Berne Convention today enjoys a membership of more than 120 countries. Its key characteristics are the following:

- A set of minimum rights that must be provided to authors. Generally speaking, these are the rights of reproduction and adaptation, and moral rights, as well as various forms of communication to the public, including live performance and broadcasting.[3]
- Restrictions on the scope of permissible limitations and exceptions.[4]
- A minimum term of protection of the life of the author plus fifty years.[5]
- National treatment.[6]
- A prohibition on formalities as a condition for enjoying rights.[7]
- Retroactive protection for existing works in which copyright has not expired.[8]

It is equally important to note what is *not* covered: Berne does not contain any specific requirements as to mechanisms for right-

---

[2] Berne Convention for the Protection of Literary and Artistic Works, Sept. 9, 1886, *as last amended* Oct. 2, 1979, 828 U.N.T.S. 221 [hereinafter Berne Convention].

[3] Berne Convention, *supra* note 2, arts. 6*bis*, 11, 11*bis*, 11*ter*, 12 & 14. 828 U.N.T.S. at 227-31, 241-45.

[4] *Id.* arts. 9(2), 10(1), 11*bis*(2) & 13(1), 828 U.N.T.S. at 239-45.

[5] *Id.* art. 7(1), 828 U.N.T.S. at 235.

[6] *Id.* art. 5, 828 U.N.T.S. at 231-33.

[7] *Id.* art. 5(2), 828 U.N.T.S. at 233.

[8] *Id.* art. 18, 828 U.N.T.S. at 250.

holders to enforce rights, or provide penalties for member states that do not live up to their obligations.

Another multilateral treaty, the Universal Copyright Convention ("UCC"), which came into being in the 1950s, also has a substantial number of adherents. In the past decade, however, since the United States joined the Berne Convention, the UCC has been eclipsed in importance, due to Berne's more extensive protection and wider membership.

There is one major gap in the coverage of both Conventions: They do not protect performers or producers of sound recordings. In many other countries of the world, the contributions of performers and producers are not considered to be copyrightable subject matter, but are protected instead by what are called "neighboring rights." The preeminent treaty dealing with neighboring rights is the Rome Convention for the Protection of Performers, Producers of Phonograms, and Broadcasting Organizations ("Rome Convention").[9] The Rome Convention operates on similar principles to Berne, setting out minimum rights and requiring national treatment (albeit in a more limited form).[10] Its influence has been less pervasive, however, both because it permits countries to pick and choose among rights, and because it has a narrower membership, not including the United States.[11]

Bilateral agreements have also played a major role in international copyright. Beginning in the nineteenth century, many countries took their first steps toward protecting foreign works on a country-by-country basis. Today, bilateral treaties are of primary importance in dealing with countries that are not yet subject to the obligations set forth in the major multilateral conventions, or obtaining commitments in areas not covered by those conventions.

C. *Trade Agreements*

Another set of international links is created by trade agreements. In recent years, intellectual property has been recognized as an important component of trade between countries, and copyright provisions have been included in a number of their agreements on trade issues.

For the United States, the inclusion of intellectual property on the trade agenda led to copyright provisions in the North Ameri-

---

9 International Convention for the Protection of Performers, Producers of Phonograms and Broadcasting Organizations, Rome, Oct. 26, 1961, 496 U.N.T.S. 43 [hereinafter Rome Convention].

10 *Id.* arts. 1, 2, 4 & 5, 496 U.N.T.S. at 44-46.

11 *Id.* arts. 15-16, 496 U.N.T.S. at 54-55.

can Free Trade Agreement ("NAFTA"),[12] which entered into force in 1994. NAFTA was shortly followed by the Agreement on Trade-Related Aspects of Intellectual Property Rights ("TRIPS"),[13] which was concluded in the Uruguay Round of negotiations leading to the creation of the World Trade Organization ("WTO"), and entered into force in 1995. The NAFTA intellectual property provisions were negotiated based on an early draft of the TRIPS Agreement, so the two agreements bear a striking resemblance to each other. Although all three NAFTA signatories are WTO members subject to the TRIPS Agreement, the NAFTA intellectual property provisions remain relevant for several reasons. NAFTA exceeds the protection required by the TRIPS Agreement in important respects: NAFTA has a stronger national treatment obligation in the area of copyrights, for example;[14] NAFTA contains shorter transition periods;[15] and it establishes its own distinct dispute settlement mechanism.[16]

As a broad-based multilateral agreement on intellectual property rights, the TRIPS Agreement was ground breaking in many respects. In the copyright area, it covers both literary and artistic works and neighboring rights, with the following key characteristics:

- It incorporates the substantive norms of the Berne and Rome Conventions.[17]
- It adds to the scope of the Berne and Rome rights, primarily in the area of rental rights.[18]
- It requires retroactive protection for all subject matter, including both copyright and neighboring rights.
- It requires not only national treatment as outlined in Berne and Rome, but also most favored nation ("MFN") treatment, ruling out the possibility of giving special treatment to only certain WTO members through new bilateral agreements entered into after the WTO came into being on January 1, 1995.[19]
- It promotes "transparency," a catch-word for open and accessible information, by imposing obligations to "notify" virtually every aspect of a country's relevant laws and regulations, and institution-

---

12 North American Free Trade Agreement, Dec. 8, 1992, Can.-Mex.-U.S., 32 I.L.M. 605, 670 (1993) [hereinafter NAFTA].

13 Agreement on Trade-Related Aspects of Intellectual Property Rights, Apr. 15, 1994, 331 I.L.M. 1125, 1197 [hereinafter TRIPS].

14 NAFTA, *supra* note 12, art. 1703, 32 I.L.M. at 671.

15 *Id.* art. 1716, 32 I.L.M. at 677-78.

16 *Id.* art. 1715, 32 I.L.M. at 677.

17 TRIPS, *supra* note 13, arts. 9(1), 10(1), 14(3) & (6), 331 I.L.M. at 1201-02.

18 *Id.* arts. 11 & 14(4), 331 I.L.M. at 1201-02.

19 TRIPS, *supra* note 13, art. 4, 331 I.L.M. at 1200.

alizing a formal process to exchange questions and answers on those laws and regulations.[20]

The most important aspect of TRIPS, however, is that it supplies the elements lacking in Berne. The Agreement sets out a long list of detailed enforcement mechanisms that countries must make available to right holders.[21] And last but surely not least, it utilizes the WTO dispute resolution system, giving teeth to the treaty's requirements.[22] A WTO member alleging that another member has not fully implemented TRIPS can request the formation of a panel to settle the matter, and the panel's decision can be appealed to an appellate body.[23] If a member is found to be not in compliance with one of its obligations, it must either implement the obligation, provide equivalent trade concessions, or face equivalent trade sanctions from the complaining party.[24] Grace periods are provided for developing and least developed countries, which are not obligated fully to implement the copyright provisions of TRIPS until the years 2000 and 2006, respectively.[25]

Fully in force for developed countries only since January 1996, the TRIPS Agreement has already proved quite effective. The United States has filed a number of disputes against other countries, one in the copyright field (dealing with Japan's failure to provide a full fifty year term of retroactive protection for sound recordings). After consultations, Japan agreed to change its law, and the dispute was resolved before proceeding to a panel. Additional cases dealing with the implementation of the copyright provisions, or with the required enforcement mechanisms, may be instituted shortly.

D. *Bilateral Trade Relations*

A critical element in the pattern of international copyright is the interaction between individual countries relating to trade. In the context of such interactions, including the establishment of watch lists under U.S. trade laws,[26] the United States has convinced other countries to adopt treaty norms and generally increase their

---

20 *Id.* art. 63, 331 I.L.M. at 1221.

21 TRIPS, *supra* note 13, art. 41-61, 331 I.L.M. at 1213-20.

22 *Id.* art. 64, 331 I.L.M. at 1221.

23 WTO. Understanding on Rules and Procedures Governing the Settlement of Disputes (1994) [hereinafter DSU] arts. 17-19, Annex 2, 331 I.L.M. at 1236-37.

24 DSU, *supra* note 23, art. 22, 331 I.L.M. at 1241-42.

25 TRIPS, *supra* note 13, arts. 65-66, 331 I.L.M. at 1222.

26 The Omnibus Trade and Competitiveness Act of 1988, Pub.L. No. 100-418, 102 Stat. 1107, which amended section 182 of the Omnibus Trade Act of 1974, requires the U.S. Trade Representative to identify countries that do not adequately and effectively protect intellectual property rights, or deny fair market access to United States persons that rely on

levels of protection and enforcement in several ongoing initiatives. The United States and other countries are working on the regional level to develop additional norms for intellectual property rights protection. The most notable of these are the negotiations leading to the Free Trade Agreement of the Americas ("FTAA") and discussions in the Asia Pacific Economic Cooperation ("APEC") forum.

III. Around the Corner

Given this extensive existing structure, what can be expected for international copyright in the short range? A number of issues are on the horizon, with work either completed or scheduled for the near future.

A. *Digital Issues*

Public attention has been devoted lately to the issue of adapting copyright to digital technologies. Individual countries and regions have begun to study this issue over the past few years. So far, the conclusion has been that existing copyright laws are generally adequate to the task, and need minor revisions rather than major overhauls.

On the international level, discussion has centered on the need to update the major international treaties. The current texts of Berne and Rome date back to more than a quarter century ago. The culmination of these discussions was the conclusion of two new World Intellectual Property Organization ("WIPO") treaties in Geneva in December 1996, dealing with copyright and neighboring rights. Among other things, these treaties and their interpretive statements require that right holders enjoy exclusive control over on-demand electronic dissemination of their works, and confirm that the reproduction right is fully applicable in the digital environment. They also require member countries to provide legal protection for technologies used to prevent infringement, and for the rights management information that right-holders may choose to provide in digital form.

Perhaps equally notable is one subject the treaties do not address: the question of on-line service provider liability. Traditionally, the question of which parties in a chain of distribution of an infringing work are liable for the infringement has been left to the national laws of individual countries. Since the new treaties are

intellectual property protection, and certain foreign countries determined to be "priority" foreign countries. 19 U.S.C. § 2242 (1994).

silent on this question, for now national legislatures remain free to grapple with shaping the answer in the Internet context. As answers begin to emerge, there may be renewed calls for international harmonization.

The treaties are not yet in effect; they require ratification by thirty countries, which will not happen overnight. Once the treaties come into force, it is possible that they will be incorporated into the TRIPS Agreement.

B. *Future WIPO Work Schedule*

Four other copyright-related issues are currently on the WIPO agenda: (1) protection for audiovisual performers; (2) *sui generis* protection for databases; (3) protection for expressions of folklore; and (4) the rights and liabilities of broadcasters. The first two issues are holdovers from the December 1996 Diplomatic Conference. Negotiators were unable to agree on an appropriate form of protection for audiovisual performers, and agreed to continue discussions with an eye toward a possible protocol to the neighboring rights treaty. A draft treaty on *sui generis* protection for databases was never reached at the Conference. In September 1997, both topics were discussed at WIPO meetings in Geneva, and work on the issues will continue through 1998.

Folklore and broadcasters' rights were the subjects of conferences held by WIPO in 1997, in Thailand and the Philippines, respectively. Future meetings may be scheduled on these topics as well.

C. *Multilateral Agreement on Investment*

Copyright is also becoming important in agreements dealing with the protection of investment. The United States is currently a party to a number of Bilateral Investment Treaties ("BITS") that define intellectual property as a form of investment, subject to significant national and MFN treatment obligations, requiring foreign investors to be treated as well as domestic investors. In the Organization for Economic Cooperation and Development ("OECD"), negotiations have been underway for some time on a Multilateral Agreement on Investment ("MAI"), which would extend this concept to a multilateral agreement among the world's most developed countries. The critical issue for copyright has been the relationship to the existing intellectual property treaties, and the application of national treatment and MFN obligations to both present and future rights.

IV. Longer Term

What is the outlook for the longer term? I will now venture to make a few predictions.

A. *Increased Level of Satisfactory Laws*

First, the trend toward satisfactory protection will continue. In the not-so-distant future, more and more countries will accept the emerging international consensus on basic copyright principles, with modern and balanced copyright laws becoming standard around the world.

This trend is rooted in a rational self-interest. Within their borders, countries may be persuaded that copyright protection will lead to more creation overall, and encourage foreign investment and technology transfer, advancing the domestic culture and economy. In the international arena, countries see the benefits they can obtain for their citizens by joining treaties on copyright and trade. Once they reach the stage of development where they perceive themselves as exporters of copyrighted works, not primarily users of works imported from abroad, the value of membership in a copyright treaty becomes clear. Even before that point, the trade-related benefits that may be obtained from joining a club like the WTO can outweigh any perceived drawbacks of adopting a new copyright law. Outside the parameters of the WTO, other countries like the United States may condition special trade treatment for developing countries on satisfactory protection of copyrighted works.

Major changes in copyright seem unlikely, however. The international norms embodied in legal systems around the world now reflect an accepted balance, ensuring that copyright owners can control economically significant uses of their works while allowing room for appropriate uses outside that control. The structure of the multilateral treaties permits and encourages this balance, by setting out only minimum rights and leaving considerable flexibility to national legislatures to determine what limitations on those rights are appropriate to their own conditions. This framework has stood the test of time and technological change; there is no reason why it should not continue to do so.

I do not believe that the list of copyright rights and subject matter will grow significantly. The future is likely to bring consolidation rather than expansion, with standards established on national levels being exported to more countries and eventually percolating upward into treaties. And of course, periodic adjustments will be required to adapt existing rights to new types of works and new forms of exploitation.

Now I will go out on a limb and make one truly long-term prediction. At some point, the pace of the adjustments required by the development of technologies may outstrip the ability of the law to keep up. After all, even today the state of the art in digital technology looks completely different every year, while the process of amending legal systems is slow and ungainly. Eventually a greater simplification of the system of rights may become desirable. Instead of specifically delineated rights tailored to particular techniques of exploitation, it might be preferable to provide authors with a general right to exploit the work in any manner, with an appropriate balance provided through exceptions relating to the purpose and economic effect of a use.

Some steps in this direction can already be seen in certain countries' laws that provide to copyright owners a general right to exploit a work or make it available. Similarly, the new WIPO Copyright Treaty pulls together a number of detailed and specific rights from the Berne Convention into a broad and general right of communication to the public.

B. *Issues of the Future*

Accordingly, the focal point of international copyright is likely to shift. Rather than conceptual questions of subject matter and scope of rights, more practical issues will take center stage. These issues are not new, but are already the subject of considerable discussion today. They arise from the nature of a global, digital marketplace, and relate to enforcement, the operation of the market, and choice of law. I will outline a series of questions:

1. Enforcement

• How can rights be effectively enforced when works are made available electronically across national boundaries?

Customs authorities will no longer be able to assist in enforcement by seizing physical copies at borders. As in the analogue world, law enforcement agencies will need to work together to develop cooperative approaches in order to deal with pirates operating in more than one jurisdiction. Copyright owners must be able to take action against these pirates without the impossible burden of suing in every country. In this context, the issue of who is legally responsible in the chain of an unauthorized dissemination of a copyrighted work may take on heightened significance.

2. The Market

• How can a market for the licensing and sale of copyrighted works operate safely and efficiently over the Internet?

The solution will involve a combination of many elements, including protection of the integrity of the information used to make the market function, as required by the new WIPO treaties; protection of the authenticity of the works communicated; adequate and internationally compatible information systems; and the technology to allow permissions to be given and payments to be made electronically.

One topic related to both enforcement and the operation of the market is the future role of collecting societies. On the one hand, the new technologies could increase the need for copyright owners to rely on collecting societies; on the other hand, they could make it easier for copyright owners to administer and enforce rights individually.

3. Choice of Law

• Which country's law applies when a work is made available by a distributor in one country to users in several other countries simultaneously?

While it is often noted that the Internet creates tensions for the traditional territorial basis for copyright protection, I believe it is premature to predict its demise. The principle of territoriality is too deeply embedded in the copyright system, as part of the basic foundation. As long as copyright protection remains a function of each country's own law, it will be necessary to devise rules for choosing applicable laws in different settings. This problem has become a fashionable topic for examination at conferences, and a number of scholars have begun to develop possible solutions.[27]

At the same time, the trend toward greater harmonization means that choice of law is less critical in determining outcome. Professor Jane Ginsburg, the leading U.S. commentator on this issue, has suggested an approach requiring courts to presume that a particular country's laws reflect the international consensus, placing the burden on the parties to prove otherwise. The international consensus could be established by the obligations of existing

---

[27] *See, e.g.,* Jane C. Ginsberg, *Copyright Without Borders? Choice of Forum and Choice of Law for Copyright Infringement in Cyberspace,* 15 CARDOZO ARTS & ENT. L. J. 153 (1997); Paul Edward Geller, *Conflicts of Laws in Cyberspace: Rethinking International Copyright in a Digitally Networked World,* 20 COLUM.-VLA J.L. & ARTS 571 (1996); Jane C. Ginsburg, *Global Use/Territorial Rights: Private International Law Questions of the Global Information Infrastructure,* 42 J. COPYRIGHT SOC'Y U.S.A. 318 (1995).

multilateral treaties, plus the contents of negotiated treaties reflecting widespread agreement, even if not yet in force. For example, the provisions of the two new WIPO treaties were adopted by consensus by the more than 100 countries participating in the 1996 Diplomatic Conference, and therefore can be seen as representing standards generally accepted as appropriate.

C. *Process and Players*

It is not only the substantive issues, but the process and the participants that are evolving.

One such direction is the intertwining of domestic and international concerns. In today's global market, it is no longer possible to evaluate changes to national law without considering the international implications. In weighing proposed legislation, Congress regularly considers questions of consistency with treaty obligations and the likely impact on other countries.

This is not simply an abstract exercise; questions posed to the United States at meetings of the TRIPS Council have made clear that every copyright bill introduced in Congress is under scrutiny by our trading partners. Nor is our interest purely defensive. U.S. legislation is inevitably part of an ongoing international mutual education process, and can serve as a starting point for discussion or a model for change. As countries grapple with issues posed for copyright by new technologies, they look to proposals developed elsewhere, particularly in the United States, for possible solutions. This is not a one-way street; debate on such issues at the Diplomatic Conference in Geneva was a valuable process, shedding further light on the problems and on the scope of evolving consensus.

Another path characterizing the process is the intertwining of intellectual property with other issues on the international agenda. For copyright, these include trade, protection of investment, and access to government data.

It has become increasingly clear in the past two years that the participants in the process have also changed. The days are over when international copyright was the province of a small club of copyright experts operating with a high degree of common language and mutual understanding. New players are involved in both the domestic and international debates, primarily as a result of the famed convergence in communications technologies in the digital age. Most notable is the involvement of the telecommunications industry, and providers of Internet services generally. At a relatively late date in the development of the WIPO treaties, these interests became quite active in the discussions, and were extensively represented at the Diplomatic Conference in Geneva.

Although these players are here to stay, their identities and interests, like those of the copyright industries, are metamorphosing over time. Their businesses are highly dynamic, marked by shifts in the nature of their activities and increasing consolidation. The lines between industries, and between content and service providers, may become increasingly blurred. The impact on copyright is hard to predict.

One final significant change is the role of the developing countries. The division between the developed and developing worlds is no longer as distinct as it once was. A number of shifts in attitudes and alignments have taken place since the 1960s and 1970s. I believe these shifts can be attributed in substantial part to the impact of technology. Even though most developing countries may not yet be fully adapted to the latest digital technology, they see the future rapidly approaching. These technologies promise to level the playing field by making it possible to create and disseminate works around the world with a minimum of investment. All that is needed is creative minds with a basic level of training—not an expensive infrastructure of factories or physical distribution facilities.

Other influences include the increased and unavoidable globalization of markets, and the related rise of international conglomerates doing business around the world. Every country today is subject to both the lure and the pressure of potential investment from these businesses. The lobbying in Geneva was by no means limited to delegations from the developed world.

Finally, it is no longer possible to characterize developed countries as favoring a high level of rights across the board, with developing countries favoring a lower level. Positions today are more complex among particular regions of the developing world, which in WIPO has been organized into an Asian group, a Latin American and Caribbean group, and an African group. Even within those regions, there is little unanimity. It is clear, however, that in some areas, developing countries are seeking stronger rights than certain countries in the developed world, including the United States. This is particularly true in the areas of moral rights, protection for performers, and protection of folklore.

THE 1996 FEDERAL ANTI-DILUTION STATUTE

J. THOMAS MCCARTHY*

I. AN ANALYSIS OF THE STATUTE

A. *History and Background*

Why is the 1996 Federal Anti-Dilution Act[1] ("1996 Act") so important to intellectual property law that I chose it as the subject of my Tenzer Lecture? I think it is important because this law represents a radical and fundamental break with prior federal trademark law. While twenty-six states have had for some years their own, local anti-dilution laws, they were, while much discussed, very seldomly useful or effective. Only a very few trademark cases were ever won solely on the basis of a state anti-dilution act. By enacting the controversial anti-dilution theory into a nationwide law, Congress significantly changed the way trademarks are selected and the scope of exclusivity that trademarks possess. This law has the potential to change in a meaningful way the basic rules of free and fair competition under which the American business community must operate. In addition, a number of foreign countries are closely observing the U.S. experience with this new law to see if they should also enact an anti-dilution law. Thus, this new statute has global implications.

The 1988 Trademark Law Revision Act, as enacted and signed into law effective in 1989, did *not* contain any provisions relating to dilution of famous marks.[2] A federal anti-dilution law was contained in the *Trademark Review Commission Report* as well as in a bill introduced in the Senate. A modified version of an anti-dilution law was passed by the Senate in May of 1988, and would have appeared as Lanham Act section 43(c). However, in 1988, the House of Representatives was not receptive, and no anti-dilution provision

---

* Professor of Law, University of San Francisco. J. Thomas McCarthy is the author of MCCARTHY ON TRADEMARKS AND UNFAIR COMPETITION (4th ed. 1997); THE RIGHTS OF PUBLICITY AND PRIVACY; and MCCARTHY'S DESK ENCYCLOPEDIA OF INTELLECTUAL PROPERTY (2d ed. 1995). Copyright 1998 by J. Thomas McCarthy.

This article expands on the Herbert Tenzer Distinguished Lecture in Intellectual Property Law, given at the Benjamin N. Cardozo School of Law, October 28, 1997.

1 Federal Trademark Dilution Act of 1995, Pub. L. No. 104-98, 109 Stat. 985 (1995) (codified as amended at 15 U.S.C. §§ 1125, 1127 (West 1996)).

2 See discussion of the background and history of the 1996 legislation at 3 J. THOMAS MCCARTHY, TRADEMARKS & UNFAIR COMPETITION §§ 24:85-24:87 (4th ed. 1997).

was contained in the bill as it finally emerged from House and Senate negotiations in the fall of 1988.[3]

In one sense, the 1996 Act, passed in 1995 and effective in 1996, cleaned up "unfinished business" left over from the 1989 revision of the Lanham Act. Therefore, to the extent that the language is the same, two sources provide useful legislative history for interpreting the 1996 Act: (1) the *Trademark Review Commission* report of 1987;[4] and (2) the Senate Judiciary Committee report of 1988.[5] The 1996 Act directly descended from these two sources. This is important because the 1996 Act passed rapidly through Congress with minimal hearings in the House and no hearings in the Senate. The 1996 Act thus has very little legislative history and these two prior sources are helpful to shed light on the sometimes ambiguous language of the 1996 Act.

The International Trademark Association ("INTA") was the prime mover in promoting the enactment of the law that is almost the same as the provision that failed enactment in Congress eight years earlier. The legislation was supported by the American Bar Association ("ABA"), American Intellectual Property Law Association ("AIPLA"), Patent and Trademark Office ("PTO"), and industry groups. The statute became effective on January 16, 1996.

B. *The Elements of a Prima Facie Case for an Injunction*[6]

The elements of a prima facie case for an injunction under the Lanham Act section 43(a)[7] can be summarized as follows. Under section 43(c), plaintiff must plead and prove that:

(1) the plaintiff is the owner of a mark which is a "famous" mark as measured by the totality of the eight factors listed in section 43(c)(1);

(2) the defendant is making commercial use;

(3) in interstate commerce;[8]

(4) of a mark or trade name;

(5) and defendant's use began after the plaintiff's mark became famous;

---

3 *Id.*

4 *The United States Trademark Association Trademark Review Commission Report and Recommendations to USTA President and Board of Directors,* 77 Trademark Rep. 375 (1987) [hereinafter *Commission Report*]. *See* Babson Bros. Co. v. Surge Power Corp., 39 U.S.P.Q.2d (BNA) 1953, 1954 n.5 (T.T.A.B. 1996) (the 1987 Trademark Review Commission Report is relevant legislative history in interpreting the 1996 Anti-Dilution statute).

5 S. Rep. No. 100-515, at 41-43 (1988).

6 3 McCarthy, *supra* note 2, § 24:89.

7 15 U.S.C. § 1125(a) (1994).

8 Or in U.S. import or export trade that can be regulated by Congress.

(6) and defendant's use causes dilution by lessening the capacity of the plaintiff's mark to identify and distinguish goods or services.[9]

C. *Significant Points about the Federal Anti-Dilution Statute*

A Famous Mark Can be Diluted Without any Likelihood of Confusion. The 1996 Act enacts into a national law the principle of anti-dilution law that no one can make a diluting use of a famous mark, even though there is no likelihood of customer confusion of source, sponsorship, or approval under traditional trademark infringement law. While traditional trademark (or passing off) law rests primarily on a policy of protection of customers from mistake and deception, anti-dilution law more closely resembles an absolute property right in a trademark. Anti-dilution law has a strong resemblance, not to the law of consumer protection, but to the law of trespass.

There is no Federal Preemption. The 1996 Act adds to and does not replace existing state anti-dilution laws.[10]

Federal Registration is not Needed. To invoke the 1996 Act, the plaintiff does not need a federal registration. However, one of the statutory factors to weigh in considering whether a mark is "famous" is whether it is registered.[11]

Only Defendant's Use Need be in Interstate Commerce. The use in interstate commerce requirement is linked to defendant's activity, not to the famous mark owner's activity. However, one of the statutory factors to weigh in considering whether a mark is "famous" is the geographic extent of the plaintiff's trading area.[12]

The Anti-Dilution Statute is not Relevant to Ex Parte or Inter Parte Application Matters in the PTO. Trademark examiners in the PTO will not cite the federal dilution doctrine in ex parte examination under Lanham Act section 2(d), nor can it be a ground of opposition or petition to cancel.[13]

There is no Register of "Famous" Marks. There is no place to go to find out if a particular mark is "famous." There is no special register for famous marks. Fame must be determined on a case by case

---

9 15 U.S.C. § 1125(c).

10 This was one of the aspects of the bill that I personally opposed. I could not see the point of imposing a federal layer of law *on top of*, rather than in place of, the 26 state statutes. I had thought that one of the goals of the federal legislation was to make the selection and adoption of new marks *less* risky and *more* predictable. It has achieved just the opposite result.

11 *Factor H. See infra* Part I.E.2.

12 *Factor D. See infra* Part I.E.2.

13 Babson Bros. Co. v. Surge Power Corp., 39 U.S.P.Q.2d (BNA) 1953 (T.T.A.B. 1996).

basis in litigation. This uncertainty introduces the major source of unpredictability applying the law and giving legal advice and counseling.

The Federal Act Applies as Between Competitors. The 1996 Act is not limited to the traditional non-competitive setting in which the concept of "dilution" was first envisioned by its creators.[14]

Retroactivity of the 1996 Legislation. Consider this hypothetical: UNITED AUTO REPAIR opened in San Jose, California in 1994. It receives in 1997, a cease-and-desist letter from UNITED AIR LINES, accusing it of dilution by blurring, in violation of the federal anti-dilution law. Does first use of the accused mark before the January 16, 1996 date of the 1996 Act mean that the Act does not apply? The cases hold that the 1996 Act does *not* apply, for to do so would be to improperly give retroactive effect to the statute. In the leading *Officemax* decision,[15] the court held that the 1996 Act does *not* apply to defendant's marks first used before January 16, 1996, because there can be no retroactive application of the federal anti-dilution statute.[16] The court held that the senior user, OFFICEMAX, could not sustain a federal anti-dilution claim against the junior user, CARMAX, who first began use of the mark in 1993, two and one-half years before Lanham Act section 43(c) became law: "Relying on the law as it existed in 1993, CarMax selected and, for over two years, advertised and promoted a valid legal mark. Enforcing the Dilution Act under these circumstances would be tantamount to 'reaching back' to deny CarMax the substantial benefits its past legal conduct has reaped."[17] Other cases agree,[18] but one does not.[19]

14 Because the statutory definition of the word "dilution" includes situations where the parties are in competition, this, I think, opens up the federal statute for application in cases that do not fit into the traditional "blurring" mode of the same mark being used on non-competing and widely different goods. Inventive attorneys will use the new law in ways that INTA did not envision.

15 Circuit City Stores, Inc. v. Officemax, Inc., 949 F. Supp. 409, 42 U.S.P.Q.2d (BNA) 1194 (E.D. Va. 1996).

16 *Id.*

17 *Circuit City*, 949 F. Supp. at 418, 42 U.S.P.Q.2d (BNA) at 1203.

18 *See, e.g.*, Viacom, Inc. v. Ingram Enters., Inc., 965 F. Supp. 1278, 1281, 43 U.S.P.Q.2d (BNA) 1148, 1151 (W.D. Mo. 1997) ("The Court believes the analysis used by the *Circuit City* court was correct in all respects." The section 43(c) claim was dismissed because defendant's mark pre-dated enactment of section 43(c)); Resorts of Pinehurst, Inc. v. Pinehurst Nat'l Dev. Corp., 973 F. Supp. 552, 557, 43 U.S.P.Q.2d (BNA) 1746, 1750 (M.D.N.C. 1997) ("This Court is persuaded that the *Circuit City Stores* court's analysis of the Landgraf principles in the context of the Dilution Act is an appropriate standard to use.").

19 Fuente Cigar, Ltd. v. Opus One, Nos. Civ.96-2389-CIV-T-24(E), 97-346-CIV-T-24(E), 1997 WL 725962, at *5 (M.D. Fla. Nov. 4, 1997) ("This Court declines to follow the Circuit City court in holding that prospective relief under the anti-dilution statute, premised on conduct or events occurring before its enactment, has a retroactive effect.").

The Degree of Similarity of the Conflicting Marks is not Defined. The 1996 Act is silent on the crucial question of how similar the conflicting marks must be to create the requisite "dilution." The familiar test of similarity used in the traditional likelihood of confusion test cannot be the guide, for likelihood of confusion is not the test of dilution. It has been held that identity of the marks is not required.[20] One should recall the famous 1989, *LEXIS v. LEXUS* case[21] where the challenged LEXUS was held not close enough to LEXIS to be diluted by blurring.[22] Applying the *Lexis* case "very" or "substantially" similar test, it was held that defendant's mark THE GREATEST BAR ON EARTH did not dilute by blurring plaintiff's famous circus slogan THE GREATEST SHOW ON EARTH because, among other reasons, the marks were not similar enough.[23]

Federal Registration is a Complete Defense only to a Charge Under a State Anti-Dilution Law. Section 43(c)(3)[24] states that ownership of a valid federal registration of a mark on the Principal Register is a complete defense to a claim that the registered mark is illegally diluting another's mark under *state* law. But this means that ownership of a federal registration is *not* a defense to a federal charge of diluting a famous mark.

D. *The Two Prongs of Dilution: Blurring and Tarnishment*

Section 45 of the Lanham Act[25] defines "dilution" as "the lessening of the capacity of a famous mark to identify and distinguish goods or services, regardless of the presence or absence of" competition and likelihood of confusion.

1. Dilution by Blurring

Blurring is the classic, or "traditional," type of dilution theory as envisioned by its original proponents. Even though no confusion as to source, sponsorship, affiliation, or connection has occurred, the unique link between that designation and a single source has been "diluted" or "blurred." The dilution theory presumes *some kind of mental association* in the reasonable buyer's

---

20 Ringling Bros.-Barnum & Bailey Combined Shows, Inc. v. Utah Div. of Travel Dev., 955 F. Supp 605, 42 U.S.P.Q.2d (BNA) 1161 (E.D.Va. 1997) (holding THE GREATEST SNOW ON EARTH does not dilute THE GREATEST SHOW ON EARTH).

21 Mead Data Cent., Inc. v. Toyota Motor Sales, U.S.A., Inc., 875 F.2d 1026 (2d Cir. 1989).

22 *Id.*

23 Ringling Bros.-Barnum & Bailey Combined Shows, Inc. v. B.E. Windows Corp., 937 F. Supp. 204, 40 U.S.P.Q.2d (BNA) 1010 (S.D.N.Y. 1996).

24 Lanham Act 15 U.S.C. § 1125(c)(3) (1994).

25 *Id.* § 1127.

mind between the two parties and the mark. Not that the mark links the two parties, but that it now links two distinct sources.

An example is something like the hypothetical "TOYOTA brand candy bars" made by a company having nothing to do with the Japanese Toyota car people. Customers or prospective customers will see the plaintiff's mark used on a plethora of different goods and services. If "TOYOTA brand candy" is permitted, then there will be others who will adopt Toyota brand for bread, Toyota brand cola, and Toyota shoes. The unique and singular significance of the mark to identify and distinguish only *one source* might be diluted and weakened. But there is no confusion as to source, sponsorship, affiliation, or connection.

The challenge to plaintiffs is how to muster evidence in court to prove that there has in fact been, in the words of the statute, a "lessening of the capacity of a famous mark to identify and distinguish goods or services."[26] Or will judges be willing to presume such a "lessening" merely by the defendant's usage of the same designation as its own mark?

The assumption is that the relevant public sees the junior user's use, and intuitively knows, because of the context of the junior user's use, that there is no connection between the owners of the respective marks. For example, if I believe that the company that makes ROLLS ROYCE autos is *not* operating or sponsoring the hypothetical ROLLS ROYCE bakery on upper Broadway in New York City, then there is no confusion of source—only the possibility of dilution. Thus, a given unauthorized use by a defendant can cause confusion in some people's minds and cause dilution by blurring in other people's minds. But in no *one* person's mind can both perceptions occur at the same time. Either a person thinks that the similarly branded goods or services come from a common source (or are connected or affiliated), or not. In that sense, they are inconsistent states of customer perception.

It is important to see that as legal theories, a traditional likelihood of confusion claim and a dilution claim look to separate and distinct harms to a trademark and can be pleaded as alternative legal counts. But both infringement by a likelihood of confusion *and* dilution can coexist as legal findings if it is proven that a significant number of customers are likely to be confused *and* that among a significant number of customers that are not confused, the defendant's use will illegally dilute by blurring or tarnishment.

---

[26] Lanham Act § 45.

How could there be any "whittling away" if the buyer, upon seeing defendant's mark, would *never*, even unconsciously, think of the plaintiff's mark? For example, if the person who sees the hypothetical ALBERT FORD brand hiking boots would not even think of FORD autos, then there is no dilution. This could be proven in court only by a consumer survey.

2. Dilution by Tarnishment

Dilution by tarnishment exists where the effect of the defendant's unauthorized use is to dilute by tarnishing or degrading positive associations of the mark and thus, to dilute the distinctive quality of the mark. For example, in the *SPAM* case,[27] the Second Circuit said that: "The *sine qua non* of tarnishment is a finding that plaintiff's mark will suffer negative associations through defendant's use."[28] No tarnishment to the trademark SPAM was found from the use of the character name "Spa'am" in a Muppets movie.[29]

But does the new 1996 Act cover dilution by tarnishment of a mark? While some commentators have argued that it does not,[30] the case law to date has held that it does.[31] However, it has been held that a junior user's use of a similar mark on an allegedly

---

27 Hormel Foods Corp. v. Jim Henson Prods., Inc., 73 F.3d 497, 507, 37 U.S.P.Q.2d (BNA) 1516, 1523 (2d Cir. 1996).

28 *Id.*

29 *Id.*

30 *See, e.g.*, Robert C. Denicola, *Some Thoughts on the Dynamics of Federal Trademark Legislation and the Trademark Dilution Act of 1995*, 59 L. & CONTEMP. PROBS. 75, 88-90 (1996) (The history of the 1996 legislation requires that it be limited to dilution by blurring. "Unlike broader state dilution acts with their references to 'injury to business reputation' as well as to 'dilution of the distinctive quality of a trademark,' the federal dilution statute is limited to uses that blur the source significance of the mark.") (footnote omitted); Miles J. Alexander & Michael K. Heilbronner, *Dilution Under Section 43(c) of the Lanham Act*, 59 L. & CONTEMP. PROBS. 93, 124-25 (1996) ("Under a strict constructionist view like Justice Scalia's, the omission in the federal statute of the 'injury to business reputation' language that is contained in most state dilution statutes may mean that a claim for tarnishment is not available under the federal statute.").

31 *See, e.g.*, Hasbro Inc. v. Internet Entertainment Group Ltd., 40 U.S.P.Q.2d (BNA) 1479 (W.D. Wash. 1996) (holding CANDYLAND for children's game diluted by tarnishment by the "candyland.com" web site showing sexually explicit pictures); Anheuser-Busch Inc. v. Andy's Sportswear Inc., 40 U.S.P.Q.2d (BNA) 1542 (N.D. Cal. 1996) (granting temporary restraining order ("TRO") against use of BUTTWEISER on T-shirts as tarnishing BUDWEISER for beer); Toys "R" Us Inc. v. Akkaoui, 40 U.S.P.Q.2d (BNA) 1836, 1838 (N.D. Cal. 1996) (TOYS "R" US held tarnished by use of ADULTS R US as domain name for sale of adult sexual products: "adultsrus.com." "'Adults R Us' tarnishes the "'R Us" family of marks by associating them with a line of sexual products that are inconsistent with the image Toys 'R' Us has striven to maintain for itself."). *See* 3 McCarthy, *supra* note 2, § 24:95.

"cheap knock-off" product does not fit within the meaning of "tarnishment."[32]

E. *What is a Famous Mark?*

To be eligible for the extraordinary scope of protection and exclusivity offered by the new 1996 Act, the plaintiff's mark must be "famous." Section 43(c)(1)[33] of the 1996 Act has a "list of eight" factors for a court to ponder and weigh to determine if a mark is "famous." But there is little predictability of how these factors will be balanced and applied.

1. Examples under the 1996 Act

a. Some marks held to be "famous" under the 1996 Act:

BUDWEISER for beer[34]

CANDYLAND children's game[35]

DON'T LEAVE HOME WITHOUT US slogan for traveler's checks and credit cards[36]

THE GREATEST SHOW ON EARTH slogan for a circus[37]

INTERMATIC electrical products[38]

NAILTIQUES fingernail care products[39]

---

32 [Defendant] is not attempting to associate [plaintiff's skin care] products with obscenity or sexual or illegal activity, the [defendant's cheaper skin care] product line is neither shoddy nor unwholesome, and no evidence suggests that [plaintiff's] trademark or trade dress will suffer negative associations through [defendant's] use of [its] mark.

Clinique Lab., Inc. v. DEP Corp., 945 F. Supp. 547, 562 (S.D.N.Y. 1996).

33 Lanham Act 15 U.S.C. § 1125(c)(1) (1994).

34 *Anheuser-Busch,* 40 U.S.P.Q.2d (BNA) at 1542 (granting a TRO against the use of BUTTWEISER on T-shirts).

35 *Hasbro,* 40 U.S.P.Q.2d (BNA) at 1479 (holding that a trademarked children's game was diluted by tarnishment by the "candyland.com" web site, which shows sexually explicit pictures).

36 American Express Co. v. CFK, Inc., 947 F. Supp. 310, 41 U.S.P.Q.2d (BNA) 1756 (E.D. Mich. 1996) (failing to grant summary judgment for plaintiff against use of DON'T LEAVE HOME WITHOUT ME POCKET ADDRESS BOOK registered mark for pocket-sized address books).

37 Ringling Bros.-Barnum & Bailey Combined Shows v. B.E. Windows Inc., 937 F. Supp. 204, 40 U.S.P.Q.2d (BNA) 1010 (S.D.N.Y. 1996) (holding that the mark was not diluted by THE GREATEST BAR ON EARTH); Ringling Bros. Barnum & Bailey Combined Shows, Inc. v. Utah Div. of Travel Dev., 955 F. Supp. 605, 42 U.S.P.Q.2d (BNA) 1161 (E.D.Va. 1997) (holding that the mark was not diluted by THE GREATEST SNOW ON EARTH).

38 Intermatic Inc. v. Toeppen, 947 F. Supp. 1227, 40 U.S.P.Q.2d (BNA) 1412 (N.D. Ill. 1996), *approved,* 41 U.S.P.Q.2d (BNA) 1223 (N.D. Ill. 1996) (holding that the mark was diluted by cyber-squatter).

39 Nailtiques Cosmetic Corp. v. Salon Sciences Corp., 41 U.S.P.Q.2d (BNA) 1995 (S.D. Fla. 1997) (finding fame without analyzing the eight statutory factors on a motion for preliminary injunction).

PANAVISION movie and television cameras[40]

TOYS "R" US toy stores[41]

WAWA chain of 500 convenience stores in five eastern states, in use for ninety years[42]

b. Some marks held not to be "famous" under the 1996 Act:

COLUMBIA university[43]

PETRO truck stop services[44]

WE'LL TAKE GOOD CARE OF YOU slogan for retail drugstore chain[45]

STAR MARKET chain of eight supermarkets only in Hawaii[46]

2. What is Fame? The "List of Eight"

Factor (A): *The degree of inherent or acquired distinctiveness of the mark.* This factor requires an evaluation or measure of exactly just how strong and famous the mark is.

Factor (B): *The duration and extent of use of the mark in connection with the goods or services with which the mark is used.* These criteria are similar to those traditionally used to determine if a non-inherently distinctive designation has achieved that minimum degree of distinctiveness needed to qualify as a mark. This is usually referred to as acquiring "secondary meaning" through use.

Factor (C): *The duration and extent of advertising and publicity of the mark.* This is similar to *factor (B)* and requires evidence of the quantity and quality of promotion and advertising of the mark. This kind of evidence is the same as that traditionally used in trademark law to prove that a mark is relatively "strong." While *factor (B)* focuses on sales, *factor (C)* focuses on advertising and publicity.

---

40 Panavision Int'l L.P. v. Toeppen, 945 F. Supp. 1296, 40 U.S.P.Q.2d (BNA) 1908 (C.D. Cal. 1996) (holding that the mark was diluted by cyber-squatter).

41 Toys "R" Us Inc. v. Akkaoui, 40 U.S.P.Q.2d (BNA) 1836 (N.D. Cal. 1996) (finding dilution by being tarnished by use of ADULTS R US as domain name for sale of adult sexual products).

42 Wawa Inc. v. Haaf, 40 U.S.P.Q.2d (BNA) 1629 (E.D. Pa. 1996), *aff'd*, 116 F.3d 471 (3d Cir. 1997) (holding that a mark was diluted by the HAHA market in Pennsylvania).

43 Trustees of Columbia Univ. v. Columbia/HCA Healthcare Corp., 964 F. Supp. 733, 750, 43 U.S.P.Q.2d (BNA) 1083, 1097 (S.D.N.Y. 1997) ("The plaintiff has also failed to prove that the COLUMBIA mark is a unique identifier of the plaintiff's service such that the defendant's use of its mark [to provide healthcare services] undermines the identifying character of the plaintiff's mark.").

44 Petro Shopping Ctr. L.P. v. James River Petroleum, 41 U.S.P.Q.2d (BNA) 1853 (E.D. Va. 1997).

45 Genovese Drug Stores, Inc. v. TGC Stores, Inc., 939 F. Supp. 340 (D.N.J. 1996).

46 Star Markets, Ltd. v. Texaco, Inc., 950 F. Supp. 1030 (D. Haw. 1996) (one state is not enough).

Factor (D): *The geographical extent of the trading area in which the mark is used.* The 1995 legislative history of the 1996 Act contains statements by both Senator Hatch and Congressman Moorhead repeating the view of the Trademark Review Commission to the effect that "a Federal trademark dilution statute is necessary, because famous marks ordinarily are used on a nationwide basis."[47] Similarly, the House Report section by section analysis opined that "[t]he geographic fame of the mark must extend throughout a substantial portion of the U.S."[48] While use in only one state has been held to be insufficient,[49] use in five states for ninety years has been held sufficient.[50]

Factor (E): *The channels of trade for the goods or services with which the mark is used.* This factor merely requires the court to define the product or service line or market within which the plaintiff's mark is used and has become famous.

Factor (F): *The degree of recognition of the mark in the trading areas and channels of trade used by the mark's owner and the person against whom the injunction is sought.* This factor requires that the court determine the extent to which the fame of the mark in plaintiff's product line *A* extends to the defendant's product line *Z*. Unlcss the mark is famous among a significant percentage of the potential purchasers in the defendant's market or product line, there can be no dilution.

The Trademark Review Commission gave the example of a use of a mark on fish oil sold only to the food processing trade as being non-diluting, where the mark was the same as a famous mark used on microbiological chemicals sold to research laboratories.[51] The assumption of this hypothetical is that persons in these two customer groups do not overlap. If there is no overlap, then a less than substantial portion of people in the fish oil and food processing trade are aware of the mark, which is famous in the bio-tech field. If this is the fact, then the fame of the bio-tech mark is not

---

47 141 CONG. REC. H14317 (daily ed. Dec. 12, 1995) (statement of Rep. Moorhead in House). *See also* 141 CONG. REC. S19310 (daily ed. Dec. 29, 1995), *reprinted in* 51 Pat. Trademark & Copyright J. (BNA) No. 1259, at 345 (Jan. 4, 1996) (statement of Sen. Hatch) (stating similar sentiments as Representative Moorhead).

48 H.R. REP. No.104-374, at 7 (1995), *reprinted in* 1996 U.S.C.C.A.N. 1029, 1034.

49 *Star Markets*, 950 F. Supp. at 1030 (one state is not enough).

50 Wawa Inc. v Haaf, 40 U.S.P.Q.2d (BNA) 1629 (E.D. Pa. 1996), *aff'd*, 116 F.3d 471 (3d Cir. 1997) (holding that the mark was diluted by the HAHA market in Pennsylvania).

51 Commission Report, *supra* note 4, at 460-61. "Dilution is possible with respect to one purchaser universe but not another. For example, if a mark is famous at the industrial level but not at the consumer level, protection may be appropriate at the industrial level but not at the consumer level." *Id.* at 461.

diluted when used in the food processing trade. On the other hand, if there is some overlap, then dilution becomes a possibility.

Assume that the hypothetical mark NEW WAVE is a registered trademark used by the Babbitt Company in Texas for commercial farm equipment used to pick fruit. Babbitt NEW WAVE equipment is sold to commercial fruit growers around the United States. Among persons in portions of the farming industry, NEW WAVE is a strong and famous mark. Assume that our client Frita-Hay wants to use NEW WAVE as the trademark for its new brand of snack chips, aimed at the general population of consumers. Because of our concern over the NEW WAVE farm equipment registration, we commission a telephone survey of 500 households, asking, "Have you or have you not ever seen or heard of a product or service sold under the name 'NEW WAVE?'", with follow-up probing questions. The results are that only 2 of the 500 respondents (0.4%) associated NEW WAVE with farming equipment. Does this mean that our client's NEW WAVE illegally dilutes because there is some overlap in the customer markets? The issue is whether a *significant number of persons* in the market for *defendant's product* are aware of the fame of the mark in the specialized field.

In my view, there is no dilution in the NEW WAVE hypothetical. The *Restatement* supports this view, taking the position that a mark famous only to a sub-group of purchasers is protectable against dilution only in that particular sub-market, not protectable in a broader market of overall consumers.[52] The famous *LEXIS* case also supports this view. In the *LEXIS v. LEXUS* case,[53] while LEXIS was a strong mark in the field of attorneys and accountants, only 1% of the general public recognized LEXIS as a mark.[54] Thus, the court concluded that: "For the general public, LEXIS has no distinctive quality that LEXUS will dilute."[55] Blurring was unlikely in the minds of a significant percentage of the general public who were potential buyers of a LEXUS auto, for the LEXIS mark was

---

[52] A mark that is highly distinctive only to a particular class or group of purchasers may be protected from diluting uses directed at that particular class or group. For example, a mark may be highly distinctive among purchasers of a specific type of product. In such circumstances, protection against dilution of the mark's distinctiveness is ordinarily appropriate only against uses specifically directed at that particular class of purchasers; uses of the mark in broader markets, although they may produce an incidental diluting effect in the protected market, are not normally actionable.

RESTATEMENT (THIRD) OF UNFAIR COMPETITION § 25 cmt. e (1995).

[53] Mead Data Cent., Inc. v. Toyota Motor Sales, U.S.A., Inc., 875 F.2d 1026, 1028 (2d Cir. 1989).

[54] *Id.*

[55] *Id.* at 1031 ("[S]uch distinctiveness as LEXIS possesses is limited to the narrow field of attorneys and accountants.").

not known to them. The court said that blurring would occur only where the plaintiff's mark is so famous in its own field that it is also famous for a "significant percentage of the defendant's market."[56] The court did not try to define what is a "significant percentage," but presumably 1% was not "significant."[57]

Factor (G): *The nature and extent of use of the same or similar marks by third parties.* Evaluating mark strength and fame by the degree of third party use is a method often used in traditional infringement analysis. A mark that is merely one in a "crowd" of similar marks will not usually be "famous."

Factor (H): *Whether the mark was registered under the Act of March 3, 1881, or the Act of February 20, 1905, or on the Principal Register.* While federal registration as a prerequisite for protection under the 1996 Act was deleted in congressional hearings, this factor permits a court to find that a mark is not "famous" because, among other reasons, it was not federally registered.

F. *Defenses. There are Three Statutory Defenses:*

1. Fair Use in Comparative Advertising.[58]

For example, assume that we represent the hypothetical client Bay Burgers, a local chain of fast food outlets. Our client just put up a sign on the same pole that its big BAY BURGERS sign appears, the new sign reading: "Better burgers. Faster Service than Burger Queen." We receive a cease-and-desist letter from the competitor Burger Queen, claiming that this use "dilutes" their famous mark. In my opinion, on behalf of our client, we could tell the attorney for Burger Queen that there is no basis for the claim of dilution. This kind of use of a competitor's trademark is entirely proper and constitutes fair comparative advertising. In addition, our client is using the Burger Queen designation, not as a mark to identify the client, but as a mark to truthfully identify the competition.

2. Noncommercial Uses.[59]

The intent of Congress appears to be that the 1996 Act cannot be used as a legal riposte to uses of a trademark in negative product reviews in the media or negative opinions expressed about

56 *Id.*

57 If we changed the facts so that our client was not selling NEW WAVE snack chips, but NEW WAVE farm tractors, the whole equation changes to a different result, with probable dilution by blurring being the result.

58 Lanham Act § 43(c)(4)(A), 15 U.S.C. § 1125(c)(4)(A) (1994).

59 *Id.* § 43(c)(4)(B). This statutory "defense" is probably redundant in view of the requirement in section 43(c)(1) that the challenged use be a "commercial use."

company policies.[60] So when our angry client calls and demands that we threaten a product review web site or an electronics magazine with an anti-dilution claim because of an unfavorable product review, we should urge the client to cool off and not send a letter threatening an anti-dilution claim.

3. All Forms of News Reporting and News Commentary.[61]

This statutory defense includes all forms of news reporting and news commentary. This was obviously inserted to satisfy the free speech concerns and the lobbying of the media that stopped the anti-dilution bill in the House in 1988. This category of exempted uses seems self-explanatory and was inserted to assure the media that the federal anti-dilution law would not be used as a weapon against media use of trademarks in the context of conveying news and other forms of socially useful information. This section also ensures that the statute does not apply to allegedly tasteless or nasty modifications of famous marks in the media, in newspaper cartoons, magazine stories, Internet home pages, and the like. The commitment to free speech means that media parody does not generally trigger the anti-dilution laws.

G. *Remedies*

Injunction is the normal remedy, while the usual Lanham Act remedies of damages and profits require the predicate finding that the defendant "wilfully intended to trade on the owner's reputation or to cause dilution of the famous mark."[62]

II. Conclusion

Soon this shiny new federal law will become encrusted with court decisions, narrowing the scope of my speculations and predictions. But the difficulty of determining what marks are "famous," will, I think, continue and the definitional process will be vague and imprecise.

This is a very potent piece of legislation. All who do business in the United States will have to deal with it either as a sword or will be looking for a shield against claims under the new law. Other nations are pondering whether to enact such a law. The world is

60 See the case law interpreting Lanham Act section 43(a)'s requirement that an allegedly false representation be in "*commercial* advertising or promotion" and misrepresent the nature of "goods, services or *commercial* activities." *See* 3 McCarthy, *supra* note 2, § 27:71.

61 Lanham Act § 43(c)(4)(c).

62 *Id.* § 43(c)(2).

watching what the U.S. courts will do with this new approach to expanding the exclusionary scope of trademarks.

YET ANOTHER FOX IN THE HEN HOUSE: GOVERNMENT PROTECTION OF ARTISTIC EXPRESSION WITHIN PRIVATELY OWNED PUBLIC SPACES

DAVID RUDENSTINE*

To what extent should the state be empowered to regulate privately owned public spaces, such as shopping malls, for the purpose of protecting artistic expression? As framed, the issue does not necessarily focus our attention on either federal or state governments, even though *Pruneyard Shopping Center v. Robins*[1] made clear that the powers of federal and state governments to protect free expression within privately owned public spaces are not identical.

This subject marks the enormous distance First Amendment jurisprudence has traveled during this century. Traditional First Amendment problems concern potential government censorship of quintessential political speech. Our topic differs from the traditional paradigm in two respects. First, the topic suggests that we consider the government a potential ally, as opposed to a potential opponent, of free expression. Second, the topic focuses our attention on the public display of art as opposed to written or verbal speech.

The idea that the government should be empowered to regulate privately owned public spaces in the name of artistic expression is menacingly seductive. It takes little effort to conjure up images of private entities censoring art which is to be displayed in privately owned public spaces. The suggestion almost seems to ask: what is wrong with permitting the state to limit the influence of prejudice, intolerance, ignorance, and stupidity, at least as it is aimed at curtailing horrible abuses by private orthodoxies in our privately owned public spaces? But like so many tempting apples in the Garden of Eden, this one is poisoned.

Before explaining why the government should not have the power to regulate privately owned public spaces in the name of protecting artistic expression, one must note two problems of defi-

---

* Dr. Herman George & Kate Kaiser Professor of Constitutional Law, Benjamin N. Cardozo School of Law. B.A., 1963, M.A.T., 1965, Yale University; J.D., 1969, New York University.

1 447 U.S. 74 (1980).

nition inherent in the proposal. First, distinguishing art from other modes of expression may be quite difficult. Consider this example. On New Year's Day, I saw the Robert Rauschenberg Retrospective at the Guggenheim Museum. Rauschenberg, who created "Combines," which are three-dimensional colored objects inscribed with painted images, tells this story.[2] When he exhibited these stunning works with artists who worked in a two, as opposed to a three-dimensional format, he was told that his "Combines" were sculptures, not paintings. When he displayed his "Combines" in an exhibition featuring conventional sculptures, he was told that his "Combines" were paintings, not sculptures. As the anecdote suggests, it can be difficult to distinguish painting from sculpture, even though they are two traditional modes of artistic expression. If this is true, as it was in Mr. Rauschenberg's case, it is questionable whether we can reach a workable consensus about the concept of art. Thus, by art, do we mean only paintings, or do we include sculptures, architecture, drawings, photography, films, performance art, and possibly cartoon drawings? To the extent that we consider empowering the government to protect free expression of artists, we put a premium on defining the concept of art, which would be quite difficult.

The second definitional problem concerns the concept of "privately owned public spaces." If we are going to consider empowering the government to intrude into zones previously free of regulation in order to protect artistic expression, then we must first define the concept of "privately owned public spaces." The proposal to the panel suggests that shopping malls are the prototypical example of a privately owned public space that would be subject to such regulation. But what other privately owned public spaces will be encompassed? Surely a lawful regulation cannot be written which applies solely to shopping malls, enclosed or not. Consider two examples. A Park Avenue office tower houses the international headquarters of a major corporation. In its entrance lobby, art is routinely exhibited. This art is fully visible from the sidewalk and street. Should the State of New York have a say in what art is hung in this highly visible space? Alternatively, should Governor George E. Pataki of New York, who hit the Achille's heel of intellectual freedom recently when he criticized State University officials for sponsoring a conference which discussed controversial sex issues,[3]

---

[2] For a brief review of Rauschenberg and his "Combines" see Robert L. Pincus, *Artist Still Combines Known Ideas, Original Vision,* THE SAN DIEGO UNION-TRIBUNE, March 29, 1998, at 2.

[3] Governor George E. Pataki, state lawmakers, and conservative groups criticized the

be empowered to review judgments of curators at the Metropolitan Museum of Art to assure that the Museum does not improperly censor what is exhibited? I doubt that many, who might otherwise favor government regulation of shopping malls, would favor the government sticking its nose into the museum tent to assure that artistic expression is not limited. Are there differences among these forums that warrant limiting government regulation to the shopping malls? Perhaps there are, but I am not convinced.

Having raised these few problems of definition, I do not wish to rest on them. I have more significant concerns that prompt me to be skeptical about giving the state a role in protecting artistic expression in privately owned public spaces.

I begin with the important tenet that there is no necessary connection between individual liberty, or more precisely, the public display of art, and a democratic order.[4] As Isaiah Berlin has reminded us, the answer to the question "[w]ho governs [us]?"[5] is logically distinct from the question, "[h]ow far does government interfere with [us]?"[6] Thus, it is conceivable that an intolerant majority in a democracy could deprive some citizens of many liberties, and that an enlightened despot might allow her subjects a large measure of personal freedom. Because there is nothing intrinsic to a democratic order that guarantees a preconceived zone of individual liberty, any democratic order must structure and limit government power to preserve and protect liberty.

In the United States, we seek to accomplish this end by using many familiar devices. We divide governmental power horizontally into "Our Federalism,"[7] and vertically by the Separation of Powers doctrine. We curtail the reach of government power, most notably by the Bill of Rights,[8] and we empower a press, under the First Amendment,[9] to report on public matters and to search out abuses of power. We maintain a powerful private sector that counter-balances public power. We assume that government power to regulate expression should be sharply limited, because free expression is important to the flourishing of the individual, the vigor of the democratic process, and the general welfare of society. These as-

---

State University of New York at New Paltz after details emerged regarding a conference held on November 1, 1997 which included seminars about lesbianism, sadomasochism, and sex toys. *A $350,000 Gift for SUNY*, N.Y. TIMES, Dec. 14, 1997, at 1, *available in* 1997 WL 8016532.

4 *See* Isaiah Berlin, *Two Concepts of Liberty*, in FOUR ESSAYS ON LIBERTY 118, 130 (1969).

5 *Id.*

6 *Id.*

7 *See generally* Younger v. Harris, 401 U.S. 37, 44 (1971).

8 U.S. CONST. amend. I-X.

9 *Id.* amend. I.

sumptions do not give rise to an absolute right of expression, but they support the imposition of sharp limitations on the power of government to regulate expression, artistic or otherwise.

It is against these considerations that we must assess the proposal that the government be empowered to regulate private spaces previously immune from regulation in order to assure artistic expression. When I do that, I find the proposal flatly inconsistent with our traditional axiom. Traditionally, government regulation of expression in private spaces is considered an encroachment on — not an enhancement of — liberty. But the proposal flips the traditional formula on its head and urges that we consider government power to regulate expression within private spaces as an ally of free expression. From my perspective, this would be letting the fox in the hen house.

The proposal may not be an oxymoron, but I have a hard time thinking of it as otherwise. Only two reasons come to mind that might cause me to reconsider this conclusion. First, if it were clear beyond doubt that narrow-minded private entities had overwhelming control over important public spaces and were seriously stifling the public display of art, I might be more open to find ways in which the government might assist in protecting free expression. I do not, however, think that we face such a serious condition of repression. Second, if I were convinced that legal criteria could be defined to limit government power so that its exercise would enhance the public display of art in privately controlled public spaces, I might be more sympathetic to the proposal. Allow me to explain why I am not so persuaded.

It is proposed that the government have the power to prevent mall owners from improperly censoring the images they display publicly. But what is obnoxious censorship? If we were concerned with political speech, we might feel confident that offensive censorship by mall owners could be defined as censorship based on content. Thus, as in *Pruneyard Shopping Center v. Robins*,[10] California required mall owners to permit the distribution of pamphlets within the mall, subject only to time, place, and manner restrictions. However, what comparable standard would the government employ in deciding whether a mall owner improperly declined to permit the display of a particular exhibition? Consider the following example. A mall owner regularly mounts exhibitions celebrating the wilderness, in the hope that the art will enliven public awareness about the value of the wilderness. Now suppose an artist

10 447 U.S. 74 (1980).

whose works celebrate industrialization, especially in developing economies, wants to mount an exhibition of his works in the mall. The mall owner rejects the proposed exhibition. What position should the state assert if it used *Pruneyard* as its guide? If the mall owner rejects the proposed exhibition because he disagrees with the artist's political claim that industrialization benefits developing economies, perhaps the state should intervene on the ground that the mall owner discriminated against the proposed exhibition because of the content of its message. But if the rejection results from aesthetic considerations, perhaps the state should allow the mall owner's judgment to stand.

Neither result seems satisfactory. Sustaining mall owner judgments when they are ostensibly based on aesthetic grounds would only invite rejections by mall owners based on these grounds. In contrast, reversing mall owner judgments based on the content of an artist's work, puts a premium on defining what constitutes content in art, and on differentiating content from aesthetic judgments. These two matters would be difficult to define and defend.

If we did not use *Pruneyard* as our guide, we might direct the government to sustain any discriminating judgment that was reasonable. This deferential standard would insulate mall owners' judgments from reversal. The result would be that government efforts at protecting artistic freedom in public spaces controlled by private entities would be ineffective.

The area between these two extremes, one requiring the mall owner to display more or less whatever art is presented, the other essentially requiring the government to defer to a mall owner's decision, is likely to be treacherous. I cannot imagine what the standard might be. I suspect that all it would accomplish would be to substitute the judgment of government officials for that of mall owners in deciding what art should be displayed. I do not perceive any virtue in such a regime. However, I can perceive a distinct disadvantage, at least as far as artistic expression is concerned. If malls are preserved as private havens, there will likely be some diversity of judgment as to what type of art should be hung. Indeed, if I am correct, the idea that government intervention into privately controlled public spheres for the purpose of curtailing the tyranny of orthodoxy will likely boomerang and result in the imposition of the government's orthodoxy.

If we should not trust the government with protecting the display of art in privately owned public spaces, whom should we trust? I believe that we should trust our culture. I will make this point somewhat indirectly.

A central problem of free speech jurisprudence is whether free speech rights should be extended to political groups whose beliefs are antithetical to a democracy and who might destroy a democratic order if properly elected. Justice Jackson, fresh from his experience at the Nuremberg trials, thought that such an idea was ludicrous. As he wrote in his dissenting opinion in *Terminiello v. Chicago*,[11] protesting the Court's reversal of a breach of the peace conviction: "[I]f the court does not temper its doctrinaire logic with a little practical wisdom, it will convert the Constitutional Bill of Rights into a suicide pact."[12] Not surprisingly, Justice Black had a different attitude. As he wrote in his dissent in *Dennis v. United States*:[13] "I cannot agree that the First Amendment permits us to sustain laws suppressing freedom of speech and press on the basis of Congress' or our notions of mere 'reasonableness.' . . . The Amendment as so construed is not likely to protect any but those 'safe' or orthodox views which rarely need its protection."[14]

In commenting on this free speech problem, the journalist I.F. Stone wrote that the issue presented "two dangers."[15] On the one hand there is "the danger that fascist or revolutionary movements may utilize the basic freedoms of the Constitution to destroy it."[16] On the other hand, there is the risk that government officials "will abuse this power [to censor] and limit the open discussion which is the foundation of a free society."[17] Stone conceded that the choice was "difficult" because . . . the dangers either way are real enough. But you cannot have freedom without the risk of its abuse. The men who wrote the Bill of Rights were willing to take their chances on freedom."[18] In this passage Stone sounds like a student of Holmes' dissent in *Gitlow v. People of New York*,[19] in which Holmes wrote: "If in the long run the beliefs expressed in the proletarian dictatorship are destined to be accepted by the dominant forces of the community, the only meaning of free speech is that they should be given their chance and have their way."[20]

In the debate over whether to grant freedom of speech to groups who might use it to destroy the Constitution, I side with Justices Holmes and Black, as well as I.F. Stone. I do so, not only

---

11 337 U.S. 1 (1949).
12 *Id.* at 37 (Jackson, J., dissenting).
13 341 U.S. 494 (1951).
14 *Id.* at 580 (Black, J., dissenting).
15 I.F. STONE, THE TRUMAN ERA 109 (1972).
16 *Id.*
17 *Id.*
18 *Id.* at 110.
19 268 U.S. 651 (1925).
20 *Id.* at 673 (Holmes, J., dissenting).

because of the dangers inherent in entrusting the government with the power to censor political speech, but because there is a more effective way to nurture freedom and free institutions than permitting the government to limit freedom in the name of security. This point was eloquently made by Judge Learned Hand in a speech he delivered in Central Park on May 21, 1944, when the Nazi threat to liberty was still alive. He said:

> I often wonder whether we do not rest our hopes too much upon constitutions, upon laws, and upon courts. These are false hopes; believe me, these are false hopes. Liberty lies in the hearts of men and women; when it dies there, no constitution, no law, no court can save it; no constitution, no law, no court can even do much to help. While it lies there it needs no constitution, no law, no court to save it.[21]

We should take Judge Hand's advice to heart. If we trust our culture (as opposed to relying on government regulation) to preserve our democratic order in the face of extremist groups who speak freely and peacefully, though they might seek to subvert the constitutional order if elected, I see no reason not to trust our culture (as opposed to government regulation) to provide substantial forums that display art in such variety that it infuses our culture with freshness and challenge.

Government orthodoxy is the quintessential oppressor of free expression, artistic or otherwise. The *Pruneyard* decision sought to avoid that pitfall by allowing the government to intrude into the private sphere, only to enforce a neutral stance by mall owners with regard to the content of the message of people who wish to distribute pamphlets within malls. There is no comparable position for the government to take with regard to the public display of art in privately owned public spaces. Although the values of the private sector leave much to be desired, I do not see government intrusion in the name of artistic freedom as enhancing the public display of artistic expression. Indeed, it would have the opposite consequence.

---

21 LEARNED HAND, *The Spirit of Liberty*, *in* THE SPIRIT OF LIBERTY: PAPERS AND ADDRESSES OF LEARNED HAND 189, 189-90 (3d ed. 1960) (address given at the "I am an American Day" Ceremony held in Central Park, New York City, May 21, 1944).

ART AND THE MARKETPLACE OF EXPRESSION

MARCI A. HAMILTON*

How do we engineer a marketplace of ideas to our liking? I think many of us would agree unthinkingly that the appropriate goal in a free society is to effect a marketplace of expression that is wide-ranging and diverse. The question is how. My thesis today is that the Constitution's Copyright Clause constructs the marketplace and that the First Amendment police government interference with that market construction. By expanding our vision from the First Amendment alone to the First Amendment coupled with the Copyright Clause, we can better apprehend what sorts of suppression are possible and, more important which are permissible.

I am inclined to agree with David Rudenstine's choice: if one must trust one or the other, I would place my trust in the market rather than the government.[1] But, I believe that the discussion of the marketplace of ideas in First Amendment doctrine too frequently oversimplifies the issues.

When discussing the freedom of speech, or art, we tend to speak in either/or categories. Speech is either suppressed or free. The government is either oppressor or not. The speaker is either engaging in protected speech or not. Suppression is bad; freedom is good. Government is dangerous; speech is not. We use these either/or categories to construct decision trees to reach answers in particular cases. The problem with the either/or methodology here, as elsewhere, is that it oversimplifies the actual operation of the law and the societal forces underlying the law. My purpose today is to prod discussion by complicating the analysis.

The marketplace of ideas is a subset of the marketplace of expression. The marketplace of *expression* is governed simultaneously by the interlinked forces of the First Amendment and the Copyright Clause. The Copyright Clause sets the ground rules for the market and the First Amendment reinforces the market's inherent limits on government interference with speech.

The marketplace of expression generated by the Copyright Clause's partnership with the First Amendment is considerably more complicated than the dualism of suppression/freedom ad-

---

* Professor of Law, and Director, Intellectual Property Law Program, Benjamin N. Cardozo School of Law. B. A. 1979 Vanderbilt University; M.A. 1982, M.A. 1984, Pennsylvania State University, J.D.; 1988; University of Pennsylvania.

1 *See* This volume at 159.

mits. Under the Copyright Clause, the federal government may grant authors of original works the right to keep others from repeating or using their expression for limited times. This is a government-sanctioned right to suppress expression, but it has palpable limits. This power of suppression does not extend to the entire "thing" holding the expression. Only original expression trumps other expression. And the *ideas* in any work cannot be suppressed by government or private individual.

Moreover, the right to suppression does not exist in perpetuity.[2] Once the expression reaches its majority, it is available to all.

The Copyright Clause appears midway in Article I's listing of Congress's enumerated powers. In the midst of clauses granting Congress power to collect taxes, borrow money, coin money, and declare war, the Copyright Clause states: "The Congress shall have power to promote the progress of Science and useful Arts, by securing for limited times to Authors and inventors the exclusive Right to their respective Writings and Discoveries."[3]

The Framers believed that they were crafting an ingenious governmental scheme that would avoid tyranny and therefore engender liberty. There is precious little in the Debates at the Constitutional Convention that would indicate precisely why the Framers inserted the Copyright Clause into the Constitution. The Copyright Clause was passed as a matter of course, prompting no debate, let alone any dissent.[4]

We hardly need Convention history, however, to realize that the *only* way in which the first draft Constitution sent to Congress addressed expression was through the Copyright Clause.[5] It is worthwhile to sit back for a moment to absorb the fact that the Framers endorsed, without question, the notion of government-sanctioned private suppression of expression (copyright law) but they thought that it was unnecessary to mention rights-protection for speech, religion, or any matter touching upon conscience. They inserted the Copyright Clause as though it was an obvious choice for this new polity. But they refused to include a bill of

---

2 The Copyright Clause permits copyright only for "limited times." U.S. CONST. art. I, § 8, cl. 8. Unfortunately, Congress recently formed to industry pressure to increase the term to approximately 100 years. *See* The Sonny Bono Copyright Term Extension Act, Pub. L. No. 105-298, 112 Stat. 2827 (1998). Marci A. Hamilton, *Copyright Duration Extension and the Dark Heart of Copyright*, 14 CARDOZO. ARTS & ENT. L.J. 655 (1996).

3 U.S. CONST. art. I, § 8, cl. 8.

4 *See* Journal of James Madison (Sept. 5, 1787), *in* THE RECORDS OF THE FEDERAL CONVENTION of 1787, vol. II, at 505 (Max Farrand ed.) (1986).

5 *See* JAMES MADISON, NOTES OF DEBATES IN THE FEDERAL CONVENTION 1787, 608 (1981).

rights on the ground that it was unnecessary. Liberty, apparently, would be secure, at least in part, if the federal government were limited to the exercise of enumerated powers, if one of those powers permitted authors to suppress the expression of others for limited times, and if there were no independent articulation of rights against the government. The view should be understood against the backdrop of British history. In England, the Stationers Company, the Crown and the established Church aggressively censored works with the aid of the Star Chamber. The American genius lay in the decision to detangle the powers that worked together to suppress liberty.[6]

Drawing upon the history of publishing and censorship in Britain, one can find three features of the United States Copyright Clause that shape the character of the marketplace of expression that is then policed by the First Amendment. First, the clause tends to decentralize control over expressive works. (Authors, not publishers, the government or an established Church, hold rights.) Second, the clause fosters original works. An expanding array of works is necessary to ensure liberty. Third, the clause encourages the commodification of expressive works. I will focus on the first two factors—decentralization and originality.

Let us return to the question about private ownership of public spaces and what to do. There are now three potential suppressors of a particular artwork: the author of the work, the government, and the private owner of a publicly shared space. The Constitution permits, even encourages, the author to censor or chill others' speech for a limited time. By giving enforceable property rights in her expression, Article I simultaneously makes it possible for her to receive a return on her investment of time, energy, and resources, and encourages her to disseminate her work, making it possible for others to benefit.[7] Moreover, by giving the author power over her original work for a limited period, the clause forces contemporary authors to create their *own* new works, and therefore, engenders more quantity, quality and diversity in the marketplace. In sum, for utilitarian purposes, the clause annoints authors with censorship powers.

The Constitution does *not* grant the federal government the same censorship power over art works,[8] because the government's centralized power is too likely to be used coercively to the detri-

---

6 *See* Marci A. Hamilton, Copyright and the Constitution (forthcoming) (manuscript at 15-17, on file with *Cardozo Law Review*).

7 *See* U.S. Const. art. I, § 8, cl. 8.

8 *Id.*

ment of the people. While the government ought to have free rein to purchase art for its own purposes, it cannot engage in viewpoint discrimination when it finances the creator of the new works.[9]

The utility of the private owner's power to censor presents a harder question. The private owner can operate as both a purchaser, (such as the shopping mall owner who purchases statuary, architectural designs, and graphics to decorate the space), or as a provider of works (in the case of the mall, by permitting artists to sell their works on his premises, or in the case of the Internet, by displaying and distributing copyrighted works). Because works eventually fall into the public domain, older works are largely free while newer works must be purchased. This might argue that new works will not receive airing in these fora and, therefore, intervention-funding, for example, is needed. But the seemingly insatiable appetite for the "new" which is characteristic of American culture and which is a value embedded in our constitutional scheme (and highlighted in the Information Era) is likely to drive such space-owners to use their resources to invest in new works to attract the public. Those works run the gamut from architecture, graphics, and sculpture to motion pictures, concerts, and plays performed on the owner's premises or through the Internet.

The argument that private owners will use their resources in a way that positively contributes to the quantity, quality, and diversity of artworks available to the public turns on the extent of industry *centralization.* As long as there is a meaningful variety of owners, we can expect the mix of art available to the public to be fairly diverse and even interesting. What happens, though, when a single conglomerate owns a significant percentage of the shopping malls, when airports are privatized and owned by a bare handful of air service conglomerates, or when only a small number of companies control the vast majority of the spaces visited by the public on the Internet? What happens when one of the media multinationals starts investing in malls, or the Internet, and plays only its music, displays only its graphics, and shows only its movies? Economies of scale suggest that such concentration of ownership will result in less variety, less originality, and more conformity. The dangers of centralized government control over expressive works are just as real when we have centralized private control. This is the lesson of the stationers Company, the Star Chamber and the Statute of Anne.[10]

---

9 *See Finley* discussion, *Speech Art Law Symposium*, New Orleans (Jan. 8, 1999).

10 *See* Hamilton, *supra* note 6, at 15-17.

If centralization of control over artistic works is the cardinal fear, and the Copyright Clause tells us it is,[11] then turning to the government to solve the problem posed by consolidated private power is backward to say the least. Why turn to one centralized power to fix another centralized power's errors? Federal or state laws that would force private arts purchasers to open their doors to particular works or types of works, or that would force diversity in their art choices are misguided. Such a solution simply compounds the problem posed by oligopolistic private owners.

The better answer, if we intend to foster the marketplace of expression, lies in the rigorous enforcement of the antitrust laws. As the current dispute between Microsoft and the Justice Department over Microsoft's web browsers implies,[12] the antitrust laws[13] can be important tools in engineering the marketplace of expression. Where were they when our media companies consolidated their world domination over the marketplace of expression?

Keeping the government from censorship and private owners from monopolistic behavior is not enough, however, to ensure healthy development of the marketplace of expression. The Copyright Clause rewards only that expression that is demonstrably original.[14] It transforms what could be a static set of expressions into an ever expanding array. Assuming the proprietors of space frequented by the public do not have monopolistic power, that ever-expanding array, or at least a significant portion, is likely to find its way to the public. Without the Copyright Clause, the market in expression would *not* be a free market and it would not be a diverse market.

In sum, the Copyright Clause establishes criteria by which we can judge how the marketplace of expression is faring. It is not enough to ask whether art is being suppressed, for the Copyright Clause empowers the federal government to permit authors to suppress those works that copy theirs. We should be asking instead whether the market is subject to decentralized control and whether it contains an ever-expanding variety of original, creative works.

---

11 *Id.*

12 *See* Michelle M. Flores, *Gathering Clues on Microsoft*, SEATTLE TIMES, Sept. 22, 1996, at F1.

13 15 U.S.C. §§ 1-27 (1996).

14 *See* U. S. CONST. art. I, § 8, cl. 8.

NEW LYRICS FOR AN OLD MELODY: THE IDEA/ EXPRESSION DICHOTOMY IN THE COMPUTER AGE*

HONORABLE JON O. NEWMAN**

The computer era has presented new challenges to all segments of society, so it should come as no surprise that these challenges arise in the domain of law in general and copyright in particular. It should also not be surprising that our initial efforts to meet these challenges have not been entirely successful. After all, if the programmers could not anticipate that the year 2000 would not be just one year after 1999 but in another century[1] — one in which computers would be thinking that 2000 is 1900 — the legal community ought to be forgiven for not immediately adapting its doctrines to the demands of cyberspace.

Among the major challenges the computer age poses for copyright law is how to draw the line with respect to digital materials — mostly software[2] — between what is protectable by copyright and what is available to be copied. The instinct of many judges, lawyers, and commentators has been to start with the idea/expression dichotomy and then struggle to adapt this basic continental divide to digital materials. The effort has thus far led to two deficiencies in our approach — deficiencies that have been recognized insufficiently, if at all. Moreover, unless we begin to notice what has happened and seriously consider whether our approaches are sound, we risk not only a deficient approach to copyright issues concerning digital materials, but also an unwise corruption of previously sound approaches to copyright issues concerning non-digital materials.

These two deficiencies of decision-making in the copyright

---

* This Article is adapted from the Sixth Annual Herbert Tenzer Distinguished Lecture in Intellectual Property Law, given at the Benjamin N. Cardozo School of Law, October 22, 1998.

** Circuit Judge, United States Court of Appeals for the Second Circuit.

1 Purists would no doubt point out that the year 2000 is the last year of the twentieth century, not the first year of the twenty-first century, just as it is the last year of the second millennium, not the first year of the third millennium. But as others have observed, those who wait until midnight on December 31, 2000, to celebrate the start of the new century and the new millennium will have missed a lot of excitement on December 31, 1999.

2 I say "mostly software" because the 1s and 0s of object code that make source code readable by a computer can be embodied either in software on floppy disks or CD-ROMS, or in the hardware of a computer itself. *See* Pamela Samuelson et al., *A Manifesto Concerning the Legal Protection of Computer Programs*, 94 COLUM. L. REV. 2308, 2319 (1994).

field pose potential difficulties both for litigants and for the orderly evolution of copyright law. On the one hand, some courts are taking doctrines developed in the traditional context of writings and applying them forceably in non-traditional contexts involving emerging computer technologies.[3] On the other hand, and sometimes simultaneously, some courts are taking new doctrines, or at least refinements of old doctrines, developed in non-traditional computer-related contexts and applying them broadly to traditional contexts.[4] We need to examine how these trends have developed before we can consider what, if anything, to do about them.

From the beginning of copyright law, courts have properly recognized the obvious truth that a line must be drawn between what is protectable and what is not. For those who create, we want to maintain the incentive of receiving a financial reward for the socially useful task they perform in contributing, as our Constitution puts it, to "the Progress of Science and the Useful Arts."[5] At the same time, for the public at large, we want to recognize that some results of an intellectual process ought to be available for copying and use because such copying and use also contribute to the progress of science and the useful arts. As the Supreme Court noted in *Sony Corp. of America v. Universal Studios, Inc.*,[6] copyright law seeks to achieve a balance between "the interests of authors . . . in the control and exploitation of their writings . . . on the one hand, and society's competing interests in the free flow of ideas . . . on the other hand."[7] An important part of this balance is permitting — even encouraging — the public to copy unoriginal material. As the Court made clear in *Feist Publications, Inc. v. Rural Telephone Service Co.*,[8] "[r]aw facts may be copied at will. This result is neither unfair nor unfortunate. It is the means by which copyright advances the progress of science and art."[9]

When courts were dealing with writings such as ordinary prose texts, they attempted to strike that balance by distinguishing between ideas and expression. Ideas remained in the public domain, even though it took the working of one person's mind to articulate the idea and thereby make it available to the world. Courts recog-

[3] *See, e.g.,* Computer Assocs. Int'l v. Altai, Inc., 982 F.2d 693 (2d Cir. 1992); *infra* text accompanying notes 16-28.

[4] *See, e.g.,* Country Kids 'N Slicks, Inc. v. Sheen, 77 F.2d 1280 (10th Cir. 1996); *infra* text accompanying notes 34-37.

[5] U.S. CONST. art I, § 8, cl. 8.

[6] 464 U.S. 417 (1984).

[7] *Id.* at 429.

[8] 499 U.S. 340 (1991).

[9] *Id.* at 350.

nized that if an idea could be protected, intellectual progress would be slowed. However, courts also recognized that there was usually a sufficient number of alternative ways of expressing an idea such that requiring payment for copying one person's expression of the idea left ample opportunity for others to use and to apply the idea itself with their own creative expressions of it.[10]

Recognizing the two broad categories, however, was only the first insight. What remained was to provide some guidance as to how the categories would be distinguished in close cases. As in most areas of law, the easy cases presented no problem. It would not be difficult, on the one hand, to tell Einstein that when he had the idea that $E=MC^2$, others could copy and use that idea without payment of license fees or infringement damages, and, on the other hand, to tell Shakespeare that when he wrote *Romeo and Juliet,* others could not sell copies of his play without his permission (and a royalty payment to him). But the close cases proved more difficult, and where courts draw the line between idea and expression, or at least where courts place the somewhat narrow range of seriously disputed cases, ultimately determines whether we have protected too much or too little and thereby risked serving either of the broad purposes we set out to serve to such a great extent that the other is insufficiently served.

I suppose we might have approached the line-drawing task simply by asking in each case where protection was claimed for a particular writing whether there was available a sufficient number of alternative ways of saying what the claimant had said. If so, we would grant protection. That approach would enable us to determine what is copyrightable, but would not be of assistance in determining whether a somewhat similar work infringed, because in order to determine infringement, we have to isolate the "what" in our inquiry — what is it that the claimant has said? *Romeo and Juliet* is undoubtedly a work entitled to copyright protection, but does another playwright infringe with a play about a boy who loves a girl, about a boy from one ethnic background who loves a girl from another ethnic background, about a boy from one ethnic background who mistakenly believes that the girl of another ethnic background whom he loves is dead and therefore commits suicide?

---

10 In rare instances where the number of ways of expressing an idea was so limited that protecting expression of the idea equaled, or at least substantially approached, protection of the idea itself, we said that the idea had "merged" with its expression, and in that limited circumstance denied protection to the idea-encapsulating expression. *See, e.g.,* CCC Info. Servs. v. Maclean Hunter Mkt. Reports, Inc., 44 F.3d 61, 70-73 (2d Cir. 1994); Kregos v. Associated Press, 937 F.2d 700 (2d Cir. 1991).

In *Nichols v. Universal Pictures Corp.*,[11] Judge Learned Hand famously noticed the difficulty when he observed, in a passage more often cited than read:

> Upon any work, and especially upon a play, a great number of patterns of increasing generality will fit equally well, as more and more of the incident is left out. The last may be no more than the most general statement of what the play is about, and at times might consist only of its title; but there is a point in this series of abstractions where they are no longer protected, since otherwise the playwright could prevent the use of his "ideas," to which, apart from their expression, his property never extended. Nobody has ever been able to fix that boundary, and nobody can. . . . In such cases we are . . . concerned with the line between expression and what is expressed. As respects plays, the controversy centers upon the characters and sequence of incident, these being the substance.[12]

There are several points to note about this well known passage. In the first place, Judge Hand manifestly did not think of his observations as the enunciation of anything that might be called a "test." His disclaimer (for himself and everyone else) of the ability to "fix the boundary" should have been sufficient caution that no "test" capable of yielding a result was intended. Second, he observed that the line between "expression" and "what is expressed" might well be drawn differently depending on the subject matter. In *Nichols*, Judge Hand was concerned with a play and a film (Hand called it a "motion picture play") — *Abie's Irish Rose* and the *Cohens and the Kelly* (the copyright on *Romeo and Juliet* had long since expired). The context of plays was worth identifying as such, he usefully pointed out. Third, he thought it useful to identify those elements that would normally be significant in determining, within the context of plays, whether one play so closely resembled another as to copy protectable elements. With plays, he observed, "the controversy centers upon the characters and sequence of incidents."[13]

Regrettably, Judge Hand's careful expression has not been sufficiently read, and his idea has been often misunderstood. Starting in 1971, courts began referring to an "abstractions test,"[14] thus per-

---

11 45 F.2d 119 (2d Cir. 1930).

12 *Id.* at 121.

13 *Id.*

14 *See* Bevan v. CBS, Inc., 329 F. Supp. 601, 605 (S.D.N.Y. 1971). A Westlaw search reveals that the phrase "abstraction test" was used in the copyright context in 5 opinions during 1970-80, in 15 opinions during 1980-1990, and in 30 opinions since 1990. Candor

verting Judge Hand's sensible thought that the boundary between idea and expression cannot be fixed — not by judges and surely not by anything to be called a "test."[15] Next, courts applied *Nichols* and what they unfortunately called an "abstractions test" to areas of intellectual achievement wholly different from plays, indeed, wholly different from writings. Thus, courts have tried to apply an "abstractions test" to copyright issues beyond the context of written texts and are now trying to apply it to computer programs.[16] In doing so, they have very likely been influenced by this sweeping assertion in *Nimmer on Copyright*:[17] "Although the abstractions test was created for use with literary works, it is readily adaptable to analyzing computer software."[18] In *Computer Associates International v. Altai, Inc.*,[19] our Court joined the chorus: "While the abstractions test was originally applied in relation to literary works such as novels and plays, it is adaptable to computer programs."[20]

Proceeding from this observation, *Altai* then advised courts to "dissect the allegedly copied program's structure and isolate each level of abstraction contained within it."[21] This is to be done, we are told, by charting the program into a hierarchy of modules, each identified, apparently, by the function it performs.[22] Having stratified the program into these levels of abstraction or modules, we are then to move on to what Nimmer calls, and *Altai* embraces, a "'successive filtering method' for separating protectable expression from non-protectable material."[23] We are to make the separation by determining whether what the opinion calls "the structural components at each level of abstraction"[24] is an idea, which would be unprotectable, or is covered by any of three other inquiries, which if satisfied, would also render the component unprotectable. The first is whether the component was "dictated by considerations of efficiency, so as to be necessarily incidental to that idea."[25] The

---

obliges me to admit my own contribution to this unfortunate series of usages. *See* Warner Bros. v. American Broad. Cos., 720 F.2d 231, 240 (2d Cir. 1983).

15 As Judge Easterbrook has observed, "Hand's insight is not a 'test' at all. It is a clever way to pose the difficulties that require courts to avoid either extreme of a continuum of generality." Nash v. CBS, Inc., 899 F.2d 1537, 1540 (7th Cir. 1990).

16 *See* Computer Assocs. Int'l v. Altai, Inc., 982 F.2d 693, 706-07 (2d Cir. 1992).

17 4 MELVILLE B. NIMMER & DAVID NIMMER, NIMMER ON COPYRIGHT §13.03 [F][1] at 13-121 (1998).

18 *Id.* (footnote omitted).

19 982 F.2d 693.

20 *Id.* at 706-07.

21 *Id.* at 707.

22 *See id.*

23 *Id.* (quoting 3 MELVILLE B. NIMMER & DAVID NIMMER, NIMMER ON COPYRIGHT § 13.03[F] (1991)).

24 *Id.*

25 *Id.*

second is whether the component was "required by factors external to the program itself."[26] The third is whether the component was "taken from the public domain."[27] Once this "filtration" has occurred, the allegedly infringing program is compared to the protectable elements that have survived filtration to determine whether protectable elements have been copied and to assess the relative importance of the copied elements to the plaintiff's overall program.[28]

The seductive three-step progression of *Altai's* structured approach has not escaped criticism, notably by Professor Patry. He believes that the Court misapplied an infringement test designed for plays as a copyrightability test for computer programs.[29] He described *Altai's* approach as sounding and acting "more like a water purification process than a copyright infringement analysis."[30] The result, he concluded, is that the "whole" of a computer program is viewed as "considerably less than the sum of its parts."[31] In fairness, however, I should note that although *Altai* is open to criticism for promulgating an overly structured approach, it represents an important and useful advance over the Third Circuit's approach in *Whelan Associates v. Jaslow Dental Laboratory, Inc.*,[32] which proceeded on the unwarranted assumption that a computer program could have only one idea and that everything else must be expression.[33]

While our Court was endeavoring to apply an "abstractions test" to computer programs, and in the process formulating an "abstraction-filtration-comparison" mode of analysis, other courts were taking the newly refined approach to computer programs and invoking it to decide cases far removed from computer programs.[34] In this effort, they were again doubtless influenced by the Nimmer treatise, which introduced its discussion of the filtration component of what was now labeled the "abstraction-filtration-comparison test" by stating: "Although the discussion in this subsection illustrates the application of the filtration test [sic] solely in the context of computer software, there is no reason to limit it to that

---

26 *Id.*

27 *Id.*

28 *See id.* at 710.

29 *See* 1 WILLIAM F. PATRY, COPYRIGHT LAW & PRACTICE 224 (1994).

30 *Id.* at 221.

31 *Id.* at 224.

32 797 F.2d 1222 (3d Cir. 1986).

33 *See id.* at 1236-37.

34 *See, e.g.*, Country Kids 'N City Slicks, Inc. v. Sheen, 77 F.2d 1280 (10th Cir. 1996).

realm."[35] Thus, the Tenth Circuit used the "filtration test" to determine what features of wooden dolls were protectable,[36] and whether the advertisements in a telephone directory were protectable.[37]

I do not deny that all of these subject matters required courts to determine whether the first work was copyrightable and whether the second infringed protectable elements. What I question is whether courts should be making those determinations with the same modes of analysis and even the same vocabulary that was appropriate for writings. As I shall try to indicate, it is not just a matter of vocabulary. Words convey concepts, and if we use identical phrases from one context to resolve issues in another, we risk failing to notice that the relevant concepts are and ought to be somewhat different.

I tried to point this out many years ago in an opinion that considered the issue of whether the character of Ralph Hinckley, protagonist of the television series *The Greatest American Hero* infringed the copyright in the well-known Superman character.[38] I first noted that copyright law has enunciated two somewhat opposing propositions — that differences between an allegedly infringing work and a copyrighted work will not preclude infringement,[39] and that, as Nimmer puts it, "a defendant may legitimately avoid infringement by intentionally making sufficient changes in a work which would otherwise be regarded as substantially similar to that of the plaintiff's."[40]

Then, in an effort not to apply uncritically our prior approaches in text cases to the different context of graphic images, I wrote the following:

> The tension between these two propositions perhaps results from their formulation in the context of literary works and their

---

[35] 4 MELVILLE B. NIMMER & DAVID NIMMER, NIMMER ON COPYRIGHT §13.03 [F][1] at 13-119 (1998).

[36] *See Country Kids,* 77 F.2d 1280. *Country Kids* quoted from an earlier version of the Nimmer treatise, which had advised, even more expansively than the current version, that the successive filtration test "should be considered not only for factual compilations and computer programs but across the gamut of copyright law." *Id.* at 1284 n.5 (citing 3 MELVILLE B. NIMMER & DAVID NIMMER, NIMMER ON COPYRIGHT § 13.03[E] at 13-96-97 (1991).

[37] *See* Transwestern Publ'g Co. v. Multimedia Mktg. Assocs., 133 F.3d 773 (10th Cir. 1998).

[38] *See* Warner Bros. v. American Broad. Cos., 720 F.2d 231, 241 (2d Cir. 1983).

[39] *See id.* ("'It is entirely immaterial that in many respects plaintiff's and defendant's works are dissimilar if in other respects similarity as to a substantial element of plaintiff's work can be shown.'") (quoting 3 MELVILLE B. NIMMER & DAVID NIMMER, NIMMER ON COPYRIGHT § 13.03[B] at 13-38 (1991)).

[40] *Id.* (quoting 3 MELVILLE B. NIMMER & DAVID NIMMER, NIMMER ON COPYRIGHT § 13.03[E] at 13-38.1-38.2 (1991)) (internal quotations omitted).

> subsequent application to graphic and three-dimensional works. A story has a linear dimension: it begins, continues, and ends. If a defendant copies substantial portions of a plaintiff's sequence of events, he does not escape infringement by adding original episodes somewhere along the line. A graphic or three-dimensional work is created to be perceived as an entirety. Significant dissimilarities between two works of this sort inevitably lessen the similarity that would otherwise exist between the total perception of the two works. The graphic rendering of a character has aspects of both the linear, literary mode and the multi-dimensional total perception. What the character thinks, feels, says, and does and the descriptions conveyed by the author through comments of other characters in the work episodically fill out the viewer's understanding of the character. At the same time, the visual perception of the character tends to create a dominant impression against which the similarity of a defendant's character may be readily compared and significant differences readily noted.[41]

Thus, I was saying, to borrow what later would be *Altai*'s formulation, one cannot divide a visual work into neat layers of abstraction in precisely the same manner one could with a text.

In another context, that of compilation of facts, I have also suggested that simply calling something an "idea" will not necessarily help locate the dividing line between an unprotectable idea and a protectable expression of it. In *Kregos v. Associated Press,*[42] our Court considered whether copyright protection was available for a selection of nine statistical categories for use on a baseball pitching form.[43] In ruling that such protection was available, or at least could be found to be available by the trier of fact, I pointed out that for copyright purposes, simply labeling an aggregation of facts as an idea does not help decide whether a particular aggregation is protectable.[44] All ideas are not created equal. The unprotectable category includes those that undertake to advance the understanding of phenomena or the solution of problems, while the protectable category includes those that reflect the author's taste and opinion. We placed the pitching form in the latter category.[45] Our Court later followed this approach in *CCC Information Services v. Maclean Hunter Market Reports, Inc.*,[46] to accord protection to a

41 *Id.* at 241-42.
42 937 F.2d 700 (2d Cir. 1991).
43 *See id.* at 701-02.
44 *See id.* at 706.
45 *See id.* at 706-07.
46 44 F.3d 61 (2d Cir. 1994).

compilation of used car valuations.[47] Ultimately, what we ruled in both *Kregos* and *CCC Information Services* was that the particular compilations in those cases were not instances appropriate for application of the merger doctrine.

Indeed, the Nimmer treatise, despite its fondness for an "abstractions test" and an "abstraction-filtration-comparison test," has usefully recognized that in the area of computer programs the line for distinguishing an unprotectable idea from a protectable expression "is a pragmatic one, drawn not on the basis of some metaphysical property of 'ideas,' but by balancing the need to protect the labors of authors with the desire to assure free access to ideas."[48] That sensible thought has been embraced by our Court in *CCC Information Services.*[49]

Unfortunately, however, even some of the knowledgeable commentators who are offering useful insights as to how courts should analyze the scope of copyright protection for computer software,[50] fall victim to the old terminology. For example, Professor Samuelson, though sensibly urging that "[c]opyright law should describe computer programs and user interfaces in a technically appropriate manner,"[51] wants us, when considering a claim of infringement of a program or a user interface, "to determine whether what has been copied is 'expressive' in a copyright sense."[52] As a result, we find courts solemnly considering whether the use of the key on a computer keyboard that produces a virgule — a forward-leaning slash mark — to invoke a series of menu commands is protectable "expression."[53] Now, I have nothing against a virgule, but is it really the sort of "expression" that Judge Hand wanted us to consider when Shakespeare had Romeo say, "It is the east, and Juliet is the sun"?[54] Now, that's "expression"! Fortunately, Judge Keeton declined to protect the virgule,[55] but his inquiry and his ultimate decision invoked all the vocabulary from the cases considering written texts.

In the area of computer programs, I think we might be better

---

47 *See id.* at 63.

48 4 MELVILLE B. NIMMER & DAVID NIMMER, NIMMER ON COPYRIGHT § 13.03[F][1], at 13-125 (1998).

49 44 F.3d at 72 n.24.

50 *See, e.g.*, Pamela Samuelson et al., *A Manifesto Concerning the Legal Protection of Computer Programs*, 94 COLUM. L. REV. 2308 (1994).

51 Pamela Samuelson, *Computer Programs, User Interfaces, and Section 102(b) of the Copyright Act of 1976: A Critique of Lotus v. Paperback*, 6 HIGH TECH. L.J. 209, 268 (1992).

52 *Id.*

53 *See* Lotus Dev. Corp. v. Paperback Software Int'l, 740 F. Supp. 37, 67 (D. Mass. 1990).

54 WILLIAM SHAKESPEARE, ROMEO AND JULIET, act 2, sc. 2.

55 *See Lotus Dev.*, 740 F. Supp. at 37.

off to recognize that, although we need to separate protectable "expression" from unprotectable "ideas," a somewhat different vocabulary might assist us in properly balancing the ultimate values we seek to advance. Thus, I do not consider it helpful, in considering the protection accorded source code, to ask whether it is the written expression of an idea embodied at some higher level of abstraction within the computer program. I would rather begin the process of labeling the protectable and unprotectable elements of computer programs with terms peculiar to the realm of software. For example, I might move away from referring to source code as the "expression" of an "idea," a phrasing that all too readily enlists the doctrines and case law developed in cases involving written texts, and instead call these arcane writings what they are called in cyberspace — namely, source code. Then, I could consider which source codes or which portions of source codes were protectable. Also, I might not call the unprotectable aspects of a computer program "ideas," which again evokes the written text cases, but instead call them something like "program purposes" or "program objectives." After all, you don't see many cases involving copyrights in musical works talking about the "expression" of some musical "idea." Why should we force upon copyright cases involving computer programs the same vocabulary we use for cases involving written texts?

Then, I might begin to recognize that a computer program, unlike a play, is not easily reduced to a hierarchy of abstractions, ranging vertically from the most to the least abstract. A computer program can and should be analyzed in several ways, along dimensions that do not constitute a neat downward vertical progression. One example of the different ways of analyzing a computer program, for purposes of copyright protection, was recently suggested to our Court in an amicus brief filed by an able group of computer scientists.[56] Since the case in which they filed their brief has now been settled, I feel free to comment on their suggested analysis which, in any event, is set forth in their publicly available brief. They point out, using as an example a program for check-book management, that there are several different ways in which even a simple program can be analyzed for purposes of separating the protectable from the unprotectable.[57] Starting with the vocabulary

---

[56] *See* Amicus Brief in support of Computer Scientists, Harbor Software, Inc. v. Applied Sys., Inc., (2d Cir. 1998) (No. 97-7197) [hereinafter Amicus Brief]. The professors are Hal Abelson, Roy Campbell, Randall Davis, Lee Hollaar, and Gerald J. Sussman. Their brief was filed by Marc M. Arkin, Esq.

[57] *See id.* at 8-9.

we have forced upon them, they call these various dissections "abstractions,"[58] but they might better be called something like "program elements." For the check-book program, they point out that "abstractions" (or, as I prefer, "program elements") might include "control structure" — "the sequence of operations that [the program] carries out;"[59] "data structures" — indications of "the way in which individual items of information are stored in the program;"[60] "data flow" — "a description of how information flows through the program;"[61] and "information architecture" — an indication of "the overall organization of the data used by the program, often in the form of the organization of databases."[62] They also point out that a complete set of "control structures" might have many levels of detail.[63] These terms might not be appropriate for all programs, but such terms, or similar ones, will be far more helpful to a court than just "expression" and "ideas."

By using terms appropriate to the subject matter, I might begin to realize that what is relevant in applying the idea-expression dichotomy to computer programs is not necessarily the same as what is relevant in other areas. Judge Hand observed that with plays, characters and the sequence of incidents were especially important. Well, there are no characters in software, at least not literary characters. There are, I suppose, what might be called "incidents," but we ought not blithely equate the sequence of incidents that combine to form the plot of a play with the sequence of steps that the computer program instructs the computer to perform on data.

So one day when I consider a play, I will be considering the characters and sequence of incidents of the plays, and the next day, when I consider a computer program, I will be looking at entirely different elements. With plays, I have a fairly clear idea, gained from reading and watching many of them, how to strike the balance so that today's playwrights have adequate incentive to write new plays and tomorrow's playwrights have adequate freedom to build upon what has preceded them. With computer programs, I lack the familiarity to strike the balance of competing purposes from my own experience, so I will have to be educated to the task.

---

58 *See id.*

59 *Id.* at A-10.

60 *Id.* at A-11.

61 *Id.* at A-10.

62 *Id.* at 23-24.

63 *See id.* at 23-24.

I will need expert witnesses if I am the trier of fact, and skillful briefs if I am considering an appeal.

These professionals would be well advised not to tell me simply that the source code is or is not protectable expression. Their opinions are relevant, but, as with all opinions, what renders them persuasive is not the vehemence of their assertion and not even the credentials of those asserting them; it is the cogency and persuasive force of the reasons they give for their respective positions. These reasons had better relate to the specifics of the computer software field. For example, as *Altai* indicates, even with its overly structured mode of analysis, it will be very important for me to know whether the essential function being performed by the copyrighted program is a function that can be accomplished with a wide variety of source codes, which will strengthen the case for protection, or, on the other hand, is a function capable of execution with very few variations in source code, or variations of such triviality as to be disregarded, in which event protection will be unlikely. For me, this mode of analysis is essentially what in other contexts we call the merger doctrine — the expression is said to have merged with the idea because the idea can be expressed in such limited ways that protection of the plaintiff's expression unduly risks protecting the idea itself.

Beyond this inquiry as to merger, I will want to think about what aspects of a computer program need protection in order to keep a proper balance between the incentive of programmers to create new programs, and the useful contribution that subsequent programmers can make if they are free to copy existing programs, or at least aspects of them. Clearly, I will need the help of knowledgeable experts in making this sort of determination.

Some have suggested that what is needed in this area is a either a new form of copyright of limited term or some sort of subcopyright protection, while others have suggested a new form of right, limited in duration and subject to compulsory licensing, that would be available for technological innovations including computer software.[64] Others have suggested that Congress can authorize a new form of protection for digital materials, such as the pending bill to protect electronic databases.[65] Whether Congress

---

64 *See* J.H. Reichman, *Legal Hybrids Between the Patent and Copyright Paradigm*, 94 COLUM. L. REV. 2432, 2504-57 (1994).

65 *See* Collections of Information Antipiracy Act, H.R. 2652, 105th Cong. (1998), which was passed by the House on May 19, 1998, *see* 144 Cong. Rec. H2298-H3404 (daily ed. May 19, 1998); Collections of Information Antipiracy Act, S. 2291, 105th Cong. (1998). A version of the Collections of Information Antipiracy Act was included as Title V in the Digital Millennium Copyright Act, H.R. 2281, 105th Cong (1998), as it passed the House in Au-

has power to protect under the Commerce Clause what might not be protectable under the Copyright Clause, thereby arguably impairing the latter clause's implied grant to the public to copy what is not copyrightable, is a fair issue for future debate. Possibly, a requirement of compulsory licensing of whatever new right is created under the Commerce Clause might meet the objection based on the Copyright Clause. That, too, remains for future debate.

However we come out on these broader public policy and even constitutional issues, I hope that as lawyers, commentators, and courts analyzing copyright issues in the computer field under existing statutes, we will recognize that the analysis appropriate to written text is not transferable wholesale to the realm of computer software and hardware, and that seductively phrased "tests" are, at most, only an aid to understanding and not a mechanical process that can readily yield answers. There is no "abstractions test," and I am not sure we ought to have something called an "abstraction-filtration-comparison test." Moreover, I am quite sure that whatever approaches we develop to help us decide copyright cases in the computer field should not be uncritically imported back into traditional areas of written text, music, or audio-visual works.

At a most abstract level, we can continue to recognize that ideas are not copyrightable and that the expression of ideas is copyrightable. At a less abstract level of thought, however, what we must strive for is a recognition that the differences among modes of expression oblige us to eschew anything like "tests" that can yield answers across all fields. It is at this less abstract level that copyright cases will be decided. We will need the help of all knowledgeable students of copyright so that we can proceed as well as possible to balance the need for creation with the need to copy — all toward the ultimate Progress of Science and the Useful Arts.

---

gust 1998, but it was excised from the Digital Millennium Copyright Act that became law in October 1998. *See* Digital Millennium Copyright Act, Pub. L. No. 105-304, 112 Stat. 2860 (1998).

SOFTWARE AS DISCOURSE: THE POWER OF INTELLECTUAL PROPERTY IN DIGITAL ARCHITECTURE*

BRIAN F. FITZGERALD**

ABSTRACT

As software increasingly facilitates our living, we are drawn more and more to conceptualize software as discourse. While this may sound trite, it is a fundamental point to appreciate.

One of the most significant intellectual developments of the latter part of the twentieth century has been the poststructuralist writing of thinkers like Foucault, Derrida, and Baudrillard, who explain the multitude of power relationships we experience in our daily lives, the indeterminacy of law, the construction of meaning, and the role of language, or discourse, in the construction of meaning and identity. According to the post-structuralists, we live in an environment constructed from many elements—one of the dominant ones being language, or discourse, which contains inherent biases and tendencies. This philosophy has given rise to the development of identity politics—a space in which arguments are made for and against the construction of identity through language and other circum-

* *Publisher's Note*: This Article is adapted from the Seventh Annual Herbert Tenzer Distinguished Lecture in Intellectual Property Law, given at the Benjamin N. Cardozo School of Law, October 14, 1999. The *Cardozo Arts & Entertainment Law Journal* is proud to publish this Article and thanks the author for his patience and generous assistance during the editorial process. The *Journal* has verified most of the sources cited in the Article; however, some sources were unavailable, obtainable only in foreign countries, or written in foreign languages. The author stands by the accuracy of the information presented herein.

** BA (GU), LLB (Hons.) (QUT), BCL (Oxon.), LLM (Harv.), Dean of the School of Law, Southern Cross University, Australia: bfitzger@scu.edu.au. My sincere appreciation and heartfelt thanks to Marci Hamilton and Editors Willard Knox, Rebecca Morris, Jessica Stern, and Mark Kravitz from the *Cardozo Arts & Entertainment Law Journal* for inviting me to give this paper as the Seventh Annual Tenzer Lecture, and to those attending earlier and later presentations of this paper: in October of 1999, at Hamline University Law School, St. Paul, Minnesota; Berkman Centre for Internet and Society, Harvard University Law School; Baker McKenzie Law Offices, Chicago; Norwegian Centre for Computers and Law, Law School, University of Oslo; Institute for Information Law, University of Amsterdam; in particular thanks to David Post, Jonathan Zittrain, Fern Nesson, John Willbanks, Alexander Macgillivray, Ken Salzberg, Joseph Daly, Dennis Ahlburg, Tom Smedinghoff, Sam Kramer, Brian Arbetter, Olav Torvund, Peter Lodrup, Bernt Hugenholtz, and Lodewijk Asscher; and to those attending a presentation of this paper at the Australian Law and Society Conference in Byron Bay on December 7, 1999, in particular thanks to Anne Fitzgerald, Larry Lessig, and Scott Beattie.

stances. In the end, the poststructuralists have allowed us to appreciate and conceptualize our circumstantial being. We are witnessing the exponential growth of a new form of social structure known as the information society. The quintessential element of discourse, of language, of speech, in this information society is (soft)ware. Software is now a key part of our social structure—we sense it in our cars, in our supermarkets, in our televisions, in our computers. We sense it everywhere: it is a ubiquitous, undulating, architectural, air-like, water-like commodity that infiltrates our daily lives. More interesting is that software, through its various forms of (coded) structure can act to construct meaning and identity in much the same way as speech. Software in the information society is discourse. It is not simply a literary text (a copyright law categorization); it is fundamental to communicative architecture. The fierce debate over open code versus proprietary code software is intimately connected with this construction of identity through software.

If a software engineer has the tools—fully or partially—to construct discourse and identity in the digital world, then the principles of law that mediate power relations (especially those between individuals, often described as "private law") need to mediate such a construction process. Otherwise, technological determinism will see me as simply another cyborg programmed to mediocrity and slavery. Laws that will play an important role in this process are those that will govern the construction of the new discourse known as software.

Already, battle lines have been drawn. Major choices that will impact upon the value of our lives are being hidden beneath the veil of private law rhetoric. The role and function of software will be mediated initially by a blend of intellectual property law, contract law, competition law, and privacy law, which I would term informational law or informational constitutionalism. It is the development of the principles of these areas of law in their relation to software that will determine much about the way we live in the future.

As we enter the digital millennium, it is ever more pressing for us to fathom the genetic structure/code (natural and manufactured) of life. Here, I have highlighted how software will act to construct us and how the law will facilitate such a process.

Introduction

With the coming of the information age, we are represented continually through digital architecture constructed through digital wares.[1] The contours of this new digital landscape are yet to be fully realized but we are sufficiently entrenched in the information age[2] to know that conceptualizing the digital environment is a new and challenging task.

The aim of this paper is to conceptualize software as discourse, thereby allowing us to better understand the power of intellectual property rights in digital architecture. This simple, if not trite, point—software is discourse—is not readily appreciated in legal (and much other) analysis of the digital environment. I suspect this emanates from sheer ignorance and our practice of blind faith[3] in the ethical integrity of (digital) architecture; in our belief that the medium or the pathway is always acting in our best interests like some sort of virtual fiduciary.

My role is to challenge this complacency and to open up a framework of analysis that is sorely needed for social and cultural enhancement. If software is a form of discourse, a way of making things known or manifest, or letting them be seen, then the ability to create and hold proprietary rights in software (in discourse) is a fundamental determinant of social construction. The power to

---

1 *See* Michael Madison, *Legal-Ware: Contract and Copyright in the Digital Age,* 67 FORDHAM L. REV. 1025, 1031 (1998).

2 *See generally* Esso Australia Resources Ltd. v. The Comm'r of Taxation [1999] 67 HCA at para. 101 (Dec. 21, 1999) (Kirby, J.) (acknowledging the information revolution), (visited Apr. 13, 2000) <http://www.austlii.edu.au/>; F. BLOCK, POST-INDUSTRIAL POSSIBILITIES: A CRITIQUE OF ECONOMIC DISCOURSE (1990); MANUEL CASTELLS, THE INFORMATION AGE: ECONOMY, SOCIETY AND CULTURE chs. 1-3 (1996); NIGEL DODD, SOCIAL THEORY AND MODERNITY (1999); N. GARNHAM, COMMUNICATION TECHNOLOGY AND POLICY, MASS COMMUNICATIONS REVIEW YEARBOOK 285 (M. Gurevitch & M.R. Levy eds., Sage Books 1985) (considering the pervasive nature of information society and its never-ending expansion into the more private and less commercial spheres of life); ANTHONY GIDDENS, THE CONSEQUENCES OF MODERNITY (1990); DAVID HARVEY, THE CONDITION OF POSTMODERNITY (1990); GREG HEARN ET AL., THE COMMUNICATION SUPERHIGHWAY: SOCIAL AND ECONOMIC CHANGE IN THE DIGITAL AGE ch. 2 (1998) (discussing the notions of "technological determinism" versus "social constructivism"); AGNES HELLER, A THEORY OF MODERNITY (1999); TIM JORDAN, CYBERPOWER: THE CULTURE AND POLITICS OF CYBERSPACE AND THE INTERNET (1999); JOHN B. THOMPSON, THE MEDIA AND MODERNITY (1995); LESTER C. THUROW, BUILDING WEALTH: NEW RULES FOR INDIVIDUALS, COMPANIES AND NATIONS IN A KNOWLEDGE-BASED ECONOMY (1999); JOHN TOMLINSON, GLOBALIZATION AND CULTURE (1999); SHERRY TURKLE, THE SECOND SELF: COMPUTERS AND THE HUMAN SPIRIT (1984); JUDY WAJCMAN, FEMINISM CONFRONTS TECHNOLOGY (1991); FRANK WEBSTER, THEORIES OF INFORMATION SOCIETY (1995); Brian F. Fitzgerald, *Commodifying and Transacting Informational Products Through Contractual Licences: The Challenge for Informational Constitutionalism, in* INTELLECTUAL PROPERTY AND THE COMMON LAW WORLD ch. 3 (C.E F. Rickett & G.W. Austin eds., 2000); Esther Dyson et al., *A Magna Carta for the Knowledge Age,* 11 NEW PERSP. Q. 26 (1994); Lester C. Thurow, *Needed: A New System of Intellectual Property Rights,* 75 HARV. BUS. REV. 5, 95 (1997).

On business models for information society, see JILL H. ELLSWORTH & MATTHEW V. ELLSWORTH, THE INTERNET BUSINESS BOOK (1995); DANIEL S. JANAL, ONLINE MARKETING HANDBOOK (1998); RAVI KALAKOTA ET AL., E-BUSINESS: ROADMAP FOR SUCCESS (1999); PATRICIA B. SEYBOLD, CUSTOMERS.COM (1998); ELAINE LAWRENCE ET AL., INTERNET COMMERCE: DIGITAL MODELS FOR BUSINESS (1998).

3 *See* GIDDENS, *supra* note 2, at 33-34; BARBARA A. MISZTAL, TRUST IN MODERN SOCIETIES: THE SEARCH FOR THE BASES OF SOCIAL ORDER (1996).

construct and control channels of communication through law is a most serious question in the digital era.

In order to assert my argument with clarity and authority, this article will perform the following steps: define software; explain the notion of discourse; posit software as discourse; explore how software acts to construct identity; examine how the law regulates intellectual property rights in software and impacts on discursive formation; introduce the notion of power; and posit the new constitutionalism. To clarify things from the outset, I am not arguing that all information should be free. Rather, my basic point is that when we commodify (or propertize)[4] information through property rights recognized by law, we must hold in the balance and appreciate the value of free and open discourse. The quest for value in the digital economy challenges us to understand the boundaries that law will draw around the digital estate.[5] On one side stands the school of thought that believes information as the basic building block of knowledge should (and wants to) be free.[6] On the other side stands the idea that in a market economy, value added to raw information has been, and inevitably will be, commodified and sold in the market. The end point lies somewhere between the extreme reaches of each argument.[7] My argument is that commodification of information has and will continue to occur—digital informational products will be propertized in our market

---

4 *See generally* Felix Cohen, *Transcendental Nonsense and the Functional Approach*, 35 COLUM. L. REV. 809, 814-17 (1935); Michael A. Heller & James E. Krier, *The Tragedy of the Anticommons: Property in the Transition from Marx to Markets*, 111 HARV. L. REV. 621 (1998); Ejan Mackaay, *The Economics of Emergent Property Rights on the Internet, in* THE FUTURE OF COPYRIGHT IN A DIGITAL ENVIRONMENT 13 (P. Bernt Hugenholtz ed., 1996); Pamela Samuelson & Kurt Opsahl, *Licensing Information in the Global Information Market: Freedom of Contract Meets Public Policy*, EUR. INTELL. PROP. REV. 387 (1999).

5 *See* Rochelle Cooper Dreyfuss, *We Are Symbols and Inhabit Symbols, So Should We Be Paying Rent? Deconstructing the Lanham Act and Rights of Publicity*, 20 COLUM.-VLA J.L. & ARTS 123 (1996); Brian F. Fitzgerald, *Commodifying and Transacting Informational Products through Contractual Licences: The Challenge for Informational Constitutionalism, in* INTELLECTUAL PROPERTY AND THE COMMON LAW WORLD ch. 3 (C.E.F. Rickett & G.W Austin eds., 2000); Brian F. Fitzgerald, *Conceptualising the Digital Environment, in* GOING DIGITAL 2000: LEGAL ISSUES FOR E-COMMERCE, SOFTWARE AND THE INTERNET 1 (Anne Fitzgerald et al. eds., 2000); Brian F. Fitzgerald & L. Gamertsfelder, *Protecting Informational Products through Unjust Enrichment Law, in* THE FUTURE OF COPYRIGHT IN THE DIGITAL ENVIRONMENT 244 (P. Bernt Hugenholtz ed., 1998) *European Intellectual Property Review*; Brian F. Fitzgerald & E. Sheehan, *Trademark Dilution and the Commodifictaion of Information: Understanding the "Cultural Command,"* 3 MAC. L. REV. 61 (1999); CARL SHAPIRO & HAL VARIAN, INFORMATION RULES: A STRATEGIC GUIDE TO THE NETWORK ECONOMY (1999).

6 *See* John Perry, *Selling Wine Without Bottles: The Economy of Mind on the Global Net, in* THE FUTURE OF COPYRIGHT IN THE DIGITAL ENVIRONMENT 244 (P. Bernt Hugenholtz ed., 1998).

7 *See* Fitzgerald, *Conceptualising*, *supra* note 5, at 1; Brian F. Fitzgerald & M. Head, *Introduction to Law and Digital Frontiers*, 3 MAC. L. REV. 1 (1999); Mackaay, *supra* note 4, at 13.

economy[8]—but we must infuse this process with respect and appreciation for free and open discourse.

I. The Traditional Definition of Software

The first element needed to underpin my explanation of software as discourse is a working definition of software.

Software may be described as a computer program, which facilitates the operation of a computer system.[9] The relationship between a computer and a program has been described as follows:

> A program is executed by the central processing unit (CPU) of the computer, which is the [center] of control for arithmetical and logic operations within the microprocessor. The CPU consists of an arrangement of electronic circuits which are activated by impulses of electric current. A logic gate within the CPU is either turned on or off depending on the presence or absence of such pulses.
>
> The presence or absence of pulses of current is represented by binary digits ('bits'). The CPU [recognizes] '1' as indicative of the presence of a pulse, and '0' as indicative of its absence.

---

8 *See* CAPITAL FOR OUR TIME: THE ECONOMIC, LEGAL, AND MANAGEMENT CHALLENGES OF INTELLECTUAL CAPITAL (Nicholas Imparato ed., 1999); THOMAS A. STEWART, INTELLECTUAL CAPITAL: THE NEW WEALTH OF ORGANIZATIONS (1999); DON TAPSCOTT, THE DIGITAL ECONOMY: PROMISE AND PERIL IN THE AGE OF NETWORKED INTELLIGENCE (1995).

9 *See* 17 U.S.C. § 101 (1999) ("A 'computer program' is a set of statements or instructions to be used directly or indirectly in a computer in order to bring about a certain result."); Australian Copyright Act 1968, Section 10 (Cth).

> "[C]omputer program" means an expression, in any language, code or notation, of a set of instructions (whether with or without related information) intended, either directly or after either or both of the following:
>
> (a) conversion to another language, code or notation;
>
> (b) reproduction in a different material form,
>
> to cause a device having digital information processing capabilities to perform a particular function.

Id. Amendments to the Australian Copyright Act 1968 (Cth) propose to replace the current definition of "computer program" in section 10(1) with the following: "computer program means a set of statements or instructions to be used directly or indirectly in a computer in order to bring about a certain result." *See* Copyright Amendment (Digital Agenda) Bill 1999 (Cth) (Austl.); Copyright Law Review Committee ("CLRC"), *Computer Software Protection* ("Final Report") (Attorney General's Department, Canberra, Apr. 1995) (visited Apr. 13, 2000) <http://www.aph.gov.au/house/committee/laca/digitalagenda/contents.html>; Data Access Corp. v. Powerflex Servs. Pty Ltd., [1999] HCA 49 (Sept. 30 1999) (visited Apr. 14, 2000) <http://www.hcourt.gov.au>; Alcatel USA Inc. v. DGI Techs. Inc., 166 F.3d 772, 778 (5th Cir. 1999) ("[F]irmware . . . is software embedded in a memory chip on the card."); Pamela Samuelson et al., *A Manifesto Concerning Legal Protection of Computer Programs*, 94 COLUM. L. REV. 2308, 2315-30 (1994) ("[P]rograms are, in fact, machines (entities that bring about useful results, i.e., behavior) that have been constructed in the medium of text (source code and object code)."); *see also* B. GAZE, COPYRIGHT PROTECTION OF COMPUTER PROGRAMS 2-12 (1989); Marci A. Hamilton & Ted Sabety, *Computer Science Concepts in Copyright Cases: The Path to a Coherent Law*, 10 HARV. J.L. & TECH. 239 (1997); Michele C. Kane, *When is a Computer Program Not a Computer Program? The Perplexing World Created by the Proposed UCC Art. 2B*, 13 BERKELEY TECH. L.J. 1013 (1998).

> A computer program is a series of bits, each bit representing the presence or absence of a pulse. The program operates within the CPU as a series of pulses in a prearranged sequence in accordance with the order of bits devised by the computer programmer. Accordingly, the 'instructions' of a computer program represent a series of impulses which operate within the computer to make the machine perform certain predefined functions.
>
> Each instruction is held in a memory location within the computer, which has an address, by which the location may be identified. The addresses of the memory locations in which program instructions are to be found are held in the program counter. The CPU locates the address of each instruction of the program, accesses it from the memory location, from where it is reproduced and executed in the instructions register. The program counter may contain a 'jump' instruction, which makes the CPU jump beyond the next instruction in sequential order in the software, to access and execute a subroutine.[10]

In the Australian case of *Computer Edge Pty Ltd. v Apple Computer Inc.*,[11] Chief Justice Gibbs explained the traditional notion of a computer program in these terms:

> Computer science makes much use of jargon and metaphor, and to enable the matters in issue to be understood it seems desirable to attempt a brief explanation of the meaning of some of the expressions used in that science and to describe the manner in which a computer program is developed. *A computer program is a set of instructions designed to cause a computer to perform a particular function or to produce a particular result.* A program is usually developed in a number of stages. First, the sequence of operations which the computer will be required to perform is commonly written out in ordinary language, with the help, if necessary, of mathematical formulae and of a flow chart and diagram representing the procedure. . . . Next there is prepared what is called a source program. The instructions are now expressed in a computer language—either in a source code (which is not far removed from ordinary language, and is hence called a high level language) or in an assembly code (a low level language, which is further removed from ordinary language than a source code), or successively in both. Sometimes the expression source code seems to be used to include both high level and low level language. In the present case, the source

---

10 Data Access Corp. v. Powerflex Servs. Pty Ltd., (1999) 166 A.L.R. 228 (quoting CARR & ARNOLD, COMPUTER SOFTWARE: LEGAL PROTECTION IN THE UNITED KINGDOM 1-2 (2d ed. 1992)), *available at* <http://www.austlii.edu.au> (visited Apr. 13, 2000).

11 Computer Edge Pty Ltd. v. Apple Computer Inc. (1986) 161 C.L.R. 171.

programs were written in an assembly code, comprising four elements, viz.—

(a) labels identifying particular parts of the program;
(b) mnemonics each consisting of three letters of the alphabet and corresponding to a particular operation expressed in 6502 Assembly Code (the code used);
(c) mnemonics identifying the register in the microprocessor and/or the number of instructions in the program to which the operation referred to in (b) related; and
(d) comments intended to explain the function of the particular part of the program for the benefit of a human reader of the program.

The writing has been destroyed, although it is possible to reconstruct the mnemonics, but not the labels and comments, which were comprised in it.

The source code or assembly code cannot be used directly in the computer, and must be converted into an object code, which is 'machine readable', i.e., which can be directly used in the computer. The conversion is effected by a computer, itself properly programmed. The program in object code, the object program, in the first instance consists of a sequence of electrical impulses which are often first stored on a magnetic disc or tape, and which may be stored permanently in a ROM ("read only memory"), a silicon chip which contains thousands of connected electrical circuits. The object code is embodied in the ROM in such a way that when the ROM is installed in the computer and electrical power is applied, there is generated the sequence of electrical impulses which cause the computer to take the action which the program is designed to achieve. The pattern of the circuits in the ROM may possibly be discerned with the aid of an electron microscope but it cannot be seen by the naked eye. Obviously, the electrical impulses themselves cannot be perceived. However the sequence of electrical impulses may be described either in binary notation (using the symbols 0 and 1) or in hexadecimal notation (using the numbers 0-9 and the letters A-F), and it is possible to display the description on the visual display unit of the computer, and to print it out on paper. And, as has been said, it is also possible to reconstruct the mnemonics in the source code. It will have been seen from this account that a program exists successively in source code and in object code, but the object code need not be written out in binary or hexadecimal notation in the process of producing and storing the program.[12]

This traditional definition of software (admittedly designed for copyright law) highlights its functional nature: a set of instructions that tell a computer how to operate.[13] My argument is that software is much more than this—it acts as a medium for communication—it is a form or variant of discourse.[14] Before developing this argument, though, it is important to consider more closely the notion of discourse.

II. Discourse, Software and the Construction of Identity

A. *What Is Discourse?*

A chain of European ("linguistic") philosophers through this century, from de Saussure,[15] Heidegger,[16] Gadamer,[17] and Fou-

---

12 *Id.* at 178-79 (emphasis added).

13 *See* Larry Long & Nancy Long, *Software: Telling Computers What To Do, in* COMPUTERS (6th ed. 1999). "Software refers to any program that tells the computer system what to do." *Id.* at C73. A suggestion that software is not solely focused on directions to the computer is given when the authors note that "we interact with software to direct the overall activities within a computer program." *Id.* at C72.

14 Consider Eben Moglen, *Anarchism Triumphant: Free Software and the Death of Copyright*, THE NATION (1998) (Apr. 13, 2000)), *available at* <http://emoglen.law.columbia.edu/my_pubs/anarchism.html>.

15 *See* FERDINDAND DE SAUSSURE, GENERAL COURSE ON LINGUISTICS (Charles Bally & Albert Sechehaye eds., English ed., Collins 1974) (1916); MARGARET DAVIES, ASKING THE LAW QUESTION 229-35 (1994); EMILE DURKHEIM, RULES OF SOCIOLOGICAL METHOD (English ed., Collier-MacMillan 1966) (1895); GEOFFREY SAMPSON, SCHOOLS OF LINGUISTICS (1980).

16 *See* 1-2 THE PHILOSOPHY OF DISCOURSE (Chip Sills & George H. Jensen eds., 1992).

17 *See* HANS-GEORG GADAMER, PHILOSOPHICAL HERMENEUTICS (David E. Linge, trans., Univ. of Cal. Press 1976); S. Feldman, *Diagnosing Power: Postmodernism in Legal Scholarship and Judicial Practice*, 88 N.W. U. L. REV. 1046, 1060-62 (1994).

> Philosophical hermeneutics, contrary to foundationalism, maintains that no matter what we do, we are always and already interpreting. All experience, perception, and understanding are interpretive. Thus the text is not an object in the foundationalist sense. No uninterpreted source of meaning stands outside of an interpretive act. And since the text does not exist in an independent and uninterpreted state, its meaning cannot be derived through some mechanical technique or method. As Hans-Georg Gadamer, one of the foremost interpretivist philosophers, writes: "[O]ur perception is never a simple reflection of what is given to the senses." Nonetheless, according to philosophical hermeneutics, this reflection of objectivity does not mean that understanding or interpretation is purely subjective or capacious. The reader (or interpreter) is never an independent and autonomous subject who freely or arbitrarily imposes meaning on a text (or text-analogue). To the contrary, the interpreter is always situated in a "tradition" . . . from which we inherit prejudices and interests that constrain and direct our understandings of texts. One's life within a community and its traditions necessarily limits one's range of vision—what one can possibly see or understand in a text. As Gadamer says, the traditions of one's community help to shape the interpreter's "horizon": "the range of vision that includes everything that can be seen from a particular vantage point." Furthermore, the notion of an interpretive community underscores that we are historical beings who live in tradition: [W]e are always situated within traditions . . . [which are] always part of us . . . Thus, tradition is not a thing of the past; rather it is something in which we constantly participate. As Gadamer noted:

cault[18] to Derrida[19] and Baudrillard[20] have explored and explained the ways in which discourse (including language) can act to construct our existence. One of the most significant intellectual moments for legal and constitutional theory has been the development of understanding of discourse by these philosophers to explain the multitude of power relationships we experience in our daily lives, the indeterminacy of law, the construction of meaning, and the role of language, of discourse, to the construction of meaning and identity.[21]

The "linguistic turn" of these philosophers has led to the realization that discourse, which is usually but not always language, does not simply point to an external reality but rather mediates and represents such external reality.[22] We only understand through prevailing discourse, which carries with it a complex web of determinants having the ability to stereotype existence through lines/labels of nationality, race, gender, class, and more recently, software products. I will discuss this constructive capacity of discourse in more detail at a later point. For the moment, we need to move toward a more exacting definition of discourse.

Discourse may be considered in the following manner:

> A discourse is a group of statements which provide a language for talking about—i.e., a way of representing—a particular kind of knowledge about a topic. When statements about a topic are

---

> "Tradition is not simply a permanent precondition; rather, we produce it ourselves inasmuch as we understand, participate in the evolution of tradition, and hence further determine it ourselves." A crucial element of philosophical hermeneutics is the recognition that although communal traditions and the concomitant prejudices constrain our possibilities for understanding, they simultaneously enable us to communicate and to understand. Our traditions, prejudices, and interests actually open us to meaning, understanding, and truth.

Id.

18 Michel Foucault posits that "language consists of vast tectonic discursive formations embodying sinister power plays that dictate texts and predetermine authorship." MICHEL FOUCAULT, *Archaeology of Knowledge*, *in* POWER/KNOWLEDGE: SELECTED INTERVIEWS AND OTHER WRITINGS, 1972-1977, at 25 (Colin Gordon ed. & Colin Gordon et al., trans., 1980).

19 *See* JACQUES DERRIDA, OF GRAMMATOLOGY (Gayatri C. Spivak, trans., John Hopkins Univ. Press 1977); JACQUES DERRIDA, WRITING AND DIFFERENCE (Alan Bass, trans., Chicago Univ. Press 1978).

20 *See* JEAN BAUDRILLARD, SIMULACRA AND SIMULATION (1981) (Sheila F. Glaser, trans., Mich. Univ. Press 1994); JEAN BAUDRILLARD, THE CONSUMER SOCIETY: MYTHS AND STRUCTURES (1998).

21 *See* KENNETH J. GERGEN, THE SATURATED SELF: DILEMMAS OF IDENTITY IN CONTEMPORARY LIFE (1991); JEAN-FRANCOIS LYOTARD, THE POSTMODERN CONDITION: A REPORT ON KNOWLEDGE (1979); MARK POSTER, THE MODE OF INFORMATION: POSTSTRUCTURALISM AND SOCIAL CONTEXT (1990); J.M. Balkin, *Deconstructive Practice and Legal Theory*, 96 YALE L.J. 743 (1987); *see also* KENNETH J. GERGEN, AN INVITATION TO SOCIAL CONSTRUCTION (1999); DOUGLAS E. LITOWITZ, POSTMODERN PHILOSOPHY AND LAW (1997); Feldman, *supra* note 17.

22 *See* ALAN HUNT & GARY WICKHAM, FOUCAULT AND LAW: TOWARDS A SOCIOLOGY OF LAW AS GOVERNANCE 7-8 (1994).

> made within a particular discourse, the discourse makes it possible to construct the topic in a certain way. It also limits other ways in which the topic can be constructed. A discourse does not consist of one statement, but of several statements working together to form what Foucault called discursive formation. Discourse is about the production of knowledge through language. But it is itself produced by a practice: discursive practice—the practice of producing meaning. So discourse enters into and influences all social practices.[23] *Discourse constitutes, not merely describes, its object.*[24]

Martin Heidegger, a German philospher whose academic reputation was later put into question due to his involvement with the Nazi regime, explained in *Being and Time*[25] that we construct knowledge through the three concepts of Situatedness, Understanding, and Discourse. He explained:

> We—humankind—are a conversation. Because language is the medium in which reality is constituted, language is at once the house of being and home of human beings. Discourse is the literal translation of the Greek word *logos* which means *to make manifest or to let something be seen.*[26] Discourse is the articulation of intelligibility.[27] It therefore underlies both interpretation and assertion.[28] Discourse refers to the way we express ourselves as a being towards entities. . . .[29]

As Heidegger's words capture the essence of what is meant by discourse in a concise and understandable manner, I adopt his words as my working definition—discourse means to make something manifest or let it be seen.[30] My next step then is to break with the traditional definition of software as a program of directions to a computer system and to posit software as a form of discourse, something that allows things to be seen or appreciated.

---

[23] S. Hall & B. Gieben, Formations of Modernity 291 (1992).

[24] Foucault, *supra* note 18, at 49 (emphasis added).

[25] Martin Heidegger, Being and Time (Joan Stambaugh, trans., State Univ. of N.Y. Press 1997) (1927).

[26] *Id.* at 55-56 (emphasis added).

[27] Charles B. Guignon, *Heidegger: Language as the House of Being, in* Formations of Modernity, *supra* note 23, at 183. "Language is the medium through which our most basic sense of life comes to articulation and expression. Language constitutes our sense of reality and indeed our own identity as speakers employing sign systems." *Id.*

[28] Heidegger, *supra* note 25, at 203.

[29] *Id.* at 266; *see also* Jessica Prinz, Art Discourse/Discourse in Art (1991).

[30] Discourse in a broader sense is a context for constructing meaning. As Scott Beattie pointed out to me in reference to the work of Judith Butler on feminism and discourse, discourse, like law (and like context for that matter), is both a noun and a verb. Throughout this article, discourse should be conceived of as an inclusive concept which represents any part of the communicative architecture. *See* Judith Butler, Bodies that Matter: On the Discursive Limits of "Sex" (1993).

B. *Software Is Discourse: The Architecture of Knowledge*

The *raison d'etre* of operating and application systems software[31] is to construct meaning or let something be seen. In this sense, software is a discourse that acts to construct meaning amid the new digital architecture of knowledge.

Much the same way as the linguistic philosophers explain that I experience meaning through the discourse or language employed, I now experience meaning through software. It is an interpretive filter that mediates my digital communication with things external to myself. For example, if I were to pick up off the shelf and use the Australian, Italian, Chinese, or Irish language as if speaking through a loud speaker, meaning flowing in and out of me and others would be constructed in accordance with the channel or speaker (discourse) I was using. Or, closer to home, imagine me as a lay person in a court trying to speak to a judge, where often legalese, the official language of lawyers, will defeat my attempts to construct legal meaning. This power of discourse, or language, is now regarded as obvious. However, we should be mindful to translate this effect of discourse to the digital environment. For example, my use of a particular Internet browser, search engine, or other software product acts as a channel to my construction of meaning. Many of us assume that when we look into the monitor, the communication in which we are engaging is pure. Most of us are unaware of the elaborate coding structure (labyrinth) that mediates our digital world of communications.

Software, which acts as the customizing agent of information technology, has become so integral to our daily lives that I am moved to conceptualize it as a form of discourse that in turn informs my understanding of how the law might regulate software.[32] Software provides us with a framework for understanding and knowing; it is a representational framework. At the most basic level, software in object or source code is seen to be a literary (discursive?) text for the purpose of copyright law. Software, though, is much more than a literary text. In a broader and more abstract way, software is seen to be a mode of understanding or a methodology for constructing meaning: it is part of the architecture of

---

[31] On this distinction, see Long & Long, *supra* note 13, ch. 3. The broader issue of the construction of Internet protocols also raises interesting questions. *See* TIM BERNERS-LEE ET AL., WEAVING THE WEB (1999). On the notion of protocols, see Long & Long, *supra* note 13, at C165 ("Communication protocols are rules established to govern the way data are transmitted in a computer network.").

[32] *See* Brian F. Fitzgerald, *Software as Discourse? A Constitutionalism for Information Society*, 24 ALTERNATIVE L.J. 144 (1999); Brian F. Fitzgerald, *Software as Discourse: The Challenge for Information Law?*, EUR. INTELL. PROP. REV. 47 (2000).

knowledge. The following case questions the level of appreciation of this dynamic communicative and constructive power of software.

1. *Bernstein v. United States Department of Justice*[33]

> Daniel Bernstein, a professor in Computer Science at the University of Illinois in Chicago developed encryption[34] software that he dubbed "Snuffle."
>
> Seeking to present his work on Snuffle within the academic and scientific communities, Bernstein asked the State Department whether he needed a license to publish Snuffle in any of its various forms. The State Department responded that Snuffle was a munition under the International Traffic in Arms Regulations ("ITAR"), and that Bernstein would need a license to "export" the paper, the source code, or the instructions.[35]

Bernstein then challenged the constitutional validity of the regulations, claiming they were facially invalid as a prior restraint on speech.[36] The Ninth Circuit Court of Appeals held that the regulations "(1) operat[ed] as a prepublication licensing scheme that burdens scientific expression, (2) vest[ed] boundless discretion in government officials, and (3) lack[ed] adequate procedural safeguards. Consequently, [the court held] that the challenged regulations constitute[d] a prior restraint on speech that offend[ed] the First Amendment."[37]

Much of the controversy involved in this case concerned the question of whether software is speech protected by the First Amendment. The court specifically addressed the issue of whether the Export Administration Regulations ("EAR") restrictions on the export of encryption software in source code constituted a prior restraint in violation of the First Amendment. In his opinion, Judge Fletcher, with whom Judge Bright concurred, began by looking at the definition of source code:

> "Source code," at least as currently understood by computer

---

[33] 176 F.3d 1132 (9th Cir. 1999), *vacated*, 192 F.3d 1308, 1309 (9th Cir. 1999) (en banc). *See also* Junger v. Daley, 209 F.3d 481 (6th Cir. 2000).

[34] "Encryption . . . involves running a readable message known as 'plaintext' through a computer program that translates the message according to an equation or algorithm into unreadable 'ciphertext.' Decryption is the translation back to plaintext when the message is received by someone with an appropriate 'key.'" *Bernstein*, 176 F.3d at 1137.

[35] *Id.* at 1136. This is based on the view that the power of encrypting software to secure information raises issues of national security. *See id.*

[36] The district court found that the source code was speech protected by the First Amendment and subsequently granted summary judgment to Bernstein on his First Amendment claims. *See* Bernstein v. United States Dep't of State, 922 F. Supp. 1426 (N.D. Cal. 1996).

[37] *Bernstein*, 176 F.3d at 1135.

> programmers, refers to the text of a program written in a "high-level" programming language, such as "PASCAL" or "C." The distinguishing feature of source code is that it is meant to be read and understood by humans and that it can be used to express an idea or a method. A computer, in fact, can make no direct use of source code until it has been translated ("compiled") into a "low-level" or "machine" language, resulting in computer-executable "object code." That source code is meant for human eyes and understanding, however, does not mean that an untutored layperson can understand it. Because source code is destined for the maw of an automated, ruthlessly literal translator—the compiler—a programmer must follow stringent grammatical, syntactical, formatting, and punctuation conventions. As a result, only those trained in programming can easily understand source code.
>
> Also important for our purposes is an understanding of how source code is used in the field of cryptography. . . . By utilizing source code, a cryptographer can express algorithmic ideas with precision and methodological rigor that is otherwise difficult to achieve. This has the added benefit of facilitating peer review—by compiling the source code, a cryptographer can create a working model subject to rigorous security tests. The need for precisely articulated hypotheses and formal empirical testing, of course, is not unique to the science of cryptography; it appears, however, that in this field, source code is the preferred means to these ends.[38]

In light of this evidence, the court held that "encryption software, in its source code form and as employed by those in the field of cryptography, must be viewed as expressive for First Amendment purposes . . ."[39] The government had argued that because source code was primarily functional, it was not protected by the First Amendment. The court rejected this claim, saying that source code could be read and understood by humans, and that, furthermore, an ounce of functionality does not negate the First Amendment.[40] The government also contended that the challenged regulations were immune from prior restraint analysis because they were "laws of general application" (e.g., a law requiring a building permit) rather than being "directed narrowly and specifically at expression."[41] The court rejected this argument, saying that in the cryptography field, source code is utilized as a means of expres-

---

38 *Id.* at 1140-41.
39 *Id.* at 1141.
40 *See id.* at 1141-42.
41 *Id.* at 1142.

sion, and because the regulations apply to encryption source code, they necessarily burden a particular form of expression directly through unbridled discretion vested in government officials.[42]

The court emphasized the narrow scope of its holding, saying that it was not suggesting that all software is expressive.[43] This assertion is very interesting, yet somewhat vague.

Judge Nelson dissented, explaining that the majority judgment failed to recognize "the basic function of encryption source code [, which] is to act as a method of controlling computers."[44] He wrote:

> [S]oftware engineers generally do not create software in object code—the series of binary digits (1's and 0's)—which tells a computer what to do because it would be enormously difficult, cumbersome and time-consuming. Instead, software engineers use high-level computer programming languages such as "C" or "Basic" to create source code as a shorthand method for telling the computer to perform a desired function. In this respect, lines of source code are the building blocks or the tools used to create an encryption machine. Encryption source code, once compiled, works to make computer communication and transactions secret; it creates a lockbox of sorts around a message that can only be unlocked by someone with a key. It is the function or task that encryption source code performs which creates its value in most cases. This functional aspect of encryption source code contains no expression; it is merely the tool used to build the encryption machine.
>
> This is not to say that this very same source code is not used expressively in some cases. Academics, such as Bernstein, seek to convey and discuss their ideas concerning computer encryption. As noted by the majority, Bernstein must actually use his source code textually in order to discuss or teach cryptology. In such circumstances, source code serves to express Bernstein's scientific methods and ideas.
>
> While it is conceptually difficult to categorize encryption source code under our First Amendment framework, I am still inevitably led to conclude that encryption source code is more like conduct than speech. Encryption source code is a building tool. Academics and computer programmers can convey this source code to each other in order to reveal the encryption machine they have built. But, the ultimate purpose of encryption code is, as its name suggests, to perform the function of encrypt-

---

42 *See id.* at 1142-43.

43 *See id.* at 1145.

44 *See id.* at 1147.

> ing messages. Thus, while encryption source code may occasionally be used in an expressive manner, it is inherently a functional device.[45]

The activity or conduct at issue here is the export of encryption source code. As I noted above, the basic nature of encryption source code lies in its functional capacity as a method to build an encryption device. Export of encryption source code is not conduct commonly associated with expression. Rather, it is conduct that is normally associated with providing other persons with the means to make their computer messages secret. The overwhelming majority of people do not want to talk about the source code and are not interested in any recondite message that may be contained in encryption source code. Only a few people can actually understand what a line of source code would direct a computer to do. Most people simply want to use the encryption source code to protect their computer communications. Export of encryption source code simply does not fall within the bounds of conduct commonly associated with expression such as picketing or handbilling.[46] This conceptualization of software as conduct, at points, betrays understanding of the expressive or discursive nature of software and also too narrowly focuses on the act of export.

The *Bernstein* opinions failed, in general, to appreciate the representational and discursive competence of software. Software is a medium for communication, for representing meaning. No matter how embedded or hidden the function of software, it is simply to construct meaning—to make something obvious. That is discourse.

To contrast the expressive nature of source code with the functional industrial processes of technology is not convincing. The dichotomy collapses when we conceptualize software as the medium for communication, for expression. Function, then, is seen to be an integral part of building the communicative framework. How would the *Bernstein* court react to a suggestion that the mechanism of voice, of speaking, or the mechanism of the brain of thinking, is not protected by the First Amendment because it is functional, in that it just tells the body what to do? Software is digital speak. The *Bernstein* court failed to appreciate that the (functional) medium can also make up the message.[47]

---

[45] *Id.* at 1147-48 (citations omitted).

[46] *Id.* at 1149.

[47] *See* Gary Genosko et al., The Masters of Implosion (1999); Marshall McLuhan, Understanding Media: Extension of Man 7-21 (1964).

Cryptography is a great example of this—it allows us to construct a private and secure identity and discourse that is otherwise not available. In this case, in essence, the court was dictating how we might speak—the discourse or dialect through which we might speak. How would one react if the government said we could not whisper or send secret notes? Or said we must talk to others in English only?

There is also a question of remoteness.[48] As the court pointed out, a building regulation does not infringe the First Amendment, even though in an abstract way a building is part of the medium and will construct meaning in some sense.[49] The "feel" of a building and its location may act to construct expression.

The proximity of code to communication, though, convinces us that software is discourse. Its primary purpose is to construct meaning and that is what the First Amendment is all about. By controlling code, one has the power to control thought processes. In this digital environment, the ability to distort the construction of meaning in any pure sense is immense, and it is in the mechanism of distortion that bias and prevailing prejudices can be invoked.[50] The protectors of speech must be vigilant.

Should all software be protected by the First Amendment? *Primae facie*, the answer must be "yes" but the process of scrutiny could well find justifiable regulation.[51] For instance, the protec-

---

[48] *See* City of Lakewood v. Plain Dealer Publ'g Co., 486 U.S. 750, 759 (1988) (holding that not every law involving discretion may be challenged as censorship by the press or a speaker, but only laws that have a close enough nexus to expression, or to conduct commonly associated with expression to pose a real and substantial threat of the identified censorship risks).

[49] *See id.* at 761.

[50] *See* JÜRGEN HABERMAS, THE STRUCTURAL TRANSFORMATION OF THE PUBLIC SPHERE (1996); *see also* JÜRGEN HABERMAS, COMMUNICATION AND THE EVOLUTION OF SOCIETY (1984); JÜRGEN HABERMAS, MODERNITY AND LAW (PHILOSOPHY & SOCIAL CRITICISM) (Mathieu Deflem ed., 1996); JÜRGEN HABERMAS, MORAL CONSCIOUSNESS AND COMMUNICATION ACTION (1990); JÜRGEN HABERMAS, PHILOSOPHICAL DISCOURSES OF MODERNITY (1987); JÜRGEN HABERMAS, A THEORY OF COMMUNICATIVE ACTION (1984 & 1987); JÜRGEN HABERMAS, TOWARD A RATIONAL SOCIETY (1971); MARK POSTER, THE SECOND MEDIA AGE (1995).

[51] At a number of the presentations of this paper (particularly at Cardozo (New York), Baker McKenzie (Chicago) and the Institute for Information Law (Amsterdam)) some members of the audience were disturbed at the thought that software designed to be purely functional (e.g., software that assists in the operation of a steel mill) should be regarded as discursive. My claim is that functionality cannot automatically negative the discursive aspect of software—even in the steel mill, software is used to construct meaning. A court, in assessing the constitutionality of regulating this kind of speech, would consider whether the regulation is content based or content neutral and accordingly, weigh the discursive value of the software through the balancing or scrutiny process. To resile from the notion that all software is discursive would be tantamount to saying that not all speech is discursive. *See* LAURENCE TRIBE, AMERICAN CONSTITUTIONAL LAW 825-32 (2d ed. 1988). A number of people also pointed to the fact that copyright law regards software as a literary text and that this adds to the argument that all software is discursive.

tion of national security or the prevention of crime may justify well-reasoned regulation.

The *Bernstein* facts also raise the further issue of "transnational constitutionalism."[52] The facts of the case concern exporting cryptography—the sending of a commodity out into the sea of transnational space beyond state borders. This is a completely different topic concerning the process of law in the midst of transnational civil society and the consequent question of the protection of speech in this space; and this is no doubt why the act of export was an important criterion in the dissenting opinion.

In summary, while the majority opinion in *Bernstein* gave much support to the view that software is discourse, its inability to articulate clearly this point (conceptualization) and its hesitancy in fully embracing "all software" limit the persuasiveness of its argument. The holding that software in its coded forms can be expressive for First Amendment purposes is only one small step toward recognizing that we are talking not just about a (digital) text but also about a (digital) discourse or lanaguage. Flowing through this coded format is a constant stream of communicative activity that acts to construct meaning. It is this broader facilitative (or discursive) notion that must inform First Amendment analysis and other areas of law.

The dissenting judge, while understandably concerned with the functional aspects of software, fell prey to questionable reasoning through a lack of appreciation of the architectural capacity of software.

C. *Constructing Identity: Rethinking the Traditional View of Software*

As software possesses such deep discursive capabilities, it has a

---

52 "Trans"national symbolizes a notion of movement and cross-border activity. Transnational society inhabits a global space and to this extent extends beyond territory, sovereignty, and the state. "Inter"national symbolizes a static notion rooted in territory and sovereignty. If I draw a picture of the international, I might draw the blocks of stone (the buildings) in Harvard Yard, stationary in their territory, controlling whoever walks in the door. While if I draw a picture of the transnational, I might draw Harvard Yard as a space filled with a swirling mass of things, humans, corporations, blocks of stone (buildings), or states. The transnational is a space "beyond or without borders"; it does not seem to be merely a society of states, rather it is a society that inhabits spaces beyond borders, beyond territory and sovereignty; it is a space that is ever moving and not static, and one that fills every corner of the earth. *See* Regina v. Bow St. Stipendiary Magistrate, *ex parte* Pinochet Ugarte, 4 All. E.R. 897 (H.L. 1998), Regina v. Bow St. Metro. Stipendiary Magistrate, *ex parte* Pinochete Ugarte (No. 2), 1 All. E.R. 577 (H.L. 1999); Jerry Everard, Virtual States: The Internet and the Boundaries of the Nation-State (2000); Global Law Without a State (Gunther Teubner ed., 1997); David Held et al., Global Transformations (1999); Michael P. Ryan, Knowledge Diplomacy (1998); Brian F. Fitzgerald, *Trade-Based Constitutionalisms: A Framework for Universalising Substantive International Law*, 5 U. Miami Y.B. Int'l L. 111 (1996-97); Anne-Marie Slaughter, *International Law in a World of Liberal States*, 6 E.J. Int'l L. 1 (1995).

tremendous capacity to construct our digital identities.[53] It is, in essence, the womb from which digital discourse is born.[54]

Understanding this capacity alerts us to the power of software developers to construct communication pathways and, consequently, identity. Since software is the quintessential element of discourse, of language, of speech, in information society, the intentions of the software creator and their accountability are crucial issues. In case you have not noticed, software is now a key part of our social structure—we sense it in our cars, our supermarkets, our televisions, and our computers. We sense it everywhere; it is a ubiquitous, undulating, architectural, air-like, water-like commodity that infiltrates our daily lives. Even more interesting is that software, through its various forms of (coded) structure,[55] can act to construct meaning and identity in much the same way as we understand speech can do. Software in the information society is discourse. It is not simply a literary text (a copyright law categorization); it is fundamental to communicative architecture.[56] The fierce debate over open code versus proprietary code software is intimately connected with this construction of identity through

---

[53] In much the same way, Gadamer saw tradition impacting upon the construction of meaning. *See* GADAMER, *supra* note 17; *see also* Feldman, *supra* note 17.

[54] It is the framework of construction; a digital interpretative community. *See* STANLEY FISH, IS THERE A TEXT IN THIS CLASS? (1980); *see also* STANLEY FISH, DOING WHAT COMES NATURALLY (1989).

[55] *See* LAWRENCE LESSIG, CODE AND OTHER LAWS OF CYBERSPACE (1999); *see also* Lawrence Lessig, *Constitution and Code*, 27 CUMB. L. REV. 1 (1997); Lawrence Lessig, *Intellectual Property and Code*, 11 ST. JOHN'S J. LEGAL COMMENT. 635 (1996); Lawrence Lessig, *Law of the Horse: What Cyberlaw Might Teach* (visited Apr. 15, 2000) <http://www.cyber.law.harvard.edu/works/lessig/finalhls.pdf.>; Lawrence Lessig, *The Limits in Open Code: Regulatory Standards and the Future of the Net*, 14 BERKELEY TECH. L.J. 758 (1999); Wired Magazine, *Tyranny in the Infrastructure* (visited Apr. 13, 2000) <http://www.wired.com/wired/5.07/cyber_rights.html>. On the notion of "open code," see David Bollier, *The Power of Openness: Why Citizens, Education, Government and Business Should Care About the Coming Revolution in Open Source Code Software* (visited Apr. 13, 2000) <http://cyber.law.harvard.edu>. The call for open code or free software, as opposed to proprietary software, is intimately connected with the construction of identity in the digital environment.

[56] *See* HABERMAS, A THEORY OF COMMUNICATIVE ACTION, *supra* note 50; *see also* HABERMAS, COMMUNICATION AND THE EVOLUTION OF SOCIETY, *supra* note 50; HABERMAS, MORAL CONSCIOUSNESS AND COMMUNICATION ACTION, *supra* note 50. On digital architecture, see generally F. BAR ET AL., DEFENDING THE INTERNET REVOLUTION IN THE BROADBAND ERA: WHEN DOING NOTHING IS DOING HARM E-CONOMY (Berkeley Roundtable on the Int'l Economy (BRIE) Working Paper No. 12 Aug. 1999); JERRY FITZGERALD, BUSINESS DATA COMMUNICATIONS chs. 8-9 (4th ed. 1993); ANTHONY WILDEN, SYSTEM AND STRUCTURE : ESSAYS IN COMMUNICATION AND EXCHANGE (1972); Mark A. Lemley & Lawrence Lessig, *Ex Parte Petition to FCC re Proposed Merger of AT&T and Media One* (visited Apr. 13, 2000) <http://cyber.law.harvard.edu/works/lessig/MB.html>; Charles R. Morris & Charles H. Ferguson, *How Architecture Wins Technology Wars*, HARV. BUS. REV. 86 (Mar.-Apr. 1993); David Reed et al., *Comment on Active Networking and End to End Arguments*, IEEE NETWORK, May/June 1998, at 69-71; Jerome Saltzer et al., *End to End Arguments in System Design* (visited Apr. 13, 2000) <http://www.citeseering.nj.nec.com/did/83743.html>.

software.[57]

Software, then, is not just a passive text that tells a computer what to do. It is an integral part of our lives that informs a process of knowledge and identity construction. Like law, it is not just a thing, but also a practice. It is in this aspect that we are challenged to fully comprehend the construction of meaning in the digital environment.

1. The Multiplicity of Meaning: The Antitrust of Knowledge

Foucault, under the influence of Nietzschean philosophy, invoked the concept of genealogy to expose humanity as a series of interpretations.[58] The notion that there is diversity of knowledge and viewpoints nowadays seems commonplace. Whether we like it or not, the monopoly of knowledge by any one entity (at least in theory) is not acceptable. The Internet is said by some to be an agent for such diversity by ushering in an era of semiotic democracy where possibilities of self-determination are increased. Interestingly, this development of virtual social and political communities is implemented through a discourse of software.[59]

To augment diversity, it is vital that law and information policy ensures that the discourse of software is open to investigation, re-

---

[57] The arguments are that in an environment of free (meaning freedom to change source code not free in price) or open, as opposed to proprietary, software we are guaranteed a freedom to construct our own identity. For an argument similar to the sociological and communication theories of the seventies that we need to value and open public space where discourse can be pure and not systematically distorted see *supra* note 50. Who could forget Marshall McLuhan's cry that the medium is the message! *See* MARSHALL MCLUHAN, UNDERSTANDING MEDIA: THE EXTENSIONS OF MAN 7-21 (MIT Press 1994) (1964). The new medium of software, aptly described as the new silk road, has inherent characteristics that act to mold our lives, our identities. The open code movement urges us to support free software, as it allows the user to modify and build on the distributed software, thereby facilitating diversity. To prevent developers using the open code software to build a modified product which they could copyright, Richard Stallman from MIT popularised the notion of copyleft. The open code software is copyrighted, but licensed on terms that it or any product derived from it may be distributed only in accordance with the terms of the original distribution. In this way, it is argued, copyright is used to guarantee user freedom rather than to reduce user freedom, as happens with copyright protection of proprietary code. *See* Greg Aharonian, *Linux Gurus Debate Impact of Crappy Patent on Linux* (visited Apr. 13, 2000) <http://lpf.ai.mit.edu/Patents/ipns/ipns-19991122.txt> (considering how this license might intersect with patent claims); Bryan Pfaffenberger, *The Coming Software Patent Crisis: Can Linux Survive?* (visited Apr. 13, 2000) <http://www.2linuxjournal.com/articles/currents/003.html>. The push for open code, then, is argued to be a push for a greater self-determination of identity in the digital environment. The law will need to play a similar role in the context of proprietary software.

[58] *See* Michel Foucault, *Theatrum Philosophicum*, 282 CRITIQUE 899 (1970); Michel Foucault, *Hommage a Jean Hyppolite*, *in* NIETZCHE GENEALOGIE ET L'HISTOIRE 146 (1971).

[59] *See The Palace, Visual Chat/Communities* (visited Apr. 13, 2000) <http://www.communities.com> (demonstrating the notion of virtual communities); *see also Web Raven* (visited Apr. 13, 2000) <http://www.webraven.com.au/splash1.cfm>.

newal, and reconstruction.[60]

2. Software as an Agent of Simulation

To highlight the notion of construction of identity through software, let me refer to the writings of Jean Baudrillard, who in *Simulacra and Simulation*[61] introduced us to the notion of simulation.[62] Baudrillard wrote primarily in the context of television and aimed to highlight the layers of representation that serve to hide the origin of events through simulation. In the early 1990s, he ignited some controversy by suggesting that the Gulf War was not a real war but merely a product of simulation designed for network television.[63] A simple example of simulation can be found in the nature of televised field sports. These sports are played under lights, on artificial surfaces, in covered stadiums, filled with statistics and player profiles, instant replay, and so on. The original notion of the sport is now buried beneath layers of representation and commodification. Software, in its constructive or discursive capacity, has an immense power to augment simulation (from simple digitized versions of the hard copy items such as diaries, books, letters, clocks, etc., to fully functioning virtual reality) and thereby impact upon digital identity.

Without moving too far off point, let me recount some of the basic points of Baudrillard's theory, as it allows us to see more clearly the potential of software to construct or represent (let it be seen) digital identity. While Baudrillard, writing (initially) in the 1970s (and in part as a critique of Marxist philosophy), may have seen simulation as pernicious and questionable,[64] the digital era, the Internet, and virtual reality have found positive uses for simulation, although the overriding question of accountability remains.[65]

---

60 *See* Associated Press v. United States, 326 U.S. 1, 20 (1945); Turner Broad. Sys., Inc. v. Federal Communications Comm'n, 512 U.S. 622, 662-64 (1994) (plurality opinion as to Part IIIA, Kennedy, J., Rehnquist, C.J., Blackmun, Stevens & Souter JJ); Turner Broad. Sys., Inc. v. Federal Communications Comm'n, 520 U.S. 180, 225-26 (1997) (Breyer, J., concurring). "The basic tenet of national communication policy is that the widest possible dissemination of information from diverse and antagonistic sources is essential to the welfare of the public." *Turner Broad.*, 512 U.S. at 663-64.

61 *See* BAUDRILLARD, SIMULACRA AND SIMULATION, *supra* note 20.

62 "Computers lead us to construct things in new ways. With computers we can simulate nature in a program or leave nature aside and build second natures limited only by our powers of imagination and abstraction." SHERRY TURKLE, LIFE ON THE SCREEN: IDENTITY IN THE AGE OF THE INTERNET 47 (1995).

63 *See* JEAN BAUDRILLARD, THE GULF WAR DID NOT TAKE PLACE (1995).

64 The primary purpose of Baudrillard's work was to critique rationalist political theory like Marxism for going beyond the manifest to the latent and thereby, ignoring the surface—the layers of simulation. *See* JEAN BAUDRILLARD: SELECTED WRITINGS 4-7 (Mark Poster ed., 1988).

65 *See* Brian F. Fitzgerald, *Life in Cyberspace: A Simulating Experience*, 3 COMPUTER &

Kenneth Gergen explains that "for Baudrillard, media portrayals of the world are driven not by the way the world 'is', but by the steadily emerging histories of portrayal itself. As these histories unfold, each new lamination is influenced by the preceding, accounts are layered upon accounts, and reality is transformed into hyperreality."[66]

Howard Rheingold further explains that:

> in Baudrillard's historical analysis, human civilization has changed itself in three major stages, marked by the changes in meaning we invest in our symbol systems. . . . According to Baudrillard, during the first step of civilization, when speech and then writing were created, signs were invented to point to reality. During the second step of civilization, which took place over the past century, advertising, propaganda, and commodification set in, and the sign begins to hide reality. The third step includes our step into the hyperreal, for now we are in an age when signs begin to hide the absence of reality.[67]

Baudrillard, in his own words, introduces simulation in this way:

> To dissimulate is to pretend not to have what one has. To simulate is to feign to have what one doesn't have. One implies a presence, the other an absence. But it is more complicated than that because simulating is not pretending . . . pretending, or dissimulating, leaves the principle of reality intact . . . whereas simulation threatens the difference between the "true" and "false," the "real" and the "imaginary."[68]
>
> By crossing into a space whose curvature is no longer that of the real, nor that of truth, the era of simulation is inaugurated by a liquidation of referentials—worse: with their artificial resurrection in the system of signs, a material more malleable than meaning, in that it lends itself to all systems of equivalences, to all binary oppositions, to all combinatory algebra. It is no longer a question of imitation, nor duplication, nor even parody. It is a question of substituting the signs of the real

---

TELECOMM. L. REV. 136, 139 (1997); *see also* MARK TAYLOR, IMAGOLOGIES (1994); TURKLE, *supra* note 62; SHERRY TURKLE, THE SECOND SELF: COMPUTERS AND THE HUMAN SPIRIT (1984).

66 GERGEN, THE SATURATED SELF, *supra* note 21, at 121-22. Baudrillard's theory can be better understood by positing two words, "origination" and "simulation", which are meant to act as labels, as metaphors, and as themes. Origination is the notion that things have origin or creation (centering). Simulation is the notion that things have no origin, they exist in an imaginary way, they are make believe (decentering). *See* Fitzgerald, *supra* note 65, at 136, 139.

67 HOWARD RHEINGOLD, THE VIRTUAL COMMUNITY: HOMESTEADING ON THE ELECTRONIC FRONTIER 298-99 (1994).

68 BAUDRILLARD, SIMULCRA AND SIMULATION, *supra* note 20, at 3.

> for the real . . . .[69]
>
> Representation stems from the principle of the equivalence of the sign and of the real . . . . Simulation, on the contrary, stems from the utopia of the principle of equivalence, *from the radical negation of the sign as value*, from the sign as the reversion and death sentence of every reference. Whereas representation attempts to absorb simulation by interpreting it as a false representation, simulation envelops the whole edifice of representation itself as a simulacrum.[70]
>
> On the contrary, it is as hyperreal events, no longer with a specific content or end, but indefinitely refracted by each other . . . it is in this sense that they cannot be controlled by an order that can only exert itself on the real and the rational, on causes and ends, a referential order that can only reign over the referential . . . but that cannot do anything against this indefinite recurrence of simulation, against that nebula whose weight no longer obeys the laws of gravitation of the real . . . .[71]

Baudrillard's notion of simulation highlights how discourse can act to distort and reconfigure an appreciation of events.[72] Software is very much an agent of simulation in that it has tremendous capacity to reinvent reality through digitization. In understanding software and the regulation of it through law, we must be alert to its ability to distort and structure communication and to the power of those that create software to structure our identities through this process.

III. Legal Regulation of the Digital Architecture (Software): Intellectual Property

The role and function of software will initially be mediated by a blend of intellectual property law, contract law, competition law and privacy law,[73] which I would term informational law or informational constitutionalism. It is the development of the principles of these areas of law in their relation to software that will determine much about the way we live in the future.

---

69 *Id.* at 2.

70 *Id.* at 6 (emphasis in original).

71 *Id.* at 21. *See also* BAUDRILLARD, *supra* note 63.

72 *See* GENOSKO ET AL., *supra* note 47.

73 Law can play an important role in ensuring diversity. *See* Turner Broad. Sys., Inc. v. Federal Communications Comm'n, 512 U.S. 622, 662-64 (1994) (discussing the importance of ensuring public access to a multiplicity of information sources where the issue is whether or not a must-carry provision is unconstitutional).

A. *Copyright and Reverse Engineering*

Intellectual property law in the form of copyright protects computer software as if it were a literary text, allowing the copyright owner exclusive rights in relation to the reproduction of that text.[74] The rationale of copyright is that it will protect the expression of information but not the ideas supporting such expression. An example of the way in which copyright law will serve to shape our identity through the way it treats the expressive language of software is found in the context of reverse engineering and decompilation of software.

If a software engineer or developer constructs software that becomes an industry standard, that software acts as architecture for communication; it becomes, in essence, a discourse that allows me to speak to you. Copyright law then bears upon its shoulders the need to mediate the power given to the copyright holder to monopolize rights in discourse that may have become an industry standard—in other words, a common form—with the needs of the user or speaker. Herein lie the battles over reverse engineering and the decompilation of software. In order to develop complementary and improved software products (speech), software developers have reverse engineered the industry standard software to make software that can be interoperable (conversant) with the industry standard. In many cases, in order to reverse engineer software, you need to copy (and in some cases "borrow" parts of) the software, which technically is an infringement of the copyright owner's exclusive rights over reproduction. In the United States, the courts have employed the fair use doctrine[75] to mediate this issue, while in Australia, the government has enacted a (part) legislative solution through amendment to the Copyright Act.[76] Fair

---

74 Copyright Act of 1968, § 31 (Austl.); 17 U.S.C. § 106 (1995).

75 *See* 17 U.S.C. § 107 (1998); Sega Enters. Ltd. v. Accolade, Inc. 977 F.2d 1510 (9th Cir. 1992) (applying fair use doctrine to reverse engineering); Sony Computer Entertainment Inc. v. Connectix Corp. 203 F.3d 596 (9th Cir. 2000); *see also* Brian F. Fitzgerald, *Underlying Rationales of Fair Use: Simplifying the Copyright Act,* 2 S. CROSS U. L. REV. 153 (1998). On reverse engineering and decompilation, see generally Anne Fitzgerald & Cristina Cifuentes, *Interoperability and Computer Software Protection in Australia,* 4 COMPUTER & TELECOMM L. REV. 271 (1998); Cristina Cifuentes & Anne Fitzgerald, *Reverse Engineering of Computer Programs: Comments on the Copyright Law Review Committee's Final Report on Computer Software Protection,* 6 J.L. & INFO. SCI. 241 (1995); Anne Fitzgerald & Cristina Cifuentes, *Pegging Out the Boundaries of Computer Software Copyright: The Computer Programs Act and the Digital Agenda Bill, in* GOING DIGITAL 2000: LEGAL ISSUES FOR E-COMMERCE, SOFTWARE AND THE INTERNET (Anne Fitzgerald et al. eds., Prospect Publ'g, Sydney, Austl. 2000).

76 *See* Copyright Act of 1968, §§ 47 D-F *introduced by* Copyright Amendment (Computer Programs) Act of 1999 (Austl.); *cf.* Digital Millennium Copyright Act of 1998 § 1201(f), Pub. L. No. 105-305, 112 Stat. 2860 (1998); Universal City Studios, Inc. v. Reimerdes, 82 F. Supp. 2d 211; *see also* Attorney General D. Williams & Senator R. Alston, *Copyright Changes to Help Australian Software Industry* (visited Feb 23, 1999) <http://www.dcita.gov.au>.

use defines the appropriate balance between a monopoly right given as an incentive for innovation, and the public interest in the free flow of information for a variety of cultural reasons.[77] In Australia, the Copyright Law Review Committee ("CLRC") has recommended that we adopt a more broad-based fair use right, similar to the United States model, in place of our narrower and more specific fair dealing exceptions.[78]

The following case, which was decided by the High Court of Australia (Australia's equivalent to the United States Supreme Court) on September 30, 1999, suggests that the legality of reverse engineering for interoperability purposes will be quite narrow. This raises concerns for the vitality and diversity of digital discourse.

1. *Data Access Corp. v. Powerflex Services Pty Ltd.*[79]

Data Access Corp., a company incorporated under the law of the State of Florida in the United States, claimed to own copyright in an application development system, Dataflex, which had been in use in Australia since 1982. Dataflex was designed to develop computer programs that establish, manage, and manipulate databases by providing facilities for the storage, organization and retrieval of information and for computation and comparison with respect to the information. Dataflex also included developed computer programs that the purchaser could use instead of developing her own programs. Dataflex incorporated a "run time" program that enabled computer programs and databases developed by means of the system to operate or "run." Data Access charged a license fee for the run time program.

The third respondent, Dr. David Bennett, aspired to create an application development system that would be highly compatible with Dataflex so that persons who had been using the Dataflex application development system would be persuaded to acquire the

---

[77] *See* Fitzgerald, *Underlying Rationales of Fair Use, supra* note 75, at 153; *see also* Campbell v. Acuff-Rose Music Inc., 510 U.S. 569 (1994); PAUL GOLDSTEIN, COPYRIGHT'S HIGHWAY ch. 5 (1994); JOHN S. LAWRENCE & BERNARD TIMBERG, FAIR USE AND FREE INQUIRY (1989); WILLIAM PATRY, THE FAIR USE PRIVILEGE IN COPYRIGHT (1985); William Fisher III, *Reconstructing the Fair Use Doctrine*, 101 HARV. L. REV. 1659, 1700-04 (1988); Wendy J. Gordon, *Fair Use as Market Failure: A Structural and Economic Analysis of the Betamax Case and its Predecessors*, 82 COLUM. L. REV. 1600 (1982).

[78] *See Report on the Simplification of the Copyright Act 1968, Part 1, Exceptions to the Exclusive Rights of Copyright Owners* (Copyright Law Review Committee) (1998) (visited June 8, 2000) <http://law.gov.au/clrc/gen_info/clrc/rep_index.html/>. For examples of Australia's fair dealing exceptions, see Copyright Act, 1968, §§ 40- 42 (Austl.).

[79] (1999) 166 A.L.R. 228, *available at* <http://www.austlii.edu.au> (visited Apr. 13, 2000).

system. By December 1987, when he purchased the latest version of Dataflex, Dr. Bennett had gained a profound understanding of that system and was steadily preparing his own system. By early 1989, he had so refined the system that he procured members of the Victorian Dataflex Users' Group, a voluntary association of persons who used or were otherwise interested in the Dataflex system, to test and report on his system. In September 1989, he and his wife, Margaret Ann Bennett, (the fourth respondent) caused the second respondent (Powerflex Corp. Pty Ltd.) to be incorporated, and that company began selling Dr. Bennett's system under the name "Powerflex," which in 1990 was changed to "PFXplus." PFXplus was marketed as fully compatible with existing Dataflex files, thereby eliminating the need for payment of Dataflex run time fees.

Out of the 225 words of Dataflex language (excluding twenty-nine words relating to graphics), 192 are in the PFXplus language. The use of each of those 192 words causes a device having digital information processing capabilities to perform the same function it performs in Dataflex. Yet, there is no objective similarity between the expression in the source code of PFXplus and the expression in the source code of Dataflex, except that in each case the word is found in that expression.

The key issue for determination was whether the use of the same word in the two computer programs to perform the same function was in contravention of the copyright owner's exclusive rights bestowed pursuant to the Australian Copyright Act 1968. Further copyright issues were raised in relation to macros and a compression table. The High Court of Australia held that copying command words associated with the Dataflex program (such as "AUTOPAGE," PAGEBREAK," and "FILELIST") was not a breach of copyright. It also held that copying three Dataflex macros (i.e., "REPORT," ENTERGROUP," and "ENTER") in the same program did not infringe Australian copyright law. However, on the issue of the compression table, it found the product of Dr. Bennett's act of black box reverse engineering to be a breach of copyright.

a. Huffman Compression Table

In relation to the compression table, the High Court explained:

> Data Access alleged that part of the PFXplus program called "Runtime Program" reproduced part of the Dataflex runtime program containing the Dataflex Huffman Compression

> Table which is a system by which characters in a file expressed in a code of eight bits for each character are represented by much shorter strings of numbers. The shortest string is assigned to the most frequently occurring character and the length of each string is inversely proportional to the probability of occurrence of the character. Thus the saving of space required for the storage of data on memory devices such as hard disk drives and tapes is very great. It was common ground that the two tables, Dataflex and PFXplus, of the compressed code and corresponding character in eight bit code are identical and that Dr. Bennett intentionally caused them to be identical.
>
> The respondent in the case, Dr. Bennett, needed to "replicate precisely the . . . compression table" (used to compress data and therefore save disk space) in a competitor's database application (called Dataflex) because he wanted his database (called Powerflex) to interoperate with the Dataflex program. In order to achieve interoperablity, Dr. Bennett did not sit down and literally copy the internal code used in the Dataflex program. He used a technique called black box reverse engineering. Black box reverse engineering means that Dr. Bennett did not make a direct copy of the compression table. He indirectly copied it by observing the behaviour of the Dataflex program and deducing the exact contents of the Dataflex compression table.[80]

The High Court ruled that black box reverse engineering and subsequent literal representation of a compression table in another database application was a breach of copyright. The fact that the defendant used black box reverse engineering to determine the contents of the compression table was irrelevant for the purposes of copyright law. The Court said: "the fact that Dr. Bennett used an ingenious method of determining the bit string assigned to each character does not make the output of such a process any less a 'reproduction' than if Dr. Bennett had sat down with a print-out of the table and copy-typed it into the PFXplus program."[81]

This raises a major issue for reverse engineering in Australia as the recent amendments to the Copyright Act, expressly allowing reverse engineering for interoperability security testing and error correction purposes, require the activity to be undertaken on behalf of the owner or licensee of the copy of the program from which the reproduction or adaptation is made.[82] This can be con-

---

[80] *Id.*

[81] *Id.*

[82] The Australian Copyright Act provides the following:

> 47B Reproduction for normal use or study of computer programs
>
> . . . .
>
> (3) Subject to subsection (4), the copyright in a literary work that is a

trasted with the Digital Millennium Copyright Act[83] and fair use doctrine in the United States, which allow for reverse engineering without the consent of the owner or licensee of the copy of the program.[84]

---

computer program is not infringed by the making of a reproduction of the work if:

(a) the reproduction is made in the course of running a copy of the program for the purpose of studying the ideas behind the program and the way in which it functions; and

(b) the running of the copy is done by, or on behalf of, the owner or licensee of the copy.

(4) Subsection (3) does not apply to the making of a reproduction of a computer program from an infringing copy of the computer program.

. . . .

47D Reproducing computer programs to make interoperable products

(1) Subject to this Division, the copyright in a literary work that is a computer program is not infringed by the making of a reproduction or adaptation of the work if:

(a) the reproduction or adaptation is made by, or on behalf of, the owner or licensee of the copy of the program (the *original program*) used for making the reproduction or adaptation; and

(b) the reproduction or adaptation is made for the purpose of obtaining information necessary to enable the owner or licensee to make independently another program (the *new program*), or an article, to connect to and be used together with, or otherwise to interoperate with, the original program or any other program; and

(c) the reproduction or adaptation is made only to the extent reasonably necessary to obtain the information referred to in paragraph (b); and

(d) to the extent that the new program reproduces or adapts the original program, it does so only to the extent necessary to enable the new program to connect to and be used together with, or otherwise to interoperate with, the original program or the other program; and

(e) the information referred to in paragraph (b) is not readily available to the owner or licensee from another source when the reproduction or adaptation is made.

(2) Subsection (1) does not apply to the making of a reproduction or adaptation of a computer program from an infringing copy of the computer program.

Copyright Act, 1968, §§ 47B, 47D (Austl.) (emphasis in original). On the nuances of these terms, see Brian F. Fitzgerald, *Commodifying and Transacting Informational Products Through Contractual Licences: The Challenge for Informational Constitutionalism, in* INTELLECTUAL PROPERTY IN THE COMMON LAW WORLD (G. Austin & C. Rickett eds., 1999); Mark A. Lemley, *Beyond Pre-emption: The Law and Policy of Intellectual Property Licensing,* 87 CAL. L. REV. 111, 128-31 (1999); David Nimmer et al., *The Metamorphosis of Contract into Expand,* 87 CAL. L. REV. 17, 32-40 (1999).

The Australian House of Representatives Standing Committee on Legal and Constitutional Affairs, following a submission by Anne Fitzgerald, has recommended this requirement be removed in relation to security testing to bring Australian law into line with the DMCA. *See Advisory Report on the Copyright Amendment (Digital Agenda) Bill 1999* (1999) paras. 4.65-4.66 (visited Apr. 13, 2000) <http://www.aph.gov.au/house/committee/laca/digitalagenda/contents.htm>; *see also* Fitzgerald & Cifuentes, *Pegging Out the Boundaries, supra* note 75, at 37, 45-46.

83 Pub. L. No. 101-305, 112 Stat. 2860 (1998).

84 The Digital Millennium Copyright Act of 1998 states:

(f) REVERSE ENGINEERING—(1) Notwithstanding the provisions of subsection (a)(1)(A), a person who has lawfully obtained the right to use a copy of a computer program may circumvent a technological measure that effectively controls access to a particular portion of that program for the sole

A question also remains as to the extent to which reverse engineering rights can be contractually prohibited.[85] The degree to which reverse engineering can survive the contractual license is seen by many software developers as being of the utmost significance. The commentary to the Uniform Computer Information Transaction Act ("UCITA"), while not being definitive, suggests contractually prohibiting reverse engineering in some cases will fall foul of section 105(b).[86] In Australia, the current law as amended by the Copyright Amendment (Computer Programs) Act 1999 (Cth), provides in section 47H that an agreement that has the effect of limiting sections 47D-F (which permit reverse engineering for certain purposes on certain conditions) is of no effect.[87] However, as sections 47D-F are conditioned on the activities being undertaken by, or on behalf of, the owner or licensee of a copy of the program and on the copy of the software not being an infringing copy,[88] there may be scope for arguing that the software manufacturer still has the capacity to license the product on terms that do

---

purpose of identifying and analyzing those elements of the program that are necessary to achieve interoperability of an independently created computer program with other programs, and that have not previously been readily available to the person engaging in the circumvention, to the extent any such acts of identification and analysis do not constitute infringement under this title.

(2) Notwithstanding the provisions of subsections (a)(2) and (b), a person may develop and employ technological means to circumvent a technological measure, or to circumvent protection afforded by a technological measure, in order to enable the identification and analysis under paragraph (1), or for the purpose of enabling interoperability of an independently created computer program with other programs, if such means are necessary to achieve such interoperability, to the extent that doing so does not constitute infringement under this title.

(3) The information acquired through the acts permitted under paragraph (1), and the means permitted under paragraph (2), may be made available to others if the person referred to in paragraph (1) or (2), as the case may be, provides such information or means solely for the purpose of enabling interoperability of an independently created computer program with other programs, and to the extent that doing so does not constitute infringement under this title or violate applicable law other than this section.

(4) For purposes of this subsection, the term 'interoperability' means the ability of computer programs to exchange information, and of such programs mutually to use the information which has been exchanged.

Id. § 1201.

85 Under the European Software Directive, contractual prohibition of reverse engineering for interoperability purposes is not allowed. *See* Council Directive 122/42 of 14 May 1991 on the Legal Protection of Computer Programs, arts. 6(1), 9(1) 1991 O.J. (L 122).

86 Commentary of the NCCUSL Drafting Committee on Uniform Computer Information Transaction Act ("UCITA") (visited Apr. 14, 2000) <http://www.law.upenn.edu/bll/ulc/ucita/citaam99.htm>.

87 *See* Copyright Amendment (Computer Programs) Act 1999 (Cth) (Austl.); Copyright Act of 1968 § 47H, *available at* <http://scaletext.law.gov.au/html/pasteact/0/244/top.htm> (visited June 8, 2000).

88 *See* Copyright Act of 1968 §§ 47D-F, *available at* <http://scaletext.law.gov.au/html/pasteact/0/244/top.htm> (visited June 8, 2000).

not permit reverse engineering, thereby defeating sections 47D-F and circumventing 47H.

In summary, it is suggested that a well reasoned and evenly balanced view of the legality of reverse engineering (analyzed through the framework of software as discourse) is vital to a diverse and vibrant digital communicative architecture/discourse (premised on interoperable or conversant standards) and should be vigorously asserted.

B. *Intellectual Property: Patent Law*

A patent gives a very strong form of protection (monopoly right for up to twenty years) over the using and selling of inventions. It is now clear that software (in the form of algorithms and data structures) can be patented,[89] even though under the TRIPs Agreement, the preferred form of protection is through copyright.[90] The role of copyright in this area has now been overtaken by events.

During the last decade, the number of software patents granted in the United States has increased tremendously. Over 13,000 software patents were issued in 1997; 17,500 are estimated for 1998; and 22,500 are estimated for 1999. In fact, ten times the number of patents granted in 1992 and 1993 will be granted in 1998 and 1999.[91]

In recent times, there have been more and more extensive claims to (monopoly) patent rights in the kinds of software that act as the basic architecture of electronic commerce. There have been a number of claims in the United States that methods of transacting electronic commerce (including digital cash) are patented and

---

89 *See* J. Swinson & G. Middleton, *Patents in Cyberspace: Electronic Commerce and Business Methods Patents, in* GOING DIGITAL 2000: LEGAL ISSUES FOR E-COMMERCE, SOFTWARE AND THE INTERNET 71 (Anne Fitzgerald et al. eds., 2000); *cf.* European Patent Convention art. 52(2)(c) (1978) 13 I.L.M. 270; E. Liesegang, *Software Patents in Europe*, 5 COMPUTER & TELECOMM. L. REV. 48 (1999).

90 Article 10(1) of the Agreement on Trade-Related Aspects of Intellectual Property Rights ("TRIPS"), part of the World Trade Organization Agreement of 1994 and binding on all members of the World Trade Organization, provides that: "Computer programs, whether in source or object code, shall be protected as literary works under the Berne Convention (1971)." Agreement on Trade-Related Aspects of Intellectual Property Rights, Part II, § 1, art. 10, *available at* <http://www.wto.org/wto/intellec/4-ipstan.htm#1> (visited June 8, 2000). *See also* Brian F. Fitzgerald, *Computer Copyright: Same Words, Different Source Code: Data Access v. Powerflex* 2 COMPUTER & TELECOMM. L. REV. 120 (1996); Brian F. Fitzgerald, *Lotus Development Corporation v. Borland International Inc.: Is the Lotus 1-2-3 Menu Command Hierarchy Copyrightable*, 6 J. L. & INFO. SCI. 277 (1995).

91 *See* Gregory Aharonian, INTERNET PATENT NEWS, Oct. 18, 1998, *available from* <http://www.bustpatents.com>; *see* Fitzgerald & Cifuentes, *Interoperability and Computer Software Protection, supra* note 75, at 271.

cannot be replicated without a license.[92] Here the very foundations of the information society, the commercial structure or architecture, are being monopolized by the patent holder. We aspire to the patent monopoly in order to reward inventors for the public good, but the patent monopoly is troubling where the basic building blocks of action or speech are patented. As the following case demonstrates, in defining the patenting of software, we will be defining accessibility to new forms of discourse.

1. *State Street Bank*[93]

This case concerned the validity of a patent for a system that allowed a bank administrator to monitor and record the financial information flow and make all calculations necessary for maintaining a partner fund financial services configuration. A partner fund financial services configuration essentially allows several mutual funds, or "Spokes," to pool their investment funds into a single portfolio, or "Hub," allowing for consolidation of, inter alia, the costs of administering the fund and providing the tax advantages of a partnership. The court was asked whether the claimed subject matter fell into one of two alternative judicially-created exceptions to statutory subject matter; the "mathematical algorithm" exception and the "business method" exception.[94]

---

92 *See, e.g.*, State St. Bank & Trust Co. v. Signature Fin. Group Inc., 149 F.3d 1368 (Fed. Cir. 1998) (discussing patent on computing financial data); Teresa Riordan, *A Dangerous Monopoly? Paying Computer Users to Read Internet Ads and then Storing Their Data*, N.Y. TIMES, Feb. 1, 1999, at C1 (discussing Cybergold's patent on paying to view Internet advertisements and SightSound.com's patent for downloading audio or visual material for a fee transmitted over the network). For a list of recent e-commerce software patent claims see League of Programming Freedom, *Software Patents*, (visited Apr. 14, 2000) <http://lpf.ai.mit.edu/Patents/patents.html>. In Amazon.com, Inc. v. Barnesandnoble.com, Inc., 73 F. Supp. 2d 1228 (W.D. Wash. 1999), a district court judge in Seattle granted a preliminary injunction prohibiting Barnes & Noble from using one-click technology in the online shopping process. Paragraph One of the complaint read:

> Amazon.com brings this suit to redress Defendants' willful infringement of Amazon.com's patent encompassing its 1-Click method for processing on-line shopping orders. Amazon.com's 1-Click system is a major innovation in e-commerce: it allows customers to order, pay for, and arrange for delivery of any item Amazon.com sells, all with a single click of the mouse. The 1-Click method is popular with customers because it gives them a faster, more convenient, more efficient, and more pleasant shopping experience. In May 1998, Defendants meticulously copied Amazon.com's 1-Click process, dubbed it "Express Lane," and introduced it on their barnesandnoble.com website. Defendant's Express Lane ordering system infringes Amazon.com's United States Patent No. 5,960,411 (the "411 patent").

Complaint for Patent Infringement and Demand for Trial, Amazon.com v. Barnesandnoble.com, 73 F. Supp. 2d 1228 (W.D. Wash. 1999), *available at* <http://lpf.ai.mit.edu/Patents/amazon-vs-bn.html>.

93 State St. Bank & Trust Co. v. Signature Fin. Group, 149 F.3d 1368 (Fed. Cir. 1998).

94 Section 101 of the U.S. Patent Act reads: "Whoever invents or discovers any new and useful process, machine, manufacture, or composition of matter, or any new and useful

The court explained that the plain and unambiguous meaning of section 101 of the Patent Act meant that any invention falling within one of the four stated categories of statutory subject matter may be patented, provided it meets the other requirements for patentability set forth in sections 102, 103, and paragraph two of section 112. They further explained that repetitive use of the expansive term "any" in section 101 evidenced Congress's intent not to place any restrictions on the subject matter for which a patent could be obtained beyond those specifically recited in the section. The court stated that the Supreme Court has acknowledged that Congress intended section 101 to extend to "anything under the sun that is made by man,"[95] and that therefore it would be improper to read limitations into the statute restricting the subject matter that may be patented.[96]

Addressing the claim that a mathematical algorithm exception invalidated this patent, the court reasoned:

> The Supreme Court has identified three categories of subject matter that are unpatentable, namely "laws of nature, natural phenomena, and abstract ideas." Of particular relevance to this case, the Court has held that mathematical algorithms are not patentable subject matter to the extent that they are merely abstract ideas. . . . [T]he Court explained that certain types of mathematical subject matter, standing alone, represent nothing more than abstract ideas until reduced to some type of practical application, i.e., "a useful, concrete and tangible result."
>
> Unpatentable mathematical algorithms are identifiable by showing they are merely abstract ideas constituting disembodied concepts or truths that are not "useful." From a practical standpoint, this means that to be patentable an algorithm must be applied in a "useful" way. . . .
>
> Today, we hold that the transformation of data, representing discrete dollar amounts, by a machine through a series of mathematical calculations into a final share price, constitutes a practical application of a mathematical algorithm, formula, or calculation, because it produces "a useful, concrete and tangible result"—a final share price momentarily fixed for recording and reporting purposes and even accepted and relied upon by regulatory authorities and in subsequent trades.[97]

improvement thereof, may obtain a patent therefore, subject to the conditions and requirements of this title." 35 U.S.C. § 101 (1984).

95 Diamond v. Chakrabarty, 447 U.S. 303, 309 (1980); Diamond v. Diehr, 450 U.S. 175, 182 (1981) (quoting S. Rep. No. 1979, 82d Cong., 2d Sess., 5 (1952); H.R. Rep. No. 1923, 82d Cong., 2d Sess., 6 (1952), 1952 U.S.C.C.A.N. 2394, 2399).

96 *See State St. Bank*, 149 F.3d at 1372-73.

97 *Id.* at 1373 (citations omitted).

Regarding the claim that a business method exception invalidated the patent the court held:

> As an alternative ground for invalidating the . . . patent . . . the [lower] court relied on the judicially-created, so-called "business method" exception to statutory subject matter. We take this opportunity to lay this ill-conceived exception to rest. Since its inception, the "business method" exception has merely represented the application of some general, but no longer applicable legal principle, perhaps arising out of the "requirement for invention"—which was eliminated by § 103. Since the 1952 Patent Act, business methods have been, and should have been, subject to the same legal requirements for patentability as applied to any other process or method.
>
> The business method exception has never been invoked by this court, or the CCPA, to deem an invention unpatentable. Application of this particular exception has always been preceded by a ruling based on some clearer concept of Title 35 or, more commonly, application of the abstract idea exception based on finding a mathematical algorithm. Illustrative is the CCPA's analysis in *In re Howard*, wherein the court affirmed the Board of Appeals' rejection of the claims for lack of novelty and found it unnecessary to reach the Board's section 101 ground that a method of doing business is "inherently unpatentable."
>
> Similarly, *In re Schrader*, while making reference to the business method exception, turned on the fact that the claims implicitly recited an abstract idea in the form of a mathematical algorithm and there was no "transformation or conversion of subject matter representative of or constituting physical activity or objects." . . . *Maucorps* dealt with a business methodology for deciding how salesmen should best handle respective customers and *Meyer* involved a "system" for aiding a neurologist in diagnosing patients. Clearly, neither of the alleged "inventions" in those cases falls within any § 101 category. However, closer scrutiny of these cases reveals that the claimed inventions in both *Maucorps* and *Meyer* were rejected as abstract ideas under the mathematical algorithm exception, not the business method exception.
>
> Even the case frequently cited as establishing the business method exception to statutory subject matter, *Hotel Security Checking Co. v. Lorraine Co.*, did not rely on the exception to strike the patent. In that case, the patent was found invalid for lack of novelty and "invention," not because it was improper subject matter for a patent. The court stated "the fundamental principle of the system is as old as the art of bookkeeping, i.e., charging the goods of the employer to the agent who takes

> them." "If at the time of [the patent] application, there had been no system of bookkeeping of any kind in restaurants, we would be confronted with the question whether a new and useful system of cash registering and account checking is such an art as is patentable under the statute." This case is no exception.[98]

The court pointed out that the district court, while explaining the rationale of the business method exception as set forth in several treatises, actually gave as the primary reason for its decision the following statement:

> If Signature's invention were patentable, any financial institution desirous of implementing a multi-tiered funding complex modelled [sic] on a Hub and Spoke configuration would be required to seek Signature's permission before embarking on such a project. This is so because the '056 Patent is claimed [sic] sufficiently broadly to foreclose virtually any computer-implemented accounting method necessary to manage this type of financial structure.[99]

The appeals court explained that whether the patent's claims were too broad to be patentable was not to be judged under section 101, but rather under sections 102, 103, and 112 and had nothing to do with whether what was claimed was statutory subject matter.[100]

In summary, the court rejected the existence of judicially created exceptions to the statutory subject matter and confirmed the validity of the patent in what has been seen as a landmark decision for e-commerce software patents.

One may ponder whether the business method would have been patentable without the software. What made the claim patentable? One interpretation of the case is that the business method was patentable because it was wrapped up in software (in digital speak) and that digitizing the business method has some magical legal effect.[101]

The ever-increasing number of e-commerce business method

---

98 *Id.* at 1374-76 (citations and footnotes omitted).

99 *Id.* at 1376-77 (quoting State St. Bank & Trust Co. v. Signature Fin. Group, Inc., 927 F. Supp. 502, 516 (D. Mass. 1996)).

100 *Id.* at 1375-76.

101 As one writer points out, the real space non-digital "drive through" business method for delivery of fast food would not have been patentable in the past. *See* Claus D. Melarti, Note, State Street Bank Trust Co. v. Signature Financial Group Inc*: Ought the Mathematical and Business Method Exceptions Return to Business as Usual?*, 6 J. INTELL. PROP. L. 359 (1999). This real space business method could be protected to some extent through contract (e.g. franchise agreement), trademark, and unfair competition law.

software patents, especially those involving fundamental e-commerce architecture is making it impossible to move (speak) in digital space without fear of patent infringement.

This is a matter of serious concern, as a method of doing business is a discourse. The way we communicate to transact commercial affairs is a discursive practice. How would one react to a claim that they had to pay a license fee to say, "The item costs five dollars; please hand over your money"? As can be seen from this example, digital architecture is inherently discursive, so the more we allow proprietary rights in it, the more we impact upon the freedom of communication or discourse. The incentive to build digital architecture, however, is intertwined with the enforcement of intellectual property rights.

This interconnection raises an interesting question. The development of digital discourse is an expensive business; and, if we aspire to build the best digital communicative architecture, we may be expected to pay for such development. The difficulty is that more traditional elements of discourse, like speaking the English language, are not proprietary but open; they are not subject to a patent. I do not expect to have to pay someone a license fee to speak to you here today. My dilemma is that I strongly believe that if we are to fully exploit the amazing opportunities inherent in information society, we need to reward inventors and to understand the importance of commodifying informational products. On the other hand, I shudder at the thought that when e-commerce becomes the norm, the basic communicative architecture of business will become proprietary.[102]

Audiences to these arguments have given various responses. One person suggested that a solution might well lie in more effective patent claim processes that accord more attention to the prior art, thereby protecting the fundamental value of free and open discourse.[103] Others suggest use of compulsory licensing or the patent misuse defense to allow access to the essential architecture.[104]

---

[102] *See* Robert P. Merges, *As Many as Six Impossible Patents Before Breakfast: Property Rights for Business Concepts and Patent System Reform*, 14 BERKELEY TECH. L.J. 577 (1999); *see also* G. DREWS, THE PATENT RIGHT IN THE NATIONAL ECONOMY OF THE UNITED STATES (1952); Mark D. Janis, *Second Tier Patent Protection*, 40 HARV. INT'L L.J. 151 (1999); Francisc Marius Keeley-Domokos, Note, *Intellectual Property*, 14 BERKELEY TECH. L.J. 153 (1999); Melarti, *supra* note 101.

[103] *See* Merges, *supra* note 102.

[104] For an overview of patent misuse cases, see DONALD S. CHISUM, 6 CHISUM ON PATENTS: A TREATISE ON THE LAW OF PATENTABILITY, VALIDITY AND INFRINGEMENT § 19.04[3] (1999). *See also infra* note 124. In the future we may see stronger arguments for application of the antitrust-based essential facilities doctrine to proprietary digital architecture, although current case law would suggest this is not an easy route to take. *See* Australian

Some have queried whether we have a right to expect the business infrastructure to be free—after all, phone lines are not free! Although, in reply, the English language is not proprietary, software patents have the potential to exclude competitors who invest resources, not just free riders (as the District Court pointed out in *State Street*), and no one is claiming that you do not have to pay for a business service provided. These issues are complex and deserve more thought, but an immediate response is that they can be accommodated if we remember that free and open discourse is a fundamental value, but not the only value to be weighed in the balance.

In summary, the conceptualization of software as discourse makes us aware of the broad-reaching power of e-commerce software patents and of our need to consider carefully the proprietary nature of digital discourse/architecture.

C. *Contract Law: The Software License*

We distribute software primarily through a software license—shrink-wrap or click-wrap. Software is not distributed through the sale of a tangible good but rather through the licensing of an intangible commodity. The license is the product.[105]

"Shrink-wrap licenses" are normally used where the software is shrink-wrapped and sold in a store. The license is disclosed only

Trade Practices Act, 1974, Part IIIA (Austl.); MCI Communications Corp. v. American Tel. & Tel. Co, 708 F.2d. 1081 (7th Cir. 1983), *cert. denied by* American Tel. & Tel. Co. v. MCI Communications Corp., 464 U.S. 891 (1983); Byars v. Bluff City News Co., Inc., 609 F.2d 843 (6th Cir. 1980); Hecht v. Pro-Football Inc., 570 F.2d 982 (D.C. Cir. 1977), *cert. denied,* 436 U.S. 956 (1978); Cyber Promotions Inc. v. AOL, 948 F. Supp 456 (E.D. Pa. 1996); AOL v. Cyber Promotions Inc., (E.D Pa. 1996); Intergraph Corp. v. Intel Corp., 3 F. Supp. 2d 1255 (N.D. Ala. 1998), *vacated* 195 F.3d 1346 (Fed. Cir. 1999); Data Gen. Corp. v. Grumman Sys. Support Corp., 36 F.3d 1147 (1st Cir. 1994); Aspen Skiing Co. v. Aspen Highlands Skiing Corp., 472 U.S. 585 (1985); Eastman Kodak Co. v Image Technical Servs., Inc., 504 U.S. 451 (1992); Image Technical Servs., Inc. v. Eastman Kodak Co., 125 F.3d 1195 (9th Cir. 1997); *In re* Independent Serv. Orgs. Antitrust Litig., 203 F.3d 1322 (Fed. Cir. (Kan.) 2000); Melway Publ'g Pty Ltd. v. Robert Hicks [1999] FCA 664, *available in* <http://www.austlii.edu.au/> (visited Apr. 14, 2000); Hamersley Iron Pty Ltd. v. Nat'l Competition Council, [1999] FCA 867, *available in* <http://www.austlii.edu.au/> (visited June 8, 2000); Radio Telefis Eireann & Indep. Television Publications Ltd. v. E.C. Comm'n (Magill Case), [1995] 4 C.M.L.R. 718; Oscar Bronner v. Mediaprint Zeitungs- und Zeitschriftenverlag GmbH & Co. KG C-7/97, *available in* <http://curia.eu.int/> (visited Apr. 14, 2000); Phillip Areeda, *Essential Facilities: An Epithet in Need of Limiting Principles,* 58 A.B.A. ANTITRUST L.J. 841 (1990); Allen Kezsbom & Alan V. Goldman, *No Shortcut to Antitrust Analysis: The Twisted Journey of the "Essential Facilities" Doctrine,* 1 COLUM. BUS. L. REV. 1 (1996); W. Greg Paciak, *Essential Facilities Doctrine:* Intergraph Corp. v. Intel Corp., 14 Berkeley Tech. L.J. 323 (1999).

105 *See* Robert W. Gomulkiewicz, *The License Is The Product: Comments on the Promise of Article 2B for Software and Information Licensing,* 13 BERKELEY TECH. L.J. 891 (1998); *see also* G. Evans & Brian F. Fitzgerald, *Information Transactions Under UCC Article 2B: The Ascendancy of Freedom of Contract in the Digital Millennium,* 21 U. NEW S. WALES L.J. 404 (1998); Nimmer et al., *supra* note 82, at 17.

after the purchaser opens the package. "Click-wrap licenses" are used in an online environment, such as the Internet. The user accepts the terms and conditions of a software license by clicking on a button prior to using a program. After the decision in *ProCD, Inc. v. Zeidenberg*,[106] shrink-wrap, and arguably, click-wrap, licenses are enforceable in parts of the United States.[107]

In the digital world, the essential transaction consists of licensing information commodities, rather than the transferring of a tangible product. The value of the commodity is the information, and the right to control and exploit it. In this regard, the rights that are assigned in conjunction with the license, set out as terms of the contract, are crucial, as they define the product the licensee receives. The more restrictions are placed on the licensee's use of the software, the less its value will be to the licensee, and the greater the value retained by the licensor to use the same information in future transactions. The proposed Uniform Commercial Code ("UCC") Article 2B in the United States, which has become the Uniform Computer and Information Transactions Act ("UCITA"), adopted by the National Conference of Commissioners on Uniform State Laws ("NCCUSL") on July 29, 1999,[108] is an attempt to provide guidelines for software licensing. At this point in time, it has not achieved total support.[109]

Yet, this licensing mechanism, said to be necessary to protect investment in innovation, is mooted to allow privately legislated informational property rights to arise. It is even suggested that the public domain rights currently recognized by copyright law can be ousted by the contractual software license. Contract law then, needs to be infused with some notion of public interest in relation to informational goods such as software; and if software is discourse, we need to factor that into the rights that private ordering will allow.[110]

---

106 86 F.3d 1447 (7th Cir. 1996).

107 *See id.* at 1453.

108 *See* commentary at <http://www.badsoftware.com>.

109 *See id.*

110 *See generally* JAMES BOYLE, SHAMANS, SOFTWARE, SPLEENS (1996); Yochai Benkler, *Free as the Air to Common Use: First Amendment Constraints on Enclosure of the Public Domain*, 74 N.Y.U. L. REV. 354, 429-40 (1999); David Lange, *Recognizing the Public Domain*, 44 LAW & CONTEMP. PROBS. 147 (1981); Charles R. McManis, *The Privatization (or Shrink-Wrapping) of American Copyright Law*, 87 CAL. L. REV. 173 (1999); Madison, *supra* note 1, at 1025 (1998); Nimmer et al., *supra* note 82; Lemley, *supra* note 82; J.H. Reichman & Jonathan A. Franklin, *Privately Legislated Intellectual Property Rights: Reconciling Freedom of Contract with Public Good Uses of Information*, 147 U. PA. L. REV. 875 (1999); *cf.* Raymond T. Nimmer, *Breaking Barriers: The Relationship Between Contract and Intellectual Property Law*, 13 BERKELEY TECH. L.J. 827 (1998).

D. *Competition/Antitrust Law*

In an ideal world, competition law will balance the monopolies that copyright, patent, and contract create in software. It will define the scope of the grant of intellectual property rights. Originally, the approach in the European Union was that dealings within the scope of the intellectual property rights granted by the relevant intellectual property law were immune from competition law, while other dealings were subject to competition law. This approach was questioned in a decision that looked primarily at the anti-competitive effect of intellectual property rights—in other words, the scope of the grant as defined by intellectual property and competition law.

The appropriate interplay between competition law and intellectual property law, which is of utmost importance to the construction of our digital identity, is currently being played out in the *United States v. Microsoft* case.[111]

In an ideal world, competition law will balance the monopolies that copyright, patent, and contract create in software. It will define the scope of the grant of intellectual property rights. Originally, the approach in the European Union was that dealings within the scope of the intellectual property rights granted by the relevant intellectual property law were immune from competition law, while other dealings were subject to competition law. This approach was questioned in a decision that looked primarily at the anti-competitive effect of intellectual property rights—in other words, the scope of the grant as defined by intellectual property and competition law.

The appropriate interplay between competition law and intellectual property law, which is of utmost importance to the construction of our digital identity, is currently being played out in the *United States v. Microsoft* case.[112] In Australia, much focus has been

[111] *See* JOSEPH TAUBMAN, COPYRIGHT AND ANTITRUST (1960).

[112] *See* United States v. Microsoft Corp., ___F. Supp. ___ (D.D.C. June 7, 2000), *available in* 2000 WL 726757; <http://www.microsoft.com>. Judge Jackson concluded that Microsoft violated antitrust law (sections 1 and 2 of the Sherman Act and section 1 of the Clayton Act) in the Internet browser software market. *See* United States v. Microsoft Corp., 87 F. Supp. 2d 30 (D.D.C. April 3, 2000). He subsequently ordered that Microsoft be split into an Operating Systems Business and an Applications Business. *See* United States v. Microsoft Corp., 97 F. Supp. 2d 59 (D. D.C. June 7, 2000). This judgment has been stayed, subject to an appeal to the Supreme Court. *See Court Stays Final Judgment, Sends Microsoft Case to Supreme Court* (Microsoft press release) (visited June 28, 2000) <http://www.microsoft.com/presspass/trial/Jun00/062000.asp>

On the notion of copyright misuse, which at this point is seen as being distinct from general competition law, see Alcatel USA, Inc. v. DGI Techs., Inc., 166 F.3d 772 (5th Cir. 1999); Practice Management Info. Corp. v. American Med. Ass'n, 121 F.3d 516 (9th Cir. 1997); Lasercomb Am. v. Reynolds, 911 F.2d 970 (4th Cir. 1990); Lemley, *supra* note 82.

placed on section 51(3) of the Trade Practices Act 1974 (Cth), which exempts licensing of certain intellectual property rights from the full application of the Act.[113] Section 51(3) was targeted for reform in accordance with the Draft Report[114] published by the National Competition Council.[115] The proposal to remove the licensing of intellectual property rights from the section 51(3) exemption[116] would have made competition lawyers even more eager

---

[113] *See* Trade Practices Act 1974 § 51(3) (Cth) (Austl.), *available from* <http://www.austlii.edu.au/> (visited June 8, 2000).

[114] NATIONAL COMPETITION COUNCIL, DRAFT REPORT, REVIEW OF SECTIONS 51(2) AND 51(3) OF THE *Trade Practices Act 1974*, at 93-132, *available at* <http://www.ncc.gov.au/nationalcompet/section%2051%20review/section%2051.htm> (visited Apr 14, 2000).

[115] *See* National Competition Council (visited Apr. 14, 2000) <http://www.ncc.gov.au>; *see also* J. Fung, *The Case of an Awkward Interface—Patents versus Competition*, 21 U. NEW SOUTH WALES L.J. 757 (1998).

[116] Section 51(3) does not prevent application of section 46, which covers abuse of market power. *See* Trade Practices Act 1974 § 46 (Cth) (Austl.), *available from* <http://www.austlii.edu.au/> (visited June 8, 2000). It is suggested that section 46 can be infringed through exercise of property and contract rights. *See* QWI Pty Ltd. v. BHP Co. Ltd., (1989) 167 C.L.R. 177, 202 (Dawson, J.); *cf.* Warman Int'l Ltd. v. Envirotech Australia Pty Ltd., (1986) 11 F.C.R 478. For a general introduction to Australian law, see S. CORONES, COMPETITION LAW IN AUSTRALIA (1999); A. BRUCE & E. WEBB, TRADE PRACTICES LAW (1999). Section 46 reads:

> Misuse of market power
>
> (1) A corporation that has a substantial degree of power in a market shall not take advantage of that power for the purpose of:
>
> (a) eliminating or substantially damaging a competitor of the corporation or of a body corporate that is related to the corporation in that or any other market;
>
> (b) preventing the entry of a person into that or any other market; or
>
> (c) deterring or preventing a person from engaging in competitive conduct in that or any other market.
>
> (1A) For the purposes of subsection (1):
>
> (a) the reference in paragraph (1)(a) to a competitor includes a reference to competitors generally, or to a particular class or classes of competitors; and
>
> (b) the reference in paragraphs (1)(b) and (c) to a person includes a reference to persons generally, or to a particular class or classes of persons.
>
> (2) If:
>
> (a) a body corporate that is related to a corporation has, or 2 or more bodies corporate each of which is related to the one corporation together have, a substantial degree of power in a market; or
>
> (b) a corporation and a body corporate that is, or a corporation and 2 or more bodies corporate each of which is related to that corporation, together have a substantial degree of power in a market;
>
> the corporation shall be taken for the purposes of this section to have a substantial degree of power in that market.
>
> (3) In determining for the purposes of this section the degree of power that a body corporate or bodies corporate has or have in a market, the Court shall have regard to the extent to which the conduct of the body corporate or of any of those bodies corporate in that market is constrained by the conduct of:
>
> (a) competitors, or potential competitors, of the body corporate or of any of those bodies corporate in that market; or
>
> (b) persons to whom or from whom the body corporate or any of those bodies corporate supplies or acquires goods or services in that market.
>
> (4) In this section:

to look at the monopolies created through intellectual property legislation. Such scrutiny would be aimed particularly at the monopolies imposed by a contractual license of intellectual property such as software,[117] but the Final Report on the matter recommends against removing the licensing of intellectual property rights from the section 51(3) exemption.[118] Nevertheless, the Australian Intellectual Property and Competition Review Committee are currently undertaking another government inquiry into the interplay of intellectual property and competition law.[119]

In 1995, the United States Department of Justice and the Federal Trade Commission issued the *Antitrust Guidelines for the Licensing of Intellectual Property,* which govern the interaction of intellectual property and competition law. The guidelines' three main principles set forth:

> (a) for the purpose of antitrust analysis, the Agencies [the DOJ and FTC] regard intellectual property as being essentially comparable to any other form of property;
> (b) the Agencies do not presume that intellectual property creates market power in the antitrust context; and
> (c) the Agencies recognize that intellectual property licensing

---

(a) a reference to power is a reference to market power;

(b) a reference to a market is a reference to a market for goods or services; and

(c) a reference to power in relation to, or to conduct in, a market is a reference to power, or to conduct, in that market either as a supplier or as an acquirer of goods or services in that market.

(5) Without extending by implication the meaning of subsection (1), a corporation shall not be taken to contravene that subsection by reason only that it acquires plant or equipment.

(6) This section does not prevent a corporation from engaging in conduct that does not constitute a contravention of any of the following sections, namely, sections 45, 45B, 47 and 50, by reason that an authorization is in force or by reason of the operation of section 93.

(7) Without in any way limiting the manner in which the purpose of a person may be established for the purposes of any other provision of this Act, a corporation may be taken to have taken advantage of its power for a purpose referred to in subsection (1) notwithstanding that, after all the evidence has been considered, the existence of that purpose is ascertainable only by inference from the conduct of the corporation or of any other person or from other relevant circumstances.

Trade Practices Act 1974 § 46 (Cth) (Austl.).

117 *See* David McGowan, *Free Contracting, Fair Competition and Draft Art. 2B: Some Reflections on Federal Competition Policy, Information Transactions and "Aggressive Neutrality"*, 13 BERKELEY TECH. L.J. 1173 (1998); Ronald A. Cass, *Copyright, Licensing, and the "First Screen"*, 5 MICH. TELECOMM. & TECH. L. REV. 35 (1999).

118 *See* Final Report, Review of Sections 51(2) and 51(3) of the Trade Practices Act 1974, *available at* <http://www.ncc.gov.au/nationalcompet/section%2051%20review/section%2051.htm>.

119 *See further* Intellectual Property & Competition Review Committee (visited Apr. 14, 2000) <http://ipcr.gov.au/>.

> allows firms to combine complementary factors of production and is generally procompetitive.[120]

These guidelines, along with the European approach and the call for reform in Australia, are a good indication that competition law will act to inform the scope of intellectual property rights in the future and mediate attempts by any one entity to dominate the construction of informational discourse and identity. Furthermore, the fact that digitization facilitates the merging of communication and distribution channels (through a discourse of software) demands that competition/antitrust law act to preserve the multiplicity of meaning and the antitrust of knowledge.[121] This will be no easy task, as the Microsoft case demonstrates; the allegation of technology tying and the digital converging of two software products challenges the ability of antitrust law to fathom new business methods.[122]

The intention of making competition law more prominent in the digital environment in order to open access to discourse is evidenced by the wide-reaching decision in *Alacatel v. DGI.*[123] This decision overrides the copyright owner's right in the name of misuse.[124] This doctrine is said to derive from the equitable notion of clean hands[125] (and seems to invoke constitutional enumerated

---

120 Antitrust Guidelines for the Licensing of Intellectual Property § 2.0.

121 The tradition of antitrust law in the United States and the important role it is likely to play in the digital environment highlights the fact that while it is not formally entrenched as a constitutional principle it will certainly act like one, especially in relation to intellectual property rights in software where speech restrictions have been legitimated and First Amendment challenges negatived. In this last instance antitrust law has the potential to act as a surrogate champion of open and free (digital) speech/discourse.

122 *See* United States v. Microsoft Corp., 147 F.3d 935 (D.C. Cir. 1998).

123 166 F.3d 772, *reh'g denied,* 180 F.3d 267 (5th Cir. 1999).

124 The patent of architecture is vitally important and will necessarily invoke competition law. On patent misuse and associated anti-competitive conduct, see Vitamin Technologists, Inc. v. Wisconsin Alumni Research Found., 146 F.2d 941, 946-47, 956 (9th Cir.), *cert. denied* 325 U.S. 876 (1945); United States v. General Elec. Co., 272 U.S. 476 (1926); United States v. Line Materials Co., 333 U.S. 287 (1945); General Talking Pictures Corp. v. Western Elec. Co., 304 U.S. 175, *reaff'd on reh'g,* 305 U.S. 124 (1938); Herbert Hovenkamp, Federal Antitrust Policy: The Law of Competition and its Practice 218-25 (1994); Philip E. Areeda & Louis Kaplow, Antitrust Analysis: Problems, Text and Cases 182-85 n.428 (4th ed. 1988); Intergraph Corp. v. Intel Corp., 3 F. Supp. 2d 1255 (N.D. Ala. 1998), *vacated* 195 F.3d 1346 (Fed. Cir. 1999); Data Gen. Corp. v. Grumman Sys. Support Corp., 36 F.3d 1147 (1st Cir. 1994); Image Technical Servs., Inc. v. Eastman Kodak Co., 125 F.3d 1195 (9th Cir. 1997); *In re* Independent Serv. Orgs. Antitrust Litig., 203 F.3d 1322 (Fed. Cir. (Kan.) 2000).

125 *See* Morton Salt Co. v. G.S. Suppiger Co., 314 U.S. 488, 492 (1942) ("It is a principle of general application that courts, and especially courts of equity, may appropriately withhold their aid where the plaintiff is using the right asserted contrary to the public interest."); SEC v. United States Realty Co., 310 U.S. 434, 455 (1940); United States v. Morgan, 307 U.S. 183, 194 (1939); Virginian Ry. Co. v. System Fed'n No. 40, 300 U.S. 515, 552 (1937); Central Ky. Natural Gas Co. v. Railroad Comm'n of Ky., 290 U.S. 264, 270 (1933);

powers rhetoric[126]) inherent in copyright and patent law. While the doctrine of misuse is said not to emanate directly from competition/antitrust law, such law surely defines its motivation.

1. *Alcatel USA, Inc. v. DGI Technologies, Inc.*: Copyright Misuse[127]

The facts of the case concerned telephone switching systems that were designed, made, and sold by DSC (which later became Alcatel) to long-distance telephone service providers, such as MCI and Sprint.[128] DSC switches were controlled by its copyrighted operating system software that, unlike the switches, was not sold but licensed to users on the following terms:

> (1) the operating system software remains the property of DSC; (2) the customer has the right to use the software only to operate its switch; (3) the customer is prohibited from copying the software or disclosing it to third parties; and (4) the customers are authorized to use the software only in conjunction with DSC-manufactured equipment.[129]

DSC's customers frequently needed to expand the call-handling capacity of their switches and often achieved the expansion by adding groups of "cards" to the switch. In 1989, DGI was founded to design and sell expansion cards for use with DSC switches. Prior to 1989, however, DSC was the only manufacturer of such cards.[130]

DGI claimed that it developed its cards by reverse engineering DSC's unpatented products and then duplicating their functionality to achieve a better-designed card using newer-generation electronics and including additional features. DSC asserted that "DGI

Harrisonville v. W.S. Dickey Clay Mfg. Co., 289 U.S. 334, 337 (1933); Beasley v. Texas & Pac. Ry. Co., 191 U.S. 492, 497 (1903).

126 *See Morton Salt*, 314 U.S. at 492.

> The grant to the inventor of the special privilege of a patent monopoly carries out a public policy adopted by the Constitution and laws of the United States, 'to promote the Progress of Science and useful Arts, by securing for limited Times to . . . Inventors the exclusive Right . . . .' to their 'new and useful' inventions. But the public policy which includes inventions within the granted monopoly excludes from it all that is not embraced in the invention. It equally forbids the use of the patent to secure an exclusive right or limited monopoly not granted by the Patent Office and which it is contrary to public policy to grant.

Id.

127 For a detailed introduction to this topic, see P. Goldstein, Copyright ch. 9.6 (2d ed. 1999); Melville B. Nimmer & David Nimmer, Nimmer on Copyright § 13.09, at 13-284 (1999).

128 *See Alcatel*, 166 F.3d at 777-80. "A telephone switch routes long distance telephone calls to their destinations." *Id.* at 777.

129 *Id.*

130 *Id.*

did not engage in legitimate reverse engineering, but rather misappropriated DSC's intellectual property by wrongfully obtaining schematics and manuals provided only to DSC customers on the express condition that there be no disclosure to third parties."[131]

> [B]etween 1992 and 1994, DGI developed and introduced four DSC-compatible cards—the Digital Trunk Interface ("DTI"), the Bus Terminator ("BT"), the Digital Tone Detector ("DTD"), and the Pulse Code Modulation Interface ("PCMI"). None of these initial DGI cards were microprocessor cards. . . .
>
> When installed in a switch, a microprocessor card controls the "boot up"—that is, it downloads DSC's copyrighted operating system software into its random access memory ("RAM"). A DTI, DTD, or BT card alone cannot expand the capacity of a switch; a customer must install a group of cards together with a microprocessor card to achieve expansion. For this reason, DGI obtained DSC microprocessor cards—then known as MP-2s—in the used market to sell along with three DGI cards. This enabled DGI to offer a customer a complete expansion card complement, which it did.
>
> In 1995, as a result of a new dialing plan implemented by the Federal Communications Commission ("FCC") and customer demands for new features, DSC revised and expanded its operating system software. These changes required DSC customers to upgrade to a new microprocessor card—the MP-8. As few MP-8 cards were available on the used market, DGI was no longer able to offer a complete card complement. Its marketing problems were exacerbated by DSC's practice of offering substantial discounts to customers who purchased whole complements of cards from DSC, but charging much higher prices for individual MP-8 cards. This motivated DGI to develop its own microprocessor card—the DMP-2800.
>
> To develop a microprocessor card, DGI had to overcome several difficulties. First, DGI needed to understand DSC's firmware. For this purpose, DGI purchased an MP-8 card and, using a "burner" to remove the DSC firmware from a memory chip, obtained the machine-readable object code. DGI engineers then used a process called "disassembly" to convert the firmware into human-readable form. In this way, DGI was able to write its own firmware—which it claims is not substantially similar to DSC's firmware—for its DMP-2800 microprocessor card. DSC asserts that DGI violated the copyright on its firmware when it copied DSC's firmware several times in this process.

[131] *Id.*

> Second, the DGI microprocessor card had to accept a download from the switch of the DSC operating system. To obtain the software needed for this function, several DGI engineers took an MP-8 card to NTS Communications ("NTS"), a DSC switch owner/ software licensee and DGI customer. There, Ernie Carrasco, an NTS employee who also consulted for DGI, placed the MP-8 card into an NTS switch and copied the operating system to a laptop computer. DGI engineers then took the laptop back to DGI. DSC maintains that DGI never told NTS that it was copying and removing DSC's copyrighted software, only that it was "testing" MP-8 cards.
>
> DGI engineers returned to NTS several times to test MP-8 cards containing versions of DGI's firmware. To avoid having to perform all this testing at NTS, DGI modified an MP-8 card to include a device called a "punch" card or "snooper" card, which monitored the firmware during the operating system download. Using this snooper card, DGI was able to understand which parts of the DSC firmware were accessed during the "boot" of the operating system. DSC maintains that DGI used this snooper card to copy the messages contained in DSC's copyrighted operating system software. It insists that, but for DGI's "theft" of DSC's operating system, it would have been extremely expensive and time-consuming for DGI to develop its own microprocessor card.
>
> DGI counters that the copy was used only to discern the size of the operating system download to the MP-8 card, as it was investigating the possibility of upgrading the older MP-2 card. DGI insists that, as the content of the software was irrelevant in determining its size, it never even disassembled the operating system software from unreadable machine language. DSC filed suit in 1994, alleging that DGI had misappropriated its trade secrets and engaged in unfair competition . . . .[132]

DGI counterclaimed, asserting among other things, that DSC had breached the Sherman Act "by monopolizing the relevant product market for expansion products compatible with DSC telephone switches."[133]

In 1995, DSC filed a supplemental complaint, asserting direct and indirect copyright infringement claims. . . . After a three week trial, the jury returned a mixed verdict, finding that DSC violated the Sherman Act . . . and that DGI infringed certain DSC copyrights, engaged in unfair competition by misappropriating DSC's time, labor, skill, and money, and misappropriated DSC's trade

---

[132] *Id.* at 778-79.
[133] *Id.*

secrets. The jury also determined that both parties had "unclean hands."[134]

Nine months later, in November 1997, the district court entered its Final Judgment and Permanent Injunction dismissing DGI's antitrust claim. The court stated that DGI had "failed to prove the relevant product market" as required under *Eastman Kodak Co. v. Image Technical Services, Inc.*[135] It "permanently enjoined DGI from developing any new microprocessor cards with the assistance of DSC's operating system software and from selling any other DGI microprocessor card designed to use DSC's software."[136] The court further ordered DGI to turn over all DMP-2800 microprocessor cards to DSC for destruction, staying the order pending resolution of any appeal. DGI appealed, and DSC cross-appealed.

a. Copyright Misuse

On appeal to the Fifth Circuit Court of Appeals, DGI reasserted its claim that even assuming that it committed acts of copyright infringement, the "copyright misuse" doctrine precluded injunctive relief based on that infringement.[137] In accepting this argument, the court explained the doctrine and its application in this way:

> This doctrine—which has its historical roots in the unclean hands defense—"bars a culpable plaintiff from prevailing on an action for the infringement of the misused copyright." It "forbids the use of the [copyright] to secure an exclusive right or limited monopoly not granted by the [Copyright] Office and which it is contrary to public policy to grant." The copyright misuse defense is analogous to the patent misuse defense, which was originally recognized by the Supreme Court in *Morton Salt Co. v. G.S. Suppiger.* The Fourth Circuit was the first to extend

---

[134] *Id.* at 779-80.

[135] *Id.* at 780. "The offense of monopoly under § 2 of the Sherman Act has two elements: (1) the possession of monopoly power in the relevant market and (2) the willful acquisition or maintenance of that power as distinguished from growth or development as a consequence of a superior product, business acumen, or historic accident." *Id.* at 781 (quoting Eastman Kodak Co. v. Image Technical Servs., Inc., 504 U.S. 451 at 481 (1992)) (internal quotes omitted).

[136] *Alcatel*, 166 F.3d at 780.

[137] *Id.* at 794. DGI's antitrust claim was also dismissed on appeal. The court explained:

> We are convinced that DGI, like the plaintiff in *United Farmers*, is trying to define the market as narrowly as possible (in order to make it look as if [defendant] had market power). Because (1) DGI did not present legally sufficient evidence that DSC's customers faced significant information and switching costs, and (2) DGI's proffered relevant market does not comport with market realities, its aftermarket monopoly claim fails as a matter of law.

Id. at 784.

the rationale behind patent misuse to copyrights. In *Lasercomb America, Inc. v. Reynolds*, the Fourth Circuit explained that, whereas "copyright law [seeks] to increase the store of human knowledge and arts by rewarding . . . authors with the exclusive rights to their works for a limited time . . ., the granted monopoly power does not extend to property not covered by the . . copyright."

. . . .

We agree with the *DSC I* panel's conjecture and the jury's finding that DSC's licensing agreement for its operating system constitutes misuse. The district court instructed the jury, in pertinent part:

> If DSC has used its copyrights to indirectly gain commercial control over products DSC does not have copyrighted, then copyright misuse may be present. The grant to the author of the special privilege of a copyright carries out a public policy adopted by the Constitution and laws of the United States, "to promote the Progress of Science and useful arts, by securing for limited Times to [Authors] . . . the exclusive Right . . ." to their "original" works. But the public policy which includes original works within the granted monopoly excludes from it all that is not embraced in the original expression. It equally forbids the use of the copyright to secure an exclusive right or limited monopoly not granted by the Copyright Office and which is contrary to public policy to grant.

A reasonable juror could conclude, based on the licensing agreement, that "DSC has used its copyrights to indirectly gain commercial control over products DSC does not have copyrighted," namely, its microprocessor cards. The facts on which we based our misuse prediction in *DSC I* have not changed substantially. As we reasoned then:

> Any competing microprocessor card developed for use on DSC phone switches must be compatible with DSC's copyrighted operating system software. In order to ensure that its card is compatible, a competitor such as DGI must test the card on a DSC phone switch. Such a test necessarily involves making a copy of DSC's copyrighted operating system, which copy is downloaded into the card's memory when the card is booted up. If DSC is allowed to prevent such copying, then it can prevent anyone from developing a competing microprocessor card, even though it has not patented the card.

Under these facts, DSC's assertion that its licensing agreement does not prohibit the independent development of compatible software is simply irrelevant. Despite the presence of

> some evidence—the testimony of a DSC executive—that DGI could have developed its own software, there was also evidence that it was not technically feasible to use a non-DSC operating system because the switch has a "common control" scheme in which each microprocessor card in a network of such cards runs the same operating system. Hence, without the freedom to test its cards in conjunction with DSC's software, DGI was effectively prevented from developing its product, thereby securing for DSC a limited monopoly over its uncopyrighted microprocessor cards. Furthermore, the jury instructions never mentioned that misuse could only be present if DSC's agreement prohibited the independent development of software. Consequently, we conclude that the district court abused its discretion in awarding injunctive relief based on DGI's infringing acts.[138]

This doctrine has the potential to play a significant role in determining the scope of proprietary rights in software. It will normally arise as a defense to an action for copyright infringement, and it is apparently broader in scope than antitrust law. The copyright misuse defense, is idiosyncratic yet potentially broad-reaching in its operation, and will most likely take its primary (but not sole) definition from fundamental principles of antitrust law. *Alcatel* highlights how effective copyright misuse will be in defining the ambit of copyright in software, and provides an avenue for assessing the property right and associated actions against other fundamental values, such as free and open discourse.

IV. POWER[139] AND THE NEW CONSTITUTIONALISM

Traditionally, constitutionalism (which means the regulation of power) has focused on regulating or limiting the vertical exercise of government or public power over the citizen.[140] On the other hand, the horizontal exercise of power between citizens has occurred in the private sphere and has been rarely analyzed in terms of power or constitutionalism, although the (largely common) law has played a mediating role.

The writing of Michel Foucault informed us that power was not just something exercised by sovereign entities like the state, but that power relations were everywhere. As Foucault explained:

---

138 *Id.* at 792-94 (internal cites and footnotes omitted).

139 *See generally* JORDAN, *supra* note 2.

140 "Constitutionalism refers to implicit and or explicit limits on political or state decision making, limits which can be procedural or substantive. Constitutionalism defines the proper forms and limits of state action." D. Held, *The Development of the Modern State, in* FORMATIONS OF MODERNITY 71, 89 (S. Hall & B. Gieben eds., 1992).

> What I mean is this: in a society such as ours, but basically in any society, there are manifold relations of power which permeate characterise and constitute the social body, and these relations of power cannot themselves be established, consolidated nor implemented without the production, accumulation, circulation and functioning of a discourse. . . . We are subjected to the production of truth through power and we cannot exercise power except through the production of truth. . . . Power never ceases its interrogation, its inquisition, its registration of truth: it institutionalises, professionalises and rewards its pursuit. In the last analysis, we must produce truth as we must produce wealth, indeed we must produce truth in order to produce wealth . . .[141]

This redefinition of power raises our awareness that power is ubiquitous in our daily lives and demands a reassessment of the mechanism, methodology, or epistemological framework that we invoke for understanding the role and effect of power within our world.

It seems that the nature and role of corporate power, combined with the information revolution (especially increasing reliance on digitized information) and the growth of transnational civil society, have motivated arguments that talk about the exercise of power in the private sphere in terms of the regulation of power or constitutionalism. Interestingly, the three-dimensional process of Congress/Parliament regulating (vertical) the power relations of private citizens (horizontal) is starting to be more vigorously questioned (at least in the United States) in terms of constitutionalism.

In the United States, the First Amendment, along with a generous view of the notion of state action,[142] has the potential to intersect with legislatively mediated power relations between individuals[143] in the private sphere.[144] In other countries, like my

---

141 FOUCAULT, *supra* note 18, at 93.

> Every relation of force implies at each moment a relation of power (which is in a sense its momentary expression) and every power relation makes a reference, as its effect but also as its condition of possibility, to a political field of which it forms a part. To say that 'everything is political,' is to affirm this ubiquity of relations of force and their immanence in a political field . . . .

Id. at 189.

142 *See, e.g.*, Shelley v. Kraemer, 334 U.S. 1 (1948) (holding that state court enforcement of restrictive covenants excluding certain races from purchasing real property was sufficient state action); *cf.* Flagg Bros., Inc. v. Brooks, 436 U.S. 149 (1978) (holding that a proposed sale by a warehouseman made pursuant to the New York Uniform Commercial Code did not constitute state action); TRIBE, *supra* note 51, at n.1711.

143 This could be categorized as horizontal, as opposed to vertical, constitutionalism. *See* P. Bernt Hugenholtz, *Copyright and Freedom of Expression in Europe*, Paper presented at the NYU Law School Engelberg Centre in Florence (Spring 1998) (copy on file with author of paper) (publication forthcoming).

own, the statutory (e.g., copyright) or common law (e.g., contract) rules that mediate relations between individuals in the private sphere are largely beyond constitutional review by the courts.[145] In Australia, this is a product of the Westminster notion of parliamentary sovereignty: Parliament can make or unmake any law and it is through Parliament and the common law that rights are protected. I am trying to convince my colleagues that power relations in the private sphere—in particular, those defined by information law—are fundamental constitutional issues that should be informed by fundamental constitutional principles, like freedom of discourse.[146] In the United States, a new generation of scholars is showing that the First Amendment will inform the private sphere in this regard by arguing that the DMCA, proposed database legislation, and UCITA are infringing principles of free speech[147] (although I do not think they have got to the Patent Act—yet!).[148]

---

144 It has been suggested that the First Amendment to the U.S. Constitution, the right to free speech, will play a role in determining the constitutional validity of database legislation; as will the limiting scope of Article 1, Section 8, Clause 8 of the U.S. Constitution (in part, the copyright head of legislative power). *See* Marci A. Hamilton, *Database Protection and the Circuitous Route around the United States Constitution, in* INTERNATIONAL INTELLECTUAL PROPERTY AND THE COMMON LAW WORLD (Charles Rickett & G. Austin eds., 2000); William Patry, *The Enumerated Powers Doctrine and Intellectual Property: An Imminent Constitutional Collision*, 67 GEO. WASH. L. REV. 359 (1999). On the limiting scope of Article 1, Section 8, Clause 8, see Bonito Boats, Inc. v. Thundercraft Boats, Inc., 489 U.S. 141, 146 (1989); Graham v. John Deere Co., 383 U.S. 1, 5 (1966).

145 For an excellent overview of the position in Europe, see Hugenholtz, *supra* note 143.

146 *See* Brian F. Fitzgerald, *Software as Discourse? A Constitutionalism for Information Society*, *supra* note 32, at 144; *see also* Associated Press v. United States, 326 U.S. 1, 20 (1945) ("Freedom of the press from governmental interference under the First Amendment does not sanction repression of that freedom by private interests."); EUGEN EHRLICH, FUNDAMENTAL PRINCIPLES OF THE SOCIOLOGY OF LAW (W.L. Moll, trans., Arno Press 1975) (1936); BRIAN F. FITZGERALD, AUSTRALIAN CONSTITUTIONALISM (manuscript on file with author); ANTHONY GIDDENS, THE CONSTITUTION OF SOCIETY (1984); ALAN HUNT, FOUCAULT AND LAW: TOWARDS A SOCIOLOGY OF LAW AS GOVERNANCE (1994); ALLAN C. HUTCHINSON, WAITING FOR CORAF: A CRITIQUE OF LAW AND RIGHTS (1995); Brian F. Fitzgerald, *Principles of Australian Constitutionalism*, 1(2) *Proceedings of the 49th ALTA Conference* 799 (1994), *available from* Australasian Law Teachers Association, <http://www.austlii.edu.au/au/special/alta/index.html>.

147 *See, e.g.*, Benkler, *supra* note 110, at 354; Hamilton, *supra* note 144; LESSIG, CODE AND OTHER LAWS OF CYBERSPACE, *supra* note 55; *cf.* Netanel, *Copyright and a Democratic Civil Society*, 106 YALE L.J. 283 (1996). For an overview of arguments, see GOLDSTEIN, *supra* note 127, at ch. 103; NIMMER & NIMMER, *supra* note 127, § 1.10. For established case law arguably in conflict with this view, see San Francisco Arts & Athletics, Inc. v. United States Olympics Comm'n, 483 U.S. 522 (1987); Harper & Row Publishers Inc. v. Nation Enters., 471 U.S. 539 (1985); Zacchini v. Scripps-Howard Broad. Co., 433 U.S. 562 (1977).

148 On challenges to the Patent Act, see Bloomer v. McQuewan, 55 U.S. 539 (1852); Jordan v. Dobson, 13 F. Cas. 1092, 1095-96 (C.C.E.D. Penn. 1870); The Fire-Extinguisher Case, Graham v. Johnston, 21 F. 40, 42 (C.C.D. Md. 1884); Bloomer v. Stolley, 3 F. Cas. 729 (C.C.D. Ohio 1850); Blanchard's Gun-Stock Turning Factory v. Warner, 3 F. Cas. 653, 657 (C.C.D. Conn. 1846); Blanchard v. Sprague, 3 F. Cas. 648 (C.C.D. Mass. 1839); Evans v. Jordan, 8 F. Cas. 872 (C.C.D. Va. 1813); Richard M. Cooper, *Legislative Patent Extensions*, 48 FOOD & DRUG L.J. 59 (1993). I owe thanks to Jonathan Zittrain and members of the Berkman Center at Harvard Law School for pointing out these authorities. For an Austratian perspective on this issue, see The Grain Pool of Western Australia v. The Commonwealth,

The pervasiveness of the digital environment of the information age and its discursive nature (along with the ever-increasing importance of corporate power and globalization) has forced a reassessment of where constitutionalism starts and finishes. The interesting question is how far the United States Supreme Court, through the act of balancing or scrutiny, will travel into civil society to determine constitutionality (of legislation like the Copyright Act or the Patent Act, which impose restrictions on digital speech).[149] In the challenge to and subsequent scrutiny of this type of legislation, we will see the U.S. Supreme Court draw the boundaries of (public) constitutionalism for the information age. In other countries the new constitutionalism will depend on courts realizing that fundamental issues of copyright, patent, contract, and competition/antitrust laws are the constitutional questions of the information age. In these other countries, shepherding constitutional lawyers from atoms to bits may not ride on the back of or enter through the spectrum of First Amendment jurisprudence[150] but rather will come from a broader appreciation of the dynamic constitutive choices to be made in adjudicating upon issues of interpretation of the private law.

The limits of information law and, in particular, rights in digital architecture, raise important issues of constitutionalism. In appreciating software as discourse, we start to see the importance of the new communicative structures to our social and cultural being and to the question of constitutionalism.

Conclusion: The Challenge

As we enter the digital (discursive?[151]) millennium, it is ever

[2000] HCA 14 para. 133 n.218 (March 23, 2000) (Kirby, J.) (visited June 28, 2000) <http://www.austlii.edu.au>.

149 Like an arm reaching out, the First Amendment, along with the notions of state action and enforceable judicial review, gives public constitutionalism the potential in the digital era to touch what traditionally may have been regarded as private rights/affairs between two citizens. The growth of corporate power and its pivotal role in ordering the digital environment mean this further exploration of private power relations will be fiercely pursued.

150 In the sense that the digital environment is a new discourse, in the United States, the First Amendment has the potential to play a dominant role. However, this should not blind people in the United States to the fact that other areas of (non constitutional) law such as antitrust law have an important role to play, especially where First Amendment challenge has been negatived by lawful commodification of software/information through intellectual property rights. And in this instance the constitutional principle of a free and open discourse will be implemented through interpretation of non-constitutional antitrust law.

151 It may be more appropriate to say we are entering the discursive millennium as convergence and digitization make us ever more reliant on digital discursive frameworks like software. And this suggests that our paradigm of thought will rapidly and necessarily move

more pressing for us (especially as lawyers) to fathom the genetic structure/code (natural and manufactured) of life. Here I have highlighted how software will act to construct us and how the law will facilitate such a process. The task is for us to appreciate this perspective in the development of (information) law.

beyond (as it no doubt has started to do) the sacred yet rudimentary notion of freedom of speech to something more intimately concerned with the free and open nature of discursive frameworks and practices. Ultimately then, the spectrum—or should I say the transporter—that will move constitutional scholars from atoms to bits may not be the First Amendment but a broader understanding of communicative architecture and how software, digitization and informationalism are coming to inhabit most everything we do!

CULTURAL PROPERTY, INTERNATIONAL TRADE AND HUMAN RIGHTS

JOHN HENRY MERRYMAN*

"Cultural Property Trade Law" is a phrase that some might think anomalous. Most source nations[1] have laws that, in practice, prohibit or sharply limit the export of cultural objects. The primary purpose of these retentionist laws is to keep cultural objects from leaving the national territory.[2] Such laws *oppose* trade in cultural property.

Although history reveals earlier examples, laws restricting international trade in cultural property were widely adopted by source nations only in the present century, and an international group of scholars seriously interested in the field did not begin to coalesce until the 1970s. The first major international legislation on the topic, the *UNESCO Convention on the Means of Prohibiting and Preventing the Illicit Import, Export, and Transfer of Ownership of cultural Property*,[3] was promulgated in 1970 and was supplemented in 1994 by the *UNIDROIT Convention on Stolen or Illegally Exported Cultural Objects*.[4] The leading scholarly journal, the *International Journal of Cultural Property*,[5] began publication only in 1992. Cultural property trade law is still an infant.

---

* Sweitzer Professor of Law and Affiliated Professor of Art, Emeritus, Stanford University. I am grateful to Sabino Cassese, Antonio d'Atena, Erik Jayme and Miriam Siekevitz for their suggestions and criticisms.

1 "Source nations" are the sources of cultural objects for which there is a world market. When they leave source nations, cultural objects flow to "market nations." Many nations, obviously, are both exporters and importers of cultural objects, but if the trade were unimpeded by export controls it would seldom be in balance. Thus, under present world conditions Italy would be a heavy net exporter of cultural property and Switzerland a substantial net importer.

2 *See* John Henry Merryman, *The Retention of Cultural Property,* 21 U.C. DAVIS L. REV. 477 (1988) (discussing retentionism in cultural property policy), *reprinted* in John Henry Merryman, *Thinking About the Elgin Marbles: Critical Essays on Cultural Property, Art and Law* 122 (2000) [hereinafter *Critical Essays*].

3 *See* Convention on the Means of Prohibiting and Preventing the Illicit, Import, Export, and Transfer of Ownership of Cultural Property, Nov. 14, 1970, 823 U.N.T.S. 231, 10 I.L.M. 289 (1971), *available at* http://www.unesco.org/culture/laws/1970/html_eng/page1.htm (last visited Nov. 27, 2000) [hereinafter 1970 UNESCO Convention].

4 *See* Convention on Stolen or Illegally Exported Cultural Objects, *opened for signature* June 24, 1995, *reprinted in* 34 I.L.M. 1322 (1995), *available at* http://www.unidroit.org/english/conventions/c-cult.htm (last visited Nov. 27, 2000) [hereinafter 1995 UNIDROIT Convention].

5 The *International Journal of Cultural Property*, published by Oxford University Press since 1998, is "a major forum for the discussion of all questions relating to cultural prop-

As a new field of study, cultural property trade law understandably lacks consistency, coherence and elegance. Key concepts have not been refined. Important questions await legislative, judicial and scholarly attention. Interested parties take stances that harden into inflexible positions, and there is little fruitful dialogue between them.[6] As signs of a possible escape from this *impasse,* I will describe some foreign developments that may significantly affect international cultural property law in the coming decades. Two oddly paired forces are driving these developments. One is the international commitment to free trade. The other is the international commitment to protect human rights and fundamental freedoms. We look first at free trade.

Free Trade

In discussing trade in cultural objects, it is important to understand that we deal only with the voluntary transfer of privately held works. Art works, antiquities, historical objects and other articles of cultural property in museums, monuments, public collections and storehouses do not figure significantly in international trade. It is trade in cultural objects in private hands—principally private individual and corporate collections and the stocks of dealers and auction houses—with which we are here concerned.[7]

National Treasures. What is (and what is not) a "national treasure?" The answer to that question has been made important by the growing international commitment to free trade and by the awkward position that cultural objects occupy in relation to that commitment. The two major international agreements underlying trade liberalization, the European Union Treaty ("EU Treaty")[8]

erty policy, ethics, preservation, economics and law." *International Journal of Cultural Property, at* http://www3.oup.co.uk/intjcp/scope (last visited Nov. 27, 2000).

6 *See* John Henry Merryman, *The Free International Movement of Cultural Property,* 31 N.Y.U. J. Int'l L. & Pol. 1 (1998) (describing the ideologies and discourses at play in the cultural property dialogue), *reprinted in Critical Essays, supra* note 2.

7 I do not here focus on the special problems raised by trade in archaeological objects, which are discussed in an earlier article: John Henry Merryman, *A Licit International Trade in Cultural Objects,* 4 Int'l J. Cultural Prop. 13 (1995), *reprinted in both* International Chamber of Commerce, Legal Aspects of International Trade in Art 3 (Martine Briat & Judith A. Freedberg eds., 1996), and *Critical Essays, supra* note 2.

8 *See* Treaty on European Union, Feb. 7, 1992, 31 I.L.M. 247 [hereinafter EU Treaty]. The EU Treaty renamed and amended the Treaty of Rome, Treaty Establishing the European Economic Community, Mar. 25, 1957, 298 U.N.T.S. 11, and established the Economic and Monetary Union (EMU). The EU Treaty required ratification by member states, which sometimes was politically difficult (in France, the referendum passed by 51%, and Denmark rejected it, and hence the EMU, by referendum). It entered into force on November 1, 1993. Further amendments to the EU Treaty were made in the Treaty of Amsterdam, Oct. 2, 1997, 1977 O.J. (C340)1.

and the World Trade Organization ("WTO"),[9] both prohibit export controls on "goods," which the European Court of Justice ("ECJ") has expressly held includes works of art and other cultural objects.[10]

While generally prohibiting export controls, both treaties—the EU Treaty in Article 30 and WTO in Article XX—make an express exception for restrictions "imposed for the protection of national treasures[11] possessing artistic, historic, or archaeological importance."[12] Cultural property export controls that "protect national treasures" accordingly do not violate European Union or World Trade Organization members' treaty obligations. Restrictions on the export of cultural objects that do not meet the definition of "national treasures," however, would presumably be found invalid by the ECJ. And so we need to know what is a "national treasure." For convenience I will discuss the EU Treaty and assume that similar considerations apply to the equivalent, and practically identical, WTO provisions.

One arguable approach is to accept whatever the source nation's authorities designate to be a "national treasure." After all, the argument might go, who is better qualified to decide what has the kind of national importance implied by the term "treasure" than the representatives of that nation itself? That approach would avoid the necessity, difficulty and uncertainty cost of making and justifying distinctions between one cultural object and another. Is it likely that such a *laissez-faire* approach to the problem will prevail?

Treasures? As yet there have been no decisions on the meaning of "treasures" by the ECJ. We do, however, have a number of scholarly contributions to the subject, including a leading article by

---

9 *See* General Agreement on Tariffs and Trade 1994 ("GATT"), Apr. 15, 1994, Marrakesh Agreement Establishing the World Trade Organization ("WTO"), Annex 1A, Final Act Embodying the Results of the Uruguay Round of Multilateral Trade Negotiations 21, 33 I.L.M. 1125, 1154 [hereinafter WTO].

10 The European Court of Justice held in Case 7/68, Commission v. Italy, [1968] E.C.R. 617 [1969] C.M.L.R. 1 at 8, Common Mkt. Rep. (CCH) 8057, at 7881 (1968), that works of art are "goods" within the meaning of the EU Treaty and thus, in principle, subject to the same trade liberalizing rules as other "goods."

11 The English version of the EU Treaty uses "national treasures," as does the French version. The German version is *nationales Kulturgut* and the Italian is *patrimonio nazionale. See* Andrea Biondi, *The Merchant, the Thief & the Citizen: The Circulation of Works of Art within the European Union*, 34 COMMON MKT. L. REV. 1173 (1997) (commenting on this difference in nomenclature). "However, there is no doubt that the definition should be uniform, and considering the ECJ's case law on other exceptions, it might be argued that the expression 'national treasures' should be preferred as it is narrower." *See id.* at n.27.

12 EU Treaty, *supra* note 8, at art. 30; WTO, *supra* note 9, at art. XX.

Pierre Pescatore, published while he was a Judge of the ECJ.[13] Judge Pescatore's position is clear and firm: "exceptions from the rules barring export controls are to be strictly construed."[14] The term "treasures" must be treated as restrictive. It cannot apply to the generality of cultural objects, but only to those having unusual value because of their uniqueness and their importance to a people. The purpose of the exception, according to Judge Pescatore, is not to preserve the totality of an artistic patrimony, but to safeguard its "essential and fundamental elements."[15] In speaking of works of art another scholar, Professor Biondi, states that: "[o]nly when the object is of outstanding artistic importance, can it qualify as a 'national treasure, regardless of its connection with a certain country.'"[16] A third scholar, Dr. Carducci, draws attention to the principle of proportionality:

> Les mesures de protection nationales sont conditionnées au principe de proportionnalité entre la nécessité de la mesure et son résultat effectif, eu égard surtout à l'interdiction que ces mesures aboutissent à des discriminations arbitraires ou des restrictions déguisées.[17]

Assuming that these observers are right, would an ancient vase of no particular distinction, one of many that for most purposes are unremarkable and fungible, be considered a "treasure?" What about the allegedly huge numbers of redundant antiquities in storehouses in major source nations? Picasso made thousands of paintings and sculptures. Is every one of them a "treasure?" Every

---

13 *See* Pierre Pescatore, *Le commerce de l'art et le Marché commun*, 21 REVUE TRIMESTRIELLE DE DROIT EUROPEEN 451 (1985).

14 *Id.* at 455. Judge Pescatore was a member of the Court when it decided *Commission*, [1969] C.M.L.R. 1 at 10 (deciding that Article 30 exceptions must be strictly interpreted); *see also* Biondi, *supra* note 11, at 1178-79 (adding that the burden is on the nation to justify the reliance on the exception).

15 Pescatore, *supra* note 13, at 456. We are given additional guidance concerning the effective scope of the Article 30 exception for "treasures" by European Council Directive 93/7 of 15 Mar. 1993, which provides for "the return of cultural objects unlawfully removed from the territory of a member state." Council Directive 93/7 1993 O.J. (L 74) 74. The Annex to the Directive lists categories to which objects classified as national treasures "within the limits of Article 30 of the Treaty" must belong in order to qualify for return. For example, an oil painting must not only meet the Article 30 definition of a "national treasure," but it must also be more than fifty years old, must not belong to its creator, and must have a value of at least 150,000 ecus. *See* Biondi, *supra* note 11, at 1182ff.

16 Biondi, *supra* note 11, at 1181. *See* MANLIO FRIGO, *Gli Aspetti Giurdici*, *in* ISTITUTO REGIONALE DI RICERCA DELLA LOMBARDIA, IL MERCATO DELLE OPERE D'ARTE ED I PROBLEMI DELLA CIRCOLAZIONE A LIVELLO EUROPEPO 77 (Franco Angeli ed., 1995) (providing a discussion that adopts a less strict interpretation of the Article 30 exception).

17 GUIDO CARDUCCI, LA RESTITUTION INTERNATIONALE DES BIENS CULTURELS ET DES OBJECTS D'ART (1997) at 90 ["National protective measures involve balancing the need for the measures and their efficacy with the need to ensure that such measures do not result in arbitrary discrimination or disguised restrictions."].

Fra Angelico? Every Monet? Or, as Dr. Carducci, in speaking of France, has put it: *La question reste posée de savoir si ce vaste ensemble d'objets peut rentrer dans la notion, en soi assez élitaire, de "tresor national" au sens de [l'article 30].*[18]

Perhaps the matter is better approached from another direction. Suppose we were called upon to list the "treasures"—the "essential and fundamental" elements of the artistic patrimony of a nation? How would we go about it? Recall that we are talking about privately held objects. How many cultural objects in private hands in the United States would be considered "essential and fundamental" elements of the American artistic patrimony? Thousands? Hundreds? A dozen or two? A mere handful?

National? The term "national" adds another problem of interpretation. Does "national" refer to the State territory in which the object was created? Where it was found? The nationality of its creator? The place it represents or to which it refers? Is a gold platter made in Greece, but found in Sicily, Greek or Italian or both?[19] Whatever "national" is taken to mean, could water colors of Austrian scenes painted by Adolf Hitler, held in a private Italian collection, be considered Italian national treasures? Was Italy's refusal to permit export of the Hitler watercolors justified under the EU Treaty?[20] How about Italy's *notificazione* of a Matisse painting of a French interior, painted in France,[21] or the van Gogh painting *le Jardinière,* also painted in France?[22] Would the ECJ agree with the French authorities that a painting of a Turkish scene by the Swiss artist Jean-Etienne Liotard was a French national treasure?[23] How about a Chinese jar of the Yuan period,[24] and a group of drawings by Italian artists[25] for which export permits were refused by French authorities? Were they French national treasures?

We do not know the definitive answers to these questions,

---

18 *Id.* at 92-93 ["The question still remains as to whether this vast group of objects can be included in the selective notion of 'national treasure,' in the sense of article 30."].

19 These are the facts in United States v. An Antique Platter of Gold, 184 F.3d 131 (2d Cir. 1999).

20 *See* Alan Cowell, *Hitler's Watercolors Too Hot for Italy's Comfort,* N.Y. TIMES INT'L, Nov. 20, 1992, at A4.

21 *See* Jeanneret v. Vichey, 693 F.2d 259 (2d Cir. 1982).

22 Verusio ed altri v. Ministero per i beni culturali ed ambientali ed altri, Italy, Corte cost., (14 giugno) 20 giugno 1995 n. 269, 40 Giur. It. 1918 *note* Scino *id.* 1930, Illari *id.* 3704.

23 *See Export Ban Rocks Paris,* ARTNEWSLETTER, Sept. 7, 1993, at 5.

24 *See Ministre de la culture c. Consorts Genty,* Conseil D'Etat 7 Oct. 1987, 1988 D. Jur. 269, note J. Laveissière.

25 *See Talleyrand-Périgord,* Conseil D'Etat, Ass. 12 Déc. 1969, J.C.P. 1972.II.17105, note A.-H Mesnard.

since these cases have not been taken to the ECJ,[26] which has the ultimate power to distinguish between "treasures" and other cultural objects, and to decide whether a disputed object, even if it is a "treasure," is also "national." If and when they occur, such cases will provide clamorous litigation, and the ultimate decisions will excite strong emotions. It will be interesting to see what happens.

Protection. Recall that in the EU Treaty the exception from trade liberalization rules applies to restrictions imposed for the "protection" of national treasures. That makes it necessary to consider what "protection" means. Here again it seems possible that the ECJ might decide to accept national usage and decline to impose a uniform rule or standard. In fact, however, it has already done otherwise. In *Commission v. Italy,*[27] in response to Italy's claim that the export tax on works of art was a protective measure, the Court disagreed, stating that the tax had "the sole effect of rendering more onerous the exportation" of works of art "without ensuring attainment of the aim intended by [Article 30], which is to protect the artistic, historical or archaeological heritage."[28] The Court thus recognized that retention and protection are quite different concepts.

Normally, when we speak of "protection," we mean taking measures to preserve something or keep it safe from harm. When we say we want to "protect" cultural objects, it would seem that we want to: (1) preserve them from physical damage or destruction; (2) preserve meaning and information that would be lost by removal of an object from its context; and (3) preserve the integrity of complex objects by preventing their dismemberment.[29] "Protec-

---

26 In 1997, in a casual conversation with an official of the EU Commission I was told that the Commission had encouraged litigation to supply meaning to the exception for national treasures but that, for unexplained reasons, the collectors and dealers involved were reluctant to do so. Nor did he comment on the possibility that the Commission itself might bring an action, as it did in the Italian Tax case.

27 [1968] E.C.R. 617 [1969] C.M.L.R. 1 at 8, Common Mkt. Rep. (CCH) 8057, at 7881 (1968).

28 *Id.*

29 As originally drafted by the UNIDROIT Working Group, Article 5 (3) of the UNIDROIT Convention, listing the categories of illegally exported cultural objects that a foreign court should order returned to the source nation, specified two additional categories: objects of ritual/ceremonial importance to living cultures (exemplified by the U.S. Native American Graves Protection and Repatriation Act of 1990, 25 U.S.Code §§2001ff., which provides for retention by and return of cultural objects to indigenous American Indian tribes and Native Hawaiian organizations), and objects "of outstanding cultural importance for the . . . nation." *See* Merryman, *supra* note 7, at 13 (providing a fuller discussion of special treatment of ritual objects of living cultures), *reprinted in Critical Essays, supra* note 2. The logical appeal of each of these special cases is evident. When finally promulgated, however, "outstanding" had been reduced to "significant," a pallid term that deprived the clause of meaning, justifying retention of anything a State chooses. Can one conceive of an object that has "insignificant importance?" *See* John Henry Merryman, *The*

tion" clearly seems to be an appropriate term for such cases. But suppose, as is often the case, that the export of an easel painting by Tintoretto, or a coin collection or an antique ceramic offers no significant threat of physical damage, loss of information or dismemberment. If export is prohibited in such a case, is "protection" the proper term, or would "retention" be more accurate? If the question were properly presented to the ECJ, would it be likely to find that Italian denial of an export permit would "protect" the Hitler watercolors, or the Matisse or van Gogh paintings?

Of course the court might approach the meaning of "protection" in a different way, treating the totality of objects classified as "national treasures" under Article 30 as a coherent collectivity of related objects, using such terms as "cultural patrimony" or "cultural heritage" (compare the Italian version of the Treaty, in which the term is "*patrimonio nazionale,*" rather than "national treasures"). The argument would be that export restrictions protect the patrimony or heritage by keeping it whole; any removal is a dismemberment, and retention equals protection. That appears to be the basic cultural property retentionist position, but it clearly is inconsistent with the impressive scholarly interpretation of Article 30 of the EU Treaty described above.

Consider the case of the Cleveland Poussin. The Director of the Cleveland Museum bought a Poussin painting from a French collector and had it shipped to the Museum, where it now hangs. The French government protested that the painting was removed from France without an export permit and charged the Director with criminal violation of French law (the Director had impressive expert legal advice that an ambiguous passage in the French law, properly interpreted, made such a permit unnecessary, but the French authorities obviously disagreed). Eventually the matter was settled,[30] but observe what had in fact happened. A great work of art from a private collection in France, where it was unavailable for public viewing, today hangs in a public room in a great museum, where it is properly identified as a Poussin and honored as a great work of art by the important French artist. In the Cleveland Museum, the Poussin is still a Poussin. What harm has been done to this French "national treasure?" In what way would retention in the French private collection have "protected" the Poussin?

UNIDROIT Convention: Three Significant Departures from the Urtext, 5 INT'L. J. CULTURAL PROP. 7 (1996), *reprinted in Critical Essays, supra* note 2.

30 The Cleveland Poussin *affaire* never reached the courts. *See Dispute with Louvre Ends,* N.Y. TIMES, Mar. 28, 1987, at L11, col. 4 (providing a discussion of the case and its resolution).

Compare the case of the proposed export of one of Egon Schiele's most important paintings, which was being sold by its Austrian owner to a major American museum. The competent Austrian Ministry denied export permission. In overruling the Ministry, the Austrian Administrative Court said that it should have considered that the State's interest in retaining the Schiele was outweighed by its interest in propagating Austrian art abroad.[31] Such examples are of course rare. In most source nations, cultural nationalism[32] prevails; the sentiment and the rhetoric generally support the retention of cultural goods in the name of "protection." When the proper case arrives before the ECJ, will it agree? We do not know and can only speculate. Perhaps, but perhaps not.

National Ownership Laws. Up to this point we have been discussing the exception for "national treasures" in Article 30 of the EU Treaty and Article XX of WTO. We now leave those treaties and turn to another topic. In the latter half of the twentieth century, an increasing number of nations have adopted legislation declaring that broad categories of cultural objects, including those in private hands, are property of the state, or the nation, or the people. These "national ownership laws" raise interesting and as yet, unresolved questions.

Some of these laws were adopted for a reason that may not be obvious to the casual observer. It is an established principle of private international law that nations will judicially enforce foreign private law rights, including rights of ownership.[33] If a thief steals my Jackson Pollock painting in California and takes it to Canada, I can sue him in a Canadian court and recover my Pollock. In the absence of a treaty, however, a court will not enforce another nation's export controls. It is a principle of international law, ultimately based on the principles of the independence and equality of states, that courts have no obligation to enforce foreign public laws, of which export controls are obvious examples. Thus, if an Italian collector moves to New York and takes his Matisse painting with him without obtaining export permission, the American court will not, in the absence of a treaty, enforce Italy's claim for return

---

[31] *See* Austria, Administrative Court, Decision No. 2031 (A)/1951.

[32] *See* Merryman, *The Retention of Cultural Property, supra* note 2 (discussing Cultural Nationalism).

[33] Kunstsammlungen zu Weimar v. Elicofon, 678 F.2d 1150 (2d Cir. 1982) is a leading case illustrating this point. This rule is universally recognized but is, of course, subject to the rules protecting good faith purchasers. *See* French Minister of Cultural Heritage v. Italian Minister of Cultural Heritage and De Contessini, Cass. Sez. I, 24 Nov. 1995.

of the Matisse.[34] The painting was removed from Italy by its owner. No theft had occurred. No private law right was at stake.

This clear distinction between theft and illegal export becomes cloudy in the face of national ownership laws. Consider two American decisions. In the first, *U.S. v. McClain,*[35] archaeological objects taken from an undocumented Mexican site were brought by Americans into the United States for sale. This looks like a simple case of illegal export, but the applicable Mexican law states that all pre-Columbian objects found anywhere in Mexico are property of the Mexican people. The U.S. Government brought a criminal proceeding against the McClains under an American law, the "Stolen Property Act,"[36] making it a crime to transport "stolen" property in interstate or foreign commerce.

Were these objects "stolen" within the meaning of the U.S. statute? The court, looking to the Mexican law declaring that all such objects were owned by the Mexican State held that they were stolen, and the looters went to prison.[37] Despite its arguable inconsistency with the language of the 1970 UNESCO Convention[38] and with the principle that one state will not enforce another's public laws, the *McClain* case has not been overruled.

In a later case, *The Government of Peru v. Johnson,*[39] Peru brought a civil action to recover Moche objects in an American collection, alleging that they were "stolen" under Peru's law declaring such objects to be property of the State. This was clearly an attempt to extend the *McClain* doctrine. In *McClain,* the criminal action was based on the federal statute, and the Court looked to

---

34 These are the facts in an American case, Jeanneret v.Vichey, 693 F.2d 259 (2d Cir. 1982).

35 593 F.2d 658 (5th Cir. 1979) (challenging the second round of convictions for having received, concealed and/or sold stolen goods in interstate or foreign commerce and also for conspiracy to do the same).

36 *See* 18 U.S.C. § 2314 (1994).

37 *See generally McClain,* 593 F.2d 658. An earlier case, *United States v. Hollinshead,* 495 F.2d 1154 (9th Cir. 1974), concerning a Mayan Stela illegally removed from Guatemala, had resulted in a similar conviction, but the *McClain* decision more fully considered the legal questions and is the leading precedent. Observe that the United States had, in 1972, ratified the 1970 UNESCO Convention on the Means of Prohibiting and Preventing the Illicit Import, Export and Transfer of Ownership of Cultural Property. *See* 1970 UNESCO Convention, *supra* note 3. Under Article 7(b)(I), parties to the Convention agreed to prohibit the import of cultural property "stolen from a museum or a religious or secular public monument . . . provided that such property is documented as appertaining to the inventory of that institution." *Id.* This definition of "stolen" obviously would not have included the *McClain* objects and probably would not have included the *Hollinshead* Stela.

38 *See* 1970 UNESCO Convention, *supra* note 3. In 1983, Congress finally enacted legislation implementing U.S. adherence to the Convention: the Convention on Cultural Property Implementation Act, 19 U.S. Code §§2601ff. (1999). The definition of "stolen" cultural property in this legislation parallels that in the UNESCO Convention.

39 720 F.Supp. 810 (C.D. Cal. 1989). The trial court decision was affirmed on other grounds in an "unpublished" opinion at 1991 U.S. App. LEXIS 19385.

the Mexican law to help it determine the meaning of the key term "stolen" in that statute. In the *Peru* case, the action itself was based on the foreign law. This distinction was not discussed by the *Peru* Court. Instead, in considering the Peruvian law claiming national ownership, the Court stated:

> [T]he domestic effect of such a pronouncement appears to be extremely limited. Possession of the artifacts is allowed to remain in private hands, and such objects may be transferred by gift or bequest or intestate succession. There is no indication in the record that Peru has ever sought to exercise its ownership rights in such property, so long as there is no removal from the country. The laws of Peru concerning its artifacts could reasonably be considered to have no more effect than export restrictions . . . .[40]

Since the Court would not enforce Peru's export restrictions, relief was denied.

Other civil actions to recover illegally exported objects brought in US courts by foreign nations on the basis of their national ownership laws, had ended in settlements or were decided on other grounds until the *Steinhardt* case,[41] in which the Government of Italy intervened as a civil claimant, alleging ownership of the antiquity in question, a gold Phiale from Sicily.[42] The trial court held for Italy, but the appellate court affirmed on other grounds, and the question whether the *McClain* doctrine properly extends to civil actions remains open.

I have found only one case in which a nation successfully brought an action in a foreign court to assert a right of ownership based on its own national ownership law. This was a civil action by Ecuador to recover archaeological objects exported without permission to Italy, where they found their way into a private collection. Basing its decision on the language of Ecuador's antiquities legislation, the Tribunal of Torino ordered the artifacts returned to Ecuador.[43]

These three cases: *McClain, Peru* and *Danusso,* raise a host of unanswered questions about the foreign legal effects of national

---

40 *Id.*

41 *See* United States v. An Antique Platter of Gold, 184 F.3d 131 (2d Cir. 1999).

42 *See id.*

43 *See Repubblica dell'Ecuador c. Danusso, Matta ed altri,* Trib.Torino, 25 marzo 1982, 18 Riv. dir. int. priv. proc. 625 (1982). The language of the Ecuador law actually fell short of claiming ownership and was interpreted by the Italian court to create a right of *dominio eminente* in the Ecuadorian State. There is an extensive discussion of the case in Manlio Frigo, La Protezione dei beni culturali nel diritto internazionale 315ff (Milano 1986).

ownership laws. Do such laws mean what they say? Should the forum look behind the words of the foreign law to determine its meaning in application in the source nation, as the court did in *Peru*? Do such laws actually convert private property to public ownership? If so, do they satisfy constitutional requirements of notice, hearing and compensation? If the source nation seeks to exert its ownership in a foreign action, should the defendant be permitted to question the constitutionality, and thus the validity, of the law on which the plaintiff's action is based? It is time to consider individual rights and freedoms.

Individual Rights and Fundamental Freedoms

We can begin with a Costa Rican case. According to Article 3 of the Costa Rican Law on National Archaeological Patrimony of 28 December 1981, "[a]ll archaeological objects that are discovered in any way after this Law takes effect are property of the State." Does it surprise you to learn that in 1983, the Costa Rica Supreme Court found this law unconstitutional because it sought to expropriate private property without observing the procedural requirements and without awarding the compensation required by the Costa Rican Constitution?[44]

Many other nations have adopted laws declaring large categories of cultural property to be state property. If enforced, they significantly affect the market value of privately held cultural objects. Indeed, the mere prohibition of export itself reduces value, since cultural objects generally bring higher prices on the international market than on the national market. Although collectors complain, courts in source nations often reject the claim that such laws are expropriative. In Italy, for example, the Constitutional Court has on several occasions rejected such arguments.[45] The Costa Rica decision is unusual.

The topic is a very large one, which arises in every constitutional jurisdiction, since almost any public measure produces both winners and losers, and the losers naturally would prefer to be compensated. Such a question recently came before the European Court of Human Rights, under Article 1 of the First Protocol to the *European Convention for the Protection of Human Rights and Fundamental Freedoms*,[46] which provides:

---

[44] *See* Costa Rica, *Boletín Judicial* No. 90 of 12 May 1983.

[45] *See, e.g.*, Italian Constitutional Court decisions 55/1968, 56/1968, 79/1971, 202/1974 and 245/1976.

[46] *See* European Convention for the Protection of Human Rights and Fundamental Freedoms, *opened for signature* Nov. 4, 1950, Eur. T.S. No. 5, 213 U.N.T.S. 221.

> Every natural or legal person is entitled to the peaceful enjoyment of his possessions. No one shall be deprived of his possessions except in the public interest and subject to the conditions provided for by law and by the general principles of international law.[47]

The case of *Beyeler v. Italy*,[48] decided January 5, 2000, concerned a van Gogh painting, *Portrait of a Young Peasant*, in a private collection in Italy. The painting had been classified by the Italian Government as a work of historical and artistic interest. The owner sold it in 1977 for 600 million Italian Lire (less than $1 million) and reported the sale to the appropriate Ministry as required by law. The statutory two-month period for exercise of the Government's right of preemption under section 32 of the law expired without exercise.

There then ensued a remarkable series of events set out in detail in the court's decision. The Ministry disingenuously employed evasions, formalisms, contradictory reasons, administrative inertia and other bureaucratic devices to frustrate efforts by the painting's owner, Swiss dealer Ernst Beyeler, to export the picture or to sell it to the Peggy Guggenheim Collection in Venice. In 1988, Beyeler finally succeeded in selling the painting to the Peggy Guggenheim Collection for $8,500,000 and gave the required notice of the sale to the Ministry, which then announced that it "exercised its right of preemption in respect of *the 1977 sale*"[49] (emphasis added) and offered Mr. Beyeler 600 million Italian Lire (which was now worth less than $600,000).

Mr. Beyeler sued the Italian Government, and the case eventually reached the European Court of Human Rights. That Court held for Beyeler, finding a violation of the right of property in Article 1 of the First Protocol, and reserved judgment for six months on the amount of damages in order to give the parties an opportunity to reach an agreed resolution. The six months expired June 5, 2000.

The expropriation of value question was earlier faced in non-

---

47 *Id.*

48 App. No. 33202/96, Eur. Ct. H.R. (2000). For a discussion that antedates this important decision, *see* E. Llana Nakonechny, *Protection of Property Rights Under the European Convention for the Protection of Human Rights and Fundamental Freedoms: Recent Cases*, 3 CAN. INT'L LAW 89 (1998). The author briefly discusses six Article 1 decisions of the Commission/Court (none of which involved cultural property) and concludes that: "[t]he cases have created a criteria [sic] for examining the restriction of property rights by States, and in particular, have acknowledged the need for appropriate compensation when an expropriation takes place." *Id.* at 93.

49 *Beyeler*, App. No. 33202/96 Eur. Ct. H.R.

constitutional form in France in the *Walter* litigation.[50] M. Walter, owner of yet another van Gogh painting, *Jardin á Auvers,* applied for an export permit to send it to London for sale. When the permit was denied, M. Walter sold the picture at a French auction, where he received a price of something less than $10 million. He then sued the State for the difference between that amount and the price he would have received on the world market, basing his action on a seldom-used 1913 French Law. In the *Tribunal,* he won an enormous judgment for over $70 million, which was reduced on appeal to approximately $24 million.[51]

Subsequently, the French adopted new legislation (law of 31 Dec. 1992 and Decree of 29 Jan. 1993),[52] which provides that a first application for an export permit for a work of art may be denied without State liability. After thirty months, a second application may be made, at which time the State must either grant export permission or offer to buy the work. The price the State must offer is determined by a panel of experts, "taking account of prevailing prices on the international market."[53] This statutory development has brought the French much closer to the widely admired British and Canadian schemes, which give public or private institutions a limited time–usually a few months–within which to buy an important work offered for export, failing which export permission must be granted.

A different possibility is suggested by a recent Italian decision. On July 22, 1999, the Court of Cassation dramatically changed Italian administrative and tort law by discarding a doctrinal distinction between "subjective rights" and "legitimate interests," by expressly subjecting the public administration to liability for the consequences of their actions, and by adopting the principle that liability should be based on injury, rather than conduct.[54] Although the decision had nothing to do with cultural property, it raises the interesting possibility that Italian courts may, for the first time, find that an export prohibition produces a compensable injury, *a la* the *Walter* decision in France.[55]

Finally, the European Human Rights Convention in Article 2

---

50 There is an interesting discussion of the *Walter* case and its implications in CARDUCCI, *supra* note 17, at 69ff.

51 *See id.* at 69ff.

52 *See* Lois 477 of 31 December 1992, *as amended by* Lois 643 of 10 July 2000.

53 *Id.*

54 *See* Cass., sez. un. 22 luglio 1999, n. 500, 5 Giornale di diritto amministrativo 832 (n. 9, 1999). There is an accompanying comment on the decision by Luisa Torchia. *See id.* at 843.

55 *See, e.g.,* CARDUCCI, *supra* note 17, at 69ff.

of the Fourth Protocol, states that "[e]veryone shall be free to leave any country, including his own."[56] Professor Erik Jayme of Heidelberg has suggested that this right of travel necessarily includes the right to take along one's goods, because one who must leave her goods behind if she leaves a country is not truly free to leave it: "*Die Freizügigkeit der Person wird behindert, wenn sie die in ihrem Eigentum stehenden Kulturgüter nicht in die neue Heimat mitnehmen darf.*"[57] According to Professor Jayme's reasoning, a Peruvian collector who for business or personal reasons moves to Spain, and an Italian dealer who decides to reestablish his business in Switzerland, should be free to take their cultural property out of the country when they leave it.

If Professor Jayme's view were accepted, it would be necessary to consider Article 3 of the Protocol.[58] Article 3 states that the permissible restrictions on the freedom to leave a country are those that "are necessary in a democratic society in the interests of national security or public safety for the maintenance of '*ordre public*,' for the prevention of crime, or for the protection of rights and freedoms of others."[59] Is a law prohibiting the export of cultural property by its emigrating owner "necessary in a democratic society in the interests of national security or public safety, for the maintenance of public order, for the prevention of crime or for the protection of the rights and freedoms of others?"[60] Perhaps, but perhaps not. Once again, the answers to such questions must await clarifying litigation. Until then we can only speculate.

A More Basic Question

This discussion has identified questions that, when pursued, demonstrate how thin and porous is the fabric of the law applicable to international trade in privately held cultural objects. These questions will eventually have to be answered by scholars, courts and legislatures. I will conclude by introducing the more basic questions that are implied by those we have already discussed: Why should a nation's law prohibit the export of privately held works of

56 Protocol (No. 4) to the European Convention for the Protection of Human Rights and Fundamental Freedoms, Securing Certain Rights and Freedoms Other Than Those Already Included in the Convention and in the Protocol Thereto, Sept. 16, 1963, E.T.S. 46, 7 I.L.M. 978 (1986), 58 A.J.I.L. 334 (1964) [hereinafter Fourth Protocol].

57 Erik Jayme, Nationales Kunstwerk und Internationales Privatratrecht (Gesammelte Schriften Band I) 201 (1999) ["A person's freedom of movement is restricted if he cannot take his cultural property with him to his new home."].

58 *See* Fourth Protocol, *supra* note 56.

59 *Id.*

60 *Id.*

art? Why should other nations be expected to recognize and enforce such laws?

The obvious response is the traditional one: there is a public interest in cultural property,[61] and the State, as guardian of the public interest, acts to protect it. We have seen, however, that this answer raises a variety of troubling questions.

Its acceptance is further undermined by such modern developments as the international liberalization of trade in the WTO and the EU Treaty,[62] the decision in the *Walter* case[63] and the post-*Walter* French legislation,[64] the Austrian Administrative Court and the Costa Rican Supreme Court cases,[65] the decision of the European Court of Human Rights in *Beyeler*,[66] and a significant, growing body of scholarship. The traditional position is ripe for reconsideration.

Suppose that a deceased Italian collector owned important paintings by Goya and Caravaggio. The heirs, who live in New York, would like to sell the Goya at auction in London and donate the Caravaggio to the Boston Museum of Fine Arts. The paintings are moveable without significant threat of injury or destruction. Neither is germane to a context that is important to its study and enjoyment.

Given these premises, why should the Goya not be allowed to go to London for sale? The artist was not Italian. The work was painted in Spain and does not have an Italian subject. In private hands it has been unavailable to the public for enjoyment or study. So what remains? The painting is a very valuable object. If it remains in private hands in Italy, it may eventually fall into public ownership by gift or in settlement of taxes, or the State may be able to buy it at a reduced value. Once it leaves Italian territory these opportunities are lost. Is this an acceptable basis for refusal to allow export of the painting? Judge Pescatore thought not:

> Il n'est pas exclu que l'interdiction d'exporter l'oeuvre d'art fasse partie d'une manoeuvre combinée, destinée à permettre à l'État d'acquérir le bien en question à des conditions plus favorable que le seraient celles d'un marché internationalement ouvert. En d'autres termes, dans un tel cas se pose le question de savoir si le recours à larticle 30 ne sert pas plutôt l'intérnèt

61 This question is discussed at some length in John Henry Merryman, *The Public Interest in Cultural Property*, 77 CAL L. REV. 339 (1989), *reprinted in Critical Essays*, *supra* note 2.

62 *See generally* WTO, *supra* note 9, at 188; EU Treaty, *supra* note 8, at 28.

63 *See* CARDUCCI, *supra* note 17, at 69ff.

64 *See id.*

65 *See* Costa Rica, *Boletin Judicial* No. 90 of 12 May 1983.

66 *See* App. No. 33202/96, Eur. Ct. H.R. (2000).

économique et financier de l'État que la protection du patrimoine culturel.[67]

The Caravaggio painting would seem to present a more congenial case for retention. If an important painting by a great Italian artist is not "protected" by a prohibition against export, what remains of the traditional position? Still, we should remember that Caravaggio is already well represented in Italian public collections. In a private collection this painting adds nothing to the publicly accessible body of his work. The painting would be added to the collection of one of the world's great museums where, properly identified as a Caravaggio, it would represent and glorify Italy and the work of a great Italian artist to the millions of viewers and scholars who now would have access to it. In what sense could it be said that export of the Caravaggio painting would impair the Italian cultural heritage or cultural patrimony?

Suppose we look at the question from a different direction. It certainly is reasonable for Italians to favor the eventual addition of major works of art, now in private hands, to the collections of national museums. That is not in question. What is in question is the use of export prohibitions and the rhetoric of cultural nationalism[68] to advance that interest at the expense of private collectors and dealers.

Two well-established and widely accepted legal procedures are already available to governmental authorities to assert the governmental interest in eventual acquisition of privately held works of art: expropriation and preemptive purchase of works offered for sale or export. Both have the disadvantage (to the public administration) that they require compensation to the owner. Both have the arguable advantage that, by requiring compensation, they provide a check on bare retentionism, unrelated to any genuine protective purpose. The impact on the fisc now becomes a factor in the decision to refuse to license export. In contrast, under the traditional approach, the cost to the State is negligible. The obligation to compensate has a disciplining effect: if it is truly important for public reasons that a privately held work of art remain within the territory of the State, then the public authorities are justified in

[67] Pescatore, *supra* note 13, at 455-56 ["It is not unlikely that the prohibition against exporting works of art is part of a plan aimed at permitting the State to acquire the objects in question on terms more favorable than would be available in an open international market. In other words, in some cases, the question arises as to whether recourse to article 30 better serves the economy and financial interest of the state, rather than the protection of its cultural patrimony."].

[68] *See* John Henry Merryman, *The Retention of Cultural Property*, *supra* note 2 (discussing Cultural Nationalism).

allocating public funds to acquire the appropriate interest in the work—ownership or a servitude—from its owner. If not, not. That is the direction that the British, the Canadians and, more recently, the French have taken. Are they indicators of the future shape of the law in major source nations?

Finally, if the traditional position is indeed in crisis at home in source nations, what does that suggest about international efforts to control the traffic in works of art? Consider privately held easel paintings, free-standing sculptures and loose drawings whose export does not threaten their damage or destruction or the impairment of contextual values, does not incur the dismemberment of complex works and does not deprive a living culture of objects of ritual or ceremonial importance? Should the 1970 UNESCO and 1995 UNIDROIT Conventions,[69] the EU Treaty and WTO be interpreted to support the retention of such works?[70] If such works escape from the source nation's territory, should the courts of other nations be expected to order their return? Why?

Conclusion

I am encouraged by these foreign developments. As some readers may know, I have written, with perhaps wearying frequency and at possibly excessive length, about source nation cultural property laws.[71] Some of those laws appear to me, and to a few others in this country and abroad, to be overly inclusive and overly restrictive. The justifications for these excesses have seemed to us to be sustained more by passion and rhetoric than by principled, evidence-based reason. And to some of us in the United States, our nation's eager responses to the concerns of source nations seem occasionally to lack discrimination and proportion.

How interesting it is that the disparate imperatives of free trade and human rights, so far apart in their ideological origins and objectives, appear to be aligning themselves with us in this mutually supportive way. How interesting cultural property law is.

69 *See generally* 1970 UNESCO Convention, *supra* note 3, at 289; 1995 UNIDROIT Convention, *supra* note 4, at 1322.

70 *See generally* EU Treaty, *supra* note 8, at 28; WTO, *supra* note 9, at 188.

71 The relevant articles are collected in *Critical Essays, supra* note 2.

E-COMMERCE, BUSINESS METHOD PATENTS, AND THE USPTO: AN OLD DEBATE FOR A NEW ECONOMY*

Q. TODD DICKINSON**

INTRODUCTION

I am honored to be here today, and honored that you have invited me to become a part of what is a very distinguished program. As everyone here knows, Cardozo has one of our country's finest intellectual property programs. Those of us in Washington are proud to work with, and call upon, Cardozo's resources. Marci Hamilton, your IP program director, was co-chair of a United States Patent and Trademark Office ("USPTO") conference this year, and just a few months ago Professor Hamilton testified before Congress on some important copyright issues.

On our side, Lynne Beresford, our Deputy Commissioner of Trademarks for Trademark Policy and chair of the World Intellectual Property Organization's ("WIPO") trademark committee, was a speaker at Cardozo last year, and Justin Hughes from our office uses his personal time to teach Cyberlaw at Cardozo, which I understand was one of the school's most popular courses in the last academic year. So, I am very proud to have an opportunity to contribute to this cross-pollination of ideas about intellectual property.

I want to start tonight by saying that within the past two decades it has become abundantly clear to most observers that the United States is making an important transition from a mature industrial and manufacturing economy to an emerging entrepreneurial/innovation-driven knowledge based economy.[1] E-

---

* *Editor's Note.* This Article is adapted from the Eighth Annual Herbert Tenzer Distinguished Lecture in Intellectual Property Law given at the Benjamin N. Cardozo School of Law on October 24, 2000. The Lecture was produced by the United States Patent and Trademark Office; no copyright is claimed by the United States in this speech or associated materials.

** At the time the Lecture was given, Mr. Dickinson was Under Secretary of Commerce for Intellectual Property and Director of the United States Patent and Trademark Office. Mr. Dickinson is currenly a Partner and Co-Chair of Howrey Simon Arnold & White's Intellectual Property Practice. Allegheny College, B.S., 1974; University of Pittsburgh, J.D., 1977.

[1] *See* CRAIG JOYCE, WILLIAM PATRY, MARSHALL LEAFFER & PETER JASZI, ET AL., COPYRIGHT LAW 1 (5th ed. 2000).

commerce, the Internet, and business method patents are basic elements of this transition. And when I was approached to give this lecture, I was pleased to be given the opportunity to discuss them. So tonight, I will endeavor not only to talk about business method patents and software, I also look forward to discussing their place in the broader context of the intellectual property issues we are now confronting.

Really, "An old debate for a new economy" is actually a good subtitle of this talk because it summarizes almost all, if not all, of the burning questions in intellectual property today. The intellectual property system, while retaining basic principles, is also dynamic, constantly evolving to respond to changing technologies, changing social norms, and changing business practices.[2] These changes most often take the form of court decisions, international treaties, legislation from Congress, as well as new or revised procedures at the USPTO.

When any one of these changes touches off a policy debate, it is almost always about whether the intellectual property system is drawing the proper balance between two policy goals—the two pillars on which the whole system is built. The first is that economic incentives are needed to get people to invest in the development of new innovations, creations, and information. In our society, we provide those incentives through copyrights, patents, and trade secrets, as well as special forms of legal protection for semiconductor masks, plant varieties, and the like. Some call these rights "monopolies," but that's too strong a word, with its own inherent, negative connotations; what is really granted is a limited property right, a property right whose economic value will be determined by the market, not by government fiat.

Balanced against this need to have incentives to spur creativity, innovation, and investment in information, the other pillar of the intellectual property system is the need for new works and inventions to be distributed as widely as possible, subject to maintaining effective incentives for the works and inventions to be created in the first place. When a group of people disagree about intellectual property policy, they almost always disagree about where to draw the line, how to achieve the optimal balance between distribution and incentives.

That's why tonight I want to talk about a whole variety of changes in the intellectual property system—some exciting, some mundane—to see how they will impact this debate, our informa-

---

2 *See id.* at 2.

tion economy, and information society, in which we are going to live. Along the way, one of the things I hope to emphasize about the American intellectual property system, something in which I truly believe, is its progressive nature, flexibility, and adaptability. Let me start with a more mundane area, changes in the day to day functioning of the USPTO.

I. Overview: The USPTO and Recent Reform

A. *AIPA*

No agency of the U.S. Government has to respond to the full range of our society's technological changes more quickly than the USPTO. Other agencies are not under constant pressure to upgrade their computers; other agencies, like the Food and Drug Administration ("FDA") or the Federal Trade Commission ('FTC"), have the *option* to master specific new technologies or business practices. At the USPTO, we don't have that luxury. Every patent application that arrives challenges our existing knowledge—that's the whole idea of a patent being for "new" and "non-obvious" innovations.[3] Needless to say, the "new economy" has compelled us to implement dramatic changes in our agency. The raw speed of technological change has forced us to innovate in every respect.

Many such changes were realized by the passage of the American Inventors Protection Act[4] ("AIPA"). The transformations we are seeing at the USPTO as a result of that law are manifold, but it was certainly the Performance Based Organization aspect that gives us the greatest hope for significant reform of the day to day operations of the United States intellectual property system. Changing from a regular government agency to a "performance based organization" has freed us to utilize the same kinds of practices that American businesses use in order to compete effectively in the information age. In fact, we now enjoy full autonomy in decision-making about the management and administration of our operations in areas such as budgeting, personnel, and procurement.

There are other substantial changes that AIPA has brought to the USPTO. For example, AIPA provides for the publication of patent applications eighteen months after a patent application is filed, a change that will have a great impact on our internal opera-

---

[3] *See* Michael A. Epstein, Epstein on Intellectual Property § 5.02 (4th ed. Supp. 2000).

[4] American Inventors Protection Act of 1999, Pub. L. No. 106-113, 113 Stat. 1501 (codified in scattered sections of 35 U.S.C.).

tions.[5] These published applications will be electronic and full text searchable. Because patent applications represent the cutting edge of any technology, what this means in practical terms is that applications will likely become the predominate form of prior art used by examiners.[6] This will help us in ensuring that high quality patents are consistently issued.

But notice that the publication of patent applications after eighteen months also affects that fundamental balance between incentives to innovate and dissemination of information. These published patent applications will disseminate vast amounts of technological information even before the patent system issues any property rights in the form of patents. The published applications will help companies determine where they should invest research dollars and, to some degree, avoid the problem of "submarine patents," patents that are issued after a long examination process and threaten to slow down or unduly burden an industry that has already grown up around a set of innovations. The law also protects the published application through the grant of provisional rights, actual damages for actual notice of infringement of a published claim.

Another critical aspect of the pregrant publication that is especially important in the debate over business methods is the possibility of additional art finding its way to the examiner through Rule 99,[7] either in paper or even on Internet sites. Another important feature of the recent patent law reforms[8] is new reexamination provisions. We now provide for optional inter-parties reexamination for reviewing patent validity, allowing third parties to participate fully in reexamination proceedings. This is a change that will give us the chance to respond to new prior art, overlooked or unavailable on first examination. Although, considering today's topic, I'd like to mention that since we've broadened reexamination, there have only been three third party requests in Class 705,[9] the group responsible for technology and business method patents.

Partnering with private sector, a point I'll return to later, is another significant part of the AIPA initiative, and a vital compo-

---

5 *See* 35 U.S.C. § 122(b)(1)(A) (2000).

6 *See id.* § 102 (e)(1).

7 37 C.F.R. § 1.99 (2001).

8 *See, e.g.*, Scott Erickson, *Patent Law and New Product Development: Does Priority Claim Basis Make a Difference?*, 36 AM. BUS. L.J. 327-28 (1999) (discussing the 1992 Advisory Commission on Patent Law Reform).

9 *See Class 705*, United State Patent and Trademark Office, *available at* http://www.uspto.gov/web/menu/busmethp/class705.htm (last modified July 27, 2001) (citing statistics as of June 2001).

nent of the USPTO's activities as we continue to keep pace with new technologies. We've established opportunities to work with varied members of the IP community through the creation of two new USPTO advisory panels, the Patent Public Advisory Committee and the Trademark Public Advisory Committee. These panels advise the USPTO on agency operations, goals, performance, budget issues, and user fees. And it is our hope that continued work with these two committees will help us see "around the corner," or do a better job of anticipating challenges that the new economy will throw at us.

These are just some of the ways in which the USPTO is handling the demands of the new economy. Our organization is simply enacting reforms much as any other business would in this day and age. We, too, have been affected by the Internet and the possibilities of e-commerce. We, too, see that if we want to continue having the best intellectual property system in the world, it is our responsibility to recognize the realities of the future.

B. Globalization

Those are some of the ways the intellectual property system is changing domestically, but "e-commerce" is one of the points on which we are focusing today. Before we get to a specific topic like business method patents, we should talk about some of the broader legal trends being fueled by the Internet and the rise of e-commerce. The broader legal trend spurred by the Internet can be described by the same word used to describe real world commerce in the past twenty years: globalization. While in some quarters a pejorative term, in the case of the legal system, "globalization" means the need to develop international norms for all kinds of laws—ranging from the protection of personal privacy to contract law to the laws by which national courts exercise jurisdiction, in order to meet the demands of the globalized economy.[10]

With the technological and commercial advances of the past few years, we've seen an unprecedented integration of intellectual property in trade treaties, practices, and agreements. For example, the last four years alone has seen a total of five treaties: the Trademark Law Treaty,[11] the Patent Law Treaty,[12] the two WIPO Copy-

---

10 *See* Christopher W. Rudolph, *Globalization, Sovereignty, and Migration: A Conceptual Framework*, 3 UCLA J. Int'l L. & Foreign Aff. 325, 328 (1998) (stating that "[g]lobalization, as its name suggests, refers to structural and other changes manifest in the international system, and as such, operates largely beyond the domestic sphere").

11 Oct. 27, 1994, Hein's No. KAV 5200, *available at* World Intellectual Property Organization, www.wipo.int/treaties/ip/index.html (last visited Aug. 6, 2001).

right Treaties,[13] and the Hague Agreement on Industrial Designs.[14] All are hallmarks of the trend towards global IP integration. And this trend is continuing. In December, the USPTO will take part in another Diplomatic Conference to negotiate a treaty that protects the rights of audio-visual performers.[15] The protection of these rights is particularly relevant because, in the digital era, a performer's image can be altered and exploited in ways over which they have no control or involvement. We also continue to work on the Madrid Protocol,[16] which will streamline trademark practice. In the fall of 2000, we were very close to ratifying this treaty, but once it reached the Senate it was caught in the crossfire over the "Havana Club" dispute, a trademark disagreement involving the Government of Cuba. However, when the United States is finally able to join the Protocol, a U.S. trademark owner may apply to register its mark in any of the sixty-five Madrid counties by filing a single application, in English, in the USPTO.

Operationally, our Office and IP offices around the world have also responded to globalization. Our embrace of automated systems, for example, is not only about improving service. It's also an acceptance of the fact that at some point IP offices will cease to be independent units only equipped to deal locally with IP rights; they will instead become smaller units of a greater whole as economies become increasingly service-based and need an integrated IP network with which to work. This is an exciting concept. The potential for almost instantaneous, global protection of intellectual property rights through harmonization and automation is a reality that would revolutionize the way IP offices conduct business and the way we view IP rights entirely.

We are on the right path; electronic filing of patents have begun, and we already offer electronic filing for trademarks and implementation of on-line systems that allow our customers to check on the status of their patents and trademark applications, or trade-

---

12 May 11 – June 2, 2000, 39 I.L.M. 1047, *available at* World Intellectual Property Organization, www.wipo.int/treaties/ip/index.html (last visited Aug. 6, 2001).

13 World Intellectual Property Organization Copyright Treaty, Dec. 20, 1996, 36 I.L.M. 65, *available at* World Intellectual Property Organization, www.wipo.int/treaties/ip/index.html (last visited Aug. 6, 2001); World Intellectual Property Organization Performances and Phonograms Treaty, Dec. 20, 1996, 36 I.L.M. 76, *available at* World Intellectual Property Organization, www.wipo.int/treaties/ip/index.html (last visited Aug. 6, 2001).

14 Nov. 6, 1925, 74 L.N.T.S. 343, *available at* World Intellectual Property Organization, www.wipo.int/treaties/ip/index.html (last visited Aug. 6, 2001).

15 *See Diplomatic Conference on the Protection of Audiovisual Performers*, World Intellectual Property Organization, *available at* http://www.wipo.org/eng/document/iavp/index.htm (last visited Aug. 6, 2001).

16 *See* James N. Palik, *Failure by U.S. to Join Madrid Protocol Proves Costly*, N.Y.L.J., June 23, 1997, at S4.

mark registration. There is also the Electronic Filing System in Biotechnology, or EFS-BIO. EFS-BIO is our response to the advent of genomic inventions and gives us the capability to handle gene sequence listings that typically are hundreds of thousands of pages long.

Increased availability to the public of our automated systems in Public Search Facilities is also a part of this movement we're making towards complete access.[17] As it stands, we are the first national intellectual property office in the world to offer this depth and breadth of automation—digitized, networked access to information. We are working on two levels, with both domestic and international activities and policies working towards a global system that will be a virtual requirement in the twenty-first century. For example, it is clear to me that we need to see a substantive patent law treaty during the next decade if we are to recognize the full potential of our intellectual property.

We have indeed, already addressed the harmonization of patent formalities under the Patent Law Treaty; now the international community needs to come together and enact substantive harmonization, instituting a treaty that encompasses all aspects of patent application and postgrant procedure. This is the kind of reform[18] that will be necessary if we are to remain true to our mission of helping spur innovation and, thereby, improve the well being of people's lives.[19]

II. Greater Appreciation of IP in Developing Countries

We also see a greater appreciation of intellectual property in developing countries. Again, this is another place where the new, global economy provides a stage setting for the old debate about the proper balance between incentives to create new knowledge and, on the other hand, unfettered distribution of knowledge. The Trade-Related Aspects of Intellectual Property Agreement[20] ("TRIPS") requires developing countries to improve their intellectual property protection as part of their joining the World Trade Organization. In the early days of TRIPS, many people criticized

---

[17] *See generally* United States Patent and Trademark Office, *at* http://www.uspto.gov (last modified July 16, 2001).

[18] *See generally* Erickson, *supra* note 8.

[19] *See* U.S. Const. art. I, § 8, cl. 8 ("Congress shall have Power . . . to promote the Progress of Science and useful Arts, by securing for limited Times to Authors and Inventors, the exclusive Right to their respective Writings and Discoveries.")

[20] *See* Agreement on Trade-Related Aspects of Intellectual Property Rights, 33 I.L.M. 1197 (1994) [hereinafter TRIPS Agreement].

this as "too much" IP protection[21]—that intellectual property laws would stifle growth in developing countries and would only amount to royalties checks being sent from economically poorer societies back to U.S., Japanese, and European companies.

But that view is changing—changing rapidly in the last few years. In their desire to move away from economies grounded in unreliable commodities and their concern that they not be left behind in this new phase of economic growth, leaders in many developing economies are increasingly recognizing the important role IP protection plays in economic development.[22] Serious, empirically based economic studies have now shown that properly calibrated intellectual property rights—again, properly balancing incentives to create with the need to distribute information widely—have positive effects on a developing country's economic advancement.[23]

The USPTO has been committed to assisting countries to improve their intellectual property systems. We have sponsored regional conferences in countries like Senegal and Kenya in order to teach and learn from foreign governments, governments that are equally as committed to bringing their IP systems up to speed. We've met with the top leaders of IP offices throughout Asia, including China and Vietnam. In the last two years, we've sent experts to provide technical assistance to Egypt, Albania, China, Namibia, Nigeria, Botswana, and Uzbekistan—just to name a few places. Very recently, we sponsored special symposia on intellectual property enforcement, one in Washington D.C., which was geared toward our trading partners in the Western Hemisphere, and one in Thailand, where we partnered with WIPO. Of course we can still do more. We have to make a promise to all developing nations that we will support them in their efforts to create a strong intellectual property rights system and, in doing so, contribute to

---

21 *See, e.g.,* Eric J. Schwartz, *The Impact of Technological Change in the Canada/U.S. Context: Protecting and Exploiting U.S. and Canadian Intellectual Property Abroad in a Technologically Changing World Economy – A U.S. Perspective,* 25 CAN.-U.S. L.J. 97, 102 (1999) (commenting that the most important part of the TRIPS Agreement was the addition of enforcement standards in Articles 41 through 61.)

22 *See, e.g.,* Jeffrey Lax, Note, *A Chile Forecast for Accession to NAFTA: A Process of Economic, Legal, and Environmental Harmonization,* 7 CARDOZO J. INT'L. & COMP. L. 97, 110 (1999) (discussing that, among Latin American countries, Chile is the prime candidate for joining the North American Free Trade Agreement).

23 *See* Robert M. Sherwood, *Human Creativity for Economic Development: Patents Propel Technology,* 33 AKRON L. REV. 351, 352 (2000) (noting that the economic development in developing countries is largely a function of the availability of protection for intellectual property).

their socio-economic growth and competitiveness in the marketplace.

III. Intellectual Property: At a Crossroads

Now I want to return to my original point regarding intellectual property in the new economy. If nothing else is clear, it's at least obvious that new technologies demand new responses. Internet technologies and business method patents, like gene patents, have engendered controversies that are, in many ways, but new chapters in the old debate about whether the intellectual property system properly balances incentives to creators with distributional goals, whether it optimally fuels innovation and the diffusion of innovation or, whether, as some critics charge, it actually slows down innovation and imposes unnecessary costs on people and institutions.

But I think that there are some "atmospherics" we have to recognize too. The innovations we are dealing with today are almost unimaginable, and that people assume the *unimaginable* must therefore be *unmanageable*. Not too long ago, a concept like the Internet was unimaginable. Genetics, an unexplored terrain.

So people have become concerned that our government, through the USPTO, is ill-equipped to handle the special concerns these unimaginable creations have spawned. Will we stifle innovation as we try to protect it? Will we kill competition even as we claim that we are encouraging a diverse marketplace? Do we have the expertise to handle these inventions? These are serious concerns in any economy, but even more so in the United States, a country literally built upon the ideal and ideas of the American dream.

Let us now touch upon the controversy surrounding subject matter and patentability. Plainly speaking, there are many people who think that patents should not be issued on methods of doing business on the Internet, that is, on computer and/or network-enabled business systems or processes. My view on this specific question must be understood in a broader context. Part of that context is a patent system specifically designed to absorb new technologies. Our patent system has responded to wave after wave—some small waves, some tidal waves—of new technologies. It has provided patent protection for these new technologies without seeming to slow America's economic progress. Would the people who oppose patenting a method of shopping on the Internet also have opposed, a century ago, a patent on a cash register, since it is just a way of using a machine to do a well known activity—adding purchase prices? If we have no empirical evidence to show that patents retard progress in a particular field of endeavor, then shouldn't the presumption, as a matter of policy, be in favor of providing patent protection? In fact, the evidence is that our patent system stimulates research and new products; one only has to compare the United States biotech industry with that of Europe.[24] Further, it has been demonstrated that expanding subject matter, and the introduction of new products based on these changes, is something that our IP system, with its flexibility and ability to adapt to new technologies, is well equipped to handle.

The second part of my answer is not a policy perspective, but a perspective on the law. Today I want to say this regarding business method patents: the USPTO is following the *State Street* decision[25] and accepts the patentability of business methods and software. In the *State Street* decision, the Federal Circuit concluded that § 101 of the patent law does not encompass an exception from patentability of "business methods."[26] Since the Supreme Court decided not to review the *State Street* decision,[27] that is the interpretation of the law that the USPTO must follow.

Now let me say that we are not hiding behind the robes of the Federal Circuit judges. It is not just that *State Street* is law, it is that the *State Street* decision is a reasonable and proper interpretation of § 101's statutory language.[28] Section 101 states unequivocally that "[w]hoever invents or discovers any new and useful process, machine, manufacture, or composition of matter" may obtain a patent if he or she meets the standards of novelty and non-obviousness.[29] There is nothing in the statute that says methods of doing business should be excluded.[30] If an Internet-enabled method of selling widgets is a "new and useful process" *and* it meets the law's required levels of "novelty" and "non-obviousness," it is appropriate matter for a patent.

Now the USPTO's job with business method patents, as with all patents, is to issue quality patents—to do the best we can to

---

24 *See* Michael J. Malinowski, *Legal Development: Globalization of Biotechnology and the Public Health Challenges Accompanying It*, 60 ALB. L. REV. 119, 123-24 (1996) (noting that the British biotechnology industry is not as developed as that of the United States).

25 *See* State St. Bank & Trust Co. v. Signature Fin. Group, Inc. 149 F.3d 1368 (Fed. Cir. 1998).

26 *See id.* at 1375.

27 *See* State St. Bank & Trust Co. v. Signature Fin. Group, Inc., 525 U.S. 1093 (1999) (denying writ of certiorari).

28 *See State Street*, 149 F.3d at 1372.

29 35 U.S.C. § 101 (2000).

30 *See id.*

ensure that patents issue only when the innovation is useful and truly new and non-obvious in relation to all that was known before. To address concerns, including our own, about business method patents being issued by the office, we launched a Business Method Action Plan in March 2000. The program is explained in great detail in our White Paper, which, of course, is online.[31] This initiative included revised examination guidelines and a business methods roundtable, another example of our work on fostering partnerships with the private sector.

One of the components of our revised procedures for business method patents is that we have instituted a second-level review of all allowed applications in this area by an additional examiner beyond the Primary Examiner signing the case. This "second pair of eyes" will be very helpful in ensuring the quality of these patents. The USPTO has also doubled the size of end-product quality review sampling of these applications.

On the issue of genomics, there are also few brief points that I need to make. One, under United States law, and this is identical to our position on business method patents, gene patents are allowed. When the USPTO issues patents on genomic inventions, we are following precedent set by the U.S. courts, specifically 1980's *Chakrabarty* case,[32] which firmly established the legitimacy of gene patents, in this case for a new strain of bacteria.[33] And, number two, the USPTO does not issue patents on *raw genetic data.* The USPTO is not in the business of issuing patents on this basis; we demand actual invention. We can look to history and see the same standards applied to numerous other naturally occurring chemicals. One of my favorite examples is penicillin—originally starting life as a mold, but eventually generating an entire generation of patentable antibiotics. This is just one obvious example. But it's important for people to understand that the USPTO's approach has been consistent. We follow United States patent law; we insist on innovation; and we work to make sure that the highest of standards are met when we issue a patent.

Still, the controversy remains, and we want to respond to that, always. There will probably be controversies of this nature as long as there exists an inventor, an idea, and an intellectual property system. That is to be expected when we are dealing with emerging

---

31 *See White Paper,* United States Patent and Trademark Office, *available at* www.uspto.gov/web/menu/busmethp/index.html (last visited Aug. 2, 2001).

32 Diamond v. Chakrabarty, 447 U.S. 303 (1980).

33 *See id.* at 309.

technologies, and we welcome the opportunity to work with the IP community on these questions.

A. *Domain Name/Privacy*

Those of you interested in trademarks and Internet issues are no doubt quite familiar with the challenges posed by domain name registration and privacy issues. One viewpoint on obtaining information from the Whois database, the database that contains ownership and contact information for all of the domain names in the generic top-level domains (for example, dot com, dot net, and dot org), is that, in order to protect privacy, ownership information should not be readily available to trademark and copyright owners.[34] However, access to this information is vital. Only by obtaining such information can the trademark and copyright owner effectively pursue remedies against infringers and cybersquatters.[35]

Clearly there is a conflict here; and, although protecting the privacy of individuals is extremely important, the United States believes that it is also important to allow the owners of copyrights and trademarks to have quick and effective means to stop cybersquatting, infringement, and unlawful copying.[36] Owners of valid trademarks and copyrights must be able to obtain accurate and current ownership and address information in order to stop those who are using the Internet to infringe valid trademarks or unlawfully copy protected material.[37] Hopefully, further international cooperation will be able to remedy diverging philosophies while at the same time respecting privacy appropriately.

B. *Database Protection*

Additional legal protection for databases, beyond what is provided by copyright law, is another area where the new economy has rekindled the old debate over where to draw the line between adequate incentives and adequate access.[38] There is no question that digitization and the Internet environment make it possible for large databases that are the result of substantial investment to be

---

34 *See Register.com Seeks End to Alleged Misuse of Whois Database,* 18 (No. 2) ANDREWS COMPUTER & ONLINE INDUSTRY LITIG. REP. 12 (2000).

35 *See* Dale M. Cendali & Rebecca L. Weinstein, *Intellectual Property and the Internet,* 1998 A.B.A CENTER FOR CONTINUING LEGAL EDUC. A-137-38.

36 *See* Navin Katyal, *The Unauthorized Dissemination of Celebrity Images on the Internet . . . in the Flesh,* 46 CLEV. ST. L. REV. 738, 753 (1998).

37 *See* Cendali & Weinstein, *supra* note 35, at A-138.

38 *See* J. Ryan Mitchell, *If at Feist You Don't Succeed, Try, Try Again: An Evaluation of the Proposed Collections of Information Antipiracy Act,* 78 NEB. L. REV. 900, 901 (1999).

pirated in the blink of an eye.[39] But it is also clear that too strong a form of legal protection might stifle the use of information in research, the sciences, downstream commercial applications, and society at large.[40] For that reason, in 1998, the Administration laid out six principles that we believe should govern legal protection of the investment in databases. Those principles both recognize the need for such protection and the need for a wide range of "fair uses" analogous to what is provided in copyright law. I believe that we need to move forward domestically on the basis of those principles to ensure that the global intellectual property community does not move ahead without us.

C. *Ethical Issues: Technology and Culture/Folklore*

There are also many questions regarding globalization, technology, and the effects on traditional cultures.[41] This controversy has spawned a generation of books, lectures, and programs.[42] It's an important question: at what cost progress? This is a particularly sensitive point to developing nations that fear the total Westernization, or more specifically Americanization, of their society, especially as the Internet starts infiltrating even the most closed of cultures.[43] Furthermore, the question of folklore, and how to adequately protect it, still troubles us. There is abuse through commercialization and distortion, and copyright protection as it stands doesn't seem to be the answer. From the Berne Convention[44] to our most recent meetings with WIPO, we are still struggling to find the correct kind of protection for folklore.

D. *Enforcement*

But above all, we need to make sure that effective enforcement is implemented globally. And let me be even more specific: inexpensive methods of enforcement have to be implemented. The widespread embrace of the Internet has made this critical, as

---

39 *See id.* at 909.

40 *See* G.M. Hunsucker, *The European Database Directive: Regional Stepping Stone to an International Model?*, 7 FORDHAM INTELL. PROP. MEDIA & ENT. L.J. 700, 706 (1997).

41 *See generally* Kevin D. Brown, *Globalization and Cultural Conflict in Developing Countries: The South African Example*, 7 IND. J. GLOBAL LEGAL STUD. 225 (1999).

42 *See, e.g.*, Kevin R. Johnson, *Celebrating Latcrit Theory: What Do We Do When the Music Stops?*, 33 U.C. DAVIS L. REV. 753 (2000); Chantal Thomas, *Globalization and the Reproduction of Hierarchy*, 33 U.C. DAVIS L. REV. 1451 (2000); Chantal Thomas, *Transfer of Technology in the Contemporary International Order*, 22 FORDHAM INT'L L.J. 2096 (1999).

43 *See* Jim Chen, *Globalization and Its Losers*, 9 MINN J. GLOBAL TRADE 157, 162-63 (2000).

44 Berne Convention for the Protection of Literary and Artistic Works, Sept. 9, 1996, 25 U.S.T. 1341.

industry loses billions to piracy and infringement. All nations need to be able to protect their economies from these violations.

I spoke earlier about developing nations and the trend towards greater appreciation of IP protection and enforcement, but this is a long road, due to the sheer number of countries obligated to comply with TRIPS. On January 1, 1996, all developed countries had to have their domestic intellectual property laws and enforcement regimes in compliance with TRIPS. As of January 1, 2000, over seventy developing countries have had the same obligation to ensure that their laws are TRIPS-compliant, and by 2006 the least developed countries will be obligated to do the same.

Assisting developing countries to meet these obligations will require: (1) a great deal of technical assistance and training by developed countries, private industry, and international and regional organizations; (2) strong public-private sector cooperation; and (3) an ongoing dialogue between developed and developing countries on enforcement issues. Domestic enforcement is also critical. Clearly, the United States is not immune to the violation of IP rights. We must continue to work with the recently-established National Intellectual Property Law Enforcement Coordination Council ("the Council"), which the USPTO co-chairs along with the Department of Justice and which consists of the State Department, the United States Trade Representative, Customs, the Department of Commerce, and the Copyright Office.

With a mandate to coordinate domestic and international intellectual property law enforcement among federal and foreign entities, we look forward to a time when the Council will serve as a vehicle through which federal agencies can partner with industry to develop effective strategies for addressing Internet piracy. The Council has already begun a dialogue with industry to identify ways they can work together to create effective domestic and international enforcement regimes, and in November 2000 we will be holding a public meeting to welcome all opinions concerning this important issue. All in all, we have a full plate. Even if we answer all these concerns, rest assured that there will be different ones for us to deal with, as progress continues and intellectual property continues to lead us into the next century.

Conclusion

Let me close by reminding everyone here what the last few years have meant to the intellectual property community. Our profile, obviously raised, has reached a point where the work that we do has become the central turning point of the twenty-first century. Globalization, technology, and information have formed an entirely new way of life for every individual, and for every government. The Internet, a driving force behind these changes, has asked us to explore new avenues of management in our IP system. What an opportunity this has turned out to be. We have, as a result, seen how responsive and practical our system truly is, while at the same time we've been able to expand our capabilities in order to push our economy, and those of developing nations, to new heights.

Of course we admit that there are no absolutes here. It will never be our intention to establish a tradition of inflexibility and limited perspective; that would fly in the face of what our founding fathers envisioned when they first created our IP system. Like our Constitution, our system is strong by being flexible; and it is this adaptability that has fostered innovation, and in turn is enriched by it. I ask you to be proud of this tradition, as you are proud of the legal tradition you have chosen to join. By doing this, you are not only contributing to its success, you are also taking the crucial step of bearing responsibility and of taking care that we do not mismanage a system that offers so much to so many.

This is a concept that I cannot overstate. Throughout my tenure at the USPTO, I have stressed, by both word and deed, that our role is to sustain a balance. It is not, as I said earlier, to control terms and hand down edicts; it is to work with the people we serve to make sure that our system helps rather than hinders. The USPTO is not a typical government agency. We are not bureaucratic. We are not reactive. We are instead proactive, responsive, and a leader in government reform, acting as an example to every single IP office in the world. It is in no one's best interest to ignore change and the realities of a new era. We are responsible for far too much. If the twenty-first century is the era of technology, then the intellectual property system of the United States is leading the world into the new century well prepared.

CONTRIBUTORS

Keith Aoki is Associate Professor of Law at the University of Oregon School of Law.

Ralph S. Brown was Simeon E. Baldwin Professor Emeritus of Law and Frank E. Taplin Professorial Lecturer in Law at Yale Law School.

Rosemary J. Coombe is Canada Research Chair in Law, Communication, and Cultural Studies in the Faculty of Arts at York University.

Hon. Edward J. Damich is a judge of the United States Court of Federal Claims.

Q. Todd Dickinson is a partner of the law firm of Howrey Simon Arnold & White LLP in Washington, D.C. He was Under Secretary of Commerce for Intellectual Property and Director of the United States Patent and Trademark Office.

Niva Elkin-Koren is Senior Lecturer in the Faculty of Law at the University of Haifa.

Brian F. Fitzgerald is Dean of the School of Law and Justice of Southern Cross University, New South Wales, Australia.

Patty Gerstenblith is Professor of Law at DePaul University College of Law.

Jane C. Ginsburg is Morton L. Janklow Professor of Literary and Artistic Property Law and Director of Kernochan Center for Law, Media and the Arts at Columbia Law School.

Marci A. Hamilton is Paul R. Verkuil Chair in Public Law and Director of the Intellectual Property Law Program at the Benjamin N. Cardozo School of Law, Yeshiva University.

Justin Hughes is Visiting Professor of Law at UCLA School of Law.

Peter Jaszi is Professor of Law at Washington College of Law, American University.

Hon. Pierre N. Leval is a judge of the United States Court of Appeals for the Second Circuit.

Jessica Litman is Professor of Law at Wayne State University Law School.

Glenn B. Manishin is a partner of the law firm of Patton Boggs LLP in McLean, Virginia.

J. Thomas McCarthy is Professor of Law at the University of San Francisco School of Law. He is author of *McCarthy on Trademarks and Unfair Competition.*

John Henry Merryman is Nelson Bowman Sweitzer and Marie B. Sweitzer Professor of Law, Emeritus and Affiliated Professor in the Department of Art at Stanford University.

Neil Netanel is Arnold, White & Durkee Centennial Professor of Law at the University of Texas School of Law.

Hon. Jon O. Newman is a senior judge of the United States Court of Appeals for the Second Circuit.

David Nimmer is Of Counsel to the law firm of Irell & Manella in Los Angeles and Lecturer in Law at UCLA School of Law.

Ralph Oman is Counsel to the law firm of Dechert in Washington, D.C. He is the former Register of Copyrights of the United States.

William F. Patry is Of Counsel to the law firm of Skadden Arps Slate Meagher & Flom LLP in New York. He was counsel to the Subcommittee on Intellectual Property and Judicial Administration, Committee on the Judiciary, U.S. House of Representatives.

Shira Perlmutter is Vice President and Associate General Counsel for Intellectual Property Policy of AOL Time Warner, Inc. She was Associate Register of Copyrights for Policy and International Affairs in the United States Copyright Office.

Monroe E. Price is Joseph & Sadie Danciger Professor of Law and Director of the Howard M. Squadron Program in Law, Media & Society at the Benjamin N. Cardozo School of Law, Yeshiva University. He is Co-director of the Programme in Comparative Media Law & Policy at the University of Oxford.

J.H. Reichman is Bunyan A. Womble Professor of Law at Duke University School of Law.

David Rudenstine is Dean and Dr. Herman George and Kate Kaiser Professor of Constitutional Law at the Benjamin N. Cardozo School of Law, Yeshiva University.

Pamela Samuelson is Professor of Law and Information Management and Director of Berkeley Center for Law & Technology at the University of California at Berkeley.

Matthew L. Spitzer is Dean and Carl Mason Franklin Professor of Law at University of Southern California Law School.

Laurence H. Winer is Professor of Law and Faculty Fellow of the Center for the Study of Law, Science, & Technology at Arizona State University College of Law.

Alfred C. Yen is Associate Dean for Academic Affairs and Professor of Law at Boston College Law School.

Geri J. Yonover is Professor of Law at Valparaiso University School of Law.

Peter K. Yu is Acting Assistant Professor of Law, Executive Director of the Intellectual Property Law Program, and Deputy Director of the Howard M. Squadron Program in Law, Media & Society at the Benjamin N. Cardozo School of Law, Yeshiva University. He is Research Associate of the Programme of Comparative Media Law & Policy at the University of Oxford.

ABOUT THE PROGRAM

The Intellectual Property Law Program at the Benjamin N. Cardozo School of Law, Yeshiva University, boasts an exceptional full-time and adjunct faculty and a wide range of courses and externships for Cardozo students. In addition to offering a J.D. program, Cardozo is one of the few American law schools that offers an LL.M. in intellectual property law. The program, which consistently ranks among the top intellectual property programs in the United States, is devoted to furthering an understanding of intellectual property law in the academy and among the practicing bar and to facilitating legal reform. To this end, Cardozo publishes the *Cardozo Arts and Entertainment Law Journal*, a book series on intellectual property and technology law, and a series of occasional papers. The Law School also sponsors the Annual Tenzer Distinguished Lecture in Intellectual Property Law, runs the premier intellectual property and entertainment law moot court competition, and hosts frequent ground-breaking symposia and lectures.